Corrections in the United States

A Contemporary Perspective

Fourth Edition

Dean John Champion
Texas A & M International University

Upper Saddle River, NJ 07458

Library of Congress Cataloging-in-Publication Data

Champion, Dean J.
    Corrections in the United States : a contemporary perspective / Dean John Champion.
    — 4th ed.
      p. cm.
    Includes bibliographical references and index.
    ISBN 0-13-102736-0
1. Corrections—United States.   I. Title.

HV9471.C47 2004
364.6'0973—dc22

              2004000069

Editor-in-Chief: Stephen Helba
Executive Editor: Frank Mortimer, Jr.
Assistant Editor: Sarah Holle
Production Editor: Karen Berry, Pine Tree Composition
Production Liaison: Barbara Marttine Cappuccio
Director of Production and Manufacturing: Bruce Johnson
Managing Editor: Mary Carnis
Manufacturing Buyer: Cathleen Petersen
Creative Director: Cheryl Asherman
Cover Design Coordinator: Miguel Ortiz
Cover Designer: Amy Rosen
Cover Image: CORBIS (Royalty Free)
Editorial Assistant: Barbara Rosenberg
Marketing Manager: Tim Peyton
Formatting and Interior Design: Pine Tree Composition
Printing and Binding: Courier Companies

Pearson Education LTD.
Pearson Education Singapore, Pte. Ltd.
Pearson Education, Canada, Ltd
Pearson Education–Japan
Pearson Education Australia PTY, Limited
Pearson Education North Asia Ltd
Pearson Educaçion de Mexico, S.A. de C.V.
Pearson Education Malaysia, Pte. Ltd.

10 9 8 7 6 5 4 3 2
ISBN: 0-13-102736-0

Contents

Preface   ix
About the Author   xv

Chapter 1
An Introduction to Corrections: Philosophy, Goals, and History   1

Introduction   2

Corrections Defined   4

Early Origins of Corrections   6

The History of Corrections in the United States   10

Correctional Functions and Goals   14

Some Correctional Models   18

Types of Corrections   24

Correctional Reforms   30

SUMMARY   32   QUESTIONS FOR REVIEW   33   SUGGESTED READINGS   34
INTERNET CONNECTIONS   34

Chapter 2
Classifying Offenders, Sentencing Systems, and Sentencing Issues   35

Introduction   36

Types of Offenses   38

Classifying Offenders   39

The Sentencing Process   48

Types of Sentencing Systems   49

Sentencing Hearings   58

The Pre-sentence Investigation (PSI) and Report   59

Aggravating and Mitigating Circumstances   82

Some Sentencing Issues   84

SUMMARY   89   QUESTIONS FOR REVIEW   91   SUGGESTED READINGS   92
INTERNET CONNECTIONS   92   APPENDIX 2A: OFFENSE REPORT   93

Chapter 3
Diversion, Standard, and Intensive Supervised Probation Programs   100

Introduction   101

Civil Alternatives: Alternative Dispute Resolution and Diversion   103

Pretrial Diversion   107

The History of Probation in the United States   113

The Philosophy and Functions of Probation   117

Types of Probation   119

A Profile of Probationers   135

Shock Probation and Split Sentencing   139

Boot Camps   142

Landmark Cases in Probation Revocation   150

SUMMARY   159   QUESTIONS FOR REVIEW   161   SUGGESTED READINGS   161
INTERNET CONNECTIONS   162

Chapter 4
Community Corrections   163

Introduction   164

Community Corrections Acts and Community Corrections   167

Community Corrections Programs   172

Selected Issues in Community Corrections   191

SUMMARY   195   QUESTIONS FOR REVIEW   197   SUGGESTED READINGS   198
INTERNET CONNECTIONS   198

Chapter 5
Jails: History, Functions, and Types of Inmates   199

Introduction   200

The History of Jails in the United States   202

Jail Inmate Characteristics   206

Functions of Jails   207

Types of Jail Inmates   215

SUMMARY   219   QUESTIONS FOR REVIEW   220   SUGGESTED READINGS   221
INTERNET CONNECTIONS   221

Chapter 6
Jail Administration: Officer Training, Inmate Supervision, and Contemporary Issues   222

Introduction   223

Jail Administration   226

Selected Jail Issues   236

Jail Reforms   256

SUMMARY   269   QUESTIONS FOR REVIEW   270   SUGGESTED READINGS   271
INTERNET CONNECTIONS   271

Chapter 7
Prisons and Prisoners   272

Introduction   273

The History of Prisons in the United States   276

State and Federal Prison Systems   284

A Profile of Prisoners in U.S. Prisons   291

Types of Prisons and Their Functions   296

Inmate Classification Systems   305

Risk Assessment and Institutional Placement   308

Functions of Prisons   323

Prison Culture: On Jargon and Inmate Pecking Orders   326

Selected Prison Issues   334

SUMMARY   342   QUESTIONS FOR REVIEW   343   SUGGESTED READINGS   344
INTERNET CONNECTIONS   344

Chapter 8
Corrections Administration and the Privatization of Prisons   345

Introduction   346

The Bureaucratic Model and Legal-Rational Authority   348

Corrections and Offender Management   358

The Organization of Corrections   358

Forms of Correctional Administration   363

Prison Administrator Selection and Training   371

Prison Privatization   372

Selected Issues on Privatization   375

SUMMARY   382   QUESTIONS FOR REVIEW   384   SUGGESTED READINGS   385
INTERNET CONNECTIONS   385

Chapter 9
Jailhouse Lawyers and Inmate Rights   386

Introduction   387

What Are Jailhouse Lawyers?   390

The Constitutional Basis for Inmate Rights   391

The Jailhouse Lawyer and the Nature of Civil Remedies   414

Prisoner Rights and Selected Litigation Issues   421

The Death Penalty   427

What Compensation Is Given to Exonerated Prisoners?   453

Inmate Grievance Procedures   455

SUMMARY   457   QUESTIONS FOR REVIEW   460   SUGGESTED READINGS   460
INTERNET CONNECTIONS   460

Chapter 10
Parole, Parole Programs, and Parole Revocation   462

Introduction   463

Parole   465

Pre-Release Programs   480

Post-Release Parole Programs   487

Parole Boards: Revoking Probation and Parole   492

Measuring Parole Effectiveness Through Recidivism   505

The Parole Revocation Process   506

The Rights of Probationers and Parolees   507

Serving Time beyond Maximum Sentences   512

SUMMARY   515   QUESTIONS FOR REVIEW   518   SUGGESTED READINGS   519
INTERNET CONNECTIONS   519

Chapter 11
Correctional Officer Selection and Training   520

Introduction   521

Corrections Officers and Probation/Parole Officers: A Distinction   523

The Selection and Training of Correctional Officers   525

The Recruitment of Women in Correctional Work   540

The Organization and Operation of Probation and Parole Programs   544

Selection Requirements for Probation and Parole Officers   547

PO Caseloads   555

Volunteers in Community Corrections   558

Paraprofessionals in Community Corrections Programs   565

SUMMARY   567   QUESTIONS FOR REVIEW   570   SUGGESTED READINGS   570
INTERNET CONNECTIONS   571

Chapter 12
Women and Corrections   572

Introduction   573

Female Offenders   576

Women's Prisons   579

Co-Corrections   608

Female Probationers and Parolees: A Profile   611

Intermediate Punishments for Women   612

SUMMARY   616   QUESTIONS FOR REVIEW   618   SUGGESTED READINGS   618
INTERNET CONNECTIONS   619

Chapter 13
Juveniles and Corrections   620

Introduction   621

Juvenile Offenders   624

The Juvenile Justice System   630

Constitutional Rights of Juveniles   636

Waivers, Transfers, and Certifications   639

Juvenile Corrections   645

SUMMARY   673   QUESTIONS FOR REVIEW   676   SUGGESTED READINGS   676
INTERNET CONNECTIONS   676

Glossary   679

References   704

Case Index   737

Name Index   739

Subject Index   746

Preface

Corrections in the United States: A Contemporary Perspective (4th ed.) is about the punishment phase of the criminal justice system. When crimes are committed and suspects are apprehended, prosecuted, and convicted, correctional agencies take over. Corrections is the vast collective of persons, agencies, and organizations that manages criminals. The most visible part of corrections is prisons and jails. Various notorious prisons have been popularized by the media. Prisons, such as San Quentin, Alcatraz, Sing Sing, Leavenworth, Attica, and Marion, are familiar to the general public. But prisons and jails, though important, are only two parts of the larger corrections mosaic. Another part of corrections manages offenders who either have been granted early release from prison or have been convicted but not incarcerated. Community correctional agencies are increasingly popular as nonincarcerative alternatives for probationers and parolees. One reason for their popularity is that they are more cost-effective than maintaining inmates in prisons and jails. In some instances, less serious offenders are not prosecuted, but rather, they are diverted from the criminal justice system. They are also managed by certain corrections agencies for a specified period. Community corrections supervises two-thirds of all convicted and unconvicted offenders.

Today, correctional agencies and organizations face several significant challenges. Rising crime rates and greater numbers of criminal prosecutions are establishing new prison and jail population records. At the same time, new prison and jail construction is not keeping pace with these escalating prison and jail populations. Overcrowding is inevitable, and it fosters living conditions for inmates that are both intolerable and unconstitutional. In recent years a litigation explosion has occurred where thousands of lawsuits have been filed by prisoners against prison and jail administrators and correctional officers. Inmate rights is an increasingly important issue.

This organization of this book is as follows. Chapter 1 examines the history of corrections in the United States and contrasts several important philosophies that have influenced correctional reforms. The goals and functions of corrections are outlined and discussed. Several correctional models are presented that guide the thinking of correctional administration and staff. Chapter 2 presents several types of sentencing systems used in the United States. Offenders are profiled. The sentencing process is described, including sentencing hearings and the preparation of presentence investigation reports. Aggravating and mitigating circumstances that influence sentencing decisions are presented. Several contemporary issues associated with sentencing systems are discussed.

Chapter 3 examines some of the preliminary events following arrests of alleged offenders. Pretrial diversion is examined, where prosecutors temporarily suspend prosecutions against particular suspects. The eligibility criteria for diversion are examined. Another pretrial option is alternative dispute resolution, where selected criminal cases are diverted from the criminal justice system for possible civil resolution. The strengths and weaknesses of alternative dispute resolution are discussed, together with an examination of the types of cases that result in such outcomes. When offenders are convicted of crimes, they may or may not be incarcerated. This chapter continues with an examination of the probation option, where many offenders are sentenced to terms in their own communities. These sentences are always conditional, requiring offenders to participate in rehabilitative programs, perform community service, and/or pay fines. The philosophy and functions of probation are presented. Probationers are profiled, and typical probation programs and their conditions are examined. For some offenders, they may be sentenced to shock probation, where they may be subject to unexpected short-term confinement. This sentencing option, together with split sentencing and other sentencing variations, is examined. For many offenders, especially youthful ones, more regimentation may be required as a part of their rehabilitation and reintegration back into society. One sentencing option is boot camp, which is a military-like punishment requiring strict obedience to rules and a high degree of regimentation. The philosophy, goals, and clientele of boot camps are described. The chapter concludes with an examination of the process whereby probation is revoked. All probationers are within the original jurisdiction of sentencing judges. Judges may or may not revoke a person's probation program, depending upon the circumstances. The probation revocation process is examined in some detail, including a presentation of selected state and federal cases pertaining to this process.

Chapter 4 examines community corrections and provides a broad overview of community corrections programs. These are programs that are usually operated at the state or local levels. Community correctional clientele are described. Some of the community programs discussed in detail include home confinement, electronic monitoring, and day reporting centers. In each case, the particular program is explained, and the philosophy, goals, and functions of the programs are clearly articulated. The chapter concludes with an examination of several important issues closely associated with community corrections. Because offenders involved in community corrections are essentially free to roam about their communities, there is some concern among community residents for their safety and security. There is even some public resistance to community corrections. This issue is discussed. Furthermore, private corporations have become involved to a greater degree in offender management, particularly in communities. Not everyone supports the privatization of community corrections, and the constitutionality and propriety of private interests supervising convicted offenders is sometimes questioned. This issue will be explored. When offenders are supervised in their communities, there is a legitimate concern about public safety and security. How effective is the community supervision of offenders on probation, home confinement, or electronic monitoring? The public safety issue will be addressed. Other issues pertain to services delivery and special needs offenders. A growing community corrections clientele with diverse needs draws increasingly on more community resources and personnel for assistance and support. The quality and availability of these services are explored. Also, there are growing numbers of special-needs offenders, or persons with drug/alcohol dependencies; mental diseases, defects, or illnesses; debilitating and infectious diseases such as HIV/AIDS and tuberculosis; and ambulatory ailments. The problems posed by special-needs offenders will be discussed.

Chapter 5 examines the history of jails and jail systems. Jail inmate characteristics are described. Several important functions of jails are listed. The types of jail inmates accommodated are presented and discussed. Chapter 6 discusses the administration of jail systems. This discussion includes the selection of jail personnel and their training. Several important jail issues are presented, including jail overcrowding, jail suicides, and inmate classification problems. Chapter 7 examines prisoners and prison issues. The history of prisons in the United States is presented together with a profile of state and federal prison inmates. Several popular prison inmate classification systems are presented. A distinction between prisons and jails is provided. Several important functions of prisons are listed.

Chapter 8 looks at corrections administration. Several organizational models are presented, including the bureaucratic and human relations models. Both state and federal prison organization are described. The selection and training of prison administrators and staff is described. Selected issues in prison administration are presented, including the professionalization of administration, public accountability, public reaction to privatization, and political considerations.

In Chapter 9, the rights of prisoners are discussed, including the increasingly important role of the jailhouse lawyer and related legal issues that often prompt civil and criminal lawsuits filed by inmates against institutional staff. The constitutional basis for inmate claims against prison and jail systems is examined. Several avenues for filing lawsuits are treated, including *habeas corpus* petitions, civil rights actions, and tort litigation. Several important constitutional amendments that affect inmates are also discussed. These include the First, Fourth, Eighth, and Fourteenth Amendments. One of the most controversial punishments is the death penalty. Capital punishment has come under fire in recent years because of the fact that several condemned offenders have been shown to be innocent of their conviction offenses. In some instances, innocent persons have been executed. Technological advances in DNA testing and other scientific discoveries have caused judges and others to re-examine the original convictions of those sentenced to death. Thus, the death penalty and the philosophical underpinnings of it are critically examined. Most arguments favoring the death penalty as well as opposing it are presented. The chapter concludes with a discussion of various grievance procedures available to inmates who have complaints about their incarceration and treatment.

Chapter 10 focuses upon parole and parole programs. Parole is defined and a brief history of parole developments in the United States is presented. Included here are the philosophy and goals of parole programs. Parolees are also profiled. Whenever parolees and/or probationers violate one or more conditions of their conditional programs, their respective programs may be revoked. The revocation process is described, including some of the landmark U.S. Supreme Court decisions relating to such revocation actions. In most states, parole boards function to determine a person's early release eligibility. This decision making involves anticipating the person's future potential for public risk or dangerousness. Some of the instruments and techniques used in risk assessment will be described. The nature and functions of parole boards will be examined. Various types of parole board actions are described, including an overview of some of the programs into which prospective parolees may be directed. The quality of decision making in parole actions is assessed according to rates of recidivism among probationers and parolees. Recidivism rates are measured in different ways. Different types of recidivists are profiled. The chapter concludes with an examination of the parole revocation process. Included in this examination are the rights of parolees and several leading U.S. Supreme Court cases that have influenced this process, as well as some of the state-level parole revocation cases which have been decided.

Chapter 11 describes correctional officer selection and training. Corrections officers may work in institutions or within communities. Conventionally, corrections officers work in prisons or jails, while other types of corrections officers, known as probation and parole officers, work with offenders in their communities. The selection and recruitment of probation and parole officers will also be examined. The education, training, and role performance of these officers will be highlighted. Additionally, for those working with offenders within the community, caseload assignments are made and determine the numbers and types of offenders who will be supervised at any given time. Several important caseload assignment models will be identified and discussed. Correctional work, whether it is institutional or within the community, is stressful. Stress often leads to burnout. Therefore, some of the factors that contribute to stress and burnout will be examined, together with a discussion of some of the strategies officers use to combat and/or overcome stress. Also described in Chapter 11 is the increasingly important role of volunteers and paraprofessionals who become involved in correctional work. Some of the legal liabilities of volunteers and paraprofessionals will be examined. Also, more offenders with special needs are being supervised, both in institutions and communities. Clients with special needs include those who are alcohol or drug-dependent, the mentally ill, sex offenders, those with AIDS and other communicable diseases, and offenders with various physical handicaps. Communities have been responsive to meeting these offender needs in diverse ways.

Chapter 12 is an examination of women in corrections. Nearly 10 percent of all inmates and probationers/parolees are women. Women's prisons are generally different from male facilities in several important ways. Also, female offenders have different needs compared with their male counterparts. Some of the major differences in male and female inmates and clients will be examined. Included are selected issues relating to women's prisons, such as the problem of inmate-mothers, vocational/educational programs for women, and the general problem of co-correctional facilities.

Juvenile corrections is described in Chapter 13. A brief overview of the juvenile justice system is presented, together with the leading cases that have shaped it over the years. Various types of community corrections programs for juveniles are discussed, together with probation and parole programs and revocation actions.

As helpful study aids at the ends of chapters, questions are included that are designed to assist students in reviewing important chapter features. These questions are also useful as a means of studying chapter contents and learning important concepts and issues. Key terms important to all aspects of corrections have been boldfaced throughout each chapter. Additionally, these key terms have been defined and listed in a comprehensive glossary at the end of the book. Each chapter also contains several contemporary suggested readings for those desiring to learn more about specific chapter subject topics, for class report or paper writing and/or preparation, or for general research investigations on particular subjects. An extensive reference section is also included. Students will find these references helpful in their own research projects on various corrections topics. Finally, several important Internet sites have been listed at chapter ends to assist students in looking up important information and maximizing their learning through online means. Almost all of these sites have important links to other interesting locations on the growing cyberhighway.

Acknowledgments

The author wishes to thank the following persons for their assistance in the development of this project. I would like to thank Frank Mortimer, my editor, for his support of my ideas and proposed projects over the years. Also to be thanked is my former editor, Kim Davies, who was one of my strongest advocates. Her work and keen eye for critical details were vital to the quality of my earlier editions. My production editor, Karen Berry, has offered considerable assistance and advice as the work has progressed from final draft to the published book. Overseeing any textbook is a tedious and often thankless task, since most of this work is behind the scenes. Usually, only the book's author is intimately familiar with the meticulous details that must be addressed by production editors and their assistants as the book moves forward to publication. Also, a special thanks goes to Sarah Holle, the assistant editor who is the key facilitator throughout the entire production process. Sarah is a master troubleshooter and problem solver who has done an admirable job in seeing this project through to its completion. Finally, I would like to thank the reviewers of this fourth edition who have made valuable comments and suggestions to affect the nature and contents of the present edition. These reviewers are Barbara Sims, Pennsylvania State University, Harrisburg, PA; David McElreath, Washington University, Topeka, KS; and Michael Perna, Broome Community College, Johnson City, NY.

Dean John Champion
Laredo, TX

About the Author

Dean John Champion is Professor of Criminal Justice, Texas A & M International University, Laredo, Texas. Dr. Champion has taught at the University of Tennessee-Knoxville, California State University-Long Beach, and Minot State University. He earned his Ph.D. from Purdue University and B.S. and M.A. degrees from Brigham Young University. He also completed several years of law school at the Nashville School of Law.

Dr. Champion has written over thirty texts and/or edited works and maintains memberships in eleven professional organizations. He is a lifetime member of the American Society of Criminology, Academy of Criminal Justice Sciences, and the American Sociological Association. He is a former editor of the ACJS/Anderson Series on *Issues in Crime and Justice* (1993–1996) and the *Journal of Crime and Justice* (1995–1998). He was a contributing author for the *Encarta Encyclopedia 2000* for Microsoft. He was the Visiting Scholar for the National Center for Juvenile Justice and president of the Midwestern Criminal Justice Association.

Among his published books for Prentice-Hall include *Basic Statistics for Social Research* (1970, 1981); *Research Methods for Criminal Justice and Criminology* (1993, 2000); *The Juvenile Justice System: Delinquency, Processing, and the Law* (1992, 1998, 2001, 2004); *Corrections in the United States: A Contemporary Perspective* (1990, 1998, 2001); *Probation, Parole, and Community Corrections* (1990, 1996, 1999, 2002); and *Policing in the Community* (with George Rush) (1996). Works from other publishers include *The Sociology of Organizations* (McGraw-Hill, 1975); *Research Methods in Social Relations* (John Wiley & Sons, Inc., 1976); *Sociology* (Holt, Rinehart, and Winston, 1984); *The U.S.*

Sentencing Guidelines (Praeger Publishers, 1989); *Juvenile Transfer Hearings* (with G. Larry Mays) (Praeger Publishers, 1991); and *Measuring Offender Risk* (Greenwood Press, 1994); *The Roxbury Dictionary of Criminal Justice: Key Terms and Leading Supreme Court Cases* (Roxbury Press, 1997, 2001); *Criminal Justice in the United States, 2/e* (Wadsworth, 1998), and *Police Misconduct in America: A Sourcebook* (ABC-CLIO, 2001). Dr. Champion's primary research interests relate to attorney use in juvenile justice proceedings and plea bargaining.

CHAPTER 1 | *An Introduction to Corrections: Philosophy, Goals, and History*

London's Bridewell was similar to a debtor's prison. It confined both children and adult "vagrants."

Chapter Objectives	*As the result of reading this chapter, the following objectives should be realized:*

1. Defining corrections and specifying those agencies and organizations within the corrections rubric.
2. Identifying the goals of corrections.
3. Describing the early origins of corrections and the subsequent development of modern correctional enterprises in the United States.
4. Describing several popular correctional models that have been used as patterns for modern correctional systems and treatment programs.
5. Identifying several important correctional reforms that have shaped modern-day corrections.

INTRODUCTION

• *It was a hot day in July. The Southern prison was not air conditioned. It was designed to hold 1,500 inmates, although the actual number of confined inmates was in excess of 2,000. A crew of inmates had just returned from working in the fields, clearing the land of rocks and other debris. They were hot, sweaty, and thirsty. A correctional officer allegedly made a snide remark to one new inmate who had bloody blisters on his hands: "You think you're a tough guy. Tough guys don't get blisters. Don't worry, though. A few months of this work will give you a man's hands, although from the looks of you, you wouldn't deserve them." Other inmates who heard the remark rushed the correctional officer and quickly overpowered him. Word quickly spread throughout the prison about what the officer had said to the inmate, and the rumors became more distorted. By the end of the day, a full-fledged riot had broken out, and it took a good twelve hours for order to be restored. As a part of the negotiations, the warden promised air conditioners for the individual cell blocks. Three other correctional officers who had been taken hostage were released unharmed. No charges were placed against any of the rioting inmates. It was just another hot day in a Southern prison.* [Adapted from the Associated Press, "Guard's Remark about Inmate Blisters Sparks 12-Hour Riot," July 15, 2001].

• *The judge actually apologized. During the sentencing of a convicted offender with a record of five prior violent offenses, including rape and aggravated assault, the judge said, "You deserve to be imprisoned for at least ten years on this charge. You are a violent predator, and I have no doubt that you will strike again. But right now, there's no room in the system for you. I'm going to sentence you to three years' of intensive probation supervision, with electronic monitoring, with instructions to the probation department to keep a close eye on you. Maybe they can keep you out of trouble for three years. I seriously doubt it, but we'll give it a try." The 31-year-old offender, convicted of simple robbery, was released and ordered to report to the probation department. Another violent habitual offender would be turned loose on California streets.* [Adapted from the Associated Press, "Career Criminal Gets Three Years' Probation for Robbery," July 3, 2002].

• *"Your honor, in my own behalf, I just want to say that I only stole two slices of pizza. I didn't hurt anybody. I don't think I deserve a ten-year sentence for this crime." The comments from the convicted offender fell on deaf ears. The judge imposed the ten-year sentence anyway, because it was the law. The offender had previously been convicted of sixteen separate felonies, mostly property crimes. His crime spree had occurred throughout eight states, and he had done time in at least seven different state prisons for various terms. This time, however, he chose to commit his crime, armed robbery, in Minnesota, where he had been convicted of three prior property offenses. Under Minnesota's habitual offender statute, the judge has the discretion to impose a sentence of life imprisonment for repeat offenders who are convicted of felonies. The judge said, "You didn't need to steal pizza at the point of a gun. You had other options if you were hungry. Armed robbery is no excuse. And I don't care if it was $2 worth of pizza or a $1 million. You've been convicted and you're going to do the time."* [Adapted from the Associated Press, "Pizza Robbery Nets Robber Ten Years," December 13, 2001].

These scenarios are indicative of a nationwide crisis that is growing in its seriousness. Chronically overcrowded and old-fashioned prisons are contributing to inmate frustration over the conditions of confinement. Prison and jail overcrowding is correlated highly with growing prison violence. Despite the best efforts of correctional administrators to remedy existing problems with older prisons and jails, the fact is that there are insufficient funds to bring many of these facilities into compliance with contemporary guidelines for inmate security and safety.

Another problem facing corrections is that many offenders who should be incarcerated for committing serious crimes are being placed on probation. California is one of a growing number of states that has little or no room to house rising numbers of serious felons. Despite their personal feelings and the laws they are sworn to uphold and implement, judges must often sentence serious convicts to probation and community corrections rather than institutionalize them. There simply is not enough existing prison space to accommodate newly convicted offenders. And in some states where prison overcrowding is not as chronic as it is in California, some felons who commit relatively minor offenses are incarcerated for extraordinarily long periods, given the nature of their instant offenses.

Corrections is in trouble and haunted by many problems. And these problems are getting worse. One pervasive and continuing problem is jail and prison overcrowding. As overcrowding both continues and increases, other jail and prison problems are created and/or aggravated. The annual growth rate of offenders entering correctional facilities and institutions each year is considerably greater than the growth rate of the U.S. population.

By the beginning of 2002, 6.6 million persons were under some form of correctional supervision in the United States. This compares with 5.1 million persons who were under some form of correctional supervision in 1994 and 6 million persons in 1997 (Glaze 2002, 1). About 32 percent (1.96 million) of these persons were incarcerated in jails and prisons. The offender population has been growing about 3.6 percent per year. Supervising these offenders were over 650,000 personnel in adult and juvenile corrections (American Correctional Association 2002). About 40 percent of these were correctional officers working in prisons and jails, and about 10 percent of all personnel worked in juvenile corrections. There were 2,725 administrators of adult and juvenile correctional facilities (American Correctional Association 2002).

Whatever the causes of crime, our courts are glutted with record numbers of criminal cases, and U.S. prisons and jails are well above their maximum capacities. On the average in 2001, state prisons were operating on the average of 107.2 percent of their rated capacities. Even the Federal Bureau of Prisons was operating at 131.2 percent of its rated capacity in 2001 (Camp and Camp 2002, 86). Many local, state, and federal incarcerative facilities are under federal court order to reduce their inmate populations to more healthy and safe levels. Most correctional programs and facilities are inadequately staffed and underfunded. One result is that offenders frequently leave these programs without receiving proper treatment or assistance and quickly return to crime as a way of life. Thus, a vicious cycle recurs to perpetuate and aggravate many types of correctional problems.

This chapter is an introduction to corrections in the United States and has three objectives. First, corrections is defined and a brief history of corrections is presented. The early origins of corrections are described, together with an overview of correction's critical components. Influencing corrections in the United States was a strong religious influence that was pervasive in early English correctional systems. Social and economic conditions of earlier times have also influenced the nature and direction of present-day corrections in the United States. The views of several important criminological theorists, philosophers, and social reformers are presented as they pertain to correctional philosophy. Since the inception of the United States, corrections has undergone significant transformation. Important stages or eras in U.S. correctional development are described, including the formation of various organizations that subsequently developed contemporary policies related to offender treatment.

Second, several contrasting correctional philosophies are described. Generally, corrections is guided by several important models. These models pertain to retribution, deterrence or prevention, incapacitation or isolation, rehabilitation, reintegration, and control. Depending upon the theme that is most dominant in any given era, political interests have oriented themselves toward offenders in particular ways. These relationships are explored briefly.

Several important functions of corrections are outlined and discussed, together with an examination of certain correctional alternatives and reforms. These models suggest ways of approaching the problem of crime and its causes, including various strategies that might be useful in reducing or preventing crime. Correctional models are best understood in particular contexts. Thus, various important subdivisions of corrections are discussed in a broad overview. Institutional corrections, which includes jails and prisons, is described. In contrast, community corrections is presented and discussed briefly. The chapter concludes with an examination of several correctional reforms. These reforms relate to changing sentencing practices, the appropriateness of particular punishments, and architectural and operational features of prison and jail systems.

CORRECTIONS DEFINED

The term **corrections** means many different things to the average citizen. Some of these connotations have created several myths about what corrections is and does. Ideally, criminals assigned to correctional agencies are "corrected." That is, they are punished and reformed. However, a significant part of corrections is unrelated to punishment or reformation. In fact, some investigators question whether any correctional institution corrects or reforms (Sarre 2001).

Corrections is the vast number of persons, agencies, and organizations that manage accused, convicted, or adjudicated criminal offenders and juveniles (Utting and Vennard 2000). Although prisons and jails are the most visible correctional institutions, the vast majority of correctional personnel, agencies, and organizations are less obvious and blend in with many other community agencies and organizations. A fifth of all convicted criminals are placed in jails and prisons. The remainder of all offenders are involved as **clients** in a variety of community programs and services that manage offenders in different ways. When prison **inmates** are granted early release from incarceration or paroled, or if convicted offenders are given nonincarcerative sentences, such as probation, they are usually supervised by **parole officers,** probation officers, or public and private agencies for varying periods (Alarid and Cromwell 2002). These offenders live within the community, lead reasonably normal lives, are employed in diverse occupations or professions, support their dependents, and otherwise blend in with other community residents. The conditions of their supervision (e.g., observance of curfews, periodic drug or alcohol tests, and random checks of their residences) are only a few of the unobtrusive program rules and regulations that differentiate them from others in their communities.

The services provided by correctional agencies are diverse (Byrne, Byrne, and Howells 2001). While correctional institutions manage primarily those persons convicted of crimes, other categories of offenders are supervised as well. Those charged with minor offenses (e.g., shoplifting, petty theft, vandalism, public drunkenness) in some communities may be placed in **diversion programs.** These programs are usually operated by correctional employees and are designed to monitor program participants for short probationary periods. If offenders in these programs obey the rules and comply with all conditions of their diversion programs, they usually avoid further involvement with prosecutors and the courts and their records are often expunged (Kelly et al. 2001).

When persons are arrested by **law enforcement officers** for more serious crimes or for violations of local ordinances such as loitering or freeway hitchhiking, they are usually confined in jails temporarily for investigation and released, or they may be charged with one or more crimes. Sometimes important witnesses are housed in jails until they are called to testify in criminal trials. When juveniles are arrested or cited for whatever reason, they, too, may be placed in jails or detention facilities temporarily until their disposition can be properly managed by juvenile authorities. Thus, corrections is not limited to the management of adult offenders (Houston 2001).

Despite public relations campaigns and the mass distribution of informative materials by correctional officials and organizations, offenders and the programs designed to manage and help them both inside and outside of prison walls are grossly misunderstood by many citizens. Few people want prisons in their communities, and even fewer citizens like the idea of having community-based offender services operating in their neighborhoods to house criminals while they are on work release, **furloughs,** parole, or probation (Gowen 2001). Some citizens are terrified by the idea of criminals roaming freely within their communities.

Arrests of suspects begin the criminal justice process, which may lead to convictions for serious offenses.

EARLY ORIGINS OF CORRECTIONS

Imprisonment as a punishment is found in ancient Greece and Rome. In 640 B.C., the **Mamertine Prison** was constructed by Ancus Martius. This was a vast series of dungeons constructed under the main sewer of Rome called the *Cloaca Maxima,* and it housed a variety of offenders. In addition to this facility, rock quarries and strong cages were often used by the Romans and others to incarcerate political dissidents, social misfits, and criminals (Farrington 1996). Particularly targeted for incarceration in subsequent centuries in Europe and throughout the rest of the modern world were the poor and political dissidents. Today, a similar pattern exists, according to some observers (Wacquant 2001). Viewed within a neoliberal framework, social disorders that are created among the lower classes of society are managed and regulated to an extent through incarceration. Although this is not a widely held position, it does furnish us with at least one explanation for why some discrimination according to social class is leveled against U.S. penal systems and why our corrections systems are sometimes considered to be prisons of poverty (Wacquant 2001).

Religion and Corrections

The role of religion in the development of prisons and punishments throughout the world is particularly evident from ancient times through the Middle Ages (U.K. Home Office 2001). The Spanish Inquisition, a religious tribunal reorganized after earlier thirteenth century inquisitions to suppress and punish nonconformists for assorted heresies, existed for many years and was widely feared as a severe sanctioning medium. Joan of Arc (1412–1431) was an early victim of such inquisitions and was burned at the stake for alleged witchcraft. She had professed to have visions from God instructing her to lead the French people away from British occupation and control. A bothersome troublemaker for the British (a fact that was more likely the reason for her execution than allegations of witchcraft), Joan of Arc was pronounced innocent by the Pope in 1456, and she was declared a saint in 1920 (Thomas 1995).

Religious institutions have influenced the structure and functioning of punishment systems in many countries throughout the world including the United States (Brettschneider 2001). Religious nonconformists were often confined in dungeons for long periods in order to induce them to recant their dissident religious beliefs. The Apostle Paul was confined under a type of house arrest, during which time he was given the opportunity of repenting and appealing to his captors for forgiveness. Until the Middle Ages, wrongs committed against the state and citizens were frequently handled privately under the principle of *lex talionis* or the law of retribution or retaliation. Revenge was the usual remedy, particularly during the feudal period.

During the Middle Ages, particularly in Scotland and England, the first examples of what are currently recognized as elements of contemporary corrections began to appear. Although there was little administrative organization or coordination among cities and counties and their incarcerative facilities, large numbers of debtors' prisons existed to confine those who couldn't pay their bills. Many debtors died in prison, either because they or their families or friends were unable to pay for their release. Debtors' prisons were not correctional institutions in any sense, primarily because no efforts were made by guards and others to correct or rehabilitate the inmates.

These penal facilities also housed social misfits and criminals and were exclusively designed to segregate them from society. Again, no consideration was given to offender treatment or rehabilitation. These early institutions were principally custodial. Conditions under which prisoners were confined were miserable, inasmuch as it was deemed wasteful to feed and clothe outlaws who were either going to die a natural death or be executed anyway. The Church of England was particularly adept at punishing persons for vague crimes such as offenses against morality. Thus, it is important to recognize that early uses of prisons and other incarcerative facilities were exclusively punishment-centered and not synonymous with what is currently meant by corrections.

Scottish and English prisons eventually were transformed into profitable enterprises by influential mercantile interests. In the 1500s houses of correction were nothing more than slave labor camps designed to exploit prison labor and produce marketable goods cheaply. **Bridewell Workhouse** was established in 1557 to house London's undesirables, although more often than not, this facility and others like it were designed to train prisoners to acquire special skills and where they would labor as craftsmen in the service of private interests (Roberts 1997). This thinly disguised private profiteering was passed off as work for the development and improvement of an offender's social skills and moral habits. Interestingly, whenever there was an excess in the labor supply, execution was often used as a punishment. In later years, England transported many vagrants, petty criminals, and dissidents to the American colonies as **indentured servants.** Indentured servants were obligated to work for certain wealthy businessmen for seven-year periods. In some respects, indentured servants were the voluntary equivalent of the involuntary slave pattern that emerged in the United States in the early 1800s. However, indentured servants entered into these servile work arrangements for a period of years in exchange for the cost of their passage to the American colonies. After their period of servitude, they were granted freedom, whereas black slaves and their offspring remained slaves for life or until slavery was abolished at the end of the Civil War.

Banishment and Other Punishments

Banishment. Regardless of the primitiveness of any society, sanctions have always been applied against offenders who violate societal rules. Imprisonment has not always been the primary punishment of choice in most social systems. In Biblical times, **banishment** was frequently used and often amounted to capital punishment. Food and shelter would be denied those banished within a distance of 400 or 500 miles, thus dooming them to certain death. In later centuries, banishment was used for other purposes. Probably the first recorded case where banishment was used as a punishment was Adam and Eve (Duff and Garland 1994).

During the eighteenth and nineteenth centuries, banishment was used as a punishment in various Chinese provinces, such as Xinjiang (Waley-Cohen 1991). The Chinese ranked banishment second only to death as the most serious punishment they could impose. Eventually, the Chinese used banishment as a form of colonization for newly discovered regions. The use of convicts as colonists was also economically expedient, since China could profit from low-cost colonial goods.

Banishment has also been used in more recent times. In 1993, for instance, two Everett, Washington, teenagers, Simon Roberts and Adrian Guthrie, were banished to a desolate Alaska island for several months as their punishment for a 1993 robbery (Associated Press 1994, A7). Tlingit Indian tribal law governing these youths decreed that banishment should be imposed, and the courts did not intervene to prevent their banishment. The youths were forced to live in one-room cabins heated with wood-burning stoves. They were given shotguns, an ax, a pitchfork, a knife, and some other basic tools to survive off of the land. They ate wild foods supplemented by fish and canned food. The banishment and solitary living was intended to transform them and cause them to feel remorse and regret. Additionally, a milder form of banishment is **parental banishment,** where some parents of delinquent youths have expelled children from their homes more or less permanently. This "Don't come home again!" phenomenon is occurring with increasing frequency.

Transportation.   During the post-Reformation period and the next few centuries, England found it practical to export large numbers of prisoners to their possessions in remote parts of the world through banishment. Between 1600 and 1776, England exported thieves, vagrants, political undesirables, and religious dissidents to the American colonies through **transportation,** a form of banishment (Lynn and Armstrong 1996). Although estimates vary, 2,000 or more convicts were transported to the American colonies during this period.

Transportation was either a temporary or permanent removal of an offender from England, coupled with a condition that the offender would never return to England or would not return within a specified time period. When the American colonies separated from British domination, England sought other locations to banish some of their offenders. From 1788 to 1868, over 160,000 prisoners were exiled through banishment or transportation to Australia or Africa for work in labor colonies (Strange 1996).

Corporal Punishment.   Besides banishment, England and many other countries used **corporal punishments** as sanctions for various offenses. Corporal punishment is the infliction of pain on the body by any device or method. Corporal punishment included branding, flogging, dismemberment, stretching on a device known as the rack, and other forms of mutilation. Pickpockets and thieves often had their hands cut off and adulterers would be branded with the letter "A" on their arms or faces. Perjurers or liars would lose their tongues. Stocks and pillories were also used for the public display of offenders. Stocks and pillories were wooden frames through which one's head and hands would protrude. Offenders would be made to stand in these devices for several days for such obscure offenses as lying or spousal disobedience. Execution was also a common sanction for minor offenses. In the early 1800s, England used the death penalty as punishment for over 200 crimes, ranging in seriousness from murder to disturbing the peace (Duff and Garland 1994).

Early penal philosophy stressed punishment for deterrence, retribution, and revenge. Theoretically, potential wrongdoers in France would be deterred from crime if they believed there was a good chance they would be caught and beheaded by the guillotine. Ideally, prospective thieves, robbers, and murderers would be deterred if they knew corporal punishments would be inflicted such as mutilation or death. Convicted offenders suffering corporal tortures would think seriously about the unpleasant consequences if they should commit new offenses. In the United States today, capital punishment in two-thirds of all states exists, in part as a form of vengeance against those who kill others. While the deterrent value of capital punishment is questionable, the vengeance and retribution functions of the death penalty are undeniable.

Enlightenment and Social Reforms

During the 1700s and early 1800s, several French, English, and Italian philosophers and social reformers achieved prominence through their criticisms of corporal punishments. One of the more influential humanitarians was the Frenchman **Montesquieu** (Charles-Louis de Secondat, Baron de La Brede et de Montesquieu, 1689–1755). He was a lawyer, philosopher, and writer whose book, *The Spirit of the Laws*, criticized the French penal code and inhuman punishments suffered by prisoners. Montesquieu believed that punishments should fit the crimes committed and that more humane conditions should be provided for incarcerated offenders.

Another French philosopher and social critic, **Voltaire** (François-Marie Arouet Voltaire, 1694–1778), was appalled by French injustices meted out to criminals. Voltaire believed that judges were capricious in their sentencing practices. Secret trials were conducted and equal protection under the law for citizens was nonexistent. A less influential French encyclopedist and anarchist, Denis Diderot (1713–1784), also campaigned strongly for political penal reforms he believed to be cruel and inhuman.

English penal philosophy during the late 1700s was influenced by **Jeremy Bentham** (1748–1832). Bentham's work, *An Introduction to the Principles and Morals of Legislation*, described a scheme where the punishment inflicted would offset the pleasure offenders achieved from their crimes. His hedonistic reasoning was that criminals engage in crime for pleasure. Thus, a utilitarian philosophy would be useful in deterring crime by minimizing or eliminating the pleasures offenders derived from wrongdoing. Criminals would therefore calculate the gains and losses or pleasures and pains associated with criminal conduct. Offenders would be deterred from crime by rational thought, since they would believe that punishment would likely be swift, certain, and painful. Bentham also advocated several reforms and architectural changes that are still used today. He pioneered the panopticon or circular design for prisons where correctional officers may monitor many offenders from one central location (Skolnick 1995).

The most influential writer of that period was **Cesare Beccaria** (Cesare Bonesana, Marchese di Beccaria, 1738–1794), an Italian jurist and economist. Beccaria developed the **classical school of criminology.** The classical school is a synthesis of penal philosophies that derive largely from Montesquieu and Voltaire. This philosophy assumes that persons are rational beings, act on the basis of reason and intelligence, and are capable of being responsible for their own behavior. Accordingly, punishment should be rational and fitting for whatever crimes are committed. Like Voltaire, Beccaria was aware of judicial tyranny and injustice and the torturous corporal punishments that included dismemberment, branding, stoning, and crucifixion. Beccaria's work, *An Essay on Crimes and Punishments*, contained the basic elements of the classical school (Beirne 1994). These include:

1. The best approach to crime is prevention rather than punishment. Prevention is maximized by establishing legal codes that define prohibited behaviors and the punishments for them.

2. Law serves the needs of society rather than enforce moral virtues. Therefore, law should be limited only to the most serious offenses.

3. All persons should be considered innocent until proven guilty.

4. Punishment should be swift and certain, with no regard for offender personalities or social characteristics.

5. Since those who violate the law should be punished, their punishment should be retributive. The degree of retribution should fit the seriousness of the crime.

Several of Beccaria's principles have been incorporated into the present-day jurisprudence of many countries. When his ideas were first suggested, they were considered antithetical toward the existing legal system. Legal rights and privileges were most often extended to those with wealth, property, and political influence, while those without wealth or political power were often denied the same rights. Many of the founders of the U.S. Constitution were influenced by Beccaria's ideas, and the statutory language of some of our current criminal laws reflect Beccaria's thinking (Hirsch 1992).

In this context of social and legal inequality, Beccaria may not have been quite the humanitarian he appeared to be. Some observers have suggested that Beccaria's classical school of criminology advocated equal access to legal rights primarily for the purpose of controlling citizen unrest and preventing revolution. Interestingly, the radical school of criminology and penology argues that basic inequalities continue today as they existed during the time of Beccaria, and for many of the same reasons (Beirne 1994). The radical view is that economic and political groups create laws that perpetuate their possession of wealth and property and preserve the socioeconomic status quo.

Regardless of their motives, Beccaria and Voltaire were instrumental in shaping the future correctional policies and philosophies of several countries including the United States. Also influential in bringing about major correctional changes were religious groups such as the Quakers. Additionally, corporal punishments had failed to reduce crime or to deter offenders from committing new offenses.

THE HISTORY OF CORRECTIONS IN THE UNITED STATES

There are several uniquely American innovations associated with corrections in the United States. However, many U.S. penal practices were also derived from procedures and policies developed by other countries. The system of punishments used during the American colonial period was patterned after English penal methods, largely because most colonists emigrated from England and continued those punishment practices most familiar to them. However, there were several important differences. England continued to execute large numbers of misfits and political and religious nonconformists because of their labor supply excesses, while the American colonies reserved execution only for the most serious offenses. The colonists perpetuated the pillory, flogging, mutilations, branding, and even banishment (to the West known as the wilderness) as corporal solutions to crime and as sanctions for other forms of deviant behavior. Banishment to the Western territories meant almost certain death at the hands of hostile Indians who dominated these territories and were intolerant of intruders.

The colonists used a variety of corporal punishments. One punishment was the **ducking stool,** where offenders were placed in a chair at the end of a long lever and dunked in a nearby pond until they almost drowned. These offenders were often town gossips or wife beaters. Branding irons were also used to brand both serious criminals and petty offenders. Thieves were branded with a "T," while drunkards were branded with a "D" (Roberts 1997).

These punishments continued to be used in the colonies until the Quaker and founder of Pennsylvania, **William Penn,** commenced several correctional reforms in 1682. Under the **Great Law of Pennsylvania,** Penn abolished corporal punishments and gradually introduced fines and incarceration in facilities known as jails, named after their **gaol** (pronounced *jail*) British counterparts. Penn commissioned each county in Pennsylvania to establish jails to accommodate offenders. Local constables or **sheriffs** were appointed to administer these county jails.

The sheriff concept emerged in the aftermath of the Norman Conquest, the conquest of England by the Normans in 1066. William the Conqueror introduced the feudal system, which lasted for several centuries. During this period, England counties known as **shires** were administered by **reeves** or political appointees. Reeves collected the taxes, kept the peace, and operated gaols on behalf of the King. In effect, each shire had a reeve or peace officer, and eventually these terms combined into sheriff (**shire-reeve**). Today the sheriff designation denotes the chief law enforcement officer of many U.S. counties in different states.

Penn's ideas about correctional reform were unpopular with Pennsylvanians, and when Penn died in 1718, his colony quickly reverted to corporal punishment. Pillories were reestablished, floggings and lashings were reinstituted, and other corporal punishments were reintroduced. Every colony practiced these punishment methods for many decades preceding the Revolutionary War.

Adamson (1984) divides penal developments in the United States after 1790 into six distinct periods. These are:

1. The post-revolutionary period, 1790–1812
2. The recession following the War of 1812
3. The Jacksonian period, 1812–1837
4. The mid-century period, 1837–1860
5. The post-bellum South, 1865–1890
6. The industrial Northeast, 1890–1914

These periods coincide with U.S. economic, political, and social conditions and trends. Prison policies were often modified as the demand for cheap labor increased. In fact, many early jails and prisons in the United States were designed to exploit prisoners and secure forced slave labor. Profits from prison labor often were diverted to wealthy interests and the private sector. Prisoners were given sufficient food for survival and strength to produce goods for others.

An example of private profiteering from prison labor is North Carolina's state prison operations during the period 1741–1868. Private business interests were largely in control of North Carolina inmates, because both state and local governments attempted to evade the responsibility for their confinement and maintenance. From the end of the Civil War to 1933, the responsibility for containing North Carolina's inmate population gradually shifted from private enterprises to state legislature–approved operations, although prison labor continued to be exploited by North Carolina as a revenue source. However, North Carolina was not alone in its prison exploitation of inmate labor. Oklahoma and Louisiana were two of several other states that had histories of exploiting prisoner labor, not only for greater revenue, but also for political patronage (Hawkins 1984).

These periods delineated by Adamson (1984) do not necessarily mean that in 1790, for instance, suddenly there were major changes in prison construction and operations in the post-revolutionary period. Rather, they are general date ranges which encompassed several penal reforms. In fact, a review of relevant literature shows that several different historians and penologists have devised their own date categories to emphasize particular reforms or penal developments. For example, Frank Schmalleger and John Smykla (2001, 193–196) have distinguished nine stages of prison development. Some of these stages parallel those outlined above by Adamson. But Schmalleger and Smykla offer considerably more detail, referring to specific events in prison development in the time periods they have designated. Their stages are:

Penitentiary Era (1790–1825): Construction of at least thirty state prisons, as well as large jails in Philadelphia and other large cities.

Mass Prison Era (1825–1876): At least thirty-five more prisons were constructed, mainly as warehouses for criminals; little thought given to rehabilitation or reintegration.

Reformatory Era (1876–1890): Invention of reformatories in various jurisdictions, where emphasis was placed on rehabilitating prisoners and teaching them marketable skills.

Industrial Era (1890–1935): Characterized by use of prison labor to manufacture cheap goods for public consumption.

Punitive Era (1935–1945): Emphasis on maximum-security prisons with a focus upon inmate isolation and control.

Treatment Era (1945–1967): Greater differentiation among prisoners according to their needs; attention given to different types of prisoners with particular problems that could be treated through individual or group therapy, counseling, or vocational/educational training.

Community-Based Era (1967–1980): Emphasis upon community corrections and the use of community resources to meet social, economic, and psychological needs of less serious offenders; focus upon community reintegration.

Warehousing Era (1980–1995): Focus of prisons upon containment and control of large numbers of inmates; overcrowded conditions and limited access to programs and services for rehabilitation.

Just Deserts Era (1995–present): Due process is emphasized, as well as deserved punishment, as states and the federal government seek to equate the punishment with the seriousness of the crime committed.

Although the eras profiled by Schmalleger and Smykla are more detailed than most, they serve to highlight the general weaknesses of *all* "era" schemes. For instance, the community-based era did not end in 1980. Rather, there is widespread interest in community-based correctional programming, and it is growing today at a phenomenal rate in the United States. Also, we have been in a warehousing era since the 1700s. It is interesting to compare the industrial era with the warehousing era. The industrial era was characterized with a growing incidence of prisoner labor. This era did not end in 1935. Prison industries and prisoner-made goods are operating at an all-time high. However, only about 20 percent of all U.S. prisoners qualify for or become involved in prison labor. There is simply not enough work for all prisoners to do in all prisons. Thus, inmate idleness is the norm rather than inmate industriousness. The vast majority of prison and jail inmates, therefore, do not perform jobs in prisons. They are warehoused, and in some respects, just as they were during the late 1700s and 1800s.

We also remain in a treatment era, where considerable time and attention are devoted to classifying offenders and assigning them to programs and services where their needs can be met. Since the 1940s, we have been in a just deserts era, as inmates in various state and federal institutions have successfully won lawsuits against prison officials and institutions. The rights of prisoners are a very important part of the prison landscape today. The American Civil Liberties Union and Amnesty International, Inc. have been two of the more visible organizational advocates for fair treatment of prisoners. Substantial sentencing reforms have occurred since the 1960s, and many jurisdictions are currently experimenting with diverse sentencing methods geared to equate punishment with offense seriousness.

In all fairness to Schmalleger and Smykla, as well as to Adamson, it should be noted that these eras are merely designed to categorize time periods during which particular events have been emphasized. Thus, there is much overlap among these eras, with some special events continuing rather than terminating.

At the federal level, offender sentences in early U.S. district courts were served in their entirety. Early release from prison was unknown. However, between 1790 and 1815, the federal inmate population escalated, and prison officials were faced with a dilemma that continues to be the most serious corrections problem: overcrowding. Soon, federal district judges were permitting prison administrators to grant prisoners early release or **parole,** simply to make room for new and more serious prisoners. Sometimes prison administrators made these decisions on their own without court approval. State prisons and local jails were both experiencing overcrowding problems during this period, despite the fact that by 1840 the national inmate population was only 4,000. Thirty years later, in 1870, the national inmate population had grown to 33,000, which meant that there were about 83 inmates for every 100,000 persons in the United States. Prison and jail construction had not kept pace with the growing inmate population.

The **National Prison Association** was founded in 1870, with **Rutherford B. Hayes** (a later U.S. president) selected as its first president. Its name was later changed to the **American Prison Association.** By 1954, as its membership increased, it was eventually renamed the **American Correctional Association (ACA)** (Roberts 1997). By 2002, the ACA had a membership of over 31,000 members, more than triple the 10,000 members enrolled about a decade earlier in 1992 (American Correctional Association 2002; telephone communication, September, 2002). These members represent a cross-section of many corrections-related professions, including correctional officers, teachers, prison and jail administrators, probation/parole officers, and court personnel. When originally formulated, the goals of the ACA were to (1) provide technical assistance to correctional institutions, (2) provide training and publications to any interested agency, (3) work toward establishing a national correctional philosophy, and (4) design and implement high correctional standards and services (Roberts 1997).

Probation and parole were established as nonincarcerative strategies for managing offenders during the early 1800s. Evidence of the early use of parole is found in the 1820s, while probation was used informally during the 1830s in selected jurisdictions. By 1944, all states had parole. Parole is the early release of inmates from incarcerative sentences that were originally imposed by judges. This decision is usually, though not always, made by parole boards consisting of prison administrators, other correctional personnel, and prison psychiatrists or group counselors. Probation is a sentence in lieu of incarceration. Offenders are assigned to **probation officers** or to community programs where they must comply with several stringent conditions. Probationers are responsible to judges for their conduct during their probation period, while parolees are accountable to the parole boards.

Today corrections is at a crossroads (Sarre 2001). Rising crime rates together with numerous correctional experiments have led some professionals to conclude that nothing works. The late Robert Martinson (1976) noted caustically that the history of corrections is a graveyard of abandoned fads. His own disenchantment with the current state-of-the-art in corrections has generated much debate among correctional professionals and others about the proper role of corrections in the United States. In order to understand the debate and why it persists, several contrasting and often competing correctional philosophies must be examined.

CORRECTIONAL FUNCTIONS AND GOALS

Most authorities agree that corrections oversees the punishment of criminals. However, disagreement persists about how and why offenders should be punished. Several functions of corrections have been identified. These include (1) retribution, (2) deterrence or prevention, (3) incapacitation or isolation, (4) rehabilitation, (5) reintegration, and (6) control.

Retribution

Retribution or revenge is probably the oldest goal of corrections. It is rooted in the ancient doctrine of *lex talionis* or an eye for an eye and a tooth for a tooth. Retribution means getting even. The death penalty is the ultimate retribution, and it has been used in many countries as retribution for serious crimes such as murder and kidnapping. As we have seen in nineteenth-century England, many less serious offenses such as theft and burglary were punishable by death (Cavadino and Dignan 1997).

Corporal punishments practiced by England and the American colonies were based on retribution. Among Beccaria's complaints about the legal system was that, often, punishments imposed for crimes far exceeded the seriousness of them. The major character in the novel, *Les Miserables*, was sentenced to twenty years' hard labor for stealing a loaf of bread to feed his starving family. This and other fictional portrayals of punishments in the 1700s and 1800s were real reflections of life in those times.

The **retributionist philosophy** is apparent in the sentencing practices of contemporary U.S. courts, decisions of state legislatures, and rules and regulations of various correctional programs. Restitution, fines, and victim compensation for losses, pain, and suffering resulting from crimes are common punishments in many jurisdictions. Offenders are required to perform hundreds of hours of public service as restitution to the state in partial payment for the losses resulting from their crimes. Although it is not invoked on a large scale, the death penalty is used in many states as the punishment for first-degree murder. The Florida execution of serial murder Ted Bundy in January 1989 was hailed by many of the families of his victims as just punishment. However, other relatives of his victims were opposed to death as a punishment for Bundy on any grounds. Thus, there is considerable disagreement about whether this punishment form should be used as a retributive criminal sanction (Pojman and Reiman 1998).

Deterrence or Prevention

Another goal of punishment is **deterrence.** The rationale underlying deterrence is that if punishment is sufficiently severe enough for crimes, offenders will be deterred from committing those crimes. Thus, **prevention** is a major concomitant of deterrence. However, extensive research on the severity of punishment as a deterrent to crime has been disappointing. Nothing seems to deter offenders from committing crimes, not even capital punishment. Both incarcerative and nonincarcerative correctional strategies have been found ineffective for reducing crime in most U.S. jurisdictions. Evidence for this view is found in rising crime rates that are disproportionately higher than the corresponding general population increase. Furthermore, many criminals who have already been punished for previous offenses continue to commit new crimes.

Incapacitation and Isolation

By isolating criminals from society through confinement, incarceration is the most direct method of crime prevention. **Incapacitation** and **isolation** mean the restriction of movement or liberty. For many offenders, incapacitation is psychologically painful, and it is seen by the public as a legitimate correctional function. Although public sentiment is difficult to gauge accurately by any poll, some evidence indicates that incapacitating criminals through incarceration is seen as a mechanism for social defense. Containing offenders in prisons and jails means that they cannot harm others or damage their property. Such isolation is viewed as beneficial and as a sound defensive strategy that the public can use to combat crime. However, many criminals remain undetected, unapprehended, and unrestrained. Thus, the defensive value of incarceration may be limited or overrated (Riveland 1999).

Rehabilitation

Rehabilitation has always been promoted as a key correctional goal. However, the effectiveness of corrections as a rehabilitative medium has been controversial (Sarre 2001). At times, researchers are inclined to dismiss the rehabilitative value of prisons, while at other times, other investigators reaffirm it (Lehman

2001). The National Congress on Penitentiary and Reformatory Discipline convened in Cincinnati, Ohio, in 1870, and rehabilitation through reformation was officially recognized as a valid and useful correctional function. However, almost a century earlier, the Quakers had established the Philadelphia Society for Alleviating the Miseries of Public Prisons in 1787. While this was private philanthropy, the goals it espoused paralleled closely those of the 1870 National Congress. They considered the main objective of jails and prisons to be reformation, not retribution. Religious instruction in the Quaker faith and elementary education were key elements of the Quaker jail plan.

The **Walnut Street Jail** in Philadelphia was constructed in 1776 to handle the overflow from the already overcrowded **High Street Jail.** Primarily through the efforts of the religious reformer and physician, **Dr. Benjamin Rush** (1745–1813), the Quakers successfully incorporated their ideas into the organization and operation of the Walnut Street Jail with positive results. Prisoners worked at various tasks, and a portion of their wages were applied to pay for court costs, fines, and inmate maintenance. Gardening was permitted, and inmates grew much of their own fresh fruit and vegetables.

In 1876, the **Elmira Reformatory** in New York was established and administered by **Zebulon Reed Brockway** (1827–1920), an advocate of rehabilitation and reformation. Although historians disagree about the true rehabilitative value of the Elmira Reformatory, it is undisputed that the **reformatory** movement was greatly stimulated by Brockway and his management philosophy (Rafter 1997). Between 1876 and 1920, a fourth of the states used the Elmira model for their own construction and operation of reformatories. Like Elmira, these institutions emphasized educational training and the cultivation of vocational skills as worthwhile inmate activities to facilitate their eventual rehabilitation and reformation.

During the lawless decades and Prohibition Era of the 1920s and 1930s, prison populations increased dramatically beyond their capacities. Prison overcrowding has always interfered with the proper administration of educational and vocational programs, and the Prohibition Era was no exception. Unable to operate their prison rehabilitative programs effectively, many officials discontinued these programs or offered them on a limited scale to small numbers of prisoners. During the next several decades, the public grew increasingly disenchanted with these rehabilitation programs.

During the 1960s, 1970s, 1980s, and well into the 1990s, changes in sentencing and correctional practices were introduced in an effort to stem the rising tide of crime. The courts were considered too lenient on offenders. Parole was discontinued in several states. Incarcerative punishments were increased for certain types of offenses. Sentencing practices have been modified by state legislatures so that the emphasis today is adjusting punishments to fit crime seriousness. Thus, several of Beccaria's ideas have been revived and applied to contemporary offender sentencing (Burke 2001).

Reintegration

Reintegration as a punishment goal is particularly relevant for offenders who have been incarcerated for long prison terms. Prison life means strict adherence to rules and regulations that are alien to community residents on the outside. Prisons foster their own subculture among inmates, and this subculture is pervasive and long-lasting (Petersilia 2001). For some incarcerated offenders, especially those with undiagnosed mental illnesses, the adverse effects of prison life can be critical to their future adjustment (Swanson et al. 2001). Certain symptoms of mental illness may manifest themselves in ways that cause prison officials to overclassify some mentally ill persons and place them in maximum-security settings where they will not receive the institutional treatment they deserve. Such persons may eventually emerge from prison life with impressions of themselves that are much worse than when they were initially confined. Many inmates find it difficult to adjust to life outside of prison when they are released, because the suddenness of freedom is so overwhelming. The highly regimented and violent milieu of prison environments is so coercive that many parole-eligible inmates are more than a little anxious about the prospect of living with minimal restrictions in community settings (Motiuk et al. 2001).

Besides the use of direct parole or early release, many prison systems gradually accustom parole-eligible inmates for the outside world through a variety of pre-release programs. Within prisons, inmates have the opportunity to acquire vocational skills and earn academic degrees. Some of these inmates may be permitted to attend classes at nearby colleges or universities during their last year or so before being paroled. Psychological services, vocational and employment counseling, and experiences intended to heighten one's self-awareness and responsibility also contribute to enhancing one's community adjustment prospects (Petersilia 2001).

Control

Another important goal of corrections is to **control** offenders through intensive supervision or monitoring. Annually, large numbers of offenders are released into communities where intensive supervision programs exist. Some of these programs involve **shock incarceration,** where some offenders are placed in jail for up to 130 days and then placed on probation. The shock experience of confinement is intended to acquaint these clients with the undesirability of confinement. While the public is generally skeptical of the value of such programs and naturally apprehensive about having convicted felons roaming their streets freely, the other alternative is increasingly costly incarceration. Society currently lacks the resources and means to lock up all offenders and is reluctant to pay the price of such large-scale incarceration.

Considerable experimentation has been undertaken in various dimensions of corrections. Such experimentation has often involved varying the levels of supervision or control over offenders, different programs with diverse components or elements, and a variety of other control strategies. More intensive supervised probation programs and boot camps for more youthful offenders have been promoted strongly in the 1990s as viable interventions that have the best chance of deterring offenders and reducing recidivism. Programs that attempt to equip clients with useful skills to make them more employable are also positively viewed by corrections professionals. However, some researchers caution that despite this considerable experimentation and programming to rehabilitate, control, and/or reintegrate offenders, the growth of corrections has not been particularly beneficial socially or economically (Illinois Department of Corrections 2000). The effectiveness of correctional programs and program evaluation generally is difficult to assess, since vast differences in program planning and implementation make assessments of outcomes either premature or unreliable. Furthermore, the ready availability of drugs, alcohol, and other controlled substances, together with the conditional release of greater numbers of mentally disordered offenders, make program effectiveness an elusive goal in many jurisdictions.

SOME CORRECTIONAL MODELS

The functions of corrections are best understood by examining several competing philosophies of punishment. These philosophies have evolved into models and/or schemes used to construct and operate various correctional programs (Singh and White 2000). Usually, a close inspection of any correctional program will reveal the influence of a particular correctional model. Each model makes different assumptions about criminals and the reasons they become criminals. The logic is that if a specific process exists whereby persons become criminals, then there must be a specific remedy or solution that will counter or reverse this process. Five models are examined. These are (1) the medical or treatment model, (2) the rehabilitation or reform model, (3) the community model, (4) the just deserts or retribution model, and (5) the justice model.

The Medical or Treatment Model

The **medical model** or **treatment model** assumes that criminal behavior is the result of psychological or biological conditions that can be treated. If we accept the premise of the medical model that criminals are criminals because they have particular biological or psychological conditions or problems, then the identification of cures is vital to remedying these criminal behaviors.

The medical model was officially recognized by the National Prison Association in 1870 through its Declaration of Principles. Moral regeneration of criminals was emphasized through the administration of appropriate treatments. Thus, researchers sought psychiatric and biological solutions. Experiments were conducted where offender diets were controlled, since it was believed that the improvement of physical health was the basis for criminal reform. Psychiatrists examined thousands of prisoners, attempting to find significant psychological clues to explain their criminal condition.

One application of the medical model is for sex offenders (Scheela 2001). Many convicted sex offenders have been placed on chemical therapies or drug treatments that function to control their sexual urges. Therefore, if proper medical treatment is applied when the need for such medication exists, then the circumstances that trigger sexual misconduct are less likely to occur. Unfortunately, many sex offenders who undergo such drug treatment programs and therapy have somewhat higher relapse rates when they eventually leave their programs or discontinue their medication (Tierney and McCabe 2002).

Group therapy, behavior modification, and counseling have been considered as essential tools to effect behavioral changes (Bazemore, Nissen, and Dooley 2000). Since few significant long-range behavioral changes among prisoners were observed over the years, correctional personnel became disenchanted with the medical model. The medical model was popular until the 1950s, but it was eventually replaced by more popular alternative explanations and solutions.

Corrections has several goals, including rehabilitation, where useful skills such as carpentry are acquired by offenders. Courtesy of Custer Youth Correctional Center.

The Rehabilitation or Reform Model

Closely related to the treatment or medical model is the **rehabilitation model** or **reform model.** This model stresses rehabilitation and reform (Lightfoot and Fraietta 2002). Although rehabilitation may be traced to William Penn's work in correctional reform, the most significant support for the rehabilitation orientation came from Zebulon Brockway's Elmira Reformatory in 1876. Eventually, federal recognition of rehabilitation as a major correctional objective occurred when the Federal Bureau of Prisons was established on May 14, 1930. Although the first federal penitentiary was built in 1895 in Leavenworth, Kansas, it took thirty-five more years for an official federal prison policy to be devised. The original mandate of the Bureau of Prisons called for rehabilitating federal prisoners through vocational and educational training, as well as the traditional individualized psychological counseling that was associated with the treatment model. In later years, encounter groups, group therapy, and other strategies were incorporated into federal prison operations and policy as alternative rehabilitative methods (Bazemore, Nissen, and Dooley 2000).

Prison settings have been criticized because of their inability to rehabilitate offenders. However, some prison settings have been modified to create conditions more conducive to rehabilitation. In 1962, for instance, Grendon was established in England. Grendon was known as a therapeutic prison. It was designed to receive and treat prisoners with mental disorders. These disorders, although serious, were deemed insufficient to justify transfers of these inmates to mental hospitals. Subsequently, Grendon established three wings to provide a more therapeutic milieu for those inmates with mental health needs. Interestingly, the maintenance of order and control at Grendon was achieved without coercion or force. Grendon made it a point to hire only those personnel who

 **BOX 1.1**

Agustin Dovalina, III

Chief of Police, Laredo (TX) Police Department

Statistics

A.A.S., Laredo Junior College; B.S.C.J. & M.S.C.J., Texas A & M International University; FBI National Academy; International Association of Chiefs of Police (IACP); Texas Police Chiefs Association (TPCA); National Criminal Justice Association (NCJA)

Background and Interests

I am currently the Chief of Police of the Laredo (TX) Police Department and have served as chief since July 1996. I served as the interim police chief until August 1997 when I was named the police department's ninth chief of police. I am a 24-year law enforcement veteran who oversees an agency of more than 400 sworn officers, 80 civilians, and a $30 million budget. I'm a native Laredoan, and I began my career with the Laredo Police Department as a patrolman back in 1978. I rose through the ranks of Laredo's finest via promotion from street cop/patrol officer to detective, to sergeant, to lieutenant, and finally, to captain. I'm a firm believer in problem-oriented, community-based policing philosophies that are evident in the Laredo Police Department's organizational makeup and its operational strategies.

I am a graduate of the 178th session of the FBI National Academy, as well as an active member of the Texas Chapter of the FBI NA Associates. I belong to the International Association of Chiefs of Police (IACP), National Association of Police Chiefs (NAPC), and the National Criminal Justice Association (NCJA), where I serve as the Southern Regional Representative, among numerous other organizations.

Experiences

I entered into this law enforcement career purely by accident. I come from very humble origins—a product of Laredo's low-income municipal housing projects or barrios, and I was once told by one of my high school counselors that I'd never make it in an academic setting, much less get a college degree. Even though I was an all-state musician and member of our high school marching band, I was told by the school counselor that it'd be best if I took a class in air-conditioning maintenance and become a certified air conditioning technician instead.

Well, despite his words of discouragement, I applied to the University of Texas at Austin, where I not only enrolled as a student, but I became a proud member of the University of Texas Longhorn Marching Band. I was a concert soloist who played the euphonium and trombone with both the University and Austin Symphonies as well. I also made extra money as a guitarist and string bassist playing with several area rock bands. In fact, I majored in music in college and was going to be a music educator/band director.

Well, halfway into my final semester of college, I went home and decided to take brief sabbatical from school. On a whim, I took the police entrance exam with several friends of mine who had just returned from serving in the armed services. I had no interest in law enforcement whatsoever, but I was talked into going with the group to take the test. Well, as luck would have it, I'm the only one from our group who passed the police entrance test, and I ended up staying in the police department. I never imagined that I'd be a police officer, much less the police chief. Yet, I rose through the ranks of Laredo's finest and the rest is history. Incidentally, the school counselor who told me I'd never make it in academia came by to see me a few years ago. He asked me for a job.

Insights

I'm certainly no golf professional, but I can readily improve my golf score with the likes of Tiger Woods any day. I'd liken this assessment to the present state of corrections in our country, in my opinion. Picture this: One Saturday morning, a golfer sliced his tee shot into the bushes. As the golfer bent to place his ball on the tee again, a man in the group muttered, "For gosh sakes, do something different!"

As a veteran law enforcement officer and a less-than-mediocre golf enthusiast, I'd liken the state of our country's corrections efforts to this analogy. The penal system in this nation keeps swinging, slicing, and wondering why repetition doesn't improve anything. Sure, it's logical to counter crime with tougher sentencing, more prisoners, and tighter parole laws—but the slice "ain't leavin'." More, not fewer people, walk out of prison with what seems to be an advanced degree in anger, criminal networking, and hardened criminality, but with minimal job skills, literacy, and dedication to personal responsibility. And we wonder why most of these victimizers default to more crime. And then, what do we do with our convicted felons? We literally "warehouse" them, which I believe costs more money in housing than it would be to rehabilitate them.

One need ask, "What business endeavor could conceivably succeed with the rate of recall of its products that we see in the 'products' of our prisons?" It seems that about two out of every three released felons are rearrested within three years, and these charges mean that half of them eventually return to prison. Arrests, of course, are only the visible tip of the criminal iceberg.

And just when you think you've heard it all in the area of corrections, experts reportedly have a revolutionary plan for setting up a faith-based prison somewhere in our great state. I understand that the concept would go beyond the Christian prison wing in Sugar Land, Texas, with a faith-based program teaching personal responsibility and self-support, backed up by inmate employment with private industry to help defray operating costs. This special-purposes prison should reportedly furnish everything at 10 percent or more under current state costs per prisoner per day, a novel concept in prisons, more for less!

According to these revolutionary thinkers, a Christian prison is not a 24-hour Sunday school, but a rigorous mental, physical, and spiritual program that will teach criminals how to deal with life responsibly, primarily through example, but also through explicit instruction. Internal change, a new way of thinking, alone empowers a human being to start a new life. Men and women rarely step behind bars and resolve to stick to responsible choices and respect the equal rights of others. Most should be pushed and taught how to do it, and they should be supplied with the tools to begin. Post-release counseling and aftercare are integral parts of the program. But what is the downside? Failure of Christian prisons would give us what we've got already, lots of slices into the rough. Success, on the one hand, will straighten out many more lives, putting more down the fairway of life. But will it work? The jury will surely be out on that one for quite some time before we know.

Nevertheless, it is opined that we must punish the criminal for his or her egregious acts, mostly by denying him or her freedom. But if we want criminals to change, I believe we should teach them a new picture of how to cope responsibly with life's challenges, as well as real skills through work. But the pressing question remains, how do we accomplish this? In 1997, the Texas Senate passed Concurrent Resolution No. 44 to restore order, security, and protection to Texas neighborhoods, "because nearly one-half of released inmates are soon jailed again, often for more serious and violent crimes." The resolution urged "all methods effective at breaking the expensive and tragic cycle of criminal behavior and in seeing that criminals get changed, not just released," to help them "re-enter society as contributing, self-sufficient citizens, which benefits all Texans." I can't add much more to that. The question is, "Should we get started and

(continued)

BOX 1.1 *(Continued)*

support the first-ever faith-based prison taking the fight against crime to criminals' minds, the only battleground for lasting victories?" Everyone knows what is not working. Perhaps we should try a different "stroke."

Advice to Students

At the risk of sounding clichéd, I firmly believe that education is the key to success. I went back to school to obtain a post-graduate degree—and after almost 25 years with a full-time job, a family, a mortgage, bills, and even a dog to support. And, although it seemed like a daunting endeavor, it has continued to pay off. I've got a great job and an excellent career. And so the best advice I'd offer you is to stay in school. It will always pay off in great dividends for you if you do—no matter what *anyone* says!

were deeply committed to offender therapy and assistance. The positive attitudes they reflected were soon adopted by the inmates themselves, and a therapeutic prison community was established. Elements contributing to the therapeutic environment were a free flow of staff and inmate communication, a general atmosphere of safety, encouragement for inmates to find solutions to their problems, and prior encouragement of the prison system. While at Grendon, inmates achieved many beneficial changes in their attitudes and behaviors. These changes produced a marked reduction in reoffending among at least a third of all released offenders, while the institutional performance of about half of those transferred to other prisons was also unproblematic (Genders and Player 1995). Therapeutic prison community programs have subsequently been established in states such as California (Prendergast, Farabee, and Cartier 2001).

The Community Model

The **community model** is a relatively new concept based on the correctional goal of inmate reintegration into the community (Lehman 2001). Sometimes called the **reintegration model,** the community model stresses offender adaptation to the community. The primary strengths of the community model are that offenders are able to reestablish associations with their families, and they have the opportunity to work at jobs where a portion of their wages can be used for victim restitution, payment of fines, and defrayment of program maintenance costs. Furthermore, offenders may participate in psychological therapy or educational and vocational programs designed to improve their work and/or social skills (Taxman and Bouffard 2000).

The community model also encourages citizen involvement in offender reintegration. Often, paraprofessionals and community volunteers may assist probation officers in their paperwork. These volunteers also assist offenders by performing cleaning and kitchen work. With such community support, offenders have a better chance of adapting to community life. In recent years, operators of community-based offender programs have been keenly aware of the importance of cultivating links with the community, especially with community leaders (Taxman and Bouffard 2000). The community model is applicable to both adult and juvenile offenders, regardless of whether they are nonviolent or violent (Polaschek and Dixon 2001; Richman and Fraser 2000).

The Just Deserts or Retribution Model

The **just deserts model, deserts model,** or **retribution model** emphasizes equating punishment with the severity of the crime. In this respect, Beccaria's ideas are evident in the development of just deserts as a punishment orientation (Blomberg and Cohen 1995). Offenders should get what they deserve. Therefore, retribution is an important component. Just deserts dismisses rehabilitation as a major correctional aim. It alleges that offenders ought to receive punishments equivalent to the seriousness of their crimes. If rehabilitation occurs during the punishment process, this is not undesirable, but it is also not essential (J. Miller 1996).

Applying the just deserts philosophy, offenders sentenced to prison would be placed in custody levels fitting the seriousness of their crimes. Petty offenders who commit theft or burglary might be sentenced to minimum-security facilities or honor farms with few guards and fences. Accordingly, robbers, rapists, and murderers would be placed in maximum-security prisons under close supervision. If offenders are sentenced to probation, their level of supervision would be adjusted to fit the seriousness of their offenses. The more serious the offense, the more intensive the supervision (U.S. National Institute of Justice 2000).

The just deserts model has emerged in recent years as a popular alternative to the rehabilitation model, which influenced correctional programs for many decades. Penal and sentencing reforms among jurisdictions are currently consistent with the just deserts approach (J. Miller 1996). Public pressure for applying the just deserts orientation in judicial sentencing, including greater severity of penalties imposed, has stimulated the get-tough-on-crime movement.

The Justice Model

Like the just deserts model, the **justice model** rejects rehabilitation as the major objective of punishment. By the same token, sentencing disparities for offenders convicted of similar crimes are opposed. A key proponent of the justice model is David Fogel (1979, 1981) who argues all persons should receive equitable treatment under the law. Sentencing disparities attributable to race, ethnic origin, gender, or socioeconomic status should not to be tolerated (Chan and Mirchandani 2002).

Cesare Beccaria's ideas were influential in establishing the foundations of the justice model. Offenders should be punished for their crimes (just deserts), and these punishments should vary according to the crime's seriousness (Pease 2001). An offender's prior record should be considered as an important factor influencing the severity of punishments for current offenses. The principle of distributive justice should be used as the basis for administering punishments, and these punishments should reflect the community sense of social condemnation (Pedahzur and Ranstorp 2001). Everyone is responsible for his or her own conduct. Through rational thought, persons decide whether to commit crimes. Those who decide to commit offenses are blameworthy, and the state must ensure that they are appropriately sanctioned. Deterrence and rehabilitation are not essential. The public deserves to be protected, however, and therefore the sanctions imposed should be within constitutionally permissible severity ranges. Thus, punishment guidelines for all criminal offenses should be established and adhered to by the courts (Stinchcomb and Hippensteel 2001).

Fogel (1981) has endorsed the principle of justice as fairness. Sentencing for crimes should be scaled proportionately according to the crime's seriousness. The justice model also contains the fundamental concept that sanctions should be influenced by past, proven criminal behavior rather than on predictions of future illegal acts. In this respect, the justice model requires a backward-looking perspective in applying sanctions. Sanctions should be clear, explicit, and highly predictable (Helfgott et al. 2000). This would overcome the indefiniteness associated with rehabilitation-oriented and individually based sentencing schemes currently used by judges in a majority of jurisdictions. Perhaps a comparison of these models in terms of the etiology of the correctional client problem and proposed solution would be helpful. Below are the different models contrasted in terms of the nature of the client problem, as suggested by the model, and the proposed cure, remedy, or action to be taken.

Model*	Cause of Behavioral Problem	Suggested Solution
Medical/treatment model ⟶	Psychological or social maladjustment or biological illness	Group or individual therapy, curative medicines, drugs
Rehabilitation/reform model ⟶	Poor social adjustment to society	Vocational/technical courses and training, anger management courses, behavior modification through group/individual therapy
Community model ⟶	Poor concept of social accountability, ineffective early childhood socialization	Obligate offenders to make restitution to victims; reconciliation; involvement with volunteers/paraprofessionals in community projects
Just deserts/ retribution model ⟶	Crimes vary in seriousness; lack of offender accountability; lack of remorse over crimes committed	Strict punishment proportional to crime committed; revenge
Justice model ⟶	Rational thought and decision to commit crimes as choice over law-abiding behavior	Due process and equitable treatment as punishment; stress on understanding motives for crime commission; state-enforced sanctions

*Compiled by author.

TYPES OF CORRECTIONS

Whenever the term *corrections* is used, people usually think of jails and prisons. Jails and prisons conjure up thoughts of facilities with high perimeter walls, barbed wire fencing, guard towers, locked cells, lots of steel bars, and armed correctional officers who enforce harsh rules. Those held in such facilities are most often referred to as inmates, and it is assumed that all of them have been convicted of serious crimes. Thus, jails and prisons contain hardened, convicted offenders who are separated from the rest of society because they have been convicted of serious crimes. Actually, jails and prisons account for only about a third of all facilities and programs designed as corrections. Jails and prisons are the most visible manifestations of what are referred to more specifically as **institutional corrections.** Institutional corrections are any incarcerative facilities where persons are held in custody for more or less lengthy time intervals. Furthermore, not everyone confined in institutional corrections has been convicted of a crime. Some inmates haven't even been charged with a crime, nor are they considered suspects in any crime that has been committed. In 2000, for example, only 43.6 percent of all jail inmates were serving time for criminal convictions. About 56 percent of the nation's adult jail inmates were awaiting court action on their current charges or serving time for a probation or parole violation. Less than 1 percent of all jail inmates were juveniles being held for various reasons in 2001 (Beck, Karberg, and Harrison 2002:9).

In fact, corrections is a broad term that encompasses both institutional corrections, such as jails and prisons, and **community corrections,** a collection of agencies, organizations, and programs that manages and supervises large numbers of both juvenile and adult offenders and nonoffenders for various lengths of time, in most cities, towns, and neighborhoods throughout the United States (Byrne, Byrne, and Howells 2001). The major differences between institutional and community corrections are explained in the next two sections.

Institutional Corrections

The two major components of institutional corrections are jails and prisons. Both types of organizations contain inmates, by virtue of the fact that all persons confined in jails and prisons have been taken into custody for a variety of reasons and are held for widely different time periods under diverse circumstances.

Jails and Prisons: Some Differences.   **Jails** are mostly locally operated, short-term facilities. They are designed to hold misdemeanants; those awaiting trial; probation and parole violators; fugitives from other jurisdictions; persons in protective custody; more serious juvenile offenders awaiting transfer to juvenile detention facilities; runaways, truants, and curfew violators; vagrants and homeless persons; drunks and derelicts; and others charged with summary offenses. Most jail inmates who are serving sentences for criminal convictions are usually serving jail terms of less than one year.

Prisons are state- or federally operated facilities designed to accommodate long-term offenders who usually are convicted of more serious offenses compared with those housed in jails. Almost all inmates in prisons have been convicted of one or more felonies or serious crimes. It is important to recognize some major differences between jails and prisons and the types of inmates accommodated by each.

1. Compared with prisons, jails have a greater diversity of inmates, including witnesses for trials; suspects or detainees; defendants awaiting trial unable to post bail or whose bail was denied; juveniles awaiting transfer to

 **BOX 1.2**

Dave Compomizzo

Lieutenant, Shasta County (CA) Sheriff's Office

Statistics

A.A., Shasta Community College; B.S., Sacramento State University

Background and Interests

I am 42 years of age and have worked for the Shasta County Sheriff's Office for 22 years. I am presently assigned to the Custody Division as a Jail Manager. Our facility houses approximately 400 inmates both sentenced and unsentenced, and I oversee the supervision of 110 employees. Our annual budget is about $10 million. The Shasta County Sheriff's Office has designed and implemented several programs as alternatives to custody. These programs were implemented to alleviate overcrowding in the jail and include home electronic confinement, work release, community corrections, and a 90-bed detention annex for low-risk inmates. As a result of the above, the jail houses dangerous and high-risk offenders. I truly feel that I have one of the most important jobs with the Shasta County Sheriff's Office.

I have been married 18 years and have two boys, ages 15 and 16. My wife, Peggy, has been involved with the majority of my law enforcement career. I have been extremely fortunate that my wife is a caring, supportive, and loving person. We have been fortunate in the fact that we are a single-income family and my wife has been able to play a large role in raising our two boys. I was born in Yuba City, California, which is an agricultural community, and moved to Redding, California, at age 10. I have had the privilege of living in northern California my whole life and would not consider myself a well-traveled person. My hobbies include waterfowl hunting and tournament bass fishing on the amateur level. I enjoy golfing and the recreational opportunities of Northern California.

I attended Shasta Community College and Sacramento State University with the intention of obtaining a degree in business, ultimately changing my pursuit to a degree in criminal law. I was hired by the Shasta County Sheriff's Office during my second year of college, so I remained in Shasta County and ended my college experience at only three years. As a result, I obtained an associate of arts degree in business and one in the administration of justice. At this point, I have never regretted my decision concerning my formal education; however, I feel that a four-year degree is a valuable tool in today's society.

During my course of employment with the Shasta County Sheriff's Office, I have been assigned to boating patrol, custody (at a 43-year-old jail just prior to its being condemned), Crystal Creek Minimum Security Facility, patrol (as a resident deputy in northeastern Shasta County), investigations, evidence and ID, and most recently the custody division. I have always enjoyed being involved in the function and training of the sheriff's office and as a result, I have been assigned as an assistant search and rescue coordinator, swift-water rescue-dive team specialist, firearms instructor, field training officer, hostage negotiator, and narcotics K-9 handler.

During the course of my career, I have been involved in almost all of the major events that have taken place within the sheriff's office jurisdiction as well as those in surrounding counties. Some of these events have been rewarding, such as rescues, presidential security, coordination of events in natural disasters, not to mention the day-to-day needs of the public that we meet and soon forget about. I am not a person who is talented at remembering jokes and passing them on, and sometimes I feel that I have the same quality when remembering past events or special moments. For most civilians, when they experience what an officer experiences once in their civilian career—such as a pursuit, apprehension, or a close call—it becomes imprinted and very memorable. For people who are fortunate enough to do what we do, it often becomes day-to-day and not as significant. Unfortunately, in my job there are those moments I wish I could forget. These include burying a fellow officer and calling yourself a dive-rescue specialist, but, in fact, you are really a deep-water body recoverer. This is especially true in the case of infants. I don't know how many times doing my job has caused me to think about my family, especially my children.

I probably have a dozen tales I could tell that would keep readers on the edge of their seats desiring to know more. These entail rescues, running into my captain head-on with my detective vehicle, pursuits, being electrically shocked in a flood and getting the nickname "lightning," wild land fires, floods, shootings, homicides, getting mauled by a fellow officer's police dog, and many more incidents. Due to space restrictions, I will share one event that took place in my career in December 1984, just two weeks after I was married. Northeastern California can get very cold during the winter. As a matter of fact, I have seen it snow on the Fourth of July. This was the case on the day in question. I had ended my swing shift at 11:00 P.M., and after the usual small talk and horseplay with the oncoming graveyard shift, I was preparing to leave about 11:30. As I was saying my goodbyes, dispatch radioed of a drive-by shooting approximately one mile from our station. I, together with another officer, responded to the scene of a vehicle sitting in front of a grocery outlet. The driver's window was shattered, and glass was lying on the pavement below the broken window. A male in his late teens was seated behind the wheel, slumped over. The male was unresponsive, had labored breathing, and was bleeding from his head and arms. This scene had all the characteris-

tics of a drive-by shooting. It was during these initial few moments that I discovered this was not the case. A female companion of the shooting victim had been placed in an arriving highway patrol car. Upon contacting her, I found her to be dressed in her underwear. This companion, in a state of shock, then relayed that she and the victim had been parked in the woods on a secluded dirt road talking when the driver's side window shattered from gunfire, striking the victim. The companion was then sexually assaulted. And after the assault, she was told to get back into the vehicle where she, too, believed she was going to be shot. After a period of time and realizing the suspect was no longer present, the companion attempted to drive the vehicle into town to summon assistance. The companion was unsuccessful in getting the victim to respond to her and move over in the seat. Due to the companion's inability to move the victim, she was forced to drive the vehicle into town while seated on the victim. The companion was successful in driving the vehicle into town and summoning a highway patrol officer. As my attention was directed to the male victim seated behind the wheel, my first-aid training kicked into gear and I began thinking about the ABCs of first aid. I attempted to correct the victim's breathing by holding his slumped head up and monitoring any vital signs. It was going through my mind that I was probably holding the head of a dead man and only preventing the inevitable. It was during this time that I began to catch my thoughts and remember back to the scene. As I looked at the car, I began noticing similarities to my new sister-in-law's car. I then realized that the person's head I was holding was her son. You can probably figure out how the rest of the night went. The case has yet to be solved.

Advice to Students

As you go throughout your law enforcement career, someone will always be telling you "when you mature." That person will inevitably be older than you and, to them, you will never be as mature as they are. You will find yourself saying the same thing to

BOX 1.2 *(Continued)*

people younger than you. Welcome to the world of the generation gap. Sometimes I feel I've seen as many as five of these "gaps" in my career. In this fast-paced world, things change fast. If I were to give a new recruit one word of advice, it would be "attitude." By this I am not concerned with personality. Personalities are what make the world go around. Attitudes stop it. By this I am saying do not come to work with a chip on your shoulder, looking for a fight or mad at the world. Be responsible for your behavior and don't look to place blame. Everyone around you is affected by a negative attitude, and it only erodes any concept of a team environment. I have always said that I would take an 80 percent personality and a 100 percent attitude any day of the week over a 100 percent personality and an 80 percent attitude. By this I am saying to accept people for who they are and sell your agency just as if you owned your own store and survived on word-of-mouth and repeat business.

juvenile facilities or detention; those serving short-term sentences for public drunkenness, driving while intoxicated, or city ordinance violations; mentally ill or disturbed persons awaiting hospitalization; and overflow from state and federal prison populations.

2. Compared with prisons, jails usually do not have programs or facilities associated with long-term incarceration, such as vocational, technical, or educational courses to be taken by inmates, jail industries, recreation yards, or psychological or social counseling or therapy.

3. Compared with prisons, the quality of jail personnel is lower, with many jail personnel untrained, undertrained, or otherwise less qualified to guard prisoners compared with their counterparts, prison correctional officers.

4. Compared with prisons, jails are not as elaborately divided into maximum-, medium-, or minimum-security areas. Guard towers are not usually found, where armed correctional officers patrol regularly. Jails are ordinarily not surrounded by several perimeters, with barbed wire areas, sound-detection equipment, or other exotic electronic devices.

5. Compared with prisons, jail inmate culture is less pronounced and persistent. There is a high inmate turnover in jails, with the exception of the state and federal convict population.

6. Compared with prisons, the physical plant of jails is poorer, with many jails under court order to improve their physical facilities to comply with minimum health and safety standards.

This list of differences is not exhaustive, since there are also administrative, operational, social, and a host of other features that serve to distinguish prisons from jails. Probably the most significant difference between prisons and jails is admission rates. In general, new prison commitments account for 50 percent of the prison population. In contrast, there are between 10 and 13 million jail admissions and releases annually. This means that it takes two years for the nation's prison population to turn over once, while the jail population turns over twenty to twenty-five times each year.

Community Corrections: Some Alternatives

Community corrections comprise a broad array of alternatives to incarceration that are based in cities and towns. These alternatives include supervision and monitoring programs for both convicted and unconvicted offenders (Dickey and McGarry 2001). The vast majority of community corrections clients are probationers and parolees. Both probationers and parolees have been convicted of one or more crimes. In most cases, however, probationers have been sentenced to serve their time in their own communities, under the supervision of probation departments and personnel. Parolees are those who have served some amount of time in prison or jail and are freed into their communities under supervisory conditions similar to those of probationers (Petersilia 2001).

A small portion of community corrections clientele are also under probation supervision, although they have not been convicted of a crime. These are persons who have been charged with one or more crimes, although it is believed that a civil, rather than a criminal, solution is more consistent with community interests. In short, freedom within the community, with restrictions, is believed superior to incarceration in either a jail or prison for reasons of rehabilitation and reintegration. Most unconvicted persons under some form of public or private community supervision are either **divertees** who are participating in a **diversion program** or simply **diversion,** or those who have undergone **alternative dispute resolution (ADR).**

Diversion is an action whereby a criminal case is removed temporarily from the criminal justice system, usually at the recommendation of the prosecutor, and with judicial approval. Divertees must remain law-abiding and conform to certain rules and other diversion program requirements for specified time periods, such as one year. Once they have completed their diversion programs successfully, divertees may have the original criminal charges against them dismissed or downgraded (Bottoms, Gelsthorpe, and Rex 2001).

Those who participate in ADR agree to have their criminal cases resolved through civil means, where a third-party arbiter decides the punishment to be imposed. Usually, there is a victim and a perpetrator. The perpetrator may be required to make restitution to the victim for losses incurred. Community service may be required. Other conditions may be imposed. Both parties must agree to all of these conditions. If all conditions are subsequently satisfied, criminal charges against the perpetrator are dismissed. If either party does not consent to these conditions, then the case is pursued in criminal court and resolved through a criminal trial.

However, most community corrections clients are probationers and parolees. Depending upon the jurisdiction, these offenders are supervised more or less intensively. Less intensively may mean monthly check-ins or visits to probation offices by probationers or simply filling out a form and mailing it to the local probation office. Parolees may be similarly monitored by parole officers. "More intensively" may mean frequent (e.g., daily, weekly) face-to-face visits with probationers or parolees and intermittent and random drug and/or alcohol testing or urinalyses. Both less intensively and more intensively monitored probationers and parolees may also be required to be employed, to participate in social and/or psychological counseling or therapy, participate in vocational/educational programs, perform community services of different types, pay fines, and/or make restitution to victims.

Community corrections may include restricting clients' movements and whereabouts during nonworking hours to their homes. Electronic surveillance also may be used to monitor their movements. Some clients may be obligated to report to certain homes or agencies located in neighborhoods on a regular basis, where they can receive employment assistance and other forms of aid from community correctional staff, paraprofessionals, or volunteers.

Some community correctional clients may be prison or jail inmates who are released for brief periods for educational or vocational reasons to participate in local high school or college courses or perform part-time work. Some of these clients may be permitted short periods of release from confinement for weekend conjugal visits with their families. Furthermore, some of these clients may be obligated to live in certain temporary group homes or transitional residences in communities where their whereabouts and behaviors can be monitored during nonworking hours.

It is apparent that community corrections represents a wide variety of programs and services available to either convicted or unconvicted persons as an alternative to incarceration. About two-thirds of all persons under some form of correctional supervision are community corrections clientele. Community corrections services are largely publicly operated, although private community corrections agencies, organizations, and personnel are gradually increasing their presence in this growing correctional enterprise.

CORRECTIONAL REFORMS

The history of corrections is a history of reforms (U.S. National Institute of Justice 2000). The Quakers sought extensive reforms in Pennsylvania and other colonies in the 1700s and continued their efforts well into the twentieth century. These reforms were directed at inhumane prison conditions, and several religious and other philanthropic interests have engaged in social experiments and instituted innovations designed to eliminate and/or alleviate inmate suffering.

In his analysis of the history of sentencing reforms in the United States, David Rothman (1983) has described in great detail specific time periods associated with different punishment emphases. During the period 1790 to 1820, the wholesale use of capital punishment was gradually replaced by lengthy incarceration. By 1870 and during the next few decades, offender imprisonment became less popular as rehabilitation and reform gained prominence. During 1900 through 1960, rehabilitation programs dominated the correctional scene, and sentencing patterns were closely identified with and influenced by rehabilitation as the major correctional objective. In recent years, there has been a major shift toward justice-oriented sentencing schemes. Despite these major reforms in corrections and sentencing, their effectiveness has been debated by researchers.

Some observers say that sentencing reform laws as they were originally conceived were designed to prevent or decrease crime and crime rates and reduce incarceration rates. However, under existing sentencing reforms in most jurisdictions, crime rates have continued to climb and prison and jail populations have escalated (Bottoms, Gelsthorpe, and Rex 2001; Utting and Vennard 2000). For example, California and many other states have revised their laws to include a Three Strikes and You're Out! provision, which means that if offenders commit three or more serious felonies, they will receive mandatory life prison terms. For some observers, three-strikes laws are a common and costly response to concerns about crime. Broadening the definition of what constitutes a strike makes the laws more effective in the sense that they take a bigger bite out of crime but are less cost-effective in the sense that criminal justice costs to taxpayers per crime averted rise with expanding scope (Caulkins 2001). Often, the sentences for repeat offenders under California law are also too long from the perspective of efficient crime reduction. Despite this get-tough posturing by California and other states, there has been no discernible effect on the crime rates in these jurisdictions as the result of adopting this new sentencing provision (Maguire and Pastore 2002).

Quite often, policymakers create sentencing reforms before thinking through their long-range impacts or implications. The results are often disastrous. In many jurisdictions, sentencing reform laws have driven overcrowding in jails and prisons further upward, with little or no meaningful planning about how these inmate population increases can be accommodated. However, in other jurisdictions, new sentencing laws are only indirectly responsible for rising inmate populations. Some investigators have attacked policymakers for changing sentencing laws to enhance their cosmetic value rather than for any direct crime prevention benefits (Caulkins 2001). Politicians often take credit for implementing get-tough policies so that they appear to be tough on crime. But the implemented reforms often create more problems than they resolve.

The United States is not unique in making sweeping changes in sentencing policies. Other countries, such as the United Kingdom, Canada, Sweden, and Australia, have implemented similar sentencing reforms. In many instances, these countries have not achieved the desired effects of their sentencing reforms and have abandoned them (Bottoms, Gelsthorpe, and Rex 2001).

Present problems of prison and jail overcrowding raise serious questions about policies and reforms that will increase prison and jail inmate populations rather than decrease them. Originally intended to reduce sentencing disparities among federal judges, the **U.S. Sentencing Commission** guidelines implemented in 1987 and the abolition of federal parole have been labeled by some critics as aggravating federal prison overcrowding in future years rather than alleviating the problem. In 1976, for example, Maine abolished parole. But soon, Maine prisons became overcrowded, and Maine officials had to devise alternative strategies such as good-time adjustments to compensate for an escalating inmate population. Despite the bad luck Maine had with its parole abolition, 15 other jurisdictions since 1976 abolished parole (Camp and Camp 2002, 228–229).

During the 1990s, architects and correctional officials have been working to devise new schemes for prison construction, organization, and operation. But new prison and jail construction does not solve the overcrowding problem. We fill our jails and prisons as fast as they are built (Maguire and Pastore 2002). This fact has caused criminal justice professionals to examine nonincarcerative alternatives such as community-based programs, especially for those designated as low-risk offenders. Experiments are underway in most states to target the most successful programs for managing growing offender populations. While it is presently unknown where these reforms are leading, few critics question the need for them (Okun 1997). Considerable disagreement exists among correctional researchers over which sentencing systems are best; which nonincarcerative alternatives are most workable and fair to both society and offenders; and how much discretion prosecutors, judges, and corrections officials should have in decisions affecting offender life chances (Wooldredge 1996).

SUMMARY

Corrections is the vast number of persons, agencies, and organizations that manage accused, convicted, or adjudicated criminal offenders and juveniles. The most visible correctional organizations are prisons and jails. Prisons accommodate long-term inmates who have committed particularly serious offenses, whereas jails are ordinarily designed to manage short-term offenders and pretrial detainees. In recent years, however, jails have accommodated the overflow from prisons as the courts have mandated that inmate populations should be reduced to comply with constitutionally permissible health and safety standards. Thus, many jails house increasing numbers of long-term offenders. This, in turn, has aggravated jail overcrowding.

Incarceration as a punishment dates to ancient Greece and Rome, particularly the Mamertine Prison constructed by Ancus Martius in 640 B.C. Religious institutions have been influential on the nature and growth of prison systems, as many religious dissidents were confined as a form of punishment. Mercantile interests during the Middle Ages in Scotland and England exploited prison labor for profit. Another form of punishment, banishment, has been used since Biblical times. During the late 1700s and 1800s, Great Britain banished thousands of prisoners to remote British-controlled colonies, including Australia, through transportation. These prisoners worked in the colonies for menial wages and aided mercantile interests in profit-making. Corporal punishment or the infliction of pain was used to sanction offenders as well. Corporal punishments included branding, whipping, pillories, rack-and-screw devices, and dunking.

In the colonies William Penn, a Quaker and founder of Pennsylvania, instituted many correctional reforms to humanize incarcerative environments. Corporal punishments were temporarily abandoned and more treatment-centered programs were instituted. When Penn died, corporal punishments were reinstituted for a period. Early U.S. prisons were poorly managed and operated on substandard health and safety levels. Quickly, jail and prison overcrowding became epidemic throughout the states. Gradually, probation and parole were introduced to alleviate prison overcrowding. These programs also were consistent with the reform movement which was, in part, religiously based.

The gradual professionalization of corrections occurred through organizations such as the National Prison Association (later the American Correctional Association), whose first head, Rutherford B. Hayes, later became U.S. President. As improvements throughout correctional organizations occurred, functions and goals of corrections were delineated. These goals and functions, both past and present, include retribution, deterrence or prevention, incapacitation and isolation, rehabilitation, reintegration, and control. Until the 1960s rehabilitation and reintegration were emphasized and dominated correctional thought. In subsequent decades, more punitive programs and policies were implemented because of the ineffectiveness of rehabilitation and reform. These reforms included more mandatory sentencing and longer terms for various offenses, usually related to drugs, firearms use, and accompanying violence.

Several correctional models exist that serve to guide the efforts of correctional authorities in supervising and providing services for offenders. These include the medical or treatment model, which considers crime to be a disease that can be treated much like an illness. Another model is the rehabilitation or reform model. This model probably best reflects the most powerful stimulus at work throughout all correctional areas, since offenders are expected to change their behaviors through the application of different correctional practices. Other models are the community model, which stresses reintegration; the just deserts or retribution model, which stresses variable offender punishments according to the nature and seriousness of the offense committed; and the justice model, which seeks to administer fairness in punishment, regardless of the offense. Presently, the just deserts correctional model is dominant, although the other models are evident in different correctional practices among the states and federal government.

Today corrections is divided into two large categories: institutional corrections and community corrections. Institutional corrections includes jails and prisons. Theoretically, at least, only the most serious offenders are incarcerated in jails and prisons. The larger division of corrections is community corrections. Community corrections encompasses probation, parole, and a host of programs ranging from diversion to intensive supervised probation or parole. Community corrections also includes alternative dispute resolution, restorative justice, furloughs, home confinement, electronic monitoring, work/study release, halfway houses, and conditions such as community service, fines, and restitution.

Correctional reforms are always occurring. In fact, some observers have concluded that the history of corrections is the history of reforms. Several interested organizations and individuals have promoted changes in correctional systems throughout the United States. These changes have sought improvements in offender accommodations in prisons and jails and an observance of inmate and client rights. Other reforms pertain to changing sentencing schemes to further fairness in sentencing. Thus, more serious offenders are punished more severely, depending upon the nature of the offense. One obvious area of correctional reform pertains to sentencing. Many changes have occurred and are occurring with respect to how offenders are sentenced. Numerous jurisdictions have shifted to sentencing schemes that promote greater equity in treatment but more consistent and harsher penalties for lawless behaviors. Other reforms pertain to how offenders are supervised, both in institutions and in communities.

QUESTIONS FOR REVIEW

1. What is the general meaning of corrections? What are two major correctional subdivisions? What are some of their characteristics?

2. Compare the medical or treatment model with the rehabilitation model. What are some of their respective strengths and weaknesses? Why have these models been criticized in recent years?

3. How have religion and philanthropic interests changed corrections over the past several centuries?

4. What were some significant accomplishments of William Penn and the Quakers?

5. What are four functions of corrections? Which function do you think is the most relevant for our society today? Why do you think this?

6. What were some popular methods England used for punishing their offenders? What are some of the primary characteristics of these methods?

7. What are the major assumptions and ideas associated with the justice model? How has the justice model influenced our sentencing practices? Give an example.

8. How were Beccaria, Voltaire, and Montesquieu influential in helping to bring about penal reforms?

9. What are five important eras that typify different stages in the development of U.S. corrections? What are some defining characteristics of these eras?

10. What are some major differences between jails and prisons? What reforms have occurred that influence jail and prison design and operation?

SUGGESTED READINGS

Blomberg, Thomas G. and Karol Lucken. *American Penology: A History of Control.* Hawthorne, NY: Aldine de Gruyter, 2000.

Lilly, J. Robert, Francis T. Cullen, and Richard A. Ball. *Criminological Theory: Context and Consequences.* Thousand Oaks, CA: Sage Publications, 2002.

Moyer, Imogene. *Criminological Theories: Traditional and Non-Traditional Voices and Themes.* Thousand Oaks, CA: Sage Publications, 2001.

Roth, Mitchel P. *Crime and Punishment: A History of the Criminal Justice System.* Belmont, CA: Wadsworth/Thomson Learning, 2002.

Van Ness, Daniel and Karen Heetderks Strong. *Restoring Justice.* 2d ed. Cincinnati, OH: Anderson Publishing Company, 2002.

INTERNET CONNECTIONS

American Bar Association
abanet.org/crimjust/links.html

American Community Corrections Institute
http://www.acci/lifeskills.com/

American Correctional Association: Past, Present, and Future
http://www.corrections.com/aca/pastpresentfuture/history.htm

American Probation and Parole Association
http://www.appa-net.org

Criminal justice links
http://www.lawguru.com/ilawlib/96.htm

Federal Judicial Center
http://www.fjc.gov

History of Federal Bureau of Prisons
http://www.bop.gov/lpapg/pahist.html

Legal Resource Center
http://www.crimelynx.com/research.html

National Institute of Justice
http://www.ojp.usdoj.gov/nij

New York Corrections History Society
http://www.correctionshistory.org

Probation agency links
http://www.cppca.org/link

Probation and parole sites
http://www.angelfire.com/md/ribit/states

State court links
http://www.doc.state.co.us/links

State criminal justice links
http://www.statesnews.org/other_resources/law_and_justice.htm

U.S. Department of Justice
http://www.usdoj.gov/02organizations/02_1.html

Vera Institute of Justice
http://www.vera.org

CHAPTER 2

Classifying Offenders, Sentencing Systems, and Sentencing Issues

Source: John Neubauer, PhotoEdit.

Chapter Objectives   *As the result of reading this chapter, the following objectives should be realized:*

1. Describing traditional offender categorizations, including property and violent offender types, first offenders, recidivists, and career criminals.
2. Describing particular types of specialized offenders, including drug/alcohol-dependent, mentally ill, and sex offenders.
3. Describing the sentencing process and discussing various types of sentencing and their implications for sentenced offenders.
4. Discussing several major sentencing issues, including sentencing disparities according to race, gender, socioeconomic status; prison and jail overcrowding; cor-

rectional resources and their limitations; and systemic constraints.
5. Describing presentence investigation reports, their contents, and functions.
6. Describing the sentencing hearing and sentencing procedures.
7. Discussing aggravating and mitigating factors that judges use in sentencing offenders.
8. Highlighting various sentencing issues including jail and prison overcrowding, sentencing disparities, and the effectiveness of rehabilitation/reintegration.

INTRODUCTION

• *He was a 26-year-old convicted of six counts of sexual assault against four children under the age of 8. At his sentencing hearing, he asked for the judge to place him in solitary confinement, away from the rest of the prison population where he would be sent. The judge rejected his request, and he was subsequently incarcerated in a prison for eleven years. After being processed and classified, the prisoner was celled with another inmate in the general population. One week after arriving at the prison, the convicted child molester was found stabbed to death in an obscure part of the recreation yard. His penis and scrotum had been cut off and stuffed in his mouth. According to the prisoners, no one saw anything, and no one had any idea who murdered the inmate. But one inmate made an observation: "Child molesters don't last long around here. The cons don't like 'em and neither do I. He got what he deserved, if you ask me."* [Adapted from the Associated Press, "Convicted Child Molester Dies after Two Weeks in Georgia Prison," September 15, 2002].

• *At the man's sentencing hearing, many people testified for and against him. He was convicted of murdering a young couple, who had given him a ride during a heavy rainstorm in Nebraska. According to his own version of events, he hitched a ride with the young couple, who had recently been married. It was raining hard, and he professed to them that his car had been disabled down the road. When he got into their car, he pulled out a gun and forced them to drive to a service road beside the interstate highway. There, he made them get out of the car and walk into the woods where he shot both of them to death. He took their money and valuables and drove off in the stolen car. Coincidentally, the brother-in-law of the woman was a Nebraska state trooper who recognized the car. He stopped the car and, at gunpoint, made the man exit the vehicle. A search turned up the stolen watches, pocketbook, wallet and other personal effects of his relatives. Investigators who subsequently arrived at the scene had the man show them where he had hidden the bodies. It turns out that the man had a lengthy prison record and was on parole for burglary and larceny. He was charged with first-degree murder in the deaths of the two victims and convicted. The judge listened to both sides, one side appealing for leniency, the other side wanting the maximum penalty under the law. The judge allowed the victims' parents to read a victim impact statement into the record. A parole officer testified about the man's behavior while on parole. The man's mother, brother, sister, and a priest testified that he was basically a good man and should be granted leniency. In the end, the judge sentenced the double murderer to life without the possibility of parole.* [Adapted from the Associated Press, "Double Murder in Nebraska Draws Life Without Parole," February 16, 2002].

• *The 19-year-old man standing before the judge had just been convicted of vehicular theft. It was his first offense. A pre-sentence investigation report revealed a good employment record, good comments from teachers, the man's pastor, and work associates. He seemed to be a likely candidate for probation. He had a bachelor's degree in social science. The judge didn't feel that prison would be in the man's best interests. Therefore, he sentenced the man to three years' probation. The man was ordered to house arrest for 90 days, together with electronic monitoring. Three days after being sentenced and while under the supervision of the probation department, the man committed another burglary late one night and bludgeoned to death two elderly women who were sleeping in a bedroom he entered. He carried a lead pipe for "self-defense." The public was perplexed. How could a judge let such a dangerous person off with probation? The judge was equally puzzled. All of the indicators suggested that the man was an ideal candidate for probation. A prediction was made that he would succeed on probation, complete his probationary term, and lead a law-abiding life. Obviously, the prediction was in error.* [Adapted from the Associated Press, "Probationer Murders Two Elderly Women During Burglary," January 19, 2002].

We are often perplexed over the types of sentences criminals receive. In some cases, we might applaud judges for doing the right thing and imposing what we think are just sentences. In other cases, we may feel strongly that the sentencing **judge** didn't do enough to punish the offender. For instance, we might read about a woman in Ottawa, Ohio, who steals over $400,000 from her church and who receives a sentence of two years. We know that she will probably only serve one year at the most and that this will be followed by her conditional release into the community. What sentence would you impose on someone who steals nearly a half million dollars from a church? We might also read about a man in Seattle, Washington, who steals $40 and gets life without parole. This seemingly excessive sentence may seem unwarranted. But not all crimes and punishments parallel closely the amounts of money stolen or embezzled. Many other factors and circumstances cause judges to increase or decrease accordingly the punishments they impose. These and the real scenarios above are indicative of the diversity of **sentencing** among U.S. judges.

When offenders enter corrections, they are classified in various ways. In order to understand the nature and purposes of correctional **classification,** we must first describe the types of offenders who enter corrections. These include traditional offender categorizations, such as first offenders, property, and violent offenders. Other offender categories are described, including drug/alcohol-dependent offenders, the mentally ill, sex offender and child sexual abusers, physically handicapped offenders, and those with AIDS and other communicable diseases. These offenders commit either misdemeanors, or minor offenses, or more serious felonies. Misdemeanor and felony offenses are defined and described. Crimes are also divided according to whether they are property or violent offenses. This distinction is discussed. Further, an important feature of the classification process is to describe offender personalities and social characteristics. Several instruments are described that assist corrections authorities in classifying offenders in different ways.

Several types of sentencing systems used today in various U.S. **jurisdictions** are described. Sentencing is the penalty phase of the **criminal justice system** where incarcerative and nonincarcerative punishments are imposed. Every criminal statute in every jurisdiction is accompanied by possible fine and incarceration guidelines. The sentencing process is described, commencing with a description of pretrial alternatives available to **prosecutors** and judges. Several sentencing systems are identified and discussed. These include indeterminate sentencing, determinate sentencing, presumptive or guidelines-based sentencing, and mandatory sentencing. Each of these sentencing schemes is defined and discussed.

By either legislative mandate or court request, presentence investigation reports are prepared for particular offenders and are used during a **sentencing hearing.** These reports are usually prepared by probation officers, although private organizations may sometimes prepare them for more affluent offenders. Such reports, their contents, and functions will be described.

Judicial sentencing discretion and the latitude many judges have in sentencing convicted offenders will be examined. The criteria for sentencing offenders will be discussed, including the **risk** or dangerousness posed by particular offenders to their communities and the seriousness of their crimes. Consideration is given to certain factors that might intensify punishments if offenders are convicted of the crimes alleged. These are aggravating factors. Other factors may lessen the severity of punishments. These are mitigating factors. All jurisdictions throughout the United States consider both aggravating and mitigating factors when determining the most appropriate punishment for any given offender. The chapter concludes with an examination of selected sentencing issues. These issues include sentencing disparities that may occur, where race/ethnicity, gender, age, socioeconomic status, or some other extralegal factor is considered; correctional resources and their limitations; the economics of systemic constraints; and jail and prison overcrowding and the pervasive problems such overcrowding creates.

TYPES OF OFFENSES

Misdemeanors and Felonies

Crimes are divided into two general categories: (1) misdemeanors and (2) felonies.

Misdemeanors.   **Misdemeanors** are minor or petty offenses. These types of offenses carry less severe penalties compared with major crimes or felonies. Misdemeanor offenses may result in fines and/or incarceration for less than one year. **Misdemeanants,** or those who commit misdemeanors and are incarcerated, usually spend their period of incarceration in a local jail. Examples of misdemeanors include making a false financial statement to obtain credit, prostitution, shoplifting, and trespass.

Felonies.   **Felonies** are major crimes that carry more severe penalties. A **felon** is a person who commits a felony. Usually, statutory penalties associated with felonies are fines and/or incarceration in a state or federal prison for one or more years. Felonies include arson, murder, rape, burglary, robbery, vehicular theft, and aggravated assault. Both misdemeanor and felony convictions create criminal records for offenders. In some jurisdictions, there is a third class of crimes known as **summary offenses.** These are petty crimes that ordinarily carry penalties of fines only. Also, convictions for these petty offenses will not result in a criminal record. Examples of summary offenses are speeding or dumping litter from an automobile on a public highway.

Each state has a compilation of criminal statutes different from other states. Acts defined as crimes in one state may not be crimes in other jurisdictions. Because of these interstate differences, it is difficult to apply standard criteria suitable for defining misdemeanor and felony offenses across all states. You can be convicted of rape in California, but not in North Dakota. This is because North Dakota uses "gross sexual imposition" instead of "rape." Furthermore, felony offenders often enter guilty pleas to less serious misdemeanors in exchange for leniency through **plea bargaining** (Dickey and Stiebs 1998).

Violent and Property Crimes

Crimes may be distinguished also according to violent crimes and property crimes.

Violent Crimes.   **Violent crimes** usually involve injury to one or more victims. Violent crimes include robbery, aggravated assault, homicide, and rape.

Property Crimes.   **Property crimes** are considered nonviolent, because their commission does not ordinarily cause physical injuries or death to crime victims. Examples of property crimes are larceny, burglary (of an unoccupied dwelling), and vehicular theft.

CLASSIFYING OFFENDERS

Classifying offenders is more complex than it appears. Objectively classifying criminals according to their crimes is one way of differentiating between offenders. Felons are in one category, misdemeanants are in another. Further simplified breakdowns are possible where the *Uniform Crime Reports' (UCR)* index offenses such as robbery, larceny, aggravated assault, arson, or burglary are utilized. Classification schemes are used by prison and jail authorities to decide which **level of custody** is most appropriate for particular prisoners. Placing prisoners in optimum custody levels enables officials to control their institutions more effectively and regulate the level of inmate violence (Reitzel and Harju 2000). Psychological inventories, such as the **Minnesota Multiphasic Personality Inventory (MMPI)** and the **Psychological Inventory of Criminal Thinking Styles (PICTS)** for female offenders, are often used in assessments of inmate personalities in order to make more effective placement decisions (Walters and Elliott 1999). Such devices are believed to be helpful in predicting an inmate's future adjustment, institutional performance, and post-release recidivism (Weiss 2000).

During the 1990s, the incidence of **AIDS (Acquired Immune Deficiency Syndrome)** among prisoners increased dramatically (Welch 2000). Confirmed AIDS cases in federal and state prisons more than doubled—from 1,682 cases in 1991 to 3,765 cases in 1993 (Vaughn and Smith 1999). And by the beginning of 2001, the number of confirmed AIDS cases among state and federal prisoners had risen to 5,528 (Maruschak 2002:1). Female inmates were nearly twice as likely to be HIV positive or have AIDS than male inmates. One way of transmitting AIDS is receiving blood from others who have AIDS. Anal intercourse among prisoners is often linked with the transmission of this deadly virus. Semen contains the AIDS virus as well, and oral-genital contact may result in new AIDS victims among inmates. Thus, those diagnosed as having AIDS are often segregated from those who do not test positively for this virus. Favorably, AIDS-related deaths among inmates have decreased significantly, from 1,010 in 1995 to 174 in 2001. Also, segregating those who are HIV positive from those who aren't seems to be slowing down the incidence of both those who are HIV positive and those who are confirmed AIDS cases (Maruschak 2002:1,5). For instance, there were 25,801 HIV-positive inmates in both state and federal prisons in 1999; this figure declined to 25,088 in 2000. Furthermore, the estimated number of confirmed AIDS cases declined from 7,039 in 1999 to 6,520 in 2000. It should be noted that there are discrepancies between actual *confirmed* AIDS cases and *estimated* numbers of AIDS cases because, each year, several states do not report this information. Thus, estimates are based on projections from the most recent years when such information was provided by these nonreporting states.

Increasing proportions of inmates in prisons and jails annually are women (Maguire and Pastore 2002). As more women enter correctional institutions, special problems are created relating to how and where such offenders will be accommodated. More creative solutions are required as the jail and prison in-mate population grows and continues to be more diverse. Corrections officials also want to know which offenders should be placed in maximum-security cus-tody and which ones should be confined in minimum-security facilities. Certain prisoners pose a physical threat to other prisoners and should be isolated from them. Sometimes prisoners can endanger themselves and are potential suicide risks. Other prisoners are low-risk and are cheaper to supervise, often requiring only minimal supervision by one or two correctional officers. Classification is an ongoing process, as offenders are reassessed periodically to determine whether their custody level should be changed or their treatments modified.

Traditional Offender Categorizations

Most criminals fit into a limited number of standard classifications used by cor-rections professionals. These classifications are useful for investigating settings within which criminals are placed, whether those settings are jails, prisons, or probation/parole programs (Austin et al. 1997). Besides violent and low-risk of-fenders, three additional classifications include (1) first offenders, (2) situa-tional offenders, and (3) recidivists and career criminals.

First Offenders.   **First offenders** are those who commit one or more crimes but have no previous history of criminal behavior. There is nothing especially unique about first offenders (Veneziano et al. 2000). They may commit violent crimes or property crimes. They may be male or female. They may be old or young. They may or may not have records as juvenile delinquents. No useful blanket generalizations can be made about first offenders other than the fact they have no previous criminal history. However, even this statement may be inaccurate. For example, a first offender in Colorado may have a prior record in Utah or California. Additionally, first offenders may have committed previous crimes and escaped **arrest.** Depending on the sophistication of the police ad-ministration in the jurisdiction where offenders are arrested, computer checks with other jurisdictions may or may not disclose whether any offender has a prior criminal history.

Situational Offenders.   Those first offenders who commit only the offense for which they were apprehended and prosecuted and who are unlikely to commit future crimes are called **situational offenders.** Situational offenders commit se-rious crimes or petty offenses. Usually, the situation creates the unique condi-tions leading to the criminal act. A heated argument between husband and wife over something trivial may lead to the death of one of the spouses. Serious fi-nancial pressures or setbacks may prompt situational offenders to commit rob-bery or theft. Situational offenders seldom need rehabilitation or counseling, and they respond favorably to authorities whether on probation or incarcerated. Precisely because of the uniqueness of their act and their lack of criminal histo-ries, it is difficult to prescribe treatment for them. Jail and prison officials often consider some of these situational offenders good candidates for early release and believe they contribute unnecessarily to overcrowding.

Recidivists and Career Criminals.   Generally, a **recidivist** is an offender who reverts to criminal behavior after being convicted of a prior offense. However, recidivists may also be (1) parolees who violate one or more terms of their parole and are returned to prison; (2) probationers who violate one or more terms of their probation and are sentenced by the judge to jail or prison; (3) those who fail to complete their rehabilitation or vocational/technical training programs; (4) those who are rearrested for new offenses but not necessarily convicted; (5) those simply returned to prison; or (6) those who are convicted of new offenses (Dana 2001). **Recidivism** is the reversion of an individual to criminal behavior after he or she has been convicted of a prior offense, sentenced, and (presumably) corrected. Recidivism rates as high as 70 percent have been reported among those who have been granted early release from incarceration in different state prisons (Baumer et al. 2002).

Career criminals are those offenders who earn their living through crime. They go about their criminal activity in much the same way workers or professional individuals engage in their daily work activities. Career criminals often consider their work as a craft, since they acquire considerable technical skills and competence in the performance of crimes (Piquero and Mazerolle 2001). Reckless (1961) suggests that career criminals expect to get arrested and convicted occasionally as one of the risks of their criminal behavior. The career criminal has been epitomized by Edwin H. Sutherland's description of the professional thief (1972).

Special Types of Offenders

Correctional agencies must manage a wide range of offenders including those with special problems or needs (Oritz et al. 2000). These include: (1) drug- and alcohol-dependent offenders, (2) mentally ill offenders, (3) sex offenders and child sexual abusers, (4) physically handicapped offenders, and (5) offenders with AIDS and other communicable diseases.

Drug- and Alcohol-Dependent Offenders. Drug and alcohol abuse are highly correlated with crime. In the late 1990s, 80 percent of federal, state, and jail inmates had used drugs as frequently as once a week during the period preceding their conviction offenses. One of the leading causes of correctional program failures is drug and/or alcohol dependencies (Turnbull et al. 2000).

Those considered **drug/alcohol-dependent offenders** present several problems to correctional personnel. The most prevalent types of problems linked with drugs and alcohol among inmates involve discipline, aggression, and insubordination. Jails are usually unable to deal with or control an inmate's drug/alcohol withdrawal symptoms. Also, the symptoms themselves are most often dealt with rather than the social and psychological causes of these dependencies. Thus, when offenders go through an alcohol detoxification program or are treated for drug addiction, they leave the program and are returned to similar circumstances that caused their original drug or alcohol dependencies (Peyton and Gossweiler 2001).

The pervasiveness of drug and alcohol problems among jail and prison inmates has caused several national organizations to experiment with a variety of drug/alcohol treatment programs. These programs have been implemented in all types of correctional facilities. Available evidence suggests that drug treatment programs currently offered in these correctional facilities can impact recidivism, perceptions of self-efficacy, and mood states such as depression and anxiety. Some of these drug treatment programs reporting favorable results include:

1. Jail Education and Treatment (JET) Program, Santa Clara County, California.
2. Deciding, Educating, Understanding, Counseling and Evaluation (DEUCE) Program, Contra Costa County, California.
3. Rebuilding, Educating, Awareness, Counseling, and Hope (REACH) Program, Los Angeles County, California.
4. Substance Abuse Intervention Division (SAID) Program, New York City Department of Correction.
5. New Beginnings, Westchester County, New York (Tunis et al. 1996:i–ii).

Because the use of illegal substances is so prevalent in state and federal prisons, the **Federal Bureau of Prisons (BOP)** revised its regulations to permit random urinalyses of high-risk inmates who are known to have been involved with drugs prior to their incarceration. The abuse of drugs is not strictly confined to inmates. It has been found that corrections employees are often about as likely as prisoners to abuse drugs. Most state, local, and federal agencies conduct routine urinalyses to detect and/or deter drug abuse among corrections employees as well as inmates (Martin and Bryant 2001; Vanyur and Strada 2002).

Interestingly, England, Australia, Canada, and several South American countries have experimented with stimulant maintenance programs in recent years. Thus, instead of promoting complete drug withdrawal and abstinence, drug offenders are placed on methadone maintenance as a first step toward stimulant maintenance. However, some addiction professionals oppose stimulant maintenance on the basis of its possible effects on drug abstinence and the fact that it sends the wrong message to society. However, advocates of stimulant maintenance in other countries have countered that, in the United States, a prohibition on illegal drugs has compromised basic human rights, created and sustained a black market for illicit drugs, multiplied the prison population, and exacerbated an epidemic spread of AIDS among intravenous users (Alexander and Tsou 2001).

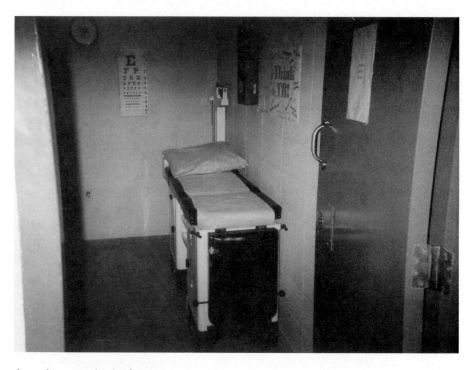

A medium-sized jail infirmary.

Mentally Ill Offenders. It is estimated that of the 7 million people jailed annually for short periods, about 600,000 of these are mentally ill. On any given day, 86 percent of our nation's jails hold mentally ill individuals for varying periods (Cornelius 1997:31). The mentally ill exhibit a range of mental problems from psychoses and emotional disruptions to dysfunctions in their abilities to work with or relate to others (Davison and Taylor 2001). Concern about the prevalence of mental illness in prisons is not unique to the United States. Other countries, such as Argentina and Canada, have studied mental illness in their custodial institutions for many years (Brink, Doherty, and Boer 2001; Crisanti and Love 2001; Folino and Urratia 2001).

A survey of U.S. prisons shows that about 63,000 inmates were involved in some type of mental health treatment program in 2001 (Camp and Camp 2002:134). Mentally ill inmates often exhibit a high degree of socially disruptive behavior. Such inmates often behave in ways atypical to the general jail/prison population. Because they respond differently to correctional officer commands, they are often unfairly disciplined for insubordination. In addition to their behavioral peculiarities, mentally ill inmates often cannot deal with the stresses of confinement; they may pose a danger to themselves, other inmates, or jail/prison staff; and their symptoms may worsen if they remain untreated (Dennison, Stougt, and Birgden 2001). There may be as many as 250,000 untreated and undiagnosed mentally ill inmates in U.S. prisons today (American Correctional Association 2002).

Inadequate jail and prison staffing makes diagnoses of inmates and their problems difficult. Mentally ill inmates often disguise their mental illnesses and are highly susceptible to prison culture and manipulation by other inmates. Also, they are often unresponsive to traditional rehabilitation programs available to other inmates. Advocates for developmentally disabled inmates argue that proper classification systems should be established to identify them. These inmates also need appropriate legal representation, with serious consideration given to dispositional alternatives for them other than incarceration (Williams and Arrigo 2002).

One state, Washington, has attempted to meet the needs of mentally ill prisoners aggressively. At McNeil Island, for instance, a program for mentally ill inmates has been established that provides medication monitoring, skills training, and a supportive milieu to help inmates cope with life in prison. Between 1994 and 1999, 448 inmates were admitted into the program for treatment. The program itself has been depicted as a intermediate-care residential program that isolates mentally ill prisoners from the general population. Those inmates who have been treated in this program have emerged with largely prosocial attitudes and conduct. Significant reductions in staff assaults have been reported, as well as fewer infractions and higher rates of work and school participation. The program does not work for all mentally ill inmates, however. A small minority continue to be difficult to manage despite the program intervention. But Washington authorities believe that they are making a difference by allocating their scarce resources in ways that benefit the majority of inmates designated as mentally ill (Lovell et al. 2001).

Sex Offenders and Child Sexual Abusers. Receiving special emphasis from corrections are **sex offenders** including **child sexual abusers.** Some researchers classify these offenders the same as criminals who are mentally ill and deserve special services (Dennison, Stougt, and Birgden 2001). Since many sex offenses are committed against victims known by the offender as a friend or family

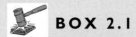

BOX 2.1

William L. Cox

Captain and Chief Deputy Coroner
Shasta County (CA) Sheriff's Office

Statistics

B.S. (physical education and business administration), California State University-Dominguez Hills

Background

Presently, I am a captain with the Shasta County Sheriff's Office, serving in the capacity of chief deputy coroner. I have been with the sheriff's office for the last thirteen years. I began my tenure in Shasta County as a patrol deputy in a residency post in the eastern portion of the county. The beat area was in excess of 540 square miles. Since that time, I have held positions of detective, custody sergeant, and chief deputy coroner. Prior to Shasta County, I was a police officer for the Hermosa Beach Police Department from 1978–1988. My assignments included patrol and detectives.

How I got into law enforcement was anything but a planned event. I had gone on a couple of ride-alongs with a local police department where I was raised in Southern California when I was in my early twenties. I could tell the police officer was not thrilled about having a ride-along, and my first impressions were not very affirming. I decided law enforcement was not my calling. During my last year of college I began applying for firefighter positions throughout Southern California. During those times, there were usually no more than three positions available and anywhere from 700 to 1,200 applicants taking the exams. I called the City of Hermosa Beach to see if they were giving a firefighter examination. I was advised that they were not, but that particular day was the last day they were taking applications for police officer. Well, as you can guess, I rushed down and submitted an application. It was a great fit for me and I've been at it over twenty-three years.

Work Experiences

In 1980 while working for the Hermosa Beach Police Department, I had the opportunity to transfer to investigations. I was assigned along with my partner to investigate a series of sexual assaults that had occurred over the prior two and a half years. There were in excess of twenty assaults believed to have been committed by the same suspect. Many hours went into investigating these unsolved cases with no results. This included surveillance and bike patrols during nighttime hours in areas where the suspect had committed the assaults. One evening, a man wearing men's underwear as a mask was observed by a witness outside a residence window. He appeared to be stretching and doing warmup exercises in preparation for the assault. The witness called the police, and the suspect was eventually caught by a police K-9 after a foot pursuit. My partner Tony Altfeld and I conducted the investigation and the suspect eventually pleaded guilty to several counts of burglary and sexual assault.

As the result of this investigation, I was hooked. I learned about the frustrations associated with ongoing, unsolved, dead-end after dead-end investigations. I learned about the anxiety associated with knowing that if we could not stop this individual, there would be more victims. I also learned of the elation associated with bringing someone to justice after experiencing all of the above emotions associated with that type of investigation. The greatest reward I personally felt was a simple comment one of the victims made to me during a telephone conversation. She had been victimized a year before the suspect's capture. She was visiting someone in New York during the followup investigation. I sent a videotape of a lineup to a detective in New York and had asked him to make contact with the woman and have her view the video. The detective contacted me and advised that she had positively identified the person we had in custody as the suspect in her case. When I telephoned for a followup interview, the first words from her were "You guys are great." There was a tone of relief and sincere appreciation in her voice. Those words have stuck with me ever since. It made me realize how much of a difference we can make.

Since 1997 I have been assigned to the coroner's office as chief deputy. Simply put, I am the administrator, not to be confused with the forensic pathologist who actually performs the post-mortem examinations. The role of the coroner is distinctly different from anything I have ever done in law enforcement. In the grand scheme of law enforcement, it seems like a minor role. However, nothing could be farther from the truth. We are the last people to speak for the decedent. We are responsible for determining why people die in sudden, unexpected, or unattended circumstances. We are responsible for ruling out foul play. In the case of a homicide, one of the single most important pieces of evidence is the decedent. From the deceased victim we may be able to determine the number and direction of gunshot or knife wounds, evidence of sexual assault, and even locate latent evidence from the suspect. With advancements in DNA, we are able to match saliva, semen, blood, skin cells, or hair follicles left on the victim back to the suspect. I recall one case where a suspect who strangled a little girl even left latent fingerprints on her skin.

Advice to Students

Law enforcement is a very comprehensive, demanding endeavor that will test your mettle. Never settle for anything less than excellence from yourself. If at all possible, obtain at least a bachelor's degree in a law enforcement–related field. Maintain balance in life. Remember that your badge is loaned to you by society for the purpose of serving them. Keep your faith in God and your commitment to family a higher priority than your job. Always keep a positive attitude about everything. Treat all people as you would want to be treated. Serve justice with malice toward none. Look upon the peace officer code of ethics as a standard by which to adhere. Enjoy the precious gift of life!

member, a large number go unreported to the police. Thus, it is impossible to obtain an accurate picture of the actual number of sex offenders in the United States (Peugh and Belenko 2001).

Sex offenders make up about 2 percent of the prison population in the United States (Camp and Camp 2002). About 20 percent of all state prison inmates have reported victimizing children. More than half of all violent crimes committed against children have involved child victims under the age of 12. Two-thirds of all prisoners convicted of rape or sexual assault had committed their crime against a child. While a majority of child sexual abusers are men, a small but significant number of child sexual abusers are females, and these numbers are growing (Kolton, Boer, and Boer 2001).

Child sexual abusers are generally adults who involve minors in virtually any kind of sexual activity ranging from intercourse with children to photographing them in lewd poses. A small portion of sex offenders who abuse young children are juveniles (Kenny, Keogh, and Seidler 2001). Over 3 million cases of general child abuse and neglect are reported to various government agencies each year, although the actual number of unreported cases is no doubt much higher. About 1 million of these cases are subsequently confirmed (Ericson 2001:1).

 **BOX 2.2**

MAN KILLS WITH HIV

Paul Leslie Hollingsworth

It happened in Austin, Texas. Paul Leslie Hollingsworth, 46, was HIV positive and had AIDS, a highly infectious disease. Hollingsworth had been diagnosed with AIDS in 1987. At the time Hollingsworth was diagnosed, he was donating blood at a local blood bank. Subsequently, Hollingsworth began to manifest AIDS symptoms. One symptom was a fungal infection in his mouth known as thrush. Ironically, Hollingsworth was working at the Austin State Hospital. Between 1987 and 1997, Hollingsworth had several sexual encounters with women. He knew that he had AIDS, but he did not inform his sexual partners of his condition. In 1997, one of the women Hollingsworth had sex with, a hospital co-worker, noticed the fungal infection in Hollingsworth's mouth. She had herself tested for AIDS and tested positive for HIV. She also inquired of another female co-worker who had dated Hollingsworth whether the woman had ever tested positive for HIV. The other woman said that she had contracted HIV from Hollingsworth in a previous year. At that point, prosecutors filed criminal charges against Hollingsworth, alleging that he had committed aggravated assault with a deadly weapon, namely the AIDS virus. Hollingsworth's case was the first of its kind in Texas where a person had been charged with knowingly transmitting HIV during consensual sex. The Travis County, Texas Assistant District Attorney, Bill Mange, said, "He knew he had HIV, he didn't tell her, he didn't use protection, and he knew that he was putting her at serious risk." Furthermore, Hollingsworth denied that he had ever been tested for AIDS, but his mother confirmed that he had, indeed, been tested, and that he knew that he was HIV positive. Police located at least four other women with whom Hollingsworth had had unprotected sex. Only one later tested positive for HIV.

In a subsequent plea bargain, Hollingsworth entered a plea to aggravated assault with a deadly weapon. The judge sentenced Hollingsworth to nine months' deferred adjudication, a form of probation. Prosecutors said that Hollingsworth had received the lenient sentence since he was in the advanced stages of AIDS and likely wouldn't live long enough to face a jury trial. Hollingsworth's defense counsel, David Frank, said that Hollingsworth did not admit to intentionally transmitting the virus and that he should not bear the full responsibility. He said that "these were two consenting adults having consensual heterosexual sex. They weren't exercising caution—neither one of them was." Frank also argued that prosecuting someone who knowingly transmits HIV could discourage people from getting tested and could open the floodgates for prosecuting the transmission of other diseases. However, Sandy Bartlett, an education coordinator with AIDS Services of Austin, said that AIDS educators have recently shifted their focus from making people aware of their responsibility to avoid contracting the disease to focusing more on the responsibility of those who have HIV. Being able to prosecute reckless behavior is critical to that message. Bartlett added that the responsibility is not equal. HIV-infected people know that they are infected, and it is their obligation first to exercise that responsibility. The case also raises questions about whether police officers should be allowed to seize medical records and use them as evidence in court. Under Texas law, police can investigate a person's HIV status only in sexual assault cases.

Should knowingly transmitting the AIDS virus to others be a crime? How should judges punish such a crime? What do you think?

Source: Adapted from the Associated Press. "Man Pleads Guilty to Using HIV as a Deadly Weapon," April 15, 2001.

Sex offenders, especially child sexual abusers, pose serious problems for jail and prison authorities. A majority of sex offenders have histories of being abused as children (Peugh and Belenko 2001). Attempts have been made to evaluate sex offender risks and needs. For instance, the Sex Offender Need Assessment Rating (SONAR) has been designed to assess sex offender risk. SONAR consists of five relative stable factors, including intimacy deficits, negative social influences, tolerance of sex offending, sexual self-regulation, and general self-regulation, together with four acute factors (i.e., substance abuse, negative mood, anger, and victim access). Tests of the scale's validity have been conducted on samples of 272 child-victim molesters and 137 adult-victim rapists who have been on probation or parole. Results thus far indicate that the test discloses interventions and social service strategies that might prove useful in meeting offender needs (Hanson and Harris 2001).

Child sexual abusers are often abused themselves by other inmates when their crimes become known to others. Other sex offenders become the prey of stronger inmates who use these offenders for their own sexual satisfactions. Because of limited resources and space, jail and prison officials cannot segregate these offenders effectively from other inmates. When placed in communities under some form of community correctional supervision, sex offenders may be more difficult to manage. But the research about sex offender recidivism is mixed. At least some research reports lower recidivism rates among sex offenders compared with other offender categories (Firestone et al. 2000; Jockusch and Keller 2001). In 1998 there were over 234,000 sex offenders under the authority of corrections in the United States, with 60 percent supervised in communities. Because of the diversity of personalities and social makeup of sex offenders, they pose unique challenges to probation and paroling authorities for supervision (Brink, Doherty, and Boer 2001; Peugh and Belenko 2001).

Physically Handicapped Offenders.   Those offenders with physical handicaps are a neglected but growing part of the offender population. Some offenders are confined to wheelchairs, and therefore special facilities must be constructed to accommodate their access to probation or parole offices or community-based sites. Other offenders have hearing or speech impairments that limit them in various ways. More than a few violent offenders, including some murderers, are deaf or have severely limited communication skills. In these instances, problems are generated pertaining to being able to understand the charges against them and/or being able to participate in their own defense (Vernon, Steinberg, and Montoya 1999).

Physically challenged offenders often require greater attention from their POs. Acquiring and maintaining employment is sometimes difficult for persons with different types of physical handicaps, such as the parolee-client managed by Kay McGill. Many POs become a **broker** between their own agencies and community businesses who are encouraged to employ certain of these clients with special problems. Community volunteers are increasingly helpful in assisting probation and parole agencies with physically handicapped clients (Motiuk et al. 1994).

HIV/AIDS: A Growing Problem.   **AIDS** or Acquired Immune Deficiency Syndrome is a growing correctional problem. Inmates living in close quarters are highly susceptible to the AIDS virus because of the likelihood of anal-genital or oral-genital contact. Since the mid-1980s, AIDS education in incarcerative settings has been expanded to provide inmates with a greater understanding of the causes and spreading of this disease (Keeton and Swanson 1998).

If AIDS is prevalent and increasing among jail and prison inmates, then it is prevalent and increasing among probationers and parolees as well. In view of the various circumstances under which AIDS has been transmitted in recent years, from saliva or blood residue from dentists and others working in different health professions, probation and parole officers have perceived that their risk of being infected with the AIDS virus has increased greatly. Many probationers and parolees are former drug offenders. Drug-dependent clients represent a special danger, since AIDS is known to be easily transmitted when drug addicts share their needles used to inject heroin and other substances. Thus, there have been increased efforts to coordinate AIDS treatment between prison and community-based corrections agencies in recent years.

Either voluntary or mandatory AIDS testing has been undertaken in many jails and all prisons. While the U.S. Supreme Court has not ruled definitively on the constitutionality of such mandatory testing, the results of these tests have helped limit the spread of AIDS in selected jurisdictions. For correctional officers who must work around inmates with AIDS, there is clear apprehension. A survey of correctional officers has revealed that requiring inmates to undergo AIDS testing would assuage their own feelings while working within a potentially medically dangerous population. At the same time, educational programs have been or are being established in various jurisdictions for the purposes of enabling correctional officers to learn more about how HIV is transmitted and to dispel some of the myths associated with AIDS (Mahaffey and Marcus 1995). AIDS education is a major issue in contemporary corrections.

THE SENTENCING PROCESS

Purposes of Sentencing

The purposes of sentencing are (1) retribution, (2) deterrence and prevention, (3) just deserts and justice, (4) incapacitation and control, (5) and rehabilitation and reintegration.

Retribution.   Sentences are designed to exact retribution for crimes committed. Perpetrators must be punished in some way in order to comply with criminal laws. Punishments include jail or prison time, fines, or both. Proportionality is sought so that the greater the offense, the greater the punishment. This objective is not always fulfilled perfectly, and the system is replete with examples of disproportionality in sentences imposed (Bessette 1997).

Deterrence and Prevention.   When the public sees offenders punished for their crimes and given harsh sentences, an element of deterrence is introduced whereby potential criminals are deterred from committing crimes because of the penalties they may suffer if caught. To some extent, at least, some crime is prevented and criminals are deterred because of the sentences others receive. Sentences, especially those involving confinement in a jail or prison, are generally unpleasant (Ashe 2001). If potential offenders avoid committing crimes because of the painfulness of prospective punishments, then some deterrence and prevention are accomplished.

Just Deserts and Justice.   Judges attempt to match sentences imposed with the nature and seriousness of conviction offenses. The public seems satisfied whenever criminals are punished in ways that equate with their crime seriousness. The public is dissatisfied whenever criminals receive leniency or light sentences that do not seem justified in view of one's crime. Prosecutors seek penalties that satisfy the law, both technically and morally.

Incapacitation and Control.   Whether criminals are sexual predators, embezzlers, murderers, or petty thieves, citizens wish to be protected from them. Thus, placing criminals in some type of confinement facility such as a jail or prison effectively removes them from society. But not all convicted offenders can be incarcerated because of chronic **jail and prison overcrowding.** Therefore, alternative methods are used to supervise and control these criminals. Probation and community corrections are punishments that place a large proportion of offenders under the supervisory auspices of probation departments. Various behavioral restrictions and conditions are also imposed in order to minimize the likelihood that these criminals will reoffend.

Rehabilitation and Reintegration.   In a perfect world, corrections corrects behavior of offenders and makes former criminals law-abiding and respectful of the rights of others. However, two-thirds or more of all convicted offenders recidivate and commit new offenses. The offending rate varies according to the type of offense and other variables. There is sufficient recidivism among criminals that true rehabilitation does not occur in a majority of cases. Nevertheless, a continuing objective of corrections is to provide offenders with the means and opportunity to become law-abiding and rehabilitated. There are numerous reintegrative programs available to criminals of all types, including vocational-educational curricula, individual and group counseling, and a variety of social services. Offenders are encouraged to participate in these programs, whether they are offered in jails, prisons, or communities (Burke and Vivian 2001). One indicator that rehabilitation occurs is the amount of remorse expressed by convicted offenders. Offender remorse is expected, although expressions of remorse by convicted criminals often have little impact on the sentences they receive (Bagaric and Amarasekara 2001).

TYPES OF SENTENCING SYSTEMS

In 2000, there were 905,957 felony convictions obtained in state courts (Maguire and Pastore 2002:457). About 45 percent of these convicted felons were incarcerated in state prisons, while about 29 percent were confined in local jails. For every one of these felony convictions, sentences were imposed by judges according to one of four sentencing schemes. These include (1) indeterminate sentencing, (2) determinate sentencing, (3) presumptive sentencing, and (4) mandatory sentencing.

Indeterminate Sentencing

Indeterminate sentencing is used by a majority of state courts (Connelly and Williams 2000). Indeterminate sentencing is when the judge sets upper and lower limits on the time to be served, either on probation or in jail or prison. If offenders are incarcerated under indeterminate sentencing, a parole board determines their early release. Usually, offenders must serve at least the minimum sentence as prescribed by the judge before parole can be granted. This is known as the minimum-maximum sentence. An example of indeterminate sentencing might be where a judge sentences an offender to "not less than one year nor more than ten years" for robbery. The offender must serve at least one year of this sentence before a parole board can grant early release. Indeterminate sentencing provides a strong inducement for inmates to behave well while confined. Inmates who disrupt the prison or jail or who otherwise cause correctional staff or other inmates problems will seriously jeopardize their early-release chances. Inmates who are continually disruptive may never be paroled. But after they serve their maximum sentence of ten years, the state must release them.

Another version of indeterminate sentencing is **fixed indeterminate sentencing.** Under this scheme, judges sentence offenders to a single prison term, which is treated as the maximum sentence for all practical purposes. The implied minimum might be zero for all sentences, one year for all sentences, or a fixed proportion of the maximum. In either the **minimum/maximum determinate sentencing** or fixed indeterminate sentencing systems, parole boards determine an inmate's early-release date (U.S. Bureau of Justice Assistance 1998).

Determinate Sentencing

In the last few decades, all states have revised or reformed their sentencing schemes. In nearly half of all state jurisdictions, a shift has occurred from indeterminate to **determinate sentencing** (Getty 2000). Determinate sentencing prescribes that judges fix the term of an offender's incarceration, which must be served in full, less any **good-time credits** that might be applicable. Good-time credits are days earned and deducted from one's maximum sentence as the result of good institutional behavior.

For example, in 2000, most U.S. state correctional systems awarded either 15 days, 20 days, or 30 days a month off of an inmate's maximum sentence for every 30 days served in prison. Thus, if an inmate was sentenced to a maximum of ten years, under a 30-day-per-month good-time scenario, it is possible that the inmate would serve only half of the original maximum sentence of ten years. Essentially, an inmate would have an equivalent amount of time deducted from his sentence for every month or year served. A five-year incarcerative period would earn five years' worth of good-time credit. Under this determinate sentencing scheme, good-time credit accumulations would determine one's specific release date. This is a key reason such a scheme is called determinate sentencing, because inmates know approximately when they must be released from custody (Maguire and Pastore 2002).

The most generous good-time credit allocation is Alabama, which permitted 75 days of good-time credit for every 30 days served. Prior to 1988, Oklahoma provided 137 days of good-time credit for every 30 days served. The U.S. Federal Bureau of Prisons awards up to 54 days a year to federal inmates for every year served (U.S. Bureau of Justice Assistance 1998).

The basic distinction between indeterminate and determinate sentencing is that judges must impose a fixed sentence under determinate sentencing and early release is governed by the accumulation of good-time credit; under indeterminate sentencing, parole boards make early-release decisions following a minimum-maximum sentence imposed by the sentencing judge. Theoretically, at least, determinate sentencing reduces or minimizes the abuse of judicial and parole board discretion in determining early release for inmates. It is arguable, however, whether judicial discretion has been affected seriously by determinate sentencing (Stolzenberg and D'Alessio 1997).

Presumptive or Guidelines-Based Sentencing

One way of making sentencing more objective is to establish a sentencing commission to study sentencing and its deterrent effects. The use of sentencing commissions was first proposed in the United States in the early 1970s, with the first sentencing commission being established in 1978 (Heikes and Martinez 2001). Sentencing guidelines have reduced disparities and gender differences in sentencing in most jurisdictions where they have been established.

The U.S. Sentencing Commission and eighteen other state jurisdictions, such as Minnesota, have shifted to **presumptive or guidelines-based sentencing** schemes (Givelber 2000). Presumptive sentencing is based upon predetermined guidelines accompanying each offense. For instance, the presumptive guidelines formulated by the U.S. Sentencing Commission arrange offenses into 43 levels, with 6 criminal history categories. Table 2.1 is the sentencing guidelines table devised by the U.S. Sentencing Commission.

A formula is used to arrive at the specified range of numbers of months imposed by the sentencing judge. The formula is based on an offender's prior record or criminal history, mitigating and/or aggravating circumstances, the length of previous incarcerations, and other factors. For example, the base offense level for the crime, insider trading, is 8. Transporting a minor for the purpose of prostitution has a base offense level of 16. From here, the level is increased by one of several possible aggravating circumstances such as the amount of money involved or whether victim injury resulted from the crime. Thus, an offender convicted of insider trading but with no prior record is in offense level 6 and criminal history category I. Where these values intersect in the body of Table 2.1 shows the number of months possible incarceration, 0–6 in this instance. The judge may sentence the offender to probation ("0") or a maximum of six months. Career offenders are always placed in category VI, regardless of the offense level associated with the crime they have committed.

Several states, including Minnesota, have adopted presumptive sentencing guidelines for judges to follow. Interestingly, Minnesota's sentencing guidelines scheme has allowed many chronic offenders to avoid lengthy incarcerations. Chronic offenders in Minnesota average eight times more convictions for property offenses and six times more convictions for violent offenses compared with other offenders. However, Minnesota's sentencing guidelines do not address habitual or chronic offenders aggressively. In contrast, Tennessee groups offenses into various ranges such as a Range I offense or a Range II offense. Class X felonies are also identified with accompanying serious punishments. Rather complex calculations are used by Tennessee judges in arriving at sentences imposed on offenders. If offenders are recidivists, a separate set of calculations is necessary to determine numbers of years or months of incarceration.

Presumptive sentencing guidelines supposedly curb judicial discretion by obligating judges to stay within certain boundaries (expressed in terms of

TABLE 2.1

U.S. Sentencing Guidelines (months)

Offense Level	Criminal History Category					
	I 0 or 1	II 2 or 3	III 4, 5, 6	IV 7, 8, 9	V 10, 11, 12	VI 13 or more
1	0–1	0–2	0–3	0–4	0–5	0–6
2	0–2	0–3	0–4	0–5	0–6	1–7
3	0–3	0–4	0–5	0–6	2–8	3–9
4	0–4	0–5	0–6	2–8	4–10	6–12
5	0–5	0–6	1–7	4–10	6–12	9–15
6	0–6	1–7	2–8	6–12	9–15	12–18
7	1–7	2–8	4–10	8–14	12–18	15–21
8	2–8	4–10	6–12	10–16	15–21	18–24
9	4–10	6–12	8–14	12–18	18–24	21–27
10	6–12	8–14	10–16	15–21	21–27	24–30
11	8–14	10–16	12–18	18–24	24–30	27–33
12	10–16	12–18	15–21	21–27	27–33	30–37
13	12–18	15–21	18–24	24–30	30–37	33–41
14	15–21	18–24	21–27	27–33	33–41	37–46
15	18–24	21–27	24–30	30–37	37–46	41–51
16	21–27	24–30	27–33	33–41	41–51	46–57
17	24–30	27–33	30–37	37–46	46–57	51–63
18	27–33	30–37	33–41	41–51	51–63	57–71
19	30–37	33–41	37–46	46–57	57–71	63–78
20	33–41	37–46	41–51	51–63	63–78	70–87
21	37–46	41–51	46–57	57–71	70–87	77–96
22	41–51	46–57	51–63	63–78	77–96	84–105
23	46–57	51–63	57–71	70–87	84–105	92–115
24	51–63	57–71	63–78	77–96	92–115	100–125
25	57–71	63–78	70–87	84–105	100–125	110–137
26	63–78	70–87	78–97	92–115	110–137	120–150
27	70–87	78–97	87–108	100–125	120–150	130–162
28	78–97	87–108	97–121	110–137	130–162	140–175
29	87–108	97–121	108–135	121–151	140–175	151–188
30	97–121	108–135	121–151	135–168	151–188	168–210
31	108–135	121–151	135–168	151–188	168–210	188–235
32	121–151	135–168	151–188	168–210	188–235	210–262
33	135–168	151–188	168–210	188–235	210–262	235–293
34	151–188	168–210	188–235	210–262	235–293	262–327
35	168–210	188–235	210–262	235–293	262–327	292–365
36	188–235	210–262	235–293	262–327	292–365	324–405
37	210–262	235–293	262–327	292–365	324–405	360–life
38	235–293	262–327	292–365	324–405	360–life	360–life
39	262–327	292–365	324–405	360–life	360–life	360–life
40	292–365	324–405	360–life	360–life	360–life	360–life
41	324–405	360–life	360–life	360–life	360–life	360–life
42	360–life	360–life	360–life	360–life	360–life	360–life
43	Life	Life	Life	Life	Life	Life

Source: U.S. Sentencing Commission, *U.S. Sentencing Guidelines*, Washington, DC: U.S. Government Printing Office, 1987.

months) when sentencing offenders. The intent of presumptive guidelines is to create greater consistency among judges in the sentences they impose on different offenders convicted of the same offenses under similar circumstances. However, judges may depart from these statutory ranges by as much as a year or more (Shane-Dubow et al. 1998). But if judges impose a harsher or more lenient sentence, they must furnish a written explanation to justify these departures.

The results of presumptive sentencing among state jurisdictions are inconsistent. In various jurisdictions where guidelines-based sentencing has been implemented, it has been found that sentences are more often influenced by a judges' attitudes and defendant racial/ethnic and socioeconomic factors than strictly legal criteria (Hanbury 2000). Generally, however, after new sentencing guidelines have been imposed in different jurisdictions, sentencing disparities have been reduced as sentencing has become more systematic for similar offense categories. Newly implemented screening mechanisms for prosecuting cases have reduced case processing time in various jurisdictions, although the types of case dispositions and sentences continue to be influenced by one or more extralegal factors (Taxman and Elis 1999).

As the result of massive sentencing reforms, the percentage of prison sentences among convicted state felons has significantly changed. About 68 percent of all convicted felons received incarceration in 1994, but this figure had climbed to 83 percent in 1999 (Maguire and Pastore 2002:443). However, the average prison sentence has decreased from 67 months in 1994 to 62 months in 1999 (Maguire and Pastore 2002). But for certain types of offenses such as distribution of drugs, the incarceration of drug traffickers has steadily risen.

While these various sentencing schemes have changed the average sentence lengths of prison inmates, sentencing disparities have also been minimized in more than few jurisdictions. Stolzenberg and D'Alessio (1997) have found that in Minnesota, for instance, there has been a 22 percent reduction in disparity for nonprison/prison outcomes and a 60 percent reduction in sentencing inequality for overall sentence lengths for persons of different races and ethnicities convicted of identical offenses. Reductions in disparities according to racial factors also occurred over time in Pennsylvania among convicted felons (Gorton and Boies 1999). However, disparities in types of sentences and sentence lengths attributable to extralegal factors such as race, gender, or socioeconomic status continue to be found in various jurisdictions, including federal courts (Cole 1999; Everett and Nienstedt 1999).

Mandatory Sentencing

Mandatory sentencing is a sentencing system where the judge is required to impose an incarcerative sentence, often of a specified length, for certain crimes or for particular categories of offenders (Renzetti 2001). There is no option of probation, suspended sentence, or immediate parole eligibility. Michigan and many other states have mandatory sentencing provisions for specific offenses, such as using a dangerous firearm during the commission of a felony. Michigan adds two years to whatever sentence judges might impose otherwise. For example, if the conviction offense is armed robbery, the judge may impose a sentence of five to ten years. However, an additional mandatory two-year sentence is imposed to run consecutively with the five to ten year sentence as a punishment for using a dangerous weapon. Thus, if the offender becomes parole-eligible after serving six years of his or her sentence, then an additional two-year sentence must be served in its entirety before parole can be considered by the parole board. Clearly, Michigan wants offenders who commit felonies not to use dangerous weapons. Mandatory sentencing is intended to deter them from using such weapons.

Most states have mandatory penalties for particular offenses, especially for drug trafficking (Gest 2001). The most well-known mandatory penalty is life imprisonment for being convicted as an habitual offender. Habitual offenders are punished under **habitual offender laws,** which usually carry life-without-parole sentences. Recidivists, especially those who commit violent crimes, are targeted by habitual offender legislation, such as that enacted in Florida (Kovandzic 2001). Offenders convicted of a third felony may receive life imprisonment as a mandatory sentence. One clear intent of mandatory penalties is to deter criminals from committing crimes. But do such laws have this impact? In Florida, at least, there is little evidence that the habitual offender law has changed crime rates. Over an extended period of time, slight reductions in rape, robbery, assault, burglary, larceny, and auto theft have occurred in Florida, but this almost negligible decline has been attributable to longer prison terms served by habitual offenders rather than to the actual deterrent value of the law.

Mandatory sentencing laws have been severely criticized (Fradella 2000). Some observers say that mandatory sentencing should be abolished outright, since it does not reduce recidivism. The absence of a noticeable incapacitation impact is supported by the fact that the laws have resulted in little or no prison population growth. Furthermore, the three-strikes laws have had few, if any, compensating crime reduction effects through deterrence or incapacitation, and thus they have no justification for continued use (Marvell and Moody 2001; Zimring, Hawkins, and Kamin 2001). One possible explanation for the lack of prison population growth during the period immediately following the enactment of three-strikes-and-you're-out legislation is that many prosecutors are not charging these offenses. Instead, they may be using the threat of mandatory penalties to elicit guilty pleas to lesser charges from criminal defendants. This scenario is quite common in most jurisdictions with such statutes.

Some observers have hypothesized that because of three-strikes laws and their accompanying mandatory penalties, an increase in homicides may result. This is because a few criminals, fearing the enhanced penalties, will murder their victims and witnesses to limit resistance and subsequent identification. An analysis of fifty states for the period 1970–1998 revealed that passage of three-strikes legislation in various states was accompanied by a 10 to 12 percent increase in homicides in the short run and a 23 to 29 percent increase in homicides in those jurisdictions in the long run (Marvell and Moody 2001).

Further, extensive prison overcrowding has occurred in those jurisdictions where mandatory sentencing policies have been enforced. Interestingly, this overcrowding has occurred in large part due to the incarceration of numerous nonviolent offenders who also happen to be chronic recidivists. It has been estimated that over 1 million nonviolent recidivists have been incarcerated for lengthy prison terms, some for life without the possibility of parole, for less serious and nonviolent felonies. The theft of a slice of pizza from a Pizza Hut by someone who has been convicted of two previous felonies may cause that person to be prosecuted as a habitual offender and be incarcerated for life. Are these the types of offenders who should be targeted by habitual offender statutes and mandatory prison terms? Some critics have suggested that the states and federal government should abolish mandatory sentencing schemes

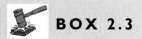 **BOX 2.3**

STATE AND FEDERAL PUNISHMENTS FOR THREE-TIME FELONY OFFENDERS WHO COMMIT NONVIOLENT PROPERTY CRIMES AS THEIR THIRD OFFENSE

State or Federal Jurisdiction	Punishment
Federal	12–18 months, presumptive 15 months
Alaska	3–5 years, presumptive term of 3 years
Arizona	4–6 years
Connecticut	1–10 years
Delaware	Not more than 10 years; recidivist offender penalty not applicable
District of Columbia	Not more than 10 years; recidivist offender penalty not applicable
Florida	Not more than 10 years
Georgia	10 years
Hawaii	20 months
Idaho	1–14 years; recidivist/habitual offender penalty 5 years to life imprisonment, with exceptions
Illinois	2–5 years; recidivist offender penalty not applicable
Indiana	18 months; possible 18 additional months for aggravating circumstances; recidivist offender penalty not applicable
Iowa	3–5 years
Kansas	9–11 months; recidivist offender penalty not applicable
Kentucky	5–10 years
Maine	Less than 1 year; recidivist offender penalty not applicable
Massachusetts	Not more than 5 years; recidivist offender penalty not applicable
Minnesota	Not more than 5 years; recidivist offender penalty not applicable
Mississippi	Not more than 5 years; recidivist offender penalty not applicable
Nebraska	Not more than 5 years; recidivist offender penalty not applicable
New Jersey	5–10 years
New Mexico	30 months
New York	3–4 years
North Carolina	4–25 months; recidivist offender penalty not applicable
North Dakota	Not more than 10 years
Ohio	6–12 months; no general recidivist statute
Oregon	Not more than 5 years; no general recidivist statute
Pennsylvania	Not more than 5 years; recidivist offender penalty not applicable
Rhode Island	Not more than 10 years; recidivist offender penalty not applicable
South Carolina	Not more than 5 years; recidivist offender penalty not applicable
Tennessee	4–8 years
Utah	Not more than 5 years; recidivist offender penalty not applicable
Washington	Not more than 14 months; recidivist offender penalty not applicable
Wyoming	Not more than 10 years; recidivist offender penalty not applicable

Not more than 15 years in prison

Colorado	4–12 years; recidivist offender penalty not applicable
Maryland	Not more than 15 years; recidivist offender penalty not applicable
New Hampshire	Not more than 15 years; recidivist offender penalty not applicable
Wisconsin	Not more than 11 years; after 2/2003 up to 2 years

(continued)

BOX 2.3 *(Continued)*

State or Federal Jurisdiction	Punishment
Not more than 20 years in prison	
Arkansas	3–20 years; eligible for parole after one-third of sentence served
Missouri	Not more than 20 years; eligible for parole after one-fourth of sentence served
Texas	2–20 years; eligible for parole after one-fourth of sentence served
Virginia	1–20 years; under sentencing guidelines, 6 years, 3 months to 15 years, 7 months; recidivist offender penalty not applicable
25 years or more	
Alabama	Life or any term of not less than 20 years; eligible for parole after the lesser of one-third of sentence or 10 years served
California	25 years to life; eligible for parole after 25 years
Louisiana	Life without the possibility of parole; recidivist statute triggered with violent felony and at least two prior violent felony convictions; 6⅔–20 years for petty theft as third offense
Michigan	Imprisonment for life or for a lesser term; eligible for parole following minimum term set by sentencing judge
Montana	5–100 years; not more than 5 years for third offense of petty theft
Nevada	Life without the possibility of parole; or life with the possibility of parole after serving 10 years; or a definite term of 25 years with eligibility for parole after serving 10 years
Oklahoma	Not less than 20 years; eligible for parole after serving one-third of sentence
South Dakota	Maximum penalty of life imprisonment with no minimum term; eligible for parole after serving one-half of sentence
Vermont	Up to and including life, or not more than 10 years; court has discretion to sentence habitual offender to sentence specified for grand larceny alone; eligible for parole after 6 months
West Virginia	Life imprisonment, with parole eligibility after 15 years

Source: Ewing v. California, _____ U.S. _____, 123 S.Ct. 1179, at 1202–1205 (2003).

that send nonviolent offenders to prison for lengthy periods and concentrate their energies and resources on more serious violent offenders (Irwin, Schiraldi, and Ziedenberg 2000).

Another charge against mandatory sentencing is that the criminal statutes targeted for mandatory sentences are typically associated with street crimes. Street crimes are overrepresented by criminals in the lower socioeconomic levels, and thus there is inherent class discrimination whenever such mandatory laws are implemented (Steffensmeier and Demuth 2001). Thus, mandatory sentencing provisions have applied to and targeted powerless and marginal groups in U.S. society.

In sum, mandatory sentencing provisions, such as the three-strikes-and-you're-out law passed in California, are considered enormously overrated by some critics (Zimring, Hawkins, and Kamin 2001). In fact, analyses of various data sets for several aggregates of criminal offenders in California and other states where habitual offender laws have been enacted have shown that these laws have had very little impact, if any, on state crime rates. This is largely because these statutes are infrequently used (Chen 2000). If they are infrequently used, why were they passed in the first place? One answer is that the passage of such laws appeals to public interest and reflects a get-tough stance toward crime by legislators. With these laws in place, indeed, state and federal criminal justice systems are equipped to deal more severely with repeat offenders. But most often these laws are used as leverage by prosecutors who accept guilty pleas to lesser crimes from defendants who are in jeopardy of being charged as habitual offenders. Thus, more than a few prosecutors advise defendants that if they don't plead guilty to lesser crimes, then they will be prosecuted as habitual offenders where life imprisonment is a definite possibility. In fact, this is how many convictions are elicited, especially from chronic recidivists (Chen 2000; Meehan 2000).

The Federal Violent Crime Control and Law Enforcement Act of 1994 and Sentencing Reforms.   Also known as the Federal Crime Bill, the 1994 Anti-Crime Bill, or simply the Crime Bill, the Federal Violent Crime Control and Law Enforcement Act of 1994 was designed to accomplish many things, including putting more police officers on the streets, investigating and experimenting with new crime prevention techniques, and exploring ways of attacking gangs and juvenile delinquency (Wilson and Petersilia 2002). The Crime Bill was also intended to modify the present sentencing practices and policies of individual states and to get tough on criminals. One way of getting tough on criminals would be to impose more severe sentences on them and to make offenders serve greater portions of their sentences. Short-term federal monies would be made available to any state agreeing to ensure that sentenced offenders would have to serve at least 85 percent of their maximum sentences. In 2000 the average sentence was about 35 percent of the maximum sentence imposed (Maguire and Pastore 2002). Making offenders serve at least 85 percent of their maximum sentences would cause most inmates to be confined for longer periods than they presently serve.

But this aspect of the Crime Bill has its drawbacks, particularly the problem created by greater prison and jail overcrowding. In states such as North Dakota, for example, offenders have served about 40 percent of their maximum sentences in the past. Thus, if a ten-year sentence was imposed, offenders were ordinarily paroled after serving four years. But under the Crime Bill, inmates would have to serve eight and a half years of a ten-year sentence, or 85 percent of the maximum sentence imposed. While the North Dakota State Penitentiary did not have an overcrowding problem in 1995, by 1996 the operational capacity of the penitentiary was exceeded (American Correctional Association 2002). Some legislators considered new prison construction for North Dakota, which would impose a substantial tax burden on state residents. It doesn't take a lot of math to project growing inmate populations in those states accepting federal money. Because the federal money given to states is only short-term money, the burden of paying for additional prison and jail space eventually shifts to taxpayers, many of whom already feel overtaxed.

One other aspect of the Crime Bill worth mentioning is its ban on a group of military-style semiautomatic firearms or assault weapons, as well as magazines capable of holding more than 10 rounds. The intent of this ban was to reduce the homicide rates in those types of crimes involving firearms. Throughout the remainder of the 1990s and beyond 2000, available evidence suggests that the Crime Bill has not significantly reduced either multiple-victim homicides or multiple-gunshot-wound victimizations as a result of the assault-weapon ban (Koper and Roth 2001). This result is likely attributable to ineffective enforcement methods and the ready availability of such firearms through black markets in most large cities in the United States.

SENTENCING HEARINGS

For almost every serious felony conviction, a sentencing hearing is held. This hearing is usually scheduled six to eight weeks following one's conviction. A sentencing hearing is a formal proceeding where the sentencing judge hears pleadings and arguments from both the prosecution and defense to either impose the maximum sentence under the law or show leniency by imposing a lesser sentence. The sentencing hearing is arguably the most critical stage in the criminal justice process (Konradi and Burger 2000). Sentencing hearings may be conducted exclusively by the judge or with a **jury.** In murder cases where the death penalty might be imposed, juries find defendants guilty in a first phase, deliberating at the conclusion of a **trial.** Then the same juries must convene again in a second phase, the sentencing hearing, and determine whether the death penalty should be imposed.

Sentencing hearings are usually held in the same courtrooms where the convicted offender's trial was conducted. Defense counsel may present friends and relatives of the offender who can testify about the offender's past, his or her good qualities, and his or her likelihood of behaving in a law-abiding fashion in the future. An attempt is made by the defense to influence the judge so that a lighter sentence will be imposed. Significant others in the convicted offender's past are called to make favorable remarks about the offender. However, the prosecution is able to call as witnesses against the offender the victims, their relatives and friends. These persons can make statements and give testimony about why the judge should impose the maximum sentence. They can speak out against showing the offender any leniency.

For instance, Richard Allen Davis, 42, was convicted in June 1996 of kidnapping and murdering a 12-year-old girl, Polly Klaas, in Petaluma, California, on October 1, 1993 (Associated Press 1996:A4). In August 1996, a sentencing hearing was held for Davis to determine whether he should receive life without parole or the death penalty. Polly Klaas's father, Marc Klaas, spoke in favor of Davis's execution. Many other relatives and friends of Polly Klaas spoke out against any leniency for Davis. However, Davis showed his contempt for the proceedings by making vulgar gestures at television cameras. At one point, Davis spoke on his own behalf, apologizing to the Klaas family in open court. But he ruined this exhibition of contrition by insinuating that Polly Klaas had been sexually abused by her own father and that she had disclosed this fact to Davis shortly before he killed her. Davis was sentenced to death (Locke 1996:A1).

Essentially, sentencing hearings enable both victims and offenders an opportunity to be heard. In the Davis hearing, the event was clearly cathartic for the family and close friends of Polly Klaas. In less emotionally charged hearings, some victims and their families may actually ask the judge to show the offender leniency. In short, the victims and/or the friends and family of victims may speak about how the offender's crime has affected their lives. The loss of a loved one is most grievous, and statements can be given to indicate the extent of this loss. For convicted offenders, sentencing hearings provide them with a brief forum to show judges that they have accepted the responsibility for their own actions and that they are sorry. While their apologies cannot replace the loss of life, they can attempt to mitigate or lessen the harshness of the penalty contemplated by the sentencing judge.

Besides hearing from the defense and prosecution orally, letters and other documents are introduced both for and against convicted offenders. Psychiatrists may provide additional testimony, either favorable or adverse to offenders. However, this information is not always accurate. It has been found, for instance, that mental health professionals have erred in various ways when giving testimony in sentencing hearings. These observed errors include (1) inadequate reliance on base rates, (2) failure to consider context, (3) susceptibility to illusory correlation, (4) failure to define severity of violence, (5) overreliance on clinical interviews, (6) misapplication of psychological testing, (7) exaggerated implications of antisocial personality disorder, (8) ignorance of the effects of aging, (9) misuse of behavior patterns, (10) neglect of preventive measures, (11) insufficient data, and (12) failure to express the risk estimate in probabilistic terms (Cunningham and Reidy 1999). Unfortunately, we have no way of estimating the incidence of such errors in testimony given by these experts. Despite the possibility of such errors, sentencing hearings do permit ample opportunity for both sides to present inculpatory and exculpatory information to the judge from a variety of sources.

Judges also request a **presentence investigation.** A presentence investigation is a thorough background check of a convicted offender by a probation officer, usually at the direction of the sentencing judge. This background check includes a description of the conviction offense; the educational, familial, and social background of the offender; indication of any prior record; a report of any prior juvenile offending; and other relevant information. Pre-sentence investigations almost always involve the preparation of **pre-sentence investigation reports (PSIs).** These documents, usually prepared by probation officers at court request or order, are submitted to the judge during the interval between conviction and the sentencing hearing. Thus, an additional written statement, evaluation, and recommendation is a part of the documentation judges consider when imposing sentences.

THE PRE-SENTENCE INVESTIGATION (PSI) AND REPORT

The pre-sentence investigation report is an informational document prepared by a probation officer that contains the following personal data about convicted offenders, the conviction offense(s), and other relevant data:

1. Name
2. Address
3. Prior record including offenses and dates
4. Date and place of birth
5. Crime(s) or conviction offense and date of offense

6. Offender's version of conviction offense
7. Offender's employment history
8. Offender's known addiction to or dependency on drugs or alcohol or controlled substances of any kind
9. Statutory penalties for the conviction offense
10. Marital status
11. Personal and family data
12. Name of spouse and children, if any
13. Educational history
14. Any special vocational training or specialized work experience
15. Mental and/or emotional stability
16. Military service, if any, and disposition
17. Financial condition, including assets and liabilities
18. Probation officer's personal evaluation of offender
19. Sentencing data
20. Alternative plans made by defendant, if placed on probation
21. Physical description
22. Prosecution version of conviction offense
23. Victim impact statement prepared by victim, if any
24. Codefendant information, if codefendant is involved
25. Recommendation from probation officer about sentencing
26. Name of prosecutor
27. Name of defense attorney
28. Presiding judge
29. Jurisdiction where offense occurred
30. Case docket number and other identifying numbers (e.g., Social Security, driver's license, etc.)
31. Plea
32. Disposition or sentence
33. Location of probation or custody

Pre-sentence investigation reports are written summaries of information obtained by the probation officer through interviews with the defendant and an investigation of the defendant's background (Stinchcomb and Hippensteel 2001). An alternative definition is that PSI reports are narrative summaries of an offender's criminal and noncriminal history, used to aid a judge in determining the most appropriate decision as to the offender's sentence for a crime. These documents are often partially structured in that they require probation officers to fill in standard information about defendants. PSIs also contain summaries or accounts in narrative form highlighting certain information about defendants and containing sentencing recommendations from probation officers. In some instances, space is available for the defendant's personal account of the crime and why it was committed.

Regardless of whether convictions are obtained through plea bargaining or a trial, a pre-sentence investigation (PSI) is often conducted on instructions from the court (Kellough and Wortley 2002). This investigation is sometimes waived in the case of negotiated guilty pleas, because an agreement has already been reached between the prosecution and defense concerning the case disposition and nature of sentence to be imposed.

Sample PSI Reports: State

A sample pre-sentence investigation report from Texas for a convicted female drug offender is shown below. Although the report is genuine, the convicted offender's real name has been changed to a fictitious name, "Maria Guerra," for privacy. Accompanying the PSI report is an offense report or investigative report that was completed by the Texas Department of Public Safety Criminal Law Enforcement Division, Narcotics Service. This investigative report details the offense and the sequence of events that led to the arrest of the offender.

****

PRE-SENTENCE INVESTIGATION REPORT
ON
MARIA GUERRA, #1234567

****

TO: THE HONORABLE MANUAL R. FLORES, JUDGE
49TH DRUG IMPACT COURT
LAREDO, WEBB COUNTY, TEXAS

FROM: ROBERTO MEZA, DIRECTOR
COMMUNITY SUPERVISION & CORRECTIONS DEPARTMENT
LAREDO, WEBB COUNTY, TEXAS

PROBATION OFFICER CONDUCTING PRE-SENTENCE INVESTIGATION REPORT

****

I RESPECTFULLY SUBMIT THE FOLLOWING PRE-SENTENCE INVESTIGATION REPORT REQUESTED BY YOUR HONOR IN THE ABOVE ENTITLED AND NUMBERED CAUSE.

IF THE COURT SHOULD NEED ANY ADDITIONAL INFORMATION CONCERNING THIS CASE, PLEASE LET US KNOW AND WE SHALL BE HAPPY TO OBLIGE.

****

TEXAS DEPARTMENT OF CRIMINAL JUSTICE
COMMUNITY JUSTICE ASSISTANCE DIVISION
PRE/POST SENTENCE INVESTIGATION REPORT

<u>GENERAL INSTRUCTIONS</u>: Pursuant to provision of Art. 42.12 Sec. 9, a presentence investigation report shall be completed prior to the imposition of sentence by the court. Type or print all requested information. If the information is not available at the time the report is prepared, please state "not available" in the space provided. The source of information for each section should be reflected in the appropriate space. Additional comments and/or source documents for any section may be attached to this report, as local jurisdictions dictate.

DISP: _____   CS: _____   CS REV: _____Y _____N   PEN: _____

SAFPF: _____   JAIL: _____

Date PSI   Sentence

Completed: _05/09/2002_____   Begin date: _06/06/2002__

STATE JAIL ONLY
SJF: (SJ UP FRONT)
Cumulative with ID sentence?
Concurrent with ID sentence?
Special Medical Needs:

I. COURT/LEGAL INFORMATION: Report information regarding the court of original jurisdiction, and identification of attorneys assigned to the case.

County: _Webb_____   Sentencing Judge: _Manuel R. Flores_____   Court #: _49th Drug Impact__

Prosecutor: _GARZA_____ ERNESTO_____   Defense Counsel: _RAMIREZ_____ DAN_____
                    (Last)   (First)   (MI)   (Last)   (First)   (MI)

Source of Information: COURT DOCKET_____

II. DEFENDANT INFORMATION: Provide demographic and/or other identifying information on the defendant in this section.

Cause #: _____   TRN# _NOT AVAILABLE_____   TRS# _NOT AVAILABLE_____

NAME: _____   aka (if known): _____
                (Last)   (First)   (MI)   (Last)   (First)   (MI)

Current Address _____   Permanent Address: _____

                    _____LAREDO, TEXAS_____   _____

Phone#: _____   Phone #: (__)_____

Age: _40_____   Gender: _Female_____   Marital Status: _Married_____

DOB: _____   Ethnicity: _Hispanic_____   No. of Dependents: _3_____

Place of Birth: _LAREDO_____ TEXAS-USA_____   Citizenship: _U.S._____
                    (City)   (State-Country)

Alien #: _N/A_____   Alien Status: _N/A_____   INS notified: _____ Yes _____ No

SSAN: _____   Driver's License: _N/A_____   DPS/SID No.: _____   _____

FBI No.: _NOT AVAILABLE_____   TDCJ-ID#: _N/A_____   Other: _____

Source of Information: _SELF-DISCLOSURE, NCIC REPORT AND WEBB COUNTY SHERIFF'S DEPARTMENT_____

III. CURRENT OFFENSE: Provide information relative to the circumstances of the primary offense. A copy of the offense report may be attached. If the report is not attached, briefly describe the offense.

Offense _POSSESSION OF A CONTROLLED SUBSTANCE,_   Offense Date _06/07/00_____   Arrest Date _06/07/00___

            _F/1_____

Circumstance _SEE APPENDIX "A"_____

Weapon Used: _____ __X__   If yes, type: _____
                            yes   no

*Guilt acknowledged _X_____   *Guilt minimized _____   *Declined to discuss _____

Source of Information: _OFFENSE REPORT_____   *Optional Fields

Defendant's Name:
Cause No.:

TDCJ-CJAD approved: 1-17-97

IV. CUSTODIAL INFORMATION: Report whether the defendant is currently under correctional supervision.

Status: _Released_   Release type: _BOND_   County/State _WEBB/TEXAS_____

Detainers/Pending Charges   NONE

Source of Information: _____

V. CRIMINAL HISTORY: Report both juvenile and adult criminal histories on the defendant. If available, attach either a DPS, FBI rap sheet or NCIC-TCIC report <u>and</u> answer the following questions:

A. JUVENILE: Criminal Record: _____ yes   _____ no   __X__ unavailable

If yes, number of probations: _____   Number of adjudications: _____   Number of arrests _____

Source of Information: _Defendant_____

B. ADULT: Criminal Record: ___X___ yes   _____ no   _____ unavailable

Indicate the number of incidences regarding the defendant in the appropriate box(es):

	Arrests	Pretrial Intervention	Conviction(s)	Community Supervision(s)	Intermediate Sanctions(s)	Community Supervision Revocation(s)	Parole/MS	Parole/MS Revocation(s)
Felony	1							
Misdemeanor	1							

Previous incarceration(s):

Jail: __X__ yes   _____ no   # _____ Charge(s):   _SEE APPENDIX "A"_____

Prison: _____ yes   _X_ no   # _____ Charge(s):   _____

State Jail: _____ yes   _X_ no   # _____ Charge(s):   _____

SAFPF: _____ yes   _X_ no   # _____ Charge(s):   _____

Source of Information: _WEBB COUNTY SHERIFF'S DEPARTMENT, TEXAS DPS AND NCIC REPORT_____

C. STATUS AT TIME
OF OFFENSE   __X__ Previous criminal history   County/State _FORT WORTH/TEXAS_____

_____ No Previous criminal history   County/State _____

_____ Bond Supervision   County/State _____

_____ Community Supervision   County/State _____

_____ Parole/Mandatory Supervision   County/State _____

Age at 1st conviction: __40__

Current gang affiliation: _____ yes   __X__ no   If yes, name: _____

Past gang affiliation: _____ yes   _____ no   If yes, name: _____

Suspected gang affiliation: _____ yes   If yes, name of city/state _____

Reasons(s)   _____

Source of Information: _SELF-DISCLOSED, WEBB COUNTY SHERIFF'S DEPARTMENT_

Defendant's Name:
Cause No.:

VI. VICTIM INFORMATION: If an offense is attached, please respond to the questions pertaining to restitution only. If no offense report is attached, please answer all questions in this section. If there were no direct victims or property loss associated with the offense, then skip the remaining questions in this section.

Victims associated with offense: _____ yes ___X___ no   If yes#: _____

Relationship to victim: _____

Victim(s) age at time of offense: _____ (Sex Offense Only)

Type of injury suffered/property loss: _____

Restitution: Amount claimed: __$0_____

Source of Information: __SELF-DISCLOSED, WEBB COUNTY SHERIFF'S DEPARTMENT, NCIC REPORT_____

VII. SOCIAL HISTORY: Provide information regarding the defendant's status.

A. HEALTH STATUS

Has a psychological evaluation of the defendant been prepared? _____ yes ___X___ no   If yes, attach.

Has the defendant ever been treated at a psychiatric hospital? _____ yes ___X___ no   If yes, location. _____

Has the defendant ever been treated at an MHMR facility? _____ yes ___X___ no   If yes, location. _____

Does the defendant presently have a physical or medical or mental impairment? ___X___ yes _____ no

If yes, specify: __THE DEFENDANT HAS HIGH BLOOD PRESSURE_____

Is the defendant currently taking any medications, including psychotropic? ___X___ yes _____ no

If yes, please list: __TOPROL-XL, LIPITOR, MICARDIS HCT_____

Has the defendant ever attempted suicide? _____ yes ___X___ no   If yes, date of last attempt: _____

B. EDUCATIONAL STATUS: __Not in school_____ Highest grade completed: __9TH GRADE_____

High School diploma:	_____ yes ___X___ no	Special classes:	_____ yes ___X___ no
GED:	_____ yes ___X___ no	Some college:	_____ yes ___X___ no
Vocational training:	_____ yes ___X___ no	College graduate:	_____ yes ___X___ no

Type: _____   Job Skills: _____

Provide information regarding any educational/psychological test(s) administered and the results:

Test: _____   Results: _____

_____   _____

_____   _____

_____   _____

Principal Language __English and Spanish_____   Secondary Language _____

Does the defendant appear to be literate? ___X___ yes _____ no   _____ yes _____ no

Source of Information: __SELF-DISCLOSED_____

Defendant's Name:
Cause No.:

C. EMPLOYMENT STATUS: _____ employed   _____X_____ unemployed

If unemployed: SIX MONTHS   length: Amount of income N/A _____
                                                     Source of income _____

Answer the following:
  Current employer:

  N/A _____   Job type: _____
  (Name)

  _____   Status: _____
  (Address)

  _____   Date of employment: _____
                                                                          mm dd yy
  ( ) _____   Amount of income: _____

Reason for leaving: _____

Is the defendant paying child support? _____ yes   X no   Comments:

Source of Information: Defendant _____

VIII. SUBSTANCE ABUSE: Provide information regarding the defendant's reported use of drugs.

Indicate the type and frequency of drug(s) used by placing an "X" in the appropriate space.

	Daily	Weekly	Monthly	Occasionally	Age First Used	Date Last Used	Denied Use
01 Alcohol/Beer	____	____	____	X	17	4/2002	____
(How many drinks—shots or beers—do you have in one sitting ____ 1–4 drinks _X_ 5–8 ____ 9 or more)							
02 Cocaine	____	____	____	____	____	____	X
03 Crack	____	____	____	____	____	____	X
05 Heroin	____	____	____	____	____	____	X
06 Marijuana	____	____	____	____	____	____	X
10 Amphet/Methamphetamines	____	____	____	____	____	____	X
07 LSD	____	____	____	____	____	____	X
08 PCP	____	____	____	____	____	____	X
09 Inhalants	____	____	____	____	____	____	X
10 Other Drugs:	____	____	____	____	____	____	X
_____	____	____	____	____	____	____	____

Substance Abuse screening/evaluation (SASSI, ASI, etc): _____ yes   X no
If yes, tool and score: N/A _____

Were any of the drugs noted above taken intravenously: _____ yes   _____ no

Indicate the type and number of incidents of drug counseling or treatment received:

_____ DWI education   _____ AA/NA, etc.

_____ individual counseling   _____ drug education classes

_____ out-patient group counseling   _____ residential treatment

Was the defendant under the influence of drugs or alcohol at the time the offense was committed: _____ yes   X no

Did the defendant commit the offense in order to obtain funds for the purchase of drugs or alcohol: _____ yes   X no

Source of Information: SELF-DISCLOSED _____

Defendant's Name:
Cause No.:

IX. SUPERVISION PLAN: The programs/supervision types identified by an "X" are available to the courts for this individual. The department may attach their individual plan if the items outlined below are addressed.

PROGRAMS

_____ Alcohol/Drug Education

_____ Alcohol/Drug Evaluation

_____ Alcohol/Drug Treatment

_____ Urinalysis

_____ Adult Basic Education (ABE)

_____ GED

_____ English as a Second Language (ESL)

_____ Community Service Restitution (CSR)

_____ DWI School/Drug School

_____ Victim Impact Panel

_____ Community Supervision Violator Trusty Camp

_____ Vocational Intervention Program

_____ Life Skills Training

_____ Intensive Supervision Program

_____ Electronic Monitoring

_____ CCF _____ type

_____ CCC _____ type

_____ Restitution of <u>$0</u>

_____ Specialized Caseload; (specify type)

_____ Surveillance

_____ Employment _____

_____ Jail

_____ Sex Offender Counseling

_____ Other; (specify) _____

COMMUNITY SUPERVISION TYPES

_____

_____ Pretrial Intervention Supervision

_____ Deferred Adjudication

_____ Regular Community Supervision

_____ DWI Community Supervision

_____ Shock Community Supervision

_____ State Jail Felony

Legal Requirements:

_____ Ignition Interlock (per T.C.C.P. Article 42.12, Section 13(i))

_____ Sex Offender Registration (per T.C.C.P. Article 42.12, Section 11(e))

Respectfully submitted,

<u>Braulio Gloria</u>   <u>5/09/02</u>
Supervision Officer   Date   Telephone

_____
Assisting   Date

Defendant's Name:
Cause No.:

X. NARRATIVE *(Optional)*

The defendant is a married, forty year old Hispanic female and mother of three children. The defendant suffers from high blood pressure and has no signs of mental/emotional disorders. The defendant is unemployed and has a 9th grade level of education. The defendant is currently residing in Laredo, Texas.

A. EVALUATION / SUMMATION:

Since the defendant did not finish high school and did not obtain a GED, the defendant would benefit from some type of educational program. Furthermore, the defendant may deviate from further criminal behavior if she becomes gainfully employed.

B. RECOMMENDED TREATMENT / SUPERVISION PLAN:

SHOULD THIS HONORABLE COURT GRANT THE DEFENDANT PROBATION, THIS OFFICER RESPECTFULLY MAKES THE FOLLOWING RECOMMENDATION:

1. The defendant is to perform 320 hours of community service within three years of her probated sentence.

2. The defendant is to submit to a drug/alcohol evaluation within 90 days of sentencing.

3. The defendant is to submit to drug testing at her own expense and at the discretion of the Supervision Officer.

4. The defendant is to attend and successfully complete an educational program on the dangers of drug abuse approved by TCADA at her own expense within 180 days of sentencing.

5. The defendant is to obtain a GED within three years of her probated sentence at her own expense.

6. The defendant is to report to a job counselor or employment agency as directed by the Supervision Officer until gainfully employed and will tender any and all financial documents as directed by the Supervision Officer.

Respectfully Submitted,

Braulio Gloria _____   _____

Supervision Officer   Date: 5/09/02   Telephone

Sample Federal Pre-Sentence Investigation Report

In this section, an example of a federal PSI report is presented. Depending upon the seriousness of the offense, these reports are more or less lengthy. In this instance, a fictitious example has been provided involving a PSI report for a petty offense, assault by striking, beating, or wounding, on a military base.

* *

SAMPLE PSI REPORT

IN THE UNITED STATES DISTRICT COURT
FOR THE WESTERN DISTRICT OF ATLANTIS

UNITED STATES OF AMERICA)
　　　　　　　　　　　　　　　)
　　　　　　　　　　　　　　　)　　　PRESENTENCE INVESTIGATION REPORT
　　　　　　　v.　　　　　　　)
　　　　　　　　　　　　　　　)
　　　　　　John Rich　　　　　)　　　Docket No. CR 02-221-KGG

Prepared for:　　　　　　　　The Honorable Alice B. Gray
　　　　　　　　　　　　　　　United States District Judge

Prepared by:　　　　　　　　 Craig T. Doe
　　　　　　　　　　　　　　　United States Probation Officer
　　　　　　　　　　　　　　　(123) 111-1111

Assistant U.S. Attorney　　　　　Defense Counsel
Mr. Robert Prosecutor　　　　　　Mr. Arthur Goodfellow
United States Courthouse　　　　　737 N. 7th Street
Breaker Bay, Atlantis　　　　　　 Breaker Bay, Atlantis
(123) 111-1212　　　　　　　　　 (123) 111-1313

Sentence Date:　　　　　　　　October 3, 2002 at 9:00 a.m.

Offense:　　　　　　　　　　　18 U.S.C. §113, Assault by striking, beating, or
　　　　　　　　　　　　　　　wounding, on a Military Base—6 months/$5,000 fine

Release Status:　　　　　　　　Released on $2,500 secured bond

Detainers:　　　　　　　　　　None

Codefendants:　　　　　　　　None

Related Cases:　　　　　　　　None

Identifying Data:

Date of Birth:　　　　　　　　April 12, 1980
Social Security Number:　　　　123-45-6789
Address:　　　　　　　　　　　18 Peachtree Lane
　　　　　　　　　　　　　　　Breaker Bay, Atlantis

Detainers:　　　　　　　　　　None.

Codefendants:　　　　　　　　None.

Date report prepared: September 22, 2002

PART A. THE OFFENSE

Charge(s) and Conviction(s)

1. On July 23, 2002, a three-count Criminal Information was filed in the Western District of Atlantis against Ann Chesnut. Count one charges that on March 3, 2002, the defendant slashed the front screen door of Quarters 999H Armory Court at the Sandy Beach Military Base, in violation of 18 U.S.C. § 1361. Count two charges that on March 3, 2002, the defendant assaulted Jane Walsh at the Sandy Beach Military Base by cutting her on the ring finger with a knife, in violation of 18 U.S.C. § 113(d). Count three charges that on or about March 3, 2002, Ann Chesnut engaged in disorderly conduct by participating in a fight at the Sandy Beach Military Base, in violation of 18 U.S.C. § 13 and Atlantis Revised Statute (ARS) 525.060.

2. On June 19, 2002, pursuant to an oral plea agreement, the defendant entered a plea of guilty to Count two assault, in violation of 18 U.S.C. § 113(d). According to the plea agreement, in exchange for a plea or guilty to Count two, the Government will recommend probation, and the remaining counts are to be dismissed.

3. The defendant agrees to pay a $500 fine on the date of sentence, which is scheduled for October 3, 2002.

Offense Conduct

4. At the time of the offense, the defendant and the victim, Jane Walsh, were neighbors in military housing on the Sandy Beach Military Base. On March 3, 2002, Jane Walsh and the defendant became involved in a verbal altercation over neighborhood friends. Ms. Chesnut went into her residence, retrieved a baseball bat, and swung the bat at Ms. Walsh, missing her. Ms. Walsh took the bat away from Ms. Chesnut and hit the defendant on the left arm with the bat. After being struck by the bat, Ms. Chesnut pulled a knife from inside her pants and cut Ms. Walsh on the right finger. Ms. Walsh then returned to her residence. The defendant went to her own residence, obtained a butcher knife and a barbecue fork, and returned to Ms. Walsh's residence. Upon arriving at Ms. Walsh's apartment, the defendant slashed the screen door with the knife, but never gained entrance to the residence.

5. Following arrest, the defendant was taken to the U.S. Army medical facility, Sandy Beach, where she received medical treatment for a bruised and swollen arm. There were no broken bones and a blood specimen taken from the defendant revealed the presence of alcohol.

6. At the time of her treatment at the medical facility, Ms. Chesnut made several statements to hospital staff about her altercation with Ms. Walsh. Ms. Chesnut admitted that she tried to hit Ms. Walsh with a baseball bat but missed. She admitted also that she then tried to stab Ms. Walsh with a knife.

7. A subsequent investigation by Military Police elicited an admission by Ms. Chesnut that she had assaulted Ms. Walsh with both a baseball bat and a knife. Military Police filed a report with base security.

Adjustment for Obstruction of Justice

8. The probation officer has no information suggesting that the defendant impeded or obstructed justice.

Adjustment for Acceptance of Responsibility

9. During the interview with the probation officer, Ms. Chesnut was distraught and tearful regarding the offense. She stated that she was sorry for any harm caused to Ms. Walsh.

Offense Level Computation

10. Base Offense Level: The guideline for an 18 U.S.C. § 113(d) offense is found in Section 2B1.1(a) of the Guidelines. The base offense level is 2.   2

11. Specific Offense Characteristics: Section 2B1.1(b) provides that if physical injury is sustained by one or more victims, the offense level is raised by 5.   5

12. Adjustment for Role in the Offense: None   0

13. Victim-Related Adjustment: None   0

14. Adjustment for Obstruction of Justice: None   0

15. Adjustment for Acceptance of Responsibility: Based on the defendant's admission of guilt, her payment of a fine, and her acceptance of responsibility, pursuant to Section 3E1.1(a), two levels are subtracted.   −2

16. Total Offense Level: 5

PART B. THE DEFENDANT'S CRIMINAL HISTORY

Juvenile Adjudications

17. None

Criminal Convictions

18. None

Criminal History Computation

19. The defendant has no criminal convictions. Therefore, she has zero criminal history points and a criminal history category of I.

Other Criminal Conduct

20. None

PART C: OFFENDER CHARACTERISTICS

Personal Characteristics

21. Ann Chesnut is a lifelong resident of Ocean County, Atlantis. The defendant currently resides in a small apartment with her 2-year-old daughter in Breaker Bay, Atlantis which she rents for $190 per month. She has lived at this address for the past six months.

22. Ms. Chesnut is the older of two children. She related that her formative years were uneventful. Her mother and sister also reside in Breaker Bay, Atlantis, and Ms. Chesnut has a close relationship with her sister. Her parents are separated and her father's whereabouts are unknown.

23. The defendant married Mike Beavers on December 19, 1999 in Breaker Bay, Atlantis. Subsequent to the instant offense, the defendant was divorced on October 14, 2001. She has custody of a 2-year-old daughter born during the marriage. Mr. Beavers pays $250 per month in child support.

24. Ms. Chesnut graduated from high school on June 13, 1998. She is presently unemployed and has not maintained employment for the past two years. In the past, she has held several jobs as a waitress, which typically lasted only a few months. These jobs paid minimum wage plus tips. Ms. Chesnut stated that she would quit a job after a few months because she would grow tired of the work.

25. The defendant married Arnold Chesnut, a lieutenant in the U.S. Army, on January 13, 2002.

Mental and Emotional Health

26. According to the defendant, she has never suffered from any mental or emotional problems that would require professional intervention. It was obvious to the probation officer during the interview with Ms. Chesnut that she is extremely remorseful about the outcome of this case. Her sister confirmed that the defendant has no history of mental or emotional problems but recently has been very anxious about the instant case.

Physical Condition, Including Drug Dependence and Alcohol Abuse

27. Ms. Chesnut reports that she is in good health and has never suffered from any serious illnesses or injuries. She states that she has never used illicit drugs and consumes alcohol occasionally.

Education and Vocational Skills

28. A transcript from Monroe High School of Cleveland indicates that Ann Chesnut was graduated in June, 1998 with a grade point average of 2.7.

Employment Record

29. At the present time, Ms. Chesnut is unemployed.

PART D. SENTENCING OPTIONS

Custody

30. Statutory Provisions: The maximum term of imprisonment is 5 months. 18 U.S.C. § 113(d).

31. Guideline Provisions: Based upon a total offense level of 5 and a criminal history category of I, the guideline imprisonment range is 0 to 5 months.

Supervised Release

32. Statutory Provisions: If a term of imprisonment is imposed, the court may impose a term of not more than 5 months pursuant to 18 U.S.C. 3583(b)(2).

33. Guideline Provisions: If a sentence of imprisonment is imposed within the guideline range, a term of supervised release is not required but is optional.

Probation

34. Statutory Provisions: The defendant is eligible for probation by statute. Because the offense is a misdemeanor, 18 U.S.C. 3563(a)(2) requires that one of the following be imposed as a condition of probation: a fine, restitution or community service.

35. Guideline Provisions: The defendant is eligible for probation. If the court were to impose probation, the term may be up to one year. Section 5B1.2(a)(1).

PART E. FINES AND RESTITUTION

Statutory Provisions

36. The maximum fine is $5,000. 18 U.S.C. 3571(b).

37. A special assessment of $50 is mandatory. 18 U.S.C. 3013.

38. Restitution is owed to Ms. Jane Walsh for her injuries and costs of medical treatment.

Guideline Provisions About Fines

39. The fine for this offense is $5,000 less any restitution ordered with a minimum of $500 (Section 5E4.2(c)(1)(B).

40. Subject to the defendant's ability to pay, the court shall impose an additional fine amount that is at least sufficient to pay the costs to the government of any imprisonment, probation, or supervised release. Section 5e4.2(i).

Defendant's Ability to Pay

41. Based upon a financial statement submitted by Ms. Chesnut, a review of her bank records and a credit bureau check, the defendant's financial condition is as follows:

Assets

Cash

Cash on hand	$ 50
Checking account	150
U.S. Savings Bond	75

Unencumbered Assets

Stereo system	$ 200

Equity in Other Assets

1992 Toyota Cresida	$2,000 (equity based on Blue Book value)
TOTAL ASSETS	$2,575

Unsecured Debts

Loan from sister	$ 500
Attorney fees balance	2,500
TOTAL UNSECURED DEBTS	$3,000

Income

Net salary	$ 0.00
TOTAL INCOME	$ 0.00

42. Based upon Ms. Chesnut's financial profile, it appears that she has the ability to remit restitution if she makes monthly installments. However, her income is rather modest, and it does not appear that she could also pay a fine.

PART F. FACTORS THAT MAY WARRANT DEPARTURE

43. The probation officer has not identified any information that would warrant a departure from the guidelines.

Recommendation

It is respectfully recommended that sentence be imposed as follows:

Pursuant to the Sentencing Reform Act of 1984, it is the judgment of the court that the defendant, ANN CHESNUT, is hereby placed on probation for a term of 1 year.

While on probation, the defendant shall not commit another federal, state, or local crime, shall not possess a controlled substance, shall not possess a firearm or destructive device, and shall comply with the standard conditions of supervision that have been adopted by this court, and shall comply with the following additional conditions:

> The defendant shall participate in a program of testing and treatment for alcohol abuse, as directed by the probation officer, until such time as the defendant is released from the program by the probation officer.

> The defendant shall perform 40 hours of community service as directed by the probation officer.

The defendant shall make restitution to Jane Walsh in the amount of $236, and that the defendant pay a special assessment in the amount of $50, both to be paid immediately.

Respectfully submitted,

JOHN JAY FREDERICK
CHIEF PROBATION OFFICER

By

_____

CRAIG T. DOE
U.S. Probation Officer

Reviewed and Approved:

_____

ORLANDO W. WILSON
SUPERVISOR

ADDENDUM TO THE PRE-SENTENCE REPORT

The probation officer certifies that the pre-sentence report, including any revision thereof, has been disclosed to the defendant, her attorney, and counsel for the Government, and that the content of the Addendum has been communicated to counsel. The Addendum fairly states any objections they have made.

OBJECTIONS

By the Government

The Government has no objections.

By the Defendant

The defense attorney maintains that the defendant's youth, lack of a prior record, and her remorse are characteristics that should be considered for probation. He will present argument at the sentencing hearing that community confinement is not necessary in this case and that the court should depart by a sentence of probation with restitution.

The probation officer does not believe that a departure is warranted. Remorse and lack of a prior record are factored into the guidelines. The Sentencing Commission policy statement on age (Section 5H1.1) suggests that youth is not a valid reason for departure.

CERTIFIED BY

JOHN JAY FREDERICK
CHIEF PROBATION OFFICER
By

_____

Craig T. Doe
U.S. Probation Officer

Reviewed and Approved

_____

ORLANDO W. WILSON
SUPERVISOR

SENTENCING RECOMMENDATION

United States v. Ann Chesnut, Dkt No. CR-02-221-KGG,
U.S. District Court for the Western District of Atlantis

CUSTODY

Statutory maximum:	5 months
Guideline range:	0 to 5 months
Recommendation:	One year probation

Justification:

According to the Guidelines, the defendant is eligible for probation. Ms. Chesnut is a good candidate for probation because she has no prior record and is willing to make restitution to the victim. A prison sentence does not appear to be necessary in this case since the defendant does not need to be incapacitated to deter her from further crime and other sanctions will provide sufficient punishment.

FINE

Statutory maximum:	$5,000
Guideline range:	Up to $5,000.
Recommendation:	$0

Justification:

Restitution to the victim is recommended as a condition of probation. The defendant's lack of income will necessitate that the restitution be paid in monthly installments. At this point, Ms. Chesnut does not have the ability to pay both restitution and a fine.

PROBATION

Statutory term:	Maximum of 1 year
Guideline term:	Up to one year
Recommended term:	1 year

Recommended conditions:

1. That the defendant not commit any crimes, federal, state, or local.

2. That the defendant abide by the standard conditions of probation recommended by the Sentencing Commission.

3. That the defendant will report to the U.S. Probation Office once per month during the term of her probation.

4. That the defendant pay restitution to Jane Walsh in the amount of $236.

5. That the defendant be assessed a special assessment of $50.

6. That the defendant provide the probation officer with access to any requested financial information.

Justification:

A sentence of probation contingent upon payment of restitution will provide sufficient punishment for Ms. Chesnut as well as a general deterrence to others. Conditions of supervision requiring financial disclosure to the probation officer and a provision against consuming any drugs or alcohol.

SPECIAL ASSESSMENT $50

VOLUNTARY SURRENDER

If the court imposes a custodial sentence, Ms. Chesnut appears to be a good candidate for a voluntary surrender.

Respectfully submitted,

JOHN JAY FREDERICK
CHIEF PROBATION OFFICER

By

_____

Craig T. Doe
U.S. Probation Officer

Reviewed and Approved:

_____

ORLANDO W. WILSON
SUPERVISOR

Date: September 28, 2002

* *

Functions and Uses of PSI Reports

Why Are PSI Reports Prepared?   No standard format exists among the states for PSI report preparation. The PSI report was adopted formally by the **Administrative Office of the U.S. Courts** in 1943. Since then, the PSI has been revised several times. The 1984 version reflects changes in correctional law that have occurred in recent decades. Prior to 1943, informal reports about offenders were often prepared for judges by court personnel. Probably the earliest informal PSI was prepared in 1841 by **John Augustus,** the father of probation in the United States.

Although the U.S. Probation Office represents federal interests and not necessarily those of particular states, their PSI report functions are very similar to the general functions of PSI reports in most states. The PSI report for the U.S. district courts and the U.S. Probation Office serves at least five important functions. These are:

1. To aid the court in determining the appropriate sentence for offenders.
2. To aid probation officers in their supervisory efforts during probation or parole.
3. To assist the Federal Bureau of Prisons and any state prison facility in the classification, institutional programming, and release planning for inmates.
4. To furnish the U.S. Parole Commission and other parole agencies with information about the offender pertinent to a parole decision.
5. To serve as a source of information for research. (Administrative Office of the U.S. Courts 1984:1)

Providing information for offender sentencing is the primary function of a PSI. It continues to be an important function, since judges want to be fair and impose sentences fitting the crime. If there are mitigating or aggravating circumstances that should be considered, these factors appear in the report submitted to the judge. Frequently, investigative reports are appended to PSI reports for the purpose of furnishing more specific arrest details for judicial consideration. Such a report is shown in Appendix 2A at the end of this chapter.

Aiding probation officers in their supervisory efforts is an important report objective because proper rehabilitative programs can be individualized for different offenders. If vocational training or medical help is needed, the report suggests this. If the offender has a history of mental illness, psychological counseling or medical treatment may be appropriate and recommended. This information is also helpful to ancillary personnel who work in community-based probation programs and supervise offenders with special problems such as drug or alcohol dependencies. PSIs assist prisons and other detention facilities in their efforts to classify inmates appropriately. Inmates with special problems or who are handicapped physically or mentally may be diverted to special prison facilities or housing where their needs can be addressed by professionals. Inmates with diseases or viruses such as AIDS can be isolated from others for health purposes.

The fourth function of federal PSIs is crucial in influencing an inmate's parole chances. In those jurisdictions where parole boards determine an inmate's early release potential, PSIs are often consulted as background data. Decisions about early release are often contingent upon the recommendation of the probation officer contained in the report. For instance, if the prospective parolee is a sex offender, it is important for the parole board to know the likelihood that the person will reoffend if released (Danni and Hampe 2000). Finally, criminologists and others are interested in studying those sentenced to various terms of incarceration or probation. Background characteristics, socioeconomic information, and other relevant data assist researchers in developing explanations for criminal conduct. Also, research efforts of criminologists and those interested in **criminal justice** may be helpful in affecting the future design of prisons or jails. Special needs areas can be identified and programs devised that will assist offenders with their various problems. Since most inmates will eventually be paroled, research through an examination of PSIs may help corrections professionals devise more effective adaptation and reintegration mechanisms, permitting inmates to make a smoother transition back into their respective communities.

When Are PSI Reports Conducted?   In all felony convictions in local, state, and federal trial courts, a pre-sentence investigation is conducted usually between the time an offender is convicted and the date of the sentencing hearing. These reports are designed to assist judges in their sentencing decisions. The Administrative Office of the U.S. Courts uses standardized PSIs that include five core categories that must be addressed in the body of the report. These are (1) the offense, including the prosecution version, the defendant's version, statements of witnesses, codefendant information, and a victim impact statement; (2) prior record, including juvenile adjudications and adult offenses; (3) personal and family data, including parents and siblings, marital status, education, health, physical and mental condition, and financial assets and liabilities; (4) evaluation, including the probation officer's assessment, parole guideline data, sentencing data, and any special sentencing provisions; and (5) recommendation, including the rationale for the recommendation and voluntary surrender or whether the offender should be transported to the correctional institution on his or her own or should be transported by U.S. marshals.

Who Prepares PSI Reports?   When requested by federal district judges, PSIs are usually prepared within a 60-day period from the time judges make their requests. While there is no standard PSI format among states, most PSIs contain similar information. Pre-sentence investigation reports are usually prepared by probation officers. Although it was much more informally prepared contrasted with contemporary PSIs, John Augustus has been credited with drafting the first one in 1841. It has been estimated that over 1 million PSI reports are prepared by probation officers annually in the United States (Norman and Wadman 2000).

Specific duties of probation officers relating directly to PSI report preparation include the following:

1. Probation officers prepare pre-sentence investigation reports at the request of judges.
2. Probation officers classify and categorize offenders.
3. Probation officers recommend sentences for convicted offenders.
4. Probation officers work closely with courts to determine the best supervisory arrangement for probationer-clients.
5. Probation officers are a resource for information about any extralegal factors that might impact either positively or adversely on the sentencing decision.

There are at least three legal approaches to PSI report preparation. In forty-three states, PSI report preparation is mandatory for all felony offense convictions (Camp and Camp 2002:214–215). Other factors may initiate PSI report preparation in these jurisdictions, such as when incarceration of a year or longer is a possible sentence, when the offender is under 21 or 18 years of age, and when the defendant is a first offender. In nine states, statutes provide for mandatory PSI report preparation in any felony case where probation is a possible consideration. When probation is not a consideration, then the PSI report preparation is optional or discretionary with particular judges. Finally, in seventeen states, a PSI report is totally discretionary with the presiding judge. Examples of various state policies governing the preparation of PSI reports follows.

New Jersey

PSI report = required in all felony cases; suggested in misdemeanor cases involving one or more years incarceration

Connecticut

PSI report = mandatory for any case where incarceration is one or more years

Pennsylvania

PSI report = mandatory for any case where incarceration is one or more years

District of Columbia

PSI report = required unless offenders waive their right to one with court permission

California

PSI report = mandatory for all felony convictions; discretionary for misdemeanor cases

Most probation officer work involves PSI report preparation and writing, and client contacts consume less than half of their time on the job. Courtesy of Custer Youth Correctional Center.

Arizona

PSI report = mandatory for anyone where incarceration is a year or more; may be ordered in other cases

Texas

PSI report = totally discretionary with the judge (Clear, Clear, and Burrell 1989:174)

Can Private Organizations Prepare PSI Reports?   Yes. Sometimes PSIs are prepared by private corporations or individuals. Criminological Diagnostic Consultants, Inc., Riverside, California, founded by brothers William and Robert Bosic, is a corporation that prepares privately commissioned PSIs for defense attorneys and others (Kulis 1983:11). William Bosic is a former prison counselor and probation officer, while his brother, Robert, is a retired police officer. Their claim is, "We don't do anything different than (sic) the probation department; we just do it better." The average cost of a government-prepared PSI report is about $250, while privately prepared PSIs cost from $200 to $2,000 or more. The cost varies according to the PSI contents and thoroughness of the investigation and whether psychiatric evaluations and other types of tests of offenders are made. Increasing numbers of PSIs are being prepared privately, often by ex-probation officers or others closely related to corrections.

The advantages of privately prepared PSI reports are that the preparers can slant the facts about the offender and the offense in such a way so as to increase the chances of leniency from sentencing judges. Public servants, probation officers, may not take the time to include mitigating details about the offense. Therefore, when offenders can afford to have PSI reports prepared, they are at an advantage in that the judge will likely see their side more clearly. However, no one knows how much value judges place on PSI reports, regardless of who prepares them (Fruchtman and Sigler 1999).

How Long Does It Take to Prepare PSI Reports?   PSI report preparation may take as little as a few hours, while a majority of PSI reports might take several working days to prepare properly. Investigative time and interviewing must be factored in when considering how long probation officers require to complete reports for any particular offender. In many jurisdictions, it is not unusual to discover that over half of a probation officer's time is spent preparing such reports. It takes time for officers to verify employment, check educational records, interview family members, obtain victim and/or witness information, analyze court records, review police reports of the arrest and crime details, and a host of other bits and pieces of necessary and relevant information. And this activity is only a preliminary step in the process of PSI report preparation. Then officers must sit down and type up these reports. Many probation agencies do not have adequate secretarial staff where such information can be dictated and subsequently transcribed and committed to a written report by someone else, so probation officers must often write their own reports. Knowing how to type or use a word processor or computer is an essential skill for probation officers to acquire.

How Confidential Are PSI Reports?   California permits an examination by the public of any PSI report filed by any state probation office for up to ten days following its filing with the court. Under exceptional circumstances, however, even California courts may bar certain information from public scrutiny if a proper argument can be made for its exclusion. Usually, a good argument would be potential danger to one or more persons who have made statements or declarations in the report. Further, some witnesses or information-givers do so only under the condition that they will remain anonymous. This anonymity guarantee must be protected by the court. But as has been previously indicated, most jurisdictions maintain a high level of confidentiality regarding PSI documents and their contents.

Ordinarily, however, only court officials and others working closely with a particular case have a right to examine the contents of these reports. All types of information are included in these documents. Convicted offenders are entitled to some degree of privacy relative to a PSI report's contents. The federal government requires the disclosure of the contents of PSIs to convicted offenders, their attorneys, and to attorneys for the government at least ten days prior to actual sentencing (18 U.S.C., Sec. 3552(d), 2003). At state and local levels, this practice varies, and the PSI report may or may not be disclosed to the offender. Under 18 U.S.C., Fed.R.Cr.Proc. 32(c)(3)(B) (2003), some information in the PSI may be withheld from the defendant. The report may contain confidential information such as a psychiatric evaluation or a sentencing recommendation. The presiding judge determines those portions of the PSI report to be disclosed to offenders and their counsels. Anything disclosed to defendants must also be made available to the prosecutors.

In some jurisdictions, these provisions have been interpreted to mean that convicted offenders should have greatly restricted access to these PSI reports. Many federal prisoners have filed petitions under the **Freedom of Information Act (FOIA)** in order to read their own PSI reports in some judicial districts (Casarez 1995). This Act makes it possible for private citizens to examine certain public documents containing information about them, including IRS information or information compiled by any other government agency, criminal or otherwise.

The Offender's Sentencing Memorandum and Version of Events

An essential part of the PSI report is the offender **sentencing memorandum.** Sentencing memorandums are a written account of how and why the crime occurred, including the offender's explanation and apology. This memorandum is especially crucial in most sentencing decisions, since the offender uses this occasion to accept responsibility for the crime committed. This is an obligatory component and must be written convincingly. If judges honestly believe that offenders have accepted the responsibility for their actions and are ready to accept the consequences, then they might impose a more lenient sentence. Too many convicted offenders blame others: "I had a bad childhood; my mother and father beat me!"; "I was sexually abused as a child"; "Society did this to me. It's society's fault that I'm here."; "Everybody was against me, and no one gave me a chance." The classic line from convicted offenders is, "I'm not guilty; I'm really innocent; I shouldn't be punished." When judges see or hear offenders make these claims, this is a clear indication that the offenders have not accepted responsibility for the crimes. Of course, there are innocent convicted offenders out there who express righteous indignation over their plight—but they can't do much about it except appeal the verdict. In the meantime, judges must sentence them and rely in part on the information they put in their sentencing memorandums (Herman and Wasserman 2001).

Victim Impact Statements and the Victim's Version of Events

Many U.S. jurisdictions today request victims of crimes to submit their own versions of the offense as a **victim impact statement** (Lynett and Rogers 2000). The victim impact statement is a statement made by the victim and addressed to the judge for consideration in sentencing. It includes a description of the harm inflicted on the victim in terms of financial, social, psychological, and physical consequences of the crime. It also includes a statement concerning the victim's feelings about the crime, the offender, and a proposed sentence. Victim participation in sentencing is increasingly encouraged, and a victim impact statement is given similar weight compared with the offender's version of events. While victim participation in sentencing raises certain ethical, moral, and legal questions, indications are that victim impact statements are used with increasing frequency and appended to PSI reports in various jurisdictions. In capital punishment cases where the death penalty may be imposed, for example, victim impact evidence has increased the likelihood of receiving the death penalty for some crimes (Aguirre et al. 1999).

Victim impact statements may be in the form of an attachment to a PSI report. Victims provide a written account of how the crime and offender influenced them. Victims may also make a speech or verbal declaration during the offender's sentencing hearing. This is ordinarily a prepared document read by one or more victims at the time offenders are sentenced (Herman and Wasserman 2001). The admission of victim impact statements is controversial. Defense attorneys may feel that these statements are inflammatory and detract from objective sentencing considerations. Victim impact statements may intensify sentencing disparities in certain jurisdictions with sentencing schemes that rely more heavily on subjective judicial impressions compared with those jurisdictions where more objective sentencing criteria are used, such as mandatory sentencing procedures or guidelines-based sentencing schemes. Proponents of victim impact statements believe that such statements personalize the sentencing process by showing that actual persons were harmed by certain offender conduct. Also, victim's rights advocates contend that victims have a moral right to influence one's punishment (Erez and Laster 1999). In recent years, the U.S. Supreme Court has ruled victim impact statements are constitutional in *Payne v. Tennessee* (1991).

What Influence Do PSI Reports Have on Judicial Sentencing Decisions?

Judges may treat the PSI the same way they treat plea agreements. They may concur with probation officer sentencing recommendations, or they may ignore these reports. However, since most convictions occur through plea bargaining, the only connection a judge usually has with the defendant before sentencing is through the PSI report (Davis and Smith 1994). In federal district courts, judges may decide not to order PSIs if they feel there is sufficient information about the convicted offender to "enable the meaningful exercise of sentencing discretion, and the court explains this finding on the record" (18 U.S.C., Rule 32(c)(1), 2003). Sometimes defendants may waive their right to have a PSI report prepared as long as the court approves.

It would be foolish to conclude that PSI reports have no impact on judicial sentencing decisions. The contents of PSI reports furnish judges with a detailed account of an offender's prior record. However, the influence of socioeconomic,

---

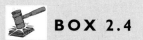 **BOX 2.4**   **VICTIM IMPACT STATEMENTS**

On the Constitutionality of Victim Impact Statements

Booth v. Maryland, 482 U.S. 496, 107 S.Ct. 2529 (1987)

Booth was convicted of first-degree murder in a Baltimore, Maryland, court. During his sentencing hearing, a victim-impact statement (VIS) was read so that his sentence might be enhanced or intensified. Following the sentence of death, Booth appealed, alleging that the VIS was a violation of his Eighth Amendment right against cruel and unusual punishment. The U.S. Supreme Court agreed and said that during sentencing phases of capital murder trials, the introduction of VISs is unconstitutional. Among its reasons cited for this opinion, the U.S. Supreme Court said that VISs create an unacceptable risk that a jury may impose the death penalty in an arbitrary and capricious manner. Thus, VIS information may be totally unrelated to the blameworthiness of the offender. However, the U.S. Supreme Court changed its mind in *Payne v. Tennessee.*

Payne v. Tennessee, 501 U.S. 808, 111 S.Ct. 2597 (1991)

Payne was convicted of a double murder. At the sentencing hearing, Payne introduced various witnesses on his behalf to avoid the death penalty. During the same hearing, the victims' relatives introduced their victim impact statement, pressing the jury to impose the death penalty on Payne. The death penalty was imposed and Payne appealed, contesting the introduction of damaging evidence and opinions expressed in the victim impact statement. The U.S. Supreme Court upheld Payne's death sentence, holding that victim impact statements do not violate an offender's Eighth Amendment rights. The significance of this case is that it supports and condones the use of victim impact statements against convicted offenders during sentencing hearings.

gender, and racial or ethnic differences on judicial attitudes and sentencing severity is pervasive, although we do not know for sure how heavily these factors influence particular judges. Most judges weigh one's prior record heavily when imposing prison terms or nonincarcerative alternatives (Luginbuhl and Burkhead 1995). While many judges believe themselves to be fair and impartial when imposing sentences on offenders of different genders or races, their actions strongly suggest that these variables do influence their decisions, although the impact of these variables is not consistent for judges across all jurisdictions. Good predictors of sentence type and sentence length are case facts; offender characteristics such as age, educational level, and employment history; and prior record of other criminal activity. Crime seriousness and victim injury also figure prominently when judges calculate the most appropriate sentences for offenders (Weinrath and Gartrell 2001).

Judges have considerable sentencing power under most sentencing schemes. Mandatory sentences must be imposed on offenders for specific conviction offenses, although prosecutors decide in advance which crimes will or will not be prosecuted. Judges see only the conviction offense rather than other charges that have been dropped. The fairest scenario for convicted offenders is for judges to have a knowledge of both the bad and good information about offenders and their crimes. Bad information (unfavorable to offenders) is often expressed as aggravating circumstances, while good information (favorable to offenders) consists of mitigating circumstances. These circumstances are most often detailed in the PSI report.

AGGRAVATING AND MITIGATING CIRCUMSTANCES

Aggravating Circumstances

Aggravating circumstances are those factors that may increase the severity of punishment. Some of the factors considered by judges to be aggravating include:

1. Whether the crime involved death or serious bodily injury to one or more victims.
2. Whether the crime was committed while the offender was out on **bail** facing other criminal charges.
3. Whether the offender was on probation, parole, or work release at the time the crime was committed.
4. Whether the offender was a recidivist and had committed several previous offenses for which he or she had been punished.
5. Whether the offender was the leader in the commission of the offense involving two or more offenders.
6. Whether the offense involved more than one victim and/or was a violent or nonviolent crime.
7. Whether the offender treated the victim(s) with extreme cruelty during the commission of the offense.
8. Whether the offender used a dangerous weapon in the commission of the crime and the risk to human life was high.

Whenever PSI reports or sentencing hearings disclose one or more aggravating circumstances about the offender or crime committed, judges are likely to intensify the punishment imposed. This might mean a longer sentence, incarceration instead of probation, or a sentence to be served in a maximum security prison rather than a minimum- or medium-security institution. Mitigating circumstances may influence judges to be lenient with offenders and place them on probation rather than in jail or prison. A sentence of a year or less may be imposed rather than a five-year term, for example.

Mitigating Circumstances

Mitigating circumstances are those factors considered by the sentencing judge to lessen the crime's severity. Some of the more frequently cited mitigating factors in the commission of crimes might be the following:

1. The offender did not cause serious bodily injury by his/her conduct during the commission of the crime.
2. The convicted defendant did not contemplate that his or her criminal conduct would inflict serious bodily injury on anyone.
3. The offender acted under duress or extreme provocation.
4. The offender's conduct was possibly justified under the circumstances.
5. The offender was suffering from mental incapacitation or physical condition that significantly reduced his or her culpability in the offense.
6. The offender cooperated with authorities in apprehending other participants in the crime or in making restitution to the victims for losses suffered.
7. The offender committed the crime through motivation to provide necessities for him- or herself or his or her family.
8. The offender did not have a previous criminal record.

Judges weigh the mitigating and aggravating circumstances involved in an offender's conviction offense. If the aggravating circumstances outweigh the mitigating ones, then the judge is justified in intensifying sentencing severity. However, if the mitigating circumstances outweigh the aggravating ones, then judges may exhibit greater leniency in their sentencing decision. Judges have considerable discretionary power when sentencing offenders. How particular aggravating or circumstances might be evaluated are highly individualized according to particular judges. More than a few judges are especially severe when sentencing child sexual abusers, for example (Craissati and Beech 2001). They may impose especially harsh sentences even though there may be extensive mitigating circumstances, simply because they don't like child sexual abusers. Other judges have similar inclinations, depending upon the nature of the offense and attitude of the offender. Besides these factors, judges also consider the risk or dangerousness posed by particular offenders (Brock, Sorensen, and Marquart 2000). If judges contemplate placing some of these convicted offenders on probation and allowing them freedom to move about within their communities, then these judges will want to have some objective criteria to assist them in their probation decision.

SOME SENTENCING ISSUES

No matter which sentencing schemes states or the federal government use, there are an unending list of criticisms leveled against them. Criticisms of one type of sentencing system have led to the establishment or enactment of an alternative sentencing scheme. Eventually, critics will mass evidence to show why the new sentencing scheme is unworkable, and thus a never-ending cycle is set in motion for the constant reassessment of how offenders should best be punished. No one has yet devised a universally acceptable answer to the question of how offenders should be sanctioned and which sentencing system is best (Kilty and Joseph 1999).

The sentencing reforms implemented by most states have been prompted by various sentencing issues. These issues include: (1) sentencing disparities: race, gender, age and socioeconomic factors; (2) correctional resources and their limitations; (3) the economics of systemic constraints; and (4) jail and prison overcrowding problems.

Sentencing Disparities: Race/Ethnicity, Gender, Age, and Socioeconomic Factors

When judges are accused of unfairness in their sentencing practices, they are quick to take offense and claim they do not discriminate between convicted offenders according to extralegal variables, such as race, gender, age, and socioeconomic status. Most judges believe their decisions about offenders to be made impartially and free of any overt bias or prejudice (Tonry 1998). However, an examination of judicial sentencing patterns in various jurisdictions in some instances reveals substantial disparities in sentencing offenders who have similar records and have been convicted of identical offenses. These disparities have often been explained by racial or ethnic factors more than legal factors, such as prior record or offense seriousness (California Administrative Office of the Courts 2001). Even among the federal judiciary, the U.S. sentencing guidelines have failed to curb **sentencing disparities** according to extralegal factors (Cole 1999; Everett and Nienstedt 1999).

In the federal system, for instance, more power has shifted to prosecutors and probation officers and away from judges. Thus, actors in the federal system exert considerable influence over the life chances of offenders before they are sentenced. Judges are only able to impose sentences based upon the factual information they are provided by the prosecution and U.S. Probation Office. If plea agreements have been worked out in advance and federal probation officers have provided their own spin on an offender's conviction offense and the circumstances of it, then judicial discretion in sentencing has obviously been diminished. It is easy to see how earlier decision making in the plea agreement phase of a prosecution can take on extralegal dimensions and how such decision making is attributable to one's race, ethnicity, gender, age, and/or socioeconomic status.

Sentencing disparities are pervasive even under sentencing schemes that are presumably fair, such as sentencing guidelines (Gallagher, Poletti, and MacKinnell 2001). It has been found, for example, that Maryland courts tend to sentence black and Hispanic offenders to longer sentences than white offenders with similar criminal histories and who are convicted of the same offenses

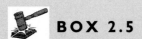 **BOX 2.5**

Hugo D. Martinez

Attorney at Law

Statistics

B.S. (business administration), St. Edward's University; J.D., University of Texas

Background and Interests

I received my bachelor's degree in business administration and finance from St. Edward's University in 1981. Two days later, I started my classes at the University of Texas School of Law. I received my J.D. in 1983.

In May 1984 I began working with a local firm that engaged mainly in corporate banking law. While I was very fond of my co-workers, I soon realized that corporate law was not for me. After two years, I left to become the legal officer for Excel Banc.

Thereafter, I worked as a staff attorney for the Laredo, Texas Legal Aid Society, Inc., where I became the acting interim director of the program. After a brief stint as an Assistant Webb County Attorney, I took a job with the Webb County Public Defender's Office. I have been with the Webb County Public Defender's Office for approximately eight years.

I had become interested in practicing criminal law while I was enrolled in the Criminal Defense Clinic in law school. Unfortunately, I was not able to pursue this area upon my graduation. I had become so dissatisfied with the corporate and banking area that I seriously considered changing professions. In fact, that was one of the reasons I took a position with Excel Banc.

Fortunately, my love and passion for the law was restored once I started working as an assistant public defender. As I see it, my job is to maintain the integrity of those constitutional rights given to us by our founding fathers against those who would seek to diminish them, i.e., the state.

Doing defense work has given me an enormous amount of personal satisfaction and it has also given me some insight as to some of the problems plaguing our great country. The majority of our cases (e.g., robberies, burglaries, and assaults) are drug and/or alcohol related. I hope that our leaders will make battling drug and alcohol abuse one of their main priorities.

Advice to Students

The legal profession is a tough one, and it can be extremely taxing if you do not have a passion for it. I was once ready to make a sweeping indictment of the profession simply because I did not like the area of law I practiced. If you intend to study law, find that one area of law that interests you so that you may always have a love for your work, so that you may always prove yourself helpful to those who seek your guidance. This is a great profession. This is a great country.

(Souryal and Wellford 1997). Interestingly, the effect of race on sentence length varied by crime category, with black and Hispanic offenders convicted of drug offenses more likely to receive longer sentences than white defendants. Race also influenced the incarceration decision, regardless of whether the sentence was consistent with the sentencing guidelines.

In order to foster greater accountability and democracy among judges during the sentencing process, nationwide parameters for sentencing in similar situations have been recommended, the establishment of requirements for judges to submit written reasons for the sentences selected, and opening up judicial decisions to direct and indirect citizen review (Houston 2001). But such requirements are often unwieldy and not easily implemented. Judicial cooperation is required, and few judges are interested in creating more paperwork for themselves.

Correctional Resources and Their Limitations

There is only so much that corrections can do to accommodate the growing and increasingly diverse offender population. New prison and jail construction was originally believed to be a practical way of housing and treating greater numbers of offenders. Indeed, the prison space available in 2000 was six times greater than the prison space that existed in 1965 (Camp and Camp 2002). Despite this expansion of prison space, we would need at least four times as much space as exists today to accommodate the current population of offenders who should be incarcerated. Where does the money come from for new prison construction? Prison space isn't cheap. In 2001, for example, the average construction cost per bed was $93,020 for maximum-security space, $56,414 for medium-security space, and $39,121 for minimum-security space (Camp and Camp 2002:91).

In October 1994, for example, Governor Robert P. Casey of Pennsylvania authorized the expenditure of $60.5 million in contracts for the construction of a new, 640-inmate medium-security state correctional institution near Chester, Pennsylvania (*Corrections Digest* 1994:27). Unfortunately, by the time this facility is completed (the seventh and last prison constructed in Pennsylvania under a prison-expansion initiative commenced in 1990 to add 10,000 beds to the state correctional system), there will be a continuing demand for more prison space as new offenders are sentenced and enter Pennsylvania corrections. In 2001, despite its massive prison construction program, the entire Pennsylvania prison system was operating at 109.2 percent of its rated capacity, housing 36,282 inmates in rated space for only 33,180 inmates (Camp and Camp 2002:85). But the Pennsylvania prison system was not the worst among state prisons. In 2001, Nebraska housed 3,810 inmates in facilities rated to hold 2,371 inmates, thus operating at 160.7 percent of its rated capacity.

The Economics of Systemic Constraints

Some researchers examine the economics of incarceration by comparing the costs saved by offender incapacitation and crime reduction with the direct cost of prisoner maintenance (Marvell 1996:1–2). Using a cost-benefit analysis, investigators compare the actual costs of prisoner maintenance in prison with the potential cost to victims if these inmates were placed on probation instead. Thus, if we incarcerate Offender A for five years, it will cost X dollars. However, if Offender A is placed on probation and not incarcerated, the future crimes Offender A might commit are estimated and compared with Offender A's incarceration costs.

Several cost-benefit studies have been conducted to examine whether the cost of incarcerating offenders is worth the benefits accruing to victims and general public. Using data from the **National Crime Victimization Survey (NCVS)** and *Uniform Crime Reports (UCR)*, considering the average cost of particular index offenses, such as burglary, theft, auto theft, rape and robbery, the reduced cost to victims by incarcerating a single offender per year is about $19,000 (Marvell and Moody 1994). Additionally, crime entails losses such as suffering by victims' families, increased fear of crime by acquaintances, loss to victims' employers for sick leave, and commercial declines in high-crime neighborhoods (Marvell 1996:2–3). These costs were estimated at about $18,000 per prisoner per year. Together, the cost savings per prisoner per year was about $37,000. Average incarceration costs per prisoner per year, using 1994 dollars, were about $29,000. Thus, the gain accruing to victims and the public was about $8,000 per prisoner per year. Using 2003 dollars as the basis for our estimates, the gain would be much greater than in 1994.

These estimates are difficult to verify because we have no way of predicting which offenders will commit any particular amount of crime if placed on probation instead of being incarcerated. We do know that the results of cost-benefit analyses disclose that relatively few offenders commit disproportionately high amounts of crime during their criminal careers. Therefore, **selective incapacitation** is one possible solution to the problem of deciding which offenders should be incarcerated for greater or lesser lengths than others. But the state of the art regarding predicting risk and future dangerousness is not particularly sophisticated even beyond 2000. Thus, the potential use of selective incapacitation raises more issues than it resolves.

Specific types of offenders, such as child sexual abusers and other kinds of sex offenders, have often been targeted in different jurisdictions for enhanced sentencing to prolong their incarceration and heighten their accountability. However, crime control for this particular offender aggregate is made difficult by ineffective crime reporting and a lack of law enforcement and prosecution resources (Applied Research Services 2001). Furthermore, these persons vary significantly in their personality systems and have complicated social histories that often require modifications in standard treatment modalities. Many jurisdictions simply fail to make such modifications, and as a result, unacceptable recidivism figures are generated (Schlank 2001).

Louisiana is one of many states plagued with the problem of prison overcrowding. One solution to this overcrowding has been to establish risk review panels through what is called Act 403 of 2001 (Foster 2002:101). These panels consist of a Department of Public Safety secretary or designee, a board-certified psychologist, the warden or deputy warden, a retired judge with criminal law experience, and a probation and parole officer with at least ten years' experience. Many of these members are gubernatorial appointments. The responsibility of the risk review panel is to screen all inmates sent to it for release consideration. A risk review questionnaire is completed for each inmate, and the review panel may order a psychological evaluation of particular prisoners. The risk review panel subsequently makes a recommendation to the parole or pardon board to either grant or deny parole. Several types of offenses bar certain offenders from being considered for early release. These include violent crimes, certain sex offenses involving minors, and serious violations of substance abuse laws.

The intent of Act 403 was to target less serious offenders for early release as a way of easing prison overcrowding in the state. Thus, it authorized an alternative method of crime control and provided for an informed buffer, the risk review panel, between parole-eligible offenders and parole board action. As of March 2002, 11,036 inmates in Louisiana had filed applications for early release. However, 35 percent of these were identified as ineligible because of their crimes. Only 4.8 percent of these inmates were recommended for panel hearings, while 60 percent either had pending psychological and risk evaluations or had been placed on a defer docket for subsequent consideration. But critics of Act 403 continue to support lengthy incarceration as the preferred method of crime control, despite the exorbitant costs of incarceration. Supporters of the Act believe that it is a healthy first step toward resolving Louisiana's prison overcrowding problem through selective release by an informed risk review panel (Foster 2002:101).

It seems that correctional systems at all levels—local, state, and federal—will continue to face the twin challenges of providing more beds while competing for scarcer government resources (Higgins 1996:8). These conflicting forces will place increasing demands on those working within systems as well as for those providing services to support these programs. Also, within the federal prison system, at least, it is ordinarily assumed that the life expectancy of a prison facility is between twenty and thirty years. However, most major federal prison construction occurred during the 1930s, and many of today's federal prisons are sixty or more years old. It is likely that many of these sixty-year-old structures will be with us for perhaps another sixty years or longer. Nevertheless, new prison construction and design within the federal system may enable the Federal Bureau of Prisons to manage and cope more effectively with the growing population of federal inmates (Abramsky 2002). In the future, however, most state and federal officials are exploring less costly community-based approaches to offender management.

Jail and Prison Overcrowding Problems

In 2001, Nebraska was operating at 160.7 percent of its rated prison capacity, while the District of Columbia was operating at the lowest rated prison capacity of 77.7 percent (Camp and Camp 2002). Jail and prison overcrowding conditions influence judicial discretion in sentencing offenders (Roman and Harrell 2001). Judges have many sentencing options, including incarceration or a nonjail/prison penalty such as fines, probation, community service, restitution to victims, halfway houses, treatment, or some combination of these; or judges may even suspend or stay the execution of sentences. It is precisely because of this broad range of discretionary options associated with the judicial role as well as the independence of other actors in the criminal justice system that has led to jail and prison overcrowding becoming the most pressing problem facing the criminal justice system today.

Judges are not solely to blame for jail and prison overcrowding, however. The responsibility for overcrowding problems is shared also by the police, magistrates, prosecutors, parole boards, jail and prison officials, and even probation personnel (Tonry and Frase 2001). Judges must balance several interests in the sentencing process. First, they must consider the offender and the seriousness of the crime committed. Should the offender be incarcerated or sentenced to some nonincarcerative alternative? Second, they must be responsive to both the prosecutor and probation officer and their recommendations, whether such recommendations stemmed from plea agreements or PSI reports (Stinchcomb and Hippensteel 2001). Third, they must consider public interests. Will the public good be served by imprisoning an offender, or will these interests be better served by placing offenders in nonincarcerative probation programs where they can perform constructive services and possibly become rehabilitated? Finally, what will be the impact upon jail or prison populations if judges sentence offenders to incarceration, even for short periods?

One controversial solution to the problem of prison overcrowding is exporting prison inmates to jails, often in other states. For several years, several Texas jails have advertised to accommodate federal and state prisoners from other jurisdictions experiencing overcrowding problems. Ordinarily, state and federal prison inmates do not have a choice in deciding where they will be housed for the duration of their sentences. Many county jails in different states are used to house a portion of their state prison overflow. The Knox County Jail in Tennessee, for example, houses federal and state prisoners serving lengthy sentences together with other offenders convicted of misdemeanor offenses and who are serving short jail terms. Taking advantage of Texas jail space are at least two states, Virginia and Hawaii. In 1995, Virginia placed at least 450 of its prison inmates in Texas jails. In May 1995, Virginia authorities sent an additional 154 prison inmates to Texas to be housed in jails. In 1995, over 100 Hawaii state prison inmates were also serving their time in Texas jails (*Corrections Today* 1995:28–29). Besides using Texas jail facilities, Virginia prison officials were also making use of their own county jail facilities in order to control their inmate overflow. Some Virginia county sheriffs were not pleased with these arrangements since this meant overcrowding in their own jail facilities.

Following numerous lawsuits filed by inmates and jail officials against the Virginia prison system, a Virginia circuit judge ruled on May 2, 1995 that Virginia was violating the law by "illegally stuffing local jails with felons who should be held in state prisons instead" (*Corrections Today* 1995:30). Jail officials in Alexandria, Richmond, and Virginia Beach collectively alleged that Virginia was causing its county jails to become overcrowded by ordering state prisoners to be housed in county jail facilities. The ruling from the circuit court meant that Virginia would have to look elsewhere in order to accommodate its growing inmate population. As a followup, by 2000, Hawaii was using private contractors to house 1,200 of their inmates in-state, while Virginia had 1,728 prisoners supervised in-state privately (Camp and Camp 2002:93).

SUMMARY

Crimes are differentiated according to felonies or major offenses and misdemeanors or minor offenses. Felonies are generally punishable by incarcerative terms of one or more years, whereas misdemeanors are punishable by incarcerative terms of less than one year. Convicted felons ordinarily spend their terms in prisons, whereas misdemeanants spend their time in jails. However, prison overcrowding has caused many of the nation's jails to be used as confinement facilities for long-term felons. Another offense category is the summary offense, which includes petty crimes that can be tried quickly by a magistrate or justice of the peace. Summary offenses also include traffic violations, misrepresentations of mileage on a motor vehicle, or dumping litter on public highways.

Crimes are further distinguishable according to whether they are property crimes, where items of value are taken from others, and violent crimes, where persons are directly involved as victims of criminals. Property crimes include larceny, burglary, and vehicular theft, whereas violent crimes include robbery, forcible rape, homicide, and aggravated assault. Violent crimes, or crimes against the person, usually involve physical injuries or death to one or more victims.

Criminals are classified in different ways when they are apprehended and charged with one or more crimes. Some offenders with no prior criminal records are called first offenders and are generally treated more leniently by prosecutors and judges compared with recidivists, who have prior criminal records. Some offenders are labeled as career criminals because they make their livelihood from crime. There are also several special offender categorizations. These include drug- or alcohol-dependent criminals, the mentally ill, the physically handicapped or challenged, and sex offenders. Some offenders have highly contagious diseases, such as tuberculosis or HIV/AIDS. Significant attempts have been made by corrections authorities to isolate those with these diseases from the general offender population. Special-needs offenders often receive medical treatment and/or individual or group counseling in addition to the traditional punishments of incarceration and/or fines. Those with drug or alcohol dependencies tend to have higher failure rates when placed on probation or parole. In some jurisdictions, a deinstitutionalization movement has occurred to place special offenders, such as the mentally ill or retarded, into categories other than criminal, where they can be hospitalized and treated rather than incarcerated and punished.

Convicted offenders are sentenced in a sentencing hearing. This is a proceeding conducted by a judge where sentences are imposed. Usually, judges explain the reasons for their decisions to offenders, their attorneys, and prosecutors. The purposes of sentencing are to insure retribution, promote deterrence and crime prevention, impose just deserts and justice, impose incapacitation and enhance offender control, and promote rehabilitation and reintegration where necessary. Sentencing variations include indeterminate sentencing, where parole boards determine early release of offenders short of serving the full term imposed by judges; determinate sentencing, where inmates serve their full terms less good-time credit; presumptive sentencing or guidelines-based sentencing, where judges rely on sentencing ranges and guidelines to gauge the length of incarceration; and mandatory sentencing, where judges impose a statutory term in cases of habitual offenders or those who use firearms during the commission of a felony. These sentences are flat sentences and must be served in their entirety, exclusive of good-time credit. Judges have considerable discretion under most sentencing schemes, and they base their decisions in part on the anticipated dangerousness of offenders and their degree of public risk. Affecting the sentencing decision are issues relating to jail and prison overcrowding, disparities in sentencing, and ineffectiveness of rehabilitation. Those who reject rehabilitation as a genuine correctional aim, or those who do not regard it as effective, favor more punitive-oriented sentences to coincide with the seriousness of offenses committed. Either during trial or plea bargaining, mitigating circumstances and aggravating circumstances are considered by prosecutors and judges to lessen or intensify punishment. Sentences are imposed when defendants are found guilty or enter guilty pleas.

Assisting judges in their sentencing decisions are presentence investigation reports (PSIs), usually prepared by probation officers or private corporations. These PSIs are useful and contain much background information about convicted offenders. Mitigating and aggravating circumstances associated with the offense are included, and judges often rely heavily on probation officer recommendations contained in these PSIs. Aggravating circumstances include whether there was serious bodily injury or death, whether there were multiple victims, whether the offender committed the offense while on probation or pa-role, whether the offender had a prior criminal record, whether a dangerous weapon was used, and whether the criminal played a leadership role in the crime's commission. Mitigating circumstances include no physical injuries to victims; cooperation with law enforcement to apprehend other criminals who participated in the crime's commission; whether there was mental incapacita-tion, disease, or defect; whether the criminal was a first offender; and whether the offender was somehow justified in committing the crime.

PSIs function to aid the court in determining appropriate sentences, they aid probation officers in supervising offender-clients, they assist various prison systems in classification decisions about inmates, and they furnish parole boards with information relevant to early release decisions. PSIs are not re-quired for all offenders, but most jurisdictions require their preparation where convictions for serious offenses have been obtained. The length and complexity of PSIs varies according to each jurisdiction, offense seriousness, and the par-ticular protocols followed by different probation departments and courts. Often appended to these PSIs are victim-impact statements, where victims or their relatives explain how they were harmed by the offenders' actions. The criminal also furnishes an account of what occurred through a sentencing memorandum. Judges may or may not be persuaded to impose particular punishments based on a PSI report's contents. These PSI reports are also used subsequently by pa-role boards whenever they must make early-release decisions about incarcer-ated inmates.

Several sentencing issues include sentencing disparities, where widely different sentences have been imposed on different persons for reasons of race, ethnicity, gender, socioeconomic status, age, or some other extralegal factor; correctional resources and their limitations, where many jails and prisons are old and have poorly designed physical plants, thus posing health and safety risks to both inmates and those supervising them; and jail and prison over-crowding. Most jails and prisons in the United States are overcrowded. Jail and prison overcrowding is a major correctional issue. Overcrowding causes prob-lems in other dimensions of the correctional system.

QUESTIONS FOR REVIEW

1. What are felonies and misdemeanors? What are some primary distinguishing char-acteristics of these types of offense categories? Are all felonies violent crimes? Why or why not?

2. Who are situational offenders? How do they differ from recidivists and first offenders?

3. What are five different purposes of sentencing? Which purpose do you believe is most important and why?

4. What are four major types of sentencing? What type of sentencing is used most frequently among the states? What are some explanations for this sentencing preference?

5. In what ways do presumptive sentencing guidelines limit the sentencing discre-tion of judges?

6. What are several aggravating factors? How do they differ from mitigating factors? What weight is assigned to these factors by judges when sentencing particular offenders?

7. Do sentencing disparities exist among judges? What factors are frequently associ-ated with sentencing disparities? How have presumptive and mandatory sentenc-ing schemes influenced sentencing disparities?

8.   What are four types of special-needs offenders? Why do they pose problems for prison and jail administrators?

9.   What is a presentence investigation report? Who prepares these reports? How are such reports used by judges and parole boards? What are some of the contents of PSIs?

10. What are victim impact statements? How are they used in sentencing hearings?

SUGGESTED READINGS

Felson, Marcus. *Crime in Everyday Life.* 3d ed. Thousand Oaks, CA: Sage Publications, 2002.

Holmes, Ronald M. and Stephen T. Holmes. *Sex Crimes: Patterns and Behavior.* Thousand Oaks, CA: Sage Publications, 2002.

Lyman, Michael D. and Gary W. Potter. *Drugs in Society: Causes, Concepts, and Control.* 4th ed. Cincinnati, OH: Anderson Publishing Company, 2003.

Rex, Sue and Michael Tonry, eds. *Reform and Punishment: The Future of Sentencing.* Portland, OR: Willan Publishing, 2002.

Spohn, Cassia C. *How Do Judges Decide? The Search for Fairness and Justice in Punishment.* Thousand Oaks, CA: Sage Publications, 2002.

INTERNET CONNECTIONS

Bureau of Justice Statistics
http://www.ojp.usdoj.gov/bjs/correct.htm

National Association of Pretrial Services
http://www.napsa.org

National Criminal Justice Reference Service
http://www.ncjrs.org

Punishment and Sentencing
http://www.uaa.alaska.edu/just/just110/courts4.html

Sentencing Project
http://www.sentencingproject.org/

U.S. Courts
http://www.flmp.uscourts.gov/Presentence/presentence

U.S. Sentencing Commission
http://www.ussc.gov/ANNRPT/1999/sbtoc99.htm

Vera Institute of Justice Projects: State Sentencing and Corrections Program
http://www.vera.org/project/project1_1.asp?section_id=26

APPENDIX 2A

Offense Report

TEXAS DEPARTMENT OF PUBLIC SAFETY
CRIMINAL LAW ENFORCEMENT DIVISION
NARCOTICS SERVICE

INVESTIGATIVE REPORT

REPORT TITLE: LAREDO, TEXAS	**THIS REPORT IS THE PROPERTY OF THE CRIMINAL LAW ENFORCEMENT DIVISION - NARCOTICS SERVICE. NEITHER IT NOR ITS CONTENTS MAY BE DISSEMINATED OUT-SIDE THE AGENCY TO WHICH LOANED.**

ACCESS: MAA/Multi-Agency Access
DISSEM: 2/Release Data Elements and Pointer
SUBMITTED BY: Inv Mickey Hadnot
STATIONED: Laredo, TX

DISSEMINATED TO:

Cross Related Info? [N]   Disseminations? [N]

REPORT RE:

DEFENDANTS

Offense: Poss CS pg 2>=400g — 481.116(e) HSC, F*   **Offense Date:** 06/07/2000

Offense: Poss CS pg 2>=400g — 481.116(e) HSC, F*   **Offense Date:** 06/07/2000

SYNOPSIS

On 6/7/00, Sergeant Leo Perez received information from a confidential informant that a Hispanic female by the name of _____ and another Hispanic female would board the 8:00 p.m. El Conejo Bus headed for Dallas Texas. The confidential informant further advised Sergeant Perez that both of the females would have hidden on their bodies, approximately 2 kilos of cocaine each. Agents of the Texas Department of Public Safety and U.S. Customs conducted surveillance on the El Conejo Bus Company and observed two Hispanic females board the bus matching the description given by the confidential informant. The bus was checked at the IH-35 North Immigration checkpoint and as the result, both females identified as _____ Date of Birth: _____ and _____ Date of Birth: _____, were arrested for Possession of a Controlled Substance after they were checked and found to be in possession of approximately 2 kilos of cocaine each.

DPS SENSITIVE
INVESTIGATIVE

JUL 11 2000

DETAILS

1. On Tuesday, 6/6/00, Sergeant Leo Perez was advised by a confidential informant that a Hispanic female by the name of _____ and four (4) small children would board the 8:00 p.m. El Conejo Bus.

2. The informant also gave a full description of _____ and the clothing she would be wearing. The informant further stated that _____ would be carrying 2 kilos of cocaine hidden on her body.

3. On Tuesday, 6/6/00 at approximately 7:00 p.m., Agents from the Texas Department of Public Safety and U.S. Customs set up surveillance on the El Conejo Bus Terminal.

4. At approximately 7:55 p.m., Sergeant Perez was contacted by the informant and advised that there was a change in plans and _____ would not be arriving at the bus station on this date.

5. At approximately 8:10 p.m., surveillance was terminated at this location.

6. On Wednesday, 6/7/00, Sergeant Perez was again contacted by the same informant who advised that _____ would board the El Conejo Bus at approximately 8:00 p.m. on this date headed for Dallas Texas.

7. The confidential informant stated that two small children would accompany _____ and another adult Hispanic female identified as _____.

8. The informant gave a complete description of _____ and _____ and the clothing they were wearing.

9. According to the informant, both adult females were carrying, hidden on their person, 2 kilos of cocaine each.

10. At approximately 7:00 p.m., Agents with the Texas Department of Public Safety and U.S. Customs again began surveillance on the El Conejo Bus Station.

11. At approximately 7:44 p.m., a white, early model, 4-door Chevrolet, driven by a Hispanic male, arrived at the El Conejo Bus Station. A small Hispanic female and two small children exited. This female was wearing the exact clothing as described earlier by the informant.

12. Sergeant Hadnot watched as the adult Hispanic female and two small children entered the bus station and approached the ticket counter.

13. At approximately 7:50 p.m., a gray Dodge sports utility vehicle, driven by a Hispanic female, pulled up to the bus station. In the vehicle, another Hispanic female was in the front passenger side.

14. After a brief conversation with the driver, the front passenger exited and entered the bus station. This female was also wearing the exact clothing as described by the informant as the second person to be carrying cocaine hidden on her body.

15. As both Hispanic females and the small children loaded onto the bus, Sergeant Hadnot left this location and proceeded to the IH-35 North Border Patrol checkpoint and further advised them of the situation.

16. At the checkpoint, Sergeant Hadnot spoke with Special Agent Ruben Garza Jr. and asked if he could check the El Conejo Bus with his canine once it arrived at that location. SPA Ruben Garza Jr. agreed to the inspection.

17. At approximately 8:15 p.m., the El Conejo Bus arrived at the checkpoint where SPA Ruben Garza Jr., using his canine (Sonia), checked it.

DPS SENSITIVE
INVESTIGATIVE

18. While checking the baggage compartment of the bus, Sonia alerted high to the roof of the storage compartment just below where the two suspects were now sitting (see ATTACHMENT #1, U.S. Border Patrol form I-44, prepared by SPA Ruben Garza Jr.).

19. Garza entered the bus and after a short interview with the occupants, he exited with the two adult females and two small children I had observed arrive at the bus station earlier.

20. The first female to exit the bus was later identified by Texas Identification card _____ as _____ Date of Birth: _____

21. _____ was wearing a very loose fitting blue denim blouse and blue jean pants with black velcro sandals.

22. The Second female from the bus was later identified by Texas Identification card _____ as _____ Date of Birth: _____

23. _____ was also wearing a very loose fitting blue denim blouse with a large black shirt underneath and blue jeans and black sandals.

24. _____ was carrying a small child, several jackets and a large white towel in her arms as she exited the bus and entered the checkpoint station.

25. As she walked into the room, _____ walked over to a far wall and dropped all the contents of her arms onto the floor. _____ then picked the small child up from the floor and walked over and sat in a chair leaving the jackets and towel on the floor.

26. _____ took a seat opposite _____ as they were both detained awaiting the arrival of a female agent to conduct a search for contraband.

27. At approximately 8:45 p.m., female Border Patrol Agent Kerry Daniel arrived to conduct the search of _____ and _____

28. Agent Daniel first escorted _____ to the ladies room and conducted a search.

29. At approximately 8:50 p.m., Agent Daniel exited the restroom with _____ and advised that she did not find any illegal substance on _____

30. Agent Daniel then escorted _____ into the ladies room and conducted a search.

31. At approximately 8:54 p.m., Agent Daniel and _____ exited the restroom with Daniel holding EXHIBIT #1; two (2) cellophane wrapped packages believed to contain cocaine.

32. _____ was then placed under arrest for possession of a controlled substance.

33. Sergeant Hadnot then checked the area where _____ had been seated, and the contents she had placed on the floor as she entered the trailer.

34. Inside the large white towel, which _____ had carried in her arms as she entered the trailer, was located EXHIBIT #2; four (4) cellophane wrapped bundles believed to contain cocaine.

35. _____ was also placed under arrest for possession of a controlled substance.

36. Both _____ and _____ were read the Miranda Rights by Sergeant Victor Escalon.

37. _____ AND _____ were transported to the Laredo DPS Office for debriefing. Both were photographed and fingerprinted before being asked if they wished to give a statement.

38. Both _____ and _____ gave written statements concerning them being in possession of the cocaine. (See ATTACHMENT #2, Voluntary Written Statement signed by _____, dated 06-08-00 and ATTACHMENT #3, Voluntary Written Statement signed by _____ dated 06-08-00.)

DPS SENSITIVE
INVESTIGATIVE

39. _____ and _____ were transported to the Webb County Jail and remanded to their custody for violation of the Texas Health and Safety Code 481.116 Possession of a Controlled Substance.

40. On Thursday, 6/8/00, Justice of the Peace Hector Liendo assessed bond on _____ and _____ at five hundred thousand dollars ($500,000.00) each for the charge of Possession of a Controlled Substance.

41. On Thursday, 6/8/00, Sergeant Hadnot marked, initialed, dated, photographed and weighed Drug Exhibits #1 and #2. The approximate weight including packaging was 5.72 kilograms.

42. At approximately 1:00 a.m., Sergeant Hadnot submitted Drug Exhibits #1 and #2 to Texas Department of Public Safety Crime Laboratory in Laredo Texas for analysis and preservation. Exhibits #1 and #2 will be analyzed for latent prints. Exhibits #1 and #2 were issued Laboratory #L3L-4970, (see ATTACHMENT #4, Lab Submission form prepared by Sergeant Hadnot).

43. This file should remain open and all evidence should be retained pending final disposition on the criminal charges against _____ and _____.

44. This investigation will continue.

WITNESSES - OFFICIAL
TX DEPT. OF PUBLIC SAFETY
Sgt./Inv. Mickey Hadnot
1901 Bob Bullock Loop
Laredo, Texas 78043-9771
956/728-2243

WILL TESTIFY TO
Having located 4 bundles of cocaine in a large white towel which had been discarded on the floor by the defendant, and having placed both defendants under arrest.

WITNESSES - OFFICIAL
Sgt./Inv. Leo Perez
As above.

Sgt./Inv. Victor Escalon
As above.

UNITED STATES BORDER PATROL
Special Agent Ruben Garza Jr.
207 W. Del Mar Blvd
Laredo, Texas 78041
956/723-4367

Agent Kerry Daniel
As above.

WILL TESTIFY TO
Having been contacted by a confidential informant who gave the description of the defendants who would have the cocaine in their possession.

Having given each defendant their Miranda Warning and to have taken a written statement from each.

He and his canine partner "Sonia" checking the luggage compartment of the El Conejo Bus and to "Sonia" alerting to the presence of Narcotics.

Having searched both female defendants and locating 2 kilos of cocaine on the body of one and nothing on the other.

DPS SENSITIVE
INVESTIGATIVE

SUBJECTS

Physical Description
Race: White   **Sex:** Female   **DOB:** _____   **Hair:** Black   **Eyes:** Brown   **Facial Hair:** Other
Height: 4′ 11″   **Weight:** 210

Identifying Numbers
ID#: (TX)   **SSN#:** (TX)

Addresses
IH35 N
Laredo, TX (Arrested)

Laredo, TX (Residence)

Laredo. TX (Observed)

Physical Description
Race: White   **Sex:** Female   **DOB:** _____   **Hair:** Brown   **Eyes:** Brown   **Facial Hair:** Other
Height: 5′ 01″   **Weight:** 115

Identifying Numbers
ID#: (TX)   **SSN#:** (TX)

Addresses
IH35 N
Laredo, TX (Arrested)

Laredo, TX (Residence)

Laredo, TX (Observed)

DESCRIPTION AND CUSTODY OF SEIZURE/EVIDENCE

Exhibit # 1 (Drug)
Description
Quantity: 4.95 Pound(s)   **Court:** DPS Laredo NARC - Texas
Cocaine
2 bundles of white powdery substance wrapped in cellophane

Exhibit # 2 (Drug)
Description
Quantity: 6.3 Pound(s)   **Date Submitted to Lab:** 06/08/2000
Cocaine
4 bundles of white powdery substance wrapped in cellophane

DPS SENSITIVE
INVESTIGATIVE

ANIMALS

SONIA (Canine - German Shepard)

ATTACHMENTS

US Border Patrol Report

Description
Date: 06/07/2000   **Location:** DPS Narcotics - Laredo   **Custodian:** Hadnot, Mickey (Inv)
Ref: U.S. Border Patrol form I-44 submitted by Special Patrol Agent Ruben Garza and Agent Kerry Daniel.

Voluntary Statement of Accused

Description
Date: 06/08/2000   **Location:** DPS Narcotics - Laredo   **Custodian:** Hadnot, Mickey (Inv)
Ref: Voluntary Written Statement signed by _____

Voluntary Statement of Accused

Description
Date: 06/08/2000   **Location:** DPS Narcotics - Laredo   **Custodian:** Hadnot, Mickey (Inv)
Ref: Voluntary Written Statement signed by _____

Lab/c-1 (Controlled Substance Submission Form)

Description
Date: 06/07/2000   **Location:** DPS Narcotics - Laredo   **Custodian:** Hadnot, Mickey (Inv)
Ref: #L3L-4970, Submission of 2 bundles of white powdery substance wrapped in cellophane believed to be cocaine and 4 bundles of a white powdery substance wrapped in cellophane also believed to be cocaine.

CHAPTER 3 | Diversion, Standard, and Intensive Supervised Probation Programs

Courtesy of Custer Youth Correctional Center.

Chapter Objectives

As the result of reading this chapter, the following objectives should be realized:

1. Describing the process of pretrial diversion, the forms of diversion, who qualifies for diversion, and the effectiveness of diversion as a nonincarcerative option.
2. Discussing the nature and functions of alternative dispute resolution.
3. Discussing probation, its history, philosophy, and effectiveness.
4. Describing the functions of probation, including punishment, deterrence, community reintegration, and crime control.
5. Discussing intensive supervised probation and the reasons for its use.
6. Describing shock probation, split sentencing, and boot camps as punishment options.
7. Describing those who qualify for probation.
8. Describing the probation revocation process, including discussing important U.S. Supreme Court cases that have impacted the rights of probationers regarding the revocation of their probation programs.
9. Showing variations among the states according to the different conditions that might result in probation revocation.

INTRODUCTION

• *Robert was very familiar with the area. It was known as good hunting territory. In fact, on weekends, many hunters would drive through a large hole in a high fence surrounding the land and hunt for deer. The only problem was that the area encircled by a high fence was a military post. The woods where hunters hunted were located on government property. But hunters hunted there anyway. One Sunday, Robert drove his pickup truck onto the site and hunted all day. Frustrated with not finding any deer, Robert started to drive off. However, he noticed a large pile of 2" × 4" boards. The weeds had grown up around them, and some of the boards were beginning to rot. Robert didn't think anyone would miss the boards, and so he piled them into his pickup truck and drove away. Later, he sold the boards at a flea market for $50. Two weeks later, two government agents appeared at Robert's door and placed him under arrest for misdemeanor theft of government property. Robert was assigned a public defender who discussed his case with the U.S. Attorney's Office. It was disclosed that Robert, a part-time custodian at a local grammar school, had no prior criminal record. Robert had explained that he had no intention of stealing anything. He just saw the rotting wood and didn't want it to go to waste. He didn't think that what he did was wrong. The Assistant U.S. Attorney suggested diversion, meaning that Robert's case would be taken out of the criminal justice system temporarily and he would be placed on a form of probation for a period of one year as a divertee. If he stayed out of trouble and paid a monthly maintenance fee of $30 from his wages, the government would drop its case against Robert. Robert agreed and became a divertee. After one year, his record was expunged and Robert was free of the criminal justice system. In the meantime, the hole in the military post fence was repaired and signs were posted to keep out hunters.* [Adapted from the Associated Press, "Favorite Hunting Spot on Military Base Closed to Local Hunters," March 30, 2002].

• *It was another bar fight. Two men, both drunk, were seated at separate tables with their girlfriends. Suddenly, one man took offense at the other man's looking at his girlfriend. A fight ensued. One man suffered a broken nose, while the other had three teeth knocked out. Sheriff's deputies arrested both men and charged them with assault. After posting bond, the men were offered an opportunity to settle their cases through civil means. They were brought together in a deserted school classroom about a month later, where a retired judge presided. The judge heard each man's version of events. Then he concluded that each man would have to pay for the other man's lost wages and medical bills. Otherwise, there would be criminal charges filed, and the men would have to go to criminal court. Neither man wanted that. They agreed to the settlement worked out by the judge, and over the next few months, each man paid the medical expenses and lost wages of the other. The judge filed a report with the local state's attorney and the matter was concluded. Alternative dispute resolution had just occurred. No criminal records were acquired. Everyone seemed satisfied with the result. This was an example of alternative dispute resolution in action.* [Adapted from the Associated Press, "Alternative Dispute Resolution Works in Vermont," April 20, 2002].

• *James has serious alcohol and drug dependency problems. Over the years, he has had several drunk driving arrests. Also, he has mugged people to get money for drugs. Some of these muggings have resulted in arrests, and he has at least one conviction for assault. His most recent arrest was for buying cocaine from an undercover police officer. At his subsequent trial, testimony revealed that his alcohol and drug dependencies were serious and that without proper treatment he would continue to pose problems for society. After a finding of guilty by a jury, James was interviewed by a probation officer who conducted a pre-sentence investigation and filed the report with the judge. The judge decided to place James on intensive supervised probation, subject to frequent face-to-face drug and alcohol checks. Furthermore, James was ordered to undergo treatment for his drug and alcohol dependencies and attend Alcoholics Anonymous and Narcotics Anonymous meetings. He was also ordered to undergo counseling for his addictions. The period of probation specified for James was four years. If James violated one or more probationary terms, his probation would be revoked and he would be incarcerated. However, James turned out to be a model probationer, complying with all program requirements. He observed curfew, performed well at his job, provided for his family, and attended the required meetings and counseling sessions. During his probationary period, James developed a close bond with his probation officer, a twenty-year veteran who specialized in supervising cases involving drug/alcohol dependencies. The officer was very effective in providing James with various forms of assistance when necessary. James served his probationary term and has lived a law-abiding life for the past three years. James's case appears to be a success story, according to the probation department.* [Adapted from the Associated Press, "Success on Probation Attributed to Probation Officer Actions," November 12, 2002].

This chapter describes various punishments that may be applied to either unconvicted or convicted offenders. Some crimes seem best resolved without formal court action. In some instances, prosecutors decide to divert these cases to a civil forum for resolution. Thus, **diversion** or alternative dispute resolution may be used. Diversion occurs prior to any formal adjudication of offender guilt and is best described as a type of pre-conviction probation. Although those granted diversion may never be prosecuted, convicted, or incarcerated, diversion is included as a part of corrections because it is ordinarily administered by various correctional agencies in most jurisdictions.

Another pretrial resolution of an offense is through alternative dispute resolution. In these cases, the unconvicted offender meets with the victim(s) in the presence of a third-party arbiter. Hopefully, a civil resolution to the problem can be obtained, where both the perpetrator and the victim agree as to the punishment. Usually, diversion or alternative dispute resolution does not result in a criminal record for the perpetrator. The weaknesses, strengths, and particular conditions under which these different programs are used will be discussed.

In contrast, **probation** is often imposed after a conviction has been obtained in court. Probation is a sentence imposed by the judge, whereby the offender usually resides in his or her community and is required to abide by certain probation conditions for a designated time interval. Probation in the United States dates back to the 1830s. Over a century later, in the 1940s, all states and the federal government had probation programs of different kinds. Various goals and functions of probation will be described and discussed. The history of probation will also be examined briefly, together with an evaluation of its effectiveness. Community reaction to probation will also be examined.

Different types of probation are described. Although all probation programs have conditions, most probation programs have standardized behavioral requirements. These programs are referred to as standard probation. Other types of probation include probation with special conditions and intensive supervised probation. Usually, the nature and frequency of contact between probationers and their supervising probation officers is increased in these latter types of programs. Intensive supervised probation is more expensive to use compared with standard probation. Thus, some attention is given to the types of offenders who are usually recommended for more intensive supervision. Several probation programs and their varying conditions are described. Both the strengths and weaknesses of these programs are discussed.

Probationer-clients are also profiled. The characteristics of probationers are constantly changing, usually in response to changes in the manner of sentencing used in particular jurisdictions. Some of these offenders are sentenced to shock probation or incarceration, a form of split sentencing. Shock probation will be described, as well as its philosophy, functions, weaknesses, strengths, and applications. Various other types of split sentencing will be discussed.

The chapter next discusses boot camps, their philosophy and goals, and some general characteristics of boot camp programs. Boot camp clientele are profiled. While most boot camps are tailored for youthful offenders, older offenders are sometimes sentenced to them for short periods. Boot camps have not been without their critics, and several criticisms of boot camps will be examined. The chapter concludes with an examination of the probation revocation process. The U.S. Supreme Court has issued decisions in several important cases that have affected how judges must conduct probation revocation hearings. The rights of probationers are examined in this regard. There is much state variation concerning the grounds for revoking one's probation program. Therefore, several important state probation revocation cases will be examined, and the issues involved in each probation revocation case will be highlighted. Although states vary according to their rules for revoking one's probation program, there is a great deal of similarity among jurisdictions, where state policies have been influenced largely by U.S. Supreme Court and circuit court decisions.

CIVIL ALTERNATIVES: ALTERNATIVE DISPUTE RESOLUTION AND DIVERSION

Pretrial Services

Whenever someone is arrested and charged with a crime, all jurisdictions initiate processes known as **pretrial services.** Pretrial services exist for both the states and federal government. One example of the array of pretrial services provided defendants is the Santa Clara County, California, Superior Court Pretrial Services (Santa Clara County Superior Court 2003). Defendants arrested and booked at the Santa Clara County Jail are the subjects of an investigative report prepared by the Pretrial Services Jail Division for the Superior Court. This report is compiled at the time of booking, and it consists of an interview with the defendant, reference verification, criminal records, and an affidavit describing the alleged offense. The report is used both to assess eligibility for release on one's own recognizance and to assist the court in setting bail. Defendants who are eligible for release consideration also receive a recommendation as part of the report. In order to be considered for release, defendants must provide any information requested in an interview, and they must give their permission for authorities to contact their personal references.

The court may determine that some cases require further documentation and investigation. Pretrial Services may have to determine the extent of injuries suffered by an alleged victim, verify the safe placement of an alleged victim who is a minor, or determine whether the defendant has secured an alternate address for the duration of the case. Some substance abuse treatment may be required in the interim between arrest and subsequent trial. Other supervision services provided by Pretrial Services include ensuring that defendants comply with any and all court-ordered conditions, such as mental health treatment, domestic violence counseling, or substance-abuse testing. Pretrial Services may meet with defendants to determine their individual needs for services, and referrals may be made to the appropriate community treatment programs. Defendants are required to make regular contact with Pretrial Services officers to chart their progress, reinforce the conditions of pretrial release, discuss problematic issues, and receive information about future counseling or court appearance dates and times (Santa Clara County Superior Court 2003).

The Pretrial Services Resource Center, headquartered in Washington, D.C., has outlined several important functions for pretrial services in most jurisdictions. The mission of the Pretrial Services Resource Center is to improve the quality, fairness, and efficiency of the criminal justice system at the pretrial stage by promoting systemic strategies that improve court appearance rates, reduce recidivism, provide appropriate and effective services, and enhance com-

---

 **BOX 3.1**  **PERSONALITY HIGHLIGHT**

Maria Teresa Salazar

U.S. Pretrial Services Officer, Laredo, TX

Statistics:

M.S. (criminal justice), Texas A & M International University; B.S. (criminal justice), Laredo State University

Work History and Experience

My first employment in the law enforcement field was as a detention officer with the Webb County Juvenile Department. My plans were to obtain my degree and work as a juvenile probation officer. I obtained my bachelor's degree in May 1992 from Laredo State University. Subsequently, I was employed with the Webb County Adult Probation. It was a real challenge for me, because it was something new. Most of my experience had been working with juveniles, where the laws are different. I began my career preparing pre-sentence investigation reports and later transferred to a supervision caseload. I was employed as a probation officer for seven and a half years. My experience as a probation officer made me realize that I had made the right career choice. I learned that it is not always easy to try to help a defendant to become a productive citizen. The role of being a probation officer is not just making sure the defendant complies with the conditions of probation imposed

by the court, but also to assure that the defendant is rehabilitated to be able to function in society. In addition, I have been able to gain the knowledge necessary to expand my horizons in the criminal justice field.

Currently, I am employed with the U.S. Pretrial Services Agency in the capacity of an officer, where I have been for the past three years. The main goal of the department is to conduct investigations to determine if a defendant should be released on bond or be detained pending his or her criminal case. My recommendations are based on the Federal Criminal Code and Procedure and the defendants' backgrounds.

Advice to Students

Life has many challenges and one must always want to be successful. Obtaining one's goals will not come instantly. Rather, hard work, dedication, and love for what you do can prove to be the beginning of a rewarding career.

munity safety (Pretrial Services Resource Center 2003). This mission is accomplished through the achievement of the following goals:

1. To provide accurate and current information on pretrial issues.
2. To identify and evaluate emerging trends in the pretrial stage.
3. To provide technical assistance in the pretrial area.
4. To improve and advance the pretrial services profession.
5. To identify and promote best practices in pretrial release, including effective techniques and practices to supervise pretrial defendants and detention decision making.
6. To promote the use of conditions for pretrial release that are not inappropriately dependent on financial circumstances.
7. To identify and promote best practices in achieving timely dispositions.
8. To identify and promote best practices in pretrial diversion decision making (Pretrial Services Resource Center 2003:1).

At the beginning of offender processing and depending upon the particular jurisdiction, several options exist for prosecutors as alternatives to a full-fledged prosecution of the defendant. Two options are presented here. These are alternative dispute resolution and pretrial diversion.

Alternative Dispute Resolution

An increasingly used option by the prosecution in both adult and juvenile cases is **alternative dispute resolution (ADR)** (Hadley 2001). ADR is a community-based, informal dispute settlement between offenders and their victims (Ostermeyer and Keilitz 1997). Misdemeanants, or those who commit minor crimes, are most often targeted for ADR. However, some first-offender felons might also be included in such programs. More ADR programs are being established throughout the United States annually. ADR is also known as **restorative justice** (Karp 2001). ADR involves the direct participation of the victim and offender, with the aim of mutual accommodation for both parties.

The emphasis of ADR is upon restitution rather than punishment (Van Ness and Strong 2001). Someone might get drunk in a tavern and break up furniture or assault another patron, one who might also be drunk. The fight leads to property loss for the tavern owner as well as physical injuries to both fighting parties. Grounds exist for a criminal prosecution of the drunk patron who broke furniture and provoked a fight. But under certain circumstances, if both the offender and victim agree, ADR can be used to resolve these crimes by civil means rather than criminal ones (Maxwell and Morris 2001). The drunk patron can agree to pay the damages he caused in the tavern and reimburse the injured patron for any medical expenses and time lost from a job. If both parties agree, the case is concluded and no criminal action is taken. ADR programs have been established in over 200 U.S. jurisdictions, 60 in Norway, 50 in France, 50 in Canada, 40 in Germany, 28 in England, 30 in Finland, 20 in Belgium, and 25 in Australia (Harley 1999).

When criminal cases are removed from the jurisdiction of criminal courts, not everyone views this alternative favorably. There are those who insist that criminals should receive their just deserts (Bazemore and Schiff 2001). Mediation or victim-offender reconciliation has been studied extensively. One study evaluated the effects of participation in victim-offender mediation on reoffense in order to determine whether such interventions were successful at reducing of-fender recidivism. While those investigated were 1,298 juveniles in four different jurisdictions, there were overall similar results among the different sites. In short, the perpetrators who participated in victim-offender mediation reoffended at a rate of 32 percent less than those youths who did not participate in victim-offender mediation programs. Thus, the difference in reoffense rates was more than three times larger than the average effect associated with interventions for delinquency in other studies (Nugent et al. 2001). The clear implication of this re-search is that it is also workable for adult offenders. Mediation has been used in other countries besides the United States with favorable results (Spapens 2001).

Restorative justice is not limited to communities. Quite often, persons are victimized within jails and prisons (Braithwaite 2002). When victimizers are other inmates, probationers, or parolees, everyone in the corrections community is af-fected. Tensions rise, personal and collective safety are jeopardized, and distrust and pervasive fear abound. When an inmate (or even a staff member) harms an-other, that harm has a domino effect that ripples far beyond the scene of the crime. Everyone in the corrections community must be informed and involved in design-ing and implementing restorative justice approaches to crime (Seyko 2001). Bene-fits to the community—including staff, inmates, and their families—must be tangible. Expected outcomes should include a safe environment, remorse by the perpetrator(s), and opportunities to repair the harm done (Sullivan and Tifft 2001).

Victim-Offender Reconciliation Projects

Another type of alternative dispute resolution is victim-offender reconciliation (Johnstone 2002). Victim-offender reconciliation is a specific form of conflict reso-lution between the victim and the offender. Face-to-face encounter is the essence of this process (Mlinarzik 2001). A **Victim-Offender Reconciliation Project (VORP)** was established in Kitchener, Ontario, in 1974 and subsequently repli-cated as **PACT (Prisoner and Community Together)** in northern Indiana near Elkhart in 1987. VORP has several objectives, including (1) making offenders more accountable for their wrongs against victims, (2) reducing recidivism among participating offenders, and (3) heightening responsibility of offenders through victim compensation and repayment for damages inflicted (Roy and Brown 1992).

During the 1987–1991 period, an investigation of ADR and its effectiveness was undertaken and the results evaluated (Roy and Brown 1992). The VORP sig-nificantly reduced recidivism among offenders. Results suggest that it will be continued. Caution is recommended, however, when interpreting the results of ADR programs in selected jurisdictions, because it is believed that net-widening occurs, where a state's political policy agenda is furthered by expanding state control over larger numbers of people (Palumbo, Musheno, and Hallett 1994).

In 1995 Orange County, California, implemented an extensive Victim/Offender Reconciliation Program. The program targeted juvenile delinquents. Two samples of delinquents were studied. There were 131 VORP graduates and 152 youths who were referred to VORP but never participated. Among the 131 graduates of the VORP, 49 percent of the cases resulted in written agreements between offenders and their victims. These cases were resolved without any type of restitution paid. Thus, not all victims were participating simply to re-coup their monetary losses. The remainder of the resolved cases involved some amount of restitution. When recidivism rates were compared between those participating and those not participating in the VORP, there were no significant differences. Nevertheless, the process resulted in a better understanding between the victims and the offenders—a less tangible but no less important aim of the program (Niemeyer and Shichor 1996).

Victim/offender reconciliation projects and alternative dispute resolution programs are increasingly compared with restorative justice, where the intent is to reform and rehabilitate offenders by heightening their accountability, and improving general conditions for victims, including restoring their material possessions or losses as well as fulfilling their sense of justice (Walgrave 2001). However, critics of restorative justice suggest that little meaningful effect on offender recidivism will occur (Miers 2001; Miers et al. 2001). Nevertheless, restorative justice does hold the promise of fulfilling somewhat intangible goals of achieving mediation between offenders and victims that enhances accountability and understanding between parties (Crawford and Enterkin 2001).

PRETRIAL DIVERSION

Diversion or **pretrial diversion** is the temporary and conditional suspension of the prosecution of a case prior to its adjudication usually as the result of an arrangement between the prosecutor and judge (Mahoney 2001). Diversion is not new. It has been used as an informal sanction against offenders for many centuries. During the mid- to late-1970s, for instance, the Kalamazoo, Michigan, Citizen's Probation Authority (CPA) made **deferred prosecution** available to 200 to 300 persons per year. Under CPA directives, formal criminal proceedings against these criminal defendants were conditionally suspended for one year to allow suspects an opportunity to complete successfully a pretrial period of informal probation supervision. When the informal probationary period was completed, then the individual's record for that offense was expunged. Prosecutorial discretion determined whether particular defendants would be included in the CPA program. In followup investigations of those persons who participated in the CPA program, 83 percent of the participants were not involved in further criminal activity, whereas only 17 percent were rearrested for new offenses.

Diversion is frequently used in cases involving first offenders who are arrested for nonviolent property offenses. *Source:* Bob Daemmrich, Stock Boston.

Who Qualifies for Diversion?

Divertees, or those placed on diversion, are selected according to whether they are first offenders and if their crimes are minor ones. Violent offenders and career criminals do not qualify for diversion programs. If some of those charged with crimes have mental illnesses or are psychologically disturbed or retarded, then they might be diverted into mental health systems in their communities (Braswell, Fuller, and Lozoff 2001). For example, selected numbers of charged offenders in a Canadian province between 1990 and 1992 were diverted to mental health services on the basis of their (1) minor **offense seriousness;** (2) court jurisdiction, where the court was remotely located; and (3) psychiatric evaluations and potential for rehabilitation or recovery. Some jurisdictions, such as Montgomery County, Pennsylvania, have established **jail diversion** for persons who are mentally ill or are substance abusers. An integrated program of collaboration with law enforcement agencies, mental health agencies, and social services allows Montgomery County officials to place many arrestees into jail diversion where they can be closely monitored and receive needed treatments and services (Draine and Solomon 1999). Jail recidivism is avoided among those clients who receive adequate supervision and effective treatment.

Forms of Diversion

Several different kinds of diversionary programs are categorically referred to as pretrial diversion. Pretrial diversion programs are either publicly or privately operated. These programs include (1) standard or unconditional diversion (2) conditional diversion (3) youth services, and (4) treatment services.

Standard or Unconditional Diversion.   All diversion programs involve one or more conditions. No specific program of treatment is usually indicated. The primary obligations of offenders are to conduct themselves properly, behave as good citizens, and not get into trouble. After a period of six months or a year, the case is reviewed by the prosecutor. Usually, **unconditional diversion** or **standard diversion** is distinguished from conditional diversion by the number of special conditions added to one's diversion program.

Conditional Diversion.   In some instances, divertees have problems with drugs or alcohol or have mental problems. Thus, one or more greater obligation added to a diversion program, such as drug treatment, mental health counseling, or observance of curfews and periodic drug/alcohol checks, changes a divertee's program from standard or unconditional to conditional. These types of diversion are known as **conditional diversion.**

Functions of Diversion

Some of the more important functions of diversion are:

1. To permit divertees the opportunity of remaining in their communities where they can receive needed assistance or treatment, depending upon the nature of the crimes charged.
2. To permit divertees the opportunity to make restitution to their victims where monetary damages were suffered and property destroyed.

3. To permit divertees the opportunity of remaining free in their communities to support themselves and their families and to avoid the stigma of incarceration.

4. To help divertees avoid the stigma of a criminal conviction.

5. To assist corrections officials in reducing prison and **jail overcrowding** by diverting less serious cases to nonincarcerative alternatives.

6. To save the courts the time, trouble, and expense of formally processing less serious cases and streamlining case dispositions through informal case handling.

7. To make it possible for divertees to participate in self-help, educational, or vocational programs.

8. To preserve the dignity and integrity of divertees by helping them avoid further contact with the criminal justice system and assisting them to be more responsible adults capable of managing their own lives.

9. To preserve the family unit and enhance family solidarity and continuity (Law Enforcement Assistance Administration 1977).

Factors Influencing Pretrial Diversion

Whether any particular defendant is eligible for pretrial diversion is up to individual prosecutors in each jurisdiction. Under most circumstances, diversion may be granted with judicial approval and oversight. Pretrial diversion is not a constitutional right available to anyone charged with a crime. Those most likely to qualify for diversion have no previous criminal record and are charged with petty offenses. Another consideration is **overcrowding, prison or jail.** If there are serious overcrowding problems at either local jails or state prisons where diversion programs exist, then diversion becomes a more attractive consideration for prosecutors, since they would view the diversion option as a temporary, front-end solution to such overcrowding. Less serious offenders, especially first offenders, would contribute unnecessarily to jail or prison overcrowding, especially if their period of diversion is successful and causes them to desist from future criminal conduct.

Are there sufficient resources within the community to operate a diversion program? After all, divertees most often report to or make periodic contact with probation departments and/or courts by furnishing evidence that they have complied or are complying with diversion program requirements. In some communities, the caseload of probation officers may be such that the additional responsibility for supervising numerous new divertees is overwhelming.

Not everyone approves of diversion. **Court-watchers** often sit in courtrooms and observe judicial decision making in progress. If they observe judges granting diversion to persons, such as those charged with driving while intoxicated (DWI), they may feel that justice is not being properly dispensed. In Knox County, Tennessee, for example, those first offenders charged with DWI whose blood alcohol level was between .10 and .16 (where .10 was the level at which intoxication was presumed) would typically be diverted to a one-year program. The program obligated DWI divertees to send in a monthly report, showing their continued employment and problem-free driving record. They also paid a nominal monthly program maintenance fee. At the end of their year on diversion, they returned to court where the judge dismissed the DWI charges against them and eradicated or expunged the DWI charge from state records. Thus, if such persons were ever stopped by police in future months or years, the state departments of motor vehicles or public safety would have no record of their previous DWI charge. Court-watchers were outraged by this use of diversion. Mothers Against Drunk Drivers (MADD) representatives wrote letters to the local paper, criticizing this diversion leniency. They pressured judges to impose harsher penalties on those charged with DWI and to eliminate the use of diversion for them. Eventually, public pressure caused prosecutors and judges to suspend the diversion program insofar as it applied to DWI cases. Thus, the nature of the offense became a major consideration in whether diversion would be granted. No one complained when diversion was used for first-offender exhibitionists or bad check writers in that same Tennessee jurisdiction. Therefore, diversion itself was not attacked by these interest groups as wrong—only certain types of offenses where diversion was applied. Actually, one positive outcome was the establishment of victim impact panels sponsored by MADD, which those convicted of DWI were required to attend. Victim impact panels are emotionally charged meetings where victims who have been harmed by DWI offenders speak out on the dangers of drunk driving. However, in subsequent years, little evidence has been generated to show that DWI offenders change their behaviors any more often when attending victim impact panels or attending a DWI school (Polacsek et al. 2001).

Profiling Divertees

There are no definitive criteria describing U.S. divertees. Because diversion means a temporary cessation of a criminal prosecution while a conditional program of diversion is undertaken, record expungements upon successfully completing these programs mean that we have no access to data regarding divertee characteristics. Despite this lack of definitive information about divertees, some of the selection criteria used in most jurisdictions where diversion exists are as follows:

1. The age of the offender
2. The residency, employment, and familial status of the offender
3. The prior record of the offender
4. The seriousness of the offense
5. Aggravating or mitigating circumstances associated with the commission of the offense

A majority of divertees are first offenders and pose a low risk to their supervising officers (DeMore 1996:34–37). They are typically employed, have relatively stable families, and have no serious prior records; there are often mitigating circumstances associated with their instant offense. While almost all divertees have the ability to pay their monthly maintenance fees for their diversion programs, their inability to pay such fees cannot disqualify them from these programs. Thus, persons of lower socioeconomic statuses cannot be rejected from diversion programs because of their financial circumstances (*State v. Jimenez* 1991).

Some of the characteristics of divertees can be deduced by examining the criteria that exclude certain offenders from diversion programs. For instance, in California diversion programs, the following types of persons are not eligible for diversion:

1. Those with prior drug offense convictions, former drug offense divertees, and/or who traffic in drugs.
2. Those convicted of a felony within the previous five-year period.
3. Those whose current offense involves violence.
4. Those who are past or present probation or parole violators (Galvin et al. 1977).

Diversion Outcomes: What Should Divertees Expect?

Essentially, there are two primary outcomes resulting from the successful completion of a diversion program. One outcome is expungement of one's criminal record relating to the diversion offense. Expungement is offered as an incentive to comply with program requirements for the duration of the program. Once the program is completed, divertees expect that the charges originally filed against them will be expunged and that they will continue to have a crime-free record. In several Canadian cities between 1990 and 1992, 232 criminal suspects with mental disorders were diverted to mental treatment and hospitalization with the understanding that charges against them would be dropped following successful treatment. A majority of these divertees had their records expunged upon receiving the appropriate mental health treatment (Davis 1994).

Another possible outcome is a reduction of charge seriousness or some mitigation of sentence. More than a few jurisdictions cause the charges against successful divertees either to be decreased from a more to less serious misdemeanor or felony, or the actual sanctions imposed by judges upon conviction will be less severe. A divertee may ultimately be convicted of a crime, but the sentence may be one year in jail instead of a five-year prison sentence. For those who fail to complete their diversion programs successfully (e.g., who test positive for drugs or alcohol, are rearrested for another crime, or fail to abide by curfew or other technical program conditions), the original criminal charges are reinstated and prosecutors seek convictions against these defendants.

The Effectiveness of Diversion and Recidivism

Because diversion removes certain cases out of the criminal justice system temporarily and because it may result in the expungement of criminal charges against defendants, it is often considered too lenient an option by the skeptical public. However, those who have been granted diversion and have conformed their behaviors to the requirements of the law consider this alternative advantageous in several respects. Offenders may continue their employment without the taint of a criminal conviction. Some diversion programs include victim compensation and restitution by offenders. Therefore, offenders can do much good work while on diversion. There is also the real possibility that treatment programs such as Alcoholics Anonymous (AA) and **Treatment Alternatives to Street Crime (TASC)** can curb or cure alcohol and/or drug dependencies for many clients (Shaw and Robinson 1998).

A benefit to prosecutors is that those cases slotted for diversion make it possible to concentrate on more serious and important cases. Diversion may also be used by prosecutors as a weapon against defendants to elicit guilty pleas. Defendants themselves often consider diversion as a better option than obtaining criminal records.

Criticisms of Diversion.   The most frequent criticism of diversion is the charge of net-widening. Diversion widens the net by drawing persons into diversion programs who would not be processed by the criminal justice system if the diversion programs did not exist. For example, Hepburn et al. (1992) describe a pretrial diversion program operated in Maricopa County, Arizona, for drug users. Under a general TASC initiative, first-time felony drug users were placed in a drug treatment program in lieu of criminal prosecution. Because of the program's existence, many drug offenders were drawn into the program who would not have been prosecuted by the criminal justice system. While the program itself attracted considerable attention by the media and drug community, the overall results were disappointing. The level of drug use and trafficking in the areas targeted, as well as the recidivism rates among program participants, remained about the same. Perhaps the program was not as selective as it should have been when drawing in prospective serious drug-using clientele.

More recently, drug courts have been established in numerous jurisdictions at a mushrooming rate (Bavon 2001; Listwan, Shaffer, and Latessa 2002). Drug courts are special courts that deal exclusively with those charged with drug offenses (Kassebaum and Okamoto 2001). They are designed, in part, to alleviate the glutted dockets of criminal courts, where largely non-drug-related offenses are adjudicated. But a prominent characteristic of these drug courts is a focus on aftercare and treatment within the community as a part of the punishment (Leukefeld, Tims, and Maiuro 2001). One experimental drug court treatment program has been described in Las Cruces, New Mexico. The treatment program is aimed at those convicted of driving while intoxicated or DWI. Court personnel conduct evaluations of first- and second-time offenders for symptoms of alcoholism. Then offenders who qualify are placed in a treatment program for alcoholism, which encompasses individual, group, and family counseling sessions. Based on data from 152 DWI offenders who were tracked up to 24 months following their initial DWI convictions, there were significantly fewer reconvictions when compared with a control sample of DWI convicts who did not participate in the program (Breckenridge 2000).

Another criticism is that the application of diversion may be discriminatory. There is inconsistency regarding how diversion is applied among jurisdictions. Because of the inconsistent application of diversion, some investigators have labeled it as discriminatory. Socioeconomic, race/ethnic, or gender factors may influence whether diversion will be used or if alleged offenders will be formally charged with crimes and prosecuted. Informal diversion is highly individualized. Alleged offenders are not brought into the criminal justice system but rather, they are diverted from it, often without participation in any systematic treatment program or penalty. Since offenders who become divertees do not have their cases resolved in court, their guilt is assumed without benefit of trial. Thus, diversion is an admission by divertees that the criminal allegations against them are true.

Summarizing the major criticisms of diversion, we may include the following:

1. Diversion is soft on criminals.
2. Diversion is the wrong punishment for criminals.
3. Diversion leads to net-widening.
4. Diversion excludes female offenders.
5. Diversion ignores due process.
6. Diversion assumes guilt without a trial.

Nondiverted criminal cases that are prosecuted result in either convictions or acquittals. Frequently, plea bargaining yields guilty pleas in exchange for certain prosecutorial concessions. The vast majority of criminal convictions involve probation as a contingent condition. Probation is the release of a convicted offender into the community to avoid incarceration, under a suspended sentence, with good behavior, and generally under the supervision of a probation officer (Black 1990:1152).

THE HISTORY OF PROBATION IN THE UNITED STATES

Probation means forgiveness or a period of trial, and its use originated in ancient times. Religious and political dissidents were often placed on probation so that their ideas could be brought into line with official church or political policies. Probation originated in the United States in 1841 through the pioneering work of John Augustus (1785–1859), a Boston shoemaker and philanthropist.

Augustus was noted for his affiliation with the Temperance Movement, a religiously based organization dedicated to reforming alcoholics. Together with **Rufus R. Cook** and **Benjamin C. Clark,** other social reformers and philanthropists, Augustus frequented the Boston Municipal Court to offer his services to those charged with public drunkenness and petty crimes. One morning in 1841, Augustus was in the courtroom observing offenders being sentenced by the municipal judge. A man convicted of being a common drunkard was about to be sentenced to the Boston House of Corrections when Augustus intervened and asked the judge to assign the drunkard to his own supervision for three weeks. Augustus guaranteed the man's appearance in court later and agreed to pay all court costs. The judge consented to Augustus's proposal. Three weeks later, Augustus returned with the first probationer in the United States. The judge was so impressed with the reformed drunkard that he fined the offender a nominal amount and suspended the six-month sentence. From 1841 to 1859 when Augustus died, he supervised 1,956 offenders on probation. Only one person ever violated his trust, according to Augustus (Lindner and Savarese 1984).

Although the Boston courts permitted Augustus and others the opportunity of privately supervising certain offenders convicted of petty crimes, these probation efforts were not particularly popular with various vested interests. One group opposed to the early use of probation in Boston were corrections personnel, jailers, and jail administrators. Their opposition had little or nothing to do with the rehabilitative benefits to offenders derived from probation. Quite simply, they were opposed to probation because it decreased their profits from city funds allocated to them for inmate food and housing. Regularly, jail guards and administrators would divert a large portion of Boston funds intended for prisoner food and accommodations. This is one reason why the Boston House of Corrections was regarded by observers as a rat-infested hellhole (Probation Association 1939).

The public-at-large was not supportive of probation either (Lindner and Savarese 1984). The press and others considered probation as excessive leniency toward offenders who ought to be punished for their misdeeds. Today, similar criticisms are directed toward the probation concept and programs associated with it (Cushman and Sechrest 1992). Several charitable and religious organizations continued the work of Augustus in Boston and other large cities. Between 1860 and 1900, much of the privately funded philanthropic work in probation was directed at juvenile offenders. The **Boston Children's Aid Society,** sponsored in part by Rufus R. Cook, was established in 1860 and saw to the needs of orphans and other youngsters who did not have adequate adult supervision. Many children were helped by this philanthropy and voluntary work.

In 1878, Massachusetts passed the first probation statute in the United States. The statute authorized the mayor of Boston to hire probation officers and operate a small-scale probation program. The Boston Superintendent of Police was placed in charge of all appointed probation officers. Between 1878 and 1938, 38 states, the District of Columbia, and the federal government passed probation statutes. Table 3.1 shows these states and jurisdictions according to the years when probation statutes were passed.

In the meantime, New York and Chicago were sites of **settlement houses** between 1886 and 1900. Settlement houses were operated privately and furnished food and lodging to wayward or disadvantaged youths. **Jane Addams** established **Hull House** in Chicago in 1889, an experimental settlement house that provided employment assistance and shelter to needy juveniles and others. Addams was instrumental in achieving several important reforms in juvenile laws in Illinois, and she spent many hours helping the children of immigrant families.

TABLE 3.1

The Adoption of Probation Statutes by Jurisdiction and Year

Year	States/Jurisdictions
1878	Massachusetts
1897	Missouri
1898	Vermont
1899	Rhode Island
1900	New Jersey
1901	New York
1903	California, Connecticut, Michigan
1905	Maine
1907	Kansas, Indiana
1908	Ohio
1909	Colorado, Iowa, Minnesota, Nebraska, North Dakota, Pennsylvania, Wisconsin
1910	District of Columbia
1911	Delaware, Illinois
1913	Arizona, Georgia, Montana
1915	Idaho
1918	Virginia
1921	Washington
1923	Utah
1925	Federal government
1927	West Virginia
1931	Oregon, Tennessee, Maryland
1934	Kentucky
1937	Arkansas, North Carolina
1938	New Hampshire

Source: Compiled by author.

James Bronson Reynolds, an early prison reformer, was the headworker of **University Settlement** in New York City in 1893. Although this settlement was created to provide job assistance and referral services to disadvantaged community residents, it also served as a community-based probation agency to supervise those placed on probation by New York courts. University Settlement was privately financed and operated in its early years. However, by 1906, New York State had authorized nominal payments to those working with **probationers,** including University Settlement volunteers. University Settlement was unsuccessful at rehabilitating offenders, largely because it lacked clear goals and a definite purpose, and it was soon forced to close its doors (Lindner and Savarese 1984).

The federal government formally adopted probation for convicted federal offenders in 1925, although probation in federal district courts was practiced on a limited basis prior to 1925. The administrative control of probation officers was shifted to the U.S. Attorney General in 1930. Ultimately, the responsibility for probation officers was assigned the Administrative Office of the U.S. Courts. In 1938, Congress passed the **Federal Juvenile Delinquency Act** which permitted those juveniles within federal jurisdiction the option of probation.

All states had probation statutes by 1957 (Coffey et al. 1974). By 2001, over 4.7 million convicted state and federal offenders were on probation or parole. The total federal, state, and local adult correctional population, incarcerated or in the community, reached a new high of 6.6 million by January 2002 (Glaze 2002:1). Table 3.2 shows all probationers by jurisdiction for 2001.

TABLE 3.2

Adults on Probation, 2001

Region and jurisdiction	Probation population, 1/1/01	2001 Entries	2001 Exits	Probation population, 12/31/01	Percent change, 2001	Number on probation per 100,000 adult residents, 12/31/01
U.S. total	3,826,209	2,110,550	1,999,164	3,932,751	2.8%	1,849
Federal	31,669	13,828	13,893	31,561	−0.3%	15
State	3,794,540	2,096,722	1,985,271	3,901,190	2.8	1,834
Northeast	573,280	232,600	209,691	596,189	4.0%	1,462
Connecticut	47,636	22,752	20,556	49,832	4.6	1,928
Maine	7,788	7,179	6,028	8,939	14.8	906
Massachusetts	45,233	39,871	40,985	44,119	−2.5	904
New Hampshire[a,b]	3,629	2,798	2,762	3,665	1.0	385
New Jersey	130,610	55,010	52,774	132,846	1.7	2,075
New York	186,955	43,199	33,319	196,835	5.3	1,374
Pennsylvania[b]	121,176	48,245	43,493	125,928	3.9	1,344
Rhode Island[a]	20,922	8,g482	4,645	24,759	—	3,049
Vermont	9,331	5,063	5,128	9,266	−0.7	1,988
Midwest	896,061	569,740	550,868	914,606	2.1%	1,903
Illinois	139,029	62,911	60,432	141,508	1.8	1,532
Indiana	109,251	90,845	87,395	112,701	3.2	2,481
Iowa	21,147	18,870	19,220	20,797	−1.7	950

(continued)

TABLE 3.2   *(Continued)*

Region and jurisdiction	Probation population, 1/1/01	2001 Entries	2001 Exits	Probation population, 12/31/01	Percent change, 2001	Number on probation per 100,000 adult residents, 12/31/01
Kansas	15,992	21,338	22,080	15,250	−4.6	769
Michigan[b]	170,276	118,999	112,536	176,406	3.6	2,385
Minnesota	115,906	62,194	64,487	113,613	−2.0	3,081
Missouri	53,299	25,741	23,273	55,767	4.6	1,327
Nebraska	21,483	14,570	15,206	20,847	−3.0	1,651
North Dakota	2,847	1,782	1,728	2,901	1.9	613
Ohio[b]	189,375	123,269	117,247	195,403	3.2	2,302
South Dakota	4,214	3,404	3,156	4,462	5.9	805
Wisconsin	53,242	25,817	24,108	54,951	3.2	1,362
South	1,573,215	921,288	874,971	1,616,358	2.7%	2,117
Alabama	40,178	16,019	15,580	40,617	1.1	1,215
Arkansas	28,409	11,308	13,159	26,558	−6.5	1,319
Delaware	20,052	11,792	11,849	19,995	−0.3	3,321
District of Columbia	10,664	8,542	8,738	10,468	−1.8	2,291
Florida[b]	296,139	245,593	244,827	294,626	−0.5	2,304
Georgia[b,d]	321,407	203,155	166,532	358,030	—	—
Kentucky	19,620	11,255	8,884	21,993	12.1	716
Louisiana	35,854	11,857	11,967	35,744	−0.3	1,101
Maryland	81,523	42,602	43,417	80,708	−1.0	2,006
Mississippi	15,118	8,074	7,757	15,435	2.1	741
North Carolina	105,949	61,596	56,869	110,676	4.5	1,776
Oklahoma[a,b]	30,969	15,086	15,786	30,269	−2.3	1,179
South Carolina	44,632	14,815	17,039	42,408	−5.0	1,388
Tennessee	40,682	24,374	23,070	41,089	1.0	946
Texas	441,848	202,476	200,640	443,684	0.4	2,873
Virginia	33,955	29,642	25,715	37,882	11.6	694
West Virginia[b]	6,216	3,102	3,142	6,176	−0.6	441
West	751,984	373,094	349,741	774,037	2.9%	1,630
Alaska	4,779	908	832	4,855	1.6	1,091
Arizona	59,810	39,464	36,192	63,082	5.5	1,598
California[a]	343,145	157,440	149,817	350,768	2.2	1,388
Colorado[b]	50,460	29,125	23,018	56,567	12.1	1,702
Hawaii	15,525	5,813	5,757	15,581	0.4	1,675
Idaho[c]	35,103	30,324	29,757	35,670	1.6	3,747
Montana	6,108	3,526	3,376	6,258	2.5	928
Nevada	12,189	5,528	7,263	10,454	−14.2	654
New Mexico	10,461	7,735	6,561	10,335	−1.2	782
Oregon[a]	46,023	17,419	16,902	46,540	1.1	1,770
Utah	9,800	5,036	4,505	10,331	5.4	667
Washington[b]	154,466	68,401	63,748	159,119	3.0	3,551
Wyoming	4,115	2,376	2,014	4,477	8.8	1,223

Note: Because of incomplete data, the population for some jurisdictions on December 31, 2001, does not equal the population on January 1, 2001 plus entries, minus exits.

—Not calculated.

[a]All data were estimated.

[b]Data for entries and exits were estimated for nonreporting agencies.

[c]Counts include estimates for misdemeanors based on annual admissions.

[d]Counts include private agency cases and may overstate the number under supervision.

Source: Glaze 2002: 3.

THE PHILOSOPHY AND FUNCTIONS OF PROBATION

Philosophy of Probation

The general philosophy of probation can be gleaned from examining the original intent of its pioneer, John Augustus. Augustus wanted to reform offenders. He wanted to rehabilitate common drunks and petty thieves. Thus, rehabilitation was and continues to be a strong philosophical aim of probation. But somewhere over the years, probation changed from how Augustus originally conceived it. Let's look at how Augustus supervised his probationers. First, he stood their bail in the Boston Municipal Court. Second, he took them to his home or other place of shelter, fed them, and generally looked after them. He may have even provided them with job leads and other services through his many friendships as well as his political and philanthropic connections. In short, he provided his probationers with fairly intensive supervision and personalized assistance, financial and otherwise.

Augustus supervised approximately 100 probationers a year between 1841 and 1859. We know that Augustus kept detailed records of his client progress. In this respect, he compiled what are now called pre-sentence investigations, although he usually made extensive notes about offenders and their progress after they had been convicted. He showed intense interest in their progress, and no doubt many of these probationers were emotionally affected by his kindness and generosity. According to his own assessment of his performance, rehabilitation and reformation were occurring at a significant rate among his clients, and his own efforts were largely responsible.

Present-day probation has become streamlined and bureaucratic. While there are exceptions among probation officers, relatively few take interest in their clients to the extent that they feed and clothe them and look after their other personal needs. No probation officers sit in municipal courtrooms waiting for the right kinds of offenders who will be responsive to personalized attention and care. No probation officers eagerly approach judges with bail bonds and assume personal responsibility for a probationer's conduct, even if for brief periods.

Today, probation officers assess their work in terms of client caseloads and officer/client ratios. Extensive paperwork is required for each case, and this consumes enormous amounts of time (American Probation and Parole Association 1993:31). If we have strayed far afield from Augustus's original meaning of what probation supervision is and how it should be conducted, it has probably been largely the result of bureaucratic expediency. There are too many probationers and too few probation officers. It is hardly unexpected that the public has gradually become disenchanted with the rehabilitative ideal probation originally promised.

Some investigators have characterized today's probation officer as a **ROBO-PO** (Cosgrove 1994). Cosgrove (1994) says that in the 1970s, rehabilitation was the primary aim of probation supervision. In the 1980s, reintegration replaced rehabilitation as a probation goal. By the end of the 1980s, community needs became primary. Public safety and security caused many probation agencies to devise more effective client supervision strategies. Probation officers in the 1990s acquired a broader range of duties and responsibilities such that the nature of probation work today is multifaceted and more complex.

Despite these changes and philosophical shifts in the nature of probation work, the rehabilitative aim of probation has not been entirely rejected. Rather, it has been rearranged in a rapidly growing list of correctional priorities. One dominant, contemporary philosophical aim of probation is **offender control.** If we can't rehabilitate offenders, at least we can devise more effective strategies for controlling their behavior while on probation. Thus, this priority shift in probation's philosophical underpinnings has prompted the development of a string of nonincarcerative **intermediate punishments,** each connected directly with increased offender control by one means or another. Researchers generally agree that the future of probation is closely aligned with the effectiveness of intermediate punishments. And virtually every intermediate punishment established thus far contains one or more provisions for controlling offender behavior (Sluder, Sapp, and Langston 1994).

Functions of Probation

Probation has the following aims and functions: (1) punishment, (2) deterrence, (3) community reintegration, and (4) crime control.

Punishment.   Probation seems to send mixed messages to probationers and the public. Some citizens don't think probation is much of a punishment. They see probationers free from imprisonment, living in their communities, moving about freely. To some citizens, at least, this is the same as no punishment (Robinson 2001). Some probationers have similar sentiments. However, the courts and a majority of probationers identify with probation as a punishment. It does have conditions that limit a probationer's rights. Probationers must allow probation officers entry into their homes or apartments at any time. Often, these probationer-clients must submit to on-the-spot drug and alcohol checks. If probationers are employed, they must maintain a satisfactory work record. Probation officers check up on these things. These standard requirements of probation are somewhat constraining to most probationers. But most probationers have the strong incentive of avoiding imprisonment by behaving well while on probation (Spelman 1995).

Deterrence.   There is disagreement about the deterrent effect probation serves. The deterrent value of probation is measured most often by recidivism figures among those placed on probation. Because of the low degree of offender control associated with standard probation supervision, recidivism rates are proportionately higher than those associated with those of offenders in more intensively supervised intermediate punishment programs. For instance, one low-level crime with a high recidivism rate is prostitution. A study of female street prostitutes during 1998–1999 found that jailing arrested prostitutes and subsequently placing them on probation makes it more difficult for them to leave prostitution (Norton-Hawk 2001). Fifty interviews were conducted with street prostitutes who had been arrested and served three months to one year in jail for their offenses. Following their release from jail and being placed under a period of supervision by the probation department, many of these prostitutes re-entered prostitution because they didn't know any other ways to make a living. In this instance, jailing these prostitutes was counterproductive because the arrest and incarceration policy made it difficult for them to leave prostitution. It has been recommended that such a punitive approach should be replaced with a community-based rehabilitative model that incorporates such innovations as diversion, education and job training, drug rehabilitation, medical intervention and health education, psychological counseling, and outreach (Norton-Hawk 2001).

A major problem with using recidivism rates as a measure of the success of probation is that quite different probationer aggregates are studied and erroneously compared. For instance, there is a 75 percent success rate (25 percent recidivism) among misdemeanants who are placed on probation. These are low-level offenders initially, and they are often placed back in their communities with little or no supervision. Thus, when they "go straight," they do so either of their own accord or the probation program provided a slight deterrent effect. More serious probationers, felony probationers, have a recidivism rate of 65 percent. Many of these felony probationers have prior criminal records, and thus their greater rates of recidivism are not unexpected (Petersilia 1998:43). For the most dangerous offenders placed on probation, these are often more closely supervised. Many of these offenders have long histories of chemical dependencies, drug and alcohol abuse, and violence, which are often interrelated. Under more intensive probation supervision, these offenders are less likely to reoffend during the course of their programs. However, these programs are costly, particularly if substance abuse treatment programs are offered contemporaneously for affected probationers (Chermack and Blow 2002).

Community Reintegration.   One benefit of probation is that it permits offenders to remain in their communities, work at jobs, support their families, make restitution to victims, and perform other useful services. It is not so much that offenders need to be reintegrated into their communities; rather, probationers can avoid the criminogenic influence of jail or prison environments. Also, the community reintegration function of probation is most closely associated with its rehabilitative aim. Apart from the idea that retribution deters, probation appears to fulfill at least two distinct reintegrative aims. Probation is a means of providing rehabilitation for society; at the same time, probation assists in the rehabilitation of clients.

Crime Control.   Precisely how much crime control occurs as the result of probation is unknown. When offenders are outside the immediate presence of probation officers, they may or may not engage in undetected criminal activity (Horn 1992). Probation officers are obligated to make periodic checks of workplaces, and conversations with an offender's employer disclose much about how offenders are managing their time. Michigan probation officers, for example, conduct frequent mandatory screenings of probationer-clients for drugs and alcohol (Blevins, Morton, and McCabe 1996:38–39). Since problem drinkers and others who are drug-dependent tend to have higher reoffending rates compared with those who don't drink or use drugs, it is especially important for probation officers to effectively supervise this aspect of probationers' lives. The Michigan Alcohol Screening Test is increasingly used by federal probation officers as well. The results have been favorable. Those clients with drinking problems can be given special assistance and placed in the proper programs within their communities. While these programs don't cure everyone, some offenders are helped in ways that deter them from future offending.

TYPES OF PROBATION

There are two types of probation: (1) standard probation, and (2) intensive supervised probation.

Standard Probation

Standard probation involves minimal contact with a probation officer. A probationer may or may not be expected to report to the probation department monthly. The probationer probably fills out a monthly report. This report probably includes the probationer's current address, workplace, statement of earned wages, an open-ended question or two about any specific probationer needs that can be met by action on the part of the probation officer, and several other related items. Together with fees ranging from $10 to $50, the report is either hand-delivered or mailed to the probation officer in charge of the offender (Olson and Ramker 2001). The probation officer may or may not have face-to-face contact with the offender. While probation officers sometimes make periodic checks of police records, they rely on police to keep them advised should their client be arrested or interrogated about new crimes within the jurisdiction.

Standard probationers have most of the same freedoms as other community citizens. Probation is so common in certain jurisdictions that community residents are often unaware that their neighbors are felony probationers under minimal supervision. In California, for example, 1 percent of the entire population is on probation. Standard probation in many jurisdictions may involve a complete absence of supervision of any kind. Even telephone or mail contacts between probation officers and clients are minimal (Petersilia 1997).

In Marion County (Indianapolis), Indiana, for example, a high-tech tool for monitoring short-term, low-risk probationers is now in use by the Marion Superior Court Probation Department. It is called **PAM (Probation Automated Monitoring System),** and it was developed by the AutoMon Corporation. It allows specific probationers to report to probation kiosks located throughout Marion County using an ID card then verifying their identity by placing their fingerprint into a fingerprint reading device. This combination triggers an ATM-type machine to complete an interview with the probationer. During that interview, the probationer is asked to verify some specific information, which includes any changes in employment, address location, and police contact. Questions about drug use may also be included. Probation officers who supervise such offenders can leave email messages for them. Depending upon a probationer's answers to various questions, a visit from the supervising PO may be required. PAM is also designed to accommodate Spanish-speaking offenders. Probationers who use the kiosk for check-ins are required to pay a maintenance fee of $5 per month to defray the costs of machine operation (Marion Superior Court Probation Department 2002). PAM is also helpful if a PO is temporarily absent from the jurisdiction on business or for probationers who have completed a majority of their probation conditions and are eligible for minimum reporting. Since the late 1990s when PAM was initiated, this expedited caseload method has taken more than 650 cases that would otherwise have gone to regular PO caseloads. This is a savings of between 15 and 20 cases per PO over a two-month period. Approximately 8 to 10 hours of work have been reduced for POs who would otherwise have to supervise these offenders more intensively.

In some jurisdictions, the most important aspect of an offender's term of probation is the regular payment of the maintenance fee. Late payments result in officer-initiated contacts with clients. The ever-present threat is the revocation of probation because of client failure to observe one or more technical probation conditions, especially the payment of the monthly maintenance fee. One probationer said his probation officer spent 45 minutes of a one-hour conference at the beginning of the offender's probation term reminding the probationer of the importance of paying this fee. The probationer never saw the officer again until his two-year probationary term was concluded successfully.

Standardless Standard Probation?   Regardless of its standardless appearance, standard probation involves conditions to the same extent as standard pretrial diversion. Probationers are expected to adhere to a list of rules and regulations, and most probationers consider their probation terms as true sentences with penalties. An example of these rules and regulations is provided in Box 3.2.

For many probationers, however, the intensiveness of supervision may have little deterrent value as a behavioral intervention. Several studies involving both adult and youthful offenders have shown that the intensity with which these clients are supervised matters little in whether they will eventually reoffend or recidivate. In fact, some studies show that intensively supervised offenders had about the same recidivism rates as standard probationers. However, during the terms of their closer supervision, those probationers who were more closely supervised had higher rearrest rates compared with standard probationers. Many of those intensively supervised clients were also cited with more technical program, noncriminal violations than standard probationers. This finding simply suggests that if we watch certain probationers more closely than others, we will detect more technical program violations. Thus, for many probationers at least, standard probation functions as an adequate general deterrent to future offending.

The Effectiveness of Standard Probation.   Probation programs offer nonincarcerative alternatives to offenders. The avoidance of a jail or prison environment and its stigma are considered significant as a deterrents to future criminal activity. Of course, no program is perfect, and there will always be recidivism among ex-offenders. Thus, it is unrealistic to expect that probation alone will function as the major means of crime control. The major question is how much recidivism is observed before a program is declared ineffective? An informal standard of 30 percent or lower has evolved in the criminal justice research literature, meaning that if a probation program has a demonstrable recidivism rate among its clients of 30 percent or less, then it is considered successful. This doesn't necessarily mean that if a program has a 31 percent recidivism rate, it will be judged unsuccessful. The informal standard exists as a yardstick of program success. And success is a relative term. One factor that may assist probation officers in being more effective, and thus conceivably bring about a reduction in the recidivism rates of probationers, is to perhaps orient themselves differently toward male and female probationers. These offenders have different needs, and while the advertising slogan, "One size fits all" may apply to some extent in the business world, the fact is that different approaches may be required when supervising female compared with male probationers (Johnstone 2001).

During the 1980s, numerous programs were established and experiments conducted designed to effect greater nonincarcerative control over a growing offender population. Because of prison and jail overcrowding in many jurisdictions, solutions have been sought by legislators and others that strike a balance between standard probation, which often involves little or no control over offenders, and total control through confinement. The result has been the creation of a series of intermediate punishments, broadly defined as those sanctions that exist somewhere between incarceration and probation on the continuum of criminal penalties (Petersilia 1997).

The chief distinguishing feature of intermediate punishments is presumably the high degree of monitoring and control exerted by program officials over offender behaviors. Other characteristics of intermediate punishments include curfews that offenders are expected to observe and frequent monitoring or contact

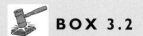 **BOX 3.2**

The State of New York has established general probation conditions for courts to follow when imposing probation. These are known as Conditional Release Conditions.

Conditional Release Conditions

Local Conditional Release Commissions shall establish at a minimum mandatory conditions whenever granting conditional release to an individual. These conditions shall require that an individual shall:

a. Report as directed by the probation officer or the Local Conditional Release Commission.

b. Remain within the county of supervision unless granted permission to leave by the probation officer. For purposes of this regulation, the county of supervision for conditional release cases in New York City shall include all five boroughs.

c. Permit the probation officer to visit him at his residence, place of employment, or elsewhere; discuss with his probation officer any proposed changes in residence, employment, or program status; and notify the probation officer prior to any change in residence, employment, or program status.

d. Answer all reasonable inquiries by his probation officer.

e. Notify his probation officer immediately any time there is contact with or he is arrested by any law enforcement agency.

f. Refrain from being in the company of or fraternizing with any person having a criminal record or adjudicated a youthful offender unless granted permission by his probation officer.

g. Obey any law or order to which the individual is subject.

h. Comply with any restitution order and/or mandatory surcharge previously imposed by a court of competent jurisdiction.

i. Submit to a search of his person, residence, vehicle, or property whenever a probation officer has reasonable grounds to believe that a conditional releasee has illegal drugs, drug paraphernalia, deadly or prohibited weapons, or stolen property in his possession, is engaging or has engaged in any unlawful activity.

j. Be prohibited from owning, possessing, or purchasing any shotgun, rifle, or firearm of any type without the written permission of his probation office and owning, possessing, or purchasing any deadly weapon defined in the Penal Law (loaded weapon, switchblade knife, gravity knife, pilum ballistic knife, dagger, billy, blackjack, metal knuckles), electronic dart gun, cane sword, bludgeon, chuka stick, sand bag, wristbrace type slingshot or slingshot, dangerous knife, dirk, razor, stiletto, imitation pistol, shirken or kung-fu star, or any other dangerous weapon. In addition, agree not to own, possess or purchase any instrument readily capable of causing physical injury without a satisfactory explanation for ownership, possession, or purchase.

k. Be prohibited from owning, possessing, or purchasing drug paraphernalia and from using or possessing illegal drugs without proper medical authorization.

Other conditions of conditional release

Other conditions of conditional release that may be imposed at the time of release or if modification occurs include:

a. Work faithfully at a suitable employment or faithfully pursue a course of study or of vocational training that will equip him for suitable employment.

b. Undergo medical, psychiatric, alcohol, or drug treatment as determined by the probation officer and remain in a specified institution, when required for that purpose.

c. Participate in an alcohol or substance abuse program or an intervention program as determined by the probation officer.

d. Abstain from alcohol and/or drugs and submit to periodic alcohol or drug testing to determine abstinence.

e. Support his dependents and meet other family responsibilities.

f. Satisfy any other conditions reasonably related to his rehabilitation or public safety.

Source: New York Division of Probation and Correctional Alternatives (2002).

with program authorities, usually probation officers (Texas Department of Criminal Justice 2002). The amount and type of frequent monitoring or contact varies with the program, although daily visits by probation officers at an offender's workplace or home are not unusual. The ultimate aim of more intensive supervision over probationers is that their recidivism will be less than those supervised by standard probation supervision methods. This is not always the result, however.

Ideally, intermediate punishments are intended for prison- or jail-bound offenders. Although offenders are given considerable freedom of movement within their communities, it is believed that such intensive monitoring and control fosters a high degree of compliance with program requirements. It is also believed that such intensive supervision acts to deter offenders from engaging in new criminal behaviors. In the following section, we will examine several **intensive probation/parole supervision (IPS)** programs and assess their effectiveness (Bazemore and Griffiths 1997). It should be noted in advance, however, that despite the legacy of a decade of experimenting with intermediate sanctions of any kind is the strong message that no one program—surveillance or rehabilitation alone—and no one agency—police, probation, mental health, or schools alone—nor any of these agencies without the community can reduce crime or fear of crime on its own (Petersilia 1999:44).

Intensive Supervised Probation (ISP)

No common standard exists for deciding when a supervision program for probationers becomes intensive. A comparison of intensive supervised probation programs in most states discloses a range from 2 contacts per month by probation officers with offenders in Texas to as many as 32 contacts per month in Idaho (Texas Department of Criminal Justice 2002). Generally, **intensive supervised probation/parole (ISP)** consists of the following:

1. Low client-officer caseloads, no more than a 10 to 1 ratio.
2. Weekly face-to-face contacts between officers and clients.
3. Regular field visits at an offender's workplace, perhaps weekly or monthly.
4. Frequent and random drug and alcohol testing.
5. Administrative review and revocation procedures for violating one or more probation conditions (Petersilia 1999).

One of the positive features of ISP programs is that a wider variety of services and programs exist to meet client needs. Often, these needs are specific to certain types of deficiencies, such as poor reading ability. A program that compels offenders to enroll and participate actively in a reading program, therefore, would attempt to remedy reading deficiencies of program clients. The program itself is not a cure-all or panacea for a client's problems. Rather, client weaknesses and strengths are assessed and appropriate therapies or treatments are recommended. One reading program involving numerous male probationers is Changing Lives through Literature, offered by a Texas probation organization. An assessment of the Texas program showed a recidivism rate of 19 percent among program clients compared with a recidivism rate of 45 percent among a control group of probationers who did not participate in the reading program (Jablecki 1998). This same reading program was implemented in Massachusetts for a sample of probationers. The recidivism results were similar to the Texas program, where 18 percent of the Massachusetts probationers who became involved in the Changing Lives through

Literature program recidivated compared with a 45 percent recidivism rate for a comparison group that did not participate (Jarjoura and Krumholz 1998).

Other types of needs, including chemical dependencies, need to be treated as well. Many probationers have serious alcohol and drug abuse problems (Office of National Drug Control Policy 2000). Thus, drug treatment is an integral part of their community therapy program. An examination of 183 male property felons who were placed on probation and ordered as a condition to undergo drug treatment revealed that those who successfully completed the drug treatment program were less likely to be rearrested later compared with those who did not complete the program. Drug treatment tended to reduce the recidivism of these property offenders while on probation (Benedict, Huff, and Corzine 1998). Given the greater intensity of supervision received by ISP clientele by POs and the more extensive networking with community treatments and services, ISP clients stand a greater chance of succeeding on probation compared with standard probationers, especially when offenders have substance abuse problems that require special community services (Zold 1999). Other types of offenders who probably need ISP include those convicted of domestic violence (Johnson 2001).

Numbers of ISP Clients. In 1992 there were over 48,000 offenders under some form of ISP in 41 state jurisdictions (Davis 1992). This was a 48 percent increase in the number of ISP clients compared with a similar survey conducted in 1988. By 2001 there were 190,000 persons under ISP, nearly a 300 percent increase since 1992 (Maguire and Pastore 2002).

The average caseload of offenders supervised under ISP was about 35 in 2001 (Camp and Camp 2002:195). Nebraska and Minnesota had the smallest ISP PO caseloads of 10 to 12 clients, while Rhode Island had the largest ISP caseloads at 62 per probation officer. While ratios were not computed, it is clear that considerable variation exists among the states concerning the proportion of probationers who are in ISP programs compared with the total number of state probationers.

Sample ISP Programs

Two programs are examined here. These are the New Jersey Intensive Supervision Program and the Florida Community Control II Program.

The New Jersey Intensive Supervision Program (ISP). The New Jersey Intensive Supervision Program (ISP) was established in June 1983. Technically, it is a form of parole, since only incarcerated offenders are eligible as possible clients. This program has been influenced by the traditional, treatment-oriented rehabilitation model and is targeted to serve certain less serious incarcerated offenders (Ciancia and Talty 1999). The New Jersey ISP program was established largely in response to chronic overcrowding in New Jersey's prisons and jails. Probation officer caseloads are limited to 20 offenders. The ISP program goals are:

1. To reduce the number of offenders serving state prison sentences by permitting them to be resentenced to an intermediate form of punishment.
2. To improve the utilization of correctional resources by making additional bed space available to violent criminals.
3. To test whether supervising selected offenders in the community is less costly and more effective than incarceration.

The New Jersey ISP program's primary expectations include:

1. Offender participation in the ISP for a minimum term of 16 months. If one's original sentence was for more than five years and/or if one violates any program condition, a longer period of supervision may be ordered by the court.

2. Offenders must participate in selected treatment and counseling programs, including Alcoholics Anonymous, Narcotics Anonymous, and/or Gamblers Anonymous.

3. Offenders must have weekly contact with their ISP officer and permit the officer access to their residences at any time for the purpose of conducting searches of their person, places, or things under their control.

4. Each month, the offender will have at least twelve face-to-face visits and eight telephone contacts with the ISP officer.

5. Offenders must comply with a 6:00 P.M. curfew until employed. Once employed, curfews may be changed to times between 8:00 P.M. and 10:00 P.M.

6. Offenders must obtain a job within 30 days of their release from prison. They must notify their employers that they are on ISP within 30 days after finding a job.

7. Offenders must pay all fines, victim compensation or restitution, and other miscellaneous fees associated with program maintenance. Those with dependents must support them as well as meet other family responsibilities.

8. Offenders must submit to random checks for drug use through urinalysis tests or alcohol abuse through breathalyzer tests. Drug and alcohol screenings are conducted at least three times per week.

9. Community service work must be performed a minimum of 16 hours per month. Community service requirements may be increased if an offender is unemployed. Community service hours may be increased also for program violations.

10. A daily diary must be maintained by the offender to show periodic accomplishments.

Becoming involved in New Jersey's ISP program is strictly voluntary. Not all volunteers are chosen. All persons sentenced to a state prison term are eligible for program consideration unless they have been convicted of homicide, a sex offense, a crime of the first degree, or robbery or are sentenced to life without the possibility of parole. Applications for the ISP program are available at all of New Jersey's prisons and jails. Any applicant's pre-sentence investigation report and judgment of conviction are reviewed by ISP staff to determine eligibility. Subsequently, applicants deemed eligible are interviewed by program staff. Potential participants must develop detailed case plans establishing goals and objectives for achieving program success. Participant goals include remaining free from abusive substances, strengthening relationships, maintaining steady employment, resolving legal problems, and paying required financial obligations. Applicants must obtain a community sponsor and develop a network team.

An ISP screening board reviews the suitability of recommended applicants. The screening board consists of three citizens appointed by the Chief Justice, representatives of the Commissioner of the Department of Corrections, and designated ISP representatives. The screening board interviews all applicants to determine their level of motivation to participate in the program and follow program rules. Accepted applicants are immediately released from prison into ISP. They must agree to all program conditions as outlined by a form (see Box 3.3) that they sign.

The screening requirements are stringent. Of the 30,000 applicants through 1999, only 19 percent were accepted into the ISP program. Participants are initially released into ISP on a 90-day trial basis. The progress of each offender is evaluated every 90 days. After 180 days of successful supervision, offenders are resentenced by a Resentencing Panel consisting of three judges. If any program rule is broken, the offender may be returned to prison. At any time following the sixteen-month minimum ISP program involvement, offenders may meet with their Resentencing Panel. The Resentencing Panel determines whether any particular offender is eligible to graduate. Those who successfully complete the program are presented with a certificate signed by the Panel and the ISP Court Executive.

According to official sources, the cost of the New Jersey ISP program averages about $7,100 per offender per year, compared with $31,000 per offender per year for state prison inmates. Furthermore, ISP participants contribute at least $4,100 per year to the economy, thus reducing overall program costs to $3,000. In 1999 there were 1,133 participants in the New Jersey ISP program. A majority of participants had been convicted of drug and property offenses. About 40 percent were first-time offenders. Approximately 85 percent of all program participants in 1999 were male. The average age of participants was 30, while the average original sentence length was four years. Two-thirds of all participants were high school graduates, and about the same percentage were employed prior to being convicted of their present offenses (Ciancia and Talty 1999).

The successfulness of the New Jersey ISP program may be assessed by the recidivism rate of its graduates. Of the 2,720 offenders who successfully completed the ISP program in 1997, only 13 percent were convicted of new offenses during a two-year followup. Overall program figures indicate that of the 7,154 offenders released into ISP by 1999, 40 percent were returned to prison, largely because of violating program rules. Only 8 percent of those whose ISP program was revoked were returned to prison for new criminal convictions (Ciancia and Talty 1999).

The Florida Community Control II Program.   The Florida Community Control II Program (FCCP) was created by the Florida Legislature in 1983 and implemented by the Florida Department of Corrections. Originally, the program was considered a "house arrest" operation, and it was created primarily to reduce serious prison overcrowding and the increasing numbers of offenders being sentenced to prison. Selectively, low-risk, prison-bound offenders were given alternative community corrections sentences, where they would be confined to their homes during nonworking hours. They were also expected to perform specific numbers of community service hours, participate in self-improvement programs as approved by their community control officers, participate in individual or group counseling if needed, and/or participate in other activities under the auspices of various social service agencies (Florida Department of Corrections 2002).

In 1987 the Florida Legislature approved the implementation of the **Community Control II Program,** which expanded greatly the surveillance of offenders through the use of electronic monitoring devices and more frequent face-to-face contacts with community control officers. Today, **community control** refers to a form of intensive, supervised custody in the community, including surveillance on weekends and holidays, administered by officers with restricted caseloads. Community control is an individualized program in which

 **BOX 3.3**

Conditions of the Intensive Supervision Program (ISP)

You have been placed in the Intensive Supervision Program (ISP) by the ISP Resentencing Panel for a trial period of 90 days subject to your compliance with your case plan and the conditions listed below. If you are arrested for a new offense, the ISP Resentencing Panel may issue a warrant to detain you in custody, without bail, to await disposition on the new charges.

1. I will obey the laws of the United States, and the laws and ordinances of any jurisdiction in which I may be residing.
2. I am required to promptly notify my ISP Officer if I am arrested, questioned, or contacted by any law enforcement official whether summoned, indicted, or charged with any offense or violation.
3. I will report as directed to the Court or to my ISP Officer.
4. I will permit the ISP Officer to visit my home.
5. I will answer promptly, truthfully, and completely all inquiries made by my ISP Officer and must obtain prior approval prior to any residence change. If the change of address or residence is outside the region in which I am under supervision, I will request approval at least 30 days in advance.
6. I will participate in any medical and/or psychological examinations, tests, and/or counseling as directed.
7. I will support my dependents, meet my family responsibilities, and continue full-time (35 hours or more per week), gainful employment. I will notify my ISP Officer prior to any change in my employment or if I become unemployed.
8. I will not leave the State of New Jersey without permission of my ISP Officer.
9. If I abscond from supervision (keep my whereabouts unknown to my ISP Officer), I may be charged with a new crime of Escape under 2C:29-5, which may subject me to an additional sentence of up to five years consecutive to any ISP violation time.
10. I will not have in my possession any firearm or other dangerous weapon.
11. I will perform community service of at least 16 hours per month, unless modified by the ISP Resentencing Panel.
12. I will participate in ISP group activities as directed.
13. I will maintain a daily diary of my activities and a weekly budget while under supervision.
14. I will not borrow any money, loan any money, or make credit purchases without permission of my ISP Officer. I may be required to surrender any credit cards in my possession to my officer.
15. I will maintain weekly contact with my community sponsor and network team.
16. I will comply with the required curfew from 6:00 P.M. to 6:00 A.M. unless modified by my ISP Officer. If unemployed, I will abide by a 6:00 P.M. curfew unless modified by my ISP Officer.
17. I will submit at any time to a search of my person, places, or things under my immediate control by my ISP Officer.
18. I will abstain from all illegal drug use and consumption of alcohol (including nonalcohol beer) and submit to drug and/or alcohol testing as directed. I also will not ingest any product containing poppy seeds. I will not use any medications, including over-the-counter medications, that contain alcohol.
19. I will notify my employer of my participation in ISP within 30 days after commencing employment.
20. I will not ingest any medication prescribed to someone else and will inform my ISP Officer of any medication prescribed to me by a physician or dentist.
21. I will file my Federal and State tax returns by the lawfully proscribed date and provide copies of the returns to my ISP Officer.

(continued)

BOX 3.3 *(Continued)*

23. I will maintain telephone service at my approved residence. If the telephone service is discontinued, I will notify my ISP Officer immediately. I am not permitted to have a caller ID or call forwarding services on my telephone.
24. I cannot collect unemployment benefits, disability assistance, or welfare benefits without permission.
25. I cannot possess a pager (beeper) and/or cellular telephone unless approved by my ISP Officer.
26. I cannot visit inmates in county or state correctional facilities until I have completed six months of satisfactory ISP supervision and with the permission of the ISP Regional Supervisor.

27. I may not serve in the capacity of an informant for a law enforcement agency. If requested to do so, I must decline and inform my ISP Officer of the request.
28. I will not engage in any gambling, including the purchase of lottery tickets. I will not enter a gambling establishment (casino) unless employed at such an establishment or given permission to visit such establishment by my ISP Officer.
29. I will turn in to my ISP Officer my driver's license (if driving privileges have been revoked), firearms ID card, and hunting license, if any of them are in my possession.
30. I will comply with any and all directives from the ISP Resentencing Panel or my officer.

Source: Ciancia and Talty (1999:7–8).

the freedom of the offender is restricted within the community, home, or noninstitutional residential placement, and specific sanctions are imposed or enforced (Florida Department of Corrections 2001). **Community Control II** refers to an intensive supervision program by officers with restricted caseloads with a condition of 24-hour-a-day electronic monitoring and a condition of confinement to a designated residence during designated hours.

Furthermore, in recent years Florida has commenced using **Global Positioning Satellites (GPS)** to track offenders under community control supervision. The GPS system has been made possible because of the extensive use of global satellites for military and communications uses. Thus, it is possible to track the locations of individual offenders in near real time and provide mapping for retrieval upon demand. For example, in cases where offenders have been convicted of sex offenses and have been ordered to avoid contact with their victims, it is possible to set exclusionary boundaries at whatever distance is deemed appropriate by the court around the victim's residence or place of work. If these perimeters are broken by an offender, an early warning can be sent to the victim, and the offender can suffer sanctions, such as program termination (Florida Department of Corrections 2002).

Program eligibility extends to any charged or convicted misdemeanor or felony offender, who, in the opinion of the court, is not likely to engage in further criminal activity, and where it is believed that the ends of justice and the welfare of society do not require that the offender should suffer the actual penalty prescribed by law. Those offenders specifically excluded from community control include (1) those convicted for a forcible felony (e.g., rape, aggravated assault, robbery, murder), (2) those previously convicted of a forcible felony, and (3) those under sentence of death. Some sex offenders may be eligible for inclusion in the community control program under a special form of sex offender community control. The goals of community control are (1) rehabilitation, (2) reintegration, (3) crime control, and (4) public safety. Community control officer caseloads are limited to 25 (Florida Department of Corrections 2001).

The program goals of Community Control II are to:

1. Impose strict noninstitutional sanctions in the local community for those found guilty of a crime.
2. Provide a diversionary alternative to prison confinement and the courts.
3. Provide protection to the community through surveillance and control of cases.
4. Identify and involve appropriate community resources to accommodate supervision objectives.
5. Establish public service programs in the community and enforce participation, when ordered by the court.
6. Enforce confinement to residence, curfew, and other restrictions.
7. Develop team as well as individual supervision.
8. Provide surveillance after normal weekday business hours and on weekends and holidays.
9. In order to ensure an appropriate level of supervision, restrict caseloads to a maximum of 25 cases per Community Control Officer, inasmuch as department resources, management, and geographic considerations permit (Florida Department of Corrections 2001).

Many community corrections clients are supervised from central offices where their whereabouts are tracked by sophisticated computer systems. Courtesy of BI, Inc.

The terms and conditions of Community Control II are outlined in Box 3.4. These conditions are rigorous and strictly enforced. Any offender may have his or her program revoked for any program violation, whether it is a technical one (e.g., violation of curfew, failing a drug/alcohol check) or a criminal one (e.g., an arrest or conviction).

There are also elaborate provisions that prescribe the nature of public service to be performed; the nature and amount of restitution or victim compensation; the amount of fines and other fees to be assessed; the nature and amount of participation in community programs to deal with sex offenders and those who are mentally disturbed in any way; and the specific grounds for program termination. All community controllees must agree to all of these conditions and signify their acceptance of them by signing a formal document in court.

By the beginning of 2001, the Florida Department of Corrections had 151,356 offenders on active community supervision. Of these 145,000 offenders were originally sentenced to standard probation, while approximately 6,300 offenders were placed in community supervision from prison. Only 711 offenders were on electronic monitoring, with 427 offenders being monitored by global positioning systems. There were 145 special types of offenders, such as sex offenders, placed on community control, with another 841 sex offenders placed on standard probation.

Actually, global satellite tracking has been extended in recent years and used by other states, such as Maryland, to augment what have become known as geographic information systems (GIS) (Harries 2002:27). GIS enables various jurisdictions to map crime incidents and link them with the whereabouts of certain offenders who are being electronically monitored. GIS is best visualized as a series of infinitely flexible map layers representing agency caseloads, agency field offices, agency administrative districts, treatment centers, schools, subjects of protective orders, bus routes, offenders classified by crimes for which they have been convicted, caseload classified by level of supervision, caseload for a specific probation officer, locations where law enforcement officers have been threatened or injured, liquor licenses, recidivists, locations of persons with sexually transmitted diseases, substandard housing, abandoned buildings, and drug markets (Harries 2002:27). Ultimately, supervised offenders can be linked rather rapidly to particular crimes wherever and whenever they occur in particular jurisdictions.

Property offenders (e.g., burglary, theft, forgery, fraud, weapons, other nonviolent) made up 73 percent of the community controllees, while those convicted of violent offenses, including murder/manslaughter, sex offenses, and robbery, made up the remaining 23 percent. The average amount of time served in the community control program for all offenders was 3.7 years. About 35 percent of all community controllees were first offenders, while about 49 percent were those who had one or two prior supervision commitments. Eighty-one percent of all community controllees had no prior state prison commitments.

Demographically, approximately 80 percent of all community controllees were male and 61 percent were white. The predominant age range of offenders ranged from 18 to 49, with an average age of 32 (Florida Department of Corrections 2001).

Successfulness of the Community Control II Program.   The Florida Community Control II program has been somewhat successful, with a recidivism rate among offenders of about 28 percent. In large part responsible for such low rates of recidivism is the high degree of program compliance among community controllees. For instance, at the beginning of 2001, the number of pending

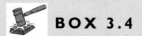

BOX 3.4

FLORIDA'S COMMUNITY CONTROL II PROGRAM REQUIREMENTS

Terms and Conditions of Probation or Community Control

The court shall determine the terms and conditions of probation or community control. These conditions may include among them the following, that the probationer or offender in community control shall:

1. Report to the probation and parole supervisors as directed.
2. Permit such supervisors to visit him or her at his or her home or elsewhere.
3. Work faithfully at suitable employment insofar as may be possible.
4. Remain within a specific place.
5. Make reparation or restitution to the aggrieved party for the damage or loss caused by his or her offense in an amount to be determined by the court.
6. Make payment of debt due and owing to a county or municipal detention facility for medical care, treatment, hospitalization, or transportation received by the felony probationer while in that detention facility.
7. Support his or her legal dependents to the best of his or her ability.
8. Make payment of any debt due and owing to the state subject to modification or change of circumstances.
9. Pay any application fee assessed and attorneys' fees and costs assessed, subject to modification based on change in circumstances.
10. Not associate with persons engaged in criminal activities.
11. Submit to random testing as directed by the correctional probation officer or the professional staff of the treatment center where he or she is receiving treatment to determine the presence or use of alcohol or controlled substances.
12. If the offense was a controlled substance violation and the period of probation immediately follows a period of incarceration in the state correctional system, the conditions shall include a require-

ment that the offender submit to random substance abuse testing intermittently throughout the term of supervision, upon the direction of the correctional probation officer.

13. Be prohibited from possessing, carrying, or owning any firearm unless authorized by the court and consented to by the probation officer.
14. Be prohibited from using intoxicants to excess or possessing any drugs or narcotics unless prescribed by a physician. The probationer or community controllee shall not knowingly visit places where intoxicants, drugs, or other dangerous substances are unlawfully sold, dispensed, or used.
15. Attend an HIV/AIDS awareness program consisting of a class of not less than two hours or more than four hours in length, the cost for which shall be paid by the offender, if such a program is available in the county of the offender's residence.
16. Pay not more than $1 per month during the term of probation or community control to a nonprofit organization established for the sole purpose of supplementing the rehabilitative efforts of the Department of Corrections.
17. The court shall require intensive supervision and surveillance for an offender placed into community control, which may include but is not limited to:
   a. Specified contact with the parole or probation officer.
   b. Confinement to an agreed-upon residence during hours away from employment and public service activities.
   c. Mandatory public service.
   d. Supervision by the Department of Corrections by means of an electronic device.
   e. Electronic monitoring 24 hours per day.
   f. Confinement in a designated residence during designated hours.

Source: Florida Department of Corrections (2001).

violations—cases in which a violation report was initiated and which signified an alleged violation of one or more program conditions—averaged about 25 percent. Among the different regions, these pending violations varied from a low of 20.4 percent to a high of 28.1 percent. In many instances, community controllees who are found guilty of having violated one or more program requirements are not necessarily returned to prison or placed in prison. Rather, they are subjected to more intensive supervision by their community control officers (Florida Department of Corrections 2001). Positive outcomes of this program are that a majority of participating offenders have been able to obtain the counseling and therapy needed to function in law-abiding ways in society, and most have been able to support their dependents with sustained employment. Many have earned high school diplomas and associate's degrees from colleges. In these respects, the rehabilitative aspects of community control are quite apparent.

Local ISP Programs   Virtually every state and the federal government has some type of ISP program. The behavioral conditions and regulations accompanying these different programs vary among jurisdictions, as each state adds or deletes relevant requirements for the clientele. But it would be misleading to say that all ISP programs are operated exclusively at the state level. Many cities and counties have their own versions of ISP and are virtually independent of state control or supervision. For example, Indianapolis, Indiana, and the surrounding Marion County vicinity established an intensive supervision program in 1994. The former Marion County Municipal Court Probation Department obtained grant funding through Marion County Community Corrections for one probation officer position dedicated to the intensive supervision of up to 30 D-felony offenders. The goal of this program was to divert offenders from commitment to the Department of Corrections through the provision of intensive supervision services. By 1998 the program had focused almost exclusively on high-risk probationers recently released from incarceration in the Department of Correction or Community Corrections who were largely unemployed or undereducated (Marion Superior Court Probation Department 2002).

Furthermore, in 1998 a second ISP was established to deal with repeat violent offenders. This program became known as **VIPER (Violence Impact Program Enhanced Response),** and it required close monitoring of violent clients to reduce violence in the community. With each caseload, the components of the program include weekly meetings with the supervising PO as well as regular urine drug screens. A minimum of two contacts per month must occur in the field (i.e., the probationer's home, employment location, or other community site). Special emphasis is placed on ensuring that the needs of the probationer are met in a timely manner and that all possible resources are utilized in providing the services necessary to help the offender be successful in the community (Marion Superior Court Probation Department 2002). Two years earlier, in 1996, **Operation Probationer Accountability** was established by the Marion Superior Court Probation Department. This program is a partnership between local law enforcement agencies and the probation department to conduct random field investigations and searches at the residences of high-risk probationers convicted of drug, violent, or weapons offenses. The program has helped to deter and detect further criminal activity by those individuals under court supervision. During 1999 alone, 29 operations were completed, targeting a total of 1,204 high-risk probationers. Items found during these investigations included handguns and illegal drugs, including marijuana, cocaine, and crack. A high degree of program compliance has been reported (Marion Superior Court Probation Department 2002). Numerous counties and cities in other jurisdictions have their own versions of ISP (Texas Department of Criminal Justice 2002).

In 2001, North Carolina had almost 110,000 probationers and about 5,000 parolees. The North Carolina Department of Corrections operated several community corrections programs, including regular probation/parole, intensive probation, electronic house arrest, and drug screening programs. The program requirements of North Carolina ISP are very similar to both the New Jersey and Florida models. North Carolina officials have reported favorable success experiences with their ISP program (North Carolina Department of Corrections 2001). Especially significant is the savings of community corrections programs and ISP compared with the cost of incarcerating offenders in prisons. For instance, North Carolina officials report that in 2000, the following costs of different types of supervision were incurred on the basis of security level per inmate per day:

Prison-close custody	$75.32
Prison-medium custody	$68.13
Prison-minimum custody	$52.52
Average prison cost	$63.65
Regular probation/parole	$1.89
Intensive probation	$12.23
Electronic house arrest	$6.41
Drug Screening Program	$4.12

It is clear from these figures that the cost of ISP in North Carolina is less than 20 percent of the average cost of incarcerating offenders in prison.

Some ISP programs are directed at specific offender populations, such as sex offenders (Stalans, Seng, and Yarnold 2001). In Cook County, Illinois, the Adult Sex Offender Program (ASOP) has been established as an intensive supervision, specialized probation program for felony sex offenders. It is believed by Cook County authorities that sex offenders must be closely monitored. As an important part of its surveillance efforts, the ASOP has increasingly networked with sex therapists and various community agencies in an effort to increase program effectiveness as well as stricter offender monitoring (Stalans et al. 2001).

Criticisms of Intensive Supervised Probation. All ISP programs can be faulted because they do not achieve their stated goals. Some say that victims are ignored in probation decision making. Others contend that ISP programs contribute to net-widening by bringing certain offenders under the ISP program umbrella who really do not need to be intensively supervised. Many critics praise ISP programs for alleviating prison inmate overcrowding and providing a meaningful option to incarceration. One aspect of ISP programs in certain jurisdictions that has drawn some criticism has been the imposition of supervision fees on ISP program clients. These costs are normally incurred by probationer-clients. Despite the fact that it is unconstitutional to deny any client admission to an ISP program because of a client's inability to pay supervisory fees, there continues to be considerable controversy about requiring such fees.

The different ISP programs described have been used by other states as models for their own ISP program development. Several elements of the New

Jersey model have been adopted by Arizona, Colorado, Illinois, Indiana, Iowa, Kentucky, Louisiana, Nevada, and North Carolina. These states have not copied New Jersey precisely in their probation guidelines, but their newly developed programs resemble the New Jersey program to a high degree. In Kentucky, for example, ISP is used exclusively with parolees as a condition of their supervision.

Some positive comments on the Florida program are that it has shown low rates of recidivism and has alleviated the prison overcrowding in Florida to a degree. However, New Jersey officials who operate the program are alleged to be too selective about which clients can become involved in the program. The program includes those offenders most likely to be successful. With only 29 percent of the offenders exhibiting maximum risk scores, it is believed by critics that the program is self-serving and thus not a true indication of how effective intensive supervised probation can be. The process of selecting only those most likely to be successful clients is known as **creaming.** In order to be of greatest service, the program should probably target more offenders who are risks and difficult to manage.

New Jersey's ISP program has been criticized because client involvement is strictly voluntary. While volunteers are not automatically included in the program, there is an inherent bias introduced. The most serious types of felons are excluded, again reflective of creaming. However, the screening process used by New Jersey is considered one of the most rigorous of all existing ISP programs.

The Florida Community Control II program has a low rate of recidivism among its clientele. Compared with the New Jersey program, this program relies on the use of risk assessment instruments for recruiting clients and determining their level of intensive supervision. Also, the combined use of house arrest and electronic monitoring, together with frequent face-to-face visits and checks by supervising POs, greatly heightens offender control.

Summary of ISP Program Components.   Several program components are shared among states. These components include electronic surveillance, community sponsorship, payment of probation fees, and split-sentencing respectively (Wiebush 1991). Fulton and Stone (1993:43–44) have identified the following criteria as essential program components of ISP programs:

1. High risk/need population targeted for ISP.
2. Reliable risk/need instruments used to select clients.
3. Small caseloads (no more than 20-30 offenders).
4. Frequent substantive contact with probationers.
5. Phase or level system used.
6. Systematic case review for program evaluation.
7. System of sanctions for program violators.
8. Available range of correctional interventions.
9. Restitution to victims.
10. Community involvement of clients.
11. ISP officers as facilitators and advocates.
12. Objectives-based management used.
13. Sound means of program evaluation.

The successfulness of any one or more of these programs for assisting probationers rests, in part, on evaluation research. This research tests program effectiveness by analyzing essential elements or components, the amount of money needed to establish programs and operate them, and the success rates of clients. One prevalent criticism of many programs for probationers is that they are often too small and the funding cycle too short. Thus, unless a good process or program analysis is done at the same time, the findings are somewhat ambiguous. Or the findings from outcome studies take a great deal of time to generate and disseminate in professional outlets such as journals and books. In many cases, the results of outcome studies are of little value to agents or administrators of the original projects (Zedlewski 1999).

In 1998 a Correctional Program Assessment Inventory was devised by the International Community Correction Association. The Inventory was designed to raise numerous crucial questions of agency leaders and staff in order to sensitize them to the clarity and effectiveness of their own programs. The areas covered by the Inventory include: (1) Program Elements, (2) Client Pre-Service Assessment, (3) Program Characteristics, (4) Therapeutic Integrity, (5) Relapse Prevention and Follow-Up, and (6) Staff Characteristics. Was a thorough literature review conducted, and was the need for the program systematically assessed? Is there a rational inclusion and exclusion process in place for selecting clients? Are criminogenic needs set as intermediate targets? Is there more intense service for high-risk cases? Is the training or treatment monitored? Do most staff have BA degrees and adequate training? These and other questions enable program staff to do a better job by anticipating their program weaknesses and strengths. While compliance with these program requisites may not guarantee success, major noncompliance certainly portends failure (Holt 1998:18).

A PROFILE OF PROBATIONERS

Probationer Characteristics

The profile of probationers in the United States is changing annually. Table 3.3 shows several salient characteristics of probationers compared for the years 1990, 1995, and 2001.

Each year, the probation population includes increasing numbers of felony offenders. For example, in 1990, for instance, 48 percent of all probationers were convicted felons. In 2001 this figure had grown to 53 percent. The percentage of probationers convicted of misdemeanors declined from 52 percent to 45 percent between 1990 and 2001 (Glaze 2002:4). These changes suggest that the probationer population is consisting of more dangerous offenders, or at least of persons convicted of more serious crimes. One indication of the increasing dangerousness of probationers POs must supervise is that larger numbers of probation offices are using metal detectors to screen entering probationers before they are admitted into POs' offices (Thornton 2002:19).

About 55 percent of all probationers in 2001 were white, compared with 52 percent white in 1990. Approximately 12 percent of these probationers were Hispanic in 2001, compared with 18 percent in 1990. Black probationers increased slightly from 30 percent to 31 percent between 1990 and 2001. Most probationers were male (78 percent). The percentage of females on probation increased from 18 percent to 22 percent between 1990 and 2001 (Glaze 2002:4).

TABLE 3.3

Characteristics of adults on probation, 1990, 1995, and 2001

Characteristic	1990	1995	2001
Total	100%	100%	100%
Gender			
Male	82%	79%	78%
Female	18	21	22
Race[a]			
White	52%	53%	55%
Black	30	31	31
Hispanic	18	14	12
American Indian/Alaska Native	1	1	1
Asian/Pacific Islander[b]	—	—	1
Status of supervision			
Active	83%	79%	74%
Inactive	9	8	11
Absconded	6	9	10
Supervised out of State	2	2	2
Other	**	2	3
Adults entering probation			
Without incarceration	87%	72%	76%
With incarceration	8	13	17
Other types	5	15	7
Adults leaving probation			
Successful completions	69%	62%	62%
Returned to incarceration	14	21	13
With new sentence	3	5	3
With the same sentence	9	13	7
Unknown	2	3	4
Absconder[c]	7	**	3
Other unsuccessful	2	**	11
Death	—	1	1
Other	7	16	10
Type of offense of adults on probation[d]			
Felony	48%	54%	53%
Misdemeanor	52	44	45
Other infractions	1	2	1
Most serious offense			
Driving while intoxicated	21%	16%	18%
Drug law violations	**	**	25
Minor traffic offenses	**	**	7
Domestic violence	**	**	7
Other	79	84	43

(continued)

TABLE 3.3   (Continued)

Characteristics of adults on probation, 1990, 1995, and 2001

Characteristic	1990	1995	2001
Status of probation			
Direct imposition	38%	48%	54%
Split sentence	6	15	9
Sentence suspended	41	26	25
Imposition suspended	14	6	10
Other	1	4	1

Note: For every characteristic there were persons of unknown status or type. Detail may not sum to total because of rounding.
**Not available.
—Less than 0.5%.
[a]In 2001 race/Hispanic origin was collected as a single item. For comparison, percents were recalculated for prior years.
[b]Includes Native Hawaiians.
[c]In 1995 absconder status was reported among "other."
[d]In 2001 type of offense was limited to three categories. Driving while intoxicated was reported among the most serious offense. For comparison, percents were recalculated for prior years.
Source: Glaze, 2002: 4.

 **BOX 3.5**    **PERSONALITY HIGHLIGHT**

Braulio Gloria

Adult Probation Officer, Webb County, TX

Statistics

M.A. (in progress, public administration), Texas A & M International University; B.A. (political science/sociology), Texas A & M International University; Texas Department of Criminal Justice Probation Officer Training; Texas Department of Criminal Justice Residential Service Training

Background

I am currently employed as an Adult Probation Officer or Community Supervision Officer for the State of Texas, County of Webb. I have been employed as a probation officer for about seven months. Prior to this position, I was employed as a Shift Supervisor for a local halfway-in house, or community residential facility, called the Webb County Court Residential Treatment Center (CRTC), for about five years.

I first became interested in the criminal justice field while employed at the CRTC. The CRTC was my basic training ground for my current occupation as a probation officer due to the daily interactions I had with probationers residing in this facility. This facility housed approximately 45 adult male probationers with drug/alcohol addictions. My job entailed monitoring the probationers residing at the CRTC via several techniques,

(continued)

BOX 3.5 *(Continued)*

such as surveillance, searches, drug screens, and the like. Within six months of being employed at the CRTC, I decided to enroll at Laredo Community College to pursue an Associate's Degree with a major in criminal justice. This feat proved to be very tough, since it required working graveyard shifts to continue my schooling during the day. After graduating from this two-year college, I continued with the same concept (working nights to go to school during the day) at Texas A & M International University (TAMIU) in Laredo, Texas. It took all of four and half years, but I finally graduated, *summa cum laude*, with a Bachelor of Arts with a major in political science and a minor in sociology. Shortly thereafter, I was hired as an Adult Probation Officer. I am currently pursuing a Master's Degree in public administration at TAMIU and am aspiring to either move up in rank at my current place of employment or obtain a better position within the criminal justice field.

Work Experiences

I encountered several challenging situations while employed at the CRTC, but the most severe situations had to do with suicidal probationers. You really do not know what to expect when dealing with a suicidal person, and working with a population that is alcohol/drug dependent heightens the situation. Furthermore, most probationers residing at the CRTC have gone through a life full of difficult obstacles preventing them from having a normal life, and some find suicide as the only solution to overcome their problems. On more than one occasion, I have received calls from ex-probationers, whom I assumed were under the influence, threatening to kill themselves. In these situations, I have found myself trying to counsel them throughout most of the night. However, sometimes you do not

get an opportunity to do even that. On one afternoon shift, a probationer slit one of his wrists while in his dormitory. He did not notify any staff member that he was depressed or contemplating suicide, and none of us (the staff) saw any of the warning signs. Fortunately, the situation was quickly controlled and the probationer lived.

I believe that the worst situation ever in the history of the CRTC was when an employee became romantically involved with a probationer residing in the facility. The probationer was successfully released from the CRTC and the employee decided to resign and live with the released offender. About a year and a half later, the ex-employee was murdered by the ex-probationer. The ex-probationer dismembered the ex-employee's body and scattered the body parts in different areas around Laredo. The ex-probationer was subsequently arrested, only to commit suicide in jail. Although I have not painted a pretty picture, these situations are rare and far between. In addition, this line of work can be very rewarding. I am proud to call myself a probation officer because I know that I am helping to keep my community safe. Moreover, it is very rewarding when you actually see a probationer turn his or her life around to become a productive citizen.

Advice to Students

Prepare, prepare, prepare. Even though this may sound like a cliché, in this field, you need to get as much experience as possible. Also, do not be discouraged if you do not land the career you want right off the bat. You will soon learn that elite criminal justice agencies are hard to get into. You need to be persistent, and in order to have a competitive edge, you need to *prepare*. Last, continue to develop yourself by continuing your education.

Recidivism figures of probationers are contrasted for 1990 and 2001. Slightly fewer numbers of probationers were returned to prison or jail in 2001 (13 percent) compared with 1990 (14 percent). About half of these probationers were returned to incarceration with the same sentence, suggesting that program violations rather than new crimes were responsible for most of these revocations of probation. A significant number of probationers have their probation programs revoked because of substance or alcohol abuse (Lurigio and Swartz 1998).

SHOCK PROBATION AND SPLIT SENTENCING

Shock probation refers to planned sentences where judges order offenders imprisoned for statutory incarceration periods related to their conviction offenses. However, after 30, 60, 90, or even 120 days of incarceration, offenders are taken out of jail or prison and resentenced to probation, provided they behaved well while incarcerated. The shock factor relates to the shock of being imprisoned initially. Theoretically, this trauma will be so profound that inmates will not want to return to prison later. Therefore, a strong deterrent factor is associated with these terms.

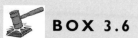 **BOX 3.6**

IS IT SHOCK PROBATION WHEN YOU ASK FOR SHOCK PROBATION?

Felipe de Jesus Del Bosque, 29

It happened in Laredo, Texas. On April 7, 2000, a man, Rolando Alarcon, attempted to run down another man with his car. The intended victim was Felipe de Jesus Del Bosque, 29. Del Bosque pulled out a firearm and shot at Alarcon, wounding him. Then Del Bosque robbed Alarcon and fled the scene. Police caught up with Del Bosque, and he was subsequently convicted of robbery and theft, then sentenced to seven years in the Texas penitentiary.

After serving several months in prison, however, Del Bosque requested to reappear before the judge and speak to her regarding the possibility of receiving probation. He advised the judge that he suffered back injuries from being hit by Alarcon's car. Furthermore, he said he was drunk the night of the shooting and that he had also taken some pills. In his own behalf, Del Bosque told the judge, Elma Salinas Ender, that since he's been incarcerated, he's participated in drug rehabilitation and a walk-a-thon to raise money for the September 11th victims and goes to Bible studies. He told the court that he wants to change his life and wants to help his father, who is a mechanic and who is also recovering from surgery and is in failing health. Del Bosque added that he would be willing to make restitution to pay for damage to the car and comply with any further drug rehabilitation the judge might order. "I know Jesus's love and he wants me to be a better person," Del

Bosque told the judge. Under cross-examination by the prosecutor, Del Bosque admitted that he had mingled with the "wrong crowd" in past years, and that the crowd did not make him drink, take pills, or commit crimes. The district attorney also reminded the court that Del Bosque had a lengthy criminal record, including a prior robbery of a convenience store. Furthermore, Del Bosque had prior convictions for resisting arrest and drug possession.

Judge Ender made her decision. She denied Del Bosque's request for shock probation, saying that "you got the message that you could get away with it. If I granted your motion for shock probation, what kind of message would I be sending?" She said that the only reason she allowed him back into court for a probation hearing was that she believed he had the right to state his case. The judge added that she hoped that Del Bosque's religious conversion would be sustained and that she hopes that his wishes to change his life are genuine. She said that maybe God's message for bringing him to the hearing was so that the community could understand that people couldn't persist in committing crimes and getting away with them.

Should persons such as Del Bosque with lengthy prior records be placed on probation following a robbery and a shooting? Was the judge acting appropriately by denying Del Bosque's motion for shock probation? What do you think?

Source: Adapted from Laurel Almada and the Associated Press, November 21, 2001.

The key to understanding shock probation is knowing that offenders are not told in advance that they are only being confined for short terms. Judges sentence offenders to five years in prison (or jail), and offenders enter confinement thinking that they are commencing the first day of a five-year sentence. Suddenly, after 30, 60, 90 or 120 days, they are taken out of confinement and brought before the judge again. The judge suspends the rest of their jail/prison time and imposes probation. Yes, these offenders are relieved. Further, they are shocked as they realize they will not have to serve more time in jail.

Ohio introduced the first shock probation law in 1965. Several other states have adopted similar laws in recent years (Vito 1984). In 1988, 1,056 offenders participated in 9 shock incarceration programs throughout the country (Yurkanin 1988:87). By 1994, 41 shock probation programs were being operated in at least 25 states (MacKenzie and Souryal 1994:1). In 1998 there were 6,492 shock probationers in 25 programs in the United States (American Correctional Association 2002). One of these shock incarceration programs is operated by the U.S. Federal Bureau of Prisons at the Intensive Confinement Center at Allenwood, Pennsylvania. A study of 271 inmates who participated in the shock incarceration program compared with 106 traditional minimum-security inmates showed that shock incarceration program participants tend to hold more positive attitudes and to be better adjusted than traditional inmates during their incarceration. Despite these positive results, it has been recommended that in subsequent applications of shock incarceration to federal prisoners, each shock incarceration component should be carefully planned and implemented so that participants observe a direct connection between what they are experiencing and how it supports their future change. This is especially true in relation to programs designed to get tough on offenders by including both punishment and rehabilitation in the same program (Lutze 2001).

The use of shock probation has increased substantially since 1990. In 1990 only 8 percent of all probationers received probation with some incarceration, usually a short-term jail sentence. By 2000, however, 20 percent of all probationers received probation with a short-term jail sentence (Maguire and Pastore 2002). Thus, it would appear that shock probation is gradually growing in popularity. Reasons for this trend are lower recidivism rates among shock probationers in various jurisdictions, including New York, and greater responsiveness to treatments for substance abuse among probationer/clients (New York State Division of Parole 1998).

The Philosophy and Objectives of Shock Probation

Crime Deterrence. Ideally, persons who are locked up in jails for brief periods are literally shocked into becoming law-abiding, since they do not want to do more time in jails in the future (Lutze 1996). This is because of the unpleasantness of the jail experience. Thus, deterrence is a key objective of shock probation. However, not everyone is affected the same way by short-term incarceration. Depending upon the jurisdiction, the length of jail time varies from one month to four months. For some offenders, this jail time is relatively lenient relative to the crime they have committed.

Rehabilitation. While shock probation is intended to be traumatic, it is also considered rehabilitative to a degree. After all, shock probationers are ultimately released from jails after serving short jail terms and released into their communities. While in their communities, shock probationers can perform jobs, live with their families, and otherwise lead normal lives. This scenario is much better for their rehabilitation than being confined in prison for one or more years.

Creative Sentencing.   In some cases, judges are encouraged to be creative in their sentencing options. Thus, judges may sentence offenders to short jail terms, followed by the inmate's release into the community. Judges may vary such sentences to include intermittent confinement, such as weekend incarceration. Judges may also add conditions to these sentences, including victim compensation, restitution, community service, counseling, and vocational/educational training (Horn 2001).

Jail/Prison Overcrowding.   One result of shock probation in some jurisdictions has been to alleviate some degree of jail and prison overcrowding. Shock probation in South Carolina, for example, has diverted about one-third of its offenders from prison during the first few years of its operation since 1987 (South Carolina State Reorganization Commission 1990). Similar results have been found in other jurisdictions, as shock probation is increasingly used as a front-end solution to jail and prison overcrowding (Vaughn 1993). Interestingly, while shock probation eases prison overcrowding to a degree, it strains jail inmate populations by sending larger numbers of offenders to jails where they must be housed for short periods. However, if shock probation deters some offenders from reoffending, then perhaps some temporary jail population increase is justified.

Punishment.   The fact of locking up shock probationers, even if the periods of confinement are relatively brief, is evidence that some punishment is being imposed. While the incarcerative terms served by shock probationers are not entirely consistent with what the public thinks ought to be served, confinement is equated with punishment. Thus, shock probation programs have citizen appeal to that extent.

Offender Needs.   When offenders are brought out of jails following short incarcerative terms, judges may impose conditions that include group counseling or individual therapy or treatment for those with special needs. Some offenders are drug- or alcohol-dependent and require medical intervention and assistance as well as employment guidance. The flexibility of shock probation facilitates meeting offender needs more effectively (Lutze 1998).

Shock Probation and Offender Accountability.   The most important components of shock probation programs are those that heighten offender accountability. Offenders who are made to pay restitution to victims or perform some community service are painfully aware of the problems and suffering they have caused others. For many shock probationers, these experiences make them feel more accountable, since they are being made to do something constructive to make up for their crimes.

Community Safety.   Citizens want to feel safe. They do not especially like the idea that criminals are being freed within their communities short of serving their full incarcerative sentences (Gilling 2001). Some citizens do not understand the rehabilitative or reintegrative value of shock incarceration programs. Nevertheless, the corrections system believes that for some offenders, at least, the shock probation option is better in the long run that long-term imprisonment. Thus, only those most likely not to reoffend are included in shock incarceration programs. Typically, these include low-risk first offenders. It would be inconsistent with shock probation philosophy, for example, to include career criminals or violent offenders in such programs. Some amount of common sense is necessary to understand why certain offenders are included while others are deliberately excluded from program participation (Boutellier 2001).

The Effectiveness of Shock Probation

Extensive research has been conducted of existing shock probation or shock incarceration programs. MacKenzie and Souryal (1994) investigated eight shock probation programs in 1992. These were programs operated in Oklahoma, Georgia, Texas, Florida, New York, Illinois, Louisiana, and South Carolina. They found that the programs shared certain similarities, including rigorous military drills and a daily schedule of physical training and hard labor. In the programs they studied, the program lengths varied from 90 to 180 days. Most participants were youthful male nonviolent offenders with little or no criminal history.

The rates of recidivism for offenders in these shock probation programs were relatively low and varied among the states. A one-year followup of the New York program found that only 10 percent committed new crimes and were imprisoned (Clark, Aziz, and MacKenzie 1994:9). However, in Louisiana, about 43 percent of the shock probation clients did not complete their programs successfully for one of several reasons, including program violations and new crimes (MacKenzie, Shaw, and Gowdy, 1993).

One observation by researchers is that the effectiveness of shock probation programs may depend, in part, on who selects shock probationers as clients. In some jurisdictions, judges select offenders, while in other jurisdictions, client selection is the duty of corrections officials. Thus, it is entirely possible that less-than-rigorous selection methods may lead to net-widening, where offenders who would never have been incarcerated initially upon conviction are included in shock probation programs anyway, simply because they show the most promise for completing the program successfully. Further, there is substantial program variation pertaining to the amount of emphasis placed on education, vocational training, discipline, and rehabilitation. All of these factors influence program effectiveness (Lutze 2001). Generally, shock probation serves useful rehabilitative and reintegrative purposes. Shock probation programs have been shown to be effective in deterring offenders from recidivating. It is likely that we will see greater expansion of shock probation programs in future years, as more states establish such programs.

BOOT CAMPS

Another program that is sometimes confused with shock probation is shock incarceration or **boot camps.** As in shock probation, convicted offenders are confined in a secure setting, but their confinement resembles a military boot camp. Shock probation involved sentencing offenders to a short jail term, with no participation in any military-like programs. In contrast, shock incarceration or boot camp programs do provide military-like regimentation and regulation of inmate behaviors.

Boot Camp Instruction, Custer Youth Corrections Center, Custer, South Dakota.

Definition

Boot camps are highly regimented, military-like, short-term correctional programs (90 to 180 days) where offenders are provided with strict discipline, physical training, and hard labor resembling some aspects of military basic training. When successfully completed, boot camps provide for transfers of participants to community-based facilities for nonsecure supervision. By 2001, boot camps had been formally established in over half of the states (Zachariah 2002).

The first juvenile boot camp was developed in Orleans Parish, Louisiana, in 1985. Boot camps for adult offenders were officially established in 1983 by the Georgia Department of Corrections Special Alternative Incarceration (SAI). The general idea for boot camps also originated in Georgia in the late 1970s (Koch Crime Institute 2002).

In 2001, there were 24 state systems operating 44 boot camp programs for adult offenders, with more states planning to establish similar programs (American Correctional Association 2002:26). Also in 2001, there were 22 juvenile boot camps operated in 11 state jurisdictions (American Correctional Association 2002:28). The usual length of incarceration in boot camps varies from three to six months. During this period, boot camp participants engage in marching, work, and classes that are believed useful in rehabilitation. Usually, youthful offenders are targeted by these programs.

Rationale

The rationale for boot camps includes the following:

1. Some youths who get into trouble are unsupervised by adults and/or lack discipline to control their emotions, such as anger and hostility. Boot camps structure a youth's environment in ways that promote discipline and emotional control.

2. Controlled environments are necessary for some youths who lack social and psychological capacity to live around others. Boot camps train offenders in responsible living techniques to help them become law-abiding citizens.

3. Boot camps force offenders to learn vocational skills and attain higher educational levels that enable them to function more productively within their communities.

4. The sufficient punishment involved in boot camp involvement tends to reduce offender recidivism. Boot camps deter offenders from further offending by making them more fearful of prison-like environments.

Goals

The goals of boot camps are to (1) foster rehabilitation/reintegration; (2) promote discipline; (3) deter crime; (4) ease prison/jail overcrowding; and (5) provide vocational, educational, and rehabilitative services.

To Provide Rehabilitation and Reintegration.   Boot camps are intended to assist offenders in living in a law-abiding manner with other offenders. Clientele learn to respect one another's property and to be considerate of others.

To Promote Discipline.   The military-like regimen of boot camp training instills discipline in most participants. It has been found that many boot camp clientele have never had discipline in their homes and families. They have been disruptive in their schools. Thus, the boot camp experience teaches them about rules and the importance of abiding by them.

Promoting Deterrence.   A certain amount of punishment is inherent in boot camps. Having to adhere to rigid and demanding physical and educational schedules is something these clients have never had to do in the past. The boot camp experience is a shocking one for most participants. After they have graduated from boot camp, most participants never want to go through boot camp again. The experience is both rewarding and punitive.

Easing Prison/Jail Overcrowding.   It is uncertain as to how much prison and jail overcrowding is alleviated by boot camp programs. It is clear that if the goals of boot camps are followed closely, only prison- or jail-bound offenders should be targeted for boot camp participation. To the extent that such persons are actually singled out for boot camp experiences, then prison and jail overcrowding are eased somewhat. Additionally, the relatively low rates of recidivism of a majority of boot camp participants suggests that most of these former clients will be law-abiding in their future years and not be drawn again into the criminal justice system. Therefore, this should be considered a long-term fringe benefit of boot camp experiences (Tonry and Hamilton 1995).

Providing Vocational and Rehabilitative Services.   An integral part of most boot camp programs is the provision of vocational and educational services for clients. Not only must boot camp clients adhere to strict physical regimens, but they must also participate in educational and vocational programs designed to equip them with skills that will make them more employable. Many of these clients were either unemployed or underemployed when they committed their

 **BOX 3.7**

The North Carolina IMPACT Boot Camp Program

North Carolina operates several boot camps for both male and female youths and young adults. IMPACT means Intensive Motivational Program of Alternative Correctional Treatment. IMPACT instructors are trained to seek to instill discipline, a sound work ethic, and self-confidence through the administration of a strictly regimented, work-intensive, paramilitary system. The boot camp provides youthful offenders incentives to change their behaviors and develop new and positive attitudes.

Both young men and women are sent to IMPACT for a 90-day boot camp experience. They must be:

1. 16 through 30 years of age.
2. Eligible to serve a prison sentence of one year or longer.
3. Certified as medically fit.

IMPACT provides a highly regimented routine of physical exercise, hard work, and continued education. A typical day is as follows:

4:30 A.M.	Wake up
4:30–5:30 A.M.	Personal training
5:30–5:50 A.M.	Physical training
5:50–6:00 A.M.	March to breakfast
6:00–6:30 A.M.	Breakfast
6:30–6:45 A.M.	Return to dormitory
6:45–7:45 A.M.	Clean rooms/ inspection
7:45–8:00 A.M.	Reveille (flag raising)
8:00 A.M.–12:00 noon	Work/drill
12:00–12:30 P.M.	Lunch (pack out)
12:30–4:00 P.M.	Work/drill
4:00–4:45 P.M.	Personal hygiene
4:45–5:00 P.M.	Retreat (flag lowering)
5:00–5:10 P.M.	March to dinner
5:10–5:30 P.M.	Dinner
5:30–5:45 P.M.	Return to dormitory
5:45–6:00 P.M.	Preparation for school
6:00–10:30 P.M.	School

IMPACT trainees are required to exercise, drill, work, and attend school. They begin each day with 30 to 45 minutes of calisthenics. In their first two weeks, they devote more than 30 minutes a day to marching drills. The trainees spend at least seven hours a day at work. Much of the work involves clearing land or cleaning property for federal, state, or local government agencies. They also work on conservation projects at state wildlife resources sites, clear lands around fire stations, and renovate buildings and campsites.

A major aspect of the program is the ropes challenge course, a physically challenging series of tasks divided into two areas: the low course and the high course. The low course emphasizes tasks such as getting all members of a group over a 12-foot high wall, a task that teaches the value of working as a group to solve problems. The high course focuses more upon building an individual's self-confidence. All high ropes tasks—walking a balance beam, crossing a wire bridge, and four-foot jump—are performed 30 feet above the ground. The course encourages personal, physical, and psychological growth.

Trainees are given a battery of tests upon arrival. A determination is made of their educational level and background. Teachers from the local community college provide individualized instruction for those who do not possess a high school diploma. Trainees who have graduated are put to work in a tutoring program. More than two hours are devoted to these education programs four nights a week. Trainees also receive counseling; instructors help them develop social, job, and financial skills. A chaplain presents weekly self-development discussions, offers counseling, and conducts religious services. Trainees also receive 16 hours of substance abuse education. Trainees who successfully complete the 90-day program are awarded certificates of completion and recognized for their achievements. Family members are invited to attend these graduation ceremonies. After completing the program, successful trainees are released into the custody of a probation officer to complete a term of probation in the community.

(continued)

Source: North Carolina Department of Correction (2002).

BOX 3.7 (Continued)

The New York High Impact Incarceration Program (HIIP)

Operating since 1990, the New York High Impact Incarceration Program (HIIP) is a boot camp operated at Rikers Island. It is a voluntary, 61-day, 200-bed residential program for technical parole violators and some city-sentenced adult inmates convicted of nonviolent offenses. It provides these inmates with an opportunity to change their lifestyle.

HIIP seeks to achieve the following objectives:

1. Learn military drill and ceremony.
2. Receive vocational and educational training.
3. Receive substance abuse counseling.
4. Perform community service.

These objectives are accomplished through a behavior modification plan based on a highly disciplined regimen like the military model. It emphasizes behavior modification and community responsibility through the teaching of the Five Basic Needs, Five STEPS of Decision Making, Four Elements of Social Control, Control Theory, and Six Criminal Tendencies. HIIP operates out of a compound at the Correctional Institution for Men on Rikers Island and is believed to be the nation's first urban boot camp. Instruction is provided by corrections officers and counselors who have volunteered for this assignment and received special training in military drill-instructor techniques as well as various counseling methodologies. Many HIIP officers went through their own boot camp experiences at the Marine base at Quantico, Virginia. At Quantico for three weeks, they were on the receiving end of the same kind of strict discipline, intense physical activity, precision drills, and no-nonsense, gut-checking counseling that they continue to enforce as HIIP drill instructors.

Inmate participation in HIIP is voluntary. In order to qualify, inmates—or teammates, as they are called—must, among other requirements, be at least 19 years of age, pass a physical examination, and not have a record for violent crimes or sex offenses. Technical parole violators who successfully complete the program satisfy their parole warrant and are released from custody, but they continue to be supervised by the New York State Division of Parole.

Teammates are required to have their hair cut in a short-cropped military fashion; wear special green uniforms; and wear no jewelry other than a religious medal or wedding band. There are other restrictions about when and to whom they may speak and on the correct forms for addressing officers, teammates, and others. Another component of HIIP involves work details on Rikers Island, such as landscaping, painting, and other housekeeping responsibilities.

HIIP teammates begin their day with wake up at 4:45 A.M., followed by military marching drills, classes, and counseling sessions daily. After a full day of exercises, school, work details, counseling, and no television, they must be in bed by 10:00 P.M., when lights go out. Community service from HIIP includes details at the Partnership for the Homeless, various community roadways, which include graffiti removal and cleanup, and details for the U.S. Coast Guard. HIIP also facilitates weekly aftercare support groups within the community. HIIP has several integral rehabilitative components, including substance abuse seminars, life skills sessions, and network meetings.

Island Academy is a part of the academic and vocational segments, conducting pre-G.E.D., G.E.D., and construction workshops. John Jay College of Criminal Justice and LaGuardia Community College, both of the City University of New York system, have provided several important educational components such as computer training, pesticide removal, and asbestos removal, as well as providing college preparatory classes.

Source: New York Department of Correctional Services (2002).

first crimes. If most of these clients can acquire skills that make them more attractive to employers, then they can hold down jobs and provide for their families more effectively. The need to resort to crime to make ends meet will either not exist or be diminished. Employment is almost always a strong factor influencing whether former offenders will reoffend.

A Profile of Boot Camp Clientele

What are the characteristics of those who participate in boot camps? Most boot camp participants are prison-bound youthful offenders convicted of less serious, nonviolent crimes who have never been previously incarcerated. Depending upon the program, there are some exceptions. Participants may either be referred to these programs by judges or corrections departments or they may volunteer. They may or may not be accepted, and if they complete their programs successfully, they may or may not be released under supervision into their communities. For example, the State of Virginia operates a boot camp that was established by the 1990 General Assembly. The program runs for 13 weeks and includes military-style training, drill, and ceremony. It also includes short haircuts, no smoking, no speaking without permission, and limited telephone privileges. Program eligibility includes (1) conviction for a nonviolent offense; (2) no minimum age, although juveniles must have been tried and convicted as adults in criminal court; (3) no more than one prior incarceration stemming from a conviction on a state charge and cannot be classified as a state-responsible inmate; (4) mentally and physically capable of participating in all program activities or events; (5) mandatory and one year probation supervision upon release, including intensive supervision. The usual means of entering the Virginia boot camp are court referrals resulting from sentencing, and revocation of probation. In 2001, Virginia had 259 boot camp participants, with 108 graduates. Twenty youths earned their G.E.D. The remainder were terminated from the program because of medical or disciplinary problems or voluntary withdrawal (Virginia Department of Corrections 2002:1–2).

Although the programs operated in each jurisdiction vary in their minimum-age eligibility requirements, the age range targeted for adult boot camps is 25 to 35. Several programs have no age limitations. Voluntary participation is a requirement for enrollment in a majority of these programs. Further, recidivists and violent offenders are automatically excluded from about half of these programs.

Private Boot Camps

Increasingly, private organizations are operating several boot camps in different jurisdictions. Short-term private boot camps have helped thousand of teenagers during the past decade. Parents generally spend thousands of dollars for these short-term camps. The camps generally last from 14 to 90 days, and they include a highly structured schedule. Private boot camp activities include drills, military exercises, cooking, and some academics. Unlike state boot camps, private boot camps do not require a criminal record to attend. Most likely, teenagers in these private camps may face criminal charges that are not severe, but most judges will allow them to complete boot camp training in lieu of incarceration. Private behavioral modification programs are operated as an alternative to detention or youth corrections. Those qualifying for such private boot camps have the following characteristics:

1. Teens from ages 12–18.
2. Teens who are falling behind in school.
3. Teens abusing drugs and/or alcohol.
4. Teens that are defiant or who resist authority.
5. Teens who are on probation or have committed minor crimes (Boot Camps Advisor 2002).

Jail Boot Camps

Several jurisdictions operate boot camps through city or county jails. These are called **jail boot camps** and are short-term programs for offenders in a wide age range. For example, those jail boot camps in New York and New Orleans have age limits of 39 years and 45 years respectively. Most existing jail boot camps target probation or parole violators who may face revocation and imprisonment (Koch Crime Institute 2002).

The age range for inclusion is highly variable among jurisdictions. The jail boot camps are almost equally divided according to whether judges or jail officials select inmates for boot camp participation. Six of the ten programs permit voluntary withdrawal. Finally, all of these jail boot camps have drug education counseling and physical training. Most provide vocational education, work, and general counseling.

Four of these jail boot camps include women in special programs. New York City and Santa Clara, California, operate jail boot camps designed for women. The number of women participants is small. The bed capacity, for instance, ranges from 12 in Brazos, Texas, to 384 in Harris, Texas. The average length of stay ranges from 5 days to 275 days in Ontario, New York, and Orleans Parish, Louisiana, respectively. The American Correctional Association has established a set of standards whereby boot camps can be evaluated and rated. Professional standards are rigorously observed to ensure that all boot camps are operated without violating anyone's constitutional rights and in accordance with due process (Koch Crime Institute 2002).

The About Face Program is a male boot camp operated by the Orleans Parish Criminal Sheriff's Office in New Orleans, Louisiana. It provides an innovative approach toward helping male inmates learn how to redirect their lives. Admission to the program is by referral by a judge, family member, or attorney. Some inmates may be self-referred. All inmates admitted to the program are carefully screened and must adhere to a strict code of conduct.

The program was developed in 1986 and became the nation's first regimented life-changing program operated at the parish/county level. In 2003 the program consisted of three basic segments, each 12 weeks in length. A new class begins every 45 days. The initial phase operates within a strict boot camp environment that places heavy emphasis upon self-discipline, responsibility for one's actions, education, and some physical activity. All inmates are tested at entry to determine their educational level, the average of which for both reading and mathematics is fifth grade. The goal for each inmate is that he attain his GED. The second and third phases of the program operate according to a modified therapeutic community modality of substance abuse treatment. During these phases, individuals learn about addictions of all forms and are encouraged to confront the behaviors that led to their criminal activity. They are taught that alternatives exist and are urged to use these when faced with problematic situations that could lead them back into destructive behaviors. The emphasis is upon education, self-discipline, and some physical activity. Subsequently, inmates move into the re-entry phase, which emphasizes skills necessary for successful re-entry into society. At the end of their incarceration, inmates may be eligible to move to a work tier in which they are taught a skill they can use to attain gainful employment such as various food service jobs, auto mechanics and body repair, horticulture, and electrical and plumbing repair. The About Face Program also provides aftercare for its graduates, offering weekly drug and/or alcohol treatment meetings with a member of the counseling staff. The About Face Program has become one of the largest jail-based therapeutic communities in the country. A similar program for female inmates was established in 2001 (Kennedy 2003:78,81).

The Effectiveness of Boot Camps

Are boot camps or shock incarceration programs successful? Most programs use the recidivism rate standard of 30 percent or less as a measure of program success. If this standard is applied to existing adult boot camp programs, then the results are not particularly impressive. For instance, the Delaware Department of Corrections Boot Camp for adults includes a six-month program of intense, military-type discipline employing physical exercise, basic education, life and work skills development, and substance abuse treatment. Successful graduates are given intensive community supervision. However, a study of 255 graduates eighteen months following their graduation disclosed that the total rearrest rate was 78 percent, while the reincarceration rate was 49.5 percent. One positive outcome was that the offenses committed by these former boot camp clients were less serious than their previous offenses and posed a much lower risk to public safety. Nevertheless, the rearrest and reincarceration figures are indicative of program failure (Delaware Statistical Analysis Center 2001). Other states, such as Washington, have reported similar nonsignificant differences in recidivism rates between those placed in boot camps and those paroled through more traditional mechanisms (Poole and Slavick 1995).

While boot camps and shock incarceration programs have grown phenomenally during the 1990s, they have not have the desired effect on reducing recidivism among boot camp participants compared with those subjected to traditional nonincarcerative programs, such as parole and probation. However, it was found that some programs, such as the Nevada Program of Regimental Discipline, have therapeutic integrity. Therapeutic integrity has to do with the competency and commitment of staff members and their ability to implement the program as originally conceived. Thus, military training as such does not appear to be either a necessary or sufficient element in the rehabilitation of boot camp participants. But most boot camp participants changed positively and significantly in their attitudes toward themselves, those around them, and their future (McCorkle 1995:373).

Additional negative feedback concerning boot camps is a study of 331 North Carolina boot camp participants and a stratified random sample of 369 regular probationers who were tracked for a three-year period. Compared with standard probationers, boot camp clients had a significantly greater record of rearrests, particularly for drug offenses (Jones and Ross 1997b). We don't know how representative the North Carolina sample of boot camp participants is, but this evidence seems consistent with other negative reports about it.

Evaluation studies of boot camps and their effectiveness are sometimes faulted because of a failure to distinguish between different boot camps with conflicting goals (Colledge and Gerber 1998). Thus, if we evaluate certain boot camps using criteria that are inconsistent with the particular boot camp program goals or emphases, then our interpretations of program effectiveness will be erroneous or misleading. Thus, some researchers have devised a typology of boot camps to separate them according to the different goals of incapacitation, deterrence, punishment, reduction of cost and crowding, and rehabilitation. The Multiple Goal Typology has been devised by Dale Colledge and Jurg Gerber for this purpose. Colledge and Gerber applied their typology to existing boot camps and their program goals. They found that the typology enhanced the generalizability of evaluative research on boot camp facilities. Other researchers have made similar criticisms of boot camp research (Zhang 1998). The implication is that boot camps should be evaluated cautiously and continuously evaluated to identify elements that tend to influence program success (Stinchcomb and Terry 2001).

There are obvious exceptions among states regarding recidivism rates of boot camp graduates. Among New Hampshire boot camp graduates, for example, Bourque, Han, and Hill (1996:9) found a recidivism rate of only 17 percent during a two-year follow-up. This compared with a 47 percent recidivism rate among a comparable aggregate of New Hampshire parolees during the same study period. It would seem, therefore, that generalizations about boot camp effectiveness are unwarranted. This is because of the wide diversity of boot camp program elements among the states. Even in those states with high boot camp participant recidivism rates, such as Georgia, the attitude of public officials such as Governor Miller seems to be "I don't give a damn what they say, we're going to continue to do it in Georgia" (Burns 1996:46). Georgia Governor Miller also said that "Nobody can tell me from some ivory tower that you take a kid, you kick him in the rear end, and it doesn't do any good." And for good measure, the massive allocation of federal resources to boot camp programs from the 1994 Crime Bill has greatly underscored the political support from the federal government. Burns (1996:45) notes that William Jenkins, Jr., the Assistant Director of Justice Issues for the General Accounting Office, has stated that "most people on the Hill believe that boot camps ought to be expanded." For better or worse, this is precisely what is happening beyond 2000.

LANDMARK CASES IN PROBATION REVOCATION

Two-thirds of all probationers will violate one or more conditions of their probation programs or reoffend within two years of their probationary sentences. Some of these program violations are new crimes. Other violations may be technical ones, such as failing a drug or alcohol screen or missing curfew. Regardless of the seriousness of the program violation, whenever such probationers come to the attention of their supervising POs, certain actions may be taken, including a recommendation to revoke probation (Harris, Petersen, and Rapoza 2001).

For instance, a PO may determine that an offender has violated her curfew, but the probationer explains that she missed the bus to her apartment and had to take a later bus. The reason for missing the first bus was that her boss at work asked her to do some last-minute chores. Since the PO knows the offender has never violated curfew before and is otherwise law-abiding and conscientious, the PO may decide to overlook this minor infraction.

But in another case, suppose a PO appears at the residence of a probationer unannounced and proceeds to administer a drug test. The probationer tests positive for cocaine use. This is a serious violation and one that should not be overlooked. Almost always, the PO will make a report of this incident, which will be forwarded to the judge for possible revocation action.

It is important to note that *any* probation program violation may be grounds for revoking a person's probation program. But as can be seen from these two examples, which happen all too often, some program violations are more serious than others. Formally, a PO is under a duty to report any program infraction to the supervising probation office. There are specific rules that guide an officer's conduct in cases where probation program violations are apparent. In New York, for instance, the following rules govern PO actions:

RULES

1. Each local probation director shall establish local written procedures governing handling of new offense violations and technical violations of probationers under his or her department's supervision and court notification of alleged violation(s) of probation.

2. In the absence of court direction, a court shall be notified upon a conviction of crime, absconder status, or a significant violation of technical conditions of probation, within seven business days of the probation department's knowledge of the conviction or determination of absconder status or significant violation.

3. Where a probationer ceases to participate in or is unsuccessfully terminated from an alcohol or substance abuse program ordered as a condition of probation, the probation officer shall immediately notify the local probation director or his or her designee. Each director shall, within 90 calendar days, report the cessation or termination to the court, unless the probationer has resumed participation in an alcohol or substance abuse program, with the approval of the director.

4. These procedures provide for graduated sanctions. When determining the appropriate action to institute with respect to any violation of probation, the department shall consider which sanction is most suitable to achieve rehabilitation and/or offender accountability consistent with public safety.

5. Prior to recommending a revocation of probation, the probation department shall consider the feasibility of enlarging the conditions of probation, extending the probation term as authorized by law, and/or intensifying the level of supervision to address the misconduct consistent with public safety. When revocation is recommended, the department shall further consider whether to propose a sentence of imprisonment coupled with probation as authorized by law, where the original sentence of probation contained no condition of imprisonment (New York State Division of Probation and Correctional Alternatives 2002).

It is important to recognize the profound influence POs have on the lives of their probationer-clients. While POs themselves do not have the authority to revoke one's probation program, POs can *recommend* such revocations. Furthermore, POs can propose a sentence of imprisonment to the judge. Judges are at liberty to consider whatever is recommended by the supervising PO and choose to impose whatever is recommended or not impose it. Judges themselves are creative entities. They may impose additional conditions not originally contemplated or recommended by the PO. They have broad discretionary powers in this regard.

In instances where probationers have committed new crimes and have acquired new convictions, they will be sentenced by other judges accordingly. But these judgments do not prohibit judges who are the primary controllers of a probationer's program from imposing separate punishments of their own. Suppose a probationer commits a burglary while on probation. The probationer is caught and convicted. The judge sentences the probationer to four years in prison for the burglary conviction. In the meantime, the judge overseeing the probationer's program conducts a revocation hearing on the matter of the program violation (e.g., the criminal conviction). A decision from that revocation hearing may be that the probationer shall be returned to prison for a period of years.

Decisions Affecting Probation Revocation

Mempa v. Rhay (1967).   The first case involved a probation revocation rather than a parole revocation, although the decision eventually influenced parole proceedings significantly. Jerry Mempa was convicted of joyriding in a stolen vehicle on June 17, 1959. He was placed on probation for two years by a Spokane, Washington, judge. Several months later, Mempa was involved in a burglary on September 15, 1959. The county prosecutor in Spokane moved to have Mempa's probation revoked. Mempa admitted participating in the burglary. At his probation revocation hearing, the sole testimony about his involvement in the burglary came from his probation officer. Mempa was not represented by counsel, was not asked if he wanted counsel, and was not given an opportunity to offer statements in his own behalf. Furthermore, there was no cross-examination of the probation officer about his statements. The court revoked Mempa's probation and sentenced him to ten years in the Washington State Penitentiary.

Six years later, in 1965, Mempa filed a writ of *habeas corpus*, alleging that he had been denied a right to counsel at the revocation hearing. The Washington Supreme Court denied his petition, but the U.S. Supreme Court elected to hear it on appeal. The U.S. Supreme Court overturned the Washington decision and ruled in Mempa's favor. Specifically, the U.S. Supreme Court said Mempa was entitled to an attorney but was denied one. While the Court did not question Washington's authority to defer sentencing in the probation matter, it said that any indigent (including Mempa) is entitled at every stage of a criminal proceeding to be represented by court-appointed counsel, where "substantial rights of a criminal accused may be affected." Thus, the U.S. Supreme Court considered a probation revocation hearing to be a critical stage that falls within the due process provisions of the Fourteenth Amendment. In subsequent years, several courts also applied this decision to any **parole revocation hearing.**

Gagnon v. Scarpelli (1973).   Since the matter of representation by counsel was not addressed directly in Morrissey's case, and since it had been the subject of previous U.S. Supreme Court action in the case of Jerry Mempa, it was only a matter of time that the U.S. Supreme Court made a decision about a parolee's right to court-appointed counsel in a parole revocation proceeding. This decision was rendered by the U.S. Supreme Court in the case of *Gagnon v. Scarpelli* (1973), a year following the *Morrissey* ruling (*Morrissey v. Brewer,* 1972).

Gerald Scarpelli pled guilty to a charge of robbery in July 1965 in a Wisconsin court. He was sentenced to fifteen years in prison. But the judge suspended this sentence on August 5, 1965, and placed Scarpelli on probation for a period of seven years. The next day, August 6, Scarpelli was arrested and charged with burglary. His probation was revoked without a hearing and he was placed in the Wisconsin State Reformatory to serve his fifteen-year term. About three years later, Scarpelli was paroled. Shortly before his parole, he filed a *habeas corpus* petition, alleging that his probation revocation was invoked without a hearing and without benefit of counsel. Thus, this constituted a denial of due process. Following his parole, the U.S. Supreme Court acted on his original *habeas corpus* petition and ruled in his favor. Specifically, the U.S. Supreme Court said that Scarpelli was denied his right to due process because no revocation hearing was held and he was not represented by court-appointed counsel within the indigent claim. In effect, the Court, referring to *Morrissey v. Brewer* (1972), said that "a probation revocation, like parole revocation, is not a stage of a criminal prosecution, but does result in loss of liberty. . . . We hold that a probationer, like a parolee, is entitled to a preliminary hearing and a final revocation hearing in the conditions specified in *Morrissey v. Brewer.*"

The significance of this case is that it equated probation with parole as well as the respective revocation proceedings. While the Court did not say that all parolees and probationers have a right to representation by counsel in all probation and parole revocation proceedings, it did say that counsel should be provided in cases where the probationer or parolee makes a timely claim contesting the allegations. While no constitutional basis exists for providing counsel in all probation or parole revocation proceedings, subsequent probation and parole revocation hearings usually involve defense counsel if legitimately requested. The U.S. Supreme Court declaration has been liberally interpreted in subsequent cases.

Bearden v. Georgia (1983).   Other more recent cases of interest involving probationers and whether to revoke their respective programs are *Bearden v. Georgia* (1983) and *Black v. Romano* (1985). In the *Bearden* case, Bearden's probation was revoked by Georgia authorities because he failed to pay a fine and make restitution to his victim as required by the court. He claimed he was indigent, but the court rejected his claim as a valid explanation for his conduct. The U.S. Supreme Court disagreed. It ruled that probation may not be revoked in the case of indigent probationers who have failed to pay their fines or make restitution. They further suggested alternatives for restitution and punishments that were more compatible with the abilities and economic resources of indigent probationers such as community service. In short, the probationer should not be penalized where a reasonable effort has been made to pay court-ordered fines and restitution.

A more recent case illustrates that one's probation cannot be revoked because of an inability to pay child support, which was an original probation program requirement. In the case of *Gomez v. State* (1998), Gomez's probation was revoked for failure to make child support payments, which were a part of her probation program conditions. She appealed, contending that she lacked the ability to make such payments. Subsequent information revealed that she did, indeed, lack the ability to pay the child support. Her probation program was reinstated. Courts cannot revoke one's probation program because of an inability to pay restitution or other monetary obligations, such as child support, which are a part of one's probation conditions.

Black v. Romano (1985).   In the *Black v. Romano* (1985) case, a probationer had his probation revoked by the sentencing judge because of alleged program violations. The defendant had left the scene of an automobile accident, a felony in the jurisdiction where the alleged offense occurred. The judge gave reasons for the revocation decision, but did not indicate that he had considered any option other than incarceration. The U.S. Supreme Court ruled that judges are not generally obligated to consider alternatives to incarceration before they revoke an offender's probation and place him in jail or prison. Clearly, probationers and parolees have obtained substantial rights in recent years. U.S. Supreme Court decisions have provided them with several important constitutional rights that invalidate the arbitrary and capricious revocation of their probation or parole programs by judges or parole boards. The two-stage hearing is extremely important to probationers and parolees, in that it permits ample airing of the allegations against offender, cross examinations by counsel, and testimony from individual offenders.

United States v. Bachsian (1993).   Offender indigence does not automatically entitle them to immunity from restitution orders. In *United States v. Bachsian* (1993), Bachsian was convicted of theft. He was required to pay restitution for the merchandise still in his possession under the Victim Witness Protection Act. Bachsian claimed, however, that he was indigent and unable to make restitution. The 9th Circuit Court of Appeals declared in Bachsian's case that it was not improper to impose restitution orders on an offender at the time of sentencing, even if the offender was unable to pay restitution then. In this instance, records indicated that Bachsian was considered by the court as having a future ability to pay, based on a pre-sentence investigation report. Eventually, Bachsian would become financially able and in a position to make restitution to his victim. His restitution orders were upheld. Also, bankruptcy does not discharge an offenders obligation to make restitution, although the amount and rate of restitution payments may be affected (*Baker v. State* 1993; *State v. Hayes* 1993).

Other Probation Conditions and Revoking Probation

Conditions of probation, including victim restitution payments, are legitimate; however, there are situations when offenders may or may not be able to pay restitution declared by the court. In the case of *Bearden v. Georgia* (1983), an inability to pay restitution does not alone entitle judges to revoke one's probation program. In Bearden's case, the judge had not examined other options, such as community service, in lieu of the restitution order. More recent cases have upheld *Bearden*, and some interesting spins have been added. For instance, a Florida man, Moore, was convicted of purchasing a stolen truck (*Moore v. State* 1993). The original truck's owner, the victim, claimed that there were tools worth $500 in the truck when it was stolen initially by the one who sold the truck to Moore. Nevertheless, the judge imposed a sentence of probation, with a restitution condition that Moore repay the victim $500 for the loss of the tools. A Florida Court of Appeals set aside this condition, since it did not (1) show that the loss was caused by Moore's action; and (2) that there was a significant relation between the loss and the crime of purchasing a stolen vehicle.

In Illinois, a judge revoked the probation of Bouyer, who was ordered to pay $300 a month toward restitution (*People v. Bouyer* 2002). Bouyer fell behind in his court-ordered restitution payments because he was unable to find work. Although the judge expressed the opinion that Bouyer was not a threat to society, the judge also declared that Bouyer's probation deserved to be continued as long as Bouyer continued paying restitution. Subsequently, the judge revoked Bouyer's probation program and imprisoned Bouyer for a five-year term. Thus, it was clear that Bouyer's imprisonment was for failure to pay restitution. Bouyer appealed the probation revocation and an Illinois appeals court reversed the judge's decision. Probation programs cannot be terminated based solely on the fact that offenders are unable to pay restitution.

Probationers must permit their probation officers to search their persons, vehicles, or premises at any time, without a search warrant, if there is reasonable cause for such a search.   Almost every probation agreement contains a provision wherein the probationer agrees to unrestricted searches of his or her person, vehicle, or dwelling by the probation officer, at any time, day or night, provided that there is reasonable cause or suspicion. Ordinarily, citizens are protected from warrantless searches by law enforcement personnel if probable cause does not exist to justify these searches. However, probationers are serving sentences of probation, and these sentences are always conditional. In the case of *United States v. Stokes* (2002), Stokes was on probation in Montana for the crime of felony intimidation. His probation carried various conditions, including that he not consume alcoholic beverages, that he not possess firearms, and that he submit to searches of his person, vehicle, personal effects, and residence by the supervising probation officer, at any time, without a warrant, if there was reasonable cause for the search. During his probation, Stokes met a co-worker outside of his workplace, and the co-worker showed Stokes some firearms that the co-worker kept in his car. Later, the co-worker saw Stokes put something in the trunk of Stokes's car, and the co-worker heard a sound of metal hitting metal. When the co-worker went to his car after work, he discovered that the firearms were missing. He reported the theft to the police and identified Stokes by giving police his name and description. Subsequently, police officers found an abandoned vehicle at a local convenience store. The vehicle was traced to Stokes. When Stokes showed up to claim his car, the officer smelled alcohol and asked Stokes if he had been drinking. Stokes replied that he had "had a few drinks," and Stokes's probation officer was notified. The probation officer arrived at the scene, searched the car, and found a firearm, which turned out to be one of the missing weapons. Stokes was then arrested for possession of the firearm. Prior to his trial on the charge, Stokes moved to suppress the firearm, claiming that the probation officer did not have reasonable suspicion to search his car and therefore required a search warrant. The court disagreed, noting that Stokes had agreed to such searches when he accepted the probation sentence. Further, there was sufficient reasonable suspicion, in view of the co-worker previously showing firearms to Stokes, Stokes's suspicious behavior putting something in his car trunk, the subsequent theft report and identification of Stokes by his co-worker. Also, Stokes admitted to the police and the probation officer that he had been drinking. The court held the warrantless search to be reasonable.

Committing new offenses may not be sufficient grounds to terminate one's probation program.   In the case of *Conforti v. State* (2001), Conforti was a Florida probationer who was surreptitiously observed by an undercover police officer masturbating while sitting in his vehicle. Conforti was arrested and charged with this new offense. Subsequently, the probation officer alleged that this new offense was an unnatural and lascivious act and that because this was a clear violation of the law, Conforti's probation should be revoked. On the basis of testimony from the probation officer, the judge terminated Conforti's probation, and Conforti appealed. The appellate court reversed the judge's action, holding that the plain wording of the "lewd and lascivious act" statute included "with another person," and that it cannot be said that Conforti's masturbation was committed by a person with "another person."

Self-incriminating statements made by probationers can be used to revoke their probation programs if made during court-ordered polygraph examinations as a probation program condition.   In the case of *Marcum v. State* (1999), Marcum was originally placed on probation resulting from a conviction for sexual assault. One condition of his program was that he was to submit to periodic polygraph examinations. During one of these examinations, he admitted to two other sexual assaults that had been committed by him subsequent to his original conviction. A report was made by the polygraph operator to the probation officer and the probation officer recommended that Marcum's probation should be revoked. A judge revoked Marcum's probation. Marcum objected, contending that the statements he had made violated his *Miranda* rights. However, it was held that his statements were admissible and that he had freely and willingly entered into an agreement to make admissions, regardless of their incriminating nature.

Probation supervision fees may be imposed on probationers even if such fees are established following one's conviction and sentence.   In the case of *State v. Oliver* (1998), Oliver was a probationer who was required to pay probation office supervision fees. He objected to these fee payments, since they were established following his conviction and probation sentence. However, the court ruled that he must pay such fees, since they are imposed for the purpose of offsetting the costs of probation supervision and are not considered punitive. Fees imposed, even in an *ex post facto* manner, are lawful so long as they are not imposed for purposes of punishment.

Judicial Actions and Rights

Judges often impose various sentences that differ from those provided or recommended by statute. Sometimes these sentences contain special conditions of probation, involving victim compensation, community service, or participation in group or individual therapy. Below are some of the decisions made by judges at the time of sentencing and whether these decisions are valid.

Judges who impose probation in lieu of mandatory sentences for particular offenses may have their probation judgments declared invalid.   In a New York case, a plea bargain was worked out between the state and a defendant, Hipp (*People v. Hipp*, 1993). Hipp was determined by the court to be addicted to gambling. The nature of the conviction offense and the gambling addiction compel the Court under mandatory sentencing to prescribe a jail term as well as accompanying therapy for the addiction. In this instance, the judge simply accepted a plea agreement, accepting the defendant's guilty plea in exchange for a term of probation. The New York Court of Appeals overruled the judge in this case, indicating that New York statutes do not authorize a trial court to ignore clearly expressed and unequivocal mandatory sentencing provisions of the New York Penal Law. However, in Florida, a judge imposed probation on an offender convicted under a Habitual Offender Statute (*McKnight v. State*, 1993). McKnight, a habitual offender, was convicted of being a habitual felony offender. Ordinarily, this conviction carries a mandatory life-without-parole penalty. However, the judge in McKnight's case imposed probation. While the Florida Court of Appeals did not like the judge's decision, the Court upheld it anyway, supporting the general principle of judicial discretion.

Defendants can refuse probation if the court imposes probation as a sentence. In the case of Cannon, Cannon was convicted of criminally negligent homicide after entering a guilty plea (*Cannon v. State*, 1993). However, in open court, after probation was imposed, Cannon refused the probation and demanded to be incarcerated instead. The judge insisted that the probation sentence be accepted by Cannon. Cannon appealed. In an Alabama Court of Appeals decision, the Court upheld Cannon's right to refuse probation, and he was remanded to prison instead. This is not as bad as it sounds, however. Cannon had been incarcerated for some time prior to his criminally negligent homicide conviction. By accepting probation, Cannon would have been obligated to adhere to certain restrictive conditions for a period of time far in excess of the time remaining to be served. In effect, he had only a few more months to serve of his original sentence, counting the many months he had been behind bars before his trial and conviction. Thus, a probation sentence in Cannon's case would have involved a longer term of conditional freedom rather than the number of months remaining before his unconditional release from prison. The Court said that "Our holding merely recognizes a convict's right to reject the trial court's offer of probation if he or she deems it to be more onerous than a prison sentence."

Defendants cannot refuse probation if the court must impose probation under a mandatory probation statute.   Some states, such as Arizona, have **mandatory probation** for certain types of offenses, such as drug violations. In 1996 Arizona passed Proposition 200, which made probation mandatory for nonviolent persons convicted of personal possession or use of drugs and provided that they undergo court-supervised treatment. Thus, Proposition 200 would free up space in prisons for violent offenders. Subsequently, in the case of *State v. Tousignant* (2002), Tousignant pleaded guilty to solicitation to possess narcotics. Tousignant was placed on mandatory probation and ordered to participate in a drug court program. Tousignant later failed to contact his probation officer. Furthermore, he failed to attend the court-ordered drug treatment program, claiming that he had a right to reject probation and its conditions, including the court-ordered drug treatment program. The judge revoked Tousignant's probation and ordered him to prison. However, an appellate court reversed the judge, holding that (1) Tousignant could not refuse mandatory probation, and (2) the judge was not authorized to terminate Tousignant's program for the probation program violation. In this case, a statute provides that anyone who violates his or her probation program shall have new conditions established by the court. These new probation conditions may include intensified drug treatment, community service, intensive probation, house arrest, or any other such sanctions short of incarceration.

Judges may revoke one's probation program or supervised release and impose a new sentence, which may include imprisonment, or an extension of the original term of probation. A federal probationer, Levi, was under supervised release (*United States v. Levi*, 1993). During his first 11 months of supervised release, Levi committed one or more probation violations. The Judge revoked his probation and declared that he must spend the remaining 13 months incarcerated. The 8th Circuit Court of Appeals upheld the judge's action, since the 13-month imprisonment was within the two-year sentence of probation originally imposed by the same judge.

In the case of *United States v. Kremer* (2002), Kremer was placed on supervised release for a specified term, which was less than the maximum probationary term as provided by statute. Subsequently, Kremer was found in violation of his probation and the judge imposed an additional probation condition of house arrest as well as extending his probationary term. Kremer appealed, arguing that the judge did not have the power to change the original probation conditions or extend his probationary period. An appellate court upheld the judge's decision, holding that the judge may extend a term of supervised release if less than the maximum authorized term was previously imposed and that the judge is authorized to modify, reduce, or enlarge the conditions of supervised release.

Probation officers cannot compel their probationer-clients to perform services, participate in programs, or do work apart from whatever has been specified in probation orders. Under Texas law, for instance, probation orders or conditions imposed on probationers that are in addition to one's program requirements and conditions are unconstitutional. In the case of *Lemon v. State* (1993), Lemon, a probationer convicted of misappropriation of property, was required by a judge to perform community service. However, it would be up to the probation officer to determine the nature of the community service to be performed. This feature of the sentence was appealed by the probationer. The Texas Court of Appeals reversed this condition of his probation, since the nature of community service had not been articulated by the judge. It is improper for correctional officers to determine the nature of one's community service to be performed under a sentence of probation with conditions.

In *Wade v. State* (1998), Wade's probation office advised Wade that he must complete a certain amount of community service by a specified deadline. However, the deadline was one not originally imposed by the sentencing court. The deadline was beyond Wade's probationary term, and when it expired, the community service had not been completed. The probation office moved to have Wade's probation revoked. The court ruled that the probation office did not have the authority to impose a deadline upon Wade inconsistent with what the court had originally declared. Therefore, his probation could not be revoked for failure to comply with a probation office–imposed deadline for community service.

Probationers who are indigent and are denied counsel in their probation revocation hearings cannot have their probation revoked. In *State v. Christian* (1999), Christian was arrested for a probation violation, and a revocation hearing was scheduled. Christian was incarcerated and applied for court-appointed counsel because he was indigent. The court denied him counsel, contending that Christian had previously been employed and was not indigent. The appellate court disagreed, saying that there was sufficient evidence to conclude that Christian was indigent and could not afford telephone calls to contact attorneys whose names he had been given. Because Christian had been denied due process by being denied counsel when indigent, his probation program was reinstated.

SUMMARY

Prosecutors have several options in the prosecution of offenders. They can decide to dismiss cases, or they may recommend pretrial diversion. Pretrial diversion is a conditional nonincarcerative option where offenders must comply with various terms for a specified period, usually a year. Successful completion of diversion may result in dropping charges against defendants and removing the record of arrest from their file. For less serious cases, alternative dispute resolution is used, whereby cases are diverted to civil courts for disposition. Impartial judges, often retired judges or part-time attorneys, function as arbiters to settle disputes between criminals and victims, including restitution and/or community service.

Criminal charges filed against suspects do not always mean those suspects will be prosecuted. However, whenever prosecutions are pursued against defendants and convictions are obtained, it does not automatically mean that the convicted offenders will be incarcerated. About two-thirds of all convicted offenders in the United States receive a sentence of probation. There are several types of probation. These include standard probation, probation with conditions, and intensive supervised probation. Standard probation is similar to diversion, where probationers are required to comply with minimal behavioral conditions and restrictions. Probation officers may supervise as many as 200 or more probationers under standard probation. Standard probation is ordinarily imposed as a sentence where offenders are nonviolent and inclined to benefit by remaining free in their communities to provide for themselves and their dependents. Standard probation with conditions means that besides the standard features of one's probation program, additional requirements of probation have been added. These usually include restitution, community service, fine payments, and/or required participation in individual or group counseling. Sometimes vocational programming is required. Depending upon the jurisdiction, some convicted offenders may refuse probation if it is offered. Probation is sometimes refused because the offender would rather do time in jail or prison for a relatively short period rather than be subjected to stringent probation conditions in their communities. In some cases, however, probation is mandatory and must be accepted by the convicted offender.

In less than 10 percent of all probation cases, some offenders will receive more intensive supervision. Thus, intensive supervised probation subjects these offender-clients to more frequent face-to-face visits with their supervising probation officers, more frequent drug/alcohol checks, curfew, and various other conditions. Those supervised under ISP are considered more likely to recidivate. They often have prior drug problems, or they may have serious prior criminal records. Thus, it is in their best interests as well as for community safety and security that they are closely monitored for a period of time.

Probation was introduced in 1841 in the United States by John Augustus, a Boston shoemaker and philanthropist. Currently, all jurisdictions in the United States have probation programs. The primary functions of probation are rehabilitation, community reintegration, deterrence, crime control, and punishment, although some citizens believe that any punishment not including incarceration is not punitive. However, behavioral restrictions and conditions of probation suggest that probation is, indeed, punitive. Recidivism among probationers varies according to the particular program. California has a high recidivism rate of 65 percent among its probationers. However, most California probationers receive little or no direct supervision and control from probation officers. The principal advantages of probation are that (1) offenders remain free in their communities to perform functional work roles and (2) the taint of criminality and the criminal label is largely avoided, especially when contrasted with those who are incarcerated for various periods in jails and prisons.

Several probation programs were described. The community control program in Florida is one of the more ambitious probation programs in the United States. It uses electronic monitoring and global positioning satellites to monitor offender whereabouts. Program eligibility requirements are stringent, although those admitted into this program have been reasonably successful when subsequently released back into their communities unsupervised.

Some offenders are sentenced to shock probation. Shock probation originated during the 1960s and involves the temporary incarceration of particular offenders in a local jail, usually for periods ranging from 30 days to 120 days. After these short incarceration periods, these offenders are brought back before the sentencing judge where they are often sentenced to standard probation. It is unusual for offenders to know when they are sentenced to shock probation, since the incarceration experience is believed to be sufficiently traumatic to cause offenders to remain law-abiding if subsequently placed in traditional probation programs. Shock probation is considered one type of creative sentence. Other variations are split sentencing, intermittent sentencing, jail as a condition of probation, and mixed sentencing.

Some offenders, particularly youthful offenders, require more structure and discipline in their lives. Many of these offenders are sentenced to boot camps for short periods. Boot camps are military-like programs that require clients to follow orders, drill, and participate in required educational and/or vocational programming. Several boot camp programs were described. Boot camps were originally regarded as a panacea for preventing further crime and delinquency, because of their disciplinary features. However, boot camps have some amount of recidivism and are believed by some authorities to be about as effective as probation in its different forms. Other professionals believe that boot camps, if operated properly, can make a significant difference in one's life. Thus, there are mixed opinions about boot camp effectiveness thus far.

When probationers violate one or more conditions of their probation programs, they may be reported to the original sentencing judge who retains jurisdiction over them. They are subject to a probation revocation hearing, where it is decided whether their probation program should be revoked. The U.S. Supreme Court has decided several probation revocation cases and has vested probationers with certain rights. These include the right to a two-stage probation revocation hearing, where their guilt must be determined, together with an appropriate penalty. The penalty imposed may or may not be incarceration. In many instances, probation program violators are simply placed under more restrictive supervision or intensive supervised probation. Other rights include the fact that probationers cannot be disqualified from probation programs because of their inability to pay program operating fees, failure to make restitution or fine payments, or failure to meet other financial obligations. Judges must consider other options rather than incarceration for certain of these offenders.

Suspected probation violators also have the right to testify in their own behalf, to have witnesses testify at their revocation hearings, and to cross-examine those testifying against them. They also have the right to a written notice of charges against them, and they must be advised in writing of the reasons for their probation program termination, if that occurs. State variations in probation revocation hearings were examined to illustrate the many different grounds that may be used for revoking one's probation program.

QUESTIONS FOR REVIEW

1. What is diversion and what are some positive benefits of it for offenders?

2. What is alternative dispute resolution? Which types of offenders are most likely to be offered alternative dispute resolution if that is an option in any given jurisdiction? What are the weaknesses and strengths of ADR for particular offenders?

3. What is meant by probation? How does standard probation differ from intensive supervised probation?

4. What are some functions of probation? How well does probation achieve these functions?

5. Who qualifies for diversion and probation? What are some of the offender characteristics favoring a diversion or probation decision?

6. Who invented probation in the United States? Generally, how successful is probation in terms of the recidivism of various probationers throughout the states and federal system?

7. What are some of the major features of intensive supervised probation programs? What is the community control program used by Florida? What are some of its primary characteristics?

8. What are boot camps? Who are the most likely boot camp clientele and how effective are boot camps at reducing recidivism?

9. What is shock probation? What are the general goals of shock probation? How does shock probation differ from other types of split sentencing?

10. What are three leading U.S. Supreme Court cases pertaining to probation revocation? What is the significance of each of these cases? Do all states follow the same probation revocation rules? Why or why not? What are some examples of interstate differences pertaining to probation revocation?

SUGGESTED READINGS

Backlar, Patricia and David L. Cutler. *Ethics in Community Health Care: Commonplace Concerns.* Norwell, MA: Kluwer Plenum, 2002.

Bazemore, Gordon and Mark Schiff, eds. *Restorative Community Justice: Repairing Harm and Transforming Communities.* Cincinnati, OH: Anderson Publishing Company, 2001.

Clear, Todd and Eric Cadora. *Community Justice.* Belmont, CA: Wadsworth/Thomson Learning, 2003.

Farrall, Stephen. *Rethinking What Works with Offenders: Probation, Social Context, and Desistance from Crime.* Portland, OR: Willan Publishing, 2002.

Mosher, Clayton J., Terance D. Miethe, and Dretha M. Phillips. *The Mismeasure of Crime.* Thousand Oaks, CA: Pine Forge Press, 2002.

INTERNET CONNECTIONS

American Arbitration Association
http://www.adr.org/index2.1.jsp

Association of Pretrial Professionals of Florida
http://www.appf.org/

Colorado Council of Mediators
http://www.coloradomediation.org/

CPR Institute for Dispute Resolution
http://www.cpradr.org/home1.htm

History of American Probation and Parole Associaton
http://www.appa-net.org/about%20appa/history.htm

Massachusetts Council on Family Mediation
http://www.divorcenet.com/ma-mediators.html

Montana Mediation Association
http://www.mtmediation.org/

National Association for Community Mediation
http://www.nafcm.org/

National Association of Pretrial Services Agencies
http://www.napsa.org/

National Association of Probation Executives
http://www.napchome.org/

Pretrial Procedures
http://www.uaa.alaska.edu/just/just110/courts2.html

Pretrial Services Resource Center
http://www.pretrial.org/

Courtesy of Custer Youth Correctional Center.

| **Chapter Objectives** | *After reading this chapter, the following objectives will be realized:* |

1. Examining community-based corrections, the purposes of these programs, and some of the major characteristics of community-based programs.
2. Defining community corrections acts and their impact on local community corrections programming.
3. Describing the philosphy of community corrections, as well as the goals, characteristics, and functions of community corrections programs.
4. Describing electronic monitoring, including various types of monitoring systems, as well as the goals, strengths, and weak-

nesses of electronic monitoring and a description of its clientele.
5. Describing house arrest or home confinement and the conditions under which it is used as a community-based sanction.
6. Examining day reporting centers and their uses.
7. Describing the use of community service orders, restitution, and fine payments.
8. Discussing selected issues related to community-based corrections, including the NIMBY syndrome, offender needs versus public safety, and services delivery.

INTRODUCTION

• *In Texas, at least, they have what is known as "super-intensive supervision" for sex of-fenders as a part of their probation and parole services. Probationer/parolee clients are supposed to wear electronic monitoring devices as a part of their program requirements. These devices enable supervising probation/parole officers (POs) to detect their where-abouts or determine whether they are at home. In 2001, there were 10 to 15 parolees as-signed to the super-intensive supervision program or SISP. One of these clients was Lawrence James Napper, 42, a convicted rapist. Napper was supposedly being tracked by a satellite in outer space, known as a Global Positioning Satellite System (GPSS). Accord-ing to authorities, the GPSS is capable of monitoring whenever clients leave their homes, what streets they travel, how fast they drive, and where they park their cars. In the fall of 2000, Napper was tracked by the GPSS on at least eight different occasions during a two-month period from October to December cruising through a south-central Houston neigh-borhood that was not a part of his approved daily activity schedule. Following the period of being tracked by the GPSS, Napper was removed from that program and affixed with an electronic bracelet as a part of an electronic monitoring program. This electronic bracelet would enable authorities to determine only whether Napper was at home.*

In February 2001, a 6-year-old boy was abducted from a convenience store parking lot in the south-central neighborhood that Napper had been cruising. The boy had left his babysitter's home and was walking to the store with his 8-year-old brother and some friends when a stranger lured him into a car with the promise of a $10 bill. Police later determined that the boy was taken to a residence where he was tied to a bed overnight and sexually assaulted. He was released the following day and walked home. An anony-mous tip several days later led to Napper, and the child identified him from a lineup. Additionally, DNA at the scene of the assault matched Napper's. The main question in the minds of authorities was, How did this happen in the first place? Wasn't the GPSS supposed to keep track of Napper's movements? Shouldn't the travel into the prohibited neighborhood have been reported? Unfortunately, none of this information was ever re-layed to Napper's parole officer. Therefore, early intervention couldn't have been ac-complished before the 6-year-old boy was assaulted.

The chairman of the Texas Board of Criminal Justice, Alfred "Mac" Stringfellow, ordered an internal audit of the GPSS program. Pulling out old information from the fall of 2000, tracking charts showed that, indeed, Napper had traveled through the forbid-den neighborhood in question, and on several occasions. Why this information was never reported by officials working with the GPSS equipment is unclear. More than a few people are under the mistaken impression that electronic monitoring of any kind is a device that can prevent someone from doing something. Rather, electronic monitoring, even GPSS, is capable only of tracking an offender's whereabouts and not controlling his or her behavior. Such devices are useful for POs who are interested in determining whether their clients are in their homes during evening hours or if they are in desig-nated locations where they are supposed to be. These devices were never intended to control one's behavior. Who is at fault in Napper's case? What policies and protocols should have been in place to report Napper's travel into restricted areas? Do we expect too much from electronic monitoring? What do you think? [Adapted from the Associ-ated Press, "Monitoring Did Not Stop Sex Offender from Cruising," June 4, 2002].

• *She didn't look like a murderess. Although it is impossible for anyone to describe what a murderess or murderer should look like. Marie Noe, a 70-year-old mother of ten, is a con-fessed murderess. She killed one of her children in 1949. Over the next twenty years, she killed seven more of her children. For some unexplained reason, two children were per-mitted to live. They have since died of natural causes. In June 1999, Marie Noe admitted that she smothered the eight children, earlier diagnosed with sudden infant death syn-drome or SIDS. It was fifty years ago that Mrs. Noe smothered her first infant, leading police investigators to believe that the baby had simply died in the crib. Crib deaths were increasingly common during the 1950s and 1960s. Later, SIDS was the expression coined to describe such deaths. In subsequent years, more than a few parents escaped prosecution as murderers of their own infants because of SIDS. The cases of the deaths of the Noe children were never closed. Investigators suspected that factors other than chance were at work in the deaths of eight infants from a single family. In 1998 a book was published, entitled* The Death of Innocents, *about sudden infant death syndrome. Mrs. Noe's children and their deaths were described in the book. Investigators renewed their efforts to consider Mrs. Noe as the murderess when a retired Philadelphia medical examiner expressed his suspicions about her role in her infants' deaths. Under questioning and as the result of a liberal plea bargain with state authorities, Mrs. Noe confessed to four of the murders. She could not remember the other four murders, although she could not deny that she had killed her other children. One by one, the judge asked Mrs. Noe if she had killed each child named. She simply declared, "Yes," to each question. She offered no explanation for why she had killed the children. Police were unable to disclose a viable motive. The judge was exceptionally lenient in Mrs. Noe's case. He sentenced the 70-year-old to probation for twenty years. Furthermore, she must serve the first five years of her probation sentence under house arrest and electronic monitoring. She must also undergo mental health treatment sessions with a psychiatrist to determine the cause of her repeated homicides. An explanation by the court suggested that the light sentence had to do with the unusual circumstances and age of the case. Further, it was not believed by the defense attorney, David Rudenstein, that "we have the heart of a killer." Mrs. Noe has spent the last ten years caring for her wheelchair-ridden husband, Arthur Noe, 77. He was not charged in the case and has always believed his wife was innocent of any wrongdoing, at least until she confessed to these crimes. Authorities believe that they can learn much from studying Mrs. Noe. The Philadelphia District Attorney, Lynne Abraham, said, "We needed to get this matter finalized. Is it perfect? We don't always get a perfect outcome." Deputy District Attorney Charles F. Gallagher said, "It's important for the medical community and the legal community that she admit these murders and . . . something good will come out of this analysis." If this were a 25-year-old male serial killer who murdered eight people, do you think the system would impose probation, house arrest, and electronic monitoring? What do you think?* [Adapted from Jennifer Brown, "'Heart of a Killer': Woman Pleads Guilty to Killing Eight of Her Young Children Decades Ago," June 29, 1999].

• *It occurred in Upper Darby, Pennsylvania. A man walked into a bank and told a teller that he had a bomb. He demanded money or he would detonate the bomb. The teller handed him $1,500 and he walked out. Less than two hours later, police had identified and arrested former Mayor Daniel F. Devlin, 51. What would prompt someone like Devlin to rob a bank? For starters, Devlin lost the recent mayor's race after serving a previous four-year term. Evidently, Devlin became depressed because of the lost income from the mayor's position. At about the same time, he lost his position with the Pennsylvania State Lottery. Eventually, he surrendered to police and returned the money. When he robbed the bank, he wore sunglasses and a baseball cap. He had no bomb. Apparently, no one in the bank recognized him, and it was only from surveillance cameras that others were able to identify him. Devlin was charged with terrorism, robbery, and related charges. He was released on a $15,000 bond. What do you think should happen to Devlin? It is clear that he had no criminal record prior to this bizarre activity. Is Devlin a good candidate for a community corrections program?* [Adapted from the Associated Press, "Ex-Mayor Charged with Robbing Bank," December 19, 1997].

This chapter examines community corrections acts and the types of programs that are encompassed within community corrections. The first part of this chapter defines community corrections acts, which most frequently enable communities to establish various programs for probationers and others who serve some or all of their sentences in the community. Several key elements of community corrections acts are described.

The philosophy, goals, and functions of community corrections are described. The general thrust of community corrections is toward rehabilitation and reintegration, seeking to preserve an offender's contact with the community. Community corrections seeks also to heighten the offender's accountability and preserve public safety. Rehabilitative elements include participating in various programs and receiving services. These programs and services are geared to addressing particular offender problems, such as illiteracy, unemployment, and addictions to various substances. These programs and services are especially valuable to offenders because, often, they are not made available in prisons and jails. Offenders may hold jobs, support their families and other dependents, pay restitution to victims, and participate in relevant programming of an educational or counseling nature, depending on their particular conviction offenses.

This chapter next describes several important community corrections programs, including electronic monitoring and home confinement or house arrest. Often, electronic monitoring and home confinement are used in tandem, and offenders must abide by curfews and other related conditions. Electronic monitoring involves the use of technology and electronic mechanisms, such as electronic wristlets or anklets, that emit signals that can be received by probation or parole officers at central office locations. Electronic monitoring technology may make use of the offender's telephone for programmed contact. Or supervising officers may simply drive by an offender's residence and capture electronic signals emitted from these devices, which are worn by offenders. Home confinement requires that offenders stay in their homes during particular hours, especially at night. Offenders must observe curfews or particular times when they must be at their residences. Failure to abide by these curfews may result in the termination of a probation program. The overall purpose of electronic monitoring is to assist probation or parole officers in the verification of a person's whereabouts at particular times. The specific behaviors of offenders, criminal or otherwise, are uncontrolled by either electronic monitoring or house arrest. Thus, these programs deter more than prevent additional crime by participating clients.

Another community corrections program is the day reporting center, where offenders may receive employment assistance and/or employment referrals or be tested for drugs, alcohol, and other controlled substances.

Besides these programs, offenders may have additional conditions, such as fine payments, community service orders, or restitution requirements. Fines are not assessed against offenders in any consistent fashion. Furthermore, collecting fines has proven problematic for certain types of offenders who may be unemployed or underemployed. Thus, although all criminal statutes provide for fines, their use varies according to the offender and the jurisdiction. Community service orders involve manual labor from convicted offenders who are unable to obtain legitimate employment. They may be obligated to clean city parks or do other labor, where a portion of their earnings is set aside to defray probation program operating costs. In many instances, a portion of their earnings from community service may be applied toward restitution to victims.

The chapter concludes with an examination of several important issues pertaining to community corrections. One of these issues is the NIMBY syndrome, which means "not in my backyard." This issue has to do with the opposition to community corrections programs being established within communities. Some residents believe that having such programs located within their communities will lower property values and in some way endanger residents because of the increased presence of convicted offenders. Government interests contend that these community programs are valuable rehabilitative and reintegrative tools and that offenders must have the chance to prove themselves and receive needed services.

Another issue pertains to whether community corrections is actually a punishment. How much of a punishment is it to require some offenders to stay home instead of go to prison or jail? Compelling arguments for and against community corrections as a punishment are examined. Ultimately, a balance is sought between respecting community interests and the rehabilitative and reintegrative potential of community corrections programs. Essentially, this conflict is over the needs of offenders versus the public safety of community residents. Another issue is the adequacy of services delivery. What services should be provided to offenders, and how will these services be delivered? Should private interests become involved in the provision of such services? Another issue addresses special-needs offenders and the unique problems they pose for those supervising them. What types of special-needs offenders benefit from community corrections programs? The nature and types of services for special-needs offenders are examined.

COMMUNITY CORRECTIONS ACTS AND COMMUNITY CORRECTIONS

Community Corrections Act Defined

A **community corrections act** is the enabling medium by which jurisdictions establish local community corrections agencies, facilities, and programs. It is a statewide mechanism through which funds are granted to local units of government to plan, develop, and deliver correctional sanctions and services at the local level. The overall purpose of this mechanism is to provide local sentencing options in lieu of imprisonment in state institutions. Community corrections acts in various states are designed to make it possible to divert certain prison-bound offenders into local, city-, or county-level programs where they can receive treatment and assistance rather than imprisonment. In selected jurisdictions, such as Ohio, "community solutions acts" have been passed. In 2001, for instance, Ohio enacted the Community Solutions Act for the purpose of expanding and supporting recruitment efforts of the state to attract faith-based personnel and organizations to assist indigents, troubled juveniles, and ex-jail and prison inmates with drug/alcohol problems (Watts 2002:84). It should be noted that community solutions acts are different from community corrections acts, in that there are no provisions for supervising offenders in communities under the correctional rubric. Community solutions acts, therefore, target persons in need of financial or social assistance, counseling, and other forms of treatment for their problems. In contrast, community corrections acts enable communities to establish agencies to supervise offenders on a continuous basis.

Eight Elements for Community Corrections Effectiveness

Eight common elements essential to community corrections acts' success are:

1. Prison/jail-bound offenders are targeted, rather than adding additional punishments to those who would have otherwise remained in the community.

2. Financial subsidies are provided to local government and community agencies.

3. A performance factor is implemented to ensure funds are used for the act's specific goals.

4. Local advisory boards in each local community assess local needs, propose improvements in the local criminal justice system, and educate the general public about the benefits of alternative punishments.

5. Advisory boards submit annual criminal justice plans to the local government.

6. There is a formula for allocating funds.

7. Local communities participate voluntarily and may withdraw at any time.

8. There are restrictions on funding high-cost capital projects as well as straight probation services.

The Philosophy of Community Corrections

The philosophy of community corrections is to provide offenders with a rehabilitative and reintegrative environment where their personal abilities and skills are improved. Community-based programs established through community corrections acts include halfway houses, outreach centers, furlough monitoring facilities for parolees, and halfway-in houses. The objectives of these programs are intended to heighten offender accountability through effective community networking in an effort to promote community justice (Evans 1999:73).

Offender Reintegration. **Community-based corrections programs** assist probationers in becoming reintegrated into their communities, although parolees are assisted by such programs as well. Some offender-clients, such as compulsive gamblers, may not need to be reintegrated as much as they need to be helped with some type of addiction problem, whether it be drugs, alcohol, or gambling. Compulsive gambling is a growing problem among probationers, and this addiction leads to further crimes, such as embezzlement, fraud, robberies, and larcenies. When compulsive gambling is combined with drug and/or alcohol addiction, the relation between gambling and crime increases by five or ten times. Thus, community corrections is the ideal means whereby treatment and services can be provided for addicted clients (Clear and Corbett 1999).

Alleviating Prison and Jail Overcrowding.   Community-based programs also help alleviate prison and jail overcrowding by accepting those offenders who are not dangerous and pose the least risk to society. Of course, the difficulty here is attempting to sort those most dangerous offenders from those least dangerous. Community corrections acts recognize that:

1. States should continue to house violent offenders in secure facilities

2. Judges and prosecutors need a variety of punishments

3. Local communities cannot develop these programs without additional funding from such legislatures (Huskey 1984:5).

Characteristics of Community Corrections Programs

Community-based corrections programs vary in size and scope among communities, but they tend to have in common the following characteristics:

1. One or more large homes or buildings located within the residential section of the community with space to accommodate between 20 and 30 residents are provided within walking distance of work settings and social services.

2. A professional and paraprofessional staff on call for medical, social, or psychological emergencies.

3. A system is in place for heightening staff accountability to the court concerning offender progress.

4. Community-based program administrators have the authority to oversee offender behaviors and enforce compliance with their probation conditions.

5. These programs have job referral and placement services where paraprofessionals or others act as liaisons with various community agencies and organizations to facilitate offender job placement.

6. Administrators of these programs are available on-premises on a 24-hour basis for emergency situations and spontaneous assistance for offenders who may need help.

Goals of Community Corrections

The goals of community corrections programs include (1) facilitating offender reintegration, (2) fostering offender rehabilitation, (3) providing an alternative range of offender punishments, and (4) heightening offender accountability.

Counseling services are offered in a variety of community corrections programs.
Courtesy of Custer Youth Correctional Center.

Facilitating Offender Reintegration.   Although the major aims of community corrections have been strongly linked with diversion, advocacy, and reintegration, the emphasis upon reintegration has been replaced in recent years by an emphasis upon offender control, surveillance, and monitoring. There seems to be a new emphasis upon punitive-restrictive restraint rather than therapeutic-integrative considerations.

Fostering Offender Rehabilitation.   Community-based corrections programs assist first-time nonviolent offenders. Through probation, diversion, halfway houses, and parole, community-based programs are thought to have considerable success in rehabilitating offenders. The importance of job development and assistance in job placement is underscored by the fact that those without jobs or who are underemployed tend to recidivate and cause programs to be less effective.

Offender Punishment.   Community corrections is a continuation of punishment. Not all punishment must be served in institutions such as prisons or jails. One aim of community corrections is to punish offenders. Victim compensation and restitution are used to compel offenders to repay their victims for losses sustained as the result of crimes.

Heightening Offender Accountability.   Community corrections strongly emphasizes heightening offender accountability by ensuring that one's program conditions are complied with fully. Criticisms that community corrections programs are soft on offenders because of the lack of institutionalization are simply without merit. Probation or parole revocation are consequences that await those unwilling to comply with their program requirements. Support services and various community agencies are designed to enable offenders to seek needed treatment, education, or counseling (Robinson 2001).

It is significant to note that community corrections programs are not unique to the United States. In fact, many countries throughout the world have established community corrections programs in recent years. The Scandinavian countries of Sweden, Finland, Denmark, and Norway have evolved different types of community corrections programs for offenders. Although there are several differences among these programs, the overall goals of U.S. programs are generally shared by them (Kyvsgaard 2001a, 2001b; Lappi 2001; Larsson and Dullum 2001; Traskman 2001).

Functions of Community Corrections

Community corrections has the following functions: (1) monitoring and supervising clients, (2) employment assistance, (3) alleviating prison and jail overcrowding, (4) vocational and educational training, and (5) public safety.

Monitoring and Supervising Clients.   Placing offenders in their communities requires that one or more agencies accept responsibility for their supervision. This supervision is more or less intense, since probation or parole programming usually contains conditions requiring treatments or services. Monitoring may include electronic monitoring or home confinement, together with frequent face-to-face visits with POs (Johnson et al. 1994). Close supervision of offenders enhances their compliance with program requirements.

Employment Assistance.   Community corrections provides offender-clients with job assistance. Often, these clients do not know how to fill out simple job application forms. One successful employment assistance program tailored for female offenders was established in Pennsylvania in 1974 (Arnold 1992). Known as the **Program for Female Offenders, Inc.,** the program was guided by two goals: reforming female offenders and creating economically independent women. The program started with a job placement service. Training centers were eventually created and operated by different counties on a nonprofit basis. Training center offerings have included remedial math instruction, English instruction, and clerical classes such as word processing, data entry, and telecommunications skill training. Psychological counseling has also been provided for those women with various types of problems.

Alleviating Jail and Prison Overcrowding.   Community-based corrections functions to alleviate jail and prison overpopulation. One short-term benefit is reducing jail and prison populations by diverting a substantial number of offenders to community-based supervision. A long-term benefit is that offenders in community-based programs tend to have lower rates of recidivism compared with paroled offenders who have served time in prison.

Vocational and Educational Training.   Community corrections agencies help offender-clients in many useful ways. Many of these agencies provide education services for offenders with language deficiencies or who have dropped out of school previously. Many offenders do not know how to fill out job placement forms or applications. Community corrections staff offer assistance in this regard. In addition, offender-clients may participate in study release through local schools. A task force in Arizona investigated the literacy level of Arizonans and found that over 400,000 of them were functionally illiterate. Another 500,000 did not have a high school diploma. About 60 percent of Arizona's prison inmates had a reading level at about the sixth grade (O'Connell and Power 1992). Arizona has attempted to remedy this situation by implementing L.E.A.R.N. labs, or Literacy, Education, and Reading Network. The general program purpose is to raise the educational and reading level of offender-clients so that they will be more competitive in the workplace.

   One of the problems facing many parolees, however, is that they are not as marketable and cannot find work equivalent with that performed before they were originally arrested and convicted, regardless of how much they retrain and receive employment assistance. A survey of ex-inmates suggests that their earning power as parolees will be between 10 to 30 percent lower than it was before they were originally arrested. For some offenders, especially older and white-collar offenders, their future earnings may be far lower (Western, Kling, and Weiman 2001).

Public Safety.   Crime control is a major concern for community corrections administrators. An obvious concern of community residents is for their safety in view of the fact that recently convicted felons are roaming their neighborhoods more or less freely and in relatively large numbers. Although probationers and parolees have relatively high recidivism rates, recidivism most often is in the form of a program violation rather than the commission of a new crime. Contributing to high recidivism rates among parolees is ready access to drugs and relapses among those with former drug dependencies (Hagan and Petty 2001). Also, public safety is jeopardized by ineffective planning by many probation and parole departments and where there are insufficient or even nonexistent services to meet the needs of the growing probationer and parolee populations (Hammett, Roberts, and Kennedy 2001). Female parolees are particularly in need of services, especially pertaining to drug treatment and family counseling (Richie 2001).

Numbers of Community Corrections Clients

In 2000, there were approximately 1,800,000 offenders in state community corrections programs (Maguire and Pastore 2002). About 85 percent of these offenders were obligated to pay supervision fees, court costs, and fines. Thirty percent were ordered to pay restitution to victims, and 25 percent had to perform community service. Forty-one percent of these offenders had to participate in mandatory substance abuse treatment programs and were subject to random drug and alcohol checks. Less than 5 percent of these clients were restricted in their movements about the community, with 4 percent placed on electronic monitoring and/or house arrest with curfews.

Conditions of Community Supervision

Many citizens have misconceptions about community corrections and the general nature of community supervision. Some citizens think that because certain offenders are permitted the freedom to live among them in their communities, then community corrections must not be much of a punishment. Only incarceration in a jail or prison seems like a fitting punishment for someone who has been convicted of one or more crimes. From the point of view of the courts and corrections, however, community corrections is very much a punishment, although it has its obvious rehabilitative and reintegrative features. One example of the conditions accompanying most community corrections programs and the nature of supervision community corrections clients receive is from Webb County, Texas. This form is illustrated in Box 4.1. In this hypothetical case, a convicted offender, George Marlow, was convicted of driving while intoxicated, a Class B misdemeanor.

COMMUNITY CORRECTIONS PROGRAMS

The most prevalent types of community corrections programs are described in this section and include (1) electronic monitoring, (2) home confinement or house arrest, and (3) day reporting centers. Several additional conditions are described, including fines, community service orders, and restitution.

Electronic Monitoring

Definition.   **Electronic monitoring** is the use of telemetry devices to verify that offenders are at specified locations during particular times (Dodgson et al. 2001). Electronic devices such as wristlets or anklets are fastened to offenders and must not be removed during the duration of their parole or probation. In 1987, there were 800 offenders under some type of electronic monitoring program in the United States. By 2000, that figure had increased to 90,000 (Maguire and Pastore 2002). This is only an estimate, however. Some observers say that the true number of clients on electronic monitoring in various U.S. jurisdictions is unknown (Schmidt 1998:11). Several manufacturers, such as GOSSlink, BI Incorporated,

 **BOX 4.1**

TEXAS COMMUNITY CORRECTIONS SUPERVISION CONDITIONS

THE STATE OF TEXAS
VS.
NAME: George Marlow
D.O.B.: September 1, 1975
A.K.A.:
CAUSE NUMBER: 1234567

OFFENSE: Driving While Intoxicated, Class B

❏ **REGULAR**   ❏ **DEFERRED ADJUDICATION**

On the 2nd day of July, A.D. 2002, you were granted community supervision for a period of 12 months with the following terms and conditions, as denoted below by X in left margin:

❏   **ORDER ALTERING AND AMENDING TERM OR CONDITIONS OF COMMUNITY SUPERVISION**
On the _____ day of _____, A.D., _____, you were placed on Community Supervision in the above numbered and entitled cause for a period of _____ months.

❏   All of your conditions will remain in full force and effect, except as may be specifically altered and amended by the following changes or additional condition(s): #_____

❏   As an alternative to incarceration, the term of Community Supervision is extended _____ month(s) from _____ until _____.

❏ 1. Commit no offense against the Laws of this State or of any other State or of the United States.

❏ 2. Avoid injurious or vicious habits and abstain from the illegal use of controlled substances, dangerous drugs, or use alcoholic beverages; submit to drug testing as directed by the Court or Supervision Officer and pay a urinalysis fee of $10 for each test (four [4] times per year). Submit as directed to an alcohol/drug evaluation and follow through with any recommended treatment.

❏ 3. Avoid places and persons of harmful or disreputable character, including places where controlled substances and dangerous drugs are illegally possessed, sold, or used and not associate with persons who illegally possess, sell, or use controlled substances and dangerous drugs as well as not associate with persons who have criminal records.

❏ 4. Obtain and keep gainful employment in a lawful occupation and show proof of employment. If unemployed, you will report to a job counselor or employment agency as directed by the Court or Supervision Officer until gainfully employed. You will tender any and all financial documents as directed by the Court or the Supervision Officer.

❏ 5. Report, in person, to the Supervision Officer of Webb County, Texas, once a month/week/day as directed by the Court or Supervision Officer and conduct yourself in a proper and orderly manner while reporting.

(continued)

BOX 4.1 *(Continued)*

❏ 6. A. Permit the Supervision Officer, or his or her Assistants, to transport you as needed and to visit you in your home or elsewhere.

B. Consent to search of your person, or residence, or of any vehicle in which you are operating at any time by your Supervision Officer without prior notice or search warrant, to determine if you are in compliance with the Conditions of Community Supervision. Any contraband found to be in your possession is subject to confiscation.

C. Not possess any contraband in your home, vehicle, or on your person, including, but not limited to: prohibited or illegal weapons, controlled substances or illegal drugs, pornographic materials, and obscene devices.

❏ 7. Remain within Webb County, Texas, unless permitted in writing to depart by the Court or by the Supervision Officer.

❏ 8. Not leave the State of Texas, unless permitted in writing to depart by the Court or by the Supervision Officer.

❏ 9. Support any dependents that you now have or that you may acquire during the term of your probated sentence or as ordered in a decree of divorce or civil order.

❏ 10. Provide proof of residence and report any change of address, change of job, or arrest to the Supervision Officer within 48 hours.

❏ 11. Pay the following, in one of several sums, through the Webb County Community Supervision and Corrections Department, in whatever sum that the Court shall determine during the term of your Community Supervision, until all fees have been paid in full.

❏ A. RESTITUTION of $1,000.00, at a rate of $_____ each month, beginning 7/02.

❏ B. SUPERVISION FEE of $40.00 per month, beginning 7/02.

❏ C. COURT COSTS of $301.00.

❏ D. FINE of $500.00.

❏ E. ATTORNEY'S FEE of $_____ (❏ Public Defender)

❏ F. TIME PAYMENT FEE of $25.00 if FINE, COURT COSTS, and RESTITUTION are not paid within 30 days of sentencing.

❏ G. EXTRADITION FEE of $_____.

❏ H. CRIME STOPPERS PROGRAM FEE of $50.00.

❏ I. WOMEN'S SHELTER FEE of $_____.

❏ J. CHILDREN'S ADVOCACY PAYMENT of $_____.

❏ K. LAB FEES of $_____.

❏ L. SEXUAL ASSAULT PROGRAM FEE of $5.00 per month, under 420.008, Government Code sixty days after the granting of Community Supervision, beginning: _____.

❏ 12. Not purchase, receive, possess, or transport any weapon, including but not limited to a club, explosive device, firearm, ammunition, illegal knife, martial arts weapon, brass knuckles, or chemical dispensing device during your term of Community Supervision.

❏ 13. EXTRADITION You will waive extradition to the State of Texas from any jurisdiction in or outside the United States where you may be found and also agree that you will not contest any effort by any jurisdiction to return you to the State of Texas.

❏ 14. Not operate a motor vehicle without a valid Texas Driver's License.

❏ 15. NO CONTRACT ORDER

❏ A. GENERAL ORDER: You will neither contact nor attempt to contact _____, or any of his/her family members by phone, mail, or in person, either directly or indirectly. Should you find yourself inadvertently in contact with said individual, you will immediately leave and not threaten, assault, or verbally abuse him/her.

❏ B. STALKING

1. You are prohibited from following, stalking, or communicating

BOX 4.1 *(Continued)*

in person, verbally, telephonically, in writing, or in any other manner with the victim _____.

2. You are prohibited from being within 500 feet of _____ residence, place of employment, or the school of the victim's children.

❑ C. GANG AFFILIATION You will neither contact or attempt to contact _____ or any other gang, and should you find yourself inadvertently in contact with said individual/gang or any other gang, you will immediately leave and not threaten, assault, or verbally abuse them.

❑ 16. DAY REPORTING CENTER

A. You are to be admitted to the Webb County Day Reporting Center for a period of no more than eighteen (18) months, beginning on or about the _____ day of _____, 2002.

B. Your supervision fees will be waived while an active participant in the Day Reporting Center.

❑ 17. DRIVING WHILE INTOXICATED

A. Attend and complete D.W.I. school within 180 days of sentencing at your own expense.

B. Complete eight (8) hours of counseling through Bridging the Gap Program at your own expense within 90 days of sentencing.

C. Complete twenty (20) community service hours through Texans Against Drunk Driving Program within 90 days of sentencing.

❑ 18. IGNITION INTERLOCK You will immediately enroll and participate in the ignition interlock program as directed by the Court, in that:

A. You are instructed to immediately report to: _____   _____
           Agency   Address
Make an appointment as well as necessary financial arrangements to have the interlock device installed in your vehicle(s) within 24 hours of placement on Community Supervision.

B. You will have the ignition interlock device installed in your personal motor vehicle(s), to include any and all vehicles you operate within 24 hours from _____, and will not drive the vehicle(s) until one is installed.

C. You will only operate a vehicle with an ignition interlock installed.

D. You will not adjust, tamper, alter, or circumvent the ignition interlock device installed, or the electrical wiring to the unit, or to the ignition system, or remove the unit from the designated vehicle. If any other individual tampers or alters the ignition interlock device, you will report the tampering to the Webb County Community Supervision and Corrections Department immediately.

E. You will abide by all the policies and procedures of the ignition interlock program. Upon rejection or nonacceptance of any phase of this program, you will immediately report to the Webb County Community Supervision and Corrections Department.

❑ 19. SERVICE RESTITUTION Perform 25 hours of Community Service Restitution. You will fully comply with all rules, regulations, and instructions as directed by the head or authorized personnel of this agency. You will work faithfully at the Community Service task assigned and the number of hours ordered by the Court are to be performed at a minimum rate of _____ hours per _____, to be completed no later than 07-02-03. Proof of Community Service hours performed is to be provided to the Webb County Community Service Restitution Coordinator as directed.

❑ 20. COURT RESIDENTIAL TREATMENT CENTER You shall be committed to the Webb County Court Residential Treatment Center for a period of not less than successful completion of the six levels of treatment required and not more than 24 months commencing upon availability. You will comply with the rules, regu-

(continued)

BOX 4.1 *(Continued)*

lations, and instructions as directed by the Court and/or Court Residential Treatment Center personnel and be financially responsible for any required medical attention and/or prescriptions. You will pay a daily fee of $10.00. Payments will be made while at the facility with remaining balances due upon release.

☐ 21. BOOT CAMP As a sentencing and in lieu of incarceration in an institutional division, you are hereby committed to the Homer Salinas Rehabilitation Center (Boot Camp) located on M Road and Richardson Road, in Edinburg, Hidalgo County, Texas, for a period not to exceed six (6) months, commencing on the date directed by the Center. You shall remain committed on the date directed by the Center. You shall remain committed to the Center, cooperate fully with the program, and abide by all program rules until released by Order of the Court. Upon release, you may be assigned to any program under the continuum of sanctions of the Cameron County Supervision and Corrections Department.

A. While an active participant in the Boot Camp, your supervision fees will be suspended.

☐ 22. SUBSTANCE ABUSE TREATMENT PUNISHMENT FACILITY

☐ A. Pursuant to Art. 42.12 C.C.P., Section 14, the Court finds: (1) this defendant has been placed on community supervision under this Article; (2) the defendant is charged with or convicted of a felony other than a felony under Sec. 21.11, 22.011, 22.021, or 25.06 of the Penal Code; and (3) the Court affirmatively finds that (a) drugs or alcohol abuse significantly contributed to the commission of the crime or violation of community supervision; and (b) the defendant is a suitable candidate for treatment, as determined by the suitability criteria established by the Texas Board of Criminal Justice

under Section 493.009(b) of the Government Code. As a condition of community supervision, the defendant is required to serve a term of confinement and treatment in a substance abuse treatment facility under this section for a term of not less than three months or more than one year and, upon release, the defendant is required to participate in a drug or alcohol abuse continuum of care treatment plan and will comply with all rules, regulations, and instructions of the assigned treatment providers as directed by the Court/Supervision Officer/treatment provider personnel until successfully discharged.

☐ B. You are to be transferred by the Webb County Sheriff's Department to said agency.

☐ C. The Court further finds that the defendant has been charged with or convicted of a felony other than a felony under Sec. 21.11, 22.011 of the Penal Code, that drugs or alcohol abuse significantly contributed to the commission of the crime in violation of Community Supervision, that the defendant has previously been placed in a substance abuse felony punishment facility operated by the Texas Department of Criminal Justice, under Section 493.009(b) of the Government Code.

It is therefore ordered by the Court that the term of Community Supervision to the above-styled and numbered cause be continued and the following conditions be imposed. The defendant is required to serve a term of confinement and RELAPSE TREATMENT in a substance abuse treatment facility under this section, abiding by all rules and regulations of said program for a term of not less than 90 days or more than 1 year. Upon successful completion of the program, the defendant is required to

BOX 4.1 *(Continued)*

participate in a drug or alcohol abuse continuum of care treatment plan as developed by the Texas Commission on Alcohol and Drug Abuse, abiding by all rules and regulations of said treatment plan until discharged by the staff of the continuum of care program or as directed by the Court/Supervision Officer.

❏ 23. JAIL TIME

❏ A. Serve a term of imprisonment in the Webb County Jail for _____ days/months; this period of detention shall begin _____. If allowed to participate in the Work Release Program, you will comply with all rules, regulations, and instructions as directed by the authorized personnel of this program.

1. Upon release from the Webb County Jail, you will report to the Webb County Community Supervision and Corrections Department, 1110 Victoria Street, Suite 104, Laredo, Texas, within 48 hours or the next working day if said day falls on a Saturday, Sunday, or legal holiday.

❏ B. Serve a term of confinement in a State Jail Felony Facility for a period of _____ days, said term to begin upon admission of the defendant into the facility, and abide by all rules and regulations, and participate in the rehabilitative programs of said facility until discharged from the facility.

1. Upon release from the State Jail Facility, you will report to the Webb County Community Supervision and Corrections Department, 1110 Victoria Street, Suite 104, Laredo, Texas, with 48 hours or the next working day if said day falls on a Saturday, Sunday, or legal holiday.

❏ C. Serve a term of confinement in a State Jail Felony Facility for a period of no less than 120 days and not more than 180 days; obey all rules and regulations of the State Jail until discharged; participate in the Substance Abuse Program at the State Jail upon availability; follow all guidelines and instructions until successfully discharged or until further ordered by the Court; and follow all aftercare recommendations. This term is to begin upon actual admission to the State Jail Felony Facility without credit for any time spent in the county jail.

1. Upon release from the State Jail Facility, you will report to the Webb County Community Supervision and Corrections Department, 1110 Victoria Street, Suite 104, Laredo, Texas, within 48 hours or the next working day if said day falls on a Saturday, Sunday, or legal holiday.

❏ 24. Beginning _____ you will report to your Supervision Officer on a weekly basis and submit to urinalysis until you are accepted into this specialized program as designated by Condition No. _____.

❏ 25. EDUCATION

❏ A. If you do not have an educational skill level that is equal to or greater than the average skill level of students who have completed the sixth grade in public schools in this state, then you are required to attain that level of educational skill through Literacy Classes.

❏ B. You shall participate in the following educational or vocational program, to wit: _____ to be completed within _____.

❏ 26. DEPORTATION

❏ A. Should you be deported, you will be placed on unsupervised supervision. You are not to re-enter the United States illegally.

❏ B. If you legally re-enter the United States during the term of your su-

(continued)

BOX 4.1 (Continued)

pervision, you will immediately report to and notify the Webb County Community Supervision and Corrections Department and this Court; and upon doing so reporting, the Conditions of Community Supervision will be amended to conform to the requirements of this Court.

27. SEX OFFENDER PROGRAM AND INSTRUCTIONS

A. You will immediately report to the appropriate law enforcement agency and register with that agency pursuant to Article 6252-13c.1 of the Revised Texas Civil Statutes. You will comply with all registration instructions as directed by the authorized personnel of this agency and provide verification of such registration to your Supervision Officer. Any intended change of residence will be reported to and approved by the Court or Supervision Officer PRIOR TO any such move. You will immediately register with the law enforcement agency for that jurisdiction.

B. Attend and participate in a sex offender treatment program (to include aftercare) with a Court and Community Supervision and Corrections Department approved sex offender treatment provider until supervision completion and/or further orders of the court. Program participation is defined as attendance at all meetings, prompt payment of fees, admission of responsibilities for his/her offense, and progress toward reasonable treatment goals. [Texas CCP Art. 42.12, Sec. 13(B)].

C. Do not go to, frequent, or seek employment in a sexually oriented establishment (topless bars or clubs) or places where pornographic materials (sexually explicit videos, magazines, etc.) are sold, possessed, or displayed. Do not own or possess any form of pornographic material.

D. Have no contact or communication, directly or indirectly, whether in person, by telephone, in writing, via electronic communication, or through a third person, with the victim of your offense _____ (name optional) or with the family of the victim unless authorized by the Court or Community Supervision and Corrections Department.

E. Pay for all therapy, treatment, and medical expenses incurred by the victim as a result of your offense.

F. Submit, at your own expense, to any psychosocial assessment, and/or a clinical polygraph when scheduled by the sex offender treatment provider, to determine whether you are in compliance with the Conditions of Community Supervision.

G. Provide a blood sample for a DNA database, in compliance with Texas CCP 42.12, Sec. 11(23) in conjunction with the Texas Government Code Chapter 411.

H. Not enter the premises or act as an employee or volunteer at any place or activity where minor children under the age of seventeen (17) are gathered or known to congregate. This prohibits the defendant from working at any primary or secondary school, public or private, coaching Little League, being a scout leader, teaching junior Bible study, baby-sitting, or entering parks, zoos, recreational centers, fairs, video arcades, and theme parks such as, but not necessarily restricted to, Six Flags, Fiesta Texas, Seaworld, Splashtown, etc.

I. Have no direct contact with or enter onto the premises where the victim or ANY minor children, including your own children, or stepchildren, reside or are present. Exceptions to this must be approved in writing by the Court/Supervision Officer IN ADVANCE

BOX 4.1 *(Continued)*

and ONLY in the presence of an adult chaperon approved by the Court/Supervision Officer. At no time will the supervised contact include physical contact with any minor child (such as having a child sit on the defendant's lap, holding hands, bathing, etc.).

J. Not reside or go within 1,000 feet of any school, day care center, or other area where children congregate unless all living arrangements and locations have been reported to and approved by the Court and/or Supervision Officer [Texas CCP Art 42.12, Sec. 12(B)].

K. Do not reside, or attempt to reside, in a household where minor children live without the approval of the Court.

L. Not possess any videotape cassette unless you provide said cassette upon request to a Supervision Officer for inspection and examination at reasonable times and places.

M. Not possess, have access, or view any journalistic, photographic, video, electronic, compact disc, Internet or World Wide Web, or computer-based material that is sexually oriented and/or portrays the nudity of a child or an adult. Upon request you will permit a Supervision Officer to review any journalistic, photographic, video or computer-based material in your house. You must also provide upon request, a computer generated list of the Internet/World Wide Web sites you visited in the past month. You will not engage in any sort of communication including in person, through another person, telephone, letters, email, Internet, "chat room," or faxes, with any person under the age of 18.

N. Notify third parties of possible risks resulting from your criminal record, personal history or characteristics. You will also permit your Supervision Officer to make such notification and to confirm your compliance with such notification requirements.

O. Pay the costs of providing notice for publication to a newspaper as required by law through the Webb County Community Supervision and Corrections Department.

P. As per House Bill 1939, you are required to maintain a "special" driver's license and/or identification card issued by the Texas Department of Public Safety, to be renewed annually.

❑ 28. T.A.I.P. PROGRAM

A. As a special condition imposed by this Court, you are to be committed to La Buena Salud for participation in the AIR Program.

B. Participate with the AIR program in such requirements as initial assessment, detoxification, intensive residential, residential, group outpatient and individual outpatient.

C. While a participant in the program, you are expected to comply with all the rules, regulations, and instructions of said facility.

D. Continue to abide by your Conditions of Community Supervision upon release from the Program.

E. While an active inpatient in the AIR Program, your Court assessed fees will be suspended.

❑ 29. DRUG OFFENDER EDUCATION PROGRAM

A. Attend and successfully complete an education program on the dangers of drug abuse approved by the TCADA at your own expense.

❑ 30. STOP THE VIOLENCE PROGRAM

A. Participate and remain in the Department's Stop the Violence Program until completion or discharged by the Court.

❑ 31. CASE SUPERVISION TRANSFER

A. Your case will be transferred to _____ County for supervision.

(continued)

BOX 4.1 *(Continued)*

B. You will report by mail on a monthly basis to the Webb County Supervision and Corrections Department until your case has been accepted for supervision.

C. Should supervision of your case be rejected, you must return to Webb County immediately.

❏ 32. INTERSTATE COMPACT SERVICES

A. Your case will be transferred through the Interstate Compact Services to the State of _____. The supervision fee of Webb County is waived during your absence from this State. Upon returning to this State for completion of Community Supervision, you are required to pay a monthly supervision fee of $_____.

❏ 33. Reside at Address: _____; City: Laredo; State: Texas; County: Webb, and not depart said County without the written permission from the Court or Supervision Officer.

❏ 34. _____

❏ 35. _____

_____

JUDGE PRESIDING

_____

DATE

You are hereby advised that under the Laws of this State, the Court shall determine the Terms and Conditions of your Community Supervision and may, at any time during the period of your community supervision, alter or modify the terms and conditions of your community supervision. THE COURT ALSO HAS THE AUTHORITY, AT ANY TIME DURING THE PERIOD OF YOUR COMMUNITY SUPERVISION, TO REVOKE SAME FOR VIOLATION OF ANY OF THE CONDITIONS OF YOUR COMMUNITY SUPERVISION SET OUT ABOVE. The Court has placed you on Community Supervision believing that, if you sincerely try to obey and comply with these Conditions, your attitude and conduct will improve to the benefit of the public and yourself.

I acknowledge receipt of a copy of the Conditions of Community Supervision and fully understand same.

CONDITIONS AND GUN CONTROL ACT WERE EXPLAINED, CONDITIONS WERE FINGERPRINTED AND SIGNED. I ALSO ACKNOWLEDGE THAT I MUST REPORT IN PERSON WHETHER OR NOT I HAVE MONEY FOR FEES.

_____

Defendant's Signature

_____

Defendant's Address

_____

Supervision Officer
Webb County Community Service and Corrections Department
1110 Victoria Street, Suite 104
Laredo, Texas 78040

A copy furnished to the above-named Defendant and noted on the docket this day _____ of _____, A.D. 2002.

_____

Clerk, County Court at Law 2 of Webb County, Texas

BY: _____
                    Deputy

and Controlec, Inc., produce tamper-resistant wrist and ankle bracelets that emit electronic signals and are often connected to telephone devices and are relayed to central computers in police stations or probation departments.

The Establishment of Electronic Monitoring Programs.   Electronic monitoring devices were originally used in 1964 as a means of monitoring certain mental patients and parolees (Roy 1997). In later years, electronic monitoring was extended to include monitoring office work, employee testing for security clearances, and

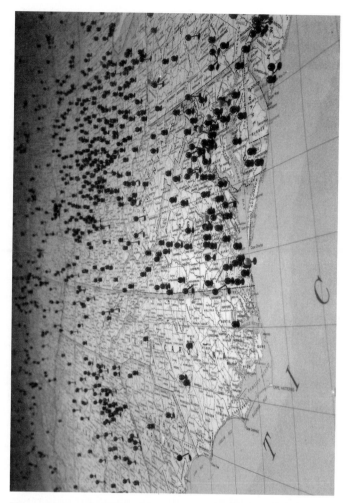

Electronic monitoring centers on the East Coast operated by
BI, Inc. are widespread, as indicated by numerous map pins.
Courtesy of BI, Inc.

many other applications. For instance, in 2001 the Suffolk County, Massachusetts, Women's Resource Center commenced using electronic monitoring as a part of its broader substance abuse treatment program for women (Johnston 2001). The feasibility of using electronic devices to monitor probationers was investigated by various researchers during the 1960s and 1970s (Rasmussen and Benson 1994).

New Mexico Second Judicial District Judge Jack Love established a pilot project in 1983 to electronically monitor persons convicted of drunk driving and various white-collar offenses. The New Mexico Supreme Court examined the program and approved it subject to the voluntary consent and participation of offenders as a condition of their probation and as long as their privacy, dignity, and families were protected. Offenders were required to wear anklets or wristlets that emitted electronic signals that could be intercepted by probation officers conducting surveillance operations. This practice continues presently with similar offender populations (Lucker et al. 1997). Today, electronic monitoring programs are in use throughout the world, in countries such as Canada, Australia, and England (Mortimer and May 1997).

Types of Electronic Monitoring Systems.   Four basic categories of electronic monitoring equipment used for surveillance of offenders include (1) **continuous signaling devices,** which emit a continuous signal that can be intercepted by telephonic communication from a central dialing location such as a probation office or police station; (2) **programmed contact devices,** where telephonic contact is made at random times with the offender and the offender's voice is verified electronically by computer; (3) **cellular telephone devices,** which are transmitters worn by offenders that transmit a signal that can be intercepted by local area monitors; and (4) **continuous signaling transmitters,** which are also transmitters worn by offenders that emit continuous signals that may be intercepted by probation officers with portable receiving units. Probation officers need only to drive by an offender's home to verify the offender's presence during random hours, thus eliminating the need for face-to-face contact (Virginia Department of Criminal Justice Services 1998).

Electronic Monitoring Costs.   The initial startup costs associated with electronic monitoring range from $25,000 to $50,000 or more, depending upon the sophistication of the electronic monitoring system and how many clients are to be monitored. Once the system is in place, electronic monitoring is a cheap means of verifying an offender's whereabouts. Costs for monitoring one client per day range from $3.00 in Arkansas to $28.60 in Maryland (Camp and Camp 2002). On the average, it costs $9.32 per day per client for electronic monitoring in the United States. This compares with $4 per day per client for regular probationer or parolee supervision. However, only those offenders requiring the most intensive supervision are placed in electronic monitoring programs. Electronic monitoring costs compare very favorably with the costs of incarcerating offenders in state or federal prisons at an average of $55.50 per day per inmate (Camp and Camp 2002).

CrimeTrax: The Latest Florida Electronic Monitoring Experiment.   In 2000 the Florida Department of Law Enforcement, the Florida Department of Corrections, and the Tallahassee Police Department teamed up on a pilot project to address the problem of felony recidivists. Based on previous research, these agencies believed that over two-thirds of all probationers commit new crimes within a three-year period following their original sentences. Many of these offenses are serious (Russo 2002:16). Florida implemented the use of standard electronic monitoring for supervising offenders during the 1980s, and its use has continued to the present. However, improvements in technology have afforded Florida and other jurisdictions the capability of more effective offender monitoring (Kelly et al. 2001).

CrimeTrax was established on an experimental basis in 2000. It is essentially an information system that collects data from local law enforcement agencies, the Florida Department of Corrections, and Global Positioning Satellite (GPS) tracking. The system retrieves local law enforcement agencies' crime location data on offenses and incidents nightly, no matter what local software is being used. The data is scrubbed and standardized with other data to eliminate duplicate data entries. Offender demographics are entered, including offender reporting requirements, activity schedules, and exclusion zones, which indicate locations where offenders are prohibited from being. The GPS tracking system transmits each offender's nightly location history points. All of this data is integrated, and then offender GPS location data and crime incident data are compared to assist investigators and corrections personnel solve and prevent crimes and to hold offenders more accountable for their actions (Russo 2002:16).

CrimeTrax functions as a powerful deterrent to further criminal activity by those offenders under electronic monitoring. One factor leading to criminal behavior is the probability that the act will not be detected by authorities. If offenders know that they can be placed at the scene of a crime with certainty, they will be less likely to commit new offenses. Therefore, the crime prevention benefits of CrimeTrax cannot be overstated. In 2002 there were 560 offenders being tracked via GPS at a cost of $9.17 per day per offender. Florida officials are the first to acknowledge that CrimeTrax is not suitable for all types of offenders. Public safety and offender accountability require that some selectivity occurs so that only the most eligible offenders are screened and included in the CrimeTrax tracking program. Thus far, the program has served 22 local law enforcement agencies representing 20 percent of Florida's population and 23 percent of all reported crime. Florida officials believe that the operational capabilities of CrimeTrax have been proven and that all agencies presently involved in its use have enthusiastically accepted it as an effective supervising medium (Russo 2002:16).

Strengths and Weaknesses of Electronic Monitoring Programs. The strengths of electronic monitoring are:

1. Assisting offenders in avoiding criminogenic atmosphere of prisons or jails and helping reintegrate them into their communities (e.g., avoids labeling as criminals).
2. Permitting offenders to retain jobs and support families.
3. Assisting probation officers in their monitoring activities and having the potential for easing their caseload responsibilities.
4. Giving judges and other officials considerable flexibility in sentencing offenders (e.g., persons in halfway houses or on work release).
5. Having the potential for reducing recidivism rate more than existing probationary alternatives.
6. Potentially useful for decreasing jail and prison populations.
7. More cost-effective in relation to incarceration.
8. Allowing for pretrial release monitoring as well as for special treatment cases such as substance abusers, the mentally retarded, women who are pregnant, and juveniles.

The weaknesses of electronic monitoring are:

1. Some possibility exists for race, ethnic, or socioeconomic bias by requiring offenders to have telephones or to pay for expensive monitoring equipment and/or fees.
2. Public safety may be compromised through the failure of these programs to guarantee that offenders will go straight and not endanger citizens by committing new offenses while free in the community.
3. Electronic monitoring may be too coercive, and it may be unrealistic for officials to expect full offender compliance with such a stringent system.
4. Little consistent information exists about the impact of electronic monitoring on recidivism rates compared with other probationary alternatives.
5. Persons frequently selected for participation are persons who probably don't need to be monitored anyway.
6. Technological problems exist, making electronic monitoring somewhat unreliable.
7. Electronic monitoring may result in widening the net by being prescribed for offenders who otherwise would receive less costly standard probation.

8. Use of electronic monitoring raises right to privacy, civil liberties, and other constitutional issues, such as Fourth Amendment search and seizure concerns.

9. Much of the public interprets this option as going easy on offenders and perceives electronic monitoring as a nonpunitive alternative.

10. The costs of electronic monitoring may be more than published estimates (Smykla and Selke 1995).

11. Clients can access the Internet where they may come into contact with other convicts and/or engage in illegal activities or acquire illegal contraband (Gaines 1998:20).

 **BOX 4.2**    **PERSONALITY HIGHLIGHT**

Richard N. Irrer

Manager, Michigan Department of Corrections Electronic Monitoring Program

Statistics

B.A. (multidisciplinary social science with a secondary teaching certificate), Michigan State University; M.A. (learning, guidance, and criminal justice), Michigan State University

Present Situation and Interests

I am currently the manager of Michigan's Electronic Monitoring Program (EMP). This program includes a monitoring center, which is a 24-hour operation that utilizes custom-designated software to monitor the curfews of over 3,000 probationers, prisoners, and community-based prisoners throughout the state. Michigan's program is the largest state program in the country, and it is also the largest government-operated monitoring center in the United States. In addition to curfew monitoring, remote alcohol monitoring is also conducted for over 300 offenders. I am also responsible for the evaluation of various community supervision systems such as kiosk reporting systems, Global Positioning, and other remote alcohol monitoring systems.

Background and Experiences

When I graduated from college, I tried unsuccessfully to find a high school teaching position. My wife was employed by the Department of Corrections, and I learned about an opening. I applied and was hired as a State Probation Officer. I was later put in charge of a program that diverted offenders from prison, and then I worked in a prisoner halfway house program. In 1986 I became involved in establishing the electronic monitoring program for community-based prisoners and was named the manager of the program in 1997 when the three regional centers were consolidated into a single site. I eventually did find that teaching job, on a part-time basis at Lansing Community College.

Throughout my career with the Department of Corrections I have been involved in a wide variety of programs, primarily in the area of community corrections. One of the major challenges facing corrections in the late 1970s and early 1980s was a drastic increase in prisoners with no significant increase in funding. As one result, many innovative community-based programs were introduced during this time period. In Michigan we experienced a prison building boom in the late

The Constitutionality of Electronic Monitoring.   Certain legal issues about electronic monitoring are presently unresolved to everyone's satisfaction, although the constitutionality of electronic monitoring has never been successfully challenged (Roy 1997). Many of the legal arguments raised question the constitutionality of electronic monitoring and whether it violates client rights. However, all offenders placed in electronic monitoring programs must agree to abide by all electronic monitoring program conditions. The consensual nature of offender participation in such programs undermines virtually all challenges they may raise about whether such program conditions are constitutional (Corbett and Marx 1994). If certain offenders don't want POs to intrude in their homes at any time of the day or night without warrants to search for illegal contraband or

1980s, during which time our population doubled over a five-year period of time. Prison overcrowding is a continuing problem, and we must constantly explore new ways to carry out our mission more efficiently.

I have been fortunate to have had the opportunity to evaluate various technologies and build programs around those that have proven to be worthwhile. Because of my experience in the field, I have given presentations at a variety of state and national conferences and was one of eight electronic monitoring managers nationwide to be named to the Working Group on Electronic Surveillance Technologies, sponsored by the National Institute of Justice and the American Probation and Parole Association. The group developed a comprehensive manual for agencies to develop successful monitoring programs.

Electronic equipment may work well in a controlled laboratory environment, but once it is placed in the real world, unforeseen problems can surface. One manufacturer found that offenders in warm climates who used a lot of suntan lotion had a greater chance of having a malfunction in the strap that held the transmitter on the ankle. Staff soon found out that people with waterbeds had problems, as the water would block the transmission of radio waves to the receiver. When the signal faded in and out rapidly, staff had a good time speculating on offenders' nocturnal activities.

Cockroaches were another problem in the first monitoring receivers. The early models were easily penetrated by these insects, who found them to provide a warm, dry place to live. Further problems developed when they defecated on the wiring and shorted it out. For a long time, field agents would have to de-roach units by leaving them inside a plastic bag filled with insecticide. Later models manufactured were new and improved roachproof models.

One thing to keep in mind with all technology is that it is not infallible: People can beat electronic monitoring systems if they have enough time, money, and resources, just as a prisoner can escape from any prison. In fact, a Michigan inmate once did so by using a helicopter. Monitoring is not a program in itself, but it is a tool that can enhance supervision. Probation and parole officers must be thoroughly aware of how these systems work, and they must be on guard for new attempts to compromise the equipment.

Advice to Students

Corrections can be very interesting and rewarding. It consists of a wide variety of occupational career tracks. If you are interested in corrections, talk to others in the field and participate in an internship if possible. Professional organizations, such as the American Correctional Association and the American Probation and Parole Association, have a great deal of valuable information. If you have an interest in new technologies in corrections, the National Law Enforcement and Corrections Technology Center has a regular periodical and also sponsors an annual workshop on innovative technologies.

evidence of program violations, then they can accept a jail or prison sentence. In fact, some offenders reject electronic monitoring and any other probationary sentence in favor of jail or prison, simply to get their sentence over with.

Another constitutional issue is the Fifth Amendment right against self-incrimination (Payne and Gainey 1998). Some offender-clients have alleged that the fact of electronic monitoring is self-incriminating, since clients must disclose to correctional officers information about themselves at random times. This allegation lacks constitutional support, since physical incrimination, such as a drug or alcohol check or search for and discovery of illegal contraband, is not protected as a Fifth Amendment right (Roy 1997).

Criticisms of Electronic Monitoring Rights Violations Muted by Offender Consent to Be Monitored.   Most, if not all, of these constitutional questions are undermined by the fact that one's participation in electronic monitoring is voluntary. Offenders are not forced to wear anklets or wristlets if there are other sentencing options that may be imposed. In view of this voluntariness, therefore, it is peculiar that some of these program volunteers have sought relief in court for alleged infringements of their constitutional rights (Conway 2001). Supposedly, these offender-clients sign rights waivers, submitting themselves to random visits and searches of their premises by their supervising POs.

Home Confinement or House Arrest

Definition.   **House arrest, home incarceration,** or **home confinement** is an intermediate punishment consisting of confining offenders to their residences for mandatory incarceration during evening hours, after a specified curfew, and on weekends (Gowen 2001). Home confinement was used to punish St. Paul the Apostle, who was detained under house arrest in biblical times. During the 1600s, Galileo, the astronomer, was made to live the remaining eight years of his life under house arrest. In 1917, Czar Nicholas II of Russia was detained under house arrest until his death (Meachum 1986:102). And during Czar Nicholas II's reign, Lenin was placed under house arrest for a limited period. St. Louis, Missouri, first used house arrest in 1971. Florida was the first state to adopt home confinement as a statewide intermediate punishment through its Correctional Reform Act of 1983 (Rackmill 1994). By 2002, more than 30,000 offenders were under house arrest and supervision by probation officers in the United States (Maguire and Pastore 2002). House arrest is a growing sentencing option, especially for low-risk first offenders.

Goals of Home Confinement.   The goals of home confinement programs include the following:

1. To continue offenders' punishment while permitting them to be confined to their personal residences.
2. To enable offenders the freedom to hold jobs and earn a living while caring for their families and/or making restitution to victims.
3. To reduce jail and prison overcrowding.
4. To provide a means for ostracism while ensuring public safety.
5. To reduce the costs of offender supervision.
6. To foster rehabilitation and reintegration by maintaining offenders' controlled presence within the community.

Eligibility Requirements for Home Confinement.   Probationers and parolees sentenced to home confinement meet the following requirements:

1. Clients tend to be first offenders.
2. Clients tend to be nonviolent and/or have been convicted of nonviolent property offenses.
3. Clients tend to be those with fairly strong family ties, are married, and live with their spouses in a structured living arrangement.
4. Clients do not have drug or alcohol dependencies.
5. Clients have jobs or good prospects of becoming employed and maintaining their employment over time.
6. Clients tend to have higher levels of education and vocational skills.
7. Clients tend to be older, age 30 and over.

Advantages and Disadvantages of Home Confinement Programs.   The advantages of home confinement include the following: (1) It is cost effective; (2) it has social benefits; (3) it is responsive to local citizen and offender needs; and (4) it is easily implemented and is timely in view of jail and prison overcrowding. The disadvantages of home confinement are: (1) House arrest may actually widen the net of social control; (2) it may narrow the net of social control by not being a sufficiently severe sentence; (3) it focuses primarily upon offender surveillance; (4) it is intrusive and possibly illegal; (5) race and class bias may enter into participant selection; and (6) it may compromise public safety (Petersilia 1988a, 1988b:2-4).

Home Confinement Issues.   Several issues concerning home confinement are (1) punishment versus rehabilitation and reintegration, (2) public safety, and (3) crime control and deterrence.

Punishment versus Rehabilitation and Reintegration.   One of the most frequent criticisms of home confinement is that it does not seem to be much of a punishment (Lucken 1997). The public sees offenders confined to their homes and considers this incarceration more of a luxury rather than just deserts. One reason for regarding home confinement as something less than a true punishment compared with institutional incarceration is that the courts do not often equate time served at home with time served in prison (Rackmill 1994). In 1990 an Illinois defendant, Ramos, was placed at his parents' home for a period of weeks under house arrest while awaiting trial for an alleged crime. He was not permitted to leave the premises except for work or medical care. Subsequently, he was convicted of the crime and requested the court to apply the time he spent at home toward the time he would have to serve in prison. The court denied his request, holding that his confinement at home did not amount to custody (*People v. Ramos* 1990). Subsequent court decisions have been consistent with the *Ramos* ruling. Several federal cases have held that the amount of time offenders spend in house arrest cannot be counted against jail or prison time to be served (*United States v. Zackular* 1991; *United States v. Insley* 1991; *United States v. Arch John Drummond* 1992; *United States v. Edwards* 1992; and *United States v. Wickman* 1992).

Also, when offenders leave their residences without permission while under house arrest, they are not guilty of escape from prison; rather, they are guilty of a technical program violation. Lubus, a convicted Connecticut offender, was sentenced to house arrest. At some point, he failed to report to his supervising probation officer. The officer claimed this was the equivalent of an escape and sought to have him prosecuted as an escapee. The Connecticut Supreme Court disagreed, indicating that unauthorized departures from community residences are not the same as unauthorized departures from halfway houses, mental health facilities and hospitals, and failures to return from furloughs or work release (*State v. Lubus* 1990).

Public Safety.   In any community corrections program, corrections staff consider as paramount the need for public safety. This is why great care is taken to restrict the eligibility requirements of those who become involved in home confinement programs. If offenders are first-timers without prior records, and if their conviction offenses are nonviolent, they are considered for inclusion (Vigorita 2001). An absence of a prior record is no guarantee that an offender will automatically qualify, however. Furthermore, the public is not the only concern. Often, families of home confinement clients may have strong reservations about having these persons in their midst. The client's presence may create more problems for the family than are resolved for the client (U.S. General Accounting Office 1997).

Crime Control and Deterrence.   Does home confinement function as a crime deterrent? No. It isn't supposed to function as a crime deterrent (Jones and Ross 1997a). Jail or prison incarceration doesn't deter some offenders from exploiting and victimizing other inmates. Why should we view home confinement differently? The primary function of house arrest is to enable POs to maintain some amount of supervisory control over an offender's whereabouts (Buddress 1997).

Day Reporting Centers.   **Day reporting centers** are operated primarily during daytime hours for the purpose of providing diverse services to offenders and their families. Day reporting is defined as a highly structured nonresidential program utilizing supervision, sanctions, and services coordinated from a central focus. Offenders live at home and report to these centers regularly, and daily.

Day reporting centers are like invisible jails, or halfway houses without the houses. In a way, they are jails on an outpatient basis. Actually, they are a hybrid of intensive probation supervision, house arrest, and early release. Many participants serve out their last few weeks or months of jail still in the government's custody, but technically on their own—living at home, perhaps working at a regular job in the community (Roy and Grimes 2002).

Fines

Definition.   An integral part of sentencing in an increasing number of cases is the use of **fines.** The use of fines as sanctions can be traced to preindustrialized and non-Western societies (Winterfield and Hillsman 1993:1). Ordinarily, state and federal criminal statutes provide for various incarcerative lengths upon conviction. Additionally, various fines are imposed and/or conditions exercised at the discretion of sentencing judges. For instance, if law enforcement officers were to violate one's civil rights by the unlawful use of physical force or excessive force in making an arrest, they might be subject to penalties, including confinement in a state penitentiary for up to five years and a fine of not more than $10,000. This means that if these law enforcement officers are convicted of violating one's civil rights, the judge can sentence them to prison for up to five years and impose a fine of $10,000. This would be within the judge's discretionary powers. Estimates are that over 14 million persons are arrested each year in the United States, and that most of those who are convicted are fined (Maguire and

Pastore 2002). However, these estimates may be exaggerated. For instance, a study of a random sample of felony sentences drawn from 28,000 cases showed that only 9.6 percent of those convicted were fined as a punishment for their offenses. The use of fines as a punishment also varies according to whether the jurisdiction is urban or rural, whether the convicted offender is employed or unemployed, and whether the offender is male or female (Vigorita 2002:3).

Types of Fines and Fine Collection Problems.   Different types of fine scenarios include (1) fines plus jail or prison terms; (2) fines plus probation; (3) fines plus suspended jail or prison terms; (4) fines or jail alternatives ($30 or 30 days); (5) fines alone, partially suspended; and (6) fines alone (McDonald, Greene, and Worzella 1992:1). The arguments for and against the use of fines as sanctions have also been clearly delineated. For instance, it is argued that (1) fines are logically suited for punishment because they are unambiguously punitive; (2) many offenders are poor and cannot afford fines; (3) because the poor cannot afford fines as easily as the rich, there is obvious discrimination in fine imposition; (4) someone else may pay the fine other than the offender; (5) often, fine payments are unenforceable because of offender absconding; (6) courts lack sufficient enforcement capability; and (7) fines may actually increase crime so that the poor can get enough money to pay previously imposed fines. The problems of fine collection are such that less than half of the fines imposed are ever collected in most U.S. courts. Billions of dollars are involved in fine nonpayment. In New York City, for instance, a sampled jurisdiction disclosed that the fine payment rate upon conviction was 19 percent. In other jurisdictions, the fine payment rate at conviction was only 14 percent (Parent 1990).

Aggravating and Mitigating Factors Influencing Judicial Decisions to Impose Fines.   As we have seen, the imposition of fines varies greatly among jurisdictions. Furthermore, a variety of factors influence judicial decision making and whether fines are actually imposed. Research has disclosed that certain aggravating and mitigating factors are considered when deciding whether to impose fines. Aggravating factors include (1) the nature and circumstances of the offense and the role of the actor, including whether it was committed in an especially heinous, cruel, or depraved manner; (2) if the victim was particularly vulnerable or incapable of resistance; (3) the risk that the defendant will commit another crime; (4) the risk that the lesser sentence will depreciate the seriousness of the offense; (5) the likelihood that the defendant is involved in organized crime; (6) the extent of the defendant's criminal record and the seriousness of the offense of which he or she has been convicted; (7) whether the defendant has paid or agreed to pay for the commission of the offense; (8) if the offense is against a law enforcement officer or public official; (9) the need for deterring the defendant and others; (10) the fraudulent or deceptive practices against the state; (11) whether the imposition of the fine or restitution without imprisonment would be perceived by the defendant as a part of the cost of doing business; and (12) if the offense is against the elderly.

Mitigating factors include (1) if the conduct neither caused nor threatened serious harm; (2) if the defendant did not contemplate that conduct would cause or threaten serious harm; (3) if the defendant acted under strong provocation; (4) if there are substantial grounds to excuse or justify the conduct; (5) whether the victim induced or facilitated the crime's commission; (6) if the defendant has compensated or will compensate the victim or will perform community service;

(7) if the conduct was the result of circumstances unlikely to recur; (8) if the character and attitude indicate that it is unlikely that the defendant will commit another offense; (9) if the defendant is likely to respond affirmatively to probationary treatment; (10) if incarceration would entail excessive hardship for the defendant or family; (11) the willingness of the defendant to cooperate with law enforcement agencies; and (12) whether the conduct of youthful defendant was substantially influenced by another person more mature than the defendant (Vigorita 2002:27). Presumably, judges consider these different factors when deciding to impose fines, although it is presently unknown how much weight is given to these factors or whether some judges arbitrarily ignore fines when sentencing offenders.

Community Service Orders and Restitution

Under the Victim and Witness Protection Act of 1982 (18 U.S.C. Sec. 3579–3580, 2003), restitution to victims was incorporated as an option in addition to incarceration at the federal level. Community service is different from restitution in that usually, though not always, offenders perform services for the state or community. The nature of community service to be performed is discretionary with the sentencing judge or paroling authority through the issuance of **community service orders.** In some jurisdictions, prisoners must perform a specified number of hours of community service such as lawn maintenance, plumbing and other similar repairs, or services that fit their particular skills (Tonry 1999). The philosophy underlying community service is more aligned with retribution than rehabilitation. Few judges in any jurisdiction offer community service sentences as alternatives to imprisonment, however.

Community service orders are symbolic restitution, involving redress for victims, less severe sanctions for offenders, offender rehabilitation, reduction of demands on the criminal justice system, and a reduction of the need for vengeance in a society, or a combination of these factors. Community service orders are found in many different countries and benefit the community directly (Bottoms, Gelsthorpe, and Rex 2001). Further, when convicted offenders are indigent or unemployed, community service is a way of paying their fines and court costs. Donnelly (1980) summarizes some of the chief benefits of community service: (1) The community benefits because some form of restitution is paid; (2) offenders benefit because they are given an opportunity to rejoin their communities in law-abiding responsible roles; and (3) the courts benefit because sentencing alternatives are provided. Typically, offenders sentenced to community service should be individually placed where their skills and interests can be maximized for community benefit. Usually, between 50 and 200 hours of community service might be required for any particular convicted offender (Albrecht and van Kalmthout 2002).

Restitution Programs for Victims

An increasingly important feature of probation programs is **restitution.** Restitution is the practice of requiring offenders to compensate crime victims for damages offenders may have inflicted. Restitution may also be viewed in the broader context of mediation, where third-party arbiters resolve disputes between victims and perpetrators (Kleiboer et al. 2000). Several models of restitution have been described by Patel and Soderlund (1994). These include (1) the financial/community service model, (2) the victim/offender mediation model, and (3) the victim/reparations model.

The Financial/Community Service Model.   The **financial/community service model** stresses the offender's financial accountability and community service to pay for damages inflicted upon victims and to defray a portion of the expenses of court prosecutions. It is becoming more commonplace for probationers and divertees to be ordered to pay some restitution to victims and to perform some type of community service. Community service may involve cleanup activities in municipal parks, painting projects involving graffiti removal, cutting courthouse lawns, or any other constructive project that can benefit the community. These community service sentences are imposed by judges. Probation officers are largely responsible for overseeing the efforts of convicted offenders in fulfilling their community service obligations. These sentencing provisions are commonly called community service orders.

The Victim/Offender Mediation Model.   The **victim/offender mediation model** focuses upon victim-offender reconciliation. Alternative dispute resolution is used as a mediating ground for resolving differences or disputes between victims and perpetrators. Usually, third-party arbiters, such as judges, lawyers, or public appointees, can meet with offenders and their victims and work out mutually satisfactory arrangements whereby victims can be compensated for their losses or injuries.

The Victim/Reparations Model.   The **victim/reparations model** stresses that offenders should compensate their victims directly for their offenses. Many states have provisions that provide **reparations** or financial payments to victims under a Crime Victims Reparations Act. The Act establishes a state-financed program of reparations to persons who suffer personal injury and to dependents of persons killed as the result of certain criminal conduct. In many jurisdictions, a specially constituted board determines, independent of court adjudication, the existence of a crime, the damages caused, and other elements necessary for reparation. Reparations cover such economic losses as medical expenses, rehabilitative and occupational retraining expenses, loss of earnings, and the cost of actual substitute services (Umbreit 2001).

SELECTED ISSUES IN COMMUNITY CORRECTIONS

There are several unresolved and controversial issues associated with community corrections. These issues relate to (1) the NIMBY syndrome, (2) punishment versus rehabilitation and reintegration, (3) offender needs and public safety, (4) services delivery, and (5) special-needs offenders.

The NIMBY Syndrome ("Not In My Back Yard")

When community corrections agencies are proposed for different communities, the problem of where to locate these facilities arises. Community officials may desire community corrections programs in theory, anticipating that the community will acquire additional external resources from state or federal funding agencies. Community corrections organizations will provide new jobs for the community. Certain community businesses will anticipate additional revenue from these corrections agencies. However, the matter of locating these facilities becomes a sensitive one. This has become a major issue in many communities and persists today as the **NIMBY syndrome.** The NIMBY syndrome means "Not In My Back Yard." No one seems to want a halfway house or community corrections agency next door or across the street (Wicklund 2000). Thus, public reaction to community corrections is often the same as the reaction toward locating prisons near communities (Quinn, Gould, and Holloway 2001).

Punishment versus Rehabilitation and Reintegration

The true aims of community-based correctional programs are punishment and rehabilitation-centered, although there is some disagreement over these stated objectives. It is unsettling for some citizens to know that 1 percent of California's population is on probation and that one's next door neighbor might be a convicted felon involved in a community-based probation program, for example (Petersilia 2002). But the advantages and strengths of community-based programs need to be considered together with their disadvantages and weaknesses.

 **BOX 4.3**

A NEW PRISON? NOT IN MY BACKYARD!

The New Prison Proposal for Tolar, Texas

Tolar, Texas, is a small farming and ranching town of 500 near Dallas. In 2001 Texas prison authorities approached the community with an offer to build a new prison nearby. The prison offered the community at least 150 new jobs and $1 million in revenue per year. Town leaders were elated. Mayor Gayle Meyer and other city council persons were very much in favor of having a new prison in their midst. They believed that the new prison would bring unprecedented growth to the community and enable the town to pay off its debts. What Texas officials contemplated was the construction of a medium-security prison facility capable of holding 1,500 inmates. They selected Tolar since it was near Dallas and yet was remote enough to effectively isolate prisoners. Negotiations with city leaders commenced and everything seemed OK.

But the town had another opinion. At a town meeting, a majority of residents expressed opposition to the new prison construction. They alleged that building the new prison would be tantamount to a payoff for selling out small-town values and lifestyle. The mayor was stunned. She said, "I'm a little naive. I felt like people would see the improvements, the wonderful jobs created with no environmental impact. I was stunned that people weren't thinking their neighbors needed jobs or the city needed money." In the end, the plan to construct a prison in Tolar was rejected outright by angry citizens. The opposition also alleged that the new prison would create a danger that the community did not presently have. Citizens believed that a prison would expose them to escapes of dangerous prisoners who might bring harm to them. Despite the financial benefits touted by the prison authorities, the citizens didn't want a prison in their community. In the end, plans to build a prison in Tolar were set aside. The State of Texas would look elsewhere for a site to build its new prison.

Are citizens justified in believing that a prison nearby poses undue risks and dangers? How can citizen fears be overcome? How can the state and prison officials better market the idea of a new prison in this community? What does this incident say about the importance of public relations in corrections–community interactions? What do you think?

Source: Adapted from the Associated Press. "Small Town Rejects Prison Possibility," April 16, 2001.

Some societal reintegration occurs as one of community-based corrections' key goals, although some critics say we are moving toward operations that have deterrence and control as priorities (Tonry 1998). Some researchers have examined regular U.S. population growth and compared these figures with the concurrent growth of prison populations.

Offender Needs and Public Safety

A continuing issue regarding community corrections is public safety from dangerous offenders. Neighborhoods don't like the idea that convicted felons are roaming freely among residents. Some of this fear is overcome through the inclusion of low-risk inmates for community placement. For example, in January 1989, inmate work crews were put to the task of renovating Lake Murray State Park in Ardmore, Oklahoma. Ten inmates lived, ate, and slept in buildings on the park grounds. They were supervised by five correctional officers from the Lexington Assessment and Reception Center, about 75 miles south of Ardmore. Subsequent inmate work crews expanded the scope of their original renovation activities by doing additional building renovation, trail and bridge construction and improvement, and picnic table fabrication and placement. Some inmates performed routine maintenance functions. The general public soon learned about what the inmates had accomplished and were more receptive to the idea of permitting ex-convicts into their communities.

Services Delivery

Services delivery can be improved to the extent that the goals for specific offenders are individualized (Tonry 1998). In Grant County, Wisconsin, parole officers identify through interviews various offender needs, such as help with economic and/or social stresses to cope with life. Some offender-clients have family problems or problems living in their communities. Certain problems can be targeted for treatment with proper parole officer–client interactions. Certain innovative programs in other states are responsive to particular community resources that exist.

Special-Needs Offenders

Community-based corrections will invariably have to deal with and make provisions for special-needs offenders. Special-needs offenders include physically, mentally, psychologically, or socially impaired or handicapped offenders who require extraordinary care and supervision. Major problems have been identified for special-needs offenders, including lack of access to adequate mental health services, inadequate information and training among court and corrections personnel, and insufficient interagency coordination and cooperation.

It may not be possible for community corrections to provide the degree of protection needed for persons who are disabled. Mentally ill persons may not be able to function normally in their communities. Some offenders who are mentally impaired may require constant monitoring and supervision, primarily for their own protection. It may be necessary for entire Departments of Correction to examine the problems of special-needs offenders in greater detail (Arrigo 2001).

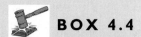 **BOX 4.4**

Ricardo Acosta

Lieutenant, Webb County Sheriff's Office, Laredo, TX

Statistics

A.A. (criminal justice), Laredo Community College; B.S. (criminal justice), Texas A & M International University; Master Peace Officer Certification; Texas Commission of Law Enforcement Certified Instructor; Certified State Firearms Instructor; NRA Certified Police Firearms Instructor; Texas Commission on Private Security Certified Instructor

Background and Interests

I am presently Lieutenant in charge of the Webb County (Texas) Sheriff's Office training division. My duties include providing training for over 250 peace officers and correctional officers and keeping all personnel in compliance with state-mandated training. Most of our officers have dual licenses. That is, they have peace officer and jailer licenses. I also supervise personnel attending the Police Academy and in-service training. I am responsible for certifying all peace officers in firearms proficiency and keeping training records up to date on all personnel. I am a part-time instructor at Laredo Community College Police Academy. I have trained personnel on firearms, defensive tactics, expandable baton, chemical mace, cultural diversity, use of force, defensive driving, and pursuit driving. In addition, I teach security officer courses. The training division is also in charge of all traffic citations and traffic warrants issued by sheriff's deputies and justices of the peace.

I was born in Laredo, Texas. I am the second oldest of seven brothers and four sisters. I joined the U.S. Naval Reserves after graduating from high school and attended a Naval Radar School and became a radar man. My interest in law enforcement first began when I was assigned to military police duties in Da Nang, Vietnam. I was a shore patrolman in camp Tien Shay at the base of Monkey Mountain in Da Nang. Later I was transferred in-country to Chu Lai, Saigon, and Binh Thuy in the Mekong Delta, working in the Naval Operations Center. After my tour of duty in Vietnam, I returned and obtained my Associate of Arts degree from

Laredo Junior College. After working as a roughneck, security guard, cook, teacher's aide, school bus driver, coach's aide, and part-time at the telephone company, I realized that I needed a more stable occupation. Another reason was that I was married and had a son. I passed the written and physical agility test for the Laredo Police Department. I spent fifteen years with the Laredo Police Department, six years as a patrol officer. Later, I became an investigator in charge of the training division. Then I spent two years as an instructor with Laredo Community College Regional Police Academy. I have 23 years of law enforcement experience and have attended over 40 training schools, obtaining over 1,900 hours of instruction.

Training

In the State of Texas, to become a licensed jailer, one has to be 18 years of age and have a high school diploma or G.E.D. Also, an extensive background check is conducted, as well as a physical and drug test. Applicants must have no felony convictions; no class B misdemeanor convictions or above for the last ten years; must pass a psychological exam; must not be currently under indictment for any criminal offense; must never have been convicted of any family violence offense; must not have been prohibited by state or federal law from operating a motor vehicle or possessing firearms or ammunition; and must not be on court-ordered supervision or probation for any criminal offense above a class B misdemeanor. The person (if employed by the agency) will receive a temporary jailer's license for one year. During that year, he or she must attend a Basic County Corrections course of 80 hours and pass a state licensing examination. The individual has three opportunities to pass the examination.

Experiences

One very important thing I learned about being a law enforcement officer is to always listen. Listening is very important to us. An incident occurred early in the morning on New Year's Day a few years ago while I was on patrol. We had received an emergency call about a family disturbance. The first officer to arrive at the scene was a rookie police officer with less than one year of experience. I was the backup unit and arrived shortly after him. The young officer encountered a gruesome scene: A woman was lying on her back with her throat cut, and a hysterical man was yelling, wielding an open 5-inch jackknife in his right hand. The young officer quickly drew his .357 magnum revolver and pointed it at the suspect. As I was approaching the doorway where the officer was, I also drew my .357 magnum revolver. Somehow, through all of this commotion, we were able to make out what this suspect was yelling. The suspect was shouting in Spanish that he was going to kill him. He kept yelling this as he ran toward us with knife in hand. We quickly created more reactionary distance from the charging suspect. The suspect kept coming toward us with the knife, yelling, "I am going to kill him." As the suspect reached the doorway, we backed up with our weapons and aimed at him but didn't fire because of what he kept yelling. He was not saying that he killed the woman, but that he wanted to kill "him." The suspect rushed past us with the knife, heading for the street, still yelling in Spanish that he was going to kill "him." At this time, our sergeant arrived at the scene and saw the suspect running toward him with the knife. The sergeant quickly used the patrol car for cover and got his shotgun out and aimed it at the suspect. The sergeant was also listening and held his fire. We all chased the suspect and kept talking to him until he finally stopped and dropped the knife as instructed. The suspect then told us that his father-in-law had killed his mother-in-law. Apparently, the father-in-law, who was a very docile man, had freaked out and committed this hideous crime. The father-in-law was not intoxicated or under any influence of drugs. He quickly admitted that he had murdered his wife and came peacefully with us under arrest.

Advice to Students

The art of being a good listener, no matter under what circumstances, is a good trait every officer needs.

SUMMARY

Community corrections is responsible for supervising over two-thirds of all convicted offenders, as well as unconvicted offenders who may be participating in diversion or alternative dispute resolution programs. Besides probation and parole programs, community-based corrections involves extensive networking among different community agencies for the purpose of meeting the needs of the community corrections clientele. Enabling legislation for community-based corrections and related services is established through community corrections acts. The acts provide state and federal monies to local jurisdictions to establish what will eventually become self-sustaining community corrections programs designed to reintegrate and rehabilitate offenders. Most often targeted for participation in community corrections programming are jail- or prison-bound offenders who might profit more from community punishments rather than institutional incarceration. Thus, the philosophy of community corrections is largely offender reintegration. An additional benefit is that such correctional programming alleviates jail and prison overcrowding to a great degree.

Goals of community corrections include facilitating offender reintegration, fostering offender rehabilitation, providing an alternative range of offender punishments, and heightening offender accountability. The goals are achieved as the result of strategic offender monitoring, employment assistance, vocational and educational training, skill development, and individual and group counseling. Public safety is also stressed, since offenders serve their time in the community rather than behind bars in a prison or jail. Nearly 2 million offenders were involved in community-based programs in 2000, with a significant portion of these clients ordered to pay restitution to victims, perform community service, and participate in mandatory drug and alcohol testing and counseling.

Several community-based corrections programs include electronic monitoring, home confinement or house arrest, and day reporting centers. Electronic monitoring uses wristlets or anklets that emit electronic signals. These devices are tamper-resistant and can be removed by clients, although there are severe penalties for tampering with electronic monitoring equipment. Tampering is easily detected and conceivably punished by program termination and incarceration. Electronic monitoring has been used since the 1960s and is a primary method for determining and verifying an offender's whereabouts. Electronic monitoring does not control a client's behavior. However, such provisions as curfew are more easily enforced, as probation officers may conduct drive-bys of one's residence at all hours and verify that the offender is on the premises. Some electronic monitoring devices are connected with telephone systems, where offenders have telephones. Random dialing is accomplished from a central headquarters, and the offender must be home at particular times and verify his or her identity by using sensor equipment provided by the probation department. Other types of electronic monitoring use global positioning satellite tracking for ascertaining an offender's location in the community.

Electronic monitoring is advantageous in that face-to-face visits with clients are not usually required to verify one's whereabouts at particular times. However, some critics have said that electronic monitoring is intrusive and violates one's privacy. But the U.S. Supreme Court has not ruled decisively concerning the unconstitutionality of this monitoring method. Some critics believe that electronic monitoring widens the net by bringing certain persons under supervision who would not ordinarily be subject to such scrutiny on standard probation. However, the lower cost and minimally intrusive features of electronic monitoring more than compensate for any potential inconveniences to clientele who are supervised with such equipment.

Home confinement, which is often used in tandem with electronic monitoring, is another option. This program uses one's residence as the site for client confinement at particular times under curfew conditions. Although some people believe that home confinement isn't much of a punishment, others have found that it is much harsher for offenders than it appears. Some of the goals of home confinement include offender reintegration, reducing prison and jail overcrowding, and enabling offenders to maximize their rehabilitation and reintegration chances. Not everyone can be admitted into home confinement programs. Once the stringent eligibility requirements are met, various conditions are imposed. All home confinement clientele must make their residences available to warrantless searches by probation officers at any time, for whatever reason. This is a punishment many clients would like to avoid.

Day reporting centers are located in central points in neighborhoods. Clients may report to these centers during the day, where they can receive valuable assistance relating to job applications, vocational or educational training, individual or group counseling, and/or referrals to necessary community treatments or services. Sometimes termed invisible jails, these centers also monitor offenders by conducting alcohol and drug screens at random times. Other conditional punishments might include fine payments, community service orders, and restitution. These conditions are intended to heighten offender accountability. Furthermore, offenders do not need to pay for the community services they perform. Thus, if they are financially unable to pay fines, then they can be assigned to community service as an alternative punishment. Several restitution models were also examined. These include the financial/community service model, the victim/offender mediation model, and the victim/reparations model.

Community corrections raises several important issues. One of these issues has to do with the negative reaction of community residents to having criminals in their neighborhoods. If day reporting centers are located in particular neighborhoods, some residents believe that their property values are adversely affected. This is the NIMBY syndrome, or "not in my back yard" reaction. Citizens want offenders to be rehabilitated and law-abiding, but some citizens are unwilling to have correctional facilities located in close proximity to their own dwellings. This raises another issue—the delicate balance between offender needs and public safety. In order for offenders to maximize their rehabilitation and reintegration chances, they must be permitted some freedom of movement within their communities. But there is also a legitimate concern for citizen safety, since these offenders are often not monitored closely by probation officers and others. However, the effectiveness of community corrections programming is such that most offender-clients remain law-abiding while in their community programs and pose no significant risk to community residents. Other issues pertain to the nature and quality of services provided to these offenders, and whether some of these offenders have special needs. Many offenders are former drug addicts or alcoholics. Therefore, it is believed that they must be monitored or supervised more closely compared with those without drug or alcohol dependencies. Considerable effort must be made by any community corrections agency to ensure that effective coordination exists between different community service providers, and that offender-clients, including certain special-needs offenders, receive their needed services.

QUESTIONS FOR REVIEW

1. What is a community corrections act? What types of programs are established through these acts?

2. What are five important elements of community corrections effectiveness?

3. What is the philosophy of community corrections? Are the goals of community corrections realized in most communities? Why or why not?

4. How does community corrections alleviate prison and jail overcrowding? What are four goals of community corrections?

5. Who are community corrections clientele? What are some of their characteristics? Are there particular types of offenders who might be excluded from community corrections? If so, what are their characteristics?

6. What is electronic monitoring? What types of electronic monitoring systems are there? What are some of the issues that have been raised about the use of electronic monitoring in communities? Are these legitimate issues? Why or why not?

7. What is home confinement? What is its philosophy? What are several weaknesses and strengths of home confinement programs? Under what circumstances might electronic monitoring be used with home confinement?

8. What is a day reporting center? What services does it provide for clientele?

9. Under what circumstances might someone be ordered to pay fines, make restitution, or perform community service?

10. What are three major issues relating to community corrections? How does each of these issues hinder or assist community corrections planners in implementing community corrections programming?

SUGGESTED READINGS

Bottoms, Anthony, Loraine Gelsthorpe, and Sue Rex. *Community Penalties: Change and Challenges.* Portland, OR: Willan Publishing, 2002.

Braswell, Michael, John Fuller, and Bo Lozoff. *Corrections, Peacemaking, and Restorative Justice: Transforming Individuals and Institutions.* Cincinnati, OH: Anderson Publishing Company, 2001.

Cromwell, Paul F., Rolando V. del Carmen, and Leanne Fiftal Alarid. *Community-Based Corrections.* 5th ed. Belmont, CA: Wadsworth/Thomson Learning, 2002.

Perry, John, ed. *Repairing Communities through Restorative Justice.* Lanham, MD: American Correctional Association, 2002.

INTERNET CONNECTIONS

Addictions page
http://www.well.com/user/woa

Alcoholics Anonymous
http://www.alcoholics-anomymous.org

American Community Corrections Institute
http://www.accilifeskills.com/

BI Incorporated
http://www.bi.com

Center for Community Corrections
http://www.communitycorrectionsworks.org/aboutus

Center for Restorative Justice
http://www.ssw.che/.umn.edu/rjp

Citizen Probation
http://www.citizenprobation.com/

Fairfax County Pre-Release Center
http://www.g2.to/fairfax/departments/prc/prc

Federal Prison Consultants
http://www.federalprisonconsultants.com

Home Confinement Program
http://thwp.uscourts.gov/homeconfinement.html

International Community Corrections Association
http://www.iccaweb.org

National Institute on Drug Abuse
http://www.nida.nih.gov

New York State Probation Officer's Association
http://www.nyspoa.com/

Shadow Track Technologies
http://www.shadowtrack.com/?sources=Overture

Smart Recovery
http://www.smartrecovery.org

U.S. Probation Office, District of New Mexico
http://www.nmcourt.fed.us/pbdocs/

CHAPTER 5 | Jails: History, Functions, and Types of Inmates

Source: Damian Dovarganes, AP/Wide World Photos

Chapter Objectives | *As the result of reading this chapter, the following objectives should be realized:*

1. Describing the history of jails in the United States, workhouses, and other short-term detention facilities.
2. Describing and presenting jail inmate characteristics and admission-release data.
3. Delineating the diverse functions of jails.
4. Describing the types of inmates who are held in jails.

INTRODUCTION

• *A Jefferson County, Texas, grand jury indicted four persons on charges relating to sexual misconduct in the Jefferson County Jail. All were women. All were jail officers. The women involved are Latisha Trahan, 25, Chastity Broussard, 21, Ingrid Fisk, 21, and Monica Mahoney, 22. There were indications that some jail officers were committing various sex acts with several of the female prisoners, according to official sources. Surveillance cameras were installed in specific areas without the knowledge of the officers involved. Subsequently, video surveillance revealed that several of these staff members were having sex with different offenders. One jail officer, Broussard, was charged with assisting, promoting, and encouraging another officer, Fisk, to have sexual contact with an inmate as well as another employee in the control room of the jail facility. The sexual contact allegedly occurred on December 22, 2001. What punishment should be imposed, if these women are found guilty of the charges? What can be done to prevent jail officer misconduct in the future? Should video surveillance be in place in all U.S. jails and prisons? What do you think?* [Adapted from the Associated Press, "Guards Accused in Prison Cases," February 11, 2002].

• *Inmates thought it was funny. They made it look easy enough. On January 28, 2002, four dangerous felons escaped from the Montague County (Texas) Jail. Two inmates, Curtis Gambill, 23, and Joshua Bagwell, 24, were convicted murderers. Two other inmates, Michael Vick, 28, and Michael Ray West, 34, were being held awaiting trial, also on murder charges. The inmates were on the run for about two weeks. They fled to Oklahoma where they were eventually recognized and apprehended. While these dangerous prisoners were being held in Oklahoma awaiting extradition back to Texas, they joked with their Oklahoma jailers about how easy it was to break out of the Texas jail. According to one Oklahoma jail officer, "They were saying they had never seen a jail that was so easy to get out of. . . . they said it was a joke." A district attorney, Tim Cole, of Montague County, Texas, said, "I guess the truth is, that's probably correct. It wasn't all that difficult for them to get out." Two of the escapees said, "It wasn't that hard. It was easier than it should be, obviously." County officials who were contacted after these remarks said that they were taking steps to beef up jail security and plug the holes through which inmates had made good their escape. A sheriff's spokesman said, "They may laugh about it now, but they won't be laughing when we go to court. The humor will be gone then." How serious is the problem of jail security throughout the United States? How escape-proof should jails be? What do you think?* [Adapted from the Associated Press. "Inmates Laughed at Ease They Broke Out of Jail," February 11, 2002].

• *It happened in a small jail in Texas. Carl Franklin, 38 and homeless, was arrested by local police for loitering in a public park late at night. He appeared intoxicated and officers detected the odor of alcohol on Franklin's breath. Suspecting that Franklin was drunk, Franklin was taken to the local jail where he was fingerprinted and photographed. Jail officials confined him to a cell with four other inmates. Franklin was discovered dead the next day. A subsequent autopsy revealed that Franklin was a former mental patient who suffered from several physical ailments, including diabetes. When arrested by police, Franklin was probably in a diabetic coma. No effort was made by jail deputies to determine Franklin's intoxication level, which may have involved a simple blood analysis with kits available at the jail. Franklin had no relatives, according to sheriff's department sources. Subsequently, he was buried in a pauper's grave near Dallas. No one attended his funeral and no charges were ever brought against the jail for negligence or for the wrongful death of Franklin.* [Adapted from the Associated Press, "Homeless Man Dies in Jail from Diabetic Coma," February 28, 2002].

Jails in the United States are one of the most maligned and forgotten components of the criminal justice system. This chapter is about jails in the United States, their history, evolution, and reforms. With some exceptions, a **jail** is a confinement facility that is usually administered and operated by a local law enforcement agency, such as a county sheriff's office or county department of corrections; jails are intended to confine adults, but they may hold juveniles for brief periods (Cornelius 1997:1).

Jails are an integral feature of U.S. corrections. In 2001, there were an estimated 13 million admissions to and releases from U.S. jails, with an average daily jail population of 625,966 (Beck 2002:11). At midyear in 2001 there were 702,000 jail inmates, with 631,240 inmates housed in local jails. The remainder were supervised by jail authorities in alternative programs outside of jail facilities. The rated capacity of the nation's jails in mid-year 2001 was estimated at 699,309, indicating an occupancy of 90 percent of rated capacity. Between 1990 and mid-year 2001, the jail population grew by 53 percent (Beck 2002:12–13).

This population increase has created serious overcrowding problems in city and county jails in most jurisdictions. In turn, jail overcrowding has been directly or indirectly responsible for numerous inmate deaths and extensive violence, much offender litigation challenging, among other things, the constitutionality of the nature of confinement and treatment, and administrative and/or supervisory problems of immense proportions.

This chapter begins with an historical overview of jails in the United States. Jails are an outgrowth of gaols in England, incarceration facilities in English counties or shires. These early jails were workhouses, where inmates were assigned to various business interests for cheap labor. Early workhouses were known for their cruel and inhumane treatment of prisoners, many of whom were incarcerated for petty offenses. Pennsylvania was a pioneer in early jail developments in the newly formed United States, and jails were patterned after those in England. However, in 1790, the Walnut Street Jail was built in Philadelphia, and it quickly became a model for jails that was emulated by other jurisdictions. Subsequent jail developments are described, including the various attempts to identify different types of jails through surveys and census data. There have always been problems defining jail features, however, since many diverse types of facilities have been labeled as jails. Lockups, drunk tanks, and temporary huts or caves have been included within the jail rubric in past years. This conceptual Tower of Babel has made it difficult to obtain an accurate picture of the actual number of jail facilities in the United States. Most jails are locally administered, usually by sheriff's departments in U.S. counties, although some jail systems are state-operated.

The chapter next examines different kinds of jail inmates. Jails house a mixed clientele, including both short- and long-term offenders, adults and juveniles. The diversity of the jail population is linked closely with the different functions of jails and who they are intended to house. Thus, jails accommodate pretrial detainees; witnesses in protective custody; those serving short sentences for petty crimes; some juvenile offenders; convicted offenders awaiting sentencing; persons held on detainer warrants; drunks, derelicts, or the homeless; the mentally ill; state and federal contract prisoners; and probation and parole violators. These types of jail inmates are described. Some writers have suggested that jails hold society's rabble under the rabble hypothesis, suggesting that jails are comprised of mostly detached and disreputable persons. In recent years, greater attention has been given to jail design and function, and many jail improvements have occurred that have remedied various jail problems to a degree.

THE HISTORY OF JAILS IN THE UNITED STATES

The term *jail* is derived from old English term, *gaol* (also pronounced "jail"), which originated in 1166 A.D. through a declaration by Henry II of England. Henry II established gaols as a part of the Assize or Constitution of Clarendon (Roberts 1997). Gaols were locally administered and operated, and they housed many of society's misfits. Paupers or vagrants, drunkards, thieves, murderers, debtors, highwaymen, trespassers, orphan children, prostitutes, and others made up early gaol populations. Since the Church of England was powerful and influential, many religious dissidents were housed in these gaols as a punishment for their dissent. This practice continued for several centuries.

Local Political Control

Local control over the administration and operation of jails by shire-reeves in England was a practice continued by the American colonists in later years. Most jails in the United States today are locally controlled and operated similar to their English predecessors. Thus, political influence upon jails and jail conditions is strong. In fact, changing jail conditions from one year to the next are often linked to local political shifts through elections and new administrative appointments. Also, the fact that local officials controlled jails and jail operations meant that no single administrative style typified these facilities. Each locality (shire) was responsible for establishing jails, and the way in which jails were operated was left up to local official discretion. Again, current U.S. jail operations in each jurisdiction are characterized by this same individuality of style.

Jails in England were originally designed as holding facilities for those accused of violating local laws. Alleged law violators were held until court could be conducted and the guilt or innocence of the accused was determined. Today, pretrial detainees make up a significant proportion of the U.S. jail population. Shire-reeves made their living through reimbursements from taxes collected in the form of fees for each inmate housed on a daily basis. For instance, the reeve would receive a fixed fee, perhaps 50 or 75 cents per day for each inmate held in the jail. Therefore, more prisoners meant more money for reeves and their assistants. Such a reimbursement scheme was easily susceptible to corruption, and much of the money intended for inmate food and shelter was pocketed by selfish reeves. Quite logically, the quality of inmate food and shelter was very substandard, and jails became notorious because of widespread malnutrition, disease, and death among prisoners.

Workhouses

These cruel and inhumane jail conditions continued into the sixteenth century, when **workhouses** were established largely in response to mercantile demands for cheap labor. A typical workhouse in the mid-sixteenth century was Bridewell, created in 1557. This London facility housed many of the city's vagrants and general riffraff (Roberts 1997). Jail and workhouse sheriffs and administrators quickly capitalized on the cheap labor these facilities generated, and additional profits were envisioned. Thus, it became commonplace for sheriffs and other officials to hire out their inmates to perform skilled and semi-skilled tasks for various merchants. While the manifest functions of workhouses and prisoner labor were to improve the moral and social fiber of prisoners and train them to perform useful skills when they were eventually released, most of the monies collected from inmate labor was pocketed by corrupt jail and workhouse officials. This inmate exploitation continued a pattern that was widespread throughout early European corrections (Spierenburg 1991).

In the New England area and throughout the colonies, jails were commonplace. Sheriffs were appointed to supervise jail inmates, and the fee system continued to be used to finance these facilities. All types of people were confined together in jails, regardless of their gender or age. Orphans, prostitutes, drunkards, thieves, and robbers were often contained in large, dormitory-style rooms with hay and blankets for beds. Jails were great melting pots of humanity, with little or no regard for inmate treatment, health, or rehabilitation.

The Walnut Street Jail

The religious influence of the Quakers in Pennsylvania remained strong in the wake of abandoning Penn's jail reforms. Shortly after the Revolutionary War, the Quakers were able to reinstitute many of Penn's correctional philosophies and strategies through the creation in 1787 of the **Philadelphia Society for Alleviating the Miseries of Public Prisons.** This society was made up of many prominent Philadelphia citizens, philanthropists, and religious reformers who believed prison and jail conditions ought to be changed and replaced with a more humane environment. Members of this Society visited each jail and prison daily, bringing food, clothing, and religious instruction to inmates. Some of these members were educators who sought to assist prisoners in acquiring basic skills such as reading and writing. Although their intrusion into prison and jail life was frequently resented and opposed by local authorities and sheriffs, their presence was significant and brought the deplorable conditions of confinement to the attention of politicians. One particularly disturbing feature of both jails and prisons of that period was the extensive use of common rooms for men, women, and children. Little or no thought was given to housing these inmates in private or separate accommodations.

In 1790, the Pennsylvania legislature authorized the renovation of a facility originally constructed on Walnut Street in 1776, a two-acre structure initially designed to house the overflow resulting from overcrowding of the High Street Jail. The Walnut Street Jail was both a workhouse and a place of incarceration for all types of offenders. But the 1790 renovation was the first of several innovations in U.S. corrections. Specifically, the Walnut Street Jail was innovative because (1) it separated the most serious prisoners from others in sixteen large solitary cells; (2) it separated other prisoners according to their offense seriousness; and (3) it separated prisoners according to gender. Therefore, the Walnut Street Jail was the forerunner of minimum-, medium-, and maximum-security prisons in the United States as well as **solitary confinement.**

Besides these innovations, the Walnut Street Jail assigned inmates to different types of productive labor according to their gender and conviction offense. Women made clothing and performed washing and mending chores. Skilled inmates worked as carpenters, shoemakers, and other artisans. Unskilled prisoners beat hemp or jute for ship caulking. With the exception of women, prisoners received a daily wage for their labor that was applied to defray the cost of their maintenance. The Quakers and other religious groups provided regular instruction for most offenders. The Walnut Street Jail concept was widely imitated by officials from other states during the next several decades (Okun and Thomas 1997). Many prisons were modeled after the Walnut Street Jail for housing and managing long-term prisoners.

Jail Developments Since Walnut Street

Information about the early growth of jails in the United States is sketchy. One reason is that many inmate facilities were established during the 1800s and early 1900s serving many functions and operating under different labels. Sheriffs' homes were used as jails in some jurisdictions, while workhouses, farms, barns, small houses, and other types of facilities served similar purposes in others. Thus, depending on who did the counting, some facilities would be labeled as jails and some would not. Limiting jail definitions only to locally operated short-term facilities for inmates excluded also those state-operated jails in jurisdictions such as Alaska, Delaware, and Rhode Island. Another reason for inadequate jail statistics and information was that there was little interest in jail populations.

Another problem was that it was difficult to transmit information from jails and jail inmates to any central location during that period of time. Often, local records were not maintained, and many sheriff's departments were not inclined to share information about their prisoners with others. Streamlined communications systems did not exist, and information was compiled very slowly, if at all. State governments expressed little or no interest in the affairs of jails within their borders, since these were largely local enterprises funded with local funds. Even if there had been a strong interest in jail information among corrections professionals and others, it would have been quite difficult to acquire.

The U.S. Census Bureau began to compile information about jails in 1880 (Cahalan 1986:73). At ten-year intervals following 1880, general jail information was systematically obtained about race, nativity, gender, and age. Originally, the U.S. Census Bureau presented data separately for county jails, city prisons, work-houses, houses of correction, and leased county prisoners. But in 1923, these figures were combined to reflect more accurately what we now describe as jail statistics. A special report was prepared by the U.S. Census Bureau entitled *Prisoners, 1923*. And in that same year, Joseph Fishman, a federal prison inspector, published a book, *Crucible of Crime*, describing living conditions of many U.S. jails. Comparisons with 1880 base figures show the jail population of the United States was 18,686 in 1880 and eventually reached 631,240 by mid-year 2001.

Historically, reports about jail conditions in the United States have been largely unfavorable. The 1923 report by Fishman was based on his visits to and observations of 1,500 jails, describing the conditions he saw as horrible. More recent reports suggest these conditions have not changed dramatically since Fishman made his early observations (Kerle 1998). Of course, there are exceptions, but these are few and far between. It was not until 1972 that national survey data about jails became available. Exceptions include the years 1910, 1923, and 1933, where jail inmate characteristics were listed according to several offense categories. A majority of jail inmates each of those years had committed petty offenses such as vagrancy, public drunkenness, and minor property crimes (Cahalan 1986:86). Even since 1972, jail data have not been regularly and consistently compiled.

There are several reasons for many of the continuing jail problems in the United States. While some of these persistent problems will be examined in depth later in this chapter, it is sufficient for the present to understand that (1) most of the U.S. jails today were built before 1970, and many were built five decades or more before that; (2) local control of jails often results in erratic policies that shift with each political election, thus forcing jail guards and other personnel to adapt to constantly changing conditions and jail operations; and (3) jail funding is a low-priority budget item in most jurisdictions, and with limited operating funds, the quality of services and personnel jails provide and attract is considerably lower compared with state and federal prison standards and personnel.

How Many Jails Are There in the United States?

Currently, no one knows for sure the exact number of jails in the United States at any given time. One reason is that investigators disagree about how jails ought to be defined. Some survey researchers count only locally operated and funded, short-term incarceration facilities as jails, while other people include state-operated jails in their figures. In remote territories such as Alaska, World War II quonset huts may be used to house offenders on a short-term basis. Work-release centers, farms for low-risk inmates, and other facilities may be included or excluded from the jail definition. Sometimes, **lockups** (drunk tanks, holding tanks) are counted as jails, although these facilities exist primarily to hold those charged with public drunkenness or other minor offenses for up to 48 hours. These are not jails in the formal sense, but rather, they are simple holding tanks or facilities.

Several different federal agencies have reported different numbers of jails for any given year. For instance, in 1970, the Census of Institutional Population estimated there were 2,317 jails in the United States, while the Law Enforcement Assistance Administration reported 4,037 U.S. jails. Furthermore, a 1923 study conducted by the U.S. Census Bureau reported there were 3,469 U.S. jails in operation. And in 1984, the Advisory Commission on Intergovernmental Relations reported there were 3,493 jails in the United States. These widely disparate figures are confusing to most readers.

There has been a substantial decrease in the number of jails in the United States between 1970 and 2002, with 4,037 jails reported in 1970 and 3,365 jails reported in 2002 (Beck 2002:11). How can existing jails accommodate such inmate population increases? One answer is that many old jails have been destroyed or drastically remodeled and expanded, while many new jails have been constructed. Newer jails are generally designed to accommodate several times the number of jail inmates that were accommodated in the old jails.

Because many jails are small, it has been difficult to stimulate interest among local officials to accredit them through certification from any national organization. The American Correctional Association Division of Standards and Accreditation reports that, often, hesitancy on the part of jail officials and sheriffs to apply for accreditation is due to a lack of funds (Thompson and Mays 1991). The primary benefits of accreditation include (1) protecting life, safety, and health of both jail staffs and inmates; (2) assessing the strengths and weaknesses of jails to maximize their resources and implement necessary changes; (3) minimizing the potential for costly, time-consuming litigation through negligence and other liability; (4) enhancing the jail's credibility with courts and the public; (5) achieving professional and public recognition of good performance; and (6) improving staff and inmate morale (Washington 1987:15).

Most county jails throughout the United States have sought accreditation from organizations such as the American Jail Association and the American Correctional Association (Bittick 2003:8). The El Paso County, Colorado, Sheriff's Office, for instance, is devising policies and procedures designed to enhance inmate programs and officer safety in compliance with nationally accepted standards evolved from the ACA (Hilte 1998:33–34). Recommendations are solicited from both the private sector and various corrections agencies to improve jail officer effectiveness with various forms of jail training in jurisdictions such as Alameda County, California (Ryan and Plummer 1999). And at the Albany County Jail in New York, various initiatives have been adopted to deal with the problem of chronic jail overcrowding and facility improvement (Chapman 1998:9). Private contractors have also been consulted for their input and assistance in alleviating various types of jail problems and providing certain kinds of services for jail inmates.

Studies have been conducted to determine whether there are any definitive patterns associated with the rate of male and female incarcerations (Senese 1991). Admission records were examined from a large midwestern jail for a five-year period from 1982 to 1986. There appeared to be a cyclical occupancy pattern in the jail for men and women. It has been suggested that certain peak days can be predicted and that budgeting and staffing needs can be adjusted accordingly so that jail operations can proceed more smoothly. Thus, both jail operations and staff effectiveness issues are increasingly important as most jails in the United States are attempting to meet inmate needs adequately (Senese 1991).

JAIL INMATE CHARACTERISTICS

Some general characteristics of jail inmates are shown in Table 5.1 in the form of distributions of selected sociodemographic characteristics of jail inmates compared for the years 1990, 1995, 2000, and 2001.

In 2001 there were 625,966 jail inmates in the United States. Approximately 90 percent of these inmates were males. Jail admissions average between 10 million and 13 million inmates per year. This means that the jail population turns over twenty to twenty-five times a year (Weedon 2003:18). There is a growing proportion of female inmates, increasing from 9.2 percent in 1990 to 11.6 percent in 2001 (Beck, Karberg, and Harrison 2002:9). There are disproportionate numbers of blacks in jails compared with their proportionate distribution in the population. Blacks in 1990 accounted for 42.5 percent of all jail inmates. By 2001, blacks made up 40.6 percent of the U.S. jail population. In contrast, whites made up 43 percent of the 2001 jail inmate population, up from 41.8 percent in 1990. The proportion of Hispanic jail inmates remained fairly constant from 1990 (14.3 percent) through 2001 (14.7 percent). About 41.5 of all jail inmates in 2001 had previously been convicted of a crime, down from 48.5 percent in 1990. Thus, jails are holding increasing numbers of unconvicted offenders.

Additional characteristics of jail inmates apart from those disclosed in Table 5.1 are that fewer juveniles are being held in jails each year. In 1990, for example, there were 2,301 juveniles held in local jails. By 2001, this number had diminished to 856 juveniles. This is the result of the **jail removal initiative,** which seeks to prevent the detention of juveniles in adult jails for any length of time (Snell and Grabowski 2003:79–81). Another interesting trend is that increased numbers of jail inmates are being supervised outside of jails. Various types of noncustodial jail supervision include electronic monitoring, home detention, day reporting, community service, weekender programs, pretrial supervision, and assorted work and treatment programs (Beck, Karberg, and Harrison 2002:8). In 1995, there were 34,869 persons under jail supervision but not confined in jails.

TABLE 5.1

Gender, Race, Hispanic Origin, and Conviction Status of Local Jail Inmates, Midyear 1990, 1995, 2000–2001

| | Percent of Jail Inmates | | | |
Characteristic	1990	1995	2000	2001
Total	100%	100%	100%	100%
Gender				
Male	90.8%	89.8%	88.6%	88.4%
Female	9.2	10.2	11.4	11.6
Race/Hispanic origin				
White, non-Hispanic	41.8%	40.1%	41.9%	43.0%
Black, non-Hispanic	42.5	43.5	41.3	40.6
Hispanic	14.3	14.7	15.1	14.7
Other*	1.3	1.7	1.6	1.6
Conviction status (adults only)				
Convicted	48.5%	44.0%	44.0%	41.5%
Male	44.1	39.7	39.0	36.6
Female	4.5	4.3	5.0	4.9
Unconvicted	51.5	56.0	56.0	58.5
Male	46.7	50.0	50.0	51.9
Female	4.8	6.0	6.0	6.6

Note: Detail may not add to total because of rounding.
*Includes American Indians, Alaska Natives, Asians, and Pacific Islanders.
Source: Allen J. Beck, Jennifer C. Karberg, and Paige M. Harrison. *Prison and Jail Inmates at Midyear 2001.* Washington, DC: U.S. Department of Justice, 2002, p. 8.

In 2001 this number had grown to 70,804. Although jail incarceration rates have steadily risen during the period 1990–2001 (163 inmates per 100,000 U.S. residents in 1990; 222 inmates per 100,000 U.S. residents in 2001), larger numbers of jail inmates are being supervised in their communities rather than incarcerated. This suggests that jail space, like prison space, is being reserved increasingly for more serious types of offenders (Beck, Karberg, and Harrison 2002).

FUNCTIONS OF JAILS

Jails have the following functions:

Holding Pretrial Detainees

Those arrested for various offenses who cannot afford or are denied bail are housed in jails until a trial can be held. These persons are called **pretrial detainees.** In some jurisdictions, such as Blackhawk County Jail, Iowa, the duration of **pretrial detention** has lengthened. Thus, there is a greater time interval between the time a person is arrested and tried for an offense. As a result, the Iowa jail inmate population has increased and has exacerbated existing jail overcrowding problems (Hunter and Sexton 1997).

Jail recreation room.

Housing Short-Term Offenders

Convicted offenders in local courts are typically housed in jails for periods of less than one year. Maximum incarcerative sentences for misdemeanors in almost every jurisdiction are less than one year. Furthermore, many convicted felons serve short sentences in jails, despite the fact judges may impose longer incarcerative sentences (Harlow 1998).

Holding Witnesses in Protective Custody

In more serious criminal cases, material witnesses may be housed in jails temporarily until trials can be held. These witnesses may be reluctant to testify and often are placed in protective custody. In some cases, threats have been made against certain witnesses, and their lives are in jeopardy. The popular image of Mafia organized crime figures disposing of witnesses who can incriminate them or link them with criminal activity is more a reality than a myth. Often, jails are designed so that these witnesses can be segregated from the general inmate population in special areas.

Holding Convicted Offenders Awaiting Sentencing

Convicted offenders awaiting sentencing are usually held in local jail facilities. These offenders may be federal, state, or local prisoners. When these offenders are housed in local jails, the jurisdiction is ordinarily reimbursed for offender expenses from state or federal funds.

Temporarily Housing Juvenile Offenders

Although most jails in the United States are designed to accommodate adult offenders, some arrested juveniles may be housed in jails for brief periods. The jail removal initiative has been used to restrict admissions of juveniles into jails whenever jail confinement can be avoided, even if the confinement period is brief. A federal provision applicable to states accepting federal funds for jail improvements states that when juveniles must be held in jails for short times, they must be segregated from adult offenders by both sight and sound. This is one of several stringent provisions set forth in the Juvenile Justice and Delinquency Prevention Act of 1974 and its various subsequent amendments. However, not all jails are able to comply with this stringent initiative. Thus, there are occasions in some jails where juveniles are celled adjacent to or with adult offenders for brief periods. But, as has been noted earlier, the numbers of juveniles held in adult jails has steadily diminished during the years 1990 through 2001. Only 856 juveniles were held for brief periods in U.S. jails in 2001 (Beck, Karberg, and Harrison 2001:9). However, more juveniles are being held in U.S. jails as adults. These are youths who have been designated as adults for the purpose of prosecution in criminal courts. In 1995, for instance, 5,900 juveniles were being held in U.S. jails as adults, while in 2001, this figure had increased to 6,757. This is largely the result of the get-tough movement, which seeks to punish certain juveniles more harshly for committing more serious offenses. All states presently have provisions to waive juvenile court jurisdiction over certain types of juvenile offenders, especially those charged with violent crimes such as murder, rape, robbery, or aggravated assault (Myers 2001).

Thus, the confinement of juveniles in jails, either as adults or juveniles, is often unavoidable. Many youths possess false identification, or they may appear to be much older than they really are. Both male and female runaways may engage in prostitution to earn survival money on city streets (Kingree, Braithwaite, and Woodring 2001). They may be arrested by police and confined in jails temporarily until it can be determined who and how old they really are. When it is discovered that they are juveniles, they are often taken to the available community social services or agencies for subsequent disposition. While some persons oppose the placement of juveniles in jails, even for brief periods, the U.S. Supreme Court has upheld the constitutionality of their temporary jail detention.

In 1984, the U.S. Supreme Court ruled in the case of *Schall v. Martin* that juveniles may be subject to the same pretrial detention as adults, especially if it is the opinion of the court that the juvenile would otherwise pose a risk or danger to society if released. This is **preventive detention,** and it is designed to control offenders, adult or juvenile, who are high escape risks or who might pose a danger to themselves or others if released from jail prior to trial.

Confining Misdemeanants, Drunks, and Derelicts

About a fourth of all jail inmates in 2000 were convicted of property offenses, such as burglary, larceny/theft, motor vehicle theft, fraud, and stolen property charges. Another fourth were held on public-order offenses, such as weapons charges, traffic violations, driving while intoxicated, and violations of probation or parole. Many jail inmates were being held on drug charges, including the use of or trafficking in illegal narcotics. A majority of these were convicted of misdemeanors, where sentences imposed were less than one year. About 25 percent of all jail inmates were held on charges involving violent offenses, such as rape, homicide, robbery, and aggravated assault (Maguire and Pastore 2002).

Large numbers of jail arrestees include transients, the homeless, and other derelicts who are picked up for loitering or sleeping in city parks, store entrances, and alleys. Police officers who pick up these persons often refer to these arrests as mercy bookings, since they know such persons will die if left out on the streets. At least in jail, even for temporary periods, these persons will receive shelter and something to eat.

Housing the Mentally Ill

In recent years, jails have held increasing numbers of persons who are mentally ill or suffer from some type of mental disorder (Dekleva 2001). Not all mentally ill arrestees enter insanity pleas or offer mental illness as a defense, however. One reason is that most states have difficult tests for insanity to be sustained if claimed (Wheatman and Shaffer 2001). Also, if persons are successful in being acquitted of criminal charges by reason of insanity, they are nevertheless possibly subject to an indeterminate length of confinement in a mental institution (Kirschner and Galperin 2001). It has been estimated that of the more than 10 million jail admissions annually, at least 650,000 of these inmates have mental disorders (Ventura et al. 1998). Many of these mentally ill inmates remain incarcerated for long periods before their cases are processed.

Since jail staff are not ordinarily trained to deal effectively with mentally disordered arrestees, it is often difficult to detect which inmates have mental disorders, which ones are pretending to be mentally ill, and which ones are free of any dysfunctional mental disturbance. Lupton (1996:49) says that mentally ill inmates are highly unpredictable, and they may abruptly begin to exhibit bizarre behaviors. Under circumstances in which jail inmates act in peculiar ways, jail staff often call in mental health professionals to diagnose these inmates. Presently, more than a few jail staff are untrained to deal with these sorts of problems. Thus, some mentally ill inmates are criminalized rather than hospitalized (Reiss et al. 2001).

Often, physicians are available only on an on-call basis from local clinics in communities, and no rehabilitative programs or activities exist. Most jails have no facilities such as outdoor recreation yards where inmates may exercise. Vocational, educational, and therapeutic programs are almost nonexistent, since jail inmates are considered short-term occupants. Some jurisdictions have explored the possibility of training police officers to recognize mentally ill arrestees so that they can be diverted from jails to hospitals or mental institutions where they can receive treatment rather than jail confinement (Simonet 1995:30). However, this alternative has generally been found to be prohibitive and unworkable (Wood 1995).

For larger jails with more services and personnel, physicians and paramedics are available to administer one of several mood-altering medications that will calm disturbed inmates. However, it takes time to report disruptive behavior and to locate staff to make on-the-spot diagnoses of inmate problems. Subsequent to a psychological examination by trained personnel, medications may be ordered for them. These medications are supposed to treat specific mental illnesses temporarily. In jail settings, this means that certain drugs may be prescribed for and administered to particular inmates in the interests of institutional or individual safety. The case of *Washington v. Harper* (1990) involved the right of a prison inmate, Harper, to refuse psychotropic medications under the due process clause of the Fourteenth Amendment. However, the U.S. Supreme Court said that compulsory

BOX 5.1

Robyn M. Pope-Burgess

Student Assistant, California Department of Justice

Statistics

A.A. (general education), Shasta Community College; B.S. (criminal justice), California State University-Sacramento; M.A. (criminal justice management and administration), University of Alaska-Fairbanks

Background and Interests

Currently, I am a graduate student assistant with the California Department of Justice (DOJ), Bureau of Forensic Services (BFS), Latent Print Program in Sacramento, California. I began my career with California as a student assistant in June 1997 at the DOJ, BFS, Redding Criminalistics Laboratory in Redding, California. Upon completion of my A.A. degree from Shasta Community College, I transferred to California State University-Sacramento (CSUS) and was also able to transfer within the Department of Justice. I graduated with honors from CSUS in December 2001, with my B.S. in criminal justice. Immediately following graduation, I began working toward my M.A. in criminal justice management and administration via the Internet through the University of Alaska-Fairbanks.

My interest in the area of law enforcement stems back to my father. I was raised in a law enforcement environment in rural northern California and have been involved with various related activities my whole life. My father, Jim Pope, has been the sheriff of Shasta County, California, for the past twelve years and has worked in the area of law enforcement for forty years. I am an associate member of the California State Sheriff's Association and have attended many annual conferences held throughout California and also a National Sheriff's Association Conference in the past.

I met my husband, Jody, on a blind date in May 1997. Both reluctant to go, we soon found we were complete opposites, but we became inseparable from day one. He is also from northern California and was raised with a law enforcement background. My father-in-law is a recently retired Cali-

fornia Highway Patrol Traffic Officer of the Trinity River Division. My husband is a 1998 criminal justice graduate of CSUS and a 2002 graduate of the University of the Pacific, McGeorge School of Law. His inspiration and encouragement has motivated me to continue my educational career. In June 1999, Jody and I were married.

As a graduate student assistant, my regular duties encompass a variety of areas in the office. Under the direct supervision of a Latent Print Analyst, I have accompanied analysts to and assisted with processing major crime scenes; assisted with processing evidence submitted to the laboratory; assisted with processing and obtaining fingerprints from submitted hands and fingers of deceased "John Doe" victims; and have observed analysts giving court testimony. Other duties include maintaining and organizing the evidence locker; compiling monthly attendance records; typing case reports; updating and maintaining training records; and, at the request of a supervisor, generating memorandums and other documents containing sensitive and confidential information. I really enjoy my current position and have learned so much by having the opportunity to see hands-on the various stages from examining a crime scene, collecting relevant evidence, processing evidence, distributing the results, and observing court testimony that oftentimes results in convictions. I was able to participate in events such as attending Attorney General's Zone Meetings, volunteering in the Attorney General's Megan's Law Booth at the California State Fair, and attending formal training courses. I was also very fortunate that my department

(continued)

BOX 5.1 (Continued)

supported me and allowed me to focus my education as my number one priority.

Now that I have a degree, I have tested and am pursuing a permanent position with California as a Criminal Intelligence Specialist. I soon will be transferring to the DOJ, Bureau of Narcotic Enforcement, Redding Field Office, and I will continue in my current student position while I finish graduate school. Although I have recently graduated with a bachelor's degree, I feel that I have not yet reached my level of academic potential. I have observed through my current occupation that most administrators today would not hold their current positions if the standards they were hired in accordance with were set as high as today's standards. I realize that further advancing my education will be beneficial to me in the future in the event a promotional opportunity were to become available.

Advice to Students

My advice to fellow students would be to persevere and continue to work hard. Completing your educational goals while you are young will leave you with endless career opportunities free from interruptions and missed promotions due to a lack of education. If possible, I would recommend getting involved with a law enforcement agency that will work with you while you are in school. You will gain valuable knowledge and experience and form networks that can prove beneficial when you begin to seek permanent employment. I would also recommend to go above and beyond what is expected and to always reflect a friendly and welcoming demeanor. Impressions can last a lifetime, and you never know whose path you may once again cross down the road.

medication may be administered to unruly inmates of both prisons and jails if their behaviors pose a reasonable threat to institutional safety and order (Glade 1996).

One complication affecting how the mentally ill in jails are treated is that many of them have assorted chemical dependencies, such as cocaine or heroin addictions or chronic alcoholism (Atkins, Applegate, and Hobbs 1998). When such persons are deprived of these addictive substances, even for short periods of time, they may become suicidal and their behaviors may become increasingly violent and unpredictable (Haddad 1993). Some of the larger jails, such as Orange County Jail, Florida, have established central assessment units, with both voluntary and involuntary entrances. These facilities are also equipped with detoxification units for those with substance abuse problems. Both community volunteers and professional health-care workers are able to manage effectively the relatively large numbers of mentally ill substance-abusing inmates who are processed by the Orange County Jail (Atkins, Applegate, and Hobbs 1998:71). However, the Orange County Jail in Florida is exceptional and by no means portrays how the average jail deals with mentally ill offenders. Considerable community networking and cooperation is necessary in order for any jail to establish these types of provisions for inmates with problems (Kaufman 1998).

Holding Prisoners Wanted by Other Jurisdictions on Detainer Warrants

Jails must often accommodate prisoners wanted by other jurisdictions in other states on the basis of a **detainer. Detainer warrants** are notices of criminal charges or unserved sentences pending against prisoners (Harlow 1998). Even though these types of prisoners will eventually be moved to other jurisdictions when authorities from those jurisdictions take them into custody, detainees take up space and time when initially booked and processed.

Holding Probation and Parole Violators

When probationers or parolees are picked up by local authorities and others for alleged violations of the terms of their programs, they are usually taken to jail. Under the law, probationers and parolees are entitled to a hearing regarding whether their probation or parole conditions have actually been violated. These hearings take time to arrange, and in the interim, these prisoners often remain jailed until these matters can be concluded.

Accommodating State and Federal Prison Inmate Overflow

In some jurisdictions, such as Tennessee, Texas, and Utah, state and federal prison authorities enter into contracts or leasing arrangements with local city or county jails to accommodate excessive numbers of state or federal prisoners. In 2000, for example, over 63,000 state and federal inmates were being held in jails or other locally operated facilities (Norman and Locke 2002:13). Texas has contracted with state and federal authorities to house a portion of its prison inmate overflow. For example, Denton County Jail in Texas houses 232 Oregon prisoners (Lucas 1996). What does Denton County get out of it? The county receives about $250,000 per month for inmate maintenance. Oregon inmates don't especially like being confined in a county jail for up to two years. In fact, some Oregon inmates, known as **contract prisoners,** have gone on hunger strikes and engaged in other disruptive behavior while confined at the Denton County Jail. These incidents have been suppressed. However, once jail officials announced that "no prisoner will be returned to Oregon because of misbehavior, but he will be dealt with according to Denton County Jail rules," the disruptive incidents and protests ended fairly quickly.

Other Miscellaneous Jail Functions

The diversity of functions fulfilled by jails accounts for many of their present problems. A jail in a large city or even a small one must accommodate all types of people. It is apparent that not everyone who is processed through a county or city jail has violated the law. Witnesses may be held to testify later in court against various defendants. Or some juveniles, indigents, and others are held temporarily until a community agency can provide alternative services. Those arrested for public drunkenness may be held overnight, where they will be released the following morning after payment of a fine or some other penalty. Interstate hitchhikers may be picked up by county or city police and taken to jail. It is necessary to log or book each detainee or arrestee, especially in the larger jails where routines have become more formalized. Even in less formal jail settings, people-processing takes time.

The Rabble Hypothesis.   John Irwin (1985) argues that jails are more likely to receive, process, and confine mostly detached and disreputable persons rather than true criminals. Irwin has referred to such persons as rabble. He says that many noncriminals are arrested simply because they are offensive and not because they have committed crimes. Irwin worked as a caseworker in several

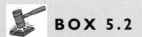

BOX 5.2

CONTRACT PRISONERS IN ARIZONA

Hawaiian Inmates in Arizona

Arizona prisons accommodate about 1,100 Hawaiian inmates per year. Corrections Corporation of America (CCA), a private firm, operates various prisons throughout the United States on a "for-profit" basis. Increasingly, states and the federal government are turning to privatization in order to solve the growing problem of institutional overcrowding. One site housing at least 1,100 Hawaiian inmates is the Florence, Arizona, prison operated by CCA. Hawaii pays CCA about $17 million per year to house these inmates. This is relatively cheap, considering what Hawaiian prison officials must spend to accommodate their prisoners in Hawaiian institutions.

As the state contract was about to expire with CCA, Hawaiian officials flew to Florence, Arizona, to conduct an inspection of the prison system. In recent months, two Hawaiian prisoners died while in CCA custody. These deaths were unrelated to CCA negligence, however. One inmate died of natural causes, while the other inmate died of a drug overdose when he swallowed a package of drugs in an attempt to smuggle them into the facility. Despite the nature of these deaths, CCA has been criticized anyway.

According to the monitoring team sent to inspect the Florence prison, there was widespread drug use among inmates. Furthermore, the inspection team did not tour the entire prison because of what they perceived to be a hostile environment. The hostile environment was attributable to gang activity and menacing prisoners. Gang presence in prisons throughout the United States is pervasive. No one denies that. Can it be prevented or controlled? Probably not. Attempts are made to break up gang members by segregating them or shipping them to different prisons within various states. But somehow, gangs persist. Furthermore, almost every prison has drug problems. Inmates get drugs smuggled in to them by different means, often by corrupt prison correctional officers (Marquart, Barnhill, and Balshaw 2001). Thus, drug use among inmates is extremely difficult to control or eliminate.

Despite the hostility encountered by the Hawaiian inspection team, the CCA contract was renewed. CCA authorities indicated that they are establishing new drug treatment programs and counseling sessions. Further, they plan to establish educational and various rehabilitative programs in future years. Typical inmate complaints are that they lack educational, sex offender, and drug treatment programs or opportunities to work at prison jobs. Hawaii has been sending some of its inmates to mainland prisons and jails since 1995. Most of the inmates they send to the mainland are "problem prisoners" that many systems reject. One Hawaiian prison official said, "We send them to Arizona because Arizona accepts them. We didn't have too many alternatives. We know these were problem inmates."

What do you think of prison privatization? Should it be minimized? How can we accommodate growing numbers of offenders who deserve to be incarcerated without privatization? What do you think?

Source: Adapted from the Associated Press, July 1, 2001.

county jails in San Francisco, California, during the early 1980s, and he based his conclusions on personal observations as well as conversations and interviews with county pretrial release and public defender personnel.

Subsequently, researchers sought to determine whether Irwin's observations were valid. Testing the **rabble hypothesis,** Backstrand, Gibbons, and Jones (1992) studied all bookings at the Multnomah County (Portland, Oregon) Jail for a period of time as well as all bookings in Skamania County, Washington, during a one-week period in 1991. These investigators found that although Irwin may have overstated his case, there was some support for the idea that many jail bookings, at least in these jurisdictions, involved marginal, nonserious offenders. The investigators did determine that greater proportions of bookings involved persons charged with or convicted of serious offenses.

TYPES OF JAIL INMATES

The large volume of people admitted to and released from jails annually, over 10 million, together with the average daily jail population of 625,966 in 2001, suggests that most admissions are extremely short-term, probably 24 to 48 hours or less (Beck, Karberg, and Harrison 2002:9). A hitchhiker might be picked up by a state trooper and taken to the nearest jail for a brief investigation. The hitchhiker is warned about local ordinances prohibiting hitchhiking; his or her name, address (if any), and other information may be recorded for future reference; and the person is soon released. These types of arrests and jail bookings account for many of these 10 million jail admissions. If juveniles are taken to jail because of suspicious behavior, their brief stay before being turned over to parents is also included in jail admission figures.

Reports received from citizenry about suspicious persons in their neighborhoods or those walking the streets late at night without explanation may result in arrests and temporary detentions, where brief investigations of suspicious people are conducted. Again, these arrests and detentions usually result in releases several hours later. Persons wandering about in high-crime areas of cities are prime targets for arrest by police, especially if they are vagrants or indigents. Those sleeping in alleyways at night or in unoccupied buildings or dwellings are also subject to arrest and detention for violating city or county ordinances.

Pretrial Detainees

In 2001, for instance, over 50 percent (339,461) of all adults being held in jails were pretrial detainees awaiting trial (Beck, Karberg, and Harrison 2002). Most local jurisdictions have established policies governing how long these persons will be detained. Much depends upon the seriousness of the offense and court efficiency. Sometimes, court calendars are clogged and inmates must be held beyond periods outlined in city or county policy. In some jurisdictions, a 30-day period is the maximum interval between one's arrest and trial for petty offending and city or county ordinance violations. Inmates may be held for longer periods if sufficient justification exists.

Of the average daily jail inmate population in 2001, the average length of stay for pretrial detainees in a majority of U.S. jails was 67 days (Maguire and Pastore 2002). For sentenced prisoners, including federal and state prisoners, the average length of stay in these same jails was 143 days. The average length of stay for all jail inmates was 86 days (Maguire and Pastore 2002).

Convicted Offenders: Local, State, and Federal Prisoners

Some jails contract with state and federal prison systems to house a portion of their overflow. In fact, evidence suggests that in recent years, these overflow numbers in U.S. jails have been increasing (Gilliard and Beck 1998). While accommodating state and federal prison overflows increases jail revenues in these jurisdictions, such contracting only serves to aggravate existing jail overcrowding problems in these same jurisdictions (Cole and Call 1992:36–37).

One of the nation's largest jails, the Shelby County Division of Correction in Memphis, Tennessee, has space available for 3,572 inmates (Schellman 1996:27). For the past several years, space has been made available for 252 prisoners from the Tennessee Department of Corrections. During the time that Shelby County has made jail space available to state prisoners, there has been an average daily bed occupancy of at least 200 state prisoners (Schellman 1996:27–28). One of the major problems experienced by state prisoners being held at the Shelby County facility is boredom. Tennessee Department of Corrections inmates most often are not enrolled in a treatment or vocational program. Most do not have a jail job. As a result, they do slow time. Nevertheless, state inmates have blended fairly easily into the general population of jail inmates, and problem incidents have not been frequent.

In some cases, contract prisoners are more trouble than they are worth. In December, 1988, for instance, 50 prisoners from the District of Columbia were shipped to the Spokane County Jail in Washington (Zupan 1993:22). Rejecting outright this transfer some 3,000 miles away from their home, the inmates proceeded to threaten and assault jail officers, clog toilets, throw food trays, and destroy other jail property. After only three months, Spokane authorities sent these prisoners back to the District of Columbia. During the 1990s and beyond 2000, the numbers of contract prisoners have been steadily growing. At the beginning of 2001, for instance, there were 112,854 contract prisoners reported in a survey of 35 jurisdictions (Camp and Camp 2002:93). This figure is considered an underestimate of the total number of contract prisoners in the United States today, inasmuch as 15 jurisdictions were not included in the survey.

Increasingly, jail and prison cells include tamper-resistant sinks, cots, and commodes to minimize destructive actions by inmates.

Drunk and Disorderly Persons, Transients

There were about 260,000 convicted offenders serving terms of various lengths in U.S. jails in 2001, according to an annual survey of jails (Beck, Karberg, and Harrison 2002:9). A majority of these offenders were serving short terms for misdemeanor convictions. However, included in these figures are those prisoners from state or federal facilities representing prison overflow, those being held who are wanted by jurisdictions in other states, and those convicted by federal or state courts and not as yet sentenced.

However, a significant proportion of jail inmates consists of those who are indigent, transients, or vagrants (Beck, Karberg, and Harrison 2002). These people pose additional problems to jail staff, because in most small jails, there are no separate facilities for segregating these inmates from more serious offenders. Historically, jails have housed a variety of transient persons (e.g., inebriates, homeless) in calabooses or small lockups (Green et al. 1997). All kinds of people are processed through jails every day. If juveniles are taken to jail because of suspicious behavior, their brief stay before being turned over to parents is counted as a jail admission. Neighbors may complain about loiterers in their neighborhoods. Persons wandering about in high-crime areas of cities are prime targets for arrest by police, especially if they are vagrants or indigents. Persons who sleep in alleyways, public parks, or unoccupied buildings at night are also subject to arrest and detention for violating city or county ordinances. Police officers may bring loiterers and vagrants to jail and hold them temporarily until they can establish their identity and account for their conduct (Shelden and Brown 1991). These arrests and detentions most often result in releases several hours later. Drunk drivers are taken to jails by police officers every evening, and they are released in the morning, after they have sobered up.

The Mentally Ill or Retarded

Many jail inmates are mentally ill or retarded. Various clinical studies suggest that at least 15 percent or more of those incarcerated in jails and prisons have severe mental illnesses. Psychologically disturbed inmates may prove bothersome or disruptive to other inmates (Simonet 1995). These people pose additional problems to jail staff, because in especially small jail facilities, there are no separate facilities for segregating them from serious offenders.

There are several reasons for why so many mentally ill persons are being confined in jails. First, there has been extensive deinstitutionalization of the mentally ill throughout the United States, especially during the 1980s and 1990s. Many of these people who should be institutionalized or hospitalized are permitted to roam city streets and create greater enforcement problems for police. More rigid criteria govern civil commitments of mentally ill persons. Further, there are increasing barriers that prevent the mentally ill from receiving needed community treatment for their disorders. There is also the general attitude of the police and society toward the mentally ill, where low priority is assigned to their numbers and treatment (Wettstein 1998).

A blanket solution to the problem of greater numbers of mentally ill who commit minor offenses is to divert them to community programs. However, outpatient treatment of such persons is difficult to supervise and enforce. Community agencies frequently lack the time and/or personnel to oversee the treatments these persons should receive (Faiver 1998). There is some evidence to show that whenever persons with mental disorders are properly supervised in their communities with effective case management systems, their recidivism declines significantly and they are able to sustain law-abiding behaviors for longer periods before rearrests (Ventura et al. 1998).

Alcohol and Chemically Dependent Offenders

Drug and alcohol abuse are highly correlated with criminal conduct. Large numbers of pretrial detainees are characterized as having drug and/or alcohol dependencies. Furthermore, there is evidence that many offenders suffer from polysubstance abuse (Morris and Steadman 1994).

Offenders with drug or alcohol dependencies present several problems for correctional personnel (Kaufman 1998). Often, jails are not equipped to handle their withdrawal symptoms, especially if they are confined for long periods. Also, the symptoms themselves are frequently dealt with rather than the social and psychological causes for these dependencies. Thus, when offenders go through alcohol detoxification programs or are treated for drug addiction, they leave these programs and are placed back into the same circumstances that caused the drug or alcohol dependencies originally.

Those re-entering the community on parole after years of incarceration are especially vulnerable to drug dependencies during the first six months following their release (Bean 2002). Individual or group counseling and other forms of therapy are recommended for drug- or alcohol-dependent clients, although many clients are considered treatment-resistant (Dawson 1992). Since 1972, various community-based treatment programs have been implemented to treat and counsel drug-dependent clients. These community-based programs have been collectively labeled Treatment Alternatives to Street Crime (TASC) and currently are being operated in numerous jurisdictions throughout the United States to improve client abstinence from drugs, increase their employment potential, and improve their social/personal functioning.

Some jail programs are gender-specific. This is because at least half a million women are locked up in jails annually (Muraskin 1997:27). In the San Francisco Sheriff's Department, a program was established in 1993 known as the SISTER Project. SISTER stands for Sisters in Sober Treatment Empowered in Recovery. It is a substance abuse treatment and recovery program for incarcerated women. It was the first in-custody women's therapeutic community in the nation (Shapiro 2001). The SISTER Project is an in-jail drug treatment program that is modeled after a more typical postrelease therapeutic community. Drug treatment is addressed through a variety of disciplines, including individual counseling, group counseling, basic education, parenting classes, health classes, acupuncture, life skills workshops, and peer counseling by ex-offenders. A prison participant is involved in organized therapeutic activities at least eight hours a day. SISTER Project participants, female jail inmates who are substance and alcohol abusers, remain in the program an average of 46 days. The program adds $38 per day to incarceration costs, although the lower recidivism rate among female participants justifies this greater expense. A highlight from the SISTER Project is that most women who are rearrested later are arrested on charges unrelated to drugs or alcohol. Thus, SISTER Project officials claim the following beneficial effects: (1) longer time intervals between arrest, (2) general reduction in recidivism, and (3) reduction in the propensity to be rearrested on drugs/alcohol charges (Hennessey 1997:43). In subsequent years, the therapeutic community concept directed toward female offenders has been established in states such as Florida, Idaho, Illinois, and Texas (Blount and Jalazo 2002; Shapiro 2001).

Juvenile Offenders

A growing number of jail inmates are offenders age 17 or younger. Regardless of how long these persons are accommodated in adult jails, some investigators believe it is too long. But despite jail removal initiatives and the lure of federal money for jail programs, the number of juvenile jail inmates has increased rather than decreased over the last few decades. The most obvious problems with celling juveniles in adult lockups or jails are that (1) youths are subject to potential sexual assault from older inmates, and (2) youths are often traumatized by the jailing experience (Kerle 1998). This latter problem leads to another problem that is even more serious—jail suicides. Juveniles are especially suicide-prone during the first 24 hours of their incarceration in jails. Thus, it is little consolation that several states have passed laws prohibiting a juvenile's confinement in adult jails for periods longer than 6 hours (Austin, Johnson, and Gregoriou 2000).

There are several organized movements in many jurisdictions to mandate the permanent removal of juveniles from adult jails, even on temporary bases. Civil rights suits as well as class action claims are being filed by and on behalf of many juveniles currently detained in adult facilities. In the Iowa case of *Hendrickson v. Griggs* (1987), a federal district judge, Donald E. O'Brien, ruled that the Juvenile Justice and Delinquency Prevention Act could be used as the basis for a lawsuit seeking the permanent removal of juveniles from adult jails. There is much remaining to be done to change a situation that seems more within the jurisdiction of the juvenile justice system than within the criminal justice system (Reddington and Anderson 1996).

SUMMARY

Jails are short-term incarcerative facilities designed to hold those offenders serving sentences of less than one year or those awaiting trial. Pretrial detainees are often housed in jails. While no accurate estimates exist about how many jails there are in the United States, it is likely that there were 3,365 jails in 2002. Jails are subject to local political control in most jurisdictions, although some of them may be state-operated. Increasingly, some jails are privately operated and administered. Workhouses were used in early England as a source of cheap labor, and inmates were often exploited by mercantile interests. In the United States, the Walnut Street Jail was an innovative enterprise in 1790. It separated prisoners according to their offenses and gender. It also introduced solitary confinement to corrections. Several functions of jails include holding pretrial detainees, holding witnesses in protective custody, housing some of the federal and state prison inmate overflow, and housing those awaiting sentencing. Jail administration is generally in the hands of county sheriffs who hire jailers and other jail personnel.

The jail population in the United States is fluid, with an estimated 10 million or more persons admitted to and released from jails annually. In 2001 the jail population in the United States was over 600,000. Although some juveniles are a part of the jail population every year, the jail removal initiative has operated to reduce the number of juveniles held in adult jails. Jail functions include holding pretrial detainees and persons who have been convicted but who are awaiting sentencing. Jails also house those serving short-term sentences. In the last several decades, some of the nation's larger jails are housing state and federal prisoners for longer periods under a contracting system. These contract prisoners are accommodated in jails with extra space and are intended to alleviate prison overcrowding.

Other jail functions include holding witnesses in protective custody; holding probation and parole violators; holding those wanted by other jurisdictions on detainer warrants; and confining drunks, derelicts, and various misdemeanants. Often, some of the homeless population are housed in jails temporarily, simply because there is no other place to confine them. Jails are also repositories for the mentally ill, who often wander the streets aimlessly and get into trouble.

Closely connected with these different jail functions is an interesting mix of jail inmates. These include persons awaiting trial, who are known as pretrial detainees. They are held in jails because it is believed that they might otherwise escape or flee the jurisdiction to avoid prosecution. Other inmates have been convicted of one or more crimes in court and are awaiting sentencing, perhaps subsequently being transferred to prison. When probationers or parolees violate their probation or parole program conditions, police officers or sheriff's deputies may bring these persons to jails where they are held pending a revocation hearing. Some jail inmates are fugitives from other jurisdictions. These other jurisdictions issue detainer warrants, authorizing jails to hold these persons until someone from these other jurisdictions can transport the prisoners back to be tried for their crimes.

Numerous jail inmates have drug or alcohol dependencies, or they may be mentally ill. Because of their unusual behavior, they attract the attention of law enforcement officers, who bring them to jails until decisions can be made about them. Some of the homeless population, including drunks and derelicts, are brought to jails. In some instances, these persons are the result of mercy bookings, because police officers believe that if they are in jails, they will be protected from severe weather in certain areas of the country. Some jail inmates are actually state or federal prisoners. Entering into contracts with various local jurisdictions with larger jails, state and federal officials place some of their long-term offenders under jail supervision for extended periods. These are known as contract prisoners. Thus, it is not entirely unexpected that some persons have referred to the jail population as rabble, and that the rabble hypothesis seems to have some validity in describing this diverse collection of jail inmates.

QUESTIONS FOR REVIEW

1. How many jails are there in the United States? Why is it difficult to determine precise numbers of jails that exist at any given time?

2. What are some characteristics of jails? How does local political control influence jail policies?

3. What are workhouses? What is the Bridewell Workhouse and how did it exploit inmates?

4. What are detainer warrants? What types of offenders are held in jails on detainer warrants?

5. Why are there so many mentally ill persons in local jails?

6. What was the Philadelphia Society for Alleviating the Miseries of Public Prisons? How did this society improve jail conditions?

7. What are six functions of jails? In each case, explain the importance of each function.

8. What is meant by the jail removal initiative? Why is it important?

9. What was the Walnut Street Jail and why was it important in jail history?

10. What is the rabble hypothesis? How does it describe the general nature of the jail population?

SUGGESTED READINGS

Alarid, Leanne Fiftal and Paul F. Cromwell. *Correctional Perspectives: Views from Academics, Practitioners, and Prisoners.* Los Angeles: Roxbury, 2002.

Austin, James and John Irwin. *It's About Time: America's Imprisonment Binge.* 3d ed. Belmont, CA: Wadsworth/Thomson Learning, 2002.

Bradford, Michael and Paul Perrone. *Incarcerated Juveniles and Recidivism in Hawaii.* Honolulu, HI: Crime Prevention and Justice Assistance Division, Department of the Attorney Genera, 2001.

Cunniff, Mark A. *Jail Crowding: Understanding Jail Population Dynamics.* Washington, DC: U.S. Department of Justice, National Institute of Corrections, 2002.

Martin, Jamie S. *Inside Looking Out: Jailed Fathers' Perceptions about Separation from Their Children.* New York: LFB Scholarly Publishing LLC, 2001.

INTERNET CONNECTIONS

American Correctional Health Services Association
http://www.corrections.com/achsa/indexl.html

American Jail Association
http://www.corrections.com/aja

American Service Group, Inc.
http://www.asgr.com/

Citizens for Legal Responsibility
http://www.clr.org/

Connections: A Correctional Education Program Serving Offenders with Special Learning Needs
http://www.theconnectionsprogram.com/MainPageText.htm

Cook County Boot Camp
http://www.cookcountysheriff.org/bootcamp/

CSS Special Supervision Services
http://www.csosa.gov/css_specialsupervision.htm

Female Special Needs Offenders
http://www.stars.csg.org/slc/special/2000/female_offenders.htm

Gamblers Anonymous
http://www.gamblersanonymous.org/

International Association of Correctional Training Personnel
http://www.iactp.org/

International Institute on Special Needs Offenders
http://www.iisno.org.uk

Koch Crime Institute
http://www.kci.org/publications/bootcamp/docs/nij/Correctional_Boot+Camps/chpt17.htm

Narcotics Anonymous
http://www.na.org

Narcotics Complete Recovery Center
http://www.drugrehab.net

Recovery Resources Online
http://www.soberrecovery.com

CHAPTER 6 | *Jail Administration: Officer Training, Inmate Supervision, and Contemporary Issues*

Chapter Objectives | *As the result of reading this chapter, the following objectives should be realized:*

1. Describing jail administration and the background of those administering jails.
2. Describing jail correctional officer recruitment and training, including the professionalization process.
3. Examining the nature of lawsuits against jails and jail staff and administrators and the bases for these lawsuits in the context of the lawsuit syndrome.
4. Highlighting various contemporary jail issues, including overcrowding, the quality of jail personnel, and the quality of jail life.
5. Identifying various problems associated with classifying jail inmates.
6. Examining some of the major problems associated with inmate management and providing necessary services for prisoners, including health care and other treatments and services.
7. Describing the special problems of small jails and the lack of necessary services.
8. Describing a typology of jails according to their size.
9. Examining the development of regional jails and new-generation or direct-supervision jails.
10. Describing the problem of jail suicides and the preventive measures taken by jails to minimize them.
11. Examining jail reforms including jail architecture and design and the privatization movement.

INTRODUCTION

• *A sheriff in a Tennessee county was indicted on charges of accepting bribes from drug traffickers who would land their planes loaded with drugs on a remote airfield in the sheriff's county. Allegedly, the sheriff would accept payment of $2,000 per shipment permitted to land in his county. The smugglers unloaded several bales of marijuana, large quantities of cocaine and heroin, and other drugs. Their Tennessee contacts would arrive in trucks at an appointed time, offload the illegal drugs and narcotics, and leave soon thereafter for different towns and cities, where they would distribute their illicit products to street dealers for sales to the public. The FBI and Tennessee Bureau of Investigation coordinated a sting operation involving over fifty officers and law enforcement personnel at the county and federal levels. An undercover FBI agent posed as a drug smuggler and approached the sheriff in his office concerning the possibility of landing planes on the remote airfield in exchange for financial consideration. After a sum was agreed upon, the undercover agent arranged for several shipments of illegal drugs to be delivered by air to the remote field under the watchful eye of the sheriff. All of these transactions were videotaped from concealed positions around the airfield. Subsequently, payment to the sheriff was made with marked bills by undercover FBI agents who tracked the sheriff to a cabin where he deposited his money. Over $300,000 in cash and a quantity of drugs were seized when FBI and Tennessee Bureau of Investigation officers obtained a search warrant for the sheriff's remote cabin and surrounding premises. The sheriff was released on $500,000 bond pending a trial.* [Adapted from the Associated Press, "Tennessee Sheriff Nabbed in FBI Sting," April 12, 2002].

• *In a Florida county jail, John Merrill, 31, was placed in a cell and kept in custody for nearly seven months before being charged with a crime. Merrill was stopped by a sheriff's cruiser in late November 2001 for speeding. Officers searched Merrill's vehicle and discovered a bag containing what appeared to be marijuana. They transported Merrill to the jail where he was booked and confined. Merrill's automobile was impounded and kept in a jail impound parking lot. Merrill made no effort to determine when he should be released and never requested an attorney to represent him. After seven months of confinement in the jail, Merrill asked a jail deputy one day when his trial was going to occur. The deputy reportedly answered, "What trial?" Merrill explained that he had been held in the jail for seven months and expected to come to trial on speeding charges. The deputy reported Merrill's query to the chief jailer. Subsequently, it was determined that the substance seized was an herbal tea, not marijuana. A check of booking records indicated that Merrill had been "lost" in the system. Had it not been for his question to the jail deputy, Merrill may have languished in the jail for more months. Merrill was immediately released and brought before a magistrate for the charge of speeding. The case was dismissed when the original arresting deputy could not be found. He had resigned from the sheriff's department and moved to another state during the period Merrill was confined. Merrill is now considering civil action concerning his wrongful detainment on an unfiled charge of possessing a substance believed to be marijuana. However, a spokesman for the sheriff's department said that the deputy who arrested Merrill initially had acted in good faith and that Merrill's subsequent unchallenged detention in the jail, although prolonged, was proper.* [Adapted from the Associated Press, "Man Held in Jail for Seven Months for Possessing Herbal Tea," May 10, 2002].

• *It happened in Everett, Washington. A young woman was involved in a serious traffic accident. Investigating at the accident scene was Deputy Chuck Adams, 35. The accident occurred when a youth who was driving while intoxicated drove his car into a ditch, rolling the car. The occupants were injured, although not critically. Adams was given charge of a 17-year-old girl, who was a passenger in the wrecked vehicle. She was intoxicated. Adams said he would drive her to a sheriff's substation some miles from the accident scene. When they got to the sheriff's substation, Adams says that the girl initiated sexual contact by groping him and removing her clothes. Adams says that he escorted the girl to a restroom at the back of the sheriff's substation, where he had sex with her. He said that the sex was consensual. Subsequently, the girl was charged with public drunkenness. In retaliation, she claimed that she had been raped by Adams. She described the events, but not in the same way Adams did. She claimed that Adams groped her and suggested that she could get out of the drunkenness charge by having sex with him. It was then that she agreed to follow him to a restroom where he raped her, she said. Adams was charged with rape and a jury listened to testimony from both sides. Ultimately, they convicted Adams, a six-year veteran with the sheriff's department. Under standard sentencing, Adams would face from six months to one year. However, prosecutors said they would ask the judge for a longer term because of the circumstances. Should officers of the law receive longer prison terms for violating laws that would draw shorter sentences for civilians?* [Adapted from the Associated Press, "Deputy Convicted of Rape," May 10, 2001].

• *A young woman was brought to a local jail one afternoon in Indiana following her arrest for shoplifting. Her ID identified her as "Jane Smith," age 21, from South Bend. She had been arrested following a shoplifting incident involving some cosmetic products. After being fingerprinted and photographed, she was placed in a jail cell down a long corridor where she could not be observed directly. About two hours later, a passing jail officer looked into her cell and saw her hanging from some water pipes that ran across the top of the cell. "Jane Smith" had hung herself, using her pantyhose to form a noose. Subsequently, it was revealed that she was a 16-year-old runaway from Iowa, and she had been reported missing for two weeks. Jail officials claim that they believed that she was 21 years old and that she gave them no impression that she intended to commit suicide. One observer commented that the jail was old, built in 1929, and it lacked adequate observation posts where persons in all cells could be observed directly. Local initiatives to remodel the old jail had failed in recent years because of excessive cost estimates and the low priority of jail funding for the Indiana county. A local businessman, Mark Brewer, said, "We never would have had that problem if we had spent the money to build us an up-to-date jail."* ["16-Year-Old Hangs Self in Jail Cell After Arrest for Cosmetics Theft," April 2, 2002].

These incidents are only a few of the many cases that occur in jails across the nation annually. Some jail officials are corrupt and engage in illicit enterprises, profiting from their positions of authority. Arrestees are admitted and forgotten or mistreated. Misclassifications of inmates are made. Large numbers of mentally ill are scooped up as a part of jail rabble. Jail suicides continue unabated.

This chapter is about jail organization and administration. In most jurisdictions, sheriffs administer jails and are responsible for selecting jail personnel and establishing jail policies. Because sheriffs are most often elected positions, their backgrounds are not especially uniform. Many persons become sheriffs who have had little or no previous law enforcement experience. Thus, their lack of understanding about jail operations sometimes impairs effective jail operations and contributes to various types of jail problems. Various sheriff's responsibilities are described, and sheriff characteristics are typified.

Jail correctional officer recruitment and training is examined. Jail officers, who are not paid well in most jurisdictions, usually have little or no previous experience in working with inmates. Labor turnover among jail personnel is fairly high. Almost every county jail has its own training standards, and there is great variation among U.S. jails pertaining to quality of jail personnel. In recent years, however, the American Jail Association and other interested organizations have attempted to professionalize jail staff by establishing programs that will upgrade their education and training. Some of these training programs will be described. At the organizational level, jail standards have been promulgated, and in-service training for jail officers has been offered in selected jurisdictions. One stimulus to promote greater professionalism among jail staff has been the flood of lawsuits filed against jail personnel and administration. The lawsuit syndrome has had a crippling effect on jail operations and services delivery for many jail systems. The lawsuit syndrome and the different bases for lawsuits against jails and their officers and administrators will be examined.

Several selected jail issues are examined. One issue has to do with the quality of jail personnel and the sorts of incentives offered to improve jail officer performance and effectiveness. Today's jail officer must confront and deal with several serious inmate problems, since many jail inmates have drug/alcohol dependencies, are illiterate, and/or are mentally ill. It is difficult to classify jail inmates, and it is even more difficult to provide necessary services that will meet their needs effectively. Most jails are not equipped to handle the many problems inmates present to jail staff. Another issue pertains to jail programs and what types of skills and experiences jail officers should have in order to maximize their effectiveness in supervising inmates. Some jail inmates are contract prisoners from state and/or federal jurisdictions who pose more serious supervision problems compared with less serious, short-term offenders or those who are awaiting trial or sentencing. More emphasis has been placed in recent years on social skills and the human relations approach in jail officer training, in order that jail officers may confront and deal with more culturally diverse inmate populations. Another issue examined pertains to health-care services in jails. A majority of U.S. jails are small and poorly equipped to deliver necessary health-care services. A portion of the jail inmate population has some serious communicable diseases, such as tuberculosis or HIV/AIDS, and therefore, there are serious problems posed for inmates who interact closely with those infected with these diseases.

Some of the more serious types of small jail problems will be described and discussed. Jail overcrowding is another important issue. Jails have little or no control over the volume of offenders who must be processed on a day-to-day basis. Chronic overcrowding means that it is difficult if not impossible to provide high-quality services to jail inmates when necessary. The problem of jail overcrowding is described, and some of the outcomes of jail overcrowding are indicated.

The chapter next explores ways of measuring the size of jails. Several typologies of jails have been established as a means of defining jails more precisely. One type of jail is the regional jail, and this particular jail development will be discussed. Jail features have also undergone significant change in the last several decades. New-generation or direct-supervision jails are described and contrasted with more traditional jail patterns, which are carryovers from older jail organizations and operations. Another issue examined is the incidence of jail suicides. While there are not substantial numbers of jail suicides annually, there are sufficient numbers of them so that jail suicide has received national attention. In response, many jails have established programs that attempt to detect those most likely to commit suicide while jailed. Existing and proposed policies for dealing with jail suicide problems will be described.

The chapter concludes with a discussion of several important jail reforms. Some of these reforms have occurred as the result of court-ordered jail improvements. Thus, many of the larger jails have been ordered by courts to reorganize their structures and operations and to provide services more consistent with humane treatment. The result of such reforms has been a general improvement in inmate accommodations and services. Increasing numbers of inmates have special needs. These special-needs offenders may require special accommodations, particularly if they are physically handicapped or suffer from various mental or drug/alcohol-related problems. Changes in jail architecture, as well as changes in the nature of jail organization and supervision, are described. One result of these changes has been an improvement in the effectiveness of jail officer supervision and the delivery of services to offenders in need.

JAIL ADMINISTRATION

In a majority of jurisdictions, jails are county-operated and funded from local sources. Most large cities in the United States also have jails. These city jails are staffed by the local police department. Thus, a duality of jurisdiction characterizes most city and county jail operations, with sheriffs in charge of county jails and police chiefs in charge of city jails.

The growth of jail populations has been affected by changing crime trends, shifting patterns of offending, changes in criminal justice policies, and the increasing willingness of local governments to fund construction and operation of local jails (Beck 1999:10). For example, changing drug enforcement policies and dealing more harshly with drug offenders have escalated the number of jail inmates held for various drug crimes. This also holds true for other countries, such as Australia and Canada (Beyer, Reid, and Crofts 2002) Punishment severity and greater sentence lengths under new truth-in-sentencing provisions have meant that more persons are confined in jails and prisons for longer periods. Greater numbers of states have adopted more stringent drunk-driving policies by lowering the legal limit for intoxication from a .10 to .08 blood-alcohol level. This simple change in the DWI standard has resulted in a dramatic increase in drunk driving arrests. These arrestees are usually confined in jails, even if for short periods. Despite decreasing crime rates reported by the FBI and other agencies, the jail population has steadily increased. Called upon to manage these growing offender populations are county sheriffs and their jail personnel and staff (Hunter and Sexton 1997).

Traditionally, the chief executive officer in charge of jail operations is the county sheriff. This is most often an elected position. In most jurisdictions, no special qualifications exist for those who aspire to be sheriffs. They may or may not have previous law enforcement experience (Hayes 2001). Because these posts are most often filled by elected officials, some of these persons may be ex-police officers, ex-sheriff's deputies, ex-restaurant managers, or even ex-school superintendents. While there is a National Sheriffs' Association that disseminates information to its membership about jails and jail problems, there is not much more to foster national sheriff professionalism, unity, or consistency of performance. Furthermore, the functions of local jails are gradually changing, causing additional problems for administrators (Beck 2002).

Jail Management and Operations

Most jails in the United States are locally operated by sheriff's departments. In some states, such as Alaska, jail operations are contracted for with the state. Thus, for many lockups and jails in Alaska, particularly in remote rural regions, a state agency allocates funds and staffs jails, including provisions for housing inmates on short- or long-term bases. Local jail managers transfer the management and administration of local jails to state agency personnel. New standards are established for jail operations and inmate health and safety, including revised provisions for inmates who may suffer from posttraumatic stress disorders or other psychiatric problems (Kokorowski and Freng 2001). Liability insurance is provided by the state and protects against suits by detainees, public inebriates, mentally incapacitated, and juveniles in protective custody. The state also provides for jail officer training and education.

Sheriff Responsibilities

Sheriffs are responsible for appointing chief jailers and jail staff. They are also administratively responsible for monitoring the health and safety of jail inmates. But they have other duties as well. They must protect their counties from criminals and do their best to ensure public safety. This requires hiring and retaining deputies who can patrol, make arrests, serve **warrants,** respond to citizen complaints, keep the peace, and exercise discretion. Given the budgets provided by county authorities, they often find it difficult to attract, hire, train, and retain high-quality deputies to perform these various chores.

Jail Correctional Officer Recruitment and Training

Those hired to perform jail duties frequently have little or no formal training in any kind of law enforcement (Jones and Carlson 2001). Sheriff's deputies generally receive low pay and have low prestige compared with their officer counterparts on city police forces, although some jurisdictions such as California and Nevada pay their deputy sheriffs much better than average salaries in other jurisdictions. An indication of the low status and prestige of jail correctional officers is that some sheriffs assign their regular deputies to jailer duty as a punishment for violating one or more sheriff's department rules or disciplinary infractions. In some jurisdictions, sheriffs supplement their force of deputies with auxiliary personnel made up of community volunteers. These volunteers receive little or no training in law enforcement. Often, they are assigned correctional duty at the jail, with little or no training in prisoner management.

Stringent minimal educational requirements are nonexistent, since such requirements would rapidly deplete the ranks of job applicants for correctional officer positions. Minimum educational requirements are often a high school diploma or GED. Whenever jail inmates are permitted visits from families or close friends, jail staff often are unskilled in matters such as search and seizure and the protocol of visitation. With the low degree of security these types of officers create, much contraband is smuggled into jails. Some materials (e.g., knives, saws, or other tools) reaching jail inmates are used to facilitate escapes (Sturges 2002).

Jail Officer and Administrative Salaries and Labor Turnover.   One major reason it is difficult for jails to recruit and retain high-quality jail personnel is low pay. In 2000, for example, the average starting salary for jail officers nationwide was $24,706, ranging from a low annual salary of $17,000 in McCracken, Kentucky, to $32,856 in Ramsey, Minnesota (Camp and Camp 2002). The average turnover rate was 13.1 percent, with the largest jails having the lowest turnover with 8.9 percent and the smaller jails having the greatest turnover of 16.4 percent. The differences in labor turnover rates are likely attributable to better pay and working conditions in the larger jails compared with the smaller ones.

BOX 6.1

Jim Pope

Sheriff-Coroner
Shasta County Sheriff's Office
Redding, CA

Statistics

AA degree (police science), Shasta College, 1968; B.A. (public administration), Chico State University, 1972; graduate of FBI National Academy, 1983; president, California State Sheriffs' Association, 1995; past president, Western States Sheriffs' Association, 2001.

Background

I was born and reared in the Redding area of Shasta County and attended elementary schools there. My mother became a single parent when I was 6 years old. Being the oldest of four children, I was taught to do my share and more. My work ethic was developed at a young age and has served me well in my law enforcement career. I joined the military and completed boot camp at the age of 17 and spent the next four years in the U.S. Navy. I decided very early in my career that I wanted to become a law enforcement professional and set out to obtain the educational background needed to pursue this goal soon thereafter. I have never regretted that decision and believe it is an honorable and rewarding career choice.

When elected to the office of Sheriff for the first time in 1990, I had gained over 27 years of law enforcement experience between the Shasta County Sheriff's Office and the Anderson Police Department in Shasta County where I obtained my first job in law enforcement.

Experiences

Presently, I am serving my twelfth year as the elected sheriff-coroner of Shasta County and my thirty-ninth year as a full-time law enforcement officer. Shasta County is located in northern California about 160 miles north of

Despite these low salaries, some researchers think that the recruitment process has been successful at bringing in well-qualified officers and retaining a significant proportion of them in various jurisdictions (Slatkin 1994:77).

The average jail administrator's salary is $71,014, with a low annual salary of $48,000 in Broome, New York, to a high of $104,104 in San Luis Obispo, California. Average starting lieutenant's annual salaries were $49,470. One ad for a superintendent of jails for Monroe County, New York, placed in *Corrections Today* in 2003, sought someone to supervise an inmate population of 1,300, a staff of 500, and work with an annual budget of $46.5 million. The applicant must have a bachelor's degree, master's preferred, with seven to ten years experience in corrections, three of which must be in an administrative or supervisory capacity. The advertised salary range was $73,642 to $94,970. Another ad in the same issue of *Corrections Today* advertised for a director of the Harris County Community Supervision and Corrections Department in Houston, Texas, with a salary ranging from $95,000 to $105,000, depending upon qualifications and experience. Qualifications for this position included a graduate degree preferred in criminology, counseling, social work, psychology, business, or a closely related field. At least ten years of administrative or managerial experience, with demon-

Sacramento. The office of sheriff is a state constitutional office in the State of California. I also serve as Shasta County Emergency Services Director, California Office of Emergency Services. As such, I have overseen several major disasters in the county, such as fires, floods, and a major chemical spill from a railroad car into the Sacramento River that flows through the county (Cantara Spill). This spill received worldwide attention. During my term I also oversaw one of the largest manhunts ever conducted in northern California when a deputy sheriff from my department was murdered by two suspects he was transporting to the jail. The suspects were apprehended and subsequently convicted of the murder. In 1972 I worked a major homicide case featured on the front cover of *True Detective* magazine. This was an extremely violent murder case where the suspect butchered the victim at a campground picnic on Shasta Lake. Three days later the suspect was captured in the Sacramento area and convicted of first-degree murder.

Recently, I was re-elected to a fourth term as sheriff-coroner. Prior to being elected sheriff, I served as undersheriff of Shasta County, an at-will position that serves at the pleasure of the sheriff. I held that position for eight years. Immediately prior to my appointment as undersheriff, I served as a lieutenant in the Shasta County Sheriff's Office where I was commander of the Crystal Creek

Rehabilitation Center, a 120-bed minimum-security facility. Other assignments within the Shasta County Sheriff's Office included sergeant, Jail Division; sergeant, Patrol Division; and detective sergeant in the Major Crimes Division. I also had assignments as a patrolman and in the Custody Division in the jail early in my career.

Advice to Students

Good police officers and all public officials must maintain a commitment to their communities and a caring attitude toward its citizens. This has been my trademark for all my years in law enforcement. Wherever you go during your lifetime, there is one thing you will always leave behind—your influence. This is especially true in law enforcement. Influence is that invisible force to your personality that causes others to act. A career in law enforcement requires you to become a leader. Leadership is the act of leading by example: walking the talk, standing up for what you think is right, and embracing positive beliefs. These are the principles that will be required of you in law enforcement. Courage, integrity, and caring for others will become a part of your lives as you strive to do what is right and strengthen others with your positive influence. With these principles and appropriate educational background, you can succeed in this profession.

strated leadership in a department or business with more than 200 employees was desired (*Corrections Today* 2003:19). Titles for jail administrators vary among jurisdictions. For example, 52 percent of all jail systems in the United States are administered by sheriffs, 19 percent by directors, and the rest by wardens, captains, superintendents, and chief deputies (Camp and Camp 2002).

Table 6.1 shows a distribution of selected sociodemographic characteristics for U.S. jail staff for 2000. There were approximately 190,000 jail personnel in 2000, with about 70 percent of these performing roles as jail officers. In 2000 about 65 percent of all jail officers were male, while 74 percent were white (Maguire and Pastore 2002). However, newly hired jail officers in 2000 indicated that over 72 percent were male and 70 percent were white. Additionally, 71 percent of all jail officers have been in their positions for two years or less. Approximately 33 percent of all officers are over age 30. About 82 percent of all jail officers have had some college experience.

Jail Officer Attitudes and Work Performance.   Many jails are plagued with morale problems among existing jail staff. In a majority of instances, the good-old-boy network seems to operate, where promotional opportunities and

TABLE 6.1

Jail Officer and Administrator Characteristics 2000[*]

Characteristic	Officers (%)	Staff/Administrators (%)
Gender		
Male	71.6	68.4
Female	28.4	31.6
Race/Ethnicity		
White	69.7	74.3
Black	28.4	18.7
Other	1.9	7.0
1997 Hires		
Male	68.4	74.6
Female	31.6	25.4
White	66.3	68.7
Black	29.9	27.6
Other	3.8	3.7
Education		
High school or less	18.0	8.0
Some college	42.0	36.0
College graduate +	40.0	56.0
Length of Time in Jail Corrections		
Less than 1 year	34.0	28.0
1–2 years	37.0	35.0
3–4 years	19.0	21.0
5 or more years	10.0	16.0
Age		
21 or younger	16.0	4.0
22–25	22.0	21.0
26–30	29.0	33.0
31–40	25.0	26.0
40+	8.0	16.0

[*]*Sources:* Compiled by author from Camille Graham Camp and George M. Camp. *The Corrections Yearbook, Adult Systems 2001.* Middletown, CT: Criminal Justice Institute, Inc., 2002; Kathleen Maguire and Ann Pastore. *Sourcebook of Criminal Justice Statistics.* Albany, NY: The Hindelang Criminal Justice Research Center, 2002; American Correctional Association. *2002 Directory.* Lanham, MD: American Correctional Association, 2002.

advancements are based on whom one knows and not how well one performs. Such arrangements are often stressful and cause jail officer burnout. Beyond the traditional bureaucratic network are numerous interrelated and often contradictory factors at work to influence jail officer role performance. For instance, jail officers must be counselors, diplomats, caretakers, caregivers, disciplinarians, supervisors, and crisis managers simultaneously (Griffin 2001). This role conflict generates a high degree of officer stress, sometimes disabling the best officers so that their work effectiveness is adversely affected.

Ken Kerle has studied the morale and training of jail officers. He has indicated that poor training of jail employees, the lack of clear jail policies, and inequality among male and female officers regarding wages are impediments to

Sheriff's department work involves close coordination between supervisors and staff as well as strict adherence to inmate-officer policies.

overall efficiency in jails and to personal job satisfaction. Kerle notes that opportunities for promotion are often thwarted primarily by relegation of female officers to work only with female inmates. He suggests that behind the effort to hold back the advancement of female jail officers is a political agenda, where local officials believe that female officers lack experience in supervising male prisoners and cannot relate to their particular problems. Many county governments seem reluctant to change, and this reluctance is a substantial roadblock to the promotion of female jail officers. Kerle believes that more jail administrators will have to give up their former stereotypes of female officers in order for significant change to occur. Strong leadership is the key to the advancement of all qualified jail personnel, according to Kerle (1998). These and similar concerns are voiced by other corrections critics (Moynahan 2001).

The Mecklenburg County Jail Experience.   Some jail administrators and county sheriffs have implemented new awareness programs designed to improve communications between all jail staff. In December 1994, for example, at the Mecklenburg, North Carolina, County Jail, Sheriff Jim Pendergraph became the new administrator for a 614-bed direct supervision facility, outfitted with the most up-to-date state-of-the-art security equipment, a massive kitchen designed to feed 10,000 persons, and a centralized agency training facility (Emerick 1996:53). Immediately, Pendergraph sensed that morale among his jail staff was incredibly low. The attrition and labor turnover rate among his jail staff was high, a bad sign. He found that many jail staff were unaware of what was expected of them. They had no idea about how they could be promoted within the system or who to report to for advice and information. Most jail officers simply reported for their 12-hour shifts, stayed there for 12 hours, and left.

Pendergraph decided to change things. In December 1995 he organized small focus groups with his jail. He selected fifty officers at random and divided them into groups of ten each. These five groups met for one hour per week for four weeks. They shared information about their work, who they were, what they did, and shared their personal interests outside of the jail. Subsequent meetings led to a venting of complaints, grievances, and concerns. The sheriff met with each group and encouraged all persons to open up to the group and to him. He had each group devise a list of problems and possible solutions for them. Subsequently, he involved all jail personnel in decision making affecting their particular areas and brought each officer into a catalyst role. Pendergraph implemented many of the group's suggestions and distributed memos and other communication to advise and inform all jail officers of changes brought about as the result of these focus groups. Thus, he reinforced the idea that individual officers were having significant input in jail affairs.

In 1996, Pendergraph and his officers were working together on other strategic ideas for improving communications within the jail (Emerick 1996:58). Pendergraph believes that his efforts have been rewarded by more positive attitudes among his staff. Employee morale has improved, and labor turnover has decreased. The good-old-boy network has been replaced with a more objective system of rewards for promotions and recognition.

Upgrading Jail Officer Education and Training. Jails are most frequently staffed by local personnel (Peak 1995). The actual amount of formal training received by jail officers varies considerably from no training to considerable training (Koren 1995:43–44). Durkee (1996:58) says that prior to the 1970s, training and education for jail officers in the United States was virtually nonexistent. Subsequently, correspondence courses were offered in jail management. In the 1980s, state and local training services were implemented in various jurisdictions, such as Michigan, where prospective jail officers were given 160-hour basic training courses and experiences through the Michigan Corrections Officers Training Council (Durkee 1996:60). Some training programs for jail officers have been offered in collaboration with nearby colleges and universities (Heim 1993). Lansing Community College in Michigan offers courses in prisoner behavior, first aid, stress management, sexual harassment, ethics, correctional law, booking/intake, cultural diversity, defensive tactics, inmate suicides, and custody/security. All of this formal training is designed to professionalize jail staff and provide them with a better understanding of jail clientele (Durkee 1996:59–60).

The Lansing Community College has the following curriculum, which leads to acquiring the County and Local Detention Vocational Certificate:

Code	Title	Credit Hours
WRIT 117	Writing Prep II	4
CJUS 130	Local Detention	3
CJUS 135	Legal Issues in Corrections	3
CJUS 242	Unarmed Defense	3
CJUS 245	Report Writing	2
CJUS 251	Correctional Clients	3
CJUS 255	Human Relations in Criminal Justice (Client Relations)	3
CJUS 001	Special Subjects	4
Total		25

This certificate is designed to provide entry-level skills for the person who wishes to enter the job market as a corrections officer at a jail or local lockup after two semesters of study. Besides this academic preparation, a 160-hour Local Corrections Basic Training program was developed in Michigan in the late 1980s (Durkee 1996:58). This training provided useful skills for officers who were already employed at one of the local county jails or city police lock-ups. The training was an important step and signified a substantial upgrading of skills for participating officers. Similar programs have been incorporated into the curricula at participating colleges and universities in other jurisdictions, such as Washburn University of Topeka, Kansas (Heim 1993:18–19).

A concerted effort has been made to upgrade and improve the quality of jail correctional officers and other correctional personnel generally (Tartaglini and Safran 1996). Few corrections professionals dispute the fact that additional education and training for jail personnel is good and that both their **professionalization** and self-concepts are bolstered as a result (Koren 1995:43). Further, additional training will make these officers more effective in dealing with the diversity of inmates entering jails annually. Proposals have been made that specify certain minimal criteria for those monitoring prisoners or jail inmates. In past years, the selection of correctional officers has emphasized physical attributes rather than the behavioral and educational skills these officers should possess to perform their work adequately. However, contemporary jail officer training programs emphasize person skills, including human relations and writing effectively (Blowers 1995). In fact, increasing numbers of jails are seeking various types of accreditation from organizations such as the American Jail Association and American Correctional Association (Ryan and Plummer 1999). Further, the National Institute of Corrections Jails Division provides direct services to jail staff, including technical assistance, training, and information. This information pertains to issues including new jail planning, jail operations, and jail management (Hutchinson 1999:15).

Emerging on the heels of discussions at the 1970 American Correctional Association Professional Education Council was a formal standardized corrections curriculum and approved by the International Association of Correctional Officers (IACO). IACO has now established minimum standards for corrections-related higher education programs. Since 1990 the IACO has sponsored and approved increasing numbers of standardized curricula in major colleges and universities. Through such formalized programs, corrections institutions in the United States are accredited and corrections officers acquire a higher degree of professionalization to perform their jobs more effectively (Hahn 1995:45–47).

The IACO has approved the following correctional officer curriculum as a model for training centers and schools to follow:

I. **Corrections in the Criminal Justice System:** History; Total Systems Overview; Philosophies and Goals; Police, Courts, and Corrections; Corrections in Institutions and the Community; Contemporary Issues.

II. **Correctional Practices:** Safety, Security and Supervision; Classification and Programming; Institutional Procedures; Jail Operations; Alternatives to Incarceration; Probation and Parole; Contemporary Issues.

III. **Basic Communications in Corrections:** Verbal Skills, Nonverbal Skills and Writing Skills; Cross-Cultural Communications; Practical Skills Exercises.

IV. **Offender Behavior and Development:** Types of Offenders; Women's Institutions; Offenders with Special Needs; Origins of Criminal Behavior; Subcultures; Offender Change and Growth; Contemporary Issues.

V. Juvenile Justice and Corrections: Distinction from Adult System; Evolution of Juvenile Justice System; Youthful Offender in the Adult System; Legal Issues; Control and Intervention; Current Practices; Contemporary Issues.

VI. Ethical and Legal Issues in Corrections: Constitutional Issues; Basics of Criminal Law; Offender Rights and Responsibilities; Staff Rights, Responsibilities and Liabilities; Legal Procedures and Grievances; Professional Ethics; Contemporary Issues (Hahn 1995:45–46).

In 1993, a Commission on Correctional Curriculum in Higher Education was established, comprised of the President of the IACO, the Executive Directors of the American Correctional Association, the American Jail Association, and the National Sheriff's Association; the Commissioner of Corrections in the state of Maine; an administrator from the U.S. Bureau of Prisons; and four academicians. The mission of this Commission is as follows:

The mission of the Commission on Correctional Curriculum in Higher Education is to promote recognition of corrections as a profession by ensuring relevant higher education of correctional officers. In support of this mission, this Commission shall (1) evaluate the corrections curriculum component in programs of higher education offering degrees in criminal justice and related fields and (2) certify that the standardized curriculum (18 semester hours) recognized by the International Association for Correctional Officers is incorporated in such curriculum (Hahn 1995:47).

Jail Standards. By 2000, most states had developed and implemented jail standards that address issues of mandatory minimum training (Rosazza and Nestrud 2000). Most of these states make it mandatory for all jail personnel to participate in annual in-service training. In Kentucky, for example, jail officers must undergo annual training and certification from the state corrections cabinet. Although

County sheriff's department control rooms are not that different from penitentiary control rooms.

much of this training is tactical or inmate control oriented, there have been efforts to provide personnel with a more formal or academic set of skills—communication, crisis intervention, interpersonal problem solving. As a result, line officers who work in jails that have mandatory standards enjoy more pay and job satisfaction than those working in jails without standards (Howerton 2001).

Not only is jail officer training a key priority, but substantive concerns relating to inmate mental health are also viewed as critical areas for improvement (Walsh 1998). Some attention has been given to diverting certain types of offenders from jails before they become jail problems (Atkins, Applegate, and Hobbs 1998). In some cases, day reporting centers have been suggested and used for low-risk offenders in lieu of jail incarceration (Roy and Grimes 2002).

Not all jail officer improvement takes place in classrooms. In many of the larger jails throughout the United States, occasional inmate disturbances are encountered. Sometimes, hostages are taken and the lives of correctional officers and other inmates are jeopardized (Romano 2003). On these occasions, jails may have to call in outside agencies to quell such disturbances. However, some jails have created **tactical response teams** to cope with serious jail problems. Also known as Correctional Emergency Response Teams or Hostage Recovery Teams, tactical response teams are special units trained in various types of hand-to-hand combat, firearms, and other skills to neutralize hostile jail inmates and perform rescue missions within jails (Webb and Alicie 1994:16–17).

Increased attention is also being paid by different jurisdictions regarding jail upgrading and systemic improvements. Many jails have sought to improve services delivery in different areas, such as better food service. Fire protection and life safety have also been improved in many jurisdictions. Regular procedures for inspecting jail facilities have been established in many of the larger jurisdictions with desired results. Greater compliance with federal standards for jail operations has been observed (Slatkin, Wimbs, and Sidebottom 1994:47–48).

Jail Lawsuits.   About a third of all jails in the United States are involved in one or more lawsuits or some type of legal action. A **lawsuit syndrome** seems to be crippling both prison and jail systems (Hunter and Sexton 1997). It is believed that many of the jail lawsuits are triggered by insensitive jail officers who bring **street attitudes** to work with them. Street attitudes include failing to work within one's job description and failing to follow established policies and procedures; personal biases and prejudices are included. Jail lawsuits can be minimized by (1) hiring the right staff; (2) providing staff training with greater emphasis on development and self-understanding; and (3) using participatory management, where jail officers are involved more in decision making affecting their work. Professionalizing the jail work force can do much to reduce the incidence of jail lawsuits (Koren 1995).

In growing numbers of county jurisdictions, jail officers are receiving training equivalent to police officers in P.O.S.T. (Peace Officer Standards and Training) curricula. In states such as Texas, for instance, jail officers must undergo P.O.S.T. training in a state-run academy. Further, they are required to acquire annual in-service training as a part of their growing professionalism. The thrust of this training is to professionalize jail staff and make them sensitive to inmate needs. All jail inmates should receive proper care and be supervised by a well-trained staff cognizant of correctional law. One positive outcome of such training is the minimization of lawsuits filed by inmates against jail officers or supervisors for different kinds of misconduct (Etter and Birzer 1997:67).

In many instances, certain inmates have challenged jail policies that limit their religious practices (Cohn 1998). Telephone systems have been the target of legal challenges by some inmates (Townsend and Eichor 1995). Older inmates may require special handling, although jail staff may not be sufficiently trained to recognize some of the problems that afflict older inmates (Morton 2001). Some inmates require special religious artifacts to perform their rituals, while others require special diets and are forbidden from eating certain kinds of foods. Under various theories, different constitutional amendments have been used to launch successful lawsuits against both prisons and jails. Thus, it is critical that jail officers receive some training in the rights of inmates under their control (Cohn 1998).

Also, it is important that jail officers know how much force to apply when moving prisoners from place to place within jails. Various lawsuits have been filed against jail administrators under the theory that these administrators have failed to train their officers adequately. In some cases, jail inmates who suffer physical injuries may not receive immediate treatment, because some jail officers may not believe that they are injured or simply ignore these injuries. Thus, these inmates may sue under a theory of **deliberate indifference.** Many of these lawsuits are successful. Thus, these suits underscore the importance of acquainting jail staff with the use of physical force for any institutional purpose (Drapkin and Klugiewicz 1994a, 1994b). Critical contact points between jail officers and inmates include (1) stabilizing inmates with handcuffs or other restraint devices; (2) monitoring inmates, debriefing; (3) searching inmates; (4) escorting inmates; (5) transporting inmates (e.g., to hospitals or schools); and (6) turnover (e.g., turning inmates over to other authorities, such as state corrections officials for movement to other facilities) (Drapkin and Klugiewicz 1994b).

Private Jail Operations.   Considerable attention has been given in recent years to the constitutionality of jail operations and jail environments generally. **Privatization** of jails and some prisons in the United States has occurred, where private enterprises contract with state or local governments to provide supervisory and operational services in lieu of publicly authorized organizations. While some persons oppose privatization and question the constitutionality of it relating to any correctional enterprise, there is nothing inherently unconstitutional about private organizations operating and managing prisons or jails. Private interests are authorized by state departments of corrections to act on their behalf and under their scope of authority, and thus they are vested with the necessary credentials to run correctional institutions (Shichor and Gilbert 2001).

SELECTED JAIL ISSUES

The leading cause of court-ordered inmate population reductions or jail improvements is jail overcrowding (Roberts 1994). Whenever any jail population exceeds its rated or design capacity, overcrowding occurs. Most jails in the United States, especially those in larger jurisdictions, have serious overcrowding problems. In 2000, U.S. jails were operating at 97 percent of their rated capacity (Maguire and Pastore 2002). The sheer density of jail inmate populations generates a milieu for fostering increasing numbers of assaults among inmates and other problems requiring special intervention by jail staff (Maguire and Pastore 2002). There are many other problems caused by jail overcrowding. Beyond overcrowding, growing offender populations require more effective management and supervision (Hunter and Sexton 1997).

This section examines briefly six jail issues cited by corrections professionals as major problems. This list is not exhaustive. It seeks to highlight certain issues that either aggravate other jail problems or are themselves growing problems. These issues include (1) the quality of jail personnel, (2) inmate classification problems, (3) health-care services for jails, (4) small jails and small-jail problems, (5) jail overcrowding and megajails, and (6) jail suicides.

The Quality of Jail Personnel

Corrections is the fastest growing profession in the criminal justice field (Hansen 1995:37). Because of intense prison overcrowding and the increasing incapacitation of offenders, even for brief periods, jails have experienced a disproportionately high amount of strain. The average daily population of jails is increasing annually, as jails are used as holdover sites until inmates can be transferred to prisons. This strain has greatly increased the need for competent jail supervisors (Wittenberg 1998). Today's jail supervisor may have to perform one or all of the following responsibilities:

1. Setting and maintaining jail standards.
2. Keeping up with changes in modern jail operations.
3. Conducting routine jail inspections.
4. Assisting jail administrators with policy changes.
5. Providing proactive risk management to reduce liability.
6. Training and mentoring line staff (Hansen 1995:37).

Ken Kerle (1995:5) says that supervision in the world of corrections encompasses a much wider area compared with the vast majority of government agencies and businesses operating today. Line officers in jails are supposed to supervise and manage inmates. But competent inmate management and supervision is acquired only through an effective training program where various skills are transmitted. Kerle believes that jail managers and staff should receive more training relative to ethics and responsibility, human relations skills, progressive staff discipline, and jail management techniques. All too often, Kerle indicates, jail supervision of inmates is nothing more than monitoring cell blocks every half hour or so. Giving staff more responsibilities for managing inmates means greater participatory management. Empowering more staff to act on their own, especially when accompanied by more effective human relations training, can do much to improve staff effectiveness and make jail organization and operation run more smoothly.

Gary Cornelius (1995:62) has described the nature of training jail supervisors and staff receive. Cornelius has encouraged jail staff to adopt a **human services approach** during their periods of inmate supervision. First, jail staff must recognize that there is considerable inmate diversity and that this diversity goes well beyond ethnic, racial, and gender differences. Many jail inmates cannot handle being confined, some constantly complain, and some anger easily. Coupled with overcrowding, budget constraints, manipulative inmates, and lawsuits, these different dimensions of jail supervision and inmate diversity make inmate management more complicated than it might appear (Cornelius 1995:62).

Cornelius suggests that one approach for jail officers to adopt is to accept inmates as human beings and not just entities housed in cells for particular time periods. Thus, jail officers will profit more from their work if they view themselves as human service providers rather than keepers. Inmates have needs, human needs, and jail officers are in the position of supervising these inmates in ways that will minimize disruptions and other inmate problems. Thus, Cornelius indicates that jail officers should be more sensitive to inmate issues and immediate needs by doing the following:

1. Providing goods and services: Frustrations and tensions among inmates can be reduced to the extent that jail officers can provide inmates with their basic necessities, such as food, clothes, clean linens, and proper medication.

2. Helping inmates to adjust: All inmates feel powerless, anxious, or depressed at given times. Human service-oriented officers take the time to talk with inmates, check on them, and make sure that they are all right. These officers must listen to inmates. If there are potential fights brewing, jail officers can intercede and mediate.

3. Providing referrals and advocacy: In bureaucratic and overcrowded inmate environments, officers can assist inmates by permitting them telephone calls or putting them in touch with certain inmate services, counseling, or consultation.

4. Being a part of a helping network: Jail officers should be a part of a team that performs various mental health, classification, and program functions. They should attempt to reduce fear and tension in the jail environment.

5. Avoid the power struggle: If inmates want to be argumentative, jail officers should not take this type of encounter personally; rather, they should remain calm, take a mature attitude, and walk away, telling such inmates that they will return when they are acting more appropriately. Many inmates are highly manipulative and know the right buttons to push to trigger defensive reactions from jail staff. These provocations can be minimized with the right type of jail officer response.

There are three essential components in jail inmate control: effective planning, close cooperation with other criminal justice system components, and the development of an array of intermediate sentencing options and alternatives to pretrial incarceration. Planning is crucial to maximizing a jail's effectiveness. Good jail managers can anticipate future jail growth and potential problem areas. They can take a proactive approach to imminent overcrowding by developing tools to analyze their inmate population. Jail supervisors form the foundation for effective jail operations. Good supervisors need to be thoroughly familiar with jail operations as well as have exceptional interpersonal skills. The right kinds of supervisors can make all the difference in the world whether a jail is effective or ineffective. Poor supervision leads to employee dissatisfaction and poor security (Sigurdson 1996:9–11).

Jail Training Programs.   One way of equipping jail staff with useful skills that will improve their supervisory effectiveness is to establish jail officer training programs. Often, local universities may be the ideal sites for such training programs. At Winona State University in Minnesota, for example, a useful training program was established for jail officers. This program was the first higher education program certified by the International Association of Correctional Officers (IACO). A grant from the National Institute of Justice assisted the university in acquiring the staff and developing an appropriate curriculum. The program stressed applied or practical experiences as well as theory (Flynt and Ellenbecker 1995:57–58).

In Texas, the Texas Jail Association cooperated with Stephen F. Austin State University in Nacogdoches to initiate the most comprehensive jail training program in the organization's history (Boyd and Tiefenwerth 1995:59). The ongoing program provides a 40-hour annual jail officer certification, including verbal and nonverbal communication skills and the proper use of force. The topics covered are handling mentally ill inmates/confinees, HIV/AIDS inmates, cultural sensitivity, security procedures, correctional officer stress: recognition and reduction, and other relevant areas. Updating existing programs is encouraged, especially as the jail work environment becomes more complex technologically and the use of computers increases.

Cornelius (1997:51–52) reported that in 1990, at least 120 hours of correctional training were required of most state correctional officers. By 1993, an average of 5.7 weeks of training was required of these officers. A 2000 survey found that jail officers were required to have an average of 7 weeks of training or 274 hours of jail basics (Maguire and Pastore 2002). For jail officers, Cornelius specifies that the American Correctional Association recommends training in each of the following subject areas:

1. Security procedures: key control, head counts, searches
2. Inmate supervision
3. Use of force regulations/procedures
4. Report writing
5. Inmate rules, regulations, discipline, due process
6. Inmate rights and responsibilities
7. Emergency procedures: fire, escape, hostages
8. Weapons training: firearms, nonlethal weapons
9. Interpersonal communications/relations
10. Inmate social/cultural lifestyle
11. Constitutional law and legal issues
12. Ethics
13. Suicide prevention
14. Special management for inmates (mentally ill)
15. On-the-job training

An annual average of 33 hours of in-service training were required of all jail officers in most jurisdictions in 2000 (Maguire and Pastore 2002). One additional facet of jail officer training has increasingly included how to deal with AIDS inmates and those with tuberculosis, hepatitis, and other diseases (Buckley 1998). Also, no matter how well trained jail staff may be, they need state-of-the-art equipment if they are to do the best job in treating inmates with physical ailments or dealing with emergency life-saving situations. Many of the nation's jails, particularly the smaller ones, lack sophisticated medical equipment to use in the event of inmate emergencies. This problem is addressed locally through additional funding, which is often difficult to obtain. Sometimes state, federal, or private agencies may provide grants for the purpose of obtaining necessary equipment for jail personnel to do their jobs more effectively (Lowe 2002).

Managing Offenders from Other Jurisdictions.   Managing offender populations from other jurisdictions is another facet of jail officer training that is increasingly important. As we have seen, more jail systems in the United States
are making space available to state prisoners in other jurisdictions. The Albany
County Jail and Penitentiary in New York is one example. The Albany County
Jail has an average daily inmate population of 783 and a capacity of 834
(Szostak 1996:22–24). The jail began to receive prisoners from other jurisdictions in the mid-1970s. The outside inmate population grew steadily each year.
Apart from the financial rewards of accepting prisoners from other jurisdictions, the jail has had to become increasingly diverse in its approach to managing inmate problems and dealing with controversial inmate issues. Substantial
expansion of the Albany County Jail was undertaken during the 1980s and early
1990s, although the increased revenue generated by accommodating prisoners
from other jurisdictions helped to offset construction costs. But jail officers
have had to receive extra training. With appropriate planning and staff improvements, the Albany County Jail has been both profitable and effective at inmate management.

Working with Other Jail Officers.   Working around other jail officers is also an
important dimension of staff effectiveness. Jail officers must acquire a respect
for one another and get along. If there are tensions among jail officers, often
these tensions will be sensed by jail inmates, triggering interpersonal problems.
Interactions between jail officers of different genders may be difficult under certain circumstances. Occasionally, some officers will harass others because of
their gender. Female deputies in some jurisdictions report that some of their
male co-workers engage in paternalism and exclusion, while creating stress and
diminishing their career prospects (Pogrebin and Poole 1998).

   Sexual harassment of female deputies by their male counterparts often takes
the form of gender slurs. In one case, a male deputy continued to label a female
deputy as "PMS." The female deputy told the male officer that he had "MSB"

Larger numbers of women are performing correctional officer roles.

(Massive Sperm Buildup). She said, "I have to slam them back." Another female deputy said, "I think some of these (male) officers have their heads up their ass with the things they say. . . . I've told a few off in no uncertain terms and they've learned to keep their distance." Another female deputy said, "Male officers are intimidated by us, so they act like juveniles with gutter mouths. I have to treat them like my own kids in setting limits on their behavior." One woman said, "I sometimes reply, 'Not on your best day,' or 'You're not my type.' But the trash they talk really wears you down, so most of the time I just ignore it." One female deputy remarked, "They (male deputies) know all the right buttons to push, but you have to keep your cool. . . . I'm not about to let them get to me or let it show if I do get upset about something" (Pogrebin and Poole 1997:17).

It is imperative for all jails to have in place workable sexual harassment statements and policies to minimize or prevent such instances from ever occurring. Specific two- or three-day **gender courses** have been implemented in some jurisdictions, such as the one pioneered by the Washington Criminal Justice Training Commission in Spokane, Washington (Gurian 1994:29,33).

Inmate Classification Problems

A contemporary jail issue is how to effectively measure and classify jail inmates so that they can be managed in optimum ways, given existing jail resources and personnel (Sullivan, Cirincione, and Nelson 2001). Despite the short-term nature of jail confinement, many jails can offer various types of programs and services to assist certain offenders in coping with one or more of their problems. Some persons believe that because jails are intended as short-term facilities, the classification of jail inmates is not particularly important. Especially for many small county jails, this may be true. Short periods of confinement of several days would not seem to justify any type of elaborate classification procedure. However, growing numbers of jails are housing more diverse types of offenders for longer periods. In many jurisdictions, prisoners are housed for periods of one or two years, or even longer. Thus, it is imperative for such jails that functional classification procedures should be established and implemented to promote smoother jail operations and inmate control.

Since the early 1980s, there have been concerted efforts by many of the nation's jail systems to devise more effective inmate classification procedures (Wells and Brennan 1992:59). Such procedures have been consistent with the movement to professionalize jail environments and provide for more effective staffing and inmate control mechanisms. An early program was operated in Michigan in 1981. It was known as the Community Justice Alternatives and was operated in a ten-county region. The services provided by this program included offender support services such as self-help programs, substance abuse education, employability and life skills, and re-entry job placement.

In mid-1984 Michigan jail officials devised an experimental Jail Inmate Classification system (JICS) to be used as a decision tree for screening incoming inmates. The screening instrument for incoming inmates was designed to detect medical and suicide risks and to justify some type of temporary cell assignment and observation. Eventually, computerized and automated versions of these screening procedures were devised to accommodate growing numbers of inmates. The Michigan project yielded a standardized classification system that was being used in over twenty-five jail jurisdictions by 1992. The JICS instruments have been used successfully throughout Michigan to facilitate jail organization and planning. Brennan and Wells (1992:50) have suggested several important reasons for jail inmate classification. These are to:

1. Provide greater inmate safety
2. Provide greater staff safety
3. Provide greater public safety
4. Provide for greater equity, consistency, and fairness among inmates and where they are placed
5. Provide for more orderly processing and discipline
6. Protect the agency against liability
7. Provide data for planning, resource allocation, and greater jail efficiency

The project also promoted the Michigan Jail Population Information System, which is a statewide reporting system for Michigan jail inmates. The system is being used to monitor trends and patterns of jail utilization (Wells and Brennan 1992:61).

The Santa Clara County Jail (California) has implemented **B.A.C.I.S. (Behavior Alert Classification Identification System** (Stack and Dixon 1990:45). According to Stack and Dixon (1990:45–46), classification systems must identify inmates within the jail to ensure that the appropriate housing decision is made. Classification systems based entirely on risk factors are inadequate, because they will not result in appropriate inmate placement for new direct supervision styles. B.A.C.I.S. begins at intake, with booking personnel separating medically and mentally ill inmates from the main population and segregating assaultive, high escape risk, and extreme protective custody inmates into high-security housing units. The overall objective of B.A.C.I.S. is the safety and security of the facility, staff, and inmates. During the first 72-hour period of an inmate's entry into jail, the following will happen:

1. Custody staff report on in-custody behavior.
2. Classification admissions/orientation staff evaluate prior risk assessments, administer psychological behavioral instruments, document in-custody behavior.
3. Establish a recommended classification code.

An examination is also made of behavior factors based upon psychological instrumentation, housing placement, a custody profile/risk assessment, judicial status (inmate's judicial status at time of assessment or reassessment), special conditions (identifies special handling protective custody, medical, mental health, gang status), and bail and current tracking of an inmate's bail amount. Stack and Dixon report that since B.A.C.I.S. was implemented, the incidence of jail inmate violence, extortion, and gang activity has decreased substantially and jail operations are running more smoothly.

The American Jail Association has established specific resolutions to improve jail operations and provide for more effective inmate processing and safety. Among the principles espoused by the American Jail Association are the provision for better inmate classification and orientation (Ingley 1993:7). Increasing numbers of jail jurisdictions have attempted to fulfill this objective in different ways. For instance, the Multnomah County (Oregon) Jail created a population release matrix system (Wood 1991:52–53). This matrix cross-tabulates an inmate's offense seriousness with prior record and other factors. A score is yielded that enables jail officers to place particular inmates in the best jail surroundings for a particular supervision level. Behavior alerts include assaultiveness, escape risk, unstable personality system, gang membership, and other psychological problems. Thus, jail staff can supervise and transport inmates more safely and overall jail security is enhanced.

Subsequently, more jails have implemented automated management information systems (MIS) in order to record offender data for basic record keeping and to facilitate basic inmate management routines. The primary uses of MIS are to (1) identify and correctly classify the high risk and predatory inmates and keep them separated from the general population; (2) drive the inmate housing decision consistent with the goals of classification, facility policy, and housing plan; (3) drive eligibility for inmate programs (assessed needs) and privileges; (4) identify and isolate offender subpopulations for early release, community corrections screening, and facilitate crowding control; and (5) collect, store, and easily retrieve appropriate and relevant classification-related inmate-specific data for management, planning, and policy applications (Wells and Brennan 1997:58).

Although gangs are more commonly associated with prisons than jails, a gang presence in jails is pervasive (Huff 2002). Thus, in the interests of jail security and good correctional management, it is important for jail officials to identify gang members and deal with their presence in positive ways. There is an adage that says, "Gangs are only as strong as the community or institution allows them to be." This is true of U.S. jail environments where large numbers of gang members are housed. As most gangs are deceptive in nature, it is important for staff to control situations where inmate gangs may attempt to rule other inmates. Therefore, some classification of jail inmates early in their jail placement should ascertain whether they are gang members. Once these detainees have been identified, they should be closely monitored. Some of the supervisory suggestions include: (1) Rap music, rap videos, and other programs that promote violence on television should be excluded; (2) massive movements of detainee population that could include large numbers of gang members should be discouraged, since this will assist in preventing open-area and other confrontations; (3) a no-gang tolerance policy that encourages the consistent application of rules will deter gang operations; and (4) staff should be encouraged to become familiar with gang identifiers as well as the identifiers of other groups that are potential threats to security or are otherwise disruptive (Moore 1997:84).

Health-Care Services for Jails

Because of the increasing longevity of jail inmates and the changing composition of the jail inmate population, a greater need for health services has been created (Smith et al. 1994). Communicable diseases, such as tuberculosis and AIDS, have caused increased concern among jail officials as they attempt to devise methods for controlling the spread of these and other diseases (Buckley 1998). It has been found, for instance, that jail and prison populations are three times more likely to have tuberculosis and other related diseases compared with the general population. But because of the confined nature of the inmate population, appropriate management methods can be implemented to provide for greater violence and disease control, surveillance, containment, and assessment (Potter and Saltzman 1999).

One solution to improving the general health standards of jails is to liaison with local health and medical services to arrange for long-term contracting. Because health-care costs are increasing, it is important for jail staff to plan effectively to provide for nursing and medical services for those inmates suffering from various injuries and illnesses. On-site pharmacy services may be required, especially for some of the nation's largest jail systems. Correctional health and detention administrators can conduct cost evaluations of needed services and plan accordingly. In Maricopa County, Arizona, such planning has been implemented effectively. A workbook has been produced to provide jail officials with jail health-care costs and guidelines (Maricopa County Arizona Correctional Health Services 1991).

In some jails, exercise programs have been established to alleviate the boredom and routine of jail living. Physical exercise was found to be effective in decreasing inmate psychological stress and depression in several Missouri jail sites (Libbus, Genovese, and Poole 1994). Existing jails without adequate facilities for exercise and other recreational activities have been encouraged by the federal government to make structural changes with supplemental funds.

In those jails where inmates with HIV are housed, separate and segregated facilities have been established for the purpose of isolating healthy inmates from sick ones (Hammett and Maruschak 1999). Such segregation facilities have been found to be constitutional as well as useful for the effective administration of treatments and medications. Professional societies, such as the American Medical Association, have recommended the establishment of more effective screening mechanisms for early detection of medical problems and sexually transmitted diseases.

Beyond HIV and tuberculosis, there are many other types of medical problems that characterize large numbers of jail inmates. Many of them are drug or alcohol dependent (Buckley 1998). Thus, adequate screening mechanisms must be in place to determine which entering inmates should receive priority regarding treatment of their particular chemical dependencies. Cornelius (1997:29) estimates that at least 58 percent of all entering jail inmates annually are chemically dependent on either drugs or alcohol or both.

Many of the larger jails have established detoxification programs, 12-step programs such as Alcoholics Anonymous, and group or individual therapy for specific offenders (Keeton and Swanson 1998; Welch 2000). Some of these programs involve educational presentations to inform those who are chemically dependent of ways to cope with these dependencies.

Small Jails and Small Jail Problems

Jails are unique institutions in criminal justice and U.S. society (Kingery 1994). According to early jail researchers, small jails were defined as having a rated capacity of ten or fewer inmates. In the 1983 National Jail Census, for instance, there were 355 jails that met this small-jail criterion. Using 1997 jail figures, jails with this rated capacity accounted for about 12 percent (400) of all U.S. jails. At the beginning of 2001, the proportion of small jails in the United States rated for 10 or fewer inmates appeared largely unchanged (Maguire and Pastore 2002). But the most widely accepted definition of a small jail is any jail rated for housing fewer than 50 inmates (Kerle 1998). Using this criterion, a survey of jails conducted in 1992 showed that there were 1,584 small jails in the United States, accounting for nearly half of all jails (Cornelius 1997:19). A subsequent examination of jail sizes in the United States in 2000 has continued to show a similar proportion of small jails (Maguire and Pastore 2002).

Most of these local jails have no on-site medical facilities. For medical services and health needs, local agencies are used on an as-needed basis. Screening procedures for entering inmates are almost nonexistent. Thus, the potential for suicide and other threats to inmate well-being are greatly increased. Death

Many jails offer a no-frills environment, which minimizes inmate interaction as well as access to various amenities found in prisons.

rates, suicide rates, and homicide rates in small jails are many times larger than their large-jail counterparts (Hoefle 1995).

Small jails are plagued with assorted health and safety problems. Because of these problems, there is greater risk for liability suits filed against counties where such jails are located. The bases for lawsuits range from unconstitutional housing conditions to mistreatment and misconduct by jail staff. The fact that such jurisdictions often lack financial resources to adequately equip their jails does not defend well against such lawsuits by jail inmates and their families (Garza 1994).

A key problem confronting small jails is how to separate juveniles from adult offenders. Often, small jails do not have elaborate housing and segregation facilities. Rather, they are equipped with a few general holding cells for overnight occupants. Inmate security problems are chronic and persistent. Compared with larger jails, smaller jails are dangerous places (Mays and Thompson 1988:436–437). In Meade County, Sturgis, South Dakota, a small jail was originally started as a mom-and-pop operation (Kaiser 1994:77). The family resided in quarters connected to the jail. Mom did the laundry and helped keep the kids in line. Dad was responsible for processing inmates and dealing out discipline whenever required. In the mid-1980s the Meade County Jail was renovated and updated. Juveniles were held during a four-year period (1985–1989), but they posed more problems than existing jail staff could handle. When they came into the custody of Meade County jail officers, they were separated from adult inmates. However, they were from homes where they were not welcome; they had so much unspent energy that they spent most of it fighting among themselves in jail cells. They destroyed anything they got their hands on. Eventually, Meade County Jail refused to accept juvenile offenders, even for short periods, because of their destructive propensities (Kaiser 1994:81).

Pete Garza, Jr. (1994:71) provides some interesting insight into how at least one small jail is operated. After three days of training, Garza was placed as the sole jail officer in charge of 22 prisoners and 6 work releasees in the Sunnyside Jail near Yakima, Washington. Garza says that there were 18 beds allocated for

BOX 6.2

PERSONALITY HIGHLIGHT

Gary F. Cornelius

First Lieutenant, Programs and Recreation Supervisor, Fairfax County Adult Detention Center, Fairfax County Sheriff's Office, Fairfax, VA

Background and Interests

I grew up outside of Pittsburgh, Pennsylvania, in the suburb of Bethel Park, where my family taught me that hard work pays off. I wanted at different times to be a variety of things: a radio broadcaster, a historian, and I even thought about astronomy. When I went to Edinboro, I, like many others, did not have definitive idea about what I wanted to do. In 1973 I entered a new Criminal Justice Focus Program where I began taking courses in constitutional law, evidence, and corrections. From then on, I was hooked into law enforcement. As any veteran law enforcement officer will tell you, once it (law enforcement) gets into your blood, it is hard to get it out. I also worked as an intern in the Erie County Volunteers in Probation program where juvenile offenders are matched up with citizens who will work with them to try to keep them from committing offenses. Even back then, I could see the value of volunteers. Being an intern gave me some good "hands-on" experience, and today I am glad to bring college interns into our jail to work. It gives them a feel for correctional work, and the agency can make use of their dedication, energy, and hard work.

Experiences

My first law enforcement job was being a radio dispatcher/desk operator at a substation for the Allegheny County (PA) police in 1973. It was a summer job, but it taught me a lot about police being important public servants. I graduated from college and went to work for the Executive Protective Service (EPS) of the United States Secret Service. EPS is now called the United States Secret Service Uniformed Division. Its responsibilities included, and still do include, the protection of the President, the Vice President, their offices and residences, and the protection of foreign diplomats, embassies, and chanceries in the District of Columbia or as assigned by the director of the Secret Service.

I must say that I received excellent training in firearms, arrest procedures, and security. I took the job seriously—wearing a badge and firearm impresses that upon you. I did some on-the-job training at the White House, but I was assigned to the Foreign Missions Division. I was involved in several protection details at different embassies, the Blair House (the residence for visiting heads of state), and the Vice President's residence.

After two years, I served on a small-town police force in Virginia, where I attended my second law enforcement academy and picked up some more experience. But corrections—the people, the security, and the teamwork—continued to interest me. And so, in 1978 I was hired by the Fairfax County Sheriff's Office and started to work in the jail. Back then, the jail was an old, three-floor "clanging bars" type of building—hot as an oven in the summer and very cold in the winter. In the twenty-five years that I have been with the Sheriff's Office, I have worked in literally four different institutions. The old jail that I described gave way to a linear, more modern jail in 1978, and that building has been added to over the years. A podular addition was built in 1987. Also in 1987, a pre-release center was added. In 2000, we opened up a large 750-bed direct supervision expansion that includes a substance abuse unit and a mental health unit.

I have been fortunate enough to have had many different job assignments over the years: confinement, classification, work release, planning and policy development, community programs, and treatment programs supervisor. I will never call myself an expert—just a correctional worker who has seen a lot in the field, both good and bad.

Early in my career at the jail, I worked at the booking desk and receiving. It was a sobering experience to see firsthand the effects of incarceration on people and to be on the front line: handling mentals, substance abusers, uncooperative people, and others. Classification taught me a lot about handling problems among inmates in the population, the disciplinary process, making proper housing decisions, helping inmates to adjust to the jail, and seeing how their lives have been affected by breaking the law. Transitioning from the jail to work release was interesting—from keeping them locked up to trusting them to go out into the community.

The most challenging, rewarding, while at the same time the most difficult, job that I have had is being a jail programs director, an assignment that I have had since October 1995. I have come to realize several things: There *are* some inmates who really want to live crime-free lives when released. Not all, but some do feel this way, and they will try. The second thing that I have learned is that there are dedicated people—teachers, counselors, and volunteers—who will make a difference. Corrections is about change—while we have the offender under our control, we must try to promote change, all the while knowing that sometimes our efforts will be in vain. Programs, one-on-one involvement, and volunteer activities can accomplish this. Taking an idea and building it into a program is rewarding. I am fortunate to work with a great team in our section.

The largest aspect of my work experience is how I have channeled what I have seen and learned into writing and teaching. I have found it rewarding to teach several different subjects to jail personnel; my two favorite subjects are inmate manipulation and stress management. In 1986 I became an adjunct faculty member at George Mason University, where I teach Sociology of Punishment and Corrections, Community Corrections, and supervise college interns who work in the jail. I have been blessed enough to write five books on correctional issues, and I have performed teaching and consulting for organizations such as the American Correctional Associa-

tion, the American Jail Association, the National Institute of Justice, and the National Institute of Corrections.

My writing and teaching have made me see the importance of not only sharing with people in the field what I have learned and experienced, but often I learn from students, correctional staff, and others that I meet. I enjoy taking an idea and watching it blossom into something that can help others. In every class or seminar, or while doing research, I pick up an idea, a fact, or a different perspective that I did not know before. We can learn from each other.

Advice to Students

As I head toward retirement (and I will still keep active in the field), I would like to pass this advice on to the new group of corrections professionals:

1. Jail work is not the "bottom." It is a valuable public service; it is interesting; and it can be rewarding.
2. Practice good ethics and moral behavior. You wear a badge and uniform, and the public trusts you. Be proud of your agency and do not do anything to cast a negative light on it.
3. Some inmates do want rehabilitation. Encourage program involvement and proper behavior; be a role model. Treat inmates as you would want to be treated; remember that they are people, too.
4. Control your stress. I am a former burnout, and I learned the hard way that unmanaged stress is harmful. I am fortunate to have a wife, Nancy, and two great children, Gary Jr. and Amber, who support what I do and listen when I feel that I must talk and unwind. Practice stress management. Keep healthy, both mentally and physically.
5. Keep getting training and education, no matter how long you have been in the field. Corrections is a constantly changing field. Keep your options open by keeping informed. Take advantage of classes, seminars, college courses, and correspondence courses. Read the literature.
6. Practice teamwork. Operating a jail takes many people working together. Get some insight as to what others do.

Good luck!

male prisoners, and 4 beds allotted to female prisoners. However, there were seldom any female offenders in his facility. At one point in time, Garza's jail became overcrowded as the result of having to accommodate additional prisoners from an adjacent jurisdiction. New arrestees would be taken to the Sunnyside Jail where they would be held. The Washington State Highway Patrol entered into an agreement with the Yakima County Sheriff's Office providing that arrestees would be held for up to 30 days in the Sunnyside Jail. After 30 days, these prisoners would be transferred to the Yakima County Jail by a van.

At the same time, judges would see the same offenders again and again appearing in court before them. Disgusted with the high rate of recidivism among these persons, judges would impose longer jail sentences on them. This meant that the Sunnyside Jail would have to accommodate more inmates for longer periods. Eventually, Garza was able to hire one and one-half more deputies to assist him. Despite this additional personpower, jail inmates could not be continually supervised by jail officers. Periods during evening hours were spent where the only supervision maintained over inmates was through a closed-circuit camera in the dispatcher's office. Thus, the dispatcher became a jail officer by default. Garza notes that his budget was never increased during the overcrowding period. "We were running the same budget size as we were when we had only three prisoners. During the first and second year, we ran out of money to run the jail" (Garza 1994:71).

The Sunnyside Jail was equipped with only one shower, located on the male side of the jail. The shower lacked water pressure so that hot water was inadequate. If female offenders were jailed, then in order for them to shower, the complete male inmate population had to be moved from that portion of the jail to another area during the female showering period. The city attempted to provide Sunnyside Jail with additional jail space. However, a small building provided by the city lacked metal doors, which had been removed earlier. Garza tracked down the metal doors, which were being used by a local farmer to plow his fields. Garza negotiated the return of the metal doors, which were welded back into place to secure jail inmates in the newly created space. While all of this was going on, Garza had to contend with the fact that the city police department had taken over two cells in the original jail area for office space, shared with the parks department. Two other cells had been converted into a kitchen and a detective's office. Garza eventually succeeded in freeing up this space for jail use exclusively. Garza's frustrations with the system are quite apparent in his account of his jail officer experience. Evidence from other sources suggests that Garza's experiences are not unique to Sunnyside Jail (Oldenstadt 1994).

Jail Overcrowding and Megajails

Jail overcrowding is the major cause of inmate lawsuits in federal and state courts (Pontell and Welsh 1994). In California, for instance, lawsuits against jail systems last an average of 55 months. Whenever litigation is favorable for inmates, court orders are issued against general jail operations. In 79 percent of the cases involving county jails in California during 1975 through 1989, for instance, overcrowding was the most frequently cited problem to be rectified by court action. Other issues cited in these lawsuits included inadequate medical care, sanitation problems, hygiene, access to courts, food services, and ventilation (Welch and Gunther 1997a, 1997b).

California is not alone in its jail overcrowding problems. In Texas, for instance, there was a statewide epidemic in 2003 of overcrowded prisons with a state deficit that led to packed county jails, with no apparent relief in sight

(Almada 2003:A1). Problems at the state level tend to trickle down to county jails and cause them to become overcrowded. In Texas's case, the Texas Department of Criminal Justice is not accepting those who have already been convicted of crimes, and so the felons must be housed at the county level. For Webb County Jail in Southwest Texas, for instance, this has become an especially problematic issue. Webb County Jail has traditionally housed numerous federal inmates, contract prisoners, in order to help the Federal Bureau of Prisons ease their overcrowding problems. But with new overcrowding problems of their own, the Webb County Jail has been forced to expel more than 120 federal prisoners from the jail in order to make room for newly convicted local inmates. The Webb County Sheriff, Juan Garza, said that he had 718 inmates in the jail in February 2003, well above the 570 capacity set for the jail by the Texas Jail Commission. One possible solution is to contact with private facilities, such as the Corrections Corporation of America, in order to accommodate inmate overflow.

In many jurisdictions, police arrest policies have been changed to ease jail overcrowding. Thus, police officers are less inclined to take minor offenders to jail for less serious infractions because these persons would exacerbate existing overcrowded jail conditions (Welsh 1993a, 1993b). But no matter how much planning jail officials can muster, there is no way to predict correctly optimum jail capacity from one day to the next. There is some seasonal variation in jail inmate populations. But there are frequent unpredictable peaks in jail inmate populations that must somehow be accommodated (Murray and Bell 1996:61). Overall averages regarding daily jail occupancy are deceptive, because unanticipated peak occupancy periods cannot be predicted. Nevertheless, jail officials are expected to accommodate rising and falling inmate populations no matter how unusual these daily fluctuations.

In Washington state, for example, a persistent jail overcrowding problem was partially resolved through effective planning and interaction between jails and the courts. A jail capacity study was conducted to explore ways to maximize the use of existing jail space and beds. Three strategies were examined: (1) Increase capacity and accommodate the added demand; (2) reduce admissions and lengths of stay and mitigate the effects of demand; or (3) add correctional options and divert demand to other types of placements.

Experiments in several Washington counties showed that increasing the use of bail in minor offense cases greatly alleviated jail overcrowding. Police officers were advised not to bring the following types of persons to these jails: (1) out-of-county misdemeanant warrant arrest, (2) misdemeanor charges except those required under the district court bail schedule or state law, and (3) traffic charges other than driving under the influence. With this policy in effect, the Spokane County Jail admission rate decreased by 29 percent. Further, many postconviction misdemeanants and traffic offenders were diverted from jail, while the average length of stay for the average jail inmate was decreased from fourteen to twelve days. These strategies were effective in controlling the fluctuating inmate population and alleviating serious overcrowding problems (Murray and Bell 1996:62–63).

Megajails are jails with 1,000 or more beds (Cornelius 1997:19). In 2001, for example, the nation's 50 largest jails housed 33 percent of all jail inmates (Beck, Karberg, and Harrison 2002:11). Table 6.2 shows the 50 jails in the United States with the largest jail populations for 1999–2001.

When jails equal or exceed 1,000 or more beds, there are more complex logistical problems that must be dealt with on a daily basis. Greater coordination among the individual parts of such jails is required. Greater formality between jail officers and inmates is expected. Inmate control becomes an increasingly

TABLE 6.2

The 50 Largest Local Jail Jurisdictions: Number of Inmates Held, Average Daily Population, and Rated Capacity, Midyear 1999–2001

Jurisdiction	Number of Inmates Held[a]			Average Daily Population[b]			Rated Capacity[c]			Percent of Capacity Occupied at Midyear[d]		
	1999	2000	2001	1999	2000	2001	1999	2000	2001	1999	2000	2001
Total	206,794	206,713	205,875	207,814	207,481	206,619	227,351	226,833	228,554	91%	91%	90%
Los Angeles County, CA	20,398	18,957	19,944	20,683	19,662	19,327	24,320	24,320	24,440	84%	78%	82%
New York City, NY	16,321	14,349	14,249	17,562	15,530	14,490	22,584	22,558	22,574	72	64	63
Cook County, IL	9,047	10,000	10,356	9,430	9,801	10,212	9,677	9,798	9,798	93	102	106
Harris County, TX	8,419	7,854	6,197	7,772	8,234	7,124	8,700	8,602	8,602	97	91	72
Maricopa County, AZ	6,502	7,012	6,951	6,770	6,660	7,055	7,671	5,293	5,194	85	132	134
Philadelphia City, PA	6,272	6,568	7,047	6,270	6,484	7,041	5,600	5,600	5,600	112	117	126
Dade County, FL	6,862	6,402	6,720	7,127	6,851	6,410	8,127	8,140	8,179	84	79	82
Dallas County, TX	6,492	6,900	6,354	6,400	7,299	6,275	7,666	8,187	6,585	85	84	96
Orleans Parish, LA	6,624	6,293	5,899	6,935	6,381	5,875	7,250	7,250	7,477	91	87	79
San Bernardino County, CA	4,752	5,581	5,220	4,924	5,124	5,300	4,754	4,957	4,957	100	113	105
Shelby County, TN	6,091	5,428	4,721	5,840	5,795	5,176	6,470	6,901	6,392	94	79	74
San Diego County, CA	5,495	5,335	4,790	5,666	5,317	4,895	5,994	6,104	4,726	92	87	101
Orange County, CA	4,853	4,982	4,498	5,194	4,807	4,792	3,812	3,821	4,109	127	130	109
Broward County, FL	4,358	4,861	5,008	4,424	4,813	4,745	5,130	5,280	5,562	85	92	90
Orange County, FL	4,197	4,063	4,228	3,880	4,131	4,172	3,905	3,940	3,940	107	103	107
Santa Clara County, CA	4,817	4,114	4,132	4,748	4,343	4,122	4,094	3,910	3,629	118	105	114
Alameda County, CA	4,562	4,216	3,844	4,333	4,229	3,856	4,809	4,354	4,354	95	97	88
Hillsborough County, FL	3,275	3,528	3,463	3,213	3,350	3,502	3,369	3,369	3,373	97	105	103
Tarrant County, TX	3,462	3,626	3,024	3,693	3,807	3,484	4,546	4,548	5,089	76	80	59
Milwaukee County, WI	3,366	3,378	3,398	2,747	3,394	3,444	4,066	3,790	3,790	89	89	90
Bexar County, TX	3,517	3,672	3,448	3,536	3,561	3,418	3,670	3,670	4,231	96	100	81
Baltimore City, MD	3,149	3,467	3,648	3,544	3,193	3,287	3,744	3,777	3,861	84	92	94
Sacramento County, CA	3,097	3,172	3,183	3,318	3,020	3,217	4,218	4,732	4,488	73	67	71
De Kalb County, GA	2,734	3,070	3,119	3,005	2,948	3,146	3,636	3,636	3,636	75	84	86

Jacksonville City, FL	2,846	2,892	2,850	2,758	2,730	3,025	3,113	3,200	3,089	91	90	92
King County, WA	2,406	2,484	2,929	2,345	2,400	2,885	2,143	2,143	3,641	112	116	80
Allegheny County, PA	2,171	2,405	2,402	2,086	2,288	2,868	2,713	2,757	2,923	80	87	82
Fulton County, GA	3,380	2,869	2,813	3,692	3,008	2,785	2,330	2,550	2,550	145	113	110
Pinellas County, FL	2,525	2,488	2,771	2,432	2,504	2,728	2,261	3,183	3,303	112	78	84
Wayne County, MI	2,588	2,650	2,619	2,650	2,800	2,680	2,643	2,668	2,874	98	99	91
Travis County, TX	2,516	2,915	2,827	2,531	2,572	2,659	1,958	1,958	2,246	128	149	126
Riverside County, CA	2,552	2,619	2,790	2,582	2,574	2,641	2,879	2,468	2,659	89	106	105
Kern County, CA	2,568	2,591	2,672	2,025	2,553	2,621	2,698	2,684	2,698	95	97	99
Davidson County, TN	—	2,752	2,790	—	2,794	2,615	—	2,868	2,866	—	96	97
Clark County, NV	2,245	2,262	2,538	2,312	2,378	2,538	1,488	1,488	1,488	151	152	171
Marion County, IN[e]	2,343	2,521	2,514	2,303	2,425	2,451	2,389	2,390	2,403	98	105	105
Essex County, NJ	1,648	2,084	2,526	2,016	1,771	2,408	1,756	1,503	2,410	94	139	105
Palm Beach County, FL	2,574	2,448	2,353	2,543	2,565	2,353	3,255	2,619	2,619	79	93	90
Fresno County, CA	2,220	2,301	2,331	2,254	2,250	2,346	2,382	2,348	2,482	93	98	94
Suffolk County, MA	2,448	2,297	2,360	1,800	2,312	2,300	1,798	2,452	2,452	136	94	96
Cobb County, GA	1,970	2,074	2,274	1,931	2,053	2,274	2,229	2,224	2,224	89	93	102
Franklin County, OH	—	2,216	2,405	—	2,156	2,271	—	2,639	1,681	—	84	143
El Paso County, TX	2,049	2,102	2,046	2,059	2,000	2,148	2,464	2,464	1,978	83	85	103
Multnomah County, OR	1,990	2,001	1,884	1,893	2,036	2,036	2,073	2,073	2,073	96	97	91
Cuyahoga County, OH	1,840	1,914	2,135	1,750	1,980	2,000	1,777	1,749	1,749	104	109	122
Hamilton County, OH	2,073	2,041	1,916	2,007	2,093	1,985	2,465	2,465	2,465	84	83	78
Reeves County, TX	1,131	1,142	2,007	1,080	1,125	1,968	1,085	1,168	2,185	104	98	92
York County, PA	1,550	1,647	1,911	1,358	1,558	1,931	1,600	1,725	1,950	97	95	98
Salt Lake County, UT	1,480	1,745	1,888	1,500	1,522	1,875	2,400	1,930	1,960	62	90	96
Oklahoma County, OK	2,136	2,425	1,883	2,100	2,300	1,863	2,410	2,580	3,000	89	94	63

Note: Jurisdictions are ordered by their average daily population in 2001.—Not available.

[a] Number of inmates held in jail facilities. Totals for 1999 include estimates for Davidson County, TN, and Franklin County, OH.

[b] Based on the average daily population for the year ending June 30. The average daily population is the sum of the number of inmates in jail each day for a year, divided by the number of days in the year.

[c] Rated capacity is the number of beds or inmates assigned by a rating official to facilities within each jurisdiction.

[d] The number of inmates divided by the rated capacity multiplied by 100.

[e] Figures for 1999 and 2000 have been updated to include Marion County Jail II-CCA.

Source: Allen J. Beck, Jennifer C. Karberg, and Paige M. Harrison. *Prison and Jail Inmates at Midyear 2001.* Washington, DC: U.S. Department of Justice, 2002, p. 11.

important problem as well. The following breakdown of jail sizes gives us some perspective about how jail capacities are defined (Cornelius 1997:19):

Megajails = 1,000 or more beds

Large jails = 250 to 999 beds

Medium jails = 50–249 beds

Small jails = 49 or fewer beds

In some respects, some megajails operate similar to prison systems. These jails are large enough to hire full-time medical and support staff to be on call for jail inmate emergencies. Greater segregation among prisoners is achieved with more massive jail size. Some of these megajails have their own commissaries, where prisoners may purchase personal items, articles of clothing, and snacks. These jails are also equipped with weight rooms, small tracks, and other amenities usually found in large prison systems. But despite these amenities, megajails can be overcrowded as well, with all of the problems accompanying overcrowding.

Cornelius (1997:64) indicates that during the next decade, megajails will generate the following:

1. Epidemics of AIDS and tuberculosis
2. Expansion of jail industries
3. Diminishing revenues with which to fund jail operations
4. Privatization
5. Increase in inmate programs
6. Continuing searches for alternatives to incarceration
7. Employee incentives
8. Inmate populations becoming more institutionalized and sophisticated

One solution to chronic jail overcrowding is to regionalize jail operations. **Regional jails** have the potential to deal with the overcrowding in existing jails at reduced costs per prisoner when compared to other jails within their states. Regional jails also offer greater capacity for more prisoners, a wider array of inmate services, updated and more secure facilities, and a safer environment for both staff and inmates (LaMunyon 2001). Regional jails are multijurisdictional corrections facilities in which two or more jurisdictions share in both the initial capital construction and ongoing operating costs. Representatives of the jurisdictions jointly organize, administer, operate, and finance the facilities through an annual budget (National Institute of Corrections, 2003).

Virginia is one of several states that has constructed several regional jails. Two exemplary facilities include Henrico County Regional Jail East in New Kent County and Henrico County Jail West located in Richmond. Jail East was built as a part of a regional agreement between Goochland, Henrico, and New Kent counties and is maintained and secured by the Henrico County Sheriff and the Henrico County Sheriff's Office. Jail East is a state-of-the-art new-generation jail that uses the direct supervision approach and holds the distinction of being the first campus-style jail in Virginia. Direct supervision offers a barrier-free environment between deputies and inmates to encourage communication and more effective supervision. This style helps to promote a proactive approach to solving problems. Jail East also features training and rehabilitation by offering a wide range of mental health and substance abuse services as well as educational and vocational training. Classes, programs, and services are provided to assist the inmates to achieve their educational and vocational goals upon their release. These programs are offered through the cooperative effort of staff, community volunteers, and outside agencies.

In contrast, Jail West was opened in 1980 and renovated in 1996. It is a maximum-security facility that houses both pretrial and post-trial inmates. It is also the headquarters of the Office of Sheriff, Administrative Services, Court Services, and Human Resources. Deputies assigned to Jail Security and Jail Services maintain the safety and order of the facility. They provide security to the community by preventing jail disturbances and escapes. Jail Security staff move inmates throughout the facility and see to their safety and well-being. The Intake and Release Booking section uses state-of-the-art imaging technology to assist in the processing and releasing of inmates. Jail Services staff provide programs and services to the inmate population. These programs and services include laundry, recreation, visitation, property control, mail delivery, religious services, a wide range of mental health/substance abuse services, and education. These programs are offered through the cooperative effort of staff, community volunteers, and outside agencies. Specific programs offered include G.E.D. preparation and testing; computer technology; parenting and fatherhood classes; substance abuse and relapse prevention; and group and individual counseling (Henrico County 2003).

Jail Suicides

Jail suicides are a significant problem confronting jail administration and staff. In 2000, 147 inmates committed suicide, while 124 inmates committed suicide in 2001 (CEGA Services, Inc. 2002:6). Many of those who killed themselves while jailed were under the influence of either drugs or alcohol. It is not unusual for suicide survivors to sue jail systems for not properly monitoring them. One problem with many jails is that there are insufficient policies in place governing the supervision of potentially suicidal inmates. The following suicide prevention policies have been established by many jurisdictions. The numbers in parentheses indicate the number of jails with established suicide policies as of 1996 (Cornelius 1997:33):

> Jails with no suicide prevention policy (317)
>
> Jails with a suicide prevention policy (2,628)
>
> Jails with staff suicide prevention training (1,796)
>
> Jails with risk assessment at intake (2,209)
>
> Jails with suicide watch cell (including checks every 10 to 15 minutes) (2,025)
>
> Live or remote monitoring (1,801)
>
> Special counseling (mental health staff, etc.) (1,885)
>
> Inmate suicide prevention teams (120)
>
> Other methods (removal of belts, shoelaces, issue paper gowns, transfer to psychiatric ward) (53)

Besides drugs and alcohol, other factors are responsible for contributing to jail suicides. Many arrestees are shocked or traumatized by the jail experience. Some are embarrassed by the experience and fear social exposure and ridicule (Suris et al. 2001). Some observers have suggested importation explanations, where jails attract persons more likely to consider suicide. Other explanations include deprivation, suggesting great trauma experienced through a loss of freedom or liberty (Kunzman 1995).

Virtually all large and medium-sized jails have implemented policies and procedures designed to prevent or minimize inmate suicides. While suicide training for staff is important, it is also important to realize that very few jail suicides are actually prevented by mental health, medical, or other professional staff. This is because most suicides occur during late evening hours and on weekends. Furthermore, while inmates can commit suicide at any time, research shows that most inmate suicides occur within the first 24 hours of incarceration (Winter 2000:8–9).

Many jails have established suicide plans. The Los Angeles, California, Sheriff's Department, for instance, uses a screening device for all new jail admissions, and the following risk factors are identified:

1. Suicide risk assessment
2. Relationships with family/friends
3. Significant losses
4. Worry about problems
5. Suicide of family member or significant other
6. Psychiatric history
7. Drug or alcohol abuse history
8. Shocking crime
9. Verbalization of suicide idea
10. Past suicide attempts
11. Hopelessness
12. Signs of depression
13. Expressions of anxiety, fear, or anger
14. Expressions of embarrassment or shame
15. Appearance of being incoherent, withdrawn, or mentally ill
16. Under the influence
17. No prior arrests
18. Strange behavior or comments
19. Violence of recent suicide attempt, if any
20. Detailed and feasible suicide plan (Kunzman 1995:90–91).

Arrestees who exhibit five or more of these indicators are considered more likely suicide risks and may be placed in observation areas where their actions can be closely monitored. Technological developments make it possible to monitor suicide-prone inmates through closed-circuit television monitors from a central location.

Persons with physical handicaps or limitations should not be excluded as suicide candidates. For example, a Missouri man was arrested and transported to a rural county jail after causing a disturbance. While being transported to the jail, he tried to slash his wrists with a sharp wire. Police officers were able to restrain him. The man was wearing a back brace from recent surgery, and when he was admitted to the jail, the police advised jail officers of his suicide attempt. The man was placed in a cell away from other inmates, in a housing unit normally reserved for female inmates. At 6:30 the following morning, the man was found hanging by his neck. He had used the back brace strap as a noose and attached it to a pipe that ran across the cell ceiling. He had last been checked at 3:30 A.M. by jail officers and seemed fine. This incident underscores the necessity for supervising suicide-prone inmates constantly and closely.

Several solutions have been proposed by different authorities for reducing inmate suicides and other problems. One solution is indirect and involves accrediting jails through a process that standardizes the quality of services and inmate management procedures jails exhibit. Some persons view accreditation of jails as the equivalent of professionalizing jail staff with greater amounts of education and technical assistance. However, achieving national accreditation is not required to operate a safe and effective jail (Ryan and Plummer 1999:157). One result of jail accreditation through an organization such as the American Correctional Association is national recognition and staff pride in a job well done and the likelihood that lawsuits from jail inmates will be minimized. This is because the jail staff of an accredited jail are more in touch with jail inmates, their dispositions and problems. Jail officer training is more intensive, and potential suicide risks can be spotted more easily and quickly.

Jail accreditation can also help to minimize unethical staff behavior. Unethical staff behavior can occur on or off the job (Henry 1998). Inmate-staff misconduct and unethical behavior occur on the job and often relate to interpersonal relations between staff and jail inmates. Unethical staff misconduct may involve deliberately ignoring an inmate's need for medical attention or assistance. Or the misconduct may involve physical injuries upon inmates perpetrated by jail staff. Any type of unethical staff behavior affecting jail inmates can aggravate situations where suicide-prone inmates are found. Specific policies should be in place to govern the officer-inmate relation, and these policies should be enforced.

But perhaps the best solution pertains to inmate classification. Inmate classification is the cornerstone of effective inmate management and the resulting reduction in violence, escapes, suicides, and vandalism that have been all too common in jails (Hutchinson 1999:16). The National Institute of Corrections, Jails Division (NICJD) has established a training and technical assistance program that operates on a year-round basis and is available to any jail jurisdiction interested in implementing an objective jail classification (OJC) system. The NICJD also assists jurisdictions in planning for new jails, including (1) pre-architectural activities, (2) site selection and planning, (3) architectural design, (4) construction, and (5) occupancy.

The Jails Division training targets issues specific to jails. Much of this training takes place in Longmont, Colorado. A jail officer's training manual has been developed, featuring a curriculum on suicide detection and prevention, a document on staffing analysis for jails, a document on special design issues for small jails, and others. There are four major phases of Jails Division training:

OJC Phase I: A workshop conducted to introduce participants to basic concepts in objective classification.

OJC Phase II: Technical assistance for the purpose of assessing an agency's readiness to implement objective classification.

OJC Phase III: A workshop conducted to teach participants the specifics of implementing objective classification.

OJC Phase IV: Technical assistance for the purpose of assessing how well an agency is implementing its objective classification program.

Additional Jails Division services include site visits to direct supervision in jails, training for line staff on how to run a podular direct supervision housing unit, and a training-for-trainers workshop on how to run a direct supervision housing unit (Hutchinson 1999:19). The Jails Division also runs workshops on jail mental health services and jail security.

JAIL REFORMS

Corrections generally has been undergoing various reforms in recent decades. The inmate litigation explosion has focused the attention of policymakers and others on prisoner rights and the quality of life in jail and prison settings. One result has been court-ordered improvements in jail conditions and inmate population reductions. The commitment of the American Correctional Association and other interested organizations to improve the quality of life for jail inmates extends also to improvements in the quality of correctional officers selected to perform jail tasks. Educational and training programs are now being offered in various jurisdictions for the purpose of providing more effective training of correctional recruits. Two other reforms have achieved a degree of popularity in recent years. These include jail architecture and the privatization of jail management.

Court-Ordered Jail Improvements

Jail overcrowding is at the top of a list of problems plaguing jails of any size (Cunniff 2002). Jail overcrowding has prompted numerous court-ordered improvements. However, more than a few of these court-ordered jail improvements address other important issues related directly or indirectly to overcrowding. For example, Cornelius (1997:26) notes that civil rights suits have targeted numerous areas that have generated court action. These areas include physical security (failure to protect); medical treatment; due process (improper disciplinary hearings); challenges to conviction (invalid sentences); miscellaneous (denial of parole and other reasons); physical conditions (inadequate sanitation, crowding, and other issues); denial of access to courts or attorneys; living conditions (inadequate clothing or other issues); denial of religious expression, visits, racial discrimination; and assault by jail officers.

Jail inmates do not lose their constitutional rights when entering jails. In 2000 about 16 percent of 112 of the largest jail systems in the United States reported that they were under court orders to correct various jail conditions and lack of services, including crowded living units, recreational facilities, medical services/facilities, visitation policies/procedures, disciplinary policies/procedures, food services, administrative segregation policies/procedures, staffing patterns, grievance policies/procedures, training/education programs, fire hazards, counseling programs, classification of inmates, and/or library services. Only 3 of the 15 largest jail systems were under a court monitor or special master. Six out of 28 of the larger jail systems reported that they were under court orders to cap their inmate populations. The fewest numbers of jails under court order to improve their conditions were the medium-sized and smaller jails (Camp and Camp 2002). Population caps refer to a court-ordered limit on the number of inmates that may be safely incarcerated by a jail system. Usually, court-ordered jail improvements result from civil litigation by inmates who challenge jail systems on various issues (Hanson and Daley 1995).

Accommodating Inmates with Special Needs

Jail inmates with various types of disabilities are increasingly common (Goldstein and Higgins-D'Alessandro 2001). Known as **special-needs offenders,** jail inmates with physical and/or mental disabilities create unique problems for jail officers and staff. These inmates do not act in predictable ways. They require special care and treatment. Some require continuous medication for their conditions. Others require special facilities, such as ramps, if they are confined to wheelchairs (Motiuk et al. 1994). An increasingly popular term is **special management inmates.** Special management inmates include:

1. The aggressive and assaultive: persons who must be separated for the protection of other inmates and must be managed with additional security concerns to provide for staff protection.

2. The vulnerable: persons, who because of their size, appearance, history, or behavior require protection from the general inmate population.

3. The mentally ill: persons who are unable to maintain appropriately in the general population and require assistance and professional treatment.

4. The physically ill: persons who are physically ill, require special services, and may be contagious.

5. The physically disabled: persons with disabilities that require special services and/or equipment (Wood 1995:23).

Inmates with these and related problems require jail staff to become familiar with their problems and how best to deal with them. Thus, jail staff training programs are increasingly including topics pertaining to managing inmates with special needs. Furthermore, architectural plans for new jails are including features that accommodate special-needs offenders (Gauger and Pulitzer 1991). Some of these architectural improvements are federally mandated through the Americans with Disabilities Act. This Act, passed in 1990, provides protections for disabled inmates and staff who receive government services, programs, or activities, including those provided in local jails. Changes might be required in a jail's physical plant, such as the addition of wheelchair ramps and handrails, and changes in procedures or programs that require accommodating disabled inmates, including provision of accessible housing or work. In fact, inmates are the only persons in the United States with a constitutionally guaranteed right to health care (Buckley 1998:27). Consequently, sheriffs and jail administrators are partnering with contract providers of correctional health-care services to identify and properly address health-care trends among the jail population.

The Multnomah County (Oregon) Sheriff's Office manages five jails in Multnomah County, which is located in Portland, Oregon. The five jails have a combined rated capacity of 1,416 inmates. The jail system has one of the more elaborate classification systems used by jails in the United States. The five jails are divided as follows. The maximum-security unit is the Multnomah County Detention Center (MCDC), which has 476 beds. The Multnomah County Inverness Jail (MCIJ) has 559 beds and accommodates less serious offenders in a dormitory-like atmosphere. Three other minimum-security jails accommodate general dormitory inmates, work releasees, and other inmates requiring minimal supervision. At the MCDC, however, special units have been constructed to house violent inmates under administrative segregation; those requiring disciplinary supervision; psychiatric and medical patients; close maximum and close mental patients; vulnerable inmates; and those requiring drug treatment. Other units exist for intake and preliminary inmate classification (Wood 1995:26).

The actual number of jail (and prison) inmates who suffer from various mental illnesses is unknown, although many persons familiar with jail operations acknowledge that the incarceration of severely mentally ill offenders is a serious issue for sheriffs and jail administrators (Faust 2003:6). Thomas N. Faust, Executive Director of the National Sheriff's Association, indicates that the problem of jailing the mentally ill has continued to escalate and that it is a major quality of life issue for these inmates because they are more likely to be beaten, victimized, or commit suicide than those who are not sick. The Los Angeles County Jail, for example, spends about $10 million per year on psychiatric medication. He says that the three largest *de facto* psychiatric facilities in the United States today are the Los Angeles County Jail, Rikers Island in New York City, and the Cook County Jail in Chicago. There are twice as many mentally ill people in the Miami-Dade County Jail than the South Florida Evaluation and Treatment Center. According to figures reported by the Treatment Advocacy Center, there are nearly five times more mentally ill people in the nation's jails (300,000) than there are in all of the state psychiatric hospitals (60,000) (Faust 2003:6–7). Despite the significant efforts of the largest nation's jails to devise mental health programs for inmates with mental problems, there remain thousands of inmates who go untreated by their respective jail systems.

One major factor contributing to larger numbers of mentally ill jail inmates is a series of legal reforms occurring during the 1970s, where treatment laws were changed to require that individuals be a danger to themselves or to others before they could be treated involuntarily. Thus, many of the nation's mentally ill were turned out of mental hospitals and were loosed on the streets where they attracted the attention of law enforcement officers. In effect, jails and prisons have become alternative treatment centers for many of these mentally ill persons. Faust sums up the problem by noting that "there is something fundamentally wrong when, for some families, the only way to obtain involuntary treatment for a mentally ill family member is to have that person arrested" (Faust 2003:7). Faust says that it is time to shift the responsibility for caring for the mentally ill back to the professionals who are trained to do so rather than waiting until only law enforcement and corrections can respond.

Jail Architecture: Aging Jails and Facility Deterioration

On June 6, 1993, the oldest jail in the United States closed. This jail was the Litchfield (Connecticut) Correctional Center, constructed in 1812 to hold the prisoners during that war (*Monday Highlights* 1993). The Litchfield Jail operated for 181 years. It had 16 employees and was constructed of red brick. Officials did not plan on destroying Litchfield CC. Rather, they intended to use the old facility as a 30-bed halfway house for women after some extensive remodeling. And scheduled for opening was the 2,400-bed Allegheny County (Pennsylvania) Jail on a 14-acre tract overlooking the city of Pittsburgh (L. Robert Kimball & Associates 1991). Thus, there is a continuous replacement of old jail facilities with new ones annually, as jail inmate populations continue to escalate.

Recent interest in jail architecture is accounted for, in part, by the concerns of local jurisdictions to utilize their available jail space more economically for more inmates (Powers 2002). Thus, jail overcrowding may be alleviated to some degree, and jail correctional officers will be able to more effectively monitor in-

Old-fashioned linear cell blocks are being replaced with new-generation facilities, which improve offender monitoring and minimize inmate assaults.

mate behavior where blind areas are eliminated (Waltz and Montgomery 2003). Electronic innovations such as closed-circuit television cameras and other devices have been used historically to assist guards in the performance of their prisoner management chores, but more effective jail construction can also mean more direct and effective inmate supervision by officers (Conley 2000).

A relatively new concept in jail design has been implemented for constructing the Pinellas County Jail, Florida. The jail houses 192 inmates in three interconnected, octagonally shaped buildings of a modular design. Made of precast concrete, the Pinellas Jail is an example of how new jail construction may be implemented at relatively low cost to taxpayers. The structure will eventually reach a height of five stories, the first modularly constructed jail in the nation to achieve that height. With various components of these jails prefabricated and assembled in other cities, these jails can be completed in less than a year, some in about eight months, ready for use. The initial costs range from $16,000 (one-person cells) to $29,000 (two-person cells). Statistics show that in other jurisdictions, prison and jail construction using more traditional building concepts have ranged from $39,000 to $100,000 per one-person cell, depending upon the particular security level (Camp and Camp 2002).

Despite the proliferation of prefabricated jails throughout the United States, some jails continue to be plagued with overcrowding problems, even where the physical plants of these jails have been greatly expanded and extended (Waltz and Montgomery 2003). In Minnesota, the Hennepin County Adult Detention Center, operated by the Hennepin County Sheriff's Department, has experienced dramatic jail inmate population growth since the early 1970s. Massive reconstruction programs have attempted to keep pace with the growing offender population, but overcrowding has gradually occurred. Double-bunking was approved in 1982 but this was only a temporary measure that slowed jail overcrowding. By the 1990s the facility was housing offenders far in excess of the rated jail capacity. The only feasible solution was to use other jail facilities throughout the state to house inmate overflow. Thus, Hennepin County began contracting with other jails to house their excess inmates. Soon over 2,000 Hennepin County inmates were being accommodated in other county jails at a cost of several million dollars a year. Thus, other jails began housing jail inmate overflow. One policy change has been to be more selective in the selection of prisoners to be housed in the Hennepin County Jail (Kooy 1992:68).

Modular construction is not a panacea for jail overcrowding. The Worcester County Jail and House of Correction in West Boylston, Massachusetts, is a living example of the failure of sound planning for future jail inmate population growth. A modern state-of-the-art facility was constructed in 1973. At the time it was planned to house 270 inmates. The structure was 76,000 square feet and took only 210 days to construct. However, within months following its construction, the jail had an inmate population of 350. The jail capacity was increased, again with modular units, to 478 in 1986. But again, the inmate population soared to 600 that same year. Lawsuits filed by inmates led to addi-

---

 **BOX 6.3**

FIRE IN OLD JAIL KILLS EIGHT TRAPPED INMATES

Bakersville, NC

A fire broke out in a North Carolina county jail located in Bakersville on May 4, 2002. It appeared that the fire started in a storage room on the jail's ground floor and quickly spread throughout the two-story brick-and-wood building that, not unlike many other jails in the United States, was constructed during the 1950s. At the time of the fire, seven inmates were being held in an upstairs cell. Another inmate was being held in a holding cell adjacent to the storage room where the fire started. An additional nine inmates were being held elsewhere in the jail on assorted misdemeanor offenses, while some were awaiting trial on felony charges.

When the fire broke out, a jailer smelled smoke and called for help. This was at 10:00 P.M. There was already a great deal of smoke within the old building. The jailer and an inmate trustee attempted to ascend the staircase to the upper floor to release inmates locked in their cells. But the smoke was too overpowering and they were prevented from effecting the rescue. Unlike more modern jails, the cells in this jail could only be opened, one at a time, with separate keys. About 100 firefighters converged on the old jail and, by 11:30 P.M., the fire had

been extinguished. The fire had covered the entire back of the two-story building, and heavy smoke filled the jail. When firefighters were able to enter the upper cell area, they found seven inmates dead from smoke inhalation. Another inmate was found in a locked cell adjacent to the storage room, also dead after being overcome by smoke.

A fire inspector later observed that there were no sprinklers in the jail and that it was unclear whether the jail's smoke detectors actually sounded to alert authorities that a fire had broken out. Thirteen persons, including several inmates, were injured and treated at a local medical center. A firefighter was also treated for smoke inhalation. The North Carolina State Bureau of Investigation was at the scene later to help determine the fire's cause. The storage area where the fire originated contained wiring and an electric heater.

Should national jail standards be imposed on all jail facilities throughout the United States to require minimum compliance with fire codes? Was this fire preventable? What safety measures could authorities have implemented to guard against inmate deaths? What do you think?

Source: Adapted from the Associated Press, "Jail Fire Kills 8 Trapped Inmates," May 5, 2002.

tional expansion of this facility, again through modular construction. This time, additional floors were added. It will only be a matter of time, however, before the inmate population again exceeds the rated jail capacity (Flynn 1991).

Direct Supervision and New Generation Jails

Many of the nation's jails were built prior to 1970, and many are fifty years old or more (Perroncello 2002). These jails are not only architecturally unsound and unsafe, they also are designed so that jail officers cannot always monitor inmate behaviors. One answer to escalating inmate violence is the establishment of jail and prison facilities that permit greater inmate monitoring. A new innovation in inmate management, a hybrid of architectural design and inmate management principles, is **direct-supervision jails,** sometimes called **new-generation jails** (Zupan 1993:21).

New-generation jails are a philosophy of both design and management. They attempt to use the physical plant to improve the staff's ability to manage the inmate population and are based on three architectural concepts: (1) podular design, (2) interaction space, and (3) personal space. Podular units, which are self-contained living areas, house from 12 to 24 inmates in many settings. These are composed of single-occupancy rooms for inmates to pursue their own interests and a common, multipurpose dayroom for recreational interaction. Podular living areas are complete with comfortable furniture, porcelain lavatories, tile and carpet floor coverings, and windows. Pods have telephones, radios, televisions, and an outdoor exercise area. They also have daily activities of meal service, recreation, and visitation (Bayens, Williams, and Smykla 1997:32).

Direct-supervision jails are constructed so as to provide officers with 180-degree lines of sight to monitor inmates. Direct-supervision jails employ a podular design. Modern direct-supervision jails also combine closed-circuit cameras to continuously observe inmates when celled. Correctional officers are in the same pod as inmates. These pods consist of secure dormitory-like area housing approximately 40 inmates. Inmates are monitored 24 hours a day. The first podular, direct-supervision jail was constructed in Contra Costa, California, in 1981 (Parrish 2000). It has been found that coercion and threats by inmates against others is minimized and all but eliminated through the direct supervision concept. This is because all inmate behavior is subject to correctional officer scrutiny. Also, inmates have fairly direct access to correctional officers in their central work locations. In 2000 there were over 100 direct supervision jails in the United States, with plans in many jurisdictions for building more of them (Parrish 2000:84).

Modular jail designs or new-generation jails have been used increasingly in various jurisdictions. In order to understand what is meant by new-generation jails, we must first examine earlier jail generations. Cornelius (1997:7) describes the following generations of jails during the last 200 years:

1. First-generation jails: These jails are sometimes called linear. This is because cells are aligned in rows; the correctional officer walks down a central corridor or catwalk; interactions with inmates are usually through food slots or cell bars.

2. Second-generation jails: These jails are characterized by officers stationed in a central control booth; inmate housing surrounds the officers; usual observation of inmates by officers is increased, but officer interaction with inmates is very limited.

3. Third-generation jails (new-generation jails): These types of jails are characterized as having jail officers placed inside housing units known as pods; there are no physical barriers; under this direct supervision, officers act as inmate behavior managers; jail officers have more supervisory authority in the daily operations of pods.

The Walworth County Jail in Wisconsin is an example of the application of direct supervision of correctional facilities with a new superpod architectural design to create a national model for effective management of county jails (McKenzie 1997:59). The 177,000 square foot facility has a variety of inmates requiring diverse security. The two key components of the facility's plan and design are the direct supervision model and the superpod architectural design. Under direct supervision, staff supervise inmates by being and working in the same space as inmate, requiring frequent and continuous interaction instead of intermittent inspections down double-loaded corridors with cells on each side. Direct supervision consists of the following principles: (1) effective control, (2) effective supervision, (3) competent staff, (4) safety of staff and inmates, (5) manageable and cost-effective operations, (6) effective communication, (7) classification and orientation, (8) justice and fairness, and (9) ownership of operations (McKenzie 1997:60).

The Walworth superpod design features four detention pods: the superpod, the inmate dormitory for work release inmates, and two male inmate pods. The Law Enforcement Center has seven enclosed support facilities, including a visitation area, evidence and property storage area, kitchen and laundry support facility, booking and holding area, sheriff's department, health area, and a dispatch and emergency area. Each detention area has a dayroom and surrounding cells: a male general area, a female general area, a high security area, a medical isolation area, an administrative segregation area, a disciplinary segregation area, a female special area for those requiring a higher level of security, and an inmate workers' dormitory area (McKenzie 1997:60–61). The direct-supervision concept is in place from the time inmates are admitted. The direct-supervision model assumes rational behavior of people incarcerated until proven otherwise. Master control is a self-contained unit from which one staff person can shut down the facility—electrical, heating, telephones, and locks—by pushing four buttons. All inmates are directly monitored from the master control area. Direct-supervision jails are increasingly popular and are being developed in numerous jurisdictions (Coleman and Oraftik 2001).

Vocational/Educational Provisions

Most jails are not equipped to provide inmates with any vocational/technical and educational programs (Tewksbury 1994). In fact, many prisons lack a broad variety of programs geared to enhance inmate skills and education (Schlossman and Spillane 1992). This state of affairs seems consistent with the view that the rehabilitation orientation in U.S. prisons is on the decline. For instance, it has been found that for at least some of the major state prison systems, the influence of higher education programs on graduating inmates and their subsequent rates of recidivism has been ineffective (Batchelder and Koski 2002). Special populations of inmates, such as sex offenders, have exhibited higher recidivism rates despite available treatment and educational programs in prisons and jails (Nathan and Ward 2001). For drug offenders in the U.S. Bureau of Prison's Choice program, the plan of drug treatment and intervention has been regarded as successful. Inmates with drug dependencies are subjected to a ten-month program, including intake/evaluation/followup, drug education, skills development, lifestyle modification, wellness, responsibility, and individualized counseling/case supervision (Walters et al. 1992). The emphasis in the Choice program is upon education and the development of cognitive skills rather than on treatment and insight-oriented therapy.

No guarantees exist that all jail inmates with educational deficiencies will enroll in such programs in jails where educational programs are offered. In a suburban Texas county, for instance, courses were offered to jail inmates pertaining to counseling, stress management, and education. High school dropouts and high school graduates were identified and targeted for these different programs. A disappointing 26.7 percent of the high school dropouts enrolled in self-enriching courses or utilized counseling services. Even the participation rates of high school graduates were low. Only 14 percent of them took advantage of the offered programs (Tobolowsky, Quinn, and Holman 1991).

In some jails in thirteen state jurisdictions, participation in jail or prison educational programs for both men and women is mandatory (Mullen et al. 1996). Of those states making education mandatory, those inmates most frequently targeted have obvious educational deficiencies and do not meet minimum educational criteria (Wright 2001). Reduced sentence lengths are offered as incentives to participate in educational programs. The measure of success of such programs is whether inmates continue their education in jail or prison beyond the mandatory minimum (Haulard 2001). One of the more innovative inmate literacy programs is operated by the Virginia Department of Corrections. Since September 1986, the no-read, no-release program has emphasized literacy achievement at no lower than the sixth-grade level and has made such an achievement part of the parole decision-making process. Results have been favorably viewed by various states. However, compulsory educational programs in jails and prisons have been subjected to constitutional challenges in recent years (Jurich, Casper, and Hull 2001). There is also international appeal for requiring greater amounts of education among prison inmates. In Nigeria, for instance, allocating resources for improved educational programs for Nigerian inmates has been viewed as a humanizing action where offenders are encouraged not only to acquire more education, but to develop positive social skills as well (Enuku 2001).

Some information suggests that those acquiring greater education while in prison have higher percentages of new convictions (Houchins 2001). A study examined 526 inmates who enrolled in prison and jail college, vocational, secondary, and elementary programs according to their post-release success experiences. While those who had taken college coursework and other skills courses exhibited fewer problems adjusting to life outside of prison, the more educated group had somewhat higher rates of recidivism attributable to new criminal convictions. Admittedly, it is difficult to predict precisely which inmates will be more amenable to treatment than others, although attempts have frequently been made to do so. It has been found that, generally, older and better-educated inmates seem to benefit more from prison educational programs compared with those younger offenders who perhaps are most in need of such education (Miller and Hobler 1996).

However, the importance of intervention and educational or vocational training programs should not be rejected outright. For some inmates, these experiences are quite valuable. For instance, the Sandhills (North Carolina) Vocational Delivery System (VDS) is a vocational rehabilitation program offered to offenders ages 18 to 22 (Lattimore, Witt, and Baker 1990). An experiment was conducted involving 295 youths in an experimental group who participated in the VDS program and 296 youths in a control who did not participate. A post-release analysis

A small jail library.

of the arrest records of both experimental and control group offenders showed that the experimental group had a significantly lower arrest record. Researchers attributed this success to participation in the VDS program, although further research was recommended to improve the reliability of these findings.

An aggressive program has been implemented by the Orange County, Florida, Corrections Division, which provides intensive educational and vocational programming in its 3,300-bed jail (Finn 1998b). Premised on the foundation that many inmates return to a life of crime because they have poor reading skills, poor job skills, and substance abuse problems, the Corrections Division took over the Orange County Jail from the sheriff in 1987. Funding was provided to staff the jail with 70 full-time instructors. Diverse programs were established for the general equivalency diploma (G.E.D.), vocational training, life skills development, psychoeducational groups, and substance abuse education. Courses run for short periods of time, 6 hours a day, five days a week. Direct supervision design enables monitoring of classrooms to enable maximum contact between staff and inmates without physical interaction.

When inmates are admitted to the Orange County Jail, they take a Test of Adult Basic Education (TABE), the Substance Abuse/Life Circumstances Evaluation (SALCE), to determine whether they have a substance abuse problem and a vocational needs and interests assessment to identify suitable job options after their release. After testing, inmates meet with individual assessment staff members who explain the course offerings and incentives to participate. The inmates then transfer to one of four jail facilities where certain types of courses are offered. A work release program is available for those inmates who satisfactorily complete their educational requirements. The entry into these educational/vocational programs is strictly voluntary, and other less desirable options are available for those unwilling or unable to participate. Figure 6.1 shows the educational and vocational programming process for admitted inmates at the Orange County facility.

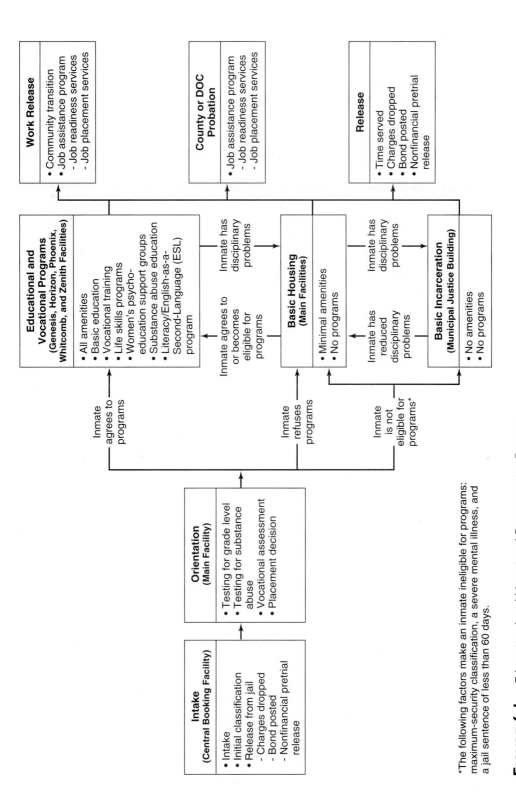

FIGURE 6.1 Educational and Vocational Programming Process.

Source: Peter Finn. "The Orange County, Florida, Jail Education and Vocational Programs." *American Jails* **12**(1998b):11 (Exhibit 1). Reprinted by permission of the *American Jails*.

*The following factors make an inmate ineligible for programs: maximum-security classification, a severe mental illness, and a jail sentence of less than 60 days.

What is the payoff for Orange County, Florida? More than 4,200 inmates have attended classes at the jail. Eighty-four percent of all inmates taking the G.E.D. test earned their diploma. Recidivism rates among program participants were significantly lower than non-participants during the period of an evaluation study conducted by researchers from the University of South Florida. Orange County officials are optimistic that the program works and assists a substantial number of inmates attain vocational and educational goals they otherwise would not attain (Finn 1998a, 1998b).

Jail Inspections from the Private Sector.   When jail policies are implemented, what agencies or personnel are in place to ensure that jails are in compliance with these policies and are operating according to county specifications? Each jurisdiction throughout the United States has accountability mechanisms, and many different strategies are used to enforce county policies in jail environments. In Arkansas, for instance, jails are subject to inspections by private political committees appointed by the governor. Arkansas enacted its first jail legislation in 1973. In 1983 a substantial legislative change occurred with the establishment of the Criminal Detention Facilities Review Committees within the 26 judicial districts within the state. Under the 1983 provisions, each county within the judicial district has a membership appointed by the chief circuit judge. Member terms are for four years, and no compensation is provided the committee membership. The committees have authority to (1) provide consultation and technical assistance to county and local government officials with respect to criminal detention facilities; (2) visit and inspect such criminal detention facilities for compliance within the standards as established under the act; (3) advise such governing officials and other appropriate persons of the deficiencies in such facilities and make recommendations for improvement; (4) submit written reports of such inspections; (5) review and comment on plans for construction or modification or renovation of such criminal detention facilities; and (6) perform such other duties as may be necessary to carry out the policy of the state regarding such criminal detention facilities. While there has been some concern that an unpaid committee of volunteers could adequately inspect jails, the system has been very effective in that out of the approximately 120 city and county jails currently operating, one-third are new jails opened after February 1988 or currently under construction. Further, some older jails have been closed by committee recommendation, while others have been extensively renovated. Thus, substantial compliance to state mandates for jail standards has been achieved by these committees (Norman 1997:66).

The Privatization of Jail Operations

A proposal that has received mixed reactions in recent years is the privatization of jail and prison management by private interests. Few proposals in corrections have ever stimulated as sharply divided opinions as the prospect of privately operated jails. Legally, there is nothing to prevent private enterprises from operating prisons and jails as extensions of state and local governments and law enforcement agencies. Few states have legislation on the subject (Chang and Tillman 2002). It is imperative that private enterprise ensures minimal standards currently guaranteed by the law and complies with basic constitutional guarantees. The private operation of incarcerative facilities appears feasible.

Given the fact that many local jails today in the United States are in a state of crisis, private sector intrusion into offender management and jail operations is not entirely unexpected (Ethridge and Liebowitz 1994:55). A study of sheriff's attitudes toward privatization was conducted in the summer of 1991 by Ethridge and Liebowitz. Questionnaires were mailed to 254 sheriffs of Texas counties. Of these, 195 sheriffs responded. Sheriffs were asked various questions about privatization and their opinions about it. Among other things, Ethridge and Liebowitz wanted to know sheriff's reactions to the pros and cons of privatization. The checklist of reasons against privatization included:

1. Private companies should not have control of inmates.
2. Too expensive for the county.
3. Will not relieve the county from liability.
4. Inmates will be abused.
5. Security risks.
6. Government agencies are more efficient and effective.
7. Private companies are only interested in making money.
8. Danger of company declaring bankruptcy.

The reasons for privatization included:

1. Relieve overcrowding.
2. Save taxpayers money.
3. Relieve county of liability.
4. Boost local economy—add new jobs.
5. Better care for inmates.
6. Better classification and evaluation.
7. Better rehabilitation (Ethridge and Liebowitz 1994:56).

These researchers found that 70 percent of all responding sheriffs were opposed to privatization. Only 25 percent of the sheriffs were for privatization. The primary reasons cited against privatization were that private companies should not have control over inmates, the county would not be relieved of liability, and privatization would be too expensive. Proponents favored privatization because, they said, it would alleviate jail overcrowding, boost the local economy, and save taxpayers money.

Cornelius (1997:49–50) notes that the privatization issue continues to be hotly debated. As of 2000, at least 120 jails in the United States were under contracts with private agencies for health care. More than a few jails were operated by private corporations. For instance, the Corrections Corporation of America operates Nashville, Tennessee's Metro Davidson County Detention Center, a medium-security facility with a capacity of 1,575 (Camp and Camp 2002). The debate over privatization continues, as proponents and opponents disagree over the nature, scope, quality of services, and appropriate roles of public and private agencies (Shichor and Gilbert 2001).

One controversial policy established in the Broward County, Florida, Main Jail in Fort Lauderdale is charging the 1,500 inmates $2 a day for a room with a New River view. In 1996 the Florida State Legislature implemented the new policy designed to collect revenue from jail inmates as a means of defraying jail operating expenses. Projected revenues from jail inmates were estimated to be $550,000 per year. More than a few jail inmates were upset by these new fees and protested by filing lawsuits. They alleged among other things that they were being charged fees without being convicted of a crime and that indigent inmates could not afford the fee. Thus far, the courts have not been sympathetic with these inmates and the suits have been unsuccessful (McCampbell 1997:39).

Jail Industries.   Besides charging inmates for their jail space, some jails put all inmates to work, whether they are convicted offenders or simply unconvicted pretrial detainees, probation/parole violators, or those held on detainer warrants. The idea of using jail inmate labor is not particularly new, although few counties used inmate labor prior to 1990. However, this idea became increasingly popular. Thus, jail inmates presently deliver 9 million hours of labor annually, the equivalent of 90,000 full-time staff (Miller 1997). Many counties are finding that it's worth the effort to put inmates to work, in terms of management benefits, cost savings, and inmate success after release. It is the latter concern that drives jail industries.

In 1993 the Bureau of Justice Assistance (BJA) created the BJA Jail Work and Industry Center, which has provided a central point of contact for counties interested in developing and expanding jail work and industry programs. BJA also funded the first national Jail and Work Industry Symposium held in Houston in March 1995. Additionally, the Jail Industries Association was established and incorporated as the first professional affiliate of the American Jail Association in April 1991 (Miller 1997:45).

The nature of jail industry work is diverse. However, it focuses largely on the types of work most useful to jail inmates upon their release. For instance, jail inmates are becoming involved in an ever-increasing diversity of work projects. More high-tech ventures will be realized, involving inmates in more sophisticated and timely activities using computers, telephones, and the Internet (McIntyre, Tong, and Perez 2001). Inmates will take on roles and responsibilities that were inconceivable in the 1980s. Service jobs will become more common, consistent with labor and employment trends in the community (Miller 1997:46).

One of the more ambitious jail industry programs is the York Street Industries (YSI), which was established by the Hampden County Jail, Massachusetts, in 1985 (Trevathan 2002). By 2001 the YSI was generating over $500,000 a year in revenues, while an average of 25 inmates were delivering 26,000 hours of labor. Inmates have also been able to earn sentence reductions as the result of their involvement with YSI. YSI has negotiated with government agencies, schools, colleges, hospitals, and private agencies in providing its diverse services. These services include (1) chair manufacturing, (2) furniture repair, (3) design and manufacture of inmate uniforms, (4) silk screening, (5) production of personal hygiene kits, (6) production of mattresses and mattress covers, (7) an alcohol center operation, and several other activities. During 2001, for instance, 51 inmates (including 4 females) were involved in the YSI. All inmates must complete all other jail programming that their counselors believe is necessary before they become eligible for working in the YSI. Inmate wages range from 50 cents to $1 per hour (Trevathan 2002:43). Future plans of YSI include establishing an Internet website, improving customer relations, and expansion and improvement of existing facilities (Miller and Trevathan 2003).

SUMMARY

Most jails in the United States are funded and administered by counties, although jail operations in some jurisdictions are state operated. Sheriff's departments are usually in charge of jail organization and administration. County sheriffs are most often elected officials. Many of them have little or no previous experiences managing offenders. More than a few sheriffs have no prior law enforcement experience. Thus, they are often elected on the basis of their political connections rather than because of their inmate management qualifications. Most jail administrators are white males with some college background. Most have fewer than three years' experience with jail organization and operations. Yet these persons are responsible for hiring jail personnel who must supervise and meet the various needs of an increasingly culturally diverse jail inmate population.

Jails have low funding priority in their respective jurisdictions. As a result, they are often poorly equipped to maintain prisoners for lengthy periods. Jail officers are often untrained or poorly trained to do perform their supervisory work effectively. Because jail officers typically receive low pay, it is difficult to attract and retain high-quality jail personnel. However, in recent years various programs have been established to improve jail officer quality. These programs, usually offered through nearby educational institutions, such as community colleges or universities, attempt to deliver educational training and hands-on practical experiences to jail officers in order to improve their professionalization. Every year more jail officers are seeking this training receiving certificates signifying the attainment of certain professional goals. The American Jail Association and the American Correctional Association are seeking to provide all jails with the means of becoming accredited through improvements in staff education and training. All of these efforts are designed to enhance the services and treatments extended to jail inmates. Thus, professionalization of jail staff through accreditation of jail programs is an ambitious plan that is slowly being realized. A concomitant feature of accreditation is the promulgation of new jail standards. These standards are being raised in an effort to provide jail inmates with higher quality services and programs.

One stimulus that has prompted greater attention to jail officer professionalization and jail program accreditation has been the lawsuit syndrome, where large numbers of lawsuits have been filed in state and federal courts. These lawsuits have alleged cruel and inhumane jail conditions and deliberate indifference in the treatment of various inmate problems. In recent years, jail improvements have eased the volume of lawsuit filings in the courts. In some jurisdictions, jail operations have been assumed by private interests that are in a position to deliver needed services and programs at a lower cost to local jurisdictions. Thus, the privatization of jail operations has been established and is a slowly growing phenomenon in the United States.

The great cultural diversity of U.S. citizens has carried over into jail populations and has affected them accordingly. It is increasingly the case that jail officers must be more sensitive to cultural diversity as a result. Thus, attempts are underway to provide exposure and training to jail officers that will enable them to more satisfactorily interact with more culturally diverse jail inmates, and a human services approach to inmate supervision has been proposed for jail officers in many jurisdictions. Jail training programs are increasingly rigorous, and jail officers are trained to deal with a greater array of inmate problems. Thus, jail officers are learning how to deal more effectively with jail security issues, the use of force, more sophisticated report writing, sensitivity to inmate rights, more weapons training, special management skills for drug/alcohol-dependent offenders and the mentally ill, and inmate social/cultural lifestyles. Interactions among jail officers themselves are also targeted for improvement by such jail officer training programs.

Several problems arise concerning classifying jail inmates and how they should be accommodated. Larger numbers of jail inmates are from state and federal prisons. Others have special needs or communicable diseases. They must be accommodated in special ways. Some inmates are at greater risk of committing suicide, and thus they must be more effectively monitored. More emphasis has been placed on classifying jail inmates in recent years in an effort to provide inmates generally with a safer jail environment. One classification system that has been used is the Behavior Alert Classification Identification System (B.A.C.I.S.), which seeks to improve inmate placement in the most appropriate accommodations depending upon offender needs and special problems exhibited. At the same time, health-care delivery has been improved. One reason for such improvement has been because larger numbers of jail inmates are being housed for longer jail terms. Some of these inmates are contract prisoners from state and federal penitentiaries. Another reason is that a portion of jail inmates have drug/alcohol dependencies or have communicable diseases such as HIV/AIDS or tuberculosis. They must be isolated from other inmates so that they will not endanger others and also so that they can receive special treatments and services. Jails are also delivering improved vocational and educational training to a segment of the jail population that is illiterate or lacking in practical job skills.

Because so many jails in the United States are small, they are unable to provide certain services that some of their inmates may require. Furthermore, some juveniles are often celled with adult offenders for temporary periods, and for various reasons. This is an adverse consequence of jail size. Nevertheless, significant efforts have been made to reduce the numbers of juveniles who are held in jails generally, even for brief periods (Snell and Grabowski 2003:79–82).

Attempts have been made to describe jails according to their size and functions. Jails have been variously described as small, medium, and large, with some jails described as megajails. Megajails hold 1,000 or more inmates and usually have the greatest number of jail problems. In sparsely populated areas where smaller jails are most abundant, regional jails have been created for the purpose of housing offenders from contiguous jurisdictions. Many jails are also old and deteriorating. These jails have been targeted for demolition or renovation. In recent years, a concomitant occurrence has been the creation of new-generation or direct-supervision jails, where jail supervision methods have been greatly modified and improved. These changes have often been undertaken together with redesigns in jail architecture. Some of these jail changes have occurred as the result of court-ordered improvements. More emphasis has been given in recent years to vocational and educational programs, especially in the larger jails. Presently, a growing number of jails are offering diverse vocational and educational services, together with more sophisticated health care delivery systems. Private interests have become increasingly involved in jail management and operations.

QUESTIONS FOR REVIEW

1. What are some of the characteristics of jail administrators?

2. Are all jails in the United States operated by counties? Who are the chief administrative officers of jails? How do these persons become jail administrators?

3. What are some of the problems facing jail administrators relating to attracting and retaining high-quality jail officers and other jail personnel?

4. How much labor turnover is there among jail staff? What are some of the remedies proposed to deal with this labor turnover and staff quality?

5. Why are there significant morale problems among jail officers and staff? What are some of the consequences of these morale problems for jail inmates?

6. How is the problem of jail suicides being addressed by jail administration? What preventive measures have been established by different jails in order to screen jail inmates more effectively? How does jail classification influence this screening process?

7. What is meant by the lawsuit syndrome? What are the bases of lawsuits against jail officers, administrators, and jail organizations?

8. How does a more culturally diverse jail inmate population contribute to the problems of jail operations and jail officer effectiveness? What remedies have been proposed to deal with these problems?

9. What are the primary components of training programs for jail officers and staff? What are accreditation and professionalization? How are these phenomena improving work effectiveness among jail officers?

10. What are direct-supervision jails? What are some of their characteristics? What are regional jails and what purposes do they serve?

SUGGESTED READINGS

Abramsky, Sasha. *Hard Time Blues: How Politics Built a Prison Nation.* New York: St. Martin's, 2002.

Griffin, Marie L. *The Use of Force By Detention Officers.* New York: LFB Scholarly Publishing LLC, 2001.

LaMunyon, James W. *Regional Jails in the State of Washington.* Olympia: Washington Association of Sheriffs and Police Chiefs, 2001.

Wilson, Doris James. *Drug Use, Testing, and Treatment in Jails.* Washington, DC: U.S. Bureau of Justice Statistics, 2000.

INTERNET CONNECTIONS

Correctional Medical Services
http://www.cmsstl.com

Federal Prison Consultants
http://www.federalprisonconsultants.com/

Jail Management
http://www.mmmicro.com/jail_management.htm

NaphCare, Inc.
http://www.naphcare.com/

National Institute of Corrections Jail Administration Training Program
http://www.nicic.org/services/training/programs/jails/jail-admin.htm

Objective Jail Classification
http://www.corrections.com/aja/training

PRC Jail Record Management System
http://www.northrupgrummanit.com

PS.NET
http://www.ps.net/cms

Tiers and cell blocks, North Dakota State
Penitentiary.

| Chapter Objectives | *After reading this chapter, the following objectives should be realized:* |

1. Describing the history and development of prisons in the United States.
2. Highlighting particular prison systems, including Auburn and Pennsylvania models and the Elmira Reformatory.
3. Contrasting federal and state prison systems and administrations, including discussing the U.S. Bureau of Prisons.
4. Profiling prisoners in the United States, including various inmate classification systems.

5. Describing different types of prison systems, including minimum-security, medium-security, maximum-security, and maxi-maxi prisons and their functions.
6. Describing prison culture and inmate jargon and customs.
7. Focusing upon and describing various prison issues, including jail and prison differences, prison overcrowding, violence, discipline, and prison design and control.

INTRODUCTION

• *Numerous federal lawsuits have been filed by or on behalf of mentally ill inmates in both state and federal prisons. Some of these lawsuits date back to 1980, when a federal district court judge ruled that the Texas prison system was unconstitutional on various grounds. During December 2001, a psychologist hired to evaluate Texas inmates being held in solitary confinement issued a report that has stimulated a reexamination of these lawsuits. The report issued from an order from U.S. District Court Judge William Wayne Justice, the same judge who declared the Texas prison system unconstitutional in 1980. Justice ordered that a psychologist should be hired to evaluate those maintained in solitary confinement and determine their mental condition or stability. Specifically, Justice wanted to know about the presence of seriously mentally ill prisoners being held in administrative segregation (solitary confinement) by the Texas prison system. The psychologist subsequently visited various prisons in Texas and interviewed prisons in isolation, conducting detailed interviews as needed. He also talked with security officers to determine if they had any concerns about any of the offenders regarding their mental illness. Based on the report filed by the psychologist, it may be that steps will be taken to move mentally ill prisoners to places more appropriate to their mental condition. Should mentally ill prisoners be placed in administrative segregation or solitary confinement? Should we expand the number of hospitals for mentally ill inmates? What do you think?* [Adapted from the Associated Press. "Fed Court Gets Report on Mentally Ill Inmates," December 5, 2001].

• *On December 13, 2000, seven dangerous prisoners escaped from a maximum-security prison in Texas. They overpowered eleven prison employees and three other prisoners, jumped two guards at a back gate, and made off in a stolen prison truck. Subsequently, the stolen truck was found abandoned in a shopping mall parking lot. Apparently, the escapees had outside assistance and had obtained new means of transportation. On their way out of the prison, they left the warden an ominous note. It said, "You haven't heard the last of us." Two days later in Houston, Texas, several of the escapees robbed a Radio Shack of police scanners, two-way radios, and a small amount of cash. On Christmas Eve, the seven escapees held up Oshman's sporting goods store in Irving, a Dallas suburb. This time, things did not go smoothly. A police officer, Aubrey Hawkins, 29, pulled up at the back of the store to investigate a report of suspicious activity. He was ambushed and shot in the head and back. He died instantly. As the men made their escape, they drove over Hawkins' body in their Ford Explorer SUV. The hunt was on. Their photographs were flashed on* America's Most Wanted, *a popular television program that features fugitives from justice weekly. For nearly twelve weeks, these men eluded police. Texas and federal officials were getting desperate. These were serious offenders. The following men were on the run, listing their offenses and sentences: Joseph Garcia, 29, 50 years for murder; Randy Halprin, 31, 30 years for beating a child; Michael Rodriguez, 38, life imprisonment for capital murder; George Rivas, 30, life imprisonment for kidnapping and armed robbery; Larry Harper, 37, 50 years for serial rape; Donald Newbury, 38, 99 years for armed robbery; and Patrick Murphy Jr., 50 years for aggravated sexual assault.*

Eventually, a tip was received that the group of seven were possibly holed up in a Pace Arrow camper at an RV park in Woodland Park, Colorado, near Colorado Springs. It seems that several of the escapees had made several trips into town to have dinner, drink, and shoot pool at Tres Hombres Tex-Mex restaurant. They had badly dyed hair, although they didn't seem to attract that much attention. The owner, Darby Howard, said, "We get a lot of guys in here with Mohawk haircuts, and so it wasn't really anything out of the ordinary." Nearly 100 law enforcement officers descended on Woodland Park on January 22, 2001, apprehending four of the seven fugitives. A fifth fugitive, Larry Harper, committed suicide rather than being taken alive. Two days later on January 24, the other two escapees were apprehended by police at a Colorado Springs motel. They were allowed to surrender peacefully. Murder charges were sought against all of the six remaining escapees in the death of Officer Hawkins.

What type of additional security should prisons adopt to keep such escapes by so many dangerous prisoners from occurring in the future? Should these types of offenders be kept in solitary confinement and not be permitted to socialize as these men? [Adapted from Bill Hewitt, Michael Haederle, Vickie Bane, and Bob Stewart. "A Clean Sweep." *People*, February 5, 2001:61–64].

• *A semi-truck rammed through four security fences at an Everglades maximum-security prison in Florida during a planned breakout on Saturday, April 11, 1998. The driver, a woman, pulled out a riot shotgun and fired numerous times at prison corrections officers. In the meantime, a prisoner jumped into the truck and the pair escaped. Later, the woman was apprehended. She turned out to be the mother of one of the inmates, Jay Junior Sigler, 31, who was serving a 20-year sentence for armed robbery. The woman was identified as Sandra Sigler, 58. She had thoroughly thought out her son's escape from the Everglades Correctional Institution, about 20 miles west of Miami, according to Miami-Dade detective Rudy Espinosa. "By all accounts, the mother had masterminded everything," said Espinoza. Sandra Sigler jumped from the vehicle and opened fire on several corrections officers with the shotgun, wounding several. Her son took advantage of the diversion to make good his escape. Police were still searching for the younger Sigler at the time of this writing. Several corrections officers were subsequently treated for gunshot injuries. What should be the punishment for Sandra Sigler who freed her son from a Florida prison? What should be the charges filed against her? What do you think?* [Adapted from the Associated Press, "Mother Helps Son Escape from Prison," April 12, 1998].

This chapter is about prisons, inmates who are incarcerated in prisons, and an overview of selected prison problems. Prisons are state or federally funded and operated institutions to house convicted offenders under continuous custody on a long-term basis. Unlike jails, prisons are completely self-contained and self-sufficient. A social scientist, Erving Goffman (1961), developed the concept *total institution* to describe the environmental reality of prisons and the absolute dominance they have over prisoner's lives. Over the years, prison life has been amply depicted in feature films and catalogued by historians. A rich folklore of American prison culture has been established. However, much of this folklore is mythical and unrelated to the real world of corrections (O'Connor 2000).

In 2001, there were 1,406,031 prisoners under the supervision of state and federal prisons (Harrison and Beck 2002:1). The incarceration rate per 100,000 persons increased by 40 percent between 1990 and 2001 from 458 to 686. State prison systems were operating between 1 and 16 percent above their capacity, while the federal system was operating at 31 percent above its capacity. Between 1990 and 2001, the federal and state inmate population increased by 82 percent. In 2001, there were 93,031 women in state or federal prisons, making up 6.6 percent of all prison inmates. Overall, the United States incarcerated 2,100,146 individuals in 2001, including local jails, territorial prisons, and juvenile facilities (Harrison and Beck 2002:1).

The first part of this chapter briefly examines the history of prisons in the United States. Prisons in the United States have had rather humble origins, with the first prison being a converted copper mine in Connecticut. Subsequently, more sophisticated prisons were established in various jurisdictions. The chapter begins with a description of several important types of prison systems that were models upon which prisons in other states were based. One of these systems was the Pennsylvania system, which incorporated various ideas about penal philosophy devised by William Penn. The influence of the Quakers in early Pennsylvania prison developments is described, including a discussion of the Great Law of Pennsylvania. The Auburn (New York) State Penitentiary is subsequently described. The innovations at Auburn, including tiers and solitary confinement, are described and discussed. During the 1870s, the reform era began, and the Elmira Reformatory in New York is examined. The reformatory concept was innovative, although it was poorly implemented. The gradual deterioration of the reformatory is described.

Next, the chapter describes federal and state prison organization. In recent years there has been extensive prison construction and expansion at both the federal and state levels. Much of this expansion is attributable to the growing offender population, which has been adversely impacted by new laws and a tougher stance on particular kinds of crimes, including drug offenses. Prison administration is described. There are many different state systems, and there are many variations in state operating systems and wide differences in expenditures for accommodating prison inmates.

Prisons are considered total institutions, because they form the entire world of each offender for more or less lengthy incarcerative periods. Elaborate classification systems have been devised, particularly during the last century, in an effort to deal with different types of offenders. Minimum-, medium-, maximum-, and supermax prisons have been established, each signifying increasingly secure facilities to house inmates who pose greater risks. These different types of prison systems are examined. Several inmate classification schemes are profiled and described. These schemes are based on various psychological, behavioral, and sociodemographic criteria. These risk instruments are constantly being revised, as scientists learn more about offenders and their behaviors. A general overview of classification and its functions is presented. Besides risk instrumentation, most jurisdictions also attempt to determine offender needs. Thus, some attention is given to needs instruments.

Several types of prediction are described. These include actuarial prediction, clinical prediction, and anamnestic prediction. None of these prediction schemes, which attempt to forecast offender risk, is perfect, and thus there are frequent prediction errors. This has given rise to categories of offenders known as false positives and false negatives. These types of offenders are described, together with the problems they create for prison systems. One of these problems is selective incapacitation, which is examined.

Several important prison functions are subsequently discussed. Prison functions include providing societal protection, offender punishment, rehabilitation, and reintegration. Prisons attempt to provide meaningful work for inmates, as well as vocational and educational programming. However, not all inmates can participate in such programming, largely because of budgetary constraints and overcrowding.

The chapter next examines prison culture and profiles prison inmates and their attitudes. Several important studies about prison culture are described. Being in prison causes prisonization to occur, where prisoners undergo a form of socialization that is often counterproductive to their eventual reintegration into society. Another counterproductive element is the increasingly adverse gang presence. Gangs in prisons are defined and examined.

This chapter concludes with a discussion of several important prison issues. One of the most pervasive issues facing prison administrators is overcrowding. Most prison systems in the United States today are overcrowded, according to various standards use to measure inmate populations. These standards are also explained. One consequence of overcrowding, which results in another issue, is growing prison violence and rioting. Some attention is given to various administrative solutions to inmate violence, including the establishment of inmate disciplinary councils, which are examined. However, not everyone agrees about how much power inmates should be given in an attempt to resolve different inmate problems.

Innovative prison designs have been explored by various jurisdictions in an attempt to foster safer prison environments for both correctional officers and inmates. These designs are described. Also examined are the issues of sexual assaults that occur in prisons, and the problems of sexually transmitted diseases, such as HIV/AIDS. Many prison systems segregate these offenders from the general inmate population, and this has triggered several constitutional challenges. This issue is explained.

THE HISTORY OF PRISONS IN THE UNITED STATES

The development and growth of U.S. prisons was influenced originally by English and Scottish penal methods (Hughes 1987). Those English and Scottish prisons that did exist to house criminals and others frequently adopted operational policies that were strongly influenced by economic or mercantile interests as well as those of the Church. An influential English prison reformer, **John Howard** (1726–1790), was critical of the manner and circumstances under which prisoners were administered and housed. He had been a county squire and later, in 1773, he became sheriff of Bedfordshire. He took his job seriously and conducted regular inspections of gaol facilities in his jurisdiction. He found that prisoners were routinely exploited by gaolers, since gaolers had no regular income other than that extracted from prisoners through their labor.

In order to get new ideas about gaol operations, Howard visited several other countries to inspect their prison systems. He was especially impressed with the Maison de Force (House of Enforcement) of Ghent, where prisoners were well-fed, adequately clothed, and humanely lodged separately during evening hours. He believed these ideas could be incorporated into British prisons and gaols, with proper lobbying. He reported his observations of prisons in other lands to the House of Commons in a lengthy and detailed document, and he succeeded in convincing British authorities that certain reforms should be undertaken. In 1779, the **Penitentiary Act** was passed.

The Penitentiary Act provided for secure and clean facilities, where prisoners could work productively at hard labor rather than suffer the usual punishment of banishment or even the death penalty, which was imposed for numerous offenses, including petty ones (Solotaroff 2001). Prisoners were to be well-fed, clothed, and housed in isolated sanitary cells during evening hours. They were to be given opportunities to learn useful skills and trades during daytime hours. Fees for their maintenance were abolished, rigorous inspections were conducted regularly, and balanced diets and improved hygiene were to be strictly observed. Howard did not believe prisoners should be cruelly treated, but he didn't believe they should be coddled, either. He felt they should be given a hearty work regimen. Through hard labor and productive work, prisoners could be made to realize the seriousness and consequences of their crimes. Thus, work was a form of penance. Howard also believed that prisoners should receive religious instruction. Furthermore, all prisoners should be provided with uniforms as a part of a general program to improve their hygiene. Qualified staff to run Howard's idea of a good prison included hiring nongambling, nondrinking men of high moral character who would be paid a sound wage (Buffardi 1999:2). Howard's ideas inspired the coining of a new word, penitentiary, which was synonymous with reform and punishment. Today, penitentiaries in the United States are regarded as punishment-centered rather than equated with reform, as significant philosophical shifts have occurred in U.S. corrections (Wacquant 2001). In any case, Howard's work inspired others—including Dr. Benjamin Rush and other U.S. reformers—in the innovations they pioneered in later years.

The First State Prison

Although authorities disagree about the first state prison, an underground prison was established in Simsbury, Connecticut, in 1773. This prison was actually an underground copper mine that was converted into a confinement facility for convicted felons. It was called Newgate Prison. It was eventually made into a permanent prison in 1790. Prisoners were shackled about the ankles, worked long hours, and received particularly harsh sentences for minor offenses. Burglary and counterfeiting were punishable in Simsbury by imprisonment not exceeding ten years, while a second offense meant life imprisonment. These punishments did not deter inmates from rioting, however. In 1774, one year after Newgate Prison was established, the first American prison riot occurred. Several injuries were recorded, but prison guards quickly quelled the disturbance and restored order to the prison (Topham 2002).

The Pennsylvania System

Historians consider the Walnut Street Jail to be the first true American prison that attempted the correction of offenders. Compared with the Newgate Prison in Connecticut, a strictly punishment-centered facility, the Walnut Street Jail was operated according to rehabilitative principles. One of the signers of the Declaration of Independence, Dr. Benjamin Rush (1745–1813), was both a physician and a humanitarian. Dr. Rush believed that the purposes of punishment were to reform offenders, to prevent them from committing future crimes, and to remove them from society temporarily until they developed a repentant attitude. Several of Rush's ideas were incorporated into the operation of the Walnut Street Jail, and eventually, the pattern of discipline and offender treatment practiced there became known popularly as the **Pennsylvania System** (Rogers 1993). Actually, this system was a reflection of the prison reforms originally proposed by the Quakers and advocated by William Penn as the Great Law of Pennsylvania in 1682. Under the Great Law, corporal punishment was discarded in favor of hard labor. Although the Walnut Street Jail Pennsylvania System was widely imitated by other jurisdictions and holds a permanent and important place in the history of American corrections, poor administration and planning caused the jail to fail as a correctional facility during the next few decades.

Consistent with his profession as a physician, Rush believed that prisoners should exercise regularly and eat wholesome foods. Thus, he encouraged prisoners to grow gardens where they could produce their own goods. Prisoner-produced goods were so successful at one point that produce and other materials manufactured or grown by inmates were marketed to the general public. Therefore, he pioneered the first prison industry, where prisoners could market goods for profit and use some of this income to defray prison operating expenses.

The Walnut Street Jail introduced outside cells with a central corridor. Solitary confinement was a permanent feature, with inmates confined to these cells during evening hours according to age, gender, and type of offense. From all accounts, this attempt to classify offenders and confine them according to their age, gender, and offense differences was probably the first step toward actual prison reform, although Walnut Street was not considered a reformatory in the strictest sense. Also, this was the first time in history that solitary confinement in such cells was used, and this architectural pattern was subsequently repeated at the Auburn State Penitentiary in New York and elsewhere throughout the United States (U.S. Bureau of Prisons 2002).

The Auburn State Penitentiary

In 1816, New York correctional authorities were authorized to establish a new type of prison, the **Auburn State Penitentiary.** Work commenced on the penitentiary in June 1816, with carpenters and brick masons constructing the facility. In April 1817, several prisoners were put to work on the prison, and by 1823, it was finally completed and ready to accommodate inmates.

The Auburn State Penitentiary was designed in **tiers,** where inmates could be housed on several different levels. The **tier system** became a common feature of subsequent U.S. prison construction, and today most prisons are architecturally structured according to tiers. The term **penitentiary** is used to designate an institution that not only segregates offenders from society but also from each other. The original connotation of penitentiary was a place where prisoners could think, reflect, and repent of their misdeeds and possibly undergo reformation (Sims 2001). Presently, the words *prison* and *penitentiary* are often used interchangeably, since virtually every prison has facilities for isolating prisoners from one another according to various levels of custody and control. Thus, each state has devised different names for facilities designed to house its most dangerous offenders. Examples include Kentucky State Penitentiary, California State Prison at San Quentin, New Jersey State Prison, North Dakota Penitentiary, and Maine State Prison.

The Auburn State Penitentiary incorporated several features of the old Walnut Street Jail concept such as solitary confinement. Prisoners were housed in solitary cells during evening hours, thus perpetuating the solitary confinement theme. Solitary confinement is an administrative segregation feature of virtually every major U.S. prison today (Rogers 1993). However, prior to the introduction of solitary confinement as a punishment, inmates were punished in other ways. In 1819, for instance, flogging of inmates was authorized. Up to 39 lashes were administered to unruly inmates in the presence of at least two prison inspectors for various rule violations. In 1821, 80 men were selected to be placed in solitary confinement, a new wing of solitary cells that had been completed. Subsequent reports indicated that solitary confinement was an unpopular punishment with many inmates, and more than a few inmates committed suicide while confined under these conditions or developed various mental illnesses or breakdowns. All prisoners were ordered to move about the prison in silence, with their heads pointing to the right and downward toward the ground. This silence was to remind them of their low place in society. Inmates who violated the silence rule were flogged. In 1845, for instance, 173 inmates were flogged for not maintaining silence and attempting to communicate with others. Officials explained that this enforced silence was for purposes of security and reformation. Actually, flogging prisoners continued at Auburn and at other New York state prisons until 1847, when it was outlawed. Other equally harmful punishments were substituted for flogging, however.

One innovation was that inmates were allowed to work together and eat their meals with one another during daylight hours. This was known as the **congregate system,** because of the opportunity for inmates to congregate with one another. Dining rooms were fashioned according to large military mess halls, and work areas were large enough to accommodate several hundred inmates. Despite being allowed to congregate in a large dining area, prisoners were obligated to maintain the rule of silence at all times.

Auburn Penitentiary also provided for divisions among prisoners according to the nature of their offenses. The different tiers conveniently housed inmates in different offense categories, with more serious offenders housed on one tier and less serious offenders housed on another. Certain tiers were reserved for the most unruly offenders who could not conform their conduct to prison policies. The most dangerous inmates were kept in solitary confinement for long periods as punishment. These periods ranged from a few days to a few months, depending upon the prison rule violated. Therefore, Auburn Penitentiary is significant historically because it provided the minimum-, medium-, and maximum-security designations by which modern penitentiaries are known.

Prisoners were provided with different uniforms as well, to set them apart from one another. The stereotypical striped uniform of prison inmates was a novelty at Auburn that was widely copied as well. Over half of all state prisons patterned their structures after the Auburn system during the next half century, including the style of prison dress and manner of separating offenders according to their crime seriousness (Spiegel and Spiegel 1998). Striped prison uniforms continued until the 1950s, when they were eventually abandoned.

One additional feature about the Auburn system was that prisoners helped to defray a portion of their housing and food costs through their labor. Prison officials contracted with various manufacturers and retailers for purchases of prison goods. Thus, prison industry was gradually recognized as a mutually beneficial enterprise—prison officials could interpret prisoner labor as worthwhile and rehabilitative, and they could also contemplate the possibilities of profits from prison-manufactured goods. These profits not only offset the costs of prisoner housing, but they also enhanced New York State revenues. While some critics may contend that exploitation of prison labor was the primary objective of the work of Auburn inmates, it is also arguable that the skills these prisoners cultivated, for whatever reason, were beneficial and assisted them in securing employment in various factories when they were eventually released. Subsequently, the Auburn system was widely imitated in other states and in Canada (Smandych 1991).

Although Auburn was primarily a facility to house male offenders, several female inmates were also housed there. However, women were placed in the attic of the prison where they were brought supplies and rations once a day by a keeper and several male prisoner assistants. The women were employed to pick wool, knit, and perform spooling. After several years, the attic was labeled a receptacle of wickedness and sin by various officials and critics. This was because it was difficult, if not impossible, to prevent some men from entering the attic at different times, surreptitiously, and having forced sexual relations with some of the female inmates. At least one female inmate became pregnant as a result of these illicit sexual encounters. By 1832, a female matron was hired at Auburn to look after these female inmates. Eventually, in 1838, the female inmates were transferred from Auburn to a new female unit constructed at Sing Sing, in Ossining, New York. However, female prisoners were returned to Auburn State Penitentiary in 1892 after the so-called lunatic asylum at Sing Sing was closed. Thus, the Auburn Prison for Women remained open until 1933, when a new women's prison at Bedford Hills was constructed.

Other Early Prison Developments

Between 1816 and 1900, many state prisons were established. One of the first successful prisons was Eastern State Penitentiary, constructed at Cherry Hill, Pennsylvania, in 1829. This prison was considered successful because it was the first to offer a continuing internal program of treatment and other forms of assistance to inmates (Kim 1999). But humanitarianism was not Eastern State Penitentiary's dominating feature. The prison was a huge fortress with thick walls. Prisoners were marched to and from their cells wearing hoods so that they could not see other prisoners. The regimentation at Eastern included lockstep marching in close-order single-file shuffling, with inmate heads turned toward the right and downward. This pattern followed similar practices at Auburn State Penitentiary. Inmates were not permitted to have visitors, and they were denied mail and newspapers. Confinement at Eastern State Penitentiary was decidedly bleak.

The first state penitentiary in Ohio was opened in Columbus in 1834. The largest state prison of that time period was established in Jackson, Michigan, in 1839. By 1998, this State Prison of Southern Michigan contained 1,530 inmates, nearly reaching its capacity of 1,562. However, the original building constructed in 1839 had been rebuilt to accommodate larger numbers of inmates in 1926. Another large state prison was built in Parchman, Mississippi, in 1900. In 1998, it housed 4,836 inmates and had a rated capacity of 5,261. Louisiana claims one of the oldest state prisons, however, being built in 1866 with a capacity of 4,532 inmates. In 1998, the Louisiana State Penitentiary in Angola housed 5,113 males, in excess of its rated capacity of 5,108 (American Correctional Association 2002).

Besides those prisons constructed in Pennsylvania and New York, many of the early state penitentiaries were built in areas with large populations. For instance, the California State Prison at San Quentin was constructed in 1852. The Illinois State Penitentiary at Joliet was built in 1860. The Massachusetts Correctional Institution at Bridgewater and the Indiana State Prison were constructed in 1855 and 1859 respectively. However, these older prisons were neither constructed nor designed to house equivalent numbers of offenders as the Louisiana and Mississippi prisons. In 1998, San Quentin housed 5,883 inmates (rated capacity 3,281); the Indiana State Prison housed 1,835 inmates (rated capacity 1,650); the Bridgewater, Massachusetts, facility housed 256 prisoners at 100 percent of its rated capacity of 256; and the Joliet, Illinois, Correctional Center housed 1,112 inmates (rated capacity of 1,180) (American Correctional Association 2002).

State prisons in other states with smaller populations were established in later years. The Civil War (1860–1865) did much to indirectly change prison structure and purpose, particularly in the South. After the Civil War, many Southern states established prisons that exploited inmate labor through various leasing arrangements with private enterprises as well as the federal and state governments. This occurred largely because the Southern economy was adversely affected by the abolition of slavery and the drastic depletion of cheap labor. Thus, many inmates of Southern prisons worked the cotton fields, formed chain gangs to repair state roads, and engaged in other constructive work (Foster, Rideau, and Wikberg 1991). Outside the South, penal authorities and others became increasingly critical of such prisoner exploitation. Although Southern prisons gradually changed their operating systems to emulate those of the North, East, and West, especially during the 1940s, an element of prisoner exploitation remains through prison industry. However, today prison inmates who engage in manual labor are paid wages commensurate with the work performed. A portion of these wages offsets the cost of inmate accommodations, although inmates may now save a portion of their wages to provide partial support for their dependents or to acquire a nest egg to use when they are eventually released.

Elmira Reformatory

The next major event in U.S. correctional history occurred in 1870 with the creation of the American Correctional Association (ACA). Rutherford B. Hayes, a future U.S. president, was elected to head the organization. The original goals of the ACA were to formulate a national correctional philosophy, to develop sound correctional policies and standards, to offer expertise to all interested jurisdictions in the design and operation of correctional facilities, and to assist in the training of correctional officers. The ACA was originally called the National Prison Association, then the American Prison Association, and finally and more generally, the American Correctional Association. Actually, the 1870 meeting was convened as the National Congress on Penitentiary and Reformatory Discipline. The meeting attracted prison and corrections officials from all over the United States as well as from other countries.

It is no coincidence that the United States was entering a new era of correctional reform with the establishment of the ACA and, subsequently, the Elmira State Reformatory in Elmira, New York, in 1876. Elmira Reformatory was innovative in that it experimented with certain new rehabilitative philosophies espoused by various penologists, including its first superintendent, Zebulon Reed Brockway (1827–1920). Brockway began his correctional career as a clerk and guard at Wethersheld, Connecticut, Prison in 1848 (Eggleston 1989). Later, he moved to New York to become superintendent of the Albany Municipal and County Almshouse, the first county hospital for the mentally ill and insane. His experience included superintendencies of prisons and houses of correction at various sites in New York and Michigan. Brockway was critical of the harsh methods employed by the establishments he headed, and he envisioned better and more effective treatments for prisoners. He had his chance in 1876 when he was selected to head the Elmira Reformatory.

Elmira was touted as the new penology and the latest, state-of-the art scientific advancement in correctional methods. Penologists from Scotland and Ireland, **Captain Alexander Maconochie** and **Sir Walter Crofton,** were instrumental in bringing about changes in European correctional methods during the period when Elmira was established in the early 1870s. These men influenced U.S. corrections by introducing the mark system, whereby prisoners could accumulate good-time credits to be applied against their original sentences. Thus, through hard work and industry, prisoners could shorten their original sentences, which earlier had to be served in their entirety (Roberts 1997).

Elmira was truly a reformatory. Concurrent with penal developments in Great Britain and other United Kingdom countries, prisoners were channeled into productive activities of an educational or vocational nature, where their good behavior and productivity could earn them time off for good behavior. Thus, parole and indeterminate sentences became distinguishing features of Elmira. Brockway established a board of managers to oversee the parole or early-release process. He employed a three-grade system, where all new inmates were placed in the middle grade. If inmates earned perfect marks in school, work, and deportment for six straight months, then they were advanced to the first grade, which gave them extra privileges. Another six months of good marks would earn them parole at the discretion of the board of managers. However, if they received unsatisfactory marks, they would be demoted to the third grade, where they would be outfitted with a red suit and required to march in lockstep, with a loss of privileges relating to correspondence and visitation.

Individualized treatment was also practiced. Actually, Zebulon Brockway attempted to classify and segregate prisoners in meaningful ways in order to improve the quality of their individualized assistance. In fact, Brockway is credited with establishing the first modern classification process for inmates. As a part of the classification procedure, Brockway interviewed each new inmate. Questions were asked about each inmate's social, economic, psychological, biological, and moral makeup. On the basis of these interviews, Brockway would determine each inmate's subjective defect or limitation, whatever it might be. This defect would be used as the means of individualizing offender programming. Also, Brockway would place each inmate in a particular grade with specific work and school assignments. He also took cranial measurements and conducted research about various criminal types. Special programs were devised for what he termed mental defectives. Inmate progress was monitored constantly, and Brockway continued to reclassify offenders as they progressed in their respective programs. The long-range impact of such classification is illustrated by the creation of a special training class for mental defectives that was commenced in 1913. About 37 percent of all Elmira inmates were considered mental defectives and placed in menial jobs, such as janitorial duties, mending clothes, and shelling peas. A few years later, in 1917, inmates were administered IQ tests and other psychological measures in an attempt to more adequately devise work and educational programs for them.

Brockway also hired several teachers and used some of his more literate inmates to teach other prisoners how to read. Elementary classes were conducted six nights a week. For advanced students, courses in bookkeeping, geography, physiology, and other disciplines were taught by professors from nearby schools, such as the Elmira Women's College. An instructor from the Michigan State Normal School was hired as the moral director in 1878, and he began teaching courses in psychology and ethics. Subsequently, history and literature were added to the Elmira curriculum. Elmira Reformatory actually began a summer school program in 1882. And in 1883 Elmira installed a printing press and began to publish *The Summary,* an eight-page weekly digest of world and local news. This digest became the world's first prison newspaper. Brockway used this paper as a propaganda device to promote Elmira and its diverse programs. Subsequently, Brockway routinely printed 3,000 copies of his annual reports and 1,500 copies of *The Summary* weekly. These were distributed to various influential persons around the state.

The military model was used at Elmira as well, as prisoners were trained in close-order drill, wore military uniforms, and paraded about with wooden rifles. This was regarded as one means of instilling discipline in inmates and reforming them. While Brockway didn't invent parole, he saw that it was used frequently as a reward for those who conformed to the new ways of Elmira. Historians credit Elmira Reformatory with introducing the individualization of prisoner treatment and the large-scale use of indeterminate sentencing.

The influence of Maconochie and especially Crofton are apparent in this regard. Crofton had invented indeterminate sentencing by establishing various work stages whereby prisoners could progress, thus shortening their original sentences. In Elmira Reformatory, however, there is evidence that Brockway and his staff resorted to corporal punishments on occasion to emphasize their principles and encourage conformity to reformatory rules and policies. Despite these drawbacks, however, Elmira Reformatory was widely imitated by other states during the next forty years.

Brockway retired from Elmira in 1900 under a cloud of unsubstantiated charges that he routinely brutalized certain inmates. Evidently, some corporal punishment was used during Brockway's administration. Paddling was detected by an investigation, where inmates were whipped with a leather strap. Furthermore, some inmates were placed in a dungeon, shackled to the door or floor, and given insufficient food and inadequate medical attention. Two separate investigations of Brockway's methods yielded contradictory findings. The second investigation exonerated Brockway, although the first investigation resulted in formal charges of cruel and inhuman punishment of inmates. Brockway dismissed these allegations as meaningless, claiming that his harmless parental discipline of inmates was grossly misrepresented. Furthermore, Brockway claimed that Elmira commenced its operations at a disadvantage. He alleged, for instance, that Sing Sing and Auburn penitentiaries sent Elmira all of their inmates with the most serious disciplinary problems. If this is true, then it explains why Brockway sometimes resorted to corporal punishments as disciplinary measures. It also helps to explain why there were so many inmates classified as mental defectives during his tenure as superintendent.

Inmate overcrowding was also a major problem contributing to ineffective programming. When Elmira was originally constructed, 504 cells were created. However, more inmates were sent to Elmira than were being paroled. By 1886, and again in 1892, substantial additions were made to Elmira's facilities to house 1,296 inmates, although by the late 1890s, there were approximately 1,500 prisoners being accommodated there. No prison administrator, regardless of how well-intentioned, could operate rehabilitative programming successfully under such overcrowded conditions.

Apparently responsive to such overcrowding, the New York legislature approved a second reformatory, the Eastern New York Reformatory at Napanoch, which was opened in 1900. The first inmates at Eastern were transferred from Elmira. These were the older and stronger inmates. Thus, Eastern became known as a repository for hardcore recidivists, parole violators, troublemakers, and incorrigibles, while Elmira accepted and concentrated on younger more hopeful cases. Over the next century Elmira underwent numerous structural and operational changes. Renamed the Elmira Correctional and Reception Center in 1970, the facility continues to offer industrial, vocational, academic, and other diverse programming for inmates, who average 35 years of age. Subsequently, services to treat substance abusers were established, together with a shock incarceration program for new offenders.

Rehabilitation was not a poor concept theoretically. In fact, it remains as one of correction's continuing goals as a part of general prison reform (M. Schneider 2001). But prison overcrowding stimulates significant changes in prison operating policies, and criminal justice procedures are changed to accommodate growing numbers of inmates. Of course, forces external to prison settings have always been at work to shape prison policies as well. Economic fluctuations over time have worked to modify the growth and development of prison industries, for example (Liebling, Elliott, and Arnold 2001). And prison industries, including the labor generated from inmates, provide training and development opportunities for prisoners that are closely connected with and facilitate rehabilitation. However, no simple causal link exists to prove a definite connection between economic change and modes of penal discipline and labor.

Many prisons have reported greater inmate idleness and violence as a result of greater overcrowding in recent years. Furthermore, many prisons are experiencing greater inmate growth than staff to properly supervise them. Accordingly, the quality of programs offered to inmates suffers as prison capacities are exceeded through higher conviction rates and changes in sentencing and parole policies. Although the link between prison population growth and program quality is unclear, overcrowding does seem to adversely influence prison practices and policies (McLennan 1999).

STATE AND FEDERAL PRISON SYSTEMS

Each state and political subdivision, including counties and cities, maintains facilities for housing offenders. There is considerable diversity in the quality of these facilities, the numbers of offenders housed, and the general conditions of confinement. Those convicted of state offenses and sentenced to a period of incarceration are normally maintained in state prisons or correctional centers. Those convicted of violating local criminal laws and sentenced to incarceration are usually housed in city or county jails.

The Federal Bureau of Prisons

There was no federal prison system until 1891, when Congress passed the **Three Prisons Act.** This act authorized the construction of a prison in Fort Leavenworth, Kansas, opened in 1895; a prison in Atlanta, Georgia, opened in 1902; and a prison at McNeil Island, Washington, in 1909 (Federal Bureau of Prisons 2002). When the prison at Fort Leavenworth was constructed, it was constructed for military prisoners (Jackson 2001). Under another act of Congress in 1895, a United States Penitentiary (USP) was authorized for construction about two miles from the military prison at Fort Leavenworth. The labor of military prisoners from Fort Leavenworth was used to construct what is now USP Leavenworth. When a portion of this new prison was completed in 1903, 418 federal prisoners were housed at the new prison site in a large facility that now serves as the laundry building. USP Leavenworth was eventually completed and opened in 1906. All of the other federal prisoners from Fort Leavenworth were housed in the new USP Leavenworth, and the military prison there was returned to the War Department (Federal Bureau of Prisons 2002). The first warden at USP Leavenworth was James W. French.

These and subsequent federal prisons were originally under the Superintendent of Prisons and Prisoners, which was subsequently changed to the Superintendent of Prisons. The first Superintendent of Prisons was R.V. LaDow, who served from 1908 to 1915. Successively, the next superintendents included Francis H. Duehay (1915–1920), Denver S. Dickerson (1920–1921), Heber H. Votaw (1921–1025), Luther C. White (1925–1926), Albert H. Conner (1927–1929), and finally, **Sanford Bates** (1929–1930) (Federal Bureau of Prisons 2002).

No central authority system existed to administer these facilities until Congress created the Federal Bureau of Prisons in 1930 (Federal Bureau of Prisons 2002). Under the direction of the Attorney General of the United States, the Bureau of Prisons was established to manage and regulate all federal penal and correctional institutions; to provide suitable quarters, subsistence, and discipline for all persons charged with or convicted of federal crimes; and to provide technical assistance to state and local governments in the improvement of their own correctional facilities (18 U.S.C., Sec. 4041–4042, 2003). The first Director of the new Federal Bureau of Prisons was Sanford Bates (1884–1972), who retained that post from 1930 to 1937. When the Federal Bureau of Prisons was established, there were eleven federal prisons in existence.

Presently, a director oversees five U.S. regions where all federal correctional institutions are located. These regional directors are headquartered in Atlanta, Dallas, Kansas City, Philadelphia, and San Francisco. The Director of the Federal Bureau of Prisons in 2002 was Dr. Kathleen M. Hawk Sawyer (American Correctional Association 2002).

Because of prison overcrowding and other factors, the federal prison system has not always been able to adequately accommodate all prisoners in its charge. Thus, contractual arrangements are frequently made between the federal government and state and local corrections to house a portion of the federal prisoner overflow (Lauen 1997). Early challenges by prisoners as to the constitutionality of such contracting upheld the right of the federal government to make such arrangements with states. In 1876, the U.S. Supreme Court declared that as long as a state permits a federal prisoner to remain in its prison and does not object to his detention, he is rightfully detained in custody under a sentence lawfully passed (*Ex parte Karstendick* 1876). States also have the right to refuse to allow the use of their jails and prisons for housing those convicted of federal crimes if they so desire (*Ex parte Shores* 1912).

In 2002 there were 101 federal correctional institutions, ranging from penitentiaries and prison camps to detention centers, medical centers, and low-security facilities (American Correctional Association 2002:508–550). These facilities and the dates of their construction are shown in Table 7.1.

Ideally, those convicted of violating federal criminal statutes and sentenced to incarceration are placed in one federal correctional institution or

TABLE 7.1

Development of Federal Correctional Institutions, 1902–2001*

Year	Type of Facility
1902	U.S. Penitentiary, Atlanta, GA
1906	U.S. Penitentiary, Leavenworth, KS
1927	Federal Prison Camp, Alderson, WV
1930	Federal Correctional Institution, Petersburg, VA
1930	Federal Prison Camp, Maxwell AFB, Montgomery, AL
1932	U.S. Penitentiary, Lewisburg, PA
1932	Federal Correctional Institution, La Tuna, Anthony, TX
1933	Federal Correctional Institution, El Reno, OK
1933	Federal Correctional Institution, Milan, MI
1933	U.S. Medical Center for Federal Prisoners, Springfield, MO
1938	Federal Correctional Institution, Tallahassee, FL
1940	Federal Correctional Institution, Ashland, KY
1940	Federal Correctional Institution, Danbury, CT
1940	Federal Correctional Institution, Englewood, CO
1940	Federal Correctional Institution, Seagoville, TX
1940	Federal Correctional Institution, Texarkana, TX
1940	U.S. Penitentiary, Terre Haute, IN
1952	Federal Prison Camp, Allenwood, PA

(continued)

TABLE 7.1   (Continued)

Development of Federal Correctional Institutions, 1902–2001[*]

Year	Type of Facility
1955	Federal Correctional Institution, Terminal Island, CA
1958	Federal Correctional Institution, Safford, AR
1959	U.S. Penitentiary, Lompoc, CA
1959	Federal Correctional Institution, Sandstone, MN
1962	Federal Prison Camp, Eglin AFB, FL
1963	U.S. Penitentiary, Marion, IL
1968	Federal Correctional Institution, Morgantown, WV
1973	Federal Correctional Institution, Oxford, WI
1974	Federal Correctional Institution, Lexington, KY
1974	Federal Correctional Institution, Pleasanton, CA
1974	Metropolitan Correctional Center, San Diego, CA
1975	Metropolitan Correctional Center, Chicago, IL
1975	Metropolitan Correctional Center, New York, NY
1976	Federal Correctional Institution, Butner, NC
1976	Metropolitan Correctional Center, Miami, FL
1977	Federal Correctional Institution, Memphis, TN
1979	Federal Correctional Institution, Bastrop, TX
1979	Federal Correctional Institution, Talladega, AL
1979	Federal Prison Camp, Big Spring, TX
1979	Federal Prison Camp, Boron, CA
1971	Federal Correctional Institution, Ft. Worth, TX
1980	Federal Correctional Institution, Otisville, NY
1980	Federal Correctional Institution, Ray Brook, NY
1982	Tucson Federal Correctional Institution, Tucson, AR
1983	Federal Prison Camp, Duluth, MN
1984	Federal Correctional Institution, Loretto, PA
1985	Federal Correctional Institution, Phoenix, AZ
1985	Federal Correctional Institution, Black Canyon, AZ
1985	Federal Medical Center, Rochester, MN
1986	Federal Detention Center, Oakdale, LA
1986	Federal Correctional Institution, Oakdale, LA
1988	Federal Correctional Institution, Marianna, FL
1988	Federal Prison Camp, Pensacola, FL
1988	Federal Prison Camp, Yankton, SD
1988	Federal Prison Camp, Bryan, TX
1988	Metropolitan Detention Center, Los Angeles, CA
1989	Federal Correctional Institution, Sheridan, OR
1989	Federal Correctional Institution, Bradford, PA
1989	Federal Prison Camp, Seymour Johnson Air Force Base, Goldsboro, NC
1989	Federal Prison Camp, El Paso, TX
1990	Federal Correctional Institution, Jesup, GA
1990	Federal Correctional Institution, Fairton, NJ
1990	Federal Correctional Institution, Three Rivers, TX
1990	Federal Detention Center, Oakdale, LA
1990	Federal Prison Camp, N. Las Vegas, NV
1990	Federal Prison Camp, Millington, TN
1991	Federal Correctional Institution, Minersville, PA
1991	Federal Medical Center, Lexington, KY

Year	Type of Facility
1992	Federal Correctional Institution, Manchester, KY
1992	Federal Correctional Institution, Fort Dix, NJ
1992	Low Security Correctional Institution-Allenwood, White Deer, PA
1993	Federal Correctional Institution-Allenwood, White Deer, PA
1993	U.S. Penitentiary-Allenwood, White Deer, PA
1993	Federal Correctional Institution, Estill, SC
1993	Federal Correctional Institution-Satellite Camp, Bastrop, TX
1993	Federal Prison Camp-Oakdale, Oakdale, LA
1993	Metropolitan Detention Center, San Juan, PR
1994	Federal Medical Center, Ft. Worth, TX
1994	United States Penitentiary, Florence, CO
1994	United States Penitentiary-Adm Max, Florence, CO
1994	Federal Correctional Institution, Greenville, IL
1994	Federal Correctional Institution, Pekin, IL
1994	Metropolitan Detention Center, Brooklyn, NY
1994	U.S. Penitentiary, Florence, CO
1994	U.S. Penitentiary-Admin Max, Florence, CO
1995	Federal Correctional Institution, Florence, CO
1995	Federal Correctional Institution, Coleman, FL
1995	Federal Correctional Institution, Miami, FL
1995	Federal Correctional Institution, Cumberland, MD
1995	Federal Correctional Institution, Waseca, MN
1995	Federal Correctional Institution, Otisville, NY
1995	Federal Correctional Institution, Ray Brook, NY
1995	Federal Correctional Institution, Memphis, TX
1995	Federal Correctional Institution, Beckley, WV
1995	Federal Detention Center, Miami, FL
1995	Federal Detention Center, Tallahassee, FL
1995	Federal Medical Center, Ft. Worth, TX
1995	Low Security Correctional Institution, Coleman FL
1995	Low Security Correctional Institution, Butner, NC
1995	Federal Transfer Center, Oklahoma City, OK
1996	Federal Correctional Institution, Beaumont, TX
1997	Low Security Correctional Institution, White Deer, PA
1997	Federal Detention Center, Seattle, WA
1997	Federal Correctional Institution, Elkton, OH
1997	Federal Correctional Institution, Forrest City, AZ
1997	Taft Correctional Institution, Taft, CA
1997	Federal Correctional Institution, Yazoo City, MS
1997	United States Penitentiary, Beaumont, TX
1999	United States Penitentiary, Beaumont, TX
1999	Federal Detention Center, Houston, TX
1999	Federal Medical Center, Devens, MA
2000	Federal Correctional Institution, Victorville, CA
2000	Federal Detention Center, Philadelphia, PA
2000	Federal Correctional Institution, Victorville, CA
2000	United States Penitentiary, Pollock, LA
2000	Federal Medical Center, Butner, NC
2001	Rivers Correctional Institution, Winton, NC
2001	United States Penitentiary, Atwater, CA
2001	United States Penitentiary, Coleman, FL
2001	Federal Detention Center, Honolulu, HI

*Compiled by author.

another, depending upon the nature of the conviction offense, the geographical area within which the federal crime occurred, and space availability. Normally, federal prisoners are housed in federal facilities, state prisoners are housed in state facilities, and local criminals are incarcerated in local facilities.

However, for many decades, some federal and state prisoners have been lodged in local correctional facilities, largely because of overcrowding in federal institutions. Under Title 18, Section 4082 of the U.S. Code (2003), the Attorney General "may designate as a place of confinement any available, suitable, and appropriate institution or facility, whether maintained by the federal government or otherwise, and whether within or without the judicial district in which the person was convicted, and may at any time transfer a person from one place of confinement to another." Also, if space is unavailable in particular localities where federal prisoners are to be housed, the Attorney General is authorized to cause to be erected in the area a house of detention, workhouse, jail, camp, or other place of confinement that can be used to house those convicted of federal crimes (18 U.S.C., Sec. 4003, 2003).

Until 1985, the establishment of new federal penal facilities was sluggish. Between 1985 and 2001, 74 new federal prisons were constructed. The oldest U.S. penitentiary still operating is the one in Atlanta, Georgia, constructed in 1902. The smallest U.S. penitentiary is the U.S. Penitentiary-Admin Max in Florence, Colorado, with a rated capacity of 490, while the largest is in Atlanta, Georgia, with a rated capacity of 2,117. These penitentiaries generally house the most serious federal offenders and those serving the longest sentences. Those federal penitentiaries designated as Admin Max house inmates with chronic misconduct problems. Their average stay is 36 months (American Correctional Association 2002). The federal correctional institutions have varying security levels. The metropolitan correctional centers and camps are designed to house short-term and low-risk federal offenders at all security levels. Federal medical centers are designed for federal prisoners who require medical, surgical, or psychiatric care. The federal prison camps are designed as minimum-security institutions with no fences, dormitory housing, and low staff-inmate ratios. These facilities are program-oriented and focused on work. Finally, federal detention centers are designed to house pretrial detainees and criminal aliens awaiting deportation hearings (American Correctional Association 2002).

State Prisons and Prison Administration

Compared with the highly centralized Federal Bureau of Prisons, state prison organization varies greatly among jurisdictions. There are some common elements associated with the internal operations of most federal and state prisons, however. All state prisons as well as comparable federal facilities have **wardens** or **superintendents** who oversee prison operations. These people have various administrative responsibilities, including hiring and firing corrections personnel, implementing new correctional policies, ensuring the safety of all prisoners as well as prison staff, and establishing internal sanctioning systems for dealing effectively with rule infractions by staff or inmates.

Prison administrators come from diverse backgrounds. Many of these officials lack legal training. Often, former correctional personnel are appointed to warden positions after many years of service in other correctional capacities (Cullen et al. 1993). In view of the increase in prisoner litigation during the 1970s and 1980s, prison administrators have become more adept at developing defensive policies and acquainting their staffs with strategies for avoiding confrontations and situations that eventually result in lawsuits. Many prison administrators have established or helped to establish prisoner grievance committees to deal with many minor prison problems internally rather than through court action (Gorton 1997).

In 1973 the National Advisory Commission on Criminal Justice Standards and Goals directed its attention upon correctional management and identified certain basic problems of correctional organizations. Subsequently, a report was issued that highlighted certain deficiencies as well several options as possible solutions to these problems. Some of the problems the Commission identified were (1) the lack of coordination and considerable fragmentation among state corrections agencies and services, (2) shifting federal and state resources allocated to corrections, and (3) changing correctional goals from rehabilitation to more punitive policies. The Commission also noted that managing people-processing organizations such as prisons is probably more difficult compared with managing other public agencies. The fact that dangerous prisoners must be managed adequately and appropriate programs must be implemented that directly serve their diverse needs means that prison administrators must continually solve logistical and practical problems that never seem to abate.

In the early 1970s, **management by objectives (MBO)** was considered the most promising strategy whereby administrators could cope successfully with their various supervisory problems. Management by objectives is achieved by effective goal-setting and creating a system of accountability by which one's performance can be measured over time. Thus, with proper feedback from higher-ups, corrections personnel can establish goals and take appropriate action to achieve them. Administrators can facilitate goal attainment by providing an accepting climate and the necessary feedback which permits officers to remedy bad habits and cultivate good ones (Flanagan, Johnson, and Bennett 1996). But the Commission also observed that prisons ordinarily do not engage in the necessary planning for management by objectives to succeed. Thus, some of the more important needs of prison administrators were highlighted, but no specific paths were outlined by which these needs could be fulfilled. Complicating the general application of specific managerial strategies is the fact that state prisons vary greatly in their sizes and functions. As we have seen, prison sizes range from a few hundred inmates to 4,500 or more. Managerial strategies that work for smaller institutions may not work for much larger ones (Kinkade and Leone 1992).

A majority of prison administrators are men. In 2001, about 35 percent of all administrative prison staff were women (Camp and Camp 2002). There are no restrictions that would prevent women from occupying these administrative posts. However, there are informal and traditional barriers that often inhibit the hiring of women to warden posts. In 1990, for instance, a *Corrections Compendium* survey disclosed that there were 53 women wardens, superintendents, or administrators overseeing men's correctional institutions, while another 64 women were either deputies or assistant administrators at other men's or co-ed institutions (Hicks 1990:7). One of the chief barriers is overcoming resistance from other male administrators responsible for making such appointments (T. Miller 1996:16–17).

Once persons are appointed to be prison wardens or administrators, they do not stay on the job for particularly long periods. For instance, the average length of service for prison wardens in 2001 was about 15.3 years (Camp and Camp 2002:149). Those wardens with the longest tenure in their posts have served over 36 years (Pennsylvania), Indiana (24.6 years), and Georgia (24.3 years), while those serving the shortest terms were in Utah (1.6 years) and the District of Columbia (1.8 years) (Camp and Camp 2002:148).

On July 1, 1982, Jennie Lancaster was promoted to warden of the North Carolina Correctional Center for women. She had begun her career by applying for a correctional internship and taking a position with the Polk Youth Center in Raleigh in 1972. Her interest in corrections had been prompted by a criminology course she had taken during her senior year at Merideth College in Raleigh. Later, in 1972, she became program supervisor at Ulmstead Youth Center. By 1980, she had become the assistant superintendent for treatment and programs at the North Carolina Correctional Center for Women. Two years later she was promoted to warden (Gursky 1988:82–83). Lancaster recalled that two years later, in 1984, she was faced with one of the most challenging tasks of her life—the supervision of Velma Barfield, a woman who had poisoned her mother and two other people and was sentenced to death by a North Carolina court. No woman had been executed in the United States since 1962. Barfield's appeals were denied consistently as she sat on death row for six years at the Women's Prison. In May 1984, Barfield's execution was ordered to be carried out within 90 days. A final appeal by Barfield was rejected by the U.S. Supreme Court in September, and a November 2 execution date was set. Barfield was executed as scheduled.

Although the Central Prison in Raleigh, a maximum-security facility for men, performs all executions in North Carolina, Barfield was housed in the Women's Prison until a few days before the date of execution. Warden Lancaster related that this most emotionally upsetting ordeal was especially difficult for her correctional staff. She said that one of her officers lamented, "We got into corrections because we thought we could make a difference in somebody's life. We have a lot of policies and training programs to teach us how to effectively work with inmates, how to encourage them to change, how to reward positive behavior and motivate inmates. Now we're being told we're going to be a part of the death of somebody and we don't know how to do that. We never anticipated this." Neither did Warden Jennie Lancaster. It bothered her also that there was a lack of consideration given to the medical, psychiatric, and religious staff who had been working with Barfield and others. Thus, as warden, she assumed additional responsibilities for informally counseling correctional officers bothered by the impending execution. In sum, she said that "the greatest irony [is] that the authentic, genuine, caring part of you is coming right to head with the professional responsibility that seems to be asking you to do something totally against what you've been doing" (Gursky 1988:78).

Since the death penalty is not used as a punishment by several states, some wardens and superintendents do not have to face the correctional pressures and responsibilities of administering capital punishment to condemned offenders. However, many other problems face these administrators daily. Solutions to these problems, some arising from inmates and others from correctional officers, are not always clear-cut. Professional improvisation is frequently required. Furthermore, it is clear that the types of inmates administrators must supervise influences the nature of supervision practiced. Fixed and limited correctional budgets impose serious constraints that prevent administrators from being fully effective in the performance of their tasks. There is no single administrative style that describes the typical prison warden or superintendent. There is no uniformity among the states or even within them about how each prison facility should be managed and what sort of correctional officer conduct is to be prescribed. For a time in the 1970s, the Law Enforcement Assistance Administration provided monies for correctional improvements, including training for those performing supervisory roles. While some monies continue to be available under different auspices, there is little indication that former expenditures resulted in substantial administrative improvements in prisons generally.

The Total Institution Concept

Erving Goffman (1961) has observed that prisons in the United States are **total institutions.** That is, they are completely self-sufficient and define a closed culture within which inmates interact. The concept of a total institution conveys the idea that prison environments are unique and distinct from other populations, such as might be found in traditional community settings (O'Connor 2000). There are similarities to communities found in prisons, however. There is a hierarchy of authority and power structure among inmates. Besides institutional rules, prisoners establish their own rules by which to conduct themselves. Thus, a culture within a culture, or **prison subculture,** is created. This **subculture** has its own status structure and authority pattern. In many prisons, inmates fear the informal prison subculture and its reprisals for rule violations more than formal administrative rules and punishments. Intra-inmate retaliation is often fatal (Cook and Davies 1999).

In order to understand how inmates behave and why they react in certain ways to external interventions, such as vocational or educational programs and counseling, we must first understand the fabric of their subculture within their total institution. Once we understand their cultural patterns, we have done much to explain why sometimes, interventions designed to achieve specific aims, such as rehabilitation, are not particularly successful. However, some researchers dispute the idea that prisons are as segregated as they appear to outsiders (M. Schneider 2001). Community-prison interactions in certain prisons, particularly in California, cause some prison settings to be less isolated than the total institution concept would imply. Later in this chapter, inmate culture will be described. Jargon peculiar to inmates will be described as well as how inmate pecking orders are established. It is expected that in such a setting with its own culture, gang formation is one logical consequence. Inmate violence and other incidents are outgrowths of this subculture and the hostility it breeds and perpetuates (Easteal 2001). Before we examine inmate culture, we will note some of the primary characteristics of today's prison populations.

A PROFILE OF PRISONERS IN U.S. PRISONS

Considerable diversity exists among prisoners in state and federal institutions. These differences include the nature and seriousness of their conviction offenses, age, and psychological or medical problems. In order to cope more effectively with meeting the needs of such diverse offenders, prisons have established different confinement facilities and levels of custody, depending upon how each prisoner is classified.

Beyond such custodial classifications, however, is a pervasive inmate characteristic. Many inmates have limited educational skills. When they are sent to prison, little attention is given to their educational deficiencies, and many prisons simply warehouse offenders. Some prisoners are illiterate. In an effort to deal with this significant problem, states such as Oklahoma have established literacy programs of various types. For instance, the Oklahoma penitentiary system has a Peer Tutoring Program and a Family Recovery Embraces Education Program. Both of these programs are designed to return offenders to their communities better equipped to cope more effectively with living in everyday society (H.C. Davis 2001).

Some inmates have learning disabilities that make it difficult to learn, even if literacy programming is provided (Taymans and Corley 2001). Thus, alternative learning arrangements must be made for learning disabled inmates (Rasmussen, Almvik, and Levander 2001). This requires some amount of teamwork for correctional staff to offer critical services for those offenders most in need of them. Ultimately, one long-range goal of literacy programs in prisons should be to assist offenders in becoming lifelong learners. Literate people learn independently, interdependently, and continuously throughout their lives. In Canada, for example, the Cognitive Enrichment Advantage has been established. This is an inmate-centered teaching method used to improve one's reading level. Other elements of the program include overcoming antisocial propensities and criminal conduct related to inadequate coping mechanisms (B. Fisher 2001). Ireland and other countries have addressed inmate illiteracy in similar ways in recent years (Kett 2001).

State and Federal Prison Population Growth

Between 1990 and 2001, the number of prisoners in custody in the United States increased from 1,148,702 to 1,962,220, or 71 percent (Harrison and Beck 2002:2). This is an average increase of 5.9 percent per year. Table 7.2 shows the number of persons held in state or federal prisons or in local jails, 1990–2001.

TABLE 7.2

Number of Persons Held in State or Federal Prisons or in Local Jails, 1990–2001

| | Total Inmates in Custody | Prisoners in Custody on December 31 | | Inmates in Jail on June 30 | Incarceration Rate[a] |
		Federal	State		
1990	1,148,702	58,838	684,544	405,320	458
1995	1,585,586	89,538	989,004	507,044	601
1996	1,646,020	95,088	1,032,440	518,492	618
1997	1,743,643	101,755	1,074,809	567,079	648
1998	1,816,931	110,793	1,113,676	592,462	669
1999[b]	1,893,115	125,682	1,161,490	605,943	691
2000[c]	1,937,482	133,921	1,176,269	621,149	684
2001[c]	1,962,220	143,337	1,181,128	631,240	686
Percent change, 2000–2001	1.3%	7.0%	0.4%	1.6%	
Average annual increase, 1995–2001	3.6%	8.2%	3.0%	3.7%	

Note: Counts include all inmates held in public and private adult correctional facilities. Jail counts for 1995–2001 exclude persons supervised outside of a jail facility.
[a]Number of prison and jail inmates per 100,000 U.S. residents at year end. Rates for 2000 have been revised using estimates based on the *2000 Census of Population and Housing.*
[b]In 1999, 15 states expanded their reporting criteria to include inmates held in privately operated correctional facilities. For comparisons with previous years, the state count 1,137,544 and the total count 1,869,169 should be used.
[c]Total counts include federal inmates in nonsecure privately operated facilities (6,515 in 2001 and 6,143 in 2000).
Source: Paige M. Harrison and Allen J. Beck. *Prisoners in 2001.* Washington, DC: U.S. Department of Justice, 2002, p.2.

The federal inmate population increased from 58,838 in 1990 to 143,337 in 2001, a 143.6 percent increase. The state inmate population increased from 664,544 in 1990 to 1,181,128 in 2001, or 77.8 percent (Harrison and Beck 2002:2). One reason for such dramatic growth in the federal prison system over these years is the passage of anti-drug legislation in the late 1980s and early 1990s. This legislation greatly increased the punishments for various drug offenses. Another factor was the enactment of new U.S. sentencing guidelines that went into effect in October 1987. These sentencing guidelines reduced the use of probation from 65 percent to about 10 percent for all convicted federal offenders. A third factor is that federal prisoners must serve at least 85 percent of their sentences before becoming eligible for supervised release (Harrison and Beck 2002).

Sociodemographic Characteristics of State and Federal Prison Inmates

Table 7.3 shows the numbers of state prisoners for 2000 according to offense, gender, and race/ethnicity. It indicates that for all state inmates, women made up 6.3 percent of the population in 2000. Fifty percent of all state male offenders

TABLE 7.3

Estimated Number of Sentenced Prisoners under State Jurisdiction, by Offense, Gender, and Race/Ethnicity, 2000

Offense	All	Male	Female	White	Black	Hispanic
Total	1,206,400	1,130,100	76,400	436,700	562,000	178,500
Violent offenses	589,100	565,100	24,000	212,400	273,400	87,100
Murder[a]	156,300	148,100	8,200	53,000	77,200	23,400
Manslaughter	17,300	15,400	1,800	6,600	6,800	2,900
Rape	30,800	30,400	300	15,400	12,100	2,300
Other sexual assault	83,100	82,200	900	50,500	20,700	10,400
Robbery	158,700	153,400	5,300	35,800	96,000	22,800
Assault	116,800	111,200	5,700	39,400	51,100	21,400
Other violent	26,100	24,400	1,700	11,800	9,600	3,900
Property offenses	238,500	219,300	19,200	108,600	96,800	28,400
Burglary	111,300	107,800	3,600	50,800	45,100	13,200
Larceny	45,700	39,900	5,800	17,900	21,100	5,300
Motor vehicle theft	18,800	18,100	700	7,700	7,100	3,700
Fraud	32,500	24,800	7,600	17,300	12,600	2,500
Other property	30,100	28,600	1,500	14,800	10,900	3,800
Drug offenses	251,100	226,400	24,700	58,200	145,300	43,300
Public-order offenses[b]	124,600	116,400	8,200	56,600	44,900	19,000
Other/unspecified[c]	3,200	2,900	300	700	1,600	700

Note: Data are for inmates with a sentence of more than 1 year under the jurisdiction of state correctional authorities. The number of inmates by offense were estimated using the 1997 Survey of Inmates in State Correctional Facilities and rounded to the nearest 100.
[a]Includes nonnegligent manslaughter.
[b]Includes weapons, drunk driving, court offenses, commercialized vice, morals and decency charges, liquor law violations, and other public-order offenses.
[c]Includes juvenile offenses and unspecified felonies.
Source: Paige M. Harrison and Allen J. Beck. *Prisoners in 2001.* Washington, DC: U.S. Department of Justice, 2002, p. 13.

were incarcerated for violent offenses, compared with 31.4 percent of all state female prison inmates. Approximately 25 percent of all female prison inmates were convicted of property offenses, compared with 19.4 percent of all male inmates. About 32 percent of the female inmates were convicted of drug offenses, compared with 20 percent of the male inmates. Thus, disproportionately larger numbers of women were serving time for property and drug offenses compared with male offenders. White inmates represented 36 percent of all state inmates, while blacks and Hispanics accounted for 46.5 percent and 14.8 percent of them respectively. Forty-eight percent of the black inmates were serving time for violent offenses, compared with 48.8 percent of the Hispanic inmates and 48.6 percent of the white inmates. Essentially, whites, blacks, and Hispanics were represented fairly equally in the violent offense category. However, disproportionately larger numbers of blacks committed robbery (17.5 percent) compared with either whites (8.1 percent) or Hispanics (12.7 percent). About 15 percent of all white offenders were in prison for rape or sexual assault compared with 7.1 percent of the Hispanic and 5.8 percent of the black inmates (Harrison and Beck 2002:13). Black inmates had a larger proportion of drug offenses (25.8 percent) compared with whites (13.3 percent) and Hispanics (24.2 percent).

Table 7.4 shows the estimated number of sentenced federal inmates, according to their most serious offense, for the years 1990, 1995, and 2000. Table

TABLE 7.4

Estimated Number of Sentenced Inmates in Federal Prisons, by Most Serious Offense, 1990, 1995, and 2000

Offense	Number of Sentenced Inmates in Federal Prisons			Percent Change, 1990–2000	Percent of Total Growth, 1990–2000
	1990	1995	2000		
Total	56,989	88,101	129,329	126.9%	100.0%
Violent offenses	9,557	11,321	12,973	35.7%	4.7%
Homicide[a]	1,233	966	1,124	−8.8	0.2
Robbery	5,158	6,341	9,450	83.2	5.9
Other violent	3,166	4,014	2,399	−24.2	−1.1
Property offenses	7,935	7,524	9,849	24.1%	1.2%
Burglary	442	164	280	−36.7	−0.2
Fraud	5,113	5,629	7,497	46.6	3.3
Other property	2,380	1,731	2,072	−12.9	−0.4
Drug offenses	30,470	51,737	73,389	140.9%	59.3%
Public-order offenses	8,585	15,762	31,855	271.1%	32.2%
Immigration	1,728	3,612	13,676	691.4	16.5
Weapons	3,073	7,519	10,652	246.6	10.5
Other public-order	3,784	4,631	7,527	98.9	5.2
Other/unknown[b]	442	1,757	1,263	185.7%	1.1%

Note: All data are from the BJS Federal Justice database. Data for 1990 and 1995 are for December 31. Data for 2000 are for September 30. Data are based on all sentenced inmates, regardless of sentence length.
[a]Includes murder, nonnegligent manslaughter, and negligent manslaughter.
[b]Includes offenses not classifiable.
Source: Paige M. Harrison and Allen J. Beck. *Prisoners in 2001.* Washington, DC: U.S. Department of Justice, 2002, p.14.

7.4 shows that of all major federal crime categories, drug offenses had the greatest percentage of total inmate growth, 59.3 percent, between 1990 and 2000. The actual percentage increase in the number of sentenced federal inmates for drug offenses was 140.9 percent between 1990 and 2000. This increase is attributable in large measure to the passage of anti-drug legislation in the late 1980s and early 1990s.

Table 7.4 also shows a dramatic increase in numbers of sentenced federal prisoners who were convicted of immigration, weapons, and other public order offenses. The Immigration and Naturalization Service, as well as other agencies, has cracked down on illegal immigrants, especially during the late 1990s. In the general public-order offense category, therefore, there was an increase of 32.2 percent of total federal inmate population growth between 1990 and 2000.

However, the percent change in federal inmates convicted of public-order offenses between 1990 and 2000 was an increase of 271.1 percent. Although there was a 35.7 percent increase in the number of federal offenders convicted of violent crimes between 1990 and 2000, this only represented an increase of 4.7 percent of total federal inmate growth during this time interval. Of the different violent offense categories, robbery had the greatest percent increase of 5.9 percent.

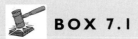 **BOX 7.1**

CAN INMATES SERVE MORE TIME THAN THEIR MAXIMUM SENTENCES?

Assault Gets Inmate One More Year beyond Maximum Term

It happened at the Ward County Jail in Minot, North Dakota. A 19-year-old man, Roland Johnson, was serving a 10-year sentence for attempted murder. He had stabbed a teenager at a downtown intersection in September 1997. He was tried and convicted, and his 10-year sentence was imposed May 18, 1998. Prior to the sentencing and while awaiting trial in the Ward County Jail, Johnson attacked a jail officer, Phil DesLauries, and cracked his nose and chipped his front teeth. According to Johnson, "I just snapped." He said he didn't know why he attacked the jail officer. Jail authorities and the district attorney said that Johnson had a history of aggressive behavior and had been both physically and verbally abusive while confined in the jail.

On Thursday, September 10, 1998, Johnson was scheduled for a jury trial on the assault charge. However, he changed his plea to guilty and received an additional year to the 10-year sentence that had been imposed by the judge in May. Under current sentencing practices in North Dakota, Johnson must serve at least 8½ years of his 10-year sentence. The assault conviction means an additional year. With time for good behavior, Johnson will serve nearly 9½ years before being released through parole.

Do you agree with the sentence imposed by the judge for Johnson's new offense? Ordinarily, assault is punishable by a sentence of 5 or more years. In Johnson's case, the additional year seemed too lenient. What do you think?

Source: Adapted from the Associated Press, "Minot Man Gets a Year Added to the Ten He's Serving," September 11, 1998.

TYPES OF PRISONS AND THEIR FUNCTIONS

There is much diversity among prisoners in state and federal institutions. Differences among them include the nature and seriousness of their conviction offenses, age, religion, and psychological or medical problems (Clear et al. 2000). In order to cope more effectively with meeting the needs of such diverse offenders, prisons have established different confinement facilities and levels of custody, depending upon how each prisoner is classified. Classification is the process of separating and confining prisoners according to various criteria, including offense seriousness, prior record, and potential for disciplinary problems.

All prisons in the United States today have classification schemes of one type or another for differentiating among prisoners and assigning them to particular accommodations (Cook and Davies 1999). The use of such schemes has varying utility depending on the purpose for the initial classification such as identifying those likely to engage in assaultive or aggressive disciplinary infractions. But regardless of the type of classification scheme employed by corrections officials in screening their inmates, prisoners are eventually channeled into one of several fixed custody levels (Cowburn 1998). These are minimum-, medium-, and maximum-security.

Minimum-Security Prisons

Minimum-security prisons are facilities designed to house low-risk, nonviolent first offenders (Hemmens and Stohr 2001). These institutions are also established to accommodate those serving short-term sentences. Sometimes, minimum-security institutions function as intermediate housing for those prisoners leaving more heavily monitored facilities on their way toward parole or eventual freedom. The Federal Bureau of Prisons operates many minimum-security facilities, including several prison camps at Eglin Air Force Base, Florida, and the Federal Detention Center in Oakdale, Louisiana. Minimum-security state facilities include a subsidiary of the New Jersey State Prison at Jones Farm in West Trenton, the Medfield, Massachusetts, Prison Project where inmates work in hospital wards in various capacities, and the Chillicothe, Missouri, Correctional Center for female offenders. In 2001 about 23.5 percent of all U.S. prison space was for minimum-security classified prisoners (Camp and Camp 2002).

Minimum-security housing is often of a dormitory-like quality, with grounds and physical plant features resembling a university campus rather than a prison (O'Connor 2000). Those assigned to minimum-security facilities are trusted to comply with whatever rules are in force. States such as California have operated honor farms where prisoners are literally placed on their honor not to attempt escape from what are lightly monitored or unmonitored facilities. Often, correctional officers are present primarily to prevent the public from entering the grounds indiscriminately.

Because of the greater trust administrators place in inmates in minimum-security institutions, these sites are believed to be most likely to promote greater self-confidence and self-esteem among prisoners. The rehabilitative potential of minimum-security inmates is high, while those in more secure detention facilities are considered more hard-core offenders and less likely to reform (Girshick 1999). The emphasis is upon prisoner reintegration into society.

BOX 7.2

William R. Brooks

Correctional Officer IV, Texas Department of Criminal Justice, Huntsville, TX

Statistics

Texas Department of Criminal Justice Academy; Texas Department of Criminal Justice Response Team training

Work History and Experiences

I grew up moving around the world as a military dependent living in places from San Antonio, Texas, to Taipei, Taiwan. After many years of living away from home, my mother moved with my sister and me back to Texas to help care for my sick grandfather. It wasn't long after that that my parents separated and divorced, leaving my father in Turkey on assignment for many years, as my mother worked and went to school full time. My grandmother raised seven children as the wife of an Air Force Tech Sergeant, which meant that every day was like serving in the military for me. I acquired my strict discipline through my everyday life activities that my grandmother patterned for my growth and maturity. She ran her home like it was from a military training manual, one that would make any visiting general proud.

After many years, my mother remarried a gentleman that she had met through some common friends of theirs. My stepfather was originally a truck driver by trade, but as many did in the early 1980s, he fell into the ranks of the unemployed. Following his father's career path, he applied to what was at the time the Texas Department of Corrections, which was in desperate need of officers at that time. Growing up living with my stepfather, I grew to have a strong respect for him, so much so that I became a third generation working for the agency.

A few years after high school, I applied for employment with the Texas Department of Criminal Justice (TDJC), and I had to wait for almost one year before I was accepted into the Academy. I attended the TDJC Training Academy in Gatesville, Texas, for a two-week

basic training. After the Academy, I was assigned to the Robertson Unit in Abilene, Texas, a maximum-security prison housing up to 2,250 offenders. It was a real culture shock, entering a male penal correctional facility where the potential for anything waits around every corner. I completed my two-week on-the-job training and served an additional four weeks working the cell blocks at the Robertson Unit before I received orders to transfer one-quarter of a mile up the road to open the Middleton Unit.

The Middleton Unit was a good experience in my short career, since this is where I was put through Response Team Training. I am assigned to the Intake-Receiving Department where I have a lot of different duty assignments. My main duties are to process in newly received offenders from the county jails into TDCJ-ID. Once I receive the newly convicted felon, I first screen him to see if he has gang connections by looking over any tattoos on his body. When I do find an offender wearing a gang-related tattoo, I begin an interrogation to help make an accurate assessment of who he may be affiliated with. Once it is determined that the offender has gang connections, then the next concern to be addressed is whether the gang affiliation is from the streets or prison. When I discover that an offender is part of a prison gang or security threat group, I then notify the Gang Intelligence Sergeant for further investigation, which will determine if he will need to be placed into Administrative Segregation to protect the offender population from recruitment, extortions, and disturbances from

(continued)

BOX 7.2 *(Continued)*

rival prison gangs claiming territory. It isn't always easy to identify members by their tattoos, because of the always-changing designs of gang markings. Some gang members go so far as camouflaging their gang tattoos by having other pictures drawn around their gang patch. To the trained eye, it is only a hurdle to overcome, but to others, it is only another tattoo of an offender's expression about his life.

I am also the Assistant Property Officer to the Holliday Unit, which brings me into some lengthy investigations. I investigate offenders who prey on the weak for their personal gain by using extortion to obtain property of value inside of prison. My office maintains records of what property an offender is authorized to possess that requires registration due to value such as, but not limited to, watches, rings, necklaces, and tennis shoes. An offender who falls victim to such an act gets in touch with me to allow an investigation and find the perpetrators, recover the stolen merchandise, and file an appropriate disciplinary report on the one who committed the theft.

As a correctional officer, I have to rely on wits and instincts to stay ahead of a crafty group that has nothing but time to plan and execute ways of hiding and transporting contraband. One afternoon, my luck was running good, and on the surface, everything seemed to be in place. But I soon found out that it wasn't. I was training a new officer on how to conduct an appropriate search of an area when I stumbled upon a clue. The clue was an empty envelope sitting on the fence of C-Building Recreational Yard. To anyone else, this may appear to be trash. But to me, it looks like an opportunity to hide something. I went over to the envelope and picked it up, looked inside, and discovered that this was used to smuggle tobacco outside to be smoked. At this time, tobacco had been banned by the agency for several years, and to use or possess it is a violation of prison policy. I looked at the front of the envelope and discovered that it was addressed to an offender assigned to C-Building. This training was becoming better by the minute. Now, with probable cause, I could search his living quarters for contraband. After we searched his locker box, it came up clean, and the rookie officer started to get discouraged. I then showed him the unsuspected areas to search where we found not only tobacco, but a lighter, a homemade tattooing gun, tattooing ink, and some whiteout that would be used as an inhalant. We put this offender out of business. He had been paid through favors or commissary-purchased items for his services to provide these outlaw items into the prison environment. After the good lesson in searches, the rookie was motivated and proud, because he saw how his training finally paid off in such a short time. The offender was found guilty in a disciplinary hearing and placed in solitary confinement, the hardest time to do while locked up in prison.

Advice to Students

To any student considering a career in corrections, take the time to learn your work environment so that you can apply your education and your intuition to better help you perform in your duties. Take pride in yourself as well as the work you do for your agency. Good luck!

Usually, a wider variety of programs is available to inmates of minimum-security facilities. Also, there are generally fewer restrictions associated with familial visits. The average cost of minimum-security prison space in 2001 is the least ($39,121 per bed) compared with the average cost of higher security levels, such as medium- or maximum-security space ($56,414 and $93,020 respectively) (Camp and Camp 2002:91).

Medium-Security Prisons

About 23.6 percent of all state and federal prisons in the United States were **medium-security prisons** in 2001 (Camp and Camp 2002:82). The Federal Bureau of Prisons uses a six-level scale ranging from Level 1 to Level 6, with Level 1 being a minimum-security facility such as the Federal Prison Camp in Big Spring, Texas, and a Level 6 being a maximum-security facility such as the Marion, Illinois, Penitentiary. Many state prisons or penitentiaries use similar classification schemes for prisoner accommodations. Medium-security facilities are really a catchall, because often both extremely violent and nonviolent offenders are placed in common living areas (Stohr et al. 2000). Visitation privileges are tighter, compared with minimum-security institutions, and privileges, freedom of movement, and access to various educational, vocational, and/or therapeutic programs are more restricted. However, medium-security facilities at both state and federal levels sometimes offer inmates opportunities for work release, furloughs, and other types of programs that increase their freedom of movement. Successful participation in different types of prison programming enables some inmates to change their classification status to a lower custody level where greater access to prison amenities is achieved (Walters 1999). In 1997 there were 120 private prisons rated at both the maximum- and medium-security levels in 27 states. These facilities supervised 120,000 inmates and operated a variety of prison programs (Moore 1998).

Maximum-Security Prisons

Approximately 13.5 percent of all U.S. prisons in 2001 were **maximum-security prisons,** classified either as "maximum" or "close/hi" (Camp and Camp 2002: 82). Ordinarily, those sentenced to serve time in maximum-security facilities are considered among the most dangerous, high-risk offenders. Those with prior

Inmate yard North Dakota State Penitentiary.

records of escape and who are violent crime recidivists often are sentenced to maximum-security institutions. Maximum-security prisons are characterized by many stringent rules and restrictions, and inmates are isolated from one another for long periods in single-cell accommodations (Farmer 1994). Closed-circuit television monitors often permit correctional officers to observe prisoners in their cells or in work areas that are limited (Patrick 1998). Visitation privileges are minimal. Frequently, these institutions are strictly custodial and make little or no effort to rehabilitate inmates (Van Voorhis et al. 1997).

One of the most notorious maximum-security penitentiaries ever constructed was the federal facility at Alcatraz in San Francisco Bay (Babyak 2001). This facility was constructed in 1934, but because of poor sanitation and the great expense of prisoner maintenance, the facility was closed in 1963. During that 29-year span, Alcatraz accommodated over 1,500 prisoners, including Al Capone and Robert "Birdman" Stroud. Escape from Alcatraz was nearly impossible, and of the eight prisoners who attempted escape during that period, only three remain unaccounted for. Maximum-security institutions are typically constructed so as to discourage escape attempts. Prisoner isolation and control are stressed, and close monitoring by guards either directly or through closed-circuit television reduces prisoner misconduct significantly. There are exceptions, however. In September 1971, the Attica, New York, Correctional Facility became the scene of a prison riot. In the next four days, state police and correctional officers stormed the facility, killing 29 prisoners and 10 officer-hostages. Following the riot, official investigations were conducted to determine why the riot had occurred.

Attica was constructed in 1931, and few physical plant improvements had been made during the next forty years. Thus, Attica had unhealthy and otherwise poor living conditions. Many prisoner rights were regularly violated by correctional officers. Medical care was inadequate. Prisoners were confined to their cells from 14 to 16 hours a day, and many inmates felt degraded and humiliated with poor food and meager clothing. Less powerful prisoners were customarily assaulted by more powerful inmates. Sodomy was common, and officials were either unable or reluctant to do anything about it.

Attica was located in a rural area of New York. Rural sites for prisons throughout the United States have been common, since many citizens are reluctant to have prisons in their backyards or nearby. Thus, the labor pool from which correctional officers are selected does not contain large numbers of highly educated and disciplined employees. In fact, the poor quality of correctional officers at Attica was cited by an investigative commission later as a contributing factor to subsequent rioting. Correctional officers were inclined to solve disagreements with prisoners by clubbing them about the head regularly rather than talk out problems. Their billy clubs or nightsticks were called nigger sticks, particularly since the all-white prison staff faced a predominantly black-Hispanic inmate contingent (Badillo and Haynes 1972:26).

Over the years, inmate gangs had formed in Attica. The Black Muslims, La Nuestra Familia, and the Aryan Brotherhood were only a few of the many racially and ethnically related gangs that formed largely for self-protection and prisoner domination, although the Attica inmate population was largely black and Hispanic. Recreational facilities were almost nonexistent, and rehabilitation programs were severely limited or did not exist. Prisoners were permitted to shower once a week. Civil rights issues were prevalent at Attica. For example, Black Muslims, black inmates who adopted the religious philosophy of Islam, were opposed to prison diets that consisted largely of pork. Furthermore, re-

BOX 7.3

SEVEN PRISONERS ESCAPE FROM TEXAS PRISON: BUREAUCRATIC SNAFU?

The Great Escape

On December 13, 2000, seven dangerous inmates escaped from the Connally Unit of the Texas Department of Criminal Justice near Kenedy, Texas. Subsequently, these inmates murdered an Irving, Texas, police officer, Aubrey Hawkins, on Christmas Eve. The inmates overpowered eleven maintenance supervisors, took control of a prison truck and a cache of weapons, and made their escape. Shortly after the escape, blame was focused upon lax security and incompetent prison correctional officers and policies. A number of security lapses allowed these inmates to escape. One of the correctional officers who was taken hostage by the prisoners and subsequently released said that the guards themselves were being made scapegoats. One guard, Alejandro Marroquin, who was taken hostage in the incident, said, "I mean I'm sorry for what happened to Mrs. Hawkins [the dead police officer's mother]. Nobody can bring his life back. I understand that, but they're making it seem like if we would have put our lives on the line, then his life would be back." One of the maintenance personnel taken hostage, Terry Schmidt, said that he doesn't believe that the escape was the fault of the prison maintenance staff or the guards. "It just seems like everything went right for them [the prisoners]," said Schmidt when interviewed. But ultimately, top administrators must absorb considerable responsibility for why the break occurred. Brian Olsen, executive director of the prison employee council within the American Federation of State, County, and Municipal Employees, said that he does not believe administrators were as-

sessed enough blame for the escape. Olsen said that "it shows that the agency does have the ability to investigate and find out what is going on. What is going to come from it from the public point of view is the Legislature is going to take a serious look at the pay and see that something is going to have to be done about this." One Texas State Senator, Carlos Truan, said that he supports pay boosts for correctional officers. He said that it boggles the mind to know that seven dangerous felons could have escaped so easily from a maximum security prison.

The Texas Department of Criminal Justice made several recommendations following a preliminary investigation of the breakout: (1) revise gate procedures posted at the Connally Unit to more specifically address rules requiring identification at gates and pickets; (2) ensure that vehicles are inside the prison compound only as long as necessary for a specific job; (3) make sure that all prison employees are aware of their responsibility to alert security staff if they notice unsupervised inmates; (4) ensure that only prison employees or authorized inmates have access to tool rooms; (5) make sure picket officers immediately notify a security supervisor of a fire alarm; (6) review the feasibility of discontinuing outside calling capabilities to telephones in areas frequented by inmates; and (7) review policies governing inmate movement into the prison compound.

Where should the blame be placed for the prison escape? How can prison officials intervene to prevent groups of prisoners from plotting escapes? What do you think?

Source: Adapted from Matt Curry and the Associated Press, "Union Boss Points Finger Back at Prison Administrators," January 12, 2001.

quests for visits by special clergy for Islam and other religions were refused by prison administration. Despite lawsuits by prisoners alleging civil rights violations and other problems, the courts were reluctant to interfere in the affairs of prison operations. In the hot summer months of 1971, several inmate leaders encouraged other inmates to demonstrate peacefully to protest these deplorable conditions. Officials attempted to break up such demonstrations by transferring inmate leaders to other prisons. But the demonstrations continued. Furthermore, several gangs of different ethnic and racial backgrounds pooled their resources and joined forces to protest what they regarded as mutually shared problems.

In early September, confrontations between inmates and correctional officers became more frequent and violent. On September 9, a general riot occurred in the breakfast hall of the facility, and several correctional officers were taken hostage. Several of the guard-hostages were beaten savagely by prisoners, and one officer died of his wounds. Prisoners attempted to call attention to their plight by demanding visits with media representatives, lawyers, and other outside observers. Negotiations progressed cautiously as the new commissioner of the Department of Correctional Services, Russell G. Oswald, attempted to meet inmate demands for prison improvements. Those inmates who had rioted also requested amnesty from prosecution, largely because of the officer death. State officials were not prepared to excuse inmates from this liability.

A poorly organized force of heavily armed state troopers and corrections officers stormed the prison, and within a few minutes, they had regained control of the facility. In the process, the other inmate and hostage deaths noted above occurred. Despite these deaths, the nation's attention was focused on Attica as well as on other similar prisons. Would other Atticas occur in the future if similar conditions existed in other prison settings? Many state prisons and correctional facilities implemented vast improvements in their physical plants and made other changes during the next few years to reduce the chances of prisoner rioting. Numerous investigations were conducted by Departments of Correction in various states during the 1970s. One result of these investigations was that prison administration, the parole concept, and prisons as rehabilitative institutions were widely criticized. It was during the 1970s that major changes occurred, not only in prison organization and administration, but in other areas of the criminal justice system as well. Extensive reforms in criminal processing, sentencing, and inmate treatment were instigated by every state jurisdiction.

Despite the improvements made by various departments of correction among states and the federal government, inmate rioting was not eliminated entirely. Riots in other state and federal prisons have occurred subsequently, some paralleling the terror of Attica. Not all of these riots have been triggered by poor prison conditions, bad food, and civil rights violations, however. Revenge against other inmates who were believed to be government informants and rats (those who squeal on others or implicate them in crimes in exchange for leniency for themselves) seemed to be largely responsible for the rioting in the New Mexico penitentiary. The Penitentiary of New Mexico in Santa Fe was overtaken by inmates in February 1980. Inmates formed death squads and systematically killed other prisoners suspected of being informants. One prisoner was beheaded, while others had their legs or arms cut off. Some were even charred beyond recognition with blowtorches. When the rioting was subdued, $80 million in damages to the prison had been sustained, 33 inmates were killed, and nearly 100 others required hospitalization.

In November 1987, the Federal Penitentiary in Atlanta and the federal detention center in Oakdale, Louisiana, were scenes of rioting by large numbers of Cuban inmates. Many Cuban exiles had entered the United States illegally to escape certain death at the hands of Fidel Castro because of their political opposition to his policies. The U.S. government took numerous Cuban refugees into custody. Over 2,400 of them were confined in large buildings on the grounds of the Atlanta penitentiary and the Oakdale facility. Rumors abounded among these Cuban exiles that they were going to be deported back to Cuba.

Desperate, fearful, and feeling that they had nothing to lose, Cuban refugees in Oakdale took 28 hostages, while 94 hostages were taken by Cubans in Atlanta.

Although these riots were less costly in terms of lives lost (one inmate was killed in early gunfire), buildings were set aflame and considerable federal property was destroyed. These riots were politically motivated because of the belief by Cuban exiles that they were going to be deported to Cuba. Over 2,400 inmates took part in the rioting. The rioting ended after eleven days and much destruction of government property, after the government agreed not to deport these Cuban refugees back to Cuba. This had been the sole issue. The prisoners contended that they would rather remain in the United States, even behind bars, rather than face Castro retaliation. The U.S. government did not agree to blanket amnesty for all Cuban refugees, however. But then-Attorney General Edwin Meese agreed to have each case reviewed on its own merits. If government investigations disclosed nothing more than petty crimes or clean prison records, Cuban exiles would not be deported (*Newsweek* 1987:38).

Rioting in U.S. prisons appears to be increasing, despite the newly implemented safeguards and policy changes made by prison administrators to minimize inmate concerns and complaints. Based on available information, there were 2,674 riots or disturbances in prisons in 2000 and 2,392 in 2001, involving 7,860 inmates. Some states, such as Tennessee, report larger numbers of disturbances because of its own defining method of noting disturbances (CEGA Services, Inc. 2002:6). There were 16 staff injuries in rioting in 2000 and 59 staff injuries in 2001.

During inmate rioting, staff assaults are commonplace. Jon Taylor reports, for instance, that while he was working in a maximum-security prison, he "survived the crucible of the maximum-security keeps." According to Taylor, "I have been threatened innumerable times, punched with fists, slashed with a razor, bashed with a pipe, and poked with a shiv by other inmates, not to mention being inadvertently shot by a tower guard. Altogether, there are a half dozen scars on my body, with an uncountable number upon my psyche" (Taylor 1996:1). Fortunately, there were no inmate or staff deaths due to rioting in U.S. prisons during 2000–2001 (CEGA Services, Inc. 2002:6).

The Maxi-Maxi Prison

For the baddest of the bad, there are prisons such as the Marion, Illinois, Federal Penitentiary. Although this facility is one of the newer federal penitentiaries—constructed in 1963 and is designed to house only 574 inmates—those incarcerated at Marion are considered the very worst prisoners in the system (Maghan 1999). Those sentenced to Marion are the most violence-prone, are inclined to escape whenever the opportunity arises, and are categorically dangerous. Marion is considered a **maxi-maxi prison,** with restrictions so severe and pervasive as to be unparalleled by any other prison in the United States (King 1999). It, too, was the scene of a major prison riot in October 1983. Two correctional officers were killed by prisoners in the Control Unit. When the riot was contained, Marion was subject to a general **lockdown,** where every prisoner was subject to solitary confinement and severe restrictions (Rosenblatt 1996). Maxi-maxi prisons represent about 5 percent of all U.S. penitentiaries for both the states and the federal government (Riveland 1999; U.S. Department of Justice Corrections Program Office 1999).

Thus, there is a wide range of prisons from those minimum-security, honor farm-type facilities to those close-custody, maxi-maxi penitentiaries like Marion. Depending upon the location of the facility, the composition of prisoners varies

Administration segregation unit,
North Dakota State Penitentiary.

greatly as well. In many prisons, gangs form according to particular racial or ethnic patterns. Membership in a gang can mean privileges for individual members, and likewise, nonmembership can expose prisoners to physical and sexual harassment or injury. In the Southwest, for example, where there are large numbers of Hispanic offenders, gangs comprised of different inmates from several ethnic backgrounds have formed within prisons to create rivalries that often lead to violence.

Less violence is associated with minimum-security facilities, although it is not entirely absent (LIS, Inc. 1997). This is due, in large part, to the fact that inmates are less dangerous and pose the least risk to the safety of correctional officers or other inmates. Each prison setting with its peculiar inmate profile means that wardens or superintendents will be presented with different kinds of problems to resolve (Halliman 2001). Few categorical statements about people management behind prison bars can be made that are applicable to all settings because of the diversity of prison culture (Evans 2001). However, some investigations of state and federal prison inmates throughout the United States suggest that a majority have been characterized as having alcohol or drug dependencies (White, Ackerman, and Caraveo 2001).

New Prison Construction: A Growing Medium-Security Trend.   A total of 24 new institutions were opened by 17 agencies in 2000, and 18,526 new beds were added as a result of this new construction (Camp and Camp 2002:87). About 3,086 were maximum-security; 5,693 were medium-security; and 1,990 were minimum-security (Camp and Camp 2002:87). If this trend in new prison construction continues, the dominant **prisoner classification** will be medium-security custody (Martin 2000). Furthermore, about 54 percent of all renovations and building additions of existing prison space was allocated to medium-security bed space (Camp and Camp 2002). This is interesting because 77 percent of all prison population growth since 1978 is attributable to nonviolent offenders who deserve to be housed in minimum-security custody levels (Irwin,

Schiraldi, and Ziedenberg 2000). However, U.S. prison systems typically operate on the questionable assumption that they are warehousing increasingly violent offenders every year (Maghan, 1999).

INMATE CLASSIFICATION SYSTEMS

Religious movements are credited with establishing early prisoner classification systems in the eighteenth century (Brown and Pratt 2000). The Walnut Street Jail in 1790 in Philadelphia attempted to segregate prisoners according to age, gender, and offense seriousness. Subsequent efforts were made by penal authorities to classify and separate inmates according to various criteria in many state and federal prison facilities. Adequate classification schemes for prisoners have yet to be devised (Walters 2001). Classification schemes are based largely on psychological, behavioral, and sociodemographic criteria. The use of psychological characteristics as predictors of risk or dangerousness and subsequent custody assignments for prisoners was stimulated by research during the period 1910 to 1920 (Roberts 1997). One risk factor that seems influential on institutional conduct is self-control and one's ability to control emotional outbursts. Some scales, such as the Five Factor Model of Personality, purportedly measure self-control and assist in more appropriate institutional placements (O'Gorman and Baxter 2002). This particular inventory utilizes the method of self-report, where inmates might disclose their intent to engage in particular types of deviant, and possibly violent, conduct.

No single scheme for classifying offenders is foolproof, although several instruments have used more frequently than others for inmate classification and placement. The **Megargee Inmate Typology** presumes to measure inmate adjustment to prison life (Bohn, Carbonell, and Megargee 1995). Several items were selected from the Minnesota Multiphasic Personality Inventory (MMPI), a psychological assessment device, to define ten prisoner types and to predict an inmate's inclination to violate prison rules or act aggressively against others. Basically a psychological tool, the Megargee Inmate Typology has been adopted by various state prison systems for purposes of classifying prisoners into different custody levels. The predictive utility of this instrument is questionable, however. One problem Megargee himself detected was that prisoner classification types based on his index scores change drastically during a one-year period. For some observers, this finding has caused serious questions about the reliability of Megargee's scale. For other observers, however, inmate score changes on Megargee's scale indicate behavioral change, possibly improvement. Thus, reclassifications are conducted of most prison inmates at regular intervals to chart their behavioral progress.

One thing is certain about risk instruments and inmate classifications resulting from applications of these instruments: How prison inmates are initially classified and housed will directly influence their parole chances (McCarthy 2001). Inmates classified as maximum security may not deserve this classification, since it means that the inmate is considered dangerous. Inmate opportunities for personal development and rehabilitation are limited in these classifications. However, inmates who are classified as minimum security have a wide variety of prison benefits and programs. They are neither supervised as closely nor considered dangerous. When minimum security inmates face parole boards, their custody levels are assets. When maximum security inmates face parole boards, their classification is a liability.

All prisons in the United States have classifications that differentiate between prisoners and cause them to be placed under various levels of custody or security. One of the main purposes for the initial inmate classification in the United States and other countries is to identifying those likely to engage in assaultive or aggressive disciplinary infractions (Hannah-Moffat and Shaw 2001; Hilton and Simmons 2001). Prisoners are eventually channeled into one of several fixed custody levels known as (1) minimum, (2) medium, and (3) maximum security.

Minimum-Security Classification

Minimum-security prisons are facilities designed to house low-risk, nonviolent first offenders. These institutions are also established to accommodate those serving short-term sentences. Sometimes, minimum-security institutions function as intermediate housing for those prisoners leaving more heavily monitored facilities on their way toward parole or eventual freedom. Minimum-security housing is often of a dormitory-like quality, with grounds and physical plant features resembling a university campus rather than a prison. Those assigned to minimum-security facilities are trusted to comply with whatever rules are in force.

Administrators place greater trust in inmates in minimum-security institutions, and these sites are believed to be most likely to promote greater self-confidence and self-esteem among prisoners. The rehabilitative value of minimum-security inmates is high. Also, family visits are less restricted. The emphasis of minimum-security classification is definitely upon prisoner reintegration into society.

Medium-Security and Maximum Security Classification

Fifty percent of all state and federal prisons in the United States are medium- and minimum-security institutions designed to accommodate medium- and minimum-security inmates (Camp and Camp 2002). About 15 percent of all U.S. prisons are exclusively maximum-security institutions. Ordinarily, those sentenced to serve time in maximum-security facilities are considered among the most dangerous, high-risk offenders. Maximum-security prisons are characterized by many stringent rules and restrictions, and inmates are isolated from one another for long periods in single-cell accommodations. Closed-circuit television monitors often permit correctional officers to observe prisoners in their cells or in work areas that are limited. Visitation privileges are minimal. Most often, no efforts are made by officials to rehabilitate inmates.

Maxi-Maxi, Super-Max, and Admin Max Classification

Only the most dangerous prisoners are held in maxi-maxi or super-max custody levels. These levels have the fewest privileges and limit physical exercise to one-half hour per day in many prisons. If an inmate is assigned to one of these types of custody, it is usually because there is a strong likelihood that the inmate will endanger others if placed in the general inmate population. In some instances, those assigned admin max custody may be placed there for their own safety (Motiuk and Blanchette 2001). The use of close custody is intended for maximum supervision of the inmate and the control of his or her behavior. Both male and female inmates are subject to confinement in admin max facilities if their prior conduct warrants. Admin max facilities are not unique to U.S. prisons. Other countries, such as Canada, use admin max for administratively segregating both male and female offenders from the general population (Martel 2001).

A good example of a supermax prison is the Wisconsin Supermax Correctional Institution, which houses up to 500 inmates and was opened in 1999 (Berge, Geiger, and Whitney 2001:105). This state-of-the-art facility maximizes technology to the fullest degree. It was designed to provide the highest level of security and the most controlled environment for the most troublesome inmates in the Wisconsin prison system. There are five 100-cell housing units, each divided into groups of 25 cells called ranges. The ranges are configured around a local control station. One unit is high security, one is transitional, and the other three are general security. An electrified perimeter fence surrounds the prison. This is the first line of defense against threats from the outside and the last line of defense for threats from inside the prison. The 12-foot high razor-wire fence is electrified for both stun and lethal modes. Cameras mounted atop each fence scan the entire perimeter. The security system includes integration of the perimeter fence, door control, door monitoring, multiple intercom systems, video surveillance, motion detection, and exterior lighting.

Entry into any of the five units is through biometric identification, which scans all inmates, staff, visitors, and emergency personnel. The biometric system includes hand-scanning, digital photography, and personal identification numbers in a secure database. Everyone must have his or her identity confirmed before admission to the facility is granted. Mechanical, plumbing, smoke control, structural systems, and architectural elements are interrelated to enhance safety and security. A central control feature monitors inmate security and staff safety. Redundant security systems provide sequential backups in the event of power failures because of storms. A hard-wired, wall-mounted redundant graphic annunciator or control panel at central control gives staff an at-a-glance picture of activity within the entire facility. Video-taped activity is recorded 24 hours a day, including inside inmate cells. None of the cells have keys. Everything is electronically controlled. All mechanical systems for the facility are located in a secure, external area where service technicians can perform repairs on the system if needed. Furthermore, the facility has an up-to-date medical facility with specially monitored cells. Thus, inmates with physical ailments can be treated without having to be moved to another facility. Any inmate movement from one part of the facility to another involves full body restraints.

The supermax facility was designed as a last resort for disruptive inmates in other Wisconsin prisons. It is used by Wisconsin corrections authorities strictly as a behavioral management tool and is not a facility where most inmates would serve their entire sentences. Inmates who enter the supermax facility are evaluated and placed at the highest level of security. They may move downward to lower security levels by exhibiting good conduct. Lower custody levels within the facility permit contact with other inmates. All inmate interaction is videotaped. Eventually, inmates may be released back into their general prison populations (Berge, Geiger, and Whitney 2001:107–108).

Early Christian Reforms and Prison Classification Systems

Christian reform movements are credited with establishing early prisoner classification systems in the eighteenth century (Roberts 1997). As we have seen, the Walnut Street Jail in 1790 in Philadelphia attempted to segregate prisoners according to age, gender, and offense seriousness. Subsequent efforts were made by penal authorities to classify and separate inmates according to various criteria in many state and federal prison facilities. One of the early pioneers in correctional reforms was Maurice Sigler, a U.S. Bureau of Prisons warden and former member of the

U.S. Parole Board. Because of his efforts, significant changes were made in both the federal system and states such as Nebraska, which resulted in separate divisions for mental health facilities and corrections, separate adult and juvenile facilities, women's reformatories, and boys' and girls' training schools (Rion 2001).

Classification schemes are based largely on psychological, behavioral, and sociodemographic criteria. The use of psychological characteristics as predictors of risk or dangerousness and subsequent custody assignments for prisoners was stimulated by research during the period 1910–1920 (American Correctional Association 1983:196). Behavioral scientists, especially psychologists and psychiatrists, were becoming increasingly involved in devising classificatory schemes for prisoners, especially those with mental problems. Eventually, devices were created based on a wider variety of personal and social criteria (Pinard and Pagani 2001). One major problem area for both prison and jail officials continues to be predicting with some degree of accuracy those inmates most likely to injure themselves or commit suicide. Efforts to typify suicides in county jails, for instance, have proved difficult. Because most jail suicides or suicide attempts occur among inmates without prior histories of mental illness and where little is known about them in advance, psychological profiles and screenings often fail to disclose who will attempt suicides (Winter 2000:8,21).

Inmate misconduct is highly correlated with being young, black, male, having a relatively high number of prior convictions, having been unemployed prior to incarceration, and having been imprisoned for a long period. But descriptions of those who engage in prison misconduct are difficult to apply in screening stages to decide the level of custody inmates should be assigned. Should all young, unemployed, black males with prior records and long sentences be placed in a high level of custody? Classifications according to these criteria would quickly be challenged as racist and discriminatory, which they would be.

The controversy over the development and use of inmate classification devices is heightened by those researchers reporting favorable outcomes when such devices are used on selected inmate populations. For example, a study was conducted of 57 general population inmates and 64 mental health unit inmates at the U.S. Medical Center for Federal Prisoners in Springfield, Missouri (Bohn, Carbonell, and Megargee 1995). The classification instrument used by the researchers was able to differentiate successfully between these two inmate samples. Generally, Bohn, Carbonell and Megargee found that psychological screenings of new admissions are more useful than attempting to distinguish between those inmates already admitted to the mental health unit. Other experiments with inmates have yielded results consistent with those of Bohn, Carbonell, and Megargee (Fazel and Danesh 2002).

RISK ASSESSMENT AND INSTITUTIONAL PLACEMENT

What Are Dangerousness and Risk?

Dangerousness and risk refer essentially to the same phenomenon: the propensities to cause harm to others or oneself. Risk (or dangerousness) instruments are screening devices intended to distinguish between different types of offenders for purposes of determining initial institutional classification, security placement and inmate management, early release eligibility, and the level of supervision required under conditions of probation or parole. Most state jurisdictions and the federal government refer to these measures as risk assessment instruments rather than dangerousness instruments (Champion 1994). There is considerable variance among states regarding the format and content of such measures (Douglas, Hart, and Kropp 2001).

Sentencing and parole decisions are based on multiple factors, including the projected risk of the offender and the danger posed to citizens if probation or parole is granted. For example, Leslie Van Houten, a convicted murderer in the deaths of actress Sharon Tate and others in the late 1960s and a former member of the Charles Manson family, has been eligible for parole in California for several decades. However, the parole board has consistently denied her request for parole on the basis of her supposed risk to the public if released. It is likely in Van Houten's case, however, that there is a hidden agenda that explains her parole denials. Her conviction offenses and how they were committed were so heinous that it is unlikely she will ever be paroled, despite the likelihood that she probably will never reoffend if released. Persistent media coverage of her parole hearings greatly increases the visibility of parole board members who do not wish to be labeled as the ones who freed one of Charles Manson's followers, regardless of her present rehabilitation, reformation, and other favorable circumstances. Van Houten is not alone. Parole-eligible and low-risk inmates in other states, such as Louisiana, are routinely denied parole, in some cases because the governors of those states have promised the victims' families that these offenders will never be paroled if they have anything to say about it. It is unfortunate and decidedly discriminatory that these and other inmates are consistently denied parole while other, more heinous criminals are freed by the same parole boards every year. However, few if any accountability measures are in place to hold parole boards accountable for these inconsistent and discriminatory actions, regardless of their transparency.

Generally, risk or dangerousness predictions are based on instruments devised by social researchers. Each instrument is methodologically flawed, and no instrument yet devised can be used with absolute confidence when sentencing offenders or determining their eligibility for early release (Weiss 2000). However, it is well known that long-term predictions of future dangerousness are used throughout the criminal justice process in investigation, pretrial detention, bail, sentencing, prison administration, and early release decision making.

In recent years, a different approach has been taken by authorities in some jurisdictions, such as Canada, for determining one's suitability for parole. In these instances, prospective parolees themselves are asked to complete a self-report questionnaire that is intended to determine their own success forecasts. In short, prospective parolees are asked to rate how they would likely succeed if granted early release by a parole board. A Self-Appraisal Questionnaire (SAQ) was administered to 68 federally sentenced Canadian male offenders prior to their early release into their communities (Loza and Loza 2001). Followup data were collected over a two-year period for these offenders. Outcome criteria measures were general recidivism, violent recidivism, and any other failure, such as negative parole reports, violation of parole conditions, incurring new charges, or a new conviction. Interestingly, prospective parolees' estimates of their own success chances were rated as effective or more effective than the standardized risk assessment measures that are normally administered. The results of this research suggest that prospective parolees themselves might be good predictors of their future behaviors if paroled.

Another self-report inventory used by corrections professionals to evaluate offenders is the Antecedents to Crime Inventory or ACI. The ACI assists clinicians in identifying individuals' antecedents to offending. A self-report questionnaire is administered to various offenders who disclose facts about themselves and what they believe caused them to engage in criminality. Subsequently, their results are used to determine individual treatment needs and may become a key part of a multimethod criminogenic need assessment. The ACI has revealed significant differences between recidivists and successful releasees in recent years. Although the validity and reliability of the ACI have not been fully investigated, uses of the ACI thus far suggest that future applications in treatment planning, sensitivity to treatment changes, and risk-management strategies will determine the usefulness of this instrument (Serin and Mailloux 2001).

Furthermore, family members of prospective parolees are becoming increasingly involved in collaborative efforts to ensure public safety and heightened offender accountability. Parole boards are involving family members to a greater degree as an important medium for managing an offender's risk to the community (Silverstein 2001).

Generally, risk assessment measures are used for the purpose of determining probabilities that inmates, probationers, or parolees will pose a risk or a danger to themselves or to others (Champion 1994). These probabilities are subsequently used for placement, program, and security decision making. Needs measures and instruments enable corrections personnel and administrative staffs to highlight client weaknesses or problems that may have led to their convictions or difficulties initially. Once problem areas have been targeted, specific services or treatments might be scheduled and provided (Maruna 2001). For instance, risk/needs indices assist officials in determining needs and proper remedies in the areas of substance abuse, marital/family problems, unemployment, and association/socialization (Dell and Boe 2000).

Risk and needs instruments were increasingly used during the 1960s. Some risk measures were used with juvenile offenders. Subsequently, numerous behavioral and psychological instruments were devised and used for the purpose of assessing client risk or inmate dangerousness. The Minnesota Multiphasic Personality Inventory (MMPI), consisting of 550 true-false items, was originally used in departments of corrections for personality assessments. This instrument is still applied in many correctional settings by researchers, such as Edwin Megargee. These researchers have extracted certain items from the MMPI for use as predictors of inmate violence and adjustment. Classifications such as Megargee's are often designated as MMPI-based assessments or classifications. Subsequent applications have extended into a variety of criminal categories, such as sex offenders, and their likelihood for readjustment and community reintegration (Geer et al. 2001). Applications of scales such as Megargee's have received mixed results and evaluations. Some studies show that these scales do not predict one's future behavior very well (Winters-Brooke and Hayes 2001).

Much of the early work with risk instruments involved juvenile delinquents. For instance, Quay devised a relatively simple typology of delinquent behavior, classifying delinquents into four categories: Undersocialized Aggression, Socialized Aggression, Attention Deficit, and Anxiety-Withdrawal-Dysphoria (Quay and Parsons 1971). Juveniles would complete a self-administered questionnaire and their personality scores would be quickly tabulated. Depending upon how certain juveniles were classified, a variety of treatments would be administered to help them. Later, Quay created **AIMS,** or the **Adult Internal Management System** (Quay 1984). Quay also used a self-administered inventory, the Correctional Adjustment Checklist and the Correctional Adjustment Life History (Sechrest 1987:302–303). His adult typology consisted of five types of inmates: Aggressive Psychopathic, Manipulative, Situational, Inadequate-Dependent, and Neurotic-Anxious.

An **I-level classification** system exists, which refers to the **Interpersonal Maturity Level Classification System.** I-level classification is based on a combination of developmental and psychoanalytic theories and is administered by psychologists or psychiatrists in lengthy clinical interviews (Phillips and Roberts 2001). Clients are classified as being at particular I-levels, such as I-1, I-2, and so on, up to I-7. Each I-level is a developmental stage reflecting one's ability to cope with complex personal and interpersonal problems. The higher the I-level, the better adjusted the client, according to its proponents. In recent years, several jurisdictions have devised special risk assessment devices for females (Dell and Boe 2000).

State corrections departments began to create and apply risk assessment schemes in the mid-1980s. For example, Arizona created its first Offender Classification System manual in 1986 (Arizona Department of Corrections 1991). Most jurisdictions are currently revising or have recently revised their risk and needs instruments (Champion 1994). An example of a classification instrument is shown in Figure 7.1, the Alaska Classification Form for Sentenced Prisoners.

Besides containing routine information about prisoners and their identifying numbers, ages, and types of cases, this form also includes whether there are any **detainer warrants** for the named prisoner. A detainer warrant is issued by another state and indicates that the named inmate is wanted, usually for other criminal charges. Thus, it is important for prison officials to know whether a given prisoner is wanted by one or more states elsewhere. Wanted prisoners do not especially want to be extradited to other jurisdictions following their incarceration in an Alaska prison. Therefore, these prisoners are considered greater escape risks than inmates who do not have detainer warrants against them.

The Alaska Classification Form for Sentenced Prisoners also measures the severity of the conviction offense; the time to a firm release date or parole; numbers and types of prior convictions; history of violent behavior; present security level; involvement with drugs or alcohol; record of disciplinary infractions while confined; responsibility demonstrated by the inmate; and family/community, which is an indication of whether there is a familial or community support system for the inmate when paroled. Many states have classification instruments such as the one used by Alaska. Among other things, the Alaska Classification Form enables prison officials to determine which custody level (e.g., minimum-, medium-, or maximum-security custody) is most appropriate for particular inmates. Officials may use the instrument to increase or decrease one's current custody level. These assessments are conducted regularly, such as every six months or year. **Overrides** are options available to prison officials who may agree or disagree with an inmate's score and potential placement in one custody level or another. Notice in Figure 7.1 the amount of detail involved in Institution Action. Recommendations for placement are made, and the superintendent approves or disapproves of the action. The inmate signs and dates the form, indicating he or she has read the document and is aware of the next review date.

Classification and Its Functions

There are several important functions served by classification instruments. These include:

1. Classification systems enable authorities to make decisions about appropriate offender program placements.

STATE OF ALASKA   **DEPARTMENT OF CORRECTIONS**

Classification Form for Sentenced Prisoners

(1) _____   (2) _____
    Institution   Prisoner Name
(3) _____   (4) _____
    Date   Date of Birth
(6) _____   (6) _____
    Type of Case: Regular or Exception   OBSCIS Number

SECTION A   SECURITY SCORING

---

1. Type of Detainer:
   0 = None   3 = Class C Felony   7 = Unclassified or Class A Felony   [ ] 1
   1 = Misdemeanor   5 = Class B Felony
2. Severity of Current Offense:
   1 = Misdemeanor   3 = Class C Felony   7 = Unclassified or Class A Felony   [ ] 2
                     5 = Class B Felony
3. Time to Firm Release Date:
   0 = 0–12 months   3 = 60–83 months
   1 = 13–59 months 5 = 84 + months   _____   [ ] 3
                                            Firm Release Date
4. Type of Prior Convictions:
   0 = None   1 = Misdemeanor   3 = Felony   [ ] 4
5. History of Escapes or Attempted Escapes:

	None	+15 Years	10–15 Years	5–10 Years	−5 Years	
Minor	0	1	1	2	3	
Serious	0	4	5	6	7	[ ] 5

6. History of Violent Behavior:

	None	+15 Years	10–15 Years	5–10 Years	−5 Years	
Minor	0	1	1	2	3	
Serious	0	4	5	6	7	[ ] 6

7. SECURITY TOTAL   [ ]
8. Security Level:
   Minimum = 0–6 points   Medium = 7–13 points   Maximum = 14–36 points

---

SECTION B   CUSTODY SCORING

---

1. Percent of Time Served:
   3 = 0 thru 25%   5 = 76 thru 90%
   4 = 26 thru 75%   6 = 91 plus %   [ ]
2. Involvement with Drugs and/or Alcohol:
   2 = Current   3 = Past   4 = Never   [ ]
3. Mental/Psychological Stability:
   2 = Unfavorable   4 = No referral or favorable   [ ]
4. Type Most Serious Disciplinary Report:
   1 = Major   3 = Low Moderate   5 = None
   2 = High Moderate 4 = Minor   [ ]
5. Frequency of Disciplinary Reports:
   0 = 5 + Reports   2 = 1 Report
   1 = 2 − 4 Reports 3 = None   [ ]
6. Responsibility Prisoner has Demonstrated:
   0 = Poor   2 = Average   4 = Good   [ ]

FIGURE 7.1   Alaska Department of Corrections Classification Form for Sentenced Prisoners.
Source: Alaska Department of Corrections (2003).

7. Family/Community:
   3 = None or Minimal   4 = Average or Good   [   ]
8. CUSTODY TOTAL: [   ]
9. Custody Change Scale:

Prisoner's Present Security Level	Consider Custody Increase if Points	Continue Present Custody if Points	Consider Custody Decrease if Points
Minimum	11–19 Points	20–22 Points	23–30 Points
Medium	11–19 Points	20–24 Points	25–30 Points
Maximum	11–19 Points	20–27 Points	28–30 Points

10: _____   _____

    PRESENT CUSTODY   RECOMMENDED CUSTODY

11. Administrative/Program Considerations:
    1. Release Plans   4. Education   7. Overcrowding
    2. Medical   5. Special Treatment   8. Judicial Recommendation
    3. Psychiatric   6. Ethnic/Cultural Consideration   9. Residence

12. Explanation:
_____

SECTION C   INSTITUTION ACTION
_____

1. Recommendation/Justification _____
_____

2. Recommendation based on: _____ Points Total   _____ Management Override
3. Community Custody Provisions (if applicable): _____
_____
_____

4. Date of Next Review: _____

5. Chair Person: _____
   Member: _____
   Member: _____

6. Superintendent's Action (if applicable): _____ Approve _____ Disapprove

   Comments: _____
_____
_____

COPY RECEIVED

_____   _____
PRISONER SIGNATURE   DATE

Notice to Sentenced Prisoners:

(1) The sentenced prisoner designation is without administrative appeal.
(2) Classification Committee action not referred to nor modified by the Superintendent may be appealed only to the Superintendent, and no higher.
(3) Classification Committee action referred to or modified by the Superintendent, except for transfer, may be appealed to the Regional Director in accordance with 760.01, Appeal Procedures.
(4) Classification Committee action regarding transfer may be appealed directly to the Deputy Commissioner for Operations in accordance with 760.01, Appeal Procedures.
(5) Forms to facilitate an appeal will be provided by institutional staff upon request by the prisoner.
(6) An appeal must be routed through the institutional staff member designated for the purpose of receiving and forwarding classification appeals.
(7) Any classification action may be commenced pending an appeal, except a transfer to an out-of-state facility.

2. Classification systems help to identify one's needs and the provision of effective services in specialized treatment programs.

3. Classification assists in determining one's custody level if confined in either prisons or jails.

4. Classification helps to adjust one's custody level during confinement, considering behavioral improvement and evidence of rehabilitation.

5. While confined, inmates may be targeted for particular services and/or programs to meet their needs.

6. Classification may be used for offender management and deterrence relative to program or prison rules and requirements.

7. Classification schemes are useful for policy decision making and administrative planning relevant for jail and prison construction, the nature and number of facilities required, and the types of services to be made available within such facilities.

8. Classification systems enable parole boards to make better early-release decisions about eligible offenders.

9. Community corrections agencies can utilize classification schemes to determine those parolees who qualify for participation and those who don't qualify.

10. Classification systems enable assessments of risk and dangerousness to be made generally in anticipation of the type of supervision best-suited for particular offenders.

11. Classification schemes assist in decision making relevant for community crime control, the nature of penalties to be imposed, and the determination of punishment.

12. Classification may enable authorities to determine whether selective incapacitation is desirable for particular offenders or offender groupings.

Incarcerative Decisions: Jail or Prison?

Should offenders be placed on probation or in jail or prison? Probation officers sometimes make these recommendations in their PSI reports. The court considers this recommendation but is not bound by it. A plea agreement may stipulate a particular sentence, and in most instances, judges approve of these stipulated sentences. The just deserts philosophy is a dominant theme in U.S. corrections today, and judges appear to be influenced by this philosophy as reflected in the sentences they impose. Generally, their interest is in imposing sentences on offenders that are equated with the seriousness of the conviction offense. However, some evidence suggests that they are influenced by other factors as well (Simourd and Hoge 2000).

Laws in most states permit pretrial detention of defendants who are considered dangerous. Judges are not prevented from using risk measures as one of several sentencing criteria. Risk assessment information is treated together with the contents of PSI reports. But some opposition exists concerning risk assessments in sentencing decisions, because it is difficult if not impossible to forecast a person's dangerousness in any absolute sense (Hollin 2001). Problems of a measure's validity, or the extent to which the measure actually measures what it purports to measure, and reliability, the consistency of the measure from one application the next, always exist and must be considered whenever risk instrumentation is used for early-release decisions or community placements (Zimmerman, Martin, and Rogosky 2001).

Offenders who are considered a risk to themselves or others also have one or more needs. Most jurisdictions have developed instruments to assess one's needs. A **needs assessment device** is an instrument that measures an offender's personal/social skills; health, well-being, and emotional stability; educational level and vocational strengths and weaknesses; alcohol/drug dependencies; mental ability; and other relevant life factors and highlights those areas for which services are available and could or should be provided. A needs assessment instrument devised by the Alaska Department of Corrections is shown in Figure 7.2. If some offenders are illiterate, they may be placed, either voluntarily or involuntarily, into an educational program at some level, depending upon the amount of remedial work deemed necessary. Psychologically disturbed or mentally ill offenders may require some type of counseling or therapy. Some offenders may require particular medications for illnesses or other maladies.

Risk and need assessments may be combined in a more lengthy instrument and labeled simply as risk-needs assessments. The Alaska Need Assessment Survey solicits information about an inmate's health, intellectual ability, behavioral/emotional problems, alcohol and/or drug abuse, educational level, vocational status, and the nature of his or her skills. On the basis of this survey, correctional officials can plan more effectively and place particular inmates into prison programs that may assist them in improving their educational or vocational skills. Appropriate group or individual counseling or therapy may be provided, if the survey shows a particular need (e.g., alcohol or drug dependency) (Simpson 2002).

However, virtually every risk or needs instrument is inherently flawed. More than a few researchers are skeptical about their application in corrections and the types of decisions they encourage officials to make concerning particular prisoners. While classifications of offenders result in separate categorizations destined to receive certain treatments and services, considerable variation exists among individual offenders within each category. Therefore, there are frequent mismatches between classification systems and the treatment programs prescribed (Shine 2001). For example, checking one category or another in a given need area can make considerable difference in the lives of offenders who are subsequently placed or misplaced in particular remedial, educational, vocational, or therapeutic programs. Scales such as the Alaska Needs Assessment Survey may result in offender/treatment program mismatches and treatment ineffectiveness.

Types of Risk Assessment Instruments

There are three different kinds of risk prediction: (1) amnestic prediction, (2) actuarial prediction, and (3) clinical prediction (Morris and Miller 1985:13–14).

Anamnestic Prediction.   **Anamnestic prediction** is a forecast of offender future behavior based upon one's past circumstances. If the past circumstances include hanging out with a gang, being a part of a dysfunctional family, being addicted to drugs and/or alcohol, and doing poorly in school and at work, then a comparison is made with present circumstances. If the present (and projected) circumstances are different, then perhaps the offender will behave in law-abiding ways. If the

STATE OF ALASKA   **NEEDS ASSESSMENT SURVEY**   **DEPARTMENT OF CORRECTIONS**

Prisoner Name: _____   Institution: _____   Date: _____

Staff member making assessment: _____; Select best description and enter number at right:

A. HEALTH:

| 1. Sound physical health, ability, able to function independently. | 2. Handicap or illness which interferes with functioning on a recurring basis. | 3. Serious handicap or chronic illness, needs frequent medical care. | _____ |

B. INTELLECTUAL ABILITY:

| 1. Normal intellectual ability, able to function independently. | 2. Mild retardation, some need for assistance. | 3. Moderate retardation, independent functioning severely limited. | _____ |

C. BEHAVIORAL/EMOTIONAL PROBLEMS:

| 1. Exhibits appropriate emotional responses. | 2. Symptoms limit adequate functioning, requires counseling, may require medication. | 3. Symptoms prohibit adequate functioning, requires significant intervention; may require medication or separate housing. | _____ |

NOTE: If number 2, or 3, is most appropriate for this prisoner for A, B, or C. above, obtain a Medical/Psychiatric Records Extract (form 20-807.060) as supplement to this form.

D. ALCOHOL ABUSE:

| 1. No alcohol problem. | 2. Occasional abuse, some disruption of functioning. | 3. Frequent abuse, serious disruption, needs treatment. | _____ |

E. DRUG ABUSE:

| 1. No drug problem. | 2. Occasional abuse, some disruption of functioning. | 3. Frequent abuse, serious disruption, needs treatment. | _____ |

F. EDUCATIONAL STATUS:

| 1. Has high school diploma or GED. | 2. Some deficits, but potential for high school diploma or GED. | 3. Major deficits in and/or reading, needs remedial programs. | _____ |

G. VOCATIONAL STATUS:

| 1. Has sufficient skills to obtain and hold satisfactory employment. | 2. Minimal skill level, needs enhancement. | 3. Virtually unemployable, needs training | _____ |

List Skills: List Skills: List possible skills to acquire:

_____   _____   _____
_____   _____   _____
_____   _____   _____
_____   _____   _____

PROGRAM RECOMMENDATION

1. Housing: _____

2. Work assignment: _____

3. Program assignments: _____

4. Other: _____

FIGURE 7.2   Alaska Needs Assessment Survey.
Source: Alaska Department of Corrections (2003).

circumstances are the same, then the prediction is that the offender will continue to recidivate. For example, a parole-eligible inmate may tell the parole board that he has a new job waiting for him in a town 100 miles from where he was originally arrested. He no longer corresponds or contacts the gang he was a part of when he was convicted. He no longer is addicted to drugs or alcohol, and he has earned a GED. He has taken several self-improvement courses while in prison and has undergone extensive counseling. The parole board will regard this inmate favorably and probably recommend his early release. This is because his circumstances in the future are different from his circumstances in the past. By the same token, another parole-eligible inmate may say that he resents teachers, hates education, has no job, doesn't know what he plans to do, still corresponds with his friends and gang members, and will probably go back to using drugs and alcohol. Further, he rejects counseling of any kind and thinks psychiatrists and counselors are stupid. It is unlikely that his present (and future) circumstances are going to be much different from his past circumstances. His parole will probably be denied.

Actuarial Prediction.   **Actuarial prediction** is based on the characteristics of a segment of offenders who reoffend (Hilton and Simmons 2001). If we study the characteristics of a large sample of recidivists who are returned to prison, for example, we may find that they are young, black, uneducated, lacking in vocational skills and training, and coming from dysfunctional families. Therefore, when parole boards or judges see new probation- or parole-eligible offenders come before them who are young, black, uneducated, lacking in vocational skills and training, and coming from dysfunctional families, the tendency is for judges and parole boards to respectively place offenders in prisons or jails or deny their early release. Studies of failures or those offenders who recidivate contain descriptions of aggregate characteristics of persons who have already failed. Theoretically, others in the future with similar characteristics are deemed more likely to reoffend than those who do not match these aggregate characteristics. However, it seems that program failures often resemble closely those who succeed as well (Silver and Miller 2002). But corrections departments focus more on failures rather than successes when considering persons for parole. Judges are inclined to decide similarly about whether to grant probation or impose an incarcerative sentence.

Clinical Prediction.   **Clinical prediction** is based on the professional training and expertise of those who work directly with offenders. Based upon extensive diagnostic examinations, the belief is that the offender will behave in a certain way. The subjectivity inherent in clinical prediction is apparent. The skills of the assessor are critical. However, such prediction is more expensive, since each clinical prediction is individualized. Both anamnestic and actuarial prediction respectively utilize situational factors and general characteristics of offenders in forecasting their future risk.

The highest degrees of validity are associated with actuarial and anamnestic predictions (for instance, those currently used by parole boards), and these types of prediction are considered more reliable than clinical prediction. Clinical prediction is more of an art and depends upon one's experience, training, and association with clients. Looking at all three types of prediction, however, we can say that no prediction method is more or less valid or reliable than the others. Further, instrument complexity doesn't seem to make much of a difference in the reliability and validity of predictions. Simple instruments seem to have about the same predictive utility compared with more complex instruments. Few studies, if any, have shown conclusively that more complex instruments are better. We may think that greater complexity should be equated with greater predictive accuracy, but comparisons of the predictive power of more complex instruments compared with simple ones are categorically disappointing. There are various limitations associated with risk prediction instruments. For instance, Morris and Miller (1985:35–37) indicate three guiding principles for parole boards to consider when making early release decisions:

1. Punishment should not be imposed, nor the term of punishment extended, by virtue of a prediction of dangerousness, beyond what would be justified as a deserved punishment independently of that prediction.

2. Provided this limitation is respected, predictions of dangerousness may properly influence sentencing decisions and other decisions under criminal law.

3. The base expectancy rate of violence for the criminal predicted as dangerous must be shown by reliable evidence to be substantially higher than the base expectancy rate of another criminal with a closely similar criminal record and convicted of a closely similar crime but not predicted as unusually dangerous, before the greater dangerousness of the former may be relied on to intensify or extend his or her punishment.

False Positives and False Negatives

It is impossible and simply not feasible to incarcerate all convicted criminals. Further, not all offenders need to be incarcerated in order to suffer punishment. Therefore, both judges and parole boards exert considerable influence over which offenders will be incarcerated and which ones will be conditionally released, either on probation or parole. However, poor decisions are often made by judges and parole boards, where some offenders are released into the community and are not considered dangerous. But some of these persons labeled as nondangerous turn out to be dangerous anyway, with some offenders committing very serious new offenses, such as rape, robbery, and murder. Also, some offenders are incarcerated by judges or are denied parole by parole boards because of the mistaken belief that these particular offenders have a strong likelihood of committing new and serious offenses if they are freed into their communities. However, some of these offenders who have been erroneously labeled as dangerous will never commit new crimes if freed. These two scenarios, therefore, describe a great correctional dilemma. Who should we lock up and who should we release? What criteria should be used in making these important decisions?

False Positives.   **False positives** are offenders who are believed to be dangerous or more likely to pose a risk to others; however, these offenders will never reoffend (Burt et al. 2000). False positives are unfairly penalized. Often they are considered dangerous because they attained a score on a risk instrument that caused officials to believe that they posed a risk to others. However, the fallibility of prediction tools is such that considerable overprediction occurs. A man who kills his wife in the heat of passion, for example, might never kill again. Circumstances associated with the murder might be that the man, a law-abiding religious person with no prior criminal record, came home unexpectedly one night and found his wife in bed with another man. The outrage and indignation prompted the husband to grab a nearby handgun and kill his wife in the heat of anger. This may be the only time in the man's life where such a crime will ever be committed. If this man were subsequently released, he might never commit another murder. This doesn't mean that we are excusing the murder of the man's wife; rather, circumstances were such that it is unlikely that the man will ever be confronted by them again.

Yet, false positives rightly object to their extra punishment, because of some score they have received on a risk instrument or from a clinical diagnosis. We are penalizing these persons for crimes they have not yet committed. Their past crimes are often easily explained, but their risk scores may tell a tale quite different from any future misconduct on their part (Piquero and Mazerolle 2001).

False Negatives.   **False negatives** are persons predicted not to be dangerous but are dangerous anyway. We are most fearful of false negatives. These are persons with low risk or dangerousness scores, persons the correctional system trusts. Again, the obvious fallibility of prediction measures lures us into making the wrong decisions for the right reasons. After all, these persons received low risk scores on these risk assessment instruments. How much trust should we have in this instrumentation?

When false negatives are placed on probation or parole, and when they commit especially heinous acts, they attract media attention. In Seattle, Washington, a man was serving time for raping a woman. At his sentencing hearing, he vowed that when freed, he would hunt down the woman and kill her for testifying against him. The woman moved to Oregon several years later. She continued to rebuild her life and acquire new friends. The man was subsequently released on parole by Washington after serving six years of his sentence. He easily located the woman out of state and murdered both her and her female companion one afternoon, thus fulfilling his earlier promise. The Washington Parole Board was shaken by this turn of events. The risk assessment tools they used indicated the man was no longer a danger or risk to others. The instrument said he would not reoffend. Even strong, supportive testimony in his behalf from friends and family was such that the parole board was willing to parole him. But the tragic consequences, the double murder, was mute testimony to the parole board error in his case. In recent years, evidence suggests that risk assessment factors have greater importance where there are major mental disorders prevalent among certain offender groups (Grann, Belfrage, and Tengstrom 2000). But mental disorders are difficult to detect and diagnose.

Risk Assessment Device Effectiveness

Risk assessment instruments are criticized because much work is needed to identify the most important criteria associated with future offending (Byrne, Byrne, and Howells 2001). This does not mean that all of the instruments presently developed are worthless as predictors of success on probation or parole. But it does suggest these measures are imperfect. Therefore, it may be premature to rely exclusively on instrument scores to decide who goes to prison and who receives probation. But in many jurisdictions, risk assessment scores are used precisely for this purpose (McCarthy 2001). Also, questions frequently arise as to whether risk assessments are more effective for predicting adult offender risk compared with risks posed by juvenile offenders. This has led to the creation of age-specific, as well as gender-specific, risk measures to assess different types of juvenile offenders, such as juvenile probationers, as well as risk instruments that target primarily older offenders (Funk 1999).

Generally, risk assessment instruments attempt to identify several crucial variables that appear to be closely correlated with offender recidivism. For instance, most of these measures identify one's prior criminal record, the nature of the current offense, various social factors (e.g., age, educational level, marital status, family relationships, living arrangements, drug/alcohol use/abuse, and prison conduct). One's prior criminal record may include all arrests as either a juvenile or an adult. Numbers of prior convictions, incarcerations, sentences of probation, years of incarceration served, the length of the present prison term, and past probation/parole violations are also included. The nature of the current offense may include aggravating and mitigating circumstances, whether a dangerous weapon was involved, and whether there were victim injuries or deaths. Prison behavior is especially important, since we cannot and should not expect someone to conform to society's rules outside of prison if they cannot abide them while in prison. Thus, much attention is given to writeups or prison rule infractions, one's escape history, and one's release plan. If enough information is gathered about these and other variables, a more informed decision may be made about whether to release a particular offender into the community. The general belief is that past behavior is a good predictor of future behavior. But as has been seen in actual practice, there are too many exceptions to this belief. Figure 7.3 is an inmate misbehavior report from a New York prison.

Some Applications of Risk/Needs Measures

One way of highlighting the most common applications of **risk-needs assessment** by various states is to inspect their own utilization criteria and objectives. The following state utilization criteria are not intended to represent all other states or typify them. Rather, they have been highlighted because of their diversity of objectives. For example, Arizona's Offender Classification System (OCS) is designed to assign all offenders to an appropriate institutional setting based on required levels of security/custody and the needs of offenders for productive work, education, and treatment during their incarceration (Arizona Department of Corrections 1991). Additionally, risk prediction tools, as utilized by the Colorado Parole Guidelines Commission (1988), are for the purposes of:

1. Concentrating secure management and/or program resources on a specific group of high-need offenders without reducing public safety.
2. Promoting greater understanding of the statistical management of the parole release process.
3. Significantly improving predictive accuracy over case review or clinical methods.
4. Addressing offender needs as they relate to reoffending in the community.

Arizona and Colorado risk prediction instrument goals are couched in the context of initial placement decisions and closely related to management objectives, including allocating scarce resources most profitably in view of system constraints. It is possible to group these diverse objectives according to several general applications. Thus, for most states, the following general applications are made of risk assessment instruments:

1. To promote better program planning through optimum budgeting and deployment of resources.

Form 2171B

STATE OF NEW YORK DEPARTMENT OF CORRECTIONAL SERVICES

Wende _____Correctional Facility

Inmate Misbehavior Report ◆ Informe De Mal Comportamiento Del Recluso

1. NAME OF INMATE (Last, First) ◆ NOMBRE DEL RECLUSO	NO. ◆ NUM.	HOUSING LOCATION ◆ CE LDA
ROSENBERG, JEROME	63A0017	AMU-4th 413-ISO

2. LOCATION OF INCIDENT ◆ LUGAR DEL INCIDENTE	INCIDENT DATE ◆ FECHA	INCIDENT TIME ◆ HORA
413-ISO	6/19/02	9:25 pm

3. RULE VIOLATIONS ◆ VIOLACIONES, 4. DESCRIPTION OF INCIDENT (DESCRIPCION DEL INCIDENTE)

122.10: Inmates shall smoke in designated areas only. 113.22: Inmates shall not use or possess authorized articles in unauthorized areas. 118.31: Inmates shall not alter, rewire, tamper, or attempt to repair electrical outlets or any electrical device. 118.30: Inmates shall maintain the cleanliness and orderliness of their living quarters, clothing, and person. 117.10: Inmates shall not cause or attempt to cause an explosion. On the above date and time, CO McGill was escorting the nurse down the East Wing, observed inmate Rosenberg #63A0017 smoking a cigarette with his oxygen on. CO Abell was then ordered to do a cell search on inmate Rosenberg's room. At which time I found four butane lighters, one in his pocket, one in his styrofoam cup, one in his small locker, and one in a Pringles can. Also found 3 cigarettes and loose tobacco in his eye glass case; also one altered extension cord in his large locker. The room had several styrofoam cups, containers of empty milk cartons, and many plastic bags in the room. The contraband was placed in the contraband locker in the captain's office. Inmate has been counseled several times about smoking in his room.

REPORT DATE ◆ FECHA	REPORTED BY ◆ NOMBRE DE LA PERSONA QUE HACE EL INFORME	SIGNATURE	TITLE
6/19/02	T. Abell	T. Abell	CO

5. ENDORSEMENTS OF OTHER EMPLOYEE WITNESSES, IF ANY   SIGNATURES _____

You are hereby notified that no statement made by you in response to the charges or information derived therefrom may be used against you in a criminal proceeding.
You are hereby notified that the above report is a formal charge and will be considered and determined at a hearing to be held.
The inmate shall be permitted to call witnesses provided that so doing does not jeopardize institutional safety or correctional goals.
If restricted pending a hearing for this misbehavior report, you may write to the Deputy Superintendent for Security or his/her designee prior to the hearing to make a statement on the need for continued prehearing confinement.

FIGURE 7.3   Inmate Misbehavior Report.

2. To target high-risk and high-need offenders for particular custody levels, programs, and services without endangering the safety of others.

3. To apply the fair and appropriate sanctions to particular classes of offenders and raise their level of accountability.

4. To provide mechanisms for evaluating services and programs as well as service and program improvements over time.

5. To maximize public safety as well as public understanding of the diverse functions of corrections by making decision making more open and comprehensible to both citizens and offender-clients (Champion 1994).

Risk includes both the danger posed by a person and the person's vulnerability to victimization. Assessment instruments are used to gather information from offenders as they enter the facility and monitor their behavior throughout the entire period of incarceration (Sabbatine 2003:67). The predators must be identified. What information can identify an offender as a potential predator? Some criteria include (1) whether a current charge is pending involving an assault or threat, (2) a past history of charges or convictions involving assaults or threats, or (3) a previous history of assault or threatening behavior within a correctional institution. Such information may be found in public sources, such as citations of new arrests or warrants, criminal history or database files, institutional history database files, information gathered by arresting officers, and/or questions asked of the offender. This information may be gathered as the offender enters the facility, at the point where it is determined that he or she will not bond out and will stay until arraignment, or periodically during incarceration. When predators are identified, several strategies have been suggested for their isolation and handling:

1. They are transported in restraints.
2. They are transported with more than one officer, where possible.
3. They are housed alone or with other predators.
4. They are not commingled with nonpredatory offenders in housing units, programs, or during visitation, meals, or recreation.
5. They are housed in single cells, if possible.
6. They receive greater levels of supervision.
7. They receive more frequent observation.
8. They are placed in a living environment void of instruments of assault as best as practical.
9. They undergo frequent shakedowns to prevent the possession of dangerous contraband (Sabbatine 2003:67).

Selective Incapacitation

Ethical, moral, and legal questions are raised when predictors of dangerousness are used resulting in one offender's incarceration and another offender's freedom when similar crimes have been committed (Dutton and Kropp 2000). This is selective incapacitation. Selective incapacitation is the incarceration of offenders who are believed to be most likely to recidivate and commit new offenses. Those offenders believed to have a low propensity to reoffend are freed, either through probation or parole. A decision to incarcerate offenders largely because of their suspected future criminal conduct is, in effect, a penalty for future behaviors that have not as yet occurred. Obviously, more research is needed before judges and others place their faith in existing prediction instruments for making sentencing decisions. But despite existing pitfalls associated with risk and dangerousness measures, they are used with increasing frequency by both juvenile and criminal courts for dispositions, sentencing, and classification (Austin et al. 2001; Feld 2001). Norval Morris (1984) suggests several useful principles when applied in tandem with judicial sentencing and probation officer PSI recommendations:

1. Clinical predictions of dangerousness should not be relied upon other than for short-term intervention.
2. Decisions to restrict offender autonomy should be made by considering the actual extent of harm that may occur and how much individual autonomy of offenders ought to be limited.

3. Predictions of dangerousness are present condition, not predictions of particular results.

4. Sufficiency of proof of dangerousness should not be confused with proof beyond a reasonable doubt, clear and convincing evidence, or on a balance of probability.

5. Punishment should not be imposed or extended, by virtue of a dangerousness prediction, beyond that justified as deserved punishment independent of that prediction.

6. Provided the previous limitation is respected, dangerousness predictions may properly influence sentencing decisions.

7. The base expectancy rate of criminal violence for the criminal predicted as dangerous should be shown by reliable evidence to be substantially higher than the rate for another criminal, with a closely similar crime, but not predicted as unusually dangerous, before greater dangerousness of the former may be relied on to intensify or extend the punishment (Morris 1984).

Selective incapacitation has been challenged in recent years. One alternative to selective incapacitation is selective release. Selective release requires an alteration of present sentencing procedures, where shorter sentences are imposed on predicted low-rate offenders. Thus, selective release is implemented much earlier in the criminal justice system at the point of sentencing. Under selective release, low-rate offenders would be identified with various prediction mechanisms and given shorter sentences. Selective release is premised on the idea that prediction scales are better at predicting low-rate offending than high-rate offending. Thus, scarce jail and prison space is reserved for more high-risk offenders who have high recidivism potential (Mathiesen 1998).

FUNCTIONS OF PRISONS

The functions served by prisons are closely connected with the overall goals of corrections. Broadly stated, correctional goals include deterrence, rehabilitation, societal protection, offender reintegration, just deserts, justice and due process, and retribution or punishment. The goals of prisons follow.

Providing Societal Protection

Locking up dangerous offenders or those who are persistent nonviolent offenders means that society will be protected from them for variable time periods. It is not possible at present to lock up all offenders who deserve to be incarcerated. Space limitations are such that we would require at least four or five times the number of existing prisons to incarcerate all convicted felons and misdemeanants. Thus, the criminal justice system attempts to incarcerate those most in need of incarceration. Obviously, this goal is not realized, since many dangerous offenders are placed on probation annually and many nonviolent offenders are incarcerated. Varying state and federal statutes and prosecutorial practices contribute to sentencing inconsistencies and peculiar incarceration policies and patterns.

Punishing Offenders

Restricting one's freedoms, confining inmates in cells, and obligating them to follow rigid behavioral codes while confined is regarded as punishment for criminal conduct (Casella 2001). The fact of incarceration is a punishment compared with the greater freedoms enjoyed by probationers and parolees (Snyder 2001). Compared with other industrialized nations, the United States has the world's largest incarceration rate (Salvatore, Aguirre, and Joseph 2001). The United States incarcerates 426 persons per 100,000 population, while South Africa incarcerates 333 per 100,000, and the Soviet Union incarcerates 268 per 100,000.

Rehabilitating Offenders

Few criminal justice scholars would agree that prisons are in the prisoner rehabilitation business. There is little support for the view that imprisonment does much of a rehabilitative nature for anyone confined. Nevertheless, many prisons have vocational and educational programs, psychological counselors, and an array of services available to inmates in order that they might improve their skills, education, and self-concept. Prisons also have libraries for inmate self-improvement.

Studies of the influence of educational degree programs for prison inmates and recidivism rates report mixed results (Eisenberg, Riechers, and Arrigona 2001). Some studies show no relation between the education an inmate receives while confined and recidivism. Other studies indicate lower recidivism rates among those inmates who acquire greater educational attainment. In Ohio, for example, 318 male inmates were studied who participated in an associate degree program offered through Wilmington College. Adjunct instructors were obtained from local businesses and universities, and inmate-students were allowed to major in business administration, social science, industrial technology, and liberal studies. The

Prison inmate dining rooms look much like school cafeterias, with many of their amenities.

college also offered extracurricular activities, including book clubs, concerts, poetry readings, and guest lectures. Inmate-students had frequent contact with instructors, and supplemental programs were provided in career planning, resume writing, and life-coping skills to assist those paroled from prison. Researchers found that inmates who completed higher levels of education had greater employment success and lower rates of recidivism over an extended followup period, compared with their less highly educated counterparts (Batiuk, Moke, and Rountree 1997:175).

More often than not, prisons also socialize inmates in adverse ways, so that they might emerge from prisons later as better criminals who have learned ways of avoiding detection when committing future crimes. There is also a physical dimension that has generated much criticism of prisons. In most prisons, facilities exist where inmates can lift weights and build up their bodies. Thus, dangerous inmates may become even more dangerous with these opportunities to improve their physical strength. Some observers have advocated exchanging barbells for books and academic courses so that inmates may improve their minds, not their bodies (Zerillo 1997). But even this view is not without its detractors. In the Netherlands, for instance, a social skills training program was introduced into various prisons. Inmate participation in this program resulted in decreased social anxiety and increased positive feelings about everyday social situations. Nevertheless, inmate aggressiveness and violence remained unaffected (Schippers, Marker, and DeFuentes 2001).

A majority of inmates who pass through prisons are not rehabilitated in the sense that they will adopt conforming, law-abiding behaviors and offend no more (Lovegrove 2001). Many inmates have drug problems that need to be treated while they are imprisoned. If these problems remain untreated, then recidivism rates are higher when these inmates are subsequently released on parole (Eisenberg et al. 2001).

Prisonization also occurs, often through inmate gang socialization (Zaitzow 1999). Gangs are important components of prison culture, regardless of what officials think about them. Gangs form, in part, for mutual protection from members of other gangs. In this prisonization milieu, inmates cannot help acquiring attitudes and knowledge from other inmates that will improve their criminal skills. Further, many of the vocational and educational programs offered to inmates are ultimately exploited by them. Participation in these programs can look good on an inmate's record, and parole boards are favorably influenced by such inmate activities. Inmates know this, and thus, they often participate in a token fashion in various prison programs for the cosmetic value it may have in favorable parole board decision making (Patterline and Petersen 1999; Reisig and Lee 2000).

Reintegrating Offenders

It might be argued that moving offenders from higher security levels, where they are more closely supervised, to lower security levels, where they are less closely supervised, helps them understand that conformity with institutional rules is rewarded (Eisenberg, Riechers, and Arrigona 2001). As prisoners near their release dates, they may be permitted unescorted leaves, known as furloughs or work release, where they may participate in work or educational programs and visit with their families during the week or on weekends. These experiences are considered reintegrative (Horn 2001). Most prisons have such programs, but they are presumably aimed at certain offenders who are believed to no longer pose a threat to society. Occasionally, officials wrongly estimate the nondangerousness

Penitentiary inmates may be offered a variety of constructive vocational and educational programs, including arts and crafts.

of certain furloughees and work releasees. In any case, the intent of reintegrative prison programs is to provide those wanting such programs the opportunity of having them. At least some inmates derive value from such programs, although some researchers believe the costs of operating them are far outweighed by the lack of rehabilitation and reintegration that actually occurs (Ashe 2001).

PRISON CULTURE: ON JARGON AND INMATE PECKING ORDERS

Descriptions of life behind prison walls are abundant. Contributing to these descriptions are Hollywood movies about prison life and inmate culture that all too often are disturbingly accurate (O'Sullivan 2001). During the last five or six decades, several classics have been written depicting prison conditions, prisoner characteristics, and the general nature of prison culture. One of the first objective and systematic studies of inmate culture occurred in 1934 with the publication of *Sex in Prison* by Joseph Fishman. Fishman, a federal prison inspector and consultant, described inmate culture vividly, indicating that prisoners devised a unique language or argot relevant only to them. Fishman focused upon the prevalence of homosexuality behind prison walls, and his work suggested to others a new and rich source in need of social description. Prison rapes involving same-sex assaults among inmates continue to be prevalent in U.S. prisons today (Human Rights Watch 2001b). Fishman used the term *subculture* to connote his observations of these unique social arrangements among prisoners.

The concept of a subculture is that a separate, smaller social system exists within the larger social system, where the smaller system contains its own special language, status structure, and rewards and punishments (Lerner 2002). Violence or an inmate's potential for aggression is a key to understanding the pecking order within any prison. Access to drugs and other scarce contraband

BOX 7.4

Troy W. Lemons Sr.

Inmate, Holliday Unit, Huntsville, TX

Experiences

Hello. My name is Troy W. Lemons Sr., and I am 35 years of age. I've been incarcerated since December 22, 1999, for an offense I committed due to my drug- and alcohol-induced lifestyle. As a result of my imprisonment, I've left behind both a wife and two small children. Upon entering the Galveston County Jail in Galveston, Texas, the judge advised me that probation was no longer an option and that the Texas Department of Criminal Justice (TDCJ) (formerly known as the TDC) would be my resting place for the next four years. Before entering the TDCJ, I had heard horrific tales in regards to what it would be like. The idea of entering TDCJ frightened me. It was like walking into a dark, unknown room in which you didn't know what to expect.

Upon entering TDCJ, my life as a human being, as well as my perception of freedom, was changed for the worse. There were so many rules, such as no talking, hands behind your back while walking, no looking staff in the eyes, which I thought were senseless. They worry about my eyeballs, while I'm suffering from an outer body experience. I was sent to the Holliday Unit located in Huntsville, Texas. I was placed in a metal building with four dorms, 50 men to a dorm. It contained both showers and toilets, which were in wide-open spaces. Due to some of the things I've heard, I knew that it would be in my best interest to mind my own business and to leave other people and their business alone.

Being in prison is like being in a totally different world. This is both life and death. Over the course of my prison stay, as I witness many fights, only the strong survive. But there are other kinds of battles to be dealt with on the inside, like the battle of the mind. Around here, guys are preyed upon like sheep, and you may have an easy-going guy in the free world (before incarceration), considerate, caring, and giving, but these traits could wreak havoc for you on the inside. And on top of that, everything is so segregated. In the free world, I have had friends of different races and cultures, but in here, everyone is for himself or with his own race. For instance, the TV, the board games, and the gymnasium/outside recreation are segregated, and that's with regard to everything. However, there is one place I know for sure these things don't exist, and that is during visitation with families on weekends. But during other times for those who aren't working or going to school, time is passed by watching TV or playing dominoes, chess, and other board games. During my incarceration, I've spent a great deal of time in the S.A.T.P. (Substance Abuse Treatment Program) classes in hopes of changing my life for the better.

I have also been fortunate enough to be involved with a program called a Prisoner for a Day. This is a program where adults are on probation and continuing to break the law. As a last resort, they are given a chance to be in prison for a day to determine if this is the lifestyle they would prefer to freedom. Being a part of this program allows me to share my experience and to strengthen my hope with others. I know I've grown because at one time in my life, seeing these men would have angered me, because I felt I

(continued)

BOX 7.4 (*Continued*)

deserved a second chance. Looking back earlier on in my life, a lot of decisions and choices I made were based on my bad attitude. I come from a single-parent home (my mother), with three brothers and a sister. It was hard having one parent, which left me unsupervised the majority of my time, to run with the wrong crowd, but I knew that if I stayed in school, received my lessons, and made the grade, then I would stay out of trouble and have a chance to make it in life. So I graduated from high school and was offered three scholarships that I later turned down, not wanting to leave my girlfriend of many years. I went to work in the steel industry for seven years, but during that time, I was selling drugs, and the majority of my clients consisted of co-workers and ended with me being my best customer. Then came my run-ins with the law.

Now, sitting here in prison, I look back over my life and wish that I could have done this differently (like graduate from college) and done what real men do, remain humble, thankful, prayerful, and take life one day at a time.

There are depressing moments in prison all the time. Like not being in control of your life, not being able to take care of your family, the loss of family and friends to death, and not being able to pay last respects. There have been many nights that I've laid in my bed crying, asking God and myself where did I go wrong. It's very painful, so today, I encourage others to do what's right.

Advice to Students

One of the most interesting things about being in prison was that I was allowed and blessed with an opportunity to get my life back, and it showed me that Troy needed to do so that he could live as an asset instead of a liability to society again. So here again I strongly encourage offenders to become more involved with a substance abuse treatment program and get involved in many classes that are offered through the chaplaincy department. Going through the many groups and programs has helped me tremendously, being able to share my problem, whether it pertains to family, prison life, and so forth. I used the group for support, and the counselors lead the pathway to a positive resource. I've developed and built bonds that come only when reality can be accepted, and this helps with rehabilitation. I pray that you don't have to go through what I've been through. If any wrong ever crosses your mind, just imagine what my prison life has been, so that you don't have to experience my pain. Remember just what my 8-year-old daughter said to me, "Daddy, when you get out of jail, I want you to be a changed man." I would like to advise students who want to avoid incarceration to stay drug-free, stay in school, go to church, obey your parents and the law. If you have a drug or alcohol problem, get help, and remember what I've been through so you don't have to come to prison and share my pain.

is rewarded and results in higher placement in the prisoner status structure, with some inmates labeled as hustlers who work the economic system (Irwin 1970). In order to understand inmate behaviors, it is essential that the inmate subculture, wherever it is located, be penetrated, described, and understood.

Six years after Fishman's research, Donald Clemmer wrote the classic *The Prison Community* (1940), which was based on his description of the Menard, Illinois, Penitentiary inmate subculture while he was a correctional officer. His description of the inmate subculture spanned three years and focused upon almost all aspects of inmate life. Especially noteworthy was his description of how new inmates were introduced into the existing prisoner subculture. Immediately upon the arrival of a new fish or inmate, other more seasoned inmates would take him aside and acquaint him with the dos and don'ts of life at Menard. This socialization process whereby new inmates learned through contact with older inmates what the rules were and who controlled the flow of scarce prisoner goods and contraband as well as certain inmate privileges was referred to by Clemmer as prisonization (Gross 1995). In reality, Clemmer was referring to socialization (i.e., learning through contact with others) applied to the prison setting. Nevertheless, prisonization quickly became a popular reference to the phenomenon whereby new prisoners learned the ropes and became acquainted with the customs among the Menard inmates. Clemmer's work stimulated a plethora of subsequent works where popular writers and criminologists became enamored with describing life among prisoners.

Perhaps the best-known and precedent-setting study of inmate subculture is Gresham Sykes's work, *The Society of Captives* (1958). Sykes has acknowledged the influence of Clemmer and Fishman in his own writings, although Sykes's work attained greater popularity among criminologists and criminal justice professionals over the years. Three reasons for this were that Sykes's description of the New Jersey State Maximum Security Prison in Trenton (1) provided rich descriptions of inmate jargon such as *merchant* (inmates who barter scarce goods for other favors), *rat* (inmates who squeal or tell authorities about illicit activities of other inmates), and *real man* (inmates who are loyal, generous, and tough in their relations with other inmates); (2) described the prevailing inmate code in detail, which outlined behaviors that either would be rewarded or punished by other inmates; and (3) provided a plausible explanation for the inmate propensity to establish solidarity and conformity among their ranks. While the terms Sykes identified as peculiar to the New Jersey State Maximum Security Prison are now dated and unlikely to be used in contemporary prison settings, his work was a masterpiece of detail to be emulated by subsequent investigators.

Three years after Sykes had written about the society of captives, criminologists Clarence Schrag, John Irwin, and Donald Cressey provided alternative typologies of inmate subcultures and advanced contrasting explanations for their emergence. Schrag, for instance, believed that prisoners developed their dispositions toward inmate life before entering prison. Reflecting his sociological background and interests, Schrag emphasized the importance of family socialization and community integration as shaping and developing attitudes of criminals consistent with the roles they eventually acquired when incarcerated. Schrag described inmates as falling into four distinct adaptive categories: (1) *right guys* (inmates who adhered to the prevailing inmate code), (2) *con-politicians* (inmates who had influence with correctional officers, had money, or who had access to scarce goods and were therefore in good bartering positions with other inmates; these inmates also had the skill and wit to manipulate other inmates), (3) *outlaws* (inmates who relied upon force and physical confrontation to get what they wanted from other inmates), and (4) *square Johns* (inmates who abided by prison rules, accepted their confinement passively, and who participated in prison vocational and educational programs) (Schrag 1961).

Irwin and Cressey differed from Schrag in that they believed some inmate roles developed within the prison setting or as the result of incarceration, while other roles were imported from the outside (Irwin and Cressey 1962). The **importation model** (implying that a part of existing prison culture is imported from the outside by new prisoners) was used by Irwin and Cressey and coincided with Schrag's notion that some inmates adapt to prison life in much the same way as they adapted to life among criminals in their communities. They identified three types of prisoners: (1) *thieves* (inmates who stick to themselves, avoid trouble, yet attempt to get what they want without getting caught), (2) *straights* (do right and conventional inmates similar to square Johns who do their time, obey the rules, and do not identify closely with any inmate subculture, and (3) *convicts* (those inmates who attempt to control other inmates and acquire power to achieve their own needs or interests). The gradual formation of inmate gangs along racial or ethnic lines has obscured these early prisoner characterizations and typologies to the extent that it is doubtful that they are universally applicable today, especially in those prisons with large ethnic or racial inmate populations (Fisher-Giorlando and Jiang 2000; Kruitschnitt, Gartner, and Miller 2000).

John Irwin's descriptions of life in prisons (*The Felon*) and jails (*The Jail: Managing the Underclass in American Society*) respectively published in 1970 and 1985, McCoy's prison profiles of inmates from the penitentiary at Walla Walla, Washington (*Concrete Mama: Prison Profiles from Walla Walla,* 1981), and Robert Johnson's *Hard Time: Understanding and Reforming the Prison* (1996) are more recent examples of attempts to describe prison life and culture. The *Concrete Mama* book is amply illustrated with Washington State Penitentiary inmates under various circumstances, and it is perhaps the best visual portrayal of life in prison that has been published thus far. Many of the photos from this work have been used to illustrate prison scenes in criminal justice-related textbooks and other publications.

The gradual influence of race and ethnicity as variables that have stimulated and heightened inmate cohesiveness and power was noted by participant observer Leo Carroll in his 1974 description of prisoner subculture at "Eastern Correctional Institution (ECI), a small state prison in a highly urban and industrial Eastern state" (Carroll 1974:11). With the consent of the prison administration, Carroll entered ECI voluntarily, for the purpose of observing and talking with prisoners about their experiences. All prisoners knew that Carroll was gathering material for a book. Although Carroll was a white male, he was accepted gradually by inmates of all races and ethnic origins (1974:11). However, his entry into prisoner culture was not entirely problem-free. Inmates regarded him as an inmate advocate and critical of the prison system, while correctional officers at first saw him as a threat for the same reason (1974:11). Eventually, he overcame prisoner suspicions and staff resentments and fears.

Carroll found that prisoners formed cohesive associations among themselves primarily along racial lines. A white Mafia was comprised of whites and vied for internal power with a black revolutionary group known as the Afro-American Society (Carroll 1974:197–206). Since Carroll's observations were made on the heels of widespread public protest of the 1960s and dramatic civil rights reforms, the emergence of a strong black inmate organization was a seemingly logical consequence. Carroll also found that both the white Mafia and the black Afro-American Society were united against prison administration and rules, although these groupings also afforded prisoners some degree of protection against assaults by other inmates.

One consistent theme running throughout all of these works is that prison culture exists as an independent entity apart from other society. Erving Goffman labeled prisons as total institutions, totally and completely self-contained communities with their own status systems, regulatory and enforcement agencies and personnel, and other phenomena ordinarily found in outside community life. In 1970 Gresham Sykes and Sheldon Messinger outlined what eventually became a widely quoted inmate code of conduct based upon their own observations of prison life (Blomberg and Cohen, 1995). Unlike the inmate argot described in studies from the 1950s and 1960s, these maxims have endured the test of time and are prevalent in virtually every prison setting. They include the following: (1) Do not rat or squeal on other inmates; (2) don't interfere with the interests of other inmates; (3) don't steal from, exploit, or cheat other inmates; (4) don't be a sucker by supporting prison policies and making a fool of yourself; (5) don't lose your head; and (6) be a man, be tough, and don't weaken. Those inmates who adhere to these implicit maxims are regarded as real men or right guys and gain the respect of other prisoners. Those inmates who fail to conform to these maxims are treated accordingly. Since these maxims have conceivably been an integral part of inmate life for many decades, we are better able to understand and appreciate earlier descriptions or typologies of inmates that have been provided by Clemmer, Sykes, Irwin, and others.

Studies have been conducted of inmate subculture in both prisons and jails, although prisons seem to be characterized more often as exhibiting subculture characteristics (Selke 1993). Each prison has its own inmate subculture, with a highly refined set of rules and regulations. These rules and regulations exist apart from those imposed on inmates by the prison administration. In several respects, these rules are enforced to a greater degree than the enforcement of the so-called official code of conduct prescribed by prison staff.

Unlike jails, where the turnover among inmates is brisk, prisons contain long-term inmates who develop and perpetuate their subculture from one prisoner generation to the next (Hasaballa 2001). New prisoners or fish are quickly oriented to the prisoner social system, sized up, and are located accordingly within the prisoner social structure (Benaquisto and Freed 1996). An inmate's strength, fighting ability, attractiveness, age, abilities and skills, conviction offense, political and social connections, race, and other criteria determine where he or she is placed socially relative to other inmates (Clemmer 1940). Access to drugs in prison is highly prized as well. Illegal drug use among U.S. prison inmates is pervasive, although such drug use is not unique to U.S. prison systems. In England and elsewhere throughout the world, prisons are places where drugs can easily be obtained (Hucklesby and Wilkinson 2001).

In recent years, more than a few prison systems in the United States have sought to create more austere living conditions for inmates and remove some of the amenities that have been routinely provided. These changes have been fostered by perceptions that the public is increasingly wary of prison settings that tend to coddle offenders rather than punish them. Some states have removed various amenities and services, such as modern aerobic exercise equipment, "R" rated movies and color television, tennis courts, softball, and certain educational and counseling programs. Where these amenities have been removed, inmate culture has been affected to a degree. Incarceration is a dehumanizing experience, and the removal of these and other amenities further dehumanizes prison settings. At the same time, the public seems to recognize that prisons need to be productive and rehabilitative. Thus, taxpayers want institutions that are humane and seek to improve inmates during their incarceration (Applegate 2001:266).

But there is only so much institutions can do to modify prison environments. No particular prison plan will have universal appeal to everyone. All U.S. prisons are different, even within a given state or system. There are not only staff differences, managerial style differences, and institutional size differences—there are also great differences in inmate diversity. It has been said that if you were to visit every correctional facility in the United States and spend a day or two talking to staff and inmates about the quality of life within their facilities, one would likely find that no two facilities, even two facilities operated by the same correctional agencies, are identical. Experienced correctional employees, and inmates as well, know that institutions operate in a manner reflecting the staff who manage them and the inmates who inhabit them. In a sense it would be fair to say that every correctional facility, ranging from state-operated community work-release centers to high security federal penitentiaries, has a distinctive way of doing things (Fleisher 2000:1). Furthermore, there are persistent forces at work within prison systems that create and perpetuate problems for any particular program to operate effectively. One of these persistent forces is the pervasiveness and influence of prison gangs.

Prison Gangs.   The influence of prison gangs formed according to racial, ethnic, or even religious affiliation has become increasingly important as a means of perpetuating and preserving inmate subculture (Decker 2001). Latin gangs in California prisons have established the Nuestra Familia (*Our Family*), while the United Chicanos and Mexican Mafia have been created in other prison settings (Miller and Rush 1996). In Texas prisons, for example, gangs formed in the 1980s include the Texas Syndicate, the Texas Mafia, the Mandingo Warriors, and the Self-Defense Family. Black inmates have formed the Black Guerilla Family and Black Muslims. Increasingly, Islamic inmates have established powerful and violent gangs in several prisons (Spalek and Wilson 2001). In many respects, these gangs have taken the control of prisoners away from prison administrators. These gangs pose more of a threat to individual prisoners than the sanctions the formal prison system can inflict. The Big Four inmate gangs that started in California prisons and have since spread in factions to correctional facilities in other states (through importation) and even into various communities are the Aryan Brotherhood, Mexican Mafia, Nuestra Familia, and Black Guerrilla Family (Miller and Rush 1996). There are increasing numbers of Asian gangs in the United States as well. These gangs are becoming more pronounced in prisons as arrests and convictions of Asian gang members increase (Tsunokai and Kposowa 2002). Another growing gang problem facing prisons in female gangs, which stem largely from the increasing numbers of female street gangs in various jurisdictions (Chesney-Lind 2001).

Few researchers contest the fact that inmate subcultures exist in virtually every prison (Richards and Ross 2001). Furthermore, it is conceded generally that these subcultures seem to share common features that operate to control inmate behavior to a high degree (Wynn 2001). The inmate riots at prisons in New Mexico, New York, and Georgia were organized to the extent that a leadership core ordered others to accomplish certain tasks, including the murders of certain inmates believed to be snitches or informants. Much violence among inmates appears prompted by racial or ethnic factors, where members of one race seek to protect themselves from members of another race. While prison administrations have not acted as yet to implement a segregation program that might help to minimize intra-inmate aggression, it has been proposed as one possible solution.

Certainly, a key to controlling prison gangs lies in a facility's ability to deal strategically with resource allocation among inmates and staff. This can be accomplished by eliminating the symptoms of disorganization and disorder, provided that the effort involves supplanting gang systems with more legitimate ones (Scott 2001). Several suppression strategies have been suggested for dealing with inmate gangs and disrupting them. Segregation, lockdowns, and transfers have been the most common response to prison gangs. However, given the complexity of prison gangs, effective intervention most likely includes improved strategies for community reentry, as well as greater collaboration between correctional agencies and researchers on prison gang management policies and practices. If communities do not structure intervention to include more than law enforcement suppression, then prison gangs are likely to gain a stronger hold in communities, rendering drug gangs more powerful forces in their neighborhoods (Fleisher and Decker 2001a, 2001b).

One major institutional problem associated with the rising presence of inmate gangs is the lack of effective interventions and assistance programs that interrupt gang formation and persistence (Davis and Flannery 2001). For instance, many former street gang members are admitted to prisons with prior histories of low self-esteem, physical and sexual abuse, substance abuse, psychiatric disturbances, posttraumatic stress disorder, cognitive deficits, and other problems. Psychological interventions include cognitive-behavioral approaches, therapeutic communities, multisystemic therapy, and recreational therapy. In order to be most effective, these treatment programs should be a part of a more comprehensive commitment by the correctional administration. But thus far, such programming and services have low priority in prison and jail funding. This is significant especially in view of the high level of social deficiencies among self-reported gang members in various prisons. A Nebraska prison study has shown, for instance, that many gang members are poorly educated with little meaningful employment history; most have a propensity toward aggressive and violent behavior; and many have high levels of drug and alcohol addiction (Krienert and Fleisher 2001). For these inmates, at least, it is difficult to implement effective programming and services unless there are remedial educational activities and substance abuse counseling provided first.

One observer notes that inmates believe that the organizational climate of a prison is influenced by the quantity of resources or number of programs; availability to staff; access to resources or the ease of getting the job an inmate desires; the quality of interaction with staffers; and the quality of interaction with inmates, where fighting and violence will fully disrupt an inmate's lifestyle and effect a disciplinary transfer to a lockdown (Fleisher 2000:18). Further, disruptive inmate cliques, gangs, and violence would most assuredly have long-range negative effects on the climate of any prison. Inmates with gang affiliations and inmates with histories of institutional violence and other types of serious disorders should be carefully screened out of the general inmate population (Fleisher 2000:19). But despite these efforts by prison staff to screen out disruptive inmates, the social climate of any prison is difficult to control and configure.

The influence of gangs operating in prison settings is potentially costly. A variety of civil actions filed by inmate gangs have claimed the following: (1) that prison/jail officials have failed to protect them from other rival gang members; (2) that their classification or placement based on their gang affiliation are unconstitutional; (3) that institutional grooming policies, partially implemented as an anti-gang measure, are unconstitutional; and (4) that officials have improperly prohibited written or audio materials believed to foster the development of prison gangs (Eckhart 2001). While the courts have been generally unsympathetic to such claims and have ruled in favor of prison administrators most of the time, the fact is that these civil actions consume valuable court time and divert many prison administrators away from their more important administrative tasks.

At the back end of the system, when inmate gang members are subsequently paroled, there are often inadequate community services to assist them in becoming reintegrated and rehabilitated. Studies of parolees who are affiliated with inmate gangs have been conducted in St. Louis and Kansas City, Missouri, Seattle, Washington, and Champaign, Illinois. There is a critical need for community involvement in the post-release integration of these gang members. These persons need a blend of services delivered in a way that meets their lifestyle. This requires an infusion of financial resources and social services. The following steps have been recommended: (1) establishment of tactical and strategic planning between senior correctional officials and law enforcement, social welfare, community college, mental health and treatment, and small business; (2) development of multimodal community-based service delivery systems; (3) use of prison workers as community mentors to strengthen local agencies' ability to design programs that fit former inmates' needs; and (4) reconfirmation publicly of the responsibility of the community for ensuring that former inmates find a lawful place within these settings (Fleisher and Decker 2001b). But there are serious gaps between policy recommendations and actual implementation of useful community programs for these and other offenders (Morton 2001).

SELECTED PRISON ISSUES

Prison Overcrowding

At the heart of many problems associated with prison operations and management is prison overcrowding. Whether a prison is overcrowded is determined by comparing present inmate populations to various criteria, such as (1) **rated capacity,** (2) **operational capacity,** and (3) **design capacity.** Rated capacity refers to the number of beds or inmates assigned by a rating official to various state institutions. Operational capacity is the total number of inmates that can be accommodated based the size of a facility's staff, programs, and other services. Design capacity is the optimum number of inmates that architects originally intended to be housed or accommodated by the facility.

Sometimes it is difficult to make valid comparisons among jurisdictions, because each prison system reports prison population excesses using one or more of these different criteria. However, most prisons report their inmate populations according to the system's operating capacity. In 2001, prisons in 51 U.S. agencies were operating at an average of 7 percent over their rated capacities (Camp and Camp 2002). Overall, state prisons were operating between 77 and 160 percent of their capacities in 2001, while the federal prison system was operating at 131 percent of its rated capacity (Camp and Camp 2002).

Overcrowding in prisons has been linked with violent deaths, suicides, psychiatric commitments, disciplinary infractions, and increased litigation by inmates (Florida Department of Corrections 1999). With the increasing threat of various communicable diseases in prison and jail settings, overcrowding is quickly emerging as a most critical issue. Another serious problem is serious injuries and assaults of inmates by other inmates, including growing numbers of inmate murders (Burns et al. 1999). Although several jurisdictions have reported new prison construction to accommodate growing numbers of convicts, official expectations are grim. It is unlikely that by the time new prison construction is completed, sufficient space will be available to house the larger offender population.

Numerous state and federal prisons contract with local jail authorities to house some of the prison inmate overflow suggests serious prison overcrowding as well. Violent deaths, suicides, psychiatric commitments, and disciplinary infractions have been linked to jail and prison overcrowding (Carter 2001). On the average, U.S. prisons were operating at 107 percent of their rated capacities in 2001. The states with the highest overcrowding according to their rated capacities were Nebraska (160 percent), Massachusetts (141 percent), Illinois (137 percent), Washington (135 percent), and Wisconsin (133 percent). The

Federal Bureau of Prisons was operating at 131 percent of its rated capacity in 2001 as well (Camp and Camp 2002:86).

Many solutions have been suggested to ease jail and prison overcrowding. Some of these solutions are labeled as **front-door solutions,** because they pertain to policies and practices by criminal justice officials who deal with offenders before and during sentencing. Other solutions are **back-door solutions,** where strategies are suggested to reduce existing prison populations through early release or parole, furlough, administrative release, and several other options.

Front-door solutions to prison overcrowding typically involve actions by prosecutors and judges, and the way they process offenders. Some investigators suggest greater use of diversion and/or assignment to community service agencies, where offenders bypass the criminal justice system altogether and remain free within their communities (Florida Department of Corrections 1999). Greater use of probation by judges and recommendations of leniency from prosecutors have also been suggested, with an emphasis upon some form of restitution, community service, victim compensation, and/or fine as the primary punishment. Some of these solutions, especially community service, are increasingly used in other countries besides the United States as a part of intermediate sanctioning programs (U. Schneider 2001). Other solutions include greater plea bargaining where probation is included, selective incapacitation, where those offenders deemed most dangerous are considered for incarceration, assigning judges a fixed number of prison spaces so that they might rearrange their sentencing priorities and incarcerate only the most serious offenders, and decriminalization of offenses to narrow the range of crimes for which offenders can be incarcerated (Boari and Fiorentini 2001).

Some of the back-door proposals by researchers include easing the eligibility criteria for early release or parole, the administrative reduction of prison terms, where the governor or others shorten originally imposed sentences for certain offenders, modifying parole revocation criteria so as to encourage fewer parole violations, and expanding the number of community programs, including the use of intensive supervised parole for more serious offender groups. Considerable work remains to be done concerning the overrepresentation of minority offenders in institutions. Some promising strategies include early intervention models aimed at education and substance abuse prevention (Hunter, Crew, and Sexton 1997).

Prison Riots, Inmate Violence, and Disciplinary Measures

Prison violence has increased dramatically during the last several decades (Carter 2001). Some prison riots have been compared with social revolutions, with an elite (corrections officers), alienation and divisions, and a widespread popular (inmate) sense of injustice and grievances regarding prison administrative actions rather than against imprisonment per se (Goldstone and Useem 1999). Because of the diversity of races, ethnicities, and ages of jail and prison inmates, coupled with chronic overcrowding, inmate violence is not an unusual occurrence. The existence of gangs is conducive to inmate violence and is something officials cannot eliminate (Riveland 1999). Interestingly, gang membership in many state prisons accounts for a small proportion of prisoners. But inmate gangs in prison systems such as New Mexico account for most of such violence (Rolland 1997).

Every prison has screening mechanisms for new inmates according to standard criteria, but misclassifications frequently occur (Boothby and Durham 1999). Dangerous offenders and the mentally retarded or ill often commit aggressive acts against other inmates. Short of using solitary confinement, most prisons lack policy provisions for segregating different classes of offenders. Even the best clinical diagnoses and personality assessment devices are unable to differentiate clearly between those who have serious sadistic personality disorders and are inclined to violence and those who share some of the personality characteristics of violent offenders but are not violent (Moore and Hogue 2000). And even when violence is accurately diagnosed for certain offenders, the treatments and counseling needed for them to adjust and improve are not provided (Gudjonsson and Moore 2001). Furthermore, there is considerable ethnic diversity in most inmate populations throughout the United States. Thus, certain types of personality assessment devices may be appropriate for certain ethnic minorities but not for others (Collier and Thomas 2001).

Correctional standards are being formulated continuously for improving the quality of life for inmates and treating those who need counseling or special services (Blackburn 2000). But policy provisions for ensuring inmate safety from other violent inmates are almost nonexistent. Often, prisoners themselves must be creative and establish their own means of self-protection within prison walls (Gendreau and Keyes 2001).

Not all prison violence is gang-sponsored or aggravated. In both jails and prisons, natural leaders emerge who may or may not be related to gangs. Sometimes the result of close interpersonal interactions among inmates cause several of them to establish social bonds. These social bonds become strong enough to challenge staff or correctional officer authority. Later, when staff are interviewed following violent or protest conduct among their inmates, officers say that the perpetrators were not "leader material," as though there is some special trait or characteristic that identifies or sets apart inmate leaders from inmate followers. Studies of inmate leadership in jail settings suggest that leadership is more of a social process arising from inmate social interactions on a continuing basis. The implication is that perhaps inmates should be shuffled regularly in order to interrupt the social influences that create disruptive inmate coalitions (McCabe 1997). Such a strategy may be workable in prison settings as well, despite the fact that prison inmates are confined for longer periods on the average, and they have greater opportunities for interaction in general recreational areas during daytime hours.

Technological innovations are increasingly used in order to monitor inmate whereabouts and identify prisoners more easily. In 2003 a handful of prisons were using TSI PRISM, a high-tech head count system that tracks inmates and correctional officers to within 20 feet. Inmates wear tamper- and water-resistant bracelets, while officers wear pager-like devices. Larry Cothran, a technology consultant with the National Institute of Justice, says that it completely revolutionalizes a prison because you know where everyone is, not approximately, but exactly (St. Gerard 2003:9). TSI PRISM conducts head counts every 2 seconds versus the old-fashioned method of five to eight times per day. Any time an inmate tampers with or removes the bracelet, it activates an alarm. Correctional officers can not only pinpoint the location of an inmate but also know who is in the vicinity. The monitoring device for officers has a red button that allows them to signal for help and an automatic "man down" alarm if the device is in a horizontal position. One state system that has implemented the TSI PRISM system is the Michigan Department of Corrections. They have discovered that such technology can assist greatly in investigations of assaults and sexual contact, common violations among inmates. However, Michigan officials acknowledge that the system is not cheap. Outfitting a prison with the system costs $1 million or more. However, if such systems were widely adopted, they could one day change the way in which correctional facilities are run and controlled (St. Gerard 2003:9).

An important tool used by prison officials to manipulate prisoners and control their violent conduct is staff reports and recommendations. Staff reports and recommendations directly influence an inmate's good-time credit. Good-time credits are earned by inmates who obey the prison rules. However, if there is an absence of incentives, such as early-release recommendations by correctional officers or officials based on a prisoner's good conduct, an important incentive for inmates to comply with prison rules is destroyed (Hollenhorst 1999).

Another strategy to reduce prison violence has been to establish anger management counseling and coursework for inmates of both prisons and jails. Anger management focuses upon preventing negative behavior arising from impulsive hostile aggression by teaching self-awareness, self-control, and alternative thinking and behaviors. It is not designed to address, and likely will have no impact on, predatory or nonemotional calculated acts of aggression. For some types of violent offenders, anger management therapy may be ineffective. For instance, anger management training by itself doesn't seem effective for domestic batterers, some animal abusers, and some nonangry violent aggressors. However, some evidence of success has been indicated for the Violent Offender Treatment Program (VOTP), where predictive accuracy of 75 percent has been reported (Ward and Dockerill 1999). Other prison interventions have included tracking gang membership, focusing on individual behaviors of gang members, dispersing gang members to different correctional institutions rather than concentrating them in a single facility, and isolating gang leaders. Such interventions have been used in the U.S. Federal Bureau of Prisons as well as in prisons in California, Texas, New York, Florida, Ohio, and Connecticut (Carlson 2001).

Inmate Disciplinary Councils.   Prisoners often form **inmate disciplinary councils.** These disciplinary councils exist apart from administrative sanctioning mechanisms. They are mechanisms whereby many inmate complaints against other inmates and even correctional officers can be resolved to the satisfaction of most parties (Toch 1995a, 1995b), informally rather than formally (Palmer 1997). All prisons at the state and federal levels currently have formal grievance procedures. These councils consist of inmates and one or two prison correctional officers. Prisoners regard the addition of the corrections officer as providing these councils with some objectivity when processing inmate grievances. These councils are similar to civil alternative dispute resolution scenarios where two grieving parties have their grievances settled by an impartial third party or arbiter.

Disciplinary infractions in all prisons are common. Racial, ethnic, and age mixtures of all types interact with overcrowding and related factors to stimulate prison violence. Although almost every prison screens new inmates and classifies them according to standard criteria, misclassifications frequently occur. Pathological offenders or those who are mentally retarded or ill often respond with aggression to their forced interaction with other inmates. In fact, several prisons have few, if any, provisions for segregating different classes of offenders, although corrections standards are improving annually and the courts are increasingly requiring such segregation for inmate safety (Memory et al. 1999).

Only the most visible prisoner violence comes to the attention of prison officials. Where certain prisoners suffer physical injuries, these incidents are almost always recorded and reported. But much prisoner violence escapes detection by prison correctional officers. And even when officers suspect or observe rule-breaking and certain forms of inmate violence, it is sometimes not reported. Correctional officers sometimes do not report the misconduct they observe, since prisoner cooperation and compliance to prison rules are dependent upon the nonreporting behavior of officers. In some respects, this gives prisoners psychological power over the correctional officers who elect not to report the violence or infractions they may observe (Boin and Van Duin 1995).

Sexual assaults and psychological harassment are frequent in these high-risk settings, although some researchers believe that our estimates about the incidence of sexual attacks in prisons are exaggerated. In 2001 there were 17,263 staff assaults by inmates and 32,831 inmate-on-inmate assaults. About 20 percent of these assaults required medical attention, and about 10 percent were referred for criminal prosecution (Camp and Camp 2002:53). The average number of assaults per state agency has increased from 1993 to 2000 from 256 to 360.

Proposals for reducing inmate violence are about as diverse as the many solutions for alleviating prison overcrowding (Wooldredge, Griffin, and Pratt 2001). One means whereby prison officials can control violent conduct of inmates is through staff reports and recommendations that affect an inmate's early release. Good-time credits may be earned by inmates who obey prison rules and do not engage in serious rule infractions. Whenever correctional officers writeup inmates for rule violations or violent conduct, this writeup becomes a part of the inmate's institutional behavior file. Parole boards consult these files when considering inmates for early release. If a particular inmate's file contains writeups of violent conduct, then early release may be denied.

Prison Design and Control

Some proposals for resolving jail and prison problems are (1) to create new jails and prisons constructed in ways that will conserve scarce space and require fewer correctional officers and (2) to reconstruct existing facilities to minimize prison violence and house more inmates. Recent prison construction has included increasingly popular modular designs. New modular designs also permit layouts and arrangements of cell blocks to enhance officer monitoring of inmates. But new prison construction is expensive, and many jurisdictions are either unwilling or unable to undertake new prison construction projects (Waid and Clements 2001). One idea is to expand existing facilities to accommodate larger numbers of prisoners. One innovation has been the use of prefabricated designs, thus shortening considerably prison construction time. Components can be assembled in other locations and transported to the building site without considering the weather factor.

New jail and prison construction, the renovation or expansion of existing facilities, and the conversion of existing buildings previously used for other purposes take into account the matter of security and safety for both staff and inmates. Stairwells and areas otherwise hidden from the view of correctional officers encourage inmate sexual or otherwise physical assaults. These areas can either be reduced or eliminated entirely with new architectural designs. It is generally conceded that reducing blind spots or areas not directly visible to officers and other corrections officials helps to reduce the incidence of inmate assaults (Conley 2000; Waid and Clements 2001).

In some jurisdictions, buildings used previously for other purposes, even school buildings, have been converted to use as minimum- or medium-security facilities by state corrections agencies. While building conversions must be ac-

Control room at a medium-sized state penitentiary.

complished selectively and carefully, they do result in substantial savings to penal authorities. Of course, such facilities adapted for incarcerative purposes are often located in communities or near residential areas where the public may object to their reconstruction. Usually, conversion projects can be more successful where aggressive public relations and citizen education programs are implemented beforehand.

Sexual Exploitation

Sexual assaults and psychological harassment are increasingly a part of the environment of jails and prisons. A study of inmates from a prison in a Midwestern state found that prison violence affects almost every inmate. The fear of victimization is especially pervasive among the inmate population, and this fear substantially and adversely impacts an inmate's well-being (Human Rights Watch 2001a). One reason growing numbers of inmates seek out gang attachments is the belief that if they are a part of a gang, their likelihood of being victimized decreases. Although it is difficult to achieve, the best policy corrections officials should adopt is to create a prison environment free from psychological and physical victimization.

Apart from gang membership as a means of self-protection, the inmate-victims of sexual exploitation are often inhibited from reporting their victimization at the hands of other inmates. There is a substantial stigma attached to being raped in prison (Scarce 1997). Often men who have been raped do not report the sexual assault. Further, they do not seek medical attention or counseling. Thus, a sense of isolation and despair permeates many prison environments (Rokach and Cripps 1999).

Sexual violence is not limited to prisons for men. Women's prisons are notorious for sexual abuses of female inmates by other inmates and prison staff. Studies of 11 U.S. state prisons conducted between March 1994 and November

1996 found that incarceration in a women's prison can be terrifying for inmates. Male correctional officers physically and sexually abuse female inmates, producing a highly sexualized and hostile environment (Human Rights Watch Women's Rights Project 1996). Younger and mentally ill offenders are particularly vulnerable, although no group appears to be disproportionately targeted for abuse. A major factor facilitating sexual misconduct is that male correctional employees are permitted to have sexual contact positions with inmates, a situation that is strongly discouraged by international correctional standards and policies. Grievance and investigatory procedures, where they exist, are often vague and ineffective. Thus, inmates who complain and report their sexual assaults may face retaliation. Correctional staff who engage in these assaults continue their conduct because they do not fear administrative or criminal accountability (U.S. National Institute of Corrections 2000).

Some states, such as Hawaii, have reported high incidences of female inmate assaults. Political pressure has been brought to bear in Hawaii in order to afford female inmates with equal protection and the guarantees of sexual assault laws applied to their victimizers. Recommendations made by those investigating female assaults in Hawaiian prisons include (1) fully investigating rumors of staff sexual misconduct, (2) enforcing laws that make any staff/inmate sexual contact a crime, (3) conducting staff training programs in cross-gender supervision and increasing staff knowledge of female inmates' vulnerability, and (4) conducting more research (Baro 1997). Staff training cannot be overemphasized, since correctional officers are often the only staff in place to prevent violence against either male or female inmates (Marquart, Barnhill, and Balshaw 2001).

Many prisons make special provisions for sex offenders as a means of isolating them from the general prison population. Not only are these offenders closely monitored while imprisoned, but they are also supervised when they subsequently leave the prison environment on parole (Friendship and Thornton 2001). The Washington State Department of Corrections operates the Sex Offender Supervision Project as a means of reducing recidivism among sex offenders and providing relapse prevention training for correctional officers. Similar sex offender treatment programs are presently being offered in other countries, such as England (Patel and Lord 2001).

Inmates with AIDS and Other Communicable Diseases

A growing problem facing prison administrators is the rapid spread of Acquired Immune Deficiency Syndrome or AIDS. AIDS is often transmitted sexually, and crowded prisons are prime settings for AIDS epidemics (Hill 2002). Despite the best efforts of prison administrators and health officials, the number of estimated AIDS cases in U.S. prisons has risen steadily from 1995 (5,157) to 2000 (6,520). At yearend 2000, 2 percent (25,088) of state inmates and .8 percent (1,014) of federal inmates were known to be infected with HIV, the virus causing AIDS. Throughout all U.S. prisons, both federal and state, there were 6,642 confirmed (not estimated) AIDS cases (Maruschak 2002:5). There were an additional 8,615 jail inmates known to be infected with HIV, with 3,081 being confirmed as AIDS cases.

AIDS is not limited to prisons for men. In 2000 there were an estimated 2,472 female HIV cases in U.S. prisons (Maruschak 2002:3). This is nearly 10 percent of all HIV cases, although women make up only 7 percent of the U.S. prison population. Although little HIV/AIDS and/or drug treatment exists in female prisons, there is substantial risk of acquiring AIDS among female inmates

(Lang and Belenko 2001). Solutions to the AIDS problem in prisons have included physical isolation of any prisoner testing positive for the AIDS virus, the distribution of condoms to prisoners who wish to engage in sexual relations with other inmates, and hospitalizing any AIDS carrier (West 2001). But isolating prisoners with AIDS in special cells is cost-prohibitive. Solitary confinement on a large scale is a luxury many prisons cannot afford. Hospitalizing AIDS prisoners is perceived by some interests as a coddling maneuver unrelated to punishment. Condom distribution is perhaps the least expensive alternative.

Besides isolating prisoners from one another, some jurisdictions have sought to educate offenders in both jails and prisons. An HIV/AIDS education program was implemented in Florida jails and prisons. After the education program had been established, an evaluation was conducted of inmate knowledge about AIDS. Four jails, involving 310 inmates, and two prisons, involving 195 prisoners, were studied. On the whole, knowledge levels were good in both offender groups, although state prison inmates scored somewhat higher than jail inmates on HIV/AIDS awareness tests. Prison inmates were also able to differentiate between levels of risk, and they were able to identify appropriate behaviors for varying risk levels (Keeton and Swanson 1998). HIV/AIDS education is an increasingly important component of prisoner education, both in the United States and in other countries with sizable inmate populations (West and Martin 2000). On a positive note, AIDS-related deaths have dropped by more than 75 percent since 1995 (Maruschak 2002:5). In fact, the rate of AIDS-related deaths among U.S. prison inmates has declined from a high of 104 per 100,000 inmates in 1994 to 14 per 100,000 inmates in 2000. This is due largely to the greater sophistication of HIV/AIDS treatments and new drug developments.

Another contagious disease prevalent in U.S. prisons and jails is tuberculosis (TB). Tuberculosis, although curable with early detection and proper treatment, is easily transmitted through the air inmates breathe. TB increased substantially among prison and jail inmates during the 1980s and early 1990s. However, TB has declined in recent years in prison and jail populations, but it continues to affect U.S. prison and jail inmates at a much higher rate than the general public. In 1997, for instance, inmate TB cases disproportionately represented 3.7 percent of all TB cases in the United States. It is impossible to know how much TB exists in jails, because these inmate populations constantly change. The Centers for Disease Control have reported that the number of new TB cases declined from 1,065 in 1994 to 729 in 1997. This is positive news for prisoners. This decline is due, in part, to aggressive screening and prevention therapy practices employed by various prison systems, such as New York, where a serious outbreak of multidrug-resistant TB occurred in 1991. Nevertheless, the long-term nature of prison confinement poses a definite threat to unaffected prison inmates who are at maximum risk of being exposed to those with active TB (Hammett and Maruschak 1999).

The Constitutionality of Segregating AIDS-Infected Inmates.   There are other problems associated with segregating AIDS-infected inmates from the general population. Many inmates with AIDS feel that they are unfairly discriminated against by such prison policies and that they lose many privileges ordinarily available to other inmates (Feeney 1995:1). One of the strongest challenges made by AIDS-infected inmates against a state department of corrections occurred in Alabama in 1991. The case, *Harris v. Thigpen,* involved a claim by inmates that the Alabama Department of Corrections segregation policy relating to AIDS-infected inmates served no useful or legitimate penological interest. However, the court ruled in favor of the Alabama Department of Corrections, concluding that the prison setting is alive with high-risk behavior that is conducive to the spread of HIV/AIDS. The courts have ruled similarly in subsequent cases filed against corrections departments by inmates (*Austin v. Pennsylvania Department of Corrections* 1991; *Gates v. Rowland* 1994; *Nolly v. County of Erie* 1991) (Feeney 1995:2).

Inmates differ in their attitudes about common correctional AIDS policies in some jurisdictions (DeGroot 2001). In Texas, for instance, samples of ex-inmates were identified and interviewed about their prison experiences relating to AIDS and segregation policies. White ex-inmates were more concerned than black ex-inmates about contracting AIDS in prison. Older ex-inmates were more concerned about contracting AIDS, but they also were less supportive of AIDS policies than younger respondents (Hemmens and Marquart 1998).

SUMMARY

Prisons in the United States were originally constructed as places for warehousing offenders. Not much attention was given to inmate amenities. However, religious organizations, such as the Quakers, and reformers, such as William Penn, made substantial improvements in prison operations in Pennsylvania and other states during the formative years of the United States. These improvements or reforms led to the Pennsylvania system, a pattern of discipline and offender treatment that influenced prisons throughout Pennsylvania and other states for many decades. Prisoners were encouraged to grow their own food and exercise regularly, while simultaneously performing useful prison labor. Subsequently, the Auburn State Penitentiary was established. This New York institution ushered in the tier system and introduced solitary confinement as a way of segregating offenders from one another for various periods. Rules of silence were implemented, and prisoners were permitted to eat together in a common area. This was known as the congregate system.

Eventually, in 1870, several prominent prison reformers and leaders convened and formed what later became known as the American Correctional Association. This organization would have a profound effect on prison developments over the next century. One innovation was the establishment of the reformatory. The Elmira (New York) Reformatory was created in 1876. The reformatory was a good concept theoretically, but it was poorly implemented. Because many prisoners left prison unreformed, the reformatory concept diminished in popularity over the next sixty years. Subsequently, the various states and the federal prison system constructed numerous penitentiaries to accomplish diverse objectives related to rehabilitation, punishment, and reintegration. During the latter half of the twentieth century, there was great prison expansion, as the offender population outpaced the nation's population growth. Revised sentencing practices and tougher laws, particularly against violent crimes and drugs, led to longer sentences for offenders and greater prison overcrowding.

Massive prison construction programs also gave rise to different experiments in prison organization and administration. Prisoners have been regarded as a society within a society, and the total institution concept was formulated. Today prison administrators must deal with a more culturally diverse inmate population, replete with its own code of conduct and prison gangs. Prisons are increasingly dangerous places, and the level of inmate violence has increased. Various efforts by prison administration to control this violence have led to the creation of risk instruments for more effective institutional placements. Prisoners are normally housed today in several identifiable custody levels, including minimum-, medium-, maximum-, and supermax security, depending upon the risk they are believed to pose for other inmates and corrections personnel.

Significant developments have occurred in the attempt to measure offender risk and predict inmate behaviors for classification and placement, but all risk instruments are imperfect, constantly being revised and retested. Prediction schemes include actuarial prediction, anamnestic prediction, and clinical prediction, and each has its preferred users. But none of these prediction methods is any better than the others at forecasting inmate dangerousness. Thus, false positives and false negatives are two unfavorable consequences of poor risk instrumentation and erroneous prediction. Attempting to predict who should be incarcerated for longer periods, selective incapacitation, has not been particularly successful. Attention has also been focused on inmate needs, and attempts to measure these needs have resulted in the creation of needs assessment devices. On the basis of needs exhibited, prisons attempt to provide the necessary vocational, educational, and counseling programs and services that will meet inmate needs more effectively. However, prison overcrowding has caused these aims to be thwarted in many institutions, since not all prisoners can be accommodated, and not all prisoners can perform prison jobs or participate in these meaningful programs. Prisonization, or prison socialization, has spawned a unique prison culture. Inmates have established status and reward systems apart from general society, with their own codes of conduct or norms. Prison gangs have been pervasive and influential in this regard, as a major means of perpetuating prison culture.

Almost every prison system is overcrowded, depending upon how prison populations are measured. Several measures of inmate populations have been established, included rated capacity, design capacity, and operational capacity. These capacities are exceeded in numerous jurisdictions. Overcrowding has created an increasingly violent and hostile prison environment, and large-scale rioting has occurred. Various methods have been attempted to deal with inmate violence. One method has been the creation of inmate disciplinary councils whose job it is to decide various inmate issues. These inmate councils are often successful at resolving minor issues between inmates or staff that might otherwise have led to lawsuits or violence. Another factor has been new prison designs that have eliminated areas where prisoner assaults are most likely to occur. Greater surveillance of prison areas has reduced somewhat the level of inmate assaults and violence (Burdett and Retford 2003). Nevertheless, various problems among inmates persist. A portion of inmates in all prisons have communicable diseases, usually from drug use or illicit sexual contacts. HIV/AIDS and tuberculosis have become major health problems for prison administrators. Various steps, including segregation, have been taken to prevent the transmission of these and other diseases among the general inmate population.

QUESTIONS FOR REVIEW

1. How were prisoners housed in early U.S. prisons during the late 1700s?
2. What is the tier system? Why is it important to corrections in the United States?
3. What were the primary features of the Pennsylvania system? What is meant by the congregate system? Where was it first used?
4. What was Elmira Reformatory? Was it successful in the attainment of its goals? Why or why not?

5. What are some general differences between minimum-, medium-, and maximum-security prisons? In what ways are these differences related to prisoner self-esteem and self-confidence?

6. What is meant by the term total institution? Do all prisons have inmate subcultures? What are some of their characteristics and functions? How do prison gangs perpetuate inmate culture?

7. What is meant by management by objectives? How do wardens use management by objectives to improve their prison operations?

8. How effective are prisoner classification schemes? What are some of the methods whereby prisoners are classified?

9. What are some front-door solutions to prison overcrowding? What are some back-door solutions?

10. How is prison overcrowding reported? What are some of the criteria for determining whether prisons are overcrowded?

SUGGESTED READINGS

Huff, C. Ronald. *Gangs in America III.* Thousand Oaks, CA: Sage Publications, 2002.

Jewkes, Yvonne. *Captive Audience: Media, Masculinity, and Power in Prisons.* Portland, OR: Willan Publishing, 2002.

Johnson, Robert. *Hard Time: Understanding and Reforming the Prison.* Belmont, CA: Wadsworth/Thomson Learning, 2002.

Ross, Jeffry Ian and Stephen C. Richards. *Convict Criminology.* Belmont, CA: Wadsworth/Thomson Learning, 2002.

Tarver, Marsha, Steve Wallace, and Harvey Walker. *Multicultural Issues in the Criminal Justice System.* Boston: Allyn and Bacon, 2002.

INTERNET CONNECTIONS

American Civil Liberties Union
http://www.aclu.org

American Correctional Chaplains Association
http://www.correctionalchaplains.com/

Amnesty International
http://www.amnesty.org

Citizens for Effective Justice
http://www.okplus.com/fedup/

Federal Bureau of Prisons
http://www.bop.gov/

Federal Bureau of Prisons Library
http://www.bop.library.net/

Federal Prison Consultants
http://www.federalprisonconsultants.com/

George A. Keene, Inc.
http://www.keenejailequip.com/

National Institute of Corrections
http://www.nicic.org/

CHAPTER 8 | Corrections Administration and the Privatization of Prisons

Chapter Objectives — As the result of reading this chapter, the following objectives should be realized:

1. Presenting contrasting models of prison management and administration, including the bureaucratic model, legal-rational authority, and the human relations model.
2. Discussing the importance of the power variable in correctional settings and reviewing various forms of correctional administration, including the authoritarian model, the bureaucratic-lawful model, the shared-powers model, and the inmate control model.
3. Describing federal corrections, including the U.S. Parole Commission, the U.S.

Sentencing Commission, and pretrial services.
4. Identifying criteria useful in the selection and recruitment of correctional administrators and their staffs.
5. Focusing upon selected recruitment issues such as the hiring of women and minorities in correctional roles.
6. Highlighting the issue of privatization of corrections, various controversies generated by the privatization movement, and the operation of prisons for profit.

INTRODUCTION

• *A bloody inmate riot occurred at a prison during the weekend of April 29–30, 2000. Subsequently, 2,000 heavily armed soldiers and police swept through the prison and overwhelmed rioting inmates with force. The high-security prison was the Modelo Prison in Bogota, Colombia. In the aftermath, police found numerous weapons, including several AK-47 automatic rifles and several moonshine distilleries. There was also sophisticated communications equipment and attack dogs. At least 26 persons lost their lives, with 16 others seriously injured. Police Chief Rosso Jose Serrano, said that "this was the center of crime, extortion, kidnapping, prostitution, even satanic acts." Twenty-six pistols, 11 pounds of plastic explosives, 8 hand grenades, and 5,000 rounds of ammunition were also found. Authorities blame corruption among prison guards who made it easy for prisoners to smuggle weapons and other contraband into the prison over time. Colombia's prison system, not unlike other prison systems throughout the world, is chronically overcrowded. The Modelo Prison has become especially crowded in recent years. In most lockups, inmate subgroups virtually control separate cellblocks. Criminals have used Colombia's prisons to organize extortion and kidnapping rings and other rackets, something President Andres Pastrana's government has vowed to stop. This was the most comprehensive sweep of any Colombian prison in the past fifteen years. If such sweeps were conducted of U.S. prisons, do you think similar contraband might be found? What administrative safeguards should be in place to ensure that prison correctional officers are monitored and refrain from smuggling contraband into prisons for inmates? How should correctional officers be punished whenever they are caught smuggling contraband for inmates? What do you think?* [Adapted from the Associated Press, "Sweep of Prison Nets an Arsenal," May 2, 2000].

• *A new warden arrived at a state prison to take over the job of running the 2,300-inmate medium-maximum-security facility. He had a background in business administration and an M.B.A. degree from a well-known school in Boston. The prison was known for its lax enforcement of prison rules. Also, large quantities of drugs were readily available to virtually any inmate. The implication was that some of the correctional officers were smuggling contraband and drugs into the prison, since they were not subject to searches by others. The first act of the new warden was to assemble his staff together for a briefing on new prison policies. All prison rules were to be enforced rigidly. Shakedowns of cells would occur at random times. Any prisoner found in violation of the rules would spend at least a month in solitary confinement. All correctional officers would be subject to searches of their personal effects and their persons, commencing with the first of the next month. There would be random drug testing among the prison staff, as well as among the inmate population. Any correctional officer testing positive for drugs would be temporarily suspended, pending a recheck within a two-week period. Otherwise, the officer would be terminated. There was a lot of grumbling among both the prison staff and inmates. About a week later, the new warden received a visit from the correctional officer's union representative, who advised the warden that his new policies, specifically those involving prison staff, were in direct violation of certain union agreements and civil laws. Subsequently, the warden issued new policies that rescinded the old policies, and the correctional staff was notified that they would not have to undergo testing or searches. However, the warden insisted on having prisoners tested at random times. After several months of random drug testing, several prisoners filed suit against the warden and staff conducting these drug tests, alleging various civil rights violations under Section 1983 of Title 42 of the U.S. Code. The warden resigned after nine months on the job for personal reasons.* [Adapted from the Associated Press, "Warden Resigns under Pressure from Inmate Lawsuits," November 5, 2001].

• *A prison superintendent in charge of a medium-security state facility hired Kermit L. to be a correctional officer. According to personnel records, Kermit L. had been a correctional officer at two other state prisons in other jurisdictions and had a good work record.*

He had six years of experience as a correctional officer. After three months on the job at his new assignment, Kermit L. became increasingly negligent in his assignments. He frequently reported for work late, by as much as two hours. He took assignments lightly, and he often failed to follow through when ordered to perform simple tasks by his supervisors. Subsequently, his conduct was reported to the superintendent. The superintendent said he would look into it. Nothing was done to remedy his behavior, and his inappropriate conduct continued. One afternoon, a prison clerk in the superintendent's office, hearing about Kermit L.'s conduct from others, decided to do some investigation on her own. She called the other prisons where Kermit L. had worked. They had no record of such a person on their previous worksheets. A check of Kermit L.'s personnel file showed several letters of recommendation from the wardens of these other prisons. It turned out that these recommendation letters were forgeries. Further investigation revealed that Kermit L. was in fact the nephew of the present superintendent, and the superintendent was aware of Kermit L.'s bogus credentials. When confronted with this information, the superintendent said that he wanted to do a favor for his sister-in-law, the mother of Kermit L. Kermit L. had both a juvenile record and a criminal record, although this information was never disclosed when Kermit L. was hired. The Department of Corrections was notified of the superintendent's actions and terminated his employment with the prison. Kermit L. was fired and is no longer a correctional officer in any prison. He was never charged for impersonating a correctional officer. What sorts of background checks should be made of persons performing correctional officer work? How could this problem have been avoided? Should the bogus correctional officer be subject to criminal prosecution? What do you think? [Adapted from the Associated Press, "Bogus Correctional Officer and Superintendent-Uncle Fired," October 3, 2001].

This chapter describes prison administration. Wardens, superintendents, managers, and other administrative personnel who oversee prison operations play a pivotal role in the corrections enterprise. They not only ensure that existing policies established by local, state, or federal authorities are carried out, but they also initiate and come to be identified with their own policies and procedures. Those who manage our correctional institutions are faced with diverse challenges. They are expected to perform many functions and make critical decisions. The decisions made by prison administrators affect both prisoners and staff. Thus, whether prison inmates file large numbers of lawsuits or small numbers of them often depends upon the nature of prison administration. Whether prison officers perform their work effectively or ineffectively and have high or low job satisfaction frequently depends on the administrative style, leadership, and goal clarity of prison managers. Like captains of large ships, these administrators are responsible for whatever transpires within the scope of their **authority.** They take the heat when prison riots occur, and they accept the praise when prison operations run smoothly.

The first part of this chapter examines the bureaucratic model and its essential features. This model is pervasive throughout most organizational systems in the United States today, including prison organization. The bureaucratic model is subsequently contrasted with the human relations model. The different emphases and priorities of each model are described and explained. Prison administration involves the use of power. Therefore, several power schemes are examined. Whenever prison administrators and wardens make policy changes or introduce organizational innovations, power clusters emerge that react to these changes; thus, power clusters are highlighted.

State and federal prison organizations are examined and contrasted. Although some states allocate similar amounts for correctional purposes, they may have quite different offender populations. Other states with similar offender populations allocate quite different monetary resources for their corrections operations.

Obviously, the quality of offender programming in these different jurisdictions is affected. The federal organizational system is also examined in some detail.

At the administrative level, several different management styles are examined. These include the authoritarian model, the bureaucratic-lawful model, the shared-powers model, and the inmate control model. These models have different implications for inmates and prison staff, and these implications are examined. Other warden leadership styles are also examined, and the participation hypothesis is explained. No prison management style is adopted as the best style by all prison administrators, however, since many factors influence how wardens will function in their respective positions. Unlike sheriffs, who are elected, most prison wardens and superintendents are appointed to their positions by governors or other officials. Most prison wardens are college graduates with some administrative experience. There is substantial longevity associated with these positions, where most wardens stay at their jobs for many years. Wardens exert a great deal of influence over the security of their prison systems. Enlisting the cooperation of their subordinates is essential to effective prison operations.

In a growing number of jurisdictions, the private sector is becoming involved in prison operations and inmate supervision. While not everyone agrees that prisoners should be supervised by private interests, there is nothing unconstitutional about privatization thus far. In fact, proponents of privatization claim that they can offer necessary services for inmates at a lower cost compared with public agencies and personnel. Privatization is controversial and has generated several important issues that are presently unresolved. One of these issues pertains to the qualifications and professionalization of those who manage private prisons. Another issue has to do with accountability. Critics of privatization are interested in the accountability process and who should be blamed when organizations supervising offenders are improperly operated. This issue is examined.

Another issue that pertains to federal prison operations and to any prison inmate enterprise that produces goods for profit is whether this activity should persist. The Bureau of Prisons operates UNICOR, or Federal Prison Industries, Inc. This is a very profitable system that generates considerable revenue. However, various economic interests believe that cheap prison labor undermines their profit making and should be discontinued. However, prison officials respond by noting the obvious rehabilitative strengths of prison inmate labor. Some critics have complained that prison labor results in substandard products. However, these claims have been largely unsubstantiated. There are mixed feelings among the public concerning privatization and whether it is a good or bad thing. Whenever something goes wrong and private interests are responsible, such as prisoner escapes or misconduct behind bars, the media and privatization critics are quick to note these shortcomings. However, these same incidents occur in the public sector and draw little if any media interest. This debate is examined, and arguments for and against privatization are presented. Presently, the privatization issue remains unresolved.

THE BUREAUCRATIC MODEL AND LEGAL-RATIONAL AUTHORITY

Prisons are organizations. They aren't Sears and Roebuck, IBM, the Ford Motor Company, the Los Angeles General Hospital, the United Mine Workers Union, or the Tennessee Valley Authority, but they are organizations in that they share many features similar to these business and service institutions. In order to understand prison operations and administration, it is important to understand some basic principles of organizations in general. An early authority on organizational phenomena, Max Weber (1864–1920), introduced the concept of **bureaucracy** to organizational writers and analysts. Weber's original intention was to advance an ideal type of organizational structure that would lead to a maximization of **organizational effectiveness.** He described what effective organizations should be like and the characteristics they ought to possess.

The Bureaucratic Model

While more elaborate discussions of Weber's **bureaucratic model** are discussed elsewhere (Champion 2003; Davis 1962), the following description lists the essential characteristics Weber devised.

1. Hierarchical authority, which means an arrangement of supervisors and subordinates with vertical differentiation and a downward flow of power.

2. A priori specification of job authority and spheres of competence or **specialization,** where each position is clearly specified by a set of predetermined rules and regulations, with duties and responsibilities to be assumed and performed by those assigned different roles, and where no overlapping responsibilities exist.

3. Separation of policy and administrative decisions, where officials are obligated to implement policies of the organization apart from their own interests, and where those interests do not conflict with those of the organization as a whole.

4. **Selection by test,** where the most qualified people are selected to perform particular tasks according to their more extensive abilities and skills.

5. Appointment and promotion on merit, where those who do the best work are rewarded through promotions to higher positions, and those who deserve recognition are recognized for their particular accomplishments.

6. Impersonal relations between superiors, subordinates, and staff, where the abstract rules and regulations can be implemented without interference by personality or interpersonal differences, friendships, or other personal qualities.

7. Task specialization, where those performing different roles are selected on the basis of their expertise and have skills that uniquely fit the position as a specialty.

8. General rules to govern relations not specified by the above dimensions, where the organization adapts to change necessitated by circumstances internal and/or external to the organization, and where the organization may create new policies or rules to apply to new or changing situations.

Weber stressed that organizations should utilize **legal-rational authority,** which is based on law, where persons are vested with rights to order others to comply with directives. Weber also suggested that employees (1) ought to view their work as a vocation, (2) should enjoy a degree of social esteem associated with their work performance, (3) should have **appointment on merit** rather than election, (4) should plan on holding their position for life as a career, and that they (5) should have a fixed salary and security benefits should accrue with each position.

The Human Relations Model

A competing organizational model was advanced in the early 1930s known as the **human relations model.** The human relations model was developed by Elton Mayo, who conducted a series of experiments dealing with factors that affect worker productivity at the Hawthorne plant of the Western Electric Company (Pennock 1930; Putman 1930; Roethlisberger and Dickson 1939). The most important of these factors was special attention workers received from plant administrators. This factor became known popularly as the Hawthorne effect, and it helped to highlight the importance of human relations in the workplace.

The principal elements of the human relations model include (1) mutual or shared interests between the employer and employees; (2) recognition of individual differences, where employees are whole persons and not just impersonal entities with a mass of separate characteristics, and where the group is secondary to the individual in importance; (3) where motivation is critical and the individual must be encouraged through various stimuli to work with others productively toward shared objectives; and (4) human dignity, where respect and consideration are shown workers and they are treated as human beings rather than as cogs or interchangeable parts in a large machine (Davis 1962:14–19).

The human relations model is relevant for correctional institutions and staff. Allison (1987:55) says, regarding prison management, that

> ... despite the achievement of management growth and architectural enhancements, problems persist with the development and deployment of mid-management supervisors. . . . correctional facilities are run by people. . . . the organization will function no better than the people who work in the organization. . . . administrators by their very nature want to promote and experience success throughout their organization. . . . networking functions both formally and informally in an organization, and flexibility is its main advantage. . . . [the] process is a powerful one and when properly used can allow the organization the opportunity to achieve efficiency and enhance morale for all staff. . . . we are dancing to a different tune and believe this tune to be a direct reflection of our management system, tapped mid-managers' resources, and proper use of knowledge and power available in the organization. Clearly, our mid-managers [are] leading a successful escape from the prison management blues.

Correctional Settings and the Power Variable

Because of the complex nature of superior-subordinate relations, writers have devised various schemes to differentiate several types of **power.** Some of the more interesting power schemes have also sought to show the nature of subordinate involvement when compliance to commands is obtained. Two popular power schemes have been developed by French and Raven (1959) and Etzioni (1961). French and Raven have identified five different kinds of power that are found in interpersonal relations between superiors and subordinates. These are (1) **reward power,** where the superior rewards subordinates in different ways or uses the expectation of reward as an incentive for compliance; (2) **coercive power,** where the superior elicits compliance by threatening to punish subordinates if they do not comply; (3) **expert power,** where superiors use their expertise or special knowledge as a device to elicit compliance from subordinates; (4) **referent power,** where friendship is used by superiors to elicit compliance from subordinates; and (5) **legitimate power,** where subordinates comply as the result of a belief that the superior has the right to compel them to do something.

These different kinds of power have prompted others to speculate about the types of involvement elicited from subordinates. For instance, Etzioni (1961) developed a scheme similar to that devised by French and Raven, but where the nature of compliance was more extensively examined and the nature of involvement elaborated. Etzioni described remunerative, coercive, and normative compliance behaviors. These roughly parallel French and Raven's power types of reward, coercive, and legitimate. But Etzioni went further in his elaboration and discussed the possible implications for subordinates where different types of power were used to elicit compliance. Known as congruent types, these include (1) remunerative-calculative, where subordinates calculate the rewards associated with complying with commands from superiors and act accordingly, (2) coercive-alienative, where subordinates comply reluctantly with superiors' requests but are alienated as a result (this is the coercive type referred to by Weber), and (3) normative-moral, where subordinates consider the position of the superior and regard compliance as natural and moral.

In prisons, compliance for staff and particularly for inmates is coercive. Prisoners must obey superiors, otherwise punishments of various sorts result. The primary means of administrative control in penal institutions of any kind is coercive control. Most prisoners do not comply with prison directives simply because it is moral to do so or because it is the right thing to do. They comply because they are forced to comply. Of course, there is an element of remunerative power involved in these relationships as well, since administrators and officers are in positions to reward inmates in various ways.

In prisons, inmate privileges to engage in one type of behavior or another are highly prized. If inmates fail to abide by institutional rules, they suffer punishments. These punishments most frequently entail a loss of privileges. Access to scarce goods is a privilege, and those prisoners with outside connections and access to scarce goods are able to wield considerable power over other inmates. Yard privileges or access to recreational facilities is also a privilege. Correctional officers are instrumental in whether these privileges are extended or denied largely because of the reports they file about inmate behavior (Wright 1998).

A relationship between inmates and correctional officers also develops along remunerative-calculative lines, where correctional officers may ignore minor infractions of rules or departures from prison policy in exchange for orderly prisoner compliance with other, more important, prison rules. Despite this power advantage correctional officers possess in relation to inmates, some reports reflect that correctional officers feel somewhat powerless in other control areas. Their inability to change inmate behavior for the better, their perceived negative public image, feeling disappointed or disenchanted with correctional work as they originally envisioned it, and lacking sufficient input in policy decision making at higher administrative levels have been cited as associated with these feelings of powerlessness among corrections personnel (Carlson 2001).

Inmate cooperation is desirable in any prison setting, and it is in the best interests of administrators to do the sorts of things that facilitate inmate cooperation without jeopardizing prison security or compromising existing policies. In fact, compliance assessments are conducted of administrators in many prisons to ensure that statutory or public policies are being enforced. One measure of administrative compliance is an absence of prisoner rioting, work stoppages, or any other form of inmate misconduct (Montgomery and Crews 1998). A frequent concomitant of prisoner cooperation is a competent and capable contingent of corrections

   **BOX 8.1**

Michael J. Gilbert

Professor of Criminal Justice
University of Texas at San Antonio

Statistics

B.A. (zoology), University of New Hampshire; M.A. (teaching), University of New Hampshire; Ph.D. (public administration), Arizona State University

Professional Experience

I have served as a part-time educator for the U.S. Navy Disciplinary Command; an Inmate Education Officer, U.S. Army Disciplinary Barracks, Executive Office, Headquarters Company; Company Commander, 172nd Direct Support Detachment, Ft. Wainwright, Alaska; Assistant Director for Staff Development and Training, Alaska Department of Corrections; Administrator for Correctional Education and Training, Arizona Department of Corrections; correctional and criminal justice consulting; and a Professor of Criminal Justice at the University of Texas at San Antonio.

Background

I have been involved, in one way or another, with military and civilian correctional systems for over thirty years as a practitioner, consultant, or academician. At present, I am an Associate Professor of Criminal Justice at the University of Texas at San Antonio and have been a professor there since 1991. I did not set out to work in the justice system or become a professor. It all happened quite by accident. Somehow the lives we lead have a way of taking us to places and careers we did not anticipate. Be flexible and enjoy the ride.

I grew up in a small town in New Hampshire and was the first in my family to earn a college degree. As far back as I can remember, I wanted to be a pediatrician, but a rocky start during my freshman year kept me from getting into medical school. Instead, I earned a Master of Arts in Teaching

degree to teach high school biology. While working on my master's degree, I took a corrections theory and practice course. It was fascinating. My professor knew that I was working toward a degree in education and suggested that I apply for a part-time position at the Naval prison to teach inmates. To my surprise, I got the job. Teaching inmates was incredibly interesting. It was such a powerful experience that it changed my entire life. All notions of going to medical school or teaching high school disappeared. The criminal justice bug had bitten me and there was no turning back. I have loved every minute since.

Experiences

After being commissioned as a Second Lieutenant in the Army, I wanted to work at the U.S. Disciplinary Barracks. However, the Army had other ideas, and the Office of Personnel Operations at the Pentagon was not interested in what I wanted. As far as they were concerned, I was going to become a supply officer. Then fate stepped in. A friend of mine had a party at his house where I happened to meet his father. During our conversation, he asked if I planned to stay in the Army. When I said, "No," he asked why. I told him of the difficulty I was having getting an assignment to the military prison at Ft. Leavenworth. Two weeks later I received a call from the Pentagon telling me that I had an assignment to the prison at Ft. Leavenworth if I wanted it. I later learned that my friend's father was a Major General and the Comptroller General of the Army. It was pure luck.

Over the next twenty-five years, I worked as an administrator with the Alaska Department of Corrections and the Arizona Department of Corrections; as a criminal justice consultant; and as a criminal justice professor. From experience and study, I have learned four major lessons about corrections work.

First, the product of correctional officer supervision of inmates is not security and control but hundreds of daily interactions with inmates. These interactions can be constructive or destructive to both inmates and staff. Constructive interactions reduce security risks and make enforcement of rules easier to carry out. Destructive interactions create unnecessary enemies, hostility, conflict, and resentments that increase security risks and threaten the safety of everyone living or working in the prison.

Second, human decency, genuine concern, fairness, and reasonableness by correctional officers in their dealings with inmates are essential attributes of effective correctional supervision because they facilitate control, security, and safety.

Third, compliance with all prison rules, all of the time, is not possible for either inmates or correctional officers. When supervisors or managers demand 100 percent enforcement of rules, it is inconsistent with the reality of prison work where most situations confronting officers don't fit the rules, and officers must make decisions about whether, when, and how to enforce these rules. Attempts to rigidly enforce rules may turn a manageable situation into an escalating confrontation. Such efforts ignore the basic reality that officers must gain the cooperation of inmates if they are to do their job effectively and safely. Inmates must perceive that they are being treated reasonably and fairly if they are to cooperate. Rigid enforcement increases incentives for inmate violence, resistance, hostility, confrontations, vandalism, escapes, and riots. None of these outcomes are consistent with the personal safety of the officer, inmate control, or institutional security. Effective officers know when to enforce and how to enforce rules so that inmates perceive their interactions with correctional officers as "just." These officers also know when to ignore or informally enforce rules.

Fourth, hierarchical and paramilitary organizational structures, used by most correctional agencies, assume that correctional workers have little discretionary power. Such organizations place excessive reliance on formal rules to govern officer conduct. They assume that officers have little discretionary power and will behave as directed or ordered. This is a fallacy. Everyone has discretionary power—including correctional officers. The discretionary power of individual officers cannot be removed by management directives and can be used in ways that are consistent or inconsistent with the law or management preferences. The challenge for management is to manage in ways that recognize this reality. This means helping officers to develop and internalize shared values consistent with law and management preferences. This is attained through values-based training, frequent discussions about the routine quandaries officers encounter, and open discussion of problems encountered on the job. These types of efforts provide a frame of reference for officers so that they make reasonable and appropriate decisions when there is uncertainty over the appropriateness or effectiveness of "going by the book."

Advice to Students

If you want to advance your career quickly, you should do two things to set yourself apart from others—complete a graduate degree and publish articles in professional or academic journals. Then, when you finally make it to a supervisory or management position, remember and apply the four lessons I have shared with you to the correctional management problems you face. If I had been accepted into medical school or had gone on to teach high school biology, I would not have enjoyed the career I have had. It has been extraordinarily fascinating, challenging, and rewarding. I wish you well in your journey.

 **BOX 8.2**

PRISON SHOE FACTORY
WORK CAN BE DANGEROUS

The Clements Unit of the Texas Department of Criminal Justice

Working with inmates as a corrections officer is considered reasonably safe by many of those performing these roles. Certainly working around inmates who have earned the right to perform prison labor and work at productive prison jobs would be considered one of the safest assignments. These inmates are literally handpicked from the total inmate population according to behavioral criteria. These are inmates who have proven track records of law-abiding conduct, are exemplary, and have demonstrated that they can obey the institutional rules and behave well. But there are occasional exceptions.

On Wednesday, January 29, 2003 at about 7:00 A.M., Stanley A. Wiley, 38, a supervisor at the Texas Department of Criminal Justice Clement Unit, a prison constructed in 1990 with an inmate capacity of 4,000, was stabbed in the throat by one of the inmates. Wiley was the supervisor of the prison shoe factory, which employed 50 inmates who earned a decent prison wage manufacturing shoes for other inmates. Wiley, from Amarillo, had joined the prison system as a corrections officer in June 1994. He worked at the Clements Unit until June 2000, when he was promoted to an industrial specialist position and assigned the job of supervising inmates working in the prison shoe factory. Following the stabbing, Wiley was first rushed to the prison infirmary and then transported by ambulance to an Amarillo hospital near the prison. He was pronounced dead shortly after being taken to the hospital. Wiley was the first corrections officer to die in the line of duty since another officer, Daniel Nagle, was fatally stabbed in a December 1999 attack at another unit, the McConnell Unit, in Beeville. Robert Lynn Pruett was convicted of Nagle's slaying and is currently on death row.

The inspector general of the Texas Department of Criminal Justice indicated that "We have several witnesses. There is significant evidence and eyewitnesses." The alleged perpetrator is Travis Trevino Runnels, 26, who is serving a 70-year term from Dallas County for aggravated robbery. Runnels is not eligible for parole until 2025. He had two prior convictions for burglary. Larry Todd, a spokesman for the Texas Department of Criminal Justice, said, "We have numerous investigators on the scene talking to witnesses and gathering information. We are conducting a criminal investigation as well as an administrative review. We are still attempting to determine how the inmate had access to the weapon, which may have been a knife used by other inmates to trim the shoes. It's very common for those inmates to be assigned cutting tools while they are working, but obviously they turn them back in at the end of the day." Overall for the year 2002, the Texas prison system reported 41 serious staff assaults, meaning that they were treated for injuries that went beyond first aid from medical staff. The prison was locked down following the stabbing incident.

Should inmates have access to dangerous weapons, such as knives, while working at prison jobs? How should prison administrators and staff screen those potentially capable of violent acts from participating in rehabilitative programs such as shoe manufacture?

Source: Adapted from the Associated Press, "Prison Guard Killed in Inmate Attack," January 30, 2003.

officers. Administrators have considerable say about who is hired and the duties they are subsequently assigned. It is no secret that an often-neglected resource is the corrections officer as a important key to understanding and dealing with inmate problems and potential subsequent litigation (Carter 2001). The prison administrator is highly dependent upon the available officer pool, however, and is not directly involved in the selection and recruitment of corrections officers.

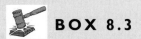 **BOX 8.3**

ATTICA RIOTING OF 1971 STILL IN COURT LITIGATION IN 2000

$8 Million Offered to Former Attica Inmates to End Lawsuit

It was one of the worst prison riots in U.S. history. In September 1971, inmates of the Attica Correctional Facility near Buffalo, New York, rioted. They were protesting many things, including how they were being treated by prison staff. There were complaints about the conditions under which they were being housed. The riots occurred over a five-day period. Nearly 1,300 inmates held numerous prison guards hostage and attempted to negotiate for improved prison conditions and inmate benefits. On the fifth day of rioting, New York state police launched an all-out assault on the maximum-security Attica facility, where more than 2,000 rounds of ammunition were fired in just six minutes. When the rioting ended, 32 inmates and 11 prison guards were dead. Hundreds more were wounded. In the years following the Attica prison rioting, many of the inmates or their relatives filed a class action suit against the state of New York, claiming they were tortured, beaten, and denied medical treatment in the aftermath of the riot. The lawsuit was filed in 1974 and sought $100 million from New York. There were also individual lawsuits filed against the state and various state officials by individual inmates who elected to take their own action. Some of these suits were settled.

One inmate, Frank "Big Black" Smith, was a leader in the rioting. Smith, who was released from prison in 1973, said that he had been forced to lie on a table while officers beat and burned him. He was also ordered to hold a football under his chin and threatened with death if he allowed it to fall.

In 1997 Smith was awarded $4 million by a federal jury. Another injured inmate, David Brosig, received $75,000 for his injuries from a similar jury decision. On January 4, 2000, New York agreed to pay inmates $8 million as an offer to settle the lawsuit once and for all. Inmates or their heirs must contact the plaintiff's lawyers to be included in the settlement. U.S. District Judge Michael Telesca was scheduled to hold hearings in February to give claimants a chance to object to the terms of the settlement, but he said that he expects a final deal to be reached by the end of 2000. Judge Telesca said, "There is no ideal time to solve a case like this, but I am assured the time is now. Any deal would not determine who was right and wrong. I will leave that to history." In agreeing to settle, New York admitted no wrongdoing. It also agreed to pay the inmates' lawyers fees up to $4 million and costs. Frank "Big Black" Smith offered his opinion. "I want to thank the judge for helping to resolve the protracted dispute. God bless you. I think where we're at today is where we need to be."

Should inmates be reimbursed for their legal fees when they initiated a major riot that left many inmates and prison guards dead or seriously injured? Was New York at fault for attempting to quell the riot in 1971? Was deadly force justified, especially when it was learned that threats had been made against the lives of guards whom the prisoners held hostage? What should be a fair compensation to surviving inmates and their families? What do you think?

Source: Adapted from the Associated Press, "Attica Riot Inmates Offered $8 Million," January 5, 2000.

Administrators are in positions where they can influence the nature of training officers receive. One important area where administrators can be beneficial is assisting officers in dealing with stress, particularly anger, resulting from inmate provocations. Even though administrative personnel are dependent upon external funding for and decisions by others about employee quality, there is still much they can do to motivate and encourage existing staff to perform their roles effectively.

Power Clusters. Despite the power of prison administrators to make policy changes within their particular prison environments, there are other powerful forces at work to influence, and in some cases control, whatever prison administrators do. Some investigators have referred to these powerful forces as **power clusters.** Power clusters are issue networks and vested interest groups that have a stake in correctional agency organization and operation and that work in partnership with other groups or individually to bring about a particular end or ensure that their interests are protected and perpetuated (Wittenberg 1996:44). Figure 8.1 shows several power clusters that are in the general environment of correctional agencies.

Figure 8.1 shows six different power clusters that appear to orbit around a correctional agency. The news media forms a power cluster, just as the executive branch, community, law enforcement, the judiciary, and the legislative branch of government form power clusters. Each of these clusters represents influence. For example, suppose a corrections department establishes a halfway house in a community and forms a liaison between the prison and the halfway house for receiving paroled inmates for community treatment. Some neighborhood residents and city government representatives join forces to oppose the placement of the halfway house in their community. The media fuels the opposition and the judiciary may provide these other power clusters with injunctive relief, effectively denying the halfway house the right to operate in that particular community. However, not all power clusters operate adversely in relation to corrections agencies. Some power clusters may assist corrections departments in their siting decision making, and the media power cluster may provide the

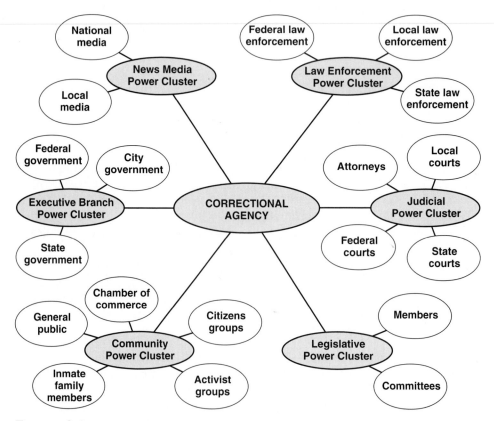

FIGURE 8.1 Power Clusters Surrounding a Typical Correctional Agency.
Source: Peter M. Wittenberg. "Power, Influence and the Development of Correctional Policy." *Federal Probation* 60 (1996): 45.

public with educational information and support. The fact is that correctional administrators do not operate in a total vacuum. Other factors are at work, whatever we may call them, including power clusters (Wittenberg 1996:44).

During the last three decades, correctional settings have been influenced increasingly by court decrees that mandate prison improvements to make these facilities more habitable. Federal district courts have been instrumental in promoting numerous prison reforms. Changes have been ordered relating to the physical condition of public facilities, staffing, reduction of institutional populations, and the quality of government services. Thus, the courts have

Gyms and weight rooms are standard features of many U.S. prisons.

effectively intruded into the realm of fashioning new policies for many prison settings (Fliter 1993). Not all prison reforms caused by court action are necessarily dedicated to the improvement of inmate amenities, however. In the United States and other countries, such as the Netherlands, prison reforms may include heightening security conditions and developing more supermax facilities to house high-risk offenders (Boin 2001).

CORRECTIONS AND OFFENDER MANAGEMENT

Supervising dangerous offenders doesn't always mean supervising offenders who will endanger others. Some offenders who are mentally ill may pose threats to themselves as well as to others (Monahan et al. 2001). Many of those released from prisons exhibit signs or characteristics of mental illness and should receive needed treatment from one or more community agencies (Harris and Lovell 2001). However, not all communities have the capacity to deal with these offenders. Mentally ill offenders may engage in self-destructive acts. They may also be unwilling to be referred to a mental health agency for treatment. It is not always the case that these persons are shuffled back to prisons (Baillargeon and Contreras 2001). Rather, community mental health agencies exist to treat these persons in limited ways.

Supervising high-risk offenders may pose other risks. Some offender-clients are dangerous and/or have a high likelihood of program failure. These persons need closer supervision or monitoring than other offenders on standard probation. Some observers suggest high-risk offender intervention strategies that incorporate accountability and acceptance of responsibility with law internalization and community expectations (Olson, Weisheit, and Ellsworth 2001).

THE ORGANIZATION OF CORRECTIONS

State Corrections Organizations

State Prison Systems and Departments of Corrections.   There is considerable variation among states in their correctional organization, operations, and budgets. No state is required to follow any federal correctional system or plan, and as a result, a mixture of agencies and organizations is found when examining differences among state correctional apparatuses. Furthermore, state budgets with similar inmate and probationer/parolee populations vary greatly, depending upon how much priority is given to corrections. Two examples of states with similar numbers of correctional officers and probation/parole officers are Arkansas and Oregon. In 2001, Oregon had 3,424 personnel in their adult correctional system, with 2,058 correctional officers. For comparison, Arkansas had 3,270 personnel and 2,847 correctional officers.

Despite these correctional personnel similarities, there are differences between the two states regarding numbers of inmates in their correctional facilities, especially their numbers of probationers and parolees. In 2001, for example, Arkansas had only slightly more prison inmates (12,429) compared with Oregon (10,722). However, Oregon's adult correctional budget was nearly twice as large as Arkansas's budget ($409.5 million compared with $252.6 million) (Camp and Camp 2002:102). Arkansas had about 50 percent more convicted offenders on probation compared with Oregon (30,353 compared with 18,483) (Camp and Camp 2002:186). However, Arkansas had almost the same number of the

The Organization of Corrections 359

parolees (9,453) compared with Oregon's parolee population (10,086). Overall, there were over 39,700 probationers and parolees under supervision in Arkansas in 2001 compared with about 28,500 probationers and parolees under supervision in Oregon. But that same year, the Arkansas probation and parole operating budget was $14.5 million compared with an Oregon probation and parole operating budget of $49.3 million. Thus, it would appear that Oregon, with a considerably smaller probationer/parolee population than Arkansas, had an operating budget for probationers and parolees in 2001 that was over three times as large as Arkansas's operating budget. This expenditure differential is attributable, in part, to the fact that in 2001, Arkansas spent an average of $1.75 per day per client under probation/parole supervision, while Oregon spent an average of $4.48 per day (Camp and Camp 2002:206–207). Perhaps one explanation for this great difference is the fact that Oregon has a more extensive array of programs for probationers and parolees compared with Arkansas.

The correctional organization of the two states also varies in complexity. Oregon has a Department of Corrections that provides correctional services through Institutions. The Department of Human Resources provides juvenile correctional services through the Oregon Youth Authority. Within Institutions, there are twelve correctional facilities including a penitentiary, six correctional institutions, a women's correctional center, two correctional facilities, and a camp. Under Juvenile Services there are two training schools and five correctional camps.

In contrast, Arkansas has a Board of Correction and Community Correction that oversees the Department of Correction, the Department of Community Correction, and a Department of Human Services. The Department of Correction is broken down into five divisions. These are the Administrative Services Division, Construction and Maintenance Division, Health and Correctional Programs Division, Institutions Division, and Operations Division. There are also twelve adult prisons or units, including one female unit. Two additional prisons, one male and one female, are privately contracted and operated by the Wackenhut Correctional Corporation. Within the Department of Community Correction, there are eight centers (e.g., work release, community punishment, and bi-state detention). Under the Department of Human Services, Arkansas has a Division of Youth Services, which is privately contracted. There are eight youth centers and programs privately contracted and operated by Cornell Corrections, Inc., Consolidated Youth Services, and South Arkansas Youth Services. Arkansas has a youth parole board, whereas Oregon does not. However, there are over three times as many wardens and administrators of adult correctional facilities in Oregon (174) compared with Arkansas (49).

Oregon has a three full-time members of the Board of Parole and Post-Prison Supervision appointed by and answerable to the governor for parole decisions. Arkansas has Post-Prison Transfer Board consisting of seven full-time members who make parole decisions as well as executive clemency and pardon recommendations to the governor. Panels of two members interview prospective parolees and make recommendations. The final parole decision is made by the full board to either approve or disapprove one's early release from custody (American Correctional Association 2002:111). In both state jurisdictions, considerable autonomy and responsibility is given to individual counties for administering detention centers, holdover facilities, and community corrections programs.

These differences in just two states suggest that it is difficult to devise a standard officer-client formula or ratio that can be applied across all state jurisdictions. Compared with Arkansas and Oregon, Maine has only a Department of Corrections, which administers the Maine State Prison, three adult correctional centers, and a youth center. Maine's Division of Probation and Parole is a part of the Department of Corrections and has six districts. Since Maine abolished parole in 1976, the Maine Parole Board consists of five part-time members who convene from time to time to hear exclusively the remaining pre-1976 cases. At yearend 2001, there were only 27 parolees in Maine, down from 57 in 1997 (Glaze 2002:5). But the abolition of parole by a state, such as Maine, doesn't necessarily mean that there is a corresponding reduction in the workload of POs in the state. In 2001, for example, Maine had the largest amount of probationer growth (14.8 percent) compared with all other states and the federal government. At yearend 2001, there were 8,939 probationers under supervision in Maine, up from 7,788 at the beginning of the year (Glaze 2002:5). In fact, Maine had approximately twice as many probationers compared with combined parolee-probationer populations of individual states such as New Hampshire, North Dakota, South Dakota, Alaska, and Wyoming.

Because of the fragmented nature of local and state correctional agencies and organizations, frequently the operation of programs and services suffers. Many state and local correctional agencies make minimal effort to coordinate their activities. An absence of effective and efficient planning is more the rule than the exception. It would be misleading to feature the correctional organization and arrangement of one state as the ideal for others to follow. The volume of offenders varies greatly among the different state and local jurisdictions. Also, the types of offenders vary. However, a careful examination of the correctional organization of various states will tell us much about the centralized or decentralized nature of these organizations.

In the Oregon–Arkansas example of correctional organizations, both Arkansas and Oregon have decentralized systems. The Arkansas Post-Prison Transfer Board can make decisions independent of the intervention of others, such as the governor. Likewise, the Oregon Board of Parole and Post-Prison Supervision consists of three full-time members who are appointed by the governor but serve as an independent body. The power relation in both states between the governor and individual board members is such that the governor may appoint and terminate parole board members at will. Generally, the greater the **decentralization** of power relative to offender management, the more difficult it is for effective coordination between organizations to occur.

Wyoming is one of the most centralized states, with four major administrative organizations to oversee all correctional operations. **Centralization** is found whenever there are few persons at the top of an organizational hierarchy who have decision-making power. The Wyoming Department of Corrections is responsible for the management of all penal institutions. A Division of Field Services operates all probation and parole activities. The Board of Parole recommends sentence commutations to the governor and controls good-time awards. Finally, the Department of Family Services oversees all juvenile functions (American Correctional Association 2002). Most of the other states have decentralized systems, since so many different boards and departments have jurisdictional authority over various facets of their corrections operations.

Federal Corrections

The **U.S. Department of Justice** exercises administrative control over all federal correctional agencies and organizations including (1) the Federal Bureau of Prisons, (2) the U.S. Parole Commission, (3) the U.S. Courts, and (4) the U.S. Sentencing Commission.

The Federal Bureau of Prisons. The **Federal Bureau of Prisons (BOP)** was established in 1930 by Congress (American Correctional Association 2002). By 2000, the BOP operated 101 correctional institutions arranged according to level of custody from maximum-security penitentiaries such as the one at Marion, Illinois, to minimum-security prison camps like Allenwood Federal Prison Camp at Montgomery, Pennsylvania (American Correctional Association 2002). Box 8.4 shows the organization of the Federal Bureau of Prisons.

In 2001, the Federal Bureau of Prisons had a budget of $4.6 billion, with $3.8 billion in operating budget and $867 million in capital budget (Camp and Camp 2002:102). There were 156,993 federal inmates in 2001, with 31,669 federal probationers and 76,089 federal parolees (Glaze 2002:3,5). Total 2001

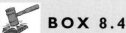 **BOX 8.4**

ORGANIZATION OF THE FEDERAL BUREAU OF PRISONS

Director (Dr. Kathleen M. Hawk Sawyer)

Administration Division (Budget development, execution, capacity planning, design and construction, facilities management, finance, management support, procurement and property, site selection and environmental review, trust fund)

Community Corrections and Detention Division (Community corrections, detention services, National Office of Citizen Participation)

Correctional Programs Division (Correctional services, chaplaincy services, psychology services, correctional programs, inmate systems management)

General Counsel and Review (Office of General Counsel, legislative and correctional issues, commercial branch, equal employment opportunity, freedom of information/privacy, ethics, rules, administrative remedies, National Legal Training Center, Staff Training Academy-Glynco)

Health Services Division (Office of Medical Director; systems, policy, planning and evaluation, health services program)

Human Resource Management Division (Labor-management relations, affirmative action, national recruiting office, examining, conference coordinator, security and background investigation, training operations, field training services, employee relations, human resources management information system, human resource research and development, policy and professional development, pay and position management, staffing)

Industries, Education and Vocational Training (Corporate management, ombudsman, management information systems, management control system, project group, human resources, plans and policy, products, marketing, procurement, engineering, financial management education, training and recreation, inmate work programs, competition, activation)

Support Divisions

Information, Policy and Public Affairs Division (Public affairs, security technology, national policy review, archives, external liaison, documents control, research and evaluation information systems)

National Institute of Corrections (Technical assistance, grants, National Academy of Corrections, National Jail Center, Information Clearinghouse)

Program Review Division (Office of assistant director, program review branch, program analysis branch, internal control branch, competition advocacy program, office of strategic planning)

Regional Offices: Mid-Atlantic (Annapolis Junction, MD); North Central (Kansas City); Northeast (Philadelphia); South Central (Dallas); Southeast (Atlanta); and Western (Dublin, CA)

Source: Compiled by author.

Federal Bureau of Prisons personnel were 32,689, with 14,063 of these as corrections officers (Camp and Camp 2002:150,152).

The U.S. Parole Commission

When the Federal Bureau of Prisons was conceived in 1930, the **U.S. Parole Commission** (USPC) was also established. It was originally called the U.S. Board of Parole (Runda, Rhine, and Wetter 1994). The USPC is under the administrative control of the U.S. Department of Justice and is responsible for the management and monitoring of all federal prisoners who are released on parole or mandatory release. The USPC is responsible for the classification and placement of parolees and maintaining reports on their progress. In order to accomplish these tasks, **community supervision officers** oversee and monitor offenders. These community supervision officers are employed by the various U.S. district courts and manage federal probationers as well as parolees (American Correctional Association 2002). In addition, these community supervision officers function as parole officers and prepare reports for the commission about parolee progress.

U.S. Pretrial Services

The U.S. Pretrial Services officers and probation officers serve in 94 judicial districts and territories (American Correctional Association 2002:817). Pretrial Services officers conduct **pretrial release** investigations for persons charged with federal offenses as well as supervise defendants released pending final disposition, including those placed on pretrial diversion (American Correctional Association 2002:817). Following federal trials, U.S. probation officers supervise convicted federal offenders who are sentenced to probation and conduct presentence investigations of offenders who are awaiting sentencing for U.S. district court judges. Federal probation officers also supervise those on supervised release imposed following a period of confinement under the Sentencing Reform Act of 1984, when the federal sentencing guidelines were enacted. The act took effect in October 1987. Until then, those placed on probation by federal judges were considered probationers. Following October 1987, these persons became known as supervised releasees.

One innovation for U.S. probation and pretrial services occurred in 1989, when the Probation and Pretrial Services Automated Case Tracking System (PACTS) was implemented (Administrative Office of U.S. Courts 1998). This new system was designed to collect and transmit valuable case information to the Administrative Office of the U.S. Courts for the purpose of tracking the progress of all ongoing federal cases. The PACTS system is regarded as largely successful in optimizing information availability, although some additional training has been required of U.S. probation officers and pretrial release officers who must access the system frequently to locate important information about specific offenders.

The U.S. Sentencing Commission

An independent agency in the judicial branch, the U.S. Sentencing Commission consists of nine members (seven voting members) and is charged with promulgating mandatory sentencing guidelines for federal judges to use when sentencing convicted federal offenders. Created under the Comprehensive Crime Control Act of 1984, the Commission's goals include reducing unwarranted disparity in sentences for offenders who commit similar offenses and ensure fairness and certainty in sentencing. New sentencing guidelines created by the U.S. Sentencing Commission went into effect on November 1, 1987. The guidelines and related sentencing provisions determine the appropriate sentence based on the specific characteristics of the offense and the offender. If incarceration is imposed, the guidelines specify a range of months from which judges must choose a specific sentence. By statute, offenders sentenced under the new guidelines are not parole-eligible. Additional responsibilities of the Commission include ongoing monitoring, amendment, and sentencing education responsibilities. The Commission members are presidential appointees with the advise and consent of Congress. The U.S. Attorney General and chair of the U.S. Parole Commission also sit on the Commission as nonvoting ex-officio members (U.S. Sentencing Commission 1997).

FORMS OF CORRECTIONAL ADMINISTRATION

One of the most common turning points reported among correctional officers relates to problems with prison administration and opening lines of communication between correctional officer staff and their supervisors (Wright 1998). If administrative personnel come largely from professional backgrounds unrelated to corrections, a conceptual Tower of Babel may exist between administrators and officers about how best to view the professionalization of correctional work. It is likely, however, that administrators quickly become attuned to their settings and make necessary adjustments to acquire the necessary skills to facilitate communication between themselves and their employees as well as the inmates.

No particular administrative style fits prison administrators, wardens, managers, or superintendents (Toch 2002). Each administrator develops a style individualized to fit the setting, staff, and inmate culture. But since administrators are in key power positions, they may choose to consolidate this power or distribute it among several staff members. Using organizational terminology, administrators either centralize or decentralize the decision-making apparatus of their institutions, and they conduct their administrative affairs according to the power scheme they have fashioned.

Centralization is the limited distribution of power for various administrative decisions among a few staff members at the top of the authority hierarchy in the prison. Decentralization is the widespread distribution of power among many staff members, perhaps extending to include some inmates as representatives of the larger prisoner aggregate. Those correctional officers who happen to be employed in a prison where the administrative philosophy is centralization of decision making will likely feel powerless in influencing prison operations. However, those who work in settings characterized by decentralization probably will be involved to a greater degree in the decision-making process.

The **participation hypothesis** says that those who participate to a greater degree in decision making, especially decisions affecting their own work, may be more satisfied with their jobs and may even be more loyal to the organization (Patenaude 2001). By the same token, those officers who are less involved in decisions affecting their work may be less satisfied and conceivably less loyal. If we were to adopt this framework for assessing correctional officer complaints about their lack of involvement in prison affairs, no doubt much of their behavior would be explained (Slate, Vogel, and Johnson 2001).

One innovation in jail officer supervision of inmates, for instance, has involved the new-generation jail. Jail officers are placed in somewhat autonomous, self-contained modules or podular areas where they can directly supervise and

BOX 8.5

PERSONALITY HIGHLIGHT

Bobby D. Lumpkin

Assistant Warden, Holliday Unit, Texas Department of Criminal Justice, Huntsville, Texas

Statistics

B.S. (criminal justice and corrections), Sam Houston State University; master's degree in progress (public administration and criminal justice), Texas A & M International University

Background and Interests

Presently I am the Assistant Warden at the Holliday Unit of the Texas Department of Criminal Justice, Huntsville, Texas. Before my current position, I served in numerous assignments, including major, captain, lieutenant, sergeant, and corrections officer. I have been employed with the Texas Department of Criminal Justice since 1990.

I grew up in the small community of Valley Mills, Texas, near Waco. Upon completing high school, I pursued my college education and began employment with an entertainment establishment in Waco. There I became night management of the establishment and found myself in charge of hiring and terminating employees as well as overseeing the entire security of a 1,500-person capacity nightclub. After a few years, I applied with the Texas Department of Corrections (later changed to the Texas Department of Criminal Justice) after ob-

serving an ad for help in a local newspaper. Upon completion of correctional training, I was assigned to the Diagnostic Unit in Huntsville. Little did I know that, eleven years later, I would find myself as the Assistant Warden after being assigned to a number of units with a variety of custodies as well as at one time working on a unit with female offenders who included death row–sentenced offenders. During these different tours, I was gradually—and at times rapidly—promoted through the paramilitary rank structure. At the same time, I spent many hours rearranging my work schedule with the blessing of my supervisors in order to complete my education.

Experiences

Throughout my career I have been involved in and dealt with many different and unique incidents. In one particular incident, I was assigned as a lieutenant at the Cotulla Unit in

respond quickly to inmates and whatever types of problems might arise. They are, in effect, mini-wardens, since they theoretically control their immediate work environment. However, it has been found that jail officers who work under these conditions do not consider themselves enriched by their jobs. Neither do they feel that they have the type of control, discretion, and autonomy that might cause their job satisfaction levels to rise. This is because they are operating in a rigid, bureaucratic environment where their every move and decision has been orchestrated by others. Thus, maximum managerial control has overridden jail officer decision making and discretion such that these jail officers feel powerless in an otherwise powerful work location (Zupan 1991). Therefore, only the illusion of participation in decision making exists in such environments. The reality is that jail officers often feel that, under such circumstances, they perceive a lack of trust from their superiors, signifying rightly or wrongly that these officers are incapable of making sound discretionary choices.

Cotulla, Texas. A neighboring unit, the Dolph Briscoe Unit in Dilley, Texas, experienced a full-level riot involving approximately 600 offenders. The riot stemmed from racial tension between black and Hispanic offenders. It so happened that I resided in Dilley at the time and was within minutes from the unit. Upon my arrival, I fully expected the disturbance to be under control. However, as soon as I arrived at the front gate and exited my vehicle, I could distinctly hear offenders hollering and screaming, numerous fire alarms wailing, and chemical agents being dispersed. With the assistance of several staff members from other units and outside law agencies, the riot was quelled within an hour.

Several months later, I was promoted to captain at the Dolph Briscoe Unit, the scene of the riot. Nervousness set in hours before reporting to the unit for my first day of work. I took the same route to the unit as I had done months earlier when responding to the disturbance. This time when exiting the vehicle, it immediately struck me how much quieter the unit was than it had been since my last visit. Regardless, I quickly reminded myself of the noises I had heard and events I had witnessed before and that the ingredients are always present for another incident if sound management and intelligence are not in place.

I would like to think that I thought of the dangers of the job before this incident; however, I am not sure that I did. Without a doubt, I have given thought to these dangers since the incident, and I try to make an assessment of the job on a day-to-day basis. One thing I have practiced while being a correctional supervisor and a correctional administrator is to never forget where I came from. My current position entails about 70 percent office work and conducting interviews and 30 percent tending to miscellaneous duties. Mixed in with all of this are attempts to spend time with staff in the trenches. Spending time with the staff makes my day-to-day job and duties less burdensome. Because as any administrator in law enforcement or corrections can tell you, if you do not surround yourself with good staff, there is no way you can accomplish your mission or goals on your own.

Advice to Students

The profession of corrections is a bustling industry. It is an employment that guarantees job security and very little if any chance of being laid off. At the same time, corrections is not for everyone. One needs to make a personal assessment before making a decision to pursue this career. It is a job that will bring you a sense of accomplishment, whether as a correctional officer who comes home to his or her family every day safely or as a member that climbs the ranks and becomes an administrator. Foremost, before entering this field or while working in this field, completing your education should be of paramount importance. A college education expands your window of opportunity. In conclusion, I live by the same motto every day and that is that you should learn something new every day. This has always held true with work and school, as well as in life.

The participation hypothesis also applies to inmates. In the last few decades, most prisons have experimented with inmate councils and committees to hear grievances and have limited input about the operations of their institutions. Grievance committees are fairly commonplace today, and these committees are often helpful at heading off court litigation over incidents that could be resolved internally to most everyone's satisfaction. Grievance committees and inmate councils are also helpful to the extent that they permit prisoner input into how the prisons ought to be operated. This is a valuable source of feedback in a cybernetics organizational context. Prison organization varies among jurisdictions, although the structure shown in Figure 8.2 seems fairly typical of many prison settings. This is a relatively simple organizational arrangement, where different deputy superintendents are responsible for selected dimensions of prison activities, including food services, security, health, and educational programs.

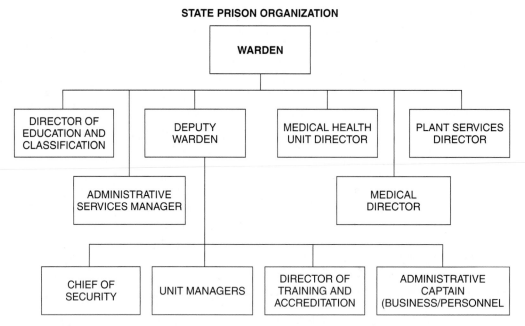

FIGURE 8.2   Formal Organization of a State Prison.

A purely bureaucratic approach to officer recruitment and job performance would suggest that those most capable of performing their roles would be selected initially and that they would orient themselves accordingly toward their different officer chores. They would perform their jobs according to a priori job specifications, and they would maintain impersonal relations between themselves, other correctional officers, and inmates. However, this seldom occurs in the real world of prison life. In fact, there is a great deal of variation among correctional officers in different prison systems concerning how they relate both among themselves and with the inmates they supervise (Toch 2002:9).

For example, a study of four different units in the Texas Department of Criminal Justice found that 366 prisoners in minimum-security, medium-security, and close-security custody reported different impressions about the corrections officers overseeing them. Close-custody inmates had the most positive attitudes toward corrections officers, and they believed that these officers would be calm and cool in problem situations, should they arise (Cheeseman, Mullings, and Marquart 2001). Although this study focused exclusively on female correctional officers and their effectiveness in supervising male offenders under different custody levels, it does raise the question about whether the level-of-custody variable makes a difference in assessing the work performance of corrections officers who work with inmates under different types of custody conditions. The interpersonal variable cannot be eliminated from any people-processing institution, especially prisons. Because of this fact, the human relations model has considerable relevance in analyses of correctional officer-prisoner interactions as well as administrator-correctional officer encounters (Farkas 2001).

The importance of the human relations element in correctional officer-inmate interactions, however, has been diminished by the utilization of computer technology in all types of penal institutions. The increased use of technology in jail and prison operations has done much to streamline organizational operations, offender processing, and inmate control. Locking or unlocking doors, inmate recognition, and other forms of prisoner control are being relegated to a few computer functions, with minimal direct staff involvement or contact with prisoners. Whether this will seriously influence the nature of officer-prisoner relationships in the future cannot be determined presently, but computerized prison settings will no doubt have impacts similar to the depersonalizing effects associated with technological change observed to occur in business or service organizations (Brenchley and Hultberg 2001).

Four Alternative Prison Management Styles

Barak-Glantz (1986) has described four prison management styles that typify how most prisons are administered by wardens and superintendents. These include (1) the authoritarian model, (2) the bureaucratic-lawful model, (3) the shared-powers model, and (4) the inmate control model. As Barak-Glantz advises, these models are viewed primarily as ideal types in much the same way as Max Weber conceived bureaucracy as an ideal type of organizational model.

The Authoritarian Model.   The **authoritarian model** is characterized by a high degree of centralization of authority and decision making. Wardens limit the amount of authority to a few trusted subordinates. Inmates have virtually no say or input regarding prison operations. This model typified early twentieth-century prisons, although many prisons in the United States today have a similar centralized scheme. Because prisoners have been excluded from any type of decision-making power in this system, it has been attacked repeatedly by civil rights groups. Eventually, lawsuits filed by inmates led to the establishment of administrative grievance procedures in all prisons whereby prisoners may register complaints about their conditions and treatment.

The Bureaucratic-Lawful Model.   Departments of Corrections in various jurisdictions have contributed to the bureaucratization of prisons and to the establishment of elaborate chains of command linking prison administrators with their subordinates. This is the **bureaucratic-lawful model.** Barak-Glantz notes that the evolution and growing importance of civil service and accompanying recruitment regulations have further bureaucratized prison settings. Control is the key to maintaining order in the prison. The courts have also contributed to the orderly and bureaucratic administration of prisons through decisions that acknowledge certain inmate rights (Anderson and Dyson 2001).

The Shared-Powers Model.   An increasingly popular scheme is the **shared-powers model,** where some degree of decision-making power is extended to inmates as well as to correctional officers and administrators. Reflecting the ideology of rehabilitation, the shared-powers model is apparent in those prisons with strong inmate councils that hear and decide inmate grievances and disputes. Prison officials acknowledge certain inmates as leaders, possessing the skills and influence to persuade other prisoners to comply with prison policies and rules. This perspective is viewed by some as democratizing prisons (Toch 1995a).

Civil rights decisions by the U.S. Supreme Court pertaining to inmates have contributed to the growth of shared-powers models in many prison settings. Prisoners are treated as citizens with rights that must be respected. Accordingly, administrators and correctional staff oblige inmates by generally following their council decisions, including recommended inmate sanctions. Of course, discretion is always exercised by top prison administrators so that abuses of inmate power will not occur or at least be minimized.

Correctional managers can do much to influence the course of events in their respective institutions (Sims 2001). **Total quality management (TQM)** is a method increasingly used, whereby inmates are viewed more as customers and consumers rather than as clients. Under TQM, inmates are involved more in decision making that most directly affects them. In a sense, TQM is similar to **participative management,** where lower-level employees, clients, or inmates are given a certain amount of regulatory responsibility and control (Gido 1998; Stevens 2001).

Furthermore, correctional administrators can direct changes that occur in their prisons toward their own ends. Cohn (1995:10) says that ordinary prison administrators tend to react to crises, fail to plan, and view their position as passive, failing to lead the organization. In contrast are those prison managers who are proactive, view the correctional setting as a system, and attempt to control the destiny of the system. Restructuring the organization of correctional setting, managing these settings more effectively with total quality management, and utilizing the benefits of technology can do much to make correctional institutions more effective.

Correctional managers can also use their positions to control the proliferation and influence of gangs in prisons. Good intelligence gathering, vigilance, sound operational procedures, and a consistent policy of discipline and firmness will enable officials to maintain control and limit the power and influence of unruly inmates (Chuda 1995).

The Inmate Control Model.   Under the **inmate control model,** prisoners form Inmate Government Councils and establish organizations such as the California Union, a prisoner union patterned after those established by Scandinavian prisons (Barak-Glantz 1986:50). While the idea of inmate unions is not a novel one, it has encouraged prisoners to act collectively to ensure that their constitutional rights are observed by prison staff. Greater weight is attached to lawsuits filed by an inmate collective, where rights violations of various kinds are alleged. Inmate unions have lobbied successfully in some jurisdictions for the abolition of the indeterminate sentence, the establishment of certain worker rights for prisoners, including the recognition of minimum wages for work performed and the right to bargain collectively.

All of these models are found in different U.S. prisons. The model most frequently observed is the bureaucratic-lawful model, although increasingly, the shared-powers model is gaining in popularity. There is a high degree of inmate participation in decision making, which is instrumental in achieving and maintaining internal social control. While some administrators don't particularly like or accept this model, they cannot deny that it is somewhat effective for maintaining order and ensuring inmate compliance with most prison regulations.

Other Warden Leadership Styles

Mactavish (1992:162–164) has profiled 283 prison managers from various jurisdictions to establish the first national database in correctional management. Mactavish has used the **Myers-Briggs Type Indicator (MBTI)** as a means of typifying correctional management behaviors and orientations. These wardens and administrators participated in a 10-day program sponsored by the National Institute of Corrections' Correctional Leadership Development Program. Tables 8.1 and 8.2 show the results of the MBTI applied to the 283 prison managers.

TABLE 8.1

Preferences of Correctional Managers

Extroversion 50%	or	Introversion 50%
Sensing 61%	or	Intuition 39%
Thinking 82%	or	Feeling 18%
Judgments 74%	or	Perception 26%

Note that sensing, thinking, and judgments are the most common traits, establishing the STJ profile.
Source: Marie Mactavish, "Are You an STJ? Examining Correctional Managers' Leadership Styles." *Corrections Today,* 1992:162. Reprinted with permission from the American Correctional Association, Lanham MD.

Sixteen personality types are derived from the four preferences. A condensed version of these preferences is:

1. People are either driven by extroversion, the outer world of actions, objects and people, OR by introversion, the world of concepts and ideas.
2. People either rely on their five senses to sense the immediate, real practical facts, OR use intuition to consider possibilities and follow their hunches.
3. People either make decisions by thinking, objectively and impersonally, OR by weighing subjective values and feelings.
4. People either live mostly by judgment, in a decisive, planned, and orderly way, OR by perception, in a spontaneous and flexible way (Mactavish 1992:164).

TABLE 8.2

The 16 Myers-Briggs Profiles

ISTJ Analytical manager, likes facts, details 23%	ISFJ Sympathetic manager, likes facts, details 2%	INFJ People-oriented innovator of ideas 1%	INTJ Logical, critical innovator 10%
ISTP Practical analyzer 5%	ISFP Observant, loyal helper 1%	INFP Imaginative, independent 2%	INTP Inquisitive analyzer 5%
ESTP Realistic adapter, stresses material items 1%	ESFP Realistic adapter, stresses human relations 2%	ENFP Warm, enthusiastic change planner 5%	ENTP Analytical change planner 4%
ESTJ Fact-minded, practical organizer 22%	ESFJ Practical harmonizer 4%	ENFJ Imaginative harmonizer 1%	ENTJ Intuitive, innovative organizer 11%

This table places correctional managers in 16 categories and shows which profiles are most common.
Source: Marie Mactavish, "Are You an STJ? Examining Correctional Managers' Leadership Styles." *Corrections Today,* 1992:164. Reprinted with permission from the American Correctional Association. Lanham, MD.

On the basis of the responses of the 182 wardens and prison superintendents, sensing, thinking, and judgment characterize the preferences of correctional managers. Those profiles most common to prison wardens are as analytical manager, likes facts, details, fact-minded; practical organizer; intuitive, innovative organizer; and logical, critical innovator (Mactavish 1992:164).

Mactavish says that most correctional managers preferred using their senses over their intuition as a way of taking in information. They preferred to work with facts, enjoyed routines and preferred to use skills they already have rather than learning new skills. They generally dislike new problems unless they can use a standard procedure for solving them. They prefer to keep things as they are, and when change is necessary, they demand to be convinced of the necessity for change by facts. These findings suggest that most prison administrators follow the bureaucratic model of structuring their own lives as prison managers as well as the lives of the inmates they manage. The Myers-Briggs Type Indicator has been applied in other types of settings, such as probation offices. In these other environments, similar positive results have been derived so as to indicate under what conditions and social circumstances probation officers can maximize their effectiveness with clients (Sluder and Shearer 1992).

It is important to note that much of the innovation relating to how prison inmates are supervised and treated has been generated by prison administrators and their peculiar or individualized views of how prisons ought to be run. Seldom has there been a master plan initiated at the state or federal level to guide prison wardens and superintendents toward particular correctional objectives. One exception is a California Department of Corrections directive that promoted rehabilitation-oriented group counseling experiments during the period 1955–1975. Such experimentation was advocated by Norman Fenton, who served as the deputy director of the California Department of Corrections during the 1950s (Toch 2002:9). During this period of experimentation, corrections officers, clerical workers, shop foremen, vocational teachers, classification teachers, and other institutional employees became active in group counseling programs that were aimed at improving inmate behaviors by heightening the general social awareness of these participants (Toch 2002). However, these and similar experiments in other jurisdictions have had variable success, and program failures have been more the norm rather than the exception.

One persistent program defect seems to be the human relations view that prisoners are people, especially people who are aggressively responsive to humane and constructive treatment and who wish to reform themselves and have a fresh start in life. Certainly, prisoners are people, but high recidivism rates among parolees (a 67.5 percent recidivism rate within a three-year followup from early release) suggest institutional program failure (*Corrections Compendium* 2002:11). Program failure, as indicated by high recidivism, has caused more than a few departments of correction throughout the United States to view their general correctional goals differently. If inmate treatment programs, counseling, and other forms of rehabilitation are ineffective, then why bother with rehabilitation at all? One response has been to create more supermax prisons intended to warehouse offenders rather than rehabilitate them. But one unanticipated consequence of supermax prisons has been to confine larger numbers of prisoners who do not deserve to be so drastically isolated from the general prison population. Often, imperfect instrumentation and unusual and nonrational criteria are utilized to justify inmate placements under high-security conditions. Suspicions of gang affiliation, an especially old prior escape attempt, or the simple notoriety of the inmate because of extensive media coverage often are used as reasons to place certain offenders in supermax isolation (Toch 2002:24).

PRISON ADMINISTRATOR SELECTION AND TRAINING

Wardens, superintendents, and other prison managers are typically hired or appointed (Camp and Camp 2002:149). In 2001 the average length of service for prison wardens was 15.3 years. States with the longest warden longevity were Oregon (37.4 years), Pennsylvania (34.6 years), Tennessee (29.9 years), and South Carolina (27.3 years). Wardens' minimum salaries averaged $54,252, while their maximum salaries averaged $86,266 (Camp and Camp 2002:149). The lowest minimum state warden's salary was in West Virginia, with $47,016. The highest state warden's maximum salary was Virginia ($122,281). The lowest and highest salaries for wardens in the Federal Bureau of Prisons were $85,024 and $133,591 respectively. Of the 7,065 wardens, superintendents, or prison managers reported by alternative sources in 2001, 78 percent were male, while 14.3 percent were black (American Correctional Association 2002:36).

Some insight into the backgrounds of prison wardens and superintendents may be gleaned from a study of Pennsylvania wardens by Whitmore (1995). Whitmore conducted both a survey and interviews with 55 Pennsylvania prison administrators. Whitmore found that most respondents, 82 percent, had completed some college, with only 14 percent possessing advanced degrees. Most respondents (96 percent) were white. The field of undergraduate study most common to these administrators was criminal justice, while 42 percent of these managers had their first corrections position in security, followed by treatment (34.5 percent). The most frequent ages of these wardens, by category, were 41 to 45 (24 percent) and over 56 (24 percent). The mean length of service of these administrators in corrections was about 17 years, with the range of service for all survey participants ranging from 3 years to 36 years (Whitmore 1995:54–55). The administrators indicated that they performed a total of 272 tasks, with the most common being:

1. Managing change within the institution
2. Providing leadership for the organization
3. Managing organizational performance
4. Conducting inspections and tours
5. Managing liability exposure and risk management
6. Maintaining professional staff (Whitmore 1995:57).

While this description is not necessarily typical of administrators in other state jurisdictions, it does give us some idea of the range of backgrounds represented as well as some of the principal duties performed by these managers.

At least some wardens influence directly the nature of prison security. For example, at the Calipatria State Prison in California, Warden K.W. Prunty has established an electrified perimeter to deter prison escapes. The electrified fence carries 4,000 volts and 650 milliamperes. Only 70 milliamperes is sufficient to kill someone. This lethal fence surrounds numerous buildings and 3,900 inmates who are being held in maximum- and medium-security custody. Some inmate rights advocates are disturbed by the presence of the fence and suggest that it is tantamount to administering the death penalty. In response,

Warden Prunty says that "The fence doesn't get distracted, it doesn't look away for a moment, and it doesn't get tired. We already had a lethal perimeter (referring to armed correctional officers in guard towers). This is simply a way to keep that same level of security while saving money." Actually, the escape rate among U.S. prisons is quite low compared with the total number of inmates incarcerated. In 2000, for instance, there were 577 actual escapes and 157 unsuccessful escape attempts from U.S. prisons, with an 87 percent capture and return. In 2001, there were 492 actual escapes and 142 escape attempts, with a 91 percent capture and return (CEGA Services, Inc. 2002:6).

PRISON PRIVATIZATION

During 2000, 24,519 lawsuits were filed against the agencies and staff of 45 prison systems. By the beginning of 2001, 265 prison institutions were affected by court orders concerning the conditions of confinement and overcrowding. Court-ordered inmate population reductions affected 82 prisons, and 141 prisons required monitoring by special masters appointed by different courts to oversee the progress of court-ordered changes (Camp and Camp 2002:75). Since 1990 and continuing to the present, prison overcrowding has been increasingly addressed by the establishment of privately operated prisons. Privatization of prisons is the financing and/or operation of prisons and other correction institutions by private, for-profit organizations. Privatization of prisons is growing in the United States and is found in other countries, such as England, Australia, and Canada (Bowery 2000; Correctional Service of Canada 2000; Moyle 2000).

Privatization is not a new phenomenon, since private business enterprises have been contracting with prisons on a regular basis for several decades for the provision of various goods, services, and prison work programs. Private enterprise operations in corrections have been particularly noticeable in the juvenile justice system, where minimum-security detention facilities are often privately organized and managed. While no state prison system was privately operated in the late 1980s, by 2001 at least 38 states had privately operated prisons to accommodate either some of their adult offenders, juvenile offenders, or both (American Correctional Association 2002). This is a significant increase from the 21 states that used private contracting for inmate confinement for either adults or juveniles in 1996.

The primary arguments advanced by those in the private sector interested in gaining control of prisons are that (1) prison operations can be run more smoothly and effectively by private enterprise than by government agencies; (2) government agencies rely on the sluggish actions of legislatures and other political bodies for appropriations and approval before implementing new policies or engaging in new prison construction; (3) private enterprise can furnish the same quality of services currently provided by governments, and these services can be furnished at lower cost to government; (4) prisons can be operated on a for-profit basis, with prisoner labor functioning to defray program operating costs and managerial expenses; and (5) the private sector is in a more advantageous position to negotiate with other private enterprises in the community to furnish necessary goods, services, and programs for offenders (Vardalis and Becker 2000; White 2001).

Opponents of privatization raise legal, moral, and ethical issues. Among these issues are (1) the accountability of private enterprise officials to government for conduct relating to prisoner management and discipline, (2) the ideological conflict between the power of the state to sanction offenders and the

 **BOX 8.6**

J. Michael Quinlan

Executive Vice President and Chief Operating Officer
Corrections Corporation of America
Nashville, Tennessee

Statistics

B.S. (American history), Fairfield University; J.D., Fordham University; Masters in Law (L.L.M.), George Washington University

Background and Experiences

I serve as Chief Operating Officer for Corrections Corporation of America (CCA), the industry leader in private sector corrections. I began working for CCA in 1993 as the head of the company's Strategic Planning Division based in Washington, DC, and in 1999, I was appointed Chief Operating Officer. I joined CCA after a 22-year career in public sector corrections.

My career began in the U.S. Air Force, where I served four years as a special investigator. I joined the Federal Bureau of Prisons in 1971. I discovered corrections while in the Air Force, while taking a course for my master's degree in law. One of my professors also served as general counsel for the Federal Bureau of Prisons, and he made the subject sound so interesting that when I was ready to leave the Air Force, I applied to the Bureau of Prisons (BOP). During my career, I served the BOP in a variety of roles, including legal counsel, warden, and director. As Director of the BOP, I was responsible for the total operations and administration of a federal agency with an annual budget of more than $2 billion, more than 26,000 employees, and 75 facilities. As COO of CCA, I oversee the operations of our 61 facilities around the nation, including 59,000 beds in 21 states and more than 14,000 employees. Our company owns, operates, and manages prisons and other correctional facilities for local, state, and federal governmental agencies, as well as provides long-distance inmate transportation services.

The corrections industry was quite different at the beginning of my career than it is today. At the time I entered the corrections industry, the BOP had 27,000 inmates in 1971, and today it supervises nearly 162,000 inmates. The corrections industry has also changed in terms of the types of facilities that are operated. In 1971, to build a new facility—of any kind—was unusual, because there was very little growth in prison populations during that decade. The growth began in the 1980s. The design of facilities began to change, too, from cell blocks to secure rooms or dormitories for inmate housing. In the early days of my career, if we *did* get to build a new facility, it would never be more than 400 or 500 beds. In later years, when I joined CCA, it was not uncommon for government agencies and private companies to routinely build structures for 1,000, 1,500, or more inmates per facility. These changes were made possible by better facility designs, coupled with the use of better-trained staff and technology.

As COO of CCA, I oversee the company's corporate and facility operations, inmate programs, and design and construction departments. My areas of specialty are strategic planning, performance assessment, and rehabilitative programming. I'm interested in ways that I can help to improve the quality of corrections, provide the chance for prisoners to successfully reintegrate into the community, and develop career opportunities for professionals in our field.

CCA is a unique and rewarding company to work for. CCA offers a high-quality, innovative service to our governmental

(continued)

BOX 8.6 (*Continued*)

partners. We provide a quality service and the flexibility to tailor our programs and customize to our clients' needs, while providing cost efficiencies to our customers. As a private business, we can move quickly to anticipate customer needs and implement creative solutions to their corrections challenges. We provide safe, secure facilities that not only ensure public safety, but also provide a safe and secure environment for inmates and our staff—an environment focused on providing opportunities for offenders in our care. The advantages that CCA bring to inmate management include a focus upon quality and on the success of the inmate. CCA provides an array of programs—educational, vocational, life skills, and counseling—in many mediums, from traditional classroom instruction to video format. We provide a hands-on work experience through a variety of vocational programs, including our PIE partnerships, which provide labor to private businesses and technical experience for our inmates. We measure their achievements on a regular basis and provide certification programs that document their work experience and endorse their achievements in a particular field so that they can apply their accrued experience toward a position in the career of their choice. We help them deal with drug and alcohol problems through substance abuse programs that teach new habits. We're proud of the performance of inmates in our facilities. We know of no other government agency that keeps as detailed information on the progression of inmates while in our care. It becomes a track record for our customers, measures inmate achievements, and, most importantly, inspires our staff to continue their commitment to the provision of quality services.

Insights

The most meaningful part of working in corrections, for me, is the opportunity to help people change their lives for the better, learn new and more productive patterns of behavior, and focus on the importance of abiding by the rules of our society and enjoying the freedoms provided to citizens in this country. I've held many different jobs in our profession, most in upper-level management, but the most meaningful ones were those I held in the field that provided daily contact with staff and inmates. It was incredibly rewarding to establish good programs and witness the positive results, to hire and promote quality staff, and to be involved in the daily operations of a correctional facility. For me, that's the most meaningful part of corrections.

Advice to Students

Corrections is not a glamorous career, but it offers great rewards. It will be misunderstood by many people, but it's a career that offers vast opportunities for individual contributions that will have great impact on both the staff you work with and the inmates you supervise. Corrections can be physically and mentally challenging at times, but the rewards far exceed the challenges. The career opportunities—particularly for college graduates—are especially good, and the rewards will be far greater than you can imagine.

Note: J. Michael Quinlan is a member of the American Correctional Association, the American Bar Association, and the National Academy of Public Administration. In 1988, he received the Presidential Distinguished Rank Award, the highest award given to civil servants for service to the United States. In 1992, he received the National Public Service Award, a distinction awarded annually to the top three public administrators in the United States by the National Academy of Public Administration and the American Society of Public Administration.

ability and/or authority of private enterprise to do so, (3) the potential for exploitation of prison labor by private interests, and (4) the potential for greatly expanding the present level of incarceration of society's offenders (Collins 2000; Shook and Sigler 2000). Unfortunately, little empirical evidence currently exists to support the arguments of either the proponents or opponents of privatization (Shichor and Gilbert 2001).

Some of the major private organizations that have offered serious proposals to state and local governments for the possible management and operation of their prison systems have been the Corrections Corporation of America, Wackenhut Corrections Corporation, Management and Training Corporation, Correctional Services Corporation, Alternative Programs, Inc., Cornell Constructions of CA, Dominion, and Marantha Production Co. (Camp and Camp 2002:114–115). These organizations bid regularly on government proposals to construct and operate new prisons in different jurisdictions. Those contracts awarded thus far have been for the management of detention centers, county and city jails, preparole transfer centers, prisons, and training centers for juveniles.

A survey of 36 states where privatization is either being used for prison operations or where enabling legislation is being proposed has shown that these states vary regarding (1) private contractor qualifications for operating corrections systems; (2) the services, both traditional and treatment, to be provided corrections operations by private contractors; and (3) the types of correctional sanctions that should be relegated to private contractors or retained by public agencies. In 2000 there were 63,575 inmates and clients under private agency supervision (Camp and Camp 2002:93). Texas used private corporations the most for managing different offender populations (11,375 inmates), followed by the Federal Bureau of Prisons (9,667 inmates), Wisconsin (4,359 inmates), Georgia (4,050 inmates), and Florida (3,936 inmates).

SELECTED ISSUES ON PRIVATIZATION

Five major issues of privatization of prisons are investigated in this section. These are (1) the professionalization of administration; (2) public accountability: who monitors the monitors?; (3) prison labor and prisons run for profit: the case of UNICOR; (4) public reactions to privatization; and (5) political and legal considerations.

The Professionalization of Administration

No state or federal statutes exist that prevent appointing private administrators for prisons in any jurisdiction. Therefore, the question is, who would do the better job—someone appointed by the governor or some independent correctional body, or someone hired by private enterprise? Many prison administrators have backgrounds unrelated to corrections. A majority have no previous experience as prison correctional officers. A majority have business or social science backgrounds, most are educated with the minimum of a bachelor's degree, and most have some managerial experience. Thus, considerable private sector involvement in prison management currently exists despite the objections of critics to private sector management of these institutions (Freeman 1999). Furthermore, by their rulings the courts have indirectly increased the professionalization of prison management, encouraging a new generation of correctional administrators amenable to reform (Feeley and Rubin 1998).

The questions in the minds of some critics are, "Should private enterprise supervise those convicted of state or federal crimes?" "Whose responsibility is it to punish state and federal criminals?" "Will private enterprise do less well in the management of prisons than public appointees who currently hold these top administrative posts?" Presently, managers of private prisons are being criticized because of the policies they have implemented and the administrative styles they have chosen to run their institutions (Vardalis and Becker 2000). However, it is unlikely that the encroachment of private enterprise into prison management on a large scale would seriously undermine the current state of professionalism among those holding these top warden, superintendent, or managerial posts. This issue is presently unresolved (Harding 1999).

Private prison operations in numerous jurisdictions including Florida have resulted in substantial savings to the state. Two private prisons were opened in Florida in 1995. These were the Bay Correctional Facility, operated by the Corrections Corporation of America, and the Moore Haven Correctional Facility, operated by the Wackenhut Corrections Corporation (Florida Legislature 1998). While the Bay Correctional Facility was constructed at a cost in excess of other similar public prisons and was not cost-effective for the first two years, the Moore Haven Correctional Facility was constructed at a lower cost and has resulted in a 7 percent savings to the state. Both facilities have ultimately saved the state over $480,000 in operating costs, despite the earlier overages due to unanticipated construction delays. In retrospect, it has been suggested that in order to make more valid comparisons of cost effectiveness of private versus public prison operations in future years, legislatures ought to establish prisons in both the public and private sectors that are comparable in size, location, types of inmates housed, and programs provided (Hodges 1997). By 2001, Florida had five privately operated prisons and accommodated the fifth largest number of privately supervised inmates compared with all other states and the Federal Bureau of Prisons (Camp and Camp 2002:93).

Public Accountability: Who Monitors the Monitors?

The issue of accountability is regarded as the most serious legal and policy concern among many opponents of privatization. The argument is that the state is solely vested with the right to sanction offenders and that the imprisonment of offenders is inherently and exclusively a governmental function. Furthermore, if private enterprise imposes criminal sanctions, including the death penalty, and disciplines inmates for rule infractions, inmates may allege successfully that their civil rights have been and are being infringed by these private interests (Lutze, Smith, and Lovrich 2000; Vardalis and Becker 2000). The legal bases for this civil rights claim are (1) whether privately operated prisons are state agencies and are therefore liable under 42 U.S.C. Section 1983 of the Civil Rights Act and (2) whether private operation of prisons is inherently constitutional. These claims have been settled by the U.S. Supreme Court as the result of lawsuits filed by inmates.

In the case of *Medina v. O'Neill* (1984), for instance, sixteen inmates of a privately operated Houston Immigration and Naturalization Service facility had been confined in a 12-by-20-foot cell originally designed to hold six inmates. They sued the private corporation as well as the Immigration and Naturalization service, alleging these conditions and the nature of their control by a private organization violated their civil rights. Tort claims arising from injury and death of inmates due to the inexperience with firearms of private security correctional officers in the facility were also made in the same suit. The U.S.

Supreme Court rejected the inmate claims and ruled that the private facility was an agent of the state. Furthermore, the Supreme Court went on to note that state action always exists when the state delegates to private parties a power traditionally and exclusively reserved to the state. Thus, they resolved the issue of whether private enterprises can perform public functions: Yes, they can.

The issue of whether a privately operated correctional facility violates the constitutional rights of any citizen was addressed in the case of *Milonas v. Williams* (1982). This case was the result of allegations by several former students of a school for youths with behavioral problems. The school had used a behavior modification program to alter their behavior, and they believed this program was a violation of the Eighth Amendment right protecting citizens from cruel and inhuman punishment. The Tenth Circuit Court of Appeals ruled in the facility's favor and held under the close-nexus test that there was sufficient close-nexus between the state and the facility that the action of the latter may be fairly treated as that of the state itself.

In a more recent test of the right of private corporations to supervise offenders under institutional and/or community conditions, the U.S. Supreme Court decided in favor of private enterprise in the case of *Correctional Services Corp. v. Malesko* (2001). The case involved John Malesko, 58, who was convicted in federal district court in December 1992 of securities fraud and sentenced to 18 months under Federal Bureau of Prisons supervision. While serving his sentence, Malesko was diagnosed with congestive heart failure, which required him to take prescription medication. Subsequently, Malesko was transferred to the LeMarquis Community Corrections Center, a halfway house in New York City operated by the Correctional Services Corporation (CSC), to serve the remainder of his sentence. Malesko was assigned to a room on the fifth floor of the facility, and he was permitted to use the elevator to gain access to his quarters. However, in March 1994, CSC established a policy requiring inmates who lived below the sixth floor to use only the staircase to travel from the lobby to their rooms. Because of his heart condition, halfway house officials permitted Malesko to continue using the elevator. On March 28, 1994, however, a CSC employee prevented Malesko from using the elevator to his apartment, insisting that Malesko use the stairs. While climbing the stairs, Malesko suffered a heart attack, fell, and injured his ear. In subsequent months, Malesko claimed that he had balance problems associated with his fall. Furthermore, CSC had failed to replenish his supply of prescription medication for his heart condition as of his injury date. Later in March 1997, Malesko filed suit against CSC and various employees, alleging that his civil rights had been violated. Malesko also sued on the grounds that CSC and its employees had violated his Eighth Amendment right against cruel and unusual punishment. A federal district court dismissed Malesko's suits, but the Second Circuit Court of Appeals reversed the district court holding that Malesko could not bring a suit against a private corporation acting under color of law. Ultimately, the U.S. Supreme Court reversed the Second Circuit and sided with the federal district court ruling. Thus, Malesko was barred from any legal claim against CSC, although the U.S. Supreme Court indicated that Malesko did have a cause of action against a particular CSC employee, the one who had barred him from the elevator earlier. However, this suit was also dismissed since Malesko had allowed the statute of limitations to expire.

It is reasonably clear that the courts view private enterprises as extensions of state and federal authority to sanction offenders (Harding 1999; Stoughton, Drowota, and Sullivan 1999). Thus, such organizations enjoy some amount of immunity from lawsuits such as the one filed by Malesko. However, private corporations do not have absolute immunity from lawsuits. A distinction has been made between federal and state prisoners and the remedies or causes of action available to offenders in each category. Businesses such as the Correctional Services Corporation may be held liable under the Federal Civil Rights Act for violating a state inmate's constitutional rights, but they may not be held liable for the very same constitutional rights violations involving federal inmates. Nevertheless, the remaining remedy available to federal inmates is to make timely claims and file lawsuits against individual members of an organization where constitutional rights violations are alleged (Adelman 2002:30).

Prison Labor and Prisons for Profit: The Case of UNICOR

The use of prison labor for profit dates back several centuries (Gabbidon et al. 2002). Great Britain exploited prison labor, not only for state benefit, but for private enterprise as well. Currently, for-profit prisoner enterprises are found in both federal and state prisons. One of the more successful federal enterprises is **UNICOR,** a profitable, government-owned corporation that sells many prisoner-made goods and products to federal agencies and employs thousands of federal prisoners (Saylor and Gaes 1991). UNICOR is the trade name for **Federal Prison Industries, Inc.**

Private for-profit prison industries are operated in many states as well (Camp and Camp 2002). In 2000, 48 states and the Federal Bureau of Prisons offered a variety of inmate-manufactured products to the general public, including agriculture and food products, garments and textiles, furniture, paper products, metal products, and various services, such as training seeing-eye dogs for the blind and taming horses (Camp and Camp 2002:128). The Utah Department of Corrections has established the Utah Correction Industries for Utah State Prison releasees (Clasby 1996). The Utah plan uses inmates who engage in profitable employment. Through this program, employee-inmates will become qualified for jobs in the private sector, and prison officials will assist them in job placements. Some of the work includes carpentry, computer programming, drafting, and electronics. The Utah Correction Industries also boasts a low recidivism rate among inmate-participants. Industries programs in Arizona, Connecticut, Delaware, Kansas, Nevada, Pennsylvania, Washington, and several other states have reported similar successes with their private prison labor programs (Camp and Camp 2002).

When inmates perform work for UNICOR, they learn many useful tasks that can get them jobs whenever they are subsequently released. The U.S. Bureau of Prisons operates a Post-Release Employment Project (PREP), which is designed to equip inmates with various useful vocational and educational skills. Studies of PREP participants have shown that compared with other parolees, they have better adjustment both in and out of prison; they have fewer misconduct reports; and they were rated as having much higher levels of personal responsibility (Saylor and Gaes 1991).

The problem of product quality has been raised by some opponents to prison labor. Is the work of prisoners comparable to product quality of major corporations? Yes. Studies comparing product quality of private corporations and prison-operated industrial and business ventures have shown that prisoner-made goods and other products are comparable in quality to those similar items manufactured by the private sector (Garvey 1998). Some myths about UNICOR have existed for several decades. However, these myths have been debunked in recent years. One popular myth is that prison-made goods cost less than goods made in the private sector, thus prison-made goods are unfair competition. In reality, prison-made goods cost more than comparable products in the private sector. An-

Prison industries include the Rough Rider Industries, which feature furniture and upholstery shops for prisoner training.

other myth is that prison industries have monopolized much of the economic market from private firms. In reality, prison-made goods make up about .16 percent of the total production of goods in the U.S. (Camp and Camp 2002).

Public Reactions to Privatization

Unquestionably, one of the most looming obstacles to overcome for the privatization movement is public reluctance to see private enterprise intrusion into correctional operations (Shichor and Gilbert 2001). However, public acceptance of privately operated facilities has been increasing. Public acceptance of prison privatization is furthered by factors such as the strong incentive among private interests to make prisons and rehabilitation work and the lower cost of prison operations compared with typically high, cost-ineffective government expenditures.

The public may be opposed to privatization because of the potential such operations have for abuses such as using unethical therapies to achieve program objectives (e.g., the extensive use of prescription drugs to control prisoner behavior) and the possibility that the quality of services would not necessarily improve. However, some critics say that public opposition is rooted in the age-old philosophy, justified or unjustified, that the state, not private enterprise, should sanction its offenders and assume all incarcerative responsibilities (Harding 1999). However, private management is delegated power to act on behalf of the state.

For more than a few critics, operating prisons of any kind for a profit seems wrong. The idea that prison growth and big business are somehow deliberately intertwined for various nefarious purposes has caused some persons to brand the $30 billion annual prison-building industry as somehow contrary to the correctional goals of rehabilitation and reintegration (Halliman 2001). At least one observer says that the consequences of prison growth are enormous. Many small towns were left behind by the current economic boom, and now they are becoming more dependent on prisons to replace jobs lost from military and factory work. One of the largest silent migrations in U.S. history is occurring as young urban men, mostly of color, enter prisons. Rehabilitative goals have been replaced with the mentality of locking up prisoners for life. Major issues include whether people are increasingly being sentenced to prison, and sentenced for longer terms, because it is big business. Has the Cold War's military-industrial complex disappeared in the wake of the contemporary prison-industrial complex? While the answers are not easy, one thing is clearly evident in the expansion of the U.S. prison system: Having failed to make prisons effective, we have learned to make them profitable (Halliman 2001).

However, a frequently overlooked counterclaim is that greater private prison construction is enabling states and the federal government to incarcerate more serious offenders who should be incarcerated rather than placing them on probation where they can offend again and harm the general public. And the cost of private prison operations is less than publicly operated facilities. If the federal government and individual states cannot afford to build enough prisons to house those who deserve incarceration as a punishment, then private enterprise should be considered as one solution. Private prisons can also help to alleviate serious prison and jail overcrowding problems that presently plague many jurisdictions. However, evaluating the cost effectiveness of private correctional enterprises and government correctional enterprises is not as easy as it might appear (Nink and Kilgus 2000:152). Not only are there different custody levels found in private and public prisons, there are also inmate population variations, where the health variable is highly unpredictable. Furthermore, different outside contractors may provide a variety of services for both public and private prison systems that affect overall operating costs of each facility.

One solution to this comparison problem is the Arizona Cost Model (ACM). The ACM identifies a prison's operating costs by custody level. The ACM also collects financial data identifying costs that have an impact on any privatization action, such as high-cost health care, substance abuse treatment, and mental health treatment. An adjustment is also made for land and buildings, as well as the local tax structure and method. A per capita cost can be identified and associated directly with the fiscal outcome for privatization actions. Two main components of the ADM are in-house costs and outside costs. In-house costs are the state's cost for providing the service, and include:

1. Direct costs—costs specifically related to the target function. If the target function ceased to exist, the direct costs also would cease. These are relevant costs such as personnel, supplies, and equipment.

2. Indirect costs—costs that are incurred for the benefit of more than one target function. These are unavoidable costs that will continue regardless of the privatization.

3. Adjustments—all adjustments must be documented in a supporting schedule. Steps should be taken to ensure that all costs included in this category are not duplicated and are relevant to service provision.

Outside costs are all the costs attributed to contracting with the outside provider, and include:

1. Contractor cost—this must be supported by a written offer submitted by the vendor in response to a request for proposals. Arizona requires that responsive offerors submit their proposals in a per capita format.

2. Contractor support—the Arizona Department of Corrections provides support for the following areas: offender records, disciplinary actions, trust accounts, and the grievance process.

3. Contract monitoring—Arizona Department of Corrections has an associate deputy warden onsite to closely monitor compliance and offer assistance at every private prison.

4. Conversion costs—the one-time conversion costs that may occur in activating a private prison, such as transportation costs to transfer inmates to the private prison (Nink and Kilgus 2000:154).

The ACM meets the need for an efficient point-in-time cost model that is both cost-effective and adaptable to most private prison comparison needs. Assumptions and cost adjustments can be made for unique programs and circumstances. The model also takes into account all cost categories, including depreciation of state equipment (Nink and Kilgus 2000:155). As the ACM illustrates, effective cost comparisons may be made between state and private correctional systems. When millions of dollars are being expended annually by various states for their correctional needs, cost savings per capita of from 15 to 25 percent are substantial. In 2001, Arizona had seven prisons and correctional centers being operated by private interests (American Correctional Association 2002:712–713). For instance, the Marana, Arizona, privately operated prison provides intensive substance abuse programming for inmates. Comparisons with facilities in other states designed to accomplish similar objectives have demonstrated that Marana was being operated at a reduced rate, by as much as 13.8 percent to 16.66 percent (Nink and Kilgus 2000:154).

Private, for-profit prisons have also outperformed their public counterparts in other jurisdictions. In Louisiana, for instance, data were collected from private and public agency records during the period 1992–1996 to determine whether there were significant differences between private and publicly operated prisons. Although only three prisons were investigated (one public and two private), the privately operated prisons significantly outperformed the public prison on the majority of measures used for comparison (Archambeault and Deis 1996). Private prisons were more cost-effective to operate; reported fewer critical incidents; provided safer work environments for employees and safer living environments for inmates; judiciously and effectively used inmate disciplinary actions to maintain order; deployed fewer security personnel while achieving higher levels of safety; had proportionately more inmates complete basic education, literacy, and vocational training courses; and equaled or surpassed the number of inmate screenings for community corrections placements. However, the public prison outperformed the private facilities in preventing escapes; having fewer aggravated sex offenses; controlling substance abuse using urine testing; consistently offering broad education and vocational adult education programs to inmates; and providing a broader range of treatment, recreation, social services, and rehabilitative services (Archambeault and Deis 1996). The private prisons were better managed than the public prison as well.

The Interstate Transportation of Dangerous Criminals Act of 2000. The federal government has been reluctant to become involved in state prison operations and contracting with private interests. However, some amount of federal intervention has occurred in recent years, especially intervention relating to the interstate transportation of dangerous criminals. In 2000, the Interstate

Transportation of Dangerous Criminals Act was passed (Title 42, U.S.C. §§13726–13726(c), 2003). This statute, also known as Jeanna's Act, was designed to enhance public safety by preventing the escape of inmates while in the custody of private inmate transportation companies (Guzzi 2001:1). Jeanna's Act is named after Jeanna North, a Fargo, North Dakota, girl who was murdered by Kyle Bell. Bell was subsequently apprehended and convicted, but he managed to escape from the custody of a private prisoner transportation company while being transported from one prison to another. He was subsequently apprehended.

The act authorizes the U.S. Attorney General, in consultation with the American Correctional Association, and the private inmate transportation industry, to promulgate regulations relating to the transportation of violent prisoners in or affecting interstate commerce. Specifically, the regulations will establish minimum standards for employee background checks and pre-employment drug testing, the length and type of training employees must have, the number of hours employees may be on duty during a specified time period, the number of staff who must supervise violent inmates, employee uniforms and identification, appropriate inmate clothing during transport, the types of restraints that must be used when transporting inmates, and the safety of violent inmates during transport (Guzzi 2001:1). It is believed that this act will promote more responsible and safe transportation policies for private as well as public organizations who move violent offenders between prisons. Failing to comply with the regulatory requirements of this act will have serious consequences for offending organizations and their employees.

Political Considerations

The political considerations associated with prison privatization center around the control factor (Harding 1997). Who should be vested with the control of prisoners? Many public officials see privatization of prisons as depriving them of prisoner control. But proponents of privatization say they can provide more client-specific services more effectively than public agencies, and they can do a better job in this regard. Therefore, any loss of control over inmates is offset by improvements in program quality and delivery services. Yet other observers say that prison privatization research is still in its infancy, and empirical tests need to be conducted in order to test the effectiveness of private enterprise intervention and control in the correctional role (Ray and O'Meara-Wyman 2000:116–122).

What is the proper scope of government relative to private prison operations? It is effectively argued that private prisons can do much to improve the quality of delivery systems in public prison operations. Some persons regard privatization as a healthy competitive intrusion into public prison operations, and that mostly beneficial consequences will result (White 2001). One thing is absolutely clear about the privatization of prisons issue, however. The debate is unresolved and continues (Nink and Kilgus 2000).

SUMMARY

Prisons are like businesses in that they are bureaucracies with various levels of authority and spans of control. The bureaucratic model is often used to assess organizational effectiveness. This model outlines a pattern of organizational structure that is believed to increase the effectiveness of both the organization and its personnel. Great attention is given to selecting personnel according to tests and ensuring that only the most qualified persons are hired. Impersonal relations between staff are emphasized to improve decision-making objectivity. Various spheres of competence are outlined, and persons perform specialized tasks. But the bureaucratic model does not always have the positive consequences it predicts.

Prison effectiveness is measured several ways, including minimal prisoner unrest and compliance with constitutional safeguards to ensure the preservation of prisoner rights. Another organizational model is the human relations model. This model stresses the importance of correctional officer/prisoner interpersonal relations as a means of preserving the status quo and minimizing conflict. Interestingly, many prison administrators have college backgrounds and experience with human relations. Thus, they are able to implement policies and procedures that might enhance their working environments and improve the safety and security of their institutions while simultaneously minimizing inmate discontent.

The power variable is quite important in correctional settings, since prisoners and correctional officers struggle to attain power over each other. Several types of power include reward power, expert power, coercive power, legitimate power, and referent power. Ideally, prison administrators have both legitimate and expert power as the bases for obtaining subordinate compliance. Their backgrounds and experience contribute significantly in this respect. But administrators do not operate in a vacuum. There are power clusters in evidence in all prison settings. These power clusters are comprised of different persons and interest groups with a state in the prison organization and operations. Thus, unilateral decision making by any warden or superintendent is affected to a degree by one or more of these power clusters.

State and federal prison organizations are quite diverse. States vary widely in their correctional expenditures. Usually, though not always, corrections is one of the lowest priorities in state budget funding. One result is that certain correctional goals are difficult to achieve under limited budget conditions. Several examples of states with similar budgets were provided, showing that widely different numbers of inmates and clients must be accommodated by similar expenditures. At the same time, there are jurisdictions with very similar inmate and client populations. These jurisdictions often allocate widely different amounts to their corrections programs. Different monetary allocations for similar inmate populations may mean reduced programming in some jurisdictions but more extensive programming and services in others. State and federal prison organizations also vary in the degree of their centralization. Greater centralization places power in the hands of fewer persons at the top of organizational hierarchies, where greater decentralization gives lower-level employees more power and involvement in decision making. One way of involving employees in their work and improving their morale and productivity is by encouraging them to participate in decisions affecting their work. This is the participation hypothesis, and it is used to one degree or another in various jurisdictions.

Wardens and superintendents use different management styles in supervising their prison operations. Several management styles include the authoritarian model, the bureaucratic-lawful model, the shared-powers model, and the inmate control model. Total quality management (TQM) is also practiced. This is similar to participative management, where both staff and inmates are given some degree of input and control over how these institutions are operated. Other warden leadership styles were described, depending upon the particular personality characteristics of prison administrators.

Wardens and other prison officials are usually appointed by governors or other officials. They are often college-educated, and they tend to stay in their jobs for fairly long periods. The responsibilities of wardens include managing change in their institutions, providing quality leadership, conducting inspections, managing liability exposure and risk management, and maintaining professionalism among the staff. It is recognized that effective recruitment of qualified correctional officers is one means of minimizing litigation against jail and prison administrations and officer staffs.

One increasingly important issue is whether private enterprises should take over the managership of prisons and jails. Privatization is increasingly popular, and those favoring privatization say they can deliver goods and resources at lower cost than the government. Accountability of private entrepreneurs is an issue raised by privatization opponents, however, who allege that the state, not private enterprise, should impose penalties on those who commit offenses against the state. Furthermore, when something bad happens, such as an inmate escape or misconduct behind bars, how can private interests be blamed? Thus, there are questions about the use and meaningfulness of sanctions as they pertain to those in charge of privately operated prisons and other correctional facilities.

Another complaint lodged against prisons by the public sector involves prison industries. Various states as well as the federal government operate enterprises where inmates produce goods for profit that are sold in the open market. Some business interests complain that prisoners, who are paid small amounts for their labor, cost these businesses money, and that this is unfair economic competition. However, proponents of prison industries contend that this work is rehabilitative and trains inmates to become more productive whenever they are eventually released back into society. Many of the arguments for and against privatization were examined. Ultimately, there are few restrictions of a constitutional nature that would bar private enterprise from operating prisons. Public opposition to privatization reflects the fear that private enterprise, seeking profits from prisons, will build more prisons and confine more people. These fears are largely unfounded, however, since incarceration decisions are made by other actors in the criminal justice process.

QUESTIONS FOR REVIEW

1. What is meant by the bureaucratic model? What are some of its important features? How should prison wardens orient themselves toward their jobs under a bureaucratic form of organization?

2. What is the human relations model, and how does it compare and contrast with the bureaucratic model?

3. What is meant by power? What are five types of power that superintendents can exercise in prison settings? Which power types seem most useful for wardens to use?

4. What is meant by a power cluster? How are power clusters influential in warden decision making?

5. What is the difference between the authoritarian model and the inmate control model?

6. What is meant by the participation hypothesis? What are some positive outcomes of the participation hypothesis for correctional officers?

7. What is meant by total quality management (TQM)? How is TQM similar to participative management?

8. What are four alternative prison management styles? What are their features or primary characteristics? What is the Myers-Briggs Type Indicator and how does it relate to one's personality?

9. How are prison administrators selected? What are some of their primary characteristics?

10. What is meant by prison privatization? What are three critical issues associated with prison privatization? How important is accountability in evaluating the effectiveness of privately run correctional programs? Is there anything unconstitutional about privatization? Why or why not?

SUGGESTED READINGS

Bosworth, Mary. *The U.S. Federal Prison System.* Thousand Oaks, CA: Pine Forge Press, 2002.

Seiter, Richard G. *Correctional Administration: Integrating Theory and Practice.* Upper Saddle River, NJ: Prentice Hall, 2002.

Shichor, David and Michael J. Gilbert. *Privatization in Criminal Justice: Past, Present, and Future.* Cincinnati, OH: Anderson Publishing Company, 2001.

Stojkovic, Stan and Mary Ann Farkas. *Correctional Administration.* Belmont, CA: Wadsworth/Thomson Learning, 2002.

INTERNET CONNECTIONS

Administrative Office of the U.S. Courts
http://www.uncle-sam.com/uscourts.html
http://www.uscourts.gov/

American Psychological Association
http://www.apa.org

Correctional Industries Association
http://www.corrections.com/industries/

Corrections Corporation of America
http://www.correctionscorp.com/

Glaser Institute on Reality Therapy
http://www.wglasserinst.com/whatisrt

National Association of Social Workers
http://www.naswdc.org

National Corrections Corporation
http://www.nationalcorrections.com

PACER Service Center
http://www.pacer.psc.uscourts.gov/

CHAPTER 9 | *Jailhouse Lawyers and Inmate Rights*

Source: AP/Wide World Photos

Chapter Objectives | *As the result of reading this chapter, the following objectives should be realized:*

1. Identifying the constitutional basis for inmate rights.
2. Highlighting selected Amendments of the Constitution as they pertain to inmate rights, including the First, Fourth, Eighth, and Fourteenth Amendments.
3. Presenting landmark cases relative to inmate rights and the evolution of these rights for those in custody in jails and prisons.
4. Describing the jailhouse lawyer and the nature of civil remedies as recourses for inmate filings and legal actions.
5. Describing several important legal avenues for filing claims against prison officials and organizations.
6. Examining and describing selected litigation issues, including cruel and unusual punishment, discrimination and racism, unreasonable or illegal searches in jails and prisons, negligence and intentional neglect by correctional officers and administrators, overcrowding, privacy issues, and the death penalty.
7. Describing the Prison Litigation Reform Act and its impact on inmate litigation.
8. Describing inmate grievance procedures leading to legal action against correctional institutions.
9. Examining the death penalty, how it is applied, and the pros and cons associated with capital punishment.
10. Describing various state and federal compensation schemes for those inmates who have been wrongly convicted of crimes.

INTRODUCTION

• *In Texas and other states with the death penalty, offenders are sentenced to death following convictions for capital crimes. But these death sentences are not carried out immediately. All death penalties are appealed automatically. The appeals process is drawn out and protracted. Appeals may be directed to state as well as to federal courts, with many death penalty cases going all the way to the U.S. Supreme Court. All of this appealing takes time. In Texas, the average amount of time for the death penalty to be imposed following one's conviction for a capital offense is ten years. However, this time interval is becoming shorter. Texas officials say that they expect that death penalties will be carried out within five or six years following legislation in 2000 designed to limit the appeals process. In the meantime, there are some inmates on death row who have been there for especially long periods. For instance, Walter Bell, 47, was on the Texas death row in 2001 for his conviction in the murders of Fred and Irene Chisum of Port Arthur in 1974. Bell was convicted and placed on death row in 1975. Thus, in 2001 he had been on death row for 26 years. One factor contributing to this lengthy time interval is that Bell's first conviction was overturned because a state psychiatrist did not tell him that his participation in an interview was voluntary or could be used against him in court. His second conviction was thrown out in 1989 because there was some question as to his mental state when the crime was committed. In another case, Jack Harry Smith, 63, has been on death row in Texas since 1978. He had to undergo major heart surgery not long after his conviction, and thus, this operation put his appeal on hold. Then his lawyer and the original trial judge died. It took his new lawyer several years to get up to speed about the facts in his case to argue effectively in his relentless appeals. In the meantime, the prosecuting attorney in Smith's case ran for a judgeship and was elected, further delaying Smith's execution. In several other cases, some prisoners on death row have slipped into dementia and cannot legally be executed. Some persons believe that persons who are on death row for many years and have aged substantially no longer pose a danger to others and should not be executed. University of Houston law professor David Dow, who opposes capital punishment, has said that "Somebody in a wheelchair who's had a stroke is hardly dangerous." However, officials in states where the death penalty is administered say that the fact that justice is not swift doesn't make the execution less relevant at time. Should the death penalty process be accelerated by eliminating excessive appeals by condemned offenders? What policy should states follow concerning the speed with which the death penalty is applied? What do you think?* [Adapted from the Associated Press. "Texas Death-Row Inmates Average 10 Years before End," April 8, 2001].

• *Florida is one of only four states that still used the electric chair in 1999 to execute those convicted of capital murder and sentenced to death. Over the years, the Florida electric chair has acquired a name—"Old Sparky." One reason for this name is that from time to time, the electric chair has malfunctioned. In a notorious case in 1997, Old Sparky malfunctioned in Pedro Medina's execution, causing flames over a foot long to flare from the mask covering his face and head. Observers were sickened by the sight, and the incident drew protests from anti-capital punishment groups to discontinue the use of the electric chair as a means of executing murderers. Old Sparky has also been used to execute serial killer celebrities such as Ted Bundy, who killed numerous young coeds. The chair was used to execute the Black Widow, Judith Buenoano, who poisoned various men in her life. Barkley Consulting Engineers, a firm that services the electric chair for the state of Florida, says that the existing electric chair shows many signs of age and wear and tear and ought to be replaced. After all, 237 men and 1 woman have been put to death at the Florida State Prison since 1923. A new chair has been constructed and has replaced Old Sparky. It is like the original one, made of oak with the same electrical system. But unlike the original, which was made by inmates, the new chair was made by prison guards. Is the electric chair cruel and unusual punishment? Should other means be used to execute prisoners in lieu of electric chairs, particularly in view of the malfunctions of previous electric chairs? What do you think?* [Adapted from the Associated Press, "Florida Replaces Its Old Electric Chair," May 9, 1999].

• *It's happened more than once. An innocent person has been executed. Following the execution, evidence emerges showing the guilt of another. Or someone else confesses to the crime. Since 1977 when the death penalty was reinstated in Illinois, for instance, 13 cases of persons on death row have been overturned when exculpatory evidence was discovered. One of the more recent cases involved a death row inmate, Anthony Porter. Porter spent 15 years on death row for a crime he didn't commit. By a fluke, a college journalism class undertook his claim of innocence and proved that he didn't commit the crime. Porter was released from prison in 1999 after the governor granted him a pardon based on the new evidence. In early 2000, a former Chicago police officer was on death row after having been convicted of a murder he didn't commit. He was convicted largely on the basis of the word of a jailhouse informant. Although his sentence was subsequently overturned, he still was serving several life terms for other crimes he had committed. Illinois Governor George Ryan says that he plans to stop executions until each can be reviewed fully and fairly. The death penalty procedures in Illinois definitely need overhauling, according to Ryan. "You have a system that's fraught with error and has innumerable opportunities for innocent people to be executed. I'm determined not to make a mistake," said Ryan. Although Ryan continues to support the death penalty, Illinois still has a problem that's too big for case-by-case review. "It's clear the system is broken," said Ryan. Ryan planned to establish a special panel to study the state's capital punishment system in general and determine what happened in the 13 cases where men were wrongly convicted. Subsequently, in late 2002, Ryan had pardoned numerous death row inmates, declaring that many convictions were obtained through police coercion and relentless interrogations. Furthermore, in some cases, other offenders later confessed to the crimes for which certain death row inmates had been convicted. In January 2003, Ryan commuted all death row inmate sentences to life-without-parole terms as he ended his term as governor. Given Illinois's action, should all other states with death penalty statutes suspend death penalties until they can give full review to inmate petitions? How can errors occur in prosecutions against persons where the death penalty is ultimately applied? What system can we use to make the system error-free? Because certain innocent persons are executed, do you think the death penalty should be abandoned in the United States? What do you think?* [Adapted from the Associated Press, "In Wake of Exonerations, Illinois Suspending Death Penalty," January 31, 2000; Associated Press, 2003].

• *A Native American prisoner at a Midwestern penitentiary sued prison officials, demanding that they provide him with a quantity of marijuana because it is essential in his religious rituals. He explained that he must have the marijuana in order to reach a state of inner peace with his God and experience repentance in order to obtain forgiveness for his crimes. Prison officials repeatedly denied his requests for marijuana. He sued the system, claiming that his religious freedoms under the First Amendment were being abridged. He also raised a claim under the "equal protection" clause of the Fourteenth Amendment, alleging that other prisoners were allowed religious artifacts for their personal religious experiences and services. A federal district court granted a motion to dismiss on the part of the state for failure to state a claim upon which relief can be granted. Should prisoners be allowed illegal drugs and other substances if such substances are considered essential to their religious services? Are lawsuits such as this one frivolous? What do you think?* [Adapted from Walter Gray and the Associated Press, "Native American Inmate Denied Marijuana for Religious Experiences," April 10, 2002].

We are in the midst of an inmate litigation explosion (Roleff 1996). In 1962, federal prisoners filed 1,500 suits alleging various complaints against prison administrators and staff. By 2000, the annual number of federal prisoner filings had increased to 58,257 (Maguire and Pastore 2002:467). In 1977, inmates of state prisons filed 14,846 petitions or suits alleging rights violations by prison staff. By 2000, the annual number of state prisoner filings had increased to 46,377 (Maguire and Pastore 2002:467).

This chapter examines some of the rights inmates have acquired in the past few decades. In the 1950s and 1960s, the authoritarian regimes of federal and state prisons as well as similar administrative modes in city and county jails were largely unchallenged. Those raising questions about inmate rights then did so in the midst of an unaccepting and insensitive public. Judges received petitions from prison and jail inmates unenthusiastically, and the presumption was almost always that prison and jail administrators had neither violated the law nor infringed the rights of any inmate. Legally untrained and uneducated prisoners found this presumption difficult to overcome. Some writers have said that during the 1960s, a **prisoners' rights movement** was established (Carlson and Garrett 1999). This movement was not highly organized and well-coordinated, but it gathered sufficient momentum over the next twenty years so that the courts were deluged by larger numbers of increasingly sophisticated inmate filings. This dramatic upsurge in lawsuits has been labeled by correctional researchers and others as the **inmate litigation explosion** or, simply, the **litigation explosion.** The litigation explosion is examined.

Next, this chapter describes jailhouse lawyers, or those who have acquired considerable legal expertise and assist themselves and others in various legal matters. Jailhouse lawyers have not always received fair treatment from prison administrations and staffs. In fact, inmate access to the courts wasn't condoned until the 1940s because of the hands-off doctrine, which is described. Subsequent U.S. Supreme Court rulings have upheld the constitutionality of jailhouse lawyers and condoned their assistance with the legal problems of others. The role of the jailhouse lawyer in prison litigation issues will be explored. Also described are the constitutional bases for inmate litigation, including several important Amendments that have frequently been cited in court actions by prisoners. The First, Fourth, Eighth, and Fourteenth Amendments are featured in this discussion. Most courts currently use a reasonableness test in resolving inmate claims against prison officials and others. This test will be explained. Several other legal issues will be examined, including the right of access by inmates to legal materials and law libraries.

Several important avenues for civil litigation by inmates are discussed. These include *habeas corpus* petitions, which challenge the fact, nature, and length of confinement; tort claims, which allege negligence and harmful acts by corrections officials; and civil rights claims, which allege unfairness and inequitable treatment of prisoners by the prison system. Each of these avenues for civil litigation is described, together with various cases that describe inmate claims and court results. One result of the rising number of inmate lawsuits has been the Prison Litigation Reform Act (PLRA) of 1995. When this act was passed, the result was a reduction in the volume of inmate claims filed in courts. This is because it required all state inmates to exhaust all of their state remedies before seeking relief in federal district courts. It also sought to have inmates consolidate their claims into single suits to minimize frivolous litigation over petty claims later. The PLRA has been modestly successful in reducing inmate claims.

Court actions by inmates have been prompted by several continuing problems. These problems are often related to the nature of prison and jail management and operation and have led to the identification of several key issues that stimulate much inmate litigation. Some of these problems are described. Racism is alleged in many prison systems, where minority offenders allege inequitable treatment on the basis of race. Other inmates allege that their right to due process is violated as the result of certain administrative actions. Some inmates claim that they have a right to rehabilitation, although the courts have not been supportive of this claim. Yet other offenders allege that they have been misclassified by their prison systems, and thus they become deprived of certain amenities and prison services as the result of this misclassification. Furthermore, they allege, they are disadvantaged by being in higher custody levels where certain programs and services are not made available to them. These claims are described. Some inmates claim that their cells are searched and valuable property is destroyed intentionally by corrections officers. These claims are usually litigated as tort actions. Yet other inmates allege cruel and unusual punishment in terms of how they are housed.

One frequent complaint stemming from prison overcrowding is that too many inmates are celled together in cells designed to hold fewer inmates. Other inmates claim that correctional officers and the administration are negligent in different respects and that the consequences of this negligence are harmful to them. Finally, some inmates are fathers or mothers, and they believe that they should be afforded the opportunity to interact with their children. A growing number of prisons are making provisions for inmate fathers and mothers to reunite with their young children under properly supervised circumstances.

Perhaps the most controversial issue in corrections today is the application of the death penalty. Capital punishment is used by two-thirds of the states and the federal government. The death penalty is constantly being challenged on constitutional grounds, although it has never been declared unconstitutional. Several death penalty cases are described that have had a profound effect on how the death penalty is determined as a punishment. These are the cases of *Furman v. Georgia* (1972) and *Gregg v. Georgia* (1976). Provisions for bifurcated trials have been established, and these procedures are explained. The pros and cons surrounding the application are examined in some detail. Recent scientific developments, such as the discovery and use of DNA, have resulted in some death row inmates being exonerated of their original crimes and freed. This has caused some critics of the death penalty to advocate its absolute abolition. This and other issues surrounding the death penalty will be closely examined. One issue is whether inmates who have been wrongly convicted of crimes should be reimbursed by the states or federal government for the time they served behind bars. Various states and the federal government have approved such remuneration, although this remains a sensitive issue. Also discussed will be the application of the death penalty to women and youthful offenders.

In recent years, all prison systems have instituted administrative procedures whereby prisoners can file grievances and complaints about the general nature of their confinement. In some prisons and jails, inmate committees have been formed to perform similar functions. Sometimes called inmate disciplinary councils, these administrative and inmate grievance mechanisms will be described and discussed.

WHAT ARE JAILHOUSE LAWYERS?

There are jailhouse lawyers and there are jailhouse lawyers. Those who file nuisance suits such as in the case of *In re Green* (1981) do a disservice to all other inmates of prisons and jails who file legitimate grievances and raise important constitutional issues. A **jailhouse lawyer** is an inmate of a prison or jail who has acquired some degree of legal expertise and assists both him- or herself or others in filing petitions and suits against their institutions (Belbot 1995). Jailhouse lawyers and lawyering have, and will continue to have, a tremendous impact on reforming jails and prisons. For many jailhouse lawyers, their efforts are a form of primitive rebellion against the system. They are exiled and power-less. However, they have several ways of resisting either the control or the conditions imposed upon them by their state keepers.

Considerable informal legal schooling frequently occurs within penitentiaries. The schooling is of all types. Prisonization imparts improved criminal skills for those desiring to acquire greater criminal expertise. Other types of schooling pertain to the law and how appeals can be filed. Jailhouse lawyers are self-taught and well-schooled in the finer points of inmate appeals. They may file appeals on their own behalf or on the behalf of other inmates who lack legal knowledge (Davidson 1995).

One of the first nationally recognized jailhouse lawyers was Caryl Chessman, author of *Cell 2455, Death Row*. Chessman was arrested and charged on January 23, 1948, with 18 counts of robbery and rape stemming from a series of incidents occurring in the Hollywood Hills area of Los Angeles, a remote region known as lover's lane. The media labeled Chessman the "Red Light Bandit," and he was subsequently convicted and sentenced to death in the San Quentin gas chamber. Before he was executed on May 2, 1960, he had filed 39 appeals and had his execution stayed or delayed eight times. Thus, he avoided execution for almost twelve years while he fought his court battles. He acquired an extensive legal library and became a legal expert on the appeals process and finding legal loopholes. Historical accounts suggest that Chessman was convicted largely on the basis of circumstantial evidence and that because he conducted his own defense in a highly inflammatory and arrogant manner, the jury was unsympathetic to his arguments, however persuasive. But the circumstantial evidence against Chessman was sufficiently persuasive to jurors. Ironically, in the wake of *Furman v. Georgia* (1972) twelve years after Chessman's execution, California suspended the death penalty temporarily and commuted all death sentences at the time to life with the possibility of parole.

Another death row inmate who eventually sprung himself out of death row in 1965 was Jerome "Jerry" Rosenberg. Rosenberg was on death row for killing a police officer. Rosenberg was a fourth-grade dropout who left his middle-class Brooklyn family for an abortive career in organized crime. Claiming he was innocent of the police officer's murder, Rosenberg began an intensive study of the law. Eventually, he convinced Governor Rockefeller to commute his death sentence to life imprisonment. Over the next three years (1965–1968), Rosenberg acquired a law degree by correspondence while at Attica State Prison. He was subsequently recognized as the nation's foremost jailhouse lawyer (Bello 1982).

THE CONSTITUTIONAL BASIS FOR INMATE RIGHTS

In some respects, the question of prisoner rights is similar to the problems of other minorities in America. Prisoners have not always enjoyed the protection of the U.S. Constitution and Bill of Rights. Their struggle to be recognized as human beings who are entitled to the same rights as those possessed by other U.S. citizens has been a long and difficult one. In 1871, for example, a Virginia judge declared that "prisoners have no more rights than slaves" (Palmer 1997:141). While this declaration was harsh, it nevertheless reflected public sentiment that imprisonment is and should be regarded as a punishment, and the loss of certain rights is a significant element of that punishment (*Ruffin v. Commonwealth* 1871).

BOX 9.1

Jerome "Jerry" Rosenberg

Inmate # 63-A-0017
Wende Correctional Facility
Alden, NY

Background

Jerome "Jerry" Rosenberg, known to his fellow inmates as "Jerry the Jew," was born on May 18, 1937. He was the third of three sons born to his parents, Lou and Rose Rosenberg. Jerry says that he became a gangster at age 13. Growing up in Brooklyn, New York, Jerry says that instead of doing things normal kids did at that age, he fought, stole, and became a young mobster. Eventually, he married his first wife, Rose Ann, and they had a daughter, Ronnie. In October 1957 he was arrested in connection with the robbery of a Brooklyn check-cashing store. He admitted to that crime (he was caught red-handed with an accomplice inside the store) and was convicted and sent to prison for four years. After he was incarcerated, his wife, Rose Ann, divorced him.

When Rosenberg was released from prison, he was allegedly involved in a New York City robbery of the Boro Park Tobacco Company with two other men in May 1962. Two men, subsequently identified as Anthony Dellernia and Anthony Portelli, pulled masks over their faces and entered the company with their guns drawn. Something went awry and gunshots were fired. Two undercover police officers nearby, Luke Fallon, 56, and John Finnegan, 29, heard the shooting and rushed to the tobacco company to see what was happening. As they entered the doorway, they were gunned down and killed. This was the first double murder of police officers in New York City in forty years. Police investigation eventually led to the arrest of Anthony Dellernia, who turned himself in to police. He confessed to being the getaway driver and was later acquitted of murder charges filed against him. A second man, Anthony

Portelli, was identified as the lone shooter and was caught in Chicago and brought back to New York where he was charged with the double murder of the police officers. Jerry Rosenberg was identified as being the other man inside the tobacco company with Portelli. After hearing that he was wanted for the murder of two police officers, Jerry Rosenberg turned himself in to police detectives at the offices of the *Daily News*. Both Portelli and Rosenberg were convicted of the double murder and sentenced to death. Subsequent changes in the death penalty statutes in New York, together with some technical arguments raised in an appeal by Rosenberg, spared him from the electric chair. His death sentence was converted to life imprisonment, which included parole eligibility. The other man, Portelli, died in prison in 1975 after serving thirteen years of a life sentence.

Actually, it was Rosenberg who taught himself about the law and learned enough to launch an appeal that eventually spared him from the electric chair. Hours away from being electrocuted in 1965, Rosenberg's appeal was heard by the New York Supreme Court. His self-taught legal knowledge was sufficient to raise the issue of whether the murder of the two police officers was premeditated. It seems that a New York statute provided that the death penalty was the punishment if one was convicted of the premeditated murder of a police officer or a prison guard. Rosenberg argued convincingly that the officers' murder could not have been premeditated. Then-governor Nelson Rockefeller commuted Rosenberg's death sentence to 20 years to life. Rosenberg was less than eight hours from execution in the electric chair when the commutation was granted.

After winning this appeal, Rosenberg went on to learn more about the law. During the next thirty years, Jerry earned three law degrees. He became the first inmate to represent a defendant from the outside. He was the first inmate to argue a case before a jury. He has successfully defended several clients. He has earned the respect of well-known attorneys such as Alan Dershowitz. His own words about his accomplishments are insightful.

In April 2002 I wrote to Jerry Rosenberg at the Wende Correctional Facility in Alden, New York. Jerry was kind enough to take the time to write to me. He said,

Dear Dr. Champion, it was an honor to receive your letter and I appreciate the nice things you said about me. It appears to be an interesting book you're putting together. First, let me inform you that I can't see too well and I am in the RMU Hospital. I'm dying and am very ill. Enclosed are medical records. So to make a long story short, I've enclosed some magazine and legal articles and some other information. To sum it up, I'm in 28 books, including my own life story entitled *Doing Life* (St. Martin's Press, 1982), by Steve Bello (paperback in 1986). I don't have a copy of the book and you can't get one from St. Martin's, since they have none. But you can get it from any library. I'm also in the following books: *A Time to Die,* by Tom Wicker (1975); *Attica: My Story,* by Oswald Chief (Seedman, 1973); *Revolt in the Mafia* by Martin (1974); *Tough Guys* (1995), and *Contract Killer* (1989) by Hoffman. All of these books can be obtained from the library. I'm in over 68 magazines and tons of newspapers, mostly national (e.g., *Washington Post, Los Angeles Times, New York Times,* etc.). I did interviews for these papers and they wrote feature stories. Plus all local papers (*New York Daily News*). I was in *People* magazine three times, *Playboy* two times, the *Star* and *Enquirer* tabloids, plus many others. I'm giving you these because you might want to research this background material. I believe this covers 45 years of my prison, criminal background, and legal matters.

As a lawyer, judges, both state and federal, speak about me, as well as very big lawyers, as you will read. You also may call any lawyer that you read about or judge about me. I'm doing this as I can't really see or write as you can tell by my writing. But I'm still intact with my mind when I go to court. As one writer said, I left behind a legacy and history concerning my achievements. There are a couple of new cases which I will try to write for you. I've been in prison for 41 years (as of 2002), since 1961. Right now I have one big murder case in federal court in Rochester, New York. I did the *habeas corpus,* and it's been pending for 2 1/2 years—the Daniels case. I will write you about that on separate pages later. It's a winner and deserving also. Although we admit the murder? Very interesting.

I did over 35 television shows, nine local, the rest national: *Good Morning, America, American Justice,* etc. Also a movie was made on the book, *Doing Life.* Tony Danza played me in the Mafia since age 13. I deny it. They claim I'm still active even though in prison. They claim I'm close with John Gotti. I am. We are friends. All my life. Well, you'll read it all. I will send you the material.

My daughter, Ronnie, died at age 41 in 1996 in Texas. I lived in Texas City and Katy, Texas in the 1950s. My ex-wife still lives there. I was just denied parole again. My ex-wife has *Doing Life,* both the book and the movie rights. Friends of mine since I started doing movies and television are Robert DeNiro, Joe Pesci, and Pat Collins. I don't know if they know that I am very sick, dying. I just lost touch with them.

On April 3, 2002, Jerry Rosenberg appeared before the New York State Parole Board to be considered for parole again. The parole board issued its repeated denial of parole with the following statement: "After a full review of the record, and noting your repeated refusal to appear before the parole board panel, the panel has determined that due to the violent nature and circumstances of the instant offense, wherein acting in concert, and during the course of a robbery, two NYC police detectives lost their lives, and that you were in absconder status from a prior conviction and incarceration, that discretionary release is not consistent with the best interests of society. We have reviewed your program and disciplinary records and all other information required by law. Following deliberation, this decision is based on review of the case record as well as the interview with parole board members."

(continued)

BOX 9.1 (*Continued*)

It is unlikely that Jerry will ever be released from prison, despite letters from judges to the state parole board recommending him for early release. For instance, New York Administrative Judge Vincent E. Doyle wrote on March 8, 2000, "I write this letter on behalf of Jerry Rosenberg to urge that he be paroled to a nursing home. As I have previously stated, in my opinion, Mr. Rosenberg meets all the criteria for release on parole and is no longer a threat to the community. He is in need of the services of a nursing home, rather than being a costly expense to the State of New York as a prisoner. I urge your favorable consideration of paroling Mr. Rosenberg to a nursing home."

Rosenberg's case is such that he is in the proverbial "between a rock and a hard place." He has consistently denied his guilt and complicity in the deaths of the New York police officers. One requirement for early release through parole board action is to accept responsibility for the crime. If Jerry were to suddenly say, "You're right, I'm guilty, I did it, I'm sorry for what I did, I accept responsibility," then the parole board would say, "Oh, you've been lying to us for the past 35 years. This deceit is sufficient to deny you parole." But continuing to deny one's guilt means that one doesn't accept responsibility for the crime. This is Jerry's endless dilemma.

In the meantime, Rosenberg has left his mark on society in many positive ways. When Rosenberg was imprisoned in Attica, New York, a riot broke out in 1971. A subsequent assault on the prison by police broke up the riot, but not before 39 persons were dead and 88 were injured. Rosenberg was involved in attempting to negotiate an amicable settlement between rioting inmates and the prison administration. His attempt at intervention was far from trivial. It led to numerous reforms throughout the New York prison system.

In 1986, Rosenberg was rushed to a hospital where he underwent open-heart surgery. Twice he died on the operating table. When he recovered from the successful operation, he filed suit seeking release from prison on the grounds that he had died, thus ending his "life" prison term. Although the suit was a novel one, appellate judges, although impressed, were unsympathetic with the argument. In 2002 Rosenberg, a heavy smoker, was confined to a wheelchair with various ailments. Yet he continues to actively represent various clients in their legal cases. At this writing Rosenberg was defending a client charged with murder. Jerry is one jailhouse lawyer who never quits.

Prisoners were often used as guinea pigs for a variety of scientific medical and social experiments. This was not considered unusual, since prisoners were not afforded rights or given serious consideration as citizens. During World War I, for example, some U.S. prisoners were used to determine the physical effects of various gases and other wartime products. Some inmates died as the result of being exposed to corrosive or poisonous gases and other chemicals. In May 1980, experimental drug research was being conducted on inmates of several prisons, including the Michigan State Prison at Jackson. The National Commission for the Protection of Human Subjects of Biomedical and Behavioral Research has made numerous recommendations, including a ban on nontherapeutic experimental drug research on prisoners. The U.S. Food and Drug Administration has sought to implement some of these recommendations and to extend to prisoners the right to participate in such experiments on the bases of informed consent and voluntariness (Hanson and Daley 1995). Also, until the early 1940s, some state prisons sterilized certain inmates, believing that their criminality was hereditary.

In 1970 the U.S. Supreme Court declared that the Arkansas state prison system was guilty of committing numerous barbaric acts against inmates, including a variety of corporal punishments (*Holt v. Sarver* 1970). Inmate compliance with prison rules was obtained by different painful and inhumane methods such as shoving needles under inmates' fingernails, starvation, flogging, and a special device called the **Tucker telephone.** The Tucker telephone (named after the Tucker, Arkansas, Prison Farm) was a crank-type apparatus, an electrical generator taken from an old-style crank telephone. Inmates were strapped to a table in the Tucker Hospital where physicians and correctional officers fastened electrodes to their penises, testicles, and toes. Turning the hand-crank on the telephone device caused its electrical generator to send a charge into the prisoner's body, inflicting unbearable shocks. So-called long-distance calls were made for especially unruly prisoners, and more than one prisoner emerged from this torture with irreparable testicle damage and psychological disorders (Murton and Hyams 1976).

For many years, Arkansas inmates had complained about the atrocities and inhumane treatment they received while in prison. However, officials were inclined to be skeptical about these complaints. In 1967, for instance, an Arkansas state representative, Lloyd Sadler, declared that he didn't believe that stuff, because "ninety-five percent of the complaints of convicts are lies." Another Arkansas official, state senator Knox Nelson, claimed that same year that Arkansas had "the best prison system in the United States" (Murton and Hyams 1976). Under a new administration, the governor appointed Thomas O. Murton, a former professor of criminology at Southern Illinois University, as the new administrator of Arkansas's prison system in 1966. Murton was charged with the responsibility of reforming the old prison system. His early efforts at reform uncovered some of the atrocities that prisoners had complained of years earlier. Because Murton's discoveries and new policies were believed to be potentially embarrassing to Arkansas, he was relieved of his administrative responsibilities in 1968. The governor claimed he had been a poor administrator. But his intervention had uncovered what came to be known as the **Arkansas prison scandal,** and the *Holt v. Sarver* decision in 1970 concluded the scandal.

Visitors of prisons and jails are searched thoroughly for contraband that might be smuggled to their inmate-relatives or friends.

Prisons are designed to incarcerate those who have violated the law. Jails fulfill this basic purpose as well, although we have seen that jails house other types of inmates besides law violators. Thus, prisons and jails have been established generally to incapacitate, control, and monitor criminals. These facilities perform other functions, including punishment, discipline, and to some extent, rehabilitation. Because prisons and jails are low-priority items in local, state, and federal budgetary allocations and because many of them are old and dilapidated, large numbers of penal facilities in the United States are considered deplorable by critics. Hundreds of prisons and jails are currently under court order to improve their physical plants and other facilities so that minimal health and safety standards can be attained (Hall 1987). Also, large numbers of penal institutions are currently operating according to minimally acceptable health and safety standards. While no court has ever declared that prisons and jails must be comfortable, numerous inmate suits have been prompted because of a variety of deprivations relating to these minimal standards.

Furthermore, it is the responsibility of prison and jail officials to operate orderly systems and to ensure that inmates comply with policies and rules. Because of the inherently coercive nature of prison and jail settings, differences of opinion and disagreements between prisoners and prison staff over the polices, rules, and conditions of confinement are inevitable. Prison and jail staff must actively seek to control the flow of contraband, since inmate access to various forms of contraband is potentially disruptive and might pose safety problems for other inmates (Logan 2001). Prison and jail regulations exist that authorize routine official body and cell searches for the purpose of discovering and seizing any illegal materials. Searches of body cavities and X-rays have yielded drugs, weapons, and other materials potentially injurious to prison staff or other inmates. **Shakedowns,** where a thorough search is conducted of an inmate's cell, also uncover illicit materials that are considered disruptive to prison or jail discipline (Gardner 1985).

Because of the coercive nature of an inmate's confinement and the tight discipline that must be maintained by prison or jail officials, inmates suffer deprivations, indignities, and other forms of treatment alien to their lives outside of institutional settings. Therefore, prisons and jails are prime sites for inmate grievances and legal action. Some inmates take radical steps to make their points about complaints concerning prison conditions. A few inmates engage in hunger strikes for brief periods, while others self-inflict wounds to attract the attention of prison staff (Bourgoin 2001). For instance, one result of hunger-strike demonstrations by inmates has been that prison officials have resorted to force-feeding them in an effort to prevent them from starving to death. Force-feeding inmates is done and justified by prison administrators who rightly cite the law that suicide is illegal. Thus, if inmates deliberately starve themselves, this is a form of suicide and illegal per se. The logical remedy is force-feeding them. Inmates contend, however, that their act of starvation is simply self-determination and a form of rebellion against prison administrators for some perceived wrong or injustice.

Some prisoners and civil rights groups have elevated hunger strikes by inmates to the level of a legitimate ethical and moral dilemma. In several instances, inmates who are serving lengthy prison sentences simply want to end their incarceration through death. In Arizona, for instance, 56-year-old Mario V. Rangel, an inmate serving 32 years for multiple counts of child abuse, refused kidney dialysis, saying he wanted to die. After rejecting kidney dialysis treatment for a week and refusing to eat, Rangel died. Subsequently, several other inmates in Arizona prisons have gone on hunger strikes for various reasons. Some of these inmates are on death row and simply want to cease their prolonged confinement. In 1998 the Arizona Department of Corrections implemented a procedure that permits force-feeding inmates who refuse to eat. Arizona Corrections Director Terry Stewart said, "Obviously, it is the Department's job to keep inmates healthy and alive by providing them with the nutrition and medical attention they require. We will, as the policy indicates, use the medical and legal means necessary to keep protesting inmates alive when they are carrying out a hunger strike or refusing medical treatment, but we also recognize, irrespective of our efforts, an inmate can succeed in dying if he so chooses" (Arizona Department of Corrections 2001).

Hunger strikes and other prisoner demonstrations are usually precipitated by a loss of privileges or actions by prison administrators that seem unreasonable. For instance, in the Arizona Department of Corrections, several prisoners, including a few death row inmates, have engaged in hunger strikes to protest such things as inadequate exercise equipment in the recreation pens; a lack of a hobby craft program to include musical instruments; a demand for more books, cassette tapes, and compact discs; more access to headphones with 10 to 12 feet of cord; not being provided sunglasses for being outside on a hard labor crew; demands for more time outside of cells; and unescorted walks to and from shower areas.

In Pennsylvania on death row, inmates have protested through hunger strikes, contending that Pennsylvania officials have established unreasonable rules relative to access to legal materials. The state has come up with a new rule requiring inmates to keep all personal property in a 12-inch by 12-inch by 14-inch box. Since inmates accumulate large amounts of legal papers, this requirement seems completely unrealistic. In one instance, when one inmate couldn't afford postage to ship his legal materials to another address, the correctional officers apparently destroyed them. Family visits have been restricted to one hour on weekdays, with no visits on weekends or holidays. Some prisons are in remote locations, requiring family and friends to drive for more than six hours for a one-hour visit. Even this amount of time has been reduced on the whims of certain correctional officers. Furthermore, prisoners have been barred from having food in their cells, or even buying food from the commissary. According to some inmates, this violated their religious freedom, since they were forbidden from eating meat. Also, inmates with diabetes were placed at risk because of denied access to certain low-calorie foods (New Abolitionist 2002).

Even in England and other countries, such as Turkey, prison officials have had to contend with prisoner-initiated hunger strikes. For example, in England, Ian Brady, an inmate sentenced to life imprisonment for a murder conviction in 1966, engaged in a hunger strike to protest his conditions of confinement. The government intervened and force-fed Brady. Subsequently, English officials passed the Human Rights Act of 1998. This act provided for more humane prison conditions. However, it also made provisions for protecting inmates in the care of the government. Presently, prison authorities have a duty to intervene and force-feed inmates as a lawful response to hunger strikers (Williams 2001).

It is difficult to achieve a balance between the responsibilities of prison and jail officials to maintain orderly premises and a reasonable social system ensuring acceptable inmate conduct on the one hand and seeing that inmate constitutional rights are fully observed on the other. Thus it is not unreasonable to find that inmates rely on one another for legal assistance at times (Hart 1995).

The Arkansas prison scandal is one extreme, representing extensive corporal cruelty to prisoners. Inhumane conditions of confinement, where prisoners were forced to sit for many days in their own excrement, naked, in solitary confinement and on starvation diets, and being tortured from time to time by the Tucker telephone and other devices represents one of the worst cases against prison administrations. The other extreme is the case of *In re Green* (1981). Green was a prison inmate who filed between 600 and 700 lawsuits on behalf of himself and other inmates during the 1970s. The courts consistently found his suits to be "frivolous, irresponsible, and unmeritorious," and one court even suggested that Green hoped to force his own release from custody by swamping the court with these frivolous suits (Knight and Early 1986:15). Large numbers of frivolous filings by inmates damage their credibility in the courts of any jurisdiction. All lawsuits, including those that are dismissed, consume valuable court time.

For many years since the judicial declaration that prisoners were slaves of the state in *Ruffin v. Commonwealth* (1871), inmates of jails and prisons were treated as second-class citizens and given little or no standing in U.S. courts. The *Ruffin* case led to the hands-off doctrine practiced by U.S. courts during the next seventy years. The courts consistently refused to intervene in the management and operation of prison affairs. This is because the U.S. Supreme Court believed that prison and jail authorities were in the best position to determine penal policies and prescribe the means whereby these policies would be implemented (Sigler and Shook 1995). However, the first major breakthrough separating the past from the present occurred in 1941 in the case of *Ex parte Hull.*

In 1941, prison and jail officials carefully screened all outgoing inmate mail, including legal documents and petitions addressed to state or federal courts. Inmate petitions to the court for virtually any grievance or complaint, founded or unfounded, were often conveniently trashed by prison officials who claimed that these petitions were improperly prepared and thus ineligible for court action. Prison and jail policies permitted the disposal of such materials. In *Ex parte Hull* (1941), the U.S. Supreme Court declared that no state or its officers may abridge or impair a prisoner's right to have access to federal courts. The court, not prison or jail officials, would determine whether petitions were properly prepared. While the original *Hull* decision pertained to a particular class of legal petitions, it was eventually extended to include categorical access to the courts (Palmer 1997:44,100). Despite the *Hull* ruling, courts have continued to take a hands-off attitude toward lawsuits filed by prisoners in later years (Milovanovic et al. 1997).

Gradually, the U.S. Supreme Court has adopted a **reasonableness test** to determine whether to hear inmate petitions. The reasonableness test contrasts inmate rights against those of the correctional institution. Any correctional institution has the right to establish policies that maintain orderly organizational operations that ensure the safety of staff and inmates. If one or more of these policies run afoul of inmate interests from time to time, they are challenged, usually when a prisoner files a petition with the court protesting the policy. The courts are inclined to side with correctional institutions rather than inmates in these matters, since institutional safety overrides perceived individual rights violations or infringements (Alexander 1994, 1995).

Inmates have continuously challenged the legality of their confinement under writs of *habeas corpus* or **habeas corpus** petitions. A **writ of *habeas corpus*** is a document that commands authorities to show cause why an inmate should be confined in either a prison or jail. It is a Latin term meaning "produce the body" or "you should have the body." While many inmate *habeas corpus* petitions are rejected by the courts, they nevertheless represent one means by which an inmate can seek relief from confinement. The *Hull* case involved an *habeas corpus* petition. In 1944, another important case was decided which

Visitors' areas of prisons are open and permit supervising correctional officers to monitor inmate-visitor interactions.

extended *habeas corpus* relief to include the conditions of confinement in addition to confinement itself. This was the case of *Coffin v. Reichard* (1944).

The *Coffin* case is significant because it is the first instance that a federal appellate court declared that prisoners do not lose their civil rights as the result of entering confinement. The **hands-off doctrine** was based on two rationales: (1) that correctional facilities were managed by the executive branch and under the **separation of powers** doctrine the judiciary should not interfere with that management, and (2) that judges were not experts in correctional administration and therefore should not interfere with the experts who ran such facilities (Sigler and Shook 1995).

Habeas corpus petitions challenge (1) the fact of confinement, (2) the nature of confinement, and (3) the length of confinement (Hanson and Daley 1995). However, the U.S. Supreme Court has determined that these writs shall only be used whenever inmates have exhausted their state remedies. Thus, state prisoners planning to file *habeas corpus* writs in federal district courts must first demonstrate that they have pursued their grievances in state courts. Otherwise, district judges will direct these suits to appropriate state courts for action. However, federal prisoners may file *habeas corpus* petitions directly in federal district courts.

An inmate challenge about the nature of confinement within the context of the federal *habeas corpus* statute must allege that by virtue of confinement the prisoner is deprived of some right to which he or she is entitled despite the confinement and that the deprivation of this right makes the imprisonment more burdensome (Palmer 1997). *Habeas corpus* relief might be sought by state or federal prisoners being incarcerated in a local jail, where the jail has contracted with the state or federal government to house a portion of prison overflow to ease overcrowding. Compared with prisons, jail facilities are particularly inadequate. State and federal prisoners rightfully feel deprived of various vocational and educational programs and other benefits otherwise available to them if they were housed in long-term prison settings (C. Smith 1995).

Today, jail and prison inmates file one out of every five civil cases in U.S. district courts (Cheesman, Hanson, and Ostrom 2000). While there are many suits filed by inmates annually, a large number of these suits are dismissed. The two most frequently used methods courts employ for dismissing these suits are (1) a **motion to dismiss** and a (2) **motion for summary judgment.** Motions to dismiss are usually granted where the plaintiff or inmate has simply failed to state a claim upon which relief can be granted. In brief, the court has read the petition and decided that no basis exists for the suit. In the latter case, motions for summary judgments are granted where prison officials offer their version of events to be considered together with the views and arguments of the prisoner. Thus, the court considers both sides of the complaint in motions for summary judgment, but it hears only the facts as outlined by the inmate in a motion to dismiss. A frequently cited reason for denying relief to prisoners when they file petitions with the court is that the filings are deemed as frivolous. Usually, a frivolous claim is considered outlandish or absurd by the courts, where the inmate is making clearly unreasonable demands or false claims (Fradella 1999). An inmate may file a lawsuit alleging that there was too much gristle in his chicken dinner. Another inmate may demand marijuana as a part of some contrived religion where a particular psychological state is required for proper communion. These types of claims are usually dismissed as frivolous. Several Amendments to the U.S. Constitution form the basis for many lawsuits against federal, state, and local penal institutions and their agents. These include the First, Fourth, Eighth, and Fourteenth Amendments.

The First Amendment

The First Amendment states that "Congress shall make no law respecting an establishment of religion, or prohibiting the free exercise thereof; or abridging the freedom of speech, or of the press; or the right of the people peaceably to assemble, and to petition the government for a redress of grievances." This Amendment has sparked numerous lawsuits by prisoners, in part because it involves the transmittal of communications with others outside of prison as well as the receipt of communications from others. Several of the scenarios at the beginning of this chapter involved First Amendment rights challenges. With the increasing popularity of the Internet, more First Amendment challenges by inmates of prisons and jails are expected (McIntyre, Tong, and Perez 2001).

The First Amendment also specifies that a prisoner's religious beliefs will be respected, so long as those beliefs do not violate existing laws and do not interfere with or pose a threat to prison discipline and operations (Opata 2001). Regarding the censorship of an inmate's mail, censorship is justified to the extent that the letter "jeopardizes security, order, or rehabilitation, and the regulations may be only as broad as is necessary to meet those goals. However, officials may not censor mail simply to eliminate unflattering opinions, factually inaccurate statements, or inflammatory racial, political, or religious views" (Bronstein 1980:30; *Procunier v. Martinez* 1974).

Prior to the *Procunier* holding, virtually every piece of inmate mail was inspected, both leaving and entering these institutions. The judgments of officials determined whether the mail would be forwarded. Many of these communications were between inmates and their attorneys. A separate case focused upon the nature of privileged communications between attorneys and their inmate-clients. This was the case of *Wolff v. McDonnell* (1974).

The *Wolff* case dealt solely with the question of whether letters determined or found to be from attorneys may be opened by prison authorities in the presence of the inmate or whether such mail must be delivered unopened if normal detection techniques fail to indicate contraband. The U.S. Supreme Court did not add a great deal of clarity to this issue in their decision. The Court indicated that attorneys must clearly identify themselves by placing their names and addresses in plain view on envelopes and that the letters should show that they came from lawyers. In any case, prison authorities may inspect and read any document leaving and entering the institution in an effort to determine whether inmates are abusing their rights by communicating about restricted matters (Bronstein 1980:29–30). Despite the *Wolff* ruling, there are continuing challenges by inmates of mail policies of various prison systems (*Avery v. Powell* 1992; *Bressman v. Farrier* 1993; *Thongvanh v. Thalacker* 1994).

The courts have been more restrictive about communications between prisoners within and between different penal institutions. Policies in many prisons and jails prohibit written communications between inmates in different institutions. Thus, if a California state prisoner in San Quentin wishes to correspond with a federal prisoner in Marion, Illinois, prison rules are in effect that prohibit such exchanges. The courts have continually upheld the right of prison officials to restrict or deny such correspondence between prisoners as potentially disruptive of prison discipline, without violating their free speech rights (*Bryson v. Iowa Dist. Court, Iowa* 1994). However, sometimes prison officials may be asked to defend why and how they believed such communications threatened the security of their prisons and presented a clear and present danger to prison discipline (*Turner v. Safley* 1987). Unsatisfactory explanations to the court by prison officials may result in such censorship being determined to be a violation of the inmate's constitutional right to free expression.

There is a general mistrust of U.S. correctional systems among federal and state inmates. Despite the legal rulings favorable to inmates in jails and prisons, some inmates have written about the informal lack of enforcement of these rulings and rights. Jerome "Jerry" Rosenberg, a "lifer" at the Wende Correctional Facility in New York, is a well-known jailhouse lawyer. In fact, his notoriety has gained him an unfavorable reputation among prison administration and staff. In 2002 Rosenberg was seriously ill and in poor health, confined to a wheelchair. Despite his infirmities, he was still assisting other inmates with their legal cases. One of his impairments is the gradual loss of his eyesight. He requested medical services to assist him in acquiring reading glasses and a magnifying glass to read his correspondence. But the doctors were slow in providing him with prescription eyeglasses. He says, "First, the doctor here refused me eyeglasses and magnifying glasses. I have sued these individuals and notified the health department. I was informed that the health department was advised by these doctors that my eyesight was not bad at all, and that I did not need any eyeglasses. They retracted these statements when confronted with a lawsuit, denying that they had examined me for my eye needs. Later, I had trouble getting someone to wheel me in my wheelchair to a room where I could be examined for chest pains. Again, after I filed another lawsuit, two inmates were requisitioned to wheel me through to the hospital where I could receive treatment for my chest pains. They didn't want guards to do it, for fear that I'd die on route to the hospital and they would be blamed. The system 'gets you' in different ways, but I have a lot of tricks of my own to 'get the system.'"

The freedom of worship issue is also the subject of numerous prisoner-initiated lawsuits. The courts have been reluctant to make decisions that restrict inmate opportunities to worship the religion of their choice, despite the fact that some religions are questionably religious. Thus, prisoners may request

 **BOX 9.2**

There's English, and Then There's Hawaiian?

The official language in Hawaii is English. The second official language in Hawaii is Hawaiian. That's right. It's official. However, it is not acceptable to speak Hawaiian at the Women's Community Correctional Center in Kailua. A social worker, Lei Kihoi, was reprimanded by prison officials recently for speaking in the traditional Hawaiian dialect as a part of an eight-step conflict-resolution program for female inmates. The conflict-resolution technique, *ho-oponopono,* is a program that means literally "to make right." Kihoi has worked in the prison since 1997 and has used the technique to assist many offenders.

The prison policy forbidding the Hawaiian language is considered a security measure to prevent female inmates from speaking in languages that prison guards cannot understand. The institution's division administrator at the Public Safety Department, Clayton Frank, said there is no official department policy against foreign languages, although non-English programs or conversations are allowed only if a warden authorizes them. "It's a security tool," says Frank.

Interestingly, more than one-third of Hawaii's prison inmates identify themselves as Hawaiian, and cultural and language programs have been promoted to boost their self-esteem and steer them away from crime. Clayton Frank says that Kihoi should be free to practice *ho-oponopono* and speak Hawaiian as long as she receives permission from the Kailua warden, Edwin Shimoda. But Kihoi's repeated requests for clarification of the Public Safety Department's foreign language policy have gone unanswered. "We are permitted to use an occasional 'Aloha' or 'Mahalo' . . . however, conversations, directives, and all other communications must be in English," said Kihoi in a memo issued by her supervisor. In October 1998, Warden Shimoda informed Kihoi that the policy prohibiting foreign language being spoken at work is not written but one that is based on good common correctional sense. Kihoi said simply, "I just want some clarity on the policy." Hawaii Civil Rights representatives contend that the prison's foreign language policy violates the state's constitutional guarantee to protect native Hawaiian rights.

Just a minute there! It took one day and a headline in order for Hawaiian prison policy to be changed. Public Safety Director Ted Sakai told officials at the Kailua women's prison that Hawaiian is an official state language and may be spoken freely by inmates and staff. "What a wonderful Christmas present," said Lei Kihoi, the social worker who was reprimanded for speaking Hawaiian. Charles Maxwell, chairman of the Hawaii Advisory Council to the U.S. Commission on Civil Rights, says that he had been poised to refer the case to the federal civil rights commission if the policy had not been changed.

Should prisons enforce an "English only" policy, especially in those prisons where there are significant numbers of non-English speaking prisoners? How much of a security risk is it to have inmates converse with one another in languages other than English? Is this a problem just in Hawaiian prisons, or can you envision such problems occurring in Southwestern prisons where Spanish is a prevalent language? What do you think?

Source: Adapted from Yasmin Anwar, "Hawaiian Banned at Jail, Worker Says." *Honolulu Advertiser,* December 23, 1998:A1, A6; Yasmin Anwar, "Hawaiian Permitted at Prison." *Honolulu Advertiser,* December 24, 1998:A1.

permission to attend regular religious services. They might grow beards or long hair in compliance with certain religious beliefs or standards. They may request visits from chaplains or other church officials representing their religious beliefs. Some inmates have sued in order to drink communion wine as a part of their religious worship services (*Corrections Today* 2002:16). In short, there is an endless string of religion-related requests generated by prisoners. Compliance with these requests often involves special custody transfers of prisoners from one area of a prison to another or some other special transportational provision. To what extent are such special religious-related arrangements potentially disruptive to prison discipline?

The courts have generally held that inmates of jails and prisons should enjoy the right to freedom of religion, but that right is subject to restrictions (*Inmates, Washington County Jail v. England* 1980; *Cooper v. Pate* 1967). In some cases, inmates claim First Amendment rights violations because their prison does not recognize their peculiar religious beliefs, no matter how bizarre they might be. One inmate, McCorkle, claimed that his faith was Satanism and that human sacrifices and eating human flesh were a normal part of his Satanic religious rituals. The appeals court denied McCorkle relief because his professed Satanic practices were inconsistent with maintaining prison order and security (*McCorkle v. Johnson* 1989). In more than a few of these cases, inmates form their own churches and establish unusual policies. In a Georgia case, a state prisoner formed his Church of the New Song and attempted to force prison officials to permit him to hold religious services. The appeals court rejected the inmate's petition, stating that the prisoner's new religion was a mockery of established religions and was nothing more than a sham unprotected by the First Amendment (*Theriault v. Carlson* 1973).

Sometimes, the near impossibility of furnishing certain materials to prisoners in order to practice their religion outweighs the prisoner's religious rights. For example, prisoners belonging to the Muslim faith requested special diets consisting of organic fruits, juices, vegetables, meats, raw milk, distilled water, and other items. This special diet was so costly to administer compared with the other foods served most prisoners that the court ruled in favor of the government by denying the inmate access to the special diet (*Udey v. Kastner* 1986). In a similar case involving a Muslim inmate, the Arkansas Department of Corrections provided sack lunches to prisoners, which consisted in part of bologna sandwiches. Again, the court ruled that constitutional right of freedom of religion was not violated because of inmate claims that bologna contained pork, which was forbidden by the Muslim faith (*Tisdale v. Dobbs* 1986).

Native American inmates in various prisons have sued prison officials and departments of corrections for rights pertaining to possession of religious artifacts used in religious rituals. In Missouri, for example, the Department of Corrections prohibited ceremonial pipes, medicine bags, eagle claws, and altar stones because of increased security risks. The courts declared that such prohibitions did not violate Native American inmate religious rights under the First Amendment (*Bettis v. Delo* 1994). However, other jurisdictions have permitted certain Native American religious items, such as ceremonial pipes (*Sample v. Borg* 1987).

For more conventional religions, such as Catholicism, Catholic inmates have been denied the use of crucifixes and rosaries in their religious practices. Wisconsin and Oregon officials have outlawed such religious items as contrary to prison safety because of their possible use as weapons (*Escobar v. Landwehr* 1993; *McClafin v. Pearce* 1990).

Inmates need haircuts. This prison barbershop accommodates 1200 inmates.

The issue of hair growth, beards, and beard length as religion-related issues has been bothersome to prison officials. In past years, prison and jail officials have claimed that permitting prisoners to grow their hair below their shoulders and to grow long beards would disrupt prison discipline because this would impair an official's ability to identify inmates easily. A case involving an Orthodox Jewish inmate's belief that he refrain from shaving, trimming, or cutting his facial hair was opposed by prison officials on several grounds, including safety, search, and identification problems posed by the lengthy beard. The court ruled in the inmate's favor, however, arguing that prison officials could take new photographs of the prisoner with long facial hair, that the prisoner could wear special protective facial gear when working around dangerous machinery or food, and that contraband could be detected in beards in a variety of ways that would not require trimming it (*Friedman v. State of Arizona* 1990). This holding is consistent with previous cases where a "no-beard rule" was rejected as unreasonable by the courts (*Moskowitz v. Wilkinson* 1977). In another case, a prisoner who had not cut his hair for twenty years because of religious beliefs was not required to comply with a New York State Department of Correctional Services directive (*People v. Lewis* 1986). However, in other cases, the use of marijuana or other illegal substances in order to complete certain religious services has been obviously prohibited. In one case, incense used by Muslim inmates was banned because its odor could be used to mask the smell of marijuana. Further, the odor might be offensive to other non-Muslim inmates (*Munir v. Scott* 1992).

The Fourth Amendment

The Fourth Amendment is that "the right of the people to be secure in their persons, houses, papers, and effects, against unreasonable searches and seizures, shall not be violated, and no Warrants shall issue, but upon probable cause, supported by Oath or affirmation, and particularly describing the place to be searched, and the persons or things to be seized." Prison officials contend that the right to privacy ends whenever an inmate enters a prison or jail (Sigler and Shook 1995). While searches are necessary to discover contraband and other materials that are either illegal or potentially injurious to inmates, including weapons and other items, some researchers disagree and contend that interfering with a prisoner's right to privacy counters any possibility for rehabilitation. The Fourth Amendment provision relating to search and seizure is quite apparent in prison and jail settings, where searches and seizures of contraband are routinely conducted. Even those not yet convicted of crimes or awaiting trial in jail settings are subjected to searches and seizures for security purposes. This is understandable. But for prisoners, violations of their privacy are sometimes regarded as discriminatory and evidences of administrative harassment (Hausser 1998).

One of the first things inmates learn when incarcerated is that prisoners do not enjoy the same rights of privacy as do ordinary citizens in their homes or offices (*U.S. v. Dawson* 1975). For example, random shakedowns of cells are permitted in either jails or prisons, without prefacing such searches with a search warrant or probable cause (*Hudson v. Palmer* 1984; *U.S. v. Cohen* 1986; *U.S. v. Mills* 1983). But while prison correctional officers do not need probable cause or a search warrant to conduct searches of prisoner cells, prisoners retain the reasonable expectation that their personal effects will not be wantonly destroyed as a result of the search (*Clifton v. Robinson* 1980).

Searches and seizures have also included visitors to prisons and jails as well as correctional officers and other institutional staff. Visitors may attempt to smuggle contraband to inmates either in their clothing or body cavities. Searches are sometimes prompted if a reasonable suspicion exists that smuggling of some sort is occurring. Of course, there are almost always disagreements between visitors and prison staff about what constitutes reasonable suspicion. Ordinarily, visitors may be subject to a pat down or general frisk in order to determine whether they are concealing contraband. A **strip search,** or bend-and-spread, is degrading and, under certain circumstances, unconstitutional. The issue of strip searches by prison officials is not peculiar to the United States. In Australia, for instance, strip-search policies of various jails and prisons have been criticized on the ground that they are often discriminatory. However, many of these criticisms have been ignored by Australian courts because they are conducted primarily to minimize institutional risks posed by volatile and threatening inmates (Queensland Criminal Justice Commission 2000).

In one case, a 68-year-old mother of an inmate was strip searched in an Arkansas prison on the basis of an informant's tip that she was smuggling drugs to her son (*Smothers v. Gibson* 1985). It was considered extraordinary by the court that the strip search was conducted one hour after she had begun the visit with her son. Furthermore, she had visited her son every week for the past eight years without incident, and she had been strip searched seven times during this interval without discovery of contraband. The court ruled in the woman's favor that the search was unreasonable.

In another similar case, a woman was subjected to a strip search when visiting her brother. The matron touched her breasts and buttocks and used a flashlight for a body cavity examination. No contraband was found nor was there ever any suspicion that she was attempting to smuggle anything to her brother. The search was determined by the court to be unreasonable and in violation of the Fourth Amendment, and the woman was awarded $177,040 in punitive damages (*Blackburn v. Snow* 1985).

Prison personnel are also subjected to searches from time to time, as they sometimes convey contraband to inmates in exchange for money or other favors. In a sense, they relinquish certain rights to privacy when they enter prison or jail settings, such as the right against searches and seizures without warrant or probable cause (*Gettleman v. Warner* 1974). However, the courts have held prison officials to a higher standard when conducting searches of prison staff.

In the New York State Department of Corrections, a handbook provided officers of prisons and jails warned that random strip searches may be conducted. When an officer was subjected to a strip search, including a visual body cavity inspection, he challenged this search on constitutional grounds. The court upheld his claim and ruled that although the state had provided a warning and notice about the possibility of such searches, it was insufficient within the context of the Fourth Amendment. In any case, the court held that **body cavity searches** of prison staff required a search warrant issued upon probable cause by a judicial officer (*Security and Law Enforcement Employees District Council #82 v. Carey* 1984). Of course, searches of employee vehicles that are accessible to inmates are permitted, as well as patdowns and frisks of employees where reasonable suspicion exists.

The Eighth Amendment

The Eighth Amendment says that excessive bail shall not be required, nor excessive fines imposed, nor cruel and unusual punishments inflicted. The **cruel and unusual punishment** provision of this Amendment is most frequently cited by prisoners who challenge the conditions under which they are incarcerated and how they are treated by prison staff. Prison overcrowding, exposure to AIDS or attacks by other prisoners, double-bunking, strip searches, heat or temperature of cells, visitation rights, banning cigarettes and smoking in cells, and adequacy of medical care are only a few of the many issues falling within the scope of the Eighth Amendment that may pertain to cruel and unusual punishment (Patrick and Marsh 2001). In some instances, certain revised prison policies have backfired. For instance, the cigarette ban in many U.S. prisons has created a black market where cigarettes have become highly prized commodities and used as currency for various forms of bartering (Lankenau 2001). Nevertheless, in 2001, 17 state jurisdictions had a total ban on smoking in their prison systems, with 34 remaining jurisdictions enforcing partial bans on smoking (Clayton 2001:2).

Under the Eighth Amendment, prisoners have exhausted practically every conceivable complaint about being incarcerated (Robertson 1999). They have sought court relief because of a state prison's failure to provide prisoners access to vocational or educational training, the failure of the prison to provide Spanish-speaking prisoners with courses in Spanish, assignment by prison staff of inmates to work camp details, failure of prison officials to make it possible for inmates to hear their favorite television programs during the day, failure of prison officials to allow inmates to exercise in any manner they see fit, and placing inmates in solitary confinement for punitive purposes where they lack companionship, intellectual stimulation, and are inactive. Prisoners have also raised issues of prison hygiene and fire safety regulations, the presence of insects in dining areas, plumbing, lighting, and even the location of the prison in relation to the prisoner's family. The effects of isolation resulting from solitary confinement have contributed to an isolation syndrome, which has been found to reduce cognitive capacity and promote depression and mental illness (Clare 2001; Gamman 2001).

Mental abuse has also been alleged as an Eighth Amendment violation in relation to correctional boot camps and shock incarceration programs. Practices

A small prison commissary.

by officials and personnel in these settings often involve verbal confrontation and summary discipline, which client-petitioners have claimed exhibit deliberate indifference and are malicious and sadistic. While most of these claims have been rejected by the courts, administrators of such programs have reduced the threat of such legal claims by making their institutional climates more supportive of a rehabilitative philosophy and by more carefully selecting and training custody and treatment staff (Lutze and Brody 1999).

Most inmate complaints alleging cruel and unusual punishment by correctional staff and/or administration have been held by courts to be without merit and not in violation of the Eighth Amendment (Sigler and Shook 1995). This does not mean that all prisoner complaints alleging such violations end in dismissals of these complaints, however. Deliberate indifference by prison officials to prisoner needs where prisoners are clearly in need of medical treatment and the wanton infliction of pain violate a prisoner's Eighth Amendment rights (*Estelle v. Gamble* 1976).

Prison and jail overcrowding has been highlighted as a major correctional issue. There are limits reached by prison and jail populations where overcrowding becomes cruel and unusual within the provisions of the Eighth Amendment. Many prisons and jails are currently under court order to reduce their populations such that overcrowding will no longer be problematic and violate inmate rights (Anderson and Dyson 2001). One of these prison systems is Texas. In 1980, the case of *Ruiz v. Estelle* was decided by the U.S. Supreme Court. The Texas Department of Criminal Justice was cited for permitting grossly deficient and unconstitutional prison conditions. A Circuit Court of Appeals condemned the deplorable conditions of the Texas prison system, including brutality by prison guards, excessive overcrowding, inadequate medical care, lack of staff training, disciplinary hearing improprieties, and interference with inmate access to the courts. Subsequently, in view of the totality of circumstances, it was determined that the Texas Department of Criminal Justice was in violation of inmate protections against cruel and unusual punishment and that their Fourteenth Amendment rights were also violated. The case initiated a series of significant reforms to improve prison conditions. By mid-2002 the *Ruiz* case was nearing its conclusion, as the Texas Department of Criminal Justice completed its various reforms as ordered by the court (Reynolds 2002:109). This case is a good example of how protracted some inmate litigation may be as well as how long it takes for some prison problems to be resolved to the court's satisfaction.

Some court decisions relating to prison and jail overcrowding have been favorable for prisoners. In the case of female pretrial detainees in a California women's detention facility, for example, it was determined that the degree of physical insecurity and psychological stress suffered by inmates as the result of noise, lack of privacy, and shortage of space constituted cruel and unusual punishment (*Fisher v. Winter* 1983). And in an Oklahoma prison, inmates were forced to sleep in garages, barbershops, libraries, and stairwells, and they were also placed in dormitories without any toilet or shower facilities. These conditions were determined by the court to be in violation of the Eighth Amendment (*Battle v. Anderson* 1977). Ordinarily, the rated capacities of prisons and jails are used as standards for determining whether they are overcrowded. In another case, a female inmate in an Alaska prison claimed that her Eighth Amendment right against cruel and unusual punishment was violated when she was placed in an all-male wing of the prison. However, the court considered the evolving standards of decency test in determining whether her Eighth Amendment rights were seriously infringed in view of the overcrowding at that particular institution (*Galvan v. Carothers* 1994).

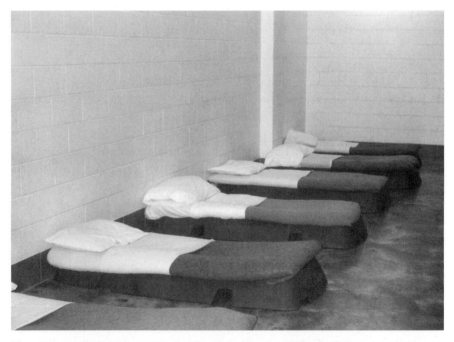

Many prison inmates are accommodated in dormitory-like facilities to maximize prison space. Courtesy of Harris County Juvenile Probation Department.

Bell v. Wolfish (1979). Two landmark cases that have been cited by correctional researchers as setbacks for inmates relate to conditions of crowding in prisons and jails. The first case, *Bell v. Wolfish* (1979), is considered to be a significant setback to the prisoner's rights movement. This case involved the minimum-security Metropolitan Correctional Center in New York City, a facility operated by the U.S. Bureau of Prisons and designed to accommodate 449 federal prisoners, including many pretrial detainees. It had been constructed in 1975 and was considered architecturally progressive and modern, generally a comfortable facility.

Originally, the facility was designed to house inmates in individual cells. But soon, the capacity of the facility was exceeded by inmate overpopulation. Inmates soon were obligated to share their cells with other inmates. This double-bunking and other issues related to overcrowding eventually led to a class-action suit against the facility by several of the pretrial detainees and prisoners. A lower court ruled in favor of the prisoners, holding that compelling necessity had not been demonstrated by prison officials in its handling of the overcrowding situation. But the U.S. Supreme Court overturned the lower court and said that the intent of prison officials should decide whether double-bunking was intended as punishment or a simple deprivation because of necessity. Since no intent to punish pretrial detainees could be demonstrated, there was no punishment. Hence, the Eighth Amendment was not violated. The suit by the pretrial detainees and prisoners was lost (Cole and Call 1992).

Rhodes v. Chapman (1981). The second case is *Rhodes v. Chapman,* an Ohio matter decided in 1981. In this instance, the single issue of double-bunking was raised and alleged to be cruel and unusual punishment prohibited by the Eighth and Fourteenth Amendments. Kelly Chapman and Richard Jaworski were two inmates of the Southern Ohio Correctional Facility and were housed in the same cell. They contended that double-celling violated their constitutional rights. Furthermore, in support of their claim, they cited the facts that their confinement was long-term and not short-term as was the case in the *Bell* case, that physical and mental injury will be sustained through such close contact and limited space for movement, and that the Ohio facility was housing 38 percent more inmates than its design capacity specified.

The U.S. Supreme Court ruled that double-celling in this long-term prison facility was neither cruel and unusual punishment nor unconstitutional per se. The court based its holding on the totality of circumstances associated with Chapman's and Jaworski's confinement. The cruel and unusual provisions of the Eighth Amendment must be construed in a flexible and dynamic manner. Thus, when all factors were considered, no evidence existed that Ohio authorities were wantonly inflicting pain on these or other inmates. These conditions, considered in their totality, did not constitute serious need deprivations. Double-celling, made necessary by the unanticipated increase in prisoners in the facility, did not result in food deprivations, a decrease in the quality of medical care, or a decrease in sanitation standards. The long-term consequences of the *Bell* and *Chapman* cases are the subjects of controversy among correctional scholars (Palmer 1997).

The Fourteenth Amendment

The relevant portion of the Fourteenth Amendment for inmates is that "no state shall make or enforce any law which shall abridge the privileges or immunities of citizens of the United States; nor shall any State deprive any person of life, liberty, or property, without due process of law; nor deny to any person within its jurisdiction the equal protection of the laws." The due process and equal protection clauses have resulted in numerous legal challenges by inmates of jails and prisons (Fradella 1998, 1999). Although there are large numbers of civil rights claims filed by inmates annually, only 3.6 percent of all U.S. inmates file such claims with the courts each year (Ross 1997). Any time inmates perceive or feel that other inmates are receiving special treatment or privileges, the Fourteenth Amendment is cited as the basis for these grievances (Worrall 2001). Any discriminatory action by penal authorities against prisoners because of their gender, race, socioeconomic status, ethnicity, or religion would be grounds for Fourteenth Amendment action (Tarver, Walker, and Wallace 2002). Section 1983 claims may also be filed outside of corrections, such as challenging police hiring decisions in certain jurisdictions (Hughes 2000).

Prisoner classifications according to minimum-security, medium-security, and maximum-security designations are frequently challenged, since they usually result in widely disparate privileges for those in different security categories. Also challenged under the Fourteenth Amendment are denial of participation in various programs such as furloughs and work release, exercise and yard privileges, and conjugal visits with spouses.

Often, female prisoners do not receive the same sorts of benefits extended to male prisoners. Prisons for male offenders are designed primarily for male offenders, with little thought given to provisions for female inmates. Services and vocational/educational programs are aimed primarily at male inmates, while female prisoners find these same programs totally unsuitable for their interests. Furthermore, these criticisms are not exclusive to women's prisons in the United States (Easteal 2001; Hannah-Moffat 2001). In 1979, however, it was held that state prison authorities must provide women inmates with treatment and facilities that are substantially equivalent to those provided men inmates (*Glover v. Johnson* 1979).

Another Fourteenth Amendment issue pertains to equal protection under the law through access to courts. In a landmark case in North Carolina in 1977, the U.S. Supreme Court declared that adequate law libraries in prisons are one constitutionally acceptable method for assuring meaningful access to courts. However, the court did not rule out other forms of access such as legal aid clinics, assistance from volunteer attorneys or law students, or some other constitutionally acceptable and equivalent plan (*Bounds v. Smith* 1977).

How successful are Section 1983 equal protection claims by inmates? Inmates prevail in less than 5 percent of the petitions they file. For instance, a study of 290 Section 1983 actions filed by inmates showed that 30 percent of the cases were dismissed as frivolous. Of the remaining 70 percent, two-thirds were dismissed by the court for reasons other than a disposition on the merits, 3.9 percent resulted in a disposition favorable to the prisoner-plaintiff, and 29.4 percent resulted in a judgment in favor of the defendant-prison officials (Fradella 1999). Thus, the actual "win rate" for the prisoners investigated in this study was only 2.8 percent.

In retrospect, jail and prison inmates have fewer rights than nonincarcerated citizens. While the courts have stated that prisoners do not lose all of their legal rights as the result of going to prison, they do lose some of them. The fact is that life behind bars is intentionally harsher than life in the free world. It would seem, however, that prisoners are entitled to equal protection under the Fourteenth Amendment when it comes to the quality of medical care they receive. Numerous civil rights claims have been filed over the years, alleging that inmates of various prisons and jails do not receive medical care equivalent to that available to free-world citizens outside of incarcerative settings. Most of these claims have been denied, in spite of the fact that less adequate medical care has been provided in correctional institutions according to the standards customarily employed by U.S. courts in evaluating medical malpractice in the free world (Vaughn and Carroll 1998).

Other Types of Legal Claims Filed by Inmates

Other constitutional amendments may be cited by jail or prison inmates in their suits against prison officials or institutions. These claims may or may not relate to their immediate confinement and treatment conditions. For instance, in a *habeas corpus* action, inmates may challenge the fact of their confinement, relying on some procedural error that may have occurred during their trial. Or they may claim ineffective assistance of counsel under the Sixth Amendment.

In recent years, a growing number of correctional institutions have established sex offender treatment programs. These treatment programs are often compulsory, requiring attendance and participation on the part of convicted offenders. Refusal to participate in such programs may result in institutional punishments and a loss of certain privileges. One important component of sex offender therapy is an admission by the offender acknowledging guilt for the sex offense committed. Furthermore, some programs require these offenders to disclose and confess to other sex crimes they have committed but for which they have not been caught or charged. More than a few of these convicted sex offenders object to these compulsory treatment programs and the fact that they must admit their culpability for their conviction offenses as well as other crimes. They regard this program component as a violation of their Fifth Amendment right against self-incrimination (Kaden 1998).

In one lawsuit filed by an inmate who alleged that his Fifth Amendment right against self-incrimination was being infringed, a test was administered to all convicted sex offenders as an eligibility requirement for their subsequent parole. The test involved penile plethysmography, where devices are attached to the offender's penis in order to determine his subsequent response, an erection, to various forms of sexual stimuli. The test is used to determine whether the offender continues to pose a threat to society. Walrath, the convicted sex offender, claimed that the test and test results were a violation of his Fifth Amendment right against self-incrimination, because the test results could be used to punish him. The appellate court rejected Walrath's claim, holding that there is no indication that any results from the plethysmograph could be used to criminally prosecute him for other acts. Furthermore, the test results, like treatment, might legitimately be used to assess whether Walrath would pose a threat to society if released (*Walrath v. United States* 1993).

Law Libraries and Other Forms of Legal Assistance

Jails and prisons are required to provide modest legal materials and aid to inmates. Most courts do not specify the nature of this legal aid or material. Each case is judged on its own merits. Some prisons hire lawyers to work with inmates as they prepare appeals and other legal documents. Some prisons have extensive law libraries, xeroxing services, and other legal amenities. However, providing any form of legal aid, whether it be books or actual attorney assistance, is costly for any department of corrections (Vogel 1995a:158; 1995b).

A prison law library.

As technology has transformed our processing of information, the solution to providing legal assistance to prisoners through computers is becoming increasingly common. West Publishing Company has converted the *Supreme Court Reporter* and *U.S. Code Annotated* to CD-ROM formats, with modest updating costs and services. Most regional reporters are available on CD-ROM as well through West and other companies. The American Association of Law Libraries has published *Recommended Collections for Prison and Other Institution Law Libraries* (1995) as a means of providing up-to-date materials for inmates.

While this particular format is not the same as actual books in library stacks, it is a more economical format for prison systems with scarce resources. It is estimated that a recommended law book collection for a prison is about $40,000, with a yearly upkeep cost of about $5,000 (Vogel 1995a:158). For a fraction of this cost, CD-ROMs from West and other companies can be obtained by prisons and maintained for modest update fees annually. Further, CD-ROMs cannot be tampered with in the sense that pages cannot be torn out or destroyed. If the CD itself is damaged, it can be replaced at a nominal charge by the company producing it.

CD-ROM information can be downloaded to floppy disks on computers, and information can be printed with conventional printers. With such computer access, inmates may be granted greater freedom to locate and use relevant materials for their appeals. Vogel (1995a:160) says that information retrieval through CD-ROMs is more rapid than conventional search methods with actual books in libraries. Additionally, online services are also available so that inmates can access other law libraries besides the volumes provided by West on CD. An additional feature of using computers is that considerable space is saved compared with the thousands of yards taken up by numerous law volumes.

Situations can be avoided such as occurred in the case of *Vandelft v. Moses* (1994). Vandelft was a prisoner housed in a segregation unit for disciplinary reasons. He was denied access to the prison's law library and could not check out hardbound books. He could only obtain copies of legal cases if he could provide prison staff with the exact citation. He filed suit against the prison, alleging an actual injury as the result of his denial of access to the law library. The court ruled in favor of prison officials, since Vandelft could not specify how he was actually injured by these rules and regulations. Further, Vandelft could not effectively challenge the prison disciplinary infraction leading to his segregative confinement. With computerized library services, it is likely that this and other prison systems might evolve more liberal access by prisoners, even those in administrative segregation for disciplinary infractions.

The actual injury rule applies if an inmate has no access to legal materials, as opposed to limited access to legal materials. Inmates must show proof of harm in their suits where rights infringements are alleged that involve access to legal materials or law libraries. The standard is difficult for inmates to meet, even where law libraries or legal materials are nonexistent in a prison or jail facility (*Hause v. Vaught* 1993; *Strickler v. Waters* 1993). Even where inmates are confined for several days without access to legal materials, they must prove some harm as the result of this inaccessibility to legal materials (*Housely v. Dodson* 1994) (Collins and Hagar 1995:26).

State and Federal Statutes

From time to time, state and federal statutes relating to prisoners and the nature of their confinement will come into conflict. Significant constitutional issues may be involved. If a state has a law that deprives any inmate of equal protection under U.S. laws or of the right to due process, that law may be challenged as unconstitutional. The successfulness of a suit by an inmate in either a state or federal court does not mean that conditions leading to court action will automatically change, however. There is a considerable lag between court declarations and policy changes, if any policy changes occur at all. Many inmate victories are empty ones, since institutional changes may strictly be forms of tokenism, paying lip service to U.S. Supreme Court decisions. The responsibility for implementing changes in accordance with court guidelines and decisions usually rests with wardens and superintendents. The law is often unclear about the nature of how these court declarations are enforced. Also, the law permits changes to be made gradually or in stages. Thus, overnight modifications of prison or jail policies are unrealistic and seldom occur.

Sometimes there are circumstances that make it difficult for jails and prisons to comply with what the court says. If adequate law libraries are to be made available for prisoner use, there must be space to locate such library facilities. If this space is lacking, it is difficult for the institution to comply with court demands. In some cases, the exigencies of the situation have caused courts to be less strict with smaller jails and prisons that lack the necessary space or personnel.

Flagrant conflicts between federal and state statutes attract more court attention, however. Despite the fact that *Ex parte Hull* applied to all jail and prison inmates and gave them access to the courts as early as 1941, the states were slow to comply with what the court said. In 1969, for example, the case of *Johnson v. Avery* brought matters to a head by forcing the issue of inmate court access. The case occurred in Tennessee and involved a prisoner, Johnson, who was serving a life sentence. Johnson studied the law diligently and on numerous occasions helped other inmates to prepare legal documents such as *habeas corpus* petitions, usually for a small fee or other reward.

Tennessee had a statute prohibiting providing legal aid from one prisoner to another. The statute read in part, "no inmate will advise, assist or otherwise contract to aid another, either with or without a fee, to prepare writs or other legal matters. . . . inmates are forbidden to set themselves up as practitioners for the purpose . . . of writing writs." Thus, Johnson was violating a Tennessee law, but he was also assisting other prisoners, many of whom were illiterate and could not prepare petitions themselves, in accessing the courts under the 1941 U.S. Supreme Court declaration. As a punishment for his legal assistance to other prisoners, Tennessee authorities placed Johnson in solitary confinement for a year. Eventually, his case was heard by the U.S. Supreme Court. The Court ruled that neither Tennessee nor any other state could prohibit the exercise of legal strategies by inmates, either on their own behalf or on the behalf of other prisoners, as means of accessing the courts. All states would be obligated to comply with this ruling unless they could demonstrate that prisoners had access to some alternative and equivalent form of legal assistance for those seeking **postconviction relief.** Postconviction relief is an attempt by prisoners to obtain some satisfaction for a grievance. This may be a challenge about the nature of their confinement, their initial conviction, or a grievance about some other matter. Thus, the Supreme Court ushered in the new age in jailhouse lawyering (Scheb and Scheb 1996).

THE JAILHOUSE LAWYER AND THE NATURE OF CIVIL REMEDIES

As we have seen, jailhouse lawyers are disliked by prison and jail officials, and sometimes officials seek revenge through withholding privileges or denying other ordinary prisoner benefits. Sometimes, retaliatory action takes other forms. In *Johnson v. Avery* (1969), Johnson suffered the punishment and deprivations of solitary confinement for nearly a year before the U.S. Supreme Court intervened. Some of the rules Johnson had violated involved furnishing other inmates with telephone numbers of attorneys they might contact for legal help or contacting a public defender on behalf of another inmate.

An illustration of the sluggishness with which various states comply with U.S. Supreme Court decisions is the Texas Department of Corrections and the case of *Novak v. Beto* (1972). At the time the *Johnson* decision was entered, all other state jurisdictions besides Tennessee were obligated to revise their correctional regulations to provide some form of acceptable legal assistance to prisoners. This acceptable legal assistance might be providing inmates with access to attorneys, law libraries, or both. Of course, other forms of legal assistance would be acceptable as well, provided that they were roughly the equivalent of these types. The Texas Department of Corrections had a prohibition similar to the one in Tennessee voided by the U.S. Supreme Court. But Texas officials maintained that they provided inmates with significant legal aid, and that this assistance brought them into compliance with the spirit of the *Johnson* decision.

The U.S. Supreme Court disagreed. While it did not accuse Texas officials of deliberate deception, it did inquire about how many of the 12,000 Texas prisoners at the time wanted legal assistance and how many were actually receiving it. The Court said that it could not be certain from the record of court proceedings whether Texas officials had not provided adequate inmate legal assistance, but they could also not ascertain whether Texas officials had provided it either. Therefore, the U.S. Supreme Court obligated Texas officials to show by clear and convincing evidence and in specific terms what the need was for legal assistance on *habeas corpus* matters in the Texas Department of Corrections and to demonstrate that Texas was reasonably satisfying that need.

This Texas case gave many of those unfamiliar with the Texas Department of Corrections an apparent example of institutionalized foot-dragging. For example, Dr. George Beto, Director of the Texas Department of Corrections during the period 1962–1972, declared that the reason he did not want some inmates setting themselves up as lawyers for other inmates was that "[those inmates] could develop unconscionable control over other inmates." Beto declared that he would "live in mortal fear of a convict-run prison." Subsequently, the issue in Texas was resolved, and jailhouse lawyers in Texas prisons are currently permitted to assist their fellow inmates without interference from prison authorities.

Sixteen years later, in 1988, Dr. Beto was a Professor of Criminology at Sam Houston State University in Huntsville, Texas. In a telephone interview with this author, Dr. Beto explained some of the reasons for his comments and actions while Director of the Texas Department of Corrections. Dr. Beto explained that the U.S. Supreme Court had made it fairly clear in the case of *Johnson v. Avery* (1969) that state prisoners were entitled to some form of legal assistance or its equivalent. At the time of the *Novak v. Beto* (1971) case, Dr. Beto had retained three full-time attorneys for the Texas Department of Corrections. Their sole responsibility was to handle inmate complaints and serve as legal advisors and inmate attorneys.

Dr. Beto noted that many inmate grievances were unrelated to general prison conditions or poor treatment by correctional officers and others. Rather, many prisoners had child adoption matters to contest with their estranged wives or inheritance questions to be resolved. In an attempt to comply with U.S. Supreme Court admonitions, Dr. Beto hired an additional seven full-time attorneys to deal with inmate legal issues and problems and to represent them in various complaints. Money allocated for correctional purposes was never an issue. Also, prison overcrowding in the Texas Department of Corrections was not problematic. The U.S. Supreme Court decision hinged mainly on the interpretation it made of Texas's attempt to provide acceptable legal assistance or some reasonable alternative.

Dr. Beto was concerned that some prisoners who acquired legal knowledge would use this information for their own personal gain. The image of the altruistic jailhouse lawyer doing only what was right to assist other inmates was not a true picture of how inmate legal assistance was being dispensed. Rather, the legal aid provided by some inmates for others, regardless of its quality, was used primarily as a means of controlling other inmates. It was an instrument whereby the inmate pecking order could be strengthened. In fact, some inmates profited from the advice they provided their fellow prisoners. Thus, Dr. Beto was interested in preventing an inmate-dominated and exploitive legal system rather than prolonging Texas compliance with U.S. Supreme Court orders for provisions for acceptable legal assistance to prisoners. Dr. Beto died in the early 1990s.

Avenues for Civil Remedies

There are three basic avenues whereby jail and prison inmates can petition the courts concerning civil wrongs. The most widely used avenue is 42 U.S.C., Section 1983 (2003), which holds that "every person who, under color of any statute, ordinance, regulation, custom, or usage, of any State or Territory, subjects, or causes to be subjected, any citizen of the United States or other person within the jurisdiction thereof to the deprivation of any rights, privileges, or immunities secured by the Constitution and laws, shall be liable to the party injured in an action at law, suit in equity, or other proper proceeding for redress" (Palmer 1997). These actions are known as **Section 1983 actions.**

A second avenue is through 28 U.S.C., Section 2674 (2003), known as the **Federal Tort Claims Act of 1946.** This Act provides that "the United States shall be liable, respecting the provisions of this title relating to tort claims, in the same manner and to the same extent as a private individual under like circumstances, but shall not be liable for interest prior to judgment for punitive damages." The U.S. Supreme Court decided in 1963 that inmates of federal prisons could file petitions against prison administrators and correctional officers under the Federal Tort Claims Act in the case of *United States v. Muniz* (1963). Until this Supreme Court action, prison officials enjoyed sovereign immunity from suits by prisoners alleging damages or injuries through administrative negligence. Currently, officials have **qualified immunity** excepting them from suits under this section alleging "any claim arising out of assault, battery, false imprisonment, false arrest, malicious prosecution, abuse of process, libel, slander, misrepresentation, deceit, or interference with contract rights" (28 U.S.C. Sec. 2680, 2003).

Like a *habeas corpus* action, Section 1983 actions may challenge the conditions of confinement, but the fact and length of incarceration are not within this section's purview (*Preiser v. Rodriguez* 1973). In order for prisoners to effectively challenge their imprisonment in court, they must file a *habeas corpus* petition under the Federal Habeas Corpus Statute (28 U.S.C., Section 2241, 2003). In recent years, *habeas corpus* petitions filed by prisoners have declined appreciably, while the number of Section 1983 petitions has systematically increased. Since state courts have concurrent jurisdiction with federal courts in deciding cases based entirely upon federal claims, state or federal prison inmates may choose either court for their litigation.

Table 9.1 shows the numbers of petitions filed by state and federal prison inmates from 1977 through 2000 (Administrative Office of the U.S. Courts 2002). These figures do not include filings by state inmates in state courts.

Civil Rights Petitions.   Federal prisoners filed 483 civil rights (42 U.S.C., Section 1983, 2003) petitions in 1977, and these filings nearly doubled to 735 in 2000. For state prisoners, 7,752 civil rights petitions were filed in 1977 in U.S. district courts, while these petitions increased to 13,415 in 2000. However, it is significant to note that the number of civil rights petitions filed by state prisoners in federal courts peaked at 40,569 in 1995, declined to 39,996 in 1996, dropped to 27,661 in 1997, and declined abruptly to 13,118 in 1998. By 2000 this figure remained relatively constant at 13,415 filings. As we will see later in this chapter, this decline is largely attributable to federal legislation passed in 1995 that obligated all state prisoners to exhaust the entire range of state remedies for their suits before bringing them to federal courts for resolution (Branham 2001). This action became known as the **exhaustion requirement.** Although this legislation affected state inmate filings through the exhaustion requirement, the sheer volume of state and federal prisoner litigation in federal courts has remained fairly constant. This suggests that state and federal inmates have modified their theories for seeking different types of relief in U.S. district courts. Also, there is a direct correlation between the rising state and federal inmate populations and the increased litigation initiated by these inmates (Cheesman, Hanson, and Ostrom 2000; Miller 1999).

TABLE 9.1

Petitions Filed in U.S. District Courts by Federal and State Prisoners, 1977–2000, by Type of Petition

	Total	Petitions by Federal Prisoners						Petitions by State Prisoners				
		Total	Motions to vacate sentence	Habeas corpus	Mandamus, etc.	Civil rights	Prison conditions	Total	Habeas corpus	Mandamus, etc.	Civil rights	Prison conditions
1977	19,537	4,691	1,921	1,745	542	483	X	14,846	6,866	228	7,752	X
1978	21,924	4,955	1,924	1,851	544	636	X	16,969	7,033	206	9,730	X
1979	23,001	4,499	1,907	1,664	340	588	X	18,502	7,123	184	11,195	X
1980	23,287	3,713	1,322	1,465	323	603	X	19,574	7,031	146	12,397	X
1981	27,711	4,104	1,248	1,680	342	834	X	23,607	7,790	178	15,639	X
1982	29,303	4,328	1,186	1,927	381	834	X	24,975	8,059	175	16,741	X
1983	30,775	4,354	1,311	1,914	339	790	X	26,421	8,532	202	17,687	X
1984	31,107	4,526	1,427	1,905	372	822	X	26,581	8,349	198	18,034	X
1985	33,468	6,262	1,527	3,405	373	957	X	27,206	8,534	181	18,491	X
1986	33,765	4,432	1,556	1,679	427	770	X	29,333	9,045	216	20,072	X
1987	37,316	4,519	1,669	1,812	313	725	X	32,797	9,542	276	22,972	X
1988	38,839	5,130	2,071	1,867	330	862	X	33,709	9,880	270	23,559	X
1989	41,481	5,577	2,526	1,818	315	918	X	35,904	10,554	311	25,039	X
1990	42,630	6,611	2,970	1,967	525	1,149	X	36,019	10,823	353	24,843	X
1991	42,462	6,817	3,328	2,112	378	999	X	35,645	10,331	268	25,046	X
1992	48,423	6,997	3,983	1,507	597	910	X	41,426	11,299	481	29,646	X
1993	53,451	8,456	5,379	1,467	695	915	X	44,995	11,587	390	33,018	X
1994	57,940	7,700	4,628	1,441	491	1,140	X	50,240	11,918	397	37,925	X
1995	60,550	8,951	5,988	1,343	510	1,110	X	54,599	13,632	398	40,569	X
1996	68,235	13,095	9,729	1,703	444	1,219	X	55,140	14,726	418	39,996	X
1997	62,966	14,952	11,675	1,902	401	974	X	48,014	19,956	397	27,661	X
1998	54,715	9,937	6,287	2,321	346	641	342	44,778	18,838	461	13,115	12,364
1999	56,603	10,859	5,752	3,590	555	642	320	45,744	20,493	513	13,441	11,291
2000	58,257	11,880	6,341	3,870	628	736	305	46,377	21,349	564	13,415	11,049
Percent change 1999 to 2000	2.9%	9.4%	10.2%	7.8%	13.2%	14.6%	– 4.7%	1.4%	4.2%	9.9%	– 0.2%	– 2.1%

Source: Administrative Office of the U.S. Courts. *Annual Report to the Director.* Washington, DC: Administrative Office of the U.S. Courts, 2002.

Habeas Corpus Actions.   *Habeas corpus* petitions made up 1,745 for prison inmates in 1977, while the number of federal inmate *habeas corpus* filings increased to 3,870 in 2000. For state inmates, *habeas corpus* petitions nearly tripled from 6,866 filed in 1977 to 21,349 filings in 2000.

Total petitions filed by federal inmates in 1977 were 19,537, while state prison inmates filed 14,846 petitions that same year. By 2000, 58,257 petitions were filed in federal courts by federal prisoners, while state prisoners filed 46,377 petitions (Administrative Office of the U.S. Courts 2002). Thus, by 2000 U.S. district courts had handled 104,634 petitions filed by state and federal inmates. This is only a fraction of all state court filings by prison and jail inmates, however. Most of these inmate petitions have been considered frivolous and a waste of court time (Maahs and del Carmen 1996:53).

The Prison Litigation Reform Act of 1995

In 1995 Congress enacted the **Prison Litigation Reform Act of 1995 (PLRA).** This Act was designed to decrease the sheer numbers of state and federal filings of inmate lawsuits in federal courts. Among other things, the PLRA was geared to prevent multiple suit filings by the same prisoners where the suits were determined to be frivolous (Cheesman, Hanson, and Ostrom 2000).

Prior to the PLRA, inmates who could not afford the filing fees for their lawsuits could rely upon the government to pay these fees for them. Further, there was no limit regarding the number of times a particular issue could be litigated by filing different lawsuits. Following the Act's passage, the PLRA pertained to all federal, state or local prisons, jails and detention centers (Fliter 2001).

The PLRA does not apply to state claims raised by inmates in state courts. However, the PLRA does pertain to federal claims raised in state courts. Section 804 of the PLRA is particularly important, since it requires inmates to be held accountable for their own filing fees. If prisoners cannot afford the filing fees for their suits against prisons, then provisions are made for deducting filing fee costs from their prison earnings on a monthly basis. Since inmates earn very little in prisons, this provision hurts them in their own pocketbooks. Thus, they will be prevented from purchasing certain goods in prison commissaries if their money is taken to cover the legal fees involved in their largely frivolous litigation.

Section 804 of the PLRA further provides that courts may dismiss prisoner-filed suits on grounds including frivolousness, maliciousness, failure to state a claim upon which relief can be granted, and immunity. Further, filing fees are not dischargeable through inmate bankruptcy proceedings. Another provision of Section 804 is that if three or more actions are dismissed on frivolous or malicious grounds, then the prisoner cannot bring an *in forma pauperis* action (claiming indigence) unless it is clearly demonstrated that there is imminent danger or serious physical injury.

Section 805 of the PLRA provides for judicial screenings of inmate suit filings. Prisoners are prevented under Section 806 from bringing tort actions against the United States government or its employees for mental or emotional injuries, unless they can demonstrate actual physical injury. Furthermore, any monetary damages awarded to successful inmates must be paid first as restitution to one's victims or to any outstanding restitution orders, and then the remainder goes to the prisoner. And last but not least, Section 809 provides that good-time credit can be revoked where prisoners bring civil actions for malicious purposes, for purposes of harassment, or if they give false testimony or present false evidence. Thus, the PLRA is a general deterrent to much of the

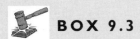

BOX 9.3

THE PRISON LITIGATION REFORM ACT (PLRA) SUMMARIZED

(Commerce—Justice—State Appropriations Bill Version)

Section 801. Title

"Prison Litigation Reform Act of 1995"

Section 8.2 Appropriate Remedies for Prison Conditions

(Amends 18 U.S.C.§ 3626)

Limits on "prospective relief" (injunctive relief and consent decrees) (§(a)(1)(A)):

- Cannot be entered unless there is a finding of a federal violation;
- Order must be narrowly drawn, extend no further than necessary to correct the federal violation, and be the least intrusive remedy;
- "Substantial weight" to any adverse impact on public safety or operation of a criminal justice system;
- Cannot violate local or state law—limited exceptions (§(a)(1)(B); BUT: Court can't order prison construction or new taxes (§(a)(1)(C)).
- Preliminary injunctions—90-day time limit (§(a)(2)).

Additional Limitations on Population Caps (§(a)(3)):

- Court must first order a "less intrusive" remedy with "reasonable time" to comply;
- In federal court: can only be ordered by three-judge panel;
- Crowding must be the "primary cause" of the federal violation and there is no other remedy that will cure violation;
- Intervention for state or local officials (prosecutors, corrections, appropriators);

Termination of Injunctions and Consent Decrees (§(b)):

- Party entitled to termination, upon motion, if injunction/consent decree is more than two years old (pre-PLRA orders terminable two years after enactment: (§(b)(1));
- Party or intervenor entitled to immediate termination where court did enter findings in accordance with PLRA

(§(2)); BUT: No termination if injunctive relief still necessary to correct current or ongoing violation (§(3)).

- Parties may still seek modification/termination under existing law (§(4)).

Settlements (§(c)):

- Consent decrees must comply with PLRA requirements (§(c)(1));
- "Private settlement agreements" (agreement provisions not court enforceable) not subject to PLRA (§(c)(2));

State Law Remedies (§(d)):

- PLRA limitations do not apply to state law claims raised in state court [Note: PLRA will apply to federal claims raised in state court].

Procedure on Motion to Modify or Terminate (§(e)):

- Injunctive relief is automatically stayed if court does not timely rule on the motion. Time limits: PLRA motions 30 days; all other motions 180 days.

Special Masters (§(f)):

- Appointment: person must be "disinterested and objective" and give "due regard to the public safety"; selected from lists submitted by parties; parties may appeal appointment order; court must review appointment every six months;
- Limited Powers and Duties; can only make proposed findings of fact based upon the record; no ex parte communications or findings; may assist in remedial plans;
- Compensation: Same rate as court appointed counsel, paid by federal funds;
- Termination of appointment; may be removed at any time, but not later than termination of relief.

Definitions (§(g)): Make Clear That PLRA Limitations:

1. Apply to any injunctive order based upon consent or acquiesce;

(continued)

BOX 9.3 (Continued)

2. Apply to all prisoner (adult and juveniles) claims except habeas; and
3. Apply to federal, state or local prisons, jails and detention centers.

PLRA Application: fully retroactive; applies to orders entered before enactment date.

Section 803. Amendments to CRIPA

- For actions by United States (on behalf of prisoners), requires Attorney General to personally sign complaints, certifications, and intervention motion;
- For suits by prisoners:
  - Must exhaust administrative remedies (even if procedures are not certified);
  - Court on own motion may dismiss civil rights action on four grounds (frivolous, malicious, fails to state claims, defendant immune);
  - Attorney's fees (under Civil Rights Act) only awarded if "directly incurred" in proving "actual" federal violation, or remedial matters [This eliminates fees for related, but unsuccessful, claims, fees for voluntary actions in response to lawsuit (known as the "catalyst" theory of recovery); and fees for ancillary litigation.]; Cannot proportionally exceed relief obtained (but later refers to 150 percent of judgment limitation); First 25 percent of monetary judgment shall be applied to attorney's fees; Maximum hourly rate 150 percent of rate for court appointed attorneys.
  - No recovery for mental/emotional injury w/o prior showing of physical injury;
  - Pretrial hearings may be conducted by telephone or video;
  - Defendant may waive the right to reply, Court may order reply, but can't grant relief w/o first requiring reply.

Section 804. In Forma Pauperis Proceedings

- Establishes a partial filing fee system;
- Prisoner must submit certified copy of prison account;
- Court must assess full filing fee;

- Court must collect initial partial filing payment (when funds exist, 20 percent of the greater of average monthly deposits or average monthly balance);
- After initial partial payment, prisoner shall make monthly payments whenever account amount exceeds $10;

BUT: Prisoner cannot be prevented from bringing action on basis that he has no assets.

- Court may appoint counsel for any person [this would also apply to indigent defendants, such as crime victims or witnesses];
- Court may dismiss on four grounds (frivolous, malicious, fails to state a claim, immunity);
- Bankruptcy exception—fees not dischargeable in bankruptcy;
- Prisoner shall be required to pay full amount of any costs assessed;
- Successive claims—if three or more actions dismissed on grounds of frivolous, malicious, fails to state a claim, prisoner cannot bring an IFP action unless imminent danger of serious physical injury.

Section 805. Judicial Screening

- Court must screen prisoner claims against government or government officials;
- Must identify cognizable claims or dismiss (if frivolous, malicious, fails to state claims, or immunity).

Section 806. Federal Tort Claims

- Prisoner can't bring action against U.S. (or employee) for mental/emotional injury w/o prior showing of physical injury.

Section 807. Payment of Damage Award in Satisfaction of Pending Restitution Orders

- Any damage award to prisoner in civil rights action must first satisfy any outstanding restitution orders; remainder then goes to the prisoner.

Section 808. Notice to Crime Victims of Pending Damage Award

- Prior to payment of compensatory damages, crime victims must be notified of pending payment.

Section 809. Revocation of Federal Good Time Credit

- Good time credit can be revoked where prisoner brings civil action—

—for a malicious purpose;
—to harass defendant;
—false testimony or false evidence by prisoner

Section 810 Severability

Sarah B. Vandenbraak
Chief Counsel, Pennsylvania
Department of Corrections

Source: U.S. Code (2003).

previously filed inmate litigation. It is likely that in future years, the sheer amount of inmate litigation will decline if these sanctions are enforced (Branham 2001).

PRISONER RIGHTS AND SELECTED LITIGATION ISSUES

Thus far, we have examined the U.S. Constitution and selected Amendments that are frequently the grounds of inmate lawsuits against prison staff and administration. In this section, several issues have been selected that pertain to each of these Amendments. This coverage is not intended to be comprehensive. Rather, it seeks to highlight briefly some of the types of cases that reach federal and state courts of appeals. Some of these issues are significant enough to reach the U.S. Supreme Court, where they become landmark cases in corrections. These issues include (1) racism, due process, and equal protection; (2) the right to rehabilitation; (3) misclassification problems and program eligibility; (4) cell searches and seizures of contraband; (5) cruel and unusual punishment; (6) double-bunking, overcrowding, and a right to privacy; (7) plain negligence, intentional neglect, and deliberate indifference; and (8) the death penalty: the whys, whos, and hows of its administration.

Racism, Due Process, and Equal Protection

Because nearly half the prison population is black and a majority of that same population is nonwhite, there is considerable legal action prompted as the result of alleged racism within the correctional system (Greenberg and West 2001). It is not particularly a phenomenon exclusively related to corrections. Sentencing disparities, plea bargain arrangements, and arrests seem closely connected with racial and ethnic factors (Baldus et al. 2001). It is not surprising, therefore, that these same disparities carry over into corrections and influence in various ways the nature and circumstances of prisoner confinement. Surveys of different prison environments and individual accounts by former correctional personnel suggest that racism in U.S. prisons is both pervasive and increasing (Kauffman 2000).

Successful legal action by inmates where racism is alleged is difficult to sustain in court. Many inmate petitions alleging discrimination or racism are categorically rejected as lacking merit or are dismissed out of hand by federal and state judges (Harrington and Cavett 2000). For instance, many incarcerated Black Muslims deluged the courts with petitions alleging denial of racial and religious equality during the 1960s (Jacobs 1980:434). According to Jacobs (1980:434), there were

66 reported federal court decisions pertaining to Black Muslims between 1961 and 1978. Despite the successes achieved by these actions, the Muslims experienced a fairly high failure or rejection rate in the suits they filed. But they emerged in the 1970s as the best organized prisoner aggregate that demonstrated for other prisoners the fruits of organized protest and the influence of solidarity in legal actions (Jacobs 1980:435). We have seen that not all actions alleging discrimination involve racial or ethnic factors. Some discrimination suits pertain to women and their equal protection under the law. Thus, the U.S. Supreme Court has stated that female prisoners are entitled to facilities and programs comparable to those enjoyed by male inmates, with the primary exceptions being hardships on prison administrations to implement comparable programs (Sharbaro and Keller 1995).

The Right to Rehabilitation

Do prisoners have a right to be rehabilitated while in prisons or jails? Unless otherwise specified by particular state jurisdictions, prisoners do not have an absolute right to be rehabilitated (Palmer 1997). Thus, if parolees commit new crimes, the state is immune from suits where it is alleged that the prison system failed to rehabilitate a given offender properly. Most prisons provide various educational and vocational services, however. Thus, if certain inmates wish to improve their skills or obtain counseling or other forms of personal assistance, such assistance can usually be provided in most prison systems.

Another important rehabilitative service is the provision of courses in applied life skills. For instance, the Delaware Department of Corrections offers a Life Skills Program, offered twice a year for up to 150 medium- and minimum-security inmates during four-month cycles. The program has three major components: academics, violence reduction, and applied life skills. The core of the initiative is Moral Recognition Therapy, a systematic, step-by-step process of raising the moral reasoning level of students through a series of moral and cognitive stages. During a first-year followup of program participants compared

Prisons often manufacture state license plates, although this activity is not considered useful for an inmate's societal reintegration when paroled.

with a control group, the life skills participants had a recidivism rate of only 19 percent compared with 27 percent for other parolees (Finn 1998a).

Female inmates are particularly affected, since their facilities typically are smaller and less well-equipped compared with men's institutions. Even when courts recognize equal protection claims raised by female inmates, identical treatment, including health care, for men and women is not mandated, and separate can be equal (Anno 2001). For instance, the TAMAR Project (Trauma, Addictions, Mental Health, and Recovery) has been established by the Maryland Community Criminal Justice Treatment Program. It offers trauma treatment to women in three different detention centers. This treatment program consists of a trauma specialist, mental health and substance abuse counselors, a medical officer, and a classification officer. The psychoeducational treatment protocol is designed to run for 12-week intervals, and it includes journal writing and art therapy. When women are released, they are encouraged to continue to meet in treatment groups in the community developed by the trauma specialist (Russell 2001).

More than a few state jurisdictions are taking the lead in developing rehabilitative programs for women, aiming these programs at the special needs of female offenders. For instance, the Massachusetts Department of Corrections has recognized the diverse needs of female offenders and has established several educational and counseling programs designed to improve their education and job skill levels. A study of female offenders revealed that many of these inmates lack economic self-sufficiency. Some inmates have substance and alcohol abuse problems. Most of the women studied had dependent children. Recommendations for improving the nature and quality of services for these women include developing an integrated treatment model that reflects relational and diversity frameworks; providing a continuing training program for staff that operationalizes these frameworks into their daily staff-to-staff and staff-to-inmate contacts; and creating linkages to agencies and services for women who are subsequently paroled (Coll and Duff 1995).

Misclassification Problems and Program Eligibility

There is a tendency in most prison systems in the United States to overclassify offenders. That is, instead of classifying an offender as minimum-security, he or she is classified as medium- or maximum-security for purposes of supervision and custody. The higher the level of custody, usually the fewer the amenities enjoyed by prisoners. Besides these restrictions, prisoners may not be eligible for certain types of programs designed for low-risk offenders. Some programs bar medium-security and maximum-security inmates, since the programs involve fewer restrictions and greater access to prison areas that are otherwise off-limits to those classified at higher security levels. Misclassifications of prison inmates are pervasive, and it appears that both male and female offenders are equally affected by faulty classification measures (Thigpen, Hunter, and Brown 2001).

Cell Searches and Seizures of Contraband

Inmates of jails and prisons have little standing in court when the issue of searches and seizures is raised (Palmer 1997). It has been determined that prisoners have absolutely no expectation of privacy when they enter prisons and jails (*Bell v. Wolfish* 1979; *Hudson v. Palmer* 1984). However, correctional officers are encouraged to exercise caution so that an inmate's personal effects, as distinguished from legitimate contraband, will not be damaged in the process of their search. Otherwise, tort liability may attach, and correctional officers may be sued for damages sustained to prisoner personal property.

Jail inmates and those incarcerated in prisons are subject to strip searches, including examinations of their body cavities, for purposes of discovering contraband. Again, no warrant is necessary for such searches, despite the psychological and physical discomforts such searches may cause prisoners. Also, if reasonable suspicion exists, searches may be conducted of correctional officers and visitors, under limited conditions (Keyser, Feucht, and Flaherty 2002). It has been determined, however, that searches of correctional officer body cavities require warrants based upon probable cause and authorized by a judicial officer (*Security and Law Enforcement Employees District Council #82 v. Carey* 1984).

Cruel and Unusual Punishment

The question of what constitutes cruel and unusual punishment within the context of the Eighth Amendment is highly subjective. The U.S. Supreme Court and lower federal and state courts have had to wrestle with this question for many decades. However, the U.S. Supreme Court has chosen never to define explicitly what this phrase means (Glazer 1996). When correctional officers or other prison staff have used force against inmates in order to induce compliance to prison rules and regulations, some prisoners have labeled this force cruel and unusual. Prison and jail overcrowding have also been labeled as cruel and unusual, although as we have seen, it takes considerable overcrowding in any institutional setting before the U.S. Supreme Court will take notice and intervene to limit or prevent it.

Virtually every type of corporal punishment has been banned in prisons and jails. The infamous **Red Hannah** whipping post used in Delaware was eventually prohibited as a sanctioning device in prisons. Other similar lashing punishments have been banned as well in other jurisdictions. Sometimes, noncorporal punishments such as placement in solitary confinement have caused prisoners to complain that this is cruel and unusual. Physical separation from others and the lack of communication are psychological painful, but the courts find little merit in prisoner complaints that this punishment form is cruel and unusual per se.

If the punishment is excessive in relation to the crime committed, the courts will probably agree that the test for cruel and unusual punishment under the Eighth Amendment is met. In the case of *Enmund v. Florida* (1982), Enmund and another defendant were convicted of first-degree murder by a Florida court and sentenced to death. However, evidence produced at the trial showed that Enmund was only incidentally related to the murders, since he was only a passenger in the getaway vehicle. Under Florida law, however, the felony murder statute prescribed the death penalty for anyone involved in the perpetration of a felony where anyone is killed, despite the fact that there may be no premeditation or intent to cause one's death. The U.S. Supreme Court decided in favor of Enmund that his sentence of death was disproportionate to his involvement in the crime. Simply put, the death penalty was too severe a punishment.

However, in another case, a habitual offender with two previous felony convictions (both fraud cases) in Texas, Rummel, was convicted of a third felony, theft by false pretenses in the amount of $120. Rummel was sentenced to life imprisonment for his third felony conviction under the Texas statute. In his case, the U.S. Supreme Court determined that the mandatory penalty of life imprisonment for habitual offenders was constitutional and not disproportionate to the crime committed (*Rummel v. Estelle* 1980). Suffice it to say that cruel and unusual punishment is an elusive concept, and that the U.S. Supreme Court has not yet dealt with the term adequately. Seemingly, injustices occur against some inmates and not against others for essentially the same or similar infractions, although the courts strive, under *stare decisis,* to be uniform in the application of judicial precedents.

Double-Bunking, Overcrowding, and the Right to Privacy

The issue of **double-bunking** (placing more than one person in a cell designed to accommodate only one person) has already been partially decided by *Rhodes v. Chapman* (1981) and earlier in *Bell v. Wolfish* (1979). In the *Bell* case, the new Metropolitan Correctional Center in New York City was the target of prisoner complaints. Specifically, numerous pretrial detainees objected to the crowding in their cells and other matters, including cell searches, strip searches, and mail censorship. Successes by prisoners in lower courts in the *Bell* case were overturned by the U.S. Supreme Court, which held that the crowding was inadvertent and not a deliberate act of punishment by jail authorities. The fact that the Metropolitan Correctional Center was considered a short-term confinement facility may have influenced their decision. However, a similar ruling was handed down by the U.S. Supreme Court in a long-term facility in the *Rhodes v. Chapman* case. It determined that 32 square feet (a 4 feet wide by 8 feet long cell shared by two inmates) was not sufficiently small to constitute cruel and unusual punishment within the context of the Eighth Amendment. When is a jail or prison overcrowded? This is subject to judicial interpretation. Some courts use the rated capacity/actual capacity ratio as a means of determining the seriousness of overcrowding. Other courts inspect the premises and determine whether overcrowding exists, on a purely subjective basis (Florida Department of Corrections 1999).

   Furthermore, there is no constitutional right to privacy for inmates of jails and prisons (Maschke 1996). The premises of facilities designed to confine and control prisoners, regardless of their status, are subject to search by authorities. If contraband, meaning any illegal goods, is found in their possession or on their premises, such contraband is subject to seizure (Alderman and Kennedy 1995). Of course, we know that correctional officers and other officers are expected to exercise some degree of care in handling an inmate's personal effects.

Plain Negligence, Intentional Neglect, and Deliberate Indifference

Because jail and prison overcrowding, inmate violence, and substandard health and safety conditions seem to characterize many U.S. penal facilities, it is often difficult for judges to distinguish between actions of administrators of these facilities that are primarily the function of these conditions, or actions that are deliberately intended to cause prisoners physical or psychological harm (Cole and Call 1992). Thus, if a prisoner is sexually assaulted by another prisoner in a cell containing four inmates but designed to accommodate only two, is this assault the fault of the prison administrator or simply the result of unanticipated overcrowding, something over which the administrator exerts little or no control (Maahs and del Carmen 1996)?

   Negligence generally is based on a duty of one person to another to act as a reasonable person might be expected to act, or the failure to act when action is appropriate. Legally, negligence is the failure to exercise reasonable care toward another (Black 1990:1033–1034). There are different kinds of negligence as well as different degrees of negligence. State and federal governments may be liable if their prison correctional officers fail to perform according to certain standards of training. Under theories of **negligent training** (where an officer is simply improperly trained or untrained), **negligent assignment** (where an officer is assigned a position for which he or she is unqualified), **negligent entrustment** (where administrators fail to monitor those officers entrusted with items they are unfamiliar with using, such as giving firearms to prison correctional officers without first exposing them to firearms training), or **negligent retention** (where those officers determined to be unfit for their jobs are kept in those jobs anyway), inmates may have grounds to sue the government or their administrative representatives (Josi and Sechrest 1998).

Degrees of negligence include slight, ordinary, and gross, although the courts regard significant degrees of care rather than degrees of negligence (Black 1990: 1033–1034). However, gross negligence includes wilful, wanton, and reckless negligence, where acts are performed that are totally unreasonable and without regard for the consequences. The standard for establishing negligence of officials or officers is a civil one, the preponderance of evidence standard. Thus, whether the plaintiff (usually the inmate) or defendant (usually administrators of a prison or jail or their agents—correctional officers or other officers) prevails is contingent upon whether the preponderance of evidence is in the plaintiff's favor or the defendant's favor. These cases become judgment calls by either judges or juries, provided the cases reach trial. And, as we have seen, few inmate cases reach the trial stage because of motions to dismiss or summary judgments granted.

It is generally conceded that if the government is negligent or if any agent or agency of the government is negligent in its treatment of prisoners, liability is incurred and damages may be sought by inmates for relief. But establishing negligence is difficult. Consider the following cases. An inmate was placed in a District of Columbia prison in a cell with another inmate who had active tuberculosis (*Sypert v. United States* 1983). The plaintiff sued the government and administrators alleging negligence, because he was placed in a cell with a tubercular inmate, and subsequent skin tests showed the presence of tubercle bacilli in his body. However, since he never developed active tuberculosis, the court ruled that he had suffered no physical injury and dismissed the case against the government.

In another case, an Oregon prison inmate was stabbed with a knife by another inmate (*Walker v. United States* 1977). The injured inmate sued Oregon officials, alleging they were negligent in the enforcement of prison rules regarding the search for contraband knives and other dangerous weapons potentially hazardous to other inmates. However, the preponderance of evidence presented in court by the injured inmate failed to show that either the correctional officers or other correctional officials were negligent.

Two interesting cases involve administrative knowledge of gang warfare and violence and prisoner safety. In one case, a prisoner alleged administrative negligence in the classification of the prisoner to a higher level of security and interaction with more dangerous prisoners. The inmate was subsequently killed by other violent inmates and his relatives brought suit against the Administrator of Corrections (*Quinones v. Nettleship* 1985). Questions were raised and affidavits presented by other inmates about general jail safety conditions, about where the correctional officers were or could have been positioned, and what steps were taken by administrators to protect other inmates from gang warfare. Again, administrative blame was not established by a preponderance of the evidence.

In a Texas case, an inmate was being held in the Dallas County Jail. He had testified briefly against another inmate held in the same jail that the other inmate had told him he had possessed and transported another's stolen automobile.

Through local newspapers distributed among other prisoners at the jail, inmates soon learned of the plaintiff's testimony. They subjected him to a severe beating, and he subsequently sued the U.S. government and jail employees, alleging that they failed to foresee the tortious and criminal acts that would occur as the result of his court testimony. The court ruled that the government had no duty to foresee such acts and absolved jail officials of blame in the incident (*Hackett v. United States* 1978). In many cases, severe overcrowding problems create serious security problems for inmates in need of protection from other prisoners.

Many authorities agree that inmates are at a considerable disadvantage in the suits they file. Whenever they win, it is difficult to determine the substance of their victory. Jail and prison officials may engage in subtle reprisals. These reprisals may involve civil rights violations or deliberate torts, but as we have seen, even seemingly flagrant tortious cases are difficult to prove, especially using the preponderance of evidence standard. And when property claims are awarded prisoners, these amounts are often token damages and very small (Josi and Sechrest 1998).

Inmate Fathers

Increasingly recognized as a significant issue for many male inmates in prisons and jails is visitation and bonding with their children (Edin, Nelson, and Paranal 2001). Since the 1960s, female inmates have made substantial progress regarding their child visitation rights. Some prisons have constructed cottages for female inmates in order for them to have their children for overnight stays and to enhance their bonding capabilities. Numerous visitation programs have been established for female inmates at most women's prisons in order to facilitate more intensive interactions with their small children (H.C. Davis 2001). For instance, Oklahoma women's prisons have implemented the Family Recovery Embraces Education program, which is targeted mainly at female inmates. However, male prisoners have not enjoyed similar luxuries (Jeffries and Menghraj 2001).

One fact disclosed by incarcerated fathers is that imprisonment of any kind is psychologically disruptive and significantly interferes with their relations with children. Their paternal behavior is evident, and it is clear that they yearn for greater contact with their families, particularly with their minor children (Kazura 2001). Their prolonged absence from their own children is frustrating, and there is some evidence that the children themselves suffer in different ways from this separation (Martin 2001). Increasingly, however, various prison systems are recognizing that male parents as well as female ones deserve to be reunited with their children from time to time, more or less frequently (Enos 2001). Thus, significant efforts are underway in different jurisdictions to provide bonding services within men's prisons as well as women's facilities to promote and maintain parent-child bonds (Seymour and Hairston-Creasie 2001).

THE DEATH PENALTY

Perhaps the most controversial of all prisoner issues is **capital punishment** and the imposition of the **death penalty.** The following discussion is not intended as a philosophical critique or examination of capital punishment. More extensive theoretical discussions of the pros and cons of the death penalty are found elsewhere (Alarid and Wang 2001; Dale 2001; J. Kelly 2001; Solotaroff 2001). Rather, the discussion is designed to highlight some of the stronger arguments for and against

BOX 9.4

Mark Turner

Intern, North Dakota State Supreme Court

Statistics

A.A. (criminal justice), *Bismarck State College;* B.S. *cum laude* (criminal justice), *Minot State University.*

Background

I hold an Associate of Arts degree from Bismarck State College. Most recently I was awarded the Bachelor of Science degree (*cum laude)* from Minot State University. My undergraduate background encompasses extensive research and writing on a number of legal and constitutional issues: search and seizure, exclusionary rule (fruits of the poisonous tree doctrine), the right to a fair trial and a free press, *habeas corpus,* capital punishment, family law, rules of the court, postverdict motions, and tribal sovereignty issues.

Interests

My inner desire and personal ambition to research the law, the judiciary, and the constitutional questions that arrive before the third branch of government led to my interests and aspirations toward a Senior Internship with an Appellate Court, the Supreme Court of the State of North Dakota. In January 1999 I began a four-month research assistantship at the North Dakota Supreme Court. During my internship with the Court I directly assisted the Court's law clerks and staff counsel in legal research for the opinions that the clerks were drafting. I was honored and privileged to work in the same area and environment as the Justices of the North Dakota Supreme Court. Even more incredible is the fact that I was directly supervised by Chief Justice Gerald W. VandeWalle, a monumental jurist, and his exceptionally brilliant, challenging, and compassionate law clerk, Jennifer Matson.

Interests in the Law

I became interested in the law as a junior in a criminal law class at Century High School in Bismarck, North Dakota. The winter of 1994 was unusually cold and bleak; however, it was the winter I fell in love with the law, the judiciary, and the U.S. legal system. The instructor, a great and wonderful high school teacher, Mrs. Jan Reisenauer, arranged several field trips for our criminal law class. After field trips to the North Dakota Supreme Court and the U.S. District Court for the District of North Dakota, and upon meeting North Dakota's first female Supreme Court Justice, the Honorable Beryl Levine, I was truly passionate about the legal system.

Upon graduation from high school I decided that I wanted with all my heart and mind to work toward going to law school. The societal impact of the law as well as the ramifications of court rulings in law enforcement, jury trials, family law, and the public-at-large has always been a source of great interest and concern to me personally. It is therefore no surprise that while a senior in college I took the Law School Admission Test (LSAT), and that upon the granting of my bachelor's degree, I did in fact apply to law school.

Most Interesting Moments While Studying and Interning

My research and writing has given me a genuine appreciation for the criminal justice system and the judiciary. As a result of my internship and legal research, I am keenly aware of the great degree to which appellate judges read and study briefs, trial transcripts, and court opinions. The position of a Supreme Court Justice is highly analytical and research-oriented in nature and is in a

(continued)

BOX 9.4 (*Continued*)

professional nature very, very similar to being a university professor. I am highly familiar with the manner in which appellate courts conduct their business, why cases are decided in various ways, how judges approach their work, and why the judiciary is by far the most mysterious and least understood branch of government. I understand that appellate judges will not always reverse a trial court judge, even if on a discretionary matter the appellate judges would have decided the procedural matter differently if they had been in the shoes of the trial court judge.

I want to address one huge misconception that the populace in general possesses concerning appellate courts and the U.S. judiciary. The misconception is that appellate judges are liberal intellectuals who, confined in their chambers, do nothing but reverse criminal convictions and thus allow brutal and violent criminals to return to the streets. This simply is not the case. Nationally, over 92 percent of the criminal convictions that are appealed are affirmed and no further appellate review is granted. We must always remember that whenever convictions are reversed, it is because of the fact that the trial itself was "fatally defective" in a constitutional sense, and thus the conviction itself is an illegal one. The other misconception is that trial judges routinely grant defense motions that set aside jury verdicts finding defendants guilty. Again, this is not the case. Motions for judgments of acquittal are in place for some extremely noble and real reasons. The reasons are obvious in the legal community, but not to the public at large. These motions exist to protect those who are truly innocent and are wrongly charged and convicted, not as a tool to set the guilty free.

Statistically, it is rare that trial judges grant such motions, and it is even more rare that a defendant is successful in appealing the trial court's denial of such a motion.

Advice to Students

If you are considering law as a profession, be serious about it. For me the law is a passion that comes from within. Taking the LSAT and sending in applications to the law school were some of the most thrilling experiences I have had since graduating from college. If the law is truly your goal, then never lose sight of that fact; work toward it each day. I also recommend that students select an undergraduate major that is useful and applicable to the world in which we live. I am adamant about the fact that a full, thorough, complete, and working knowledge of the U.S. legal system and the judiciary are essential components to an undergraduate criminal justice education.

Be intellectually honest and accurate at all times. Entering law school is serious business. One's past is heavily scrutinized in the application process, and any legal infractions, no matter how minor or trivial, must be disclosed to the law school where you apply. This information is provided to the Bar Association of the state where you desire to write the Bar Examination and thus practice law upon graduation from law school. Violation of the law by those who practice the law as a profession is not and should not be tolerated. Always be honorable and upstanding citizens, and never be afraid to hold yourself to a high standard as well as those around you. Hard work and diligence will make your goals become a reality.

capital punishment. Further, some indication will be provided of the frequency of use of the death penalty in the United States during the last several decades. Prisoners who have been convicted of capital crimes and sentenced to death contend that the death penalty is cruel and unusual punishment. As such, they claim, it violates their Eighth Amendment rights and should not be applied. Attorneys for these defendants argue similarly that while their clients should be punished, they should be punished by means other than capital punishment (Hood 2001). Religion plays an important role in whether the death penalty is administered as well.

More often than not, defense counsels will make use of religion in their closing arguments to juries who are contemplating voting for the death penalty in a capital case, hoping to persuade jurors to vote on religious grounds rather than on the facts material to the specific case (Simpson and Garvey 2001).

Death Row Inmate Characteristics

Numbers of Death Row Inmates.   The death penalty has almost always been used in the United States as a punishment for those committing capital crimes or extremely serious offenses. Not all states have death penalty provisions, however. In 2001, 37 states and the federal government had death penalty statutes, and all but one state with the death penalty had one or more inmates on death row (Snell and Maruschak 2002:1, 6).

Table 9.2 shows the status of the death penalty as of December 31, 2001. It shows the 3,581 prisoners were under sentence of death and on **death row** at year end 2001 (Snell and Maruschak 2002:1). This figure is 6 percent higher than the number of inmates on U.S. death rows in 1998. Table 9.2 also shows that during 2001 there were 66 executions. Of these executions, 63 were men and 3 were women. Executed offenders included 45 whites, 3 Hispanics, 17 blacks, and 1 Native American. All executions were carried out by lethal injection.

In 2001 California led all states with 603 death row inmates, followed by Texas, with 453, and Florida with 372. Only one state with a death penalty statute, New Hampshire, did not have any inmates on death row by the end of December 2001. Table 9.3 shows all prisoners under sentence of death, by region, state, and race, for 2000–2001 (Snell and Maruschak 2002:6).

TABLE 9.2

Status of Death Penalty, December 31, 2001

Executions during 2001		Number of Prisoners under Sentence of Death		Jurisdictions Without a Death Penalty
Oklahoma	18	California	603	Alaska
Texas	17	Texas	453	District of Columbia
Missouri	7	Florida	372	Hawaii
North Carolina	5	Pennsylvania	241	Iowa
Georgia	4	North Carolina	216	Maine
Federal Government	2	Ohio	203	Massachusetts
Indiana	2	Alabama	186	Michigan
Delaware	2	Illinois	158	Minnesota
Virginia	2	Arizona	126	North Dakota
Ohio	1	Georgia	116	Rhode Island
Arkansas	1	Oklahoma	113	Vermont
Florida	1	Tennessee	96	West Virginia
California	1	Louisiana	88	Wisconsin
Nevada	1	Nevada	86	
New Mexico	1			
Washington	1	24 other jurisdictions	524	
Total	66	Total	3,581	

Source: Tracy L. Snell and Laura M. Maruschak. *Capital Punishment 2001.* Washington, DC: U.S. Department of Justice, 2002, p. 1.

TABLE 9.3

Prisoners under Sentence of Death, by Region, State, and Race, 2000 and 2001

Region and State	Prisoners under Sentence of Death, 12/31/00			Received under Sentence of Death			Removed from Death Row (Excluding Executions)[a]			Executed			Prisoners under Sentence of Death, 12/31/01		
	Total[b]	White[c]	Black[c]	Total[b]	White[c]	Black[c]	Total[b]	White[c]	Black[c]	Total[b]	White[c]	Black[c]	Total[b]	White[c]	Black[c]
U.S. Total	3,601	1,989	1,541	155	89	61	109	61	47	66	48	17	3,581	1,969	1,538
Federal[d]	20	5	15	2	1	1	1	1	0	2	2	0	19	3	16
State	3,581	1,984	1,526	153	88	60	108	60	47	64	46	17	3,562	1,966	1,522
Northeast	269	96	162	7	5	2	6	3	3	0	0	0	270	98	161
Connecticut	7	4	3	0	0	0	0	0	0	0	0	0	7	4	3
New Hampshire	0	0	0	0	0	0	0	0	0	0	0	0	0	0	0
New Jersey	16	9	7	1	1	0	1	1	0	0	0	0	16	9	7
New York	6	4	2	0	0	0	0	0	0	0	0	0	6	4	2
Pennsylvania	240	79	150	6	4	2	5	2	3	0	0	0	241	81	149
Midwest	502	248	251	14	8	5	20	10	9	10	6	4	486	240	243
Illinois	164	60	104	1	0	1	7	2	5	0	0	0	158	58	100
Indiana	41	29	12	0	0	0	3	2	1	2	2	0	36	25	11
Kansas	4	4	0	0	0	0	0	0	0	0	0	0	4	4	0
Missouri	78	45	33	5	2	3	3	1	2	7	4	3	73	42	31
Nebraska	11	10	0	1	0	1	5	4	0	0	0	0	7	6	1
Ohio[e]	201	97	102	5	4	0	2	1	1	1	0	1	203	100	100
South Dakota	3	3	0	2	2	0	0	0	0	0	0	0	5	5	0
South	1,929	1,061	843	93	52	40	65	35	30	50	36	13	1,907	1,042	840
Alabama	185	97	87	7	6	1	6	3	3	0	0	0	186	100	85
Arkansas	40	16	24	2	1	1	1	0	1	1	1	0	40	16	24
Delaware	15	8	7	5	2	3	4	0	4	2	1	1	14	9	5
Florida[f]	371	238	132	15	8	7	13	9	4	1	1	0	372	236	135
Georgia	122	66	55	1	0	1	3	1	2	4	3	1	116	62	53
Kentucky	39	32	7	2	0	2	5	4	1	0	0	0	36	28	8
Louisiana	89	29	59	2	2	0	3	1	2	0	0	0	88	30	57
Maryland	16	6	10	0	0	0	0	0	0	0	0	0	16	6	10
Mississippi	61	28	33	2	1	1	1	0	1	0	0	0	62	29	33
North Carolina	215	85	122	14	6	7	8	3	5	5	3	2	216	85	122

(continued)

TABLE 9.3 (CONTINUED)

Prisoners under Sentence of Death, by Region, State, and Race, 2000 and 2001

Region and State	Prisoners under Sentence of Death, 12/31/00			Received under Sentence of Death			Removed from Death Row (Excluding Executions)[a]			Executed			Prisoners under Sentence of Death, 12/31/01		
	Total[b]	White[c]	Black[c]	Total[b]	White[c]	Black[c]	Total[b]	White[c]	Black[c]	Total[b]	White[c]	Black[c]	Total[b]	White[c]	Black[c]
Oklahoma	132	82	44	2	2	0	3	2	1	18	14	3	113	68	40
South Carolina	66	35	31	8	3	5	1	1	0	0	0	0	73	37	36
Tennessee	98	60	36	3	2	1	5	3	2	0	0	0	96	59	35
Texas	450	260	185	26	16	10	6	5	1	17	11	6	453	260	188
Virginia	30	19	11	4	3	1	6	3	3	2	2	0	26	17	9
West	881	579	270	39	23	13	17	12	5	4	4	0	899	586	278
Arizona	119	103	12	7	3	2	0	0	0	0	0	0	126	106	14
California	587	349	215	24	16	7	7	4	3	1	1	0	603	360	219
Colorado	6	3	2	0	0	0	0	0	0	0	0	0	6	3	2
Idaho	21	21	0	2	2	0	2	2	0	0	0	0	21	21	0
Montana	6	5	0	0	0	0	0	0	0	0	0	0	6	5	0
Nevada[g]	88	52	35	1	0	1	2	1	1	1	1	0	86	50	35
New Mexico	5	5	0	0	0	0	1	1	0	1	1	0	3	3	0
Oregon	25	24	0	2	1	1	1	1	0	0	0	0	26	24	1
Utah	11	8	2	0	0	0	0	0	0	0	0	0	11	8	2
Washington	11	7	4	3	1	2	4	3	1	1	1	0	9	4	5
Wyoming	2	2	0	0	0	0	0	0	0	0	0	0	2	2	0

Note: Some figures shown for year end 2000 are revised from those reported in *Capital Punishment 2000*, NCJ 190598. The revised figures include 20 inmates who were either reported late to the National Prisoner Statistics program or were not in custody of State or Federal correctional authorities on 12/31/00 (3 in Oregon; 2 each in Pennsylvania, Georgia, Oklahoma, California, and the Federal Bureau of Prisons; and 1 each in New Jersey, Illinois, Ohio, Florida, Tennessee, Virginia, and Colorado). The revised figures exclude 13 inmates who were relieved of a death sentence by 12/31/00 (3 in Oregon; 2 each in Indiana and Washington; and 1 each in Ohio, Missouri, Florida, Kentucky, Louisiana, and California). Data for 12/31/00 also include 1 inmate in Oklahoma who was erroneously reported as being removed from under sentence of death.

[a]Includes 17 deaths from natural causes (4 in California; 2 each in Alabama, Florida, Texas, and Nevada; and 1 each in Pennsylvania, Missouri, North Carolina, Oklahoma, and Virginia) and 2 deaths from suicide (1 each in Nebraska and Virginia).
[b]Totals include persons of races other than white and black.
[c]The reporting of race and Hispanic origin differs from that presented in tables 9 and 11. In this table white and black inmates include Hispanics.
[d]Excludes persons held under Armed Forces jurisdiction with a military death sentence for murder.
[e]Race has been changed from black to white for 1 inmate and from white to American Indian for 1 inmate.
[f]Race has been changed from white to black for 1 inmate.
[g]Race has been changed from white to Asian for 1 inmate.
Source: Tracy L. Snell and Laura M. Maruschak. *Capital Punishment 2001*. Washington, DC: U.S. Department of Justice, 2002, p. 6.

Characteristics of Death Row Inmates.   Table 9.4 shows a demographic profile of death row inmates by yearend 2001 according to race, ethnicity, education, marital status, Hispanic origin, and gender (Snell and Maruschak 2002:6,8). Most death row inmates are male (98.6 percent), 42.9 percent are black, and 11.2 are Hispanic. About 54 percent of all death row inmates never married, and about 24 percent are widowed, divorced, or separated. About 48 percent of these death row inmates had less than a high school education. (Snell and Maruschak 2002:8).

Table 9.5 shows the number of inmates on death rows at yearend 2001 according to their ages at the time of arrest and on December 31, 2001. Fifty-four percent of these inmates were between 20 and 39 when arrested, while 13.1 percent

---

TABLE 9.4

Demographic Characteristics of Prisoners under Sentence of Death, 2001

Characteristic	Prisoners under Sentence of Death, 2001		
	Year end	Admissions	Removals
Total number under sentence of death	3,581	155	175
Gender			
Male	98.6%	100%	98.3%
Female	1.4	0	1.7
Race			
White	55.0%	57.4%	62.3%
Black	42.9	39.4	36.6
All other races*	2.1	3.1	1.1
Hispanic origin			
Hispanic	11.2%	16.2%	3.8%
Non-Hispanic	88.8	83.8	96.3
Education			
8th grade or less	14.5%	15.8%	12.3%
9th–11th grade	37.2	32.5	36.1
High school graduate/GED	38.4	47.5	41.9
Any college	9.9	4.2	9.7
Median	11th	12th	12th
Marital status			
Married	22.1%	19.9%	31.7%
Divorced/separated	21.0	15.4	16.8
Widowed	2.6	0.7	3.7
Never married	54.3	64.0	47.8

Note: Calculations are based on those cases for which data were reported. Missing data by category were as follows:

	Year end	Admissions	Removals
Hispanic origin	381	13	15
Education	501	35	20
Marital status	335	19	14

*At year end 2000, other races consisted of 30 American Indians, 29 Asians, and 12 self-identified Hispanics. During 2001, 4 Asians and 1 self-identified Hispanic were admitted; 2 American Indians were removed.
Source: Tracy L. Snell and Laura M. Maruschak. *Capital Punishment 2001.* Washington, DC: U.S. Department of Justice, 2002, p. 8.

TABLE 9.5

Age at Time of Arrest for Capital Offense and Age of Prisoners under Sentence of Death at Yearend 2001

| Age | Prisoners under Sentence of Death | | | |
| | At time of arrest | | On December 31, 2001 | |
	Number*	Percent	Number	Percent
Total number under sentence of death on 12/31/01	3,311	100%	3,581	100%
17 or younger	77	2.3	0	
18–19	358	10.8	4	0.1
20–24	882	26.6	192	5.4
25–29	742	22.4	471	13.2
30–34	548	16.6	628	17.5
35–39	364	11.0	640	17.9
40–44	178	5.4	675	18.8
45–49	98	3.0	424	11.8
50–54	41	1.2	304	8.5
55–59	14	0.4	148	4.1
60–64	4	0.1	55	1.5
65 or older	5	0.2	40	1.1
Mean age	28 yrs.		39 yrs.	
Median age	27 yrs.		39 yrs.	

Note: The youngest person under sentence of death was a black male in North Carolina, born in December 1982 and sentenced to death in November 2001. The oldest person under sentence of death was a white male in Arizona, born in September 1915 and sentenced to death in June 1983.

*Excludes 270 inmates for whom the date of arrest for capital offense was not available.

Source: Tracy L. Snell and Laura M. Maruschak. *Capital Punishment 2001.* Washington, DC: U.S. Department of Justice, 2002, p.9.

of all death row inmates were under age 20 when arrested (Snell and Maruschak 2002:9). At yearend 2001, only .1 percent of those on death row were under age 20.

Table 9.6 shows the criminal histories of inmates under sentence of death for 2001 (Snell and Maruschak 2002:10). Sixty-four percent had prior felony convictions, while 8 percent (282) had prior convictions for homicide. About 35 percent of those on death row had been on probation, parole, or had charges pending against them when arrested for a capital offense. Parolees accounted for 17.5 percent (567) of all death row inmates, while probationers made up 10.3 percent (334) of them.

Numbers of Executions Since 1930 and 1977. Between 1930 and yearend 2001, there were 4,291 executions in the United States. Table 9.7 shows a distribution of these executions by state and the federal system.

Texas led all states with 553 executions since 1930 and 256 executions from 1977 through 2001 (Snell and Maruschak 2002:10). In 1972, capital punishment was suspended temporarily while the courts determined an appropriate procedure to follow in death penalty cases (*Furman v. Georgia* 1972). In 1976, capital punishment resumed following the case of *Gregg v. Georgia* (1976). The first

TABLE 9.6

Criminal History Profile of Prisoners under Sentence of Death, by Race and Hispanic Origin, 2001

	Number of Prisoners under Sentence of Death				Percent of Prisoners under Sentence of Death[a]			
	All[b]	White[c]	Black[c]	Hispanic	All[b]	White[c]	Black[c]	Hispanic
U.S. total	3,581	1,644	1,521	358	100%	100%	100%	100%
Prior felony convictions								
Yes	2,139	939	972	199	64.4%	61.5%	69.2%	59.1%
No	1,183	587	432	138	35.6	38.5	30.8	40.9
Not reported	259							
Prior homicide convictions								
Yes	282	129	126	23	8.0%	8.0%	8.5%	6.5%
No	3,224	1,484	1,357	330	92.0	92.0	91.5	93.5
Not reported	75							
Legal status at time of capital offense								
Charges pending	238	127	97	14	7.3%	8.5%	7.1%	4.3%
Probation	334	137	154	36	10.3	9.2	11.3	10.9
Parole	567	227	257	75	17.5	15.2	18.8	22.8
Prison escapee	37	21	11	4	1.1	1.4	0.8	1.2
Incarcerated	98	47	42	8	3.0	3.1	3.1	2.4
Other status	17	7	8	1	0.5	0.5	0.6	0.3
None	1,951	928	795	191	60.2	62.1	58.3	58.1
Not reported	339							

[a]Percentages are based on those offenders for whom data were reported. Detail may not add to total because of rounding.
[b]Includes American Indians, Asians, and persons of unknown race.
[c]White and black categories exclude Hispanics.
Source: Tracy L. Snell and Laura M. Maruschak. *Capital Punishment 2001.* Washington, DC: U.S. Department of Justice, 2002, p.10.

execution since the *Gregg* case was carried out in 1977, with the execution of convicted killer Gary Gilmore in Utah. Between 1977 and yearend 2001, there were 749 executions. Texas, Virginia, Missouri, and Florida led all states in the numbers of offenders executed between 1977 and 2001. Table 9.8 shows the number of inmates under sentence of death, by state, as of December 31, 2001. Figure 9.1 shows graphically the trend in U.S. death sentences from 1930 to 2001.

Time Lapse between Sentences of Death and Execution of Sentences.
There is a considerable time interval between the time prisoners are sentenced to death and when they are ultimately executed. Table 9.8 shows that the average amount of time lapsing between sentences of death and carrying out these sentences is 103 months, or 8.6 years. The reason for this nearly nine-year interval is that there are numerous appeals filed by these death row inmates. Appeals often result in stays of execution until the appeals can be decided. In most instances,

TABLE 9.7

Number of Persons Executed by Jurisdiction, 1930–2001

State	Number Executed	
	Since 1930	Since 1977
U.S. total	4,608	749
Texas	553	256
Georgia	393	27
New York	329	0
California	301	9
North Carolina	284	21
Florida	221	51
South Carolina	187	25
Virginia	175	83
Ohio	174	2
Louisiana	159	26
Alabama	158	23
Mississippi	158	4
Pennsylvania	155	3
Arkansas	142	24
Missouri	115	53
Oklahoma	108	48
Kentucky	105	2
Illinois	102	12
Tennessee	94	1
New Jersey	74	0
Maryland	71	3
Arizona	60	22
Washington	51	4
Indiana	50	9
Colorado	48	1
District of Columbia	40	0
West Virginia	40	0
Nevada	38	9
Federal system	35	2
Massachusetts	27	0
Delaware	25	13
Oregon	21	2
Connecticut	21	0
Utah	19	6
Iowa	18	0
Kansas	15	0
New Mexico	9	1
Montana	8	2
Wyoming	8	1
Nebraska	7	3
Idaho	4	1
Vermont	4	0
New Hampshire	1	0
South Dakota	1	0

Source: Tracy L. Snell and Laura M. Maruschak. *Capital Punishment 2001.* Washington, DC: U.S. Department of Justice, 2002, p. 10.

TABLE 9.8

Prisoners under Sentence of Death on December 31, 2001, by State and Year of Sentencing

State	Year of Sentence for Prisoners Sentenced to and Remaining on Death Row, 12/31/2001												Under Sentence of Death, as of 12/31/01	Average Number of Years under Sentence of Death, as of 12/31/01
	1974–80	1981–82	1983–84	1985–86	1987–88	1989–90	1991–92	1993–94	1995–96	1997–98	1999–00	2001		
Florida	23	13	26	23	36	31	53	45	32	32	43	15	372	10.2
California	13	35	39	39	52	63	63	55	76	70	74	24	603	9.5
Texas	11	5	9	15	25	27	47	65	71	71	81	26	453	7.2
Georgia	7	5	4	9	8	11	12	12	13	21	13	1	116	9.7
Illinois	6	9	12	14	13	19	14	19	20	12	19	1	158	10.4
Tennessee	3	7	6	13	13	7	8	5	8	12	11	3	96	10.8
North Carolina	3	2	1	4		4	17	50	46	37	38	14	216	6.0
Alabama	1	8	5	9	15	18	11	24	26	37	25	7	186	8.0
Nevada	1	6	9	5	8	9	4	7	18	7	11	1	86	9.9
Arizona	1	5	6	7	15	13	15	18	9	17	13	7	126	9.1
Indiana	1	2	2	3	7	2	3	3	6	4	3		36	10.4
Kentucky	1	2	5	4	2		4	5	1	5	5	2	36	9.9
Arkansas	1					2	3	9	8	8	7	2	40	6.2
Pennsylvania		6	14	22	28	22	23	38	28	27	27	6	241	9.2
Mississippi		4		2	2	5	6	10	10	14	7	2	62	7.5
Idaho		2	2	2	2	3	2	2	2	1	1	2	21	10.6
Louisiana		2	1	5	5	1	4	8	18	23	19	2	88	6.4
Missouri		1	2	3	4	1	7	13	14	13	10	5	73	6.9
Ohio			22	29	17	17	22	18	34	25	14	5	203	9.8
Oklahoma			4	8	10	9	7	11	22	26	14	2	113	7.7

(continued)

TABLE 9.8 (Continued)

Prisoners under Sentence of Death on December 31, 2001, by State and Year of Sentencing

State	Year of Sentence for Prisoners Sentenced to and Remaining on Death Row, 12/31/2001												Under Sentence of Death, 12/31/01	Average Number of Years under Sentence of Death, as of 12/31/01
	1974–80	1981–82	1983–84	1985–86	1987–88	1989–90	1991–92	1993–94	1995–96	1997–98	1999–00	2001		
South Carolina	3	2		1	1	4	7	11	16	11	10	8	73	6.4
Maryland	3				1	1	2		4	2	3		16	8.4
Utah	1	2	1	2	1	1	1	1	2	1	1		11	10.3
Nebraska	1	1	1	1					2		2	1	7	*
Montana	1		1		1		2		2				6	*
New Jersey		1		1		2		3	5	3	1	1	16	6.6
Colorado					1				2		3		6	*
Connecticut						1	2		1		3		7	*
Oregon							5	3	5	6	5	2	26	5.2
Delaware							2	3		2	2	5	14	4.4
Washington							1	2	1	2		3	9	*
Federal system								3	3	6	5	2	19	4.0
Virginia								1	1	9	11	4	26	2.6
South Dakota								1		1	1	2	5	*
New Mexico									2		1		3	*
Kansas										2	2		4	*
Wyoming										2			2	*
New York										1	5		6	*
Total	72	114	178	222	267	273	347	445	508	510	490	155	3,581	8.6

Note: For those persons sentenced to death more than once, the numbers are based on the most recent death sentence.

*Averages not calculated for fewer than 10 inmates.

Source: Tracy L. Snell and Laura M. Maruschak. *Capital Punishment 2001*. Washington, DC: U.S. Department of Justice, 2002, p. 14.

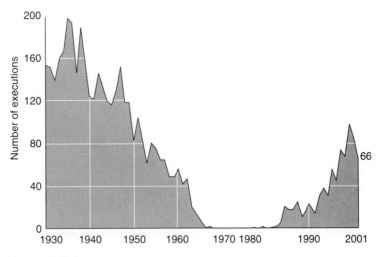

FIGURE 9.1   Persons Executed, 1930–2001

Source: Tracy L. Snell and Laura M. Maruschak. *Capital Punishment 2001.*
Washington, DC: U.S. Department of Justice, 2002, p. 11.

eventually the death sentences are imposed when all appeals have been exhausted. Actually, the time interval between conviction and execution has increased from 97 months in 1994 to 103 months in 2001. In some cases, governors
may commute death sentences to life-without-parole sentences. In 2001 Tennessee had the greatest average time interval between conviction and execution of
10.8 years, while Virginia had the shortest time interval of 2.6 years.

Methods of Execution Used by the States and Federal Government

There are five different execution methods used by the states and federal government. The most frequent method of execution is by lethal injection. Thirty-
six states and the federal government use lethal injection for executing their
prisoners. Nine states use electrocution, four states use lethal gas, three states

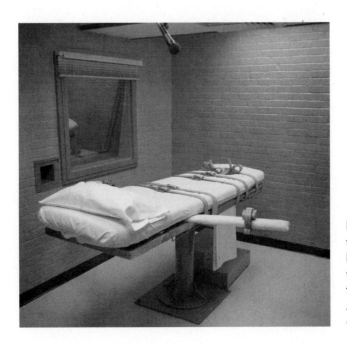

Lethal injection is used
the most in states that
have the death penalty as
the maximum punishment
for a capital offense. *Source:*
Andrew Lichtenstein/Aurora &
Quanta Productions Inc.

TABLE 9.9

Method of Execution, By State, 2001

Lethal Injection		Electrocution	Lethal Gas	Hanging	Firing Squad
Arizona[a,b]	Nevada	Alabama	Arizona[a,b]	Delaware[a,c]	Idaho[a]
Arkansas[a,d]	New Hampshire[a]	Arkansas[a,d]	California[a]	New Hampshire[a,e]	Oklahoma[f]
California[a]	New Jersey	Florida[a]	Missouri[a]	Washington[a]	Utah[a]
Colorado	New Mexico	Kentucky[a,g]	Wyoming[a,h]		
Connecticut	New York	Nebraska			
Delaware[a,c]	North Carolina	Oklahoma[f]			
Florida[a]	Ohio	South Carolina[a]			
Georgia	Oklahoma[a]	Tennessee[a,i]			
Idaho[a]	Oregon	Virginia[a]			
Illinois	Pennsylvania				
Indiana	South Carolina[a]				
Kansas	South Dakota				
Kentucky[a,g]	Tennessee[a,i]				
Louisiana	Texas				
Maryland	Utah[a]				
Mississippi	Virginia[a]				
Missouri[a]	Washington[a]				
Montana	Wyoming[a]				

Note: The method of execution of Federal prisoners is lethal injection, pursuant to 28 CFR, Part 26. For offenses under the Violent Crime Control and Law Enforcement Act of 1994, the method is that of the State in which the conviction took place, pursuant to 18 U.S.C. 3596.
[a]Authorizes 2 methods of execution.
[b]Arizona authorizes lethal injection for persons whose capital sentence was received after 11/15/92; for those sentenced before that date, the condemned may select lethal injection or lethal gas.
[c]Delaware authorizes lethal injection for those whose capital offense occurred after 6/13/86; for those whose offense occurred before that date, the condemned may select lethal injection or hanging.
[d]Arkansas authorizes lethal injection for those whose capital offense occurred on or after 7/4/83; for those whose offense occurred before that date, the condemned may select lethal injection or electrocution.
[e]New Hampshire authorizes hanging only if lethal injection cannot be given.
[f]Oklahoma authorizes electrocution if lethal injection is ever held to be unconstitutional, and firing squad if both lethal injection and electrocution are held unconstitutional.
[g]Kentucky authorizes lethal injection for persons whose capital sentence was received on or after 3/31/98; for those sentenced before that date, the condemned may select lethal injection or electrocution.
[h]Wyoming authorizes lethal gas if lethal injection is ever held to be unconstitutional.
[i]Tennessee authorizes lethal injection for those whose capital offense occurred after 12/31/98; those whose offense occurred before that date may select electrocution.
Source: Tracy L. Snell and Laura M. Maruschak. *Capital Punishment 2001.* Washington, DC: U.S. Department of Justice, 2002, p. 5.

use hanging, and three states use a firing squad. Several of these states offer prisoners the choice of lethal injection or one of the other execution methods. Table 9.9 shows the method of execution used by the different states and federal government.

Minimum Age Authorized for Capital Punishment

In 2001, 13 states had a minimum age of 16 for administering the death penalty, four states had a minimum age of 17, 15 states and the federal government had a minimum age of 18, and 7 states did not specify a minimum age. The minimum legal age for executing anyone convicted of a capital crime has previously been established as 16 in the cases of *Wilkins v. Missouri* (1989) and *Stanford v. Kentucky* (1989). Thus, it is unconstitutional to execute someone who committed capital murder and who was under 16 years of age at the time. Any state with a lower age provision for executing youthful offenders must follow the *Wilkins* and *Stanford* standard despite their statutes that specify lower ages. These states have simply failed to eliminate these statutes officially from their state codes, although eventually they will do so. Table 9.10 shows the minimum ages used by the states and federal government in 2001 for executing those convicted of capital murder.

While the U.S. Supreme Court has never held the death penalty to be cruel and unusual punishment in violation of the Eighth Amendment or ever officially abolished capital punishment, several U.S. Supreme Court decisions have interpreted the method whereby the death penalty is imposed by judges and juries to be cruel and unusual and/or unconstitutional.

One of the first significant U.S. Supreme Court death penalty cases in the 1960s challenged the manner in which jurors were selected. This was the case of *Witherspoon v. Illinois* (1968). In the Witherspoon case, the prosecution excluded all persons from the jury who expressed opposition to the death penalty. Thus, when Witherspoon was subsequently convicted and sentenced to death, it was by a **death-qualified jury.** Death-qualified juries were comprised

TABLE 9.10

Minimum Age Authorized for Capital Punishment, 2001

Age 16 or Less	Age 17	Age 18	None Specified
Alabama (16)	Georgia	California	Arizona
Arkansas (14)[a]	New Hampshire	Colorado	Idaho
Delaware (16)	North Carolina[b]	Connecticut[c]	Louisiana
Florida (16)	Texas	Federal system	Montana[d]
Indiana (16)		Illinois	Pennsylvania
Kentucky (16)		Kansas	South Carolina
Mississippi (16)[e]		Maryland	South Dakota[f]
Missouri (16)		Nebraska	
Nevada (16)		New Jersey	
Oklahoma (16)		New Mexico	
Utah (14)		New York	
Virginia (14)[g]		Ohio	
Wyoming (16)		Oregon	
		Tennessee	
		Washington	

Note: Reporting by States reflects interpretations by State attorney generals' offices and may differ from previously reported ages.

[a]See Ark. Code Ann. 9-27-318(c)(2)(Supp. 2001).

[b]Age required is 17 unless the murderer was incarcerated for murder when a subsequent murder occurred; then the age may be 14.

[c]See Conn. Gen. Stat. 53a-46a(g)(1).

[d]Montana law specifies that offenders tried under the capital sexual assault statute be 18 or older. Age may be a mitigating factor for other capital crimes.

[e]The minimum age defined by statute is 13, but the effective age is 16 based on interpretation of U.S. Supreme Court decisions by the Mississippi Supreme Court.

[f]Juveniles may be transferred to adult court. Age can be a mitigating factor.

[g]The minimum age for transfer to adult court by statute is 14, but the effective age is 16 based on interpretation of U.S. Supreme Court decisions by the State attorney general's office.

Source: Tracy L. Snell and Laura M. Maruschak. *Capital Punishment 2001*. Washington, DC: U.S. Department of Justice, 2002, p. 5.

of persons who supported the death penalty. Anyone who expressed opposition to the death penalty was systematically excluded from jury service in capital cases. Subsequently, the U.S. Supreme Court overturned Witherspoon's conviction, declaring that it was unconstitutional to exclude persons from the jury simply because they opposed the death penalty.

Three years later, the U.S. Supreme Court heard the case of *McGautha v. California* (1971). McGautha was convicted of murder by a California jury. The judge instructed the jury to decide whether McGautha should receive life imprisonment or the death penalty. McGautha's attorney challenged this discretion successfully, when the U.S. Supreme Court ruled that it is unconstitutional for juries to have the power of life or death in a capital case.

In 1972, a landmark death penalty case was decided by the U.S. Supreme Court. This was *Furman v. Georgia* (1972). For many years, Georgia and several other Southern states had used the death penalty with considerable frequency in cases such as rape and robbery. The unusual situation in Georgia was that the death penalty was being selectively applied primarily to blacks and not to whites convicted of the same offenses. This discriminatory application of the death penalty was eventually challenged. In a significant ruling, the U.S. Supreme Court declared that the death penalty was being arbitrarily applied in Georgia, and therefore, it was held to be cruel and unusual punishment.

The *Furman* case caused a suspension of the death penalty in virtually every state for a four-year period, while various state courts examined their own methods for applying it. But in 1976, another Georgia case, *Gregg v. Georgia* (1976), prompted the U.S. Supreme Court to say that the death penalty is not cruel and unusual punishment per se. Furthermore, the Court acknowledged the constitutionality of the **bifurcated trial,** a two-stage proceeding where guilt is established in one stage and the penalty decided in the other. Today, the bifurcated trial is mandatory in all capital cases where the death penalty is requested by the prosecution. The second stage of this proceeding permits the jury to consider any especially aggravating or mitigating circumstances that might influence their decision as to whether the death penalty ought to be applied.

Also during the 1976–1977 period, three other cases were decided by the U.S. Supreme Court that changed drastically the types of crimes for which the death penalty is suitable. In *Woodson v. North Carolina* (1976), a North Carolina statute called for a mandatory death penalty for any premeditated, first-degree murder case. Since a mandatory death penalty means that any aggravating or mitigating circumstances cannot be considered, mandatory death penalties were subsequently declared unconstitutional. Similarly, Louisiana had a law that had a mandatory death penalty if the convicted offender killed a police officer in the line of duty. Again, because of the fact that aggravating and mitigating circumstances could not be considered in the death penalty decision, the U.S. Supreme Court declared this statute unconstitutional on grounds similar to those in the case of *Woodson.*

In 1977, the case of *Coker v. Georgia* (1977) was decided by the U.S. Supreme Court. Coker had been convicted of rape and was sentenced to death. His appeal was eventually heard by the Supreme Court where a ruling was issued to the effect that the death penalty as a punishment for rape cases is too harsh or excessive. As noted earlier, the application of the death penalty in the United States is a highly controversial and emotionally charged issue. The primary reasons for applying the death penalty, according to its advocates, include (1) deterrence, (2) retribution, (3) justice, and (4) elimination (Cook and Slawson 1993).

Does the death penalty deter people from murdering others? While there are mixed findings on this issue, the overwhelming evidence suggests that the death penalty is not an effective deterrent (Solataroff 2001). During those years when the death penalty was temporarily suspended while different states examined their capital punishment statutes, no significant changes in the rate of homicide were observed, either nationally or in selected states (Hood 2001; Simpson and Garvey 2001).

Alternatives to the death penalty are considered in all jurisdictions. Some proposals include segregation of murderers from others in solitary confinement. Snellenburg (1986) has proposed that those convicted of capital crimes be sentenced to solitary confinement for life, without possibility of commutation or parole. However, some authorities might contend that such prolonged isolation is cruel and unusual and violative of the Eighth Amendment. Although the U.S. Supreme Court attempted to correct the administration of the death penalty in those states that use it so that racial discrimination would be eliminated, evidence suggests that some discrimination according to racial, ethnic, and gender factors continues (Arrigo and Fowler 2001).

Women and the Death Penalty

Women are the least likely to be sentenced to death in the United States. By yearend 2001 there were 51 women on death row. This is an increase from the 36 women in 1991 (Snell and Maruschak 2002:1). Also, in 2001 over 11 percent of all arrests for murder were women (Maguire and Pastore 2002). But women make up only about .1 percent of all death row inmates. Only 3 women were executed in 2001. While it is not necessarily the case that women who commit and are convicted of first-degree murder in a state with the death penalty will likely receive it as a sentence, the disproportionately small number of women on death row is not surprising.

There have always been mixed attitudes and opinions among U.S. citizens concerning executing women (Cullen, Fisher, and Applegate 2000). By the fall of 2002, only 49 women had been executed in the United States since 1900, and only 10 of these executions occurred since 1962 (Death Penalty Information Center 2002). Some observers have attempted to explain this disproportionality of punishment by attributing it largely to the **chivalry hypothesis** (Baker 1999). The chivalry hypothesis posits that generally, women in the United States benefit from the protective and paternalistic attitudes of police officers, prosecutors, and judges (Palmer 2001). However, the fact that comparatively more women convicted of capital murder have been executed in recent years suggests that attitudes about the death penalty for women may be changing (O'Shea 1999). Some persons have indicated that the pace of executing female murderers has increased because women have successfully challenged the social, political, and economic interests of the dominant male elite (Baker 1999). The Women's Liberation Movement has highlighted and helped to correct deplorable injustices to women, especially in the economic sector, where women have received considerably less compensation for their work compared with men who perform the same jobs. But in an effort to establish equal treatment with their male peers in the workplace, women have succeeded to a degree in obtaining more equal treatment in death penalty cases.

Between 1950 and 1984, the execution of women in the United States was relatively rare. Two high-profile cases from the 1950s included the execution of Ethel Rosenberg in 1953 for espionage against the United States and Barbara

Graham, who was executed in 1955 for her role in a botched robbery-murder in California. It was nearly thirty years before another woman was executed. A more recent case involved a North Carolina woman, Velma Barfield, a grand-mother who was convicted of killing her boyfriend and who also admitted to killing her mother and others. She poisoned her husband with arsenic. At first, Barfield claimed that her husband's death was the result of gastritis, since he had complained of severe stomach cramps shortly before dying. However, an autopsy demanded by his children from another marriage showed that he was poisoned with arsenic. It was later determined that Barfield had killed her mother in a similar fashion. Subsequently, she confessed to these and other murders, was convicted, and sentenced to death. She was executed in 1984.

Probably the most visible and highly publicized female death penalty case since the executions of Ethel Rosenberg and Barbara Graham occurred in Texas less than a decade following Velma Barfield's execution. This case involved a young Texas woman, Karla Faye Tucker. Tucker was convicted of killing a young man and woman with an ax. There were numerous aggravating circumstances, and it certainly did not help her case when she admitted to having an orgasm each time her ax sank into her victims. While Tucker spent time on death row, she claimed to become a born-again Christian. She attracted the attention of Amnesty International as well as Sister Helen Prejean, a woman known for her humanitarianism and work with condemned offenders on death rows in other ju-risdictions. Because of Tucker's repentance and religious conversion experience, many organizations and interested individuals sought to intercede on her behalf by encouraging the governor of Texas, then George W. Bush, to commute her sen-tence to life without the possibility of parole. Internet websites dedicated to Tucker and promoting sympathy for her plight proliferated. Even the Pope en-couraged leniency on her behalf. Despite all of her lengthy appeals and professed reforms, Tucker was executed in February 1998. On the eve of Tucker's execu-tion, large crowds of protestors assembled outside of the Texas prison where her execution by lethal injection would occur. When her execution was concluded and announced publicly, great outpourings of emotion were observed.

At least one observer has said that Tucker's execution aided in closing the gap between female and male treatment in the criminal justice system, but it also diminished the nation's sensitivity to execution and capital punishment. Applying the death penalty in a nonarbitrary manner means executing women, as well as men, who have been sentenced to death (O'Neil 1999).

Interestingly, about seven weeks following Tucker's execution, Judy "Judi" Buenoano was executed in Florida for the premeditated murders of her hus-band and son. Unlike Tucker, Buenoano's execution received almost no media coverage. It has been speculated that in Buenoano's case, she showed no re-morse for her crimes, whereas Tucker had confessed and asked for forgiveness from her victims' survivors. Further speculation was that Tucker was younger and reasonably attractive, whereas Buenoano was older and unattractive. One fact is clear, however. Today, if the name Karla Faye Tucker is mentioned, there is substantial public recognition. If the name Judy Buenoano is mentioned, people are more likely to ask, "Judy who?" Between Buenoano's execution and October 2002, seven women were executed in Texas, Arkansas, Arizona, Oklahoma, Florida, and Alabama. They included Betty Lou Beets, Christina Riggs, Wanda Jean Allen, Marilyn Plantz, Lois Nadean Smith, Lynda Lyon Block, and Aileen Pittman Wournos (Death Penalty Information Center 2002). Most of these women are unknown to the general public because there was little or no media coverage of their executions. The most visible of these other female murderers was serial killer Aileen Wournos. She was a prostitute who picked up middle-aged men and robbed and killed them. At least one television movie was made about her life and the murders she committed.

It is unlikely that the death penalty will be abolished in the United States in the near future, although groups such as the American Civil Liberties Union and many professional organizations oppose it. No doubt the Supreme Court will continue to issue opinions that will narrow the circumstances under which it can be applied (Amnesty International 1997).

Reasons for Supporting the Death Penalty

The primary reasons for supporting the death penalty in certain capital cases are threefold: retribution, deterrence, and just-deserts.

The Death Penalty as Retribution. Retribution is defended largely on the basis of the philosophical just-desert rationale (Taylor 2001). Offenders should be executed because they did not respect the lives of others. Death is the just-desert for someone who inflicted death on someone else. Retribution is regarded by some observers as the primary purpose of the death penalty (Jackson, Jackson, and Shapiro 2001).

The Death Penalty as a Deterrent to Other Capital Crimes. The deterrence function of the death penalty is frequently questioned as well. An examination of the death penalty in Tennessee was conducted. It revealed that average homicide rates for three different periods did not fluctuate noticeably. These periods included (1) times when the death penalty was allowed, (2) years when the death penalty was allowed but no executions were performed, and (3) years when the death penalty was abolished (Krzycki 2000). Persons favoring the abolition of the death penalty argue that no criminal act ever justifies capital punishment (Rivkind and Shatz 2001).

The Death Penalty as a Just-Desert for Murder. The just-deserts philosophy would argue that the death penalty is just punishment for someone who has committed murder (Williams and Holcomb 2001). The U.S. Supreme Court has not declared the death penalty to be cruel and unusual punishment.

Reasons for Opposing the Death Penalty

Some of the reasons persons use to oppose the death penalty are that (1) it is barbaric; (2) it may be applied in error to someone who is not actually guilty of a capital offense; (3) it is nothing more than sheer revenge; (4) it is more costly than life imprisonment; (5) it is applied arbitrarily; (6) it does not deter others from committing murder; and (7) most persons in the United States are opposed to the death penalty.

The Death Penalty as Barbarism. Hugo Bedau (1992) says that the death penalty is barbaric. There are other avenues whereby convicted capital offenders can be punished. The United States is one of the few civilized countries of the modern world that still uses the death penalty. Portraits of persons

BOX 9.5

WE KNOW WHO ARE THE MURDERERS. DO WE KNOW WHO ARE THE VICTIMS?

Match the murderers in the left-hand column with the victims in the right-hand column. Answers are furnished at the end of this box. In some cases, only first names and/or ages are provided where spouses/children were killed.

Murderer	Victim(s)
1. Karla Faye Tucker	a. David Spears, 43; Peter Siems, 65; Eugene Burress, 50; Dick Humphreys, 56; Walter Antonio, 60; Richard Mallory, 51
2. Heath Wilkins	b. Stuart Taylor, Lillie Bullard
3. Sean Sellers	c. Sgt. Roger Motley
4. Velma Barfield	d. Stephen Sims, 24; Tommy Temple, 17; Arden Alane Felsher, 17
5. Judy Buenoano	e. Carla Larson
6. Kevin Stanford	f. James Goodyear; Michael Goodyear, 19
7. Paul William Scott	g. Roger Tackett
8. Donald R. "Donnie" Bull, Jr.	h. Deborah Ruth, 32; David Thornton, 32; Jerry Lynn Dean, 27
9. Brandon Astor Jones AKA "Wilbur May"	i. Vonda Bellafatto, 32; Paul Bellafatto, 43; Robert Bower, 32
10. John Steven Huggins	j. Donna Tompkins, 30; Justine Tompkins, 3
11. Max Alexander Soffar	k. Baerbel Poore, 20
12. Christina Riggs	l. Nancy Allen, 26
13. Lynda Lyon Block	m. Gloria Leathers
14. Aileen Wournos	n. Justin Thomas, 5; Shelby, 2
15. Lois Nadean Smith	o. James Alessi
16. Wanda Jean Allen	p. Cindy Baillee, 21

Answers: 1h; 2l; 3i; 4b; 5f; 6k; 7o; 8j; 9g; 10e; 11d; 12n; 13c; 14a; 15p; 16m

condemned to death include accounts of their past lives by close friends and family members who oppose capital punishment in their cases. Even statements from various family members of victims express opposition to the death penalty because of its alleged barbarism. Considered especially barbaric is the administration of capital punishment to those who are mentally retarded and thus less accountable for their capital crimes (Human Rights Watch 2001a). Also, the families of executed offenders suffer in different ways. Knowing that a convicted offender has suffered the ultimate punishment may be comforting for some family members of victims, but nothing can replace their loss. Should the family members of death row inmates also be made to suffer? This is a pervasive and unresolved issue (Cross and Knauf 2002).

The Death Penalty as Unfairness. Some convicted offenders are wrongly convicted (Harmon 2001). Evidence subsequently discovered has led to freeing several persons who were formerly on death row awaiting execution (Westervelt and Humphrey 2001). One study has shown, for instance, that over 400 persons have been wrongly convicted of capital crimes and sentenced to death as miscarriages of justice in the United States. Evidence eventually discovered and used to free these persons included the confessions of the real perpetrators, reversals on appeal, and unofficial judgments when crimes were found not to have occurred (e.g., missing bodies eventually discovered and found not to have been murdered) (Mello 2001). In some instances, persons have been convicted of crimes as the result of false confessions. In short, some offenders, because of psychological problems, drug abuse, or other types of issues, confess to crimes that they did not commit. It is difficult to know in every case when a false confession is being given (Sigurdsson and Gudjonsson 2001).

Another dimension of the unfairness argument pertains to gender and the fact that although there are many female murderers, relatively few of them are ever sentenced to death. This has been referred to as gender politics, and there seem to be sound political reasons behind court actions in capital cases against women where the death penalty is not sought (Rapaport 2001).

For many capital punishment opponents, another criticism is that the death penalty is disproportionately applied to blacks compared with other race/ethnic categories. This is especially true if the perpetrator is black and the victim is white. Those convicted of capital murder where the victim is white are more likely to receive the death penalty compared with those convicted of killing nonwhite victims. Black homicide offenders who killed white victims are most likely to receive a death sentence (Williams and Holcomb 2001).

The Death Penalty as Strictly Revenge.   By condoning the death penalty, some observers argue, the U.S. Supreme Court has sanctioned vengeance, which is an unacceptable justification for imposing capital punishment (Death Penalty Information Center 2002). For persons who are retarded or intellectually disabled, it is likely that they cannot reach the level of culpability necessary to trigger the need for the death penalty.

The Death Penalty as a Costlier Penalty Than Life-without-Parole Sentences.
Opponents of capital punishment cite the cost factor to show that executing prisoners under death sentences is more costly over time than imprisoning them for life (Whitehead and Blankenship 2000). However, a key reason for the high cost of executing prisoners is that they can file endless appeals and delay the imposition of their death sentences (Palmer 2001). In 1996, Congress acted to limit the number of appeals inmates on death rows could file. Thus, it is expected in future years that the length of time between conviction and imposition of the death penalty will be greatly abbreviated. This shorter period of time will decrease the expense of death penalty appeals and undermine this particular argument.

The Death Penalty as an Arbitrary Punishment Incorrectly Applied.
Although bifurcated trials have decreased the racial bias in death penalty applications, disproportionality of death sentences according to race and ethnicity has not been eliminated (Halim and Stiles 2001). While some persons argue that some races and ethnic categories have higher rates of capital murder and thus are disproportionately represented on death row, other persons say that the death penalty continues to be applied in a discriminatory manner in many jurisdictions (Loney 2001). However, some writers have contended that there are inherent flaws associated with the death penalty. First, in rape-murder death penalty cases, a particularly gendered form of racism is perpetuated in

which the overwhelming percentage of victims are white women and black women victims are largely discounted. Second, these cases underscore the inability of death penalty schemes to ensure that the death penalty is appropriate for the individual defendant, not just the crime. The application of the death penalty to a defendant may act as a salve in an individual case, but it is a ruse that allows us to ignore the deep social problems that contributed to who the defendant is and to his raping and murdering of a woman (Crocker 2001).

The Death Penalty as a Weak Deterrent to Murder.   The literature strongly supports the idea that the death penalty apparently has no discernable deterrent effect (Sarat 2001). Persons will commit murder anyway, even knowing

 **BOX 9.6**

A DEATH ROW INMATE IS A DEATH ROW INMATE IS A DEATH ROW INMATE . . .

Huntsville, Texas, February 3, 1998

In Huntsville, Texas, on February 3, 1998, a white, attractive 38-year-old female, Karla Faye Tucker, was executed by lethal injection for the horrible ax murders of Jerry Lynn Dean and Deborah Thornton in a bloody evening in 1983. Tucker stated at her trial that she had multiple orgasms as she axed to death Deborah Thornton, a companion of Jerry Dean's, while they were in bed. The American Civil Liberties Union, Amnesty International, the Pope, Jesse Jackson, Pat Robertson, and Jerry Falwell sent strong messages to the governor of Texas to spare Tucker, presumably because she had become a "born-again" Christian while awaiting her fate on death row in the Texas prison in Huntsville. Her bid for clemency from the Texas Board of Pardons and Paroles was denied unanimously. The U.S. Supreme Court denied Tucker's eleventh-hour appeals. The governor of Texas issued a statement shortly before Tucker was scheduled to be executed, washing his hands of the affair and leaving it up to God's judgment to reckon with Tucker. Geraldo Rivera, Charles Grodin, and CNN talk shows spent a great deal of their time covering the Tucker execution. The media swarmed about the Texas prison in Huntsville, since Tucker would be the first woman to be executed by Texas since 1863. It was definitely a high-profile media event. Following Tucker's execution,

anti–capital punishment advocates spoke out on the evils of capital punishment. Proponents of capital punishment were satisfied that the laws of Texas were upheld and that equality was still alive and well, even on death row. Executions of females are rare events in the United States. In 1998, fewer than 30 women awaited execution on death rows throughout the nation. The Tucker saga was extraordinary, however, since Tucker was (1) white, (2) female, (3) attractive, and (4) had converted to Christianity. However, as proponents of capital punishment noted, the gender, appearance, and conversion experience of Tucker were all irrelevant to her fate. She had murdered two persons in cold blood, and the circumstances under which these murders occurred were particularly egregious. Tucker was being punished in accordance with the laws of Texas.

Huntsville, Texas, February 10, 1998

Exactly one week following Tucker's execution, Steven Renfro was executed at the same prison in Huntsville, Texas. Who is Steven Renfro? Renfro, 40, was convicted of killing three people in a blaze of gunfire that turned a police car into Swiss cheese. He was convicted in the August 26, 1996, brutal slayings of his live-in girlfriend, an aunt, and an acquaintance, and wounding a po-that there is a chance they may be caught eventually and executed for the crime. An examination of crime statistics and comparisons of those jurisdictions where the death penalty is applied and jurisdictions where it isn't applied show few, if any, differences in capital murder cases. Thus, the argument goes, if capital punishment fails to deter capital murder, then it should be abolished (Palmer 2001). And the death penalty is only an effective deterrent to the extent that potential murderers understand that they may suffer execution if they commit a capital crime. Some opponents of the death penalty have cited a lack of mental capacity among certain murderers and that it would be legally improper to execute them because they lack the capacity to understand the nature and consequences of their actions (Brodsky, Zapf, and Boccaccini 2001).

lice officer who pursued him. Renfro told a jury at his trial in 1997 that he "should be put to death." He felt that he would kill people in the future, injure people. Renfro was a good-looking white male. In contrast to Karla Tucker, Renfro shunned the media spotlight, refusing to speak with reporters and wanting no court actions to save his life. The prosecutor in Renfro's case was Harrison County Attorney Rick Berry, a high school classmate of Renfro's at Marshall High School.

Tallahassee, Florida, February 10, 1998

In Tallahassee, Florida, a woman, Judi Buenoano, 54, also known as the "Black Widow," was electrocuted in Florida's electric chair on March 30, 1998. Mrs. Buenoano was convicted of the 1971 slaying of her husband, Air Force Sgt. James Goodyear, by arsenic poisoning. She collected over $85,000 in insurance benefits. She also murdered her own son, Michael, 19, who was partially paralyzed and wearing leg and arm braces. She pushed him out of a canoe into a river, drowning him. Buenoano was also charged with the poisoning death of her boyfriend, Bobby Joe Morris, in Trinidad, Colorado, in 1978. However, since she received the death penalty in Florida, Colorado authorities elected not to try her on this other murder charge. Finally, she almost succeeded in killing her fiance, John Gentry, with a car

bomb in downtown Pensacola, Florida, in 1983. She had met Gentry at a mud-wrestling match in the early 1980s. At first, she tried to poison him. Gentry says that Buenoano gave him some "vitamin" pills, but the pills made him sick. The pills were laced with arsenic and led to an investigation of the circumstances of the other deaths. There was no fanfare for Buenoano as there was in the Tucker execution. Buenoano was white and, according to the media, not attractive. Further, she did not experience any religious conversion like Karla Tucker, nor did she claim to be a born-again Christian. The ACLU, Amnesty International, and the media chose to ignore Mrs. Buenoano.

Whether you are for or against the death penalty, what do these cases say about how society views persons of different genders and whether they should be executed for capital crimes? Are convicted offenders sent to death rows to be executed or rehabilitated? If states and the federal government are going to execute people for capital offenses, how important should the gender issue be? Should it make any difference whether the death row inmate is male or female? Should religious conversion be weighed in favor of commuting sentences to life-without-parole? Should physical appearance and attractiveness or unattractiveness be considered or even mentioned by the media or others? What do you think?

Source: Adapted from the Associated Press, "Man Welcomes Execution in Texas," February 9, 1998:A2; adapted from the Associated Press, " 'Black Widow' to Go to Electric Chair for Poisoning Her Husband," February 10, 1998; "Face-to-Face with Jesus." *People,* February 16, 1998:157; adapted from the Associated Press, "Poisoner Executed in Florida," April 3, 1998.

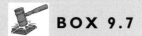 **BOX 9.7**

Amnesty International, the American Civil Liberties Union, and various other interested organizations have raised the issue of whether the death penalty should be applied to persons who are mentally ill or otherwise mentally incapacitated. Several important U.S. Supreme Court cases have addressed this issue. Some of these cases are briefed below.

- *Solesbee v. Balkcom*, 339 U.S. 9, 70 S.Ct. 457 (1950). Solesbee was convicted of murder. He filed a writ of *habeas corpus,* seeking to have a hearing on whether he was insane. Then he was sentenced to death. At the time, Georgia governors had the power of determining whether such a hearing should be convened and determining on their own authority whether convicts were mentally competent. The U.S. Supreme Court rejected Solesbee's claim that he had a constitutional right to a postconviction proceeding to determine his sanity. The U.S. Supreme Court said that persons legally convicted and sentenced to death have no statutory or constitutional right to a judicially conducted or supervised trial or inquisition on the question of insanity subsequent to sentence.

- *Ake v. Oklahoma*, 470 U.S. 68, 105 S.Ct. 1087 (1985). Ake was charged with two counts of first-degree murder. He declared that he was indigent, and counsel was appointed for him. He also requested the assistance of a competent psychiatrist to determine whether he was sane. Ake's defense was that he was insane, thus it would be the state's obligation to furnish him with a psychiatrist to examine him and make a determination. A psychiatrist did so and found Ake to be incompetent to stand trial. He was confined in a mental hospital for a period of time. After six weeks of treatment, he was found to be competent to stand trial. His attorney asked for another psychiatric evaluation, independent of the state-provided one, but the judge denied this request, claiming that the expense was prohibitive. He was convicted. No testimony was given

by psychiatrists during the sentencing phase of his trial. The death penalty was imposed when the state psychiatrist indicated that Ake's future dangerousness warranted it. Ake appealed. The U.S. Supreme Court reversed his conviction, holding that when a defendant has made a preliminary showing that his sanity at the time of the offense is likely to be a significant factor, then the state must provide access to a psychiatrist's assistance on this issue if the defendant cannot otherwise afford one.

- *Ford v. Wainwright*, 477 U.S. 399, 106 S.Ct. 2595 (1986). Ford was convicted of murder in Florida in 1974 and sentenced to death. At no time during his trial had he shown any signs of being mentally incompetent. However, when he appealed in 1982, he was examined by two psychiatrists over a period of time and determined to be mentally incompetent. His condition deteriorated to such an extent that he was almost catatonic. Nevertheless, the governor of Florida appointed three other psychiatrists to examine Ford, and they found him sane enough to be executed. However, the U.S. Supreme Court decided in Ford's favor, holding that insane persons cannot be executed. Furthermore, the U.S. Supreme Court held that Florida's procedures for determining a person's competence were inadequate. This is an interesting case, because Ford was sane when he committed the offense and was convicted of it; he became insane afterwards.

- *Penry v. Lynaugh*, 492 U.S. 302, 109 S.Ct. 2934 (1989). Penry was a mentally retarded inmate convicted of capital murder in Texas. He had an IQ of 54 and a mental age of 6 years old. He was 22 when the capital murder was committed, and he was sentenced to death. During the sentencing phase of Penry's trial, the judge failed to advise the jury that it could consider evidence of Penry's mental retardation and childhood abuse. Penry appealed his death sentence, contending that mentally retarded persons cannot be executed and that the judge had failed to give the jury proper instructions concerning mitigating circumstances including his mental retardation and childhood abuse. The U.S. Supreme Court overturned Penry's death sentence as unconstitutional, largely because the jury had not been adequately instructed with respect to the mitigating evidence. Penry was retried in 1990 and again found guilty of capital murder and sentenced to death. See *Penry v. Johnson* (2001) below for a discussion of Penry's subsequent appeal of his 1990 conviction and death sentence.

- ***Demosthenes v. Baal***, 495 U.S. 731, 110 S.Ct. 2223 (1990). Baal had attempted to rob a woman in Nevada and subsequently had stabbed her repeatedly, causing her death, stolen her car, and fled. Following Baal's subsequent arrest in Reno in February 1988, he was given his Miranda warnings and confessed. Two psychiatrists examined him in March 1988 and determined that he was competent to stand trial for the first-degree murder charges. He entered a plea of not guilty by reason of insanity. Before his trial, he was examined by other psychiatrists, who confirmed the earlier psychiatric diagnosis that Baal was "disturbed" but competent. Baal thus withdrew his not guilty by reason of insanity plea and pleaded guilty to first-degree murder and robbery, both with a deadly weapon. A three-judge Nevada panel accepted his guilty plea and sentenced him to death. On appeal he won a stay of execution from the Nevada Supreme Court. Then he tried to waive a federal review of his claim to insanity. In May 1990, Edwin and Doris Baal, his parents, filed a *habeas corpus* petition on his behalf, asserting that Baal was not competent to waive the federal review. The U.S. Supreme Court rejected the petition, concluding that federal *habeas corpus* statutes to interfere with the course of state proceedings must occur only in specified circumstances, which in this case were clearly lacking. The Nevada Supreme Court had granted the stay of execution without finding that Baal was not competent to waive further proceedings. The U.S. Supreme Court, therefore, vacated the stay of execution

and entitled Nevada to proceed with his execution as scheduled.

- ***Penry v. Johnson***, 532 U.S. 782, 121 S.Ct. 1910 (2001). Penry was convicted of first-degree murder in 1989 in a Texas court and sentenced to death. However, the conviction was overturned because it violated the Eighth Amendment. Penry was retried in 1990 and again found guilty of capital murder. During the penalty phase of the proceedings, the defense presented extensive evidence of Penry's mental impairments and childhood abuse. Prosecutors introduced and read into the record over a defense objection a 1977 psychiatric evaluation of Penry prepared at Penry's attorney's request in another court matter unrelated to the murder at issue. The report concluded in part that if Penry were released, he would be dangerous to others. Subsequently, the judge gave the jury detailed instructions including a consideration of mitigating circumstances and Penry was again sentenced to death. However, the judge provided jurors a document with the original special issues from Penry's first trial. Again a question arose about whether the judge had adequately permitted the jury to consider and give effect to the particular mitigating evidence. Penry appealed through a *habeas corpus* action, claiming in part that the introduction into evidence of his earlier psychiatric report was a violation of his Fifth Amendment right against self-incrimination. Further, Penry contended that the judge's jury instructions were inadequate because they did not permit the jury to consider and give effect to his particular mitigating evidence. The state denied Penry *habeas corpus* relief and Penry appealed to the U.S. District Court, which affirmed the Texas trial court. An appeal to the Circuit Court of Appeals resulted in a similar affirmation of the sentence. Thus, Penry appealed to the SC seeking *habeas corpus* relief. The U.S. Supreme Court heard the case and held that the introduction of the earlier psychiatric examination during Penry's sentencing phase did not warrant *habeas corpus* relief. However, the U.S. Supreme Court also held that the judge's instructions on mitigating circumstances

(continued)

BOX 9.7 (Continued)

failed to provide the jury with a vehicle to give effect to mitigating circumstances of mental retardation and childhood abuse as required by the Eighth and Fourteenth Amendments. Thus, the U.S. Supreme Court reversed in part, and affirmed in part, the decision of the trial court.

- *Atkins v. Virginia*, _____ U.S._____, 122 S.Ct. 2242 (2002). Atkins was convicted of capital murder by a Virginia jury and sentenced to death. Atkins, together with William Jones, abducted Eric Nesbitt in August 1996 and robbed and killed him. Both Jones and Atkins implicated one another at the subsequent murder trial. After a jury finding of guilt, Atkins was subjected to the penalty phase of the trial, where his defense counsel offered the testimony of Dr. Evan Nelson, a forensic psychologist, who testified that Atkins was mildly mentally retarded and had an IQ of 59. Virginia rebutted this testimony with its own expert, who gave the opinion that Atkins was not mentally retarded but rather was of average intelligence, although he had an antisocial personality disorder. Subsequently, Atkins was sentenced to death and appealed, contending that the execution of a mentally retarded offender is a violation of his Eighth Amendment right against cruel and unusual punishment. The Virginia Supreme Court affirmed Atkins's conviction and sentence, and Atkins appealed to the U.S. Supreme Court, which heard the case. The U.S. Supreme Court reversed Atkins's death sentence, holding that the execution of mentally retarded criminals will not measurably advance the deterrent or retributive purpose of the death penalty and that such punishment is excessive.
- *The Case of James Colburn, 43.* On March 26, 2003, James Colburn, 43, was strapped to a death chamber gurney in a Texas prison in Huntsville and executed by lethal injection. This was the twelfth execution of 2003 in Texas, the nation's most aggressive death penalty state. Colburn was convicted for the 1994 murder of a Conroe, Texas, woman. Colburn was on

parole at the time he entered the woman's home and stabbed her to death. Colburn admitted to the murder, was convicted, and sentenced to death. Subsequently, Colburn's defense counsels attempted to get his death sentence set aside. They requested that he be given a life-without-parole sentence instead. Their argument was based on the fact that an independent psychiatric diagnosis of Colburn revealed that he suffered from paranoid schizophrenia, that he was a ninth-grade dropout, and that because of his low educational level and mental illness, he should not be executed. Defense lawyers argued in late appeals in February 2003 that Colburn was delusional and that psychiatric results conflicted with state experts who determined that Colburn was competent. However, prosecutors retorted that while Colburn may have been suffering from this mental illness, he was competent and understood why he was facing lethal injection. "The issue was whether or not the [mental] illness kept him from knowing right from wrong," said Jay Hileman, a former assistant district attorney who prosecuted Colburn. "It didn't, and so he wasn't found to be insane," said Hileman. Colburn himself agreed. Colburn said, "None of this should have happened, and now that I'm dying, there is nothing left to worry about. I know it was a mistake. I have no one to blame but myself. It is no big deal that I knew the difference between right and wrong, and I pray that everyone involved overlooks this stupidity. Everybody has problems and I won't be a part of the problem any more. I can quit worrying now. It's [being executed by lethal injection] going to be like passing out on drugs."

Under what circumstances should persons be executed who suffer from different kinds of mental illnesses? How should one's competence be evaluated? How can we determine whether someone knows the difference between right and wrong at the time they commit capital murder? What do you think?

Source: Adapted from the Associated Press, "Mentally Ill Man Executed," March 27, 2003.

The Death Penalty as an Unpopular Punishment.   It has been suggested that there is growing lack of public support for the death penalty in the United States. However, several national surveys show that over 75 percent of those interviewed support the death penalty and its application (Rivkind and Shatz 2001).

WHAT COMPENSATION IS GIVEN TO EXONERATED PRISONERS?

No one knows the precise number of convicted offenders who are actually innocent of their conviction offenses. In recent years, technological advancements, including the use of DNA for identifying those who have committed murder, rape, and other offenses, have led to numerous exonerations of previously convicted offenders. In fact, in 2002 the U.S. Justice Department made available $500,000 in federal grants for inmate DNA tests (Klug 2002:14). These tests are expensive, averaging about $2,000 each. In a majority of states, it has been determined through a re-examination of crucial crime-scene evidence that some of those convicted of serious crimes are in fact innocent. For instance, 34-year-old Ray Krone was convicted by an Arizona court for the murder of a Phoenix, Arizona, barmaid in 1991. Krone claimed he was innocent of the crime, but circumstantial evidence pointed to his guilt. At the time, he was a U.S. Postal Service employee making $30,000 a year. He had a home, a dune buggy, and retirement savings. All of this was lost when Krone was convicted in 1992 and sentenced to death.

Krone appealed his murder conviction and won a new trial in 1995 on a technicality. The prosecution had taken too long to turn over crucial evidence to Krone's attorney prior to his trial. However, Krone was convicted again in 1996, this time receiving a life sentence. His second conviction was influenced in large part by the testimony of a bite-mark specialist who testified that Krone's teeth matched the pattern of a bite mark on the victim's neck. In 2000, Krone's attorney persuaded a judge to run DNA samples from a preserved saliva specimen from the original 1991 murder. It turned out that the DNA matched a sex offender who was already serving time in another Arizona prison. The sex offender, Kenneth Phillips, had lived just 600 yards from the site of the slaying but had not been a suspect. Krone was accused because he had gone out with the murder victim a few nights before she was killed. Following the DNA analysis, which was not readily available at the time of Krone's original murder conviction, Krone was released from prison and Kenneth Phillips was charged with the woman's murder (Willing 2002:1A–2A).

When Krone was exonerated after serving over 10 years in prison, he attempted to sue the State of Arizona for compensation for his time in prison. However, all he got for his trouble was an apology from the prosecutor and $50, the usual exit payment to the state's convicts. It is unlikely that Krone will ever collect any money from Arizona, since under Arizona law, prosecutors and other government officials, even the police, are protected from lawsuits under various types of immunity. It is estimated that during the period 1972–2002, more than 200 inmates have been deemed wrongly convicted and released from death sentences or lengthy prison terms. In 2002 only 15 states provided varying amounts of compensation to exonerated inmates. These states are shown in Box 9.8.

One of the problems with being compensated for a wrongful conviction is that the authorities (e.g., the police, prosecution, court) were merely doing their jobs. Rooted in early American history and in England, the practice of insulating public officials from lawsuits was instituted to help these officials from

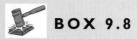 **BOX 9.8**

JURISDICTIONS THAT COMPENSATE EXONERATED OFFENDERS

Jurisdiction	Compensation Limit	When Approved	Requirements for Compensation
Alabama	$50,000 minimum per year	2001	Conviction must be reversed because of innocence
California	$100 per day incarcerated	2000	Must be pardoned by governor because of sentence
D.C.	None	1981	Reversal of conviction because of innocence
Illinois	$150,000	1945	Pardon by governor because of innocence
Iowa	$25,000 per year	1997	Conviction reversed
Maine	$300,000	1993	Pardon by governor because of innocence
Maryland	Actual damages	1963	Pardon by governor because of innocence
New Hampshire	$20,000	1977	Finding of innocence by court
New Jersey	Twice annual pay if exonerated	1997	None, other than exoneration
New York	None	1984	Pardon by governor, acquittal, or reversal of guilty verdict because of innocence
North Carolina	$150,000	1947	Pardon by governor because of innocence
Ohio	$25,000 a year	1986	Conviction must be vacated or reversed
Tennessee	Actual damages	1984	Exoneration or pardon by governor because of innocence
Texas	$500,000	2001	Pardon by governor because of innocence
West Virginia	Reasonable damages	1987	Pardon by governor because of innocence
Wisconsin	$25,000 but state board may ask legislature for more	1913	Must prove innocence to a state board
Federal government	$5,000	1948	Pardon by president because of innocence or court finding of not guilty

Source: Pace University School of Law, White Plains, New York, 2002.

being bankrupted because of their errors. Today, it is often sufficient for officials to claim that they were acting in good faith when conducting their prosecutions against the accused and/or presenting incriminating evidence in court. This principle also applies to expert witnesses, such as those who gave testimony about bite marks in Krone's case mentioned earlier.

Even in states that have established compensation guidelines for exonerated offenders, getting money from these states can prove to be quite difficult. It is often insufficient to have one's conviction overturned, particularly on one or more technicalities. The exonerated offenders must convince the governor or state board of their innocence. For instance, Jay Smith was a high school principal in Upper Merion, Pennsylvania. He was convicted in the death of a teacher and her two children, presumably in order to help her husband collect a large insurance settlement. However, the case was overturned when it was determined that police had failed to turn over crucial evidence to show that the woman's husband was more likely the killer. Smith sued the police civilly, although his case was thrown out. The court said that there was "overwhelming evidence" against Smith, including a pin that belonged to the victim that was found in his car (Willing 2002:2A).

Attorneys who have sought compensation for their exonerated clients have not had good success with their lawsuits against public officials in federal courts. Most cases seeking damages in federal court are dismissed. However, in recent years, a new class of lawsuits has originated that is directed at police officers who are accused of misconduct. In suits alleging misconduct, police officers are not immune from being sued. In Illinois, for example, four exonerated offenders brought suit against police who either ignored or hid crucial evidence that pointed to the real killers. The exonerated men were paid $36 million by Illinois to settle their case. Another case was settled for $15 million by a Chicago court where police misconduct was alleged (Willing 2002:2A).

Commuting Sentences from Death to Life without the Possibility of Parole. In more than a few instances, death row inmates have had their death sentences commuted to life without the possibility of parole for a variety of reasons. Some research has investigated the conduct of prisoners who have had their death sentences changed to life imprisonment and the potential changes in their conduct as a result. Some observers might suspect that such inmates might pose behavior problems to others when released into the general prison population. A sample of death row inmates totaling 39 was studied in Indiana between the years 1972 and 1999, for example. The disciplinary conduct while on death row was compared with their subsequent conduct while in the general prison population. Only 14 inmates became involved in 24 violent acts during this period, with 26 percent of these violent acts occurring while the inmates were on death row and 20 percent were committed while the inmates were in the general prison population. Less than a third of these acts involved serious physical injuries to others (Reidy, Cunningham, and Sorensen 2001). Thus, in this instance, there did not appear to be a significant difference in the conduct of these inmates when their status was changed from death row to the general prison population.

INMATE GRIEVANCE PROCEDURES

Although it is not a prerequisite for inmates to exhaust all state remedies before filing a Section 1983 petition in federal courts, there is an exception provided under Title 42, U.S.C., Section 1997 (2003), whereby a federal judge may refer inmate lawsuits back to the state correctional systems where they originated, if a U.S. Department of Justice–certified grievance procedure exists. Virginia was the first state to establish a certified inmate grievance procedure in 1982. The administrative procedures for inmate grievances must satisfy certain minimum standards, including the provision that inmates and employees perform advisory roles, maximum time limits are established for written replies to grievances, priority processing of grievances is made on an emergency basis where undue delay might result in inmate harm, and an independent review is made of the disposition of grievances by a person or persons not under the direct supervision or control of the correctional facility (Toch 1995b). Thus, the number of inmate petitions filed in federal courts will be affected by the presence or absence of certified administrative grievance procedures as internal remedies.

The most frequent constitutional rights violations cited in civil petitions filed by prisoners under Section 1983 are the cruel and unusual punishment provisions of the Eighth Amendment (*Pugh v. Locke* 1976; *Hutto v. Finney* 1978; *Reynolds v. Sheriff, City of Richmond* 1983), the unreasonable search and seizure provisions of the Fourth Amendment (*Burnette v. Phelps* 1985; *Hanrahan v. Lane* 1984; *Smith v. Montgomery County, MD* 1986; *Cook v. City of New York* 1984; *Gardner v. Johnson* 1977), and the due process and equal protection under the law provisions of the Fourteenth Amendment (*Owens v. Brierley* 1971; *Martinez Rodriguez v. Jimenez* 1976). Other violations upon which inmate petitions are based include but are not limited to freedom of speech, privacy, and religious practices.

Inmate Disciplinary Councils

An intervening factor influencing inmate litigation in the courts has been the large-scale establishment of alternative dispute resolution mechanisms for prisoner grievances. These mechanisms include inmate grievance procedures, ombudsmen, mediation, inmate councils, legal assistance, and external review bodies (Toch 1995b). These mechanisms were stimulated largely by the 1967 President's Commission on Law Enforcement and the Administration of Justice. Although some state corrections facilities had internal prisoner grievance mechanisms, many prisons lacked such systems. By 1982, all 50 states had established inmate grievance systems. Thus, court caseloads were eased as internal prison committees and administrative personnel responded positively to inmate grievances as an alternative to filing petitions with the court alleging civil rights violations. These internal alternative dispute mechanisms have not functioned as originally anticipated to reduce the sheer numbers of inmate petition filings in recent years, however (Contact Center, Inc. 1987).

In Texas, for instance, inmate lawsuits filed in state courts increased from 50,000 in 1990 to 132,000 in 1997 (Reynolds and Steffek 1997:5). Many of these lawsuits are frivolous, and inmates have no hope of winning them. Presently, about 25 percent of all civil filings in U.S. courts are inmate petitions.

In an effort to reduce this flood of inmate litigation, particularly frivolous litigation, the Legal Services Committee of the American Correctional Association has proposed guidelines that will establish an inmate litigation support program. The ACA recommendations include:

1. Ensuring that the inmate grievance system not only is in place and certified, but is genuinely dedicated to meaningful resolution of valid complaints.
2. Experimenting with providing attorneys for inmates, rather than access to law libraries, and supplying a filtering mechanism of legal consultation that will discourage the pursuit of fruitless claims.
3. Enacting legislation to provide disincentives to frivolous litigation, requiring exhaustion of administrative remedies (grievance procedures) and streamlining state court procedures (Reynolds and Steffek 1997:4).

Some of the disincentives contemplated by the Legal Services Committee of the ACA include imposing partial filing fees or court costs and raising the level of court scrutiny. But one of the results of closing courthouse doors to inmates is to raise their frustration level and create greater tension in their various institutions. Certification is recommended to ensure fairness in arbitrating inmate grievances. What forms of relief will the system provide? Who will review which complaints and what types of grievances will be considered? The ultimate aim of these recommendations is to establish grievance procedures that will be perceived as fair by both administration and inmates alike (Reynolds and Steffek 1997:4–5).

Administrative Review of Inmate Grievances

Some misunderstanding exists concerning the functions and origins of inmate councils that hear prisoner grievances. Some writers have erroneously concluded that inmate councils are somehow evidence of participatory management. Participatory management implies that in prison examples, inmates would have a say in the governance of prisons. This is not so. Rather, inmate councils function as buffers between the administration and prisoners. They are also designed to resolve petty disputes among inmates.

Tom Murton, a former administrator with the Arkansas prison system, has said that some persons have claimed that inmate government exists, that it is corrupting, and that it is a dysfunctional modality for prison management (Murton 1976). Murton indicates that in most participatory models where inmate councils are used, the prisoners have not been given any sort of real power in the sense that they can make decisions affecting their lives. He says that with a few notable exceptions, inmate councils have just grown. They have come into existence in response to crises, to aid in communications, or just because it seemed like a good thing to do at the time. He says that there are some obvious positive effects resulting from involving the participants in their own destiny. Inmates can sanction other inmates and provide the means of addressing various minor grievances that otherwise might result in court action.

In virtually every prison where inmate councils exist to resolve petty disputes, administrative overview or review is conducted. This is to ensure that prisoners do not exploit other inmates with abuses of discretion. Administrative review is fundamental to operating inmate councils in Texas prisons as well as other jurisdictions (Reynolds and Steffek 1997).

SUMMARY

The inmate litigation explosion began during the 1970s and 1980s and continues unabated. This litigation involves the filing of numerous lawsuits alleging violations of civil rights, torts, and *habeas corpus* petitions. The prisoner rights movement has generated considerable interest among criminal justice and corrections professionals. Assisting other inmates in the preparation of lawsuits are jailhouse lawyers, so named because of their familiarity with the law, procedural matters pertaining to inmate filings, and the rights of inmates generally. However, jailhouse lawyers don't always act out of unselfishness for others. Some jailhouse lawyers use their knowledge to exploit inmates or utilize their knowledge for a power advantage.

Courts were reluctant to become involved in jail and prison lawsuits until the 1940s. This was because of the hands-off doctrine, which caused courts, especially the U.S. Supreme Court, to view prison and jail matters as best resolved by prison wardens and county sheriffs. The thinking, though faulty, was that these persons were in the best position to understand inmate complaints and resolve them. The hands-off doctrine was abandoned during the 1940s through U.S. Supreme Court decisions in the cases of *Ex parte Hull* and *Coffin v. Reichard.* Gradually, courts have increasingly become involved in jail and prison inmate litigation and have been instrumental in ensuring that prisoners are entitled to the preservation of most of their constitutional rights. The courts have subsequently adopted a reasonableness test, which determines whether the rights of inmates are more important than the rights of correctional institutions to insure the safety of staff and other inmates.

Three major avenues for filing lawsuits against prison or jail systems were discussed. These include *habeas corpus* petitions, which challenge the fact as well as the length and nature of confinement. A second type of challenge is through the Federal Tort Claims Act. Tort actions allege wrongdoing, misconduct, or negligence on the part of correctional staff or administrators that result in physical and/or psychological damages to prisoners. Tort actions involve accusations of negligence against prison staff. These may involve a failure to act in a prescribed manner, such as a situation where inmate injury is not reported by a correctional officer. Typically, tort actions seek money from prison and jail organizations or personnel as damages.

A third avenue for filing claims is through Title 42, U.S.C. Section 1983 (2003), which is a civil rights claim. Civil rights violations involve inmates who sue under the civil rights statute. Civil rights violations may be based on race, ethnicity, or socioeconomic status, and they typically reflect possible negligence on the part of prison/jail administrators regarding each prisoner's right to equal protection under the laws, as set forth in the Fourteenth Amendment. While the majority of lawsuits filed by prisoners are *habeas corpus,* tort, or civil rights related, several other constitutional amendments have been the subject of inmate court actions. Defendants in these legal proceedings usually seek to have these lawsuits dismissed. Thus, they file motions to dismiss or motions for summary judgment with the courts. Most lawsuits filed by prisoners are dismissed or, if successful, they result in minor monetary awards or other concessions.

Several constitutional amendments were examined which are particularly relevant for inmates. The First Amendment pertains to the right of free speech and expression, as well as freedom of religion. Inmates have challenged prison officials concerning their hair length, facial hair, access to printed materials, and religious rituals involving various items, including marijuana and alcohol. Many of these claims have been dismissed by the courts as frivolous. The Fourth Amendment pertains to unreasonable searches, which in prison settings are inmate cells. Correctional officers do not require warrants to search prisoners' cells during shakedowns. Intentional destruction of inmate property by prison staff is generally unacceptable, and monetary awards have been given to inmates where their allegations of staff misconduct have been sustained in court. This amendment also includes body cavity searches. Several awards have been given, not only to inmates but to visitors, because of the unreasonable nature of body cavity searches by corrections officers.

The Eighth Amendment pertains to the matter of cruel and unusual punishment and is a favored theme of much inmate litigation. Prisoners have alleged that they have too little cell space, although the courts have never determined precisely how much cell space prisoners should have. Two significant cases involving prisoner overcrowding and celling conditions were *Bell v. Wolfish* (1970) and *Rhodes v. Chapman* (1981). In both cases, prisoners lost their claim that they should be celled separately or with fewer cell mates. Prisoners also have complained about the conditions (e.g., heat, cold, moisture) of their surroundings as well as prison food. Most of these inmate claims have been dismissed as frivolous. One especially important issue is the death penalty, which many inmates have attempted to challenge as being cruel and unusual punishment. Despite these challenges, the death penalty continues to be applied in about two-thirds of all states.

Another amendment used for inmate litigation is the Fourteenth Amendment. This is the civil rights amendment, since it guarantees equal treatment to all under the law. Thus, prisoners have seized upon the equal treatment provision and used it to their advantage in seeking relief from the courts. Other claims by prisoners that do not involve constitutional issues directly are whether they should have access to legal assistance and law libraries; whether there is racism; whether an inmate's right to due process is being infringed by particular prison policies or administrative actions; whether prisoners have a right to rehabilitation; whether inmates are entitled to participate in rehabilitative prison programs and counseling, or if they should be able to perform prison labor on request; whether seizures of their personal effects during shakedowns are justified; whether they are misclassified and assigned to a custody level for which they are unsuited; whether they are subjected to cruel and unusual punishment as the result of their confinement conditions; whether prison staff or administrators are negligent in their work performance to the extent that damages to inmates are sustained; and whether inmates with children should have visitation privileges with them for extended periods. All of these matters have been and continue to be litigated.

The death penalty was examined in some detail. The death penalty is presently used as the maximum punishment in about two-thirds of all states. Different methods for applying the death penalty include lethal injection, hanging, shooting, electrocution, and lethal gas, although lethal injection is currently the most frequently used. In 2001 there were nearly 3,600 persons on death rows in the United States. Several of these were 16 or 17 years of age when convicted. The U.S. Supreme Court has ruled that the death penalty cannot be administered to anyone who was under age 16 at the time the capital offense was committed.

Many of the reasons for applying the death penalty were examined. These included the ideas that the death penalty is retribution, a deterrent to others, and a just-desert for committing murder. Opponents of the death penalty say that it is barbaric, often applied in error to innocent persons, more costly than life imprisonment, applied arbitrarily, nothing more than sheer revenge, is not a deterrent, and that most persons in the United States oppose its use. In 2002, however, the death penalty had a 75 percent approval rating in various opinion surveys. The death penalty does appear to be applied in a discriminatory manner. A disproportionately large number of blacks are executed compared with whites. Furthermore, few female murderers receive the death penalty. Presently, the death penalty and its application is most controversial. Also, newly developed technology and advances in DNA research have resulted in some offenders being exonerated and released from prison. Many states and the federal government have adopted reimbursement policies intended to financially compensate those wrongfully convicted of crimes and imprisoned. These reimbursement programs were described.

Finally, the matter of inmate grievances within their institutions was examined. Increasingly, wardens and superintendents are establishing inmate disciplinary councils. These councils, made up exclusively of inmates, hear and decide a large number of complaints and grievances by other inmates against prison officials, staff, and other inmates. Many of these claims are amicably resolved at this level without resorting to expensive litigation through lawsuits in court. Administrative review of inmate claims may also be conducted, where the prison warden and selected staff determine through a form of participative management whether any particular inmate claim has validity and should be resolved in their favor.

QUESTIONS FOR REVIEW

1. What are three civil avenues for filing petitions with the court alleging grievances against prison or jail administration and staff?

2. Is the death penalty cruel and unusual punishment, in the opinion of the U.S. Supreme Court? What are three major cases involving the death penalty?

3. What theories of negligence might be used by inmates in lawsuits against prison or jail administrators and staff?

4. What are some of the rights prisoners have regarding search and seizure of contraband?

5. May prison and jail correctional officers seize any material possessions of prisoners, regardless of whether they constitute contraband?

6. What is meant by double-bunking or double-celling? Is it constitutional? What key cases may be cited regarding this issue?

7. What is a jailhouse lawyer? What decisions have been made by the U.S. Supreme Court condoning or approving jailhouse lawyers or some other form of legal aid for prisoners?

8. What is the hands-off doctrine? Is this doctrine still in effect?

9. What is a *habeas corpus* petition? What are two conditions it may challenge?

10. What is a shakedown? What is a strip search? Who may be strip searched and under what conditions?

SUGGESTED READINGS

del Carmen, Rolando V., Susan E. Ritter, and Betsy A. Witt. *Briefs of Leading Cases in Corrections.* 3d ed. Cincinnati, OH: Anderson Publishing Company, 2002.

Gillespie, L. Kay. *Inside the Death Chamber: Exploring Execution.* Boston: Allyn and Bacon, 2003.

Kelleher, Michael D. and David Van Nuys. *"This is the Zodiac Speaking": Into the Mind of a Serial Killer.* Westport, CT: Praeger, 2002.

Nelson, Lane and Burk Foster. *Death Watch: A Death Penalty Analogy.* Upper Saddle River, NJ: Prentice Hall, 2001.

Reiman, Jeffrey (2001). *The Rich Get Richer and the Poor Get Prison: Ideology, Class, and Criminal Justice.* 6th ed. Boston: Allyn and Bacon, 2001.

INTERNET CONNECTIONS

American Correctional Association
http://www.corrections.com/aca/index

Citizens for Legal Responsibility
http://www.clr.org

Corrections resources
http://www.officer.com/correct

Corrections Industries Association
http://www.correctionalindustries.org

Corrections industries links
http://www.corrections.com/industries

Corrections news
http://www.newstopics.corrections.com

CounterPunch
http://www.counterpunch.org

Death Row Speaks
http://www.deathrowspeaks.net/

National Institute of Corrections
http://www.nicic.org

Online Friends to Death Row Inmates
http://www.freeworldfriends.com

Social work agencies
http://www.sc.edu/swan/national

Unauthorized Federal Prison Manual
http://www.bureauofprisons.com/

Source: AP/Wide World Photos.

Chapter Objectives	*After reading this chapter, the following objectives should be realized:*

1. Describing the history and evolution of parole in the United States.
2. Listing and explaining the philosophy and goals of parole, as well as its functions.
3. Describing successful and unsuccessful parolees.
4. Describing various parole programs, including furloughs, work/study release, halfway houses, and community residential centers.
5. Describing parole boards, their composition and diversity, and their functions.
6. Describing interstate compact agreements.

7. Describing objective parole board criteria, as well as salient factor scores used for early-release decision making.
8. Elaborating different types of parole, including conditional or unconditional prerelease, standard parole with conditions, and intensive supervised parole.
9. Exploring different meaures of recidivism, including reconvictions, rearrests, and return to prison.
10. Describing the parole revocation process, including discussing different criteria used by various states for revoking parole programs.

INTRODUCTION

• *James Howard, 39, was serving seven years in prison for murder. Howard and another man had been convicted of murdering another man with a 12-gauge shotgun in Houston, Texas, in 1979. He was subsequently paroled. While on parole, he absconded to another state. On the run for several years, Howard came close to being arrested in other jurisdictions. In Illinois, for instance, Howard was stopped and arrested by police for driving while intoxicated. However, Howard gave police his brother's name. He was released the following morning on his own recognizance and left Illinois. Later, Illinois police discovered his true identity through fingerprint matches. But it was too late. In Connecticut, however, the authorities finally caught up with Howard. It happened one evening at a honky tonk on the edge of a small town, the Illusions Cafe, in Wolcott. Someone recognized Howard's photo from a wanted poster and called police. He was arrested after a night of country line dancing at the cafe. Police tracked him to the home of a friend in nearby Meriden, Connecticut. What can be done to protect the public against dangerous offenders who are placed on parole? What means can be used to track such persons if they decide to abscond? What does this case say about the usefulness of parole, if anything? What do you think?* [Adapted from the Associated Press. "Fugitive Caught Dancing," February 11, 2002].

• *The Nevada Parole Board heard the case of Ernest R., a 29-year-old robber who had several prior criminal convictions. Ernest R. was in prison for armed robbery of a convenience store, where several persons were seriously injured during his apprehension and arrest. Ernest R. had served six years of a 10-year sentence and was parole-eligible. This was Ernest R.'s third appearance before the parole board. The parole board asked Ernest R. what he had done to improve himself. Did he obtain a G.E.D. while in prison? Had he participated in prison programs? What sort of parole plan did he have if released? Had he made any contacts with employers? Was he taking anger management courses or receiving counseling and therapy for his drug dependencies? Ernest R. had several writeups or bad conduct reports while confined in the penitentiary. He had been in several fights. He was disliked by other inmates. With a smug attitude, Ernest R. told the parole board that he hadn't done any of the things they had inquired about. He hadn't taken any G.E.D. courses, he said, because he hated teachers and authority. He hadn't made any contacts with prospective employers because he thought that it would be a simple task to get a job when he got out. He didn't think he needed counseling or therapy for his drug dependencies. He said he hadn't used drugs since his confinement in the penitentiary. He had refused prison jobs because he didn't like the low wages inmates were paid. He thought that he should be paroled because, in his opinion, he wasn't the one who hurt anyone during the robbery. He said that he had just gone along with a buddy for old time's sake. The parole board rejected his parole request.* [Adapted from Earl Smith and the Associated Press, "Nevada Robber Denied Parole on Third Attempt," July 1, 2001].

• *Norris was serving a sentence of life without the possibility of parole in an Oregon prison. He petitioned the parole board to consider whether he was suitable for rehabilitation. The Oregon Board of Parole and Post-Parole Supervision convened to consider Norris's petition and found him to be suitable for rehabilitation "within a reasonable period of time," according to Section 163.105(4) of the Oregon Criminal Code. However, the Board of Parole refused to change his life-without-the-possibility-of-parole sentence to life with the possibility of parole. Norris petitioned to the Oregon Court of Appeals. On review, the Court of Appeals overturned the Oregon Parole Board's decision and ruled that they must change Norris's sentence to life with the possibility of parole if they find that the prisoner is capable of being rehabilitated. The state appealed to the Oregon Supreme Court, but the Supreme Court affirmed the Court of Appeals decision. Norris is now parole-eligible.* [Adapted from *Norris v. Board of Parole*, 13 P.3d 104 (Or.Sup.Oct.) (2000)].

Parole boards have difficult tasks and awesome responsibilities. They are in the business of attempting to forecast future behavior. Some decisions may result in the release of persons who may be dangerous to themselves or others. There are many types of criminals. We cannot put them into convenient categories and expect them to act in identical ways. Some offenders are more amenable to reform and rehabilitation than others. We don't know with certainty which ones should be granted probation or parole and which ones should be denied these punishment options.

This chapter examines the entire process of parole as it is presently used in the United States. The first part of this chapter examines parole's origins. While no one knows for sure when and where parole was originally used, Alexander Maconochie, a British penal reformer, is given credit for influencing parole in the United States. Maconochie's role as a prison reformer is examined, together with the marks of commendation he originated. The mark system, developed by Maconochie, subsequently evolved into good-time credits presently used by many prison institutions to reward certain inmates for good behavior. The work of an Irish reformer, Walter Crofton, is also examined. Crofton devised tickets-of-leave whereby prisoners could be released early from prison with conditions. These tickets-of-leave are examined. The subsequent development of parole in the United States is examined in some detail.

Next, the chapter examines the philosophy and goals of parole. Not unlike probation, parole is intended as a rehabilitative and reintegrative tool. Several important functions of parole are described. Both manifest and latent functions of parole are examined. These functions have to do with prisoner rehabilitation and reintegration, crime deterrence and control, decreasing prison and jail overcrowding, compensating for sentencing disparities, and improving public safety and protection.

The next section describes parolees and their characteristics. Both successful and unsuccessful parolees are profiled. Several important types of parole programs are featured. Furloughs are discussed, where inmates are given temporary unescorted leaves from their confinement. Work/study release is also described, where offenders may work at a job or pursue educational degrees outside of prison during daytime hours. Halfway houses are also depicted as transitional places for offenders recently released from prison. For each of these programs, the goals, functions, and weaknesses and strengths are presented.

Whenever parolees violate one or more of their parole program conditions, **parole officers** usually detect these violations and report them to parole boards. **Parole boards** usually must decide whether to revoke a parolee's parole program. Parole boards are largely gubernatorial appointments, and no special expertise is required to become a parole board member. Parole boards convene regularly and hear cases where parole-eligible inmates believe they should be released short of serving their full terms. The composition, diversity, and functions of parole boards are described. Because parole boards are imperfect and make poor early-release decisions from time to time, parole has become less popular with the public in recent years. One result of this disenchantment with parole has been to abolish it. While all states continue to have parole boards, at least a fourth of all states have abolished it, replacing it with various alternative early-release schemes, such as determinate sentencing or presumptive sentencing. In these cases, good-time credits become the major means for obtaining one's early release.

One increasingly important development in parole is the establishment of interstate compact agreements. Under such agreements, one state will supervise its residents who have been convicted of crimes in another state. Almost every state participates in this interstate compact agreement. The intent is to make it possible for offenders to be supervised in their own surroundings and be close to their families and support groups. Interstate compact agreements are described.

The chapter next explores various parole board orientations and describes objective parole criteria. The federal government uses a prediction instrument, the Salient Factor Score (SFS 81) to assist the U.S. Parole Commission in determining whether certain federal offenders should be granted early release. The SFS 81 is described. Like many other instruments that attempt to forecast inmate risk, the SFS 81 has several defects. Nevertheless, it continues to be used as one of the criteria to determine one's early-release eligibility.

The next section of this chapter examines various parole programs for offenders who have been released into their communities. These parole programs are conditional and unconditional pre-release, standard parole with conditions, intensive supervised parole, and shock parole. The weaknesses and strengths, as well as the uses of these programs, are described. Shock parole is not unlike shock probation, and it involves a short jail term followed by a period of parole. Intensive supervised parole is expensive, and thus it is used to supervise fewer than 10 percent of all parolees.

When parolees reoffend, this is regarded as recidivism. However, there are many different measures of recidivism. Another part of this chapter delves into the different meanings of recidivism and how parolee failures are determined. The chapter concludes with a discussion of the **parole revocation** process. One important U.S. Supreme Court case, *Morrissey v. Brewer* (1972), is examined in detail. This case is important because it contains several important rights that have subsequently been extended to probationers as well as parolees. Under this ruling, parolees are entitled to a two-stage revocation process and minimum due process rights. These rights are identified and the case is discussed. Several important state-level parole revocation cases are briefed, and various state supreme court or appellate court holdings are noted. While these cases are only binding on parole boards and parolees in the states where they are rendered, these should provide a good idea of the types of violations that frequently come to a parole board's attention and how they have been decided.

PAROLE

Parole is the conditional release of a prisoner from incarceration (either from prison or jail) under supervision after a portion of the sentence has been served. The major distinguishing feature between probation and parole is that **parolees** have served some time incarcerated in either jail or prison, while probationers have avoided incarceration, with limited exceptions. Some common characteristics shared by both parolees and probationers are that (1) they have been convicted of crimes; (2) they are under the supervision or control of probation or parole officers; and (3) they are subject to one or more similar conditions accompanying their probation or parole programs.

The Jurisdictional Difference between Probation and Parole

Probation is a sentence imposed and governed by sentencing judges. In contrast, parolees are under the control of parole boards who determine whether they should be released conditionally and whether their parole programs should be revoked.

The History of Parole in the United States

Parole is not unique to the United States. It has European origins, although we are not exactly sure who should have the credit for inventing it. Early release of offenders from prison for various reasons, especially reform and rehabilitation, occurred in sixteenth century France and Spain, although Great Britain and Wales also used it to some extent at about the same time (Waite 1993). Since most colonists in America originated from England and Wales, these countries have been most influential on the subsequent establishment of parole systems in the United States.

After the Revolutionary War, Great Britain directed numerous prisoners to be transported to remote islands near Australia. Two of these islands were Norfolk and Van Diemen's Land. In 1836, the lieutenant governor of Van Diemen's Land appointed Alexander Maconochie (1787–1860), a former naval officer, as his private secretary. Four years later in 1840, Maconochie was appointed superintendent of a penal colony located on Norfolk Island. Maconochie observed the extensive use of corporal punishment when he initially assumed his new duties. Very much a penal reformer, Maconochie wrote criticisms of the system he administered, and he directed these criticisms to the British Parliament and penal officials. These criticisms quickly made Maconochie unpopular with his administrators, and he was relieved of his superintendent duties at Norfolk in 1844 and returned to England (Morris 2002).

Marks of Commendation. Maconochie was transferred to various nonadministrative posts for the next several years. Eventually, he was appointed on a trial basis to the new governorship or superintendency of Birmingham Borough Prison. Again, he was dismissed from this job after less than two years for what his superiors regarded as excessive leniency in his penal policies. During his involvement with various penal systems, Maconochie consistently pushed for more humane treatment of prisoners. He firmly believed that offenders should be rehabilitated. Furthermore, he suggested an incentive system whereby prisoners could earn early release for good behavior. While he was head of Birmingham Borough Prison, he established a system where prisoners could accumulate **marks of commendation** for good work performed and for complying with prison rules. Thus, through the **mark system,** Maconochie pioneered what later came to be known as good-time credits, which are used today in U.S. prisons.

Marks of commendation resulted in the early release of prisoners. Early release was earned according to the following principles established by Maconochie:

1. Early release should not be computed on the amount of time served, but rather, upon the amount of work completed.
2. Prisoners could earn marks by hard work, better conduct, and industrious working habits. Prisoner release was determined on the basis of the number of marks accumulated.
3. Prisoners must earn everything they received.
4. Prisoners should work in small groups; the entire group would be held accountable for the conduct of individual members.
5. Prisoners would move through various stages of progressively less discipline; eventually, they would be given more rights in their own labor, in order to prepare them for release to society (Barnes and Teeters 1959:419).

Maconochie used his judgment and authority to sanction administrative releases for those more well-behaved, yet forgotten, prisoners. During the four-year period that Maconochie was superintendent of 2,000 twice-convicted prisoners on Norfolk Island, he transformed this brutal convict population into stable, controlled, and productive citizens, who on release came to be known as "Maconochie's Gentlemen" (Morris 2002). These early administrative releases granted by Maconochie to prisoners were not acceptable to the government, and they were chiefly responsible for his early dismissal. However, before his dismissal from these prison posts, Maconochie demonstrated the successfulness and potential of early release. Selectively applied, it functioned as an incentive for prisoners to comply with prison rules and policies. Furthermore, it fostered order within the prison system. Fighting and other forms of prisoner misconduct operated against an inmate's early release, and most convicts were eager to be freed at the earliest possible opportunity. Maconochie created an informal version of what later came to be known as indeterminate sentencing, although an Irishman, Sir Walter Crofton, formally introduced the concept more than a decade after Maconochie had first used it. Maconochie's persistence finally paid off in 1853, when the British Parliament passed the **English Penal Servitude Act.** This Act authorized the establishment of rehabilitative programs for inmates, and banishment was gradually eliminated. In England, at least, Maconochie is considered the father of parole (Clay 2001).

Tickets of Leave and the Irish System.   Impressed with the reforms Maconochie had instituted in British penal policies, Sir Walter Crofton, an Irish reformer and director of Ireland's prison system, gradually established the **Irish system** (Carroll-Burke 2000). The Irish system was a multistage process by which inmates could earn early release from prison. Also called the indeterminate system (the forerunner to indeterminate sentencing in the United States), the Irish system consisted of solitary confinement and hard labor for two years, congregate labor (comparable to what was later used at the Auburn State Penitentiary in New York) for an indeterminate period, limited work on outside jobs (comparable to our present version of **work furloughs**), and finally, early conditional release through **tickets-of-leave.** Tickets-of-leave were authorizations for conditional early release from prison. Violating one or more conditions of the early release resulted in revocation of these leaves and return to prison. Those granted tickets-of-leave were expected to submit regular reports of their progress while free. Tickets-of-leave are acknowledged as the first use of parole.

The American Connection.   Gaylord Hubbell, the Sing Sing, New York, prison warden, traveled to Ireland in 1863 to discuss penal reforms and prisoner rehabilitation with Crofton and to become more acquainted with the Irish system. Although massive prison policy changes were beyond the authority of Hubbell, he was nevertheless influential in bringing about eventual changes in New York sentencing and parole policies (Snyder 2001). When the National Prison Association (later the American Correctional Association) convened for the first time in Cincinnati, Ohio, in 1870, Hubbell, together with Crofton, promoted the Irish system strongly to those in attendance. The membership set forth a Declaration of Principles, including indeterminate sentencing and an elaborate offender classification system (O'Mahony 2002). Crofton was most influential in the development of these principles and the resulting classification system. This classification system is illustrated in Table 10.1.

TABLE 10.1

Mark System Developed by Sir Walter Crofton

Class and Number of Marks to be Gained for Admission to the Intermediate Prisons for Different Sentences[a]	Sentences of Penal Servitude (Years)	Shortest Periods of Imprisonment				Periods of Remission on License
		In Ordinary Prisons		Shortest Period of Detention in Intermediate Prisons		
		Years	Months	Years	Months	
Class 1st 100/00	3	2	2	0	4	The periods remitted on License will be proportionate to the length of sentences and will depend upon the fitness of each Convict for release after a careful consideration has been given to his case by the government.
			2— –6			
Class 6 A, or 6 months in A class	4	2	10	0	5	
			3— –3			
Class 14 A, or 14 months in A class	5	3	6	0	6	
			4— –0			
Class 17 A, or 17 months in A class	6	3	9	0	9	
			4— –6			
Class 20 A, or 20 months in A class	7	4	0	1	3	
			5— –3			
Class 28 A, or 28 months in A class	8	4	8	1	4	
			6— –0			
Class 44 A, or 44 months in A class	10	6	0	1	6	
			7— –6			
Class 59 A, or 59 months in A class	12	7	3	1	9	
			9— –0			
Class 68 A, or 68 months in A class	15	8	0	2	0	
			10— –0			

[a]The earliest possible periods of removal to Intermediate Prisons apply only to those of the most unexceptionable character, and no remission of the full sentence will take place unless the prisoner has qualified himself by carefully measured good conduct for passing the periods in the Intermediate Prisons prescribed by the Rules; and any delay in this qualification will have the effect of postponing his admission into the Intermediate Prisons, and thereby deferring to the same extent the remission of a portion of his sentence.
Source: Mary Carpenter. *Prison Discipline as Developed by the Rt. Hon. Sir Walter Crofton in the Irish Convict Prison* (reprint of 1872 ed.). Montclair, NJ: Patterson-Smith.

Although many corrections officials in the United States were impressed with what the National Prison Association had accomplished and recommended, it was not until 1876 that Elmira Reformatory actually established a workable good-time credit system for inmates comparable to the ones suggested and used by Maconochie and Crofton. Zebulon Brockway, the first superintendent of Elmira, was impressed with the good-time credit system, and he successfully incorporated the system for Elmira inmates. In fact, the example set by the Elmira Reformatory led to the passage of the first indeterminate sentencing law in the United States. Other states eventually adopted similar sentencing systems, and by the 1950s, every state and the federal system had indeterminate sentencing (Smykla 1981).

A version of parole was used by U.S. prisons, both federal and state, much earlier than 1876. During George Washington's administration, the U.S. prison system was designed so that all offenders had to serve their entire sentences.

Prison overcrowding quickly occurred, and administrative decisions had to be made. Wardens frequently authorized discretionary releases of certain prisoners to make room for more serious offenders, even though there was no statutory basis for their actions. Some states were so hard pressed to find space for the growing offender population that they passed good-time laws.

The first state to pass a good-time law was New York in 1817 (Bottomley 1990). This law authorized officials to commute inmate sentences to shorter lengths. Thus, early release on the basis of an inmate's good behavior occurred in the United States many decades before the official action taken at Elmira Reformatory. The distinction is that in 1817, early release through the accumulation of good-time credits resulted in an official **pardon** by the governor or other authority. A pardon is an **unconditional release,** and released inmates are no longer accountable to prison authorities or parole officers. Therefore, it was not counted as parole in the formal sense, although prisoners benefited from it similarly.

The Official Introduction of Parole in the United States.   The Massachusetts State Legislature acted to implement parole officially into its prison system in 1884 (Burke 2001; Petersilia 2001). It is significant that Massachusetts was also the first state to establish probation six years earlier in 1878. By 1900, 20 states had passed parole statutes, and by 1944, all states had established parole systems for prisoners. The U.S. Board of Parole was created by congressional action in 1930, although the federal groundwork for this board had been established in 1925. Until the mid-1970s, parole was used by every state as a back-door solution to the problem of prison overcrowding as well as a way of reintegrating prisoners into their communities. The rehabilitative ideal had been promoted in the mid-1800s, and it dominated U.S. corrections for the next century.

Rehabilitation gradually fell into disfavor with the public for various reasons, however. Parolees exhibited high recidivism rates. A second reason was political. Rehabilitation was not a sufficiently tough measure for dealing with criminals. Despite the rehabilitative programs, including vocational, educational, and technical training provided in prison settings, and despite all of the psychological and social counseling, drug and alcohol therapy and medical treatment provided by prisons and prison staff, recidivism among ex-offenders soured the public on rehabilitation. Simply, many offenders were not being rehabilitated.

Federal and State Abolition of Parole.   Maine was the first state to abolish parole in 1976. Subsequently, many states either substantially modified or abolished their parole programs. In 1984, the Comprehensive Crime Control Act was passed by Congress. This Act prescribed that parole should be abolished for federal prisoners commencing November, 1992. **Post-release supervision** was substituted for parole by the federal government in 1993 (Camp and Camp 2002). By 2000, 20 states had abolished parole and/or barred certain violent offenders from being paroled at the discretion of parole boards. The states that abolished discretionary parole by 2000 include Arizona, California, Delaware, Florida, Illinois, Indiana, Kansas, Maine, Minnesota, Mississippi, North Carolina, Ohio, Oregon, Virginia, Washington, and Wisconsin. Four additional states, Alaska, Louisiana, New York, and Tennessee, abolished discretionary parole for certain types of violent offenders (Hughes, Wilson, and Beck 2001:2). Several other states were in the process of voting to abolish their parole systems or the legislatures were discussing such legislation.

Some of the reasons for abolishing parole have to do with the unsuccessfulness of parole programs. While parolees are under supervision by parole officers, about 60 percent of them do not commit new crimes. This percentage has remained fairly constant during the 1990s through 2001 and is impressive (Austin 2002:2). However, about two-thirds of all parolees reoffend or recidivate either during or following their release from parole. These new offenses committed by parolees are not exclusively violent, but the fact that such a high percentage of parolees fails is unsettling to many citizens. Furthermore, nearly 20 percent of all death row prisoners committed their capital crimes while on parole (Snell and Maruschak 2002). Thus, there is a general mistrust among the public toward parole boards and the discretionary powers they wield (Horn 2001).

Abolishing parole seems to be supported among the general public. National polls reflect that:

85 percent of the public feels that the courts are not dealing harshly enough with criminals.

82 percent believe that parole should be made more difficult.

86 percent endorse life imprisonment for those convicted of a violent felony for the third time.

77 percent are in favor of the death penalty for a person convicted of murder (Sundt et al. 1998b:21).

However, evidence from other surveys suggests that the public may be more flexible and willing to support alternatives to incarceration, including parole, and developing community programs to keep more nonviolent and first-time offenders active and working to help reduce prison overcrowding (Sundt et al. 1998b:21). In fact, this view was favored over shortening sentences, allowing prisoners to earn early release for good behavior, giving the parole board more authority to release offenders early, and raising taxes to build more prisons.

For many parolees, especially female offenders, their successfulness for reintegrating into their communities depends upon finding shelter, obtaining employment/legal income, reconstructing connections with others, developing community membership, and identifying consciousness and confidence in self (O'Brien 2001a, 2001b). A high degree of community collaboration with parolees seems to be a fundamental prerequisite for successful reentrys (Burke 2001). There is an increased need to devise more effective interventions for parolees, interventions that will more adequately meet their individual problems and limitations (Lurigio 2001). Some of these interventions will be examined later in this chapter.

Philosophy and Goals

The original philosophy of parole was rehabilitation. Alexander Maconochie, Sir Walter Crofton, Gaylord Hubbell, Zebulon Brockway, and other penal reformers and officials were unanimous in their belief that prisoners could be rehabilitated. In some respects resembling the carrot-stick analogy, parole was used originally as an incentive for prisoners to learn to get along with others, to behave, and eventually to return to their communities. It was a reward for good behavior. But beyond that, it was an incentive to undertake various work tasks and learn new skills and to become more productive (Morris 2002).

Parole also reflected other philosophies. Some of these philosophies had nothing to do with prisoner rehabilitation. Rather, certain civil rights groups were interested in eliminating sentencing disparities according to gender, race/ethnicity, and socioeconomic status (Tarver, Walker, and Wallace 2002).

Therefore, parole reforms seemed a useful way to reduce or eliminate sentencing disparities. The discrepancy between an inmate's sentence length and type of crime committed was also considered problematic. Some offenders who committed more serious crimes were given shorter sentences, while offenders convicted of less serious crimes received longer sentences (Greene and Schiraldi 2002). Parole was viewed as a way of resolving these problems. The major aims and philosophy of parole are as follows:

1. Parole is a means whereby prisoners can be rehabilitated.
2. Parole enables inmates to become reintegrated into society. Early release through parole permits offenders to make a gradual transition back to community life.
3. Parole is an incentive for inmates to comply with prison rules and behave.
4. Parole reduces prison overcrowding.
5. Parole acts as a deterrent to further crime.
6. Parole protects the public because of the supervisory control of parole officers over parolees/clients.
7. Parole helps to reduce sentencing disparities according to race, ethnicity, gender, and socioeconomic status.
8. Parole is a continuation of punishment.

Functions of Parole

Parole fulfills both **manifest functions** and **latent functions.** Manifest functions are intended or recognized, apparent to all. Latent functions are hidden and less apparent. Three manifest functions of parole are offender rehabilitation, offender reintegration, and crime deterrence and control. Three latent functions of parole are decreasing prison and jail overcrowding, compensating for sentencing disparities, and protecting public safety.

Offender Rehabilitation.   Parole is a stage where the offender is reintroduced into his or her community. Almost every parolee is assigned to a parole department and parole officer for supervision. Depending upon the particular parole division or department, offender rehabilitation programs may or may not be stressed. In New York City, for example, the parole department has a reentry program known as La Bodega de la Familia, which offers a model for strengthening the relationship between offenders and their families (Shapiro and Schwartz 2001). La Bodega offers an array of rehabilitative services, including family case management, an inclusive process that engages the substance abuser, family members, supervision officers, and treatment providers to identify and mobilize a family's inherent strengths and resources, and to build a network of healthy relationships to support the offender. Educational and vocational training, as well as professional intervention for special needs, are critical when offenders reenter society from prison (Wilkinson 2001).

Offender Reintegration.   Parole provides a means whereby an offender may make a smooth transition from prison life to living in a community with some degree of freedom under supervision. In 1999 the National Institute of Corrections sponsored a program in two states to develop consistent and coordinated approaches to the process of offenders' transitions from prison to the community (Keiser 1999:103). A key objective was to identify specific factors that placed parolees at risk of

Parolee rehabilitation includes assistance to complete G.E.D. requirements and qualify for better jobs in the community. Courtesy of Custer Youth Correctional Center.

recidivism when released and to work with institutions and community agencies to devise strategies to minimize these risk factors for inmates. Thus, greater efforts are being made to assist parolees in their communities and making their transitions to community living more successful (U.S. General Accounting Office 2001).

Crime Deterrence and Control.   Some persons believe that keeping an offender imprisoned too long will increase an inmate's antagonism toward society and result in the commission of new and more serious offenses. Early release from prison, under appropriate supervision, implies an agreement of trust between the state and offender (Travis 2001).

Decreasing Prison and Jail Overcrowding.   Parole is considered a back-end solution to prison and jail overcrowding. Without parole, our already overcrowded prisons and jails would become even more overcrowded, many reaching unconstitutionally safe or approved levels. But in order to reduce prison and jail overcrowding, the wrong types of offenders may be released short of serving their full sentences. Supposedly, parole boards function to screen the more dangerous parole applicants and prevent their early release. But the objectivity of parole board decision making is suspect and the decisions of parole boards are not always foolproof.

Regardless of the nature of parole board decision making and discretion, there is one segment of the prison inmate population that is coming to the attention of parole boards more frequently each year. Larger numbers of aging offenders in prisons have created immense problems relative to their medical needs. Many special-needs offenders require 24-hour skilled nursing care in almost every major U.S. prison. At least one state, Texas, has established the Special Needs Parole Program, which provides for the early parole review of those offenders with special health-care needs (Texas Criminal Justice Policy Council 2000). Releasing such special-needs offenders early serves at least two useful purposes. First, it frees up prison space that can be occupied by more serious, younger offenders. Second, a greater array of social and health services is made available to these older offenders within their own communities, and they become less of a burden to the state.

Another offender class that has been targeted by officials in some states is drug offenders. In 2003 New York Governor George Pataki advocated the release from prison of large numbers of well-behaved drug offenders as well as ending parole early for others. Pataki has proposed to allow inmates incarcerated under the state's tough Rockefeller-era drug laws to be released from prison after 10 years, cutting for good behavior one-third of the 15 years to life they now serve. Those drug offenders on parole would end their parole terms after 2 years, provided they behaved well. A third Pataki proposal would expand parole rules, thus enabling parole boards to grant early release to nonviolent inmates who are serving terms up to 8 years, provided that they demonstrate good behavior. Pataki believes that $21.2 million in prison operating costs would be saved as the result of his proposals, without an accompanying risk to citizen safety (Harry 2003:14). Pataki's proposal has met with mixed reactions from prosecutors, police, and defense attorneys. Many of Pataki's critics suggest that substantial drug law reforms are needed rather than focusing upon those already convicted under such laws.

Compensating for Sentencing Disparities.   In many early-release cases, inmates are released in part to rectify previous sentencing inequities. Where an inmate has been given an unusually harsh sentence compared with other inmates who have committed similar offenses and have been paroled, parole boards can act to correct these disparities. Some disparities in sentencing have been minimized through determinate sentencing in selected jurisdictions.

Public Safety and Protection.   Can we predict with 100 percent accuracy those offenders who will or will not reoffend at the time of their early-release hearings? No. In fact, predicting an offender's future dangerousness is one of the most difficult decisions to make in the criminal justice system. However, parole boards do their best to protect society by authorizing the release only of those most likely to succeed. Parole-eligible inmates usually file a parole plan, where they have acquired a job outside of prison and furnish parole boards with other helpful information to suggest that they will be law-abiding (Wilkinson 2001).

Parolees in the United States

Numbers of Parolees under Supervision.   By 2001, 6,592,800 persons were under some form of correctional supervision in the United States. Of these, 731,147 or about 11 percent were on parole. The parole population grew in the United States by 37.5 percent between 1990 and 2001 (Glaze 2002:1). Table 10.2 shows the number of state and federal offenders on parole, according to both state and U.S. region. Table 10.2 shows that during 2001, the adult parole population grew by 1 percent.

Methods of Release from Prison.   Releases of large numbers of inmates on parole are the result of many factors. Some of these factors are prison overcrowding and good behavior of prisoners while confined. Also, prisons are attempting to manage their scarce space in order to accommodate the most dangerous offenders (Austin 2002). Another major contributing factor is court-ordered prison population reductions because of health and safety regulations and cruel and unusual punishment conditions associated with some prison facilities that have been unable to comply with federally mandated guidelines under which inmates may be confined.

TABLE 10.2

Adults on Parole, 2001

Region and Jurisdiction	Parole Population, 1/1/01	2001		Parole Population, 12/31/01	Percent Change, 2001	Number on Parole per 1,000 Adult Residents, 12/31/01
		Entries	Exits			
U.S. total	723,898	473,688	464,666	731,147	1.0%	350
Federal	76,069	28,066	25,586	78,013	2.6%	37
State	647,829	445,622	439,080	653,134	0.8	312
Northeast	159,653	69,416	66,081	162,986	2.1%	402
Connecticut	1,868	1,986	1,728	2,126	13.8	83
Maine	28	1	2	27	−3.6	3
Massachusetts	3,703	3,715	3,698	3,718	0.4	77
New Hampshire[a,b]	944	492	483	953	1.0	103
New Jersey	11,709	10,810	10,588	11,931	1.9	189
New York	57,858	25,644	26,783	56,719	−2.0	397
Pennsylvania[b]	82,345	26,015	22,122	86,238	4.7	921
Rhode Island	331	439	395	375	13.3	47
Vermont	867	313	281	899	3.7	195
Midwest	103,331	86,909	85,412	104,828	1.4%	220
Illinois	30,196	33,685	33,724	30,157	−0.1	329
Indiana[c]	4,917	5,734	5,312	5,339	8.6	118
Iowa[b,c]	2,763	3,019	2,706	3,076	11.3	140
Kansas[c]	3,829	4,492	4,330	3,991	4.2	202
Michigan	15,753	9,998	9,250	16,501	4.7	225
Minnesota	3,072	3,515	3,431	3,156	2.7	87
Missouri	12,563	8,479	8,178	12,864	2.4	309
Nebraska	476	699	645	530	11.3	42
North Dakota	110	240	234	116	5.5	24
Ohio	18,248	10,567	10,930	17,885	−2.0	211
South Dakota[a]	1,481	937	886	1,532	3.4	277
Wisconsin	9,923	5,544	5,786	9,681	−2.4	242
South	225,955	102,933	104,277	223,416	−1.1%	299
Alabama	5,484	2,403	2,224	5,663	3.3	170
Arkansas	8,659	7,928	6,286	10,301	19.0	517
Delaware	579	123	172	530	−8.5	90
District of Columbia	5,332	2,272	3,151	4,453	—	974
Florida	5,982	4,674	4,456	5,891	−1.5	48
Georgia	21,556	9,975	10,223	20,809	−3.5	346
Kentucky	4,614	2,896	2,308	5,202	12.7	171
Louisiana	22,860	13,814	13,344	23,330	2.1	718
Maryland	13,666	7,871	8,122	13,415	−1.8	340
Mississippi[c]	1,596	841	649	1,788	12.0	86
North Carolina	3,352	3,684	4,082	2,954	−11.9	49
Oklahoma[a]	1,825	2,314	733	3,406	86.6	133
South Carolina	4,378	1,132	1,410	4,100	−6.3	137
Tennessee	8,093	3,765	3,397	8,074	−0.2	188
Texas[a]	111,719	35,289	39,320	107,688	−3.6	720
Virginia	5,148	3,457	3,732	4,873	−5.3	91
West Virginia	1,112	495	668	939	−15.6	67

TABLE 10.2 (Continued)

Adults on Parole, 2001

Region and Jurisdiction	Parole Population, 1/1/01	2001		Parole Population, 12/31/01	Percent Change, 2001	Number on Parole per 1,000 Adult Residents, 12/31/01
		Entries	Exits			
West	158,890	186,364	183,310	161,904	1.9%	351
Alaska	525	311	314	522	−0.6	120
Arizona[c]	3,474	6,737	6,675	3,536	1.8	94
California[c]	117,647	156,267	156,132	117,904	0.2	479
Colorado	5,500	4,605	4,372	5,733	4.2	179
Hawaii	2,504	1,028	924	2,608	4.2	285
Idaho	1,409	1,145	868	1,686	19.7	182
Montana[c]	621	582	493	710	14.3	106
Nevada	4,056	2,957	2,494	4,519	11.4	304
New Mexico	1,670	1,744	1,510	1,742	4.3	133
Oregon	17,579	8,046	6,864	18,761	6.7	729
Utah	3,231	2,574	2,334	3,471	7.4	229
Washington[a]	160	13	18	155	−3.1	4
Wyoming	514	355	312	557	8.4	153

Note: Because of incomplete data, the population on December 31, 2001, does not equal the population on January 1, 2001, plus entries, minus exits.
—Not calculated.
[a]All data were estimated.
[b]Data for entries and exits were estimated for nonreporting agencies.
[c]Data do not include parolees in one or more of the following categories: absconder, out of State, or inactive.
Source: Lauren E. Glaze. *Probation and Parole in the United States, 2001.* Washington, DC: U.S. Department of Justice, 2002, p.5.

State prison releases by discretionary parole board decisions in 1977 accounted for 72 percent of all releasees. By 1990, this figure dropped to 56 percent, and in 1995, 50 percent of all parolees were being released through discretionary parole board action. However, by 2001, only 36 percent of all parolees were released through discretionary parole (Glaze 2002:6). However, during the period 1990–2001, the number of supervised **mandatory parole** releases rose from 41 percent to 55 percent (Glaze 2002:6). Presently, mandatory parole is the most common form of early release for inmates. Under mandatory parole, the date of release is determined by statute and supervision is provided by a parole agency after release (Piehl 2002:34).

Profiling Parolees. The characteristics of adults on parole are shown in Table 10.3. About 95 percent of these parolees for 2001 were felony offenders who had been incarcerated for periods of longer than one year. Women made up about 12 percent of all parolees, which is a significant increase in their proportion compared with 8 percent in 1990. Forty-one percent of the parolees in 2001 were black. Hispanics accounted for 19 percent of these parolees (Glaze 2002:6). Also according to Table 10.3, the successful completion rate among parolees was 46 percent, down slightly from the successful completion rate of 50 percent in 1990. However, only about 40 percent of all parolees were returned to prison for either technical or criminal violations. This compares favorably with a 46 percent return-to-prison rate among parolees in 1990. Interestingly, the percentage

TABLE 10.3

Characteristics of Adults on Parole, 1990, 1995, and 2001

Characteristic	1990	1995	2001
Total	100%	100%	100%
Gender			
Male	92%	90%	88%
Female	8	10	12
Race[a]			
White	36%	34%	39%
Black	46	45	41
Hispanic	18	21	19
American Indian/Alaska Native	1	1	1
Asian/Pacific Islander	—	—	1
Status of supervision			
Active	82%	78%	84%
Inactive	6	11	4
Absconded	6	6	7
Supervised out of State	6	4	5
Other	**	—	—
Sentence length			
Less than 1 year	5%	6%	5%
1 year or more	95	94	95
Adults entering parole			
Discretionary parole	59%	50%	36%
Mandatory parole	41	45	55
Reinstatement	**	4	7
Other	**	2	2
Adults leaving parole			
Successful completion	50%	45%	46%
Returned to incarceration	46	41	40
With new sentence	17	12	9
Other	29	29	30
Absconder[b]	1	**	9
Other unsuccessful	1	**	2
Transferred	1	2	1
Death	1	1	1
Other	**	10	1

Note: For every characteristic there were persons of unknown status or type. Detail may not sum to total because of rounding.
**Not available.
—Less than 0.5%.
[a]In 2001 race/Hispanic origin was collected as a single item. For comparison, percents were estimated for prior years.
[b]In 1995 absconder status was reported among "other."
Source: Lauren E. Glaze. *Probation and Parole in the United States, 2001.* Washington, DC: U.S. Department of Justice, 2002, p. 6.

of absconders, or those who simply left their parole programs without authorization and could not be located, rose from 1 percent in 1990 to 9 percent in 2001.

About 11 percent of all parolees were supervised intensively in 2001 (Camp and Camp 2002:191). By contrast, about 6 percent of all probationers

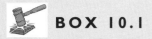

BOX 10.1

MAN PAYS OTHER MAN TO DO PRISON TIME FOR HIM: PAROLE OFFICERS DETECT HOAX

Will the Real Dexter Mathis Please Stand Up?

It happened in Atlanta, Georgia. Dexter Mathis, a young man in his 20s, was arrested and ultimately convicted of receiving $2,762 in proceeds from a bank robbery. Mathis received a 20-month sentence to be served in the federal penitentiary in Atlanta. In the meantime, while Mathis was out on bail awaiting his surrender date to U.S. marshals, he conspired with another young man, Pierre Carlton, to do his time for him. Carlton had a drug addiction, and Mathis was his drug supplier. Mathis promised Carlton that if Carlton would serve Mathis's sentence in prison, when Carlton got out, Carlton would have cash and free crack. Allegedly, Mathis also advised Carlton that there were drug treatment programs offered for free in the prison, and that Carlton could take advantage of these programs and kick his drug habit if he wanted to.

On June 7, 1999, Carlton showed up at the U.S. Marshal's Office and said that he was "Dexter Mathis." The two men were sufficiently similar in appearance that U.S. Marshals didn't question the surrender, and they escorted Carlton (posing as Mathis) to the federal prison in Atlanta. During the next 15 months, Carlton was a model pris-

oner. He earned a high school equivalency degree, kicked his drug habit, and spent most of his time reading. When he was within 47 days of being released from prison, he got tired of posing as Mathis and failed to show up at a halfway house where he had been assigned. Parole officers found him and placed him under arrest. It was then that he revealed his true identity. Later, police arrested Dexter Mathis and charged him with conspiracy, which could add five years to the 20-month sentence that the judge had originally imposed. Mathis claimed that the pretense was Carlton's idea. However, prosecutors believe that Mathis bribed Carlton with the offer of free drugs and cash.

Is the U.S. Marshal's Office to blame for this incident? You would think that U.S. marshals are competent enough to verify convicted offenders when they surrender themselves for imprisonment. Is the organization so complex that it cannot distinguish between real offenders and those pretending to be real offenders? What procedures and policies can be implemented to avoid such scenarios in the future?

Source: Adapted from Kristen Wyatt and the Associated Press. "Inmate Admits Being an Imposter," February 16, 2001.

were intensively supervised by POs the same year. One inference from these figures might be that as a general class, parolees represent more dangerous offenders or pose greater societal risks, thus requiring more intensive supervision compared with probationers.

Do Jurisdictions Charge Parolees for Their Own Supervision?   Of all states with parole programs, 19 states charged parolees supervisory fees in 2001 (Camp and Camp 2002:211). The average supervision fee was $24. Louisiana had the highest parole supervision fees assessed parolees at $53 per month, while Georgia, Kentucky, Minnesota, and Texas had the lowest parole supervision fees of $10 per month (Camp and Camp 2002:211).

Successful Parolees.   A total of 731,147 parolees were discharged from parole in 2001 (Glaze 2002:1). About 46 percent of all discharges represented successful completions of parole programs. About 40 percent of all parolees were returned to prison. About 10 percent either died or absconded while on parole. The average amount of time spent on parole was 22 months (Camp and Camp 2002:197).

Unsuccessful Parolees and Parole Violation Hearings.   Information about parole violation hearings and their results is sketchy. For instance, Camp and Camp (2002) conducted a survey of all state jurisdictions for 2000 to determine how many probation and parole violation hearings were conducted as well as the results of those hearings. Most states reported unclear and inconsistent information about their probation or parole revocation processes and results. For instance, California reported that it conducted 45,000 parole violation hearings, but it also reported that 89,346 parolees were returned to prison. No explanation was provided for these figures. Furthermore, thirteen jurisdictions, including the federal government, reported combined probation/parole revocations, without differentiating between them.

An independent analysis of these figures compiled by Camp and Camp (2002) disclosed that only six states reported complete information about their parole violation hearings for 2000. These included Maryland, New York, Oregon, Texas, Virginia, and Wyoming. Based on these reported figures, there were 57,794 parole violation hearings conducted in 2000. Of these, 13,287 (23 percent) resulted in the parolee's return to prison because of a new crime. An additional 15,086 parolees (26.1 percent) were returned to prison for technical program violations (e.g., violating curfew, failing drug/alcohol tests). Thus, it would seem that 49.1 percent of all parole revocation hearings in these jurisdictions resulted in returns to prison for these parolees. This figure seems fairly reliable, since we know from Table 10.3 that 40 percent of all parolees in all U.S.

Parolees on electronic monitoring may not comply with program requirements and be recommended for parole program termination. Courtesy of BI, Inc.

jurisdictions were returned to prison for either a new offense or technical violation in 2001 (Glaze 2002:6).

Although detailed information about parole violators is not available for 2001, we do have such information for previous years which has been compiled by the U.S. Department of Justice. Table 10.4 shows the characteristics of parole violators in all state prisons, including independent descriptions of parole violators from California, New York, and Texas. The reason California, New York, and Texas statistics are reported separately is that their combined parolee populations account for over half of all U.S. parolees.

For all states in 1997, male parolees made up 95.3 percent of all parole violators. White, non-Hispanic parolees accounted for 27.5 percent of these violators, black non-Hispanics accounted for 51.8 percent, and Hispanics accounted for 18.3 percent. Over 65 percent of all parole violators were between the ages

TABLE 10.4

Characteristics of Parole Violators in State Prisons for All States, California, New York, and Texas, 1997

Characteristic	All States	California	New York	Texas
Gender				
Male	95.3%	92.9%	96.7%	94.6%
Female	4.7	7.1	3.3	5.4
Race/Hispanic origin				
White non-Hispanic	27.5%	30.8%	11.1%	23.1%
Black non-Hispanic	51.8	33.4	54.2	50.3
Hispanic	18.3	31.9	33.1	26.0
Other	2.4	3.9	1.6	0.6
Age at prison release				
17 or younger	0.1%	0.2%	0.0%	0.0%
18–24	9.4	8.8	8.6	6.1
25–29	20.8	19.8	19.8	19.1
30–34	24.1	25.5	26.0	23.3
35–39	20.3	22.9	20.3	21.1
40–44	13.9	12.8	13.3	15.5
45–54	9.3	8.0	10.2	12.3
55 or older	2.0	2.0	1.8	2.5
Most serious offense*				
Violent	33.7%	24.4%	40.9%	33.3%
Property	30.1	25.3	15.6	36.8
Drug	23.1	27.1	33.6	21.3
Public-order	12.9	22.9	9.4	8.6
Number of prior incarcerations				
1	42.3%	28.9%	52.9%	44.1%
2	14.0	12.6	12.6	14.1
3 to 5	26.3	27.7	26.7	28.4
6 or more	17.3	30.7	7.8	13.5

Note: Data are from the *Survey of Inmates in State Adult Correctional Facilities,* 1997.
*Excludes other/unspecified offenses.
Source: Timothy A. Hughes, Doris James Wilson, and Allen J. Beck. *Trends in State Parole, 1990-2000.* Washington, DC: U.S. Department of Justice, 2001 p. 14.

of 25 and 39, and a third were violent offenders. About 42 percent had only one prior incarceration, although 28.3 percent had between 3 and 5 prior incarcerations (Hughes, Wilson, and Beck 2001:14). An inspection of Table 10.4 shows several significant departures from the statistics for all states combined for the individual states reporting. For instance, only 11 percent of the parole violators in New York for 1997 were white non-Hispanic, while 33 percent were Hispanic. Another difference is that nearly 31 percent of all California parole violators had 6 or more prior incarcerations compared with about 17 percent for all states combined. Thus, there is good reason to show overall state patterns of parole violators as well as individually reported figures for those states with the three largest parolee populations.

PRE-RELEASE PROGRAMS

Several types of pre-release programs are available to inmates. These are programs where inmates are not immediately paroled, but they are granted temporary leaves from prison for various purposes. Pre-release may be either conditional or unconditional. **Conditional releases** are further subdivided into parole board release, mandatory parole, and other conditional. Unconditional releases are divided according to expiration, commutation/pardon, and other conditional. The greatest number of conditional releases are through parole board action, where early-release decisions are made according to parole board discretion (Petersilia 2002). **Mandatory release** involves those inmates who have served their sentences less the good-time credits they have accumulated. Thus, these releases are determined by calculating the original sentence less any good behavior credits inmates acquired while in prison. These mandatory releases accounted for about a third of all conditional releases. The remainder are probation and court-ordered releases, usually to alleviate prison overcrowding (Camp and Camp 2002).

Unconditional releases comprise those whose prison terms have expired. These are **statutory releases,** since the maximum time prescribed by law for the offense has been served in its entirety. A small portion of these offenders have their sentences commuted through pardons. About 75 percent of all those paroled complete their parole terms successfully (Camp and Camp 2002). However, recidivism rates among those no longer involved in parole programs are as high as 65 percent.

In this section, we will examine two types of "other conditional" pre-release programs. These programs involve temporary prison absences. Some inmates are permitted to leave their prisons for designated time intervals, subject to various conditions. They must return to prison at prescribed times. They are not paroled, although to be eligible for a pre-release program, an inmate must be near his or her early-release date and have a clean record of institutional conduct. Usually, inmates who are granted pre-release use that time to find jobs and/or reunite with their families. Others attend school classes and work on degrees. These programs are considered transitional in that they enable those about to be paroled to have some amount of freedom in the community. They also involve a significant amount of trust, since inmates are essentially on their honor to return to their prisons when directed. Thus, when they are eventually paroled, the experience of freedom within their communities is not as abrupt as if they were to be paroled directly from prison without any transitional experiences like these. Two pre-release programs include furloughs and work/study release.

Furlough Programs

What Are Furloughs?   **Furloughs** are authorized, unescorted leaves from confinement granted for specific purposes and for designated time periods. These types of programs are considered one of several pre-release initiatives (Montana Legislative Audit Division 1998). Furloughs originated in 1918 in Mississippi. By 1970, about half the states had furlough programs (Marley 1973). Nationwide, more than 230,960 furloughs were granted in 1990 from 40 U.S. prison systems. Furloughs may be granted to prisoners for periods ranging from 24 hours to several weeks and are similar to leaves enjoyed by military personnel. But a skeptical public and state legislatures have effectively curtailed the use of furloughs. This is because some furloughees have committed high-profile crimes, heinous murders, robberies, and rapes, and the political futures of some governors and legislators have been ruined as a result. By 2001, 11,614 furloughs had been granted to inmates in 19 reporting jurisdictions (Camp and Camp 2002:147). There were 28 jurisdictions with furlough programs in 2000. Thus, we can only speculate as to the total number of offenders granted one or more furloughs during that year. At least two jurisdictions with large inmate populations, California and Texas, did not report the numbers of their furloughees. It is likely that although the true number of furloughs granted each year cannot be determined in any absolute sense, there were probably in excess of 20,000 furloughs granted throughout the United States in 2000. The rate of failures on furlough programs, where furloughees simply fail to return to prison when they are required to do so, is less than 1 percent. Considering all types of pre-release programs, including work release, study release, and furloughs, there were 4,585 inmate absences or walkaways reported in 2000 and 4,995 reported in 2001. Most of these inmates are eventually returned to their prisons (CEGA Services, Inc. 2002:6). Each year, the number of furloughs granted inmates is increasing. This is due, in large part, to growing confidence in furlough programs as helpful, reintegrative interventions (Camp and Camp 2002).

Canada has established its own type of furlough procedure, known as the Temporary Absence Program (TAP). Throughout the 1990s, Canada has had a very low failure rate with the TAP, less than 1 inmate failure per 1,000 clients. However, the use of temporary absences has declined by over 50 percent. Reasons for this decline include the less frequent involvement and participation of community volunteers as escorts and new legislation limiting the purposes of temporary absences (Grant and Johnson 1998; Grant and Millson 1998).

The Goals of Furlough Programs.   The purposes of furloughs are several. Offenders are given a high degree of trust by prison officials and are permitted leaves to visit their homes and families. Interestingly, such furloughs are beneficial to both prisoners and to their families, because they permit family members to get used to the presence of the offender after a long incarcerative absence. Sometimes, prisoners may participate in educational programs outside of prison as a type of study release. They can arrange for employment once paroled, or they can participate in vocational training for short periods.

Furloughs also provide officials with an opportunity to evaluate offenders and determine how they adapt to living with others in their community. Thus, the furlough is a type of test to determine, with some predictability, the likelihood that inmates will conform to society's rules if they are eventually released through parole (Pullen 1999).

Functions of Furlough Programs. Furloughs are intended to accomplish certain functions. These include (1) offender rehabilitation and reintegration, (2) the development of self-esteem and self-worth, (3) opportunities to pursue vocational/educational programs, and (4) aiding parole boards in determining when inmates are ready to be released.

Offender Rehabilitation and Reintegration. As has been observed with other temporary release programs such as work release, the manifest intent of furloughs is to provide offenders with outside experiences to enable them to become accustomed to living with others in the community apart from the highly regulated life in prison or jail settings. Indications are that furloughs fulfill this objective in most instances.

The Development of Self-Esteem and Self-Worth. In addition, furloughs seem to instill within inmates feelings of self-esteem and self-worth. Again, the element of trust plays an important role in enabling those granted furloughs to acquire trust for those who place trust in them. The development of self-esteem and self-worth are unmeasurable.

Opportunities to Pursue Vocational/Educational Programs. Another benefit of furlough programs for those in jurisdictions where furloughs are permitted and granted is that opportunities are available for inmates to participate in programs not available to them in prisons or jails. Thus, if inmates wish to take courses in typing, art, automobile repair, or philosophically oriented offerings in social science or related areas, furloughs permit them the time to pursue such courses.

Aiding Parole Boards in Determining When Inmates Ought to Be Released. A key function of furloughs as tests of inmate behavior are to alert parole boards which inmates are most eligible to be released and who will likely be successful while on parole.

Work/Study Release

What Is Work/Study Release? **Work/study release** is any program where inmates in jails or prisons are permitted to work in their communities with minimal restrictions and supervision, are compensated at the prevailing minimum wage, and must serve their nonworking hours housed in a secure facility (Camp and Camp 2002). The growth of work release among state correctional departments has been substantial. For instance, in 2000, New York led all states with 6,786 inmates involved in work release programs. Other states with large numbers of work releasees include Florida (1,657), and Illinois (1,397). Overall, there were 39,705 work releasees in 28 reporting state jurisdictions, up from 17,000 work releasees in 1998 (Camp and Camp 2002:144).

The first use of work release in the United States was in Vermont in 1906 where sheriffs, acting on their own authority, assigned inmates to work outside jail walls in the community. Legislation-authorized work release was first introduced in Wisconsin in 1913, and by 1975, all states and the federal system had initiated some form of work release program (Harrison 2001; Ulmer 2001). At that time, county sheriffs issued passes to certain low-risk inmates to work in the community during daytime hours, but they were obligated to return to jail at a particular curfew period. Work release is also known as **day pass, day parole, temporary release, work furloughs,** or **education furloughs** (Renzema 2000).

Some work release is labeled study release, because specific high school or college courses or other curricula are taken by eligible inmates. Prisons lacking educational facilities or programs sometimes use study release to supplement their existing resources, and only minimum-security offenders are permitted entry into such programs (Farrell 2000). Many work release and study release programs are closely connected with community-based supervisory services for ex-offenders, both probationers and parolees. One long-range advantage of work release is that it makes available employment opportunities to offenders who become acquainted with employers in the private sector while temporarily unconfined. Many Massachusetts work releasees have found employment in the private sector as the result of their work release experiences, for example (Harrison 2001).

The Goals of Work/Study Release.   The goals of work release programs are to:

1. Reintegrate the offender into the community.
2. Give the offender an opportunity to learn and/or practice new skills.
3. Provide offenders with the means to make restitution to victims of crimes.
4. Give offenders a chance to assist in supporting themselves and their families.
5. Help authorities to more effectively predict the likelihood of offender success if paroled.
6. Foster improvements in self-images or self-concepts through working in a nonincarcerative environment and assuming full responsibility for one's conduct.

Work/Study Releasee Eligibility Requirements.   Before offenders can be eligible for work release, they must meet the following criteria:

1. Inmates must have served a minimum of 10 percent of their sentences.
2. Inmates must have attained minimum custody by the date they are to begin participating in work release.
3. Inmates must not have had an escape within six months of the approval.
4. Inmates must not have had a major infraction of prison rules within three months of approval.
5. If inmates are serving a sentence for a serious sexual or assaultive crime or have such a history, the approving authority for minimum custody is the director's review committee (Witte 1973).

Weaknesses and Strengths of Work/Study Release Programs.   Generally, work release programs have been successful when client eligibility standards

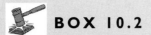

BOX 10.2

Renae Stubblefield

Administrator, Huntington Work/Study Release Center, West Virginia

Statistics

B.A. (psychology), Marshall University

Background and Interests

I was appointed as Administrator of the Huntington Work/Study Release Center in September 2001. I was tasked with the responsibility of managing and directing operational and program functions of that facility. Previously, I served as a Department of Labor apprentice and have taken a wide array of specialized courses during my 18 years' experience in the corrections profession.

I began my career at the Huntington Work Release Center as a corrections officer in 1984. In 1991, I experienced a pivotal point in my career and was promoted to a sergeant. In 1994, I became a case manager. Then I served as the facility's news reporter, business manager, interim disciplinary magistrate, institutional training coordinator, EEO officer, and institutional parole officer, as well as a third-level employee grievance evaluator.

Experiences

As I sat down to write this piece, first I wondered how I allowed 18 years to just fly by. It only seemed like a couple of years ago when I received my first uniform. I was so proud to wear it! I was so grateful to have a steady job: one that would pay the bills and leave me with a little money to play with. I was fresh out of college and needed money fast. The only way I knew to solve that dilemma was to go to work. At this point in my life, the only thing I knew for sure was that I wanted to take a break from college. I really had no idea of what I was getting into. The media shaped my perceptions of "prisoners." Therefore, I didn't have a realistic concept of inmates, the prison system, and especially work release. The next several years of my life would be a significant learning curve.

There have been several significant points of interest in my career. I have learned much through a wide variety of professional development classes offered throughout the years, but some of my most valuable lessons occurred while on the job. Unfortunately, some of life's lessons are taught the hard way. Unprofessional conduct on the job can be devastating to an organization. I truly believe that one of the most valuable lessons to learn *not* to do is compromise your position of authority by becoming intimate with inmates. I have witnessed this occurrence time and time again. It is a proven fact that everyone is affected by misconduct. Trust has been destroyed. The inmate population and co-workers are placed in jeopardy that can cause dissension, thereby creating an imbalance of control of the offenders.

I have seen literally thousands of inmates come and go through the system over the past 18 years. What saddens me the most is seeing a person become institutionalized. Prison not only contains them physically, but they have permitted a mental imprisonment that makes them feel hopeless and keeps them locked up. On the other hand, it brings me great joy to see inmates who have been paroled or discharged their sentences drop by or telephone to say "Thank you" for helping them through the rough spots because they are now leading successful lives. These experiences are what truly make the job worthwhile.

Advice to Students

During my career, I have managed to glean a few nuggets of wisdom that I would like to share.

1. Before embarking upon a career in corrections or any field for that matter, make sure you examine why you want to enter that field. If you're not sure, begin to do some volunteer work at the minimum-security level. This is the least restrictive of the four levels (e.g., minimum, medium, maximum, and supermax), but it will still provide an overview of corrections. Find a place that is well-established and has a proven track record, and then volunteer, volunteer, and volunteer! Your investment will pay off great future returns!

2. I once heard one of my mentors say, "I'd rather dream big and get a little bit than not dream at all and get nothing." Direct your career course by establishing goals. Decide who you want to be, what you want to do, and how you plan to get there. Time passing with no direction creates a fruitless routine commonly known as complacency. You will certainly establish longevity but with very little productivity.

3. If you find the business occasionally discouraging, don't allow that to deter you from having a successful corrections career if you truly enjoy what you're doing. Remember it's the nature of the business. On the other hand, if you discover that you despise the environment that you're working in, *get out!* I know this sounds elementary, but you'd be surprised how many people in the work force hate their jobs but don't leave to find something they like to do. They would rather complain and be miserable. Stay as far away as you possibly can from those people, because attitudes are contagious. If you are one of those people, find your niche in life and work at it to the best of your ability. Hard work and diligence pay great dividends.

4. No matter how much experience you have in the field, always be willing to learn. Learning new things created avenues of promotion for me.

5. Always strive to develop and maintain a professional relationship with all the people in the business (i.e., subordinates, co-workers, and especially inmates).

   a. Subordinates: In a position of leadership, learn to do the right thing instead of wanting to be right. Failing to properly supervise in order to fit in or gain friendships will not only cost your job, but will also cost your dignity and respect. That's too high a price to pay! In cases where you may already supervise friends, you should never choose friendship over properly supervising. Besides, a true friend would never place you in that position.

   b. Co-workers: Never date someone you work with. Never gossip with co-workers about other co-workers. You're setting the stage for division, animosity, and hard feelings. How would you like to supervise someone like that?

   c. Inmates: You must first remember that inmates are people! However, you should also remember that they have committed crimes and the state has entrusted you to provide adequate supervision. Never get too personal with them, because you'll begin to compromise your position of authority. Developing this habit will save you from all kinds of trouble in the future.

6. Last but certainly not least, no matter what career you embark upon, learn to be a person of integrity.

have been applied and enforced. These programs tend to have low recidivism rates compared with standard parole recidivism figures. However, some programs found little difference, if any, in recidivism among work releasees and other parolees. Usually, recidivism among work releasees is correlated highly with illicit drug use and dependencies (Simpson 2002; Ulmer 2001). When

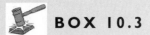

BOX 10.3

HUNTINGTON WORK/STUDY RELEASE CENTER

Try to imagine being confined in a place for a lengthy period of time as the world around you changes. In this place, your self-esteem fights to remain positive. In this place your decision-making skills are dulled because someone is always telling you what to do, when to get up, go to bed, when to eat, and when to work. Suddenly, you are released from bondage and forced to function in society just like everyone else. Imagine trying to apply for a job or a loan, finding a decent place to live that you could afford, paying not only for current bills but trying to pay back all of the debts incurred before you were confined. How about going to a grocery store and using the U-check system or even a Mastercard? If you really stop and think about it, wouldn't you feel defeated before getting to the starting gate? We really don't think much about it because we are transitioning as the world system changes. Why do we impose those same expectations of change on ex-felons who are immediately released from prison without preparing them for those changes? But for inmates who have been incarcerated for long periods of time, then forced to not only function out in society but also succeed, their futures seem bleak and hopeless. As you are well aware, hopeless people commit more crimes because prison becomes their safety net. It's commonly known as being institutionalized. This is one of the reasons why the recidivism rate is so high. It was just twenty years ago that inmates had to endure these hardships before work release centers (commonly called halfway houses) were established in West Virginia. There are currently three in the state: Beckley, Charleston, and Huntington.

Huntington Work/Study Release Center is a minimum-security facility operated by the West Virginia Division of Corrections, an agency of the Department of Military Affairs and Public Safety. The community-based program is located in the heart of downtown Huntington and houses 66 offenders (12 females and 54 males).

These offenders are carefully screened through a risk-assessment classification method for participation in the program. They are offenders convicted of nonviolent crimes and who are usually serving the last third of their sentences prior to parole or discharge. As a condition of assignment, they are required to do at least 38 hours of community service. Once community service is completed, they are permitted to seek employment in the local job market.

Our primary objective is to assist inmates in making a successful transition from incarceration to the community. Huntington Work Release Center is one of the most unique institutions in West Virginia because it was literally designed with that objective in mind. We provide inmates a better opportunity for rehabilitation by gradually readjusting them with their families, friends, and the community prior to actual release, thereby reducing some of the anxieties and frustrations often associated with immediate release back into society.

"Freedom and accountability" is the theoretical concept of work release. There is a very delicate balance of freedom while yet still being incarcerated. While offenders are allowed a more relaxed institutional environment, the rules enforced by security staff are necessary to provide discipline, safety, and proper direction until they are paroled or discharged. A disregard for those rules may result in additional work assignments, restrictions of certain privileges, or return to a more secure correctional facility.

One of the top five reasons for an inmate's return to a more secure facility is that they tend to forget they are still in prison. Their mindset changes when they've stayed too long at work release. They become too familiar with their environment and the staff. They break established rules and regulations, expecting no recourse for their actions. That is why the average stay at work release should not exceed one year. On the other hand, when residents abide by the rules, they enjoy certain freedoms or "perks," including day furloughs in town to shop, overnight furloughs with immediate family members, and attending special events out in the community.

At work release, offenders become responsible for themselves and less of a burden to West Virginia taxpayers. They are required to pay room and board, medical expenses, child support, restitution, and any fines they may have incurred. Due to the demand of taking responsibility, meaningful employment is of primary importance. Therefore, we encourage inmates to take advantage of work programs, attend educational/vocational programs, and participate in treatment programs available to them.

Treatment is another important facet at work release, because 95 percent of the inmate population has addictions. The treatment staff at Huntington Work Release Center makes a concentrated effort to address the programming needs of the residents. Treatment offered includes: Aladrue Phase III, Rational Emotive Behavior Therapy Group, AA and NA meetings, and individual and group counseling. Residents may also attend church services of their choice out in the community.

Source: Huntington (WV) Work/Study Release Center, 2003.

work/study releasees are mandated to participate in drug treatment programs, this action seems to decrease their recidivism rates, however (Leonardson 1997).

The appeal of work/study release programs is that they offer motivated offenders a chance to become reintegrated into their communities and acquire skills and educational backgrounds that will enhance their employment opportunities. Maintaining employment is a key factor in probation and parole program effectiveness and is associated with significant reductions in recidivism. Some amount of trust exists between the inmate and community, and if the program requirements are fulfilled without incident, a client's parole chances are almost guaranteed (Ulmer 2001).

POST-RELEASE PAROLE PROGRAMS

When inmates are eventually paroled, they may be directed by the parole board to participate in one of several different types of parole programs. Several types of post-release parole programs exist for parolees. All of these programs involve contact with one or more community agencies. These programs are (1) halfway houses, (2) standard parole with conditions, (3) intensive supervised parole, and (4) shock parole.

Halfway Houses

Halfway Houses Defined.   **Halfway houses** are transitional residences for inmates who are released from prison (A. Miller 2001). Ordinarily, these homes offer temporary housing, food, and clothing for parolees recently released from prison. Their assignment to one of these homes may be mandatory for a short period. In many jurisdictions, these homes offer services to offenders on a voluntary basis. They assist greatly in helping former inmates make the transition from rigid prison life to community living. It is important to understand that since halfway houses involve curfews and close supervision from halfway house staff, they are not precisely pre-release programs. However, since parolees who are assigned to these halfway houses must report at given times and stay at these homes during evening hours, they resemble furloughs and work/study release programs to a great degree.

At the beginning of 2001 there were 22,832 clients in 507 public or private halfway houses in the United States, according to 19 reporting jurisdictions (Camp and Camp 2002:143). Throughout all states, there are approximately 2,600 public and private halfway houses. An unofficial estimate is that there were perhaps in excess of 104,000 halfway house clients served by these halfway houses in 2001 (Maguire and Pastore 2002).

Halfway House Origins.   The halfway house concept probably originated in England during the early 1800s. But the first formal recommendation for the creation of a halfway house in the United States occurred in 1817 in Pennsylvania. A Pennsylvania prison riot had stirred the legislature to think of various prison reforms, including housing provisions for ex-convicts who were often poor and could not find employment or adequate housing. But these proposals were never implemented, because the public feared **criminal contamination**—if ex-offenders lived together, they would spread their criminality like a disease (Twill et al. 1998).

One of the most significant events to spark the growth of state-operated halfway houses was the creation of the **International Halfway House Association (IHHA)** in Chicago, 1964. Although many of the halfway house programs continued to be privately operated after the formation of the IHHA, the growth in the numbers of halfway houses was phenomenal during the next several decades. Today, there are numerous halfway houses for both adults and juveniles (Leon, Dziegielewski, and Tubiak 1999).

Halfway House Variations.   Because there are so many different government-sponsored and private agencies claiming to be halfway houses, it is impossible to devise a consistent definition of one that fits all jurisdictions. There is extensive variation in the level of custody for clients ranging from providing simple shelter on a voluntary basis to mandatory confinement with curfew. There are also many different services provided by halfway houses. These might include alcohol or drug-related rehabilitation facilities with some hospitalization on premises, minimal or extensive counseling services, and/or employment assistance (Walters 1999). Also, halfway house programs are designed for offenders ranging from probationers and pre-releasees to parolees and others assigned to community service with special conditions. The average cost per client per day living in state- or federally-administered halfway houses at the beginning of

2001 was $48.60. Privately operated halfway house costs averaged slightly less at $46.20 per client. Massachusetts had the highest per-client cost at $83 per day, while Kansas had the lowest per-client cost at $18 per day (Camp and Camp 2002:143).

The Functions of Halfway Houses.   The major functions of halfway houses overlap some of those associated with other programs for parolees. These include (1) parolee rehabilitation and reintegration into the community; (2) provisions for food and shelter; (3) job placement, vocational guidance, and employment assistance; (4) client-specific treatments; (5) alleviating jail and prison overcrowding; (6) supplementing supervisory functions of probation and parole agencies; and (7) monitoring probationers, work/study releasees, and others with special program conditions.

Parolee Rehabilitation and Reintegration.   The major function of halfway houses is to facilitate offender reintegration into the community. This is accomplished, in part, by providing necessities and making various services accessible to offenders. The administrative personnel of halfway houses, as well as the professional and paraprofessional staff members, assist in helping offenders with specific problems they might have such as alcohol or drug dependencies. The successful readjustment of parolees into their communities also depends on the social and emotional support received from other halfway house residents and staff. For example, a study was conducted of 37 halfway house residents in California during 1996–1997. Clients responded to several scales, including the Belief in Personal Control Scale, the Inventory of Socially Supportive Behaviors, and the Emotional/Social Loneliness Inventory. The study revealed that the parolees' halfway house experiences were enhanced through their social interactions with other clients and that their loneliness decreased substantially during their stay (Twill et al. 1998). These were believed to be positive factors that contributed to their rehabilitation and community reintegration.

Provisions for Food and Shelter.   Some parolees have acquired savings from their work in prison industries, while other parolees have no operating capital. Thus, halfway houses furnish offenders with a place to stay and regular meals while they hunt for new occupations and participate in self-help programs.

Job Placement, Vocational Guidance, and Employment Assistance.   Almost every halfway house assists offenders by furnishing them job leads and negotiating contacts between them and prospective employers.

Client-Specific Treatments.   Those offenders with special needs or problems (e.g., ex-sex offenders, drug addicts or alcoholics, or mentally retarded clients) benefit from halfway houses by being permitted the freedom to take advantage of special treatment programs.

Alleviating Jail and Prison Overcrowding.   Any program that provides a safety valve for prison or jail populations contributes to alleviating overcrowding problems. Thus, halfway houses alleviate jail and prison overcrowding in that some probationers are diverted to them, while certain inmates may be paroled to them for brief periods as transitional phases.

Supplementing Supervisory Functions of Probation and Parole Agencies.   One latent function of halfway houses is to exercise some degree of supervision and control over both probationers and parolees. These supervisory functions are ordinarily performed by probation or parole officers. However, when some inmates are released to halfway houses, halfway house staff assume a high degree of responsibility for client conduct.

Monitoring Probationers, Work/Study Releasees, and Others with Special Program Conditions.   Offender benefits accruing to halfway house residents include food, clothing, and shelter, as well as employment opportunities that serve to defray the costs of maintaining these homes (A. Miller 2001).

Weaknesses and Strengths of Halfway House Programs.   Some of the major strengths and weaknesses of halfway house programs are:

1. Halfway houses are effective in preventing criminal behavior in the community as alternatives that involve community release.
2. The placement of halfway houses in communities neither increases nor decreases property values.
3. Halfway houses assist their clients in locating employment but not necessarily maintaining it.
4. Halfway houses are able to provide for the basic needs of their clients as well as other forms of release.
5. At full capacity, halfway houses cost no more, and probably less, than incarceration, although they cost more than straight parole or outright release from correctional systems (Ely 1996; Walters 1999).

Standard Parole with Conditions

Parole accounts for about 41 percent of all time served for all offender categories. The average length of time spent on parole is 22 months (Camp and Camp 2002). Those offenses drawing the longest parole lengths include murder (38 months), kidnapping (26 months), rape (26 months), and robbery (25 months). Those offenses drawing the shortest parole lengths pertain to public order (13 percent), stolen property (15 percent), and larceny/theft (15 percent) (Maguire and Pastore 2002). Violent offenders serve substantially longer parole lengths compared with property offenders. Also, violent offenders require more intensive and longer parole supervision to refrain from recidivating when released. All parolees are subject to certain standard parole conditions. Most parole agreements contain the following generic information:

1. The defendant shall not leave the judicial district or other specified geographical area without the permission of the court or parole officer.
2. The defendant shall report to the parole officer as directed by the court or parole officer and shall submit a truthful and complete written report within the first five days of each month.
3. The defendant shall answer truthfully all inquiries by the parole officer and follow the instructions of the parole officer.
4. The defendant shall support his or her dependents and meet other family responsibilities.

5. The defendant shall work regularly at a lawful occupation unless excused by the parole officer for schooling, training, or other acceptable reasons.

6. The defendant shall notify the parole officer within seventy-two hours of any change in residence or employment.

7. The defendant shall refrain from excessive use of alcohol and shall not purchase, possess, use, distribute, or administer any narcotic or other controlled substance, or any paraphernalia related to such substances, except as prescribed by a physician.

8. The defendant shall not frequent places where controlled substances are illegally sold, used, distributed, or administered, or other places specified by the court.

9. The defendant shall not associate with any persons engaged in criminal activity and shall not associate with any person convicted of a felony, unless granted permission to do so by the parole officer.

10. The defendant shall permit a parole officer to visit him or her at any time at home or elsewhere and shall permit confiscation of any contraband observed in plain view by the PO.

11. The defendant shall notify the parole officer within seventy-two hours of being arrested or questioned by a law enforcement officer.

12. The defendant shall not enter into any agreement to act as an informer or a special agent of a law enforcement agency without the permission of the court.

13. As directed by the parole officer, the defendant shall notify third parties of risks that may be occasioned by the defendant's criminal record or personal history or characteristics and shall permit the probation officer to make such notifications and to confirm the defendant's compliance with such notification requirement.

Parole agreements are contracts between the offender and the state. Parole officers supervise offenders and insure that their clients comply with program conditions. When one or more conditions are violated, the parole officer may overlook the violation or decide to recommend parole revocation. Parole officers do not have the authority to revoke a parolee's parole.

Despite the best efforts of parole organizations throughout the United States, most state prison systems continue to be ill-equipped to ease the transition of inmates from prison to the community. A national survey and information derived from eight states have focused upon the current state of the art regarding prisoner reentry. The survey found that most of those released back into their communities on parole posed minimal risks to public safety. Thus, subsequent parole supervision frequently resulted in ex-convicts being reincarcerated for noncriminal behaviors, most often technical parole program violations. It has been recommended that in the future for parolees, reentry should be curtailed by either eliminating or substantially shortening the period of their supervision (Austin 2001).

Intensive Supervised Parole

For parolees who require more frequent supervision, intensive supervised parole (ISP) is used. ISP programs feature more frequent face-to-face contacts between POs and their clients, more frequent drug and alcohol checks, and different types of offender monitoring, including electronic monitoring and house arrest. For all practical purposes, ISP for parolees is the same as the ISP programs devised for probationers. However, because of the fact that parolees have served prison time whereas probationers have not, ISP is used in about 11 percent of all parole cases compared with 3 percent of all probation cases (Camp and Camp 2002).

Shock Parole

Shock parole, also called shock probation, refers to sentences where judges order offenders imprisoned for conventional incarceration periods related to their conviction offenses (New York State Division of Parole 1998). However, after 30, 60, 90, or even 120 days of incarceration, offenders are taken out of prison and placed on parole. This action is taken provided that the offender exhibits good institutional conduct while confined. The shock factor relates to the shock of being imprisoned. This trauma is considered so profound that inmates will not want to return to prison. Therefore, it is believed that short-term incarceration is a sufficient deterrent to further offending for those offenders placed on shock parole. The terms, shock parole and shock probation are often used interchangeably. Ohio introduced the first shock probation law in 1965. Two-thirds of all states have adopted similar laws in recent years. In 2001, 14 state jurisdictions and the Federal Bureau of Prisons operated shock parole programs (Camp and Camp 2002). About 8,000 convicted offenders participated in these programs (American Correctional Association 2002).

In some respects, shock parole is not like other conventional parole programs, since almost all shock parolees are designated as such by judges and not parole boards. As we have seen, judges retain jurisdiction over all probationers, while parole boards exercise jurisdiction over all parolees. Nevertheless, since shock parolees serve some time in jail, even though it is a short amount of time, their subsequent release from jail is treated as though they have been paroled. Judges still retain jurisdiction over them, and most are supervised by probation officers. Since most persons who are incarcerated and then released short of serving their full prison or jail terms are considered parolees, the notion of shock parole may seem a bit confusing. By the same token, one interpretation of shock probation is that it is really parole, since shock probationers have served some time incarcerated. Their subsequent release from confinement and placed in a conditional probation program is viewed by some as typifying parole. Perhaps the question of whether the program is parole or probation is best answered according to who retains jurisdiction over the offender. Where judges retain jurisdiction over them, they are probationers. If parole boards have jurisdiction over them, they are parolees.

PAROLE BOARDS: REVOKING PROBATION AND PAROLE

Cases That Parole Boards Must Review

Any prisoner who serves an indeterminate sentence must be considered for parole by a parole board from time to time. The timeliness of these early-release hearings is determined by statute. In California, for instance, prospective parolees have parole hearings every three years. The amount of time between parole hearings varies according to each jurisdiction, ranging from six months to five years. There are exceptions. When prisoners accumulate sufficient good-time credit, they may be released from prison more or less automatically, without parole board review (West-Smith, Pogrebin, and Poole 2000).

Cases That Parole Boards Do Not Have to Review

Prisoners who are sentenced to life without parole or the death penalty are not entitled to a hearing before any parole board (Proctor 1999). This does not mean that some of these life-without-parole or death row inmates will never have their cases heard by some future parole board, however. During the early 1970s, for instance, the U.S. Supreme Court heard the case of *Furman v. Georgia* (1972) and declared that the death penalty, as it was presently being applied in Georgia, was cruel and unusual punishment. California was among several states electing to suspend their application of the death penalty temporarily, until such time as an appropriate procedure for administering the death penalty could be fashioned by their state legislature. Charles Manson, a notorious murderer, had been sentenced to death in the late 1960s by a California court. Some of his cohorts, including Patricia Krenwinkle and Leslie Van Houton, were likewise under sentences of death. Therefore, California authorities commuted the sentences of Charles Manson and Leslie Van Houton to life imprisonment. This meant that Manson and Van Houton would be eligible for parole at some future date and would not face execution. Since the early 1980s, these notorious murderers have faced parole boards regularly, only to have their parole denied. It is unlikely that Manson or Van Houton will ever be paroled, although they are entitled to parole hearings every three years. There has been sufficient prosecutorial and victim input in their parole hearings that their parole chances are slight.

The case of Danny Harold Rolling is another case parole boards will not have to review. Rolling was a drifter who killed five University of Florida students in Gainesville in 1990. Rolling was convicted of their murders in early 1994. There were numerous aggravating circumstances and only a few questionable mitigating ones. Rolling had stabbed his victims repeatedly, bound them with duct tape, raped and mutilated them, and decapitated one victim. Persuasive evidence indicates that he tortured his victims prior to killing them in a brutal manner. Is there any way to murder victims kindly? In March 1994, a bifurcated jury decision recommended the death penalty for Rolling. Barring any compelling appeals, Rolling will eventually be executed by Florida authorities.

Parole Boards and the Get-Tough Movement

Most states had changed their sentencing provisions by the early 1990s. In many instances, these changes limited the discretionary power of parole boards to grant prisoners early release. This was part of the get-tough-on-crime movement among several states, known simply as the get-tough movement (West-Smith, Pogrebin, and Poole 2000). An example of the effects of get-tough policy is Pennsylvania where reductions in sentence commutations dropped from 128 in 1977 to 2 in 1981. More recent examples of the get-tough movement are President Bill Clinton's three-strikes-and-you're-out anti-crime legislation and the Crime Bill of 1994, stiffer penalties for more serious offenses, and greater certainty of punishment through mandatory prison terms for particular crimes. More states are passing habitual offender statutes, where habitual offenders will draw life-without-parole sentences for three or more serious felony convictions (Staton et al. 2000).

At the same time, there appears to be a gradual trend toward greater leniency toward inmates who are old and have serious medical problems. For example, Texas has established the Special Needs Parole Program, which provides for an early parole review for special health needs offenders who require 24-hour skilled nursing care. Between 1995 and 1999, numerous cases were identified as possibilities for consideration for early release. Over 50 percent of these cases were statutorily ineligible (e.g., serving mandatory prison terms, on death row, serving life without the possibility of parole). Of all eligible offenders, 38 percent were referred to the parole board with an early-release recommendation, and 22 percent of these were granted parole (Texas Criminal Justice Policy Council 2000).

Furthermore, greater emphasis is now placed on risk-based decision making, where parole boards consider the results of independent, objective risk assessments of individual offenders (Austin 2002). Part of risk assessment is a consideration of one's prior institutional misconduct. One belief, with considerable justification, is that past behavior is a good predictor of future behavior. Although parole boards do not rely exclusively on the results of a risk assessment instrument in their decisions to grant or deny parole to particular inmates (Turpin-Petrosino 1999), parole denials serve to encourage greater conformity with institutional rules so that more favorable early-release outcomes might occur in future parole hearings (Proctor and Pease 2000).

Parole Board Composition and Diversity

There is considerable diversity among parole boards in the United States. No graduate schools in the United States exist to offer degrees in parole board membership. Thus, it is difficult to generalize about all parole boards, the decisions they make, and the reasons for those decisions. Table 10.5 shows the size, composition, and functions of parole boards in the United States.

TABLE 10.5

Parole Board Size and Nature of Parole Board Appointments in the United States, 2001

State	Size of Parole Board	Means of Appointment	Functions
Alabama	3	Governor	Paroles adults, provides adult probation services
Alaska	5	Governor	Paroles adults
Arizona	7	Governor	Paroles adults, reviews executive clemency decisions
Arkansas	7	Governor	Paroles adults
California	8	Governor	Paroles adults, reviews disparate sentencing, considers parole for lifers
Colorado	7	Governor	Paroles adults
Connecticut	11	Governor	Paroles adults
Delaware	5	Governor	Paroles adults
District of Columbia	5	Mayor	Paroles adults and juveniles
Florida	7	Governor	Paroles adults
Georgia	5	Autonomous	Paroles adults, grants reprieves, pardons, commutations

TABLE 10.5 (Continued)

Parole Board Size and Nature of Parole Board Appointments in the United States, 2001

State	Size of Parole Board	Means of Appointment	Functions
Hawaii	3	Governor	Paroles adults
Idaho	5	Board of Correction	Paroles adults
Illinois	12	Governor	Paroles adults
Indiana	5	Governor	Paroles adults, reviews clemency applications for those serving life sentences
Iowa	5	Governor	Paroles adults
Kansas	5	Governor	Paroles adults, reviews clemency applications
Kentucky	7	Governor	Paroles adults
Louisiana	7	Governor	Paroles adults
Maine	5	Governor	Paroles adults[a]
Maryland	7	Secretary of Department of Public Safety	Paroles adults, reviews clemency applications
Massachusetts	8	Governor	Paroles adults
Michigan	10	Department of Corrections	Paroles adults
Minnesota	3	Commissioner of Corrections	Paroles adults[b]
Mississippi	5	Governor	Paroles adults
Missouri	5	Governor	Paroles adults
Montana	3	Governor	Paroles adults[c]
Nebraska	5	Governor	Paroles adults
Nevada	6	Governor	Paroles adults
New Hampshire	5	Governor	Paroles adults
New Jersey	9	Governor	Paroles adults and juveniles
New Mexico	4	Governor	Paroles adults, reviews clemency applications
New York	19	Governor	Paroles adults
North Carolina	5	Governor	Paroles adults
North Dakota	3	Governor	Paroles adults
Ohio	9	Governor	Paroles adults
Oklahoma	5	Governor	Paroles adults, reviews pardons
Oregon	4	Governor	Paroles adults
Pennsylvania	5	Governor	Paroles adults
Rhode Island	6	Governor	Paroles adults
South Carolina	7	Governor	Paroles adults
South Dakota	6	Governor	Paroles adults
Tennessee	7	Governor	Paroles adults
Texas	18	Board of Criminal Justice	Paroles adults
Utah	5	Governor	Paroles adults, reviews pardons
Vermont	5	Governor	Paroles adults
Virginia	5	Governor	Paroles adults
Washington	5	Governor	Paroles adults, fixes minimum terms
West Virginia	3	Governor	Paroles adults
Wisconsin	5	Governor	Paroles adults
Wyoming	7	Governor	Paroles adults

[a]Maine has abolished parole; the Maine Parole Board meets only to hear parole requests from pre-1976 inmates.

[b]Minnesota abolished the Corrections Board in 1982; since then, the Office of Adult Release makes recommendations concerning parole for applicants, with the exception of those serving life sentences; a special advisory panel advises the Commissioner regarding life sentence inmates who apply for parole.

[c]Montana has a Board of Pardons that is attached administratively to the Corrections Division but is autonomous in its authority to parole adults.

Source: Compiled by author.

Laurrece Carter-Hatchett   Robert W. Milburn, Jr.   Lutitia Papailler   John Coy

James D. Provence   Verman R. Winburn   Patricia A. Combs

THE KENTUCKY STATE PAROLE BOARD

All states have parole boards. Most parole board members are appointed to their posts by the governor. In most jurisdictions there are no special qualifications as prerequisites for parole board membership. Parole board members may be educators, businesspersons, retirees, or people connected with the criminal justice system in one capacity or another.

Parole boards are either full-time or part-time. Usually, those states that have abolished parole maintain their original parole boards on a full-time basis for the purpose of conducting parole hearings for all offenders convicted of crimes before parole was abolished. Abolishing parole is not retroactive. Therefore, any prisoner sentenced before parole abolition is entitled to parole consideration, with the exception of those serving mandatory sentences of specified lengths, those sentenced to life without the possibility of parole, and those sentenced to death.

A few states have part-time parole boards that do not convene on a regular basis. In 2001, for instance, there were 28 offenders on parole in Maine. Maine abolished parole in 1976, but it has maintained a part-time parole board since then to consider a diminishing number of early-release requests from parole-eligible offenders convicted of crimes prior to 1976. Presently, fewer than

25 incarcerated offenders in Maine are eligible for parole. The Maine Parole Board will continue to function as long as these inmates are still within their jurisdiction. In recent years, the Maine Parole Board's functions have expanded to include hearing juvenile parole cases from the Maine Youth Center (American Correctional Association 2002:327).

Functions of Parole Boards

The functions of parole boards in most jurisdictions are influenced by a philosophy promoting accountability, punishment, reintegration, and rehabilitation. Synthesizing the goals and philosophy statements of a cross-section of parole boards discloses the following general functions:

1. To assess parole-eligible inmates and approve or deny parole.
2. To determine whether a parolee's parole should be revoked on the basis of alleged parole violations.
3. To evaluate juveniles to determine their eligibility for release from detention.
4. To grant pardons or commutations of sentences to prisoners, where mitigating circumstances or new and exculpatory information is presented.
5. To provide for the supervision of adult offenders placed on parole.
6. To provide investigative and supervisory services to smaller jurisdictions within the state.
7. To grant reprieves in death sentence cases and to commute death penalties.
8. To restore full civil and political rights to parolees.
9. To review disparate sentences and make recommendations to the governor for clemency.
10. To review the pardons and executive clemency decisions made by the governor.

Most parole boards make parole decisions exclusively. In a few jurisdictions, additional functions are performed. Parole boards may evolve their own standards, subject to legislative approval. The Connecticut Parole Board has several standards that govern each early-release decision. These standards include:

1. The nature and circumstances of inmate offenses and the inmate's current attitudes toward them.
2. The inmate's prior record and parole adjustment if paroled previously.
3. Inmate's attitude toward family members, the victim, and authority in general.
4. The institutional adjustment of the inmate, including participation in vocational/educational programs while incarcerated.
5. Inmate's employment history and work skills.
6. Inmate's physical, mental, and emotional condition as determined from interviews and other diagnostic information available.

7. Inmate's insight into the causes of his or her own criminal behavior in the past.
8. Inmate's personal efforts to find solutions to personal problems such as alcoholism, drug dependency, and need for educational training or developing special skills.
9. The adequacy of the inmate's parole plan, including planned place of residence, social acquaintances, and employment program (Connecticut Board of Parole 1974).

Every parole board establishes criteria such as those developed by Connecticut. Sometimes psychiatric reports or examinations are used. Pre-sentence investigation reports are also considered. Victim testimony and victim impact statements are solicited. Parole boards consider written or oral victim testimony.

Parole Board Decision Making and Inmate Control

When offenders become eligible for parole, this does not mean parole will automatically be granted by the parole board. Parole boards have considerable discretionary power, and in many jurisdictions, they have absolute discretion over an inmate's early release chances. In fact, when federal courts have been petitioned to intervene and challenge parole board actions, the decisions of parole boards have prevailed (*Tarlton v. Clark* 1971). In deciding whether to grant or not grant parole for given inmates, parole boards consider the following:

1. Whether serious disciplinary infractions have been committed.
2. Seriousness of prior record.
3. Adjustment to previous probation, parole, and/or incarceration.
4. Facts and circumstances of the offense.
5. Any aggravating and mitigating factors associated with the conviction offense.
6. Involvement in institutional programs for self-improvement (e.g., individual or group counseling, alcohol or drug support groups, vocational/educational training).
7. Documented changes in self-esteem identity.
8. Documentation of personal goals and strengths or motivation for law-abiding behavior.
9. Inmate's remarks about their future behavior and the sophistication of their parole plan.
10. The contents of presentence investigation reports and reasons for the original sentence.

Parole board decision making is far from perfect. Since parole was originally established, parole boards have had to deal with both false positives and false negatives. Some prospective parolees have been deemed unsuitable for parole even though they would not reoffend if subsequently paroled. These unfortunate offenders are hampered by their prior records and other factors, such as mental illnesses or personality disorders (Hartwell 2001). Other offenders look good on paper and are paroled. However, they reoffend and are eventually returned to prison. Thus, parole board decision making is always being criticized because of the perpetual presence of false positives and false negatives.

Parole Decision Making: The Case of the Massachusetts Parole Board.

Parole boards vary in their composition and diversity throughout the United States. One variation in parole board decision making is found in Massachusetts. Massachusetts is somewhat unique in that convicted offenders are housed in either the state prison system or in county jails known as Houses of Correction, which are operated by county sheriffs. In Massachusetts, the current rule is that offenders are sent to Houses of Correction if their sentences are no longer than 2½ years for any single count, which means that county facilities in Massachusetts hold many inmates who would otherwise be sent to state prisons if they had committed the same crime in any other state (Piehl 2002:34).

The Massachusetts Parole Board is fairly active in that it releases approximately 20,000 inmates from state and county facilities per year. Nearly 90 percent of all parolees are released from Houses of Correction compared with early releases of inmates from Massachusetts prisons. In 1993 Massachusetts adopted a truth-in-sentencing provision that greatly reduced the scope of supervision for former inmates. The law eliminated the "Concord sentence," in which offenders were sentenced to terms at a state reformatory with wide latitude for the parole board to determine their actual time served. The law also eliminated the split sentence to state prison, in which inmates were given a term to be served in prison as well as a term of parole following release. Finally, the law eliminated parole eligibility at one-third or two-thirds of the minimum for state prison sentences, as well as statutory good time, in which inmates were granted a certain amount of time off of their maximum sentences. The net result of this truth-in-sentencing change was to reduce the scope for parole release, with the result being that more prisoners were released without parole supervision. More importantly, the truth-in-sentencing law discouraged incentives for inmates to conform to institutional rules and participate in rehabilitative programs while confined. Some good-time credit is still given for certain types of educational activities while inmates are serving time.

Interestingly, when the truth-in-sentencing laws were passed, minimum and maximum sentencing lengths for different offenses were substantially increased. However, judges became reluctant to impose sentences beyond the more lengthy mandatory minimums. This event was even more frustrating for the parole board, which exercised even less discretionary early-release authority than before the truth-in-sentencing law went into effect. In pre-1993 times, for instance, the parole board could use its discretion to release certain inmates short of serving their full terms, where large gaps between minimum and maximum sentences existed. However, as judges increasingly imposed sentences with shorter mandatory terms to be served, parole discretion was drastically abbreviated (Piehl 2002:34).

The most important aspect of the change in the law for the Massachusetts Parole Board pertained to the criteria the board should use to determine early-release eligibility. The law provided that the parole board must judge that there is a reasonable probability that if the prisoner is released, he or she will live and remain at liberty without violating the law, and that his or her release is not incompatible with the welfare of society. While the parole board made such choices in past years, it was not in the context of a legislative mandate. As a result, the Massachusetts Parole Board began to grant fewer parole requests. If the parole board was going to err in its early-release decision making, then it would err on the side of caution. This meant that more false positives would be denied parole when they should, in fact, be granted it. In a probabilistic context, the probability of an inmate obtaining early release from the Massachusetts Parole Board declined from 70 percent in 1990 to 38 percent in 1999.

Viewed from the standpoint of parole-eligible offenders, the percentage of those declining to have a parole hearing increased dramatically during the 1990–1999 period from 15 percent to 32 percent. This meant that more inmates who were eligible for parole were declining to have parole hearings, because they believed, rightly or wrongly, that their chances of obtaining early release were low. And being denied parole in one or more early parole hearings does not look good for parole-eligible inmates seeking parole on subsequent occasions. For various reasons, numerous inmates chose to serve out their sentences rather than seek early release through parole board discretionary actions.

One important implication of the law change for those inmates leaving prison under mandatory release was that their transition to community living would be more abrupt and probably unsuccessful. At least under parole board action, inmates granted early release were often assigned to halfway houses as transitional steps to more normal community living. Furthermore, such inmates were supervised to a degree. Parole officers were often enablers and brokers, seeking to link offenders with needed community resources, educational and vocational opportunities, and various forms of counseling, if needed. But legislatures are responsible for establishing new laws. Parole boards, such as the Massachusetts Parole Board, merely comply with the changes in laws to the best of their ability. It is clear from this discussion that both parolees and the parole board have not benefitted from the truth-in-sentencing law change in 1993. While virtually every parole board in the United States is fallible and makes mistakes in early-release decision making, it is unfortunate that both offenders and the parole board have been penalized. The rehabilitation of prospective parole-eligible offenders has been hampered substantially, while parole board discretionary authority has been drastically curtailed. Parole boards in other jurisdictions have shared the Massachusetts Parole Board experience in various ways during the past few decades (Piehl 2002).

Predicting Parolee Success and Failure.   If parole boards decide to grant parole, it is usually conditional and subject to rules and regulations. If the parole board denies parole, the reasons for this decision are made known to the inmate and become a part of the inmate's record. Most parole boards rely on inmates' past institutional conduct as a key indication of how they might behave if paroled. However, evidence suggests that good institutional behavior does not mean that an inmate will be law-abiding if early release is granted (Haesler 1992). Another indicator of parolee success is whether offenders have had vocational and/or academic training. A study of 760 parolees showed that they were largely successful, particularly if they had vocational/educational training and if they sought and maintained employment while on parole (Anderson, Schumacker, and Anderson 1991). Those whose parole programs were revoked tended to have less vocational and educational involvement than those who were more successful. Less successful parolees did not have the skills to qualify for good jobs, and they appeared unmotivated to seek work of any kind.

Three variables seem closely linked to parolee failure. First, the longer the sentence imposed on the offender, the greater the likelihood the offender will recidivate when subsequently paroled. This is logical, since longer sentences are associated with more serious offenses. More serious offenders are probably more inclined to recidivate than less serious ones. Second, if the parolee had previously been on parole, he or she was less likely to violate present parole program provisions. Although recidivist parolees may pose greater program risks compared with first-offender parolees, prior experience with parole may sensitize seasoned parolees to the expectations of POs and the importance of maintaining low-profile law-abiding behavior. Third, the PO's assessment of "high risk" often was successful in predicting parolee program violations. Thus, POs acquire some facility in predicting which parolees are more likely than others to violate one or more conditions of their parole programs. Their personal forecasts of these events are often accurate (Kronick, Lambert, and Lambert 1998).

Accessing and using community-based services for parolees assist many of them in adjusting to life in their communities. Some of these services are treatment-oriented to address one or more chemical dependencies or psychological problems of parolees (Burke 2001). In a study of 67 female Massachusetts parolees during the 1989–1991 period, for instance, these women were tracked for a two-year period following the completion of their parole programs. Over two-thirds recidivated. However, those parolees who took advantage of community-based services had a 41 percent recidivism rate compared with a 63 percent recidivism rate among those who did not use community services. The mean number of days before recidivating was 210 for those who never used community-based services, while the mean number of days to recidivism was 568 for those who did use community services (Pearl 1998). Thus, the community as well as female offenders tend to benefit when social services are incorporated into existing community punishment models.

Interstate Compact Agreements.   During the last few decades, increasing numbers of states have entered into an **Interstate Compact for Adult Offender Supervision (ICAOS)** (Humphries 2002:10). Interstate compact agreements were originally established between several states in 1937. These agreements meant that offenders who were convicted of crimes in one state, such as Minnesota, but who were legal residents of Georgia, may eventually be paroled to Georgia and be supervised by Georgia parole departments instead of Minnesota parole departments. It was believed that placing offenders in their original state environments brings them closer to their families and other social support systems. They may be able to find work more easily with the greater contacts they have already established. An alternative view is that they may have left their original states because of their criminal pasts. Furthermore, placing parolees back into their original state environments may reacquaint them with gang members and other adverse associations or relationships that gave rise to their criminal conduct. Despite this controversy, there was an informal agreement among various states for many decades to accept probationers and parolees from other jurisdictions. The informal nature of this compact meant that participating states accepted probationers and parolees on a voluntary basis and that the states could reject certain undesirable offenders if they chose to do so. Actually, all 50 states were participating in the old interstate compact in 2002, although the compact was viewed as a "toothless tiger," because any accepting state could reject any and all requests for transfers of convicted offenders from other states at any time for any reason.

During the 1990s meetings were held with the National Institute of Corrections (NIC) in an effort to formalize a nationwide compact agreement. The NIC declared that at least 35 states should pass interstate compact laws that would establish coordinating agencies. Once these interstate compact laws were passed, then a true interstate compact agreement would officially be established. Despite the public benefits of older interstate compact legislation, as well as the limitations inherent in the existing adult supervision compact agreements, the new official compact agreement would enhance legal authority and organizational capacity and empower administrators and agencies to more effectively govern the interstate movement of offenders in this age of modern transportation and communications technology (Humphries 2002:10).

An NIC Advisory Board drafted a replacement compact, and 261 state agencies and organizations were provided the opportunity to critique the compact and make recommendations and modifications. Subsequently, once the new compact had been drafted, nine states passed it in 2000 and 16 states passed it in 2001. By June 2002, 36 states had passed interstate compact agreements, and an additional four states were expected to pass such agreements by the end of 2002. The distinctive nature of the new ICAOS is that:

1. Victim representatives have participated at every stage of planning and implementation and will be an ongoing voice in the operation of the new compact. One of the messages received at public hearings is that when interstate supervision is involved, victims need and want information about where the person is who victimized them, and they have legitimate safety concerns when the offender returns and they have not been notified. They often have restitution or other monetary issues that are complicated by out-of-state supervision. Victims have generally not been afforded information or opportunity for input in the past, but their concerns will now be heard at state councils and as ex-officio members of the Interstate Commission.

2. Each state must have a State Council, which is comprised of the compact administrator, a victims' representative, representatives from each branch of state government, and any other members that a state chooses to include. Each state will define the role and responsibility of its State Council, but at a minimum, each state will provide oversight and advocacy regarding its interstate supervision policies and activities.

3. The commissioner from each state will have one vote at the Interstate Commission, the organization comprised of states that have enacted the new compact. The Commission is required to develop interstate rules that will become effective following a one-year transition period. While many of the rules adopted are likely to resemble the rules that presently exist, some existing rules are likely to be amended or deleted, while others are likely to be created. The degree of rule similarity or differences from what currently exists will be the product of decisions made collectively by member states as they exercise Commission rule-making authority.

4. Each state is obligated to financially support the Commission, which will employ staff and operate a system of year-round support and services.

5. Accountability by states will be enhanced through new enforcement provisions included in compact language.

6. A web-based information system will be developed that will expedite transfer of supervision requests and case information, permit auditing for compliance with agreed-upon time lines, and make possible an accurate compilation of relevant interstate data (Humphries 2002:10–11).

With more uniform and official standards established to govern the placement of probationers and parolees in their resident states for supervision, it is anticipated that all states will eventually accept the new compact agreement and abide by its provisions. It has been observed that as we celebrate the success and enjoy the prospect of states' enhanced ability to manage interstate movement of adult parolees and probationers, it is important to recognize that there are many difficult choices to be made by the Interstate Commission, and practices in the field will inevitably be altered in some manner. Change is not always comfortable. But the value of interstate cooperation is the achievement of shared goals, and the ultimate responsibility of the NIC is to protect the public to the greatest extent possible (Humphries 2002:11).

Parole Board Orientations

Decisions made by parole boards are increasingly standardized and professional (Austin 2002). Generally, they can be classified into six general categories, each manifesting a particular value system: (1) the jurist, (2) the sanctioner, (3) the treater, (4) the controller, (5) the citizen, and (6) the regulator (Gottfredson and Gottfredson 1988:231–233). The jurist value system sees parole decisions as a natural part of criminal justice where fairness and equity predominate. Emphasized are an inmate's rights, and parole board members strive to be sensitive to due process. The sanctioner value system equates the seriousness of the offense with the amount of time served.

The treater value system is rehabilitative in orientation, and decisions are made in the context of what might most benefit the offender if parole is granted. Thus, participation in various educational or vocational programs, therapy or encounter groups, restitution, and other types of conditions might accompanying one's early release. The controller value system emphasizes the functions of parole supervision and monitoring. The conditions are established that increase the degree of control over the offender. Perhaps electronic monitoring or house arrest might be a part of one's parole program (Whitfield 2001).

The citizen value system is concerned with appealing to public interests and seeing that community expectations are met by making appropriate early-release decisions. How will the public react to releasing certain offenders short of serving their full terms? Will public good be served by such decisions? Finally, the regulator value system is directed toward inmate reactions to parole board decisions. Will inmates acquire trust for parole board decision making? Will the integrity of parole boards be undermined if fairness and equity are not observed by parole boards?

Objective Parole Criteria

One way of enhancing fairness and equity is to devise objective parole criteria that apply to all parole-eligible inmates and not just to those who haven't captured media attention because of the sensational nature of their crimes (e.g.,

Charles Manson, Sirhan Sirhan, John Hinckley). The advantages of objective parole criteria are:

1. Presumptive release dates for inmates are known and predictable.
2. Parole boards observe and honor these presumptive release dates.
3. An impartial scoring system is used to evaluate one's early release prospects.
4. Consistent criteria and factors are applied in consistent ways in the parole-granting process.

Salient Factor Scores and Risk Assessments

A weighting system for parole prognosis was developed by Ernest W. Burgess of the University of Chicago in 1928 (Glaser 1987:256). However, the development of more contemporary objective parole decision-making guidelines can be traced to the pioneering work of Don Gottfredson and Leslie Wilkins, leaders of the Parole Decision-Making Project in the early 1970s (Goldkamp 1987:106). The National Council on Crime and Delinquency and the U.S. Parole Commission were interested in parole decision making and solicited the assistance of social scientists to examine various criteria involved in early release decisions.

SALIENT FACTOR SCORE INDEX

1. Prior convictions/adjudications (adult or juvenile):
   - None (3 points)
   - One (2 points)
   - Two or three (1 point)
   - Four or more (0 points)
2. Prior commitments of more than 30 days (adult or juvenile):
   - None (2 points)
   - One or two (1 point)
   - Three or more (0 points)
3. Age at current offense/prior commitments:
   - 25 years of age or older (2 points)
   - 20–25 years of age (1 point)
   - 19 years of age or younger (0 points)
4. Recent commitment/free period (3 years):
   - No prior commitment of more than 30 days (adult or juvenile) or released to the community from last such commitment at least 3 years prior to the commencement of the current offense (1 point)
   - Otherwise (0 points)
5. Probation/parole/confinement/escape status violator this time:
   - Neither on probation, parole, confinement, or escape status at the time of the current offense nor committed as a probation, parole, confinement, or escape status violator this time (1 point)
   - Otherwise (0 points)
6. Heroin/opiate dependence:
   - No history of heroin/opiate dependence (1 point)
   - Otherwise (0 points)

Total score = _____

FIGURE 10.1   Salient Factor Score Index, SFS 81.

Source: U.S. Parole Commission. *Rules and Procedures Manual.* Washington, DC: U.S. Parole Commission, 1983.

SFS 76 and SFS 81.   The **Salient Factor Score Index (SFS) (SFS 76 and SFS 81)** was designed to assist parole board members to make fair parole decisions. When parole boards departed from these guidelines, they were to furnish written rationales to justify these departures. At the federal level, the salient factor score was made up of seven criteria and was refined in 1976. This was called the SFS 76. In 1981, the salient factor scoring instrument was revised and a new, six-factor predictive device, SFS 81, was constructed (Hoffman 1983). Figure 10.1 shows the six-item federal Salient Factor Score instrument, SFS 81.

Scores on the SFS 81 can range from "0" to "10." The following evaluative designations accompanying various score ranges:

Raw Score	Parole Prognosis
0–3	"Poor"
4–5	"Fair"
6–7	"Good"
8–10	"Very Good"

A table of offense characteristics, which consists of categories varying in offense severity, is reviewed. Adult ranges in numbers of months served are provided for each category and are crosstabulated with the four-category parole prognosis above. Thus, a parole board can apply a consistent set of standards to prisoners who commit identical offenses.

MEASURING PAROLE EFFECTIVENESS THROUGH RECIDIVISM

Recidivism Defined

The successfulness of parole board decision making is frequently measured by the degree of recidivism among parolees. Descriptive information about recidivist-parolees is abundant, although there is considerable inconsistency about which characteristics seem most associated with recidivism (Schwaner 2000). Generally, recidivism is reoffending following a conviction for an earlier crime. However, not all reoffending involves new crimes. While there are at least 14 different definitions of recidivism (Maltz 1984), four of the more common definitions are rearrests, reconvictions, reincarcerations, and revocations of parole or probation.

Rearrests.   Any probationer or parolee has already been convicted of one or more crimes. When these persons are arrested again while on probation or parole, these rearrests are sometimes counted as recidivism. It makes no difference whether these arrestees are later released because police lack sufficient evidence to detain them. The fact of an arrest is recidivism.

Reconvictions.   The best indicator of recidivism is conviction for a new offense following a conviction for a previous offense. When probationers and parolees commit new crimes and are convicted, these convictions are used to measure their rates of recidivism. Reconvictions are considered the most accurate indicators of recidivism, since new crimes are involved. If a probation or parole program is going to be evaluated properly, then reconvictions are perhaps the best criteria to use in such program evaluations. Using any other indicator may lead to false conclusions about a program's effectiveness. If

30 percent of all parolees are revoked for technical program violations, for instance, this may mean that parole officers are more vigilant at detecting program infractions. This is because parolees are supervised more closely by parole officers in some programs. It is logical to expect that parole officers who make more frequent visits to parolee residences are going to discover more program infractions (e.g., curfew violations, failed drug/alcohol checks) compared with programs where less frequent PO visits are made.

Reincarcerations. A return to jail or prison following parole means either that a new crime was committed or alleged, or that a program violation or infraction was detected. Reincarceration doesn't mean a new criminal conviction. For this reason, the fact of reincarceration is a poor measure of program recidivism.

Revocations of Parole. Another way of measuring recidivism is to count the number of **revocations, probation or parole.** However, about 30 percent of all offenders who have their parole programs revoked are given sentences for new crimes (Camp and Camp 1999:177). Over half of these offenders are returned to prison because of program rule infractions. In all cases involving parole revocation or **probation revocation,** parolees and probationers are entitled to a **revocation hearing** before either a parole board or the sentencing judge.

THE PAROLE REVOCATION PROCESS

In 1871 a Virginia judge said that prisoners have no more rights than slaves (*Ruffin v. Commonwealth,* 1871). This pronouncement was supported by judges in other jurisdictions who favored leaving corrections in the hands of wardens and other corrections officials. This led to the hands-off doctrine, which caused appellate courts not to intervene in correctional affairs for the next seventy years. Subsequently, inmate rights have been expanded and court access is a constitutional entitlement for all inmates in prisons and jails. Despite these improvements and expansions of inmate rights, the Fourteenth Amendment was not initially interpreted by the U.S. Supreme Court to include parolees or probationers and revocations of their parole or probation programs until the late 1960s. The most significant cases influencing probation or parole revocation and all probation or parole revocation proceedings were *Mempa v. Rhay* (1967), *Morrissey v. Brewer* (1972), and *Gagnon v. Scarpelli* (1973).

Landmark Parole Revocation Cases

Morrissey v. Brewer (1972). The first landmark case involving the constitutional rights of parolees was *Morrissey v. Brewer* (1972). In 1967, John Morrissey was convicted by an Iowa court for falsely drawing checks and sentenced to not more than seven years in the Iowa State Prison. He was eventually paroled from prison in June 1968. However, seven months later, his parole officer learned that while on parole, Morrissey had bought a car under an assumed name and operated it without permission, obtained credit cards under a false name, and gave false information to an insurance company when he was involved in a minor automobile accident. Also, Morrissey had given his parole officer a false address for his residence.

The parole officer interviewed Morrissey and filed a report recommending that parole be revoked. The reasons given by the officer were that Morrissey admitted buying the car and obtaining false ID, obtaining credit under false pretenses, and also being involved in the auto accident. Morrissey claimed he was sick and that this condition prevented him from maintaining continuous contact with his parole officer. The parole officer claimed that Morrissey's parole should be revoked because Morrissey had a habit of continually violating the rules. The parole board revoked Morrissey's parole and he was returned to the Iowa State Prison to serve the remainder of his sentence. Morrissey was not represented by counsel at the revocation proceeding. Furthermore, he was not given the opportunity to cross-examine witnesses against him, he was not advised in writing of the charges against him, no disclosure of the evidence against him was provided, and reasons for the revocation were not given. Morrissey also was not permitted to offer evidence in his own behalf or give personal testimony.

Morrissey's appeal to the Iowa Supreme Court was rejected, but the U.S. Supreme Court heard his appeal. While the Court did not address directly the question of whether Morrissey should have had court-appointed counsel, it did make a landmark decision in his case. It overturned the Iowa Parole Board action and established a two-stage proceeding for determining whether parole ought to be revoked. The first or **preliminary hearing** or **preliminary examination** is held at the time of arrest and detention, where it is determined whether probable cause exists that the parolee actually committed the alleged parole violation. The second hearing is more involved and establishes the guilt of the parolee relating to the violations. This proceeding must extend to the parolee certain minimum due process rights. These rights are:

1. The right to have written notice of the alleged violations of parole conditions.
2. The right to have disclosed to the parolee any evidence of the alleged violation.
3. The right of the parolee to be heard in person and to present exculpatory evidence as well as witnesses in his or her behalf.
4. The right to confront and cross-examine adverse witnesses, unless cause exists why they should not be cross-examined.
5. The right to a judgment by a neutral and detached body, such as the parole board itself.
6. The right to a written statement of the reasons for the parole revocation.

The *Morrissey* case is significant because it sets forth **minimum due process rights** for all parolees, creating a two-stage proceeding whereby the alleged infractions of parole conditions could be examined and a full hearing conducted to determine the most appropriate disposition of the offender.

THE RIGHTS OF PROBATIONERS AND PAROLEES

There has been continuing interest in the rights of parolees. Various courts in different jurisdictions, including the U.S. Supreme Court, have issued key decisions that influence the lives of parolees (Vigdal and Stadler 1994:44). Several

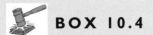

BOX 10.4

NEW PROGRAM FOR PAROLE VIOLATORS: CAMP BRANCH

Camp Branch

A new program for parolees who have had their paroles violated but who may be safely returned to parole after 180 days of programming, which includes substance-abuse treatment and cognitive restructuring, is underway at Camp Branch, Michigan. A similar program will be placed at Camp Brighton for women in the future.

The first 10 prisoners in the program arrived at Camp Branch from the Reception and Guidance Center on May 16, 2002. There are currently 16 prisoners in the program. Called the Parole Violator Diversion Program, it will try to reclaim some of the 2,880 parolees who violate annually and are returned to prison. "Many of these offenders are returned for 12 months but end up staying in prison much longer because the board is not convinced they can be safely returned," said Stephen Marschke, chairperson of the Michigan Parole Board. "We want to target those borderline cases who can return to parole after some very focused programming and opportunities and not be a danger to the public."

Between 500 and 600 parole violators are expected to be assigned to the program when it is fully operational, which will also include community service, GED completion classes, employment in camp jobs, and a life skills class. Life skills classes involve teaching offenders how to prepare resumes, find employment, prepare and live within budgets, manage checking accounts, be better parents, and generally get ready to live outside of prison.

The Parole Board will consider offenders for the program after their paroles have been violated. Early in the process, parole violators are excluded if they are classified as Very High Assault Risk, if they are serving time for a sex offense or if they had a prior conviction for a sex offense, if they are less than 18 months from their discharge date, if the crime involved a death, or if offenders have 12 or more prior criminal record points or three or more convictions for assaultive crimes using the Parole Guidelines. Further evaluation excludes those whose parole violation involved possession of a firearm or other dangerous weapon, if it involved a physical assault causing serious injury, if it involved sexual assault, including indecent exposure, or if the prisoner was convicted of a felony or has a pending felony while on parole. Only those offenders who are eligible for camp placement can be considered.

Placement of the offender in the diversion program is one of three decisions board members will make when they consider the individual after he or she has had their parole violated. The other two include a return to prison or re-parole. While in the diversion program, which is voluntary, offenders will have limited visiting, limited access to the law library, very limited personal property, and limited access to store items. They cannot receive or mail packages in general, have very limited telephone privileges, cannot smoke, cannot wear jewelry, are not paid for their work assignments inside the facility, and must adhere to very strict grooming standards.

Marschke said the offenders will be tracked to see how they do once they complete the program and are re-paroled. The new program differs from the Technical Rule Violation Program (TRV) in that the TRV participants have not actually had their paroles violated. "This new program is another chance for those who have failed parole. Many of them will have already tried the TRV program but continued to have problems while on parole," said Marschke. "We're hoping the new program will provide the kinds of additional programming and opportunities that will help the offenders finally become successful on parole."

Source: Michigan Department of Corrections, "New Program Targets Parole Violators," June, 2002.

cases are described in this section that highlight various probationer and parolee rights issues.

Parolee Rights Generally

Pardons.   Whenever governors pardon someone who may or may not be on probation or parole, the effect of these pardons is different, depending upon the jurisdiction. Generally, a pardon is an absolution for a crime previously committed. Someone has been convicted of the crime, and the intent of a pardon is to terminate whatever punishment has been imposed. In *United States v. Noonan* (1990), for instance, Gregory Noonan was convicted and sentenced in 1969 for "failing to submit to induction into the armed forces." President Jimmy Carter granted a pardon to Noonan on January 21, 1977, wherein Carter declared a "full, complete and unconditional pardon" to persons convicted during the Vietnam War for refusing induction. Noonan sought to have his record of the original conviction expunged. An expungement order has the effect of wiping one's slate clean, as though the crime and the conviction had never occurred. Noonan believed that his conviction, which remained on his record, adversely affected his employment chances. Thus, he sought to expunge his record because of the pardon he had received from Carter. However, the Third Circuit Court of Appeals, a federal appellate court, refused to grant him this request. The Court declared that "a pardon does not blot out guilt nor does it restore the offender to a state of innocence in the eye of the law." In Noonan's case, the presidential pardon was effective in removing the punishment, but it did not expunge his criminal record.

A different position has been taken regarding the influence of a pardon on one's criminal record in some appellate courts. For instance, the Indiana Court of Appeals declared in the case of *State v. Bergman* (1990) that a pardon does expunge one's criminal record. The Governor of Indiana had pardoned a convict, Berman, for a crime he had previously committed. Bergman sought to have his record expunged, in much the same way as Noonan. The Indiana Court of Appeals declared that pardons "block out the very existence of the offender's guilt, so that, in the eye(s) of the law, he is thereafter as innocent as if he had never committed the offense." Subsequent state court decisions have concurred with both Pennsylvania and Indiana.

Parolee Program Conditions.   When parolees are subject to having their programs revoked by respective authorities, what is the nature of evidence that can be used against them to support their program revocation? What are their rights concerning parole officer searches of their premises (Hemmens 1998:11)? What about the program conditions they have been obligated to follow? What about parole board recognition of and obligation to follow minimum-sentence provisions from sentencing judges?

Parole Actions and Rights.   Parole boards have considerable discretionary powers. They may deny parole or grant it. They may revoke one's parole and return the offender to prison, or they may continue the offender's parole program, with additional supervision and other conditions. Below are some of the actions parole boards may take and how parolees are impacted.

Inmates who become eligible for parole are not automatically entitled to parole. Parole boards have considerable discretion whether to grant or deny parole to any inmate. Short of serving their full sentences or completing a portion of their term less any applicable good-time credit, inmates are not automatically enti- tled to be paroled.   In 1981, for example, Franks was sentenced to life impris- onment in Texas for a violent crime he committed (*Ex parte Franks* 2001). Under the law in Texas at the time of Franks' conviction, Franks would be eligi- ble for mandatory parole when the calendar time he had served plus all good- conduct time he had accrued equaled the maximum term to which he had been sentenced. Arguing in part that the average life term served in the United States is far less than 20 years, Franks demanded a parole from the Texas Board of Par- dons and Paroles. The board refused to grant Franks early release and he ap- pealed. The appellate court rejected Franks' appeal, noting that those serving life terms are ineligible for parole, since it is impossible to calculate when "life" has been served. Thus, it is impossible to determine with certainty when the amount of time served together with good-time credits equal the unknown amount of time associated with a life sentence. One dissenting judge ridiculed the appellate decision, however, remarking that such thinking doesn't make sense, particularly in view of the fact that those serving 99-year prison terms are eligible for early release and mandatory supervision.

Another case, this time in New York, involved an offender who challenged the New York Board of Parole and the parole guidelines it had established. Douglas, a convicted offender serving time in prison, believed that he had served enough time and that the New York Board of Parole was obligated to set a specific time range for his early release (*Douglas v. Travis* 2002). The board convened and denied Douglas parole. Douglas appealed, citing several issues. However, the appellate court rejected Douglas's petition, holding that the New York Board of Parole can be compelled to act, but it cannot be compelled to act in a given way (i.e., to parole Douglas). Furthermore, the appellate court de- clared that although guidelines were required of the parole board, it was up to the parole board to interpret these guidelines in the light of other factors and evidence, such as the results of risk assessment instruments that might show the poor likelihood that Douglas would be successful if paroled.

Parole boards are not required to count the amount of time served by an of- fender while on parole as time against his or her original sentence.   In the case of *Hudson v. State* (2002), Hudson was convicted of a crime and sentenced to prison. Subsequently, Hudson violated one or more parole conditions and had her parole revoked. Later, Hudson desired another parole and wanted her time spent in her earlier parole program to count against her original sentence. The parole board rejected her request and she appealed, claiming a double jeopardy violation of her constitutional rights. An appellate court ruled in favor of the parole board, holding that time served by an offender while on parole does not equate with time served in prison. When someone violates parole, this is a for- feiture of time served while on parole. The offender is returned to prison and must serve the remainder of the original sentence, unless, of course, a parole board decides to re-parole them at a later date.

Inmates who have been paroled and who subsequently commit a new crime while on parole may have their parole programs revoked and be returned to prison to serve the remaining sentence.   Fryer, a convict, was paroled by the New York Board of Parole (*People ex rel. Fryer v. Beaver* 2002). Subsequently, Fryer was arrested for a new offense, which involved assaulting his pregnant girlfriend and inflicting facial bruises. Fryer's parole was revoked and he appealed, alleging that the board relied on hearsay testimony to find him in violation of his parole program. An appellate court rejected his appeal, holding that the determination by the parole board was supported by substantial evidence, including hearsay that was properly admitted.

Parole boards cannot discharge originally imposed sentences when resetting parole dates for offenders who are serving consecutive sentences.   Tucker, an Oregon inmate, was serving consecutive sentences of different indeterminate sentence lengths and became eligible for parole on the first sentence (*Tucker v. Lambert* 2001). The Oregon Board of Parole and Post-Prison Supervision set a parole date for Tucker on the first conviction offense. However, because of the second conviction offense, the board had to reset Tucker's parole release date and postponed his release on the first sentence. Tucker appealed, claiming that when the board set the first parole release date, it discharged his first sentence. The appellate court disagreed and rejected Tucker's petition. The court held that parole boards have the power to grant early release to inmates. They also have the power to revoke one's parole for cause. However, they do not have the power to discharge sentences imposed by courts. However, they may shorten one's sentence by discharging one from parole, where such an order for discharge occurs six months or longer after the offender has been on parole. Thus, offenders who are legally placed on parole for two separate sentences can be brought back to prison for violations of their parole on either sentence.

Parole boards cannot grant discretionary parole to inmates who are serving presumptive sentences.   In an Alaska case, Cofey was an inmate serving a presumptive sentence of a specified length (*State v. Cofey* 2001). At the time of Cofey's sentencing, the judge shortened Cofey's presumptive sentence because of several mitigating factors. Furthermore, the judge sentenced Cofey to a mitigated presumptive term. Cofey believed that the parole board should grant him discretionary early release from the mitigated presumptive sentence and the parole board denied his parole request. Cofey appealed. The appellate court determined that the parole board was within its authority to deny Cofey early release, but it set aside his sentence and remanded the case back to the original trial court for resentencing consistent with existing statutes. In sum, judges do not have the authority to order defendants sentenced to presumptive prison terms that require that they are eligible for discretionary parole release.

When clear standards for denying parole are provided by statute, parole boards are required to provide inmates with a written justification for why they deny parole consistent with those standards.   Voss was a convicted offender in Pennsylvania (*Voss v. Pa. Bd. of Probation & Parole* 2001). Voss applied for parole and was denied it. The Pennsylvania Board of Probation and Parole said simply that Voss had been denied parole on the basis of the fair administration of justice. Since this provision was not a part of the statutory language governing early-release decision making, Voss appealed. An appellate court agreed with Voss, holding that the parole board must provide a written statement articulating its reason(s) for denying him parole, referring specifically to one or more reasons set forth by statute.

SERVING TIME BEYOND MAXIMUM SENTENCES

Because of inmate misconduct and other factors, some inmates serve their entire sentences. If an offender is sentenced to 10 years, the offender serves 10 years. If the offender is sentenced to 20 years, the offender serves 20 years. If an offender serves his or her entire sentence imposed by the judge during the sentencing hearing, the offender must be freed. This process is called mandatory release, and it signifies that the offender has paid his or her complete debt to society. But there are exceptions.

One of the most obvious exceptions is an inmate who commits one or more new crimes while confined. An inmate may assault or kill another inmate. Thus, new charges are filed. The case is heard in court, like any other criminal case, and the defendant may be found guilty of the offense(s) alleged beyond a reasonable doubt. A new sentence is imposed. This new sentence runs consecutively with the original sentence being served. Thus, when an offender completes the first sentence, he or she commences the second sentence as the result of a new conviction.

A second exception is an inmate who is in a state that imposes an additional number of days beyond the original sentence imposed by the sentencing judge. The inmate may earn good-time credit and work off these additional days through law-abiding behavior, not receiving any writeups for misconduct, and otherwise being a good inmate. However, if the inmate violates institutional rules and engages in various forms of misconduct, these additional days beyond one's original sentence are not erased and must be served in their entirety.

A third exception is an inmate who has committed a crime in a state where the use of a firearm during the commission of a felony mandates an additional two-year term beyond the original sentence imposed. Thus, if the perpetrator commits armed robbery in Michigan, for instance, Michigan courts will impose a sentence of 10 years for armed robbery, as well as an additional 2 years of flat time to be served in its entirety, simply because the offender used a firearm during the crime. Therefore, when the original sentence is served in its entirety, the inmate must then commence an additional two-year sentence for the firearm sentence enhancement.

A fourth exception involves a particular offender class that is considered by the public to be dangerous. For certain types of offenders, serving their original sentences in their entirety is not considered sufficient punishment. These offenders are sex offenders, sexual predators, child molesters, pedophiles, serial rapists, and others regarded as continuing to pose a societal danger (McGrath, Cumming, and Holt 2002). How does a state keep these sorts of inmates confined beyond their maximum sentences? The answer is that the state seeks to have certain sexual predators committed to mental hospitals for observation and treatment. These civil commitments of certain sex offenders are increasingly common. However, the burden is upon the state to show that the particular sexual predator continues to pose a threat or danger to the community if released. But once a sexual predator has been civilly committed, the consequences are especially severe for that predator. The severity of these consequences is such that the offender may be committed indefinitely, provided that a psychiatric committee conducts periodic hearings to determine the suitability of the offender for release into society. If the committee decides that the offender continues to pose a societal risk, then it has the power to deny the offender's release from civil confinement. In effect, a committee at a mental hospital has the power to commit certain offenders for the duration of their natural lives. Some critics of civil commitments allege that this additional commitment is tantamount to double jeopardy and therefore is illegal. However, the courts have ruled otherwise. Furthermore, it has been argued that the "due process" nature of punishment has been served when the offender serves the original sentence for which he or she was convicted. Additional punishment is unnecessary. Again, this argument has fallen on deaf ears. The public wants to feel safe from sexual predators. Laws that perpetuate their incarceration, whether it is in a prison or a mental hospital, have general societal support (Kemshall 2001).

Although civil commitments of dangerous offenders occurred prior to 1993 in various jurisdictions throughout the United States, significant judicial notice of these commitments occurred during the early 1990s. One major reason for this notice was that certain sex offenders who had been released in their respective states after serving their full sentences committed new sex crimes, some of them especially heinous. Although recidivism among sex offenders compared with other types of criminal offenders is especially low, the media attention given to these sex offender cases prompted several states to reexamine their civil commitment options for certain sex offenders who were considered most likely to reoffend (Tierney and McCabe 2002). For instance, a study conducted by the Ohio Department of Rehabilitation and Correction involved a ten-year followup of convicted sex offenders who were released in 1989. The overall recidivism rate was 34 percent, although recidivism because of a sex-related offense was only 11 percent. Child molesters had the lowest recidivism rates of all with 7.4 percent returning to prison (Ohio Department of Rehabilitation and Correction 2001).

Four cases are discussed briefly below. These cases are chronologically ordered so that we may see how laws affecting sexual predators have become increasingly severe in their consequences.

1. The first case of note involved a simple penile plethysmography test administered to sex offenders to determine their penile response to sexual stimuli, such as pornography. This was the case of *Walrath v. United States* (1993). In *Walrath v. United States,* 830 F.Supp. 444 (1993), a penile plethysmography test was administered to Walrath, a convicted sex offender in Illinois. The test involves attaching devices to a prospective parolee's penis in order to determine his subsequent reaction to various forms of sexual stimuli. An erection is incriminating in this instance, and the offender may be denied parole. The test is also used to determine whether a sex offender continues to pose a threat to society. Walrath was required to submit to a penile plethysmography test as one condition preceding his parole by the Illinois Parole Board. Walrath claimed that such a test would violate his Fifth Amendment right against self-incrimination. The United States district court in Illinois upheld the United States Parole Commission's administration of the test to Walrath, holding that "there is no indication that any results from Walrath's plethysmography could be

used to criminally prosecute him for other acts. Instead, the results, like the treatment, might legitimately be used to assess the threat Walrath poses to society."

2. The second case established a significant precedent for civil commitments of sexual predators and squarely addressed the issue of double jeopardy as a challenge to additional civil punishment beyond criminal punishment. The case was *Kansas v. Hendricks,* 117 S.Ct. 2072 (1997). Hendricks was convicted in 1984 of sexually molesting two 13-year-old boys. Hendricks had a lengthy history of child sexual abuse convictions. In 1994, Hendricks was scheduled to be released from prison to a halfway house, but Kansas had recently enacted the Sexually Violent Predator Act, which establishes procedures for the civil commitment of persons who, due to a mental abnormality or a personality disorder are likely to engage in predatory acts of sexual violence. Kansas thus invoked the Act against Hendricks and ordered his civil commitment to a mental hospital for an indeterminate period. Hendricks challenged the civil commitment on several grounds, including double jeopardy, the prohibited application of *ex post facto* laws, and a violation of his substantive due process rights. The Kansas Supreme Court invalidated the Act, finding that the precommitment condition of a mental abnormality did not satisfy what it perceived to be the substantive due process requirement that involuntary civil commitment must be predicated on a mental illness finding. It did not address Hendricks' double jeopardy or *ex post facto* claims. Kansas officials appealed to the U.S. Supreme Court who heard the case. The U.S. Supreme Court reversed the Kansas Supreme Court, holding that the Act's definition of mental abnormality satisfies "substantive" due process requirements. Furthermore, the Act does not violate Hendricks' rights against double jeopardy or its ban on *ex post facto* lawmaking, since the Act does not establish criminal proceedings, and involuntary confinement under it is not punishment in any criminal context.

3. The third case occurred in Washington state and involved a convicted serial rapist. The serial rapist was civilly committed following his served sentence for six rapes he had committed. Again, the issue of double jeopardy was raised, as well as issues related to the rapist's treatment and potential for rehabilitation. This was the case of *Seling v. Young,* 121 S.Ct. 727 (2001). Andre Young was convicted of six rapes over three decades and was scheduled for release from prison in October 1990 in Washington state. One day prior to his release, the State filed a petition to commit Young as a sexually violent offender. A commitment hearing was held and it was determined that Young posed a threat as a sexually violent offender under Washington state's Community Protection Act of 1990, which authorizes civil commitment of such offenders. Young appealed, arguing that his civil commitment was double jeopardy and that the law was unconstitutional. Furthermore, Young alleged that the conditions of his confinement were incompatible with rehabilitation and too restrictive. Washington state courts rejected his arguments and he appealed to the U.S. Supreme Court, which heard the case. The U.S. Supreme Court upheld Young's civil commitment and rejected his double jeopardy argument. It further held that the Washington state law was constitutional. The U.S. Supreme Court did not address whether the mental health center where Young was being housed and treated was operating properly.

Rather, the U.S. Supreme Court left this determination to the Washington state courts. The U.S. Supreme Court noted that offenders have a cause of action at the state level if the mental health center fails to fulfill its statutory duty to adequately care and provide individualized treatment for sex offenders.

4. The fourth and most recent case involved a convicted Kansas exhibitionist who was convicted of sexual battery. In this instance, no rape occurred, although the offender demanded sexual favors from a victim and threatened to rape her if she didn't comply with his demands. This was the case of *Kansas v. Crane*, 122 S.Ct. 867 (2002) Michael Crane was convicted of lewd and lascivious behavior and pleaded guilty to aggravated sexual battery for two incidents occurring in 1993. He exposed himself to a tanning salon attendant and a video store clerk. In the case of the video store clerk, he demanded oral sex and threatened to rape her. Subsequently, the state court evaluated Crane and adjudicated him a sexual predator under Kansas's Sexually Violent Predator Act (SVPA). This Act permits the civil detention of a person convicted of any of several enumerated sexual offenses, if it is proven beyond a reasonable doubt that he suffers from a mental abnormality, a disorder affecting his emotional or volitional capacity, that predisposes the person to commit sexually violent acts or makes the person likely to engage in repeat acts of sexual violence. Crane was committed to civil custody. Crane appealed and the Kansas Supreme Court reversed the civil commitment of Crane, holding that the SVPA requires that the state must prove that the defendant cannot control his dangerous behavior and that the trial court had made no such finding. Kansas appealed to the U.S. Supreme Court who heard the case. The U.S. Supreme Court reversed the Kansas Supreme Court and held that (1) the SVPA does not require the state to prove an offender's total or complete lack of control over his dangerous behavior and that (2) the federal constitution does not allow civil commitment under the Act without any lack of control determination. The significance of the U.S. Supreme Court action is that a state must show that a defendant is likely to engage in sexually violent conduct in the future, but not in any absolute sense. There is no rule obligating the state to prove that any defendant must lack total control regarding violent sexual conduct. Rather, the phrase stressed is that the state must demonstrate that the defendant possesses an abnormality or disorder that makes it difficult, if not impossible, to control the dangerous behavior. Although some U.S. Supreme Court Justices disagreed with the majority opinion, the ruling was significant in that it effectively lowered the standard used by states to order the indefinite civil commitment of virtually any sex offender who merely is deemed to possess an abnormality or disorder that makes it difficult to control their sexual behavior.

SUMMARY

Parole is the conditional release of inmates from incarceration in either jails or prisons. Parole is granted primarily for good behavior exhibited during the time served as well as for the length of time served in relation to the maximum sentence originally imposed. Parole did not originate in the United States. While the true origins of parole are disputed and generally unknown, early use of parole was found in Great Britain, where Alexander Maconochie used marks of commendation and good-time marks to reward prisoners with early discharge. Sir Walter Crofton, an Irish prison reformer, also used early release from incarceration as an inmate reward for good behavior and helped to establish indeterminate sentencing in the United States through the issuance of tickets-of-leave. Tickets-of-leave authorized early release from prison. Parole was officially introduced in the United States in 1884 in Massachusetts by statute. The primary functions of parole include offender rehabilitation, offender reintegration, crime deterrence and control, decreasing prison and jail overcrowding, compensating for sentencing disparities, and public safety and protection.

In 2001 there were over 700,000 parolees in the United States. Most parolees are male, and about 60 percent are white. Presently, the successful completion rate for parole programs is about 46 percent. It is difficult to determine which factors are most responsible for parole program failures, although drug or alcohol dependencies are associated with many unsuccessful parolees. The principal philosophy of parole is rehabilitation, although in recent years it has taken on a more instrumental purpose of alleviating prison overcrowding. High degrees of offender monitoring currently characterize a growing number of parole programs in the United States. Crime control is a guiding principle of several of these programs. Under determinate sentencing schemes, mandatory parole may occur after inmates serve a fixed portion of their original sentences.

When inmates have served a portion of their original sentences, they may apply for early release. Generally excluded from early-release consideration are those under sentences of death or those serving terms of life without the possibility of parole. For the rest of the inmates, however, early release is a possibility, depending upon how well they have behaved while incarcerated. But being parole-eligible does not automatically entitle any particular inmate to parole. And exhibiting good behavior while confined does not guarantee one's early release from prison. Selective incapacitation is quite evident for certain offenders in virtually every jurisdiction. This means that paroling authorities have the power to grant or deny parole according to whatever reasonable criteria they choose to use.

As a way of easing certain inmates back into society, most states have established pre-release programs. These programs permit inmates to leave their prisons for short periods for various purposes, such as seeking employment or reuniting with their families. Two types of pre-release programs are furloughs and work/study release. Work/study release and furlough programs are generally unescorted authorized temporary leaves from prison for such participation. In essence, inmates are unsupervised during these periods and agree to return to their prisons at designated times. Usually, furloughs are granted on weekends, while work/study release is granted during weekdays. Most of the time, however, work releasees will spend their evening hours in prison, with the exception of those released for weekend furloughs.

Another category of programs applies to inmates who are granted full-fledged parole. These are considered post-release programs. Several types of post-release programs include halfway houses, parole with conditions, intensive supervised parole, community residential centers, and shock parole. Those placed on parole in these programs are supervised by parole officers who monitor their activities more or less closely. Halfway houses are especially useful, in that they provide recently released inmates with a place to stay, job placement assistance, counseling, and other services. Parole with conditions and intensive supervised parole are most often used, and the intensity of a parolee's supervision depends upon each parolee's prior record and other circumstances. Parole boards designate how much supervision each offender must receive, and this decision determines their specific program requirements. Parole officers are expected to supervise offenders and ensure their compliance with program elements. They also network with community agencies to assist their parolee-clients. Their primary aim is to assist offenders in leading law-abiding lives and readjusting in their communities.

Parole is administered through parole boards. All states have parole boards. These boards are usually comprised of laypersons who are appointed by the governor. They convene and make early-release decisions for all parole-eligible offenders. Normally, parole boards do not consider cases where offenders have been sentenced to life without the possibility of parole or who are on death row. However, there are some exceptions.

Parole boards make early-release decisions about inmates according to various criteria. Several objective parole criteria have been articulated over the years, and parole boards attempt to apply these criteria fairly for all parole-eligible offenders. Assisting parole boards in such early release decision making are projections of offender risk and future dangerousness. Salient Factor Scores are used by the federal government and some state parole boards to determine which offenders are most likely to succeed on parole and not recidivate. Almost every state has devised risk instrumentation as a means of forecasting offender dangerousness or the likelihood of future program success or failure. All of these instruments are flawed in various ways, and no prediction scheme is 100 percent reliable. Therefore, every parole board makes mistakes by paroling some inmates who should not be paroled. A portion of these parolees commit new crimes while under parole supervision. It has been estimated that about 50 percent of all those granted parole will not be successful in completing their parole programs. Thus, some amount of recidivism is expected. Recidivism is measured in different ways. Some of the more popular definitions of it include reconviction for a new offense, return to prison, and rearrests.

Parolee failures are evidence to some critics that parole is ineffective at rehabilitating and reintegrating offenders. Thus, some states have changed their parole policies and greatly restricted the conditions under which parole may be granted. More than a few states have abolished parole outright. By 2001, 20 states abolished parole, because it is believed that parole is misapplied and benefits those of particular races, genders, ethnicities, and/or socioeconomic statuses. Others criticize parole boards for faulty decision making, when certain offenders are released on parole and go on to commit more serious crimes. Alternatives to parole board discretion include determinate sentencing and the accrual of good time applied against one's maximum sentence.

Whenever parolees violate one or more of their parole conditions, these violations often come to the attention of parole officers who report their actions to the parole board. The parole board convenes and considers these violations. Depending upon the circumstances, a parolee's parole program may be revoked. Revocation of one's parole may result in return to prison. However, in a large number of parole violation cases, offenders are placed under closer supervision by parole officers, and additional behavioral conditions are imposed. Some parolees may be placed in home confinement with electronic monitoring. They may be required to submit to more frequent face-to-face visits from their parole officers. They may be expected to make restitution, perform community service, and pay a portion of their supervision costs. Drug/alcohol checks are also conducted, especially for those parolees with prior histories of substance abuse. And when parole is revoked and the offender is returned to prison, the reasons for revoking one's parole program must be specified in writing and furnished to the parolee.

Automatic parole revocation does not occur, however. Like probationers, parolees have certain constitutional rights. Parole officers cannot summarily revoke their clients' parole programs. Two-stage hearings in front of parole boards must precede any parole revocation, and parolees may have attorneys present, confront witnesses and cross-examine them, and present evidence in their own behalf. These minimum due process rights were set forth for parolees in the landmark U.S. Supreme Court case of *Morrissey v. Brewer* (1972). The first stage of parole revocation hearings, a fact-finding stage, determines the validity of charges against the parolee. The second stage determines the punishment to be imposed, if it is found that the parolee did, indeed, violate one or more conditions of their parole programs. Each state has evolved various parole revocation criteria, and presently there is some amount of uniformity throughout the states concerning the conditions under which parole can be revoked. If one's parole program is revoked, however, the parolee can appeal the decision to a state appellate court. Under certain circumstances, some parole-eligible offenders may be required to serve additional time in prison beyond their maximum sentences. These are offenders who are believed to continue to pose a serious threat to community safety. For example, some sexual predators continue to be incarcerated beyond their original maximum sentences, usually on the basis of psychological evaluations and through involuntary civil commitments to mental hospitals. The U.S. Supreme Court has upheld the constitutionality of such extended incarceration.

QUESTIONS FOR REVIEW

1. What is meant by parole? What are the early origins of parole in the United States?

2. What is the difference between marks of commendation and tickets-of-leave, and how were they originally applied? What is the relation between tickets-of-leave and indeterminate sentencing?

3. What are the philosophy and goals of parole? What are some different manifest and latent functions of parole?

4. What are some major differences between successful and unsuccessful parolees? What factors seem to be associated with parolee program failures?

5. What are furlough programs? What are their weaknesses, strengths, and applications?

6. How do work/study programs differ from furloughs? What are the primary benefits and disadvantages of work/study programs for offenders?

7. What are some major differences between pre-release and post-release programs for inmates? What are halfway houses and what are some of their goals? How successful are halfway houses?

8. What is the composition of parole boards? What kinds of criteria do parole boards use in determining one's early release? What sorts of cases do parole boards not have to consider for early release?

9. What are some major differences between standard parole with conditions and intensive supervised parole? What is recidivism and how is it measured?

10. What are the rights conveyed to parolees in the case of *Morrissey v. Brewer*? What are some of the circumstances under which parolees can have their parole pro-

grams revoked? Are all parolees who have their parole programs revoked returned to prison? Why or why not?

SUGGESTED READINGS

Braithwaite, John. *Restorative Justice and Responsive Regulation.* Oxford, UK: Oxford University Press, 2002.

Clay, John. *Maconochie's Experiment.* London, UK: John Murray, 2002.

Karp, David R. and Todd R. Clear. *What Is Community Justice? Case Studies of Restorative Justice and Community.* Thousand Oaks, CA: Sage Publications, 2002.

Petersilia, Joan. *Reforming Probation and Parole.* Lanham, MD: American Correctional Association, 2002.

INTERNET CONNECTIONS

American Probation and Parole Association
http://www.appa-net.org/

Crime Prevention Coalition of America
http://www.crimepreventioncoalition.org/

International Corrections and Prisons Association
http://www.icpa.ca/related/parole

New York State Parole Department
http://www.parole.state.ny.us/specialrelease.html

Parole boards
http://crimelynx.com/stateparole

Parole links
http://www.tbcnet.com/~salsberry/Parole%20Sites

Parole Violators
http://www.bottomlinestudios.com/ParoleViolators.html

Parole Watch
http://www.parolewatch.org

Probation and parole sites
http://www.angelfire.com/md/ribit/states

U.S. Parole Commission
http://www.usdoj.gov/uspc/

CHAPTER 11 | Correctional Officer Selection and Training

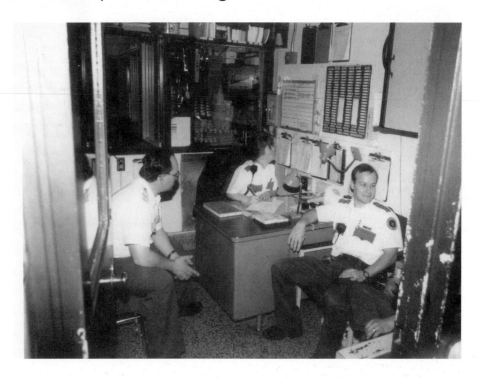

Chapter Objectives | *As the result of reading this chapter, the following objectives should be realized:*

1. Distinguishing between correctional officers, probation officers, and parole officers, and examining how different jurisdictions view these work roles.
2. Profiling probation and parole officers, describing their primary characteristics, selection, and training.
3. Describing the educational requirements of those working in corrections, including the certification and accreditation process.
4. Describing correctional officer stress and burnout, the factors contributing to these conditions, and how they can be alleviated.
5. Describing the recruitment of women in corrections, focusing upon some differences between male and female officers in terms of their job performance and general work satisfaction.
6. Describing the use of firearms by probation and parole officers and the reasons for concern for PO safety.
7. Examining different types of negligence and various liability issues associated with PO work.
8. Describing various caseload models used by probation/parole agencies.
9. Discussing the roles, responsibilities, and legal liabilities of volunteers and paraprofessionals.

INTRODUCTION

• *Rudy R. was a correctional officer at a New Jersey penitentiary. He had a high school diploma and a New Jersey driver's license. A cursory background check revealed no criminal record in New Jersey. After two years on the job, Rudy R. seemed to be well-liked by inmates. His block had fewer incidents of inmate fighting and disturbances compared with other blocks in the prison. However, an impromptu shakedown of cells one afternoon revealed that large quantities of illegal drugs and contraband were found in the cells of most inmates on Rudy R.'s cell block. Rudy R. professed ignorance about the presence of illegal drugs and other contraband. An investigation revealed that Rudy R. had a sizable bank account and lived in a large home in a New Jersey suburb. Two of his children were attending private schools with high tuition fees. His wife did not work, and it was perplexing to prison officials how someone earning Rudy R.'s salary could afford such amenities. Subsequently, it was revealed that Rudy R. was smuggling large quantities of narcotics and other contraband into the prison in his luggage and lunch box. These items were never searched by authorities because of prison policy exempting correctional officers from such searches. Rudy R. had been receiving payoffs from prisoners on a regular basis over the two years he had been with the prison system. Officials estimate that Rudy R. had accepted over $400,000 in exchange for acting as an intermediary between inmates and their drug connections on the outside. Rudy R. was suspended from his job pending further inquiry. In the meantime, a broader check of Rudy R.'s records revealed two prior criminal convictions in other states on drug charges. How closely should prospective correctional officer records be scrutinized before persons are hired into these positions? Should prison correctional officers be exempt from searches when entering the prison to work? What do you think?* [Adapted from the Associated Press, "New Jersey Prison Guard Indicted on Drug Smuggling Charges," January 2, 2002].

• *Mary M. was a prison volunteer. During the early part of 2001, she was a part of a religious group who came to various prisons on a regular basis to assist inmates in different activities. Over time, Mary M. developed an increasingly close relationship with a male inmate, Frank G., who was serving a life sentence for second-degree murder. He had convinced Mary M. that he was actually innocent of the crime and should not be imprisoned. One afternoon, Mary M. smuggled some clothing into the prison, and Frank G. changed from his prison garb into street clothing in an area hidden from correctional officer view. Mary M. had also provided Frank G. with a visitor's pass and false ID to assist him in escaping. At the end of the day when visitors and volunteers left, Mary M. and Frank G. walked through the prison gates unchallenged by anyone. Frank G. had made good his escape. Once on the outside, he had Mary stop at a drug store to obtain some medical supplies. While she was in the store, Frank G. drove off in her car. Frank G. was subsequently apprehended and prosecuted for escape. Mary M. was dismissed as a prison volunteer and charged with aiding and abetting in Frank G.'s escape from prison. She was sentenced to two years' probation. Frank G. was subsequently convicted and received an additional five years for his prison escape. How effectively should volunteers be screened before being permitted to counsel and assist prisoners? Should volunteer programs be prohibited? What do you think?* [Adapted from the Associated Press, "Prison Volunteer Assists Murderer in Prison Escape," May 11, 2002].

• *Jeffrey A. was a parole officer in Arkansas. He had a bachelor's degree in criminal justice and a master's degree in social work. Because of his social work experience, Jeffrey A. was assigned more hard-core offenders with drug and alcohol problems. Over his four-year stint as a parole officer, Jeffrey A. had seen the worst of society. He had to visit his clientele in neighborhood projects and rundown areas that were gang controlled. On more than one occasion, Jeffrey A. was shot at by drive-by gang-bangers, and he was assaulted three times while visiting parolee-clients. At no time, however, were parolees to blame for his assaults. During this time, Jeffrey A. devoted a great deal of his personal time to assisting his parolee-clients. He spent long hours networking with businesspersons to hire his parolees. With a specialized caseload clientele of 44, Jeffrey A. had quite a bit of responsibility. He had little time for his own life. He was deeply committed to helping others. However, he was on the job long enough to see half of his clientele relapse into continued drug use and alcoholism, despite his best efforts. Several of his clients had their parole programs revoked. Gradually, Jeffrey A. became disenchanted with his work and decided to quit. When his supervisor inquired as to the reasons for his resignation from parole work, Jeffrey A. said that he was "burned out,"* largely because he didn't feel he was making any difference in these clients' lives. [Personal communication with the Arkansas Department of Community Punishment and the Central Arkansas Community Punishment Center, Little Rock, Arkansas, May 14, 2002].

An estimated 6.6 million adults were under some form of correctional supervision by 2001. Local jails held about 631,240 adults, while 4.7 million adults were on probation or parole. About 1.96 million men and women were confined in prisons and jails (Glaze 2002). Supervising these offenders were an estimated 242,824 correctional officers (American Correctional Association 2002). For the 731,147 parolees and 3,932,751 probationers, there were 72,086 POs (Camp and Camp 2002:218–219).

The **caseload,** or the number of probationers and parolees supervised by probation or parole officers, averaged 133 probationers per officer and 73 parolees per parole officer (Camp and Camp 2002:195). The highest probationer caseloads were in Rhode Island, with 320 clients per officer respectively, while the highest parolee caseloads occurred in Hawaii, with 253 parolees per parole officer (Camp and Camp 2002:195).

This chapter is about the persons who work with prison and jail inmates, as well as those who supervise probationers and parolees. The first part of this chapter distinguishes between correctional officers and probation and parole officers (POs). **Correctional officers** supervise inmates in jails and prisons. These are distinguished from officers who work with probationers and parolees, known as probation officers or parole officers (POs). The methods of selecting those working in institutional corrections and community probation and parole agencies are described.

The next part of the chapter describes the education and training of correctional officers. An increasingly important part of the selection and training of these officers is professionalization. Professionalization is discussed, including the processes leading to professionalization. In recent years, greater attention has been given to certification of officers through acquiring additional skills and training. Institutions and agencies also increasingly seek accreditation from organizations such as the American Correctional Association and the American Probation and Parole Association. These activities are described. Some jurisdictions screen applicants and train prospective officers through assessment centers. Assessment centers are described. Once officers have been hired, they may be expected to acquire pre-service or in-service training as means of enhancing their professional effectiveness. The nature of these types of training is discussed.

Correctional work of any kind generates some amount of stress. Officers experience stress from various sources. The sources of stress are indicated. One negative outcome of stress is burnout. Burnout is defined and described, as well as its harmful effects. In some instances, burnout causes some officers to quit their jobs. Labor turnover among these officers is examined. Various strategies for alleviating stress and burnout are presented.

The recruitment of women and minorities into correctional officer roles is increasing. Some explanations for this phenomenon are presented. Over the years, evaluations of male and female officers have been conducted. Some of these research results will be presented, as male and female officers are contrasted in terms of their job performance, work satisfaction, and general effectiveness. The issue of sexual harassment is examined as greater gender diversity occurs in officer employment in both institutional and community corrections.

PO work is increasingly dangerous, and many jurisdictions presently require their officers to carry firearms. This important and controversial issue is examined. Also, varying training requirements and selection criteria among jurisdictions has contributed to great variations in the quality of persons who work in corrections. Thus, their competency and effectiveness vary. Some officers may not perform their jobs well, or they may not have the skills necessary to handle certain situations when they arise. Allegations of negligence arise when some officers perform poorly. Different types of negligence are described and discussed. Several liability issues associated with PO work are examined.

When POs are assigned clients to supervise, either on probation or parole, these assignments are designated as caseloads. While no ideal caseload has ever been identified, it is generally assumed that larger caseloads are associated with less supervisory effectiveness, while smaller caseloads improve one's supervisory effectiveness. Various caseload assignment models are described. These include the conventional model, the numbers game model, the conventional model with geographical considerations, and the specialized caseloads model. Each of these models has weaknesses and strengths which are discussed.

The chapter next examines the use of volunteers in corrections. Corrections volunteers work in either institutional or community corrections without remuneration, and they are generally untrained and lack professional qualities. However, they provide several useful functions. The nature of volunteers is discussed as well as their contributions to inmates and probationers and parolees. Volunteers have also been criticized for different reasons. These criticisms are outlined and examined. The chapter concludes with an examination of paraprofessionals and their work roles. Like volunteers, paraprofessionals assist corrections officers and POs in their work and provide different types of assistance to inmates and/or clients. The work roles of paraprofessionals are examined, together with an examination of some of the criticisms of paraprofessionals. The legal liabilities of both volunteers and paraprofessionals are also discussed.

CORRECTIONS OFFICERS AND PROBATION/PAROLE OFFICERS: A DISTINCTION

What should probation and parole officers be called? Technically, probation and parole officers **(POs)** are also correctional officers, because part of their responsibilities include the supervision, rehabilitation, and reintegration of offenders. This is generally considered an integral part of corrections. Labeling probation and parole officers corrections officers also makes sense because most probation and parole departments in the United States are under the general administrative rubric of Department of Corrections. Also, it is customary to refer to correctional officers in prisons and jails as correctional officers

(Patenaude 2001). The American Jail Association and the American Correctional Association have both made official statements to the effect that the term *guard* is outmoded, since it no longer reflects the skills and training required to perform correctional officer work. Furthermore, this labeling Tower of Babel is complicated and perpetuated by official state and federal reports lumping all correctional personnel (probation officers, parole officers, jail officers, prison officers, correctional officers, secretaries, jail and prison administrators, paralegals who work in jails and prisons, volunteers, and paraprofessionals who work in community corrections) into one general category (American Correctional Association 2002; Camp and Camp 2002).

One fairly easy way of differentiating between these various types of officers is to distinguish between institutional and community corrections. These are umbrella terms, with institutional corrections encompassing jails and prisons, and community corrections encompassing probation, parole, intensive supervised probation/parole, work/study release, furloughs, halfway houses, home confinement programs, electronic monitoring, diversion programs, and all other types of programs where offenders are supervised in their communities. Correctional officers are prison or jail staff and their supervisors who manage inmates, while probation and parole officers supervise and manage probationers and parolees in a variety of community programs for both unconvicted and convicted offenders (American Correctional Association 2002). Since the departments of correction in many states select correctional officers as well as prison staff and conduct training programs for all of their correctional personnel, similar criteria are often used for selecting correctional officers as well as for POs.

The Number of Corrections Personnel

It is difficult to obtain an accurate picture of the true number of institutional and community corrections personnel for any given year. Surveys are conducted by various agencies, both public and private, where information is solicited from the states and federal government. Reports and statistical information from the states are often fragmented or only partially complete, with some jurisdictions not reporting at all. Some states report aggregate data, where both institutional and community corrections personnel are combined and reported. This makes it impossible to know for sure, at any given time, how many probation officers or parole officers or corrections officers there are in the United States. Therefore, we are left with partial information that is used to make general estimates.

One certainty exists concerning these estimates, however: The number of personnel working in the area of adult and juvenile corrections is steadily increasing. In 2001, there were 401,290 corrections officers and jailers, as well as 78,640 probation/parole officers (Bureau of Labor Statistics 2002:4,7), for a total of 479,930 officers. Including juvenile corrections officers (corrections officers, probation/parole officers), estimated at 120,000, would yield a combined corrections adult/juvenile officer figure of 599,930 for 2001 (American Correctional Association 2002; Bureau of Labor Statistics 2002; Camp and Camp 2002). This is a 48 percent increase in all officers since 1998. The Bureau of Labor Statistics has reported that it estimates the number of corrections officers and jailers to be 547,900 by 2005. This would be about a 36 percent increase (Bureau of Labor Statistics 2002:7). It might be assumed that the number of new probation/parole officer positions will increase proportionally similar to corrections officers during this same time interval. Thus, the number of anticipated new positions in corrections, both institutional and community, is substantial in the near term.

Regarding the number of personnel who work for adult and juvenile corrections, there were 538,272 personnel in 2001 among reporting states and the federal government (nonreporting states included Illinois, Maine, Nebraska, New Mexico, New York, Vermont, and Wisconsin) (American Correctional Association 2002). Personnel are separate from corrections officers and probation/parole officers. These personnel include support staff, secretaries, middle-level program managers, and others. There were 7,177 adult corrections administrators in 2001, together with 2,094 juvenile corrections administrators for a combined total of 9,271 administrators among reporting agencies (American Correctional Association 2002). Nonreporting jurisdictions included Illinois, Maine, Nebraska, New Mexico, Nevada, North Carolina, Vermont, and Wisconsin. Thus, these figures are clearly underestimates of the actual numbers of administrators.

Generally, probation officers supervise probationers, while parole officers supervise parolees. In several jurisdictions, probation and parole officers supervise both types of offenders interchangeably (American Correctional Association 2002). In many states, probation and parole officers are combined in official reports of statistical information to organizations such as the American Correctional Association. For example, within the adult category, states such as Alabama, Florida, Virginia, Washington, and Wyoming report total numbers of probation and parole aftercare personnel rather than report them separately.

THE SELECTION AND TRAINING OF CORRECTIONAL OFFICERS

Correctional facilities run smoothly largely because of the professional and forward-thinking attitudes and actions of the correctional officers employed (Hemmens and Stohr 2001; Sims 2001). Of course, the administrative component plays a significant role in outlining the mission and goals of corrections facilities, and this clarity, in turn, generates the degree of enthusiasm necessary for individuals to maximize their work performance.

The traditional approach to training in most jurisdictions involves classifying recruits into several categories, subjecting each group to limited specialized training, and then moving along to the next recruit group. It is expected that recruits will learn general job responsibilities, procedures for carrying out these responsibilities, practical skills for task performance, and something about the expectations of supervisors (Liebling and Price 2001). But many recruits leave these training sessions untrained. Some recommend the inclusion of veteran correctional officers as resource persons to answer specific questions about correctional role performance and expectations.

Characteristics of Correctional Officers in the United States

At the beginning of 2001, uniformed correctional officers in prisons and jails had the following sociodemographic characteristics. Seventy-six percent were male, 65 percent were white, 23.8 percent were black, and 8.2 percent were

Hispanic. These figures are significant in that they represent substantial proportionate gains in correctional officer positions for both females and nonwhites. In 1992, for instance, female officers made up only 18 percent of the correctional officer work force. In 2001, they made up 24 percent of this work force. Nonwhite correctional officers also improved their proportionate numbers. In 1992, about 28 percent of the correctional officer work force was nonwhite. In 2001, nonwhites accounted for 35 percent of this work force (Camp and Camp 2002:154–155). Over the next ten years, it is expected that this profile will undergo additional change. For instance, in 2000 only 57 percent of those hired for correctional officer positions were male and 63 percent were white (Camp and Camp 2002:162). Thus, there is every reason to believe that greater racial and gender diversity will occur over time, as the corrections officer work force expands (Camp, Saylor, and Wright 2001).

Female correctional officer assignments have an interesting pattern. About 80 percent of all female correctional officers were assigned to male institutions in 2001, while only 3.4 percent of all officers in female correctional institutions were male. Thus, 20 percent of all female correctional officers were working in female institutions in 2001 (Camp and Camp 2002:157). During the 1990s and through 2000, there has been a steady decline in the proportionate numbers of male correctional officers working in female institutions.

Not surprisingly, the corrections industry is experiencing a growth of 38.7 percent annually compared with a U.S. labor market growth rate of 14.4 percent (Kiekbusch 2001). Translated into numbers, this means that there will be 25,300 correctional officer vacancies in the nation's prisons and jails through 2011. At the same time as a record number of vacancies is occurring, corrections officials are striving to increase the level of professionalism in the industry. Correctional agencies are becoming more assertive in attracting and retaining increasingly qualified staff. Furthermore, community/technical colleges are designing and establishing specific curricula to provide appropriate professional training and coursework for corrections. Thus, the educational requirements for correctional officers are becoming increasingly stringent (Jascor 2001:91).

Correctional Officer Education

There is considerable variation among the states regarding the amount of education required for correctional officer work. In 13 states (25.5 percent), less than a high school diploma was considered adequate in 1997 (Josi and Sechrest 1998:54). In 22 states, a GED or high school diploma was considered adequate to qualify for correctional officer employment. Only 16 states (31.4 percent) required a high school diploma or its equivalent for correctional officer work. In 1997, 38 states indicated that their current correctional staffs had less than 30 units of college. The greatest emphasis on college education was among Midwest prisons (Josi and Sechrest 1998:54).

Obtaining more education is often equated with becoming more professional. However, it is not known whether more education makes better officers (Burke, Rizzo, and O'Rear 1992:174). Generally, more education for officers is instrumental in gaining them managerial positions. Thus, those officers who aspire to middle-level or upper-level management in prison settings would probably benefit from acquiring an advanced degree. Some officers have reported that having a higher level of education enables them to understand inmate culture

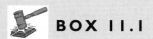 **BOX 11.1**

Jimmy D. Dugger

Training Superintendent
Texas Department of Criminal Justice

Statistics

B.B.A. (business management), Sam Houston State University; Correctional Officers Academy; F.B.I. Hostage Negotiations

Interests

Currently, I am the Texas Department of Criminal Justice (TDCJ) Superintendent for the Training Academy located in Gatesville, Texas. I supervise a staff of nine Training Sergeants. We are responsible for providing six weeks of training to new-hire employees, and we also deliver the 40-hour annual training for in-service employees. I have always stressed to the trainers that people learn more when they are having fun. The problem is, how do you make an entertaining course out of Hostage Situations, Use of Force, and Riots and Disturbances? Now, that is a challenge! I take great pride in making it known that our staff has been highly successful in fulfilling this important objective.

Background

I grew up in Killeen, Texas, best known for Fort Hood. My relatives were never directly associated with this major military base. My grandfather opened the first grocery store and hotel in Killeen. With the growth of Fort Hood, he went on to become a successful real estate agent. I was destined to go to college and then work for him. It was exciting knowing that this promising future was lined out for me. Then, my grandfather passed away when I was in my early teens. With no one prepared to take over the business, it was liquidated. With this dream crushed, I still had an interest in business. In high school, I began concentrating on an accounting career.

I worked full-time at a grocery store, which completely funded the early stages of my college education without the assistance of anyone. It was at work when I was faced

with another obstacle. The store manager informed me that my college studies were interfering with the job and that I needed to make a decision: college or work. My father advised me to work for the prison system because "they would hire anyone." I discovered that I could work in Huntsville, Texas and go to college at Sam Houston State University.

Work Experiences

I began the training academy and could recall two distinct things. First, I was scared to death. Second, I wanted to eventually become an academy instructor. There was a problem, however. I was educating myself to become an accountant.

Concerning being scared, it didn't help my situation when the academy instructors announced that the warden and farm manager had been killed by an inmate at the facility that I was assigned. I wanted to quit. I even announced it to the other students. A friend in class told me that nothing would happen to me. I replied, "But the warden was killed!" I decided to stick with it and finish the course. Another day, the instructors announced that a major search was conducted at the same facility and over 400 homemade knives had been found in the possession of the inmates. Again, I contemplated quitting, but the other students talked me into staying with the program. These incidents only verified my belief that I would be fighting knife-wielding inmates every day. Of course, I was wrong.

Following my academy graduation, and after much thought, I reluctantly arrived at the Ellis I Death Row facility to

(continued)

BOX 11.1 *(Continued)*

begin my "temporary" career as a correctional officer. My initial shock subsided on the first day. Being a people-person, I immediately loved this job. I excelled in my job abilities and my supervisors recognized it. I was surprisingly promoted to shift supervisor at the age of 23. Then I found myself becoming a successful shift supervisor, and this was recognized by administrators in our main office in Huntsville. I was contacted and asked to become a trainer at the academy. It was at this time that I decided to change my major in college towards a career in corrections. With my initial studies being in accounting, this left me with several business courses under my belt, and so I decided to attain a management degree. At the age of 25, I was offered the job of academy superintendent at Gatesville. Because of personal obligations, I turned down this promotion. Instead, I explored another route within our agency.

I was promoted to an investigator. This was extremely interesting, investigating complaints pertaining to administrative and criminal violations. The main advantage of this position was that I became privy to some of the behind-the-scenes decisions of upper-level administration. At age 30, I was once again contacted about supervising the training academy in Gatesville. This time, I accepted the responsibility and have never been disappointed with my decision.

Advice to Students

To any student trying to decide which career path to follow, I would like to suggest that there is a career that offers the ultimate in excitement and adventure. It won't be *anything* like sitting at a desk to add up numbers. Remember, to be successful in corrections, as with other law enforcement fields, the most versatile tool in your toolbox is your mind. With the addition of a college education, you can only excel within this decision-driven career. Understandably, when someone is approached concerning a career in corrections, the usual response is associated with the many perceived dangers portrayed by the media or Hollywood. Yes, in extreme and remote situations, there are dangers. But with the proper training, you can mentally and physically prepare yourself for almost anything.

better and to resolve inmate-officer conflicts more effectively (Burke, Rizzo, and O'Rear 1992). However, top-level prison managers perhaps should seek additional educational training together with their correctional staff. This will underscore the importance of training as well as improve the image of correctional officers in their respective institutions (Carter 1991:17).

In response to meeting the need for providing jail and prison corrections officers with increasing amounts of education and training, several colleges and universities have established curricula and programming that will lead to a higher degree of professionalism (Stinchcomb 2000). For example, in 1997 Mid-State Technology College (MSTC) in Wisconsin introduced a two-year associate degree in corrections science (Jascor 2001). This program catered to corrections officers who could take courses on a part-time basis. MSTC is one of four Wisconsin technical colleges to include a 120-hour training curriculum for the Basic Jail Officer and Juvenile Detention Officer as well as for other positions. While MSTC focuses upon entry-level corrections officer training, presently employed correctional officers may acquire this training and a degree. MSTC includes an on-site training facility with two jail cells equipped with institution-grade fixtures, a computer-based booking program, and a functional

In-service training is often required for correctional officers to maintain and/or improve their skills.

dayroom area. These facilities are used all year, and students gain valuable hands-on experience. A capstone course is the "Correction Officer Certification Summary," which requires students to assume the role of telecommunications dispatcher, corrections officer, or actor. An average of ten scenarios a week are staged, where arrests are made, "arrestees" are booked, and inmates are supervised (Jascor 2001:94).

Accreditation, Certification, and Professionalism.   Increasingly, correctional facilities of all types are seeking accreditation, which generally means improved services and physical plants. Generally, accreditation is a comprehensive process, incorporating numerous measures and embraces virtually every facet of the organization being assessed. A fundamental concomitant of accreditation is certification, which involves a review and evaluation of an individual's credentials and capabilities as they relate to his or her current correctional functions (Levinson, Stinchcomb, and Greene 2001:125).

The American Correctional Association (ACA) and American Jail Association (AJA) have been heavily involved in both accreditation and certification of both prisons and jails and their personnel for many years. The ACA has established a certification program to enhance professionalism of jail and prison corrections officers. Professionalism cannot be issued like a badge or uniform, and it is beyond the power of any organization to issue edicts declaring that their corrections officers are professionals (Levinson, Stinchcomb, and Greene 2001:125).

In 1978 a private, nonprofit organization was created and called the Commission on Accreditation for Corrections (CAC). Presently, it administers a national program for accrediting all components of adult and juvenile corrections. In 2001 there were 1,185 institutions and programs throughout the United States that earned CAC accreditation. In 1999 a certification program was commenced through the CAC. At about the same time, the ACA established a certification program through its Commission on Correctional Certification (CCC). Presently, there are four certification categories:

1. Certified Correctional Executives: Those at the highest organizational level who oversee development and implementation of policies and procedures; a bachelor's degree or equivalent work experience required.
2. Certified Correctional Managers: Those who manage major units or programs, have authority over supervisory staff and may contribute to, but primarily are responsible for, the implementation of agencies policies and procedures; an associate's degree or equivalent work experience required.
3. Certified Correctional Supervisors: Those who work with both staff and offenders, implement agency policies and procedures and supervise, as well as evaluate, personnel; an associate's degree or equivalent work experience required.
4. Certified Correctional Officers: Line personnel who work directly with offenders; a high school diploma or general equivalency diploma required (Levinson, Stinchcomb, and Greene 2001:127–128).

Certification requires applicants to establish their qualifications as members of one of the groups above. Detailed documentation of educational credentials, length of full-time correctional experience, time in current position, and compliance with the ACA's Code of Ethics is also required. Further, applicants must take and pass a 200-item, multiple-choice examination based on material from relevant resource publications in corrections. These source publications contain information that in the judgment of the commission best matches descriptions developed by the National Institute of Corrections for the job tasks and related competencies associated with the position (Levinson, Stinchcomb, and Greene 2001:128). Since neither accreditation nor certification are compulsory, it is up to individual jurisdictions, such as Wisconsin, to foster interest among jail and prison officers and administrators.

The recruitment and retention of good correctional officers is difficult under the best of conditions (W. Smith 2002:9). One way of recruiting more qualified and professional officers is to offer higher salaries. Indeed, in both jail and prison positions over the years, the average annual salaries of these corrections officer positions have increased. However, these salaries are somewhat low compared with salaries in the business sector. Although many jurisdictions still have a mind-set that suggests corrections officers do not necessarily have to be mature, intelligent, and capable to do adequate jobs of supervising inmates, the fact is that these corrections jobs have changed drastically. The average prison and jail officer must be increasingly proficient with computers and be able to use the new high tech equipment and technology that has been developed for better offender monitoring and supervision. Further, these officers must have human skills and cultural diversity training as inmate populations become more diverse and complex. But it is not simply a matter of money. Work environments must be improved, and the type of work performed must be made more challenging. This is where accreditation and certification become critical. Correctional institutions can be more responsive by rewarding their officers for seeking certification and advanced degrees. Encouraging and rewarding personnel for taking additional coursework and pursuing various forms of certification and education will do much to attract and retain the most qualified persons for these correctional positions (W. Smith 2002:13).

Correctional Officer Entry Requirements and Salaries

Most jurisdictions require prospective officers to be between 18 and 21 years of age, to have a high school diploma or its equivalent, and to have no felony convictions. More than a few jurisdictions require written and oral examinations, physical fitness assessments, and mental assessments (Camp and Camp 2002).

Average entry-level annual salaries in 2001 for correctional officers ranged from $15,324 in Louisiana to $36,850 in New Jersey, with an average of $23,627 for all U.S. jurisdictions (Camp and Camp 2002:168–169). These salaries are about 10 percent higher than the salaries reported in 1998. For experienced officers or those who have completed their probationary periods, salaries ranged in 2001 from a low of $17,076 in Louisiana to $40,536 in New Jersey. Maximum salaries averaged $38,232, with the lowest maximum salary of $25,000 in Maine to a high maximum salary of $57,996 in Alaska. By comparison, the federal

---

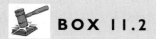 **BOX 11.2**

JOB ADVERTISEMENT FOR MIAMI-DADE CORRECTIONS AND REHABILITATION DEPARTMENT

**Miami-Dade County Corrections
and Rehabilitation Department
is now recruiting for**

CORRECTIONAL OFFICERS

Salary Entry: $28,484–Max. $49,248 Annually

What does it take to become a Correctional Officer?

- 19 years of age or older
- High school graduate or equivalent
- U.S. citizen
- No felony convictions
- No first degree misdemeanors involving perjury or false statement
- Good moral character
- Physical exam/drug test
- Basic recruit training

What are the benefits offered to Correctional Officers?

- Paid holidays
- Paid training—$926.70 Bi-weekly

- Paid vacations
- Health and dental benefits
- High risk retirement
- Night shift differential—Approximately 9%
- Hazardous duty pay—$125.00 Bi-weekly
- 50% tuition reimbursement
- Uniform Allowance
  Uniform $300
  Non-uniform $550

Apply in person at the Miami-Dade County
Employee Relations Department
140 West Flagler Street
Suite 105
Miami, Florida 33130
Open Mon.–Fri.
8:30 A.M.–4:00 P.M.

Source: American Jails, May/June 2002, Vol. XVI/Number 2, p. 69.

system had an entry-level salary of $26,354, a salary of $27,790 for those who completed their probationary training, and a maximum salary of $40,062 (Camp and Camp 2002:168–169). Standard benefits included a retirement plan, annual and sick leave, insurance programs, and deferred compensation. Officers also received uniform allowances, longevity pay, tuition assistance, and optional insurance packages and other incentives.

Pre-Service and In-Service Training

Pre-service training is provided newly hired correctional staff. It consists of both classroom instruction and on-the-job experiences. Probationary periods for correctional staff averaged 9 months, with a low of 5 months in Illinois to a high of 18 months in Utah. A majority of jurisdictions had twelve-month training programs. In 2001 the training hours for most new correctional officers averaged 262, with 38 in-service hours. Maine had the lowest numbers of required training hours with 16, while Michigan required 640 training hours (Camp and Camp 2002:166). During the 1990s the average probationary periods for state and federal correctional officers increased from 8 months to 9.9 months.

Pre-employment screenings are also conducted for illegal drug use through drug-testing of some kind. About a fifth of all jurisdictions conducted such screenings for entry-level applicants in 2001 (Camp and Camp 2002:174). Also, psychological tests and screening are administered and performed in 40 percent of all jurisdictions. Screening corrections officer applicants began in the United States in the mid-1980s, although psychological screenings of applicants for law enforcement positions were conducted during the 1950s (Culler, Byrne, and Culler 2002:92). Psychological screening through standardized instrumentation and interviews is designed to determine those eligible applicants with the most desirable characteristics for the job. The criteria pertain to motivation, intelligence, stress tolerance, potential for substance abuse, racial bias, attitudes toward work, acceptance of responsibility, practical judgment, ability to work on a team, capacity to accept criticism, ability to follow orders and a chain of command, gender bias, emotional stability, honesty, integrity, maturity, and the need to dominate others.

Because correctional officers work with inmates who are both manipulative and dangerous, probationary periods of on-the-job training and in-service hours are valuable sources of knowledge about inmate conduct and proper behaviors and officer attitudes (Camp and Camp 2002:174). Correctional officers learn proper techniques for conducting cell searches and the use of force against noncompliant inmates. They also learn about the law and their own civil and criminal liabilities. Officers learn about the full range of inmate rights, including due process and equal protection under the law. They also learn about their own rights, including affirmative action, sex discrimination and harassment, drug testing, and other relevant matters (Christensen 2002).

Prison officers have a strong professional component in the work they do. There is a marked emphasis on task outcomes and the development of standards of performance delivery within prison systems. Some features of prison officers and the profession include:

1. The profession has skills and knowledge that come from a broad knowledge base.

2. They provide a service to prisoners by means of a special relationship that consists of an attitude or a desire to help with a sense of integrity, and a bond brought about through the role relationships they have with inmates. The relationship is authorized by the prison and legitimized by public and prisoner approval.

3. They must be educated as distinct from merely trained in a narrow sense (Newell 2002:69).

The American Correctional Association, the American Jail Association, and the American Probation and Parole Association have endorsed the importance of greater officer professionalization. Greater professionalization is attained in part through an officer certification program. Certification means establishing minimum training standards and selection criteria. Among the criteria devised for recruiting correctional officers are:

1. No prior felony convictions.
2. Clearance by a search of local, state, and federal fingerprint files to reveal any criminal record.
3. At least 21 years of age.
4. Clearance by a thorough background investigation and determined to be of good moral character.
5. A high school diploma or successful passage of the General Education Development Test (GED).
6. Clearance by a physical examination to determine the absence of physical, emotional, or mental conditions that might adversely affect performance.
7. Successful passage of an oral interview by the agency head or representative prior to employment to determine suitability for correctional service.
8. Ability to read and write at the level necessary to perform the job of a correctional officer (Josi and Sechrest 1998:168–169).

Certification programs for correctional officers are growing in the United States. Incentives for pursuing one's education are an integral part of these certification programs, where the potential for advancement to higher officer levels is possible by acquiring an associate's degree, a bachelor's degree, or even a master's degree (Mall 2002; Sims 2001).

Correctional Officer Stress, Burnout, and Labor Turnover

Correctional Officer Stress.   **Stress** is a nonspecific response to a perceived threat to an individual's well-being or self-esteem (Sims 2001). These stress responses are not specific, and each person reacts differently to the same situation triggering stress, some with somatic complaints of aches and pains, and others with irritability, loss of attention span, or fatigue. What is stressful for one person may not be stressful to another. Several factors, including one's previous experiences with the event, constitutional factors, and personality may function to mediate the stress and one's reaction to the event. One indicator of stress is absenteeism. Many employees who experience a lot of stress may absent themselves from work for a variety of reasons, and these absences can be costly to the institution in many ways (Lambert 2001).

There are different kinds of stress. One investigator has distinguished between systemic workplace stress and traumatic workplace stress. Systemic stress factors include scarce resources, pay issues, conditions of work, role stress, interpersonal conflict, dysfunctional management styles, and exposure to discrimination and sexual harassment. Traumatic stress includes the direct experience of trauma, such as an assault; a threat of violence; intimidation; hearing about traumatic, violent, and distressing events; or witnessing others being subjected to a traumatic experience (P. Fisher 2001:87–88). Thus, inmate-correctional officer relationships may have an adverse impact on one's stress level (Hobbs and Dear 2000). For instance, it may be stressful whenever corrections officers have to write incident or disciplinary reports against particular inmates for minor rule infractions. While institutional rules must be enforced, some corrections officers believe that overlooking minor rule infractions will reduce officer-inmate tensions, whereas writing such reports will alienate officers from inmates to a greater degree (Fisher-Giorlando and Jiang 2000). This conflict between what the officer would like to do and what he or she must do under the circumstances generates needless stress (Kokorowski and Freng 2001).

Some stress is good. A moderate amount of stress enhances the learning and creative processes, while too little stress may induce boredom or apathy. Stress can vary according to the types of inmates supervised by correctional officers. In situations where correctional officers supervise sex offenders, for instance, the officers often perceive these offenders as more dangerous, harmful, violent, tense, bad, unpredictable, mysterious, unchangeable, aggressive, irrational and afraid (Hensley 2000). Stress may also arise when correctional officers and police officers interface at the time of booking or offender processing. Some of this type of stress relates to ensuring that offenders' constitutional rights are or have been observed throughout the duration of their processing (Paulsen and del Carmen 2000). Further, stress may arise when corrections officers experience a conflict between how they define their roles and the traditional role conceptions of corrections officers held by others (Freeman 2000; Hemmens and Stohr 2001).

While officers are generally prepared for various officer-inmate situations where personal injuries may be sustained, this does not eliminate officer stress entirely. We don't know for sure how much stress is too much. We do know that correctional officers have twice the national average divorce rate. They also have the highest heart attack rates among all types of state employees, including police officers (Josi and Sechrest 1998). These statistics appear to result directly from the stressful aspects of corrections work.

Sources of Stress.   Stress among correctional officers and other professionals emanates from several sources (Black 2001). Stress researchers have targeted the following as the chief sources of stress among POs: (1) job dissatisfaction, (2) role conflict, (3) role ambiguity, (4) high correctional officer risks and liabilities, and (5) lack of participation in decision making (Hemmens and Stohr 2001; Sims 2001).

Job Dissatisfaction.   Job dissatisfaction is somewhat unwieldy, as it occurs as the result of a variety of factors (Farkas 2001; Mitchell et al. 2000). One study of 352 Florida corrections officers investigated factors related to job satisfaction/dissatisfaction and job-related stress (Byrd et al. 2000). Self-administered questionnaires were completed by these officers and analyzed. From among the items listed below, these officers perceived the greatest job-related stress emanating from dealing with aggressive persons, being in a hazardous situation while alone, lack of agency support, the ineffectiveness of the correctional system, and racial pressures of conflict within the agency, and problems in getting along with supervisors. A more detailed listing of factors associated with job stress includes:

1. Situations requiring the use of force.
2. Dealing with aggressive groups.
3. Risk of physical attack on the job.
4. Dealing with an aggressive person.
5. Being in a hazardous situation while alone.
6. Threat of injury on the job.
7. Potential for the use of deadly force.
8. Amount of responsibility.
9. Use of discretion.
10. Making critical, on-the-spot decisions.
11. Lack of support by supervisor.
12. Lack of support by agency.
13. Problems getting along with supervisor.
14. Insufficient manpower.
15. Inadequate equipment.
16. Ineffectiveness of the judicial system.
17. Ineffectiveness of the correctional system.
18. Courts too easy with criminals.
19. Ineffectiveness of the correctional system.
20. Racial pressures or conflict within community/population.
21. Racial pressures or conflict within the agency.
22. Political pressures outside the agency.
23. Political pressures within the agency.
24. Salary.
25. Lack of adequate medical coverage.
26. Irregular hours different from regular shift.
27. Changing shifts (Byrd et al. 2000:91).

Role Conflict.   Mills (1990:3–6) summarizes many of the feelings of correctional officers who sense the frustrations of **role conflict:** "Nobody said it would be like this." "Why do you think they call them cons?" "If there is a problem, see the probation officer." "How am I doing so far?" "I never took this job to get rich." and "Will this ever end?" Mills (1990:7) says that "for the correctional officer, it is important to maintain a freshness and enthusiasm toward the career. Corrections officers themselves have described the work they do. In many respects, their view of correctional settings is similar to that of Mills (Conover 2001).

Role Ambiguity.   Closely related to role conflict is **role ambiguity.** Role ambiguity occurs whenever correctional officers have inadequate or even conflicting information about their work roles, the scope and responsibilities of the job, and the ethics of certain unwritten practices that are commonplace among many correctional officers. On-the-job training can do much to clarify a person's work role, however (Cheeseman, Mullings, and Marquart 2001). When organizational and job attributes contribute to building individual commitment to jail facilities, there appears to be less stress and turnover. Clear-cut job definitions are essential in effective administration of prisons and jails, and rewards can more easily be calculated and anticipated for work well-done (Sims, 2001).

High Correctional Officer Risks and Liabilities.   Some risk is inherent when working with dangerous inmates (Maahs and Pratt 2001). Many inmates who were convicted of aggravated assault, murder, rape, or some other type of violent crime may pose a degree of risk to the personal safety of correctional officers. Also, the risk of contracting AIDS has increased as the disease has spread throughout inmate populations in both jails and prisons (Anno and Dubler 1992).

Lack of Participation in Decision Making.   Sometimes corrections officers may believe that they should be involved to a greater degree in decisions affecting their work or how they perform their jobs. A study was conducted of 99 employees of a private, minimum-security correctional institution in the southern United States for the years 1990 and 1997. Investigators wanted to know how important it was to corrections officers to be included in decision-making. Over a period of seven years, it was found that several of these officers quit while others remained on the job. Both those who quit and those who stayed were questioned about their decisions to leave or stay. Interestingly, participation in the organizational decision-making process was cited by both groups of officers studied. Officers who quit believed that they were not included enough in organizational decision making. However, those officers who stayed said that they believed that they could freely participate in the decision-making process. Thus, the greater the perception that these officers were able to freely participate in decision making within the institution, the less they thought about leaving (Slate, Vogel, and Johnson 2001).

Burnout.   **Burnout** is one result of stress. Maslach (1982a; 1982b:30–31) has identified at least fifteen different connotations of the term. These are:

1. A syndrome of emotional exhaustion, depersonalization, and reduced personal accomplishment that can occur among individuals who do "people work" of some kind.
2. A progressive loss of idealism, energy, and purpose experienced by people in the helping professions as a result of the conditions of their work.
3. A state of physical, emotional, and mental exhaustion marked by physical depletion and chronic fatigue, feelings of helplessness and hopelessness, and the development of a negative self-concept and negative attitudes toward work, life, and other people.
4. A syndrome of inappropriate attitudes toward clients and self, often associated with uncomfortable physical and emotional symptoms.

5. A state of exhaustion, irritability, and fatigue that markedly decreases the worker's effectiveness and capability.

6. To deplete oneself. To exhaust one's physical and mental resources. To wear oneself out by excessively striving to reach some unrealistic expectations imposed by oneself or by the values of society.

7. To wear oneself out doing what one has to do. An inability to cope adequately with the stresses of work or personal life.

8. A malaise of the spirit. A loss of will. An inability to mobilize interests and capabilities.

9. To become debilitated, weakened, because of extreme demands on one's physical and/or mental energy.

10. An accumulation of intense negative feelings that is so debilitating that a person withdraws from the situation in which those feelings are generated.

11. A pervasive mood of anxiety giving way to depression and despair.

12. A process in which a professional's attitudes and behavior change in negative ways in response to job strain.

13. An inadequate coping mechanism used consistently by an individual to reduce stress.

14. A condition produced by working too hard for too long in a high-pressure environment.

15. A debilitating psychological condition resulting from work-related frustrations, which results in lower employee productivity and morale.

The importance of burnout is that it signifies a reduction in the quality or effectiveness of an officer's job performance (P. Fisher 2001). Interestingly, it has been found that older, more experienced correctional officers are often more likely to experience greater depersonalization and emotional exhaustion from their work compared with younger officers. Also, female correctional officers are less likely to reflect alienation and impersonal relationships with inmates and other staff compared with their male counterparts (Morgan, VanHaveren, and Pearson 2002). Other research is consistent with these findings (Wells 2003). Variables such as gender, age, amount and type of education, length of job-related experience, self-esteem, marital status, and the degree of autonomy and job satisfaction function as intervening ones. The social support system is made up of others who perform similar tasks as well as the frequency of contact with these people for the purpose of sharing the frustrations of work. These factors form a mosaic from which stress stems (Lambert, Hogan, and Barton 2002). Stress is manifested by physiological, psychological, and/or emotional indicators. Burnout may result. One important consequence of burnout may be labor turnover.

Labor Turnover.   Burnout and stress occur among correctional officers, especially during the first year of their duties. **Labor turnover** rates are as high as 38 percent in some jurisdictions, such as Arkansas, during the first year of an officer's employment. It has been recommended that more experienced correctional officers should be used as mentors for new recruits (Patenaude 2001). Between 1993 and 2001, turnover among correctional officers ranged from a low of 12 percent to a high of 16.1 percent (Camp and Camp 2002:171). Of all entry-level correctional officers, 25.2 percent left before completing their probationary period. Wyoming and South Carolina had the highest percentage of officers leaving prior to completing their probationary period. Wyoming had a turnover of 62.8 percent, while South Carolina had a turnover of 61.7 percent. And during 2000, 28,357 corrections officers left 45 reporting adult correctional agencies (Camp and Camp 2002:171). It is unknown why these officers left their jobs. However, burnout is a likely explanation for some of these resignations.

Recruiting the right kinds of personnel to perform correctional officer roles is designed to identify those most able to handle the stresses and strains accompanying the job. The concern about occupational stress has been rising steadily in recent years (Farkas 2001). Virtually all occupations and professions have varying degrees of stress associated with them. Probation and parole work is not immune from stress and burnout. A comparative study of 339 Canadian and 229 U.S. correctional officers found that work stresses were often dependent upon the nature of interpersonal relations among correctional officers themselves rather than job-related factors (S. Walters 1996).

Alleviating Stress and Burnout. It is believed that probation and parole organizations and agencies are at fault in creating dangerously high stress and burnout levels among correctional officers (Hemmens and Stohr 2001). But it is virtually impossible to prevent burnout among POs in all cases. However, depending on the coping strategies and mechanisms they use, it may be possible for the organization to decrease burnout or minimize it (Robinson, Porporino, and Simourd 1997). If organizational heads will recognize what causes stress and burnout, they have a better than even chance of dealing with it effectively (Tracy 2003).

One way of alleviating stress and burnout is to permit correctional officers greater input into organizational decision making, such as using their knowledge of prison culture to establish more secure inmate policies and correctional officer safety (Slate, Vogel, and Johnson 2001). This is often accomplished through participative management. Participative management is the philosophy of organizational administration where substantial input is solicited from the work staff and used for decision-making purposes where their work might be affected. Thus, subordinates' opinions become crucial to organizational decision making as lower-level participants are given a greater voice in how the organization is operated or administered (Bryans and Jones 2001).

Greater employee involvement in the decision-making process relating to offender treatment and supervision is stressed by participative management. Generally, a lack of participation in decision making is a key source of stress and burnout. Correctional officers often say that their supervisors focus only on the negative aspects of work performed. When supervisors only provide criticisms of work improperly done and leave unrewarded work of good quality, the morale of personnel suffers greatly (Flanagan, Johnson, and Bennett 1996).

Increasing numbers of correctional organizations are establishing stress reduction programs. The National Institute of Justice has implemented a Corrections and Law Enforcement Family Support (CLEFS) program. This program aims to identify and understand the stressors that officers face and find innovative ways to prevent and treat their negative effects. Traditionally, employee assistance programs have been the most common resource for officer stress, although these programs generally focus only upon the officer with little or no attention to family members. The CLEFS program emphasizes professional counseling, peer support, responses to critical incidents that include help for victims and their families, academy and in-service training that teaches stress-reduction techniques, and services for family members. Such programs are either in-house, which are operated by the correctional agency; independent contracted services, which are provided by a private, outside agency; or hybrid programs, which combine elements of both in-house and external structures (Wells 2003:24).

Supervisors are regarded as pivotal figures in most organizations for reducing employee stress. Shapiro (1982) indicates some ways by which supervisors can reduce stress levels of correctional officers:

1. Leadership that provides support, structure, and information.
2. Communication that is timely, appropriate, and accurate.
3. An environment that is efficient and orderly.
4. Rules and policies that are explicit.
5. Workers who have freedom to be self-sufficient and make their own decisions.
6. Room for staff creativity and innovation.
7. Support and nurturing from supervisory staff.
8. Manageable job pressure.
9. Peer networks of friendship and support among staff.

Assessment Centers

One method of selecting correctional personnel is the use of **assessment centers** (Page 1995). Assessment centers are not panaceas for solving the correctional officer recruitment problem. Also, they are not cookbook methods for staff selections. Rather, assessment centers, originally devised during World War II by the Office of Strategic Services (OSS), are rigorous identification and evaluation mechanisms lasting as long as one week that are geared to test thorough selected relevant attributes of prospective officers. Staffed by psychologists, veteran correctional officers, and prison administrators, these assessment centers subject prospective candidates to grueling exercises that test general mental ability, oral, written, and human relations skills, creativity, self-sufficiency, realism of expectations, tolerance of uncertainty, organization, planning, and energy, decision making ability, and interest ranges. Assessment centers also assist in the selection of managerial personnel for correctional institutions and police departments (Pynes and Bernardin 1992). A popular format used by various jurisdictions is one established by the New York City Police Department during the 1970s. The following skills areas were identified:

1. Problem-solving dimensions (problem analysis—ability to grasp the source, nature, and key dimensions of a problem; judgment—recognition of the significant factors to arrive at sound and practical decisions).
2. Communication dimensions (dialogue skills—effectiveness of discussion in person-to-person or small group interactions; writing skills—expression of ideas in writing with facility).
3. Emotional and motivational dimensions (reactions to reassure—functioning in a controlled, effective manner under stress; keeping one's head;

drive—amount of directed and sustained energy brought to bear in accomplishing objectives).

4. Interpersonal dimensions (insight into others—the ability to proceed giving due consideration to the needs and feelings of others; leadership—the direction of behavior of others toward the achievement of common goals by charisma, insights, or the assertion of will).

5. Administrative dimensions (planning—forward thinking, anticipating situations and problems, and preparation in advance to cope with these problems; commitment to excellence—determination that the task will be well-done, the achievement of high standards) (Pelfrey 1986:67).

The Florida Assessment Center.   In Dade County, Florida, the Department of Corrections and Rehabilitation was one of the first agencies to establish an assessment center to select entry-level officers (Stinchcomb 1985). While this is not a new concept, the use of these centers in corrections recruitment and training is somewhat innovative. The **Florida Assessment Center** moves beyond traditional selection mechanisms such as the use of paper-pencil measures, standard personality, interests, and aptitude/IQ tests or inventories by examining a candidate's potential on the basis of the full scope of the job. A previously established job task analysis is made of the different correctional chores to be performed by the applicants. The following skills associated with corrections work of any kind have been identified:

1. The ability to understand and implement policies and procedures.
2. The ability to be aware of all elements in a given situation, and use sensitivity to others and good judgment in dealing with the situation.
3. The ability to communicate effectively.

THE RECRUITMENT OF WOMEN IN CORRECTIONAL WORK

Women have had a particularly difficult time entering the correctional field. Until 1972, the practice of hiring men for correctional positions and excluding women for the same posts was unquestioned in most jurisdictions (Cheeseman, Mullings, and Marquart 2001). However, throughout the 1970s and 1990s, increasing numbers of women have entered fields traditionally identified with men (Farkas 2000). Among the obstacles women have had to overcome, especially in correctional work, are resentments and opposition from administrative personnel and male correctional employees (Sims 2001). In-depth interviews with a sample of male and female correctional officers reveal that some of the barriers women encounter are informal organizational resistance and the lack of administrative support in hiring, training, and on-the-job experiences. Many male correctional officers retain traditional and stereotypical views that females cannot perform the prison guard role effectively. However, objective research investigations have shown that women tend to perform as well as men.

For instance, Walters (1993a) investigated 178 male correctional officers in four state prisons. He surveyed their attitudes toward female officers and toward corrections in general. Walters found that males tended to regard their female counterparts as competent and able to perform correctional work satisfactorily. Those male officers with pro-woman attitudes stressed the quality of the working relationship they had with women officers, job satisfaction, custody orientation, educational level and prison type. In some related research, Walters (1993a, 1993b) found that a survey of 229 correctional officers yielded generally positive attitudes toward female correctional officers. Thus, it seems that at least in the jurisdictions studied by Walters, rank-and-file male attitudes toward female correctional officers are changing, and for the better.

Opposition to women as correctional officers stems from other sources besides administrators and male correctional personnel. Some male prisoners object to being supervised by females. They consider the female officer–male prisoner scenario an invasion of their right to privacy. Some court support exists for these inmate objections. In *Bowling v. Enomoto* (1981) and *Hudson v. Goodlander* (1980), lawsuits were filed by prison inmates alleging their constitutional right to privacy was violated as the result of females being posted to positions where they could view male inmates completely unclothed. In both cases, the court upheld the inmates' right to privacy and held that prisoners have a right to limited privacy in that they should be free from unrestricted observations of their genitals and bodily functions by prison officials of the opposite sex.

However, various courts have approved opposite-sex pat-down searches of male inmates by female correctional officers. For instance, inmates at the Nebraska State Penitentiary brought suit alleging that their right to privacy was violated when prison officials promulgated a rule permitting female officers to conduct pat-down searches of them. The court declared that such opposite-sex pat-down searches of male inmates by female correctional officers was not an unreasonable regulation based on security and equal employment considerations (*Timm v. Gunter* 1990). The courts have drawn the line on opposite-sex strip searches, however. Generally, female correctional officers are prohibited from conducting strip searches of male prisoners (*Kennedy v. New York State Department of Correctional Services* 1990).

Female correctional officers suffered a legal setback when the U.S. Supreme Court upheld an appeal by the Alabama Supreme Court that contended that women in maximum-security prisons present a risk to prison security. U.S. Supreme Court Justices decided in favor of Alabama and relied on the assumption that the mere presence of women in maximum-security prisons decreases prison security (Zimmer 1986:6). However, these decisions have not deterred women from seeking employment in prison settings as correctional officers. While sex stereotyping continues, evidence suggests it is lessening annually. More women are being selected for correctional officer positions, and gradually, salary discrepancies are being eliminated (Kerle 1998). About 35.5 percent of all correctional officers hired in U.S. jurisdictions in 2001 were female (Camp and Camp 2002:164). And women are entering administrative posts as well. In 2001, there were 7,177 administrators of prisons for adults in 48 reporting jurisdictions. Of these, 22 percent were women. This is an increase from 15 percent in 1996 (American Correctional Association 2002:36).

Sexual Harassment Issues

In most jurisdictions, correctional officers are subjected to mandatory courses and issues dealing with sexual harassment and management strategies to different-sex supervision of male and female prison inmates (Bergsmann 1991). Discrimination because of gender includes sexual harassment, which means unwelcome sexual advances, requests for sexual favors, and other verbal or physical conduct or communication of a sexual nature when:

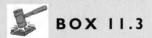 **BOX 11.3**

Managerial/Administrative Support

Warden/Jail Manager: Oversees all operations and programs within the superintendent facility.

Personnel/Human Resources Manager: Responsible for recruiting, advising, hiring, and firing staff; implements the institution's policies and procedures; provides leadership and supervision; advises and assists staff with benefits.

Employee Development Specialist: Plans, supervises, or leads programs designed to train and develop employees; consults with or guides management on employee training and development issues.

Budget Administrator: Plans and coordinates the use of resources for a facility.

Financial Manager: Maintains financial services such as auditing and credit analysis; coordinates financial policies and procedures.

Facility Manager: Manages and maintains buildings, grounds, and other facilities. Requires managerial skills and a broad technical knowledge of operating capabilities and maintenance requirements of various types of physical plants and equipment.

Safety Manager: Offers technical advice on or manages occupational safety programs, regulations, and standards. Requires knowledge of the techniques of safety and pertinent aspects of engineering, psychology, and other factors affecting safety.

Ombudsman: Acts as an unbiased liaison between inmates and facility administration; investigates inmate complaints, reports findings, and helps achieve equitable settlements of disputes between inmates and the correctional administration.

Librarian: Manages and cares for the facility's collection of books, recordings, films, and other materials.

Computer Specialist: Manages or designs use and maintenance of computer systems. This is an area of great need in the corrections field.

Researcher: Analyzes data for budgets and for projected needs and assists in the evaluation of programs.

Food Service Manager: Manages and supervises the operation of the institution's or department's food services, including the storeroom, kitchen, dining rooms, and procurement. Often requires certification as a registered dietician and familiarity with federal, state, and local health codes and sanitary standards.

Correctional Officer: Supervises the treatment and custody of offenders in correctional institutions.

Probation/Parole Officer: Advises and counsels individuals who are on probation or parole; enforces and monitors compliance with the rules imposed on the offender by either the court or parole board.

Juvenile Services Officer: Advises and counsels juveniles in aftercare; evaluates and initiates treatment plans for juveniles in aftercare and makes referrals to appropriate support agencies.

Counseling/Training

Psychologist/Counselor: Works with inmates and corrections professionals. Provides counseling and testing. Generally requires professional training. Closely allied specialists may include art therapists and drama therapists. Certified drug and alcohol counselors are in great demand.

Chaplain: Offers religious guidance and spiritual counseling to inmates. Requires ordination by a recognized ecclesiastical body; chaplains may be called on to minister to inmates not of their faith.

Recreation Specialist: Plans, organizes, and administers programs that promote inmates' physical, creative, artistic, and social development.

Vocational Counselor: Provides educational programs or career training for inmates; determines learning needs, abilities, and other facts about inmates. May participate in discussions with other staff professionals to aid in inmate rehabilitation.

Vocational Instructor: Provides both classroom and hands-on training in a variety of trades.

Industrial Specialist: Assists or manages a prison industry, such as printing, carpentry, agriculture, and sign-making programs.

Juvenile Careworker: Supervises the treatment and custody of juvenile offenders in correctional or rehabilitation facilities. Often provides support and counseling to juvenile offenders and participates in the development and implementation of treatment plans.

Teacher: Leads classes on subjects for both juveniles and adult offenders. Requires a bachelor's degree plus certification by the state education authority in a specific subject area. Teachers certified in special education in great demand.

Medical

Health System Administrator: Responsible for the administrative management of the health-care delivery system and use of outside resources to provide patient care.

Medical Officer: Performs professional aid and scientific work in one or more fields of medicine. Requires, at a minimum, the degree of Doctor of Medicine and, in most states, a current license to practice medicine. Medical support staff may include physicians' assistants, nurses, nurses' assistants, and pharmacists.

Source: Excerpted from Michael Kelly, "A Corrections Career Guide: Is a Career in Corrections for You?" *Corrections Today,* **58:**134–136 (1996); Robert C. DeLucia and Thomas J. Doyle, *Career Planning in Criminal Justice.* Lanham, MD: American Correctional Association, 1994; Stuart Henry (ed.), *Inside Jobs.* Lanham, MD: American Correctional Association, 1994.

1. Submission to such conduct or communication is made a term or condition either explicitly or implicitly to obtain employment, public accommodations or public services, education, or housing.

2. Submission to or rejection of such conduct or communication by an individual is used as a factor in decisions affecting such individual's employment, public accommodations or public services, education, or housing.

3. Such conduct or communication has the purpose or effect of substantially interfering with an individual's employment, public accommodations or public services, education or housing, or creating an intimidating, hostile or offensive employment, public accommodations, public services, educational or housing environment (Brown and Van Ochten 1990:64).

Female-Male Officer Differences in Job Satisfaction and Other Work-Related Factors

Reviews of the literature about women working as correctional officers suggest that women regard prisons as more stressful than their male officer counterparts (Wright and Saylor 1991:505). Female officers tended to feel less safe than male officers working in prison settings. Incidents of inmate assaults on female correctional officers are not uncommon (Harry 2001). Wright and Saylor (1991) mailed 8,099 surveys to about one-half of all employees working in 46 federal prisons. In all, 3,325 usable surveys were returned, with a response rate of 41 percent. The survey administered was the Prison Social Climate Survey, which sought information about numerous job dimensions and factors. Generally,

Women's Control Unit, North Dakota State Penitentiary.

female officers reported job satisfaction levels about the same as men. Women did not differ from men regarding the quality of supervision they received. Furthermore, women working in women's prisons do not have more positive work experiences compared with women working in men's prisons. Also, minority women reported no significant differences in work experiences compared with white female officers.

The differences between male and female correctional officers are less apparent in recent years (Lawrence and Mahan 1998). While women continue to face some resistance from male officers, the resistance seems to come more from experienced officers who have been on the job for many years. Younger and less experienced officers relate better with female correctional officers. Thus, it is suggested that resistance to women in corrections arises largely from entrenched biases that were acquired when staffs were mostly male. A survey of 162 male and female correctional officers in the Minnesota Department of Corrections was undertaken to determine officer perceptions of women's acceptance, safety, and perceived job performance. Female correctional officers today reveal considerable confidence in their job performance (Stohr 1997). Some differences exist between male and female officers and how they deal with stress, however. Women officers seek social support to alleviate occupational stress, where as male officers tend to use a problem-solving approach that is reflective of traditional male-female sex roles (Hurst and Hurst 1997).

THE ORGANIZATION AND OPERATION OF PROBATION AND PAROLE PROGRAMS

Probation and parole departments in various states are administered by different agencies. Although most states have departments of corrections that supervise both incarcerated and nonincarcerated offenders, these tasks are sometimes overseen in other jurisdictions by departments of human services, departments of youth services, or some other umbrella agency that may or may not have the expertise to service these clients adequately.

During the 1990s and well-beyond 2000, a growing concern has been the professionalization of all correctional personnel (Levinson, Stinchcomb, and Greene 2001). When the President's Commission on Law Enforcement and Administration of Justice made its recommendations in 1967, few standards were in place in most jurisdictions to guide administrators in their selection of new recruits. Thus, it was not unusual for critics of corrections to frequently make unfavorable remarks about and unflattering characterizations of those who manage criminals and oversee their behaviors.

Criticisms of Probation/Parole Programs

Officials believed in the early years of correctional reforms that the treatment or medical model was sound and that rehabilitation on a large scale was possible for both incarcerated and nonincarcerated offenders. Rehabilitation was projected as the direct result of proper therapeutic programs and treatments. Educational and vocational-technical programs were coupled with group and individual counseling in prisons and jails. Offenders sentenced to probation were slotted for involvement in various training courses and assigned to programs designed to improve their self-concept, skills, and marketability as jobholders and breadwinners.

Criticisms of correctional personnel generally have centered on the inadequacy of their training, lack of experience, and poor educational background. Because of their similarities to corrections officers who perform inmate management chores, PO characteristics have implications for the quality of services delivered by probation and parole agencies. If it is true that a majority of POs enter this work with little or no training, that they lack the enthusiasm and energy to perform their jobs efficiently and effectively, and that they lack basic educational skills for dealing with offender clients, then it may be that these factors significantly influence the quality of services delivered to offenders. If probation and parole officers cannot cope effectively with the demands of their jobs because of their own limited resources and experiences, then suggested reforms involving their professionalization would be justified. Often underemphasized are people skills and the ability to cope with human problems. However, some evidence suggests that POs are increasingly adept at exercising discretion in officer-client relations and that a growing number of POs desire greater participation in decision making affecting their work (Slabonik and Sims 2002). This changing profile of POs and their abilities and skills is no doubt due, in part, to greater initiatives among jurisdictions to professionalize the PO role through more stringent selection and training requirements, greater educational emphasis, and more extensive in-service experience and extended probationary periods.

Some of the major criticisms of probation and parole programs and personnel are:

1. Until the early 1980s, only one state required a college education of probation or parole officer applicants, and some states had as their only prerequisite the ability to read and write, presumably for the purpose of completing PSI reports.

2. Past selection procedures for probation and parole officers have focused upon physical attributes and security considerations.

3. Probation and parole officer training has often been based upon the military model used for police training.

4. Probation and parole programs have historically been fragmented and independent of other criminal justice organizations and agencies.

5. The general field of corrections has lacked professionalization associated with established fields with specialized bodies of knowledge.

6. Most jurisdictions have lacked licensing mechanisms whereby officers can become certified through proper in-service training and education.

Probation/Parole Officers (POs): A Profile

Interacting with ex-offenders, visiting their homes or workplaces, and generally overseeing their behavior while on probation or parole is a stressful experience (Fulton et al. 2000). One reason is that the types of offenses committed by probationers and parolees are increasingly serious. Thus, there is growing priority given to officer safety (Small and Torres 2001). The dangerousness associated with PO work is well documented, and each day exposes most POs to risks similar to those encountered by police officers (Klaus 1998; Wooten 2000). Of course, offenders are obliged to comply with probation or parole program requirements, whatever they might be, and to be responsive and accessible whenever POs wish to contact them.

The primary control mechanism operating to moderate offender behavior is the probation or parole revocation power possessed by POs. While their recommendations for a parole or probation revocation are not binding on any body convened to hear allegations of violations against an offender, it is their report that initially triggers a revocation proceeding. An unfavorable report about an offender may involve a technical violation or a serious crime allegation (D'Anca 2001). POs often overlook minor supervision violations, in part because they judge such violations not to be serious and also because they do not wish to prepare the extensive paperwork that is a preliminary requirement for a formal probation/parole revocation hearing. Despite the leverage POs have over their offender-clients, the possibility of violent confrontation with injury or death, and hostility from the public-at-large make PO work increasingly stressful and demanding.

Characteristics of Probation and Parole Officers.   Who are probation and parole officers? What are their characteristics? Although little comprehensive information about POs exists, surveys have been conducted in recent years that depict the characteristics of those performing various PO roles. These surveys indicate a gradual move toward greater PO professionalization (Burrell 2000). One indication of greater professionalization of POs has been the movement toward accreditation and the establishment of accreditation programs through the American Correctional Association (ACA) and the American Probation and Parole Association (APPA). About 50 percent of all POs are male and about 24 percent are nonwhite. A majority of POs possess bachelor's degrees and have 9 to 12 years of on-the-job experience. Thus, the labor turnover among POs is not as great as it is among correctional officers.

The average PO annual salary in 2001 for entry-level work was $26,685, with a high entry-level salary of $40,088 in Connecticut to a low of $20,244 in Tennessee (Camp and Camp 2002:225). Highest salaries for POs in 2001 averaged $48,547, with a highest high salary of $70,686 in Alabama and the lowest high salary of $36,000 in Wyoming. In the federal system, the entry-level PO salary was $29,000 with a high salary of $98,500.

Probation work pays less than parole work when departments of probation and departments of parole are compared, although the salary differences are not substantial. For instance, the average entry-level probation officer salary in 2001 was $28,881, while the average entry-level salary for parole officers was $31,465 (Camp and Camp 2002:225). However, probation officers had higher average maximum salaries of $51,536 compared with parole officers, who had average maximum salaries of $47,685. The federal system pays significantly higher salaries than most state systems at different grade levels, and thus, many POs start out in state PO work and eventually transfer to federal jobs when they are available.

SELECTION REQUIREMENTS FOR PROBATION AND PAROLE OFFICERS

Qualifications for PO Positions

A majority of POs have a bachelor's degree. At least 29 state systems required the bachelor's degree as the minimum educational level for entry-level parole officer positions in 2001 (Camp and Camp 2002). In many states, however, the general entry-level requirements for PO positions are less stringent. The minimum educational requirement in most jurisdictions for probation officer work is a high school diploma or GED.

Because probation and parole officers are often selected locally in cities and counties, there is some variation in the minimum qualifications they are expected to have to qualify for certain PO positions. In California, for instance, the minimum educational requirements for a Probation Officer I level include graduation from a four-year college or university or completion of the equivalent course work, with a major in corrections, criminal justice, political science, administration of justice, sociology, social work, psychology, or any related social or behavioral sciences field. Experience in a field related to probation may be substituted on a year-for-year basis for a maximum of two years. Further, the Butte County, California, Probation Department requires possession of, or ability to obtain, an appropriate valid California Class C driver's license and proof of valid insurance.

Additionally, one must possess or obtain a valid Certificate 832 Peace Officer Certificate and successfully complete the Basic Probation Officer Course as specified by the Board of Corrections prior to promotion to the Probation Officer II level. All prospective POs must take and pass specified training to include CPR, first aid, management of assaultive behavior, and use of chemical agents with annual requalification, if the officer requests issuance of department OC spray. Armed officers must meet additional annual training requirements consistent with state law and the Probation Department Arming policy. Any offer of employment in this classification is contingent upon taking and passing a medical examination. This examination will assess a candidate's ability to meet the physical demands of the position with or without accommodation in accordance with applicable statutes for applicants with disabilities. Applicants must be of good moral character and successfully pass a thorough background investigation, including a psychological examination, fingerprinting, criminal and other relevant records check, and pre-employment polygraph, as required by the government code. Probation officers must successfully complete forty (40) hours of annual training as certified by the California State Board of Corrections designed as continuing education to update and improve knowledge and skills in any year in which the incumbent is not enrolled in the basic course. This special requirement shall continue as long as the Butte County Probation Department participates in the State Standards and Training Program (Butte County Probation Department 2002).

For a Probation Officer II position, another California county requires the following: possession of a valid California S.T.C. Deputy Probation Officer C.O.R.E. Training Certificate and possession of a P.C. 832 Certification (and a valid copy of both must be submitted with application materials); possession of a class C California driver's license by the time of appointment with a good driving record; working knowledge of principles of applied psychology and counseling techniques as they pertain to juveniles and adults, principles of modern adult and juvenile probation, laws and codes pertaining to adult and juvenile probation, investigative techniques for juvenile and adult criminal offenses, interviewing techniques, functions and procedures of the court as they relate to probation cases, effective record-keeping procedures, community resources for juvenile and adult offenders, and familiarity with probation policies and procedures. Further, candidates must be able to communicate effectively with probationers and others in the course of work; gather and analyze facts regarding the circumstances of alleged violations of the law, and make appropriate recommendations; write clear and concise reports, letters, and recommendations; read and comprehend pertinent laws, rules, regulations, and procedures regarding probation work; speak effectively before groups and the courts; and provide excellent and courteous customer service and establish and maintain effective working relationships (Monterey County Probation Department 2002).

In DeKalb County, Illinois, the requirements for a juvenile probation officer include a bachelor of arts and sciences degree, preferably in criminal justice, social work, or education. Additionally, candidates must have good oral and written communication skills, interpersonal sensitivity, planning and organizing abilities, problem analysis capabilities, good judgment, and good oral fact finding ability. Duties of officers include supervision, counseling, and community brokering; maintaining records; providing social history reports and information to the juvenile court (DeKalb County Court Services 2002).

Qualifications for federal employment as probation officers include the following. Requirements for probation/pretrial services officers include completion of a bachelor's degree from an accredited college or university in a field of academic study, such as criminal justice, criminology, psychology, sociology, human relations, or business, or public administration, which provides evidence of the capacity to understand and apply the legal requirements and human relations skills involved in the position. Furthermore, progressively responsible experience, gained after completion of the bachelor's degree, in such fields as probation, pretrial services, parole, corrections, criminal investigations, or work in substance abuse/addition treatment are desirable. A maximum entry age of 37 is required. The supervision, treatment, and control of alleged criminal offenders requires moderate to arduous physical exercise, including prolonged periods of walking and standing, physical dexterity and coordination necessary to operate a firearm, and the use of self-defense tactics. On a daily basis, these officers face unusual mental and physical stress because they are subject to danger and possible harm during frequent, direct contact with individuals who are suspected or convicted of committing federal offenses. Applicants must be physically capable. Normal hearing ability, with or without a hearing aid, is also required. Any severe health problems, such as physical defects, disease, or deformities that constitute employment hazards to the applicant or others may disqualify an applicant (U.S. Probation Office 2002).

What Do POs Do?

POs perform diverse functions. At least twenty-three different functions are associated with PO work. These include supervision, surveillance, investigation of cases, assisting in rehabilitation, developing and discussing probation conditions, counseling, visiting homes and working with clients, making arrests, making referrals, writing PSI reports, keeping records, performing court duties, collecting fines, supervising restitution, serving warrants, maintaining contracts with courts, recommending sentences, developing community service programs, assisting law enforcement officers and agencies, assisting courts in transferring cases, enforcing criminal laws, locating employment for clients, and initiating program revocations (Campbell 1998; Rogers 1998).

For instance, the Monterey County, California, Probation Department lists the following duties for Probation Officer II positions:

1. Investigate alleged juvenile and adult offenses by interviewing the accused, parents, relatives, witnesses, police officers and others involved.

2. Write progress reports, letters and correspondence, and file court petitions.

3. Analyze facts gathered through investigation; provide written evaluations for the court that also recommend appropriate action; appear in court with recommendations on cases.

4. Supervise a caseload of juvenile and/or adult offenders placed on probation by the court to ensure the conditions of probation are met; obtain urine samples, make searches and arrests.

5. Conduct client home, school, and work visits; counsel offenders and their families.

6. Design and implement rehabilitation plans with clients and their families; encourage and persuade clients to participate in program and monitor participation (Monterey County Probation Department 2002).

The examination process for PO recruitment used in most jurisdictions has been described by the American Correctional Association. Over 80 percent of the programs require a written examination, and about 40 percent subject recruits to psychological screening. The Minnesota Multiphasic Personality Inventory and Inwald Personality Inventory appear to be those most popularly applied, when any are used. Very few programs included physical examinations, medical checks, or FBI inquiries.

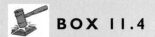

BOX 11.4

Ruben A. Foster

Probation/Parole Officer II, State of Alaska, Palmer, AK

Statistics

A.A. (justice), B.A. (justice), University of Alaska-Fairbanks; Probation Officer Academy; U.S. Army Infantry Training, Ft. Benning, GA; M.A. in progress (criminal justice administration and management), University of Alaska-Fairbanks

Background and Interests

Presently, I am an Institutional Probation/ Parole Officer at the Palmer Correctional Center in Palmer, Alaska. I spent two years as a Field Probation Officer in Fairbanks, Alaska. In addition, I was recently hired by the University of Alaska at Anchorage as a criminal justice instructor for Introduction to Justice. I am enrolled and close to completion of my first year in the master's degree in Criminal Justice Management and Administration at the University of Alaska-Fairbanks. I spent little over four years in the U.S. Army Honor Guard in Washington, DC, conducting ceremonies in the National Capital Region. For the past six years, I have served in the Alaska National Guard as an infantryman.

I grew up in Delta Junction, which is a small town in the northern area of Alaska. My parents ran a transportation business and my father was a part-time locksmith. I graduated from Delta Junction High School and left for the Army approximately two months after graduation. I had enlisted in the U.S. Army in the Delayed Entry Program one year prior to my finishing high school. I really wanted to become a military police officer, but they had no openings, and so I became an Airborne Infantryman. Fortunately, I was chosen to serve with the U.S. Army Honor Guard in Washington, DC. My time spent in Washington would not be wasted, as this played a huge part in my getting hired later in Alaska. While in the Army, I saw many neat places I had never experienced growing up in Alaska. I marched at the White House, conducted ceremonies at the Tomb of the Unknown Soldier, carried caskets, and folded the flag for presentation to families.

Upon ending my service with the military, I was accepted as a student at the University of Tennessee-Knoxville. Feeling freedom after four years in the army, my grades slipped a little as well as my focus on what I wanted to do in the future. After finishing my first year of college, my father asked me if I wanted to return to Alaska to work with his transportation company. I jumped at that chance to return to Alaska and took him up on the offer (realizing now it was important for me to get refocused). Anyway, it worked! I decided to begin college at the University of Alaska-Fairbanks (UAF) once I came back to Alaska. I was determined to get an education, since nobody in my family had attempted such a feat. I started my sophomore year in spring 1997 and received my A.A. degree that summer. I attended two more years and completed my B.A. degree. Toward the end of my senior year, I took a class entitled Community Corrections, which introduced me to the field where I currently work. Prior to that time, I had always wanted to become an Alaska State Trooper, and this was a new field I knew nothing about. Upon completion of this class, I spoke with my instructor, who just happened to be the Regional Chief Probation Officer in Fairbanks, Alaska, for the Field Probation/Parole Officers. He spoke with me about completing an internship with Fairbanks Adult Probation/Parole, which I agreed I would try. I went to the Director of the Justice Department at UAF who encouraged this as well, and he helped to set up my internship. I enjoyed the internship so much that I applied for a position with the agency upon completing my bachelor's degree. Approximately three months after graduation, I was hired as a Field Probation/Parole Officer in Fairbanks for an "off the road" caseload. During this same time, I married my college sweetheart (who is now expecting our first child). I supervised Alaskan Natives in over twenty villages in the northern region. On occasion, the opportunity presented itself to fly into the villages to check up on the offenders. This was always an interesting time, as the Alaskan Native people have an abundance of knowledge to offer a new probation/parole officer (PO). Upon completing two years in the field, I transferred to my current position as an Institutional PO at the Palmer Correctional Center (PCC) in Palmer, Alaska. PCC is a medium- and minimum-security facility, which houses approximately 400 inmates. What I have found is that Field POs and Institutional POs perform two very different jobs, but all work toward the same goal—public safety.

As a Field PO, I conducted pre-sentence investigations as well as writing the full reports for the court; prepared petitions to revoke probation as well as parole violation reports for offenders charged with violating probation/parole; appeared in court and before the Alaska Board of Parole; arrested offenders for violating their conditions; worked with offenders to get them into needed treatment; and assisted with housing, jobs, and other matters. As an Institutional PO, I designate and classify inmates, which assists in housing issues; complete furloughs and electronic monitoring applications; complete release work; and assist inmates in attempting to get out on discretionary parole. There are a lot more aspects of the job, but they are too numerous to list. Being a PO is like any other job in law enforcement: It can be extremely stressful at times, because you deal with difficult people and situations. The best part of the job is seen when one person changes because he or she decided it was time.

Experiences

My most exciting memory was an embarrassing one as well. I was a new Field PO and flew out to the village of Ft. Yukon with the Alaska State Troopers. Once we landed, I requested their assistance to conduct a home visit to one of my offenders who was a known drug user. Ft. Yukon Police Department joined us and we headed for the residence. The visit went well, and as we were leaving the residence, the Ft. Yukon police officer advised me and the trooper to look out for a dog that was chained in the front yard. I unlatched my pepper spray, thinking in case we needed to subdue the dog, I better have it ready. After advising us about the dangerous dog, the Ft. Yukon police officer walked right next to it. The officer was nipped on the leg enough to cause bleeding, and he hurried to the car we had arrived in. The Ft. Yukon officer was driving, the Alaska State Trooper was in the passenger seat, and I hurriedly jumped into the back seat. Just about the time I sat down, I heard a noise that sounded like an aerosol spray can. Suddenly, I realized that my spray had gone off and hit the trooper directly in the back of the head. I yelled, "Pepper spray!" and we all bailed out of the car. After it cleared, we all had a good laugh. The trooper was glad that I had provided that warning. The moral of this story is that any position in law enforcement is a learning experience, and it is important that we all be able to chuckle a little even in the face of adversity. Warning: Don't try this at home.

Advice to Students

My advice to anyone interested in law enforcement is to maintain your ability to laugh. Law enforcement work is serious work, and all too often, those who get caught in it lose their sense of humor. Laughter is good for the soul and heart. In addition, I would also advise those interested to obtain some level of education and attempt to get an internship. The law enforcement world is ever-changing, and college prepares you to be able to change with it. An internship is a great chance for an individual to test the waters and get your foot in the door. When hired, it will be an extremely challenging time, as you will think you can never learn everything you need to know. Don't get discouraged, because this is true of anyone in the field: We are always learning and implementing new techniques and ideas. Recognize how you personally learn and use the method that best works for you. As an old sergeant major once told me, you have to let the difficult times hit you on the head and roll down your back. Good luck, stay safe, and have fun.

These programs place considerable emphasis upon the legal liabilities of POs and other types of corrections officers. They also stress the cultivation of skills in the management and supervision of offender-clients. Programs are also offered for managing stress, crisis intervention and hostage negotiations, proposal and report writing, legal issues training, managing community corrections facilities, dealing with the mentally ill offender, and suicide prevention.

In 2001 probation officers averaged 125 introductory hours and 27 hours of in-service training. Parole officers averaged 177 hours with 48 hours of in-service training. Where probation/parole officer requirements were combined and reported, PP/Os averaged 197 introductory hours and 41 in-service hours (Camp and Camp 2002:224). Currently, most agencies require bachelor's degrees or equivalent experience, with an emphasis on a social science major. At least two states lack strenuous entry requirements. For instance, Minnesota requires applicants to pass a basic reading comprehension examination and a structured oral interview. In Nevada, POs must possess a high school diploma and have four years' experience, although the type of experience is unspecified. Nevada offers prospective recruits the option of possessing a bachelor's degree in lieu of four years' experience, however.

The Use of Firearms in Probation and Parole Work

Because the idea of POs carrying firearms is fairly new, not a great deal has been written about it. Also, it is too early to evaluate the long-range implications of PO firearms use in the field (DelGrosso 1997). More probation and parole officer training programs are featuring topics related to PO safety, especially in view of the shift from the medical model toward more proactive, client-control officer orientation (U.S. Probation Office 2002). Few professionals in criminology and criminal justice question that each generation of probationers and parolees includes more dangerous offenders. Largely because it is impossible at present to incarcerate everyone convicted of crimes, the use of probation and parole as front-end and back-end solutions to jail and prison overcrowding is increasing. Also increasing are reports of victimization from POs working with probationers and parolees in dangerous neighborhoods (Blauner and Migliore 1992:21–23). It is not necessarily the case that probationer-clients or parolee-clients are becoming more aggressive or violent toward their PO supervisors, although there have been reports of escalating client violence against their supervising POs. The fact is that POs are obligated to conduct face-to-face visits with their clients, and in many instances, these face-to-face visits involve potentially dangerous situations and/or scenarios (Butte County Probation Department 2002).

PO Work Is Dangerous.   Probation and parole work is very hazardous and stressful (Monterey County Probation Department 2002). Among other things, probation and parole officers are authorized to conduct warrantless searches of their clients' premises at any time. Sudden intrusions into the apartments or homes of clients may be unwelcome, and dangerous incidents may be created that jeopardize the lives of POs. Increasing numbers of POs are frightened by the prospect of working in high-crime areas where their lives are in danger (Lindner and Bonn 1996:22–23). The following types of assaults or attempted assaults against officers nationwide since 1980 were listed by the survey (Bigger 1993:15):

Murders or attempted murders	16
Rapes or attempted rapes	7
Other sexual assaults or attempted sexual assaults	100
Shot and wounded or attempted shot and wounded	32
Use or attempted use of blunt instrument or projectile	60
Slashed or stabbed or attempted slashed or stabbed	28
Car used as weapon or attempted use of car as weapon	12
Punched, kicked, choked, or other use of body/attempted	1,396
Use or attempted use of caustic substance	3
Use or attempted use of incendiary device	9
Abducted or attempted abduction and held hostage	3
Attempted or actual unspecified assaults	944
TOTAL	2,610

The Use of Firearms by POs Is Debatable.   Should POs arm themselves during their visits with clients? When POs are surveyed, they are often evenly divided 50–50 on the question. A study of 159 POs attending a state probation training academy in 1990 asked these officers their opinions about whether they should carry firearms during their visits with clients. The question, "Should POs be given the legal option to carry a firearm while working?" was asked of these 159 POs. Over 59 percent of the officers believed that they should be permitted to carry a firearm on the job.

Jurisdictions vary in their opinions about firearms use during PO work. In California, for example, the Parole Division adopted a firearms policy in 1979 (Sluder, Shearer, and Potts, 1991:3–5). Many officers, as well as the public, believed that PO firearms possession and display during PO/client confrontations would lead to numerous shooting incidents, even deaths of officers and/or clients. During the next twelve years, however, there were a reported seven unholsterings per month among California POs, and only one incident was reported of a gun being fired. No agents were killed or seriously injured during this period. The California Parole Division averaged 800 armed agents during this period, ranging from 250 in 1979 to 1,500 in 1990, with an average of 7,000 arrests per year (Smith 1991a). One explanation for this record is that POs are taught to deal with increasingly dangerous offenders and to use various behavior modification techniques in their client encounters (Smith 1991b, 1991c).

Some of those opposed to POs carrying firearms believe that this may escalate a situation between a PO and an armed client to the point where injuries or deaths could occur. However, other professionals claim that changing offender populations have transformed into successive generations of more dangerous, violent clientele (DelGrosso 1997). A fundamental issue at the center of this controversy is the amount and type of training POs receive who will carry these firearms. States, such as Florida, have authorized their POs to use firearms (DelGrosso 1997).

Negligent Training, Job Performance, and Retention

POs are increasingly liable for their actions taken in relation to their clients. Increasing numbers of lawsuits filed against POs are becoming more commonplace. Many of these lawsuits are frivolous, but they consume much time and cause many job prospects to turn away from PO work (Morgan, Belbot, and Clark 1997). There are three basic forms of immunity: (1) **absolute immunity,** meaning that those acting on behalf of the state can suffer no liability from their actions taken while performing their state tasks (e.g., judges, prosecutors, and legislators); (2) qualified immunity, such as that enjoyed by probation officers if they are performing their tasks in good faith; and (3) **quasi-judicial immunity,** which generally refers to PO preparation of PSI reports at judicial request (Jones and del Carmen 1992:36–37). In the general case, POs enjoy only qualified immunity, meaning that they are immune only when their actions were taken in good faith. However, there is some evidence that the rules are changing related to the types of defenses available to POs, although the limits of immunity continue to be vague and undefined. Jones and del Carmen (1992) have clarified at least two different conditions which seem to favor POs in the performance of their tasks and the immunity they derive from such conditions:

1. Probation officers are considered officers of the court and perform a valuable court function, namely the preparation of PSI reports.
2. Probation officers perform work intimately associated with court process, such as sentencing offenders.

Jones and del Carmen (1992) believe that it is unlikely that POs will ever be extended absolute immunity to all of their work functions. Subsequently, del Carmen and Pilant (1994:14–15) have described judicial immunity and qualified immunity as two types of immunity that are generally available to public officials including POs. Judicial liability is like absolute immunity described earlier. Judges must perform their functions and make decisions that may be favorable or unfavorable to defendants. Lawsuits filed against judges are almost always routinely dismissed without trial on the merits. Parole boards also possess such judicial immunity in most cases. In contrast, qualified immunity ensues only if officials, including POs, did not violate some client's constitutional rights according to what a reasonable person would have known (del Carmen and Pilant 1994:14).

Liability Issues Associated with PO Work.   A summary of some of the key liability issues related to PO work is provided below.

1. Some information about a probation/parole officer's clients is subject to public disclosure while some information isn't subject to public disclosure.
2. Probation/parole officers have a duty to protect the public; their work in this regard may subject them to lawsuits.
3. Probation/parole officer use of firearms may create hazards for both POs and their clients.
4. Probation/parole officers may supervise their clients in a negligent manner.
5. Probation/parole officer PSI report preparation may result in liability.
6. Liabilities against probation/parole officers and/or their agencies may ensue for negligent training, negligent retention, and deliberate indifference to client needs.

The above listing of potential legal liabilities of POs represents the major types of situations where POs incur potential problems from lawsuits. Jones and del Carmen (1992:36) and Sluder and del Carmen (1990:3–4) suggest at least three different types of defenses used by POs when performing their work. These defenses are not perfect, but they do make it difficult for plaintiffs to prevail under a variety of scenarios. These defenses include the following:

1. POs were acting in good faith while performing the PO role.
2. POs have official immunity, since they are working for and on behalf of the state, which enjoys sovereign immunity.
3. POs may not have a special relationship with their clients, thus absolving them of possible liability if their clients commit future offenses that result in injuries or deaths to themselves or others.

PO CASELOADS

The caseload of a probation or parole officer is considered by many authorities to be significant in affecting the quality of supervision POs can provide their clients. Caseloads refer to the number of offender-clients supervised by POs. Caseloads are the numbers of offenders supervised by POs. Caseloads vary among jurisdictions (Patrick et al. 2000). Seemingly, the larger the caseload, the poorer the quality of supervision and other services. Intensive probation supervision (IPS), for instance, is based on the premise that low offender caseloads maximize the attention POs can give their clients, including counseling, employment, social, and psychological assistance. The success of such IPS programs suggests that lower caseloads contribute to lower recidivism rates among parolees and probationers (Stalans, Seng, and Yarnold 2001).

Ideal Caseloads

No one knows what are ideal caseloads. Actual caseloads of POs vary greatly, ranging from a low of 5 or 10 clients to a high of 320 clients (Camp and Camp 2002:195). Currently, there is no agreement among professionals as to what is an ideal PO caseload. On the basis of evaluating caseloads of POs in a variety of jurisdictions, Gottfredson and Gottfredson (1988:182) have concluded that "it may be said with assurance . . . that (1) no optimal caseload size has been demonstrated, and (2) no clear evidence of reduced recidivism, simply by reduced caseload size, has been found." This declaration applies mainly to standard probation/parole supervision, and it is not intended to reflect on the quality of recent ISP programs established in many jurisdictions. Because the composition of parolees and probationers varies considerably among jurisdictions, it is difficult to develop clear-cut conclusions about the influence of supervision on recidivism and the delivery of other program services. An arbitrary caseload figure based upon current caseload sizes among state jurisdictions would be about 30 clients per PO. This is perhaps closest to an ideal caseload size (Center for Legal Studies 2000).

If POs are given the responsibility of supervising particular types of offenders, such as those with drug or alcohol dependencies, their caseloads are generally lighter. This makes it possible to devote more time and counseling to those with these addictions (Torres and Latta 2000). Sometimes special case-loads are given to officers who have exceptional education in different areas, such as counseling or languages. It is increasingly important for POs to know various foreign languages, such as Spanish, Russian, or Chinese. As the numbers of minority probationers and parolees increase, greater emphasis is placed on language skills as prerequisites for some PO positions. Some POs may be given caseloads dealing with offenders with special needs, such as deaf mute clients. Those POs who can sign are in a position to be most effective in dealing with hearing-impaired clients. Those with counseling experience may be assigned to offenders who have had convictions for domestic violence or abuse (Krmpotich and Eckberg 2000).

Changing Caseloads and Officer Effectiveness

Can Smaller PO Caseloads Increase PO Effectiveness? The frequency of contacts between POs and their clients is sometimes less important than the quality of these contacts. Frequent face-to-face contacts helps POs to determine whether clients are observing curfew and staying away from drugs and other illegal substances. POs can make a significant difference in the lives of their clients to the extent that they can connect clients with prospective employers or assist clients when filling out job application forms.

A classic study of the effectiveness of probation was the San Francisco Project, an investigation of the federal probation system, in the 1960s (Banks et al. 1977). Probationers were assigned to POs with varying caseloads. Some POs had caseloads of 20 offenders, while other POs had caseloads of 40 offenders. The ideal level of supervision was considered 40 clients, while 20 probationers as a caseload was considered intensive. The San Francisco Project showed no differences in probation supervision effectiveness as the result of increasing the intensity of supervision. Greater offender monitoring through the lower caseload assignments merely made it possible for officers to spot more technical violations committed by probationers.

However, some offenders benefited immeasurably by POs who were able to spend more time with them. Some POs are good listeners and function as emotional outlets for offenders with special problems. The primary benefit to probationers from greater contact with their POs was the more personalized attention they received. No substantial impact was made on client recidivism, however.

One explanation for these non-significant findings is that there is not much of a difference between 20 and 40 clients as a PO caseload. In many jurisdictions, these respective caseloads are considered close supervision, where POs can see their clients monthly. In those jurisdictions where POs have 300 or more clients, such as California, we might expect significant differences in recidivism rates where POs supervise 400 clients as opposed to those jurisdictions where POs supervise only 40 or fewer clients.

When we evaluate the effectiveness of POs and client success, we must remember that whatever measure of effectiveness is used, such as the recidivism rate, is best interpreted in particular contexts. What are the recidivism rates of probationer-clients and parolee-clients while they are under PO supervision? What are the recidivism rates of probationer-clients and parolee-clients when they are no longer under PO supervision? Very different recidivism rates will usually be reported if we analyze program successfulness according to these different criteria. Usually, the recidivism rates of probationers and parolees are fairly low while they are being supervised. Parolees generally have lower recidivism rates while under PO supervision compared with probationers. This is because average parole officer caseloads are much lower than average caseloads of probation officers. In short, most parolees in the United States tend to be supervised more closely than probationers; hence, their lower recidivism numbers (Basta 1995; National Council on Crime and Delinquency 1998).

However, when probationers and parolees complete their respective programs, the recidivism rates tend to increase. It is not uncommon to find, in three-year followups, for instance, that the average recidivism rates of *both* ex-probationers and ex-parolees are nearly 70 percent (Langan and Levin 2002). A government-sponsored study of 272,111 former inmates released in 1994 in 15 states was conducted. Investigators tracked these offenders over a three-year period. Within a three-year period following their release, 67.5 percent were rearrested for a new offense. Approximately 47 percent were reconvicted for a new crime, while 52 percent were back in prison for a new prison sentence or for a serious technical violation. Those with the highest rearrest rates included robbers (70.2 percent), burglars (74 percent), larcenists (74.6 percent), motor vehicle thieves (78.8 percent), those possessing or selling stolen property (77.4 percent), and those possessing, using, or selling illegal weapons (70.2 percent) (Langan and Levin 2002:1). While only about a third of all states was involved in this research, the results seem reliable and consistent with what has been reported by others in past years (Petersilia 2002).

Caseload Assignment Models

Various caseload assignment schemes for POs have been described (Carlson and Parks 1979). These include (1) the conventional model, (2) the numbers game model, (3) the conventional model with geographic considerations, and (4) specialized caseloads.

The Conventional Model.   The **conventional model** involves the random assignment of probationers or parolees to POs. The conventional model is used most frequently in probation and parole agencies throughout the United States. The major drawback is that POs must be extremely flexible in their management options, because of the diversity of clientele they must supervise.

The Numbers Game Model.   The **numbers game model** involves dividing the total number of clients by the number of POs. If there are 1,000 offenders and 20 POs, 1,000/20 = 50 offenders per PO. For offenders who require some continuing contact with an agency but not a high degree of intervention, group reporting seems to be an economical way of supervising these offenders.

The Conventional Model with Geographic Considerations.   The **conventional model with geographic considerations** is applied on the basis of the travel time required for POs to meet with their offender-clients regularly. Those POs who supervise offenders in predominantly rural regions are given lighter caseloads so that they may have the time to make reasonable numbers of contacts with offenders on a monthly or weekly basis.

The Specialized Caseloads Model.   Some POs have unique skills and knowledge relative to drug or alcohol dependencies. Some POs have had extensive training and education in particular problem-areas to better serve certain offender-clients who may be retarded or mentally ill (Leonardi and Frew 1991). Some POs by virtue of their training may be assigned more dangerous offenders. Those POs with greater work experience and legal training can manage dangerous offenders more effectively compared with fresh new PO recruits. In some respects, this is close to client-specific planning, where individualization of cases is stressed (Yeager 1992:537–544). Thus, the **specialized caseloads model** takes advantage of a PO's expertise in dealing with offenders with special problems and/or needs. Interviews with ex-offenders and clients in New York found that their interactions with parole officers were particularly helpful at assisting clients from avoiding contacts with gangs and other criminal influence for the duration of their parole programs (Duggan 1993). Their parole officer support and assistance was credited with enabling them to lead productive and law-abiding lives.

PO Labor Turnover

PO work is often not what new recruits had in mind when they commenced working for probation or parole agencies. PO work often involves meaningful interactions with offenders who want to be helped, and POs must provide counseling and assistance to offenders. They supervise offender progress and influence the course of an offender's program. They have minimal paperwork and spend most of their time in helping capacities. However, most POs spend a great deal of their time preparing PSIs, performing routine checks of their clients' premises and workplaces, and furnishing courts with periodic updated information about offender progress. One's writing skills seem more highly valued than one's interpersonal skills. This is a major disenchantment for many new PO recruits.

Many POs leave their positions during their first few years (Hurst and Hurst 1997). Estimates suggest that turnover rates among new POs range between 15 and 20 percent during their first year of service (Camp and Camp 2002). Many POs report that they considered the work temporary, as a position to be held while they seek better-paying jobs in the private sector (Cornelius 1994). Since the educational requirements are not particularly demanding, probation and parole work is fairly easy to obtain. Holding a job with some degree of responsibility is considered an asset on one's vita or resume, especially for those looking forward to working in other professions after they have acquired work experience in a related field.

VOLUNTEERS IN COMMUNITY CORRECTIONS

Who Are Volunteers?

There is little information about **volunteers** in correctional work. Winter (1993:22) says that volunteers are people helping people. Margaret A. Moore, Deputy Commissioner assigned to the Central Region of the Pennsylvania Department of Corrections, has given some breadth to Winter's definition by noting that "volunteers are integral to correctional programming. . . . they are hardworking, dedicated individuals who fill in the gaps for correctional agencies and provide much-needed services that victims, inmates, parolees, proba-tioners and their families might otherwise not receive because of limited fund-ing for programs" (Moore 1993:8).

Thus, **corrections volunteers** are any unpaid persons who perform auxil-iary, supplemental, augmentive, or any other work or services for any law en-forcement, court, or corrections agency. Corrections volunteers vary greatly in their characteristics and abilities, in their ages, and in their functions. For in-stance, Girl Scouts, ages 12 to 16, work closely with female inmates and their children at the Maryland Correctional Institution for Women in Jessup, Mary-land. Girl Scouts play with the daughters of female inmates during twice monthly Girl Scout troop meetings. Troop projects are planned as well as future activities where female inmates and their daughters may become involved and experience more intimate bonding not ordinarily possible under penal condi-tions (Moses 1993).

Some volunteers are retired schoolteachers who work with jail and prison inmates to assist them in various kinds of literacy programs. The Gray Panthers, an organization of elderly volunteers, provide various services and programs targeting older inmates specifically (Lehman 1993:84). Some volunteers, such as septuagenarian Brigitte Cooke in Huntington, Pennsylvania, work with death row inmates or those serving life sentences. Her services include spiritual guid-ance, support, and compassion (Love 1993:76–78). Some volunteers are crime victims who confront criminals who have committed crimes suffered by vic-tims (Costa and Seymour 1993:110). Some volunteers work with juvenile of-fenders and assist social workers and parents in order to reduce juvenile distress (Pierpoint 2001).

What Do Corrections Volunteers Do?

Because volunteers in corrections are largely drawn from local populations, there is no nationwide database about volunteers in the United States and their impact in different corrections areas. From time to time, however, the actions of volunteers in particular jurisdictions are reported in the professional literature. For example, Vermont citizens reported little confidence in the criminal justice system in 1994. But this lack of confidence galvanized the public to take action and get involved in various ways with offenders. By 1999, there were over 300 citizen-volunteers working with probationers and parolees to see if they could make a difference in their lives (Greene and Doble 2000). Vermont volunteers eventually established 44 community-based reparative boards. These reparative boards are designed as mediation centers between victims and their victimizers. Local reparative boards schedule meetings between convicted offenders and their victims. Judges refer these offenders to a particular board, where the crimes of offenders are reviewed. Assessments of the impact of the offender on the community and victim(s) are made, and community-based sanctions are im-posed that must be accepted by the convicted offenders. The result has been a pronounced change in the attitudes of Vermont residents toward the criminal justice system. Nearly half of those interviewed say that it works well. No doubt this favorable finding is in part attributable to greater citizen involvement in the community-based sanctioning of offenders, which seems to improve their po-tential for rehabilitation (Greene and Doble 2000).

Another reported volunteer program is the Exodus Group headquartered in Salt Lake City, Utah. This nonprofit corporation was established in 1991 to provide assistance to different types of offenders, ex-offenders, as well as their families. For instance, in 1994, 1,173 ex-offenders were interviewed by 12 Exodus Group volunteers, and 507 of these ex-offenders requested assistance. Subsequently, following volunteer intervention and assistance, a followup of these offenders was conducted. It was found that those persons receiving assistance from the Exodus Group had very low recidivism rates. Thus, it was concluded that volunteers have been of significant value in assisting ex-offenders moving from their prison environments back into society. Further, volunteer involvement in the lives of these ex-offenders does much to reduce the stigma effect of imprisonment (Celinska 2000).

Volunteers of America and Other Volunteer Organizations.   One of the most enduring volunteer organizations in the United States is the Volunteers of America. This is a nonprofit organization with numerous locally based sites that has been in operation for over 100 years. Volunteers of America is an all-encompassing voluntary organization, assisting not only convicted offenders, but also the homeless, disabled, elderly, and others (Volunteers of America, Inc. 2002). While the membership of Volunteers of America is fluid, the organization reported that, in 2001, the Volunteers of America Correctional Services programs were responsible for assisting over 58,000 persons nationwide. Volunteers of America strives to change the lives of prisoners with professional rehabilitation services and programs that provide the social, spiritual, and vocational tools needed to help persons return successfully to mainstream society and make positive contributions (Volunteers of America, Inc. 2002).

In many jurisdictions, there is public or private sponsorship of volunteer programs. In Connecticut, for example, the Department of Corrections (DOC) sponsors Volunteers in Corrections (Connecticut Department of Corrections 2002). The DOC maintains that volunteers are valued partners who assist DOC staff in the improvement of enrichment of the correctional community. Citizen involvement serves to supplement staff responsible for the coordination of inmate activities. Volunteers who support the DOC by helping to diversify and strengthen institutional activities are respected and appreciated. There are volunteer opportunities in addiction services, basic educational services, and chaplaincy services. Requirements for volunteers with the Connecticut DOC: must be a minimum age of 18, must have no current or pending significant criminal convictions; must have a structure and purpose for working with unsentenced/sentenced offenders in restrictive settings; must agree to attend a three-hour safety and security orientation; must read a volunteer handbook; and must be willing to work with assigned staff supervisors (Connecticut Department of Corrections 2002).

An example of a locally administered volunteer program is the Ramsey County, Minnesota, Volunteers in Corrections (VIC) Program. It was established in 1970 and has provided volunteers who work with clients and staff of the Community Corrections Department. VICs are currently active in every division. Each volunteer is matched with a position that most benefits the volunteer, clients, and staff. All volunteers are expected to commit to a minimum of one year and 8 hours per month of service to the program. Volunteers in VIC must complete a VIC application form, provide three character references, attend a 12-hour orientation program, undergo a criminal record check, receive a work assignment, and complete a three-month probationary period (Volunteers in Corrections 2002).

Thus, persons do not simply walk into a probation office or prison and inform officials that they want to "volunteer." As these examples illustrate, there is usually a fairly stringent application process and not everyone is accepted into volunteer work. Since volunteers work with and near federal or state offenders in different capacities, those screened from volunteer work would be anyone with a serious criminal record. Others who might be barred from doing volunteer work would be those with serious mental problems, although sometimes these are difficult to detect. Sometimes, relatives or good friends of incarcerated offenders have attempted to volunteer so as to position themselves in close proximity to these offenders. One nefarious objective might be to smuggle drugs or other contraband to inmates while pretending to do volunteer work on their behalf. Volunteer organizations wish to minimize their liabilities and build a high degree of trust with the agencies with whom they work.

A volunteer program designed for working with female offenders both in prison and in community-based programs is called The Program for Female Offenders. This program provides for volunteers who visit the Allegheny County, Pennsylvania, Jail three times a week and the State Correctional Institution at Muncy on a less frequent but regular basis (Arnold 1993:120). Incarcerated women are assisted by volunteers who help them adjust to prison life. Certain family and legal problems may be dealt with, using the volunteers as intermediaries. For those women who have been recently released, the agency operates a training center, two residential facilities, and a day treatment program. All of these facilities are located in Pittsburgh.

Arnold (1993:120–122) notes that volunteers deserve special recognition for the unpaid services they perform, including the following functions:

1. Serving as tutors at the skill training center and handling most GED preparations.
2. Providing transportation to parenting sessions at their residential centers.
3. Teaching women hobby skills such as knitting, sewing, and dressmaking.
4. Teaching computer and job search skills at the skill training center.
5. Providing gifts for women and their children every Christmas.

Often, these tasks lead to friendships between volunteers and inmate/clients. Arnold also advises that it is important to place volunteers in positions where they will feel safe and comfortable. She suggests the following guidelines:

1. Don't take offenders home or lend them money.
2. Don't share your troubles with offenders.
3. Learn to listen effectively.
4. Don't try to solve offenders' problems.
5. Don't make judgments.
6. Report irregular behavior to the agency staff. This is not being disloyal.
7. Don't provide drugs or alcohol to offenders.
8. Don't always expect to be appreciated.
9. Do have empathy and patience.
10. Do care.

How Many Correctional Volunteers Are There?

No one knows precisely how many volunteers work in U.S. institutional or community corrections. However, local and regional volunteer organizations have reported the numbers of persons who volunteer for work with various types of offenders. For example, the Alston Wilkes Society, a nonprofit agency that assists convicted offenders and their families in South Carolina, has a volunteer force of at least 5,000 persons (Walker 1993:94). Approximately 3,000 volunteers worked in various capacities with the Pennsylvania Department of Corrections in the early 1990s (Lehman 1993:84). The Federal Bureau of Prisons (BOP) used at least 4,000 volunteers in different ways for institutional and community corrections services in the mid-1990s (Walsh 1997). There are probably at least 100,000 volunteers or more assisting in various local, state, and federal programs throughout the United States today.

Criticisms of Volunteers in Community Correctional Work

While volunteers perform a valuable service for both institutional and community corrections, volunteers are not without their critics. For the most part, volunteers are untrained persons who simply wish to help others in need. Occasionally, when institutions and community organizations utilize volunteers, officials may use these persons in ways that have adverse consequences for organizations and the clients or inmates who receive assistance. Some volunteers have seasoned skills, such as retired schoolteachers who volunteer for prison or community correctional reading programs for inmates or probationers/parolees. Other volunteers may have legal expertise (e.g., lawyers or retired lawyers or judges, paralegals). Some volunteers have counseling experience with some psychological training. But a large number of volunteers are essentially unknown quantities. They may have little or no practical experience and may simply want to fill their free time by doing something productive that benefits the community in some way. We cannot discount their motives to do something useful for others. However, there are potential pitfalls whenever volunteers are used in correctional settings. Various critics of volunteer work in corrections have issued one or more of the following criticisms.

Volunteer Naiveté.   Unusual situations arise from time to time where inmates and other types of offenders might harm volunteers or be harmed by the very volunteers trying to help them. One problem that is cited frequently by critics of correctional volunteerism is volunteer naiveté. Inmates, probationers, and parolees are often effective at manipulating those who work with them in supervisory or helping capacities. It is not unusual to find that some volunteers are easily manipulated to do various favors, illegal or otherwise, for convicts. Thus, some volunteer training is necessary to deal with this criticism (Whitman, Zimmerman, and Miller 1998).

Volunteers Do Not Make Long-Term Commitments with Clients.   Because of the voluntary, unpaid nature of volunteer work, many volunteers may be in correctional settings for brief periods, tire of their activities, and leave (American Probation and Parole Association 1996).

Volunteers Do Not Work Independently.   Some volunteers are reluctant to work independently with individual probationers and parolees. Thus, a regular

PO might be required to monitor or supervise volunteer-client relations. This might necessitate a considerable and unnecessary expenditure of valuable time on the part of the supervising PO, who is often overworked with heavy caseloads and numerous other required duties.

Volunteers Lack Experience.   A chief concern of POs is that volunteers lack general knowledge about the specific rules and policies of their departments. Some volunteers do not know how to handle unusually developing scenarios between themselves and particularly troublesome clients. If offenders violate program rules, volunteers have some difficulty reporting them for these infractions. Volunteers are more easily manipulated compared with regular POs. Furthermore, special-offender populations, such as sex offenders or substance abusers, require more sophisticated counseling and assistance (Konopa et al. 2002). Some volunteers may not know how to deal effectively with such specialized populations of offenders (Lea, Auburn, and Kibblewhite 1999). However, a growing number of organizations are engaging in more selective recruiting practices for attracting volunteers, and they are providing volunteers with various types of training to render them more effective in relation to the inmates and clients with whom they will eventually interact (Godwin, Steinhart, and Fulton 1996).

Information-Sharing with Volunteers Is Limited.   A dim view is taken of disclosing confidential information about offender-clients to volunteers. Most volunteers are not credentialed. They do not carry badges and other formal documentation to initiate formal client inquiries. They may use the information they obtain in ways that harm clients rather than help them.

Volunteers Threaten Job Security.   If volunteers supplement the work performed by full-time staff, then some of the full-time staff may not be needed in the future years.

Volunteers Are Unpaid and Less Motivated.   Unpaid personnel who work with corrections agencies on a voluntary basis are under no special obligation to adhere to specific working hours or schedules.

Volunteers Contribute to Criminal Activity.   A local pastor regularly brought church members into the prison for worship services together with inmates (Bayse 1993:16). He allowed a woman from a nearby church to join the group one Sunday at the last moment. The pastor did not know that the woman was wearing two dresses and a wig. When she excused herself to go to the bathroom, an inmate discreetly followed her and outfitted himself in her extra dress and wig. Dressed as a woman, he returned with her to the church group and left with them when they exited the prison. He was apprehended a few days later.

Programs that use volunteers may attract persons who may endanger specific types of clientele, such as children. Pedophiles and child sexual abusers may volunteer to work in community corrections programs where young children are involved. If these child molesters are allowed to work around children, considerable harm might result to the children involved. Interviews with prospective volunteers who want to work with children are not foolproof.

Ogburn (1993:66) suggests the following safeguards to screen volunteers:

1. Evaluate the need for volunteers.
2. Develop goals and job descriptions for volunteers.

3. Involve staff together with volunteers as teams.

4. Actively recruit volunteers more selectively.

5. Educate volunteers about inmates and how volunteers might be manipulated.

6. Explain security needs to volunteers.

7. Give volunteers the big picture of where they fit in and how they can best fulfill the organizational mission.

8. Evaluate program effectiveness.

9. Recognize your volunteers' contributions.

Bayse (1993:48–50) adds that volunteers should observe the following rules and regulations:

1. Use appropriate language. Don't pick up inmate slang or vulgarity. Using language that isn't a part of your style can label you a phony.

2. Do not volunteer if you are a relative or visitor of an inmate in that institution.

3. Do not engage in political activities during the time voluntary services are being performed.

4. Do not bring contraband into prison. If you are not sure what is contraband, ask the staff. People who bring in contraband are subject to permanent expulsion and/or arrest.

5. Do not bring anything into or out of a facility for an inmate at any time, no matter how innocent or trivial it may seem, unless with the written permission of the superintendent. Volunteers should adopt a policy of saying no to any request by an inmate to bring in cigarettes, money, magazines, or letters. If in doubt, ask a staff member.

6. Keep everything in the open. Do not say or do anything with an inmate you would be embarrassed to share with your peers or supervisors.

7. Do not give up if you failed at your first try. Try again.

8. Don't overidentify. Be a friend, but let inmates carry their own problems. Be supportive without becoming like the inmates in viewpoint or attitude.

9. Do not take anything, including letters, in or out of a correctional facility without permission. Respect the confidentiality of records and other privileged information.

10. Do not bring unauthorized visitors or guests with you to the institution. They will be refused admission.

11. Do not give out your address or telephone number. If asked, you might say, "I'm sorry, but I was told that it was against the rules to do that."

12. Do not correspond with inmates in the facility in which you volunteer or accept collect telephone calls from them at your place of residence.

13. Be aware that the use of, or being under the influence of, alcohol or drugs while on institution grounds is prohibited.

14. Don't impose your values and beliefs on inmates. Do not let others impose a lower set of values on you.

15. Don't discuss the criminal justice system, the courts, inconsistency in sentencing or related topics. Although everyone is entitled to his or her own

opinion, what volunteers say can have serious repercussions in the dorms or with staff.

16. Ask for help. If you are uncertain about what to do or say, be honest. It is always best to tell the inmate that you will have to seek assistance from your supervisor. Inmates don't expect you to have all the answers.

17. Know your personal and professional goals. Be firm, fair, and consistent.

18. If you have done something inappropriate, tell your coordinator regardless of what happened. It is far better to be reprimanded than to become a criminal.

The Legal Liabilities of Volunteers and Agencies Using Them

Lawsuits against agencies because of volunteer conduct are not infrequent. They are diverse and may include negligence in training, hiring, assignment, supervision, entrustment, and retention (American Probation and Parole Association 1995). Officers may be liable to third parties for injuries caused by offenders or by program volunteers, and liability to offenders may occur because of unauthorized or inappropriate record disclosures, injuries in job performance, and offender physical injuries caused by volunteers (Whitman, Zimmerman, and Miller 1998). Volunteers may incur liability as the result of (1) improper record disclosures, (2) injuries inflicted on clients in job performance, and (3) injuries sustained while on the job. Some volunteers obtain liability insurance as a hedge against potential lawsuits arising in the future for any wrongful acts they might commit (Walsh 1997).

PARAPROFESSIONALS IN COMMUNITY CORRECTIONS PROGRAMS

Paraprofessionals Defined

A **paraprofessional** is anyone who possesses some formal training in a given correctional area, is salaried, works specified hours, has formal duties and responsibilities, is accountable to higher-level supervisors for work quality, and has limited immunity under the theory of agency. Agency is the special relation between an employer and an employee whereby the employee acts as an agent of the employer and is able to make decisions and take actions on the employer's behalf (Black 1990:62). Black (1990:1112) also defines a paraprofessional as "one who assists a professional person though not a member of the profession himself."

Training Paraprofessionals

Paraprofessionals perform valuable services for professionals working in the same correctional endeavors (Lea, Auburn, and Kibblewhite 1999). It is difficult to profile the education and training of all paraprofessionals as an aggregate (Dembo et al. 1999). Rather, specific categories of paraprofessionals are more easily described. Third-year law school students may clerk for attorneys as paraprofessionals, since they have acquired sufficient legal expertise to look up cases and brief them for use in courtroom arguments.

Paraprofessionals who are responsible for maintaining surveillance with various juveniles involved in a home detention program in Tuscaloosa, Alabama, in 1977 have been described by Smykla and Selke (1982). These youth workers are authorized to send juveniles directly to secure confinement when they fail to meet program requirements. These rules include regular school attendance, curfew, restraint in the use of drugs or alcohol, avoidance of companions or places that might lead to trouble, and notification of parents or workers as to their whereabouts at all times when not in school, at home, or at work. Responsibilities of paraprofessionals in this program included regular one-on-one, face-to-face visits with each juvenile daily, together with personal or telephonic contacts with parents, teachers, and/or employers (Smykla and Selke 1995).

Criticisms of Paraprofessionals

The work of paraprofessionals has been both praised and criticized for several decades (Gardner 1971). One persistent criticism of paraprofessionals is that, like volunteers, they may not be adequately trained to deal with specialized offender populations, such as substance abusers. Those who counsel drug offenders should have special counseling training and some clinical practice in order to maximize their effectiveness with clients. But, increasingly, clinical decisions are being made by legal entities such as parole, probation, and the courts. Counseling has also been influenced by a cadre of minimally trained paraprofessionals with low skill levels (Shearer 2000). Some agencies have attempted to overcome this criticism by supervising the work of paraprofessionals closely. For example, the U.S. National Institute on Drug Abuse–funded Youth Support Project has used a Family Empowerment Intervention, which is a voluntary, in-home service project requiring the participation of all members of a family or household. The intervention is delivered three times weekly by paraprofessionals, who are supervised closely by licensed clinicians (Dembo et al. 1999). With such supervision, the work of paraprofessionals under these conditions seems effective.

Since paraprofessionals are hired employees of various corrections agencies, their liability coverage is very similar to that of volunteers (Connelly 1995). Organizations using both volunteers and paraprofessionals are subject to lawsuits in the event an action by a paraprofessional or volunteer results in damages to inmates or offender-clients. These damages may be monetary, physical, or intangible, such as psychological harm. Title 42, U.S.C., Section 1983 (2003) outlines various types of civil rights violations that might be used as bases for lawsuits. The bases for different lawsuits by offender-clients are allegations of negligence, including:

1. Negligent hiring (e.g., organization failed to weed out unqualified employees who subsequently inflicted harm on an inmate or probationer/parolee).
2. Negligent assignment (e.g., employee without firearms training is assigned to guard prisoners with a firearm; firearm discharges, wounding or killing an inmate).
3. Negligent retention (e.g., an employee with a known history of poor work and inefficiency is retained; subsequently, work of poor quality performed by that employee causes harm to an inmate or offender-client).

4. Negligent entrustment (e.g., employee may be given confidential records and may inadvertently furnish information to others that may be harmful to inmates or offender-clients).

5. Negligent direction (e.g., directions may be given to employees that are not consistent with their job description or work assignment; this may result in harm to inmates or offender-clients).

6. Negligent supervision (e.g., employee may supervise prisoners such that inmate problems are overlooked, causing serious harm and further injury or death to inmate or offender-client) (Barrineau 1994:55–58).

Minimizing lawsuits against paraprofessionals and other employees of correctional agencies can be accomplished through more adequate training. Barrineau (1994:84) lists several criteria, including:

1. The training was necessary as validated by a task analysis.

2. The persons conducting the training were, in fact, qualified to conduct such training.

3. The training did, in fact, take place and was properly conducted and documented.

4. The training was state of the art and up to date.

5. Adequate measures of mastery of the subject matter can be documented.

6. Those who did not satisfactorily learn in the training session have received additional training and now have mastery of the subject matter.

7. Close supervision exists to monitor and continually evaluate the trainee's progress.

SUMMARY

Corrections officers generally include those who work directly with inmates and supervise them in prisons and jails. Other types of corrections officers include probation officers and parole officers, or, simply, POs. POs work in community corrections. Each jurisdiction strives to attract and hire better educated, higher caliber personnel for corrections work. However, relatively low pay and undesirable working conditions often frustrate these recruitment efforts.

A movement is underway to infuse the correctional field with a higher degree of professionalization. It is unclear what professionalization entails and how it is best achieved, although it often means acquiring more formal education and training as well as more in-service experiences. The American Correctional Association and National Institute of Justice have been instrumental in establishing training programs and seminars throughout the United States to provide the necessary training and skills for corrections personnel to perform their jobs adequately and professionally. Increasingly, corrections officers and POs are seeking certification through more extensive training and in-service experience. Entire institutions and community organizations are seeking accreditation in an effort to improve the quality of services provided to inmates and clients.

Correctional work of any kind generates some amount of officer stress. While stress is associated with most occupations and professions, it is particularly high for those performing correctional officer and PO roles. Stress is a nonspecific response to a perceived threat to an individual's well-being or self-esteem and it results in fatigue, somatic complaints, and other debilitating disorders. It has several sources, including job dissatisfaction, role ambiguity, high correctional officer job risks and liabilities, and a lack of participation in organizational decision making. One consequence of stress is burnout, or emotional, physical, and mental exhaustion that decreases one's effectiveness in work performed. As a result of stress and burnout, more than a few officers leave the correctional field annually. Labor turnover is fairly high, and it is usually linked with the nature of one's working conditions. Supervisors can assist employees in coping with stress by making program policies more explicit, providing opportunities for feedback and goal-setting, and permitting POs the latitude to do fruitful work with their offender-clients.

Correctional institutions and organizations strive to recruit larger numbers of women and minorities to perform different officer roles. Efforts to recruit more women have been successful. Subsequent comparisons between male and female officers have been made, using different evaluative criteria. Generally, there are no significant differences between male and female officers in terms of their competence or work satisfaction. Some amount of sexual harassment has arisen, however, as working environments have become increasingly heterogeneous according to gender. State and federal regulations governing sexual harassment issues have been promulgated, and organizations seek to minimize or eliminate sexual harassment whenever it is alleged or occurs.

Agencies and organizations such as the American Correctional Association do much to assist prospective officers to acquire the type of training that will assist them in being more effective. One intervening variable is the increasing offender population on probation and parole and the larger caseloads accompanying such population growth. While ideal caseloads have never been articulated to everyone's agreement, it is generally believed that caseloads ranging from 20 to 30 clients are optimum. A majority of POs have caseloads in excess of 90 clients, and some officers have caseloads of 200 or more.

Several caseload assignment models have been identified, including the conventional model where offenders are assigned POs on an "as-needed" basis, the specialized caseload model, where POs are assigned specific types of offenders such as drug or alcohol dependent clients, and the numbers game model, where the number of cases a PO is assigned is dependent upon the number of probationers/parolees and the number of POs in the jurisdiction. Officer-client interactions have been identified, where officers are regarded as detectors, brokers, educators, enablers, mediators, and enforcers. These different roles cause a degree of role conflict that produces emotional and psychological problems for many POs. In recent years, the PO role has undergone a transformation corresponding with certain technological and legal changes involving offender rights and supervision.

Because of low pay and long hours associated with PO work, probation and parole programs been unable to attract and retain the necessary number of qualified POs to be consistently effective in their relations with offender-clients. Probation and parole programs have historically suffered from an image problem, where the public believes that offenders are treated too leniently by the system. Probation and parole programs receive increasing numbers of offenders annually, although their budgets are not increased accordingly. Thus, more offenders must be managed with existing staffs. Recent selection and recruitment efforts by various states such as Florida have involved the establishment of assessment centers for screening potential recruits aspiring to become POs. These centers are using nontraditional selection methods including panels of evaluators who are themselves subjected to intensive training and scrutiny. In addition, various measures and inventories are administered and situational tests are conducted to provide realistic experiences for applicants in order to assess the quality of their decision making under stress.

No one agrees about how much education is desired for correctional work, although it is generally believed by corrections experts that practical, on-the-job experiences are regarded by recruits as most relevant for their interests and backgrounds. While there is high labor turnover among POs, evidence suggests that current selection practices are instilling greater commitment and motivation within new recruits to prolong their employment in corrections. In addition, more concerted efforts are being made to attract women and minorities to fulfill various corrections positions.

Assisting correctional institutions and community corrections are volunteers and paraprofessionals. Volunteers are any unpaid persons who perform auxiliary, supplemental, augmentive, or any other work or services for any law enforcement, court, or corrections agency. Corrections volunteers have diverse duties and responsibilities. Some volunteers are entrusted to help inmates or assist offenders on probation or parole. The nature of their assistance varies, although they may help offenders fill out job applications or teach them how to read and write. They may offer friendship and perform limited counseling if the situation arises. Some volunteers are recruited from schools, where students function in different voluntary capacities through internship programs. No special requirements exist for volunteers to do their work, and thus there is no consistency pertaining to volunteer qualities. Some volunteers simply have more skills than others. The services providing volunteers or the assistance they render also varies greatly among jurisdictions. The actual number of volunteers in the United States and the level of their training are unknown. Organizations, such as the Volunteers of America, indicate that the numbers of volunteers nationwide may be in excess of 100,000, although this is a crude estimate.

Not everyone agrees that volunteers should work with offenders, either in institutions or in their communities. Criticisms of volunteers come from various sources. One criticism is that volunteers work with inmates and other types of offenders and are privy to confidential information about them. Some people believe that volunteers should not have access to this information. This also says something about the lack of formal training many volunteers exhibit in various law enforcement, court, and corrections work. Sometimes, volunteers are reluctant to work with criminals unless others, such as POs or comparable professionals, are present to supervise these interactions. Further, volunteers have little, if any, incentive to stay with various programs for long periods. Thus, the turnover rate among volunteers is quite high. If some training is required of volunteers before they can perform their work properly, then turnover is costly for any correctional organization. Some believe that volunteers are incredibly uninformed about the work they do and their susceptibility to manipulation by inmates and offender-clients. Regular staff may feel threatened by volunteers in the sense that volunteers may eventually replace them. Thus, job security is an important factor in accepting volunteers in certain types of correctional work. Some volunteers may use their positions in sensitive areas to violate the law and assist or aid and abet inmates or offender-clients in illegal activities. Ample suggestions and rules exist to describe conduct that should be exhibited by volunteers when working with criminals.

Paraprofessionals are like volunteers, except that paraprofessionals are salaried and usually have more formal on-the-job and educational training and experience. Both volunteers and paraprofessionals have limited immunity from lawsuits by inmates and offender-clients similar to that enjoyed by POs. Unlike volunteers, paraprofessionals can be rewarded or punished by salary increases, changes in work schedules and assignments, and promotions or demotions. If the training of paraprofessionals is adequate, studies show that their work is comparable to their professional counterparts. The use of volunteers and paraprofessionals in corrections work in institutions and communities is increasing annually.

QUESTIONS FOR REVIEW

1. Who are corrections officers? What are some major differences between corrections officers and probation/parole officers? What are some of their respective duties and responsibilities?

2. How are corrections officers selected and trained? How much education should they possess to do effective work?

3. What is accreditation and why do organizations seek it? What is meant by professionalization and certification? Why is it important for corrections officers to gain certification?

4. What are pre-service and in-service training? What are assessment centers and how do they function to screen prospective job applications for corrections positions?

5. What is stress? What are some sources of stress?

6. What is burnout? What are some common meanings of burnout? What causes burnout and how can it be minimized? How are stress and burnout related to labor turnover?

7. Why is it important to attract larger numbers of women and minorities into correctional work roles? How do male and female corrections officers compare in terms of their work satisfaction and job performance? What is sexual harassment and what are several sexual harassment issues?

8. What do POs do? In what respects is PO work dangerous? What policies are in place for requiring POs to carry firearms? Why is this a controversial issue? What are some general types of negligence that POs might exhibit?

9. What are caseloads? What are the characteristics of four different caseload assignment models? Are there ideal caseloads? Why or why not? How does caseload size affect a PO's work effectiveness?

10. What are some major differences between volunteers and paraprofessionals? What criticisms have been leveled against corrections volunteers? Are these criticisms justified? Why or why not?

SUGGESTED READINGS

Beattie, L. Elisabeth and Mary Angela Shaughnessy. *Sisters in Pain: Battered Women Fight Back*. Lexington, KY: University Press of Kentucky, 2000.

Heymann, Philip B. and William N. Brownsberger, eds. *Drug Addiction and Drug Policy: The Struggle to Control Dependence*. Cambridge, MA: Harvard University Press, 2001.

Muraskin, Roslyn and Matthew Muraskin. *Morality and the Law.* Upper Saddle River, NJ: Prentice Hall, 2001.

Rion, Sharon Johnson. *Beyond His Time: The Maurice Sigler Story.* Lanham, MD: American Correctional Association, 2001.

Wice, Paul B. *Rubin "Hurricane" Carter and the American Justice System.* New Brunswick, NJ: Rutgers University Press, 2000.

INTERNET CONNECTIONS

International Corrections and Prisons Association
http://www.icpa.ca/home.html

Naber Technical Enterprises: Correctional Training, Correctional Consulting, Jail Research for Criminal Justice and Public Safety
http://www.nteusa.orgflyers/08.html

Probation and Parole Compact Administrators Association
http://www.ppcaa.net/

Volunteers In Prevention, Probation, and Prisons, Inc.
http://www.comnet.org/vip/

Volunteers of America
http://www.voa.org/

| Chapter Objectives | *As the result of reading this chapter, the following objectives should be realized:* |

1. Describing the characteristics of female offenders, including classification systems used in determining level of custody.
2. Understanding the history of women's prisons in the United States and major figures and events.
3. Describing the culture of women's prisons and special problems, including incarcerated mothers, squares, cools, and lifes.
4. Examining problems of administering women's correctional facilities.

5. Comparing and contrasting rehabilitative and vocational/technical facilities and programs for women and men who are incarcerated.
6. Discussing different intermediate punishments for women such as diversion, probation, and intensive supervised probation/parole.
7. Focusing upon the future of women's corrections, including the establishment of co-correctional facilities.

INTRODUCTION

• *A New York prison for women has many amenities that are not found in most men's prisons. Cottages have been constructed on prison grounds to allow inmate mothers the chance to visit with their children for periods of one week or longer. The program is believed to be therapeutic and a positive contribution toward the rehabilitation and eventual reintegration of convicted inmate mothers into society. In 2001 a lawsuit was filed by a male inmate in a southern prison, claiming that his fatherly rights were being violated. He alleged that he was not permitted visitation on prison grounds with his two children, ages 6 and 2. His ex-wife had legal custody of the children, and although the prisoner had limited visitation rights, there was no opportunity for him to bond with the children through a cottage program similar to the one established for women in New York. He has filed a Section 1983 action, alleging that his Fourteenth Amendment equal protection clause rights are being violated, since his prison had made no accommodations for inmate fathers. Should inmate fathers be permitted the same opportunities as inmate mothers to have limited visits with their children on prison grounds as they do in New York? What do you think?* [Adapted from the Associated Press, "Inmate Father Sues for Equal Time with Children behind Prison Walls," September 20, 2001].

• *During 1988 and 1989, more than a few middle-aged men were found shot to death at different locations along Florida highways and interstates. Bullets retrieved from the murder scenes revealed that they came from the same gun. Subsequently, several reports from men who narrowly escaped death at the hands of an apparent serial killer led to the arrest and conviction of Aileen Wournos, a 33-year-old prostitute who worked the Florida highways in search of prospective clients. When Wournos was first arrested, she took the position that she was merely defending herself from the unwanted advances and attacks of men who picked her up. She claimed that every time she killed, it was in self-defense because she believed that her life was in jeopardy. She was subsequently tried and convicted of six murders in 1992. Wournos was given six death sentences. Immediately, several groups opposed to the death penalty launched a massive campaign to get her off of death row in Florida. The American Civil Liberties Union and Amnesty International were among those groups seeking her reprieve from lethal injection. The story received so much publicity, in fact, that several television movies were made about her life and the deaths of her customers. In the meantime, state-appointed defense counsels sought to have her death sentences set aside, preferring that she be sentenced to life without the possibility of parole.*

    However, in a stunning development in July 2001, Wournos decided to come clean and tell the truth about the men's deaths in 1988 and 1989. She said to news reporters, "I am a serial killer. I would kill again. I'm not scared by it [death by lethal injection]. I know what the heck I'm doing. There's no sense in keeping me alive. This world doesn't mean anything to me. I killed those men in the first degree, robbed and killed them." Wournos's confession after so many years drew mixed reactions from several sources. Wournos said, "I wanted to clear all the lies and let the truth come out. I have hate crawling through my system." She requested that her state-appointed attorneys should be fired so that she can be placed on the "fast track" for her own execution. In July 2001, Florida Circuit Judge Michael Hutcheson said he would recommend to the Florida Supreme Court that Wournos is competent to make such a decision. He told Wournos it would put her on the fast track to be executed. She claimed that earlier in the 1990s and during her trial, she testified that the men she had killed had assaulted her and made her fear for her life. But in July 2001, she told reporters that she had lied in an attempt to beat the system. She apologized to the families of those she had murdered and said there was no further point in keeping her alive at taxpayer's expense. At the time of this writing, Wournos's execution date had not been set. Should serial killers like Wournos be allowed to forgo appeals and seek the penalty of death for their crimes? What do you think about Wournos? Should Florida honor her request and execute her more quickly in lieu of further appeals? [Adapted from Mike Schneider and the Associated Press, "Judge Clears Way for Woman's Execution," July 21, 2001].

• *Pamela Smart was convicted of persuading her teenage boyfriend to kill her husband, Gregory Smart. Gregory Smart was shot to death when he arrived home at the couple's condo on May 1, 1990. Pamela Smart was a teacher at a local high school. She also had a 16-year-old lover at the school, William Flynn. Flynn subsequently admitted committing the murder, but he implicated Pamela Smart, saying that they had had an affair. She had encouraged him to kill her husband, luring him with sexual favors. Flynn said that Pamela Smart helped him plan the crime to make it look like a burglary-murder. Pamela Smart has always maintained her innocence, despite the fact that explicit photos were produced showing her and Flynn engaging in sex play. Other factual information deeply incriminated her in her husband's murder. She appealed her sentence, claiming that the jury verdict against her was reached far too quickly, and that there was media-generated community pressure for her to be convicted. All of her appeals were rejected. How many appeals do you believe convicted offenders should have? Given Smart's sentence of life imprisonment, do you believe that she should ever be paroled?* [Adapted from the Associated Press, "Judge Rejects New Trial for Smart," June 14, 1997].

This chapter is about female offenders and the correctional institutions that house them. Female inmates in prisons and jails have increasingly been referred to as the **forgotten offenders** (Rafter 2000). One reason for this neglect is that women account for only about 7 percent of all jail and prison inmates. In 2001 there were 1.2 million inmates in state and federal prisons in the United States. About 76,400 of these inmates were women (Harrison and Beck 2002:13).

Because their numbers are so small, female inmates have not been given sufficient attention by state legislatures. The development of prisons and jails for women in the United States has been slow. Most prisons and jails have been designed almost exclusively for male offenders. Provisions for women, including separate accommodations, bathing facilities, and different recreational, vocational, and educational opportunities, have been slowly implemented by administrators of co-correctional institutions. And in many co-correctional institutions, programs and facilities for women are relatively limited compared with programs and facilities for their male counterparts.

Men are incarcerated more than twenty times as often as women, although women account for about 25 percent of all arrests for **index crimes** or **index offenses** (Maguire and Pastore 2002). In recent years, however, crime trends have shown increasing numbers of female arrests and incarcerations, although these numbers continue to be small in relation to proportionate numbers of arrests and incarcerations of male offenders. This does not necessarily mean that there is a new female crime wave, or that women are necessarily committing more crime than they have committed proportionately in past years. It may mean, for instance, that police are changing their attitudes about how women should be treated. It may also be the result of the women's movement, where women's ideologies have been transformed and greater opportunities now exist for them to commit more crime. And of course, it might also mean that a growing proportion of women in the U.S. population is giving the appearance of more crime among women (Harrison and Beck 2002). For instance, since 1995, the number of male prisoners has grown by 24 percent, while the number of female prisoners has grown by 36 percent. Whatever the explanation, increased numbers of female arrests and incarcerations have drawn public attention to the plight of prisons for women and to the differential treatment women receive in co-correctional institutions. These and other related issues will be examined here.

Several selected characteristics of female prisoners are described. The development of classification schemes applicable to female offenders has been slow. The classification process is described. Also discussed are some of the classification problems officials have encountered in devising appropriate programs for females. Compared with prisons for men, women's prisons have historically lacked sophisticated vocational and educational programming and other amenities. Because of this inequality, female inmates have sought and achieved greater equity in correctional treatment from the U.S. Supreme Court. The case of *Glover v. Johnson* (1979) is examined and its implications for women's prisons are explained. Several different types of programs for women are described, including the PROGRAM for Female Offenders, Inc., the Women's Prison Association, and the Women's Activities and Learning Center Program.

A discussion of the history and evolution of women's prisons in the United States is presented. As a part of this historical overview, several correctional models are described. These include the custodial model, the reformatory model, and the campus model. Several events and important persons are featured, including the National Prison Association and the English reformer, Elizabeth Gurney Fry. Construction of women's prisons in the United States was sluggish until the 1970s. Subsequently, numerous women's institutions have been constructed. Some of the reasons for this accelerated growth of women's prisons are provided, together with a discussion of American Correctional Association guidelines pertaining to institutional programming.

The chapter next examines the culture of women's prisons. Similar to prisons for men, women's prisons have a distinct subculture, which is described. Like men's prisons, women's prisons have evolved sets of norms and unwritten codes that govern inmate interactions. Many female offenders have young children. Therefore, a growing concern among these women is having the opportunity to interact closely with these children while imprisoned. In recent years, many women's prisons have established visitation facilities and programs so that inmate mothers can have closer contacts with their children on a regular basis. These facilities and programs are described.

Administrators of prisons for women believe that women's prisons are easier to administer than men's prisons. Compared with men's institutions, women's institutions are generally smaller, have fewer violent inmates and incidents of violence, and less gang presence to foment institutional problems. The advantages and disadvantages of administering women's prisons are described.

The next part of this chapter focuses upon several important issues pertaining to women's prisons. These issues include some general comparisons between institutions for men and women, the equal protection clause applied to female inmates, rehabilitative services for women, inmate mothers, and changing policies, programs, and services for female offenders. This section also examines the use of boot camps for women, as well as domestic violence prevention programs. A growing problem confronting female inmates is HIV/AIDS. This disease is more prevalent in women's prisons than in men's prisons. Several strategies for resolving this problem are examined.

One controversial solution to the problem of providing separate women's prisons and the accompanying vocational and educational programs is the establishment and operation of co-correctional prisons. These are facilities where men and women are incarcerated in separate areas but share various programs that are offered. Co-correctional or co-ed prisons are relatively recent creations, pioneered by the federal government in 1971. Several advantages and disadvantages of co-correctional prisons are discussed, together with some of the misconceptions people have about them. One important issue stemming from co-correctional prisons is whether men should guard women and whether women should guard men. This issue is discussed.

Large numbers of women are diverted from the criminal justice system and receive either diversion or probation. Probation often means assignment to some form of intermediate punishment, including intensive supervised probation, possibly electronic monitoring and/or home confinement. The chapter concludes with an examination of several of these supervision options available to women.

FEMALE OFFENDERS

Characteristics

The Number and Characteristics of Female Prison Inmates. What are the characteristics of female prisoners in the United States? Other than gender, do they differ from their male counterparts by committing less violent offenses? Are they younger? Are there more black than white females behind bars?

Of the 1,259,481 state and federal inmates in 2001, 85,031, or 6.8 percent, were female. About 53 percent of all female inmates in prison in 2001 were between 25 and 34 years of age, with nearly half (45 percent) never married. About half were unemployed at the time they were arrested. Forty-three percent were black and 12 percent were Hispanic. White female inmates made up about 42 percent of the female prison population. Sixty percent had not completed high school. A significant number of incarcerated women are from abusive households and are considered battered women (Leonard 2001). Interestingly, the general characteristics of female offenders have remained fairly constant during the period 1991–2001 (Harrison and Beck 2002; Maguire and Pastore 2002). Thus, little actual change has occurred in the profile of female prison inmates. Many female inmates have prior records of drug abuse and prostitution (Maxwell and Maxwell 2000).

Some contrasts between the profile of female prison inmates in 1991 and 2001 are in order. Females were incarcerated most frequently in 2001 for violent offenses (31.4 percent) and drug offenses (32.3 percent). By comparison, in 1991, female violent offenders made up 32 percent of female prison incarcerations, while female drug offenders accounted for 33 percent of these inmates. In 1991, 29 percent of all state prison female inmates were convicted of property crimes. By 2001, 25.1 percent of all women incarcerated in state prisons had been convicted of property crimes. These figures suggest that very little has changed regarding the profile of incarcerated females during the 1991–2001 period. Also, there are very few female murderers (2.3 percent of female state prison incarcerations) (Meyer et al. 2001). This information dispels the idea that there was a wave of female violent offending during the 1990s (Harrison and Beck 2002).

How women are housed in state and federal prisons also attests to their nonviolent behaviors. In 2002 over 60 percent of all female inmates were accommodated in minimum-security facilities, which often consisted of dormitory-like rooms holding 20 or more females. Only about 8 percent of all female inmates were held in maximum-security custody accommodations (Harrison and Beck 2002).

Classification of Female Offenders

There are relatively few risk measures designed to classify female offenders according to their dangerousness for appropriate placement in prisons or jails (Putkonen et al. 2001). This is because 90 percent or more of the studies of selective incapacitation, risk predictions, and screening decisions for determining the appropriate level of custody have simply excluded women from consideration. This exclusion is not necessarily deliberate or sexist. Rather, it is probably the result of the fact that there are so few women in prisons and jails that most researchers have not bothered to devise classification schemes or prediction devices for them (Marquart et al. 1999a, 1999b).

When prediction devices have been devised, they have usually been structured for male offenders and then tested to see whether they work for females (S. Brown 2002:105). For instance, in 1983, the Missouri Department of Corrections evaluated the reliability and validity of the Initial Classification Analysis, a device for determining the treatment plan and institutional assignments (level of custody based on risk or dangerousness) for male inmates. Inmate records were inspected, tests were administered, and interviews were conducted with the nearly 10,000 male inmates in Missouri prisons. Medical and health needs, educational needs, work skills, and proximity to residence/family ties were considered in these evaluations. Subsequently, institutional assignments were made. The following year, 120 female inmates processed at the Missouri Diagnostic Center were given the Initial Classification Analysis instrument and assigned to various Missouri penal facilities on the basis of their scores. The results disclosed that the instrument was a reliable and objective instrument for security classifications of female inmates (Robins et al. 1986). Oklahoma also uses a classification instrument for female inmate security and placement (Fletcher, Rolison, and Moon 1994).

It might be expected that those states with large female offender populations will be at the vanguard in the development of classification instruments. Yet, in states such as California (which leads all states in the absolute number of female inmates), the state-of-the-art regarding classification and prediction is at best uncertain for all offenders, male or female (Alleman and Gido 1998; Owen 1998). Recidivism figures suggest a male bias. Those types of offenders most likely to recidivate are labeled **persistent felony offenders.** Most of these are males. Little incentive exists for administrators to create elaborate schemes to differentiate female offenders from one another for assignments to various custody levels, despite the fact that some of these women are serial killers or have prior records of violent conduct (C.A. Davis 2001; Furio 2001).

DeCostanzo and Scholes (1988:108) have examined the needs of female offenders in prison settings. They note that "despite correctional policymakers' growing awareness concerning female offenders, 5 percent of a state's total inmate population is comprised of women who are handicapped, substance abusers,

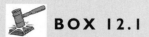

BOX 12.1

Betty Lou Beets, 62, Death Row Inmate

There aren't that many women on death rows throughout the United States. Over 99 percent of all executions are carried out against male offenders. In Gatesville, Texas, a 62-year-old woman, Betty Lou Beets, who was convicted of murdering two of her husbands, was scheduled to be executed by lethal injection on February 24, 2000. Beets would be the second woman executed in Texas since the Civil War and the fourth in the nation since the U.S. Supreme Court decided *Gregg v. Georgia* (1976). In early 2000 there were nine women on death rows throughout the United States.

Beets was convicted in 1985 of the 1983 shooting death of Jimmy Don Beets, a Dallas fire captain and her fifth husband, at the couple's trailer home near Gun Barrel City, Texas. She was also charged with but never tried for the shooting death of her fourth husband, Doyle Barker. She was also convicted of shooting and wounding her second husband. Acting on a tip, police found Jimmy Don Beets's body in a shallow grave under a wishing-well flower garden outside her trailer. Betty Lou had reported him missing on a fishing trip two years earlier. The victim's son, James Beets, said "She was watering flowers over my daddy every day for 23 months. It's not right." Both murder victims had been stuffed inside blue sleeping bags.

When Betty Lou Beets was tried for murder, she blamed a son from her first marriage for the Beets murder. She said she only helped to dispose of the body to protect her son. She blamed her second husband, now dead, for the Barker slaying. Prosecutors say that she killed her husbands to collect their pensions, including an $86,000 life insurance policy and a $760 monthly pension. Almost nothing was said at her trial about domestic violence or abuse. Suddenly, Betty Lou Beets claimed that she was the victim of spousal abuse, and that her husbands drove her to kill them. She told the *Dallas Morning News,* "I have carried a heavy burden for battered women and children and domestic violence. I'm going to be the one to put a face on that, as a real human person." James Beets shot back, "Why is she saying these things about my daddy? She had told her friends that he was the best thing that ever happened to her." He didn't buy her story.

As the former governor of Texas, George W. Bush was a proponent of the death penalty. As governor at the time, when asked about Betty Lou Beets's case, Governor Bush replied, "The thing I consider is whether or not a jury had heard all the facts and whether or not the person is guilty of the crime committed and whether or not the person has had full access to the courts. I cannot make a decision in her case until I receive a recommendation from the Texas Board of Pardons and Paroles. I will not grant clemency unless the board recommends it." In another state, Illinois, 13 inmates were released from death row over two decades when new evidence of their innocence was discovered. The Illinois governor suspended all further executions in the state until all death row inmates' cases could be re-examined for accuracy.

Should the death penalty be abolished because some death row inmates are innocent? Is the death penalty a deterrent to murder? What do you think?

Source: Adapted from the Associated Press, "Texas Woman Facing Execution Blames Domestic Abuse," February 19, 2000.

parents, the unskilled, and elderly. Each subgroup requires a unique response to its characteristics and needs. The challenges before us are complicated." Since many women's prisons in the United States are in desperate need of improvements unrelated to specific programs and plans that cater to special female offender problems, it may be expecting too much of most jurisdictions to establish fully equitable accommodations for all inmates within a short time period (Temin 2001).

Another problem that complicates the parity issue is that the female offender population in most jurisdictions changes fairly rapidly. While increasing numbers of females are incarcerated, the duration of their incarceration is shorter, on the average, compared with male offenders. This statement also holds for parolees and the length of male and female parole programs (Camp and Camp 2002). With more rapid turnovers in the types of female inmates in state and federal prisons, inmate needs change as well. Again, it is difficult for state prisons to plan for every contingency for both the male and female incarcerated populations (Farr 2000). Thus, classification devices may only be effective for short-term assessments and placements. Greater reliance upon the private sector in selected areas may be in order if these women's facilities are to offer a range of programs and services commensurate with those currently offered in all-male prison settings (Camp and Camp 2002).

WOMEN'S PRISONS

The History of Women's Prisons in the United States

Rachel Welch didn't know it at the time, but her unfortunate plight at the Auburn, New York, prison in 1826 did much to advance women's correctional reforms throughout the United States. Ms. Welch was a prisoner at the Auburn State Prison. She and many other women like her were herded into a large attic room in the prison where they were confined without benefit of recreation or even limited freedom for 24 hours a day. Food was sent up once from the kitchen daily, and slops were removed once a day as well. One of the Auburn State Prison correctional officers raped Ms. Welch, impregnated her, and, after learning that she was five months' pregnant, flogged her so severely that she died soon afterward from the wounds. A committee investigated her death, and although the facts about what had occurred were unclear and inconsistent testimony was presented, the condition of women at Auburn was publicly revealed (Hunter 1984). Several religious and philanthropic organizations intervened and pressed for various reforms that would improve significantly the conditions under which women were housed.

It is ironic that the death of a female inmate occurred in a modern prison touted for its correctional accomplishments and farsightedness in prisoner planning. Auburn Penitentiary introduced the congregate system whereby prisoners could work and socialize daily for recreational, dining, and labor purposes. During evening hours, prisoners were kept isolated from one another in solitary cells. However, these innovations were exclusively for men. Even at the modern Walnut Street Jail where separate quarters for women and men had been suggested several decades earlier, conditions had degenerated by the 1820s such that women at the Walnut Street facility were no better off than the women at Auburn.

The conditions for women at Auburn and other similar institutions were criticized initially by religious and philanthropic organizations not because of their substandard and deplorable living accommodations (Dodge 1998), but rather, because these common living areas were considered conducive to moral degeneration and widespread promiscuity. Male correctional officers had virtually unlimited social and sexual access to all incarcerated females. While increasingly segregated celling accommodations were gradually introduced for female inmates, male correctional officers continued to carry the keys to their individual cells. Thus, segregation of female prisoners from male prisoners was not a foolproof method of birth control.

At least one of the reasons for the maltreatment of women in prisons during the 1800s was that they were considered immoral women and thus unworthy of special treatment or even equal treatment compared with male offenders (Dysart 1999). Many women were separated, divorced, or had illegitimate children (Young 2001). Some observers have said that whatever the character of their legal transgressions, it was others' estimates of their own characters, and particularly their moral standing, that most often determined their fate within the criminal justice system (Brown 2001).

Three major correctional models that seem to typify women's prison conditions since 1790 have been identified (Rafter 1983). These are the custodial model, the reformatory model, and the campus model. The custodial model was emphasized during the period 1790–1870. It included features much like men's prisons, and it promoted confinement, containment, discipline, and uniformity. The **reformatory model** coincided with the reformatory movement during the 1870s and was emphasized from 1870 through 1935. Included in the reformatory model were features such as reformation, reintegration, skill acquisition, moral improvement, and social development. The campus model, emphasized from 1935 to the present, has emphasized the acquisition of diffuse goals, skill development, including cosmetology, reform, parenting, office skills, arts, and crafts.

These models are useful constructs that help us conceptualize and understand the emphasis of specific programs and objectives of women's prisons during particular time periods. Frequently, these developments coincide with correctional thinking of the period. When we attempt to explain why women and men were treated or mistreated certain ways while incarcerated, the explanation is almost always related to the dominant correctional philosophy of the period (Hovey 1971).

The first major prison for women was established in 1835 in New York, a few years after the organization of the Magdalen Society (1830), a women's prison reform-oriented movement. The facility was called the Mount Pleasant Female Prison (Rafter 1983:138). Rafter says this facility was important for at least three reasons:

1. Mount Pleasant was the first and only penal institution for women before the great era of prison construction starting in the late 1800s.

2. Mount Pleasant was managed initially by women and significant internal operational and administrative improvements were made, thus increasing the quality of life for incarcerated women.

3. Mount Pleasant was an almost exclusively custodial facility providing a place for New York's female prisoners; New York simply ran out of other places to house its female convicts (Rafter 1983:138–139).

In fact, the Mount Pleasant Female Prison typified a prevalent model for women's prisons during the 1790–1870 period: the **custodial model.** The custodial model did not offer incarcerated women much beyond the basic necessities to survive on a day-to-day basis. Women were warehoused and given limited opportunities to perform prison labor. Most of this prison labor was associated with traditional female activities, such as sewing. Women were placed in cells much like their male counterparts. Subsequently, facilities in various jurisdictions were established for women that offered more dormitory-like surroundings. Isolated cells were replaced with dormitory-like rooms with large, central recreational areas where women could sit and read. These new types of accommodations became known as the **campus model** and ushered in an era of new female correctional reforms. Nevertheless, a few U.S. prisons for women today continue to reflect predominantly custodial and reformatory policies, although the dominant correctional theme for women has shifted dramatically in the last half century.

Elizabeth Gurney Fry.   The mother of corrections for women in the United States was a Quaker Englishwoman, **Elizabeth Gurney Fry.** She traveled extensively, advocating prison reforms for women (Stewart 1993). On the basis of her experiences with women's prisons in Europe and elsewhere, she published an important work, *Observations in Visiting, Superintendence and Government of Female Prisons* in 1827. Her work was widely acclaimed by other prison reformers. Influenced by John Howard, another prominent prison reformer, she continued her reformist efforts until her death in 1845. She encouraged separate facilities for women, religious and secular education, improved classification systems for female prisoners, and rehabilitative and reintegrative programs emphasizing the learning of practical skills.

When Fry was conducting her personal visits to correctional facilities throughout the world, the custodial model was dominant. Little thought was given by prison officials to the rehabilitation of female offenders. Coincidentally, in the year of Fry's death, the Women's Prison Association was established. This philanthropic organization led to the sponsorship of the Hopper Home, a halfway house for female ex-convicts. Hopper Home, in New York City, is considered the oldest halfway house for female offenders (Creese, Bynum, and Bearn 1995). Attempts by matrons at prisons such as Sing Sing in New York to incorporate Fry's ideas met with resistance from other prison administrators, and the custodial model was continued until the early 1870s.

The National Prison Association.   The National Prison Association (later the American Correctional Association) met in Cincinnati in 1870 to consider proposals from various correctional experts about new ways of treating prisoners, both male and female (Davis 1978). The meeting was attended by prison reformers, superintendents of prisons, wardens, theorists, criminologists, academicians, and humanitarians who believed that prisons of the future ought to emphasize reform, reintegration, and rehabilitation. The Irishman, Walter Crofton, was present, as was Zebulon Brockway, the first superintendent of Elmira Reformatory in 1876. Interestingly, a major prison for women based upon the principles of the new reform era was created in Indiana in 1873, three years prior to the construction of the Elmira facility (Freedman 1981). One major difference between the Indiana Women's Prison and the Mount Pleasant Female Prison was the fact that the Indiana institution was established as a reformatory facility, not just a custodial one. Thus, using the general schema proposed by Rafter, U.S. prisons for women, although few in number, entered the reformatory period. Table 12.1 shows state and federal correctional institutions

TABLE 12.1

State and Federal Correctional Institutions for Women, By Date of Opening, 1873–1973

Date of Opening	State	Name at Opening
1873	Indiana	Women's Prison
1877	Massachusetts	Reformatory Prison for Women
1887	New York	House of Refuge for Women, Hudson
1893	New York	House of Refuge for Women, Albion
1902	New York	Reformatory Prison for Women, Bedford Hills
1913	New Jersey	State Reformatory for Women
1916	Maine	Reformatory for Women
1916	Ohio	Reformatory for Women
1917	Kansas	State Industrial Farm for Women
1917	Michigan	State Training School for Women
1918	Connecticut	State Farm for Women
1918	Iowa	Women's Reformatory
1920	Arkansas	State Farm for Women
1920	California	Industrial Farm for Women
1920	Minnesota	State Reformatory for Women
1920	Nebraska	State Reformatory for Women
1920	Pennsylvania	State Industrial Home for Women
1921	Wisconsin	Industrial Home for Women
1927	United States	Industrial Institution for Women (now Federal Reformatory for Women)
1929	Delaware	Correctional Institution for Women
1930	Connecticut	Correctional Institution for Women
1930	Illinois	State Reformatory for Women
1932	Virginia	State Industrial Farm for Women
1934	North Carolina	Correctional Center for Women
1936	California	California Institution for Women
1938	Kentucky	Correctional Institution for Women
1938	South Carolina	Harbison Correctional Institution for Women
1940	Maryland	Correctional Institution for Women
1942	Alabama	Julia Tutwiler Prison for Women
1948	West Virginia	State Prison for Women
1954	Puerto Rico	Industrial School for Women
1957	Georgia	Rehabilitation Center for Women
1960	Missouri	State Correctional Center for Women
1961	Louisiana	Correctional Institute for Women
1963	Ohio	Women's Correctional Institution
1964	Nevada	Women's Correctional Center
1965	Oregon	Women's Correctional Center
1966	Tennessee	Prison for Women
1968	Colorado	Women's Correctional Institute
1970	Washington	Purdy Treatment Center for Women
1973	Oklahoma	Women's Treatment Facility
1973	South Carolina	Women's Correctional Center

Source: Compiled by author.

for women from 1873 through 1973. Table 12.2 shows subsequent women's prisons constructed in various states and the Federal Bureau of Prisons from 1973 through 2002.

Table 12.1 shows several interesting things. First, between 1913 and 1934, nineteen women's prisons were built for various states and the federal government. Yet, for a similar two-decade period following 1934, only seven women's prisons were constructed. Many of the prisons for women during the 1913–1934 period were constructed during the height of Prohibition. This extensive construction may have been prompted by the influx of large numbers of male offenders into state and federal prison facilities because of liquor law violations or bootlegging. During the Prohibition Era, prison overcrowding at the state and federal levels was extensive, and female prison construction might have been one way of alleviating certain logistical problems such as accommodating increased numbers of female bootleggers or their companions in the same prison settings.

In any case, the construction of women's prisons during the 1920s and 1930s did much to alleviate the problems of prison administrators who were seeking solutions to the co-correctional arrangements they were increasingly obligated to provide (Rafter 1990). These new construction programs were not necessarily accompanied by new correctional innovations, however. In fact, many of the programs started in the late 1800s in women's reformatories were continued on a large-scale basis. Today, the vast majority of female offenders are housed in prisons modeled after these early reformatories.

Such massive prison construction for women during that time period had its drawbacks. Many of these prisons are still being used today (Rafter 2000). Thus, like many of the prisons for men, they are outdated, unhealthy, substandard, and inadequate for meeting the diverse needs of today's female prisoners (Kauffman 2001). Furthermore, prison conditions for women have been challenged with extensive litigation in recent years. It seems that prisons for women have bred their own jailhouse lawyers (J. Palmer 1997). This should not be taken to mean that no improvements have occurred regarding prisons for women. On the contrary. Many contemporary facilities are designed to make available a wide variety of vocational and educational programs for women that depart from stereotypical trades or occupations. In 1984, the American Correctional Association adopted a national correctional policy applicable to female offenders that has been influential in prompting legislators and others to ensure that needed reforms in female facilities are implemented. Furthermore, many female inmates are mothers, and women's prisons typically lack facilities that can accommodate inmate mothers and the special problems they create (Temin 2001). One often underreported problem is spousal violence that occurs during private family visits, which are permitted in many prisons and jails. Thus, the personal safety of female inmates should be considered when establishing such visitation programs (Toepell and Greaves 2001).

Subsequent to 1973, at least 68 new women's prisons were constructed in the United States as shown in Table 12.2. This figure does not include contemplated construction of additional women's prisons in various jurisdictions. Interestingly, this subsequent growth of women's prisons (1973–2002) has produced more prisons for women than all prisons for women constructed for the 100-year period 1873–1973.

In 2001, the female offender population in the United States was housed in largely female-only facilities. There were 113 female-only facilities housing

TABLE 12.2

Women's Prison Construction, 1973–2002

Indiana Women's Prison (1973), Indiana

Mabel Bassett Correctional Center (1974), Oklahoma

Mountain View Unit (1975), Texas

Wyoming Women's Center (1977), Wyoming

Women's Division (1978), Rhode Island

Metro Correctional Institution (1980), Georgia

Metro Transitional Center (1980), Georgia

Gatesville Unit (1980), Texas

Hilltop Unit (1980), Texas

Chillicothe Correctional Center (1981), Missouri

Women's Correctional Center (1982), Montana

Iowa Correctional Institution for Women (1982), Iowa

Tucker Unit for Women (1983), Arkansas

Fountain Correctional Center for Women (1984), North Carolina

Crane Women's Facility (1985), Michigan

Scott Correctional Facility (1986), Michigan

Black Mountain Correctional Center for Women (1986), North Carolina

Wilmington Residential Facility for Women (1986), North Carolina

Minnesota Correctional Facility (1986), Minnesota

Central Mississippi Correctional Facility (1986), Mississippi

New Mexico Women's Correctional Facility (1989), New Mexico

Northern California Women's Facility (1987), California

Women's Correctional Facility (1988), Utah

Federal Prison Camp, Bryan, TX (1988), Federal Bureau of Prisons

Raleigh Correctional Center for Women (1988), North Carolina

Hobby Unit (1989), Texas

Jefferson Correctional Institution (1990), Florida

Leath Correctional Institution-Women (1991), South Carolina

Lois M. DeBerry Special Needs Facility (1992), Tennessee

State Correctional Institution at Cambridge Springs (1992), Pennsylvania

Pueblo Minimum Center (1994), Colorado

Lockhart (1994), Texas

Janet S. York Correctional Institution (1994), Connecticut

Pulaski Correctional Institution (1994), Georgia

Washington Correctional Institution (1994), Georgia

Pocatello Women's Correctional Center (1994), Idaho

Neuse Correctional Institution (1994), North Carolina

Rockville Training Center (1995), Indiana

Neal Unit (1995), Texas

Halbert Unit (1995), Texas

Henley Unit (1995), Texas

Plain State Jail (1995), Texas

Murray Unit (1995), Texas

Plane Facility (1995), Texas

Burnet Unit (1995), Texas

Brunswick Work Center (1995), Virginia

Pocahontas Correctional Unit (1995), Virginia

Gadsden Correctional Institution (1995), Florida

Texas City Unit (1996), Texas

Pre-Release Unit for Women (1996), Maryland

Woodman State Jail (1995), Texas

North Piedmont Correctional Center for Women (1997), North Carolina

Solem Public Safety Center—SD Women's Prison (1997), South Dakota

Lemuel Shattuck Hospital Correctional Unit (1998), Massachusetts

Ronald McPherson Correctional Facility (1998), Arkansas

Women's Eastern Reception, Diagnostic and Correctional Center (1998), Missouri

New Hampshire State Prison—Women's Facility (1998), New Hampshire

Mid-State Correctional Facility (1998), New York

Fluvanna Correctional Center (1998), Virginia

Family Foundation (1998), California

Danville Center for Adolescent Females (1998), Pennsylvania

Emmanuel Youth Development Campus (1998), Georgia

Brownwood State School (1998), Texas

Corvallis House Young Women's Transition Program (1999), Oregon

Special Needs Women's Facility (1999), Iowa

Northeast Girl's Group Home (2001), Missouri

Women's Detention Facility (2002), Pennsylvania

Source: Compiled by author.

over 70,000 female offenders. There were also 57 co-ed prisons. The majority of female offenders are housed in dormitory-like facilities. Relatively few female offenders are classified as maximum-security offenders. In 2001 there were approximately 6,400 females incarcerated in maximum-security conditions. Nearly half of all female offenders were housed in minimum-security accommodations. About 60 percent of all states had work programs for women in these institutions. Eighty percent of all institutions for women had some form of educational programming, while a similar percentage had post-release vocational training (Hill 2001:8).

ACA Guidelines for Women's Prison Construction and Programming.   A guiding principle of the ACA guidelines and recommendations is the parity of services for male and female offenders. These services include traditional programs for pregnant women, child and family services, programs that aid in establishing homes and sound family relations and promoting and maintaining family ties. Increasing numbers of women's prisons are establishing conjugal visitation programs (Hensley, Rutland, and Gray 2000). Additionally, nontraditional programs have been recommended, including career counseling, nontraditional vocational training, social and economic assertiveness training, and a full range of diversion, probation, and parole services (H. Davis 2001). Evidence of the campus model is not only found in new women's prison construction, but in the layout and arrangement of women's quarters and work accommodations. The Mississippi State Penitentiary at Parchman constructed a women's facility on 17,000 acres originally designed to house male inmates in different levels of close custody. Four residential facilities for women were constructed, each with a capacity for housing 50 inmates. Besides a typical dayroom, counseling offices, and other critical prison elements, four living units have been provided specifically for mother/child visitations. These are apartment-like units that parallel closely real-life living conditions on the outside (Maxey 1986:141–142).

While there have been significant improvements in the quality of life in women's prisons, there are still gaps that are apparent among the states about how female prisoners are accommodated (Siefert and Pimlott 2001). While women have won several important legal battles in court regarding prison improvements, these improvements have either not been implemented or have been implemented very slowly. Women's prisons in other countries, such as England, have had to deal with similar issues in recent years, particularly issues having to do with inmate safety and inmate-on-inmate crime prevention (Wincup 2001).

Criticisms of Women's Prisons and Community Programs

A Minnesota study highlights some of the continuing problems associated with women's prisons and community-based treatment services. Hokanson (1986) gathered information about female inmates from 87 county correctional facilities and 31 jails. She found that the typical female offender was young; either single, divorced, or separated; educated at a level approximating the general population; lacking in work skills and dependent upon public assistance; over-representative of minority groups; and having a high probability of physical and/or sexual abuse victimization and a history of substance abuse. Similar

Women's prisons exhibit dormitory-like qualities, complete with fashionable lounge areas and other amenities.

observations have been made about women offenders by others (O'Brien 2001b; van Wormer 2001).

It is generally acknowledged that women's prisons and programming for women in community-based correctional programs have not compared favorably with programs and facilities for men (Sideman and Kirschbaum 2002). This is true of programs for female parolees in other countries besides the United States, such as England (Wilkinson, Morris, and Woodrow 2001). For instance, programs for female offenders have been poorer in quality, quantity, variability, and availability in both the United States and Canada (O'Brien 2001b). Despite these inequities, courts generally declare that men and women in prisons do not have to be treated equally and that separate can be equal when men's and women's prisons are compared (Conly 1998). There are exceptions, however.

Glover v. Johnson (1979) involved the Michigan Department of Corrections and the issue of equal programming for female inmates. A class action suit was filed on behalf of all Michigan female prison inmates to the effect that their constitutional rights were violated because they were being denied educational and vocational rehabilitation opportunities that were then being provided male inmates only. Among other things, the Michigan Department of Corrections was ordered to provide the following to its incarcerated women: (1) two-year college programming, (2) paralegal training and access to attorneys to remedy past inadequacies in law library facilities, (3) a corrected inmate wage policy to ensure that female inmates were provided equal wages, (4) access to programming at camps previously available only to male inmates, (5) enhanced vocational offerings, (6) apprenticeship opportunities, and (7) prison industries that previously existed only at men's facilities (American Correctional Association 1993:32). Several similar cases in other jurisdictions have been settled without court action (Connecticut, California, Wisconsin, and Idaho).

The *Glover* case is like the tip of an iceberg when it comes to disclosing various problems associated with women's prisons and other corrections institutions for women. The following are criticisms that have been leveled against women's correctional facilities in the last few decades. Some of these criticisms have been remedied in selected jurisdictions.

1. No adequate classification system exists for female prisoners. Women from widely different backgrounds with diverse criminal histories are celled with one another in most women's prisons. This is conducive to greater criminalization during the incarceration period. Further, most women's prisons have only medium-security custody, rather than a wider variety of custody levels to accommodate female offenders of differing seriousness and dangerousness.

2. Most women's prisons are remotely located, thus many female prisoners are deprived of immediate contact with out-of-prison educational or vocational services that might be available through study or work release.

3. Women who give birth to babies while incarcerated are deprived of valuable parent-child contact. Some experts contend this is a serious deprivation for newborn infants.

4. Women have less extensive vocational and educational programming in the prison setting.

5. Women have less access to legal services; in the past, law libraries in women's facilities were lacking or nonexistent; recent remedies have included provisions for either legal services or more adequate libraries in women's institutions.

6. Women have special medical needs, and women's prisons do not adequately provide for meeting these needs.

7. Mental health treatment services and programs for women are inferior to those provided for men in men's facilities.

8. Training programs that are provided women do not permit them to live independently and earn decent livings when released on parole (Leonard 2001; Shearer, Myers, and Ogan 2001).

Because of the rather unique role of women as caregivers for their children, many corrections professionals rule the imprisonment of women differently from the imprisonment of men (Henriques and Manatu 2001). For various reasons, female imprisonment is opposed on moral, ethical, and religious grounds. Legally, these arguments are often unconvincing. In an attempt to at least address some of the unique problems confronting female offenders when they are incarcerated or when they participate in community-based programs, some experts have advocated the following as recommendations:

1. Institute training programs that would enable imprisoned women to become literate.

2. Provide female offenders with programs that do not center on traditional gender roles—programs that will lead to more economic independence and self-sufficiency.

3. Establish programs that would engender more positive self-esteem for imprisoned women and enhance their assertiveness and communication and interpersonal skills.

4. Establish more programs that would allow imprisoned mothers to interact more with their children and assist them in overcoming feelings of guilt and shame for having deserted their children. In addition, visitation areas for mothers and children should be altered to minimize the effect of a prison-type environment.

5. An alternative to mother-and-child interaction behind prison bars would be to allow imprisoned mothers to spend more time with their children outside of the prison.

6. Provide imprisoned mothers with training to improve parenting skills.

7. Establish more programs to treat drug-addicted female offenders.

8. Establish a community partnership program to provide imprisoned women with employment opportunities.

9. Establish a better classification system for incarcerated women—one that would not permit the less-hardened offender to be juxtaposed with the hardened female offender.

10. Provide in-service training (sensitivity awareness) to assist staff members (wardens, correctional officers) in understanding the nature and needs of incarcerated women (Culliver 1993:409–410).

Other observers have recommended the establishment and provision for an environment that would allow all pregnant inmates the opportunity to rear their newborn infants for a period of one year and provide counseling regarding available parental services, foster care, guardianship, and other relevant activities pending their eventual release (Pearl 1998). Some women's facilities have cottages on prison grounds where inmates with infants can accomplish some of these objectives (Conly 1998).

The PROGRAM for Female Offenders, Inc. (PFO).   The PROGRAM for Female Offenders, Inc. (PFO) was established in 1974 as the result of jail overcrowding in Allegheny County, Pennsylvania (Vacho et al. 1994). The PFO is a work-release facility operated as a nonprofit agency by the county. It is designed to accommodate up to 36 women with space for 6 preschool children. It was originally created to reduce jail overcrowding, but because of escalating rates of female offending and jail incarceration, the overcrowding problem persists.

When the PFO was established, the Allegheny County Jail was small. Only 12 women were housed there. Nevertheless, agency founders worked out an agreement with jail authorities so that female jail prisoners could be transferred to PFO by court order. Inmate-clients would be guilty of prison breach if they left PFO without permission. While at PFO, the women would participate in training, volunteering in the community, and learning how to spend their leisure time with the help of a role modeling and parent education program for mothers and children. The program is based on freedom reached by attaining levels of responsibility (Arnold 1992:37–38). In 1984, a much larger work-release facility was constructed in Allegheny County. Currently, over 300 women per year are served by PFO. PFO authorities reserve the right to screen potential candidates for work release. During 1992, the following companion projects were implemented in Allegheny County:

1. Good-time project at the county jail.

2. Male work-release center accommodating 60 beds.

3. Development of criminal justice division in county government.

4. Drug treatment/work-release facility at St. Francis Health Center's Chemical Dependency Department.

5. Development of a male job placement program.

6. Expansion of the existing PFO Women's Center.

7. Expansion of the retail theft project.

The success of PFO is demonstrated by its low 3.5 percent recidivism rate in the community program and only a 17 percent recidivism rate at the residential facility. Over $88,000 has been collected in rent, $27,000 in fines, and $8,000 in restitution to victims of the female offenders. For the male offenders, $106,500 has been collected in rent and $107,400 in fines and restitution. Long-range plans for PFO call for a crime prevention program, including a daycare center, intervention therapy for drug-abusing families, intensive work with preschool children who are already giving evidence of impending delinquency, and a scholarship program. Plans also include expanding PFO's services to more areas throughout Pennsylvania.

The Women's Prison Association (WPA).   The Women's Prison Association (WPA) is perhaps the oldest organization dedicated to helping incarcerated women. Founded in 1844, the WPA established the **Isaac T. Hopper Home** to provide housing and training for female offenders in the mid- to late-1800s (Bacon 2000). It is estimated that over 37,000 female offenders have been helped over the years through the activities of the WPA (Conly 1998:4–5).

The mission of the WPA is to create opportunities for change in the lives of women prisoners, ex-prisoners, and their families (Women's Prison Association 1972). WPA provides programs through which women acquire life skills needed to end involvement in the criminal justice system and to make positive healthy choices for themselves and their families. They emphasize:

1. Self-reliance through the development of independent living skills.

2. Self-empowerment and peer support.

3. Client involvement in the community.

4. Assistance from dedicated staff, advisers and volunteers.

The WPA has focused considerable attention on the needs of homeless female offenders and those with AIDS or those who are HIV-positive. Also given priority for WPA concern are those with histories of substance abuse and those who are striving to reunite with their children. Some of the assumptions guiding the WPA are that (1) many women offenders are chronically ill; (2) women offenders who are HIV-positive learn about this through prison testing; and thus when they are released, this is the first time they have had to cope with the physical and emotional challenge of living with a chronic and often terminal illness; (3) many women offenders are homeless, which impairs their ability to live crime-free; and (4) reuniting with their children is of crucial importance for most female offenders (Conly 1998:6–7).

The Women's Activities and Learning Center (WALC) Program.   The Kansas Department of Corrections has established a program for women with children that has been patterned after PATCH (Parents and Their Children), started by the Missouri Department of Corrections, and MATCH (Mothers and Their Children), operated by the California Department of Corrections. The Kansas program is known as the Women's Activities and Learning Center or WALC. WALC was started with a grant from the U.S. Department of Education under the Women's Educational Opportunity Act and is based in Topeka (Logan 1992:160).

The Topeka facility has a primary goal of developing and coordinating a broad range of programs, services, and classes and workshops that will increase women offenders' chances for a positive reintegration with their families and society upon release (Logan 1992:160). A visiting area at the center accommodates visitations between female inmates and their children. Thus, women with children are given a chance to take an active part in caring for their children. Mothers acquire some measure of a mother-child relationship during incarceration. They are able to fix meals for their children and have recreation with them in designated areas. Various civic and religious groups contribute their volunteer resources to assist these women. Both time and money are expended by outside agencies and personnel, such as the Kiwanis, the Kansas East Conference of the United Methodist Church, and the Fraternal Order of Police (Logan 1992:161).

One advantage of WALC is that it provides various programs and courses in useful areas such as parenting, child development, prenatal care, self-esteem, anger management, nutrition, support groups, study groups, cardiopulmonary resuscitation, personal development, and crafts. The parenting program, for instance, is a ten-week course where inmate-mothers meet once a week to discuss their various problems. In order to qualify for inclusion in this program, female inmates must be designated as low risk, minimum security, and have no disciplinary reports filed against them during the 90 days prior to program involvement. When the ten-week course is completed, the women are entitled to participate in a three-week retreat sponsored by the Methodist Church. The retreat includes transportation for inmates, with fishing, horse-riding, hay rides, and game-playing for mothers and their children. Volunteers and a correctional officer are present during the retreat experience. Since September 1991, more than 300 women and 500 children have participated in the WALC program with a low rate of recidivism (Logan 1992:161). Programs for women that emphasize parenting and other types of family-oriented activities have been established in many other jurisdictions (Pollock 1999).

The Culture of Women's Prisons

Attempts to describe the typical women's prison are about as productive as attempts to depict the typical men's prison (Owen 1998). Hollywood portrayals of women's prisons carry provocative titles such as *Caged Heat* or *Women in Chains,* and they depict inmates as consisting mostly of lesbians or sex-starved ex-beauty queens who are the standard targets of lesbians (Faith 1987). Cases such as *California v. Lovercamp* (1974) do little to change this Hollywood stereotype.

In the early 1970s, two female inmates, Lovercamp and Wynashe, were housed in the California Rehabilitation Center. They had been confined in the facility for about two months and, according to their version of events, were continually threatened into performing a variety of sex acts with a gang of lesbian inmates that appeared to dominate the institution. "F--k or fight" was the challenge continually yelled at them by the lesbian inmates, who became more physical in their harassment. One afternoon, Lovercamp and Wynashe fled the minimum-security facility to avoid being sexually assaulted. They turned themselves in to correctional officers shortly after leaving the facility.

Although a lower California court later found them guilty of escape, their excuse was accepted by the California Court of Appeals, which overturned their conviction in 1974. The defense of necessity became a viable defense to avoid assaults by other prisoners. Prison escapes are serious matters, and the California court was careful not to issue license to all inmates, male or female, to consider escape from their institutions if they felt endangered by other inmates for whatever reason. The court advised that prisoners should report threatening behaviors of other inmates to correctional officers and prison administration. In fact, Lovercamp and her companion had complained on previous occasions to officers about the threats they were receiving from the lesbians. Their escape was even more justified when officials took no action whatsoever to safeguard them from the sexual advances of others.

Adding to depictions of female prisons as bastions of lesbianism are works such as *Women's Prison: Sex and Social Structure* by Dave Ward and Gene Kassebaum, published in 1965. Their study was concerned not only with the social behavior of female prison inmates, but with their sexual behavior as well. In fact, over half of the book is devoted to their interviews with several prisoners and their investigations of the prevalence of lesbianism among female inmates. Their study occurred at the California Institution for Women at Frontera, California. Although the sample of inmates interviewed was small, much valuable information about life in at least one women's prison was disclosed. The existence of an inmate code was revealed, although compared with the inmate codes existing in prisons for men, the one at Frontera was almost nonexistent and unenforceable. This was explained by Ward and Kassebaum as the result of a lack of solidarity and loyalty among inmates (Ward and Kassebaum 1965:53).

Regarding lesbianism, it was estimated by respondents that over 50 percent of all female inmates at Frontera were sexually involved with at least one other female inmate at least once during their incarceration. Ward and Kassebaum found this figure unremarkable, since studies by other researchers showed that lesbianism among large samples of unmarried female college graduates disclosed similar percentages of sexual encounters among one another (Ward and Kassebaum 1965:93). They also noted the absence of other comparative works examining lesbianism in other women's prisons. In short, we have a seemingly sensationalized account of rampant lesbianism in one California women's prison, based on interviews conducted with nine women selected originally by a lesbian inmate-informant picked by Ward, Kassebaum, and the warden as well as questionnaires completed by several other inmates. But according to the authors, having opinions from an articulate, experienced, yet small number of inmates was more important than a larger representative sample for hypothesis-testing purposes. More recent evidence suggests that these earlier estimates of lesbianism among females in U.S. prisons have been greatly exaggerated and that inmate-lesbians make up a small hardcore portion of female offenders. However, no one knows for sure how many lesbians there are in women's prisons (Cotten, Martin, and Jordan 1997).

In many respects, the prison experience for women is equally influential compared with male inmates. Like men, women adapt fairly quickly to the

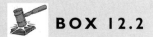

BOX 12.2

CHAIN GANGS FOR WOMEN?

The Case of Sheriff Joe Arpaio

If you don't know about Sheriff Joe Arpaio, Maricopa County (Phoenix), Arizona, by now, you will after this. Sheriff Arpaio plans a female chain gang. Implemented in September 1996, Maricopa County sheriff's deputies and armed volunteers supervised both male and female chain gangs of prisoners along Phoenix, Arizona, highways.

The idea of chain gangs is certainly not new. However, the use of chain gangs was nonexistent for many decades until Alabama renewed their use in 1995. Since then, Florida and Arizona have followed suit by pioneering the regeneration of chain gangs on their highways. Chain gangs consist of 15 inmates each, actually chained together at the ankles, where various types of work are performed each day along state highways and county roads. Typical chores include picking up trash, painting over graffiti, and breaking rocks. Leg irons hold the chains in place, limiting the movement of any given prisoner. Thus, it is impossible while working on a chain gang for a single prisoner to run away from the rest of the inmates. Armed supervision of inmates discourages inmate fights or other forms of misconduct.

More than a few observers regard Joe Arpaio's actions as attention-grabbing, and the media have been quick to give considerable coverage to his chain gangs. But Joe "doesn't believe in discrimination in [his] jail system." The sheriff says that "I feel that women should be treated just like men. These women will be placed in the same areas where I place the men, out in the streets of Phoenix where everyone can see them."

Chain gangs are popular with at least some of the inmates. In August 1996, Sheriff Arpaio had 34 volunteers signed up for chain gang duty. According to some in-

mates, it gets them outside doing something, rather than remaining in cramped cells or tent cities doing nothing. Chain gangs in Arizona are also distinctive. Sheriff Arpaio dresses his inmates in traditional black and white striped uniforms. These horizontal stripes set them apart from everyone else and remind us of the 1920s and old movies, where prisoners in stripes were chased by the Keystone Cops.

Are chain gangs unconstitutional? Not according to Sheriff Arpaio. Also, the American Civil Liberties Union has investigated Maricopa County as well as counties in Alabama and Florida, where chain gangs are used. Louis Rhodes, state director of the American Civil Liberties Union, said that Sheriff Arpaio likes to come up with headline-grabbing gimmicks, and that this is just the latest one. Rhodes says that "[Arpaio's] ideas are basically harmless. They aren't illegal or unconstitutional, [but] they end up wasting a lot of time and taxpayer money." Sheriff Arpaio has already attracted considerable media attention by banning cigarettes, coffee, and *Playboy* magazines from his Maricopa County Jail. Justice Department officials have said that some of Sheriff Arpaio's officers have been found to use excessive force with certain county inmates in the past, although the sheriff himself says that "I'm not worried about the hits. This is the right thing to do. I want to put them on the streets because I want everybody to see them, especially the prospective criminals."

What do you think of chain gangs? Do you think that public humiliation of the type this sort of chain gang activity inspires is a deterrent to potential criminals? Why or why not? Would you favor the use of chain gangs in your own state? If you were a criminal, would you want to be placed on a chain gang?

Source: Adapted from Associated Press, "Chain Gang Women: Nation's Toughest Sheriff to Put Nation's First Female Chain Gang to Work." *Minot (N.D.) Daily News*, August 26, 1996:A1, A5.

prison lifestyle. Further, those who enter prison following their convictions for nonviolent offenses may become violent as the result of prisonization. One reason is that often women are overclassified and placed in custody levels much higher than their conviction offense merits. Resentments and frustrations follow, as these women endure harsher punishments disproportional to their original offense seriousness (Cook and Davies 1999). As the result of their incarceration, more than a few women go on to commit violent crimes when released. Thus, prisonization is as salient for female inmates as for males (Stevens 1998). Although women adapt to prison life in ways similar to men, one of the most difficult aspects of doing time for women is absence from their children and families (Kruttschnitt, Gartner, and Miller 2000:711).

Incarcerated Mothers.   A majority of female inmates in U.S. prisons are mothers (Enos 2001). While this status does not shield them from sexual advances from others or prevent them from initiating such advances themselves, efforts by prison officials to maintain the family unit appear to be moderately influential for decreasing the perceived need for lesbian activity. Women in prison are much disturbed by the convict label to begin with, and arrangements by prison officials to ensure their prolonged and frequent contact with their infants and young children would seem to naturally discourage same-sex situations that would further mar their image if detected (U.S. General Accounting Office 1999). The American Civil Liberties Union (ACLU) has fought for female inmate rights involving access to their children (Seymour and Hairston-Creasie 2001). In one South Carolina case, a woman serving a 21-year sentence for armed robbery wished to keep her child with her in prison. While there are moral, ethical, practical, and logistical problems with such long-term arrangements, suits have been filed seeking such associations (Baunach 1985:124–125). In these cases, suggestions have been made for the creation of appropriate off-premises facilities where low-risk female offenders can reside with their children in reasonably normal settings. Thus, it is neither essential nor desirable that infants or young children be housed in cell areas with their mothers. The ACLU has other types of living accommodations in mind when advancing such legal actions against prison administrators and state prison systems.

Furthermore, some states, such as Florida, have permitted parent-child living arrangements in special quarters (Blinn 1997). Inmate-mothers derive positive therapy from the anticipation of resuming parenthood when eventually released. The maintenance of inmate-child ties seems to foster greater compliance with prison rules, since these offenders wish to gain early release from a favorable parole decision. Showing responsibility in caring for one's child while in prison is one way of demonstrating that a successful life may be led on the outside if released (Phillips and Harm 1997).

Excellent portrayals of female inmate culture, both inside and outside of the United States, exist in the professional literature (Hewitt 1996; Tchaikovsky 2000). Kathryn Watterson's *Women in Prison: Inside the Concrete Womb,* provides an excellent and in-depth description of what goes on inside women's prisons (Watterson 1996). Again, depending upon the source, different pictures emerge describing female interactions and life behind prison walls. A majority of jurisdictions have only a single female facility to house these prisoners (Nadel 1996). Many of these institutions do not make distinctions between female inmates other than to separate those in need of immediate medical attention from the others. For violent female prisoners, however, solitary confinement in one form or another is an option in many women's institutions.

Squares, Cools, and Lifes.   In some women's prisons, inmates have developed a jargon to depict the particular lifestyle chosen by an inmate for the duration of her incarceration (Heffernan 1985:228). Because incarcerated women often experience severe shock and a period of painful adjustment as the result of being separated from their families, friends, and children, they seek to establish temporary social relations with other inmates. In addition, they have given up many creature comforts that were associated with their identity on the outside—jewelry, certain expensive clothing, and other items (Williams and Fish 1985:215). Sometimes they establish quasi-families consisting of other inmates who play various familial roles. A new inmate may be asked to join a family as the daughter or mother. In some instances, other roles may emerge stemming from these lesbian relations. Occasionally, these unisex unions are considered binding on all parties for the period of incarceration (Owen 1998). These interactions replace temporarily those relationships on the outside that women associated with stability, security, and love.

Getting by or making it in prison requires certain adaptations. Inmate terminology in some prisons has divided women into three categories: **squares, cools,** and **lifes.** Squares are considered noncriminal. These are often first offenders who have been convicted of petty offenses, even homicide. They identify with the establishment and don't fit in with other inmates, who may be professional thieves, forgers, or drug users. The cools consist usually of women with prior records who attempt to get by with rule infractions and obtain fringe benefits within the system without getting caught. The life type is the habitual offender who engages in deviant behavior with little regard for the punitive consequences (Heffernan 1985:228–230). These designations imply three types of goal-seeking behavior and goals that lead to the formation of social networks of those inmates with similar interests (Weisheit and Mahan 1988:74).

One difficulty in applying this argot to all women's prisons is that there is considerably less continuity among female inmates than among male offenders through the importation model of inmate organization (Owen 1998). Women's sentences are generally shorter, the facilities are smaller, there is apparently greater selfishness and less loyalty, and many offenders prefer to operate independent of others. Female inmates are slow to form unions, and inmate gangs don't exist on the same scale that they exist in male facilities. This retards the development of female inmate culture, at least to the degree of sophistication and organization of male inmate cultures in state and federal prison settings. The low rate of female recidivism, except for a small offender hardcore, further interferes with perpetuating an identifiable female inmate subculture.

Administering Prisons for Women

Women's prisons are generally easier to administer than prisons for men. First, they are less organizationally complex, since there are significantly fewer services and programs ordinarily available to female inmates compared with the types of programs found in men's prisons. Second, the number of women in any prison is small. Thus, monitoring or supervision of fewer offenders involves fewer staff and less coordination between these staff compared with larger numbers of them in male institutions. And third, although some female inmates are dangerous in any prison setting, most women prisoners are low-risk offenders (Owen 1998). Even though women in prison have engaged in riots, their rioting record is quite low, again when contrasted with the rioting frequency of their male inmate counterparts. There is little unity or organization among female inmates in most prisons, and collective action is not observed with any consistency or frequency (Culliver 1993). Nevertheless, women's prisons have certain problems, such as various communicable diseases, compared with men's prisons. Incarcerated women are three times more likely to be HIV-infected and have AIDS than incarcerated men (DeGroot 2001).

Many of the facilities designed for women throughout the United States are located in remote rural areas (Rison 1996). The decision to locate many women's prisons in remote regions was based originally on the idea that women needed privacy and seclusion where they could think and reflect and thereby become rehabilitated (Fuller 1993). Another reason was that these remote locations removed them from corruption (Belbot 1995). Actually, this decision has operated to their disadvantage for several reasons. First, the spatial distance between themselves and family or close friends makes visits difficult and infrequent. As Mann (1984:203) observes, "since most of their (the inmates') families are poor, family members cannot afford the trips to visit them." Of course, even when women's prisons are located in urban areas of their respective jurisdictions, it is likely that families of inmates will still have to travel great distances to see them. Additionally, most states and the Federal Bureau of Prisons have only one all-female facility to serve their needs, and women of all security levels are housed in that same institution (U.S. General Accounting Office 1994). In short, female offenders are assigned to the nearest female prison, which may be 300 miles or more from where they were convicted.

Another limitation of the isolation of these prisons is that it is difficult to attract and retain qualified personnel to administer and operate these facilities (Quinlan et al. 1992). Usually, prison staff is recruited from among interested applicants living in those areas where women's institutions are located. Often, the prison correctional officers recruited may not be as qualified for their jobs compared with correctional officers in urban areas, where prison officials have access to a higher quality work force for their personnel selections (Owen 1998). It should be noted that this is largely an inference drawn by critics of women's prisons that are in remote areas. There are few, if any, studies directly comparing female prison correctional officer quality according to the urban-rural distinction.

A third significant disadvantage is that, compared with men's prisons located predominantly in urban areas, women's prisons are not easily accessible to vocational, educational, technical, or other services that nearby communities might otherwise be able to provide (Florida Joint Legislative Management Committee 1995). This makes it difficult for women to take advantage of nearby programs on either a furlough or work release basis, since the distance between the prison and the services is too great for the limited time allocated to furloughs or work releases.

Prison administrators must work within extremely narrow budgets. Legislators and others are inclined to allocate funds in relation to the proportionate numbers of female offenders that must be accommodated in their prisons. Thus, if their entire prison population consists of 3 percent female offenders, the women's prison budget within which the administrator must work is usually 3 percent of all correctional expenditures. Court-ordered improvements in

 **BOX 12.3**

Grace Williams Martin

Deputy Warden, Delaware Department of Correction
Delores J. Baylor Women's Correctional Institution
New Castle, DE

Statistics

Howard High School; Wilmington College; U.S. Department of Justice, National Academy of Corrections, Longmont, CO; Physical Security Training, National Institute of Corrections; University of Delaware professional development courses to enhance career; Emergency Preparedness for Correctional Institutions; Center for Substance Abuse Treatment; Prison Drug Treatment Technical Assistance Workshop, Washington, DC.

Background and Interests

I began my career in correctional administration 40 years ago as a matron at Delaware's correctional facility for women. I am considered a pioneer in the field of women's corrections in the state of Delaware. During the early 1960s, racial segregation ended in Delaware's penal system, which allowed minorities to obtain jobs as correctional employees. In October 1963, I became the second African American female hired full-time in correctional security. During my tenure, I have held numerous positions, including Acting Warden for the Baylor Women's Correctional Institution. Fifteen years ago, I became the first female deputy warden in Delaware's correctional system. My entire career has been spent working with female inmates. I have worn many hats and served as a role model in all ranks of service in my profession. I believe in the philosophy, firm, yet fair. I strive to continue my collaborative spirit and keep a professional attitude when working with others.

Experiences

My responsibilities as Deputy Warden are to support the overall mission of management and operations of the Delores J. Baylor Women's Correctional Institution. My career spans 40 years from matron to deputy warden. One memory that stays etched in my mind happened early in my career in 1965. I was the matron assigned to guard a high-profile inmate to her trial. She was a young 18-year-old involved in the murders of two Delaware state troopers. There was a lot of notoriety and national attention regarding her capture and arrest at the Delaware/Pennsylvania state line. The assignment was a challenge because there were no provisions made to prepare me for defensive training at that time. I attributed the honor of my selection to my demeanor of not being fearful, having a willingness to take on the task, and having no reservations about performing the assignment.

The inmate was part of a modern-day "Bonnie and Clyde" robbery and murder spree with her male companion. The murders and robberies took place in two states, Delaware and Pennsylvania. This event continues to be significant to me because she received three life sentences. In 1995 I began to think about her because I realized she had completed 30 years of her sentence in Pennsylvania and at some time in the future, she is expected to return to Delaware to complete the remainder of her sentence.

Advice to Students

The most profound advice that I can bestow upon you as criminal justice students is to work hard to obtain your degrees. The knowledge with which you leave the classroom will benefit you in your careers as criminal justice professionals. Academic knowledge and practical experience will help you climb the ladder in this field. Your education will enhance your professionalism, as well as keep you abreast of controversial issues that will always plague the criminal justice system, whether they are global or local community issues. Remember, proficiency is what measures your skills and abilities, thus determining your attitude in your professional endeavors. You must be proficient in whatever you do.

The criminal justice system has grown to encompass a broader perspective, especially in regard to correctional administration. In corrections today, the focus is on victim's rights and the offender making restitution to society. Many correctional facilities are developing victim sensitivity groups for offenders who have committed violent crimes. Therefore, offenders must participate in victim sensitivity groups, which place strong emphasis on empathy for victims. As students, you should include victimology and rehabilitation classes in your course of study.

As students and professionals, diversity should be paramount and become a part of you. This will allow you to create a bountiful support system. It also enables you to be resourceful, which is a powerful tool in relating to all humankind. Diversity should be second nature to you, in that you value all individuals regardless of their race, ethnicity, gender, or age. Controversial issues, such as racial profiling and hate crimes, should become nonexistent in our society. As students and criminal justice professionals, I charge you to go two extra miles to make the necessary changes so that the system is equitable and fundamentally fair for all involved. Learning and managing diversity will offer you the ability to be fair with others.

While working within the criminal justice system, you should maintain a humble spirit and mindset that enable you to work with others to get the job done. You will learn from others and they will learn from you. People will always contribute to your career and life experiences. Thus, you must remain humble, yet assertive, in your relationship with others. These attributes will guide your decision-making skills and, ultimately, elevate your professional development. Humility will allow you to place your feet in the moccasins of others, including those of the offender, while assertiveness will help you walk upright with pride and integrity, knowing that you never allowed others to take advantage of you.

As students and future criminal justice professionals, beware of the pitfalls and consequences that may threaten your integrity. It is so easy to get involved in corrupt activities within the criminal justice system. Illegal substances and money are easily accessible to some professionals who choose to jeopardize their careers and all that they have accomplished in life. You must ask yourself, "Is it worth it?" Think twice before you yield to temptation because you run the risk of losing everything you have accomplished along life's path. Don't be naive to situations that will surely lead you down a negative path because of greed or power. Your integrity is you, therefore, value it always because others will challenge it.

My integrity has been challenged, but my philosophy of being firm, fair, and consistent has prevailed and has been the focal point throughout my professional career. I learned to stand up for justice and not tolerate nonsense. It is quite rewarding to perform kind acts and good deeds unconditionally, because you will always be remembered by these acts and deeds, even if you failed in your endeavors to help others succeed.

My experience working with female offenders and for a short period of time managing a co-educational work program at the women's facility provided me with the "gutsy" stuff needed to take action whenever it appears that politics is the favorite "gig" that may get you to the top. I value hard work by coming to work, to work. As a result of going the extra mile, my professional career has been very rewarding. Hard work, diligence, and dedication have greatly contributed to my success along with the help of many persons. Finally, with the awakening of my spiritual growth, I have fulfilled my service of 40 years to the Department of Corrections. The Higher Power above has always been upon me.

women's facilities will no doubt result in larger appropriations in future years. Another administrative headache pertains to the placement of growing numbers of female offenders. Like male prisons, female facilities are faced with increased amounts of overcrowding. While the extent of overcrowding in women's prisons has not reached epidemic proportions, there are indications that in some jurisdictions, such overcrowding has resulted in a diminished quality of services available, including poorer medical care, counseling, and program staffing. Since as many as 70 percent of all female inmates entering state or federal correctional systems have some form of substance abuse, for example, there has been little concerted effort to meet this growing need among the various jurisdictions. Some states, such as Illinois, have made significant efforts to ensure that female offenders will receive proper treatment and counseling for their different substance abuse problems (Goodale, Stutler, and Klein-Acosta 2002).

Selected Issues Relating to Women's Prisons

Some Comparisons of Female Institutions with Male Institutions.   Prisons for men tend to have a greater range of vocational and educational training programs and services. They are more centrally located to urban areas, whereas women's prisons are more remotely located. Men's prisons tend to be larger and have more amenities, such as weight rooms, jogging areas, and other sports facilities. The law libraries of men's facilities tend to be better equipped, although there are substantial improvements in female facilities toward greater parity with men's institutions regarding various forms of legal assistance and materials (J. Palmer 1997).

Women tend to commit rule infractions more frequently than men, but the punishments meted out to women seem more severe compared with the punishments for men for the same types of infractions (McClellan 1994). For instance, a comparison of Texas prisons for men and women revealed that such infractions as cursing were meticulously enforced in women's prisons but routinely ignored in men's prisons. Thus, it was concluded that gender-specific rule enforcement was being practiced within the same prison system. Texas policymakers subsequently made significant changes in the nature and enforcement of these policies for both men's and women's prisons. Similar policies have been adopted and followed in Illinois (Illinois Department of Corrections 1995).

The Equal Protection Clause Applied to Incarcerated Females.   Are female inmates treated equally compared with their male counterparts? The research says that they are not treated equally. In fact, as we have already seen, there are disciplinary differentials attributable to one's gender, at least in several Texas prisons. Female offenders are sanctioned, and sanctioned more severely, for less serious types of infractions, such as swearing, compared with their male inmate counterparts who also swear extensively, but without any consequence.

Vocational and educational needs for women are not being met as well in women's institutions compared with similar programming in men's institutions (Florida Joint Legislative Management Committee 1995). Even where there are attempts to provide programming on the same level as men, the programming is often inconsistent with the real needs of women (Pollock-Byrne 1990). The remoteness of women's prisons from major urban areas makes it more difficult for family members to visit them compared with male inmates and visits with their families (Fuller 1993).

Women's prisons seem every bit as overcrowded as men's facilities. Some investigators have observed that a large proportion of incarcerated women are there for less serious crimes than male offenders. Thus, these observers argue, there may be an argument for releasing more female offenders from prison to make space for more serious types of offenders (Immarigeon and Chesney-Lind 1992). Greater rates of incarcerating women have often been the result of policy changes in state jurisdictions rather than any new female crime wave. It would seem that we have not moved very far from the way women were treated during the period 1865–1935. Persistent neglect characterized the women's prisons of that period, and the same can be said for many of the facilities for women today (Rafter 1990).

Unequal treatment of female inmates extends beyond U.S. borders. For instance, in Canada, there has been a continuing shortage of vocational and treatment programs for incarcerated women. Comprehensive community services for women compared with male offenders are conspicuously absent. Even within Canadian prison systems, there are limited opportunities and services available to women compared with their male counterparts. One area where glaring deficiencies exist pertains to risk assessment and inmate classification. Most classification systems devised by Canadian custodial institutions are designed for men. Adequate classification systems for women have not yet been devised, although Canadian prison officials are making some progress in this regard (Hannah-Moffat and Shaw 2001).

Rehabilitative Services for Women.   Some attempts have been made by prison officials in different jurisdictions to meet certain needs of their female offenders (Schram 1999). Many female inmates enter prison pregnant or having just had infants (Greene, Haney, and Hurtado 2000). According to the Bureau of Justice Statistics, in 2000 there were 1.5 million children nationwide who had at least one incarcerated parent in a state or federal prison. An additional 600,000 children had one or both parents held in local jails. At least one child in 50 has one or both parents in some form of incarceration in the United States (Bilchik, Seymour, and Kreisher 2001:108). This means that there are large numbers of incarcerated parents in U.S. prisons and jails. In order to meet their needs to maintain contact with their children, prisons and jails in various jurisdictions are establishing parent–child visitation programs.

For instance, the Massachusetts Department of Corrections has made available to women a wide variety of programs that enable them to have lengthy visits with their children under a **Visiting Cottage Program.** This program permits women to visit with their children overnight in special, on-premises cottages established by Massachusetts prison officials. The visits from children have been found quite therapeutic in assisting women to make the transition from incarceration to freedom and to lead reasonably normal lives (Massachusetts Department of Corrections 2002).

Another facility that is attempting to change the image of at least some female residents is the Bedford Hills, New York, Reformatory Prison for Women, constructed in 1902. For certain inmates with young children, Bedford officials have created a special top-floor area in an old brick building that functions as a home for both mother and child. Twenty-one cots and cribs are placed side by side, where these inmate-mothers receive parenting courses and are served by a

A female inmate reads a book with her three-year-old daughter at the Nebraska Correctional Center for Women in York, Nebraska. *Source:* AP/Wide World Photos.

resident pediatric nurse (Creighton 1988:23). And in Michigan, correctional officials have established the Women and Infants at Risk (WIAR) Program. This program is a comprehensive residential program for pregnant, drug-dependent women, whose goals are to (1) increase the availability of substance abuse prevention and treatment services to pregnant and postpartum women offenders, (2) reduce the severity and effect of drug exposure to the infants, (3) reduce the likelihood of relapse and recidivism among mothers, and (4) promote community awareness of the needs of pregnant inmates and their children (Siefert and Pimlott 2001).

If there is anything typical about women's prisons, it is that they are small. Populations of 500 or more females in one prison are considered large. Organizationally, smaller prisons are somewhat easier to manage and control. Administrators have fewer inmate problems because of fewer inmates. But there are drawbacks to small inmate populations, however. One of the major drawbacks is that smaller penal facilities receive less funding priority by state legislatures. Furthermore, it is more difficult for administrators of small institutions to justify the same range of vocational, educational, and technical programs found in large men's prisons (Wood and Grasmick 1999).

New York's Prison Nursery/Children's Center.   At the Bedford Hills, New York, Correctional Facility, a 750-woman maximum-security prison constructed in 1933, a Children's Center was established in 1989–1990. Since 1930, New York legislation provided for women in prison to keep their babies. Presently, New York is the only state that maintains a prison nursery (Roulet 1993:4).

Authorities at Bedford Hills believe that it is important for women to maintain strong ties with their families during incarceration. Further, they believe that women will have a greater chance at reintegration and lower recidivism as the opportunity for familial interaction increases. Further, there is a positive impact on babies, since they can remain with and be nurtured by their mothers. In 1993, there were two state nurseries. Besides the one at Bedford

Hills, another was opened at Taconic. This is a smaller facility, also located in Bedford Hills, housing about 400 female offenders.

Roulet (1993:4) says that not all women incarcerated at Bedford Hills are eligible to participate in the prison nursery program. A woman's criminal background, past parenting performance, disciplinary record, and educational needs are examined and assessed before they are accepted. Women who are selected are expected to make the best use of their time by developing their mothering skills and caring for their infants. They are also expected to participated in various self-help programs of a vocational and educational nature). The center's main program goal is to help women preserve and strengthen family ties and receive visits from their children as often as possible in a warm, nurturing atmosphere. They are kept closely informed of their children's physical, educational, intellectual, and emotional well-being while they are separated. Through the various classes and programs offered at Bedford Hills, women acquire a better understanding of their roles as parents and are able to reinforce their feelings of self-worth.

Inmates at Bedford Hills also participate in a Parent's Center. The primary concerns and components of the Parent's Center are:

1. Bilingual parenting (allows women to learn English while exploring issues of mothers and children; provides a bilingual parenting class).

2. Child development associate course (the CDA is a national accreditation program that prepares candidates to teach in accredited nursery schools anywhere in the country).

3. Children's advocate office (trained advocates meet with inmate mothers individually to address all child-related problems).

4. Children's library (caregivers help mothers to select age-appropriate books; occasionally films and special storytime sessions are arranged).

5. Choices and changes courses (this class helps inmates develop self-awareness and to learn the process of decision making and accountability to improve parenting).

6. Foster care committee (the committee helps women learn their legal rights and responsibilities as incarcerated women; the committee helps mothers with letter writing, direct services, monthly group meetings; provides handbooks, support groups, etc.).

7. Holiday activities (the center provides holiday activities, as directed by inmate staff members).

8. Infant daycare center (cares for the babies of nursery mothers who are programmed into school or work assignments; provides "hands-on" experience for CDA interns).

9. Mental hygiene program (inmate staff become "parents" for other less fortunate inmate parents; it is considered to be useful and relaxing therapy for these women).

10. Mothers' group (a certified social worker conducts group sessions for women who have children and want an opportunity to discuss their relationships; it also provides the services of a family therapist),

11. Nursery aides (inmate staff member works with nursery coordinators; she sews clothes for nursery babies and helps with inventory and distribution of clothes).

12. The overnight program (volunteer host parents in the community take in nursery children for a day and overnight once a month).

13. Parenting program (covers parenting from the prenatal stages to adulthood through the use of educational classes and films).

14. Prenatal center (women receive parenting classes, address their drug problems, learn sewing, crocheting, and other handiwork).

15. Records and teaching material (inmate staff member collects information on the history of the nursery program, new materials or studies on children, education, imprisoned women, drugs and their effects on children; these archival resources are used by staff and facility college students).

16. Summer program (older children spend a week during the summer with volunteer host families who live near the nursery; each day the children are brought to visit their mothers for a few hours).

17. Study corner (mothers tape-record themselves reading children's stories, which is then sent to their children).

18. Sponsor a baby (churches, temples, and other groups provide necessities for inmate mother and babies when they leave prison and the nursery and also for families of inmates not eligible for the nursery program who are unexpectedly burdened with an infant).

19. Transportation clinic (provides transportation for children of inmates to visit their mothers at the nursery and children's center).

20. Toy library (mothers select games, crafts, and toys for their children's visit; some can be taken home; others are returned to the library).

Roulet (1993:6) says that women whose babies are born while incarcerated may keep them at Bedford for up to one year. Babies are delivered in a hospital outside of prison, and the mother and infant live in the nursery for as long as the child remains. If it is likely that the mother will be paroled by the time the infant is 18 months old, then the infant may remain with the mother with special permission until that date. It is important to keep mothers and children together as much as possible while at Bedford Hills. The child's welfare is of utmost concern to authorities. Such bonding is considered significant at reducing rates of recidivism among paroled Bedford Hills women. Parenting programs for female inmates have been implemented in many other state jurisdictions, attesting to the importance of this theme for corrections officials throughout the United States and abroad (Russell 1999).

The Fluvanna Correctional Center in Troy, Virginia. The Virginia Department of Corrections commenced work on a women's correctional center in December 1995. It was to be called the Fluvanna Correctional Center (FCC) and would be located in Troy, Virginia. The original intent of the facility was to provide a medium-security center that would be designed to meet female offender needs. Officially opened in 1998, the FCC eventually accommodated 900 female felons. A dormitory-like concept was rejected, and the designers created individual cells to provide these incarcerated women with privacy. Thus, the inmates are housed at night in individual, unlocked cells. If particular inmates desire, they may request their cells to be locked during evening hours. But all cells are dry, meaning that to obtain water or use restrooms, each inmate must leave her cell and walk to a restroom nearby. Unlike community-like restrooms for men, the restrooms for these female inmates are designed with privacy in mind (Gill and Angelone 2000).

The FCC is like a large campus, although it is considered a medium- to maximum-security facility. Security fencing connects all buildings, and these buildings are surrounded by a perimeter security fence. Despite the fact that all inmate security levels are represented at the FCC, inmate interpersonal problems are minimal. For example, one incident involved the transfer of a 19-year-old inmate to FCC who had killed the son of another FCC inmate. This potential problem was defused when both women were brought together in a meeting room and advised, "Whatever you two ladies have to say to each other, say it now, because once this meeting is over, we don't want you talking to each other for the rest of your time here." They let each other have it. They went back and forth, then pulled their time, and that was it (Gill and Angelone 2000:101).

The FCC is equipped to deliver instruction in nine different vocations. Furthermore, considerable space is devoted to nursery and child visitation. A 68,000-square-foot medical building is provided, which serves a variety of physical and mental health needs. The facility deals with general medical issues, acute mental health care, and has a specialized sheltered care unit. Warden Patti Leigh Huffman, who has run FCC since 1998, says, "One of the things I truly appreciate about the design of Fluvanna is the thought that went into the medical/mental health building. To my knowledge, there is not another women's facility in this country that has the type of medical/mental health building that we have" (Gill and Angelone 2000:98).

FCC has attempted to create an environment in which inmates can learn and grow. Trades, such as cosmetology, electrical repair, computer-aided drafting and design, and computer programs, such as business application software, are taught for life after incarceration. In 2000 FCC became the first accredited state adult correctional institution in Virginia to be recognized by the American Correctional Association (Gill and Angelone 2000:101).

Changing Policies, Programs, and Services for Female Offenders. In 1992, *Corrections Compendium* published the results of a survey of 85 state-operated women's facilities in 46 states. Approximately 31,000 women were housed in these facilities at a cost of $1.5 million annually. Serious health problems were related to pregnancies, AIDS, substance abuse, and mental health (Justice Education Center, Inc. 1993). When this survey was conducted, all facilities had on-site medical staff available. Not all facilities had gynecological/obstetrical services, however. Only 68 percent of all facilities offered prenatal/postpartum services, and none of the responding institutions allowed newborn infants to remain with their mothers. In the most recent 12-month period at the time of the study, 1,445 babies were born to inmates (S. Davis 1992).

Further, more women are being convicted of drug offenses annually. Three-fourths of all women inmates were in need of substance-abuse treatment, although only 28 percent of all incarcerated women had conviction offenses involving drugs. Most offenders had dropped out of high school or had not received the GED. Most had been unable to hold a job for longer than six months. Presently, most of the surveyed institutions offer vocational and educational courses for these women. Two-thirds offer college courses and 70 have pre-release programs. Most facilities have institutional work assignments, and about half have parenting programs.

A subsequent survey conducted by *Corrections Compendium* found that in 1998 the same types of problems existed in institutions for women that existed earlier in 1992. Health care, mother-and-child program initiatives, and innovative vocational training were listed as the most pressing needs for female inmates (*Corrections Compendium* 1998:8). These programs have been difficult to implement in view of the fact that the female inmate population is growing at a much faster rate than men (6.1 percent growth for females per year compared with 4.7 percent growth for male inmates). It is difficult for various jurisdictions to find adequate accommodations for female offenders. Thus, considerable expansion of existing physical plants for women is underway in most states.

Although as a matter of right, female inmates are entitled to the same legal considerations as male prisoners (e.g., access to legal services, law libraries), historically, women's prisons have been largely ignored by the criminal justice system. Female jailhouse lawyers emerged during the 1970s and 1980s to obtain numerous concessions from prison administrators, the courts, and legislatures (Wheeler et al. 1987). A push is underway to establish a full range of programs and services for female inmates that most male or predominantly male institutions have (S. Miller 1998). Presently, programs for female offenders are poorer in quantity, quality, variability, and availability than those for male offenders. This is also true of transitional programs that affect female parolees. Female inmates are more likely to be diagnosed with personality disorders than male inmates, and these personality disorders carry over into their post-release reintegration into communities. While some jurisdictions, such as Massachusetts, have implemented social services programs such as the Department of Mental Health Forensic Transition Team program, much remains to be done in many other jurisdictions to more effectively meet the needs of mentally ill female offenders (Hartwell 2001).

One disturbing feature of many rehabilitative programs offered to women in prison is that they often reflect stereotypical views of what women should do when released (Trounstine 2001). Thus, courses are offered to make female inmates better homemakers, seamstresses, clerk-typists, and mothers (Dodge and Pogrebin 2001). Since many women in prison currently lack a high school education (15 percent have not completed elementary school), many remedial educational courses are offered to them so that they may complete their GEDs or achieve high school diplomas. Advanced courses are also available either directly or through correspondence whereby women may obtain college credits, even college degrees. Ironically, those academic courses most frequently offered to women emphasize preparation for the usual stereotypical roles, including family life education, child development, personal grooming, textiles and clothing, and consumer education (*Corrections Compendium* 1998). Comparatively few courses are available in electronic engineering, computer programming, business, law, or medicine. Even if a woman wanted to prepare for a professional career or particular occupation of a nontraditional nature when paroled or released, she would be unable to do so on the basis of what courses she had taken while incarcerated.

The Federal Bureau of Prisons has operated an exclusively female correctional facility at Alderson, West Virginia. This institution was opened in 1927, and by 1985 it was accommodating over 700 federal female prisoners (Weisheit and Mahan 1988:66). Despite the fact that the federal government has initiated large-scale prison industries programs to assist inmates in learning new vocational skills and acquiring other types of training, only 200 females from Alderson were working in these industries by 1985. Most of these women were working in a garment factory performing sewing work, while a few other female prisoners were working in graphic design in a decal shop. Thus, the leading federal female correctional institution is perpetuating traditional, stereotypical work roles for its women inmates. This same situation is mirrored in most states as well, where female inmates are offered a limited array of courses, including cosmetology, clerical work, and food services (Culliver 1993).

Mann (1984:216) suggests six reasons for the lack of vocational and educational programs for women prisoners, despite recent prison reforms and legal milestones. These reasons are:

1. Women make up such a small proportion of the prison population, so extensive programming is cost prohibitive.

2. Women prisoners are less of a threat to society compared with males; therefore, they do not require equivalent financial expenditures to fund such programs.

3. Training costs for women prisoners are too high compared with their male counterparts.

4. When programs are offered, few women participate voluntarily.

5. Women's prisons are isolated and inaccessible to many services, thus making service delivery difficult or impossible.

6. Society's traditional view of women as wage-earners is secondary to their roles as mothers and housewives.

It is insufficient to simply expand the number of services available to female inmates. Proper planning must occur, where the special needs of certain offenders are anticipated and met with adequate services and programs (Greenfield et al. 1996). One matter that is infrequently considered when designing curricula for women's prisons is whether the skill, vocation, or education is realistic in view of the criminal record the women have acquired. Many states have licensing laws and policies associated with certain kinds of jobs that prohibit hiring those with criminal records or who have served time in prison or jail.

The matter of proper health care for incarcerated women has already been resolved by the U.S. Supreme Court. Deliberate indifference to the medical needs of prisoners was determined to be cruel and unusual punishment and in violation of the Eighth Amendment in *Estelle v. Gamble* (1976). But women often require special health care, and they have gynecological needs including Pap smears and assistance with menstrual problems, obstetrical help, and other medical services (e.g., breast cancer examinations, biopsies) that may not be immediately available. Again, this is because of the remoteness of the facility and the lack of access to quality services when needed on an emergency basis. Often, these prisons cannot afford to maintain on-premises medical help to cope with anything other than minor health problems and injuries.

Those women with drug or alcohol dependencies or who may be mentally ill are at a disadvantage as well (J. Carlson 2000). Estimates vary, although it is reasonable to assume that from 10 to 15 percent of all incarcerated females have some form of mental illness or are psychologically disturbed. Over a third who are incarcerated have drug or alcohol-related problems. Many of these inmates should be hospitalized and treated with professional medical and/or psychiatric services rather than imprisoned (Casey and Bakken 2001). Yet, an unknown number of psychologically disturbed female inmates receive minimal and superficial treatment equivalent to that received by the average person in a community health clinic (Teplin, Abram, and McClelland 1996). In some jurisdictions, at least, women's treatment centers rely heavily on the use of tranquilizers to control inmates instead of more costly but necessary psychotherapy and counseling. The counseling these women do receive, whenever it is available, is of questionable quality. These insufficient treatment methods often aggravate rather than alleviate mental problems or chemical dependencies (Moon et al. 1994). Many states are establishing oversight committees intended to rectify many of these inequities between men's and women's prisons, however (U.S. General Accounting Office 1996).

One emerging perspective about incarcerating larger numbers of women, especially those with drug or alcohol dependencies, is that jails and prisons provide them with temporary safe havens where they can receive necessary treatments and services for their problems. This has been termed the **safe-haven hypothesis,** which assumes that jails and prisons provide some amount of benefit to women that they would not otherwise receive if they remained on the streets to face their various problems without critical assistance (Markowitz 2003:4). However, the "safe-haven" view of prisons for women is not a universally shared assumption. It is argued, for instance, that while jails and prisons may offer more positive experiences than those available to women on the streets, it is also true that time spent in correctional settings, rather than producing positive results, has been shown to practically guarantee a woman's return to incarceration later through recidivism. Those in favor of the safe-haven hypothesis counter by noting the destructive and negative aspects of life on the streets for many of these women. Nevertheless, this assumption may overlook some women's preferences to live as they have been socialized, risks and all, rather than in seemingly more protective, yet confining, institutions (Markowitz 2003:31). This issue is presently unresolved.

Boot Camps for Women?   Should there be boot camps exclusively for women (Clark and Kellam 2001)? At the Eddie Warrior Correctional Center in Oklahoma, a program known as the Female Offender Regimented Treatment Program (FORT) has been established (Russell, Nicholson, and Buigas 1990). This program is unique because most boot camps in the United States have been established for youthful male offenders (MacKenzie et al. 2001). FORT was established for several purposes. First, officials observed how effective comparable boot camps were for youthful offenders, and they envisioned a similar program that might be workable for certain types of female offenders. The result was FORT.

FORT consists of a substantial substance abuse treatment component; classes in parenting, decision making, and moral development; educational opportunities; and discipline. Periodic assessments were made of women in terms of their psychopathology, ego strength and self-esteem, educational achievement, behaviors and characteristics associated with substance abuse, and perceived benefits and satisfaction with the program. Regimented drills supplemented the educational and vocational activities with favorable results. Indications are that female participants have acquired sufficient self-esteem and discipline to make a better adjustment to community living once they are paroled. Investigators also indicate that participants like the program and what it has done for them (Russell, Nicholson, and Buigas 1990).

Domestic Violence Prevention Programs.   Family violence among probationers and parolees is fairly high. Often, familial disruptions are contributory to criminal acts originally committed. Family violence is not only high among offender-clients, but it has also received national recognition as a major social problem (Lockwood, McCorkel, and Inciardi 1998). A contemporary approach to family violence stresses violence prevention before it occurs (Horn and Warner 2000; Leonard 2001).

In 1988, a consortium of U.S. federal agencies asked the National Academy of Sciences to assess the understanding of family violence and the implications of that understanding for developing preventive interventions (Reiss and Roth 1993). Violence was defined as behaviors by individuals that intentionally threaten, attempt, or inflict physical harm on others. Four recommendations were forthcoming:

1. Sustained problem-solving initiatives should be undertaken on interventions related to biological and psychosocial development of individuals' propensity for violent behavior, modifying crime-prone settings and situations, and intervening to reduce public and domestic violence.

2. High priority should be given to modifying and expanding statistical information systems on violent behavior.

3. New research is needed on instrumental effects of weapons, risk factors, and comparative development sequences.

4. A new, multi-community program of developmental studies of aggressive, violent and antisocial behaviors should be launched to improve both causal understanding and preventive interventions (Reiss and Roth 1993).

One of the first problems for correctional officers is to detect spouse abuse and family violence (Hamberger 1997). This is often discovered during face-to-face visits with offender-clients and their families. However, many victims of family violence are unwilling to report such abuse to correctional officers at any time. This is a prevalent phenomenon observed by experts investigating family violence (Roberts 1996).

Family abuse victims often need legal aid, medical treatment, psychological counseling, and job readiness preparation. For sexually abused women and children, several treatment models exist that emphasize or promote child advocacy. These programs are also concerned with restructuring the legal system and developing procedures for reducing the trauma to young children, developing psychiatric and family systems orientation, and engaging in behavior modification designed to assist offenders. Some of these techniques are considered coercive, since they force offenders to enter specific treatment programs. Volunteer men's collectives, social services agencies, and women's shelters are also effective in changing offender behaviors. Because probationers and parolees are under the immediate jurisdiction of either the courts or parole boards, their participation in different kinds of intervention programs and therapies can be incorporated as a part of their probation or parole programs as an important component and requirement (Vigilante et al. 1999). Continued familial abuses of any kind can be grounds for probation or parole revocation if detected (Richie 1996).

AIDS and Female Offenders.   A growing problem among the female offender population is AIDS (Marquart et al. 1999b). Many incarcerated women know very little about AIDS or how it is transmitted (DeGroot 2001). They do not know whether they have AIDS or whether they should seek medical attention for an AIDS diagnosis. Thus, some prisons for women are instituting programs to assist inmates in their understanding of AIDS and its contagiousness (Anno 1998). Other incarcerated women have substance abuse problems that must be addressed while they are confined. Otherwise, they will leave prisons untreated and resume their drug or alcohol dependencies once again within their communities. In Oklahoma, a study was conducted of 547 female prisoners and the extent of drug use among them (Moon et al. 1994). Female drug users tended to be older than other inmates and had longer criminal histories. Those with drug dependencies tended to have histories of child abuse. White female drug users differed from black female drug users in that black drug users had lower levels of self-esteem and had multiple drug use from more extensive involvement with the criminal justice system. White drug users reported higher levels of drug use. White offenders had less multiple drug use. Thus, programs were recommended to meet the needs of those with histories of childhood abuse and chronic offending. Counseling sessions were recommended for high drug users (Cotten, Martin, and Jordan 1997).

Increasingly, designers of women's prisons are planning for areas where counseling and other women's services can be conducted (MacDonald and Watson 2001). Programming needs of women were directed toward more productive activities to make these women more competitive in the job market once they were released. Thus, there is a gradual movement away from those kinds of activities traditionally associated with women's societal roles (DeBell 2001).

CO-CORRECTIONS

The segregation of prisoners according to their gender dates back several centuries to the Walnut Street Jail, and later, to the Auburn Penitentiary in New York. Reasons given then included the improvement of inmate morality, a reduction in inmate promiscuity, and greater privacy for both sexes. In recent years, however, prisoners, both male and female, have expressed interest in co-correctional or co-ed prisons (Smykla and Williams 1996). Advocates of co-correctional prisons have used as their support the Fourteenth Amendment equal protection clause as well as U.S. Supreme Court decisions declaring the separate, but equal doctrine to be null and void as applicable to education, employment, public utilities, and other areas.

Co-Corrections Defined

Co-corrections, co-ed prisons are those where men and women prisoners live, supervised by female and male staff, and participate in all activities together, although unlike Denmark and other countries, inmates may not share the same quarters or have sexual encounters. Co-correctional prisons are not prisons that merely house male and female offenders somewhere in separate facilities on the prison grounds such as Utah and Tennessee. In traditional prison settings such as these where specific areas are assigned females, there is no interaction occurring between them. In co-correctional prisons, there is interaction, even though it may be limited to recreational periods and certain educational, counseling, or vocational programs (J. Davis 1998).

The first co-correctional prison in the United States was the Federal Correctional Institution in Fort Worth, Texas, opened in 1971 by the U.S. Bureau of Prisons (Smykla and Williams 1996). Among the states, the Massachusetts Correctional Institution at Framingham is generally regarded as the first state co-correctional facility. While the objectives of co-correctional prisons vary, generally these objectives include:

1. Permitting a more normal contact between male and female inmates as a means of alleviating the tension of gender isolation.
2. Permitting mutual access to prison services ordinarily offered to male or to female inmates.
3. Permitting male and female inmates opportunities to engage in social exchange, thus helping to ease the transition back into the community when eventually paroled.
4. Permitting more cost-effective program operations and access to more services (Feinman 1986:65–66).

The ratio of male to female inmates is recommended to be 50:50. When women outnumber men or vice versa, realistic integration is made increasingly difficult. When women are in the minority (and they usually are in most prisons), they feel conspicuous, and they tend to be treated as a minority group by their male counterparts (Mahan 1986:134). Also, jealousies among the dominant sex may arise because of greater competition for social encounters and more intimate relationships. The smallest effective proportion of women in a co-correctional prison has been recommended as 40 percent. Furthermore, keeping such facilities small means more effective monitoring and supervision by correctional officers and other staff.

A major public misconception about co-correctional prisons is that there is unchecked promiscuity, shared quarters by male and female inmates, and numerous illegitimate births (Smykla and Williams 1996). This is quite different from what actually occurs. The Kansas Correctional Institution at Lansing provides a good example of the reality of a co-correctional prison. Formerly the Kansas Correctional Institution for Women, the traditional female prison in Kansas, it was changed in September 1980, with the introduction of 27 male inmates from the Kansas State Prison (Halford 1984:44). Those male inmates transferred were low-risk offenders who had been employed earlier on a limited work-release basis. Thus, not all male prisoners were considered for integration in the new co-correctional facility.

While there were initial resentments on the part of both male and female inmates (i.e., some males felt they had been demoted by being transferred to a prison for women), these were gradually resolved. The Kansas institution is an example of a very positive experience in co-correctional imprisonment. Some of the success measures used by evaluators of the project included greater staff enthusiasm, considerable support from the Kansas Department of Corrections, positive media coverage, and privacy rights of both sexes being observed. Parolees also found it easier to gain employment when released. Also, compared with 1979, there was a 40 percent reduction in the number of violent discipline charges, a 73 percent reduction in the number of general discipline charges, and a 42 percent reduction in the number of grievances filed by inmates (Halford 1984:54).

There have been some minor problems encountered by Kansas prison authorities in that institution, but these are relatively minor considering the nature of the inmate population. Only 4 pregnancies occurred during the first 33 months of the co-correctional operation. On the positive side, according to officials, homosexuality decreased considerably. However, there were several incidents among male prisoners fighting for the attentions of certain female inmates. These have been few, however. As expected, the general public objections to the Kansas co-correctional facility are that there is widespread promiscuity (not true) and that officials are not being tough enough with inmates (Halford 1984:54).

Actually, the nature of inmate interaction in virtually every co-correctional facility today is structured and fairly closely supervised. Some researchers have found that inmates feel too closely monitored, however, compared with unisex prison settings. This causes a degree of tension and anxiety (Smykla and Williams 1996). Furthermore, the look-but-don't-touch aspect of these settings acts to aggravate sexual frustrations for both male and female inmates. But reports have largely been positive about inmate opportunities to talk to those of the opposite sex. The preoccupation of these inmates is not exclusively sexual. One inmate said, "It gives you an opportunity to have 'woman' conversations . . . verbalize frailties and inner fears . . . vent hurt and anger. . . . I don't have to act hardened. . . . Weakness won't cause me to be devoured here. . . . The primitive law of prison isn't in operation here" (Mahan 1986:138).

Some opponents of co-correctional institutions believe that women need to be physically separated from men for a time in order to regain their self-respect and identities. Also, the "look-but-don't-touch" rule of these institutions may actually encourage homosexual relationships rather than discourage them. Finally, these institutions are considered exploitive by some authorities. Women become or continue to be sexual objects of men. This view is supported by some research conducted by Amnesty International, which investigated the sexual abuse of women in custody among the 50 states and the District of Columbia in 2000. The results of the survey revealed that there is a continuing lack of laws prohibiting custodial sexual misconduct in some states; a failure of existing laws to provide adequate protection for female inmates; and the widespread lack of uniform standards to protect incarcerated women in labor from being shackled during childbirth (Amnesty International 2001).

Men Guarding Women and Women Guarding Men

A closely related issue is whether men should be placed in correctional officer positions in all-female institutions, and whether female correctional officers should be placed in all-male institutions. The question is academic at this point, since there are both types of scenarios being played out in prisons throughout the United States. In 2000, 48 agencies were surveyed. It was found that 37,834 female corrections officers were working in male institutions, while 5,459 male correctional officers were working in female institutions (Camp and Camp 2002:156). Reported in 1986 as a major breakthrough in the hiring of female correctional officers in men's institutions, opposite-gender officer assignments in corrections are now routine.

FEMALE PROBATIONERS AND PAROLEES: A PROFILE

In 2001, females accounted for 22 percent of all probationers. This is an increase from 18 percent female probationers in 1990 (Glaze 2002:4). One possible explanation for this disproportionate representation of women on probation compared with men is that women tend to do better in probation programs. They have lower recidivism rates, commit fewer crimes, and have fewer technical program violations (Olson, Lurigio, and Seng 2000). Women also tend to stay in their programs longer, secure employment, and obtain stable living arrangements when they are ready to leave their programs. These factors greatly influence their success chances (Hohman, McGaffigan, and Segars 2000).

Approximately 12 percent of all parolees were women in 2001, up from 8 percent in 1990 (Glaze 2002:6). Women comprised 10 percent of all parolees convicted of violent offenses. Overall, women made up 20 percent of all parolees convicted of property offenses. Generally, male and female offenders have different offending patterns. Males are involved to a greater degree in violent offending, while females are involved to a greater degree in property offending. Nevertheless, there is a significant contingent of violent female parolees who often pose supervisory problems for parole officers (Cherek, Lane, and Dougherty 2000). Another explanation for these sentencing differences is that judges have tended to be more paternalistic toward female offenders in the past. However, presumptive or guidelines-based sentencing schemes used by different states and the federal government have caused male–female sentencing differentials to narrow. Some observers have labeled this phenomenon *gender parity* (Steffensmeier, Kramer, and Streifel 1993).

Regarding parole, women tended to be distributed in ways similar to their conviction patterns. Female parolees tend to resemble the characteristics of female state and federal prison inmates (O'Brien 2001a). Also, female parolee distributions by conviction offense were different from their original conviction offense patterns. For instance, about 18 percent of all female parolees have been convicted of violent offenses, and 40 percent of all female parolees are property offenders. This is considerably greater than the percentage for women convicted of property offenses (28 percent). Over 37 percent of all female parolees had prior convictions for drug offenses. A similar figure accounts for the proportion of convictions for women involving drug offenses. Another interesting observation is that the female failure rate while on parole is approximately the same as it is for male parolees, about 62 percent (Maguire and Pastore 2002). One of the greatest needs of female parolees is community services that will prepare them for family responsibilities and drug treatment and resistance (Richie 2001). In many respects, parole programs in most jurisdictions are deficient relating to community programs for women recently released on parole (Cherek and Lane 1999).

In 1992, the American Correctional Association formulated a National Correctional Policy on Female Offender Services (Nesbitt 1992:7). This policy is as follows:

INTRODUCTION: Correctional systems must develop service delivery systems for accused and adjudicated female offenders that are comparable to those provided to males. Additional services must also be provided to meet the unique needs of the female offender population.

STATEMENT: Correctional systems must be guided by the principle of parity. Female offenders must receive the equivalent range of services available to other offenders, including opportunities for individualized programming and services that recognize the unique needs of this population. The services should:

A. Assure access to a range of alternatives to incarceration, including pretrial and post-trial diversion, probation, restitution, treatment for substance abuse, halfway houses, and parole services.

B. Provide acceptable conditions of confinement, including appropriately trained staff and sound operating procedures that address this population's needs in such areas as clothing, personal property, hygiene, exercise, recreation, and visitation with children and family.

C. Provide access to a full range of work and programs designed to expand economic and social roles of women, with emphasis on education; career counseling and exploration of non-traditional as well as traditional vocational training; relevant life skills, including parenting and social and economic assertiveness; and pre-release and work/education release programs.

D. Facilitate the maintenance and strengthening of family ties, particularly those between parent and child.

E. Deliver appropriate programs and services, including medical, dental, and mental health programs, services to pregnant women, substance abuse programs, child and family services, and provide access to legal services.

F. Provide access to release programs that include aid in establishing homes, economic stability, and sound family relationships.

INTERMEDIATE PUNISHMENTS FOR WOMEN

The same range of intermediate punishments exists for women as it does for men. In fact, arrest and incarceration figures suggest that proportionately more women than men are either diverted from the criminal justice system altogether or sentenced to nonincarcerative intermediate punishments. One reason is that the nature of offending among women is such that a greater proportion of them are considered low-risk and nonviolent (Lurigio 1996). These intermediate punishments may include fines, conditions for restitution and victim compensation, community service, or some other alternative provision. Even those women who are incarcerated stand a better chance of being paroled or serving shorter sentences compared with men. Parole criteria in many states include the requirements that offenders must be in minimum custody within six months' of their anticipated parole, that they committed no assaultive offense, that they had not attempted escape, and that they did not engage in major rule infractions within three months of the scheduled parole date (American Correctional Association 1995).

Intermediate punishments include intensive supervised probation, community-based correctional programs, home confinement, and electronic monitoring. More women than men, for instance, tend to be placed under house arrest in those areas where home confinement programs are available. For those offenders who are first-timers or low-risk and considered nondangerous, they may be placed in a diversion program or sentenced to probation. Women are generally considered good risks for such programs, because their success rates are much higher than for men (Pollock 1998). And when women do commit rule infractions, these are usually technical violations and noncrime related.

Women in prison may be granted furloughs, work release, or parole, where they will be subject to varying levels of supervision by parole officers (Camp and Camp 2002). This section briefly examines the use of diversion and probation, community-based supervision, and intensive supervised parole for female offenders.

Diversion and Probation

There are comparatively few diversion programs offered to female offenders (Johnston and Alozie 2001). Because of the relatively small number of female offenders compared with male offenders, the need simply hasn't existed in most jurisdictions to devise programs to accommodate those few female offenders. Of the few diversion programs that presently exist in the United States, three have achieved some visibility. These include the Women's Self-Help Center's Justice Outreach Program in St. Louis, the Community Services for Women in Boston, and the Elizabeth Fry Center in San Francisco. Each of these programs also provides assistance to female probationers as well. Thus, they are not exclusively diversion programs.

Actually, women are better candidates for diversion programs compared with men (Alozie and Johnston 2000). They tend to commit less violent offenses, are more responsive to supervision by probation officers and others, and have better records for completing these programs. If they are mothers, they often are able to continue their parenting with assistance from various community agencies. These relations with agencies are frequently mandated by their diversion programs. Thus, they receive valuable information and education that they might not have received if imprisoned.

It is presently unknown how many female divertees have characteristics similar to female inmates. Some structural features of programs such as California's statutory diversion operate to exclude those who have been charged with drug violations or who have a previous history of drug offenses. Since a fairly large proportion of female prison inmates were convicted of drug-related offenses, many of these persons probably were automatically excluded from participating in the diversion program initially. Also operating against women is the fact that diversion programs often require financial stability through gainful employment. If female arrestees share many of the same characteristics as female prison inmates (e.g., young, unemployed or underemployed, uneducated), then these factors may discourage prosecutors from considering many female offenders for diversion programs. But since diversion information either is not made public or is difficult to access by investigators, no figures are available to show whether these factors actually make a difference in diversion-granting decisions.

The major benefits of diversion for females, especially those who are mothers, are that they may maintain contact with their families and children and may receive treatment for their mental problems or drug/alcohol dependencies. They may also participate in educational programs that will lead to better-paying jobs or to the acquisition of valuable work skills, thus their self-image is enhanced. Probation for women is also a desirable option, but it means that they have been convicted of a crime. In the case of divertees, there are usually no convictions, since the case is withdrawn from prosecution. Their clean record enhances their opportunities for seeking employment and performing work requiring no prior criminal convictions.

Because of overcrowding in most prisons and jails, and because women tend to commit less serious offenses compared with men, their chances for being sentenced to probation are greater. Annual arrest, conviction, and incarceration figures for men and women support this. Furthermore, available evidence suggests that women are better probation risks, commit fewer violations of their probation conditions, and are less likely than men to be charged with technical violations even when they do commit them. Researchers say some reasons for this include certain paternalistic dispositions of probation officers, so that they resist reporting women in order to preserve their family stability. Also, factors unrelated to probation program violations, such as excessive paperwork and prison overcrowding, cause some probation officers to hesitate reporting any offender, unless the offense or violation is quite serious (Acoca and Austin 1996).

In many diversion and probation programs, one or more conditions of these programs may be the payment of fines, some amount of restitution or victim compensation, and/or community service orders (Tonry 1999). It has been found that community service has been used only infrequently as a condition of either probation or diversion. Furthermore, it is seldom used in the case of female offenders. Also, fines and other penalties are imposed with less frequency for convicted female offenders compared with male offenders. While no precise figures are available, it would appear that restitution or victim compensation orders are disproportionately assigned to male offenders compared with female offenders. It could be that since women tend to commit a greater proportion of property and nonviolent offenses, there is less victim injury associated with female criminality (Vitale et al. 2002). This would account for the disproportionate use of fines or victim compensation between male and female offenders.

Intensive Supervised Parole

Many female parolees are assigned to live in halfway houses before being completely free to live on their own resources in the community. One reason for such temporary placements of female parolees is that they provide necessary social support networks to facilitate their societal reintegration (Reisig, Holtfreter, and Morash 2002). Living in halfway houses enables female offenders to participate in valuable community programming that meets their diverse needs.

Although it is not known how many public and private halfway houses are operated exclusively for women, there are several thousand halfway houses throughout the United States operated with varying degrees of organization and sophistication. Co-ed halfway houses exist, but there is some evidence to indi-

Halfway houses for women offer a variety of services, including employment assistance, counseling, and educational opportunities. Courtesy of Custer Youth Correctional Center.

cate that many communities view these houses unfavorably. Generally, females do better on parole than males (Dowdy, Lacy, and Unnithan 2002). Not only do they comply with parole program requirements more consistently than male parolees, but their absconding rates are negligible. Absconding is minimized through effective risk/needs prediction instruments, but these instruments are often heavily biased toward male offender characteristics. Thus, attempting to predict accurately whether female parolees will abscond is a near-impossible task for parole officers and others. Ordinarily, less than 5 percent of all probationers and parolees ever abscond during any given year (Camp and Camp 2002).

Furthermore, there are some female offenders who in all likelihood will never be paroled. For instance, Leslie Van Houten, who was sentenced to death with Charles Manson and others in California for multiple murders in 1969, has faced numerous parole hearings since her death sentence was commuted to life with the possibility of parole in 1972. She has done a great deal to rehabilitate herself since she was initially incarcerated, including earning academic degrees, engaging in extensive counseling, and behaving well as an inmate. In fact, many regard her as an ideal candidate for parole. However, the California Parole Board has repeatedly rejected her early-release requests on the grounds that she has not yet become rehabilitated. In the meantime, the California Parole Board has paroled numerous murderers and others who have committed crimes more heinous than Van Houten. The most obvious explanation for why Van Houten has been turned down repeatedly for parole is that the media coverage of her crimes was so extensive that no parole board member wants to be associated with the parole board that released one of the "Manson Family" from prison. Is this fair? No. But it does suggest that even though an inmate is parole-eligible and even a good candidate for parole, early release will not necessarily be granted. And very little justification is required for a parole board's refusal to grant early release to any inmate (Faith 2001).

SUMMARY

Female inmates make up approximately 7 percent of all state and federal prisoners. Women are sometimes referred to as forgotten offenders, largely because their particular needs have been neglected by jail and prison officials. In recent years, the proportionate female inmate population has increased compared with the male inmate population. Early prison developments did not favor women, and few provisions were made by different prisons and jails to accommodate them. In some instances, they were housed together with males and juvenile offenders. The Magdalen Society was established in 1830 to ensure that women's rights were preserved and that prisons made appropriate accommodations for female prisoners. The first major prison for women, the Mount Pleasant Female Prison, was established in 1835 in New York.

Prisons for women were originally established along the same lines as reformatories for men. Several correctional models used to configure women's prisons were the custodial model, the reformatory model, and the campus model, which typifies many women's prisons currently. Elizabeth Gurney Fry was a prominent Quaker Englishwoman who succeeded in securing many rights for women as prisoners. Fry engaged in numerous philanthropic efforts designed to improve women's prisons and the conditions under which women were incarcerated. Fry was instrumental in helping to establish the Hopper Home in New York City, perhaps the oldest halfway house for women in the United States.

In 1870, the National Prison Association was formed at a conference of corrections professionals in Cincinnati, Ohio. Subsequently known as the American Correctional Association, this organization has been a leader in bringing about significant reforms for female offenders. Between 1870 and the 1940s, prisons for women were operated like reformatories. In fact, many of them were patterned after the Elmira Reformatory, which was established in New York in 1876. One such institution was the Indiana Women's Prison, which was constructed in 1873. Until 1934, there were only 19 prisons designed exclusively for women in the United States. Only 7 more women's prisons were constructed during the next 20-year period. During and subsequent to the 1970s, there was accelerated growth in women's prison construction. Some impetus to this accelerated construction was provided by the courts as more women filed lawsuits against prison systems seeking more equitable treatment compared with men's institutions. During the latter half of the twentieth century, the American Correctional Association and other interested organizations set forth clear guidelines and recommendations for women's prisons and the programs and amenities they should provide. Gradually, women's prison programming and services have shifted from traditional vocational activities to a broader range of programs and services comparable to those offered in men's prisons.

Relatively few risk measures have been devised for female offenders. Most risk assessment devices have been constructed for male offenders, although risk assessments for women are more abundant today. One reason for the lack of risk assessment instruments for women is that they comprise only a small part of the U.S. inmate population. However, as the number of women's prisons has increased, so has the need to devise more effective and adequate risk and classification instruments for women. Currently, women's prisons have similar custody levels compared with men's prisons, and women are classified and placed accordingly.

Several criticisms have been leveled against women's prisons. Historically, women's prisons have lacked comparable vocational and educational programs compared with men's prisons. Also, few provisions have been made for incarcerated mothers. Women's prisons have been remotely located in rural areas, thus making them somewhat inaccessible for family visits. Mental health and medical programs for women have been inferior to those for men. Also, women have had limited access to legal materials and services. However, the Michigan case of *Glover v. Johnson* (1979) prompted significant changes in women's prisons in all states. Several programs specifically designed for women have been established, and women now have equal access to legal materials and assistance. Moreover, institutional programming has become more sophisticated and up to date, more consistent with the programming normally found in men's facilities.

As women's prisons have evolved over time, more has been written about them. Rich descriptions of women's prisons are now abundant. It is clear that female inmates have devised status and reward systems paralleling those established in men's prisons. Female inmates have cultivated their own jargon to describe what occurs behind bars and how they refer to one another and prison staff. Female inmate terminology includes squares, cools, and lifes as depictions of different types of offenders according to their offense seriousness and other salient factors.

Women's prisons are fairly easy to administer, according to wardens and superintendents in charge of these facilities. They are small institutions compared with large male prisons. Female inmates are more controlled and do not easily riot and engage in extensive misconduct. There is also more rapid turnover in the inmate population, thus discouraging long-term relationships based on gang affiliations and other commonly shared interests and characteristics (e.g., race or ethnicity). Several issues have arisen pertaining to women's prisons. One of these is whether women are treated equally with men according to how they are housed. Like men's prisons, women's prisons are somewhat overcrowded. Thus, overcrowding is a pervasive problem, and one that is likely to continue in the future. One controversial solution to the absence of vocational and educational programming for women has been the creation of co-correctional or co-ed prisons. These are facilities where women and men share common programs. But men and women are housed separately during evening hours, and their interactions during daytime hours are closely supervised.

Since many women in prison are also mothers, greater emphasis has been placed on their relationships with minor children in recent years. Visiting cottage programs and other types of services, including New York's Prison Nursery/Children's Center, have been established. These and other related programs have assisted female inmates in meeting their needs. One especially significant problem is that female offenders are more likely to be HIV/AIDS infected. There is simply a higher incidence of this disease in women's prisons compared with facilities for men. Much of this is attributable to illicit drug use. Changes are gradually occurring to more effectively meet the medical needs of incarcerated female offenders. Women are also being exposed to boot camp experiences similar to those used to improve male offender discipline and character. Domestic violence programs are also being established, because so many incarcerated women have come from abusive relationships.

Women tend to have the same range of probation and parole programs that men have, and women also have higher program completion rates. Generally, women are more easy to supervise compared with their male counterparts, although there are exceptions. Women participate in pre-release programs, such as furloughs and work/study release. They are also paroled like men and experience standard parole with conditions and/or intensive supervised parole. The full range of probation programs is also extended to women, including home confinement, electronic monitoring, and intensive supervised probation as intermediate punishments.

QUESTIONS FOR REVIEW

1. What was the first female prison? Who was Elizabeth Gurney Fry and what were her contributions to women's prisons?

2. What are three types of correctional models that have typified women's prison conditions over the last two centuries?

3. What similarities and differences exist between prisons for men and prisons for women? How have women been successful in achieving equality with men in terms of their prison accommodations and programming?

4. What are some typical characteristics of women's prisons in the United States? Why has the classification of female offenders occurred more slowly compared with classification schemes for male inmates? How have these disparities been overcome?

5. What is the Program for Female Offenders, Inc.? What is the significance of the Women's Prison Association?

6. What are some of the reasons for establishing co-correctional prisons? Does everyone agree that co-ed prisons are desirable? Why or why not?

7. What are some characteristics of female prison inmate culture? In what ways do these characteristics parallel the culture found in men's prisons? In what ways does female inmate culture differ from men's inmate culture?

8. What are four important issues related to women's prisons and their operation?

9. What is the significance of *Glover v. Johnson* (1979)?

10. What sorts of programs are available to women who are on probation or parole?

SUGGESTED READINGS

Carlen, Pat. *Women and Punishment: The Struggle for Justice.* Portland, OR: Willan Publishing, 2001.

Chesney-Lind, Meda. *The Female Offender.* 2d ed. Thousand Oaks, CA: Sage Publications, 2003.

Grana, Sheryl J. *Women and (In)Justice: The Criminal and Civil Effects of the Common Law on Women's Lives.* Boston: Allyn and Bacon, 2002.

Joseph, Janice and Dorothy Taylor. *With Justice for All: Minorities and Women in Criminal Justice.* Upper Saddle River, NJ: Prentice Hall, 2003.

Pollock, Jocelyn M. *Women, Prison, and Crime.* Belmont, CA: Wadsworth/Thomson Learning, 2002.

Sharp, Susan F. *The Incarcerated Woman.* Upper Saddle River, NJ: Prentice Hall, 2003.

INTERNET CONNECTIONS

Caged Kittens
http://www.cagedkittens.com

Faith to Faith Friends
http://www.f2ff.com

Female Inmate Pen Pals
http://www.thepamperedprisoner.com

Very Special Women
http://www.vswomen.com

The Program for Female Offenders, Inc.
http://www.fcnetworks.org/Dir98/dir98front.html

Women Behind Bars
http://www.womenbehindbars.com/

Women in Criminal Justice
http://www.wicj.com

Women's Prison Association
http://www.wpaonline.org/WEBSITE/home.htm

CHAPTER 13 | *Juveniles and Corrections*

Courtesy of Custer Youth Correctional Center.

Chapter Objectives *As the result of reading this chapter, the following objectives should be realized:*

1. Describing various types of juvenile offenders, including status offenders and delinquents.
2. Portraying juvenile delinquency statistics.
3. Outlining and describing the juvenile justice system, including arrest, intake, and adjudication proceedings by juvenile courts.
4. Examining several landmark juvenile cases that have given juveniles substantial rights commensurate with adults.
5. Discussing the transfer or waiver process whereby juveniles are certified to the jurisdiction of criminal court.
6. Understanding the history of juvenile corrections in the United States, including key figures and events.

7. Presenting the goals of juvenile corrections, including rehabilitation and reintegration, deterrence, isolation, control, prevention, punishment, and retribution.
8. Examining several juvenile correctional alternatives including warnings, diversion, supervised probation, and youth courts.
9. Reviewing selected juvenile correctional issues, including the deinstitutionalization of status offenses, the classification of juvenile offenders, juvenile transfer hearings, violent and nonviolent juvenile offenders, capital punishment for juveniles, and the future of juvenile corrections.

INTRODUCTION

• *There is a program out there called Scared Straight. This program involves trips to prisons by juveniles, where they are confronted with several hardened criminals. These inmates curse them, belittle them, and attempt to scare them about what life is like in prison. As a result of this experience, the juveniles are expected to be shocked to the extent that they will refrain from future delinquent activity. Does this program work? Some experts say "yes," and others say "no." Certainly, it has worked for some juveniles in past years, despite its mixed reviews from critics. In Texas, a version of Scared Straight is being practiced. This time, inmates themselves travel to various cities, such as Laredo, Houston, Dallas, and San Antonio, where they visit middle school and high school students. One justice of the peace, Danny Valdez, has organized such trips by making arrangements with prison officials for escorted leaves of certain prisoners for educational purposes. It is Valdez's hope that the students who hear the inmates themselves will take their words to heart and adjust their behaviors. According to Valdez, "After listening to their stories, I hope students will take the high road and change their lives for the better." Valdez arranges trips where certain inmates, under close supervision, take temporary leaves from their prisons and visit schools to discuss their lives in prison with students. Their speeches are not limited to schools. Sometimes they visit juvenile detention centers and speak to groups of hardcore delinquent offenders. The convicts discuss their lives of crime before incarceration, their lives inside prison, and how they hope to live once they are released on parole. Valdez says that "As these youths listen to these prisoners, I hope they come to realize how valuable their freedom is and that they will decide that they should live according to the law." Valdez said that inmates also explain how their lives in prison are no longer their own and that they must follow the orders of others at all times. Usually, these sessions last about an hour. After the prisoners speak, students and delinquents have a chance to ask them specific questions. The prisoners are under constant supervision by prison guards. Do you think it is good to have prisoners visit students in schools or detention centers? What are some potential problems with such an approach to deterring delinquency? What do you think?* [Adapted from Miguel T. Ramirez and the Associated Press, "Inmates to Discuss Lives with Students," November 5, 2001].

• *Want a jail in your neighborhood? Probably not. The citizens of New England, North Dakota, don't want one there, either. As overcrowding in jails, prisons, and juvenile correctional facilities continues to grow unchecked, federal, state, and local governments are turning toward the community for short- and long-term solutions to accommodating inmate overflow. Community corrections is a growing enterprise. In southwestern North Dakota near Dickinson, federal authorities have been plagued with the problem of growing juvenile delinquency. The federal system has no juvenile court, and the Native American reservations controlled by the federal government dictate that whenever juveniles are adjudicated delinquent for serious offenses, they must be placed in secure juvenile facilities somewhere. The growing delinquency problem has caused federal agencies to consider converting unused building space into juvenile detention housing. In 1998 federal authorities moved to renovate several former school buildings in New England. New England St. Mary's School was closed in 1997, leaving approximately 57,000 square feet of space available. The federal government acquired the buildings and grounds and implemented a renovation program designed to convert the facility into a short-term detention center for juveniles. The new facility would be called the Southwest Multi-County Correction Center. Some New England citizens were outraged.*

The Citizens for a Progressive New England moved to prevent the renovation by having a federal court issue an injunction against the authorities who were initiating the conversion. Consisting of 92 members, the Citizens for a Progressive New England contended that the juvenile facility would endanger property values and the security of neighbors in the community, which is located about 25 miles south of Dickinson. An attorney for the group, Loren McCray, said that "on its face, there's a potential for property values to drop for those homes" near the former school. Proponents of the center say that the new juvenile facility will provide needed jobs and boost the local community economy. Further, they say that fears about community safety are unfounded. "These are wild assumptions that something bad will happen," said Dickinson attorney Tom Priebe, calling the injunction a pretty drastic remedy. More than a few communities oppose construction of juvenile or adult facilities in their neighborhoods. While research has generally shown that property values near these sites are unaffected, the prospect of having dangerous juveniles housed nearby may cause some community concern. What do you think about having any kind of correctional facility constructed near or within a community? Should governments convert existing schools and other public facilities into corrections centers? How would you feel if such a facility were proposed for your neighborhood? [Adapted from the Associated Press, "New England Juvenile Jail Prevails in First Round of Court Battle," November 14, 1998].

• *It happened in New Haven, Connecticut. A 13-year-old girl who was in the seventh grade in a middle school with an otherwise unblemished juvenile record was suddenly thrust into the national spotlight over truancy. For unknown reasons, the girl suddenly refused to attend her seventh-grade classes. School officials reported her truancy to a juvenile court judge, who ordered her to attend her classes. She continued to absent herself from the classroom against the judge's orders and suddenly found herself in contempt of court. Authorities were sent to pick her up and take her to juvenile detention. When she arrived at the Connecticut juvenile detention center in New Haven, a matron at the center ordered her to strip. The girl didn't know what to do. She said, "The lady told me I had to take off my clothes so that they could look for scars so that I can't go home and say that they did it and my parents can sue. I was embarrassed. I don't like having to take my clothes off in front of anyone." The following day, the girl was moved to another center for the remainder of her detention and ordered to strip again. Connecticut officials were interviewed about the incident. Apparently, it is juvenile detention center policy to strip-search all juveniles to check for drugs or weapons, as well as for signs of abuse requiring treatment. The girl strip-searched shot back, "I can see it if I was there for carrying a weapon, but for not going to school?" Strip searches are among the most invasive procedures, and considerable opinion and case law says they should be used judiciously, even with adults. In June 2001, for example, New York City settled a class-action suit filed by thousands of adults who had been strip-searched upon arrest for low-level crimes in the city.*

Connecticut officials say that some adult prisoners are exempt from strip searches. Adults held in jail prior to arraignment on misdemeanor or motor vehicle charges are not searched unless there is the reasonable belief that they are concealing contraband. Most places in Connecticut do not ordinarily strip-search children. In New York, chronic runaways and truants are not placed in detention, much less strip-searched. In New Jersey, strip searches are not routine in facilities that hold children who have committed low-level crimes. But Connecticut is different. All juveniles who are placed in detention, including runaways, truants, and those held in contempt of court, are subject to being strip-searched upon entering detention. According to William H. Carbone, executive director of court support services for the state's judicial branch, it is really for the overall security of the detainees. Carbone said that these searches are to protect children from themselves. He added, "A chronic runaway may have a razor blade taped to his foot or have barbiturates under his arm." Opponents of strip searches involving juveniles say that strip searches don't make sense in most cases. Jeanne Milstein, a child advocate, says that strip searches make sense if you are dealing with violent juvenile offenders or those accused of serious crimes. But only 12 percent of all juveniles taken into custody fit this scenario, she said. Anthony Wallace, an attorney representing the 13-year-old girl filing a lawsuit against Connecticut, said, "Why should the state force these children to bend over and show them their private parts because they didn't go to school or commit-

*ted some low-level crime?" Should status offenders be submitted to strip searches when-
ever they are taken into custody for the purpose of being held in detention? Which types
of juveniles should qualify for strip searches? What do you think?* [Adapted from
Matthew Purdy and the New York Times News Service, July 19, 2001].

Are these scenarios exceptional? Do they typify only occasional events? Or
are these youths only the tip of an iceberg of pervasive juvenile violence? In the
United States today, juvenile violence is escalating at a disturbing rate. Not
only are more youths committing violent offenses annually, but these violent
acts are being committed by younger and younger juveniles. Drive-by shootings
involving youths under age 10 are commonplace. Advocates of change want the
age lowered for transferring juveniles to criminal courts for more serious prosecutions and punishments. Juvenile court reformers want harsher punishments
meted out to those who commit heinous acts against innocent citizens. The
mushrooms are striking back, wanting to retake their streets and neighborhoods. If juvenile delinquency cannot be prevented, then it can be punished
more severely whenever it is encountered. Some experts believe that this is
where juvenile corrections can do the most good—by incapacitating and punishing more chronic, persistent violent youths.

This chapter is about corrections for juveniles. The chapter begins with a
description of different types of juvenile offenders. These include delinquent
and status offenders. **Delinquency** involves violations of criminal laws by juveniles, whereas status offenses are offenses committed by juveniles that would
not be crimes if adults committed them. Other differences between these offender categorizations are explained. Also examined is the Juvenile Justice and
Delinquency Prevention Act of 1974, which has had significant influence on
how juveniles are treated when arrested, as well as changing procedures for
their detention and confinement.

The next part of this chapter highlights the juvenile justice system and its
various components. Juveniles are arrested or taken into custody, proceed
through intake, are screened for prosecution, and subsequently adjudicated in
juvenile courts. Some juveniles are considered for prosecution as adult offenders, both because of their age and the seriousness of their offenses. Once juveniles are adjudicated, judges may consider one of several dispositional options
for their punishment, which are like sentences for adults. These dispositional
options include nominal, conditional, or custodial punishments, which are
described.

Until the mid-1960s, juveniles had few legal rights in courts. Their affairs
were administered by civil authorities, usually family or domestic courts,
chancery courts, or other exclusively civil agencies. In recent years, however,
significant advancements have been made in juvenile corrections, with substantial improvements in juvenile case dispositions. Several key U.S. Supreme
Court cases involving juvenile rights are described. These include *Kent v.
United States* (1966), *In re Gault* (1967), *In re Winship* (1970), and *McKeiver v.
Pennsylvania* (1971).

When it is decided that some juveniles should be processed as adult offenders and sent to criminal courts, this action is accomplished through waivers,
certifications, or transfers. This process is examined in some detail. Several important types of transfers are described. However, the intent of transferring juveniles to criminal courts is not always consistent with subsequent criminal court
outcomes. Both juvenile courts and criminal courts generally treat juvenile offenders leniently. This leniency will be examined and explained.

The chapter next focuses upon a historical overview of the history of juvenile corrections in the United States. Several significant events are described, such as the New York House of Refuge, children's tribunals, Hull House, the Compulsory School Act, and the first juvenile court in Illinois. Next, the goals of juvenile corrections are described. These goals include rehabilitation and reintegration, deterrence, isolation and control, prevention, and punishment or retribution. When juvenile courts find juveniles guilty of the offenses alleged, they can impose one of several different kinds of punishments, ranging from verbal warnings to incarceration or detention. Most juveniles receive verbal warnings or probation, even repeat offenders. For some juvenile offenders, however, greater discipline and harsher treatment are required, including **detention** in secure facilities. These facilities and programs will be described and assessed. Juvenile incarceration may be in either secure or nonsecure facilities. These different types of facilities will be examined. Also as an alternative, some juveniles are subjected to youth courts where they are in effect tried by their peers. Youth courts are described.

The chapter next explores several key issues in juvenile corrections. These issues involve the deinstitutionalization of status offenses, which often involves the removal of status offenders from secure confinement. Another issue pertains to the classification of juvenile offenders according to their risks and needs. Compared with the adult correctional system, juvenile corrections is less sophisticated concerning the development of risk and needs measures. However, most jurisdictions are improving the assessment procedures and instrumentation. Also examined is the issue of whether to treat some juveniles as adults through transfers or waivers. This is a hotly debated topic, and not everyone agrees that juveniles should be eligible for adult punishments. This issue is discussed.

There is also some debate about whether juvenile violence has increased in recent years. Government statistics and surveys show that juvenile violence has decreased, although the sheer numbers of juveniles who commit violent acts has increased. This issue is examined. Another issue is the privatization of juvenile corrections. Like its adult counterpart, juvenile corrections is susceptible to management by private interests. In fact, juvenile corrections is an area where privatization has been most noticeable. One of the most controversial topics is the issue of capital punishment for juveniles, which will be examined. This is especially important since the U.S. Supreme Court has determined that the death penalty cannot be administered to any juvenile under the age of 16 at the time a capital crime was committed. Several key U.S. Supreme Court death penalty cases involving juveniles will be described. These include *Thompson v. Oklahoma*, 1988; *Stanford v. Kentucky*, 1989; and *Wilkins v. Missouri*, 1989. Various arguments for and against the death penalty for juveniles will be presented. The chapter concludes with a projection about the future of juvenile corrections.

JUVENILE OFFENDERS

Types of Juvenile Offenders

Just as their adult counterparts vary according to the nature and seriousness of the offenses they commit, there is an exceptional array of offenses committed by juveniles. For instance, there are **violent offenders** and **property offenders**, or **nonviolent offenders.** But these relatively simple categorizations mask diverse personality characteristics among juvenile offenders that make it difficult to account for their behaviors in any systematic way (Glaser, Calhoun, and Petrocelli 2002).

Female juveniles commit basically different kinds of offenses than male juveniles, and it appears that both male and female delinquency rates are increasing (Palomino 2001). Regarding gender differences, for instance, a greater proportion of female juvenile offenders, as compared with their male juvenile counterparts, tend to engage in shoplifting and sex offenses, including prostitution. However, some persons believe that these differences are greatly exaggerated. A new female delinquent is emerging as one outcome of the Women's Movement, but others say this is more a function of the law-and-order phase we have entered in law enforcement. Whatever the trends in juvenile delinquency happen to be and the rationales advanced to explain them, there are two broad categories of juvenile offenders: status offenders and juvenile delinquents.

Status Offenders.   **Status offenders** are juveniles who commit offenses that, if committed by adults, would not be considered crimes. Examples of **status offenses** include truancy, running away from home, and violating curfew (Feld 2000). These offenses are considered illegal for juveniles. However, if adults enroll in courses at school and do not attend them, they are not considered truant. If adults run away from home, they are not criminals. If adults walk the streets after certain hours in particular communities, they are not arrested. In short, the status of being a juvenile, depending on the jurisdiction, places the youth in a special category as a status offender (Black 1990).

Juvenile Delinquents.   **Juvenile delinquency** is any act committed by a juvenile that, if committed by an adult, would be a crime (Black 1990). Thus, if juveniles commit either felonies or misdemeanors, then these acts are considered **delinquent acts.** These youths are known as **juvenile delinquents.** A **juvenile** is one who has not reached the age of majority or adulthood and is within the jurisdictional authority of the juvenile court. Since a civil disposition is made about juvenile offenders whenever they commit felonies or misdemeanors, their acts are classified as offenses rather than as crimes. A majority of states define age 17 as the upper limit for juvenile court jurisdiction (Reddington 2002). The remaining states use age 16 as the upper limit (8 states) or age 15 as the upper limit (4 states). While the lower age limit for juvenile court jurisdiction varies among states, age 10 is cited most frequently as the minimum age for this jurisdiction. Children under age 7 are generally presumed incapable of formulating criminal intent and in most jurisdictions are subject to the jurisdiction of civil agencies such as departments of social welfare or child and family services. In 2001 there were over 2 million youths referred to the juvenile justice system, where one or more delinquent acts were alleged (Maguire and Pastore 2002). However, self reports, where juveniles often disclose undetected or unreported crime, suggest the actual amount of delinquency may be much higher annually (Unger and Rohrbach 2002).

There are some major differences between delinquent acts and status offenses. Status offenses are not as serious as delinquent offenses. However, for many decades, more than a few states have lumped together status offenses and delinquent offenses into a single category and have processed offenders

Status offenses may include curfew violation, runaway behavior, truancy, and/or underage smoking and drinking. *Source:* Dorling Kindersley Media Library.

similarly through the juvenile courts. This means that at least in some state jurisdictions, juveniles are adjudicated as either delinquent offenders or status offenders by juvenile court judges and placed in the same programs or custodial facilities (Von Hirsch 2001).

In predominantly rural states, such as North Dakota, Montana, Nebraska, and South Dakota, for instance, both status offenders and delinquent offenders are often incarcerated in industrial schools for more or less lengthy terms. At Mandan, North Dakota, an industrial school is operated as a secure facility for both male and female juveniles. Both status and delinquent offenders are confined at the Mandan Industrial School for periods ranging from 3 to 27 months. In most other states, however, status offenders are not confined with delinquent offenders. Rather, they are managed or supervised by one or more community agencies.

The Juvenile Justice and Delinquency Prevention Act of 1974.   The passage of the **Juvenile Justice and Delinquency Prevention Act of 1974** encouraged the states to deal differently with their juvenile status offenders. The Act made monies available to various states and individual communities for the purpose of creating community-based treatment programs instead of institutionalizing juveniles in secure detention such as reform or industrial schools. Also, the Act encouraged states to divert status offenders away from the juvenile justice system entirely, where their problems could be dealt with more adequately in non-threatening settings by various community agencies. This has been referred to as the jail removal initiative, because it is aimed at preventing juveniles from being held in jails for virtually any length of time. A third aim of the Act was to provide monies to explore ways of preventing delinquency and to create various projects with this primary objective. While no states are obligated to comply with the provisions of this act, most jurisdictions have made efforts to remove juvenile status offenders from the juvenile justice system and process them differently. Also, programs in different parts of the United States have

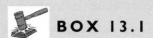

BOX 13.1

The School Bully Bill

How should school bullies be treated? What can be done to prevent bullies from ruining your day at school? Colorado thinks it has an answer. In May 2001 the Colorado state legislature signed into law a bully bill to prevent bullying at schools. The bill was prompted by the 1999 shootings at Columbine High School. The law went into effect in August 2001 and requires school districts to adopt policies against bullying and providing yearly progress reports to the state. A growing number of schools across the country have adopted similar programs. Governor Bill Owens said of the bill, "Bullying is something we think is a predictor and sometimes leads to other violence." A survey by the U.S. Centers for Disease Control and Prevention showed that 10,000 children stayed home from school in 2000 at least one month because they feared school bullies. Half of the children surveyed said that they were bullied at least once at school. Colorado Senator Penfield Tate, one of the bill's sponsors, said, "We need to create safe schools and ensure their safety in a school environment where they can grow, where they can learn, and where they can be nurtured."

Should all schools adopt bullying bills? Will such bills stop bullying behavior? Many shooters in school incidents claim that one reason they shot others was because they were bullied. Do you think that such a bill will decrease the incidence of school shootings?

Source: Adapted from the Associated Press, "School Bully Bill Inked in Colorado," May 3, 2001.

been established for the purpose of preventing delinquency or for diverting youths to various community-based services (Leiber 2002).

Children in Need of Supervision, CHINS.   A third category of juveniles is within the jurisdiction of juvenile courts. This category is neither status nor delinquent offenders. **CHINS** are **children in need of supervision.** Youths who have been abandoned by their parents, who have inadequate supervision by parents, who are unmanageable or incorrigible, or who have social or psychological problems that interfere with traditional family living, may be placed in foster homes, group homes, or some other out-of-home placement where they can receive special services. These services may include group or individual counseling (Browne 2002).

Some Characteristics of Delinquent Offenders

Table 13.1 shows the total estimated number of juvenile arrests for 2000—2,369,400 arrests (Snyder 2002). Of these, 72 percent were male offenders, while 32 percent were under age 15. Although female juveniles accounted for 28 percent of all juvenile arrests, they only accounted for about 18 percent of all juvenile violent crime arrests. The most visible violent crime arrests involving female juveniles were for aggravated assault. About 23 percent of these arrests consisted of female juveniles. However, female juveniles accounted for 30 percent of all juvenile arrests for property crimes. Among different property

TABLE 13.1

Estimated Number of Juvenile Arrests, by Offense, Percent Change, 1991–2000

Most Serious Offense	2000 Estimated Number of Juvenile Arrests	Percent of Total Juvenile Arrests		Percent Change		
		Female	Under Age 15	1991–00	1996–00	1999–00
Total	2,369,400	28 %	32 %	3 %	−15 %	−5 %
Crime Index Total	617,600	28	38	−28	−27	−5
Violent Crime Index	98,900	18	33	−17	−23	−4
Murder & nonnegligent manslaughter	1,200	11	13	−65	−55	−13
Forcible rape	4,500	1	39	−26	−17	−5
Robbery	26,800	9	27	−29	−38	−5
Aggravated assault	66,300	23	36	−7	−14	−4
Property Crime Index	518,800	30	39	−30	−28	−5
Burglary	95,800	12	39	−38	−30	−5
Larceny-theft	363,500	37	40	−24	−27	−6
Motor vehicle theft	50,800	17	26	−51	−34	−3
Arson	8,700	12	65	−7	−17	−7
Nonindex						
Other assaults	236,800	31	43	37	−1	0
Forgery and counterfeiting	6,400	34	12	−20	−24	−7
Fraud	10,700	32	18	−3	−15	−5
Embezzlement	2,000	47	6	132	48	11
Stolen property (buying, receiving, possessing)	27,700	16	29	−40	−33	−1
Vandalism	114,100	12	44	−21	−19	−4
Weapons (carrying, possessing, etc.)	37,600	10	33	−26	−28	−10
Prostitution and commercialized vice	1,300	55	13	−13	−4	−3
Sex offenses (except forcible rape and prostitution)	17,400	7	52	−4	8	5
Drug abuse violations	203,900	15	17	145	−4	0
Gambling	1,500	4	18	−27	−30	−22
Offenses against the family and children	9,400	37	38	92	−8	2
Driving under the influence	21,000	17	3	14	13	−3
Liquor law violations	159,400	31	10	20	4	−6
Drunkenness	21,700	20	13	−3	−19	−3
Disorderly conduct	165,700	28	38	33	−9	−8
Vagrancy	3,000	23	28	−33	−7	27
All other offenses (except traffic)	414,200	26	28	35	−5	−5
Suspicion	1,200	22	23	−76	−53	−29
Curfew and loitering	154,700	31	28	81	−16	−11
Runaways	142,000	59	39	−18	−29	−6

Source: Office of Juvenile Justice and Delinquency Prevention. *Statistical Briefing Book.* Washington, DC, 2002, p. 4.

offenses, female juveniles made up 37 percent of all juvenile larceny-theft juvenile arrests. They also accounted for 47 percent of the juvenile embezzlement arrests. Fifty-five percent of all juvenile arrests for prostitution and commercialized vice were females, while 59 percent of all runaways were females. Male juveniles were in the majority for all other arrest categories.

In 2000 there were an estimated 1,200 juvenile arrests for murder. Between 1996 and 2000, juvenile arrests for murder fell by 55 percent. Between 1991 and 2000, there were substantial declines in juvenile arrests for murder (65 percent), motor vehicle theft (51 percent), and burglary (38 percent), and major increases in juvenile arrests for drug abuse violations (145 percent) and curfew and loitering violations (81 percent). Youth under age 15 accounted for 65 percent of all juvenile arrests for arson in 2000 (Snyder 2002).

When arrests of juveniles are made, the youths are usually taken to the nearest jail for booking, citation, or further processing. If the arrestee is clearly a juvenile, police will take the youth to a juvenile officer. Complicating the processing of some juvenile arrestees is the fact that they may possess false identification or fake IDs. It is not always easy to determine juvenile status, since appearances can be deceptive. Underage female prostitutes often carry false identification, for instance, and their makeup makes them appear to be much older than they really are. Many male juveniles appear to be adults, and with accompanying false identification, police and jail officers may confine them in jail cells with adults for various periods.

Juveniles in Jails.   In 2001 there were 7,613 juveniles held in adult jails. Of these, 6,757 were being held as adults. These figures reflect a decrease from the 9,105 juveniles held in adult jails in 1997. Also in 2001 there were only 856 juveniles being held as juveniles in adult jails. This is less than a third of the 2,301 juveniles held as juveniles in U.S. jails in 1990. Most juveniles are held in these jails for short periods, usually for a few days or less (Beck, Karberg, and Harrison 2002:9).

Federal guidelines from the Office of Juvenile Justice and Delinquency Prevention strongly recommend the separation of juvenile offenders by both sight and sound from adult offenders while juveniles are in any type of jail custody. This means providing separate space and facilities in jails or lockups for both juveniles and adults. However, many jails are simply too small and unequipped for such separate confinement or accommodation. Nevertheless, most jurisdictions attempt to abide by these federal guidelines. But false identification, slow processing of individual cases, and jail overcrowding mean that some juveniles may not be identified as such and separated from adults when they are initially brought to jails (Benson et al. 2002). When these juveniles are eventually identified and separated, they are sent to the juvenile justice system for further processing.

Juveniles in Prisons   Table 13.2 shows the numbers of sentenced inmates in state or federal prisons in 2001. There were at least 35,800 inmates in prisons in 2001 who were in the 18 to 19 age category. While 18 is the age of majority or adulthood in a large number of states, in several others, the age of adulthood is 21. Nevertheless, these figures represent less than 3 percent of the entire state and federal prison inmate population. Several critics of the juvenile justice system are disturbed that such numbers of youths are incarcerated with adults

TABLE 13.2

Number of Sentenced Prisoners under State or Federal Jurisdiction, by Gender, Race, Hispanic Origin, and Age, 2001

| | *Number of Sentenced Prisoners* | | | | | | | |
| | **Males** | | | | **Females** | | | |
Age	*Total*[a]	*White*[b]	*Black*[b]	*Hispanic*	*Total*[a]	*White*[b]	*Black*[b]	*Hispanic*
Total	1,259,481	449,200	585,800	199,700	85,031	36,200	36,400	10,200
18–19	35,600	8,900	17,400	7,000	1,300	700	500	100
20–24	214,600	60,000	106,500	40,600	8,500	3,700	3,200	1,500
25–29	241,800	71,000	122,500	42,100	15,200	5,600	6,600	2,000
30–34	238,600	85,100	110,700	39,100	21,100	8,700	9,400	2,400
35–39	214,500	81,900	102,000	28,900	18,600	8,000	8,400	2,000
40–44	145,900	58,400	64,300	21,200	10,100	4,200	4,700	1,000
45–54	124,800	59,500	48,400	16,100	8,000	3,900	3,000	1,000
55 or older	38,400	23,300	10,800	4,100	1,800	1,300	500	100

Note: Based on custody counts from National Prisoners Statistics (NPS-1A) and updated from jurisdiction counts by gender at year end. Estimates by age derived from the Surveys of Inmates in State and Federal Correctional facilities, 1997. Estimates were rounded to the nearest 100.
[a]Includes American Indians, Alaska Natives, Asians, Native Hawaiians, and other Pacific Islanders.
[b]Excludes Hispanics.
Source: Paige M. Harrison and Allen J. Beck. *Prisoners in 2001.* Washington, DC: U.S. Department of Justice, 2002, p.12.

(Tischler 1999:1). Some of the reasons include the fact that juveniles don't receive the types of counseling and assistance they might need compared with adult offenders. Many juveniles enter prison with substance abuse problems, for example. However, 60 percent of all correctional institutions in the United States do not have adequate substance abuse programs. Thus, juvenile participation in such necessary institutional programming cannot always be guaranteed (U.S. Substance Abuse and Mental Health Services Administration 2000). Increasing numbers of mentally ill youths are entering and remaining in the juvenile justice system. More of these juveniles are eventually entering adult systems without proper mental health treatment (Boesky 2001). Further, adult prisons gear their training programs for adults and not juveniles (Austin, Johnson, and Gregoriou 2000). Thus it is questionable whether juveniles receive any meaningful training or skill development while incarcerated. Another consideration is the physical safety of youths who must associate with adult offenders (Alarid and Cromwell 2002; Burton et al. 2000). Sexual assaults are more likely in the criminogenic environment of prison.

THE JUVENILE JUSTICE SYSTEM

The **juvenile justice system** varies in sophistication, organization, and application among jurisdictions. No single diagram or model typifies the average juvenile justice system. However, there are sufficient similarities among the systems of different states to generalize about juvenile processing and dispositional

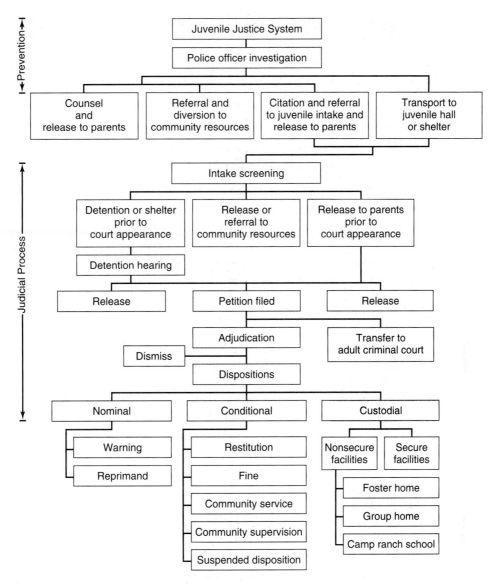

FIGURE 13.1   Procedures of the Juvenile Justice System

Source: National Advisory Committee on Criminal Justice Standards and Goals, Task Force on Juvenile Justice and Delinquency Prevention. *Report of the Task Force on Juvenile Justice and Delinquency Prevention.* Washington, DC: U.S. Government Printing Office, 1976, p. 9.

alternatives. Figure 13.1 shows a sample diagram of the juvenile justice system. The following discussion will cover briefly the significant stages of juvenile case processing.

The Jurisdiction of the Juvenile Justice System

Cases heard and decided by juvenile courts are considered within the jurisdiction of these courts. While states vary in their upper age limits for juvenile court jurisdiction, the lower age limit varies among states as well, with several states using the age of 7 as the minimum. This minimum age follows early English common law precedent, where those under the age of 7 are presumed incapable of formulating criminal intent, are not responsible for their actions, and must be

TABLE 13.3

Upper Age of Original Juvenile Court Jurisdiction, 1999

Age	State(s)
15	Connecticut, New York, North Carolina
16	Georgia, Illinois, Louisiana, Massachusetts, Michigan, Missouri, New Hampshire, South Carolina, Texas, Wisconsin
17	Alabama, Alaska, Arizona, Arkansas, California, Colorado, Delaware, District of Columbia, Florida, Hawaii, Idaho, Indiana, Iowa, Kansas, Kentucky, Maine, Maryland, Minnesota, Mississippi, Montana, Nebraska, Nevada, New Jersey, New Mexico, North Dakota, Ohio, Oklahoma, Oregon, Pennsylvania, Rhode Island, South Dakota, Tennessee, Utah, Vermont, Virginia, Washington, West Virginia, Wyoming, federal system

Source: Adapted from P. Griffin. *OJJDP Statistical Briefing Book.* Washington, DC: Office of Juvenile Justice and Delinquency Prevention, 2002.

supervised by agencies other than juvenile courts. Wisconsin, for example, has set the minimum age for juvenile court jurisdiction at 12, while other states have set the minimum age at 10. Again, no single minimum age typifies the age jurisdiction of all juvenile courts in the United States. Table 13.3 shows the upper age limit of original juvenile court jurisdiction for 1999 (Griffin 2002).

Table 13.3 shows that for most states, the upper age limit for the jurisdiction of juvenile courts is 17. Several states use age 16 as the upper jurisdictional age limit, while three states use age 15 as the upper jurisdictional age limit (Griffin 2002).

Police Actions or Other Reports

Juvenile contact with juvenile court most often occurs whenever police officers encounter juveniles committing an offense or behaving in suspicious ways on city streets (Hassell and Maguire 2001). For instance, action is taken by police who may observe juveniles breaking and entering, vandalizing automobiles or homes, joyriding in stolen vehicles, soliciting for prostitution, or committing other delinquent offenses (Taylor et al. 2001). Also, reports by neighbors of child abuse by a juvenile's parents, obvious neglect, and/or abandonment will also lead police or social services agents to investigate and intervene (Finkelhor and Ormrod 2001).

Schools are another source of juvenile **referrals** through **petitions.** Referrals are either formal or informal notifications delivered to juvenile courts and/or court officers that a juvenile has committed either a status or delinquent offense or is a CHINS (Christensen and Crank, 2001). Petitions are formal documents prepared by police officers, school officials, parents, or other interested persons who allege wrongdoing, misconduct, or a lack of supervision/control, which result in having a juvenile's case brought to the attention of the juvenile court (Black 1990:1145–1146). Thus, if a juvenile is chronically truant from school, the school principal may petition the juvenile court to hear the allegation that the juvenile is truant. This is accomplished through the filing of a petition. If a juvenile assaults another juvenile or steals something of value, a petition may be filed against that juvenile alleging the assault or theft. An investigation of the allegations will be conducted. Depending upon the sophistication of the jurisdiction, this intervention will result in juveniles being taken to a juvenile hall or other juvenile facility for further processing, to jail for further investigation, or perhaps to a community agency such as child welfare, human services, or child and family services (Clark 2001).

Whether juveniles are placed in detention centers temporarily or in jails again depends upon the elaborateness of arrangements and facilities in the jurisdiction (Butts and Adams 2001). In larger cities, **juvenile detention centers** are temporary shelters supervised by adults where juveniles may be housed and provided with food and other necessities while parents or guardians are notified. These detention centers also serve as temporary confinement facilities for juveniles who are alleged to have committed serious offenses and who must await further processing by the juvenile court. Reasons for detention include the absence of other forms of juvenile care in the particular community, the threat of the juvenile to the safety of others, the juvenile's protection, and to assure the appearance of the juvenile at a later juvenile court hearing. The length of detention varies from an hour in emergency holdover cases to two years, depending on the nature of the detention facility (Knupfer 2001).

Therefore, police or other authorities may take the following preliminary actions:

1. They may counsel juveniles and release them to the custody of their parents or guardians.
2. They may refer and divert the juvenile to the care and responsibility of community resources.
3. They may cite the juvenile, refer the juvenile to juvenile intake for further processing, and release the juvenile to the temporary custody of parents or guardians.
4. They may transport the juvenile to jail, juvenile hall or to detention center for further processing.

Intake

Intake is the first screening for juvenile offenders. This is a more or less formal procedure where a juvenile is interviewed and information is gathered about the youth's offense or condition (Glaser et al. 2001). Juveniles placed in detention centers, juvenile halls, jails, or community agencies are subsequently screened or evaluated by an **intake officer.** Intake officers are usually juvenile probation officers under the administration of the probation department of the community or county (Castellano and Ferguson 1998). It is the responsibility of intake officers to closely examine each juvenile's case and make a professional determination of what further action should be taken. On the basis of the seriousness of the offense(s) alleged, the apparent responsibility of the parents, and/or the manifest needs of the juvenile, the intake officer will take one of the following actions:

1. Intake officers will warn the juvenile and/or parents/guardians and release the juvenile to the parent's custody. This releases the juvenile from further involvement with the juvenile justice system.

2. Intake officers will release the juvenile to the custody of parents or guardians, but the officer will schedule a future juvenile court appearance where the juvenile's attendance is required.

3. Intake officers will refer and remand the juvenile to the care and supervision of some appropriate community agency or institution for particular care and treatment. This transfer of responsibility shifts the decision for releasing the juvenile to agency officials. They determine later on the basis of their own evaluations whether further juvenile justice action is warranted or whether the juvenile should be released to parents or guardians.

4. Intake officers will cause the juvenile to be detained in a detention facility or shelter to await a detention hearing, will file a petition to have the juvenile court determine the ultimate disposition of the juvenile, or both.

In a growing number of jurisdictions, community assessment centers are being established for the purpose of determining the needs of juvenile offenders and what types of services they require. These assessment centers are regarded as single points of entry and offer 24-hour centralized intake for juveniles who come into contact with the juvenile justice system. Some of the goals of these community assessment centers are to reduce law enforcement time devoted to processing juveniles, create a central booking and receiving facility specifically for juvenile offenders, accelerate a juvenile's access to treatment, pool resources from a variety of agencies, and provide referrals for parents and their children (Oldenettel and Wordes 2000:4).

Juvenile Court

All juvenile courts are civil bodies. This means that juveniles cannot acquire a criminal record directly from juvenile court actions, where the actions remain confined to juvenile courts. In most jurisdictions, juveniles are brought to the attention of juvenile courts through filing petitions. In the case of petitions directed to juvenile court, these are applications for the court to consider whether the juvenile is delinquent, neglected, dependent, or otherwise in need of a special disposition or care (Brown 1999). These petitions may be filed by anyone, including the police, who may allege serious or nonserious juvenile misconduct (misdemeanors, felonies, runaway behavior); school officials, who may allege truancy or incorrigibility; parents, who may allege unruliness or unmanageability; neighbors, who may allege child sexual abuse, neglect, or mistreatment; or intake officers, who wish official court action of some type to be taken (Horton 2002).

The actual juvenile court proceeding is quasi-adversarial, with a juvenile court prosecutor bringing specific charges against the juvenile. If the juvenile or juvenile's parents/guardians choose, the juvenile may be represented by counsel to defend against the charges alleged. Action on the petition by the juvenile judge may be a ruling that the juvenile is, indeed, delinquent. Or the ruling may result in a dismissal of charges (Lederman, Osofsky, and Katz 2001). For less serious juvenile offenders, juvenile court action may be avoided through conventional methods similar to those used for certain low-risk adult offenders in the criminal justice system. For instance, prior to any formal adjudicatory proceeding, juveniles may participate in restorative justice or mediation, where a third-party arbiter enables offenders and their victims to resolve their disputes in various ways. Restorative justice conferencing enables some low-risk youths to avoid the taint of a juvenile prosecution and the adverse effects of being labeled a delinquent (Morris and Maxwell 2001).

Adjudications and Dispositions

The action taken by a juvenile judge is an **adjudication** of the charges brought against the juvenile. An adjudication is a formal court judgment or determination. Thus, a juvenile court judge may believe the facts alleged in the petition and adjudicate the juvenile a delinquent or status offender. Or the judge may determine that the facts are not sustained as set forth in the petition. Therefore, the juvenile is adjudicated nondelinquent and is subsequently freed from the juvenile justice system. Sometimes juvenile court proceedings are called **adjudicatory proceedings.** Thus, a juvenile may be adjudicated delinquent; adjudicated dependent, neglected, or abused; adjudicated a status offender; or some other type of adjudication (Mears 2001). If a juvenile court judge adjudicates a youth as either a delinquent or status offender, then the case will be **disposed.** Several types of **dispositions** are available to judges. These are the equivalent of sentences meted out in criminal courts. But in juvenile courts, these are not called sentences; rather, these actions are called dispositions. These dispositions include: nominal, conditional, and custodial.

Nominal Dispositions.   **Nominal dispositions** consist of verbal warnings or reprimands by the judge, and these warnings normally result in the juvenile's return to the custody of parents or guardians.

Conditional Dispositions.   **Conditional dispositions** vary among jurisdictions. But the usual conditional dispositions imposed by juvenile court judges include one or more of the following: fines or restitution to victims, some form of community service, some form of community supervision such as probation under the administrative authority of juvenile probation officers, or a suspension of one or more of these conditions once they have been imposed as the sentence. Conditional sanctions may include court-ordered networking with social agencies where youths can receive help with various kinds of problems, including emotional dependency and self-definitions. A community ABC program stresses accountability, belief, and cooperation in assisting youths in acquiring better coping strategies. The ABC program is designed for especially challenging adolescents who are delinquents and court-referred (Clark 1999).

One increasingly used method for adjudicating juveniles is through **youth courts, peer courts,** or **teen courts.** These courts are comprised of one's school peers and associates, and they are designed for low-risk first offenders. Other juveniles hear one's case and decide the punishment if guilt is determined. The proceedings are overseen by a juvenile court officer, such as a juvenile court judge. Almost always the punishment is some form of probation with conditions, including restitution to one or more victims, community service, or some other activity that serves to heighten offender accountability. A great deal of conventional court protocol occurs during such proceedings, and the results have been impressive. Recidivism rates of juveniles where youth courts have determined one's guilt or innocence have been quite low. These courts are used in both the United States and Canada (Peterson, Ruck, and Koegl 2001).

Custodial Dispositions.   **Custodial dispositions** have several different forms. Youths may be placed in some type of custody for a period of time. The custody may be secure or nonsecure (Fader et al. 2001). Secure custody might be an industrial school or reform school. These are the equivalent of prisons or jails for adults. In the case of nonsecure custody, the juvenile may be assigned a foster home if the juvenile's parents are judged irresponsible or inadequate. Or the juvenile may be placed in a group home, a camp ranch, or school, where supervision and restrictions are minimal. One facility is Lakeside Center, a residential treatment program in St. Louis, Missouri. Referred youths receive job assistance training and counseling, together with other needed services (Sawicki, Schaeffer, and Thies 1999). Together with the conditional option, these custodial options make up juvenile corrections. Before we examine these correctional options, however, some of the more important constitutional rights of juveniles will be described.

CONSTITUTIONAL RIGHTS OF JUVENILES

Under the *parens patriae* doctrine, many different kinds of courts assumed responsibility for juveniles until the early 1960s. Juvenile judges and other court officials overseeing juvenile matters functioned on the basis of **in loco parentis,** meaning literally "in the place of parents," and they made important decisions about juvenile dispositions. These decisions were largely unquestioned and unchallenged. However, in recent years the U.S. Supreme Court has vested juveniles with several important constitutional rights (Butts and Sanborn 1999). At the same time, juvenile courts have been forced to acknowledge these rights under the constitution and make decisions consistent with them. When juveniles are arrested by police today for theft or some other offense, certain constitutional rights automatically attach or become relevant. Police must advise juvenile arrestees of their right to an attorney and to refrain from further questioning, if they so desire. The juvenile court trial has become an adversarial proceeding much like criminal court for adults. The path toward obtaining these rights has been long and arduous. Several important landmark juvenile cases have made these rights possible (Sanborn 2001).

Kent v. United States (1966)

Kent v. United States (1966) was the first important landmark juvenile case heard by the U.S. Supreme Court. Morris Kent was a 16-year-old residing in the District of Columbia. He was arrested by police and charged with rape, burglary, and robbery. When police first arrested Kent, they interrogated him extensively about the offenses. He was not told that he could remain silent. Under the circumstances, this was a right he did not yet have. He was also denied access to an attorney. This was another right he did not yet have. Under a lengthy interrogation, Kent confessed to the crimes. The juvenile judge in his case, on his own authority, transferred Kent to criminal court jurisdiction where Kent could be prosecuted as an adult for the crimes alleged. No hearing was held regarding the transfer and no reasons were given by the judge to explain it. But the implications for Kent were devastating. As a juvenile, if adjudicated as delinquent on any of the charges, Kent faced incarceration in a reform school until age 21, whereupon he would be released. As an adult tried on those same charges, Kent faced the maximum sentence of the death penalty under District of Columbia statutes.

In criminal court, the jury found him guilty of the crimes alleged. However, the jury also found him to be insane when the rape was committed. Thus, he was sentenced to a mental institution to be treated until sane. At that time, he would face a 30- to 90-year incarceration for the previous conviction offenses. Kent's attorney appealed to the U.S. Supreme Court. The Supreme Court overturned his conviction. The *Kent* case is significant because of why his conviction was overturned. First, the U.S. Supreme Court said, Kent was denied a hearing before he was transferred to criminal court by the juvenile judge. Second, they said, he was denied access to an attorney during his interrogation by police and later at the proceeding when a decision was made about his transfer to criminal court. Third, his attorney should have been permitted access to all reports and records relating to the transfer decision. And fourth, the judge should have furnished Kent's attorney and parents with a statement outlining the reasons for the transfer.

In re Gault (1967)

In 1967, the U.S. Supreme Court decided the case of *In re Gault*, perhaps the most important of all landmark juvenile cases. Gerald Gault was a 15-year-old who was arrested in 1964 in Gila County, Arizona, for making an obscene telephone call to a female neighbor, Mrs. Cook. Gault's parents were both working at the time and neither was notified of his arrest. Gault was interrogated extensively and detained overnight in a local juvenile detention center. Later, a petition was filed by a juvenile probation officer alleging his delinquency, although the grounds were not specified in the petition. The juvenile judge ordered a hearing several days later. The hearing was held, no witnesses were called, no one was sworn to testify, and on the basis of the limited factual information available, the judge sentenced Gault to the Arizona Industrial School (a prison for juveniles) until he reached 21 years of age. This amounted to a 6-year sentence for allegedly making an obscene telephone call. Had an adult been convicted of the same offense, the maximum penalty imposed would have been up to a $50 fine and/or a 2-month jail term.

Gault's parents obtained an attorney, and eventually through appeals, the U.S. Supreme Court heard and decided the case in 1967. The bases for Gault's appeal involved several alleged constitutional rights violations that were otherwise extended to adults. Gault's appeal alleged that he was not notified of the specific charges against him, he was not apprised of his right to counsel, he was not permitted to confront and cross-examine witnesses against him such as Mrs. Cook or the probation officer, he was not advised of his right against self-incrimination, and he was denied the right to a transcript of the proceedings against him as well as an appellate review of his case.

The U.S. Supreme Court said that Arizona was in error in denying Gault several significant rights. In their landmark decision, they established the following rights for juveniles:

1. The right to an attorney.
2. The right to be notified of charges.

3. The right to confront and cross-examine witnesses.

4. The right against self-incrimination.

Although Gault's attorney complained that a transcript was not made available of the proceedings and an appellate review provision was not prescribed according to Arizona statutes, the U.S. Supreme Court did not take action on these two points. They concluded that since they struck down Arizona's other action against Gault, the appellate review criticism was irrelevant. Furthermore, while the Supreme Court said it is not necessary for juvenile courts to furnish transcripts of their proceedings, they indicated that it would be necessary in the future for juvenile courts to bear the responsibility for reconstructing all significant events if challenged by juvenile defendants. This would mean that juvenile judges would be subject to cross-examination by defense counsel in later hearings as well as other burdensome actions. Within a few months of the *Gault* decision, the Arizona legislature issued new statutes providing for full juvenile appellate reviews, with a strong recommendation to juvenile court judges that transcripts be maintained of all proceedings before these courts.

In re Winship (1970) and *McKeiver v. Pennsylvania* (1971)

Two other landmark cases involving juveniles occurred in 1970–1971. *In re Winship* (1970) involved a 12-year-old New York juvenile, Samuel Winship, who was arrested for stealing $100 from a woman's handbag. The juvenile judge found Winship guilty of the charge, adjudicated him delinquent, and sentenced him to a New York juvenile training school for 18 months. The standard of evidence used in Winship's case was "the preponderance of evidence," a standard typically associated with civil case dispositions and tort actions.

Winship's case was appealed on the grounds that the criminal court standard, proof beyond a reasonable doubt, should have been used in his case rather than the civil standard. New York authorities contended that because juvenile court actions are civil in nature, the preponderance of evidence standard was acceptable. However, the U.S. Supreme Court overturned the verdict in Winship's case, concluding that where substantial loss of freedom may occur (such as confinement for 18 months in a juvenile training school), a more stringent standard is necessary to protect juveniles. Thus, the criminal court proof beyond a reasonable doubt standard has been mandated for juvenile courts in all cases where loss of freedom is a possible penalty.

The U.S. Supreme Court decided *McKeiver v. Pennsylvania* in 1971. In this case, Joseph McKeiver, a 16-year-old, was charged with robbery, receiving stolen goods, and larceny. His attorney requested a trial by jury but was denied one by the juvenile judge. Ordinarily, in criminal cases, if the possible incarcerative penalty for offenses alleged is 6 months or more, the defendant may request and be entitled to a **jury trial.** In previous decisions, the U.S. Supreme Court decided in *Duncan v. Louisiana* (1968) that a jury trial was mandatory if requested by a defendant where serious offenses were alleged. Many states interpreted this decision to mean felony charges against criminal defendants rather than misdemeanor charges. However, the six months or more standard was made explicit in *Baldwin v. New York* (1970). Now, any criminal defendant who may suffer incarceration of six months or more if convicted of either felony or misdemeanor charges is entitled to a jury trial in any state, if requested.

The attorney for McKeiver believed the charges would conceivably result in McKeiver's detention in a juvenile facility for a lengthy period, probably well-beyond the 6-month standard established by *Baldwin*, and no doubt this possibility influenced McKeiver's subsequent appeal. But the U.S. Supreme Court rejected the appeal and declared that juveniles do not have a right to a jury trial. They gave many reasons for their decision in McKeiver's case, but their decision was influenced largely by the fear that a juvenile right to jury trials would greatly transform the juvenile court into largely an adversarial system. This would effectively undermine any rehabilitative potential the juvenile court could invoke within the remaining parts of the *parens patriae* authority it possessed. Thus, the U.S. Supreme Court left juvenile court judges with the authority to grant juveniles jury trials only if the judge wished to grant them. In short, whether a juvenile receives a jury trial is purely discretionary on the part of the juvenile judge.

WAIVERS, TRANSFERS, AND CERTIFICATIONS

Historically, juvenile courts have sought to insulate juvenile offenders from the trappings of adult courts in an effort to minimize the possible criminogenic effects of labeling resulting from exposure to criminal-like case processing. Informally handled juvenile cases are common, and diversion is used extensively to decrease one's contact with the juvenile justice system (Sturges 2001). One reason for the greater use of diversion in juvenile cases is a suspected link to adult crime-producing processes that often emerge before the end of adolescence. Minimizing juvenile exposure to the juvenile justice system may result in less adult offending by these same juveniles later (Paternoster, Brame, and Farrington 2001). The use of probation is considerable, even where serious offenses have been committed or alleged. But during the last few decades, the public has become increasingly concerned with the apparent leniency of the courts in dealing with adult criminals as well as juveniles. The rehabilitation model of corrections has gradually ben replaced by a more punitive, just-deserts rationale that seeks to adjust the punishment to fit the crime committed. One result of this philosophical shift has been the implementation of large-scale sentencing reforms at the state and federal levels.

As the amount of violent crime committed by juveniles has increased, public disenchantment with juvenile case processing has also intensified (Snyder 2002). The result has been a noticeable policy shift toward the criminal court processing of more serious juvenile offenders and the adoption of a more punitive philosophy regarding juvenile sanctions generally (Feld 2001). There is greater use of criminal courts for punishing youthful offenders. Juveniles are sent from juvenile courts to criminal courts through actions known as **waivers, transfers,** or **certifications.** Waivers or transfers refer to relocating jurisdiction over juveniles from juvenile courts to criminal courts. Thus, juvenile court jurisdiction over particular juveniles is waived or transferred to criminal court judges. An increasing number of jurisdictions are using risk assessment devices for the purpose of waiver decision making (Hoge 2001). Once a juvenile's case has been transferred or waived to criminal courts, then the juvenile is processed as though he or she were an adult. For all practical purposes, all juveniles transferred to criminal courts are considered adults for the purpose of imposing criminal court penalties, including life without parole and capital punishment.

Certification is the process of declaring a juvenile to be an adult for the purpose of a criminal prosecution. In Texas, for instance, juveniles who have committed serious offenses may be certified as adults and sent to criminal courts for processing as though they were adult offenders (Arrigona, Hodgson, and Reed 1999). For all practical purposes, the objectives of certification, waivers, or transfers are identical (Snyder 2002). Juveniles charged with serious offenses are considered adults so that criminal courts may impose harsher punishments if these persons are subsequently convicted of crimes.

There are four types of waiver actions: judicial waivers, direct file, statutory exclusion, and demand waivers.

Judicial Waivers

The largest numbers of waivers from juvenile to criminal court annually come about as the result of direct judicial action. **Judicial waivers** give the juvenile court judge the authority to decide whether to waive jurisdiction and transfer the case to criminal court (Salekin, Rogers, and Ustad 2001). There are three kinds of judicial waivers. The first type, **discretionary waivers,** empower the judge to waive jurisdiction over the juvenile and transfer the case to criminal court. Because of this type of waiver, judicial waivers are sometimes known as discretionary waivers. The second type of judicial waiver is the **mandatory waiver.** In the case of a mandatory waiver, the juvenile court judge *must* waive jurisdiction over the juvenile if probable cause exists that the juvenile committed the alleged offense. The third type of judicial waiver is called a **presumptive waiver.** Under the presumptive waiver scenario, the burden of proof concerning a transfer decision is shifted from the state to the juvenile. It requires that certain juveniles be waived to criminal court unless they can prove that they are suited to juvenile rehabilitation.

Direct File

Whenever offenders are screened at intake and referred to the juvenile court for possible prosecution, prosecutors in various jurisdictions will conduct further screenings of these youths (Massachusetts Statistical Analysis Center 2001). They determine which cases merit further action and formal adjudication by judges. Not all cases sent to prosecutors by intake officers automatically result in subsequent formal juvenile court action. Under **direct file,** the prosecutor has the sole authority to decide whether any given juvenile case will be heard in criminal court or juvenile court. Essentially, the prosecutor decides which court should have jurisdiction over the juvenile. Prosecutors with direct file power are said to have **concurrent jurisdiction** (Feld 2001). In Florida, for example, prosecutors have concurrent jurisdiction. They may file extremely serious charges (e.g., murder, rape, aggravated assault, robbery) against youths in criminal courts and present cases to grand juries for indictment action. Or prosecutors may decide to file the same cases in the juvenile court.

Statutory Exclusion

Statutory exclusion means that certain juvenile offenders are automatically excluded from the juvenile court's original jurisdiction (Snyder, Sickmund, and Poe-Yamagata 2000). Legislatures of various states declare a particular list of offenses to be excluded from the jurisdiction of juvenile courts. A particular age range accompanies this list of offenses. In Illinois, for example, if a 16-year-old juvenile is charged with murder, rape, or aggravated assault, this particular juvenile is automatically excluded from the jurisdiction of the juvenile court. Instead, the case will be heard in criminal court. In 1997, 16 states had statutory exclusion provisions and excluded certain types of offenders from juvenile court jurisdiction. Because state legislatures created statutory exclusion provisions, this waiver action is sometimes known as a **legislative waiver** (Myers 2001). And because these provisions mandate the automatic waiver of juveniles to criminal court, they are also known as automatic waivers.

Demand Waivers

Under certain conditions and in selected jurisdictions, juveniles may submit motions for **demand waiver** actions. Demand waiver actions are requests or motions filed by juveniles and their attorneys to have their cases transferred from juvenile courts to criminal courts. One reason is that most U.S. jurisdictions do not provide jury trials for juveniles in juvenile courts as a matter of right (*McKeiver v. Pennsylvania* 1971).

Other Types of Waivers

The Reverse Waiver. The **reverse waiver** is an action by the criminal court to transfer direct file or statutory exclusion cases from criminal court back to juvenile court, usually at the recommendation of the prosecutor (Snyder, Sickmund, and Poe-Yamagata 2000). Juveniles who would be involved in these **reverse waiver hearings** would be those who were automatically sent to criminal court because of statutory exclusion. Thus, criminal court judges can send at least some of these juveniles back to the jurisdiction of the juvenile court.

The Once An Adult/Always An Adult Provision. The **once an adult/always an adult provision** is perhaps the most serious for affected juvenile offenders. This provision means that once juveniles have been convicted in criminal court, they are forever after considered adults for the purpose of criminal prosecutions. The once an adult/always an adult provision is not as serious as it seems. Each jurisdiction must keep track of each juvenile offender previously convicted of a crime. This record-keeping is difficult. Some juveniles move away from the jurisdiction where they were originally convicted. Information sharing among juvenile courts throughout the United States is extremely limited or nonexistent. Thus, often the intent of the once an adult/always an adult provision can be defeated simply by relocating elsewhere.

Although there has been a substantial increase in the rate of juvenile violence, the proportionate number of violent juveniles is relatively small (Caldwell and Van Rybroek 2001). For instance, in 2000, less than one-half of 1 percent of all juveniles in the United States ages 10 to 17 were arrested for violent crimes (Snyder 2002). About 6 percent of all juveniles were arrested in 1994. Of these, about 7 percent were arrested for violent crimes (e.g., murder and nonnegligent manslaughter, forcible rape, robbery, and aggravated assault). Public concern about juvenile violence is prompted in part by the role of juvenile gangs (McCluskey 2002). With research reporting increases in the number of juvenile gangs, important organizational changes, and the contribution of gangs to the juvenile homicide rate, reasons for this concern may be valid (Triplet and Ross 1998:29). However, certain types of violence among juveniles, such as school violence, may be somewhat exaggerated. While some school violence occurs, media sensationalism surrounding school violence events gives the impression that it is both pervasive and increasing. This is a questionable conclusion (Menifield, Rose, and Homa 2001).

All states have implemented juvenile justice reforms resulting in greater use of waivers (Snyder 2002). In fact, most states have made it easier to transfer youths to criminal courts for prosecution as adults. From 1992 through 1997, for example, 44 states and the District of Columbia passed laws making it easier for juveniles to be tried as adults. Most of these changes pertained to modifications of statutory exclusions. Seven states established exclusion provisions, while 28 states expanded the list of crimes eligible for exclusion, while 7 states lowered the age limits for exclusion (Torbet and Szymanski 1998).

Some juveniles do not want to have their cases transferred from juvenile courts to criminal courts. They may want to contest these waiver actions by juvenile court judges or prosecutors. Juveniles in all jurisdictions are entitled to a waiver or transfer hearing and the right to an attorney at such a hearing. They may present evidence in their own behalf for the purpose of defeating waivers contemplated against them. Although juveniles and their attorneys may formally oppose waivers or certification, the ultimate discretion to transfer juveniles to criminal courts rests exclusively with juvenile court judges. It is rare that transfer hearings result in favorable rulings for juveniles (Champion and Mays 1991). Essentially, if the juvenile court wants a particular juvenile transferred to criminal court, there is little or nothing juveniles or their attorneys can do to prevent such transfers or waivers.

Since the early 1990s, the number of juveniles transferred to criminal courts for processing has generally ranged between 10,000 and 13,000 cases. During the early 1990s, the amount of juvenile violent offending increased by almost 190 percent. This great increase in juvenile violence triggered an official response to transfer more juveniles to criminal courts as a get-tough measure designed to deter violent juvenile offenders. One result was to transfer proportionately larger numbers of violent youthful offenders to criminal courts for processing. However, violent juvenile offenders transferred to criminal courts have always made up less than half of all those waived. When the rate of violent juvenile offending declined slightly in the late 1990s, the emphasis upon prosecuting violent juveniles as adults also waned. In fact, between 1994 and 1999, juvenile violent offense cases waived to criminal courts declined by 52 percent. Presently, property and drug offenders account for approximately 60 percent of all transferred juveniles each year (Puzzanchera et al. 2002).

Thus, there continue to be significant inconsistencies among U.S. juvenile courts concerning which juveniles are transferred to criminal courts. The public often thinks that the most serious juvenile offenders are targeted for waivers, but this objective has never been realized. Nonserious chronic juvenile offenders who commit drug or property offenses have been transferred in larger numbers compared with violent juveniles. One reason is that these less serious offenders appear before juvenile court judges frequently. A result is that many of the most persistent nonviolent juveniles are transferred to criminal courts simply because juvenile court judges tire of dealing with them. If it is anticipated by these judges that criminal courts will deal more harshly with these less serious offenders, then these juvenile court judges are seriously mistaken.

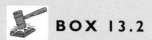 **BOX 13.2**

Who Should We Believe? Juvenile Advocates or National Institute of Justice Statistics?

According to some youth advocates at the Justice Policy Institute, juvenile violence is decreasing in the United States. Between 1988 and 1995, juvenile violence escalated by nearly 190 percent. During the next few years, there were small downward blips in juvenile violence of perhaps 10 percent. While this minuscule drop in juvenile violence is touted by some law enforcement agencies as proof of their effectiveness at combating juvenile delinquency, other sources of information suggest that the overall amount of youth violence is still increasing, despite the positive statistics to the contrary. Whether youth violence is increasing or decreasing depends on who you ask. If you ask someone from the Justice Policy Institute in Washington, DC, or the Children's Law Center in Covington, Kentucky, they will tell you that school violence is declining, and rapidly. For instance, they claim that between 1993 and 1998, a 56 percent drop in youth homicide arrests has occurred. Of course, there are other forms of violence besides homicide that attract national attention to juveniles. Juvenile advocate groups blame the media and public misconceptions that continue to fan the flames that juvenile violence is continuing to escalate and is out of control. They oppose zero-tolerance policies in schools, where mere threats of violence can get a student expelled or worse. Criminal charges have been filed against students who threaten school officials or schools with bomb scares. For instance, a 17-year-old juvenile was expelled from a Chicago high school in 1998 after he shot a paper clip at a cafeteria worker, drawing a small amount of blood. He was charged with disorderly conduct. In Arlington, Virginia, two 10-year-old boys were suspended for putting soapy water in a teacher's drink. Felony charges against them were later dismissed. One student was expelled in Madeira, Ohio, when he put graffiti on school election signs indicating that there were bombs in the student restrooms.

Public polls indicate that a majority of U.S. citizens believe that youth violence is increasing and that youths are committing increasingly violent acts at younger ages. A *Washington Post* poll in 1998 showed, for instance, that 66 percent of 1,000 persons polled believed that children are becoming more violent. According to Vincent Schiraldi of the Justice Policy Institute, "We've got kids getting kicked out of school for saying 'bang-bang' to each other. It's no more fair to stereotype them all as school shooters than to stereotype all adults as Timothy McVeigh, who bombed a federal building in Oklahoma City." While some persons believe that the zero-tolerance policies in effect in many U.S. schools are overreactions to serious juvenile violence, there is a growing use of metal detectors and more firearms and dangerous weapons are being detected. It has been found that often, verbalized threats by students about future planned violence or retaliation against other students have become a reality, with many students killed or wounded in the process. Joking about bombs in restrooms in high schools may be the equivalent about joking at airports about placing bombs in checked luggage. Presently, it is a crime to joke about such incidents in front of airlines personnel, and offenders can be arrested and prosecuted. Should the same standard apply to students in schools?

Jim Pasco, executive director of the Fraternal Order of Police, a 285,000-member police union, says that "Kids have to know there are consequences to illegal activity. The real issue is how can they (officials) be tough without creating the perception that they are oppressing these kids?"

Should the zero-tolerance policies currently in effect in many schools continue? Is an ounce of prevention worth a pound of cure? Where should officials draw the line on the type of language permitted by students in school settings? Is there such a thing as too much caution when the lives of innocent school children are at stake? What do you think?

Source: Adapted from the Associated Press, "Advocates: Youth Crimes Declining," April 12, 2000.

Criminal court outcomes of waived cases are consistently disappointing. About half of all waived cases each year are either downgraded or dismissed outright. Another 35 to 40 percent result in probation for transferred juveniles. Only about 10 to 12 percent of all transferred juveniles each year will actually serve time in jail or prison, and most will serve relatively short sentences. There are many reasons for these outcomes. Dismissed or downgraded cases often lack sufficient evidence for convictions. Police officers and criminalists may not be as rigorous in collecting and preserving evidence from crime scenes where the perpetrators are juveniles. Youthfulness is often a mitigating factor in criminal courts where juries decide the cases. Prosecutors must prioritize which cases they will prosecute, more often opting to prosecute adult offenders rather than juvenile offenders. Thus, juveniles may actually benefit from transfers to criminal courts, where they are more likely to be treated leniently (DeFrances and Strom 1997; Snyder, Sickmund, and Poe-Yamagata 2000).

Juvenile Exploitation of Juvenile Court Leniency.   Some observers claim that most juveniles who commit serious offenses know that there is a small likelihood that they will be confined in either a juvenile industrial school or adult prison following their arrest and adjudication as delinquents (Baron, Forde, and Kennedy 2001). Most often juvenile court judges impose probation on these juveniles, even repeat serious juvenile offenders. Thus, it is suggested that at least some juveniles use their status as juveniles to great advantage in violating the law. Their subsequent lenient treatment from juvenile court judges strengthens their resolve to recidivate, despite the increased chances of secure confinement, even if they are apprehended again in the same jurisdiction (Collins, Schwartz, and Epstein 2001). Compared with other countries, such as Germany, where the maximum penalty a juvenile court can impose is 10 years, it would seem that these criticisms about U.S. juvenile court leniency are somewhat warranted (Schulz 2001).

To some extent, judicial leniency toward juveniles is supported by public opinion. In 1992, for instance, telephone interviews with 681 adult householders in Georgia were directed toward determining their views about whether juvenile murderers should be tried as adults (Stalans and Henry 1994). About 76 percent of all respondents preferred juvenile court as the better place to hear these cases, where first-time offenders were involved. The respondents were divided over whether juveniles with prior records of violent offending should be tried in adult courts rather than juvenile courts, however. About 48 percent believed that such juveniles should have their cases heard in juvenile courts. Their thinking was influenced by the belief that juvenile courts would make decisions more on the basis of the best interests of youths rather than due process considerations. Unfortunately, little continues to be known about juvenile murderers and their dispositions, largely because of their infrequency (Heckel and Shumaker 2001). Much of the existing research consists of case studies of individual juvenile murderers. Thus, the generalizability of such investigations is severely limited (Myers 2002).

One reaction to this apparent juvenile court leniency where serious crimes are involved has been that many state legislatures have authorized the automatic transfer of serious young offenders from the juvenile court to the criminal court in order that more severe punishments can be imposed (Smith 2003). This is particularly true in cases where the death penalty can be applied, a sentence that is well beyond the purview of juvenile judges (Streib 1987). However, some evidence suggests that transfers of juveniles to the jurisdiction of adult criminal courts do not automatically result in more serious punishments. In fact, some authorities suggest that just the opposite results are frequently observed (Champion and Mays 1991). Further, some observers believe that automatic transfers of juveniles to criminal courts in those jurisdictions with automatic transfer provisions are overly simplistic and do not take into account mitigating factors, such as previous child abuse or other background problems (Bilchik 2003:21; Levine et al. 2001).

JUVENILE CORRECTIONS

The History of Juvenile Corrections

During the 1800s and early 1900s, juvenile matters in the United States were handled by a variety of civil courts and nonlegal institutions such as welfare agencies. The doctrine under which juveniles were managed and processed was called **parens patriae,** which means "parent of the country" (Black 1990:1114). Historically, this term was a part of English common law during the medieval period, and it meant that juvenile matters were within the purview of the King and his agents, usually chancellors and other officials in various regions. Figuratively, the King was the "father of the country" and assumed responsibility for all juveniles. Through the centuries this term was accepted by most jurisdictions. It eventually carried over into U.S. juvenile matters and influenced significantly the discretion exercised over juveniles by adult courts and other institutions (American Correctional Association 1992).

Early efforts to deal with juvenile offenders in the United States led to the establishment of the first public reformatory, the **New York House of Refuge,** organized in New York City in 1825 by the Society for the Prevention of Pauperism (Hess and Clement 1993). The manifest goals of this house of refuge were to provide poor, abused, or orphaned youths with food, clothing, and lodging, although in return, hard work, discipline, and study were expected. Since there was little centralized organization to these houses of refuge, it is difficult to determine the impact these facilities exerted on delinquency in any city area.

Charles Loring Brace set up a New York Children's Aid Society in 1853, which functioned primarily as a placement service for parentless children. The term *juvenile delinquency* was seldom used during the early 1800s, because public authorities stressed parental control of children and regarded youthful misbehaviors as lack of discipline rather than something that should be dealt with more formally (Mennel 1983:198). Many early institutions designed to care for and reform juveniles were operated under private, charitable, and religious sponsorship. The Civil War was followed by the Reconstruction Period and vast industrialization. The war had left many families fatherless, and in the years that followed, many of these families gravitated to urban areas seeking employment in factories and shops. Many children were exploited by so-called sweat shops in the absence of child labor laws, and a large number of them roamed the streets unattended while their parents worked long hours at various jobs. **Children's tribunals** were created in different states, including Massachusetts and New York, in order to deal with youths charged with committing crimes. The first statute authorizing such a tribunal to deal with juvenile matters was passed in Massachusetts in 1874 (Hahn 1984). A similar statute was passed in New York in 1892.

Jane Addams established and operated Hull House in 1889, a settlement home for children of immigrant families in Chicago. This home was financed by charitable organizations and philanthropists, and it existed to provide children with activities to alleviate boredom and monotony while their parents were at work. Many children without parents were accommodated by Addams. Teaching children morality, ethics, and certain religious precepts was an integral feature of correctional thought in Addams' day. The influence of Cesare Beccaria, the father of classical criminology, was apparent. Beccaria, an Italian criminologist, wrote in 1764 that the purpose of punishment was to deter others from committing crimes. Furthermore, the punishment should fit the crime. This theorizing was combined with humanitarianism, especially for youthful offenders (Mennel 1983).

In 1899 the Colorado legislature passed the **Compulsory School Act,** which was directed at preventing truancy among juveniles. This act included those youths who were habitually absent from school, wandered about the streets during school hours, and had no obvious business or occupation. These youths were labeled juvenile disorderly persons. Since the Act was aimed primarily at truancy, it is not considered a juvenile court act in a technical sense. The Illinois legislature created the first juvenile court act on July l, 1899. It was called **An Act to Regulate the Treatment and Control of Dependent, Neglected and Delinquent Children.** Between 1899 and 1909, 20 states had passed similar legislation for the establishment of juvenile courts. By 1945, all states had juvenile court systems. However, these systems varied greatly among jurisdictions, and the responsibility for deciding juvenile dispositions rested with a variety of courts (Fox et al. 1998).

The first census of juvenile offenders in public institutions occurred in 1880 and was conducted by the U.S. Bureau of Census. This report disclosed that there were 11,468 juvenile offenders in institutions in the United States. That figure more than doubled by 1904. By 2001 there were 365,836 juveniles under various forms of institutional and noninstitutional supervision in 41 U.S. jurisdictions. Approximately 80 percent of these juveniles were on probation or parole (American Correctional Association 2002:60).

Goals

In October 2000, the Office of Juvenile Justice and Delinquency Prevention administered the first Juvenile Residential Facility Census, and the plan is to conduct such a census every two years thereafter. The 2000 census revealed that there were 3,690 facilities, 3,061 of which held a total of 110,284 juvenile offenders younger than 21. This census does not include data relating to juveniles held in adult jails or prisons, nor does it include facilities used exclusively for mental health or substance abuse treatment or for dependent children (Sickmund 2002:2). About 40 percent of all reporting facilities said that they had more residents than available standard beds. In those cases where juvenile inmates exceeded the number of standard beds, makeshift beds were used to accommodate them. Nationwide, there was an average of nearly five empty standard beds per facility, although this figure masks a wide range—one facility with 567 residents had 124 residents for whom it did not have standard beds, and one facility with 1,207 residents reported 1,181 empty standard beds. In many respects, the various problems associated with adult corrections are re-

Youth correctional centers do much more than warehouse juveniles, such as providing computer training and other types of vocational/educational programming. Courtesy of Custer Youth Correctional Center.

flected in juvenile corrections. This has led to the identification and implementation of several important juvenile correctional goals (Sickmund 2002:1).

The goals of juvenile corrections are similar to those for adult offenders. These include rehabilitation and reintegration, deterrence, isolation and control, prevention, and punishment or retribution. In some respects, these goals are contradictory. For instance, there are those who stress delinquency prevention through keeping juveniles away from the juvenile justice system through diversion and warnings. However, an equally vocal aggregate says that the juvenile justice system is too lenient with offenders and must get tough with them through more certain and stringent penalties for the offenses they commit (Hansen, Orlando, and Backstrom 2001). And a middle ground is attempted by some juvenile correctional programs that stress discipline for punishing as well as rehabilitating (Mears 2001).

Rehabilitation and Reintegration.   Increasingly, community-based publicly and privately operated correctional programs for juveniles have a strong rehabilitative orientation (Mears and Kelly 2002). Some rehabilitative and reintegrative programs stress internalizing responsibilities for one's actions, while other programs attempt to inculcate youths with social and motor skills. Some juveniles have been known to suffer from attention deficit hyperactivity disorder (ADHD), and ADHD has been associated with juvenile violence and antisocial conduct (Vertone and Stroeber 2002). A few programs are oriented toward diagnosing and treating emotionally disturbed youths through alternative medical and social therapies. A Teaching-Family Treatment Model used in 125 group homes throughout the United States currently contains elements such as (a) teaching delinquent youths communication skills, daily living skills, survival skills, educational advancement and study skills, and career skills;

(b) breaking such skills into specific behaviorally defined components; (c) assuring that the delinquents practice the skills in the problem setting; (d) assessing each youth's skill needs; (e) developing individualized teaching plans; and (f) teaching to the individual skill deficits (Weber and Burke 1986).

In Washington, the state legislature established the Juvenile Rehabilitation Administration (JRA) to create and oversee a new rehabilitation model for adjudicated youths. The mission of the JRA is to teach juveniles accountability, provide preventive and rehabilitative programming and public protection, and reduce repetitive criminal behavior using the least restrictive setting necessary (Schmidt et al. 1998:105). The JRA has developed an initial security classification assessment to diagnose and place youths in particular community programs predicted to be beneficial for them. Also, the JRA has included several rehabilitative interventions, where several community residential facilities offer educational and/or vocational programming. A community risk assessment tool is used every three months to classify juveniles who move through the different community programs (Underwood and Falwell 2002). Objective community placement eligibility requirements have also been articulated to address the issues of public safety in relation to treatment progress and seriousness of the crimes committed. Thus, a determination is made of a person's appropriate sentence and how long that person must remain institutionalized, and when the offender is ready for community placement. High system accountability has been created by the Washington system, and the interventions proposed and implemented appear to be working. Other countries, such as England and Australia, are utilizing various types of risk assessment tools for both institutional and community placement decision making (Maguire et al. 2001; Winters-Brooke and Hayes 2001).

Deterrence.   Does the certainty and severity of punishment deter juveniles from committing various offenses? Yes and no. No program has been shown to be 100 percent effective in deterring juveniles from committing delinquent acts or recidivating (Wilson and Petersilia 2002). However, researchers suggest that significant deterrent elements of juvenile correctional programs include clearly stated rules and formal sanctions, anti-criminal modeling and reinforcement, and a high degree of empathy and trust between the juvenile client and staff (Perkins 2001). Traditional counseling, institutionalization, and diversion are considered largely ineffective, according to other investigators (Nurse 2001). The peaks in the amount of different kinds of crime for different youthful age groups suggest that many juveniles appear to grow out of the propensity to commit offenses as the become older. Thus, a natural intervention occurs apart from any particular program designed to deter (Veneziano, Veneziano, and Gill 2001).

Isolation and Control.   Isolation of juvenile offenders is achieved through apprehension and detention, although the average length of long-term youth confinement in public facilities was 9 months in 2000 (Camp and Camp 2002). Juvenile offender behaviors may be monitored or supervised to a limited degree by juvenile probation officers, but compared with adult offenders, their recidivism chances are about the same (Brownfield and Thompson 2002). In fact, there may be a self-fulfilling prophecy phenomenon occurring whenever youths are detained for any lengthy period. When youths are placed in

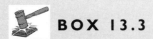 **BOX 13.3**

OPERATION KICK-IT

Is Operation Kick-It an Answer to Delinquency Prevention?

In the Texas Department of Criminal Justice, several convicted criminals are making the rounds at different elementary and high schools throughout the state in an effort to convince students that they should not take up lives of crime. Attired in their prison whites or standard prison uniforms, three inmates, Richard, 25, Ambrosio, 28, and David, 24, are escorted under guard from school to school, where they make presentations, usually in school auditoriums. Their audiences are school children of different ages. Their message—obey the law, don't wind up in prison like we did!

Texas Department of Criminal Justice (TDCJ) officials have labeled their program "Operation Kick-It," which is geared to demonstrating to students the possible consequences of making bad choices. Daniel Gorolla from the TDCJ says to students that "you all have to realize that the choices and decisions you make today can affect you and your loved ones for the rest of your lives." This message is fine, coming from a prison official. But what about messages from the prisoners themselves? Richard, serving a 15-year sentence for aggravated robbery, has been in prison for the past 7 years. He said that he began to steal when he was in high school. First, he began stealing clothes and small items that he thought he "needed" to fit in at school. But then his thefts escalated and soon included credit cards. A short time thereafter, Richard began robbing persons at gunpoint, taking their valuables. "It was a game," Richard said. "When I had the gun, I felt I could do anything." When he was 17, he stole $500 from a store. The theft landed him in jail. "This is my story. Think about your own story and if you see similarities between yours and mine, and then you know that you're headed down the wrong path."

Ambrosio, who at 21 years old was charged with intoxicated manslaughter, also talked about the events that led up to his in-

carceration. Ambrosio said that after he graduated from college, he began to work at a fluid company. He wanted to fit in. He said, "I am the type of guy who wears jeans and a buckle and cowboy boots, and I would see my boss wearing nice pants and polos, and I wanted to be like him." During a trip with his boss, Ambrosio took him to a nightclub where both of them drank a lot of alcohol. When they left the bar, Ambrosio ran a stop light and collided with another vehicle, killing the other driver. "I don't know how to live with what I have done. Yes, it was an accident, but it was a choice I made to drink and then get behind the wheel. Every time you make a choice, think about what you are doing."

David is serving two 10-year sentences for robbery and involuntary manslaughter. When he was 14, he joined a gang and began to steal. When he was 15, he and two of his homeboys robbed a pawnshop and stole five handguns. When he and his friends got home, they brandished their weapons in front of his friend's younger brother, and one of the guns went off. David didn't know the gun was loaded. "One minute I was playing with the gun, and the next minute, I am looking at my friend's 13-year-old brother who is lying on the floor dead because I shot him in the face." At age 15, David was tried as an adult and served two years in the juvenile correctional facility. At 17, he was transferred to the state prison. "When you do something," David says, "is it worth it? And think about what you're doing long and hard . . . because all it takes is one bad choice."

Operation Kick-It is increasingly popular and seems to have a positive effect on students wherever it is presented. Prisoners, especially those convicted of serious offenses, make a strong impression on school children. The TDCJ hopes that such exposure to these offenders will cause many

(continued)

BOX 13.3 *(Continued)*

youths to consider law-abiding behaviors and seek to avoid trouble and possible imprisonment themselves.

Interestingly, Operation Kick-It is similar to Scared Straight, a program started in the early 1980s in New Jersey. In Scared Straight, students from area schools would visit a prison and be confronted by menacing inmates who would talk about their prison experiences. Often, the shock value of being inside a prison and confronted by a violent inmate might literally scare straight any juvenile thinking about a career of crime. Although Scared Straight and other similar programs have had mixed reviews and limited success, prison officials in New Jersey, Texas, and other states have not given up on the idea that prisoners can help students make positive changes in their lives.

Do you think that programs such as Operation Kick-It are effective at deterring juveniles from committing crime? Should all schools expose students to the experiences of prison inmates to emphasize the realities and unpleasantness of prison life? What do you think?

Source: Texas Department of Criminal Justice. *Operation Kick-It.* Austin, TX: Texas Department of Criminal Justice, 2002.

custodial settings such as reformatories, the emphasis of the facility is more on control than rehabilitation. Thus, control for the sake of control may be self-defeating as a long-range delinquency prevention strategy (Armstrong 2002).

In Hawaii, for instance, recidivism rates of juveniles who have been confined in secure facilities have been studied. During the period 1995–1999, for example, 805 youths were released from the Hawaii Youth Correctional Facility. However, 82 percent of these juveniles were subsequently rearrested, an increase from 75 percent reported in 1984 (Bradford and Perrone 2001). Substance abuse was reported in more than 80 percent of these cases, although about half were charged with nonviolent offenses. About 80 percent were recommitted for short terms of secure confinement. Hawaii may not be typical of other jurisdictions. For instance, a study of 11,399 Florida youths released from commitment during the period 1998–1999 showed that 41 percent were subsequently readjudicated for a new offense, while 61 percent were rearrested within twelve months following their release (Florida Department of Juvenile Justice 2001). Interestingly, readjudication and conviction rates were lowest for maximum-risk youth, whereas moderate risk youth were most likely to be rearrested and recommitted within one year following their release from secure confinement.

Prevention. The influence of juvenile corrections upon delinquency prevention is currently uncertain. Delinquency prevention is a function of many factors, including preschool programs such as the 1962 Perry Preschool Project in Ypsilanti, Michigan (Berrueta-Clement et al. 1984). Nearly 70 percent of the children who participated in the program had no future reported offenses as juveniles and only 16 percent were ever arrested for delinquent acts. However, about half of the nonparticipants in the same school had future reported offenses as juveniles and 25 percent were subsequently arrested for delinquency.

Juvenile gangs play a key role in transmitting and perpetuating delinquent conduct (Brownfield and Thompson 2002; Kakar-Sirpal 2002). Thus, steps have been taken in many jurisdictions to assist vulnerable youths to resist the influence of gangs (Brandt and Russell 2002). A program known as GREAT (Gang Resistance Education and Training) is a school-based gang-prevention effort begun in Arizona in 1991. Law enforcement officers teach a nine-week curriculum to middle school students. The intent of the program is to equip students with prosocial attitudes and behaviors that will minimize the influence of gangs. Data derived from a study of 5,935 eighth graders in 42 schools in 11 states suggest that GREAT has potential for achieving its delinquency prevention aims (Esbensen 1999).

One of the key elements in many of the contemporary delinquency prevention programs is heightening offender accountability (Jackson 2002). Accountability can be incorporated as a program element in the form of restitution, community service, or victim compensation in some form. Restitution by itself may be insufficient to bring about long-term change in delinquent behaviors, however. Therefore, many current intensive supervision programs for juveniles and others include victim-offender contact, group and individual counseling, and educational and vocational support (Benda and Corwyn 2002). One program is SMART-Talk, an interactive videogame used with middle school students. Through the use of games, interactive assessment interviews, cartoons, and animation, youths are taught anger management, dispute resolution, and perspective-taking. A sample of 98 seventh graders was studied and exhibited prosocial behaviors following an experiment with SMART-Talk. Thus, there is promise for a useful multimedia violence intervention technique that is easily marketed and distributed for general delinquency prevention (Bosworth, Espelage, and DuBay 1998).

Punishment and Retribution.   One major impact of the get-tough-on-crime policy adopted by many jurisdictions is that the juvenile justice system is sending a larger portion of its serious offenders to criminal courts where they may conceivably receive harsher punishments. Whether this outcome occurs is questionable. Despite the influence of the justice model on juvenile court dispositions of youthful offenders, a highly visible and vocal public expresses opposite views. The sentiment is that rehabilitative and reintegrative efforts ought to be stressed rather than more punitive aims in juvenile correctional programs (Glick and Rhine 2001).

Alternatives in Juvenile Corrections

Juvenile court judges have several options from which to choose when deciding specific cases. They may adjudicate youths as delinquent and take no further action other than to record the event. Thus, if the juvenile appears again before the same judge, harsher measures may be taken in sentencing. Or the judge may divert juveniles to particular community agencies for special treatment (Campbell and Lerew 2002). Juveniles with psychological problems or who are emotionally disturbed, sex offenders, or those with drug and/or alcohol dependencies may be targeted for special community treatments (Goldsmith 2001; Hannon, DeFronzo, and Prochnow 2001). Judges may also impose conditions as punishments such as fines, restitution, or some form of community service. The more drastic alternatives are varying degrees of custodial sentences, ranging from the placement of juveniles in foster homes, camps, ranches, reform schools, or industrial schools. These nonsecure and secure forms of placement and/or detention are usually reserved for the most serious offenders (Martinez and Arrigona 2001).

Diversion and Deferred Prosecution. Diversion is the temporary directing of youths from the juvenile justice system, where they can remain with their families or guardians, attend school, and be subject to limited supervision on a regular basis by a juvenile probation officer. It is claimed by some authorities that diversion of offenders should be aimed at the client population that would otherwise have received formal dispositions if diversion had not occurred (Weatherburn and Baker 2001). This client population consists of youths who have committed delinquent acts and not simply status offenses. Other investigators have observed that greater recidivism rates are associated with those youths who have early encounters with the law at younger ages. Therefore, delinquent behavior is treated as qualitatively more serious when it is observed among 10- or 11-year-olds compared with 15- or 16-year-olds. The reasoning is that if younger youths are somehow diverted from the juvenile justice system, this will minimize their propensity to reoffend. Diversion is like a passive intervention and acts to minimize the adverse effects of labeling on especially young offenders (Cottle, Lee, and Heilbrun 2001).

In any case, divertees, regardless of whether they are status offenders or those who have committed delinquent acts, have some amount of recidivism. And some of these divertees do progress to more serious offenses. Many youths simply grow out of their delinquent behavior. Thus, the characteristic pattern of juvenile involvement in crime is one of high prevalence, but low frequency and persistence. This suggests that rather than attempting to control transient offending through juvenile justice diversion strategies, criminal justice agencies would be better off attempting to control the incentives, opportunities, and triggers for juvenile involvement in crime (Weatherburn and Baker 2001).

Diversion has certain logistical benefits. First, it decreases the caseload of juvenile court prosecutors by shuffling less serious cases to probation departments. Of course, this increases the supervisory responsibilities of probation departments. Another advantage of diversion for juvenile justice is that it does appear to reduce recidivism in those jurisdictions where it has been used. On the negative side, claims that diversion has widened the net by including some youths who otherwise would have received wristslaps or warnings seem justified. Much of this net widening occurs through changes in police discretion and relabeling of juvenile behaviors as more serious, however (Sturges 2001). Besides net widening, some critics have suggested that diversion and other strategies target largely white youths, while minority youths are pushed further into the juvenile justice system for more severe punishments and/or penalties (Leiber 2002). This issue is presently unresolved (Wilson and Petersilia 2002).

In 1933, a New York lawyer, Conrad Printzlien, was an Assistant U.S. Attorney in the Eastern District of New York. Subsequently, Printzlien accepted an appointment as a U.S. Probation Officer in the same district (Rackmill 1996:8). With a growing clientele of youthful offenders, Printzlien saw firsthand how prosecution and conviction both labeled youths and destroyed their lives with the stigma of criminality. Noting that many of these youths were first offenders, Printzlien helped to establish the Brooklyn Plan, a deferred prosecution program for youthful offenders in New York. The Brooklyn Program oper-

Youths performing construction work, Custer Youth Corrections Center, Custer, South Dakota. Courtesy of Custer Youth Correctional Center.

ated from 1936 to 1946 following district court approval. Deferred prosecution is temporarily halting proceedings against defendants while they are subjected to a program with particular behavioral requirements for a short period. Over 250 juvenile offenders were deferred under this program during its operation, with only 2 youths violating their program requirements.

Similar to diversion, deferred prosecution under the Brooklyn Plan involved examining a defendant's records on a case-by-case basis and determining which offenders were most likely to benefit from deferred prosecution. If an offender showed promise of being rehabilitated, then he or she would be freed on his or her own recognizance for a short period, perhaps three to six months, under the supervision of his or her parents and probation officer. Both parents and probation officers would furnish the court a written evaluation of a youth's progress following the deferred prosecution period. If youths did not reoffend during this period and behaved in a law-abiding manner in other respects, then prosecutions against them were terminated. Thus, some youths were able to avoid the adverse labeling effects of a criminal prosecution (Rackmill 1996: 8–9). During the course of the Brooklyn Plan, the length of the supervision program ranged up to two years for some offenders. The plan was also implemented in later years in other federal jurisdictions. Some states adopted the plan as well, with favorable results. Indications are that the use of diversion and deferred prosecution, for some youths at least, enabled them to recover their lives and pursue law-abiding lives as adults (Campbell and Lerew 2002).

Diversion may also involve progressive sanctions. Some jurisdictions, such as Texas, attempt to hold juvenile offenders increasingly accountable if they continue to reoffend after being treated leniently at some earlier stage of their processing. Contact rates are increased between juveniles and those supervising them. Further, they are expected to do more and have greater accountability through a process of graduated sanctions. At least for juvenile offenders in this jurisdiction, the progressive sanctioning system seems to work. Modest reductions in recidivism rates among those offenders subject to progressive sanctions have been observed (Bryl et al. 2001).

Youth Courts.   In a growing number of jurisdictions, many low-risk juvenile offenders are being processed by youth courts or teen courts, which are comprised of one's peers (Garrison 2001). These courts are often conducted in school rooms after hours. Sometimes public buildings are used, although a concerted effort is made to remove juveniles from sites associated with formal juvenile offender processing, such as courtrooms. Youth courts have been depicted as quasi-judicial forums in which adolescents pass judgments on their peers in cases involving relatively minor offenses (Acker et al. 2001).

Often, youth courts have a deeper impact on juvenile offenders than being processed and adjudicated by an adult juvenile court judge. The power of one's peers cannot be overestimated. When youths accused of crimes sit in the presence of their peers, who comprise jurors, and where the evidence is presented by other youthful peers, the resulting sanctions are those recommended and condoned by one's equals, usually one's school associates. These proceedings are overseen by a judge or other court official to ensure that proper procedures are followed. When youth courts find juvenile defendants guilty of the offense(s) alleged, then their most likely sanctioning option is some creative punishment, such as restitution, community service, or victim compensation. The intent of youth courts is to heighten offender accountability. This means that the offender is obliged to do something to repay the community and/or victim for any harm caused.

In 2001 there were over 100 teen court or youth court programs operating in different U.S. jurisdictions. One program is the Teen Court Program in Sarasota County, Florida. The Teen Court Program was studied over time. A treatment group of 111 juveniles who attended teen court and a comparison sample of 65 high school and middle school students were contrasted. One important difference was that the 111 juvenile offenders who participated in teen court emerged with a much better legal knowledge. Furthermore, their attitudes toward authority figures improved considerably. A five-month followup of the dispositions of those processed by the Teen Court Program showed a small rate of recidivism, only 12.6 percent. This program was regarded as successful at deterring future offending among those exposed to youth court (LoGalbo and Callahan 2001). Youth courts are also being used as alternatives to formal delinquency adjudications in other countries, such as Canada (Peterson, Ruck, and Koegl 2001).

Probation for Juveniles.   Placing a juvenile on probation as the result of an adjudicatory hearing is one of the juvenile judge's conditional options. Like probation for adult offenders, **juvenile probation** is a sentence of supervised conditional release for a specified period. Juvenile probation officers oversee each offender's progress through visits to homes or schools or employment sites (Giblin 2002). The juvenile judge retains control over the juvenile and may revoke probation if one or more conditions of it are violated. Not all juvenile offenders are especially good candidates for probation. For instance, those juveniles who engage in chronic delinquent behavior and who are beyond parental control may require something more than probation can provide. In Oregon, for instance, some chronic delinquents have been directed to community treatment

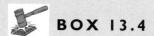

BOX 13.4

Scott B. Peterson

Program Manager, Office of Juvenile Justice and Delinquency Prevention, Office of Justice Programs, U.S. Department of Justice

Statistics

B.S. (public policy administration), State University of New York at Buffalo

Interests and Career Highlights

My interests change every few years. When you go to school in Buffalo, New York, you acquire a lifelong addiction to chicken wings. One result is that I jog a lot around the Washington, DC, area, which has a lot of sightseeing opportunities, such as the Smithsonian Museums and the National Zoo. When the opportunity arises, I like to travel to Cape Cod or Martha's Vineyard, which are my favorite vacation spots.

Some of my career highlights include being Founding Executive Director of Youth Courts of the Capital District, Inc.; Special Advisor for the United Nations Special 2002 Session on Children Ten-Year Event; receiving an American flag flown over the U.S. Capitol for my civil duty to New York; receiving the President's Award for my contribution to the Senior Citizen Community; being appointed by Governor George E. Pataki to the Juvenile Justice Board for New York; and receiving a Public Service Award from the U.S. Attorney's Office for the Northern District of New York.

Work History and Experience

Being out of college for ten years has given me quite a few interesting experiences. After graduating in Buffalo, I looked for work in the social service field. I preferred something along the lines of the Peace Corps. I sent out over 30 résumés and eventually received an interview from the Center for the Advancement of Family and Youth in Albany. My future boss asked me in that interview, "Why do you want to work here?" I told her that my family works for either social services or are on social services. She laughed and advised that she was going to hire a staff of five who would establish a runaway homeless youth shelter and transitional living program for males 16 to 21 years old. If I accepted the position, I would become a residence counselor. She also warned me that my work would be stressful and low-paying, prerequisites for high labor turnover. I was offered the job and accepted. I worked there for three years as a residence counselor, and eventually I became the Educational and Vocational Coordinator. The runaway, homeless, and throwaway population is one of the most challenging to work with in social services. Contributing to this are their transient behaviors and mental health issues. More than a few clients had prior encounters with the juvenile or criminal justice systems, which only complicated matters. During my time with the shelter, over 200 youths came and went, with many returning. We always took them back. While some of these youths were eventually reunited with their parents or guardians, many also turned to drugs, prostitution, and various types of criminal offending. Luckily for me, the staff I worked with was supportive and cared about their work and clients.

During my second year with the shelter, I was appointed to the Town of Colonie Youth Bureau Advisory Board. In our first meeting, I was asked by the board chairman to look into the growing concept of peer adjudication or youth court, also referred to as teen court or peer court. This was in 1993, and there were already about 60 youth court programs established in the United States.

(continued)

BOX 13.4 *(Continued)*

After doing some research on this topic, I found out a lot about how youth courts work and how effective they are. Little did I know that ten years later, youth courts would consume the largest amount of my time, energy, and passion.

Youth courts became interesting to me because they provided an alternative to the juvenile justice system. I discovered that in youth courts, other young people volunteer to act as judges, attorneys, and jurors in juvenile cases of their peers who commit real offenses. I found that peer pressure is a dominant and positive force in applying youth sanctions. As the result of offenders being tried by youth courts, a healthy respect for the law is acquired, since juveniles are more likely to listen to their peers than adults. Whatever the reason, youths courts became quite popular over the next decade, growing from 78 youth courts in 1994 to over 900 youth courts in 47 states and the District of Columbia by 2003. Potentially, thousands more youth courts will be established during the next decade. This type of court may well have the single greatest effect on the juvenile justice system. This type of social change is also occurring at the community level, in contrast with federal- or state-initiated programs for youth.

When I left the youth shelter in 1994, I became involved in the establishment of a nonprofit enterprise called the Youth Courts of the Capital District, Inc. I was the founding Executive Director of this new agency. The board of directors was comprised of representatives from the police department, the probation department, youth bureau, U.S. Attorney's Office, the local school district, and various social service agencies. Only a handful of people did the actual work of the agency, however. Within a year, we began to train volunteer youth to assume various youth court roles.

In 1995 the Colonie Youth Court accepted the first two juvenile cases for disposition. The first two cases were a pair of teenage girls who had been arrested for shoplifting $30 worth of merchandise from a local drug store. It was a night of anticipation as each girl had her own sentencing hearing. It is called a sentencing hearing, since most youth courts require offenders to plead guilty for admission into youth court. As the youth volunteers were assuming their roles as judge and jury in each case, evidence and other relevant information was revealed by the youth prosecutor and defender, who each questioned the girls in independent hearings. The juries in these cases deliberated and discussed each case, arriving at an appropriate number of community service hours as punishments. Interestingly, although the girls were arrested for the same theft charge, they received quite different verdicts from their respective juries. In one case, the jury gave the first girl 20 hours of community service. The second jury gave the other girl 30 hours of community service. When I asked the different juries how they arrived at their different punishments, one set of jury members who imposed more community service hours said that they were concerned that the parents did not punish the girl at home and that this explained the harsher punishment. The other jury stressed that they did not see the need to impose a large number of community service hours, since the girl's parents agreed to take her telephone away for a month and she could not go out on weekends. Three years and 300 cases later, I was always intrigued by how these young people took charge and assumed responsibility for their peers. They learned much about who they were and their civic duty to their community.

The primary targets of youth courts are youthful offenders. Youth courts offer them a chance to take responsibility and appear before their peers. Once they have completed their peer-imposed sentences, they have made restitution and repaired the harm caused to their communities. While youth courts throughout the United States vary in their models and programmatic operations, our youth court mandates that each youthful offender must come back for his or her final two hours of community service and serve as a juror in a subsequent case. Most of these youths like this aspect and see it as a final step in completing their community service, bringing them closure. The message adults who participate in youth courts deliver is, "It is not you we *don't like*, rather it is your behavior we *don't like*. You have successfully completed your peer-imposed youth court sentence and taken responsibility for your actions." We strongly encourage previously adjudicated youths to return to youth court and volunteer to participate. It is also important not to treat these first-time offenders as criminals. When we do this, we tend to cause more harm than good. At some level, we may inadvertently encourage them to continue acting like criminals if we don't positively reinforce their behavioral changes. We all make mistakes, and youth court, if implemented correctly, can be a forum where youths can learn from their mistakes. This reduces the likelihood of stigmatization. Every offense deserves a measured response.

While I was serving as Executive Director of the Youth Courts of the Capital District, Inc., I was appointed by New York State Governor George E. Pataki to the New York State Juvenile Justice Advisory Board. During this time, I assisted the governor in establishing a statewide youth court initiative, where the Colonie Youth Court served as a state model. Thousands of young people subsequently volunteered throughout New York, and as a result, New York had over 90 youth courts in 2003 with more planned for future years.

With the rapid national expansion of youth courts, there have been increased job opportunities. Director, coordinator, counselor, and case manager are all positions at local levels where youth courts always have job openings. Increasingly, there are even positions at the state and national levels. My involvement with the New York youth courts eventually drew me into federal work, and I presently work at the U.S. Department of Justice, where I manage and design the National Youth Court Initiative. Of course there are other job opportunities out there in the youth court field in organizations such as the American Probation and Parole Association, the Constitutional Rights Foundation, Street Law, Inc., and the American Bar Association. The National Youth Court Center (NYCC) is located in Kentucky and administered by the American Probation and Parole Association. Funded by the U.S. Department of Justice and Education, the NYCC has a terrific website that lists every youth court in the United States, resources available to enhance or establish youth courts, and even a national listing of job openings at youth courts across the United States and much more. It can be accessed at www.youthcourt.net.

Advice to Students

Advice is abundant, and I think that we just have to do our best to listen and determine what advice we choose and to follow that advice. I think morals and values have much to do with being able to follow advice. My own advice to students would be to remember that whatever you do for a living is not who you are; the world is what you make it; we all have issues, although some of us have more issues than others; and do not ever let anyone be oppressive to you. As often as I am asked by college students to intern for me, I always do my best to accommodate them. While internships are helpful, I also encourage students to take some fun jobs that focus on helping troubled youths. Although they often don't pay well, these jobs do provide numerous valuable learning experiences.

programs that attempt to improve parental effectiveness in their supervision practices. A program, known as Multidimensional Treatment Foster Care, has been developed by the Oregon Social Learning Center, and it focuses on the need to return adolescents to the family and community through specific treatment interventions (Moore, Sprengelmeyer, and Chamberlain 2001). These interventions include group and individual counseling, educational programming, and other useful activities.

For all practical purposes, juvenile probationers are not in the same class as adult probationers. Therefore, if their probation is revoked by the juvenile judge, they have no right to a hearing in the matter. At least the U.S. Supreme Court failed to address or clarify the rights of juveniles in probation or parole revocation hearings when these same issues were resolved for adults. They are simply informed by the judge of a new sentence and new conditions.

Conditions of probation may include supervision by juvenile probation officers or no supervision. Conditions may include restitution, if financial loss was suffered by one or more victims in cases of vandalism, property damage, or physical injury. Fines may be imposed. Or the judge may specify some form of community service. All of these conditions individually or in any combination may be a part of a juvenile's probation program (Meisel 2001). Violation of one or more conditions may result in probation revocation. Probation officers are usually the link between juvenile offenders and the courts regarding compliance with these conditions.

In jurisdictions such as Rhode Island, probation is sometimes considered a **therapeutic intervention.** Departing from traditional probation, where a probation officer might make periodic visits or inspections of the juvenile's premises and conduct checks with school officials, probation as therapy considers the **probation counselor** the good parent the child never had (Sweet 1988:90). Intervention in the Rhode Island program occurs through five distinct steps:

1. *Case review.* The probation counselor must read the behavior of the juvenile, review the case thoroughly, conduct interviews with both the juvenile and parents, and possibly discuss the juvenile's problems with other professionals.

2. *Self-awareness.* The probation counselor needs to inspect his or her own reactions to adolescents and determine whether biases exist that may influence the relation and rapport he or she establishes between him- or herself and the juvenile.

3. *Development of a relationship.* The probation counselor must establish an accepting relation between him- or herself and the juvenile, where confidence and trust are prevalent. Respect for the juvenile's feelings must be demonstrated.

4. *The critical incident.* The testing phase of the relationship occurs when the juvenile tests the honesty or consistency of the counselor. The juvenile examines carefully the response given by the counselor to the critical incident.

5. *Following through.* If the counselor passes the test, he or she will no doubt encounter other tests. But the counselor has gained the respect and rapport with the juvenile where new levels of progress can be achieved. In short, this involves a type of parenting that the parents originally failed to accomplish (Sweet 1988:90). This is considered action therapy and appears to work well, especially for those youths with family difficulties.

Restitution, coupled with probation, seems to suggest a reduction in recidivism among juvenile offenders. Roy (1995) described a juvenile victim restitution program in Lake County, Indiana. Two groups of juveniles were identified: 113 juveniles designated as the restitution group and 148 youths designated as probation only. Juvenile clients were selected from the program during 1989 and 1990. These juveniles were tracked through 1992 and compared on several salient variables, including gender, substance abuse history, prior offense history, age at first offense, and detention history. Roy found that restitution was a valuable intervention primarily for those youths considered first offenders. Recidivism rates were lowest for first offenders, regardless of whether they were involved in either probation with restitution or probation only. Similar findings have been observed in other programs (Calhoun 2001). One caution suggested by some researchers is that net-widening should be avoided. Some juveniles might be included in restitution programs simply because the programs are in place in communities. If the programs did not exist, then these offenders would likely receive probation and not recidivate. For them, involvement in a restitution program simply because the program exists would not be particularly productive as a rehabilitative tool (Pullen 1996).

Prescribing the right type of probation aftercare for juveniles is difficult. However, descriptions of those juveniles with chronic recidivism patterns reveal that the following factors are important predictors:

1. Age at first adjudication
2. Prior criminal behavior (a combined measure of the number and severity of priors)
3. Number of prior commitments to juvenile facilities
4. Drug/chemical abuse
5. Alcohol abuse
6. Family relationships (parental control)
7. School problems
8. Peer relationships (Baird 1985:36)

Probation supervision can be gauged according to the following standards, depending upon the size of the probation department and prevailing juvenile probationer caseloads:

REGULAR SUPERVISION

1. Four face-to-face contacts per month with youth
2. Two face-to-face contacts per month with parents
3. One face-to-face contact per month with placement staff
4. One contact with school officials

INTENSIVE SUPERVISION

1. Six face-to-face contacts per month with youth
2. Three face-to-face contacts per month with parents
3. One face-to-face contact per month with placement staff
4. Two contacts with school officials

ALTERNATIVE CARE CASES

1. One face-to-face contact per month with youth
2. Four contacts with agency staff (one must be face-to-face)
3. One contact every two months with parents (Baird 1985:38)

Supervising Female Juveniles.   In a growing number of jurisdictions, there are increasing numbers of female juveniles who require monitoring and supervision. Some probation agencies find adding female juveniles to their client listing to be burdensome in several respects. Female juveniles often exhibit different needs compared with their male counterparts. There is a tendency for juvenile probation officers to sexualize their behavior and follow a "one for ten" rule: "If you take this one girl from my caseload, I'll take ten of your boys" (Zaslaw 1999:33).

Female juveniles have historically been arrested and held in secure detention more than male offenders. This trend decreased during the 1980s but increased throughout the 1990s. Community agencies designed to accommodate juvenile females often find that young women will bond with agency staff. When it comes time for these females to leave the program, they may act out and run away from the facility, sometimes to avoid closeness of the social bond. When these girls have been rearrested, they have often been committed to more restrictive programs. This process is known as bootstrapping, when the juvenile justice system labels a status offense, such as runaway behavior, as the delinquent act of "escape," where the punishment is more severe (Zaslaw 1999:34).

One observation about female juveniles is that many of them have a myriad of complex problems to address. Many of them have been sexually and physically abused and tend to see bleak futures, unhappiness, and continued victimization. Typically, day treatment and residential programs are grossly underfunded and understaffed. Young women tend to respond to cognitive approaches that utilize verbal expression. They also respond to experimental learning approaches, artistic expression, role playing, and social activities. This process needs to be recognized and exploited (Zaslaw 1999:35).

Confinement or Placement.   The last resort for juvenile judges aside from transferring juveniles to criminal court is **confinement** or **placement.** Placement may be either **nonsecure placement** or **secure placement.** Nonsecure placement may involve placing the youth in a foster home if the juvenile's parents are considered unfit. Or the juvenile may be abandoned or orphaned. Foster home placement provides the youth with some semblance of a family. Other nonsecure options for juvenile judges include assignments of juveniles to group homes or camp ranches. Secure placement is placing a juvenile in a facility, such as an industrial school, where the juvenile's freedom is regulated by institution authorities. Secure-custody facilities for juveniles are the equivalent of adult prisons or penitentiaries (Research and Evaluation Associates, Inc. 2001). Some observers believe that incarcerating juveniles in prison has more disadvantages than advantages. For instance, juvenile inmate violence against other youths is sometimes ignored by correctional staff. In at least some secure facilities, it has been reported that some correctional officers have actually encouraged fighting between youths (Peterson and Koegl 2002). This does not appear to be a widespread practice, however.

One problem facing juvenile court judges is deciding which juveniles should be assigned to which programs. More often than not, juveniles are incarcerated in different secure state facilities when they do not deserve or need such confinement (Mitchell et al. 2001). This problem results from **overclassification.** This is a classification problem, and the level of accuracy associated with juvenile risk prediction instruments is about as poor as adult risk prediction devices. Other problems are that many juveniles have co-occurring disorders, such as learning disabilities, mental illnesses, and/or alcohol/drug dependencies. Risk/needs assessment inventories do not always detect the existence of multiple disorders for any given juvenile offender (Underwood and Falwell 2002). Nevertheless, judges attempt to make secure or nonsecure detention decisions on the basis of the following elements:

1. Classification based on risk of continued criminal activity and the offender's need for services.

2. A case management classification system designed to help probation and parole officers develop effective case plans and select appropriate casework strategies.

3. A management information system designed to enhance planning, monitoring, evaluation, and accountability.

4. A workload deployment system that allows agencies to effectively and efficiently allocate their limited resources (Baird 1985:34).

Juvenile Detention Centers.   When juveniles are awaiting a hearing in juvenile court or have been adjudicated delinquent, they may be placed in juvenile detention centers. A juvenile detention center is either a short- or long-term secure placement facility to house minors who require continuous supervision (Utah Legislative Auditor General 1999). In recent years, the Office of Juvenile Justice and Delinquency Prevention (OJJDP) has recognized that juvenile detention centers play increasingly important roles in assessing the needs of youths and providing training for their development (Roush and Jones 1996). Grants have been made available to various jurisdictions for the purpose of providing more effective training for staff who work in juvenile detention and corrections facilities. For instance, a Juvenile Detention Care Giver Training Curriculum Project was instituted to provide staff with a 40-hour training curriculum for new juvenile detention careworkers (Jones and Roush 1995). Such curriculums are often directly connected to specific juvenile detention functions. Figure 13.2 shows job functions and effectiveness characteristics for juvenile detention centers.

Some juvenile secure facilities have been tailored for female offenders. For instance, in Gatesville, Texas, the Hilltop Unit of the Texas Department of Criminal Justice has established Operation Outreach, a specially designed program for female juvenile offenders. Females adjudicated delinquent or convicted of one or more crimes in criminal court may be sent to Operation Outreach initially. This is a one-day program to offer these females a prison perspective and help them realize the possible results they could face if they continue their criminal behavior. Thus far, this program, which is a scaled down version of shock probation, seems to be an effective deterrent, with low recidivism rates (Bond 2001).

Group homes may be privately or publicly operated. They require juvenile clients to observe the rights of others, participate in various vocational or educational training programs, attend school, participate in therapy or receive prescribed medical treatment, and observe curfew, although the imposition of curfews for juveniles may be an ineffective juvenile management strategy in certain jurisdictions. In fact, curfew implementation and enforcement may be counterproductive in that some escalation in offending has been observed for certain minority youths (Hirschel, Dean, and Dumond 2001). Urinalyses or

Detention Functions: The "What" of Juvenile Detention

1. *Behavior management:* Using behavioral and developmental theories to establish clear expectations for residents' behavior and employing immediate positive and/or negative consequences as a result of direct involvement with residents.
2. *Crisis intervention:* Using skill and composure in order to prevent or minimize physical and emotional harm to residents and other staff members when handling a wide variety of crisis situations (e.g., physical violence, escapes, riots, and suicidal behaviors).
3. *Security:* Implementing the policy and procedures related to resident supervision and institutional security measures to ensure the physical presence of each resident in the facility.
4. *Safety:* Employing knowledge and skills in relation to emergency procedures (e.g., first aid, CPR, fire safety, and communicable disease) to assist the well-being of youth.
5. *Custodial care:* Assisting in the proper identification and treatment of problems relating to the physical and emotional health and well-being of detained youth through the use of knowledge and skills in basic health-related areas (e.g., medical and hygiene, adolescent sexuality, substance abuse, physical or emotional abuse, and symptoms of suicidal behavior and emotional distress).
6. *Record keeping:* Providing accurate and timely written documentation of both routine and special situations regarding residents, staff members, and program activities through the use of observation and recording skills.
7. *Program maintenance:* Implementing, teaching, creating, and supplementing the facility's daily program and activities (e.g., physical education, recreation, arts and crafts).
8. *Problem solving:* Creating an environment or institutional climate where a youth's personal, social, and emotional problems can be openly discussed, explored, and possibly resolved through staff use of effective interpersonal

relationship skills, communication and consultation with clinical staff, and participation in and leadership of group discussions and activities.
9. *Organizational awareness:* Understanding, supporting, and using the philosophy, goals, values, policies, and procedures that represent the daily operations of the facility.
10. *External awareness:* Identifying and keeping up-to-date with key external issues and trends likely to affect the agency (e.g., legal, political, demographic, and philosophical trends).

Effectiveness Characteristics: The "How" of Juvenile Detention

1. *Balanced perspective:* A broad view that balances present needs and longer-term considerations.
2. *Strategic view:* Ability to collect and analyze information that forms an overall longer-range view of priorities and forecasts likely needs, problems, and opportunities.
3. *Environmental sensitivity:* Awareness of broad environmental trends and their effects on your work unit.
4. *Leadership:* An ability and willingness to lead and manage others.
5. *Flexibility:* Openness to new information and tolerance for stress and ambiguity in the work situation.
6. *Action orientation:* Decisiveness, calculated risk taking, and a drive to get things done.
7. *Results focus:* High concern for goal achievement and a tenacity in following through to the end.
8. *Communication:* Ability to express oneself clearly and authoritatively and to listen clearly to others.
9. *Interpersonal sensitivity:* Self-knowledge and awareness of impact of self on others, sensitivity to the needs and weaknesses of others, and ability to empathize with the viewpoint of others.
10. *Technical competence:* Expert and up-to-date knowledge of the work methods and procedures of your work unit.

FIGURE 13.2   Job Functions and Effectiveness Characteristics for Juvenile Detention Centers.
Source: David W. Roush and Michael A. Jones. "Juvenile Detention Training: A Status Report." *Federal Probation* 60 (1996): 57.

other tests may be conducted randomly as checks to see whether juveniles are taking drugs or consuming alcohol contrary to group home policy (Garnier and Stein 2002). If one or more program violations occur, group home officials may report these infractions to the juvenile judge who retains dispositional control over the youth. Assignment to a group home or any other type of detention is usually for a definite period.

There are numerous proponents and opponents of juvenile detention of any kind. Those favoring detention cite the disruption of one's lifestyle and separation as a positive dimension, especially when chronic offenders are treated (Ogilvie and Lynch 2001). For example, a youth who has been involved with a delinquent gang or a particular circle of friends who engage in frequent law violations would benefit from detention as the result of having these counterproductive associations interrupted or terminated (Hope and Damphousse 2002). Of course, juveniles can always return to their old ways when released from detention. There is nothing the juvenile justice system can do to prevent that in any absolute sense.

However, arguments have been advanced to show that the effect of imprisonment on a juvenile's self-image and propensity to commit new offenses is negligible (Virginia Policy Design Team 1994). Thus, detention as a punishment may be the primary result, without any tangible, long-range benefits such as self-improvement or reduction in recidivism. At least there does not appear to be any substantial evidence that detention as a juvenile automatically escalates to adult crime. According to some analysts, the peak ages of juvenile criminality fall between the sixteenth and twentieth birthdays, with participation rates falling off rapidly. Thus, detention for a fixed period may naturally ease the delinquency rate, at least for some of the more chronic offenders (Puzzanchera et al. 2002).

Outward Bound and Wilderness Programs.   One productive alternative to the detention of juvenile offenders, even those considered chronic, is participation in **experience programs** or **wilderness programs** (Wilson and Lipsey 2000). Experience programs or wilderness programs include a wide array of outdoor programs designed to improve a juvenile's self-worth, self-concept, pride, and trust in others. **Project Outward Bound** is one of more than 200 programs of its type in the United States today (Salerno 1994). **Outward Bound** was first introduced in Colorado in 1962 with objectives emphasizing personal survival in the wilderness. Youths participated in various outdoor activities including rock climbing, solo survival, camping, and long-range hiking during a three-week period. Program officials were not concerned with equipping these juveniles with survival skills per se, but rather, they wanted to instill within the participants a feeling of self-confidence and self-assurance to cope with other types of problems in their communities. Other Outward Bound programs have been established in several jurisdictions (Cameron and MacDougal 2000). Some of these programs have been designed for specific youthful offender populations,

General Patrick H. Brady Boot Camp Correctional Facility, Custer South Dakota. Courtesy of Custer Youth Correctional Center.

such as sex offenders. Generally favorable results have been reported (Lambie 2000). Low recidivism rates among experience program clients of less than 30 percent are associated with many of these programs, thus attesting to their usefulness in delinquency prevention and rehabilitation (Wilson and Lipsey 2000).

Selected Issues in Juvenile Corrections

Juvenile corrections has been under attack from various sectors for many decades (Josi and Sechrest 1999). This attack comes from many quarters, and it coincides with a general attack on the criminal justice system for its apparent failure to stem the increasing wave of crime in the United States. Sentencing reforms, correctional reforms, experiments with probation and parole alternatives, and a host of other options have been attempted in an apparent effort to cure or control delinquents and criminals (Altschuler and Armstrong 2001). The United Nations and National Council of Juvenile and Family Court Judges adopted policy statements about the juvenile justice system that bear directly on juvenile corrections. The issues to be discussed in this final section may be better understood in the context of these statements. Five general recommendations have been made:

1. That continued individualized treatment of juveniles be continued, including the development of medical, psychiatric, and educational programs that range from least to most restrictive, according to individual need.

2. That the chronic, serious juvenile offender, while being held accountable, be retained within the jurisdiction of the juvenile court. As a resource, specialized programs and facilities need to be developed that focus on restorations rather than punishment.

3. That the disposition of juvenile court cases have a flexible range for restricting freedom with the primary goal focused on the restoration to full liberty rather than let the punishment fit the crime; that no case dispositions should be of a mandatory nature, but rather, they should be left to the discretion of the judge based on predetermined dispositional guidelines; that in no case should a juvenile under 18 years of age be subject to capital punishment.

4. That in situations where the juvenile court judge believes that the juvenile under consideration is nonamenable to the services of the court and based on the youth's present charges, past record in court, and his or her age and mental status, the judge may waive jurisdiction; that in all juvenile cases the court of original jurisdiction be that of the juvenile court; that the discretion to waive be left to the juvenile judge; that the proportionality of punishment would be appropriate with these cases, but the most high-risk offenders should be treated in small, but secure, facilities.

5. That policymakers, reformers, and researchers continue to strive for a greater understanding as to the causes and most desired response to juvenile crime; that research should be broad-based rather than limited to management, control, and punishment strategies (Surette 2002).

Some of the issues noted below are affected directly by these recommendations and policy statements. While these statements are not obligatory for any jurisdiction, they do suggest opinions and positions of a relevant segment of concerned citizens—juvenile court judges and juvenile corrections personnel. These issues include (1) the **deinstitutionalization** of status offenses, (2) the classification of juvenile offenders, (3) juveniles treated as adults, (4) violent and nonviolent juvenile offenders, and (5) capital punishment for juveniles.

The Deinstitutionalization of Status Offenses. The **deinstitutionalization of status offenses (DSO)** is the removal from secure institutions and detention facilities of youths whose only infractions are status offenses such as running away from home, incorrigibility, truancy, and curfew violations (MacDonald and Chesney-Lind 2001). DSO was specifically targeted as a major juvenile justice priority by Congress through the passage of the Juvenile Justice and Delinquency Prevention Act of 1974. Since 1974, many states have moved to modify their juvenile-relevant statutes to implement DSO, although the Congressional mandate was not binding on states. The major impact of DSO in various jurisdictions has been to remove from detention those juveniles charged with status offenses. Again, these are offenses that would not be considered crimes if committed by adults. However, juvenile courts continue to exercise jurisdiction over all juveniles, including status offenders. This means that although detention beyond a 24-hour period or confinement in jails is generally prohibited, it is still possible for jurisdictions to file petitions to have status offenders adjudicated as delinquent.

This is a very serious matter for affected juveniles who have not committed felonies or misdemeanors. This means, for instance, that a runaway or a curfew violator may still be labeled a juvenile delinquent according to juvenile statutes in almost every jurisdiction. Clearly, there are major differences between curfew violators, runaways, and truants contrasted with rapists, robbers, murderers, and thieves. However, they are all filtered through the same funnel and emerge with identical delinquency labels. DSO has been implemented in various jurisdictions in three different ways. First, **decarceration** may be used, where detention is prohibited, although youths may be placed in foster or group homes or on probation by the juvenile court. A second type of DSO occurs through diversion, where community-based services are used to treat juveniles for problems they may have. The juvenile court retains jurisdiction under the dependent and neglected children category. The third type of DSO is **divestiture,** where the juvenile court loses its control over status offenders and may not detain, petition, adjudicate, or place them on probation. In short, this third type of DSO results in a total loss of control by the juvenile court over the youth, since the misbehavior is a status offense.

The implications of this third DSO option are several. Police discretion is affected indirectly, since decisions by police to charge juveniles with status offenses remove those juveniles from juvenile court jurisdiction and result in youth control by community agencies instead. Juvenile judges lose control over those status offenders, and this may be interpreted as a power loss that few judges like to relinquish. DSO is considered to be a soft measure in dealing with juvenile offenders, since the power of the court to deal with them has been withdrawn. And DSO may weaken the sanctioning powers of the state where sanctions should be invoked, since it is believed by some that a link exists between status offenders and illicit behaviors (MacDonald and Chesney-Lind 2001). Several states have implemented divestiture, including Washington and Maine.

A similar outcome was observed in Connecticut, where DSO occurred through removal of juveniles from secure facilities or general detention. Rather than cut down on the number of juveniles detained, Connecticut figures disclosed a rise in juvenile detentions, where the juvenile court simply substituted noninstitutional detention for institutional detention. Instead of putting status offenders in secure detention, juvenile judges began putting them in group homes or camp ranches. Thus, DSO did not accomplish what it was designed to accomplish, at least in these jurisdictions examined.

Unfortunately for a small proportion of violent juvenile offenders who have been transferred to criminal courts for processing, they are often found guilty and incarcerated with adult offenders in prisons or penitentiaries. Many of these juveniles prove to be unruly in prison, and they become involved in fights and other aggressive behaviors. While it is important for juveniles incarcerated in adult facilities to receive individualized attention in order to meet their special needs, they frequently don't receive this attention. Some of these aggressive juveniles spend a lot of time in administrative segregation, away from the rest of the inmate population. They fail to receive any rehabilitative services. Thus, they become worse rather than better while confined (Glick 1998:99). Essentially, housing juveniles in adult institutions tends to be self-destructive and self-defeating (Ziedenberg and Schiraldi 1998:22).

The Classification of Juvenile Offenders.   Classification of any offender is made difficult by the fact that the state of the art is such in predictions of risk and dangerousness that little future behavior can be accurately forecasted. This holds for juveniles as well as adults. We know that status offenders may or may not escalate to more serious offenses, with the prevailing sentiment favoring or implying nonescalation (Glaser, Calhoun, and Petrocelli 2002).

Effective classification schemes have not been devised, although we know that on the basis of descriptions of existing offender aggregates, gender, age, nature of offense, seriousness of offense, race or ethnicity, and socioeconomic status are more or less correlated. The flaws of various classification schemes are made more apparent when program failures are detected in large numbers. Juvenile court judges make the wrong judgments and decisions about juvenile placements. Intake officers make similar errors of classification when conducting initial screenings of juveniles. However, the criteria for classification are improving and better dispositional decision making is occurring at all levels throughout the juvenile justice system (Crowe 2000).

Juveniles Treated as Adults.   The intended result of waivers is to make it possible for criminal courts to administer harsher punishments on juvenile offenders. But as we have seen, this doesn't always occur. Less than 1 percent of all juvenile offenders are transferred to criminal courts annually (Kirkish et al. 2000). And only about 10 percent of these offenders will do time in jail or prison. However, between 1990 and 1999, the proportion of delinquency cases resulting in delinquency adjudications or waivers to criminal court increased by 39 percent (Puzzanchera et al. 2002). While some progress was made in the early 1990s by sending proportionately more violent juvenile offenders to criminal courts for processing, these proportionate numbers have declined since 1994 (Snyder 2002). Nonviolent property offenders, drug-using juveniles, and public order offenders continue to make up the majority of transferred youths. These types of offenders tend to waste valuable criminal court time.

Prosecutors are not particularly interested in pursuing disturbing the peace cases or pursuing charges against juvenile drug users. Juveniles waived to criminal court for shoplifting, stealing cigarettes and alcohol from a burglary of a convenience store, or smoking marijuana do not generate as much prosecutorial enthusiasm as adult professional forgers, armed robbers, murderers, or career criminals. This should not be taken to mean that drug-use, burglary, and disturbing-the-peace cases are not serious; rather, they are not as serious as more violent types of offending (e.g., murder, rape, aggravated assault, robbery). These less serious juvenile cases should receive the full weight of the law in juvenile courts, not criminal courts. Juvenile court judges have a variety of serious dispositional options, including several conditional intensive supervision programs, community-based treatments, and secure placement.

Violent and Nonviolent Juvenile Offenders.   Investigations of violent and nonviolent youthful offenders show little evidence that escalation occurs, where those who commit nonviolent offenses eventually progress to violent offenses (Goldson 2001). Furthermore, the proportion of juvenile offenders who are violent appears to be quite small in most jurisdictions throughout the United States (Shumaker and McKee 2001). There are mixed reactions among the public about how best to deal with violent youthful offenders. The get-tough-on-delinquency trend throughout the nation is such that many violent offenders are transferred to criminal courts for potentially harsher penalties, although we are not sure how much this is occurring (Ghetti and Redlich 2001). Reducing the ready availability of firearms is also seen as a positive step toward reducing juvenile violence. Access to firearms and illicit drug use seem to be strong concomitants of juvenile violence in various jurisdictions (Ousey and Augustine 2001).

In recent years, more probation departments have become involved in sponsoring and promoting interventions that work at preventing delinquency

Violent juveniles are often affiliated with gangs, who have easy access to firearms.
Source: A. Ramsey/PhotoEdit.

and the social and educational factors that contribute to one's propensity to offend. For instance, in Pennsylvania, probation services have located themselves in schools to broker intervention and prevention services in several communities. In Phoenix, Arizona, the probation department has adopted a school and argued for more Head Start money from the city council. And in Hibbing and Chisholm, Minnesota, a probation officer spearheaded crime prevention education for and by teens through the Teens, Crime, and the Community program and won a statewide award for his efforts (Calhoun 1998:19).

The Death Penalty Applied to Juveniles.   In 2001 there were 3,581 prisoners on death row awaiting the penalty of death in 34 states and the federal prison system (Snell and Maruschak 2002:1). There were 77 death row inmates who were age 17 or younger at the time of their arrest, about 2.3 percent of all death row inmates. There were 358 inmates on death row who were 18 or 19 at the time of their arrest. In 2001 there were 4 persons on death row age 19 or younger (Snell and Maruschak 2002:9).

The first recorded execution of a juvenile occurred in 1642. Thomas Graunger, a 16-year-old, was convicted of bestiality. He was caught sodomizing a horse and a cow. The youngest age where the death penalty has been imposed is 10. A poorly documented case of a 10-year-old convicted murderer in Louisiana occurred in 1855. A more celebrated case, that of 10-year-old James Arcene, occurred in Arkansas in 1885. Arcene was 10 years old when he robbed and murdered his victim. He was eventually arrested at age 23 before being executed (Streib 1987:57).

Arguments For and Against the Death Penalty for Juveniles.   Those favoring the death penalty say it is just punishment and a form of societal revenge for the life taken or harm inflicted by the offender. It is an economical way of dealing with those who will never be released from confinement. It may be administered humanely, through lethal injection. It functions as a deterrent to others to refrain from committing capital crimes (Moon et al. 2000).

Opponents say it is cruel and unusual punishment (Kytle and Pollitt 1999). They claim the death penalty does not deter those who intend to take another's life. It is barbaric and uncivilized. Other countries do not impose it for any type of offense, regardless of its seriousness (Leiber 2000). It makes no sense to kill as a means of sending messages to others not to kill (Levin and Fox 2001). Public opinion polls in the United States suggest that 75 percent or more of the citizens surveyed are in favor of the death penalty as a punishment for a capital offense, whereas more than 50 percent of those supporting the death penalty favor its application to older juveniles (e.g., 16 and 17 years old) who commit premeditated murder. The U.S. Supreme Court ruled in 1989 that executing juveniles ages 16 and 17 at the time they committed a capital offense did not violate the evolving standards of decency (*Stanford v. Kentucky* 1989; *Wilkins v. Missouri* 1989).

For juveniles, the emotional pitch of any argument is intensified by the factor of one's age. Age functions as a mitigating factor. Thus, different factors almost always apply to adult and juvenile perpetrators (Cooke 2001). In any capital conviction, the convicted offender is entitled to a bifurcated trial where guilt is established first, and then the punishment is imposed in view of any prevailing mitigating or aggravating circumstances. Was the crime especially brutal? Did the victim suffer? Was the murderer senile or mentally ill? Or was

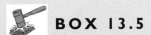 **BOX 13.5**

PERSONALITY HIGHLIGHT

Milo Colton

Professor of Criminal Justice
University of Texas-San Antonio

Statistics

B.A., M.P.A., M.A., Ph.D. (University of Colorado-Boulder); J.D. (University of Iowa)

Background and Experience

I grew up in the public housing projects in Denver, Colorado, and I spent five years at an Indian Reservation. In 1962, I enlisted for active duty in the U.S. Air Force, and I served during the Vietnam war, receiving an honorable discharge in 1968. After military service, I attended the University of Colorado at Boulder where I graduated Phi Beta Kappa with B.A., M.P.A., M.A., and Ph.D. degrees. I also graduated from the University of Iowa with a J.D. degree, and I currently hold active law licenses in Washington, DC, Nebraska, U.S. District Court in Nebraska, and the Winnebago Tribal Court.

From 1971 to 1973, I worked for the Colorado Supreme Court in the State Court Administrator's Office. From 1973 to 1975 I worked for the National Center for State Courts. From 1976 to 1977, I was a consultant to the Colorado State Patrol. From 1977 to 1980, I administered a community college program at the Winnebago Indian Reservation in Nebraska. During the same period, I taught college classes at both the Winnebago and Omaha Indian Reservations. In 1980 I was elected to the Board of Education in Sioux City, Iowa. In 1982, I was elected to the Iowa Senate where I served as a state senator from 1983 through 1987. From 1988 to 1991, I held several positions at the University of Iowa, including consultant to Native American communities. In 1991, I was recruited by the Winnebago Tribal Council to return to the Winnebago Reservation as the tribe's chief administrative officer. In 1994, I accepted a position at the University

of Texas at San Antonio, teaching legal studies in the criminal justice program and administrative law at San Antonio College, as well as at Wayne State College. I began teaching as an adjunct professor in the Criminal Justice Program at St. Mary's University in 1996, and I joined the St. Mary's faculty in the fall of 2001, teaching, among other classes, American Indians and the Law.

Living and working among Native Americans and other minorities, serving as a state senator and an attorney has made me especially conscious of the injustice of the death penalty in the United States, particularly as it applies to our children. We began executing children in Massachusetts' Plymouth Colony in 1642 when 16-year-old Thomas Graunger was hanged for having sex with animals. In 1895, a 10-year-old Cherokee Indian boy was hanged for murder, becoming the youngest on record executed in this country. In 1944, 14-year-old George Stinney, an African American, was electrocuted for murder in South Carolina, becoming the youngest executed since World War II.

Racism pervades U.S. juvenile death penalty cases. Between 1642 and 1964, African Americans represented 70 percent of the juveniles executed, whereas whites constituted only 24 percent of the juveniles executed. Nearly 90 percent of the victims were white. Of the 9 girls executed in U.S. history, 8 were African American and 1 was an American Indian. All of this bolsters the argument that, in our criminal justice

(continued)

BOX 13.5 *(Continued)*

system, which is almost exclusively controlled by whites, white lives count substantially more than those of minorities.

In 1988, the U.S. Supreme Court declared in *Thompson v. Oklahoma* that it is cruel and unusual punishment to impose the death penalty on a juvenile who commits an offense at age 15 or younger. But that has not slowed the machinery of death in this country. During the 1990s, 10 juvenile offenders who were between the ages of 16 and 18 when they committed their offenses were executed in the United States. Half of those juveniles were put to death in my newly adopted home state of Texas. There are only five other countries that also executed juveniles during the 1990s: Iran, Nigeria, Pakistan, Saudi Arabia, and Yemen. This is not the crowd with whom I want my country tied. The United States clearly is out of step with the rest of civilization and international law. At least six international treaties ban the execution of juveniles who are under 18 years of age.

When I was a state senator in Iowa, I served in a state that did not have the death penalty. Iowa's homicide rates and killings of peace officers were among the lowest anywhere in the nation. Studies have shown that the death penalty has little or no deterrent value. In states where

the death penalty is liberally used, homicides and killings of peace officers in the line of duty tend to be substantially higher than in those states without the death penalty.

The death penalty is very expensive to administer. Because of due process requirements in our criminal justice system, it costs two to three times as much to execute a person as it does to lock that person up for life without the possibility of parole. Finally, we know that mistakes are made too often in death penalty cases. Since 1976, when the U.S. Supreme Court approved the procedural protocol for determining death sentences in *Gregg v. Georgia*, 100 people sentenced to die have been released from death row because of wrongful convictions. Moreover, two-thirds of those sentenced to die had their death penalty convictions overturned on appeal.

The death penalty does not create a safer environment. It does not enhance our society or our image throughout the international community. Giving vent to an ancient ethic of revenge lowers and diminishes us all. It is time to elevate life over death. It is time for the United States to join the rest of the civilized world and abolish the death penalty for our children and for all our people.

the murderer a juvenile? Since age acts as a mitigating factor in cases where the death penalty is considered for adults, there are those who say the death penalty should not be applied to juveniles under any condition.

Early English precedent and common law assumed that those under age 7 were incapable of formulating criminal intent, and thus, they were absolved from any wrongdoing. Between age 7 and age 12, a presumption exists that the child is capable of formulating criminal intent, and in every jurisdiction, the burden is borne by the prosecution for establishing beyond a reasonable doubt that the youth was capable of formulating criminal intent.

While each case is judged on its own merits, there are always at least two sides in an issue involving the murder of one by another. The survivors of the victim demand justice, and the justice they usually seek is the death of the one who brought about the death of their own. This is a manifestation of an eye for an eye. In many respects, it is an accurate portrayal of why the death penalty is imposed for both juveniles and adults. It is supposed to be a penalty that fits the crime committed. But attorneys and family members of those convicted of capital crimes cannot help but feel compassion for their doomed relatives (Coleman 1998). Someone they love is about to lose his or her life. But hadn't that person taken someone's life in the process? But does taking another life bring back the dead victim? But does taking the life of the murderer fulfill some lofty societal purpose? Below are several important landmark cases involving the death penalty applied to juveniles.

Eddings v. Oklahoma (1982). The *Eddings* case raised the question of whether the death penalty as applied to juveniles was cruel and unusual punishment under the Eighth Amendment of the U. S. Constitution. The SC avoided the issue. The Justices did not say it was cruel and unusual punishment, but they also did not say it wasn't. What they said was that the youthfulness of the offender is a mitigating factor of great weight that must be considered. Thus, many jurisdictions were left to make their own interpretations of the high court opinion. On April 4, 1977, Monty Lee Eddings and several other companions ran away from their Missouri homes. In a car owned by Eddings' older brother, they drove, without direction or purpose, eventually reaching the Oklahoma Turnpike. Eddings had several firearms in the car, including several rifles that he had stolen from his father. At one point, Eddings lost control of the car and was stopped by an Oklahoma State Highway Patrol officer. When the officer approached the car, Eddings stuck a shotgun out of the window and killed the officer outright. When Eddings was subsequently apprehended, he was waived to criminal court on a prosecutorial motion. Efforts by Eddings and his attorney to oppose the waiver failed. In a subsequent bifurcated trial, several aggravating circumstances were introduced and alleged, while several mitigating circumstances—including Eddings' youthfulness, mental state, and potential for treatment—were considered by the trial judge. However, the judge did not consider Eddings' unhappy upbringing and emotional disturbance as significant mitigating factors to offset the aggravating ones. Eddings' attorney filed an appeal that eventually reached the SC. Although the Oklahoma Court of Criminal Appeals reversed the trial judge's ruling, the SC reversed the Oklahoma Court of Criminal Appeals. The reversal pivoted on whether the trial judge erred by refusing to consider the unhappy upbringing and emotionally disturbed state of Eddings. The trial judge had previously acknowledged the youthfulness of Eddings as a mitigating factor. The fact of Eddings' age, 16, was significant, precisely because the majority of Justices did not consider it as significant. Rather, they focused upon the issue of introduction of mitigating circumstances specifically outlined in Eddings' appeal. Oklahoma was now in the position of lawfully imposing the death penalty on a juvenile who was 16 years old at the time he committed murder.

Thompson v. Oklahoma (1988). In late 1988, the SC heard the case of William Wayne Thompson, convicted of murdering his brother-in-law on January 23, 1983. Thompson was 15 years old when the especially brutal murder occurred. Under Oklahoma law, the district attorney filed a statutory petition to have Thompson waived to criminal court where he could be tried for murder as an adult. The waiver was granted and Thompson was tried, convicted, and sentenced to death. Thompson appealed and his case was eventually reviewed by the SC. The SC concluded that "the Eighth and Fourteenth Amendments prohibit the execution of a person who was under 16 years of age at the time of his or her offense" (108 S.Ct. at 2700). Thompson's death sentence was overturned.

Thompson's attorney had originally requested the Court to draw a line so that all those under age 18 would be exempt from the death penalty as a punishment, regardless of their crimes. The SC refused to do this. However, two juvenile cases were heard in 1989 by the SC, where the juveniles were 16 and 17 respectively when they committed first-degree murder. These cases resulted in further restrictions in applying the death penalty.

Wilkins v. Missouri (1989).   Heath Wilkins was 16 when he stabbed to death a woman who was managing a convenience store. There was evidence of aggravating circumstances and torture of the woman. Wilkins was convicted of the murder after being transferred to criminal court and prosecution as an adult. He was sentenced to death and appealed, arguing that 16 is too young an age to be executed and is therefore cruel and unusual punishment. This landmark case by the SC set a minimum age at which juveniles can be executed. If juveniles are 16 or older at the time they commit a capital crime, they can suffer execution in those jurisdictions with death penalties. Previously, a case had been decided (*Thompson v. Oklahoma* [1988]) where the SC said that someone who was 15 at the time he or she committed murder cannot be executed. The *Wilkins* case effectively drew this line at age 16.

Stanford v. Kentucky (1989).   Kevin Stanford was charged with murder committed when he was 17 years old. He was transferred to criminal court to stand trial for murder as an adult. He was convicted, sentenced to death, and appealed. The appeal contended that he was too young to receive the death penalty, and that the death penalty would be cruel and unusual punishment. The SC upheld his death penalty and ruled that it is not unconstitutional to apply the death penalty to persons who are convicted of murders they committed when they were 17 years of age.

Based on the *Wilkins* and *Stanford* cases decided by the U.S. Supreme Court in 1989, the minimum age for applying the death penalty to juveniles is 16. If a youth was 16 or older at the time of committing capital murder, then a state may execute the juvenile. If juveniles commit murder when they are under the age of 16, then the death penalty cannot be applied. However, this doesn't prevent courts from imposing life-without-parole sentences for these offenders.

The Future of Juvenile Corrections

The following are indicative of future trends in juvenile corrections in the United States:

1. A greater portion of juvenile corrections will be administered by private interests. The private sector is experience the greatest gains in juvenile corrections, although adult correctional programs are feeling the encroachment of private organizations and agencies (Armstrong 2001). A critical factor is the growing numbers of adult and juvenile offenders to manage and slow adjustment of public correctional agencies to add staff commensurate to deal adequately with these offender increases.

2. The juvenile justice system will experience greater reforms in the area of juvenile rights commensurate with those enjoyed by adult offenders. Thus, we will likely see U.S. Supreme Court decisions extending to juveniles the right

to a jury trial where incarceration in secure detention facilities or even non-secure facilities of six months or more may be imposed by juvenile judges.

3. The trend in the deinstitutionalization of status offenses will likely continue, and juvenile courts will no longer have responsibility for dealing with runaways, incorrigibles, or truants. The juvenile court will become increasingly adversarial, in many respects paralleling the adult system. Plea bargaining will occur increasingly, as prosecutors and defense attorneys negotiate the best deals for their juvenile clients.

4. The increased use of transfers of juveniles to criminal courts will continue, especially for serious offenses including rape, robbery, and murder. Already, several states, including New York and Illinois, have automatic transfer statutes that result in automatic certification of juveniles in certain offender categories to the jurisdiction of criminal courts.

5. Increased use will be made of diversion and community-based probation services as alternatives to increasingly crowded juvenile court dockets. This trend will coincide with increased privatization of corrections, especially those community-based probation agencies and services (Armstrong 2001).

6. Juveniles will eventually be excluded entirely from adult facilities, including jails and lockups, even on temporary bases. Civil rights and other interest groups are attempting to see that all states remove juveniles from adult detention facilities. While this may work hardships on some isolated jurisdictions where services are not extensive, juvenile rights changes will mandate that all jurisdictions eventually comply.

7. Detention facilities for juveniles will increasingly emphasize vocational, educational, and employment-related services in order to assist youths in obtaining jobs when released. This will be a general shift from custodial to rehabilitative and reintegrative detention philosophy on a national scale.

8. There will be greater consistency among states in future years concerning the definition of juveniles and greater systematization regarding their treatment and processing. The Model Penal Code devised by the American Law Institute and other organizations is an attempt to create a high degree of uniformity in laws and regulations among the states. A similar movement is underway regarding juvenile matters.

SUMMARY

The history of juvenile corrections in the United States has been influenced by earlier events occurring in England. Originally, juveniles were within the jurisdiction of the King and his representatives or chancellors. Decisions about juvenile affairs were made by these chancellors, usually in the best interests of juveniles. This philosophy carried over into the formative years of the United States and influenced greatly how juvenile offenders were subsequently treated. This was the philosophy of *parens patriae*, and it continues to influence the nature and course of juvenile matters. During the 1700s and 1800s, juveniles were regulated largely by interests concerned about their social welfare. Protective measures were established to provide for their care if they were without adult supervision. An early public reformatory, the New York House of Refuge, was established to provide shelter and discipline for youths. During the late 1800s, children's tribunals evolved. These were forerunners of juvenile courts, which were established in 1899 in Illinois. By the 1940s, virtually all states had juvenile courts, as greater formality was incorporated into juvenile offender treatment and processing.

Presently, distinctions are made between juveniles who are delinquent and those who commit status offenses. Juvenile delinquency is any act committed by a juvenile that, if committed by an adult, would be a crime. Juveniles are traditionally within the jurisdiction of civil authorities, and all juvenile court actions are civil actions. Unlike delinquency, status offenses are not criminal acts. Nevertheless, they encompass a broad range of offenses that juveniles may commit, simply because they are juveniles. Status offenses include runaway behavior, curfew violations, and truancy. During the 1970s, a movement to deinstitutionalize these offenses occurred, and many jurisdictions subsequently deinstitutionalized status offenses (DSO) or removed status offenders from the jurisdiction of juvenile court judges. One reason for DSO is that status offenses are not as serious compared with delinquency. DSO was intended to separate status offenders from delinquent offenders. Most states today have adopted policies to separate these different types of offenders and to process status offenders differently. A majority of juvenile courts hear and decide delinquency cases, while social service agencies are frequently responsible for supervising and helping status offenders.

The juvenile justice system, exclusively a civil system, is similar to the criminal justice system for adults. Juvenile court judges preside over cases. Juveniles are typically screened by intake officers, who decide whether particular juveniles should be sent to juvenile court for an adjudicatory hearing. Juvenile court prosecutors also prioritize which juvenile offenders should be brought before the court. Subsequently, those juvenile offenders who face juvenile court judges are adjudicated, where it is decided whether the charges against them are sustained or proved. Several alternative standards are used by juvenile court judges in determining one's innocence or guilt. The civil standard of the weight or preponderance of the evidence is usually used if the possible punishment for a juvenile involves nominal or conditional punishments. The criminal standard of "beyond a reasonable doubt" is applied in deciding those cases where juveniles are in jeopardy of losing their liberty through incarceration. Several states have established youth courts as alternatives to formal juvenile court action, where less serious juveniles are judged and punished by juries of their peers. Punishments in youth courts are almost always accountability oriented and include community service and/or restitution.

Juvenile court judges have several options when adjudicating cases. They may impose nominal punishments, such as verbal warnings. Or they may impose conditional penalties, such as probation, fines, victim compensation, community service, or several other conditions. Or they may also impose nonsecure or secure confinement of various lengths. Secure custody is imposed on juveniles infrequently. Because delinquency increased substantially during the 1950s and 1960s, greater attention has been given juvenile matters by the courts. During these periods, juveniles enjoyed few legal rights. But during the 1960s and 1970s, the U.S. Supreme Court decided several important cases which afforded many legal rights for juveniles. These include *Kent v. United States*, which gave all juveniles the right to a hearing prior to being sent to criminal court to be prosecuted as adults. *In re Gault* afforded juveniles the right to cross-examine their accusers, to give testimony in their own behalf, to have an attorney, the right against self-incrimination, and the right to a notice of charges. *In re Winship* prevented juveniles from being charged with crimes in both juvenile and adult courts by ensuring them the right against double jeopardy. However, juveniles are not automatically entitled to a jury trial in juvenile court as the result of *McKeiver v. Pennsylvania*. Jury trials for juveniles are only available through judicial approval or if provided by statute in any given state.

For more serious juvenile offenders, significant legislative efforts have been made to ensure greater punishments for them. One result has been to waive or transfer them to criminal court to be prosecuted as adults, or to certify them as adults for the purposes of a criminal prosecution. Several types of waivers include the judicial waiver, the direct file or prosecutorial waiver, statutory exclusion, demand waivers, the reverse waiver, and the once an adult/always an adult provision. In recent years most states have changed their waiver statutes or modified the ways that juveniles can be processed and punished as adults. This is a very controversial area of juvenile law. One view, the traditional orientation, is that juveniles should be treated and rehabilitated, whereas another view, the due process orientation, is that juveniles who commit serious crimes should be responsible for their actions and face serious consequences, such as adult prosecution. This issue is presently unresolved.

Juvenile correctional institutions are faced with similar problems that confront adult incarcerative institutions such as overcrowding and violence. Several juvenile correctional goals include rehabilitation, reintegration, prevention, punishment, retribution, deterrence, isolation, and control. Some juveniles may also be given diversion. However, a majority of the juveniles adjudicated delinquent are placed on probation. Only a small proportion of juveniles are actually incarcerated. For juveniles who are incarcerated, short-term confinement averages about 30 days, while long-term confinement averages 6 months. Those adjudicated for serious offenses, such as murder, usually average 2 years of confinement in secure custody.

Several important issues pertaining to juvenile corrections have been identified. One issue is the deinstitutionalization of status offenses (DSO). Another involves the classification of juvenile offenders and which juveniles should be treated as adults and prosecuted in criminal courts. There is some disagreement about whether juvenile violence is increasing and whether less serious juvenile offenders will progress to more serious offending through career escalation. Little support presently exists to show that career escalation occurs to any great degree. Perhaps the most controversial topic is whether the death penalty should be applied to juveniles who commit capital murder. The U.S. Supreme Court has ruled decisively in several important death penalty cases for juveniles. It upheld as constitutional the death penalty as a punishment in the case of a 16-year-old, Monty Eddings. The *Eddings v. Oklahoma* (1982) case was precedent setting. However, a subsequent U.S. Supreme Court decision held that 15 was too young an age to sentence the guilty offender to death in the case of *Thompson v. Oklahoma* (1988). Eventually, in 1989, the U.S. Supreme Court decided in two separate juvenile capital punishment cases that the death penalty was not cruel and unusual punishment when administered to 16- and 17-year-olds respectively. These were the cases of *Stanford v. Kentucky* and *Wilkins v. Missouri*.

The future of juvenile corrections is uncertain. However, there is some indication that private interests will play an increasingly important role in operating and supervising institutions of secure confinement for juveniles as well as having a greater presence in community programs, such as probation and parole. It is also likely that the juvenile justice system will undergo additional reforms, and that the deinstitutionalization of status offenses will continue. Greater use of transfers and the gradual transformation of processing violent juvenile offenders are also likely. At the same time, more use will be made of community corrections for juveniles, and they will be exposed to more diverse types of rehabilitative and reintegrative programming. And more emphasis will be placed on heightening juvenile offender accountability, as various jurisdictions explore ways of dealing with juveniles more effectively.

QUESTIONS FOR REVIEW

1. What was the New York House of Refuge and what types of juveniles were most likely to benefit from it?

2. What are some important differences between delinquent and status offenders? What is meant by the deinstitutionalization of status offenses? How did the Juvenile Justice and Delinquency Prevention Act of 1974 influence how status offenders were eventually treated?

3. What are the major components of the juvenile justice system?

4. What are three types of dispositions that may be applied to juveniles who are adjudicated delinquent? Which dispositions are applied to juveniles most frequently?

5. What three important legal cases vested juveniles with important legal rights? What are some of the rights conveyed to juveniles in these cases?

6. What are three types of waivers or transfers that can lead to prosecutions of juveniles as adults in criminal courts?

7. What are some arguments favoring the death penalty for juveniles? What are some arguments opposing the death penalty for juveniles? What are three cases where the U.S. Supreme Court has ruled decisively in the death penalty for juveniles? What are these case outcomes?

8. What are four major goals of juvenile corrections?

9. What are some important characteristics of wilderness programs? Are these useful as alternatives to incarceration? Why or why not?

10. What are some likely trends that might occur in juvenile corrections and the juvenile justice system generally?

SUGGESTED READINGS

Armstrong, Gaylene Styve. *Private vs. Public Operation of Juvenile Correctional Facilities.* New York: LFB Scholarly Publishing LLC, 2001.

Cote, Suzette. *Criminological Theories: Bridging the Past to the Future.* Thousand Oaks, CA: Sage Publications, 2002.

Inciardi, James A. *The War on Drugs III: The Continuing Saga of the Mysteries and Miseries of Intoxication, Addiction, Crime, and Public Policy.* Boston: Allyn and Bacon, 2002.

Weis, Joseph G., George Bridges, and Robert D. Crutchfield. *Juvenile Delinquency: Readings.* Thousand Oaks, CA: Sage Publications, 2001.

INTERNET CONNECTIONS

ABA Juvenile Justice Center
http://www.abanet.org/crimjust/juvjus/home.html

Boot Camps
http://www.boot-camps-info.com/

Boot Camps for Struggling Teens
http://www.juvenile-boot-camps.com

Building Blocks for Youth
http://www.buildingblocksforyouth.org/issues/girls/resources.html

Center for Court Innovation
http://www.courtinnovation.org/

Communication Works
http://www.communicationworks.org

Council of Juvenile Correctional Administrators
http://www.corrections.com/cjca

Gender Programming Training and Technical Assistance Initiative
http://www.girlspecificprogram.org

Juvenile Boot Camp Directory
http://www.kci.org/publication/bootcamp/prerelease.htm

National Council of Juvenile and Family Court Judges
http://www.ncjfcj.unr.edu/

National Youth Court Center
http://www.youthcourt.net

North Carolina IMPACT Boot Camps
http://www.doc.state.nc.us/impact/

Juvenile Intensive Probation Supervision
http://www.nal.usda.gov/pavnet/yf/yfjuvpro.htm

Juvenile Justice Reform Initiatives
http://www.ojjdp.ncjrs.org/pubs/reform/ch2_k.html

National Girls' Caucus
http://www.pacecenter.org

Office of Juvenile Justice and Delinquency Prevention
http://www.ojjdp.ncjrs.org

PACE Center for Girls, Inc.
http://www.pacecenter.org

Rights for All
http://www.amnesty-usa.org/rightsforall/juvenile/dp/section2.html

Riker's Island High Impact Incarceration Program
http://www.correctionhistory.org/html/chronicl/nycdoc/html/hiip.html

Teen Boot Camp
http://www.teenbootcamps.com

Teen Court
http://www.teen-court.org

Texas Juvenile Probation Commission
http://www.tjpc.state.tx.us/

Wilderness Programs, Inc.
http://www.wildernessprogramsetc.com

Youth Alternatives, Inc.
http://www.volunteersolutions.org/volunteer/agency/one_177937.html

Youthful Offenders Parole Board
http://www.yopb.ca.gov/

Glossary

Absolute immunity Government officials are completely immune from lawsuits from probationers, parolees, or inmates for their actions.

Act to Regulate the Treatment and Control of Dependent, Neglected and Delinquent Children First juvenile court act passed by the Illinois State Legislature in 1899; led to establishment of first juvenile court.

Actuarial prediction Forecast of future behavior based upon a comparison of a convicted offender's characteristics with a class of offenders who are recidivists; the more the offender's characteristics match those of recidivists, the less likely it is expected that the offender will be successful while on probation or parole.

Addams, Jane Reformer who founded Hull House in Chicago in the late 1800s.

Adjudication Decision by juvenile court judge regarding the facts alleged in a delinquency petition; comparable to a determination of guilt or innocence of a defendant in criminal court.

Adjudicatory proceedings Juvenile court matters are heard and resolved; judge decides guilt or innocence of juvenile or whether the facts alleged in a petition are true.

Administrative Office of the U.S. Courts Organization that hires federal probation officers to supervise federal offenders; also supervises pretrial divertees; probation officers prepare presentence investigation reports about offenders at the request of district judge.

Aggravating circumstances Events surrounding the commission of a crime that increase its seriousness; circumstances include serious injury or death to victims; unusual or cruel punishments inflicted by defendant on victims; defendant was on probation or parole when committing new crime.

AIDS (Acquired Immune Deficiency Syndrome) Lethal virus usually spread through sexual contact.

AIMS (Adult Internal Management System) Self-administered questionnaire given to prison inmates to determine their psychological and emotional states.

Alternative dispute resolution (ADR) Removal of a criminal case from the criminal justice system temporarily, where an impartial arbiter attempts to work out an agreement between defendant and victim to their mutual satisfaction; unsatisfactory resolution places case back in system, resulting in criminal prosecution; ADR often results in financial compensation by defendant for property damage or physical injuries sustained by victim.

American Correctional Association Founded in 1870 as the National Prison Association; first president was future U.S. President Rutherford B. Hayes; had 9,000 members in 1986; provides instruction and technical assistance to correctional institutions; promotes high correctional standards; provides training and publications to any interested agency.

American Prison Association Early name given to the American Correctional Association.

Anamnestic prediction Method of forecasting one's likelihood of reoffending by considering circumstances prior to one's conviction and the circumstances of one's environment if paroled; if circumstances have changed favorably, then the offender will likely be paroled.

Appointment on merit Promotion in organizations according to one's expertise and accomplishments, not on the basis of who one knows.

Arkansas prison scandal Incident in the Arkansas State Prison system uncovered by Thomas O. Murton, appointed to administer the prison system in Arkansas by the governor; later relieved of his administrative duties when disclosures of scandal and prisoner torture and treatment became publicly known.

Arrest Taking into custody a suspect who has allegedly committed a crime.

Assessment centers Rigorous identification and evaluation mechanisms lasting as long as one week that are geared to thoroughly test selected relevant attributes of prospective corrections officers.

Auburn State Penitentiary Prison constructed in Auburn, New York, in 1816; pioneered use of tiers where inmates were housed on different floors, levels, or tiers, usually according to their offense seriousness; introduced congregate system, where prisoners had opportunities to congregate with one another for work, dining, recreation; introduced stereotypical striped prison uniforms for prisoners.

Augustus, John (1785–1859) Father of probation, which he pioneered in United States in 1841; considered first informal probation officer; Boston shoemaker and philanthropist, active in reforming petty offenders and alcoholics charged with crimes; assumed responsibility for them and posted their bail while attempting to reform them; considered successful.

Authoritarian model Prison management style characterized by a high degree of centralization of authority and decision making.

Authority Similar to power, except does not imply force to gain another person's compliance to carry out orders. (See also **Power.**)

B.A.C.I.S. (Behavior Alert Classification Identification System) Method of distinguishing between inmates according to their risk and needs; separates mentally ill jail inmates from the rest of the jail population; assessment conducted by jail officers and other personnel.

Back-door solutions Answers to prison or jail overcrowding problem after inmates have been incarcerated; court-ordered prison or jail population reductions, use of early release or parole, furloughs, work release, administrative release.

Bail A surety to obtain the release of a suspect under arrest, and to assure the court that the defendant will appear at trial later; bail is only available to those "where it is proper to grant bail," according to the U.S. Supreme Court.

Banishment A form of punishment where an offender is ostracized from the community to a remote location; Australia and the colonies were used as places for banishing Great Britain's dissidents, criminals, and undesirables.

Bates, Sanford (1884–1972) First Director of the U.S. Federal Bureau of Prisons, 1930-1937.

Beccaria, Cesare Bonesana, Marchese di (1738–1794) Developed classical school of criminology; considered "father of classical criminology;" wrote *Essays on Crime and Punishments*; believed corporal punishment unjust and ineffective; believed that crime could be prevented by clear legal codes specifying prohibited behaviors and punishments; promoted "just-deserts" philosophy.

Bentham, Jeremy (1748–1832) British hedonist; wrote *Introduction to the Principles and Morals of Legislation*; believed criminals could be deterred by minimizing pleasures derived from wrongdoing; believed punishment should be swift, certain, and painful.

Bifurcated trial Proceeding required in all death penalty cases, where first stage is to determine guilt or innocence of defendant; second stage is to determine whether death penalty should be administered, in consideration of aggravating or mitigating circumstances.

Body cavity searches Any inspection of one's private parts by jail or prison officials; includes inspections of vaginas, rectums, and any other body orifice.

Boot camps Highly regimented disciplinary programs for youthful offenders; modeled after military training camps for new recruits; these programs operate for different offenders for up to two years; objectives are to teach discipline, self-control, and to offer educational, vocational, and counseling services to disturbed youth.

Boston Children's Aid Society Privately funded philanthropic society founded by Rufus R. Cook in 1860, catering to orphans and other minors who did not have adequate adult supervision; used volunteers to assist juvenile offenders.

Brace, Charles Loring Established New York Children's Aid Society in 1853.

Brockway, Zebulon Reed (1827–1920) First superintendent of Elmira, New York, Reformatory; believed in rehabilitation and reformation; encouraged prisoners to become educated and learn vocational skills.

Broker Supervisory style of probation/parole officers where they attempt to network with other agencies and organizations to find programs or services to assist their clients.

Bureaucracy Model of organizations specifying predetermined arrangement of tasks, impersonal rules, hierarchy of authority, spheres of competence, promotion according to merit, selection by test, task specialization; invented by Max Weber (1864–1920), German sociologist.

Bureaucratic-lawful model Prison management style where elaborate chains of command are in place, where control is stressed as the means for maintaining prison order.

Bureaucratic model Organizational arrangement based upon principles of bureaucracy; appointment on merit, selection by test, hierarchy of authority, spheres of competence, specialization of tasks.

Burnout Term used to denote physical and/or psychological exhaustion associated with one's job; stressful aspects of job leading to poor work performance, labor turnover.

Campus model Pattern for detention of female offenders stressing skill acquisition, including cosmetology; parenting, office skills, arts, and crafts.

Capital punishment (See **Death penalty**)

Career criminals Those offenders who earn their living through crime.

Caseload The average number of parolees or probationers supervised by a parole officer or probation officer; computed differently, using numbers of clients divided by numbers of officers; assignments according to specialties such as mentally ill parolees or probationers, those with alcoholic or drug dependencies.

Cellular telephone devices Electronic monitoring devices that are transmitters worn by offenders that transmit signals that can be intercepted by local area monitors.

Centralization Limited distribution of power among a few top staff members of an organization.

Certifications (See **Transfers**) Act of declaring a juvenile an adult for purposes of going forth with a criminal prosecution; usually reserved for serious offenses committed by juveniles; similar to a transfer or waiver.

Children in need of supervision (CHINS) Youths who require some form of adult management and monitoring; name given to juveniles who appear in juvenile court where it is alleged that they are in need of parental or guardian supervision.

Children's tribunals Informal hearings to decide juvenile cases where offenses are alleged; used extensively in late 1880s.

Child sexual abusers Adults who involve minors in all kinds of sexual activity ranging from intercourse with children to photographing them in lewd poses.

Chivalry hypothesis Explanation for judicial leniency toward female offenders; posits that much of the criminality among females is hidden because of the generally protective and benevolent attitudes toward them by police, prosecutors, juries and judges.

Clark, Benjamin C. Social reformer and philanthropist associated with Temperance Movement; active in mid-1800s in attempting to reform alcoholics charged with crimes.

Classical school of criminology Promoted by Cesare Beccaria, this view advocated access to legal rights primarily as a way of controlling citizen unrest; punishment should be swift and certain; best approach to crime is prevention rather than punishment.

Classification Inmate classification based on measures relating to one's potential dangerousness or risk posed to public; scheme to categorize offenders according to the level of custody they require while incarcerated; measures potential disruptiveness of prisoners; measures early release potential of inmates for parole consideration; based on psychological, social, and sociodemographic criteria.

Clients Refers to probationers or parolees who are enrolled in unconditional or conditional probation or parole programs; any offender who is sentenced to a community corrections program for a period of time.

Clinical prediction Psychiatric examination of an offender to determine his or her readiness to enter community following conviction for an offense or after serving time in prison or jail for a criminal conviction.

Cloaca Maxima Old Roman prison constructed under main sewers of Rome at about 640 B.C.; vast series of interconnected dungeons.

Co-corrections, co-ed prisons Secure facilities where male and female prisoners live, supervised by female and male staff, and participate in all activities together; sharing same quarters is prohibited.

Coercive power Supervisory relation where superior elicits compliance by subordinates through threats of punishment.

Community-based corrections programs Include intensive supervised probation; privately or publicly operated facilities that provide comprehensive support for offenders, including food, clothing, shelter, counseling, job assistance, and training.

Community control Form of supervised custody in the community, including surveillance on weekends and holidays, administered by officers with restricted caseloads.

Community Control II Program An intensive supervision program by officers with restricted caseloads with a condition of 24-hour-a-day electronic monitoring, and a condition of confinement to a designated residence during designated hours.

Community corrections Collection of agencies, organizations, and programs that supervises and manages large numbers of adult and juvenile offenders and nonoffenders for various lengths of time, in most cities, towns, and neighborhoods.

Community corrections act Statewide mechanism and enabling legislation through which funds are granted to units of government to plan, develop, and deliver correctional sanctions at the local level; purpose is to provide local sentencing options in lieu of imprisonment.

Community model Correctional model stressing community reintegration; offenders are permitted brief furloughs or visits to the community from prison; work release; limited exposure to community life; eventually, their transition to the community from prison proceeds smoothly.

Community service orders Judicially imposed restitution for those convicted of committing crimes; some form of work must be performed to satisfy restitution requirements.

Community supervision officers Similar to probation officers, these personnel are responsible for the field supervision of federal parolees and mandatory releasees; they prepare periodic reports about parolee progress while under supervision, and these reports are disseminated to the U.S. Parole Commission.

Compulsory School Act Legislation passed in Colorado in 1899 directed to prevent truancy among juveniles; Act included juveniles who were habitually absent from school, who wandered the streets, and had no obvious business or occupation.

Concurrent jurisdiction (See **Direct file**)

Conditional dispositions Sanctions imposed by juvenile judge authorizing payment of fines, community service, restitution, or some other penalty after an adjudication of delinquency has been made.

Conditional diversion Temporarily ceasing a prosecution against a criminal defendant, where defendant must be law-abiding and obey conditions of probationary-type program for a period of time, usually for six months or a year; following the successful completion of this program, the charges against the defendant may be dropped or downgraded to less serious charges.

Conditional releases (See **Parole**)

Confinement (See also **Placement**) Refers to placing a juvenile in either a foster home, out-of-home group facility, agency, or non-secure or secure facility, such as a juvenile industrial school.

Congregate system Organizational pattern pioneered at Auburn, New York, Penitentiary where prisoners were allowed to congregate with one another for dining, work, and recreation but were isolated during evening hours.

Continuous signaling devices Electronic monitoring devices that emit continuous signals that can be intercepted by telephonic communication from a central dialing location such as a police station or probation office.

Continuous signaling transmitters Electronic monitoring systems that are worn by offenders and emit continuous signals that may be intercepted by probation officers with portable receiving units.

Contract prisoners Inmates held in jails or other incarceration facilities out of their own jurisdictions; Hawaiian prisoners might be housed in Texas jails, for instance, because of overcrowding; state or local jail officials contract with other jurisdictions to house a portion of their inmate overflow.

Control Close supervision or management of offenders while on probation or parole.

Conventional model Caseload assignment method for probation or parole officers where clients are randomly assigned to officers.

Conventional model with geographic considerations Method of assigning probation/parole officer caseloads on the basis of where clients live; objective is to group clients into geographical areas where they reside to decrease the amount of time spent traveling from place to place to visit clients by officers.

Cook, Rufus R. Social reformer associated with Temperance Movement in mid-1800s; dedicated to reforming alcoholics charged with crimes.

Cools Term used to describe female inmates by other inmates; "cools" are those females with prior records who attempt to violate prison rules and remain undetected.

Corporal punishments The infliction of pain on the body by any device or method; flogging, dismemberment, stretching on the rack, and mutilation are examples.

Correctional officers Guards in a prison who supervise or manage inmates.

Corrections The vast number of persons, agencies, and organizations that manage accused, convicted, or adjudicated criminal offenders and juveniles.

Corrections volunteers Any unpaid person who performs auxiliary, supplemental, or any other work or services for any law enforcement or corrections agency.

Court-watchers Private citizens who sit in courtrooms and observe judicial decision making; purpose is to ensure that justice is done and that some defendants do not escape the full measure of the law when judges punish them.

Creaming Selecting inmates or probationers/parolees for program involvement on the basis of their minor offending or first-offender status; selections include only those persons most likely to succeed, where in fact the program is supposed to help those most likely to fail; when program is successful, it is usually because only the most successful clients have been included in the program and the worst offenders have been excluded from the program.

Criminal contamination Belief by citizens that if criminals live together in halfway houses, they will breed more criminality and infect neighborhoods with their criminal behavior.

Criminal justice Investigation of decision-making bodies as they pertain to the prevention, detection, and investigation of crime, the apprehension, accusation, detention, and trial of suspects; and the conviction, sentencing, incarceration, or official supervision of adjudicated defendants; juvenile justice system is the equivalent for youthful offenders.

Criminal justice system Sometimes called a process, consisting of law enforcement, the prosecution, courts, and corrections; the system whereby offenders are processed and punished.

Crofton, Sir Walter Established Irish system (See **Tickets-of-Leave**); Irish prison reformer; Director of Ireland Prison System in mid-1800s.

Cruel and unusual punishment Unspecified by U.S. Supreme Court, subjectively interpreted on case-by-case basis; prohibited by Eighth Amendment of U.S. Constitution.

Custodial dispositions Sanctions imposed by juvenile judge following adjudication of juvenile as delinquent; includes nonsecure or secure custody; nonsecure custody may be in a foster home or community agency, farm, camp; secure custody may include detention center, industrial school, reform school.

Custodial model Pattern for housing female offenders where main interest is confinement, containment, discipline, and uniformity.

Dangerousness Measure of inmate's propensity to commit violent acts against others; index used for inmate placement and whether parole or probation should be granted to offenders.

Day parole (See **Furloughs**)

Day pass (See **Furloughs**)

Day reporting centers Community corrections agencies that supervise probationers and parolees; may conduct drug or alcohol checks, urinalyses, and collect fee payments for victim restitution or compensation.

Death-qualified jury Panel comprised of persons who can impose the death penalty despite the fact that they may be opposed to it morally; as long as their judgment to impose the death penalty is not impaired by their opposition to it, they are a death-qualified jury (See **Witherspoon v. Illinois** [1968])

Death penalty Capital punishment imposed in the United States and several other countries, where life of offender is taken; death penalty is carried out differently in various jurisdictions, including shooting, hanging, electrocution, gassing, or lethal injection.

Death row Arrangement of prison cells where inmates are housed who have been sentenced to death.

Decarceration Prohibition of detention for juveniles; removal of inmates from prisons or jails.

Decentralization Widespread distribution of power among many staff members; in prisons, limited power may be given to inmates as representatives of larger prisoner aggregate.

Deferred prosecution Temporary halting of a prosecution against a defendant while he or she is subjected to a program with particular requirements for a short period (See also **Diversion**).

Deinstitutionalization Removing juveniles from secure facilities.

Deinstitutionalization of status offenses (DSO) The removal from secure institutions and detention facilities of youths whose only infractions are status offenses, including running away from home, incorrigibility, truancy, and curfew violations.

Deliberate indifference Attitude of prison or jail officials where they ignore inmates with injuries or do not act as they should to prevent inmate abuse by other inmates; intentional tort.

Delinquency The process of committing any act by a juvenile that would be a crime if committed by an adult (See **Juvenile delinquency**).

Delinquent acts Offenses committed by a juvenile that would be crimes if committed by an adult.

Demand waiver Request and motion made by juvenile to have the case moved to criminal court from juvenile court.

Deserts model (See **Just-deserts model**)

Design capacity Optimum number of inmates that architects originally intended to be housed or accommodated by jail or prison.

Detainer, detainer warrants Notices of criminal charges or unserved sentences pending against prisoners; usually authorized by one jurisdiction to be served on prisoners held in other jurisdictions; when prisoners serve their sentences in one jurisdiction, they are usually transferred under detainer warrants to other jurisdictions where charges are pending against them.

Detention Confinement of juvenile in foster home, group home, camp as nonsecure detention; secure detention is placement of juvenile in industrial school or reform school, similar to prisons for adults.

Determinate sentencing Punishment scheme whereby judge fixes the term of an offender's incarceration that must be served in full, less any good-time credits accumulated by offender as an inmate; parole boards are not involved in any discretionary early release decision.

Deterrence Philosophy of punishment espousing that incarceration and harsh sentences will deter offenders from committing future crimes.

Direct file Type of waiver where prosecutor has the sole authority to prosecute a youth as an adult in criminal court or as a juvenile in juvenile court; also known as concurrent jurisdiction.

Direct-supervision jail Any jail facility that is constructed with a podular design, providing jail officers with a 180-degree view of inmates and that uses closed-circuit cameras to monitor inmate activities.

Discretionary waiver Type of judicial waiver empowering juvenile court judge to maintain control over a youth's case or transfer the case to criminal court.

Disposition, disposed Equivalent of a sentence imposed by a judge in a criminal court; juvenile court judge imposes one of several options upon a juvenile where it is found that the facts alleged in a petition are true; options may include nominal, conditional, or custodial sanctions.

Diversion Removing a case temporarily from the criminal justice system, while a defendant is required to comply with various conditions such as attending a school for drunk drivers, undergoing counseling, performing community service, or other condition; may result in expungement of record; a pretrial alternative to prosecution; temporary and conditional removal of the prosecution of a case prior to its adjudication, usually as the result of an arrangement between the prosecutor and judge.

Diversion program Any preconviction option whereby the prosecutor places an offender in either a supervised or unsupervised program for a period of time, usually 6 months to 1 year; following successful completion of diversion, offender either has record expunged or charges downgraded; helps to avoid criminal record in first-offender cases.

Divertee Any client of a diversion program.

Divestiture Act of juvenile court judge whereby he or she relinquishes jurisdiction over certain types of juvenile offenders, such as status offenders.

Double-bunking Practice used by jail and prison administrators of placing two or more prisoners in a single cell ordinarily designed to house one offender; used as a means of alleviating overcrowding.

Drug/alcohol dependent offenders Those with chemical dependencies, including addiction to illegal substances or drugs and alcoholic beverages.

Dunking stool Corporal punishment device where offender is placed in a chair at end of long lever and dunked in nearby pond until almost drowned; punished often for gossiping and wife-beating.

Education furloughs (See **Furloughs**)

Electronic monitoring The use of telemetry devices to determine an offender's whereabouts at particular times.

Elmira Reformatory First true reformatory built in 1876; first superintendent was Zebulon Brockway, a rehabilitation and reformation advocate; promoted educational training and cultivation of vocational skills; believed in prisoner reformation; questionably successful as a reformatory.

English Penal Servitude Act Legislation passed by British Parliament in 1853 authorizing establishment of rehabilitative programs for inmates and gradually eliminating banishment as a form of punishment.

Exhaustion requirement 1995 federal legislation designed to decrease sheer volume of federal court filings by inmates of prisons and jails; state prisoners must exhaust all available state remedies before filing their petitions in federal courts seeking relief; if they have not exhausted all state appeals, their federal suits will be dismissed.

Experience programs Various activities for juveniles who have been adjudicated delinquent or status offenders; includes wilderness experiences and other outdoors programs where youths learn self-esteem, survival skills, self-respect, and respect toward others and authority.

Expert power Authority form based on personal expertise or skills of superior.

False negatives Offenders who are predicted to be nonviolent or not dangerous according to various risk or dangerousness prediction devices but who actually turn out to be dangerous or pose serious public risk.

False positives Offenders who are predicted to be dangerous or pose serious public risk according to various prediction devices and instruments but actually are not dangerous and do not pose public risk.

Federal Bureau of Prisons (BOP) Established in 1930 by Congress; in 1987 operated 43 correctional facilities for persons convicted of violating federal laws; operates Federal Prison Industries, a business enterprise selling manufactured goods by prisoners; functions include furnishing safe custody and a humane environment for prisoners, and to provide them with educational advancement, vocational training, counseling, and personal growth experiences; also contracts with 385 halfway houses for the intermediate detention of parolees.

Federal Juvenile Delinquency Act Legislation passed in 1938 that provides for optional probation to youthful offenders within federal jurisdiction.

Federal Prison Industries, Inc. (See **UNICOR**)

Federal Tort Claims Act of 1946 28 U.S.C. Section 2674; Act providing that the United States shall be liable, respecting the provisions of this title relating to tort claims, in the same manner and to the same extent as a private individual under like circumstances, but shall not be liable for interest prior to judgment for punitive damages.

Felon One who commits a felony.

Felonies Major crimes punishable by incarceration of one year or more and/or fines; incarceration usually is in penitentiary or prison rather than jail, although jails are sometimes used to accommodate prison population overflow; FBI uses eight major felonies in *Uniform Crime Reports* for charting crime trends annually.

Financial/community service model Restitution model for juveniles that stresses the offender's financial accountability and community service to pay for damages.

Fines Financial penalties optionally imposed by judges in U.S. courts for law violations; fixed fines, day-fines, and standard fines used in Swedish courts for various types of offenses, depending on crime seriousness.

First offenders Criminals who have committed one or more crimes but who have no previous criminal record.

Fixed indeterminate sentencing Punishment scheme whereby judge sentences offenders to single prison term that is treated as the maximum sentence for all practical purposes; parole board may determine early release date for offender. (See also **Indeterminate sentencing**)

Florida Assessment Center Established in Dade County, Florida, purpose of organization is to train probation and parole officers for entry-level positions in probation and parole. (See also **Assessment centers**).

Forgotten offenders Female offenders in U.S. prisons and jails.

Freedom of Information Act (FOIA) Legislatively created mechanism whereby private citizens can obtain secret government files about them; some information is confidential and cannot be released to private citizens; most documented information must be disclosed to those making such requests, however.

Front-door solutions Answers to prison or jail overcrowding occurring at beginning of criminal justice process; includes plea bargaining resulting in diversion, probation, community service, intermediate punishment, or some other nonincarcerative alternative.

Fry, Elizabeth Gurney (?–1845) English Quaker women's prison reformer, toured United States and other countries in early 1800s attempting to implement prison reforms; encouraged separate facilities for women, religious and secular education, improved classification systems for women; reintegrative and rehabilitative programs.

Furloughs Temporary release programs; authorized, unescorted leaves from confinement granted for specific purposes and for designated time periods, usually from 24 to 72 hours, although they may be as long as several weeks or as short as a few hours; first used in Mississippi in 1918.

Gaol English term for jail.

Gender courses Classes conducted for jail and prison officers to sensitize them about how to work around women in ways that will not lead to sexual harassment; classes are oriented toward respecting the work of persons of different gender.

Global positioning satellites (GPS) Method of tracking probationers and parolees by global satellites; used for locating offenders in neighborhoods at particular times; used to enforce exclusionary geographical boundaries; helps to verify offender whereabouts.

Good-time credits Accrued days off from original sentences earned by prisoners for good behavior; introduced in early 1800s by British penal authorities, including Alexander Maconochie and Sir Walter Crofton.

Great Law of Pennsylvania Sweeping reforms that abolished corporal punishment and ushered in the use of jails (gaols) and other incarcerative facilities in 1682.

Guidelines-based sentencing (See **Presumptive sentencing**)

Habeas corpus petition Petition filed, usually by inmates, challenging the legitimacy of their confinement and the nature of their confinement; document that commands authorities to show cause why an inmate should be confined in either a prison or jail; means literally "you should have the body" or "produce the body"; also challenges the nature of confinement.

Habitual offender laws Any laws punishing persons more severely for having been convicted of previous crimes; often such laws carry mandatory life imprisonment penalties.

Halfway houses Community-based centers or homes operated either by the government or privately; designed to provide housing, food, clothing, job assistance, and counseling to ex-prisoners and others; publicly or privately operated facilities staffed by professionals, paraprofessionals, or volunteers; designed to assist parolees make the transition from prison to the community.

Hands-off doctrine Policy practiced by state and federal judiciary up until 1940s whereby matters pertaining to inmate rights were left up to jail and prison administrators to resolve; considered "internal" matters, where no court intervention was required or desired.

Hayes, Rutherford B. First president of the American Correctional Association, originally called National Prison Association; later U.S. President.

High Street Jail First jail constructed under the Great Law of Pennsylvania on High Street in Philadelphia.

Home confinement (See **House arrest**)

Home incarceration (See **House arrest**)

House arrest (also **home confinement, home incarceration**) Intermediate punishment where offender's residence is used as the primary place of custody for a fixed term; a conditional sentence requiring offender to remain confined to residence.

Howard, John (1726–1790) Early English prison reformer; sheriff of Bedfordshire, England; influenced by other European countries such as France and lobbied for prison reforms.

Hull House Settlement home established by Jane Addams, a reformer; operated as a home for children of immigrant families in Chicago; financed by philanthropists; taught children religious principles, morality, and ethics.

Human relations model Pattern of organizations devised by Elton Mayo in early 1930s, emphasizing recognition of individual differences among employees, individual motivation is critical, human dignity is important, personality characteristics are important; contrasted often with bureaucracy (See also **Bureaucracy**, for comparison).

Human services approach Philosophy of some corrections officers, either in prisons or jails, whereby they regard each inmate as a human being with feelings or emotions; actions toward inmates are in terms of how their needs can be met, apart from simply viewing inmates as objects to be guarded or confined.

I-level classification (Interpersonal Maturity Level Classification) Psychological assessment of convicted offenders; uses developmental and psychoanalytical theories to determine the appropriate level or stage where offenders can function and cope with interpersonal problems; the higher the I-level, the better adjusted the offender.

Importation model The idea that prison culture is brought into the prison by other inmates, depending upon their life experiences and outside cultural values.

Incapacitation Philosophy of corrections that espouses that offenders should suffer loss of freedom; the more serious the offense, the greater the freedom loss; belief that the function of punishment is to separate offenders from other society members and prevent them from committing additional criminal acts.

Indentured servants Persons from England who paid for their passage to the American colonies by giving up seven years of their lives as slaves to those paying for their passage.

Indeterminate sentencing Punishment scheme whereby judge, either implicitly or explicitly, sets upper and lower bounds on the time to be served in incarceration; if convicted offender is actually incarcerated, a parole board determines early release date.

Index crimes, index offenses Several crime categories used by the FBI to report crime in the United States quarterly and annually.

In loco parentis Means "in the place of parents" and indicates the fact that the state acts to decide what is best for a juvenile during juvenile court proceedings.

Inmate Prisoner of jail or prison.

Inmate control model Prison management style where inmates form governing councils for dispute resolution and processing grievances; also has input for prison or jail operations.

Inmate disciplinary councils Internal inmate grievance procedures established by inmates themselves in either prisons or jails.

Inmate litigation explosion (See **Litigation explosion**)

Institutional corrections Prisons, jails, lockups, and any other facility designed to detain either adults or juveniles for short or long periods.

Intake Process of screening juveniles who have been charged with offenses.

Intake officer Juvenile probation officer who conducts screening of juveniles; dispositions include release to parents pending further juvenile court action, dismissal of charges against juvenile, detention, or treatment by some community agency.

Intensive probation/parole supervision (IPS) (See **Intensive supervised probation/ parole**)

Intensive supervised probation/parole (ISP) No specific guidelines exist across all jurisdictions, but ISP usually means lower caseloads for probation officers, less than 10 clients per month, regular drug tests, and other intensive supervision measures.

Intermediate punishments Those sanctions ranging between incarceration and standard probation on the continuum of criminal penalties.

International Halfway House Association (IHHA) Public organization whose membership operates halfway houses throughout the world; established in Chicago in 1964.

Interstate Compact for Adult Offender Supervision (ICAOS) Agreement among states to supervise offenders on probation or parole who are residents of a given state but who have been convicted of a crime or crimes in another state; state where offenders are residents supervise those offenders, even though their conviction offenses occurred in another state.

Irish system A multistage process whereby prison inmates could earn their early release from prison by acquiring tickets-of-leave.

Isaac T. Hopper Home Halfway house established in New York City in 1845.

Isolation Complete separation of offender from society; in prisons, segregative measure designed to keep certain inmates from the general inmate population for various reasons, usually related to their dangerousness or risk; inmates are placed in single cells and kept away from other prisoners.

Jail City- or county-funded facility operated to confine offenders serving short sentences, awaiting trial, housing prison overflow, witnesses, and others.

Jail and prison overcrowding Condition existing whenever a jail or prison exceeds the recommended or rated capacity of inmate population deemed appropriate for such a facility.

Jail boot camps Programs similar to boot camps but operated for a wider age range of clientele; short-term programs designed to foster discipline and self-improvement and self-image. (See **Boot camps**)

Jail diversion Method of channeling mentally ill persons and/or substance abusers to local mental health services where they can be closely monitored and their recidivism diminished.

Jailhouse lawyer Any inmate of a jail or prison who acquires sufficient legal education while incarcerated to file petitions, submit grievances, or help other inmates in their own lawsuits and legal actions against administrators or prison staff.

Jail overcrowding (See **Overcrowding**)

Jail removal initiative Under the Juvenile Justice and Delinquency Prevention Act of 1974, congressional mandate was implemented to release all juveniles from any kind of adult prison or jail following their arrest or being taken into custody by police; states are not obligated to follow or adhere to this initiative.

Judge Court officer who hears and decides cases within his or her jurisdiction; one who is empowered to hear and decide a case.

Judicial waivers Transfer authority inherent in juvenile court judge and subsequent action taken to move youth's case to criminal court.

Jurisdictions Areas of authority, either geographical or according to type of offense, where police officers and the courts have power to make arrests and judgments against criminals; the power of the court to hear certain types of cases.

Jury Body of 6 to 12 persons who are finders of fact and determine a person's guilt or innocence in a trial.

Jury trial Adversarial proceeding where a jury, the trier of fact, decides the guilt or innocence of the defendant on the basis of the evidence presented.

Just-deserts model Correctional model stressing equating punishment with the severity of the crime; based on Cesare Beccaria's ideas about punishment.

Justice model Correctional model that rejects rehabilitation as a correctional aim; rather, persons should be punished for their crimes, and the punishments should be commensurate with the crime seriousness. (See also **Just-deserts model**)

Juvenile Anyone who has not reached the age of majority and is within the jurisdiction of the juvenile court.

Juvenile delinquency The process of a juvenile's committing any act that, if committed by an adult, would be a crime.

Juvenile delinquents Any infants or youths under the age of majority who commit an offense that would be a crime if committed by an adult.

Juvenile detention centers Places or agencies where youths are held temporarily while they await a juvenile court hearing.

Juvenile Justice and Delinquency Prevention Act of 1974 Legislation passed by Congress in 1974 encouraging states to deal differently with their juvenile offenders; promotes community-based treatment programs and discourages incarceration of juveniles in detention centers, industrial schools, or reform schools.

Juvenile justice system Process whereby juvenile offenders are processed, adjudicated, and disposed of by juvenile court.

Juvenile probation (See **Probation, Juvenile**)

Labor turnover The proportion of persons who work in an organization and who quit, retire, or die during any given year.

Large jails Short-term incarceration facilities with 250 to 999 beds.

Latent functions Hidden or unintended functions of an action.

Law enforcement officers (agencies) Local, state, or federal agencies and personnel who uphold the laws of their respective jurisdictions.

Lawsuit syndrome Similar to the litigation explosion, where jail and prison inmates deluge the courts with numerous frivolous filings of writs and motions; a means whereby inmates can harass jail and prison officials/officers.

Legal-rational authority Power based in law, where persons are vested with rights to order others to comply with directives; most common authority form for bureaucracies.

Legislative waiver (See **Statutory exclusion**)

Legitimate power Authority form based on belief that superior has a right to compel subordinates to follow orders.

Level of custody Refers to security levels where prisoners are placed according to their risk or dangerousness; includes minimum, medium, and maximum-security.

Lex talionis The law of retaliation or retribution; a form of revenge dating back to the Apostle Paul and used up until the Middle Ages.

Lifes Habitual female offenders in prison who engage in deviant behavior with little or no regard for punitive consequences.

Litigation explosion Sudden increase in inmate suits against administrators and officers in prisons and jails during late 1960s and continuing through 1980s; suits usually challenge nature and length of confinement, torts allegedly committed by administration, usually seeking monetary of other forms of relief.

Lockdown Condition in a prison when all prisoners are restricted to their cells with limited necessities; limited or no social contact; close custody or security; lasts indefinitely; used as a punishment for rule infractions such as prison riots.

Lockups Facilities sometimes counted as jails; intended to hold prisoners for public drunkenness for short periods such as 24 or 48 hours.

Maconochie, Captain Alexander (1787–1860) Considered "father of parole"; prison reformer who held various posts in British prisons such as Norfolk and Van Diemen's Land in Australia; established "good time" credits to be earned by prisoners where they could gain early release for conforming to prison rules and doing good work; credited with inventing indeterminate sentencing.

Mamertine Prison Ancient prison constructed about 640 B.C. under the *Cloaca Maxima*, the main sewer of Rome, by Ancus Martius; a series of dungeons constructed to house a variety of offenders.

Management by objectives (MBO) Organizational strategy used in early 1970s whereby administrators could cope successfully with various organizational problems; MBO achieved by effective goal-setting and creating a system of accountability whereby one's performance can be measured over time; feedback essential from higher-ups.

Mandatory parole Obligatory early-release for inmates.

Mandatory probation Conditional sentence imposed by a judge, in lieu of incarceration, that is authorized by statute and provides for an obligatory probationary term, coupled with conditions including drug treatment, house arrest, restitution, or any other punishment/condition deemed suitable by the judge; usually cannot be terminated because of one or more program violations; judges must impose additional probation conditions, depending upon the circumstances, if it is found that probationers have violated their probation program conditions.

Mandatory release Setting free of prisoners from prison or jail, ordered by court to secure compliance with health and safety codes and reduce overcrowding.

Mandatory sentencing Punishment system whereby judge is required to impose an incarcerative sentence of a specified length for certain crimes or for particular categories of offenders; habitual offenders or persons who use firearms during the commission of a felony may be subject to mandatory sentencing in certain jurisdictions.

Mandatory waiver Transfer action where juvenile court judge must transfer youth to criminal court if probable cause exists that youth committed the offense(s) alleged.

Manifest functions Intended or known functions of an action.

Mark system Arrangement devised by Sir Walter Crofton whereby inmates earned credit for time served; time applied against original sentence, thereby permitting prisoners to gain early release.

Marks of commendation Point rewards given to inmates of the Birmingham Borough Prison by Alexander Maconochie in the 1850s.

Maxi-maxi prison Institution such as federal penitentiary at Marion, Illinois, where offenders are confined in individual cells with limited freedom daily; confinement in individual cells may be up to 23 hours per day; continuous monitoring and supervision; no more than three prisoners per guard.

Maximum-security prisons Highest custody level observed in prisons; closed-circuit television monitoring of offenders, limited access to recreation or educational/vocational opportunities; segregated confinement of prisoners in single cells, solitary confinement; designed primarily for containment rather than rehabilitation.

Medical model Treatment model of corrections; assumes that criminal behavior is result of psychological or biological conditions that can be treated; led to group therapy, behavior modification, and counseling of offenders as treatments.

Medium jails Short-term incarceration facilities with 50 to 249 beds.

Medium-security prisons Most frequently observed type of prison facilities; catchall term applied to prisons housing a wide variety of offenders; less freedom compared with minimum-security; limited access to educational, vocational, and therapeutic programs.

Megajails Any jail facility that has 1,000 or more beds.

Megargee Inmate Typology Scale devised to classify prisoners; psychological assessment device. (See also **Classification**)

Minimum due process rights Privileges extended to probationers and parolees who are in jeopardy of having their probation or parole programs revoked; entitled to right to have written notice of alleged program violations; right to a hearing; right to confront and cross-examine witnesses; right to give testimony on own behalf; right to a written judgment by a neutral body, either the court or a parole board; and right to call witnesses in own behalf.

Minimum-maximum determinate sentencing Judicially imposed punishment consisting of a minimum and maximum amount of time to be served by convicted offender; following minimum sentence, offender becomes eligible for parole, which is granted by a parole board, depending upon the convicted offender's eligibility.

Minimum-security prisons Low level of custody for supervising offenders; low-risk offenders are usually placed in minimum-security prisons; fewer guards and restrictions; often dormitory-like quality; unguarded or lightly guarded facilities.

Minnesota Multiphasic Personality Inventory (MMPI) Popular measure of psychological attributes; contains over 550 true-false items that measure different personality dimensions.

Misdemeanants Persons who commit misdemeanors.

Misdemeanors Minor or petty crimes carrying small fines and penalties; incarceration is usually less than one year, if incarceration is imposed; time served is usually served in jails rather than in prisons.

Mitigating circumstances Events surrounding the commission of a crime that lessen its seriousness; includes very young or very old defendants; nature of participation in the offense; assisting authorities in apprehending other criminals; mental illness or insanity.

Montesquieu, Charles-Louis de Secondat, Baron de La Brede et de (1689–1755) wrote *The Spirit of the Laws*; lawyer, philosopher, and writer; penal reformer who wrote about inhuman punishments at Devil's Island in French Guiana.

Motion for summary judgment Judgment granted by judges who have read plaintiff's version and defendant's version of events in actions filed by inmates; decision is reached holding for the defendant, usually prison authorities.

Motion to dismiss Motions granted by judges when inmates who file petitions fail to state a claim upon which relief can be granted; court has read inmate claim and decided no basis exists for suit.

Myers-Briggs Type Indicator (MBTI) Method of determining correctional managers' leadership style, behaviors, and work orientations.

National Crime Victimization Survey (NCVS) A semiannual compilation of crimes committed against various persons surveyed; interviews conducted with national sample of household members disclosing much unreported crime; is considered more accurate than *Uniform Crime Reports* in crime estimates in the United States.

National Prison Association Founded in 1870; first president was future U.S. President Rutherford B. Hayes; later became American Prison Association; later became American Correctional Association. (See **American Correctional Association**)

Needs assessment device Paper-pencil instrument used for various purposes by community and institutional corrections to determine which types of services are needed for offenders who have psychological problems or drug/alcohol dependencies.

Negligence Tort involving a duty of one person to another to act as a reasonable person might be expected to act, or the failure to act when the action is appropriate; failure to exercise reasonable care toward another; gross negligence includes wilful, wanton, and reckless acts, without regard for consequences and are totally unreasonable.

Negligent assignment Where correctional officers or probation/parole officers or other staff members are assigned to a position for which they are unqualified.

Negligent entrustment Where administrators fail to monitor guards entrusted with items they are unfamiliar with using such as firearms.

Negligent retention Where officers determined to be unfit for their jobs are kept in those jobs by administrators anyway.

Negligent training Failure to prepare jail or prison officers for duties they must perform; failure to instruct these officers in the proper use of firearms or transporting prisoners from one area of a prison or jail to another.

New-generation jails (See **Direct supervision jails**)

New York House of Refuge Established in 1825 in New York City by the Society for the Prevention of Pauperism; goals were to provide shelter and food for abused, poor, or orphaned youths.

NIMBY syndrome "Not in my back yard"—refers to objections citizens have about having any kind of correctional facility built in or near their neighborhoods or communities.

Nominal dispositions Sanctions imposed by juvenile court where juvenile is warned or verbally reprimanded, but returned to custody of parents.

Nonsecure placement Disposition by juvenile court judge authorizing adjudicated youth to be placed in a facility where some unsupervised freedom of movement around and off of the premises is permitted.

Nonviolent offenders Persons who commit a crime that does not cause physical harm to another.

Numbers game model Method of assigning probation or parole officer caseloads where total number of clients is divided by the total number of officers—this becomes the assigned caseload.

Offender control The amount of supervision given to any probationer, parolee, or institutionalized prison inmate.

Offense seriousness Crimes with greater punishments associated with their commission; the degree of gravity of the conviction offense; e.g., felonies are more serious than misdemeanors.

Once an adult/always an adult provision Statute treating a juvenile as an adult once the juvenile has been transferred to criminal court for any offense; youth will always be treated as an adult for purposes of criminal prosecution in the future.

Operational capacity Total number of inmates that can be accommodated based on size of jail or prison facility's staff, programs, and other services.

Operation Probationer Accountability Established by Marion (Indiana) Superior Court Probation Department in 1996; program is partnership between local law enforcement agencies and probation department to conduct random field investigations and searches at the residences of high-risk probationers convicted of drug, violent, or weapons offenses.

Organizational effectiveness Measured different ways, a method of determining whether an agency is meeting its goals and fulfilling customer's/client's needs.

Outward Bound Wilderness programs for juvenile offenders; intent of programs is to teach survival skills, coping skills, self-respect, self-esteem and respect for others and authority. (See also **Project Outward Bound**)

Overclassification Practice of assigning prisoners or juveniles to higher levels of custody than they deserve; e.g., placing someone in maximum-security custody when that person could be placed in less expensive minimum-security custody instead.

Overcrowding, prison or jail Condition when prison or jail population exceeds its rated or design capacity; sometimes measured by square footage allocated per prisoner.

Overrides Decisions by prison officials to change an inmate's risk or classification or security level from that indicated by some paper-pencil testing device.

PACT (Prisoner and Community Together) (See **Alternative Dispute Resolution and Victim/Offender Reconciliation Project [VORP]**)

PAM (Probation Automated Monitoring) System Developed by AutoMon Corporation, device for keeping track of probationers; clients use ID card with ATM-type machine and verify their identity by placing their finger on a device that reads their fingerprints; triggers machine interview, where questions are asked about offender work behaviors and other factual information.

Pardon Unconditional release of inmate, usually by governor or chief executive officer of jurisdiction.

Parens patriae Meaning "parent of the country," doctrine established under early English common law that meant that King or his agents assumed responsibility for matters involving juveniles; practiced in United States in most juvenile matters until mid-1960s.

Parole Conditional supervised early release from prison granted to inmates after they have served a portion of their original sentence.

Parole boards Panels of members, usually appointed by governor of a state or other executive, to make decisions about inmate early releases; often comprised of community representatives, teachers, corrections officials, lawyers, law enforcement officers.

Parolees Inmates who have been released short of serving the full sentence; usually conditions apply, and inmate is supervised by parole officer for a specified time period.

Parole officers Officials who supervise or manage parolees while on parole.

Parole revocation (See **Revocation**)

Parole revocation hearing Due process proceeding before a parole board to determine whether parolee has violated any of the conditions of a parole program; finding of guilt in this regard may lead to termination of the program and return to prison.

Participation hypothesis Theory that says the more subordinates participate in decision making affecting their work, the more they will like their work and comply with orders from higher-ups.

Participative management Involvement of clients in determining the nature of their own supervision; method of involving subordinates in decision making affecting their work.

Peer courts (See **Youth Courts**)

Penitentiary Interchangeably used with "prison" to refer to those long-term facilities where high custody levels are observed; solitary confinement or single-cell occupancy, where prisoners are segregated from one another during evening hours.

Penitentiary Act Legislation passed by House of Commons in England in 1779; Act authorized creation of new facilities to house prisoners, where they could be productive; prisoners would be well fed, well treated, well clothed, and housed in safe and sanitary units; trained to perform skills.

Pennsylvania system Devised and used in Walnut Street Jail in 1790 to place prisoners in solitary confinement; predecessor to modern prisons; used silence to increase penitence and prevent cross-infection of prisoners; encouraged behavioral improvements.

Persistent felony offenders Habitual offenders who commit felonies; have high recidivism rates.

Petition Formal document requesting that the juvenile court hear a juvenile's case, where various offenses are alleged.

Philadelphia Society for Alleviating the Miseries of Public Prisons Society made up of prominent Philadelphia citizens, philanthropists, religious reformers, who believe prison conditions ought to be changed and made more humane; established in 1787.

Placement Removing a juvenile from the home and remanding him or her to the custody of foster parents, group homes, camps, ranches, wilderness experiences, community corrections, or nonsecure/secure institutions.

Plea bargaining Preconviction agreement whereby a guilty plea is entered by the defendant in exchange for some concession or expected leniency from the prosecution; concession may be charge reduction, recommendation for leniency to judge, or promise of not making any recommendation about sentence; accounts for over 90 percent of all criminal convictions in United States annually.

POs Abbreviation for probation officers or parole officers.

Postconviction relief Any lawsuit filed by an inmate following a criminal conviction; intent is to appeal one or more issues to seek to overturn previous conviction.

Post-release supervision Another name for parole, where states and the federal government have abolished parole but release prisoners short of serving their full sentences.

Power Person's ability to influence another person to carry out orders.

Power clusters Issue networks and vested interest groups that have a stake in correctional organizations and correctional agencies, that work in collaboration with other interest groups to bring about a particular end and ensure that their interests are protected.

Preliminary hearing, preliminary examination Hearing held to establish if there is sufficient probable cause to continue a criminal prosecution against a defendant and to bring the case to trial.

Pre-sentence investigation Publicly or privately conducted examination of convicted offender's background and sociodemographic information; contains interview summaries with persons who knew convicted offender; prior record and work history; educational background; purpose is to assist judges in determining most appropriate sentence for offenders.

Pre-sentence investigation reports (PSIs) Reports filed by probation officers, usually at the request of presiding judge; report contains information about convicted offender, the offense, victim impact statement, defendant's version of events, defendant's employment history, prior record, relatives, and social acquaintances; used both by judge and parole board to deter-

mine severity of sentence or basis for early release from prison.

Presumptive or guidelines-based sentencing Punishment scheme using predetermined guidelines for each offense; upper, middle, and lower ranges of incarceration are established for each offense; judge selects middle range of incarceration, but judge may consider aggravating or mitigating circumstances associated with offense to increase or decrease the length of incarceration.

Presumptive waiver Type of judicial waiver where burden of proof shifts from the state to the juvenile to contest whether youth is transferred to criminal court.

Pretrial detainees Those accused of committing crimes; suspects are arrested and held in local jails until their trial can be held.

Pretrial detention Maintaining a suspect in custody awaiting trial; anyone who is detained in jail awaiting a future trial.

Pretrial diversion (See **Diversion**)

Pretrial release Judicially approved release of criminal defendant prior to trial, usually on a defendant's own recognizance.

Pretrial services Various actions and functions performed by criminal justice personnel that relate to early-stage offender processing; may include identifying critical pretrial issues, supervising pretrial release of defendants released on bail or on their own recognizance, providing pretrial diversion supervision, and the compilation of important defendant background information.

Prevention Philosophy of corrections that believes that the aim of punishment should be to prevent crime.

Preventive detention Act of incarcerating an alleged offender, usually in a jail, until a trial can be held to determine one's guilt or innocence.

Prisoner classification Method of assigning inmates in prisons to different levels of custody, usually based on their conviction offense and prior record; attempts to assess risk posed by particular inmates and whether they should be isolated from or included in general inmate population; paper-pencil devices are often used to classify offenders according to various salient social and behavioral characteristics.

Prisoners' rights movement Diffuse movement among prisoners and groups supporting rights for prisoners where avenues are explored for means whereby prisoners can exercise their legal rights in court and challenge jail and prison administration policies; started in the late 1960s and continues, with growing numbers of petitions filed by inmates in state and federal courts annually.

Prisonization Social process whereby inmates determine where other inmates should be placed in the inmate subculture according to their strength, fighting ability, attractiveness, age, social connections, race, ethnicity, and other criteria.

Prison Litigation Reform Act of 1995 (PLRA) Legislation designed to decrease the sheer numbers of inmate lawsuits filed against prison systems in federal courts by limiting government subsidies for case filing fees and other litigation expenses previously paid for on behalf of prisoners by the state.

Prison overcrowding (See **Overcrowding**)

Prisons State- or federally funded and operated institutions to house convicted offenders under continuous custody on a long-term basis.

Prison subculture (See **Subculture**)

Privatization Refers to financing and/or operation or management of prisons, jails, and other corrections agencies by private enterprise, usually for profit; most noticeable in 1980s in juvenile programs.

Probation Conditional release of convicted defendant into the community to avoid incarceration, under a suspended sentence, with good behavior, and generally under supervision by a probation officer.

Probation counselor Anyone who supervises a juvenile while the juvenile is on probation.

Probationers Convicted offenders who have been granted conditional nonincarcerative release in community, usually under supervision of a probation officer, and for a specified time period.

Probation officers Officials who supervise or manage probationers.

Probation revocation (See **Revocation**)

Professionalization Process of acquiring increased education, more in-service "hands-on" training, practical work experiences, and using higher selection standards (physical, social, and psychological) for officer or staff appointments.

Program for Female Offenders, Inc. Community-based corrections program designed to reform female offenders and create economically independent clients.

Programmed contact devices Electronic monitoring system where telephonic contact is made at random times with the offender and the offender's voice is verified electronically by computer.

Project Outward Bound Established in Colorado in 1962, one of several hundred programs in United States with objectives to equip youths with survival skills in wilderness areas; also teaches personal responsibility and heightens self-awareness and self-esteem.

Property crime Felony that is nonviolent, does not result in physical injury to victims; involves criminal acts against property including but not limited to larceny, burglary, vehicular theft.

Property offender Any person who commits a crime that does not involve direct contact with another, such as theft, burglary, larceny, forgery, vehicular theft, or embezzlement.

Prosecutors State attorneys who file charges against and prosecute alleged criminal offenders.

Psychological Inventory of Criminal Thinking Styles (PICTS) A 64-item measure comprised of eight separate thinking-style scales believed to reflect current criminal attitudes and beliefs; also references past criminal attitudes and beliefs; used to predict future disciplinary and release outcomes for incarcerated offenders.

Qualified immunity Work performed in good faith by probation or parole officers may result in harm to clients; officers are entitled to some immunity from lawsuits as long as they performed their jobs in good faith.

Quasi-judicial immunity Type of insulation from lawsuits enjoyed by probation officers who work directly for judges when preparing pre-sentence investigation reports; officers may include erroneous information in their reports that may be harmful to probationers, but the officers enjoy some immunity within the scope of their duties under the power of the judges with whom they work.

Rabble hypothesis Suggested by John Irwin; theory is that persons of lower socioeconomic statuses are placed in jails to rid society of their presence; homeless, detached, or disreputable persons are often selected by police officers for confinement; objective is to remove these undesirables from society so that other social classes will not have to interact with them.

Rated capacity The number of beds or inmates assigned by a rating official to various jails or prisons.

Reasonableness test Legal test used by appellate courts to decide whether to hear inmate petitions; test evaluates whether inmate interests in personal and constitutional rights override institutional interests for safety and security, and whether the inmate petition makes reasonable claims.

Recidivism The reversion of an offender to additional criminal behavior after the offender has been convicted of a prior offense, sentenced, and presumably corrected.

Recidivist An offender who reverts to additional criminal behavior after being convicted of a prior offense; may include parolees or probationers who violate one or more terms of their parole or probation; may include persons with prior criminal records who are rearrested but not necessarily convicted; may include persons returned to prison.

Red Hannah Whipping post used by Delaware prison authorities to flog inmates; used until corporal punishment statute in Delaware was repealed in 1973.

Referent power Compliance from subordinates is obtained through friendship adhering between supervisor and subordinate.

Referral Any action taken by police officers, concerned citizens, or intake officers that alert the juvenile court that one or more juveniles has committed a serious offense or is incorrigible.

Reformatory Detention facility designed to change criminal behavior or reform it.

Reformatory model Prison prototype that emerged during reformatory movement during 1870s; prisons established during the period 1870–1935 stressed skill development, reintegration, rehabilitation, and moral improvement.

Reform model (See **Rehabilitation model**)

Regional jails Facility for holding short-term offenders, built and run using the combined resources of several contiguous jurisdictions, such as counties or cities.

Rehabilitation Philosophy of corrections that promotes educational and vocational training for prisoners, believing these skill acquisitions will bring about prisoner reform or change; the belief that corrections can be helpful in reintegrating offenders back into society to lead productive and conforming lives.

Rehabilitation model Correctional model, similar to treatment or medical model, assumes offenders can be rehabilitated through meaningful work experiences, counseling, and education.

Reintegration, reintegration model Punishment philosophy that promotes programs that lead offenders back into their communities; reintegrative programs include furloughs, work release, and halfway houses.

Reparations Monetary damages awarded to victims that must be paid by criminals for any injuries suffered or property damaged.

Restitution Conditional order by juvenile or adult courts whereby offenders must reimburse their victims for physical or property damages.

Restorative justice (See **Alternative dispute resolution**)

Retribution View of punishment that says offenders should be punished for purposes of revenge.

Retributionist philosophy View of punishment that says offenders should be punished as a form of revenge for the wrongs that have committed against others.

Retribution model (See **Just-deserts model**)

Reverse waiver Action taken by criminal court to transfer a case back to juvenile court, usually at the recommendation of the prosecutor.

Reverse waiver hearings Any official proceeding in criminal court to determine whether the transferred juvenile should be sent back to juvenile court for processing.

Revocation hearing Due process meeting with judge or parole board to determine whether probationer or parolee has committed program infraction deserving of program termination.

Revocations, probation or parole Procedures whereby parole or probation is revoked, usually because of a program violation; requires a two-stage process to determine probable cause and punishment.

Reward power Power based on ability of superior to reward subordinates.

Reynolds, James Bronson Prison reformer who established University Settlement in New York City. (See **University Settlement**; See also **Settlement houses**)

Risk An assessment of an offender's dangerousness, either on probation, parole, a community corrections program or penal institution; the potential for someone to harm him- or herself or others; assessed with psychological instruments and counseling.

Risk-needs assessment Combined items on a paper-pencil device designed to measure one's dangerousness and services required to remedy one's deficiencies, such as personality disorders, drug/alcohol dependencies, and adjustment problems.

ROBO-PO Contemporary view of probation/parole officers who see their role as law enforcers and regulators; a move away from the traditional rehabilitation and reintegrative goals practiced by many probation/parole officers.

Role ambiguity Situation where probation or parole officers lack a full understanding of their work responsibilities and duties.

Role conflict Situation arising whenever probation or parole officer wants to supervise clients one way but the agency wants them to supervise clients differently; e.g., agency may want officers to be enforcers, but officers may want to be educators or enablers.

Rush, Dr. Benjamin (1745–1813) Quaker penal and religious reformer, physician; helped organization and operation of Walnut Street Jail for benefit of prisoners; encouraged humane treatment of inmates.

Safe-haven hypothesis Assumption that women with various types of problems, such as alcohol and drug dependencies, or limited educational levels, may benefit from short- or long-term incarceration in a jail or prison, because of the services they can provide these inmates; thus street life is considered harmful, whereas institutional remedies are safe havens for women in need.

Salient Factor Score Index (SFS; SFS 76, SFS 81) Device used by U.S. Parole Commission and other jurisdictions to predict dangerousness of inmates and assist in early-release decisions by parole boards; uses prior record and other factors as predictors of future dangerousness.

Section 1983 actions Any claim filed by an inmate under the Civil Rights Act within provisions of 42 U.S.C. Section 1983; usually seeks to show unequal treatment or civil rights infringements.

Secure placement Remanding a juvenile to the custody of officials in an industrial school, which is the equivalent of a prison for adults.

Selection by test Bureaucratic principle whereby the most eligible persons are promoted to higher positions on the basis of their objective test performance.

Selective incapacitation The process of incarcerating certain offenders considered to be high risks, dangerous, or who have a high propensity to commit future crimes and freeing those considered not to be dangerous or who will not pose serious public risks; controversial procedure of incarcerating offenders selectively on the basis of test scores that some offenders are likely recidivists while others are unlikely recidivists. (See also **False Positives**, **False Negatives**)

Sentencing Judicial imposition of a punishment, usually a period of months or years, offenders must serve either incarcerated or in community corrections programs following their convictions for one or more crimes.

Sentencing disparities Any difference in sentence imposed on different offenders who have been convicted of the same offense under similar circumstances; difference in sentencing severity is usually attributable to race, gender, ethnicity, or socioeconomic status; considered discriminatory; applied to judges in their sentencing patterns; disparities also occur in early-release decisions by parole boards.

Sentencing hearing Optional hearing held in many jurisdictions where defendants and victims can hear contents of pre-sentence investigation reports prepared by probation officers; defendants and/or victims may respond to report orally, in writing, or both; hearing precedes sentence imposed by judge.

Sentencing memorandum Prepared by defendants following their conviction; contains their version of the events leading up to the conviction offense and an apology or acceptance of responsibility statement; attached to pre-sentence investigation report.

Separation of powers Doctrine indicating that judiciary should not duplicate, perform, or interfere with executive or legislative powers and duties.

Settlement houses Homes established during 1886 and 1900 to furnish food, clothing, and temporary lodging to wayward or disadvantaged youths; operated by charitable and religious organizations; staffed by volunteers.

Sex offenders Individuals who commit a sexual act prohibited by law; includes rapists, prostitutes, voyeurs, child sexual molesters, date rapists, marital rapists.

Shakedowns Procedures where correctional staff conduct thorough search of prison or jail cells for contraband and other illicit materials and weapons.

Shared-powers model Prison management style where some degree of decision making power is extended to inmates as well as to correctional officers and administrators.

Sheriffs Chief law enforcement officers of U.S. counties; derives from the word, *shire*, meaning county in England, and *reeve*, meaning law enforcement officer; combining *shire* and *reeve* equals *sheriff*.

Shire-reeve County peace officer in England; collected taxes, kept peace in shires or counties; later, the term was changed to "sheriff"; used today in U.S. counties to denote chief law enforcement official.

Shires English equivalent to modern-day U.S. counties.

Shock incarceration (See **Shock probation**)

Shock parole (See **Shock probation**)

Shock probation Program first used in Ohio in 1965; planned sentences where judges order offenders imprisoned for statutory incarceration periods related to their conviction offenses; after 30, 60, 90, or 120 days of incarceration, offenders are taken out of jail or prison and "resentenced" to probation, provided they behaved well while incarcerated; objective is to "shock" convicted offenders with imprisonment as a deterrent against committing future crime.

Situational offenders First offenders who commit only one offense for which they were apprehended and prosecuted, but who are unlikely to commit future crimes.

Small jails Short-term incarcerative facilities with 49 or fewer beds.

Solitary confinement Punishment form where prisoner is isolated in a single cell with bare necessities for survival; length of confinement varies according to seriousness of infraction committed while incarcerated.

Specialization Organizational principle of bureaucracy indicating that each person should be highly trained to perform a certain function; this specialized training enhances person's productivity and effectiveness.

Specialized caseloads model Method of supervising parolees or probationers who have certain types of chemical or alcohol dependencies or mental illnesses; probation or parole officers who supervise these clients have special training geared to working with these types of problem offenders.

Special management inmates Prisoners who are aggressive/assaultive, mentally ill, vulnerable, physical ill or disabled who pose unusual supervision problems for jailers and jail staff.

Special-needs offenders Criminal offenders who have problems of drug or alcohol dependencies, mental illness or retardation, or handicaps, or are sex offenders or child sexual abusers; diffuse category of offenders committing unusual crimes or who have serious physical or psychological problems or limitations.

Squares Term to describe female inmates who are considered by other inmates to be "noncriminal"; may be first offenders who have committed petty crimes.

Standard diversion (See **Unconditional diversion**)

Standard probation (See **Probation**)

Status offenders Anyone who commits a status offense, or an act that would not be a crime if an adult committed it.

Status offenses Infractions committed by juveniles that, if committed by an adult, would not be crimes; includes runaways, truancy, violation of curfew.

Statutory exclusion Certain juveniles are automatically excluded from the jurisdiction of the juvenile court because of the seriousness of the offense(s) alleged and/or their age.

Statutory releases State obligation to release inmates who have served their full sentences.

Street attitudes Describe feelings of jail or prison correctional officers who fail to do their jobs, follow their job descriptions, or perform their duties poorly; includes those with personal prejudices toward racial or ethnic minorities.

Stress Physical or emotional exhaustion from job pressures; real or imagined (psychosomatic) physical or psychological problems relating to job expectations and one's perceived inability to live up to those expectations. (See also **Burnout**)

Strip search Varies in thoroughness among jurisdictions, but these searches are conducted of prisoners and visitors, where these persons are asked to strip and their persons are searched; may include visual inspection of body cavities or X-rays.

Subculture Term applied to inmate culture that is separate from nonincarcerated population culture in communities; separate, smaller social system within the larger social system, with its own language, status structure, reward and punishment systems.

Summary offenses Petty crimes that usually carry penalties of fines only; Great Britain uses summary offense category as least serious crime category; punishes offense by fine; magistrate decides case and jury trial is not permitted; in United States, convictions for summary offenses do not ordinarily result in criminal records; includes traffic violations, violations of city ordinances.

Superintendents Chief executive officers of prisons or penitentiaries.

Tactical response teams Also known as Correctional Emergency Response Teams and Hostage Recovery Teams, special units trained in hand-to-hand combat, firearms, and other skills designed to put down jail or prison rioting, inmate disturbances, and rescue hostages from prisons or jails.

Teen courts (See **Youth courts**)

Temporary release, work, or education furloughs (See **Furloughs**)

Therapeutic intervention Action by juvenile probation officer where officer may make visits to juvenile's home, inspect premises, or check with school officials on juvenile's progress.

Three Prisons Act Established by Congress in 1891 and provided for the construction of three federal prisons, the first in Fort Leavenworth, Kansas; the second in Atlanta, Georgia; and the third at McNeil Island, Washington.

Tickets-of-leave Developed by Sir Walter Crofton, Director of Ireland Prison System; multistage process by which inmates can gain early release from prison; authorizations for conditional early release from prison.

Tiers, tier system Innovation at Auburn State Penitentiary where prison cell blocks were built on top of one another as different floors; often, different floors segregated prisoners according to their offense seriousness.

Total institutions Term applied to prisons by Erving Goffman; prisons are seen as completely self-contained communities for prisoners; separate status system exists; private regulatory and enforcement personnel, inmate subculture.

Total quality management (TQM) View of inmates as customers rather than clients; a different perspective toward inmates where they are viewed as human beings with needs and feelings, and not merely as objects to be guarded.

Transfers Authorization by juvenile court to change status of juvenile offender to that of an adult so that criminal court can try case and impose punishments not otherwise imposed by juvenile courts; called waivers, certifications.

Transportation A form of banishment; temporary or permanent removal of an offender from society; used by England during the 1700s and 1800s.

Treatment Alternatives to Street Crime (TASC) Series of projects sponsored by the Law Enforcement Assistance Administration during 1970s designed to treat offenders with drug dependencies.

Treatment model (See **Medical model**)

Trial An adversarial proceeding where a judicial examination and determination of facts may be made by either a judge or jury.

Tucker telephone Torture device at the Arkansas State Prison used in the 1960s to electrically shock prisoners; electrical portion of hand-crank telephone used to punish prisoners; electrodes were attached to inmates' testicles, toes, and penises; shocks were administered, often resulting in permanent physical and psychological damage.

Unconditional diversion, standard diversion Program requiring minimal or no contact with probation department; may include minimum maintenance fee paid regularly for a specified period such as one year; no treatment program is indicated. (See **Diversion**)

Unconditional release Freedom from prison without restrictions.

UNICOR Profitable, government-owned corporation that sells prisoner-made goods to the public and federal agencies and hires thousands of federal prisoners as workers or laborers.

Uniform Crime Reports (UCR) Annual compilation of crime statistics for eight major felonies and a large category of misdemeanors; compiled by the FBI on the basis of reports submitted by law enforcement agencies in cities and counties in the United States; considered an underestimate of actual amount of crime in the United States.

U.S. Department of Justice Headed by the Attorney General of the United States, department oversees Federal Bureau of Investigation and other agencies.

U.S. Parole Commission Established in 1930, the Commission is responsible for the management and monitoring of all federal prisoners released on parole; responsible for the classification and placement of parolees and maintaining reports of their progress.

U.S. Sentencing Commission Originating in 1984, established sentencing policies for federal criminal laws; determined sentencing guidelines currently in use; obligated to revise occasionally these laws and regulations and determine the proper punishments for federal convictions.

University Settlement House established in New York City in 1893 by James Bronson Reynolds; purpose of settlement was to provide job assistance and referral services to disadvantaged community residents; served as a community-based probation agency to supervise some of those placed on probation by New York courts.

Victim impact statement Oral or written document by victim of crime included in a presentence investigation report prepared by probation officer; optional in most jurisdictions; may be oral statement at sentence hearing, or a written document appended to presentence investigation report, or both.

Victim/offender mediation model Restitution model for juveniles that focuses on victim-offender reconciliation.

Victim/Offender Reconciliation Project (VORP) Form of alternative dispute resolution, whereby a civil resolution is made by mutual consent between the victim and an offender; objectives are to provide restitution to victims, hold offender accountable for crime committed, and to reduce recidivism.

Victim/reparations model Restitution model for juveniles where juveniles compensate their victims directly for their offenses.

Violent crimes Felonies involving physical injury to one or more victims; crimes include but are not limited to homicide, aggravated assault, rape, and robbery.

Violent offenders Any person who commits a crime against the person, such as rape, murder, robbery, or aggravated assault.

VIPER (Violence Impact Program Enhanced Response) Program to deal with repeat violent offenders; involves frequent face-to-face visits, urinalyses, drug screens, and weekly meetings.

Visiting Cottage Program Policy established by Massachusetts Department of Corrections where female offenders with children may have lengthy visits with their children in "cottages" on the prison premises.

Voltaire, Francois-Marie Arouet (1694–1778) French philosopher and writer who wrote about French injustices and corporal punishments.

Volunteers (See **Corrections volunteers**)

Waivers (See **Transfers**)

Walnut Street Jail Considered first American prison seeking to correct offenders; built in 1776 in Philadelphia, Pennsylvania; one of first penal facilities that segregated female from male offenders and children from adults; introduced solitary confinement of prisoners; separated prisoners according to their offense severity; operated on basis that inmates could perform useful services to defray the costs of confinement; operated one of first prison industry programs; inmates grew much of their own fruit through gardening.

Wardens Chief executive officers of prisons or penitentiaries.

Warrants Documents that direct law enforcement officers to make arrests of criminal suspects; issued by judges.

Wilderness program Any one of several experience programs designed to heighten a youth's survival skills by teaching self-reliance; outdoor experiences enable youths to improve their self-concepts and self-esteem by learning how to cope with outdoor activities; includes Project Outward Bound.

Work furloughs (See **Furloughs**)

Workhouses Early penal facilities designed to use prison labor for profit by private interests; operated in shires in mid-sixteenth century and later.

Work/study release Also called work furlough, day parole, day pass, community work, study release; any program that provides for the labor of jail or prison inmates in the community under limited supervision, and where inmates are paid the prevailing wage; used first in Vermont by sheriffs in 1906.

Writ of *habeas corpus* (See ***Habeas corpus* petition**)

Youth courts Also known as teen courts and peer courts, these informal adjudicatory proceedings are conducted under the supervision of adults with some degree of legal expertise, such as retired judges, lawyers, or others; youths accused of minor offenses are judged by a jury of their peers, usually other youths who are selected for jury membership on the basis of their integrity, scholarship, and law-abiding behavior; judgments by teen juries are binding and almost always involve some form of punishment that heightens offender accountability, such as community service or restitution; jurisdiction of teen courts does not include any type of secure confinement as a punishment; believed to be an effective deterrent to delinquency and more influential where one's peers decide cases rather than an adult judge.

References

ABRAMSKY, SASHA. *Hard Time Blues: How Politics Built a Prison Nation.* New York: St. Martin's, 2002.

ACKER, JAMES R. ET AL. "Building a Better Youth Court." *Law and Policy* 23 (2001): 197–215.

ACOCA, LESLIE AND JAMES AUSTIN. *The Crisis: The Woman Offender Sentencing Study and Alternative Sentencing Recommendations Project: Women in Prison.* Washington, DC: National Council on Crime and Delinquency, 1996.

ADAMSON, CHRISTOPHER. "Toward a Marxian Penology: Captive Criminal Populations as Economic Threats and Resources." *Social Problems* 31 (1984): 435–458.

ADELMAN, STANLEY E. "Supreme Court Rules on Potential Liabilities of Private Corrections." *Corrections Today* 64 (2002): 28–30, 119.

ADMINISTRATIVE OFFICE OF THE U.S. COURTS. *The Presentence Investigation Report: Publication 105.* Washington, DC: Probation Division, Administrative Office of the United States Courts, 1984.

ADMINISTRATIVE OFFICE OF THE U.S. COURTS. "The Probation and Pretrial Services Automated Case Tracking System: A Review of Operations." *Federal Probation* 62 (1998): 16–21.

ADMINISTRATIVE OFFICE OF THE U.S. COURTS. *Annual Report to the Director 2001.* Washington, DC: Administrative Office of the U.S. Courts, 2002.

AGUIRRE, ADALBERTO ET AL. "Sentencing Outcomes, Race, and Victim Impact Evidence in California: A Pre- and Post-Payne Comparison." *Justice Professional* 11 (1999): 297–310.

ALARID, LEANNE FIFTAL AND PAUL F. CROMWELL. *Correctional Perspectives: Views from Academics, Practitioners, and Prisoners.* Los Angeles: Roxbury, 2002.

ALARID, LEANNE FIFTAL AND HSIAO MING WANG. "Mercy and Punishment: Buddhism and the Death Penalty." *Social Justice* 28 (2001): 231–247.

ALBRECHT, HANS JORG AND ANTON VAN KALMTHOUT. *Community Sanctions and Measures in Europe and North America.* Freiburg, Germany: Max Planck Institut for Auslandisches und Internationals Stafrecht, 2002.

ALDERMAN, ELLEN AND CAROLINE KENNEDY. *The Right to Privacy.* New York: Alfred A. Knopf, 1995.

ALEXANDER, BRUCE K. AND JONATHAN Y. TSOU. "Prospects for Stimulant Maintenance in Vancouver, Canada." *Addiction Research and Theory* 9 (2001): 97–132.

ALEXANDER, RUDOLF JR. "Hands-off, Hands-on, Hands Semi-off: A Discussion of the Current Legal Test Used by the United States Supreme Court to Decide Inmates' Rights." *Journal of Crime and Justice* 17 (1994): 103–128.

ALEXANDER, RUDOLF JR. "Slamming the Federal Courthouse Door on Inmates." *Journal of Criminal Justice* 21 (1995): 103–116.

ALLEMAN, TED AND ROSEMARY GIDO, EDS. *Turnstile Justice: Issues in American Corrections.* Upper Saddle River, NJ: Prentice Hall, 1998.

ALLISON, TOM L. "Making the Most of Middle Management: Tapping a Vast Resource." *Corrections Today* 49 (1987): 54–59.

ALMADA, LAUREL. "Jails Facing Overcrowding Crisis." *Laredo Morning Times,* February 26, 2003:A1.

ALOZIE, NICHOLAS O. AND C. WAYNE JOHNSTON. "Probing the Limits of the Female Advantage in Criminal Processing: Pretrial Diversion of Drug Offenders in an Urban County." *Justice System Journal* 21 (2000): 239–259.

ALTSCHULER, DAVID M. AND TROY L. Armstrong. "Reintegrating High-Risk Juvenile Offenders into Communities: Experiences and Prospects." *Corrections Management Quarterly* 5 (2001): 72–88.

AMERICAN CORRECTIONAL ASSOCIATION. *The American Prison: From the Beginning . . . A Pictorial History.* College Park, MD: American Correctional Association, 1983.

AMERICAN CORRECTIONAL ASSOCIATION. *Juvenile Caseworker: Resource Goals.* Laurel, MD: American Correctional Association, 1992.

AMERICAN CORRECTIONAL ASSOCIATION. *The State of Corrections: Proceedings ACA Annual Conferences 1992.* Laurel, MD: American Correctional Association, 1993.

AMERICAN CORRECTIONAL ASSOCIATION. *The State of Corrections.* Laurel, MD: American Correctional Association, 1995.

AMERICAN CORRECTIONAL ASSOCIATION. *2001 Directory.* Laurel, MD: American Correctional Association, 2002.

AMERICAN PROBATION AND PAROLE ASSOCIATION. "Pros and Cons of Increasing Officer Authority to Impose or Remove Conditions of Supervision." *APPA Perspectives* 17 (1993): 31.

AMERICAN PROBATION AND PAROLE ASSOCIATION. *Restoring Hope through Community Partnerships: The Real Deal in Crime Control—A Handbook for Community Corrections.* Lexington, KY: American Probation and Parole Association, 1995.

AMERICAN PROBATION AND PAROLE ASSOCIATION. *Restoring Hope through Community Partnerships: The Real Deal in Crime Control—A Handbook for Community Cor-*

rections. Lexington, KY: American Probation and Parole Association, 1996.

AMNESTY INTERNATIONAL. *United States of America: Death Penalty Developments in 1996.* New York: Amnesty International, 1997.

AMNESTY INTERNATIONAL. *Abuse of Women in Custody: Sexual Misconduct and Shackling of Pregnant Women: A State-By-State Survey of Policies and Practices in the USA.* New York: Amnesty International, 2001.

ANDERSON, DENNIS B., RANDALL E. SCHUMACKER, AND SARA L. ANDERSON. "Releasee Characteristics and Parole Success." *Journal of Offender Rehabilitation* 17 (1991): 133–145.

ANDERSON, JAMES F. AND LARONISTINE DYSON. *Legal Rights of Prisoners: Cases and Comments.* Lanham, MD: University Press of America, 2001.

ANNO, JAYE B. "HIV Infection among Incarcerated Women." *Journal of Correctional Health Care* 5 (1998): 123–254.

ANNO, JAYE B. "Correctional Health Care: An Overview." *American Jails* 15 (2001): 15–23.

ANNO, JAYE B. AND NANCY N. DUBLER, EDS. "Special Forum: Ethical Issues in Correctional Health Care." *Journal of Prison and Jail Health* 11 (1992): 63–97.

APPLEGATE, BRANDON K. "Penal Austerity: Perceived Utility, Desert, and Public Attitudes Toward Prison Amenities." *American Journal of Criminal Justice* 25 (2001): 253–268.

APPLIED RESEARCH SERVICES. *Informing Crime Control Strategies with Criminal Career Research.* Atlanta, GA: Georgia Statistical Analysis Center, 2001.

ARCHAMBEAULT, WILLIAM G. AND DONALD R. Deis, Jr. *Cost Effectiveness Comparisons of Private Versus Public Prisons in Louisiana: Executive Summary.* Baton Rouge: School of Social Work, Louisiana State University, 1996.

ARIZONA DEPARTMENT OF CORRECTIONS. *Offender Classification System (OCS): Classification Operating Manual.* Phoenix, AZ: Arizona Department of Corrections, 1991.

ARIZONA DEPARTMENT OF CORRECTIONS. *New Policy Prompted by Hunger Strikes and Treatment Refusal.* Phoenix: Arizona Department of Corrections, 2001.

ARMSTRONG, GAYLENE STYVE. *Private vs. Public Operation of Juvenile Correctional Facilities.* New York: LFB Scholarly Publishing LLC, 2001.

ARMSTRONG, TODD A. "The Effect of Environment on the Behavior of Youthful Offenders: A Randomized Experiment." *Journal of Criminal Justice* 30 (2002): 19–28.

ARNOLD, CHARLOTTE S. "The Program for Female Offenders, Inc.—A Community Corrections Answer to Jail Overcrowding." *American Jails* 5 (1992): 36–40.

ARNOLD, CHARLOTTE S. "Respect, Recognition are Keys to Effective Volunteer Programs." *Corrections Today* 55 (1993): 118–122.

ARRIGO, BRUCE A. "Transcarceration: A Constitutive Ethnography of Mentally Ill 'Offenders.'" *Prison Journal* 81 (2001): 162–186.

ARRIGO, BRUCE A. AND CAROL R. FOWLER. "The 'Death Row Community': A Community Psychology Perspective." *Deviant Behavior* 22 (2001): 43–71.

ARRIGONA, NANCY, GARRETT HODGSON, AND TOM REED. *An Overview of Juvenile Certification.* Austin, TX: Texas Criminal Justice Policy Council, 1999.

ASHE, MARIE. "Prison-House or Prison-Houses: Incarceration in Theory and Practice." *Rutgers Law Review* 53 (2001): 437–483.

ASSOCIATED PRESS. "Teens Adjust to New Life in the Wild." *Minot (ND) Daily News,* November 16, 1994:A7.

ASSOCIATED PRESS. "Davis Convicted of Killing Klaas." *Minot (ND) Daily News,* June 19, 1996:A4.

ATKINS, HOLLY, BRANDON K. APPLEGATE, AND GILLIAN F. Hobbs. "Mentally Ill and Substance Abusing Inmates: One Jail's Solution to Traditionally Fragmented Service Delivery." *American Jails* 12 (1998): 69–72.

AUSTIN, JAMES. "The Need to Reform Parole Board Decision Making." Salt Lake City, UT: Paper presented at the Salt Lake City Conference of the APAI, 2002.

AUSTIN, JAMES, KELLY D. JOHNSON, AND MARCIA GREGORIOU. *Juveniles in Adult Prisons and Jails: A National Assessment.* Washington, DC: Bureau of Justice Assistance, 2000.

AUSTIN, JAMES ET AL. *District of Columbia Department of Corrections Long-Term Options.* Washington, DC: National Council on Crime and Delinquency, 1997.

AUSTIN, JAMES ET AL. "The Impact of 'Three Strikes and You're Out.'" *Punishment and Society* 1 (2001): 131–162.

BABYAK, JOLENE. *Breaking the Rock: The Great Escape from Alcatraz.* Berkeley, CA: Ariel Vamp Press, 2001.

BACKSTRAND, JOHN A., DON C. GIBBONS AND JOSEPH F. JONES. "What Is in Jail? An Examination of the Rabble Hypothesis." *Crime and Delinquency* 38 (1992): 219–229.

BACON, MARGARET HOPE. *Abby Hopper Gibbons: Prison Reformer and Social Activist.* Albany, NY: State University of New York Press, 2000.

BADILLO, HERMAN AND MILTON HAYNES. *A Bill of Rights: Attica and the American Prison System.* New York: Outerbridge and Lazard, 1972.

BAGARIC, MIRKO AND KUMAR AMARASEKARA. "Feeling Sorry? Tell Someone Who Cares: The Irrelevance of Remorse in Sentencing." *The Howard Journal of Criminal Justice* 40 (2001): 364–376.

BAILLARGEON, JACQUES AND SALVADOR A. CONTRERAS. "Antipsychotic Prescribing Patterns in the Texas Prison System." *Journal of the American Academy of Psychiatry and the Law* 29 (2001): 48–53.

BAIRD, S. CHRISTOPHER. "Classifying Juveniles: Making the Most of an Important Management Tool." *Corrections Today* 47 (1985): 32–38.

BAKER, DAVID W. "A Descriptive Profile and Socio-Historical Analysis of Female Executions in the United States, 1632–1997." *Women and Criminal Justice* 10 (1999): 57–93.

BALDUS, DAVID C. ET AL. *The Disposition of Nebraska Capital and Non-Capital Homicide Cases (1973–1999): A Legal and Empirical Analysis.* Lincoln, NE: Nebraska Commission on Law Enforcement and Criminal Justice, 2001.

BANKS, JERRY ET AL. *Evaluation of Intensive Special Probation Projects National Evaluation Program, Phase I.* Washington, DC: U.S. Government Printing Office, 1977.

BARAK-GLANTZ, ISRAEL L. "Toward a Conceptual Schema of Prison Management Styles." *The Prison Journal* 60 (1986): 42–60.

BARNES, HARRY E. AND NEGLEY D. Teeters. *New Horizons in Criminology.* Englewood Cliffs, NJ: Prentice-Hall, 1959.

BARO, AGNES L. "Spheres of Consent: An Analysis of the Sexual Abuse and Sexual Exploitation of Women Incarcerated in the State of Hawaii." *Women and Criminal Justice* 8 (1997): 61–84.

BARON, STEPHEN W., DAVID R. FORDE, AND LESLIE W. KENNEDY. "Rough Justice: Street Youth and Violence." *Journal of Interpersonal Violence* 16 (2001): 662–678.

BARRINEAU, H.E., III. *Civil Liability in Criminal Justice*. 2d ed. Cincinnati, OH: Anderson Publishing Company, 1994.

BASTA, JOANNE. *Evaluation of the Intensive Probation Specialized Caseload for Graduates of Shock Probation*. Tucson, AZ: Adult Probation Department, Pima County Superior Court, 1995.

BATCHELDER, JOHN STUART AND D.D. KOSKI. "Barriers to Inmate Education: Factors Affecting the Learning Dynamics of a Prison Education Program." *Corrections Compendium* 27 (2002): 1–5, 16–18, 20.

BATIUK, MARY ELLEN, PAUL MOKE, AND PAMELA WILCOX ROUNTREE. "Crime and Rehabilitation: Correctional Education as an Agent of Change—A Research Note." *Justice Quarterly* 14 (1997): 167–180.

BAUMER, ERIC P. ET AL. "Crime, Shame, and Recidivism." *The British Journal of Criminology* 42 (2002): 40–59.

BAUNACH, PHYLLIS JO. *Mothers in Prison*. New Brunswick, NJ: Transaction Books, 1985.

BAVON, A. "The Effect of the Tarrant County Drug Court Project on Recidivism." *Evaluation and Program Planning* 24 (2001): 13–22.

BAYENS, GERALD J., JIMMY J. WILLIAMS, AND JOHN ORTIZ SMYKLA. "Jail Type Makes a Difference: Evaluating the Transition from a Traditional to a Podular, Direct Supervision Jail Across Ten Years." *American Jails* 11 (1997): 32–39.

BAYSE, D.J. *Helping Hands: A Handbook for Volunteers in Prisons and Jails*. Laurel, MD: American Correctional Association, 1993.

BAZEMORE, GORDON AND CURT TAYLOR GRIFFITHS. "Conferences, Circles, Boards, and Mediations: The 'New Wave' of Community Justice Decisionmaking." *Federal Probation* 61 (1997): 25–37.

BAZEMORE, GORDON, LAURA BURNEY NISSEN, AND MIKE DOOLEY. "Mobilizing Social Support and Building Relationships: Broadening Correctional and Rehabilitative Agendas." *Corrections Management Quarterly* 4 (2000): 10–21.

BAZEMORE, GORDON AND MARA SCHIFF, EDS. *Restorative Community Justice: Repairing Harm and Transforming Communities*. Cincinnati, OH: Anderson, 2001.

BEAN, PHILIP. *Drugs and Crime*. Cullompton, UK: Willan Publishing, 2002.

BECK, ALLEN J. "Planning the 1999 Census of Jails Is Underway." *American Jails* 12 (1999): 9–14.

BECK, ALLEN J. "Jail Population Growth: National Trends and Predictions of Future Growth." *American Jails* 16 (2002): 9–14.

BECK, ALLEN J., JENNIFER C. KARBERG, AND PAIGE M. HARRISON. *Prison and Jail Inmates at Midyear 2001*. Washington, DC: U.S. Department of Justice, 2002.

BEDAU, HUGO A. *The Case against the Death Penalty*. Washington, DC: American Civil Liberties Union, Capital Punishment Project, 1992.

BEIRNE, PIERS, ED. *The Origins and Growth of Criminology: Essays in Intellectual History, 1760–1945*. Aldershot, UK: Dartmouth, 1994.

BELBOT, BARBARA A. *The Prison as a Political Community: An Analysis of Legal Issues in Classification*. Ann Arbor, MI: University Microfilms International, 1995.

BELLO, STEPHEN. *Doing Life: The Extraordinary Saga of America's Greatest Jailhouse Lawyer*. New York: St. Martin's Press, 1982.

BENAQUISTO, LUCIA AND PETER J. FREED. "The Myth of Inmate Lawlessness: The Perceived Contradiction between Self and Other in Inmates' Support for Criminal Justice Sanctioning Norms." *Law and Society Review* 30 (1996): 481–511.

BENDA, BRENT B. AND ROBERT F. CORWYN. "The Effect of Abuse in Childhood and in Adolescence on Violence among Adolescents." *Youth and Society* 33 (2002): 339–365.

BENEDICT, WILLIAM REED, CORZINE LIN HUFF, AND JAY CORZINE. "'Clean up and Go Straight:' Effects of Drug Treatment on Recidivism among Felony Probationers." *American Journal of Criminal Justice* 22 (1998): 169–187.

BENSON, ERIC ET AL. *Projection of Juvenile Justice Populations in Texas*. Austin: Texas Criminal Justice Policy Council, 2002.

BERGE, GERALD, JEFFREY GEIGER, AND SCOT WHITNEY. "Technology Is the Key to Security in Wisconsin Supermax." *Corrections Today* 63 (2001): 105–109.

BERGSMANN, ILENE R. "ACA Women in Corrections Committee Examines Female Staff Training Needs." *Corrections Today*, 53 (1991): 106–109.

BERRUETA-CLEMENT, JOHN R. ET AL. "Preschool's Effects on Social Responsibility." In *Changed Lives: The Effects of the Perry Preschool Program on Youths Through Age 19*. Ypsilanti, MI: High/Scope Press, 1984.

BESSETTE, J.M. "In Pursuit of Criminal Justice." *Public Interest* 129 (1997): 61–72.

BEYER, LORRAINE, GARY REID, AND NICK CROFTS. "Ethnic-Based Differences in Drug Offending." *Australian and New Zealand Journal of Criminology* 34 (2002): 169–181.

BIGGER, PHILLIP J. "Officers in Danger: Results of the Federal Probation and Pretrial Officers Association's National Study on Serious Assaults." *APPA Perspectives*, 17 (1993): 14–20.

BILCHIK, SHAY. "Sentencing Juveniles to Adult Facilities Fails Youths and Society." *Corrections Today* 65 (2003): 21.

BILCHIK, SHAY, CYNTHIA SEYMOUR, AND KRISTEN KREISHER. "Parents in Prison." *Corrections Today* 63 (2001): 108–111.

BITTICK, JOHN C. "Evolving Through Accreditation." *Corrections Today* 65 (2003): 8.

BLACK, HENRY CAMPBELL. *Black's Law Dictionary*. St. Paul, MN: West Publishing Company, 1990.

BLACK, SHANNON. "Correctional Employee Stress and Strain." *Corrections Today* 63 (2001): 83–85, 118.

BLACKBURN, RONALD. "Classification and Assessment of Personality Disorders in Mentally Disordered Offenders: A Psychological Perspective." *Criminal Behavior and Mental Health* 10 (2000): 8–33.

BLAUNER, PETER AND GERRY MIGLIORE. "Street Stories." *APPA Perspectives*, 16 (1992): 21–23.

BLEVINS, L. DAVID, JOANN B. MORTON, AND KIMBERLY MCCABE. "Using the Michigan Alcohol Screening Test to Identify Problem Drinkers Under Federal Supervision." *Federal Probation* 60 (1996): 38–42.

BLINN, CYNTHIA. *Maternal Ties: A Selection of Programs for Female Offenders*. Lanham, MD: American Correctional Association, 1997.

BLOMBERG, THOMAS G. AND STANLEY COHEN, EDS. *Punishment and Social Control: Essays in Honor of Sheldon L. Messinger*. Hawthorne, NY: Aldine de Gruyter, 1995.

BLOUNT, WILLIAM R. AND MICHAEL JALAZO. "Project New Attitudes: A Life Skills Program in a Therapeutic Community." *American Jails* 16 (2002): 15–24.

BLOWERS, ANITA NEUBERGER. "Improving the Writing Skills of Jail Officers." *American Jails* 8 (1995): 41–46.

BOARI, NICOLA AND GIANLUCA FIORENTINI. "An Economic Analysis of Plea Bargaining: The Incentives of the Parties in a Mixed Penal System." *International Review of Law and Economics* 21 (2001): 213–231.

BOE, ROGER ET AL. "Offender Reintegration." *Forum on Corrections Research* 10 (1998): 3–47.

BOESKY, LISA MELANIE. "Mental Health Training in Juvenile Justice: A Necessity." *Corrections Today* 63 (2001): 98–101.

BOHN, MARTIN J., JOYCE L. CARBONELL, AND EDWIN I. MEGARGEE. "The Applicability and Utility of the MMPI-Based Offender Classification System in a Correctional Mental Health Unit." *Criminal Behaviour and Mental Health* 5 (1995): 14–33.

BOIN, R. ARJEN. "Securing Safety in the Dutch Prison System: Pros and Cons of a Supermax." *The Howard Journal of Criminal Justice* 40 (2001): 335–346.

BOIN, R. ARJEN AND MENNO J. VAN DUIN. "Prison Riots as Organizational Failures: A Managerial Perspective." *Prison Journal* 75 (1995): 357–379.

BOND, EMILY L. "Operation Outreach: Reaching out to Youths Through Real-Life Experience." *Corrections Today Magazine* 63 (2001): 46–49.

BOOT CAMPS ADVISOR. *State vs. Private Boot Camps.* Washington, DC: Author, 2002.

BOOTHBY, JENNIFER L. AND THOMAS W. DURHAM. "Screening for Depression in Prisoners Using the Beck Depression Inventory." *Criminal Justice and Behavior* 26 (1999): 107–124.

BOSWORTH, KRIS, DOROTHY ESPELAGE, AND TRACY DUBAY. "A Computer-Based Violence Prevention Intervention for Young Adolescents." *Adolescence* 33 (1998): 785–795.

BOTTOMLEY, A. KEITH. "Parole in Transition: A Comparative Study of Origins, Developments, and Prospects for the 1990s." In *Crime and Justice: A Review of Research, Vol. 12,* edited by Michael Tonry and Norval Morris. Chicago: University of Chicago Press, 1990.

BOTTOMS, ANTHONY, LORAINE GELSTHORPE, AND SUE REX, EDS. *Community Penalties: Change and Challenges.* Cullompton, Devon, UK: Willan Publishing, 2001.

BOURGOIN, NICOLAS. "Self-Inflicted Injuries and Hunger Strikes in Prison." *Deviance et Societe* 25 (2001): 131–145.

BOURQUE, BLAIR B., MEL HAN, AND SARAH M. HILL. *A National Survey of Aftercare Provisions for Boot Camp Graduates.* Washington, DC: National Institute of Justice, 1996.

BOUTELLIER, HANS. "The Convergence of Social Policy and Criminal Justice." *European Journal on Criminal Policy and Research* 9 (2001): 361–380.

BOWERY, MARGARET. *Private Prisons in New South Wales: A Four-Year Review.* Sydney, Australia: New South Wales Department of Corrective Services, 2000.

BOYD, JOHN S. AND THOMAS J. TIEFENWERTH. "Jail Training on the Road in Texas." *American Jails* 9 (1995): 59–60.

BRADFORD, MICHAEL AND PAUL PERRONE. *Incarcerated Juveniles and Recidivism in Hawaii.* Honolulu, HI: Crime Prevention and Justice Assistance Division, Department of the Attorney General, 2001.

BRAITHWAITE, JOHN. *Restorative Justice and Responsive Regulation.* Oxford, UK: Oxford University Press, 2002.

BRANDT, GERRI ANN AND BRENDA RUSSELL. "Differentiating Factors in Gang and Drug-Related Homicide." *Journal of Gang Research* 9 (2002): 23–40.

BRANHAM, LYNN S. "The Prison Litigation Reform Act's Enigmatic Exhaustion Requirement: What It Means and What Congress, Courts, and Correctional Officials Can Learn." *Cornell Law Review* 86 (2001): 483–547.

BRASWELL, MICHAEL, JOHN FULLER, AND BO LOZOFF. *Corrections, Peacemaking, and Restorative Justice: Transforming Individuals and Institutions.* Cincinnati, OH: Anderson, 2001.

BRECKENRIDGE, JAMES F. "Drunk Drivers, DWI 'Drug Court' Treatment, and Recidivism: Who Fails?" *Justice Research and Policy* 2 (2000): 87–105.

BRENCHLEY, MICHAEL AND JOHN HULTBERG. "Real-World Solutions for Improving Jail Efficiencies." *American Jails* 15 (2001): 69–77.

BRENNAN, TIM AND DAVID WELLS. "The Importance of Inmate Classification in Small Jails." *American Jails* 6 (1992): 49–52.

BRETTSCHNEIDER, COREY LANG. *Punishment, Property, and Justice: Philosophical Foundations of the Death Penalty and Welfare Controversies.* Aldershot, UK: Ashgate Publishing Company, 2001.

BRINK, JOHANN H., DIANA DOHERTY, AND ALESANDRA BOER. "Mental Disorder in Federal Offenders: A Canadian Prevalence Study." *International Journal of Law and Psychiatry* 24 (2001): 339–356.

BROCK, DEON E., JON SORENSEN, AND JAMES W. MARQUART. "Tinkering with the Machinery of Death: An Analysis of the Impact of Legislative Reform on the Sentencing of Capital Murderers in Texas." *Journal of Criminal Justice* 28 (2000): 343–349.

BRODSKY, STANLEY L., PATRICIA A. ZAPF, AND MARCUS T. BOCCACCINI. "The Last Competency: An Examination of the Legal, Ethical, and Professional Ambiguities Regarding Evaluations of Competence for Execution." *Journal of Forensic Psychology Practice* 1 (2001): 1–25.

BRONSTEIN, ALVIN J. "Prisoners' Rights: A History." In *Legal Rights of Prisoners,* edited by G. Alpert. Beverly Hills, CA: Sage, 1980.

BROWN, LARRY K. *Petticoat Prisoners of Old Wyoming.* Glendo, WY: High Plains Press, 2001.

BROWN, MARK AND JOHN PRATT, EDS. *Dangerous Offenders: Punishment and Social Order.* London, UK: Routledge, 2000.

BROWN, RANDALL A. "Assessing Attitudes and Behaviors of High-Risk Adolescents: An Evaluation of the Self-Report Method." *Adolescence* 34 (1999): 25–32.

BROWN, ROBERT JR. AND MARJORIE VAN OCHTEN. "Sexual Harassment: A Vulnerable Area for Corrections." *Corrections Today* 52 (1990): 62–70.

BROWN, SAMMIE. "Are Prison Classification Systems Addressing the Diverse Inmate Population?" *Corrections Today* 64 (2002): 104–105.

BROWNE, DEBORAH. "Coping Alone: Examining the Prospects of Adolescent Victims of Child Abuse Placed in Foster Care." *Journal of Youth and Adolescence* 31 (2002): 57–66.

BROWNFIELD, DAVID AND KEVIN THOMPSON. "Distinguishing the Effects of Peer Delinquency and Gang Membership on Self-Reported Delinquency." *Journal of Gang Research* 9 (2002): 1–10.

BRYANS, SHANE AND RACHEL JONES, EDS. *Prisons and the Prisoner: An Introduction to the Work of Her Majesty's Prison Service.* London, UK: Her Majesty's Stationery Office, 2001.

BRYL, JASON ET AL. *The Impact of Juvenile Justice Reforms on the Recycling of Juvenile Offenders.* Austin, TX: Criminal Justice Policy Council, 2001.

BUCKLEY, SUE. "Best Practices: How Jails Are Addressing Evolving Inmate Health Care Needs." *American Jails* 12 (1998): 27–30.

BUDDRESS, LOREN A.N., ED. "The Federal Probation and Pretrial Services System." *Federal Probation* 61 (1997): 5–11.

BUFFARDI, HARRY C. *Beginning of the Penitentiary Movement.* Albany, NY: New York Correctional History Society, 1999.

BURDETT, GARY AND MIKE RETFORD. "Technology Improves Security and Reduces Staff in Two Illinois Prisons." *Corrections Today* 65 (2003): 108–109.

BUREAU OF LABOR STATISTICS. *National Employment and Wage Data for 2001.* Washington, DC: Bureau of Labor Statistics, 2002.

BURKE, LISA OUIMET AND JAMES E. VIVIAN. "The Effect of College Programming on Recidivism Rates at the Hampden County House of Corrections: A Five-Year Study." *The Journal of Correctional Education* 52 (2001): 160–162.

BURKE, PEGGY B. "Collaboration for Successful Prisoner Reentry: The Role of Parole and the Courts." *Corrections Management Quarterly* 5 (2001): 11–22.

BURKE, TOD W., ELAINE RIZZO, AND CHARLES E. O'REAR. "National Survey Results: Do Officers Need College Degrees?" *Corrections Today* 54 (1992): 174–176.

BURNS, RONALD. "Boot Camps: The Empirical Record." *American Jails* 10 (1996): 42–49.

BURNS, RONALD ET AL. "Perspectives on Parole: The Board Members' Viewpoint." *Federal Probation* 63 (1999): 16–22.

BURRELL, WILLIAM D. "The 'Technology' of Community Supervision." *The Journal of Offender Monitoring* 13 (2000): 14–15, 28.

BURT, GRANT N. ET AL. "Three Strikes and You're Out: An Investigation of False Positive Rates Using a Canadian Sample." *Federal Probation* 64 (2000): 3–6.

BURTON, DAVID L. ET AL. *1996 Nationwide Survey: A Survey of Treatment Programs and Models Serving Children with Sexual Behavior Problems, Adolescent Sex Offenders, and Adult Sex Offenders.* Brandon, VT: Safer Society Foundation, 2000.

BUTTE COUNTY PROBATION DEPARTMENT. *Probation Officer I.* Butte County, CA: Butte County Probation Department, 2002.

BUTTS, JEFFREY A. AND WILLIAM ADAMS. *Anticipating Space Needs in Juvenile Detention and Correctional Facilities.* Washington, DC: U.S. Department of Justice, 2001.

BUTTS, JEFFREY A. AND JOSEPH B. SANBORN JR. "Is Juvenile Justice Just Too Slow?" *Judicature* 83 (1999): 16–24.

BYRD, TERRY G. ET AL. "Behind Bars: An Assessment of the Effects of Job Satisfaction, Job-Related Stress, and Anxiety on Employees' Inclinations to Quit." *Journal of Crime and Justice* 23 (2000): 69–93.

BYRNE, STUART, MITCHELL K. BYRNE, AND KEVIN HOWELLS. "Defining the Needs in a Contemporary Correctional Environment: The Contribution of Psychology." *Psychiatry, Psychology, and the Law* 8 (2001): 97–104.

CAHALAN, MARGARET W. *Historical Corrections Statistics in the United States, 1850–1984.* Washington, DC: U.S. Department of Justice, 1986.

CALDWELL, MICHAEL F. AND GREGORY J. VAN RYBROEK. "Efficacy of a Decompression Treatment Model in the Clinical Management of Violent Juvenile Offenders." *International Journal of Offender Therapy and Comparative Criminology* 45 (2001): 469–477.

CALHOUN, GEORGIA B. "Differences Between Male and Female Juvenile Offenders as Measured by the BASC." *Journal of Offender Rehabilitation* 33 (2001): 87–96.

CALHOUN, JOHN. "Probation: Prevention's Sleeping Giant." *APPA Perspectives* 22 (1998): 17–19.

CALIFORNIA ADMINISTRATIVE OFFICE OF THE COURTS. *Report to the Legislature Pursuant to Penal Code Section 1170.45: The Disposition of Criminal Cases According to the Race and Ethnicity of the Defendant.* Sacramento, CA: California Administrative Office of the Courts, Research and Planning Unit, 2001.

CAMERON, MARGARET AND COLIN MACDOUGAL. "Crime Prevention through Sport and Physical Activity." *Trends and Issues in Crime and Criminal Justice* 165 (2000): 1–6.

CAMP, CAMILLE G. AND GEORGE M. CAMP. *The Corrections Yearbook 2001: Adult Systems.* Middletown, CT: Criminal Justice Institute, Inc., 2002.

CAMP, SCOTT D., WILLIAM D. SAYLOR, AND KEVIN N. WRIGHT. "Racial Diversity of Correctional Workers and Inmates: Organizational Commitment, Teamwork, and Workers' Efficacy in Prisons." *Justice Quarterly* 18 (2001): 412–427.

CAMPBELL, JUSTIN S. AND CHERISE LEREW. "Juvenile Sex Offenders in Diversion." *Sexual Abuse: A Journal of Research and Treatment* 14 (2002): 1–17.

CAMPBELL, RALPH JR. *Performance Audit: Department of Correction, Division of Adult Probation and Parole.* Raleigh, NC: North Carolina Office of the State Auditor, 1998.

CARLSON, ERIC W. AND EVALYN PARKS. *Critical Issues in Adult Probation: Issues in Probation Management.* Washington, DC: U.S. Department of Justice, 1979.

CARLSON, JOSEPH R. "Changing Demographics and Programs at the Nebraska Correctional Center for Women, 1982–1998." *Journal of Offender Rehabilitation* 31 (2000): 135–160.

CARLSON, PETER M. "Prison Interventions: Evolving Strategies to Control Security Threat Groups." *Corrections Management Quarterly* 5 (2001): 10–22.

CARLSON, PETER M. AND JUDITH SIMON GARRETT, EDS. *Prison and Jail Administration: Practice and Theory.* Gaithersburg, MD: Aspen Publishers, 1999.

CARROLL, LEO. *Hacks, Blacks, and Cons: Race Relations in a Maximum-Security Prison.* Lexington, MA: Lexington Books, 1974.

CARROLL-BURKE, PATRICK. *Colonial Discipline: The Making of the Irish Convict System.* Dublin, Ireland: Four Courts Press, 2000.

CARTER, DIANE. "The Status of Education and Training in Corrections." *Federal Probation* 55 (1991): 17–26.

CARTER, KEITH W. "The Casuarina Prison Riot: Official Discourse or Appreciative Inquiry?" *Current Issues in Criminal Justice* 12 (2001): 363–375.

CASELLA, RONNIE. *At Zero Tolerance: Punishment, Prevention, and School Violence.* New York: Peter Lang Publishing, 2001.

CASAREZ, NICOLE B. "Furthering the Accountability Principle in Privatized Federal Corrections: The Need for Access to Private Prison Records." *University of Michigan Journal of Law Reform* 28 (1995): 249–303.

CASEY, KAREN A. AND TIMM BAKKEN. "The Effect of Time on the Disciplinary Adjustment of Women in Prison." *International Journal of Offender Therapy and Comparative Criminology* 45 (2001): 489–497.

CASTELLANO, THOMAS C. AND MICHAEL FERGUSON. *A Time Study of Juvenile Probation Services in Illinois.* Carbondale, IL: Center for the Study of Crime, Delinquency, and Corrections, Southern Illinois University, 1998.

CAULKINS, JONATHAN P. "How Large Should the Strike Zone Be in 'Three Strikes and You're Out' Sentencing Laws?" *Journal of Quantitative Criminology* 17 (2001): 227–246.

CAVADINO, MICHAEL AND JAMES DIGNAN. "Reparation, Retribution, and Rights." *International Review of Victimology* 4 (1997): 233–253.

CEGA SERVICES, INC. "Riots, Disturbances, Violence, Assaults, and Escapes." *Corrections Compendium* 27 (2002): 6–19.

CENTER FOR LEGAL STUDIES. *An Implementation Evaluation of the Specialized Sex Offender Probation Projects in Coles, Madison, and Vermillion Counties.* Springfield, IL: Center for Legal Studies, Institute of Public Affairs, University of Illinois, 2000.

CHAMPION, DEAN J. *Measuring Offender Risk: A Criminal Justice Sourcebook.* Westport, CT: Greenwood Press, 1994.

CHAMPION, DEAN JOHN. *Administration of Criminal Justice: Structure, Function, and Process.* Englewood Cliffs, NJ: Prentice Hall, 2003.

CHAMPION, DEAN J. AND G. LARRY MAYS. *Transferring Juveniles to Criminal Court.* New York: Praeger Publishers, 1991.

CHAN, WENDY AND KIRAN MIRCHANDANI, EDS. *Crimes of Color: Racialization and the Criminal Justice System in Canada.* Lancashire, UK: Broadview Press, Ltd., 2002.

CHANG, SEMOON AND JACK S. TILLMAN. "Should County Jails Be Privatized?" *American Jails* 16 (2002): 43–48.

CHAPMAN, JACK. "Bigger, Better, Safer, Faster, and Less Expensive." *American Jails* 12 (1998): 9–17.

CHEESEMAN, KELLY A., JANET L. MULLINGS, AND JAMES W. MARQUART. "Inmate Perceptions of Security Staff across Various Custody Levels." *Corrections Management Quarterly* 5 (2001): 41–48.

CHEESMAN, FRED, ROGER A. HANSON, AND BRIAN J. OSTROM. "A Tale of Two Laws: The U.S. Congress Confronts *Habeas Corpus* Petitions and Section 1983 Lawsuits." *Law and Policy* 22 (2000): 89–113.

CHEN, ELSA YEE FANG. *"Three Strikes and You're Out" and "Truth in Sentencing": Lessons in Policy Implementation and Impacts.* Ann Arbor, MI: University Microfilms International, 2000.

CHEREK, DON R. AND SCOTT D. LANE. "Laboratory and Psychometric Measurements of Impulsivity among Violent and Nonviolent Female Parolees." *Biological Psychiatry* 46 (1999): 273–280.

CHEREK, DON R., SCOTT D. LANE, AND DONALD M. DOUGHERTY. "Laboratory and Questionnaire Measures of Aggression among Female Parolees with Violent or Nonviolent Histories." *Aggressive Behavior* 26 (2000): 297–307.

CHERMACK, STEPHEN T. AND FREDERIC C. BLOW. "Violence among Individuals in Substance Abuse Treatment: The Role of Alcohol and Cocaine Consumption." *Drug and Alcohol Dependence* 66 (2002): 29–37.

CHESNEY-LIND, MEDA. "What about the Girls? Delinquency Programming as if Gender Mattered." *Corrections Today Magazine* 63 (2001): 38–40, 43, 44–45.

CHRISTENSEN, GARY E. "Preemployment Psychological Screening among Correctional Officers: An Effective Practice?" *American Jails* 16 (2002): 9–13.

CHRISTENSEN, WENDY AND JOHN P. CRANK. "Police Work and Culture in a Nonurban Setting: An Ethnographic Analysis." *Police Quarterly* 4 (2001): 69–98.

CHUDA, THOMAS J. *A Guide for Criminal Justice Training: How to Make Training Easier for Security and Law Enforcement.* Springfield, IL: Charles C. Thomas, 1995.

CIANCIA, JAMES J. AND RICHARD B. TALTY. *New Jersey Intensive Supervision Program.* Trenton, NJ: Administrative Office of the Courts, 1999.

CLARE, EMMA. *Evaluation of Close Supervision Centers.* London, UK: Research, Development, and Statistics Directorate, UK Home Office, 2001.

CLARK, CHERIE L., DAVID W. AZIZ AND DORIS LAYTON MACKENZIE (1994). *Shock Incarceration in New York: Focus on Treatment.* Washington, DC: National Institute of Justice.

CLARK, CHERYL AND LESLIE KELLAM. "These Boots Are Made for Women." *Corrections Today Magazine* 63 (2001): 50–54.

CLARK, MICHAEL D. "The ABCs of Increasing Motivation with Juvenile Offenders." *Juvenile and Family Court Journal* 50 (1999): 33–42.

CLARK, MICHAEL D. "Influencing Positive Behavior Change: Increasing the Therapeutic Approach of Juvenile Courts." *Federal Probation* 65 (2001): 18–27.

CLASBY, RICHARD. *Recidivism Rates and UCI Participation.* Murray, UT: Utah Department of Corrections, 1996.

CLAY, JOHN. *Maconochie's Experiment.* London, UK: John Murray, 2001.

CLAYTON, SUSAN L. "U.S. Prisons Experience Trend toward Smoking Bans." *On the Line* 24 (2001): 1–3.

CLEAR, TODD R., VAL B. CLEAR, AND WILLIAM D. BURRELL. *Offender Assessment and Evaluation: The Presentence Investigation Report.* Cincinnati, OH: Anderson Publishing Company, 1989.

CLEAR, TODD R. AND RONALD P. CORBETT. "Community Corrections of Place." *APPA Perspectives* 23 (1999): 24–32.

CLEAR, TODD R. ET AL. "The Value of Religion in Prison: An Inmate Perspective." *Journal of Contemporary Criminal Justice* 16 (2000): 53–74.

CLEMMER, D.C. *The Prison Community.* New York: Holt, Rinehart, and Winston, 1940.

COFFEY, A. L. ET AL. *Juvenile Justice as a System: Law Enforcement to Rehabilitation.* Englewood Cliffs, NJ: Prentice-Hall, 1974.

COHN, ALVIN W. "The Failure of Correctional Management: Recycling the Middle Manager." *Federal Probation* 59 (1995): 10–16.

COHN, ALVIN W. "Reducing Opportunities for Civil Litigation." *American Jails* 12 (1998): 31–36.

COLE, DAVID. *No Equal Justice: Race and Class in the American Criminal Justice System.* New York: New Press, 1999.

COLE, RICHARD B. AND JACK E. CALL. "When Courts Find Jail and Prison Overcrowding Unconstitutional." *Federal Probation* 56 (1992): 29–39.

COLEMAN, JAMES E., JR., ED. "The ABA's Proposed Moratorium on the Death Penalty." *Law and Contemporary Problems* 61 (1998): 1–231.

COLEMAN, RAY AND CHUCK ORAFTIK. "Borrowed Light: The Natural Way to Improve Direct Supervision." *Corrections Today* 63 (2001): 97–99.

COLL, CYNTHIA GARCIA AND KATHLEEN M. DUFF. *Reframing the Needs of Women in Prison: A Relational and Diversity Perspective.* Wellesley, MA: Stone Center for Development Services and Studies, Wellesley College, 1995.

COLLEDGE, DALE AND JURG GERBER. "Rethinking the Assumptions about Boot Camps." *Federal Probation* 62 (1998): 54–67.

COLLIER, VIRGINIA P. AND WAYNE P. THOMAS. "Educating Linguistically and Culturally Diverse Students in Correctional Settings." *The Journal of Correctional Education* 52 (2001): 68–73.

COLLINS, MARY ELIZABETH, IRA M. SCHWARTZ, AND IRWIN EPSTEIN. "Risk Factors for Adult Imprisonment in a Sample of Youth Released from Residential Child Care." *Children and Youth Services Review* 23 (2001): 203–226.

COLLINS, WILLIAM C. *Privately Operated Speculative Prisons and Public Safety: A Discussion of Issues.*

Washington, DC: Corrections Program Office, U.S. Office of Justice Programs, 2000.

COLLINS, WILLIAM C. AND JOHN HAGAR. "Jails and the Courts: Issues for Today, Issues for Tomorrow." *American Jails* 9 (1995): 18–28.

COLORADO PAROLE GUIDELINES COMMISSION. *Report to the Legislature.* Denver: Colorado Parole Guidelines Commission, 1988.

CONLEY, JAMES R. "Design/Build: The Future of Contracting." *Corrections Today* 62 (2000): 118–120.

CONLY, CATHERINE. *The Women's Prison Association: Supporting Women Offenders and Their Families.* Washington, DC: U.S. Department of Justice, 1998.

CONNECTICUT BOARD OF PAROLE. *Standards Governing Early Release of Prisoners.* Hartford, CT: Office of Policy Management, 1974.

CONNECTICUT DEPARTMENT OF CORRECTIONS. *The ABC's for Volunteers in Corrections.* Wethersfield, CT: Connecticut Department of Corrections, 2002.

CONNELLY, CLARE AND SHANTI WILLIAMS. *Review of the Research Literature on Serious and Violent Sexual Offenders.* Glasgow, UK: Scottish Executive Central Research Unit, 2000.

CONNELLY, MICHAEL. "Mentors and Tutors: An Overview of Two Volunteer Programs in Oklahoma Corrections." *Journal of the Oklahoma Criminal Justice Research Consortium* 2 (1995): 80–88.

CONOVER, TED. *Newjack: Guarding Sing Sing.* New York: Vintage Books, 2001.

CONTACT CENTER, INC. "Inmate Grievance Procedures." *Corrections Compendium* 11 (1987): 9–13.

CONWAY, PEGGY. "The 2001 Electronic Monitoring Survey." *The Journal of Offender Monitoring* 14 (2001): 4–42.

COOK, PHILIP J. AND DONNA B. SLAWSON. *The Costs of Processing Murder Cases in North Carolina.* Durham, NC: Terry Sanford Institute of Public Policy, Duke University, 1993.

COOK, SANDY AND SUSANNE DAVIES, EDS. *Harsh Punishments: International Experiences of Women's Imprisonment.* Boston: Northeastern University Press, 1999.

COOKE, GERALD. "Patricide." *Journal of Threat Assessment* 1 (2001): 35–45.

CORBETT, RONALD P. AND GARY T. MARX. "Critique: No Soul in the New Machine: Technofallacies in the Electronic Monitoring Movement." *Journal of Offender Monitoring* 7 (1994): 1–9.

CORNELIUS, GARY F. *Stressed Out: Strategies for Living and Working with Stress in Corrections.* Laurel, MD: American Correctional Association, 1994.

CORNELIUS, GARY F. "Reducing Inmate Management Problems with the Human Services Approach." *American Jails* 9 (1995): 62–63.

CORNELIUS, GARY F. *Jails in America: An Overview of Issues.* Lanham, MD: American Correctional Association, 1997.

CORRECTIONAL SERVICE OF CANADA. *Reflections of a Canadian Prison Warden: The Visionary Legacy of Ron Wiebe: An Unfinished Conversation.* Ottawa, Canada: Correctional Service of Canada, 2000.

Corrections Compendium. "Female Offenders: As Their Numbers Grow, So Does the Need for Gender-Specific Programming." *Corrections Compendium* 23 (1998): 8–24.

Corrections Compendium. "Recidivism: Tracking, Methodology, and Reporting." *Corrections Compendium* 27 (2002): 11–19.

Corrections Digest. "Contracts Awarded for Construction of New Prison in Chester, PA." *Corrections Compendium* 19 (1994): 25–27.

Corrections Today. "Virginia Loses Jail Crowding Case." *Corrections Today* 57 (1995): 29–30.

Corrections Today. "Inmates Can Sue to Drink Communion Wine." *Corrections Today* 64 (2002): 16.

Corrections Today. "Superintendent of Jails." *Corrections Today* 65 (2003): 19.

COSGROVE, EDWARD J. "ROBO-PO: The Life and Times of a Federal Probation Officer." *Federal Probation* 58 (1994): 29–30.

COSTA, JERALITA AND ANNE SEYMOUR. "Experienced Volunteers: Crime Victims, Former Offenders Contribute a Unique Perspective." *Corrections Today* 55 (1993): 110–111.

COTTEN, OLDENBURG NIKU U., SANDRA L. MARTIN, AND KATHLEEN B. JORDAN. "Preincarceration Risky Behaviors Among Women Inmates: Opportunities for Prevention." *Prison Journal* 77 (1997): 281–294.

COTTLE, CINDY C., RIA J. LEE, AND KIRK HEILBRUN. "The Prediction of Criminal Recidivism in Juveniles: A Meta-Analysis." *Criminal Justice and Behavior: An International Journal* 28 (2001): 367–394.

COWBURN, MALCOLM. "A Man's World: Gender Issues in Working with Male Sex Offenders in Prison." *Howard Journal of Criminal Justice* 37 (1998): 234–251.

CRAISSATI, JACKIE AND ANTHONY BEECH. "Attrition in a Community Treatment Program for Child Sexual Abusers." *Journal of Interpersonal Violence* 16 (2001): 205–221.

CRAWFORD, ADAM AND JILL ENTERKIN. "Victim Contact Work in the Probation Service: Paradigm Shift or Pandora's Box?" *The British Journal of Criminology* 41 (2001): 707–725.

CREESE, RICHARD, W.F. BYNUM, AND J. BEARN. *The Health of Prisoners: Historical Essays.* Atlanta, GA: Wellcome Institute Series in the History of Medicine, Editions Rodopi B.V. Amsterdam, 1995.

CREIGHTON, LINDA L. "Nursery Rhymes and Hard Time." *U.S. News and World Report,* (August 8, 1988): 22–24.

CRISANTI, ANNETTE S. AND EDGAR J. LOVE. "Characteristics of Psychiatric In-Patients Detained under Civil Commitment Legislation: A Canadian Study." *International Journal of Law and Psychiatry* 24 (2001): 399–410.

CROCKER, PHYLLIS L. "Is the Death Penalty Good for Women?" *Buffalo Criminal Law Journal* 4 (2001): 917–965.

CROSS, MARILEE AND KEITH KNAUF. "Family Ties." *American Jails* 16 (2002): 31–36.

CROWE, ANN H. *Jurisdictional Technical Assistance Package for Juvenile Corrections.* Washington, DC: U.S. Office of Juvenile Justice and Delinquency Prevention, 2000.

CULLEN, FRANCIS T., BONNIE S. FISHER, AND BRANDON K. APPLEGATE. "Public Opinion about Punishment and Corrections." In *Crime and Justice: A Review of Research, Vol. 27,* edited by Michael Tonry. Chicago: University of Chicago Press, 2000.

CULLEN, FRANCIS T. ET AL. "Prison Wardens' Job Satisfaction." *Prison Journal* 72 (1993): 141–162.

CULLER, IRVING B., KENNETH BYRNE, AND MATTHEW CULLER. "Slashing Sick Leave/Attrition Rates Through New Recruit Screening." *Corrections Today* 64 (2002): 92–95, 140.

CULLIVER, CONCETTA C. *Female Criminality: The State of the Art.* New York: Garland Press, 1993.

CUNNIFF, MARK A. *Jail Crowding: Understanding Jail Population Dynamics.* Washington, DC: U.S. Department of Justice, National Institute of Corrections, 2002.

CUNNINGHAM, MARK D. AND THOMAS J. REIDY. "Don't Confuse Me with the Facts: Common Errors in Violence Risk Assessment at Capital Sentencing." *Criminal Justice and Behavior* 26 (1999): 20–43.

CUSHMAN, ROBERT C. AND DALE SECHREST. "Variations in the Administration of Probation Supervision." *Federal Probation,* 56 (1992): 19–29.

DALE, ELIZABETH. *The Rule of Justice: The People of Chicago versus Zephyr Davis.* Columbus, OH: Ohio State University Press, 2001.

DANA, DAVIS. *Rethinking the Puzzle of Escalating Penalties for Repeat Offenders.* Evanston, IL: Institute for Policy Research, Northwestern University, 2001.

D'ANCA, ALFRED R. "The Role of the Federal Probation Officer in the Guidelines Sentencing System." *Federal Probation* 65 (2001): 20–23.

DANNI, KRISTIN A. AND GARY D. HAMPE. "An Analysis of Predictors of Child Sex Offender Types Using Presentence Investigation Reports." *International Journal of Offender Therapy and Comparative Criminology* 44 (2000): 490–504.

DAVIDSON, HOWARD S., ED. *Schooling in a "Total Institution": Critical Perspectives on Prison Education.* Westport, CT: Bergin & Garvey, 1995.

DAVIS, CAROL ANNE. *Women Who Kill: Profiles of Female Serial Killers.* London: Allison and Busby, 2001.

DAVIS, ERNEST K. "Offender Education in the American Correctional System: An Historical Perspective." *Quarterly Journal of Corrections* 2 (1978): 7–13.

DAVIS, H.C. "Educating the Incarcerated Female: A Holistic Approach." *The Journal of Correctional Education* 52 (2001): 79–83.

DAVIS, JAMES. "Co-Corrections in the U.S.: Housing Men and Women Together Has Advantages and Disadvantages." *Corrections Compendium* 23 (1998): 1–3.

DAVIS, KEITH. *Human Relations at Work.* New York: McGraw-Hill, 1962.

DAVIS, MARK S. AND DANIEL J. FLANNERY. "The Institutional Treatment of Gang Members." *Corrections Management Quarterly* 5 (2001): 37–46.

DAVIS, ROBERT C. AND BARBARA E. SMITH. "The Effects of Victim Impact Statements on Sentencing Decisions." *Justice Quarterly* 11 (1994): 453–512.

DAVIS, SIMON. "Factors Associated with the Diversion of Mentally Disordered Offenders." *Bulletin of the American Academy of Psychiatry and the Law* 22 (1994): 389–397.

DAVIS, SU PERK. "Survey: Number of Offenders Under Intensive Probation Increases." *Corrections Compendium* 17 (1992): 9–17.

DAVISON, SOPHIE AND PAMELA J. TAYLOR. "Psychological Stress and Severity of Personality Disorder Symptomatology in Prisoners Convicted of Violent and Sexual Offenses." *Psychology, Crime, and the Law* 7 (2001): 263–273.

DAWSON, ROGER E. "Opponent Process Theory for Substance Abuse Treatment." *Juvenile and Family Court Journal* 43 (1992): 51–59.

DEATH PENALTY INFORMATION CENTER. *Women Executed in the U.S., 1900–2002.* Washington, DC: Death Penalty Information Center, 2002.

DEBELL, JOHN. "The Female Offender: Different . . . Not Difficult." *Corrections Today Magazine* 63 (2001): 56–61.

DECKER, SCOTT H. *From the Streets to the Prison: Understanding and Responding to Gangs.* Indianapolis, IN: National Major Gang Task Force, 2001.

DECOSTANZO, ELAINE AND HELEN SCHOLES. "Women Behind Bars: Their Numbers Increase." *Corrections Today* 50 (1988): 104–108.

DEFRANCES, CAROL J. AND KEVIN J. STROM. *Juveniles Prosecuted in State Criminal Courts.* Washington, DC: U.S. Bureau of Justice Statistics, 1997.

DEGROOT, ANNE S. "HIV among Incarcerated Women: An Epidemic behind the Walls." *Corrections Today Magazine* 63 (2001): 77–81, 97.

DEKALB COUNTY COURT SERVICES. *Employment Court Services.* Sycamore, IL: DeKalb County Court Services, 2002.

DEKLEVA, KENNETH B. "Psychiatric Expertise in the Sentencing Phase of Capital Murder." *Journal of the American Academy of Psychiatry and the Law* 29 (2001): 58–67.

DELAWARE STATISTICAL ANALYSIS CENTER. *Delaware's Adult Boot Camp.* Dover: Delaware Statistical Analysis Center, 2001.

DEL CARMEN, ROLANDO V. AND JAMES ALAN PILANT. "The Scope of Judicial Immunity for Probation and Parole Officers." *APPA Perspectives* 18 (1994): 14–21.

DELGROSSO, ERNEST J. "Probation Officer Safety and Defensive Weapons: A Closer Look." *Federal Probation* 61 (1997): 45–50.

DELL, COLLEEN ANNE AND ROGER BOE. *An Examination of Aboriginal and Caucasian Women Offender Risk and Needs Factors.* Ottawa, Canada: Correctional Service of Canada, 2000.

DEMBO, RICHARD ET AL. "Engaging High Risk Families in Community-Based Intervention Services." *Aggression and Violent Behavior* 4 (1999): 41–58.

DEMORE, ROSEMARY. "'I'm Not a Criminal:' Working with Low-Risk Supervisees." *Federal Probation* 59 (1996): 34–40.

DENNISON, SUSAN M., CORI STOUGT, AND ASTRID BIRGDEN. "The Big Five Dimensional Personality Approach to Understanding Sex Offenders." *Psychology, Crime, and the Law* 7 (2001): 243–261.

DICKEY, WALTER J. AND PEGGY MCGARRY. *Community Justice in Rural America: Four Examples of Four Futures.* Washington, DC: U.S. Bureau of Justice Assistance, 2001.

DICKEY, WALTER J. AND PAM HOLLENHORST STIEBS. *Three Strikes Five Years Later.* Washington, DC: Campaign for an Effective Crime Policy, 1998.

DODGE, MARY. *"Her Life Has Been an Improper One" : Women, Crime, and Persons in Illinois, 1835 to 1933.* Ann Arbor, MI: University Microfilms International, 1998.

DODGE, MARY AND MARK R. POGREBIN. "Collateral Costs of Imprisonment for Women: Complications of Reintegration." *Prison Journal* 81 (2001): 42–54.

DODGSON, KATH ET AL. *Electronic Monitoring of Released Prisoners: An Evaluation of the Home Detention Curfew Scheme.* London, UK: Research, Development and Statistics Directorate, UK Home Office, 2001.

DONNELLY, S.M. *Community Service Orders in Federal Probation.* Washington, DC: National Institute of Justice, 1980.

DOUGLAS, KEVIN S., STEPHEN D. HART, AND RANDALL P. KROPP. "Validity of the Personality Assessment Inventory for Forensic Assessments." *International Journal of Offender Therapy and Comparative Criminology* 45 (2001): 183–197.

DOWDY, ERIC R., MICHAEL G. LACY, N. PRABBA UNNITHAN. "Correctional Prediction and the Level of Supervision Inventory." *Journal of Criminal Justice* 30 (2002): 29–39.

DRAINE, JEFFREY AND PHYLLIS SOLOMON. "Describing and Evaluating Jail Diversion Services for Persons with Serious Mental Illness." *Psychiatric Services* 50 (1999): 56–61.

DRAPKIN, MARTIN AND GARY T. KLUGIEWICZ. "Use of Force Training in Jails, Part I." *American Jails* 7 (1994a): 9–12.

DRAPKIN, MARTIN AND GARY T. KLUGIEWICZ. "Use of Force Training in Jails, Part II." *American Jails* 7 (1994b): 93–98.

DUFF, ANTHONY AND DAVID GARLAND, EDS. *A Reader on Punishment.* Oxford, UK: Oxford University Press, 1994.

DUGGAN, NANCY. *So Far So Good: The Experience of Male Ex-Offenders 2–5 Years after Release from Incarceration.* Ann Arbor, MI: University Microfilms International, 1993.

DURKEE, DANIEL. "Local Detention Education and Training: A Program Developed by the Criminal Justice Center, Lansing Community College." *American Jails* 10 (1996): 58–60.

DUTTON, DONALD G. AND P. RANDALL KROPP. "A Review of Domestic Violence Risk Instruments." *Trauma, Violence, and Abuse: A Review Journal* 1 (2000): 171–181.

DYSART, MARY DIXIE. *"No Place for a Christian" : Women Inmates in Alabama Prisons, 1901–1943.* Ann Arbor, MI: University Microfilms International, 1999.

EASTEAL, PATRICIA. "Women in Australian Prisons: The Cycle of Abuse and Dysfunctional Environments." *Prison Journal* 81 (2001): 87–112.

ECKHART, DAN. "Civil Actions Related to Prison Gangs: A Survey of Federal Cases." *Corrections Management Quarterly* 5 (2001): 59–64.

EDIN, KATHRYN, TIMOTHY J. NELSON, AND RECHELLE PARANAL. *Fatherhood and Incarceration as Potential Turning Points in the Criminal Careers of Unskilled Men.* Evanston, IL: Northwestern University, 2001.

EGGLESTON, CAROLYN REBECCA. *Zebulon Brockway and Elmira Reformatory: A Study of Correctional/Special Education.* Richmond, VA: Virginia Commonwealth University, 1989.

EISENBERG, MICHAEL, LISA RIECHERS, AND NANCY ARRIGONA. *Evaluation of the Performance of the Texas Department of Criminal Justice Rehabilitation Tier Programs.* Austin, TX: Texas Criminal Justice Policy Council, 2001.

EISENBERG, MICHAEL ET AL. *The Substance Abuse Felony Punishment Program: Evaluation and Recommendations.* Austin, TX: Texas Criminal Justice Policy Council, 2001.

ELY, JOHN FREDERICK. *Inside-Out: Halfway House Staff Management of Punishment and Empathy on the Ambiguous Boundary between Prison and the Outside.* Ann Arbor, MI: University Microfilms International, 1996.

EMERICK, JEANETTE E. "Raising Morale through Communication." *American Jails* 10 (1996): 53–60.

ENOS, SANDRA. *Mothering from the Inside: Parenting in a Women's Prison.* Albany: State University of New York Press, 2001.

ENUKU, USIWOMA EVAWOMA. "Humanizing the Nigerian Prison through Literacy Education: Echoes from Afar." *The Journal of Correctional Education* 52 (2001): 18–22.

EREZ, EDNA AND KATHY LASTER. "Neutralizing Victim Reform: Legal Professionals' Perspectives on Victims and Impact Statements." *Crime and Delinquency* 45 (1999): 530–553.

ERICSON, NELS. *Healthy Families America.* Washington, DC: U.S. Department of Justice, 2001.

ESBENSEN, FINN-AAGE. "Gang Resistance Education and Training (GREAT): Results from the National Evalua-tion." *Journal of Research in Crime and Delinquency* 36 (1999): 194–225.

ETHRIDGE, PHILIP A. AND STEPHEN W. LIEBOWITZ. "The Attitudes of Sheriffs in Texas." *American Jails* 8 (1994): 55–60.

ETTER, GREGG W. AND MICHAEL L. BIRZER. "Community-Oriented: Why Training the Jail Officers?" *American Jails* 11 (1997): 66–71.

ETZIONI, AMITAI. *A Comparative Analysis of Organizations.* New York: Free Press, 1961.

EVANS, DONALD G. "Building Hope Through Community Justice." *Corrections Today* 60 (1999): 73.

EVANS, JEFF. *Undoing Time: American Prisoners in Their Own Words.* Boston: Northeastern University Press, 2001.

EVERETT, RONALD S. AND BARBARA C. NIENSTEDT. "Race, Remorse, and Sentence Reduction: Is Saying You're Sorry Enough?" *Justice Quarterly* 16 (1999): 99–122.

FADER, JAMIE J. ET AL. "Factors Involved in Decisions on Commitment to Delinquency Programs for First-Time Juvenile Offenders." *Justice Quarterly* 18 (2001): 323–341.

FAITH, KARLENE. "Media, Myths, and Masculinization: Images of Women in Prison." Unpublished paper presented at the American Society of Criminology meetings, Montreal, Canada, November 1987.

FAITH, KARLENE. *The Long Prison Journey of Leslie Van Houten: Life Beyond the Cult.* Boston: Northeastern University Press, 2001.

FAIVER, KENNETH L. *Health Care Management Issues in Corrections.* Lanham, MD: American Correctional Association, 1998.

FARKAS, MARY ANN. "A Typology of Correctional Officers." *International Journal of Offender Therapy and Comparative Criminology* 44 (2000): 431–449.

FARKAS, MARY ANN. "Correctional Officers: What Factors Influence Work Attitudes?" *Corrections Management Quarterly* 5 (2001): 20–26.

FARMER, J. FORBES. "Decentralized Management in Prison: A Comparative Case Study." *Journal of Offender Rehabilitation* 20 (1994): 117–130.

FARR, KATHRYN ANN. "Classification for Female Inmates: Moving Forward." *Crime and Delinquency* 46 (2000): 3–17.

FARRELL, AMY. "Women, Crime, and Drugs: Testing the Effect of Therapeutic Communities." *Women and Criminal Justice* 11 (2000): 21–48.

FARRINGTON, KAREN. *History of Punishment and Torture: A Journal through the Dark Side of Justice.* London, UK: Reed International, 1996.

FAUST, THOMAS N. "Shift the Responsibility of Untreated Mental Illness out of the Criminal Justice System." *Corrections Today* 65 (2003): 6–7.

FAZEL, SEENA AND JOHN DANESH. "Serious Mental Disorder in 23,000 Prisoners: A Systematic Review of 62 Surveys." *The Lancet* 359 (2002): 545–550.

FEDERAL BUREAU OF PRISONS. *A History of the Federal Bureau of Prisons.* Washington, DC: Office of the Solicitor General, 2002.

FEELEY, MALCOLM M. AND EDWARD L. RUBIN. *Judicial Policy Making and the Modern State: How the Courts Reformed America's Prisons.* New York: Cambridge University Press, 1998.

FEENEY, RENEE. "HIV/AIDS Infected Inmates Challenging DOC Policies." *Corrections Compendium* 22 (1995): 1–3.

FEINMAN, CLARICE. *Women in the Criminal Justice System.* 2d ed. New York: Praeger, 1986.

FELD, BARRY C. *Cases and Materials on Juvenile Justice Administration.* St. Paul, MN: West Group, 2000.

FELD, BARRY C. "Race, Youth Violence, and the Changing Jurisprudence of Waiver." *Behavioral Sciences and the Law* 19 (2001): 3–22.

FINKELHOR, DAVID AND RICHARD K. ORMROD. "Factors in the Underreporting of Crimes Against Juveniles." *Child Maltreatment* 6 (2001): 219–229.

FINN, PETER. *The Delaware Department of Correction Life Skills Program.* Washington, DC: U.S. National Institute of Justice, 1998a.

FINN, PETER. "The Orange County, Florida Jail Education and Vocational Programs." *American Jails* 12 (1998b): 9–28.

FIRESTONE, PHILIP ET AL. "Prediction of Recidivism in Extrafamilial Child Molesters Based on Court-Related Assessments." *Sexual Abuse: A Journal of Research and Treatment* 12 (2000): 203–232.

FISHER, BEA. "Teaching Literacy for Lifelong Learning: A New Look." *The Journal of Correctional Education* 52 (2001): 58–61.

FISHER, PATRICIA M. "Developing Initiatives to Address Workplace Stress, Burnout, and Trauma in Corrections." *American Jails* 15 (2001): 67–69.

FISHER-GIORLANDO, MARIANNE AND SHANBE JIANG. "Race and Disciplinary Reports: An Empirical Study of Correctional Officers." *Sociological Spectrum* 20 (2000): 169–194.

FISHMAN, JOSEPH F. *Sex in Prison.* New York: National Liberty Press, 1934.

FLANAGAN, TIMOTHY J., W. WESLEY JOHNSON, AND KATHERINE BENNETT. "Job Satisfaction among Correctional Executives: A Contemporary Portrait of Wardens of State Prisons for Adults." *Prison Journal* 76 (1996): 385–397.

FLEISHER, MARK. "Creating a Positive Climate in a New Federal Prison." *Corrections Compendium* 25 (2000): 1–4, 7–10, 18–19.

FLEISHER, MARK S. AND SCOTT H. DECKER. "An Overview of the Challenge of Prison Gangs." *Corrections Management Quarterly* 5 (2001a): 1–9.

FLEISHER, MARK S. AND SCOTT H. DECKER. "Going Home, Staying Home: Integrating Prison Gang Members into the Community." *Corrections Management Quarterly* 5 (2001b): 65–77.

FLETCHER, BEVERLY R., GARRY L. ROLISON, AND DREAMA G. MOON. "A Profile of Women Inmates in the State of Oklahoma." *Journal of the Oklahoma Criminal Justice Research Consortium* 1 (1994): 1–11.

FLITER, JOHN ALLEN JR. *Federal Courts and State Prisons: The Economics of Institutional Reform Litigation.* Ann Arbor, MI: University Microfilms International, 1993.

FLORIDA DEPARTMENT OF CORRECTIONS. *Time Served by Criminals in Florida's Prisons: The Impact of Punishment Policies from 1979 to 1999.* Tallahassee: Florida Department of Corrections Bureau of Research and Data Analysis, 1999.

FLORIDA DEPARTMENT OF CORRECTIONS. *Community Control: Purpose and General Requirements.* Tallahassee, FL: Author, 2001.

FLORIDA DEPARTMENT OF CORRECTIONS. *Program Types.* Tallahassee, FL: Author, 2002.

FLORIDA DEPARTMENT OF JUVENILE JUSTICE. *2001 Outcome Evaluation Report.* Tallahassee, FL: Florida Department of Juvenile Justice Bureau of Data and Research, 2001.

FLORIDA JOINT LEGISLATIVE MANAGEMENT COMMITTEE. *An Assessment of Vocational Education Needs in Florida's Women's Prisons.* Tallahassee, FL: Author, 1995.

FLORIDA LEGISLATURE. *Review of Bay Correctional Facility and Moore Haven Correctional Facility.* Tallahassee, FL: Florida Legislature Office of Program Policy Analysis and Government Accountability, 1998.

FLYNN, JOHN M. "Modular Building Techniques." *American Jails* 5 (1991): 56–59.

FLYNT, CHARLES AND MICKEY ELLENBECKER. "The Certification Experience at Winona State University." *American Jails* 9 (1995): 57–58.

FOGEL, DAVID. "*. . . We Are the Living Proof . . .*" Cincinnati, OH: Anderson, 1979.

FOGEL, DAVID. *Justice as Fairness: Perspectives on the Justice Model.* Cincinnati, OH: Anderson Publishing Company, 1981.

FOLINO, JORGE O. AND MARIA INES URRATIA. "Mental Disturbances and Criminological Characteristics in Crime-Accused Insane as Recorded at the Judiciary Office in LaPlata, Argentina for 10 Years." *International Journal of Law and Psychiatry* 24 (2001): 411–426.

FOSTER, BURK, WILBERT RIDEAU, AND RON WIKBERG, EDS. *The Wall Is Strong: Corrections in Louisiana.* Lafayette, IN: Center for Louisiana Studies, University of Southwestern Louisiana, 1991.

FOSTER, M.J. "Louisiana Changes Decades-Long Tradition." *Corrections Today* 64 (2002): 100–101.

FOX, SANFORD J. ET AL. "A Centennial Celebration of the Juvenile Court, 1899–1999." *Juvenile and Family Court Journal* 49 (1998): 110–126.

FRADELLA, HENRY F. "A Typology of the Frivolous: Varying Meanings of Frivolity in Section 1983 Prisoner Civil Rights Litigation." *Prison Journal* 78 (1998): 465–491.

FRADELLA, HENRY F. "In Search of Meritorious Claims: A Study of the Processing of Prisoner Civil Rights Cases in a Federal District Court." *Justice System Journal* 21 (1999): 23–55.

FRADELLA, HENRY F. "Mandatory Minimum Sentences: Arizona's Ineffective Tool for the Social Control of Driving Under the Influence." *Criminal Justice Policy Review* 11 (2000): 113–135.

FREEDMAN, ESTELLE B. *Their Sisters' Keepers: Women's Prison Reform in America, 1830–1930.* Ann Arbor, MI: The University of Michigan Press, 1981.

FREEMAN, ROBERT M. *Correctional Organization and Management: Public Policy Challenges, Behavior, and Structure.* Boston: Butterworth-Heinemann, 1999.

FREEMAN, ROBERT M. *Popular Culture and Corrections.* Lanham, MD: American Correctional Association, 2000.

FRENCH, J.R.P., JR., AND B. RAVEN. *The Bases of Social Power.* Ann Arbor, MI: Institute for Social Research, 1959.

FRIENDSHIP, CAROLINE AND DAVID THORNTON. "Sexual Reconviction for Sexual Offenders Discharged from Prison in England and Wales." *British Journal of Criminology* 41 (2001): 285–292.

FRUCHTMAN, DAVID A. AND ROBERT T. SIGLER. "Private Pre-Sentence Investigation: Procedures and Issues." *Journal of Offender Rehabilitation* 29 (1999): 157–170.

FULLER, LISA G. "Visitors to Women's Prisons in California: An Exploratory Study." *Federal Probation* 57 (1993): 41–47.

FULTON, BETSY AND SUSAN STONE. "Achieving Public Safety Through the Provision of Intense Services: The Promise of a New ISP." *APPA Persepctives* 17 (1993): 43–45.

FULTON, BETSY ET AL. "Moderating Probation and Parole Officer Attitudes to Achieve Desired Outcomes." *Prison Journal* 77 (2000): 295–312.

FUNK, STEPHANIE J. "Risk Assessment for Juveniles on Probation: A Focus on Gender." *Criminal Justice and Behavior* 26 (1999): 44–68.

FURIO, JENNIFER. *Letters from Prison: Voices of Women Murderers.* New York: Algora, 2001.

GABBIDON, SHAUN L. ET AL. *African American Classics in Criminology and Criminal Justice.* Thousand Oaks, CA: Sage Publications, 2002.

GAINES, MICHAEL. "Prohibiting Internet Abuse by Parolees." *APPA Perspectives* 22 (1998): 20–21.

GALLAGHER, PATRICIA, PATRIZIA POLETTI, AND IAN MACKINNELL. *Sentencing Disparity and the Gender of Juvenile Offenders.* Sidney, NSW: Judicial Commission of New South Wales, 2001.

GALVIN, JOHN J. ET AL. *Alternatives to Prosecution: Instead of Jail.* Washington, DC: U.S. Government Printing Office, 1997.

GAMMON, TOR. "The Detrimental Effects of Solitary Confinement in Norwegian Prisons." *Nordisk Tidsskrift for Kriminalvidenskab* 88 (2001): 42–50.

GARDNER, ALAN. *Paraprofessionals and Their Performance: A Survey of Education, Health, and Social Service Programs.* New York: Praeger, 1971.

GARDNER, MARTIN R. "*Hudson v. Palmer*—'Bright Lines' But Dark Directions for Prisoner Privacy Rights." *Journal of Contemporary Law and Criminology* 76 (1985): 75–115.

GARNIER, HELEN E. AND JUDITH A. STEIN. "An 18-Year Model of Family and Peer Effects on Adolescent Drug Use and Delinquency." *Journal of Youth and Adolescence* 31 (2002): 45–56.

GARRISON, ARTHUR H. "An Evaluation of a Delaware Teen Court." *Juvenile and Family Court Journal* 52 (2001): 11–21.

GARVEY, STEPHEN P. "Freeing Prisoners' Labor." *Stanford Law Review* 50 (1998): 339–398.

GARZA, PETE JR. "Sunnyside City Jail: Big Problems for a Small Jail." *American Jails* 8 (1994): 71–72.

GAUGER, GLENN AND CURTISS PULITZER. "Built to Last: Construction and Design Issue." *Corrections Today* 53 (1991): 90.

GEER, TRACEY M. ET AL. "Predictors of Treatment Completion in a Correctional Sex Offender Treatment Program." *International Journal of Offender Therapy and Comparative Criminology* 45 (2001): 302–313.

GENDERS, ELAINE AND ELAINE PLAYER. *Grendon: A Study of a Therapeutic Prison.* Oxford, UK: Clarendon Press, 1995.

GENDREAU, PAUL AND DAVID KEYES. "Making Prisons Safer and More Humane Environments." *Canadian Journal of Criminology* 43 (2001): 123–130.

GEST, TED. *Crime and Politics: Big Government's Erratic Campaign for Law and Order.* Oxford, UK: Oxford University Press, 2001.

GETTY, CAROL P. *Supervised Release Matters: A Study of Post Incarceration in the Federal System, 1994–1998.* Ann Arbor, MI: University Microfilms International, 2000.

GHETTI, SIMONA AND ALLISON D. REDLICH. "Reactions to Youth Crime: Perceptions of Accountability and Competency." *Behavioral Sciences and the Law* 19 (2001): 33–52.

GIBLIN, MATTHEW J. "Using Police Officers to Enhance the Supervision of Juvenile Probationers: An Evaluation of the Anchorage CAN Program." *Crime and Delinquency* 48 (2002): 116–137.

GIDO, ROSEMARY L., ED. "Evolution of the Concepts Correctional Organization and Organizational Change." *Criminal Justice Policy Review* 9 (1998): 5–139.

GILL, S. CARY AND RON ANGELONE. "Fluvanna: Correctional Center for women: A Model Facility." *Corrections Today* 62 (2000): 98–101.

GILLIARD, DARRELL K. AND ALLEN J. BECK. *Prisoners in 1997.* Washington, DC: U.S. Department of Justice, 1998.

GILLING, DANIEL. "Community Safety and Social Policy." *European Journal on Criminal Policy and Research* 9 (2001): 381–400.

GIRSHICK, LORI B. *No Safe Haven: Stories of Women in Prison.* Boston: Northeastern University Press, 1999.

GIVELBER, DANIEL. "Punishing Protestations of Innocence: Denying Responsibility and Its Consequences." *American Criminal Law Review* 37 (2000): 1363–1408.

GLADE, GEORGE H. "*Washington v. Harper*: An Examination of King County Correctional Facility's Decision to Not Adopt a Compelled Medications Policy." *American Jails* 10 (1996): 51–55.

GLASER, BRIAN A., GEORGIA B. CALHOUN, AND JOHN PETROCELLI. "Personality Characteristics of Male Juvenile Offenders by Adjudicated Offenses as Indicated by the MMPI-A." *Criminal Justice and Behavior* 29 (2002): 183–201.

GLASER, BRIAN A. ET AL. "Multi-Observer Assessment of Problem Behavior in Adjudicated Youths: Patterns of Discrepancies." *Child and Family Behavior Therapy* 23 (2001): 33–45.

GLASER, DANIEL. "Classification for Risk." In *Prediction and Classification: Criminal Justice Decision Making,* edited by Don M. Gottfredson and Michael Tonry. Chicago: University of Chicago Press, 1987.

GLAZE, LAUREN E. *Probation and Parole in the United States, 2001.* Washington, DC: U.S. Department of Justice, Office of Justice Programs, 2002.

GLAZER, YALE. "The Chains May Be Heavy, But They Are Not Cruel and Unusual: Examining the Constitutionality of the Reintroduced Chain Gang." *Hofstra Law Review* 24 (1996): 11–95–1224.

GLICK, BARRY AND EDWARD E. RHINE. *Journal of Correctional Best Practices: Juveniles in Adult Correctional Systems.* Lanham, MD: American Correctional Association, 2001.

GODWIN, TRACY M., DAVID J. STEINHART, AND BETSY A. FULTON. *Peer Justice and Youth Empowerment: An Implementation Guide for Teen Court Programs.* Washington, DC: U.S. Department of Transportation, 1996.

GOFFMAN, ERVING. *Asylums.* Garden City, NY: Anchor, 1961.

GOLDKAMP, JOHN S. "Prediction in Criminal Justice Policy Development." In *Prediction and Classification: Criminal Justice Decision Making,* edited by Don M. Gottfredson and Michael Tonry. Chicago, IL: University of Chicago Press, 1987.

GOLDSMITH, HERB. "The Interaction of Management and Treatment in a Residential Youth Corrections/Treatment Setting." *Residential Treatment for Children and Youth* 18 (2001): 23–32.

GOLDSON, BARRY. "A Rational Youth Justice? Some Critical Reflections on the Research, Policy, and Practice Relation." *Probation Journal* 48 (2001): 76–85.

GOLDSTEIN, HAROLD AND ANN HIGGINS-D'ALESSANDRO. "Empathy and Attachment in Relation to Violent vs. Non-Violent Offense History among Jail Inmates." *Journal of Offender Rehabilitation* 32 (2001): 31–53.

GOLDSTONE, JACK A. AND BERT USEEM. "Prison Riots as Microrevolutions: An Extension of State-Centered Theories of Revolution." *American Journal of Sociology* 104 (1999): 985–1029.

GOODALE, JEFF, MISSY STUTLER, AND DONNA KLEIN-ACOSTA. "The Prison That Drugs Built: Illinois Designs a New Women's Prison for the New Reality." *Corrections Today* 64 (2002): 88–90.

GORTON, JOE AND JOHN L. BOIES. "Sentencing Guidelines and Racial Disparity Across Time: Pennsylvania Prison Sentences in 1997, 1983, 1992, and 1993." *Social Science Quarterly* 80 (1999): 37–54.

GORTON, RONALD JOSEPH. *Organizational Change and Managerial Control During the Contemporary Post-Reform Period of the Texas Prison System.* Ann Arbor, MI: University Microfilms International, 1997.

GOTTFREDSON, MICHAEL R. AND DON M. GOTTFREDSON. *Decision Making in Criminal Justice: The Rational Exercise of Discretion.* 2d ed. New York: Plenum Press, 1988.

GOWEN, DARREN. "Analysis of Competing Risks in the Federal Home Confinement Program." *Journal of Offender Monitoring* 14 (2001): 5–11.

GRANN, MARTIN, HENRIK BELFRAGE, AND ANDERS TENGSTROM. "Actuarial Assessment of Risk for Violence: Predictive Validity of the VRAG and the Historical Part of the HCR-20." *Criminal Justice and Behavior* 27 (2000): 97–114.

GRANT, BRIAN A. AND SARA L. JOHNSON. *Personal Development Temporary Absences.* Ottawa, Canada: Research Branch, Correctional Service of Canada, 1998.

GRANT, BRIAN A. AND WILLIAM A. MILLSON. *The Temporary Absence Program: A Descriptive Analysis.* Ottawa, Canada: Correctional Service of Canada, 1998.

GREEN, DANA ET AL. "Medical Services in Jails: To Charge or Not to Charge: That Is the Question." *American Jails* 11 (1997): 85–90.

GREENBERG, DAVID F. AND VALERIE WEST. "State Prison Populations and Their Growth: 1971–1991." *Criminology: An Interdisciplinary Journal* 39 (2001): 615–654.

GREENE, JUDITH AND JOHN DOBLE. *Attitudes toward Crime and Punishment in Vermont: Public Opinion about an Experiment with Restorative Justice.* Englewood Cliffs, NJ: John Doble Research Associates, 2000.

GREENE, JUDITH AND VINCENT SCHIRALDI. *Cutting Correctly: New Prison Policies for Times of Fiscal Crisis.* Washington, DC: Justice Policy Institute, 2002.

GREENFIELD, LAWRENCE A. ET AL. "Current Issues in Prison Management." *Criminal Justice Review* 21 (1996): 4–85.

GRIFFIN, MARIE L. *The Use of Force By Detention Officers.* New York: LFB Scholarly Publishing LLC, 2001.

GRIFFIN, P. *OJJDP Statistical Briefing Book.* Washington, DC: Office of Juvenile Justice and Delinquency Prevention, 2002.

GROSS, K. HAWKEYE. *Tales from the Joint.* Boulder, CO: Paladin Press, 1995.

GUDJONSSON, GISLI H. AND ESTELLE MOORE. "Self-Deception and Other-Deception among Admissions to a Maximum-Security Hospital and a Medium Secure Unit." *Psychology, Crime, and Law* 7 (2001): 25–31.

GURIAN, MICHAEL. "Gender and Sexual Contact Training in the Criminal Justice Workplace." *American Jails* 8 (1994): 29–32.

GURSKY, DAN. "The Aftermath of an Execution—an Interview with Jennie Lancaster." *Corrections Today* 50 (1988): 76–84.

GUZZI, MARK E. "Federal Regulation of the Private Inmate Transportation Industry." *On the Line* 24 (2001): 1–2.

HADDAD, JANE. "Managing the Special Needs of the Mentally Ill." *American Jails* 7 (1993): 62–65.

HADLEY, MICHAEL L., ED. *The Spiritual Roots of Restorative Justice.* Albany: State University of New York Press, 2001.

HAESLER, WALTER T. "The Released Prisoner and His Difficulties to Be Accepted Again as a 'Normal' Citizen." *Euro-Criminology* 4 (1992): 61–68.

HAGAN, JOHN AND JULEIGH PETTY. "Returning Captives of the American War on Drugs: Issues of Community and Family Reentry." *Crime and Delinquency* 47 (2001): 352–367.

HAHN, PAUL H. *The Juvenile Offender and the Law.* Cincinnati, OH: Anderson, 1984.

HAHN, PAUL H. "A Standardized Curriculum for Correctional Officers: History and Rationale." *American Jails* 9 (1995): 45–51.

HALFORD, SALLY CHANDLER. "Kansas Co-Correctional Concept." *Corrections Today* 46 (1984): 44–54.

HALIM, SHAHEEN AND BEVERLY L. STILES. "Differential Support for Police Use of Force, the Death Penalty, and Perceived Harshness of the Courts." *Criminal Justice and Behavior* 28 (2001): 3–23.

HALL, ANDY. *Systemwide Strategies to Alleviate Jail Overcrowding.* Washington, DC: National Institute of Justice, 1987.

HALLIMAN, JOSEPH T. *Going up the River: Travels in a Prison Nation.* New York: Random House, 2001.

HAMBERGER, L. KEVIN. "Female Offenders in Domestic Violence: A Look at Actions in Their Context." *Journal of Aggression Maltreatment and Trauma* 1 (1997): 117–130.

HAMMETT, THEODORE M. AND LAURA M. MARUSCHAK. *1996–1997 Update: HIV/AIDS, STDs, and TB in Correctional Facilities.* Washington, DC: U.S. National Institute of Justice, Centers for Disease Control and Prevention, 1999.

HAMMETT, THEODORE M., CHERYL ROBERTS, AND SOFIA KENNEDY. "Health-Related Issues in Prison Reentry." *Crime and Delinquency* 47 (2001): 390–409.

HANBURY, BARBARA MICHELLE. *Are Judges Downwardly Departing from the United States Sentencing Guidelines Based on the Offenders' Personal Characteristics?* Ann Arbor, MI: University Microfilms International, 2000.

HANNAH-MOFFAT, KELLY. *Punishment in Disguise: Penal Governance and Federal Imprisonment of Women in Canada.* Toronto, Canada: University of Toronto Press, 2001.

HANNAH-MOFFAT, KELLY AND MARGARET SHAW. *Taking Risks: Incorporating Gender and Culture into the Classification and Assessment of Federally Sentenced Women in Canada.* Toronto, Canada: Status of Women Canada's Policy Research Fund, 2001.

HANNON, LANCE, JAMES DEFRONZO, AND JANE PROCHNOW. "Moral Commitment and the Effects of Social Influences on Violent Delinquency." *Violence and Victims* 16 (2001): 427–439.

HANSEN, BRIAN, FRANK ORLANDO, AND JAMES C. BACKSTROM. "Kids in Prison: Are the States Too Tough on Young Offenders?" *CQ Researcher* 11 (2001): 346–376.

HANSEN, EVAN. "Jail Supervision in the '90s." *American Jails* 9 (1995): 37–41.

HANSON, R. KARL AND ANDREW J.R. HARRIS. "A Structured Approach to Evaluating Change among Sexual Offenders." *Sexual Abuse: A Journal of Research and Treatment* 13 (2001): 105–122.

HANSON, ROGER A. AND HENRY W.K. DALEY. *Challenging the Conditions of Prisons and Jails: A Report on Section 1983 Litigation.* Washington, DC: U.S. Bureau of Justice Statistics, 1995.

HARDING, RICHARD W. *Private Prisons and Public Accountability.* New Brunswick, NJ: Transaction, 1997.

HARDING, RICHARD W. "Prison Privatization: The Debate Starts to Mature." *Current Issues in Criminal Justice* 11 (1999): 109–118.

HARLEY, D.M. *International Alternative Dispute Resolution Programs.* The Hague, Netherlands: Moorland, 1999.

HARLOW, CAROLINE WOLF. *Profile of Jail Inmates 1996.* Washington, DC: U.S. Department of Justice, 1998.

HARMON, TALIA ROITBERG. "Guilty until Proven Innocent: An Analysis of Post-Furman Capital Errors." *Criminal Justice Policy Review* 12 (2001): 113–139.

HARRIES, KEITH. "Geographic Analysis." *APPA Perspectives* 26 (2002): 26–31.

HARRINGTON, JOHN AND KATE CAVETT. *G is for Gangsta: Introductory Assessment of Gang Activity and Issues in Minnesota.* St. Paul, MN: Hand in Hand, 2000.

HARRIS, PATRICIA M., REBECCA D. PETERSEN, AND SAMANTHA RAPOZA. "Between Probation and Revocation: A Study of Intermediate Sanctions and Decision Making." *Journal of Criminal Justice* 29 (2001): 307–318.

HARRIS, VICTORIA L. AND DAVID LOVELL. "Measuring Level of Function in Mentally Ill Prison Inmates: A Preliminary Study." *Journal of the American Academy of Psychiatry and the Law* 29 (2001): 68–74.

HARRISON, LANA D. "The Revolving Prison Door for Drug-Involved Offenders: Challenges and Opportunities." *Crime and Delinquency* 47 (2001): 462–484.

HARRISON, PAIGE M. AND ALLEN J. BECK. *Prisoners in 2001.* Washington, DC: U.S. Department of Justice, 2002.

HARRY, JENNIFER L. "Michigan Inmates Rescue Female CO." *Corrections Today* 63 (2001): 12.

HARRY, JENNIFER L. "Early Release for New York's Drug Offenders." *Corrections Today* 65 (2003): 14.

HARTWELL, STEPHANIE. "Female Mentally Ill Offenders and Their Community Reintegration Needs: An Initial Examination." *International Journal of Law and Psychiatry* 24 (2001): 1–11.

HASABALLA, AIDA Y. *The Social Organization of the Modern Prison.* Lewiston, NY: Edwin Mellen Press, 2001.

HASSELL, KIMBERLY AND EDWARD R. MAGUIRE. *The Colorado Springs Juvenile Offender Unit: A Process and Impact Evaluation.* Silver Springs, MD: 21st Century Solutions, 2001.

HAULARD, EDGAR R. "Adult Education: A Must for Our Incarcerated Population." *The Journal of Correctional Education* 52 (2001): 157–159.

HAUSSER, GINGER. *The State of Corrections: Tennessee's Prisons Before and After Court Intervention.* Nashville: Tennessee Comptroller of the Treasury, 1998.

HAWKINS, DARNELL F. "State vs. County: Prison Policy and Conflicts of Interest in North Carolina." In *Criminal Justice History: An International Annual, Vol. IV.* Westport, CT: Meckler, 1984.

HAYES, COLIN. "The Office of Sheriff in the United States." *The Police Journal* 74 (2001): 50–54.

HECKEL, ROBERT V. AND DAVID M. SHUMAKER. *Children Who Murder: A Psychological Perspective.* Westport, CT: Praeger, 2001.

HEFFERNAN, ESTHER. "Making It in a Woman's Prison: The Square, the Cool, and the Life." In *Correctional Institutions,* 3d ed., edited by Robert M. Carter, Daniel Glaser, and Leslie T. Wilkins. New York: Harper and Row, 1985.

HEIKES, JOEL AND ALMA I. MARTINEZ. *The Impact of Progressive Sanction Guidelines: Trends Since 1995.* Austin, TX: Criminal Justice Policy Council, 2001.

HEIM, TED. "The Washburn Experience: The University Role in Training Jail Personnel." *American Jails* 7 (1993): 18–20.

HELFGOTT, JACQUELINE B. ET AL. "Results from the Pilot Study of the Citizens, Victims, and Offenders Restoring Program at the Washington State Reformatory." *Journal of Contemporary Criminal Justice* 16 (2000): 5–31.

HEMMENS, CRAIG. "Legal Issues in Probation and Parole." *APPA Perspectives* 22 (1998): 11–13.

HEMMENS, CRAIG AND JAMES W. MARQUART. "Fear and Loathing in the Joint: The Impact of Race and Age on Inmate Support for AIDS Policies." *Prison Journal* 78 (1998): 133–151.

HEMMENS, CRAIG AND MARY K. STOHR. "Correctional Staff Attitudes Regarding the Use of Force in Corrections." *Corrections Management Quarterly* 5 (2001): 27–40.

HENNESSEY, MICHAEL. "San Francisco Sheriff's Department SISTER Project." *American Jails* 11 (1997): 40–43.

HENRICO COUNTY. *Regional Jail Operations in Henrico County.* Richmond, VA: Henrico County Jail Services, 2003.

HENRIQUES, ZELMA WESTON AND NORMA RUPERT MANATU. "Living on the Outside: African American Women Before, During, and After Imprisonment." *Prison Journal* 81 (2001): 6–19.

HENRY, MARK A. "Unethical Staff Behavior: Good Correctional Managers Can Help Staff Succeed." *Corrections Today* 60 (1998): 108–116.

HENSLEY, CHRISTOPHER, ED. "Prison Sexuality." *Prison Journal* 80 (2000): 357–468.

HENSLEY, CHRISTOPHER, SANDRA RUTLAND, AND PHYLLIS GRAY. "Inmate Attitudes toward the Conjugal Visitation Program in Mississippi Prisons: An Exploratory Study." *American Journal of Criminal Justice* 25 (2000): 137–145.

HEPBURN, JOHN R. ET AL. *The Maricopa County Demand Reduction Program: An Evaluation Report.* Phoenix, AZ: Maricopa County Drug Abuse and Addiction Program, 1992.

HERMAN, SUSAN AND CRESSIDA WASSERMAN. "A Role for Victims in Offender Reentry." *Crime and Delinquency* 47 (2001): 428–445.

HESS, ALBERT G. AND PRISCILLA F. CLEMENT, EDS. *History of Juvenile Delinquency: A Collection of Essays on Crime Committed by Young Offenders, Vol. 2.* Aalen, Germany: Scientia Verlag, 1993.

HEWITT, BILL. "Mothers Behind Bars." *People,* December 11, 1996:95–102.

HICKS, NANCY. "When the Warden Is a Woman." *Corrections Compendium* 15 (1990): 1–7.

HIGGINS, SCOTT. "Making Sure Tomorrow's Correctional Facilities Stand the Test of Time." *Corrections Today* 58 (1996): 8.

HILL, CECE. "Female Offenders." *Corrections Compendium* 26 (2001): 5–23, 27.

HILL, CECE. "Communicable Diseases." *Corrections Compendium* 27 (2002): 8–25.

HILTE, KEN. "Writing Policy and Procedure." *American Jails* 12 (1998): 33–36.

HILTON, N. ZOE AND JANET L. SIMMONS. "The Influence of Actuarial Risk Assessment in Clinical Judgments and Tribunal Decisions about Mentally Disordered Offenders in Maximum Security." *Law and Human Behavior* 25 (2001): 393–408.

HIRSCH, ADAM J. *The Rise of the Penitentiary: Prisons and Punishment in Early America.* New Haven, CT: Yale University Press, 1992.

HIRSCHEL, J. DAVID, CHARLES W. DEAN, AND DORIS DUMOND. "Juvenile Curfews and Race: A Cautionary Note." *Criminal Justice Policy Review* 12 (2001): 197–214.

HOBBS, GAYNOR S. AND GREG E. DEAR. "Prisoners' Perceptions of Prison Officers as Sources of Social Support." *Journal of Offender Rehabilitation* 31 (2000): 127–142.

HODGES, C. MARK. *Information Brief: Comparing Costs of Private Prisons.* Tallahassee; Florida Office of Program Policy Analysis and Government Accountability, 1997.

HOEFLE, YVONNE. "National Recognition for a Small Jail Meeting Community Needs." *American Jails* 9 (1995): 65–72.

HOFFMAN, PETER B. "Screening for Risk: A Revised Salient Factor Score, SFS 81." *Journal of Criminal Justice* 11 (1983): 539–547.

HOGE, ROBERT D. "A Case Management Instrument for Use in Juvenile Justice Systems." *Juvenile and Family Court Journal* 52 (2001): 25–32.

HOHMAN, MELINDA, RICHARD P. McGAFFIGAN, AND LANCE SEGARS. "Predictors of Successful Completion of a Postincarceration Drug Treatment Program." *Journal of Addictions and Offender Counseling* 21 (2000): 12–22.

HOKANSON, SHIRLEY. *The Woman Offender in Minnesota: Profile, Needs and Future Directions.* St. Paul: Minnesota Department of Corrections, 1986.

HOLLENHORST, PAMELA STIEBS. "What Do We Know about Anger Management Programs in Corrections?" *Federal Probation* 62 (1999): 52–64.

HOLLIN, CLIVE R., ED. *Handbook of Offender Assessment and Treatment.* Chichester, UK: John Wiley, 2001.

HOLT, NORMAN. "Research Update: Assessing Correction Programs for Risk Reduction." *APPA Perspectives* 22 (1998): 18.

HOOD, ROGER. "Capital Punishment: A Global Perspective." *Punishment and Society* 3 (2001): 331–354.

HOPE, TRINA L. AND KELLY R. DAMPHOUSSE. "Applying Self-Control Theory to Gang Membership in a Nonurban Setting." *Journal of Gang Research* 9 (2002): 41–61.

HORN, JIM. "Kentucky Officers Get Involved: Political Arena." *APPA Perspectives* 16 (1992): 27–28.

HORN, MARTIN F. "Rethinking Sentencing." *Corrections Management Quarterly* 5 (2001): 34–40.

HORN, REBECCA AND SAM WARNER, EDS. *Issues in Forensic Psychology: Positive Directions for Women in Secure Environments.* Leicester, UK: British Psychological Society, 2000.

HORTON, ARTHUR. "Violence Crime: New Evidence to Consider." *Journal of Human Behavior in the Social Environment* 5 (2002): 77–87.

HOUCHINS, DAVID E. "Developing the Self-Determination of Incarcerated Students." *The Journal of Correctional Education* 52 (2001): 141–147.

HOUSTON, JAMES G. *Crime, Policy, and Criminal Behavioral in America.* Lewiston, NY: Edwin Mellen Press, 2001.

HOVEY, MARCIA. "The Forgotten Offenders." *Manpower Washington DC* (January 1971): 38–41.

HOWERTON, MIKE. "Jail Standards in 2001: Results of a 21-State Survey." *American Jails* 15 (2001): 9–11.

HUCKLESBY, ANTHEA AND CHRISTINE WILKINSON. "Drug Misuse in Prisons: Some Comments on the Prison Service Drug Strategy." *The Howard Journal of Criminal Justice* 40 (2001): 347–363.

HUFF, C. RONALD, ED. *Gangs in America.* 3d ed. Thousand Oaks, CA: Sage, 2002.

HUGHES, ROBERT. *The Fatal Shore.* New York: Alfred Knopf, 1987.

HUGHES, TIMOTHY A., DORIS JAMES WILSON, AND ALLEN J. BECK. *Trends in State Parole, 1990–2000.* Washington,

DC: U.S. Department of Justice, Office of Justice Programs, 2001.

HUGHES, TOM. "*Board of the County Commissioners of Bryan County, Oklahoma v. Jill Brown:* Municipal Liability and Police Hiring Decisions." *Justice Professional* 13 (2000): 143–162.

HUMAN RIGHTS WATCH. *Beyond Reason: The Death Penalty and Offenders with Mental Retardation.* New York: Human Rights Watch, 2001a.

HUMAN RIGHTS WATCH. *No Escape: Male Rape in U.S. Prisons.* New York: Human Rights Watch, 2001b.

HUMAN RIGHTS WATCH WOMEN'S RIGHTS PROJECT. *All Too Familiar: Sexual Abuse of Women in U.S. State Prisons.* New York: Human Rights Watch, 1996.

HUMPHRIES, KERMIT. "New Interstate Compact for Adult Offender Supervision Legally Takes Effect." *APPA Perspectives* 26 (2002): 10–11.

HUNTER, ROBERT J., B. KEITH CREW, AND TIMOTHY S. SEXTON. *Management Strategies for Long-Term Inmates.* Cedar Falls, IA: Center for Social and Behavioral Research, University of Northern Iowa, 1997.

HUNTER, ROBERT J. AND TIMOTHY S. SEXTON. "The Business of Jails: A Case Study." *American Jails* 11 (1997): 77–83.

HUNTER, SUSAN M. "Issues and Challenges Facing Women's Prisons in the 1980s." *The Prison Journal* 64 (1984): 129–135.

HURST, TIMOTHY E. AND MALLORY M. HURST. "Gender Differences in Mediation of Severe Occupational Stress Among Correctional Officers." *American Journal of Criminal Justice* 22 (1997): 121–137.

HUSKEY, BOBBIE L. "Community Corrections Acts." *Corrections Today* 46 (1984): 45.

HUTCHINSON, VIRGINIA. "NIC Jails Division: Helping Jails Meet Diverse Challenges." *American Jails* 12 (1999): 15–20.

ILLINOIS DEPARTMENT OF CORRECTIONS. *1995 Five-Year Plan for Female Inmates.* Springfield, IL: Illinois Department of Corrections, 1995.

ILLINOIS DEPARTMENT OF CORRECTIONS. *Two-Year Report on Illinois Department of Corrections' Chicago Southside Day Reporting Center.* Springfield, IL: Illinois Department of Corrections, 2000.

IMMARIGEON, RUSS AND MEDA CHESNEY-LIND. *Women's Prisons: Overcrowded and Overused.* San Francisco: National Council on Crime and Delinquency, 1992.

INGLEY, STEPHEN J. "Newly Established AJA Resolutions." *American Jails* 7 (1993): 7.

IRWIN, JOHN. *The Felon.* Berkeley: University of California Press, 1970.

IRWIN, JOHN. *The Jail: Managing the Underclass in American Society.* Berkeley: University of California Press, 1985.

IRWIN, JOHN AND DONALD R. CRESSEY. "Thieves, Convicts, and the Inmate Culture." *Social Problems* 10 (1962): 142–155.

IRWIN, JOHN, VINCENT SCHIRALDI, AND JASON ZIEDENBERG. "America's One Million Nonviolent Prisoners." *Social Justice* 27 (2000): 135–147.

JABLECKI, LAWRENCE T. "Changing Lives Through Literature." *Federal Probation* 62 (1998): 32–39.

JACKSON, JESSE L. SR., JESSE L. JACKSON, JR., AND BRUCE SHAPIRO. *Legal Lynching: The Death Penalty and America's Future.* New York: New Press, 2001.

JACKSON, JOE. *Leavenworth Train: A Fugitive's Search for Justice in the Vanishing West.* New York: Carroll and Graf, 2001.

JACKSON, YO. "Mentoring for Delinquent Children: An Outcome Study with Young Adolescent Children." *Journal of Youth and Adolescence* 31 (2002): 115–122.

JACOBS, JAMES B. "The Prisoners' Rights Movement and Its Impact, 1960–1980." In N. Morris and M. Tonry, *Crime and Justice: An Annual Review of Research.* Chicago: University of Chicago Press, 1980.

JARJOURA, G. ROGER AND SUSAN T. KRUMHOLZ. "Combining Bibliotherapy and Positive Role Modeling as an Alternative to Incarceration." *Journal of Offender Rehabilitation* 28 (1998): 127–139.

JASCOR, BARB. "Corrections Science Associate Degree Program." *American Jails* 15 (2001): 91–94.

JEFFRIES, JOHN M. AND SUZANNE MENGHRAJ. *Serving Incarcerated and Ex-Offender Fathers and Their Families: A Review of the Field.* New York: Vera Institute of Criminal Justice, 2001.

JOCKUSCH, ULRICH AND FERDINAND KELLER. "Confinement in Forensic Hospitals Under Section 63 of the German Criminal Code in Practice: Duration of Confinement and Criminal Recidivism." *Monatsschrift fuer Kriminologie und Strafrechtsreform* 84 (2001): 453–465.

JOHNSON, RICHARD R. "Intensive Probation for Domestic Violence Offenders." *Federal Probation* 65 (2001): 36–39.

JOHNSON, ROBERT. *Hard Time: Understanding and Reforming the Prison.* 2d ed. Belmont, CA: Wadsworth Publishing Company, 1996.

JOHNSON, WESLEY W. ET AL. "Goals of Community Corrections: An Analysis of State Legal Codes." *American Journal of Crime and Justice* 18 (1994): 79–93.

JOHNSTON, G. WAYNE AND NICHOLAS O. ALOZIE. "The Effect of Age on Criminal Processing: Is There an Advantage in Being 'Older'?" *Journal of Gerontological Social Work* 35 (2001): 47–62.

JOHNSTON, WENDY. "Boston Area Program Integrates Electronic Monitoring with Substance Abuse Treatment for Women." *The Journal of Offender Monitoring* 14 (2001): 20–21.

JOHNSTONE, MARK. "Men, Masculinity, and Offending: Developing Gendered Practice in the Probation Service." *Probation Journal* 48 (2001): 10–16.

JONES, JOHN R. AND DANIEL P. CARLSON. *Reputable Conduct: Ethical Issues in Policing and Corrections.* 2d ed. Upper Saddle River, NJ: Prentice Hall, 2001.

JONES, MARK AND ROLANDO V. DEL CARMEN. "When Do Probation and Parole Officers Enjoy the Same Immunity as Judges?" *Federal Probation* 56 (1992): 36–41.

JONES, MARK AND DARRELL L. ROSS. "Electronic House Arrest and Boot Camp in North Carolina." *Criminal Justice Policy Review* 8 (1997a): 383–403.

JONES, MARK AND DARRELL L. ROSS. "Is Less Better? Boot Camp, Regular Probation, and Rearrest in North Carolina." *American Journal of Criminal Justice* 21 (1997b): 147–161.

JONES, MICHAEL A. AND DAVID W. ROUSH. "Developing the NJDA Care Giver Curriculum." *Journal for Juvenile Justice and Detention Services* 10 (1995): 64–72.

JOSI, DON A. AND DALE K. SECHREST. *The Changing Career of the Correctional Officer: Policy Implications for the 21st Century.* Boston: Butterworth-Heinemann, 1998.

JOSI, DON A. AND DALE K. SECHREST. "A Pragmatic Approach to Parole Aftercare: Evaluation of a Community Reintegration Program for High-Risk Youthful Offenders." *Justice Quarterly* 16 (1999): 51–80.

JURICH, SONIA, MARTA CASPER, AND KIM A. HULL. "Training Correctional Educators: A Needs Assessment Study." *The Journal of Correctional Education* 52 (2001): 23–27.

JUSTICE EDUCATION CENTER, INC. *Court Disposition Study: Criminal Offenders in Connecticut's Courts in 1991: An Overview.* Hartford, CT: Justice Education Center, Inc, 1993.

KADEN, JONATHAN. "Therapy for Convicted Sex Offenders: Pursuing Rehabilitation without Incrimination." *Journal of Criminal Law and Criminology* 59 (1998): 347–391.

KAISER, DOUG. "Small Jails—How You Can Survive." *American Jails* 8 (1994): 77–87.

KAKAR-SIRPAL, SUMAN. "Familial Criminality, Familial Drug Use, and Gang Membership: Youth Criminality, Drug Use, and Gang Membership: What Are the Connections?" *Journal of Gang Research* 9 (2002): 11–22.

KARP, DAVID R. "Harm and Repair: Observing Restorative Justice in Vermont." *Justice Quarterly* 18 (2001): 727–757.

KASSEBAUM, GENE AND DUANE K. OKAMOTO. "The Drug Court as a Sentencing Model." *Journal of Contemporary Criminal Justice* 17 (2001): 89–104.

KAUFFMAN, KELSEY. *The Brotherhood: Racism and Intimidation among Prison Staff at the Indiana Correctional Facility-Putnamville.* Greencastle, IN: Compton Center for Peace and Justice, DePauw University, 2000.

KAUFFMAN, KELSEY. "Mothers in Prison." *Corrections Today Magazine* 63 (2001): 62–65.

KAUFMAN, GIL. "Mental Health in Corrections: Manage It or Be Managed!" *American Jails* 12 (1998): 71–74.

KAZURA, KERRY. "Family Programming for Incarcerated Parents: A Needs Assessment among Inmates." *Journal of Offender Rehabilitation* 32 (2001): 31–53.

KEETON, KATO B. AND CHERYL SWANSON. "HIV/AIDS Education Needs Assessment: A Comparative Study of Jail and Prison Inmates in Northwest Florida." *Prison Journal* 78 (1998): 119–132.

KEISER, GEORGE M. "NIC: Helping to Integrate Inmates Back Into the Community." *Corrections Today* 60 (1999): 103.

KELLOUGH, GAIL AND SCOT WORTLEY. "Remand for Plea: Bail Decisions and Plea Bargaining as Commensurate Decisions." *The British Journal of Criminology* 42 (2002): 186–210.

KELLY, BRIAN J. ET AL. "Technology and Corrections." *Federal Probation* 65 (2001): 1–70.

KELLY, JAMES. *Gallows Speeches from Eighteenth-Century Ireland.* Dublin, IR: Four Courts Press, 2001.

KEMSHALL, HAZEL. *Risk Assessment and Management of Known Sexual and Violent Offenders: A Review of Current Issues.* London, UK: Policing and Reducing Crime Unit, UK Home Office, 2001.

KENNEDY, MARY BALDWIN. "About Face Program Turns Lives Around." *Corrections Today* 65 (2003): 78–81.

KENNY, DIANNA T., TIMOTHY KEOGH, AND KATIE SEIDLER. "Predictors of Recidivism in Australian Juvenile Sex Offenders: Implications for Treatment." *Sexual Abuse: A Journal of Research and Treatment* 13 (2001): 131–148.

KERLE, KENNETH E. *American Jails: Looking to the Future.* Boston: Butterworth-Heinemann, 1998.

KETT, MARY. "Literacy Work at Wheatfield Prison, Dublin, Ireland." *The Journal of Correctional Education* 52 (2001): 63–67.

KEYSER, ANDREW, THOMAS E. FEUCHT, AND ROBERT FLAHERTY. "Keeping the Prison Clean: An Update on Pennsylvania's Drug Control Strategy." *Corrections Today* 64 (2002): 68–72.

KIEKBUSCH, RICHARD G. "The Looming Correctional Workforce Shortage: A Problem of Supply and Demand." *Corrections Compendium* 26 (2001): 1–5.

KILTY, KEITH M. AND ALFRED JOSEPH. "Institutional Racism and Sentencing Disparities for Cocaine Possession." *Journal of Poverty* 3 (1999): 1–17.

KIM, HAL, ED. *Hope Abandoned: Eastern State Penitentiary.* Philadelphia, PA: Pennsylvania Prison Society and the Eastern State Penitentiary Historic Site, 1999.

KIMBALL, L. ROBERT & ASSOCIATES. "Downtown Pittsburgh Site of New 2,400-Bed Allegheny County Jail." *Corrections Compendium* 16 (1991): 12.

KING, ROY D. "The Rise and Rise of Supermax: An American Solution in Search of a Problem?" *Punishment and Society* 1 (1999): 163–186.

KINGERY, LEROY V. "Improving the Small Jail Environment." *American Jails* 8 (1994): 99–102.

KINGREE, J.B., RONALD BRAITHWAITE, AND TAMMY WOODRING. "Psychosocial and Behavioral Problems in Relation to Recent Experience as a Runaway among Adolescent Detainees." *Criminal Justice and Behavior* 28 (2001): 190–205.

KINKADE, PATRICK T. AND MATTHEW C. LEONE. "The Privatization of Prisons: The Wardens' Views." *Federal Probation* 56 (1992): 58–65.

KIRKISH, PATRICIA ET AL. 'The Future of Criminal Violence: Juveniles Tried as Adults." *Journal of the American Academy of Psychiatry and the Law* 28 (2000): 38–46.

KIRSCHNER, STUART M. AND GARY J. GALPERIN. "Psychiatric Defenses in New York County: Pleas and Results." *Journal of the American Academy of Psychiatry and the Law* 29 (2001): 194–201.

KLAUS, JON F. *Handbook on Probation Service: Guidelines for Practitioners and Managers.* Rome, Italy: United Nations Interregional Crime and Justice Research Institute, 1998.

KLEIBOER, M.A. ET AL. "MEDIATION." *Justitiele Erkenningen* 26 (2000): 9–107.

KLUG, ELIZABETH A. "Federal Grants for DNA Tests." *Corrections Today* 63 (2002): 14.

KNIGHT, BARBARA B. AND STEPHEN T. EARLY, JR. *Prisoner's Rights in America.* Chicago, IL: Nelson-Hall Publishers, 1986.

KNUPFER, ANNE MEIS. *Reform and Resistance: Gender, Delinquency, and America's First Juvenile Court.* New York: Routledge, 2001.

KOCH CRIME INSTITUTE. *Juvenile Boot Camps: Cost and Effectiveness vs. Residential Facilities.* Topeka, KS: Koch Crime Institute, 2002.

KOKOROWSKI, FRANK AND STEVE FRENG. "Posttraumatic Stress Disorder with Co-Occurring Substance Abuse: Implications for Jails." *American Jails* 15 (2001): 33–34, 36–38.

KOLTON, DAVID J.C., ALESANDRA BOER, AND DOUGLAS P. BOER. "A Revision of the Abel and Becker Cognition Scale for Intellectually Disabled Sexual Offenders." *Sexual Abuse: A Journal of Research and Treatment* 13 (2001): 217–219.

KONOPA, JESSICA B. ET AL. "Recovery from the Inside Out: A Cognitive Approach to Rehabilitation." *Corrections Today* 64 (2002): 56–58, 112.

KONRADI, AMANDA AND TINA BURGER. "Having the Last Word: An Examination of Rape Survivors' Participation in Sentencing." *Violence Against Women* 6 (2000): 351–395.

KOOY, THOMAS J. "The Hennepin County Adult Detention Center: A Jail in Transition." *American Jails* 6 (1992): 66–69.

KOPER, CHRISTOPHER S. AND JEFFREY A. ROTH. "The Impact of the 1994 Federal Assault Weapon Ban on Gun Violence Outcomes: An Assessment of Multiple Outcome Measures and Some Lessons for Policy." *Journal of Quantitative Criminology* 17 (2001): 33–74.

KOREN, LAWRENCE. "Jail Officers and Education: A Key to Professionalization." *American Jails* 9 (1995): 43–48.

KOVANDZIC, TOMISLAV V. "The Impact of Florida's Habitual Offender Law on Crime." *Criminology* 39 (2001): 179–203.

KRIENERT, JESSIE L. AND MARK S. FLEISHER. "Gang Membership as a Proxy for Social Deficiencies: A Study of Nebraska Inmates." *Corrections Management Quarterly* 5 (2001): 47–58.

KRMPOTICH, SHARON A. AND DEBORAH A. ECKBERG. *Domestic Assault Program Evaluation.* Minneapolis, MN: Research and Systems Technology, Department of Community Corrections, 2000.

KRONICK, ROBERT F., DOROTHY E. LAMBERT, AND E. WARREN LAMBERT. "Recidivism among Adult Parolees: What Makes the Difference?" *Journal of Offender Rehabilitation* 28 (1998): 61–69.

KRUTTSCHNITT, CANDACE, ROSEMARY GARTNER, AND AMY MILLER. "Doing Her Own Time? Women's Responses to Prison in the Context of the Old and the New Penology." *Criminology* 38 (2000): 681–717.

KRZYCKI, LENNY. "A Case Study of the Death Penalty in Tennessee: History, Attitudes, and Mechanisms for Critical Interpretation." *Social Pathology: A Journal of Reviews* 6 (2000): 284–301.

KULIS, CHESTER J. "Profit in the Private Presentence Report." *Federal Probation* 47 (1983): 11–16.

KUNZMAN, E. EUGENE. "Preventing Suicide in Jails." *Corrections Today* 57 (1995): 90–94.

KYTLE, CALVIN AND DANIEL H. POLLITT, EDS. *Unjust in the Much: The Death Penalty in North Carolina.* Chapel Hill, NC: Chestnut Tree Press, 1999.

KYVSGAARD, BRITTA. "Community Sanctions and Measures in Denmark." *Nordisk Tidsskrift for Kriminalvidenskab* 88 (2001a): 94–110.

KYVSGAARD, BRITTA. "Harmony or Disharmony in the Development of Community Sanctions and Measures in the Nordic Countries." *Nordisk Tidsskrift for Kriminalvidenskab* 88 (2001b): 89–93.

LAMBIE, IAN. "Using Wilderness Therapy in Treating Adolescent Sexual Offenders." *Journal of Sexual Aggression* 5 (2000): 99–117.

LAMBERT, ERIC G. "Absent Correctional Staff: A Discussion of the Issue and Recommendations for Future Research." *American Journal of Criminal Justice* 25 (2001): 279–292.

LAMBERT, ERIC G., NANCY LYNNE HOGAN, AND SHANNON M. BARTON. "Satisfied Correctional Staff: A Review of the Literature on the Correlates of Correctional Staff Job Satisfaction." *Criminal Justice and Behavior* 29 (2002): 115–143.

LAMUNYON, JAMES W. *Regional Jails in the State of Washington: Washington Association of Sheriffs and Police Chiefs Regional Jail Study.* Olympia, WA: Washington Association of Sheriffs and Police Chiefs, 2001.

LANG, MICHELLE A. AND STEVEN BELENKO. "A Cluster Analysis of HIV Risk among Felony Drug Offenders." *Criminal Justice and Behavior* 28 (2001): 24–61.

LANGAN, PATRICK A. AND DAVID J. LEVIN. *Recidivism of Prisoners Released in 1994.* Washington, DC: U.S. Department of Justice, 2002.

LANKENAU, STEPHEN E. "Smoke 'em If You Got 'em: Cigarette Black Markets in U.S. Prisons and Jails." *Prison Journal* 81 (2001): 142–161.

LAPPI, SEPPALA TAPIO. "Community Sanctions in Finland." *Nordisk Tidsskrift for Kriminalvidenskab* 88 (2001): 111–135.

LARSSON, PAUL AND JANE DULLUM. "From Community Service to Community Punishment: Developments in the Use of Community Sanctions and Victim-Offender Mediation in Norway." *Nordisk Tidsskrift for Kriminalvidenskab* 88 (2001): 154–168.

LATTIMORE, PAMELA K., ANN DRYDEN WITT, AND JOANNA R. BAKER. "Experimental Assessment of the Effect of Vocational Training on Youthful Property Offenders." *Evaluation Review* 14 (1990): 115–133.

LAUEN, ROGER J. *Positive Approaches to Corrections: Research, Policy, and Practice.* Lanham, MD: American Correctional Association, 1997.

LAW ENFORCEMENT ASSISTANCE ADMINISTRATION. *Instead of Jail: Pre- and Post-Trial Alternatives to Jail Incarceration.* Washington, DC: Law Enforcement Administration, 1977.

LAWRENCE, RICHARD AND SUE MAHAN. "Women Corrections Officers in Men's Prisons: Acceptance and Perceived Job Performance." *Women and Criminal Justice* 9 (1998): 63–86.

LEA, SUSAN, TIM AUBURN, AND KAREN KIBBLEWHITE. "Working with Sex Offenders: The Perceptions and Experiences of Professionals and Paraprofessionals." *International Journal of Offender Therapy and Comparative Criminology* 43 (1999): 103–119.

LEDERMAN, CINDY S., JOY D. OSOFSKY, AND LYNNE KATZ. "When the Bough Breaks the Cradle Will Fall: Promoting the Health and Well Being of Infants and Toddlers in the Juvenile Court." *Juvenile and Family Court Journal* 52 (2001): 33–38.

LEHMAN, JOSEPH D. "A Commissioner's Appreciation: Pennsylvania Volunteers Build Bridges between Our Prisons and the Community." *Corrections Today* 55 (1993): 84–86.

LEHMAN, JOSEPH D. "Reinventing Community Corrections in Washington State." *Corrections Management Quarterly* 5 (2001): 41–45.

LEIBER, MICHAEL J. "Gender, Religion and Correctional Orientations among a Sample of Juvenile Justice Personnel." *Women and Criminal Justice* 11 (2000): 15–44.

LEIBER, MICHAEL J. "Disproportionate Minority Confinement (DMC) of Youth: An Analysis of State and Federal Efforts to Address the Issue." *Crime and Delinquency* 48 (2002): 3–45.

LEON, ANA M., SOPHIA F. DZIEGIELEWSKI, AND CHRISTINE TUBIAK. "A Program Evaluation of a Juvenile Halfway House: Considerations for Strengthening Program Components." *Evaluation and Program Planning* 22 (1999): 141–153.

LEONARD, ELIZABETH DERMODY. "Convicted Survivors: Comparing and Describing California's Battered Women Inmates." *Prison Journal* 81 (2001): 73–86.

LEONARDI, THOMAS J. AND DAVID R. FREW. "Applying Job Characteristics Theory to Adult Probation." *Criminal Justice Policy Review* 5 (1991): 17–28.

LEONARDSON, GARY. *Results of Early Release: Study Prompted by Passage of HB 685.* Helena, MT: Montana Board of Crime Control, 1997.

LERNER, JIMMY A. *You Got Nothing Coming: Notes from a Prison Fish.* New York: Broadway Books, 2002.

LEUKEFELD, CARL G., FRANK TIMS, AND ROLAND D. MAIURO, EDS. *Treatment of Drug Offenders: Policies and Issues.* New York: Springer, 2001.

LEVIN, JACK AND JAMES ALAN FOX. *Dead Times: Essays in Murder and Mayhem.* Boston: Allyn and Bacon, 2001.

LEVINE, MURRAY ET AL. "Is It Inherently Prejudicial to Try a Juvenile as an Adult?" *Behavioral Sciences and the Law* 19 (2001): 23–31.

LEVINSON, ROBERT B., JEANNE B. STINCHCOMB, AND JOHN J. GREENE, III. "Correctional Certification: First Step Toward Professionalism." *Corrections Today* 63 (2001): 125–129, 138.

LIBBUS, M. KAY, JOSEPH A. GENOVESE, AND MELISSA J. POOLE. "Organized Aerobic Exercise and Depression in Male County Jail Inmates." *Journal of Correctional Health Care* 1 (1994): 5–16.

LIEBLING, ALISON, CHARLES ELLIOTT, AND HELEN ARNOLD. "Transforming the Prison: Romantic Optimism or Appreciative Realism?" *Criminal Justice* 1 (2001): 161–180.

LIEBLING, ALISON AND DAVID PRICE. *The Prison Officer.* London, UK: Prison Service Journal, 2001.

LIGHTFOOT, CALVIN A. AND FRANK FRAIETTA. "The Men and Women of Truth: A Program Designed Especially for Reflective Inmates." *American Jails* 15 (2002): 9–12.

LINDNER, CHARLES AND ROBERT L. BONN. "Probation Officer Victimization and Fieldwork Practices: Results of a National Study." *Federal Probation* 60 (1996): 16–23.

LINDNER, CHARLES AND MARGARET R. SAVARESE. "The Evolution of Probation: University Settlement and the Beginning of Statutory Probation in New York City." *Federal Probation* 48 (1984): 3–12.

LIS, INC. *Supermax Housing: A Survey of Current Practice.* Longmont, CO: Information Center, U.S. National Institute of Corrections, 1997.

LISTWAN, SHELLY JOHNSON, DEBORAH KOETZLE SHAFFER, AND EDWARD J. LATESSA. "The Drug Court Movement: Recommendations for Improvements." *Corrections Today* 64 (2002): 52–54, 120.

LOCKE, MICHELLE. "Davis Sentenced to Death in Klaas Murder." *Minot (ND) Daily News,* August 6, 1996: A1.

LOCKWOOD, DOROTHY, JILL McCORKEL, AND JAMES A. INCIARDI. "Developing Comprehensive Prison-Based Therapeutic Community Treatment for Women." *Drugs and Society* 13 (1998): 193–212.

LoGALBO, ANTHONY P. AND CHARLENE M. CALLAHAN. "An Evaluation of Teen Court as a Juvenile Crime Diversion Program." *Juvenile and Family Court Journal* 52 (2001): 1–11.

LOGAN, GLORIA. "In Topeka: Family Ties Take Top Priority in Women's Visiting Program." *Corrections Today* 54 (1992): 160–161.

LOGAN, T.K. "Substance Abuse and Intimate Violence among Incarcerated Males." *Journal of Family Violence* 16 (2001): 93–114.

LONEY, RANDOLPH. *A Dream of the Tattered Man: Stories from Georgia's Death Row.* Grand Rapids, MI: William B. Eerdmans, 2001.

LOVE, BILL. "Volunteers Make a Big Difference Inside a Maximum Security Prison." *Corrections Today* 55 (1993): 76–78.

LOVEGROVE, AUSTIN. "Sanctions and Severity: To the Demise of Von Hirsch and Wasik's Sanction Hierarchy." *Howard Journal of Criminal Justice* 40 (2001): 126–147.

LOVELL, DAVID ET AL. "Evaluating the Effectiveness of Residential Treatment for Prisoners with Mental Illness." *Criminal Justice and Behavior* 28 (2001): 83–104.

LOWE, CRAIG A. "Pike County Jail: A Shocking Necessity." *American Jails* 16 (2002): 37–38.

LOZA, WAGDY AND FANOUS AMEL LOZA. "The Effectiveness of the Self-Appraisal Questionnaire in Predicting Offenders' Postrelease Outcome." *Criminal Justice and Behavior* 28 (2001): 105–121.

LUCAS, WELDON G. "Out-of-State Contract Prisoners: A Success Story." *American Jails* 10 (1996): 9–14.

LUCKEN, KAROL. "The Dynamics of Penal Reform." *Crime Law and Social Change* 26 (1997): 367–384.

LUCKER, G. WILLIAM ET AL. "Interventions with DWI, DUI, and Drug Offenders." *Journal of Offender Rehabilitation* 24 (1997): 1–100.

LUGINBUHL, JAMES AND MICHAEL BURKHEAD. "Victim Impact Evidence in a Capital Trial: Encouraging Votes for Death." *American Journal of Criminal Justice* 20 (1995): 1–16.

LUPTON, GARY L. "Identifying and Referring Inmates with Mental Disorders: A Guide for Correctional Staff." *American Jails* 10 (1996): 49–52.

LURIGIO, ARTHUR J., ED. *Community Correction in America.* Seattle, WA: National Coalition for Mental and Substance Abuse Health Care in the Justice System, 1996.

LURIGIO, ARTHUR J. "Effective Services for Parolees with Mental Illnesses." *Crime and Delinquency* 47 (2001): 446–461.

LURIGIO, ARTHUR J. AND JAMES A. SWARTZ. "Recidivism Rates of Drug Offenders on Probation." *APPA Perspectives* 22 (1998): 36–44.

LUTZE, FAITH E. Does Shock Incarceration Provide a Supportive Environment for the Rehabilitation of Offenders? A Study of the Impact of a Shock Incarceration Program on Inmate Adjustment and Attitudinal Change. Ann Arbor, MI: University Microfilms International, 1996.

LUTZE, FAITH E. "Are Shock Incarceration Programs More Rehabilitative Than Traditional Prisons? A Survey of Inmates." *Justice Quarterly* 15 (1998): 547–566.

LUTZE, FAITH E. "The Influence of a Shock Incarceration Program on Inmate Adjustment and Attitudinal Change." *Journal of Criminal Justice* 29 (2001): 207–218.

LUTZE, FAITH E. AND DAVID C. BRODY. "Mental Abuse as Cruel and Unusual Punishment: Do Boot Camp Prisons Violate the Eighth Amendment?" *Crime and Delinquency* 45 (1999): 242–255.

LUTZE, FAITH E., R.P.P. SMITH, AND NICHOLAS P. LOVRICH. "Premises for Attaining More Effective Offender Accountability Through Community Involvement: Washington State's New Approach." *Corrections Management Quarterly* 4 (2000): 1–9.

LYNETT, ELIZABETH AND RICHARD ROGERS. "Emotions Overriding Forensic Opinions: The Potentially Biasing Effects of Victim Statements." *Journal of Psychiatry and Law* 28 (2000): 449–457.

LYNN, PETER AND GEORGE ARMSTRONG. *From Pentonville to Pentridge: A History of Prisons in Victoria.* Melbourne, Australia: State Library of Victoria, 1996.

MAAHS, JEFFREY R. AND ROLANDO V. DEL CARMEN. "Curtailing Frivolous Section 1983 Inmate Litigation: Laws, Practices, and Proposals." *Federal Probation* 59 (1996): 53–61.

MAAHS, JEFFREY R. AND TRAVIS PRATT. "Uncovering the Predictors of Correctional Officers' Attitudes and Behaviors: A Meta-Analysis." *Corrections Management Quarterly* 5 (2001): 13–19.

MACDONALD, JOHN M. AND MEDA CHESNEY-LIND. "Gender Bias and Juvenile Justice Revisited: A Multiyear Analysis." *Crime and Delinquency* 47 (2001): 173–195.

MACDONALD, MARNIE AND LISA WATSON. "Creating Choices, Changing Lives: The Transformation of Women's Corrections in Canada." *Corrections Today Magazine* 63 (2001): 70–73, 127.

MACKENZIE, DORIS LAYTON, JAMES W. SHAW, AND VONCILE B. GOWDY. *An Evaluation of Shock Incarceration in Louisiana.* Washington, DC: National Institute of Justice, 1993.

MACKENZIE, DORIS LAYTON AND CLAIRE SOURYAL. *Researchers Evaluate Eight Shock Incarceration Programs.* Washington, DC: National Institute of Justice, 1994.

MACKENZIE, DORIS LAYTON ET AL. "The Impact of Boot Camps and Traditional Institutions on Juvenile Residents: Perceptions, Adjustment, and Change." *Journal of Research in Crime and Delinquency* 38 (2001): 279–313.

MACTAVISH, MARIE. "Are You an STJ? Examining Correctional Managers' Leadership Styles." *Corrections Today* 56 (1992): 162–164.

MAGHAN, JESS. "Dangerous Inmates: Maximum-Security Incarceration in the State Prison Systems of the United States." *Aggression and Violent Behavior* 4 (1999): 1–12.

MAGUIRE, KATHLEEN AND ANN L. PASTORE. *Bureau of Justice Statistics Sourcebook of Criminal Justice Statistics 2001.* Albany, NY: The Hindelang Criminal Justice Research Center, State University of New York at Albany, 2002.

MAGUIRE, MIKE ET AL. *Risk Management of Sexual and Violent Offenders: The Work of Public Protection Panels.* London, UK: UK Home Office, 2001.

MAHAFFEY, KATHERINE J. AND DAVID K. MARCUS. "Correctional Officers' Attitudes toward AIDS." *Criminal Justice and Behavior* 22 (1995): 91–105.

MAHAN, SUE. "Co-Corrections: Doing Time Together." *Corrections Today* 48 (1986): 134–165.

MAHONEY, BARRY. *Pretrial Services Programs: Responsibilities and Potential.* Washington, DC: U.S. National Institute of Justice, 2001.

MALL, MELISSA. "The Accreditation Process: An Overview." *Corrections Today* 64 (2002): 26–28.

MALTZ, MICHAEL D. *Recidivism.* Orlando, FL: Academic Press, 1984.

MANN, CORAMAE RICHEY. *Female Crime and Delinquency.* University, AL: University of Alabama Press, 1984.

MARICOPA COUNTY ARIZONA CORRECTIONAL HEALTH SERVICES. *An Evaluation of Health Care Costs in Jails.* Phoenix, AZ: Maricopa County Arizona Correctional Health Services, 1991.

MARION SUPERIOR COURT PROBATION DEPARTMENT. *Adult Services Division: Programs.* Indianapolis, IN: Marion Superior Court Probation Department, 2002.

MARKOWITZ, MICHAEL W. "There's No Place Like Home: An Empirical Test of the Safe Haven Hypothesis." *Corrections Compendium* 28 (2003): 1–4, 30–31.

MARLEY, C.W. "Furlough Programs and Conjugal Visiting in Adult Correctional Institutions." *Federal Probation,* 37 (1973): 19–25.

MARQUART, JAMES W., MALDINE B. BARNHILL, AND KATHY BIDDLE BALSHAW. "Fatal Attraction: An Analysis of Employee Boundary Violations in a Southern Prison System." *Justice Quarterly* 18 (2001): 877–910.

MARQUART, JAMES W. ET AL. "Health Risk as an Emerging Field within the New Penology." *Journal of Criminal Justice* 27 (1999a): 143–154.

MARQUART, JAMES W. ET AL. "The Implications of Crime Control Policy on HIV/AIDS-Related Risk Among Women Prisoners." *Crime and Delinquency* 45 (1999b): 82–98.

MARTEL, JOANE. "Telling the Story: A Study in the Segregation of Women Prisoners." *Social Justice* 28 (2001): 196–215.

MARTIN, JAMIE S. *Inside Looking Out: Jailed Fathers' Perceptions about Separation from Their Children.* New York: LFB Scholarly Publishing LLC, 2001.

MARTIN, RANDY. "Community Perceptions About Prison Construction: Why Not in My Backyard?" *Prison Journal* 80 (2000): 265–294.

MARTIN, SUSAN E. AND KENDALL BRYANT. "Gender Differences in the Association of Alcohol Intoxication and Illicit Drug Use among Persons Arrested for Violent and Property Offenses." *Journal of Substance Abuse* 13 (2001): 563–581.

MARTINEZ, ALMA J. AND NANCY ARRIGONA. *Limes to Limes: Comparing the Operational Costs of Juvenile and Adult Correctional Programs in Texas.* Austin, TX: Texas Criminal Justice Policy Council, 2001.

MARTINSON, ROBERT. "California Research at the Crossroads." *Crime and Delinquency* 22 (1976): 181–189.

MARUNA, SHADD. *Making Good: How Ex-Convicts Reform and Rebuild Their Lives.* Washington, DC: American Psychological Association, 2001.

MARUSCHAK, LAURA M. *HIV in Prisons and Jails, 2000.* Washington, DC: Bureau of Justice Statistics, 2002.

MARVELL, THOMAS B. "Is Further Prison Expansion Worth the Costs?" *Corrections Compendium* 21 (1996): 1–4.

MARVELL, THOMAS B. AND C.E. MOODY JR. "Prison Population Growth and Crime Reduction." *Journal of Quantitative Criminology* 10 (1994): 109–140.

MARVELL, THOMAS B. AND CARLISLE E. MOODY. "The Lethal Effects of the Three-Strikes Laws." *Journal of Legal Studies* 30 (2001): 89–106.

MASCHKE, KAREN J. "Gender in the Prison Setting: The Privacy-Equal Employment Dilemma." *Women and Criminal Justice* 7 (1996): 23–42.

MASLACH, CHRISTINA. "Understanding Burnout: Definitional Issues in Analyzing a Complex Phenomenon." In *Job Stress and Burnout,* edited by W. S. Paine. Beverly Hills, CA: Sage, 1982a.

MASLACH, CHRISTINA. *Burnout: The Cost of Caring.* Englewood Cliffs, NJ: Prentice-Hall, 1982b.

MASSACHUSETTS DEPARTMENT OF CORRECTIONS. *The Visiting Cottage Program.* Boston: Massachusetts Department of Corrections, 2002.

MASSACHUSETTS STATISTICAL ANALYSIS CENTER. *Implementation of the Juvenile Justice Reform Act: Youthful Offenders in Massachusetts.* Boston: Massachusetts Statistical Analysis Center, 2001.

MATHIESEN, THOMAS. "Selective Incapacitation Revisited." *Law and Human Behavior* 22 (1998): 455–469.

MAXEY, JOSEPH W. "Designing a Women's Prison." *Corrections Today* 48 (1986): 138–142.

MAXWELL, GABRIELLE AND ALLISON MORRIS. "Putting Restorative Justice into Practice for Adult Offenders." *Howard Journal of Criminal Justice* 40 (2001): 55–69.

MAXWELL, SHEILA ROYO AND CHRISTOPHER D. MAXWELL. "Examining the Criminal Careers of Prostitutes within the Nexus of Drug Use, Drug Selling, and Other Illicit Activities." *Criminology* 38 (2000): 787–810.

MAYER, JON'A F. "Strange Science: Subjective Criteria in Parole Decisions." *Journal of Crime and Justice* 24 (2001): 43–70.

MAYS, G. LARRY AND JOEL A. THOMPSON. "Mayberry Revisited: The Characteristics and Operations of America's Small Jails." *Justice Quarterly* 5 (1988): 421–440.

MCCABE, KIMBERLY A. "Inmate Leaders in the Jail Environment." *American Jails* 11 (1997): 53–55.

MCCAMPBELL, SUSAN W. "The Paying Prisoner: Room with a View, At a Price." *American Jails* 11 (1997): 37–43.

MCCARTHY, J. "Risk Assessment of Sexual Offenders." *Psychiatry, Psychology, and the Law* 8 (2001): 56–64.

MCCLELLAN, DOROTHY SPEKTOROV. "Disparity in the Discipline of Male and Female Inmates in Texas Prisons." *Women and Criminal Justice* 5 (1994): 71–97.

MCCLUSKEY, CYNTHIA PEREZ. *Understanding Latino Delinquency: The Applicability of Strain Theory by Ethnicity.* New York: LFB Scholarly Publishing, 2002.

MCCORKLE, RICHARD C. "Correctional Boot Camps and Change in Attitude: Is All This Shouting Necessary?—A Research Note." *Justice Quarterly* 12 (1995): 365–375.

MCCOY, JOHN. *Concrete Mama: Prison Profiles from Walla Walla.* Columbia, MO: University of Missouri Press, 1981.

MCDONALD, DOUGLAS C., JUDITH GREENE, AND CHARLES WORZELLA. *Day Fines in American Courts: The Staten Island and Milwaukee Experiments.* Washington, DC: U.S. Department of Justice, Office of Justice Programs, 1992.

MCGRATH, ROBERT J., GEORGIA CUMMING, AND JOHN HOLT. "Collaboration among Sex Offender Treatment Providers and Probation and Parole Officers: The Beliefs and Behaviors of Treatment Providers." *Sexual Abuse: A Journal of Research and Treatment* 14 (2002): 49–65.

MCINTYRE, TOM, VIRGINIA M. TONG, AND JOSEPH F. PEREZ. "Cyber Lockdown: Problems with the use of Internet Technology in correctional education." *Journal of Correctional Education* 52 (2001): 163–165.

MCKENZIE, DEAN. "Walworth County Jail Tests Direct Supervision Model by Integrating Its Concepts into 'Superpod' Design." *American Jails* 11 (1997): 59–62.

MCLENNAN, REBECCA MARY. *Citizens and Criminals: The Rise of the American Carceral State, 1890–1935.* Ann Arbor, MI: University Microfilms International, 1999.

MEACHUM, LARRY R. "House Arrest: The Oklahoma Experience." *Corrections Today,* 48 (1986): 102–110.

MEARS, DANIEL P. "Getting Tough with Juvenile Offenders: Explaining Support for Sanctioning Youths as Adults." *Criminal Justice and Behavior* 28 (2001): 206–226.

MEARS, DANIEL P. AND WILLIAM R. KELLY. "Linking Process and Outcomes in Evaluating a Statewide Drug Treatment Program for Youthful Offenders." *Crime and Delinquency* 48 (2002): 99–115.

MEEHAN, KEVIN E. "California's Three-Strikes Law: The First Six Years." *Corrections Management Quarterly* 4 (2000): 22–33.

MEISEL, JOSHUA S. "Relationships and Juvenile Offenders: The Effects of Intensive Aftercare Supervision." *Prison Journal* 81 (2001): 206–245.

MELLO, MICHAEL. *The Wrong Man: A True Story of Innocence on Death Row.* Minneapolis: University of Minnesota Press, 2001.

MEMORY, JOHN M. ET AL. "Comparing Disciplinary Infraction Rates of North Carolina Fair Sentencing and Structured Sentencing Inmates: A Natural Experiment." *Prison Journal* 79 (1999): 45–71.

MENIFIELD, CHARLES E., WINFIELD H. ROSE, AND JOHN HOMA. "The Media's Portrayal of Urban and Rural School Violence: A Preliminary Analysis." *Deviant Behavior* 22 (2001): 447–464.

MENNEL, ROBERT M. "Attitudes and Policies Toward Juvenile Delinquency in the United States: A Historiographical Review." In *Crime and Justice: An Annual Review of Research,* edited by Michael Tonry and Norval Morris. Chicago, IL: University of Chicago Press, 1983.

MEYER, CHERYL L. ET AL. *Mothers Who Kill Their Children: Understanding the Acts of Moms from Susan*

Smith to the "Prom Mom." New York: New York University Press, 2001.

MIERS, DAVID. An International Review of Restorative Justice. London, UK: Home Office, 2001.

MIERS, DAVID ET AL. An Exploratory Evaluation of Restorative Justice Schemes. London, UK: Home Office, 2001.

MILLER, ARTHUR F. "Substance Abuse Treatment for Women with Children." Corrections Today 63 (2001): 88–91.

MILLER, J. MITCHELL AND JEFFREY RUSH. Gangs: A Criminal Justice Approach. Cincinnati, OH: Anderson Publishing Company, 1996.

MILLER, MARILYN J. Changing Trends in Prisoner Petition Filings in the U.S. Courts of Appeal: A Fact Sheet. Washington, DC: Office of Human Resources and Statistics, Statistics Division, Administrative Office of the United States Court, 1999.

MILLER, MARSHA L. AND BRUCE HOBLER. "Delaware's Life Skills Program Reduces Inmate Recidivism." Corrections Today 58 (1996): 114–143.

MILLER, ROD. "Inmate Labor in the 21st Century: You Ain't Seen Nothin' Yet." American Jails 11 (1997): 45–52.

MILLER, ROD AND JOSEPH TREVATHAN. "Productive Jails Benefit Many." Corrections Today 65 (2003): 96–98.

MILLER, SUSAN L., ED. Crime Control and Women: Feminist Implications of Criminal Justice Policy. Thousand Oaks, CA: Sage, 1998.

MILLER, TEKLA DENNISON. The Warden Wore Pink. Brunswick, ME: Biddle Publishing Company, 1996.

MILLS, DARRELL K. "Career Issues for Probation Officers." Federal Probation, 54 (1990): 3–7.

MILOVANOVIC, DRAGAN ET AL. Postmodern Criminology. New York: Garland, 1997.

MITCHELL, OJMARRH ET AL. "The Influence of Personal Background on Perceptions of Juvenile Correctional Environments." Journal of Criminal Justice 29 (2001): 67–76.

MLINARZIK, JOERG. "New Roads in Criminal Policy: Offender-Victim Mediation in Criminal Law." Die Kriminalpraevention 5 (2001): 172–174.

MONAHAN, JOHN ET AL. Rethinking Risk Assessment: The MacArthur Study of Mental Disorder and Violence. Oxford, UK: Oxford University Press, 2001.

Monday Highlights. "Nation's Oldest Jail Closes After 181 Years of Service." Corrections Compendium 18 (1993): 18.

MONTANA LEGISLATIVE AUDIT DIVISION. Performance Audit: Intensive Supervision Program: Pre-Release Centers Program (PRC). Helena, MT: Montana Legislative Audit Division, 1998.

MONTEREY COUNTY PROBATION DEPARTMENT. Probation Officer II. Monterey, CA: Monterey County Probation Department, 2002.

MONTGOMERY, REID H. JR. AND GORDON A. CREWS. A History of Correctional Violence: An Examination of Reported Causes of Riots and Disturbances. Lanham, MD: American Correctional Association, 1998.

MOON, DREAMA G. ET AL. "Substance Abuse among Female Prisoners in Oklahoma." Journal of the Oklahoma Criminal Justice Research Consortium 1 (1994): 35–40.

MOON, MELISSA M. ET AL. "Putting Kids to Death: Specifying Public Support for Juvenile Capital Punishment." Justice Quarterly 17 (2000): 663–684.

MOORE, ADRIAN T. Private Prisons: Quality Constructions at a Lower Cost. Los Angeles: Reason Public Policy Institute, 1998.

MOORE, DELANCEY H. "The Complexity of Jail Classification of Gang Members." American Jails 11 (1997): 81–84.

MOORE, ESTELLE AND TODD HOGUE. "Assessment of Personality Disorder for Individuals with Offending Histories." Criminal Behavior and Mental Health 10 (2000): 34–50.

MOORE, KEVIN J., PETER G. SPRENGELMEYER, AND PATRICIA CHAMBERLAIN. "Community-Based Treatment for Adjudicated Delinquents: The Oregon Social Learning Center's 'Monitor' Multidimensional Treatment Foster Care Program." Residential Treatment for Children and Youth 18 (2001): 87–97.

MOORE, MARGARET A. "Corrections Volunteers Deserve Appreciation for a Job Well Done." Corrections Today 55 (1993): 8.

MORGAN, KATHRYN D., BARBARA A. BELBOT, AND JOHN CLARK. "Liability Issues Affecting Probation and Parole Supervision." Journal of Criminal Justice 25 (1997): 211–222.

MORGAN, ROBERT D., RICHARD A. VANHAVEREN, AND CHRISTY A. PEARSON. "Correctional Officer Burnout: Further Analyses." Criminal Justice and Behavior 29 (2002): 144–160.

MORRIS, ALLISON AND GABRIELLE MAXWELL, EDS. Restorative Justice for Juveniles: Conferencing, Mediation, and Circles. Oxford, UK: Hart, 2001.

MORRIS, NORVAL. "On Dangerousness in the Judicial Process." The Record of the Association of the Bar of the City of New York, 39 (1984): 102–128.

MORRIS, NORVAL. Maconochie's Gentlemen: The Story of Norfolk Island and the Roots of Modern Prison Reform. Oxford, UK: Oxford University Press, 2002.

MORRIS, NORVAL AND MARC MILLER. "Predictions of Dangerousness." In Crime and Justice: An Annual Review of Research, Vol. 6., edited by Michael Tonry and Norval Morris. Chicago, IL: University of Chicago Press, 1985.

MORRIS, SUZANNE M. AND HENRY J. STEADMAN. "Keys to Successfully Diverting Mentally Ill Jail Detainees." American Jails 8 (1994): 47–49.

MORTIMER, ED AND CHRIS MAY. Electronic Monitoring in Practice: The Second Year of the Trials of Curfew Orders. London, UK: U.K. Home Office, 1997.

MORTON, JOANN B. "Implications for Corrections of an Aging Prison Population." Corrections Management Quarterly 5 (2001): 65–77.

MOSES, MARILYN C. "Girl Scouts Behind Bars: New Program at Women's Prisons Benefits Mothers and Children." Corrections Today 55 (1993): 132–134.

MOTIUK, LARRY ET AL. "The Safe Return of Offenders Through Selection, Intervention, and Supervision." Forum on Corrections Research 13 (2001): 1–60.

MOTIUK, LAURENCE L., AND KELLY BLANCHETTE. "Characteristics of Administratively Segregated Offenders in Federal Corrections." Canadian Journal of Criminology 43 (2001): 131–143.

MOTIUK, MICHELE S. ET AL. "Special Needs Offenders." Forum on Corrections Research 6 (1994): 6–43.

MOYLE, PAUL. Profiting from Punishment: Private Prisons in Australia: Reform or Regression? Annandale, Australia: Pluto Press, 2000.

MOYNAHAN, J.M. "A Glimpse of Early Female Jail Officers." American Jails 15 (2001): 57–59.

MULLEN, ROD ET AL. "California Program Reduces Recidivism and Saves Tax Dollars." Corrections Today 58 (1996): 118–124.

MURASKIN, ROSLYN. "Disparate Treatment in Jails: Development of a Measurement Instrument." American Jails 11 (1997): 27–35.

MURRAY, CHRISTOPHER AND MERLYN BELL. "The 1995 Capacity Study Offender Placements in Washington State." American Jails 10 (1996): 59–63.

MURTON, THOMAS O. AND JOE HYAMS. *Accomplices to Crime: The Arkansas Prison Scandal.* New York: Grove Press, 1976.

MURTON, TOM. "Shared Decision-Making as a Treatment Technique in Prison Management." *New England Journal on Prison Law* 3 (1976): 97–113.

MYERS, DAVID L. *Excluding Violent Youths from Juvenile Court: The Effectiveness of Legislative Waiver.* New York: LFB Scholarly Publishing, LLC, 2001.

MYERS, WADE C. *Juvenile Sexual Homicide.* San Diego, CA: Academic Press, 2002.

NADEL, BARBARA A. "Designing for Women: Doing Time Differently." *Corrections Compendium* 21 (1996): 1–7.

NATHAN, PAMELA AND TONY WARD. "Females Who Sexually Abuse Children: Assessment and Treatment." *Psychiatry, Psychology, and Law* 8 (2001): 44–55.

NATIONAL COUNCIL ON CRIME AND DELINQUENCY. *Probation: An Effective Tool for the Future.* San Francisco: National Council on Crime and Delinquency, 1998.

NATIONAL INSTITUTE OF CORRECTIONS. *Regional Jails: An Overview.* Washington, DC: National Institute of Corrections Information Center, 2003.

NESBITT, CHARLOTTE A. "The Female Offender: Overview of Facility Planning and Design Issues and Considerations." *Corrections Compendium* 17 (1992): 1–7.

New Abolitionist. Resistance in the Shadow of Death. Chicago: Campaign to End the Death Penalty, 2002.

NEWELL, TIM. "The Prison Officer as a Moral Agent." *American Jails* 16 (2002): 69–70.

Newsweek. "Editorial." *Newsweek,* December 7, 1987: 38.

NEW YORK STATE DIVISION OF PAROLE. *The Eighth Annual Shock Incarceration Legislative Report.* Albany, NY: New York State Division of Parole, 1998.

NEW YORK STATE DIVISION OF PROBATION AND CORRECTIONAL ALTERNATIVES. *Conditional Release Conditions.* Albany, NY: New York State Division of Probation and Correctional Alternatives, 2002.

NIEMEYER, MIKE AND DAVID SHICHOR. "A Preliminary Study of a Large Victim/Offender Reconciliation Program." *Federal Probation* 60 (1996): 30–34.

NINK, CARL E. AND JUDITH KILGUS. "Comparing Public and Private Prison Costs." *Corrections Today* 62 (2000): 152–155.

NORMAN, BOBBY. "Arkansas Jail Inspection System." *American Jails* 11 (1997): 65–67.

NORMAN, MICHAEL D. AND HAZEN L. LOCKE. "Housing State Prisoners in County Jails: The Utah Experience." *American Jails* 16 (2002): 13–17.

NORMAN, MICHAEL D. AND ROBERT C. WADMAN. "Utah Presentence Investigation Reports: User Perceptions of Quality and Effectiveness." *Federal Probation* 64 (2000): 7–12.

NORTH CAROLINA DEPARTMENT OF CORRECTIONS. *Cost of Supervision.* Raleigh: North Carolina Department of Corrections, 2001.

NORTON-HAWK, MAUREEN A. "The Counterproductivity of Incarcerating Female Street Prostitutes." *Deviant Behavior* 22 (2001): 403–417.

NUGENT, WILLIAM R. ET AL. "Participation in Victim-Offender Mediation and Reoffense: Successful Replications?" *Research on Social Work Practice* 11 (2001): 5–23.

NURSE, ANNE M. "The Structure of the Juvenile Prison: Constructing the Inmate Father." *Youth and Society* 32 (2001): 360–394.

O'BRIEN, PATRICIA. " 'Just Like Baking a Cake': Women Describe the Necessary Ingredients for Successful Reentry After Incarceration." *Families in Society: The Journal of Contemporary Human Services* 82 (2001a): 287–295.

O'BRIEN, PATRICIA. *Making It in the "Free World": Women in Transition from Prison.* Albany: State University of New York Press, 2001b.

O'CONNELL, PAUL AND JACQUELYN M. POWER. "The Power of Partnerships: Establishing Literacy Programs in Community Corrections." *APPA Perspectives* 16 (1992): 6–8.

O'CONNOR, PATRICIA E. *Speaking of Crime: Narratives of Prisoners.* Lincoln: University of Nebraska Press, 2000.

OFFICE OF NATIONAL DRUG CONTROL POLICY. *2000 Annual Report: National Drug Control Strategy: Performance Measures of Effectiveness.* Washington, DC: U.S. Government Printing Office, 2000.

OGBURN, KEVIN R. "Volunteer Program Guide." *Corrections Today* 55 (1993): 66–70.

OGILVIE, EMMA AND MARK LYNCH. "Responses to Incarceration: A Qualitative Analysis of Adolescents in Juvenile Detention Centers." *Current Issues in Criminal Justice* 12 (2001): 330–346.

O'GORMAN, J.G. AND E. BAXTER. "Self-Control as a Personality Measure." *Personality and Individual Differences* 32 (2002): 533–539.

OHIO DEPARTMENT OF REHABILITATION AND CORRECTION. *Ten-Year Recidivism Follow-Up of 1989 Sex Offender Releases.* Columbus, OH: Ohio Department of Rehabilitation and Correction, 2001.

OKUN, PETER T.M. *Crime and the Nation: Prison Reform and Popular Fiction.* Ann Arbor, MI: University Microfilms International, 1997.

OKUN, PETER T.M. AND MICHAEL THOMAS. *Crime and the Nation: Prison Reform And Popular Fiction in Philadelphia, 1786–1800.* Ann Arbor, MI: University Microfilms International, 1997.

OLDENETTEL, DEBRA AND MADELINE WORDES. *The Community Assessment Center Concept.* Washington, DC: U.S. Department of Justice, 2000.

OLDENSTADT, STEVEN J. "Benton County Corrections." *American Jails* 8 (1994): 67–69.

OLSON, DAVID E., ARTHUR J. LURIGIO, AND MAGNUS SENG. "A Comparison of Female and Male Probationers: Characteristics and Case Outcomes." *Women and Criminal Justice* 11 (2000): 65–79.

OLSON, DAVID E. AND GERALD F. RAMKER. "Crime Does Not Pay, But Criminals Pay: Factors Influencing the Imposition and Collection of Probation Fees." *Justice System Journal* 22 (2001): 29–46.

OLSON, DAVID E., RALPH A. WEISHEIT, AND THOMAS ELLSWORTH. "Getting Down to Business: A Comparison of Rural and Urban Probationers, Probation Sentences, and Probation Outcomes." *Journal of Contemporary Criminal Justice* 17 (2001): 4–18.

O'MAHONY, PAUL. "A Critical Analysis of the Irish Penal System." *Journal of the Institute of Justice and International Studies* 1 (2002): 1–10.

O'NEIL, MELINDA B. "The Gender Gap Argument: Exploring the Disparity of Sentencing Women to Death." *New England Journal on Crime and Civil Confinement* 25 (1999): 213–244.

OPATA, JOSIAH. *Spiritual and Religious Diversity in Prisons: Focusing on How Chaplaincy Assists in Prison Management.* Springfield, IL: Charles C. Thomas Publisher, 2001.

ORITZ, MADELINE M. ET AL. "Special Needs Offenders." *Corrections Today Magazine* 62 (2000): 168.

O'SHEA, KATHLEEN A. *Women and the Death Penalty in the United States, 1900–1998.* Westport, CT: Praeger, 1999.

OSTERMEYER, MELINDA AND SUSAN L. KEILITZ. *Monitoring and Evaluating Court-Based Dispute Resolution Programs: A Guide for Judges and Court Managers.* Williamsburg, VA: National Center for State Courts, 1997.

O'SULLIVAN, SEAN. "Representations of Prison in Nineties Hollywood Cinema: From 'Con Air' to 'The Shawshank Redemption.'" *The Howard Journal of Criminal Justice* 40 (2001): 317–334.

OUSEY, GRAHAM C. AND MICHELLE CAMPBELL AUGUSTINE. "Young Guns: Examining Alternative Explanations of Juvenile Firearm Homicide Rates." *Criminology: An Interdisciplinary Journal* 39 (2001): 933–968.

OWEN, BARBARA. *"In the Mix": Struggle and Survival in a Women's Prison.* Albany: State University of New York Press, 1998.

PAGE, BRIAN T. *Assessment Center Handbook.* Longwood, FL: Gould Publications, 1995.

PALMER, JOHN W. *The Constitutional Rights of Prisoners.* 5th ed. Cincinnati, OH: Anderson, 1997.

PALMER, LOUIS J. JR. *Encyclopedia of Capital Punishment in the United States.* Jefferson, NC: McFarland and Company, 2001.

PALOMINO, AL. "The Ventura Youth Correctional Facility Provides Needed Treatment Programs to Youthful Female Offenders." *Corrections Today Magazine* 63 (2001): 66–68.

PALUMBO, DENNIS J., MICHAEL MUSHENO, AND MICHAEL HALLETT. "The Political Construction of Alternative Dispute Resolution and Alternatives to Incarceration." *Evaluation and Program Planning* 17 (1994): 197–203.

PARENT, DALE. *Day Reporting Centers for Criminal Offenders: A Descriptive Analysis of Existing Programs.* Washington, DC: U.S. National Institute of Justice, 1990.

PARRISH, DAVID M. "The Evolution of Direct Supervision in the Design and Operation of Jails." *Corrections Today* 62 (2000): 84–87, 127.

PATEL, JODY AND CURT SODERLUND. "Getting a Piece of the Pie: Revenue Sharing with Crime Victims Compensation Programs." *APPA Perspectives* 18 (1994): 22–27.

PATEL, KALPANA AND ALEX LORD. "Ethnic Minority Sex Offenders' Experiences of Treatment." *The Journal of Sexual Aggression* 7 (2001): 40–50.

PATENAUDE, ALLAN L. "Analysis of Issues Affecting Correctional Officer Retention within the Arkansas Department of Corrections." *Corrections Management Quarterly* 5 (2001): 49–67.

PATERNOSTER, RAYMOND, ROBERT BRAME, AND DAVID P. FARRINGTON. "On the Relationship between Adolescent and Adult Conviction Frequencies." *Journal of Quantitative Criminology* 17 (2001): 201–225.

PATRICK, DIANE ET AL. *How Is the Post-Conviction Polygraph Examination Used in Adult Sex Offender Management Activities? The Second National Telephone Survey of Probation and Parole Supervisors.* Denver, CO: Division of Criminal Justice, Colorado Department of Public Safety, 2000.

PATRICK, STEVEN. "Differences in Inmate-Inmate and Inmate-Staff Altercations: Examples from a Medium-Security Prison." *Social Science Journal* 35 (1998): 253–263.

PATRICK, STEVEN AND ROBERT MARSH. "Current Tobacco Policies in U.S. Adult Male Prisons." *Social Science Journal* 38 (2001): 27–37.

PATTERLINE, BRENT A. AND DAVID M. PETERSEN. "Structural and Social Psychological Determinants of Prisonization." *Journal of Criminal Justice* 27 (1999): 427–441.

PAULSEN, DEREK AND ROLANDO V. DEL CARMEN. "Legal Issues in Police-Corrections Partnerships: Can the Police and Corrections Officers Work Together without Violating Offenders' Constitutional Rights?" *Criminal Law Bulletin* 36 (2000): 493–508.

PAYNE, BRIAN K. AND RANDY R. GAINEY. "A Qualitative Assessment of the Pains Experienced on Electronic Monitoring." *International Journal of Offender Therapy and Comparative Criminology* 42 (1998): 149–163.

PEAK, KENNETH J. *Justice Administration: Police, Courts and Corrections Management.* Englewood Cliffs, NJ: Prentice-Hall, 1995.

PEARL, NATALIE R. "Use of Community-Based Social Services to Reduce Recidivism in Female Parolees." *Women and Criminal Justice* 10 (1998): 27–52.

PEASE, KEN. "Distributive Justice and Crime." *European Journal on Criminal Policy and Research* 9 (2001): 413–425.

PEDAHZUR, AMI AND MAGNUS RANSTORP. "A Tertiary Model for Countering Terrorism in Liberal Democracies: The Case of Israel." *Terrorism and Political Violence* 13 (2001): 1–26.

PELFREY, WILLIAM V. "Assessment Centers as a Management Promotion Tool." *Federal Probation* 50 (1986): 65–69.

PENNOCK, GEORGE A. "Industrial Research at Hawthorne." *Personnel Journal,* 8 (1930): 296–313.

PERKINS, ROBIN E. "Family Interventions with Incarcerated Youth: A Review of the Literature." *International Journal of Offender Therapy and Comparative Criminology* 45 (2001): 606–625.

PERRONCELLO, PETER. "Direct Supervision: A 2001 Odyssey." *American Jails* 15 (2002): 25–31.

PETERSILIA, JOAN. *House Arrest.* Washington, DC: U.S. Department of Justice, National Institute of Justice, 1988a.

PETERSILIA, JOAN. "Probation Reform." In *Controversial Issues in Crime and Justice,* edited by Joseph E. Scott and Travis Hirsch. Beverly Hills, CA: Sage, 1988b.

PETERSILIA, JOAN. "Probation in the United States." In *Crime and Justice: A Review of Research, Vol. 22,* edited by Michael Tonry. Chicago: University of Chicago Press, 1997.

PETERSILIA, JOAN. "Probation in the United States Part II." *APPA Perspectives* 22 (1998): 42–49.

PETERSILIA, JOAN. "A Decade of Experimenting with Intermediate Sanctions: What Have We Learned?" *APPA Perspectives* 23 (1999): 39–44.

PETERSILIA, JOAN. "When Prisoners Return to the Community: Political, Economic, and Social Consequences." *Corrections Management Quarterly* 5 (2001): 1–10.

PETERSILIA, JOAN. *Reforming Probation and Parole in the 21st Century.* Lanham, MD: American Correctional Association, 2002.

PETERSON, MICHELE AND CHRISTOPHER J. KOEGL. "Juveniles' Experiences of Incarceration: The Role of Correctional Staff in Peer Violence." *Journal of Criminal Justice* 30 (2002): 41–49.

PETERSON, MICHELE, MARTIN D. RUCK, AND CHRISTOPHER J. KOEGL. "Youth Court Dispositions: Perceptions of Canadian Juvenile Offenders." *International Journal of Offender Therapy and Comparative Criminology* 45 (2001): 593–605.

PEUGH, JORDON AND STEVEN BELENKO. "Examining the Substance Use Patterns and Treatment Needs of Incarcerated Sex Offenders." *Sexual Abuse: A Journal of Research and Treatment* 13 (2001): 179–195.

PEYTON, ELIZABETH A. AND ROBERT GOSSWEILER. *Treatment Services in Adult Drug Courts: Report on the 1999 National Drug Court Treatment Survey.* Washington, DC: Drug Courts Program Office, U.S. Department of Justice, 2001.

PHILLIPS, RICHARD L. AND JOHN W. ROBERTS. *Quick Reference to Correctional Administration.* Gaithersburg, MD: Aspen, 2001.

PHILLIPS, SUSAN AND NANCY HARM. *Responding to the Needs of Children of Incarcerated Mothers.* Little Rock, AR: Centers for Youth and Families, 1997.

PIEHL, ANNA MORRISON. "Inmate Reentry and Post-Release Supervision: The Case of Massachusetts." *APPA Perspectives* 26 (2002): 32–38.

PIERPOINT, HARRIET. "The Performance of Volunteer-Appropriate Adults: A Survey of Call Outs." *The Howard Journal of Criminal Justice* 40 (2001): 255–271.

PINARD, GEORGES FRANCK AND LINDA PAGANI, EDS. *Clinical Assessment of Dangerousness: Empirical Contributions.* Cambridge, UK: University Press, 2001.

PIQUERO, ALEX AND PAUL MAZEROLLE. *Life-Course Criminology: Contemporary and Classic Readings.* Belmont, CA: Wadsworth/Thompson Learning, 2001.

POGREBIN, MARK R. AND ERIC D. POOLE. "Sex, Gender, and Work: The Case of Women Jail Officers." In *Sociology of Crime, Law, and Deviance Vol. 1,* edited by Jeffery T. Ulmer. Stamford, CT: JAI Press, 1998.

POJMAN, LOUIS P. AND JEFFREY REIMAN. *The Death Penalty: For and Against.* Lanham, MD: Rowman and Littlefield, 1998.

POLACSEK, MICHELE ET AL. "MADD Victim Impact Panels and Stages-of-Change in Drunk-Driving Prevention." *Journal of Studies on Alcohol* 62 (2001): 344–350.

POLASCHEK, DEVON L.L. AND BRIAN G. DIXON. "The Violence Prevention Project: The Development and Evaluation of a Treatment Program for Violent Offenders." *Psychology and Crime and Law* 7 (2001): 1–23.

POLLOCK, JOYCELYN M. *Counseling Women in Prison.* Thousand Oaks, CA: Sage, 1998.

POLLOCK, JOYCELYN M. *Parenting Programs in Women's Prisons.* San Marcos, TX: Department of Criminal Justice, Southwest Texas State University, 1999.

POLLOCK-BYRNE, JOYCELYN M. *Women, Prison and Crime.* Pacific Grove, CA: Brooks/Cole Publishing Company, 1990.

PONTELL, HENRY N. AND WAYNE N. WELSH. "Incarceration as a Deviant Form of Social Control: Jail Overcrowding in California." *Crime and Delinquency* 40 (1994): 18–36.

POOLE, CAROL AND PEGGY SLAVICK. *Boot Camps: A Washington State Update and Overview of National Findings.* Olympia: Washington State Institute for Public Policy, 1995.

POTTER, ROBERTO HUGH AND LINDA E. SALTZMAN. "Violence Prevention and Related Activities of the Centers for Disease Control and Prevention." *Corrections Today* 61 (1999): 56–59.

POWERS, JODI. "Designing Arizona's Newest Food Factories for Maximum Efficiency and Minimum Cost." *American Jails* 15 (2002): 48–51.

PRENDERGAST, MICHAEL, DAVID FARABEE, AND JEROME CARTIER. "The Impact of In-Prison Therapeutic Community Programs on Prison Management." *Journal of Offender Rehabilitation* 32 (2001): 63–78.

PRETRIAL SERVICES RESOURCE CENTER. *Mission Statement.* Washington, DC: Pretrial Services Resource Center, 2003.

PROBATION ASSOCIATION. *John Augustus: The First Probation Officer.* New York: Probation Association, 1939.

PROCTOR, JON L. "The 'New Parole': An Analysis of Parole Board Decision Making as a Function of Eligibility." *Journal of Crime and Justice* 22 (1999): 193–217.

PROCTOR, JON L. AND MICHAEL PEASE. "Parole as Institutional Control: A Test of Specific Deterrence and Offender Misconduct." *Prison Journal* 80 (2000): 39–55.

PULLEN, SUZANNE. *Evaluation of the Reasoning and Rehabilitation Cognitive Skills Development Program as Implemented in Juvenile ISP in Colorado.* Denver: Colorado Division of Criminal Justice, 1996.

PULLEN, SUZANNE. *Pre-Release Termination and Post-Release Recidivism Rates of Colorado's Probationers.* Denver: Office of Probation Services, Research and Evaluation Unit, Colorado State Court Administrator's Office, 1996.

PUTKONEN, H. ET AL. "Female Homicide Offenders Have Greatly Increased Mortality from Unnatural Deaths." *Forensic Science International* 119 (2001): 221–224.

PUTNAM, MARK L. "Improving Employee Relations." *Personnel Journal* 8 (1930): 314–325.

PUZZANCHERA, C. ET AL. *Juvenile Court Statistics 1999.* Washington, DC: Office of Juvenile Justice and Delinquency Prevention, 2002.

PYNES, JOAN AND JOHN H. BERNARDIN. "Entry-Level Police Selection: The Assessment Center is an Alternative." *Journal of Criminal Justice* 20 (1992): 41–52.

QUAY, HERBERT C. *Managing Adult Inmates.* College Park, MD: American Correctional Association, 1984.

QUAY, HERBERT C. AND L. B. PARSONS. *The Differential Behavioral Classification of the Adult Male Offender.* Philadelphia, PA: Temple University [Technical report prepared for the U.S. Department of Justice Bureau of Prisons, Contract J-1C-22, 253], 1971.

QUEENSLAND CRIMINAL JUSTICE COMMISSION. *Police Strip Searches in Queensland: An Inquiry into the Law and Practice.* Queensland, Australia: Queensland Criminal Justice Commission, 2000.

QUINLAN, J. MICHAEL ET AL. "Focus on the Female Offender." *Federal Prisons Journal* 3 (1992): 3–68.

QUINN, JAMES F., LARRY GOULD, AND LINDA HOLLOWAY. "Community Partnership Councils: Meeting the Needs of Texas' Parole Officers." *Corrections Compendium* 26 (2001): 1–5, 18–19.

RACKMILL, STEPHEN J. "An Analysis of Home Confinement as a Sanction." *Federal Probation* 58 (1994): 45–52.

RACKMILL, STEPHEN J. "Printzlein's Legacy, the 'Brooklyn Plan,' A.K.A. Deferred Prosecution." *Federal Probation* 60 (1996): 8–15.

RAFTER, NICOLE HAHN. "Prisons for Women: 1790–1980." In *Crime and Justice: An Annual Review of Research,* edited by Michael Tonry and Norval Morris. Chicago, IL: University of Chicago Press.

RAFTER, NICOLE HAHN. *Partial Justice: Women, Prisons and Social Control.* 2d ed. New Brunswick, NJ: Transaction, 1990.

RAFTER, NICOLE HAHN. *Creating Born Criminals.* Urbana: University of Illinois Press, 1997.

RAFTER, NICOLE HAHN. *Encyclopedia of Women and Crime.* Phoenix, AZ: Oryx Press, 2000.

RAPAPORT, ELIZABETH. "Staying Alive: Executive Clemency, Equal Protection, and the Politics of Gender in Women's Capital Cases." *Buffalo Criminal Law Review* 4 (2001): 962–1007.

RASMUSSEN, DAVID W. AND BRUCE L. BENSON. *Intermediate Sanctions: A Policy Analysis Based on Program Evaluations.* Washington, DC: The Collins Center for Public Policy, 1994.

RASMUSSEN, KIRSTEN, ROGER ALMVIK, AND STEN LEVANDER. "Attention Deficit Hyperactivity Disorder, Reading Disability, and Personality Disorders in a Prison Population." *Journal of the American Academy of Psychiatry and the Law* 29 (2001): 186–193.

RAY, KENNETH A. AND KATHY O'MEARA-WYMAN. "Privatizing and Regionalizing Local Corrections: Some Issues for Local Jurisdictions to Consider." *Corrections Today* 62 (2000): 116–128.

RECKLESS, WALTER C. *The Crime Problem.* New York: Appleton-Century-Crofts, 1961.

REDDINGTON, FRANCES. "Age and Criminal Responsibility." *Journal of the Institute of Justice and International Studies* 1 (2002): 105–108.

REDDINGTON, FRANCES P. AND JAMES F. ANDERSON. "Juveniles in Jail and the Legal Responsibilities: The More Things Change, the More They Stay the Same." *Journal for Juvenile Justice and Detention Services* 11 (1996): 47–54.

REIDY, THOMAS J., MARK D. CUNNINGHAM, AND JON R. SORENSEN. *Criminal Justice and Behavior* 28 (2001): 62–82.

REISIG, MICHAEL D., KRISTY HOLTFRETER, MERRY MORASH. "Social Capital among Women Offenders." *Journal of Contemporary Criminal Justice* 18 (2002): 167–187.

REISIG, MICHAEL D. AND YOON HO LEE. "Prisonization in the Republic of Korea." *Journal of Criminal Justice* 28 (2000): 23–31.

REISS, ALBERT J. JR. AND JEFFREY A. ROTH, EDS. *Understanding and Preventing Violence.* Washington, DC: National Academy Press, 1993.

REISS, DAVID ET AL. "Casenote Assessment of Psychopathy in a High Security Hospital." *Criminal Behavior and Mental Health* 11 (2001): 27–37.

REITZEL, LORRAINE R. AND BEVERLY L. HARJU. "Influence of Locus of Control and Custody Level on Intake and Prison-Adjustment Depression." *Criminal Justice and Behavior* 27 (2000): 625–644.

RENZEMA, MARC. "Tracking GPS: A Third Look." *The Journal of Offender Monitoring* 13 (2000): 6–8, 27.

RENZETTI, CLAIRE M. " 'One Strike and You're Out': Implications of a Federal Crime Control Policy for Battered Women." *Violence Against Women* 7 (2001): 685–698.

RESEARCH AND EVALUATION ASSOCIATES, INC. *Interim Report for the Department of Labor Youth Offender Demonstration Project Process Evaluation.* Washington, DC: U.S. Department of Labor, Employment, and Training Administration, 2001.

REYNOLDS, CARL. "The Final Chapters of *Ruiz v. Estelle.*" *Corrections Today* 64 (2002): 108–109.

REYNOLDS, CARL AND TRISHA STEFFEK. "Reducing Frivolous Inmate Litigation: Committee Drafts Recommendations to Address Skyrocketing Legal Costs." *Corrections Compendium* 22 (1997): 4–7.

RICHARDS, STEPHEN C. AND JEFFREY IAN ROSS. "Introducing the New School of Convict Criminology." *Social Justice* 28 (2001): 177–190.

RICHIE, BETH E. *Compelled to Crime: The Gender Entrapment of Battered Black Women.* New York: Routledge, 1996.

RICHIE, BETH E. "Challenges Incarcerated Women Face as They Return to Their Communities: Findings from Life History Interviews." *Crime and Delinquency* 47 (2001): 368–389.

RICHMAN, JACK M. AND MARK W. FRASER, EDS. *The Context of Youth Violence: Resilience, Risk, and Protection.* Westport, CT: Greenwood, 2000.

RION, SHARON JOHNSON. *Beyond His Time: The Maurice Sigler Story.* Lanham, MD: American Correctional Association, 2001.

RIVELAND, CHASE. *Supermax Prisons: Overview and General Considerations.* Washington, DC: U.S. National Institute of Corrections, 1999.

RIVKIND, NINA AND STEVEN F. SHATZ. *Cases and Materials on the Death Penalty.* St. Paul, MN: West Group, 2001.

ROBERTS, ALBERT R., ED. *Critical Issues in Crime and Justice.* Thousand Oaks, CA: Sage, 1994.

ROBERTS, ALBERT R. "Battered Women Who Kill: A Comparative Study of Incarcerated Participants with a Community Sample of Battered Women." *Journal of Family Violence* 11 (1996): 291–304.

ROBERTS, JOHN W. *Reform and Retribution: An Illustrated History of American Prisons.* Lanham, MD: American Correctional Association, 1997.

ROBERTSON, JAMES E. "Cruel and Unusual Punishment in United States Prisons: Sexual Harassment among Male Inmates." *American Criminal Law Review* 36 (1999): 1–51.

ROBINS, ARTHUR J. ET AL. "The Missouri Classification System Applied to Female Offenders: Reliability and Validity." *Corrective and Social Psychiatry and Journal of Behavior Technology Methods and Therapy* 32 (1986): 21–30.

ROBINSON, DAVID, FRANK J. PORPORINO, AND LINDA SIMOURD. "The Influence of Educational Attainment on the Attitudes and Job Performance of Correctional Officers." *Crime and Delinquency* 43 (1997): 60–77.

ROBINSON, GWEN. "Power, Knowledge, and What Works in Probation." *The Howard Journal of Criminal Justice* 40 (2001): 235–254.

ROETHLISBERGER, FRITZ J. AND WILLIAM J. DICKSON. *Management and the Worker.* Cambridge, MA: Harvard, 1939.

ROGERS, JOSEPH W. "Seven Ideal Criteria for the Constructive Evaluation of Discipline for Parents, Teachers, and Juvenile Probation Officers." *Juvenile and Family Court Journal* 49 (1998): 27–37.

ROGERS, ROBERT. "Solitary Confinement." *International Journal of Offender Therapy and Comparative Criminology* 37 (1993): 339–349.

ROKACH, AMI AND JANICE E. CRIPPS. "Incarcerated Men and the Perceived Sources of Their Loneliness." *International Journal of Offender Therapy and Comparative Criminology* 43 (1999): 78–89.

ROLEFF, TAMARA L., ED. *The Legal System: Opposing Viewpoints.* San Diego, CA: Greenhaven Press, 1996.

ROLLAND, MIKE. *Descent Into Madness: An Inmate's Experience of the New Mexico State Prison Riot.* Cincinnati, OH: Anderson Publishing Company, 1997.

ROMAN, JOHN AND ADELE HARRELL. "Assessing the Costs and Benefits Accruing to the Public from a Graduated Sanctions Program for Drug-Using Defendants." *Law and Policy* 23 (2001): 237–268.

ROMANO, STEPHEN J. "Achieving Successful Negotiations in a Correctional Setting." *Corrections Today* 65 (2003): 114–118.

ROSAZZA, THOMAS A. AND JUDITH T. NESTRUD. "State Jail Inspection Programs: State of the Art." *American Jails* 14 (2000): 55–59.

ROSS, DARRELL L. "Emerging Trends in Correctional Civil Liability Cases: A Content Analysis of Federal Court Decisions of Title 42 United States Code Section 1983." *Journal of Criminal Justice* 25 (1997): 501–514.

ROTHMAN, DAVID J. "Sentencing Reforms in Historical Perspective." *Crime and Delinquency* 29 (1983): 631–647.

ROULET, SISTER ELAINE. "New York's Prison Nursery/Children's Center." *Corrections Compendium* 18 (1993): 4–6.

ROUSH, DAVID W. AND MICHAEL A. JONES. "Juvenile Detention Training: A Status Report." *Federal Probation* 60 (1996): 54–60.

ROY, SUDIPTO. "Juvenile Offenders in an Electronic Home Detention Program: A Study on Factors Related to Failure." *Journal of Offender Monitoring* 8 (1995): 9–17.

ROY, SUDIPTO. "Five Years of Electronic Monitoring of Adults and Juveniles in Lake County, Indiana: A Comparative Study on Factors Related to Failure." *Journal of Crime and Justice* 20 (1997): 141–160.

ROY, SUDIPTO AND MICHAEL BROWN. "Victim-Offender Reconciliation Project for Adults and Juveniles: A Comparative Study in Elkhart County, Indiana." Unpublished paper presented at the annual meetings of the American Society of Criminology, San Francisco, CA, November 1992.

ROY, SUDIPTO AND JENNIFER N. GRIMES. "Adult Offenders in a Day Reporting Center—A Preliminary Study." *Federal Probation* 66 (2002): 44–50.

RUNDA, JOHN C., EDWARD E. RHINE, AND ROBERT E. WETTER. *The Practice of Parole Boards.* Lexington, KY: Council of State Governments, 1994.

RUSSELL, BETTY G. "New Approaches to the Treatment of Women with Co-Occurring Disorders in Jails." *American Jails* 13 (1999): 21–25.

RUSSELL, BETTY G. "The TAMAR Project: Addressing Trauma Issues of Offenders in Jails." *American Jails* 15 (2001): 41–44.

RUSSELL, JEANNE, ROBERT A. NICHOLSON, AND RUDY BUIGAS. *Evaluation of the Female Offender Regimented Treatment Program at Eddie Warrior Correctional Center.* Tulsa, OK: University of Tulsa, 1990.

RUSSO, JOE. "Florida's CrimeTrax Project." *APPA Perspectives* 26 (2002): 16.

RYAN, TIMOTHY AND CHARLES C. PLUMMER. "Jail Accreditation: A Panacea or Problem?" *Corrections Today* 61 (1999): 157.

SABBATINE, RAY. "Risk Management in Jails: How to Reduce the Potential of Negative Outcomes." *Corrections Today* 65 (2003): 66–69.

SALEKIN, RANDALL T., RICHARD ROGERS, AND KAREN L. USTAD. "Juvenile Waiver to Adult Criminal Courts: Prototypes for Dangerousness, Sophistication-Maturity, and Amenability to Treatment." *Psychology, Public Policy, and Law* 7 (2001): 381–408.

SALERNO, ANTHONY W. "Boot Camps: Critique and a Proposed Alternative." *Journal of Offender Rehabilitation* 20 (1994): 147–158.

SALVATORE, RICARDO D., CARLOS AGUIRRE, AND GILBERT M. JOSEPH, EDS. *Crime and Punishment in Latin America: Law and Society Since Late Colonial Times.* Durham, NC: Duke University Press, 2001.

SANBORN, JOSEPH B. JR. "Victim's Rights in Juvenile Court: Has the Pendulum Swung Too Far?" *Judicature* 85 (2001): 140–146.

SANTA CLARA COUNTY SUPERIOR COURT. *Pretrial Services.* Santa Clara County, CA: Santa Clara County Superior Court, 2003.

SARAT, AUSTIN. *When the State Kills: Capital Punishment and the American Condition.* Princeton, NJ: Princeton University Press, 2001.

SARRE, RICK. "Beyond 'What Works'? A 25-Year Jubilee Retrospective of Robert Martinson's Famous Article." *Australian and New Zealand Journal of Criminology* 34 (2001): 38–46.

SAWICKI, DONNA RAU, BEATRIX SCHAEFFER, AND JEANIE THIES. "Predicting Successful Outcomes for Serious and Chronic Juveniles in Residential Placement." *Juvenile and Family Court Journal* 50 (1999): 21–31.

SAYLOR, WILLIAM G. AND GERALD G. GAES. *PREP Study Links UNICOR Work Experience with Successful Post-Release Outcome.* Washington, DC: U.S. Federal Bureau of Prisons, 1991.

SCARCE, MICHAEL. *Male-on-Male Rape: The Hidden Toll of Stigma and Shame.* New York: Plenum, 1997.

SCHEB, JOHN M. AND JOHN M. SCHEB JR. *Criminal Procedure.* St. Paul, MN: West Publishing Company, 1996.

SCHEELA, ROCHELLE A. "Sex Offender Treatment: Therapists' Experiences and Perceptions." *Issues in Mental Health Nursing* 22 (2001): 749–767.

SCHELLMAN, GEORGE. "Housing State Offenders in a County Correction Center: The Shelby County Experience." *American Jails* 10 (1996): 27–31.

SCHIPPERS, GERARD M., Nicole Marker, and Laura DeFuentes. "Social Skills Training, Prosocial Behavior, and Aggressiveness in Adult Incarcerated Facilities." *International Journal of Offender Therapy and Comparative Criminology* 45 (2001): 244–251.

SCHLANK, ANITA, ED. *The Sexual Predator: Legal Issues, Clinical Issues, Special Populations.* Kingston, NJ: Civil Research Institute, 2001.

SCHLOSSMAN, STEVEN AND JOSEPH SPILLANE. *Bright Hopes, Dim Realities: Vocational Innovation in American Correctional Education.* Santa Monica, CA: Rand, 1992.

SCHMALLEGER, FRANK AND JOHN ORTIZ SMYKLA. *Corrections in the 21st Century.* New York: Glencoe McGraw-Hill, 2001.

SCHMIDT, RIK ET AL. "Measuring Success: The Washington State Juvenile Rehabilitation Model." *Corrections Today* 60 (1998): 104–106.

SCHNEIDER, MICHAEL E. "A Texas Prisoner's Reaction to Faith-Based Rehabilitation Programs." *Social Justice* 28 (2001): 191–195.

SCHNEIDER, URSULA. "Community Service as an Intermediate Sanction?" *Monatsschrift fuer Kriminologie und Strafrechtsreform* 84 (2001): 273–287.

SCHRAG, CLARENCE. "Some Foundations for a Theory of Corrections." In *The Prison: Studies in Institutional Organization,* edited by Donald R. Cressey. New York: Holt, Rinehart, and Winston, 1961.

SCHRAM, PAMELA J. "An Exploratory Study: Stereotypes about Mothers in Prison." *Journal of Criminal Justice* 27 (1999): 411–426.

SCHULZ, HOLGER. "The Maximum Penalty in Juvenile Justice: An Analysis of Court Rulings." *Monatsschrift fuer Kriminologie und Strafrechtsreform* 84 (2001): 310–325.

SCHWANER, SHAWN L. " 'Stick 'em Up, Buddy': Robbery, Lifestyle, and Specialization within a Cohort of Parolees." *Journal of Criminal Justice* 28 (2000): 371–384.

SCOTT, GREGORY. "Broken Windows behind Bars: Eradicating Prison Gangs through Ecological Hardening and Symbol Cleansing." *Corrections Management Quarterly* 5 (2001): 23–36.

SECHREST, LEE. "Classification for Treatment." In *Prediction and Classification: Criminal Justice Decision Making,* Don M. Gottfredson and Michael Tonry (eds.). Chicago: University of Chicago Press, 1987.

SELKE, WILLIAM L. *Prisons in Crisis.* Bloomington: University of Indiana Press, 1993.

SENESE, JEFFREY D. "Jail Utilization over Time: An Assessment of the Patterns in Male and Female Populations." *Criminal Justice Policy Review* 5 (1991): 241–255.

SERIN, RALPH C. AND DONNA L. MAILLOUX. *Development of a Reliable Self-Report Instrument for the Assessment of Criminogenic Need.* Ottawa, Canada: Research Branch, Correctional Service of Canada, 2001.

SEYKO, RONALD J. "Balanced Approach and Restorative Justice Efforts in Allegheny County, Pennsylvania." *Prison Journal* 81 (2001): 187–205.

SEYMOUR, CYNTHIA B. AND FINNEY HAIRSTON-CREASIE, EDS. *Children with Parents in Prison.* New Brunswick, NJ: Transaction Publishers, 2001.

SHANE-DUBOW, SANDRA ET AL. "Structured Sentencing in the U.S.: An Experiment in Modeling Judicial Discretion." *Law and Policy* 20 (1998): 231–382.

SHAPIRO, BRIAN. "The Therapeutic Community Movement in Corrections." *Corrections Today Magazine* 63 (2001): 24, 55–69.

SHAPIRO, C. "Creative Supervision: An Underutilized Antidote." In *Job Stress and Burnout: Research, Theory, and Intervention Perspectives,* edited by W. Paine. Beverly Hills, CA: Sage, 1982.

SHAPIRO, CAROL AND MERYL SCHWARTZ. "Coming Home: Building on Family Connections." *Corrections Management Quarterly* 5 (2001): 52–61.

SHARBARO, EDWARD AND ROBERT KELLER, EDS. *Prison Crisis: Critical Readings.* Albany, NY: Harrow and Heston, 1995.

SHAW, MICHELLE AND KENNETH ROBINSON. "Summary and Analysis of the First Juvenile Drug Court Evaluations." *National Drug Court Review* 1 (1998): 73–85.

SHEARER, ROBERT A. "Coerced Substance Abuse Counseling Revisited." *Journal of Offender Rehabilitation* 30 (2000): 153–171.

SHEARER, ROBERT A., LAURA B. MYERS, AND GUY D. OGAN. "Treatment Residence and Ethnicity among Female Offenders in Substance Abuse Treatment Programs." *Prison Journal* 81 (2001): 55–72.

SHELDEN, RANDALL G. AND WILLIAM B. BROWN. "Correlates of Jail Overcrowding: A Case Study of a County Detention Center." *Crime & Delinquency* 37 (1991): 347–362.

SHICHOR, DAVID AND MICHAEL J. GILBERT. *Privatization in Criminal Justice: Past, Present, and Future.* Cincinnati, OH: Anderson, 2001.

SHINE, JOHN. "Characteristics of Inmates Admitted to Grendon Therapeutic Prison and Their Relationships to Length of Stay." *International Journal of Offender Therapy and Comparative Criminology* 45 (2001): 252–265.

SHOOK, CHADWICK L. AND ROBERT T. SIGLER. *Constitutional Issues in Correctional Administration.* Durham, NC: Carolina Academic Press, 2000.

SHUMAKER, DAVID M. AND GEOFFREY R. MCKEE. "Characteristics of Homicidal and Violent Juveniles." *Violence and Victims* 16 (2001): 401–409.

SICKMUND, MELISSA. *Juvenile Residential Facility Census, 2000: Selected Findings.* Washington, DC: U.S. Department of Justice, Office of Juvenile Justice and Delinquency Prevention, 2002.

SIDEMAN, LAWRENCE M. AND ELLEN KIRSCHBAUM. "The Road to Recovery: A Gender-Responsive Program for Convicted DUI Females." *Corrections Today* 64 (2002): 84–87, 112.

SIEFERT, KRISTINE AND SHERYL PIMLOTT. "Improving Pregnancy Outcome During Imprisonment: A Model Residential Care Program." *Social Work: Journal of the National Association of Social Workers* 46 (2001): 125–134.

SIGURDSON, HERBERT R. "A Difference That Made a Difference in the Administration of Justice." *American Jails* 10 (1996): 9–21.

SIGURDSSON, JON FRIDIK AND GISLI H. GUDJONSSON. "False Confessions: The Relative Importance of Psychological, Criminological, and Substance Abuse Variables." *Psychology, Crime, and the Law* 7 (2001): 275–289.

SILVER, ERIC AND LISA L. MILLER. "A Cautionary Note on the Use of Actuarial Risk Assessment Tools for Social Control." *Crime and Delinquency* 48 (2002): 138–161.

SILVERSTEIN, MARTIN. "The Ties That Bind: Family Surveillance of Canadian Parolees." *Sociological Quarterly* 42 (2001): 395–420.

SIMONET, L. JOHN. "Diverting the Mentally Ill from Jail." *American Jails* 9 (1995): 30.

SIMOURD, DAVID J. AND ROBERT D. HOGE. "Criminal Psychopathy: A Risk-and-Need Perspective." *Criminal Justice and Behavior* 27 (2000): 256–272.

SIMPSON, GARY J. AND STEPHEN P. GARVEY. "Knockin' on Heaven's Door: Rethinking the Role of Religion in Death Penalty Cases." *Cornell Law Review* 86 (2001): 1090–1130.

SIMPSON, MARK. "Are Incentives for Drug Abuse Treatment Too Strong?" *Corrections Today* 64 (2002): 64–66, 118.

SIMS, BARBARA. "Surveying the Correctional Environment: A Review of the Literature." *Corrections Management Quarterly* 5 (2001): 1–12.

SINGH, DEBBIE AND CLEM WHITE. *Rapua Te Huarahi Tika— Searching for Solutions: A Review of Research about Effective Interventions for Reducing Offending by Indigenous and Ethnic Minority Youth.* Wellington, New Zealand: Ministry of Youth Affairs, 2000.

SKOLNICK, JEROME H. "What Not to Do about Crime." *Criminology* 33 (1995): 1–15.

SLABONIK, MARIA L. AND BARBARA SIMS. "Controlling Discretion in Bureaucratic Agencies: A Survey of Adult Probation Officers." *Corrections Compendium* 27 (2002): 1–5, 22.

SLATE, RISDON N., RONALD E. VOGEL, AND W. WESLEY JOHNSON. "To Quit or Not to Quit: Perceptions of Participation in Correctional Decision Making and the Impact of Organizational Stress." *Corrections Management Quarterly* 5 (2001): 68–78.

SLATKIN, ART. "A Bad Officer Is Hard to Find." *American Jails* 7 (1994): 77–80.

SLATKIN, ART, VICKI WIMBS, AND KEVIN SIDEBOTTOM. "Jail Inspections and Audits Division: A Model for Practice." *American Jails* 8 (1994): 47–51.

SLUDER, RICHARD D. AND ROLANDO V. DEL CARMEN. "Are Probation and Parole Officers Liable for Injuries Caused by Probationers and Parolees?" *Federal Probation* 54 (1990): 3–12.

SLUDER, RICHARD D., ALLEN D. SAPP AND DENNY C. LANGSTON. "Guiding Philosophies for Probation in the 21st Century." *Federal Probation* 58 (1994): 29–30.

SLUDER, RICHARD D. AND ROBERT A. SHEARER. "Personality Types of Probation Officers." *Federal Probation* 56 (1992): 29–35.

SLUDER, RICHARD D., ROBERT A. SHEARER, AND DENNIS W. POTTS. "Probation Officers' Role Perceptions and Attitudes toward Firearms." *Federal Probation* 55 (1991): 3–12.

SMALL, SHAWN E. AND SAM TORRES. "Arming Probation Officers: Enhancing Public Confidence and Officer Safety." *Federal Probation* 65 (2001): 24–28.

SMANDYCH, RUSSELL C. "Beware of the 'Evil American Monster:' Upper Canadian Views on a Need for a Penitentiary, 1830–1834." *Canadian Journal of Criminology* 33 (1991): 125–147.

SMITH, ALBERT G. "Arming Officers Doesn't Have to Change an Agency's Mission." *Corrections Today* 53 (1991a): 114–124.

SMITH, ALBERT G. "The California Model: Probation and Parole Safety Training." *APPA Perspectives* 15 (1991b): 38–41.

SMITH, ALBERT G. "Probation and Parole Agents: Arming Officers Doesn't Have to Change an Agency's Mission." *Corrections Today* 53 (1991c): 114–124.

SMITH, CHRISTOPHER E. "Judicial Policy Making and *Habeas Corpus* Reform." *Criminal Justice Policy Review* 7 (1995): 91–114.

SMITH, LAMAR. "Sentencing Youths to Adult Correctional Facilities Increases Public Safety." *Corrections Today* 65 (2003): 20.

SMITH, ROBERT R. ET AL. "Jail Health Care: Current Issues." *American Jails* 8 (1994): 11–26.

SMITH, WALTER R. "American Jails: The Challenge of Recruitment and Retention." *American Jails* 16 (2002): 9–13.

SMITH, WILLIAM R. AND RANDALL D. SMITH. "The Consequences of Error: Recidivism Prediction and Civil Libertarian Ratios." *Journal of Criminal Justice* 26 (1998): 481–502.

SMYKLA, JOHN ORTIZ. *Community-Based Corrections: Principles and Practices.* New York: Macmillan, 1981.

SMYKLA, JOHN ORTIZ AND WILLIAM SELKE. "The Impact of Home Detention: A Less Restrictive Alternative to the Detention of Juveniles." *Juvenile and Family Court Journal* 33 (1982): 3–9.

SMYKLA, JOHN ORTIZ AND WILLIAM SELKE. *Intermediate Sanctions: Sentencing in the 1990s.* Cincinnati, OH: Anderson Publishing Company, 1995.

SMYKLA, JOHN ORTIZ AND JIMMY J. WILLIAMS. "Co-Corrections in the United States of America, 1970–1990: Two Decades of Disadvantages for Women Prisoners." *Women and Criminal Justice* 8 (1996): 61–76.

SNELL, CLETE AND MICHAEL GRABOWSKI. "The Increase of Juveniles in Adult Jails: Implications for Jail Administrators." *American Jails* 16 (2003): 78–82.

SNELL, TRACY L. AND LAURA M. MARUSCHAK. *Capital Punishment 2001.* Washington, DC: U.S. Government Printing Office, 2002.

SNELLENBERG, SIDNEY C. *A Normative Alternative to the Death Penalty.* Unpublished paper presented at the Southern Association of Criminal Justice Educators, Atlanta, GA, October 1986.

SNYDER, HOWARD N. *Juvenile Arrests 2000.* Washington, DC: Office of Juvenile Justice and Delinquency Prevention, 2002.

SNYDER, HOWARD N., MELISSA SICKMUND, AND EILEEN POE-YAMAGATA. *Juvenile Transfers to Criminal Court in the 1990s: Lessons Learned from Four Studies.* Washington, DC: U.S. Office of Juvenile Justice and Delinquency Prevention, 2000.

SNYDER, T. RICHARD. *The Protestant Ethic and the Spirit of Punishment.* Grand Rapids, MI: William B. Eerdmans, 2001.

SOLOTAROFF, IVAN. *The Last Face You'll Ever See: The Private Life of the American Death Penalty.* New York: HarperCollins, 2001.

SOURYAL, CLAIRE AND CHARLES WELLFORD. *An Examination of Unwarranted Sentencing Disparity Under Maryland's Voluntary Sentencing Guidelines.* Baltimore, MD: Maryland Commission on Criminal Sentencing Policy, 1997.

SOUTH CAROLINA STATE REORGANIZATION COMMISSION. *Evaluation of the Omnibus Criminal Justice Improvement Act of 1986, Section 3, 4 and 5 Second Year Report.* Columbia, SC: South Carolina State Reorganization Commission, 1990.

SPALEK, BASIA AND DAVID WILSON. "Not Just 'Visitors' to Prisons: The Experiences of Imams Who Work Inside the Penal System." *Howard Journal of Criminal Justice* 40 (2001): 3–13.

SPAPENS, A.C. "Mediation in Relation to Criminal Procedure." *Justiele Verkenningen* 27 (2001): 70–80.

SPELMAN, WILLIAM. "The Severity of Intermediate Sanctions." *Journal of Research in Crime and Delinquency* 32 (1995): 107–135.

SPIEGEL, ALLEN D. AND MARC B. SPIEGEL. "The Insanity Plea in Early Nineteenth Century America." *Journal of Community Health* 23 (1998): 227–247.

SPIERENBURG, PIETER. *The Prison Experience: Disciplinary Institutions and Their Inmates in Early Modern Europe.* New Brunswick, NJ: Rutgers University Press, 1991.

STACK, WILLIAM R. AND FRANK A. DIXON. "Behavior Alert Classification Identification System." *American Jails* 3 (1990): 45–47.

STALANS, LORETTA J. AND GARY T. HENRY. "Societal Views of Justice for Adolescents Accused of Murder: Inconsistency between Community Sentiment and Automatic Legislative Transfers." *Law and Human Behavior* 18 (1994): 675–696.

STALANS, LORETTA J., MAGNUS SENG, AND PAUL YARNOLD. *An Implementation and Initial Impact Evaluation of the Adult Sex Offender Probation Project in Cook County.* Chicago: Illinois Criminal Justice Information Authority, 2001.

STALANS, LORETTA J. ET AL. *An Implementation and Initial Impact Evaluation of the Adult Sex Offender Probation Project in Cook County.* Chicago: Illinois Criminal Justice Information Authority, 2001.

STATON, MICHELE ET AL. "Process Evaluation for a Prison-Based Substance-Abuse Program." *Journal of Offender Rehabilitation* 32 (2000): 105–127.

STEFFENSMEIER, DARRELL J. AND STEPHEN DEMUTH. "Ethnicity and Judges' Sentencing Decisions: Hispanic-Black-White Comparisons." *Criminology* 39 (2001): 145–178.

STEFFENSMEIER, DARRELL J., JOHN KRAMER, AND CATHY STREIFEL. "Gender and Imprisonment Decisions." *Criminology,* 31 (1993): 411–446.

STEVENS, DENNIS J. "The Impact of Time Served and Regime on Prisoners' Anticipation of Crime: Female Prisonization Effects." *Howard Journal* 37 (1998): 188–205.

STEVENS, DENNIS J. "Community Policing and Managerial Techniques: Total Quality Management Techniques." *Police Journal* 74 (2001): 26–41.

STEWART, LEE. *Women Volunteer to Go to Prison: A History of the Elizabeth Fry Society of B.C. 1939–1989.* Victoria, Canada: Orca Book Publishers, 1993.

ST. GERARD, VANESSA. "High-Tech System Improves Surveillance." *Corrections Today* 65 (2003): 9.

STINCHCOMB, JEANNE B. "Why Not the Best? Using Assessment Centers for Officer Selection." *Corrections Today* 47 (1985): 120–124.

STINCHCOMB, JEANNE B. "Developing Correctional Officer Professionalism: A Work in Progress." *Corrections Compendium* 25 (2000): 1–4, 18–19.

STINCHCOMB, JEANNE B. AND DARYL HIPPENSTEEL. "Presentence Investigation Reports: A Relevant Justice Model Tool or a Medical Model Relic?" *Criminal Justice Policy Review* 12 (2001): 164–177.

STINCHCOMB, JEANNE B. AND W. CLINTON TERRY III. "Predicting the Likelihood of Rearrest among Shock Incarceration Graduates: Moving Beyond Another Nail in the Boot Camp Coffin." *Crime and Delinquency* 47 (2001): 221–242.

STOHR, MARY K. "Noteworthy Personnel Findings from the Women's Jail Study." *American Jails* 11 (1997): 45–56.

STOHR, MARY K. ET AL. "Can't Scale This? The Ethical Parameters of Correctional Work." *Prison Journal* 80 (2000): 56–79.

STOLZENBERG, LISA AND STEWART J. D'ALESSIO. "The Impact of Prison Crowding on Male and Female Imprisonment Rates in Minnesota." *Justice Quarterly* 14 (1997): 793–809.

STOUGHTON, DON, CLAIRE DROWOTA, AND JUDY SULLIVAN. *Comparative Evaluation of Performance of Privately Managed CCA Prison South Central Correctional Facility and State-Managed Prisons Northeast Correctional Complex, Northwest Correctional Complex: Staff Report.* Nashville, TN: Tennessee Select Oversight Committee on Corrections, 1999.

STRANGE, CAROLYN, ED. *Qualities of Mercy: Justice, Punishment, and Discretion.* Vancouver, Canada: University of British Columbia Press, 1996.

STREIB, VICTOR L. *Death Penalty for Juveniles.* Bloomington: Indiana University Press, 1987.

STURGES, JUDITH E. "Westmoreland County Youth Commission: A Diversionary Program Based on Balanced and Restorative Justice." *Juvenile and Family Court Journal* 52 (2001): 1–10.

STURGES, JUDITH E. "Visitation at County Jails." *American Jails* 16 (2002): 17–22.

SULLIVAN, DENNIS AND LARRY TIFFT. *Restorative Justice: Healing the Foundations of Our Everyday Lives.* Monsey, NY: Willow Tree Press, 2001.

SULLIVAN, EILEEN, CARMEN CIRINCIONE, AND KATHERINE NELSON. *Classifying Inmates for Strategic Programming.* New York: Vera Institute of Justice, 2001.

SUNDT, JODY L. ET AL. "What Will the Public Tolerate?" *APPA Perspectives* 22 (1998b): 21–26.

SURETTE, RAY. "Self-Reported Copycat Crime among a Population of Serious and Violent Juvenile Offenders." *Crime and Delinquency* 48 (2002): 46–69.

SURIS, ALINA ET AL. "Validation of the Inventory of Depressive Symptomatology (IDS) in Cocaine Dependent Inmates." *Journal of Offender Rehabilitation* 32 (2001): 15–30.

SUTHERLAND, EDWIN H. *The Professional Thief.* Chicago, IL: University of Chicago Press (Originally published in 1937), 1972.

SWANSON, JEFFREY W. ET AL. "Can Involuntary Outpatient Commitment Reduce Arrests among Persons with Severe Mental Illness?" *Criminal Justice and Behavior* 28 (2001): 156–189.

SWEET, JOSEPH. "Probation as Therapy." *Corrections Today* 47 (1988): 89–90.

SYKES, GRESHAM. *The Society of Captives.* Princeton, NJ: Princeton University Press, 1958.

SZOSTAK, EDWARD W. "Jails and the Management of Other Agencies' Prisoners." *American Jails* 10 (1996): 22–24.

TARTAGLINI, ALDO J. AND DAVID A. SAFRAN. "Occupational Functioning of Correctional Officers: Job-Related, Organizational, and Social Considerations." *American Jails* 10 (1996): 42–44.

TARVER, MARSHA, STEVE WALKER, AND HARVEY WALLACE. *Multicultural Issues in the Criminal Justice System.* Boston: Allyn and Bacon, 2002.

TAXMAN, FAYE S. AND JEFFREY A. BOUFFARD. "The Importance of Systems in Improving Offender Outcomes: New Frontiers in Treatment Integrity." *Justice Research and Policy* 2 (2000): 37–58.

TAXMAN, FAYE S. AND LORI ELIS. "Expediting Court Dispositions: Quick Results, Uncertain Outcomes." *Journal of Research in Crime and Delinquency* 36 (1999): 30–55.

TAYLOR, JON MARC. "Violence in Prison: A Personal Perspective." *Corrections Compendium* 21 (1996): 1–12.

TAYLOR, MARK LEWIS. *The Executed God: The Way of the Cross in Lockdown America.* Minneapolis, MN: Fortress Press, 2001.

TAYLOR, TERRANCE J. ET AL. "Coppin' an Attitude: Attitudinal Differences among Juveniles Toward Police." *Journal of Criminal Justice* 29 (2001): 295–305.

TAYMANS, JULIANA M. AND MARY ANN CORLEY. "Enhancing Services to Inmates with Learning Disabilities: Systematic Reform of Prison Literacy Programs." *The Journal of Correctional Education* 52 (2001): 74–78.

TCHAIKOVSKY, CHRIS. *One Hundred Women.* Cambridge, UK: Institute of Criminology, University of Cambridge, 2000.

TEMIN, CAROLYN ENGEL. "Let Us Consider the Children." *Corrections Today Magazine* 63 (2001): 66–68.

TEPLIN, LINDA A., KAREN M. ABRAM, AND GARY M. MCCLELLAND. "Prevalence of Psychiatric Disorders among Incarcerated Women." *Archives of General Psychiatry* 53 (1996): 505–512.

TEXAS CRIMINAL JUSTICE POLICY COUNCIL. *Overview of Special Needs Parole Policy and Recommendations for Improvement.* Austin, TX: Texas Criminal Justice Policy Council, 2000.

TEXAS DEPARTMENT OF CRIMINAL JUSTICE. *Intensive Supervision Probation.* Austin, TX: Texas Department of Criminal Justice, 2002.

TEWKSBURY, RICHARD A. "Improving the Educational Skills of Jail Inmates: Preliminary Program Findings." *Federal Probation* 58 (1994): 55–59.

THIGPEN, MORRIS L., SUSAN M. HUNTER, AND SAMMIE D. BROWN. *Classification of Women Offenders: A National Assessment of Current Practices.* Washington, DC: U.S. Department of Justice National Institute of Corrections, 2001.

THOMAS, R. MURRAY. *Classifying Reactions to Wrongdoing: Taxonomies of Misdeeds, Sanctions, and Aims of Sanctions.* Westport, CT: Greenwood Press, 1995.

THOMPSON, JOEL A. AND G. LARRY MAYS, EDS. *American Jails: Public Policy Issues.* Chicago: Nelson-Hall, 1991.

THORNTON, ROBERT L. "Implementation of Metal Detector in Probation and Parole Offices." *APPA Perspectives* 26 (2002): 19.

TIERNEY, DAVID W. AND MARITA P. MCCABE. "Motivation for Behavior Change among Sex Offenders: A Review of the Literature." *Clinical Psychology Review* 22 (2002): 113–129.

TISCHLER, ERIC. "Juveniles in Prison? Solution or Problem?" *On the Line* 22 (1999): 1–2.

TOBOLOWSKY, PEGGY M., JAMES F. QUINN, AND JOHN E. HOLMAN. "Participation of Incarcerated High School Dropouts in County Jail Programs." *Journal of Correctional Education* 42 (1991): 142–145.

TOCH, HANS. "Democratizing Prisons." *Prison Journal* 74 (1995a): 62–72.

TOCH, HANS. "Inmate Involvement in Prison Governance." *Federal Probation* 59 (1995b): 34–39.

TOCH, HANS. "Trends in Correctional Leadership." *Corrections Compendium* 27 (2002): 8–9, 23–25.

TOEPELL, ANDREA RIESCH AND LORRAINE GREAVES. "Experience of Abuse among Women Visiting Incarcerated Partners." *Violence Against Women* 7 (2001): 80–109.

TONRY, MICHAEL. "Intermediate Sanctions in Sentencing Guidelines." In *Crime and Justice: A Review of Research, Vol. 23,* edited by Michael Tonry. Chicago: University of Chicago Press, 1998.

TONRY, MICHAEL. "PAROCHIALISM IN U.S. SENTENCING POL-ICY." *Crime and Delinquency* 45 (1999): 48–65.

TONRY, MICHAEL AND RICHARD S. FRASE, EDS. *Sentencing and Sanctions in Western Countries.* Oxford, UK: Oxford University Press, 2001.

TONRY, MICHAEL AND KATE HAMILTON, EDS. *Intermediate Sanctions in Overcrowded Times.* Boston: Northeastern University Press, 1995.

TOPHAM, JAMES. *Four Letters That Say So Much.* Albany, New York: Corrections Connection, 2002.

TORBET, P. AND LINDA SZYMANSKI. *State Legislative Responses to Violent Juvenile Crime: 1996–1997 Update.* Washington, DC: Office of Juvenile Justice and Delinquency Prevention, 1998.

TORRES, SAM AND ROBERT M. LATTA "Selecting the Substance Abuse Specialist." *Federal Probation* 64 (2000): 46–50.

TOWNSEND, VINCENT AND PERRY EICHOR. "Jails, Inmate Phone Service, and Call Rates . . . A Political Time Bomb Waiting to Explode?" *American Jails* 8 (1995): 27–39.

TRACY, SARAH J. "Correctional Contradictions: A Structural Approach to Addressing Officer Burnout." *Corrections Today* 65 (2003): 90–95.

TRASKMAN, PER OLE. "Community Sanctions and Measures in Sweden." *Nordisk Tidsskrift for Kriminalvidenskab* 88 (2001): 169–193.

TRAVIS, JEREMY. "But They All Come Back: Rethinking Prisoner Reentry." *Corrections Management Quarterly* 5 (2001): 23–33.

TREVATHAN, JOSEPH T. "Hampden County, Massachusetts Jail Industries: Over $500,000 in Revenues Last Year." *American Jails* 16 (2002): 41–46.

TRIPLET, RUSH AND TOBY ROSS. "Developing Partnership for Gang Intervention: The Role for Community Corrections." *APPA Perspectives* 22 (1998): 29–35.

TROUNSTINE, JEAN. *Shakespeare behind Bars: The Power of Drama in a Women's Prison.* New York: St. Martin's, 2001.

TSUNOKAI, GLENN T. AND AUGUSTINE J. KPOSOWA. "Asian Gangs in the United States: The Current State of the Research Literature." *Crime, Law, and Social Change* 37 (2002): 37–50.

TUNIS, SANDRA ET AL. *Evaluation of Drug Treatment in Local Corrections.* Washington, DC: National Institute of Justice, 1996.

TURNBULL, PAUL J. ET AL. *Drug Treatment and Testing Orders: Final Evaluation Report.* London, UK: Research and Statistics Directorate, UK Home Office, 2000.

TURPIN-PETROSINO, CAROLYN. "Are Limiting Enactments Effective? An Experimental Test of Decision Making in a Presumptive Parole State." *Journal of Criminal Justice* 27 (1999): 321–332.

TWILL, SARAH E. ET AL. "Changes in Measured Loneliness, Control, and Social Support among Parolees in a Halfway House." *Journal of Offender Rehabilitation* 27 (1998): 77–92.

ULMER, JEFFERY T. "Intermediate Sanctions: A Comparative Analysis of the Probability and Severity of Recidivism." *Sociological Inquiry* 71 (2001): 164–193.

UMBREIT, MARK S. *The Handbook of Victim Offender Mediation: An Essential Guide to Practice and Research.* San Francisco, CA: Jossey-Bass, 2001.

UNDERWOOD, LEE A. AND SALLY H. FALWELL. "Screening and Assessing Co-Occurring Disorders." *Corrections Today* 64 (2002): 22–23.

UNGER, JENNIFER B. AND LOUISE ANN ROHRBACH. "Why Do Adolescents Overestimate Their Peers' Smoking Prevalence? Correlates of Prevalence Estimates among 8th-Grade Students." *Journal of Youth and Adolescence* 31 (2002): 147–153.

U.K. HOME OFFICE. *Making Punishments Work: Report of a Review of the Sentencing Framework for England and Wales.* London, UK: UK Home Office, 2001.

U.S. BUREAU OF JUSTICE ASSISTANCE. *1996 National Survey of State Sentencing Structures.* Washington, DC: U.S. Bureau of Justice Assistance, 1998.

U.S. BUREAU OF PRISONS. *Correctional Institution Architecture and Design.* Washington, DC: U.S. Government Printing Office, 2002.

U.S. DEPARTMENT OF JUSTICE CORRECTIONS PROGRAM OFFICE. *State Efforts to Manage Violent Long-Term Offenders.* Washington, DC: U.S. Department of Justice Corrections Program Office, 1999.

U.S. GENERAL ACCOUNTING OFFICE. *Bureau of Prisons Health Care: Inmates' Access to Health Care is Limited By Lack of Clinical Staff.* Washington, DC: U.S. General Accounting Office, 1994.

U.S. GENERAL ACCOUNTING OFFICE. *Private and Public Prisons: Studies Comparing Operational Costs and/or Quality of Service.* Washington, DC: U.S. General Accounting Office, 1996.

U.S. GENERAL ACCOUNTING OFFICE. *Federal Offenders: Trends in Community Corrections.* Washington, DC: U.S. General Accounting Office, 1997.

U.S. GENERAL ACCOUNTING OFFICE. *Women in Prison: Issues and Challenges Confronting U.S. Correctional Systems.* Washington, DC: U.S. General Accounting Office, 1999.

U.S. GENERAL ACCOUNTING OFFICE. *Prisoner Releases: Trends and Information on Reintegration Programs.* Washington, DC: U.S. General Accounting Office, 2001.

U.S. NATIONAL INSTITUTE OF CORRECTIONS. *Sexual Misconduct in Prisons: Law, Remedies, and Incidence.* Longmont, CO: U.S. National Institute of Corrections, 2000.

U.S. NATIONAL INSTITUTE OF JUSTICE. *Policies, Processes, and Decisions of the Criminal Justice System.* Washington, DC: U.S. National Institute of Justice, 2000.

U.S. PROBATION OFFICE. *Requirements for Probation/Pretrial Services Officers.* Washington, DC: U.S. Probation Office, 2002.

U.S. SENTENCING COMMISSION. *1996 Sourcebook of Federal Sentencing Statistics.* Washington, DC: U.S. Sentencing Commission, 1997.

U.S. SUBSTANCE ABUSE AND MENTAL HEALTH SERVICES ADMINISTRATION. *Substance Abuse Treatment in Adult and Juvenile Facilities: Findings from the Uniform Facility Data Set.* Washington, DC: U.S. Substance Abuse and Mental Health Services Administration, 2000.

UTAH LEGISLATIVE AUDITOR GENERAL. *A Performance Audit of Utah's Juvenile Justice System: Report to the Utah Legislature.* Salt Lake City, UT: Utah Legislative Auditor General, 1999.

UTTING, DAVID AND JULIE VENNARD. *What Works with Young Offenders in the Community?* Essex, UK: Barnardo's, 2000.

VACHO, MARLA MARINO ET AL. "Women in Prison." *Forum on Corrections Research* 6 (1994): 3–48.

VAN NESS, DANIEL W. AND KAREN HEETDERKS STRONG. *Restoring Justice. 2d ed.* Cincinnati, OH: Anderson Publishing Company, 2001.

VAN VOORHIS, PATRICIA ET AL. "The Meaning of Punishment: Inmates' Orientation to the Prison Experience." *Prison Journal* 77 (1997): 135–167.

VAN WORMER, KATHERINE. *Counseling Female Offenders and Victims: A Strengths-Restorative Approach.* New York: Springer, 2001.

VANYUR, JOHN M. AND FRANK STRADA. "Moving toward a Comprehensive Drug Control Strategy in Prisons." *Corrections Today* 64 (2002): 60–62, 126.

VARDALIS, JAMES J. AND FRED W. BECKER. "Legislative Opinions Concerning the Private Operation of State Prisons: The Case of Florida." *Criminal Justice Policy Review* 11 (2000): 136–148.

VAUGHN, MICHAEL S. "Listening to the Experts: A National Study of Correctional Administrators' Responses to Prison Overcrowding." *Criminal Justice Review* 18 (1993): 12–25.

VAUGHN, MICHAEL S. AND LEO CARROLL. "Separate but Unequal: Prison versus Free-World Medical Care." *Justice Quarterly* 15 (1998): 3–40.

VAUGHN, MICHAEL S. AND LINDA G. SMITH. "Practicing Penal Harm Medicine in the United States: Prisoners' Voices from Jail." *Justice Quarterly* 16 (1999): 175–231.

VENEZIANO, CAROL, LOUIS VENEZIANO, AND ALLEN GILL. "Perceptions of the Juvenile Justice System among Adult Prison Inmates." *Journal of Offender Rehabilitation* 32 (2001): 53–61.

VENEZIANO, CAROL ET AL. "Differences in Expectations and Perceptions among Criminal Justice Officials Concerning Boot Camps." *Justice Professional* 13 (2000): 377–389.

VERNON, MCCAY, ANNIE G. STEINBERG, AND LOUISE A. MONTOYA. "Deaf Murderers: Clinical and Forensic Issues." *Behavioral Sciences and the Law* 17 (1999): 495–516.

VENTURA, LOIS A. ET AL. "Case Management and Recidivism of Mentally Ill Persons Released from Jail." *Psychiatric Services* 49 (1998): 1330–1337.

VERTONE, LEONARDO AND ROLF STROEBER. "The Correlation Between ADHD (Attention Deficit Hyperactivity Disorder) and Delinquency." *Kriminologisches Bulletin de Criminologie* 27 (2002): 5–32.

VIGDAL, GERALD L. AND DONALD W. STADLER. "Alternative to Revocation Program Offers Offenders a Second Chance." *Corrections Today,* 56 (1994): 44–47.

VIGILANTE, KEVIN C. ET AL. "Reduction in Recidivism of Incarcerated Women through Primary Care, Peer Counseling, and Discharge Planning." *Journal of Women's Health* 8 (1999): 409–415.

VIGORITA, MICHAEL S. "Prior Offense Type and the Probability of Incarceration: The Importance of Current Offense Type and Sentencing Jurisdiction." *Journal of Contemporary Criminal Justice* 17 (2001): 167–193.

VIGORITA, MICHAEL S. "Fining Practices in Felony Courts: An Analysis of Offender, Offense, and Systemic Factors." *Corrections Compendium* 27 (2002): 1–5, 26–27.

VIRGINIA DEPARTMENT OF CORRECTIONS. *Community Corrections Boot Camp.* Richmond: Virginia Department of Corrections, 2002.

VIRGINIA DEPARTMENT OF CRIMINAL JUSTICE SERVICES. *Report on Evaluation of the Richmond City Continuum of Juvenile Justice Services Pilot Program.* Richmond: Virginia Department of Criminal Justice Services, 1998.

VIRGINIA POLICY DESIGN TEAM. *Mental Health Needs of Youth in Virginia's Juvenile Detention Centers.* Richmond, VA: Department of Criminal Justice Services, 1994.

VITALE, JENNIFER E. ET AL. "The Reliability and Validity of the Psychopathy Checklist-Revised in a Sample of Female Offenders." *Criminal Justice and Behavior* 29 (2002): 202–231.

VITO, GENNARO F. "Developments in Shock Probation: A Review of Research Findings and Policy Implementations." *Federal Probation* 48 (1984): 22–27.

VOGEL, BRENDA. "Meeting Court Mandates: The CD-ROM Solution." *Corrections Today* 57 (1995a): 158–160.

VOGEL, BRENDA. "Ready or Not, Computers Are Here." *Corrections Today* 57 (1995b): 160–162.

VOLUNTEERS OF AMERICA, INC. *Volunteers of America.* Washington, DC: Volunteers of America, Inc, 2002.

VOLUNTEERS IN CORRECTIONS. *Volunteers in Corrections (VIC) Program.* St. Paul, MN: Volunteers in Corrections, 2002.

VON HIRSCH, ANDREW. "Proportionate Sentences for Juveniles: How Different Than for Adults?" *Punishment and Society: The International Journal of Penology* 3 (2001): 221–236.

WACQUANT, LOIC. "The Penalization of Poverty and the Rise of Neo-Liberalism." *European Journal on Criminal Policy and Research* 9 (2001): 401–412.

WAID, COURTNEY A. AND CARL B. CLEMENTS. "Correctional Facility Design: Past, Present, and Future." *Corrections Compendium* 26 (2001): 1–5, 25–29.

WAITE, ROBERT G. *From Penitentiary to Reformatory . . . The Road to Prison Reform—New South Wales, Ireland, and Elmira, New York, 1840–1970.* Westport, CT: Greenwood Press, 1993.

WALEY-COHEN, JOANNA. *Exile in Mid-Qing China: Banishment to Xinjiang, 1758–1820.* New Haven, CT: Yale University Press, 1991.

WALGRAVE, L. "Restorative Justice or Penal Law? Duet or Duel?" *Justitiele Verkenningen* 27 (2001): 97–109.

WALKER, S. ANNE. "Alston Wilkes Society: South Carolina Volunteer Agency Plays Vital Role in Corrections." *Corrections Today* 55 (1993): 94–100.

WALSH, ANTHONY. *Correctional Assessment, Casework and Counseling.* 2d ed. Lanham, MD: American Correctional Association, 1997.

WALSH, ARLENE. "Jail: The First Link in Our Chain of Collaboration." *American Jails* 12 (1998): 51–59.

WALTERS, GLENN D. "Short-Term Outcome of Inmates Participating in the Lifestyle Change Program." *Criminal Justice and Behavior* 26 (1999): 322–337.

WALTERS, GLENN D. "Revised Validity Scales for the Psychological Inventory of Criminal Thinking Styles (PICTS)." *Journal of Offender Rehabilitation* 32 (2001): 1–13.

WALTERS, GLENN D. AND WILLIAM N. ELLIOTT. "Predicting Release and Disciplinary Outcome with the Psychological Inventory of Criminal Thinking Styles: Female Data." *Legal and Criminological Psychology* 4 (1999): 15–21.

WALTERS, GLENN D. ET AL. "The Choice Program: A Comprehensive Residential Treatment Program for Drug Involved Offenders." *International Journal of Offender Therapy and Comparative Criminology* 36 (1992): 21–29.

WALTERS, STEPHEN. "Changing the Guard: Male Correctional Officers' Attitudes Toward Women as Co-Workers." *Journal of Offender Rehabilitation* 20 (1993a): 47–60.

WALTERS, STEPHEN. "Gender, Job Satisfaction, and Correctional Officers: A Comparative Analysis." *Justice Professional* 7 (1993b): 23–33.

WALTERS, STEPHEN. "The Determinants of Job Satisfaction among Canadian and American Correctional Officers." *Journal of Crime and Justice* 19 (1996): 145–158.

WALTZ, EMILY AND MIKE MONTGOMERY. "Fast-Track Construction in the Face of State Budget Cuts." *Corrections Today* 65 (2003): 104–107.

WARD, ANN AND JOHN DOCKERILL. "The Predictive Accuracy of the Violent Offender Treatment Program Risk

Assessment Scale." *Criminal Justice and Behavior* 26 (1999): 125–140.

WARD, DAVID A. AND GENE G. KASSEBAUM. *Women's Prison: Sex and Social Structure.* Chicago, IL: Aldine, 1965.

WASHINGTON, JEFFREY. "ACA Revaluates Small Jail Standards." *Corrections Today* 45 (1987): 15.

WATTERSON, KATHRYN. *Women in Prison: Inside the Concrete Womb.* Rev. ed. Boston: Northeastern University Press, 1996.

WATTS, J.C. JR. "Unleashing the Armies of Compassion." *Corrections Today* 62 (2002): 82–84.

WEATHERBURN, DON AND JOANNE BAKER. "Transient Offenders in the 1996 Secondary School Survey: A Cautionary Note on Juvenile Justice Diversion." *Current Issues in Criminal Justice* 13(2001): 60–73.

WEBB, DENNIS AND SONNY ALICIE. "Tactical Response Team." *American Jails* 7 (1994): 15–19.

WEBER, DONALD E. AND WILLIAM H. BURKE. "An Alternative Approach to Treating Delinquent Youth." *Residential Group Care and Treatment,* 3 (1986): 65–86.

WEEDON, JOEY R. "The Role of Jails Is Growing in the Community." *Corrections Today* 65 (2003): 18.

WEISHEIT, RALPH AND SUE MAHAN. *Women, Crime and Justice.* Cincinnati, OH: Anderson, 1988.

WEISS, JOSHUA M. "Idiographic Use of the MMPI-2 in the Assessment of Dangerousness among Incarcerated Felons." *International Journal of Offender Therapy and Comparative Criminology* 44 (2000): 70–83.

WELCH, MICHAEL. "The Correctional Response to Prisoners with HIV/AIDS: Morality, Metaphors, and Myths." *Social Pathology: A Journal of Reviews* 6 (2000): 121–142.

WELCH, MICHAEL AND DANIELLE GUNTHER. "Jail Suicide and Prevention: Lessons from Litigation." *Crisis Intervention and Time Limited Treatment* 3 (1997a): 229–244.

WELCH, MICHAEL AND DANIELLE GUNTHER. "Jail Suicide under Legal Scrutiny: An Analysis of Litigation and Its Implications for Policy." *Criminal Justice Policy Review* 8 (1997b): 75–97.

WELLS, DAVE AND TIM BRENNAN. "The Michigan Classification Project: Jail Inmate Classification System." *American Jails* 6 (1992): 59–62.

WELLS, DAVE AND TIM BRENNAN. "Designing and Selecting Automated Jail Management and Classification Information Systems." *American Jails* 11 (1997): 56–59.

WELLS, DORIS T. "Reducing Stress for Officers and Their Families." *Corrections Today* 65 (2003): 24–25.

WELSH, WAYNE N. "Changes in Arrest Policies as a Result of Court Orders against County Jails." *Justice Quarterly* 10 (1993a): 89–120.

WELSH, WAYNE N. "Ideologies and Incarceration: Legislator Attitudes toward Jail Overcrowding." *Prison Journal* 73 (1993b): 46–71.

WEST, ANGELA D. "HIV/AIDS Education for Latina Inmates: The Delimiting Impact of Culture on Prevention Efforts." *Prison Journal* 81 (2001): 20–41.

WEST, ANGELA D. AND RANDY MARTIN. "Perceived Risk of AIDS among Prisoners Following Educational Intervention." *Journal of Offender Rehabilitation* 32 (2000): 75–104.

WESTERN, BRUCE, JEFFREY R. KLING, AND DAVID F. WEIMAN. "The Labor Market Consequences of Incarceration." *Crime and Delinquency* 47 (2001): 410–427.

WESTERVELT, SAUNDRA D. AND JOHN A. HUMPHREY, EDS. *Wrongly Convicted: Perspectives on Failed Justice.* New Brunswick, NJ: Rutgers University Press, 2001.

WEST-SMITH, MARY, MARK R. POGREBIN, AND ERIC D. POOLE. "Denial of Parole: An Inmate Perspective." *Federal Probation* 64 (2000): 3–10.

WETTSTEIN, ROBERT M., ED. *Treatment of Offenders with Mental Disorders.* New York: Guilford Press, 1998.

WHEATMAN, SHANNON R. AND DAVID R. SHAFFER. "On Finding for Defendants Who Plead Insanity: The Crucial Impact of Dispositional Instructions and Opportunity to Deliberate." *Law and Human Behavior* 25 (2001): 167–183.

WHEELER, PAT ET AL. *The Woman Jailhouse Lawyer.* Unpublished paper presented at the American Society of Criminology meetings, Montreal, Canada, November, 1987.

WHITE, AHMED A. "Rule of Law and the Limits of Sovereignty: The Private Prison in Jurisprudential Perspective." *American Criminal Law Review* 38 (2001): 111–146.

WHITE, ROBERT J., ROBERT J. ACKERMAN, AND L. EDUARDO CARAVEO. "Self-Identified Alcohol Abusers in a Low-Security Federal Prison: Characteristics and Treatment Implications." *International Journal of Offender Therapy and Comparative Criminology* 45 (2001): 214–227.

WHITEHEAD, JOHN T. AND MICHAEL B. BLANKENSHIP. "The Gender Gap in Capital Punishment Attitudes: An Analysis of Support and Opposition." *American Journal of Criminal Justice* 25 (2000): 1–13.

WHITFIELD, DICK. *The Magic Bracelet: Technology and Offender Supervision.* Winchester, UK: Waterside Press, 2001.

WHITMAN, CLAUDIA, JULIE ZIMMERMAN, AND TEKLA MILLER, EDS. *Frontiers of Justice, Volume 2: Coddling or Common Sense?* Brunswick, ME: Biddle Publishing, 1998.

WHITMORE, ROBERT C. "Tasks and Duties of Superintendents and Wardens in Pennsylvania." *American Jails* 9 (1995): 53–58.

WICKLUND, CARL. "Hope in Community Corrections: Why Bother?" *APPA Perspectives* 24 (2000): 16–22.

WIEBUSH, RICHARD G. *Evaluation of the Lucas County Intensive Supervision Unit: Diversionary Impact and Youth Outcomes.* Columbus, OH: Governor's Office of Criminal Justice Services, 1991.

WILKINSON, CHRISTINE, ALLISON MORRIS, AND JANE WOODROW. "Issues of Security and Safety for Women Released from Prison." *Security Journal* 14 (2001): 63–77.

WILKINSON, REGINALD A. "Offender Reentry: A Storm Overdue." *Corrections Management Quarterly* 5 (2001): 46–51.

WILLIAMS, CHRISTOPHER R. AND BRUCE A. ARRIGO. *Law, Psychology, and Justice: Chaos Theory and the New Disorder.* Albany: State University of New York Press, 2002.

WILLIAMS, MARIAN R. AND JEFFERSON E. HOLCOMB. "Racial Disparity and Death Sentences in Ohio." *Journal of Criminal Justice* 29 (2001): 207–218.

WILLIAMS, VERGIL L. AND MARY FISH. "Women's Prisons." In *Correctional Institutions,* 3d ed., edited by Robert M. Carter, Daniel Glaser, and Leslie T. Wilkins. New York: Harper and Row, 1985.

WILLING, RICHARD. "Exonerated Prisoners Are Rarely Paid for Lost Time." *USA Today,* June 18, 2002.

WILSON, JAMES Q. AND JOAN PETERSILIA, EDS. *Crime: Public Policies for Crime Control.* Oakland, CA: Institute for Contemporary Studies Press, 2002.

WILSON, SANDRA JO AND MARK W. LIPSEY. "Wilderness Challenge Programs for Delinquent Youth: A Meta-Analysis of Outcome Evaluations." *Evaluation and Program Planning* 23 (2000): 1–12.

WINCUP, EMMA. "Managing Security in Semi-Penal Institutions for Women." *Security Journal* 14 (2001): 41–51.

WINTER, BILL. "Does Corrections Need Volunteers?" *Corrections Today* 55 (1993): 20–22.

WINTER, MELINDA M. "County Jail Suicides in a Midwestern State: A Description of the 'Typical' Suicidal Act from 1980 through Mid-1998." *Corrections Compendium* 25 (2000): 8–9, 20–23.

WINTERFIELD, LAURA A. AND SALLY T. HILLSMAN. *The Staten Island Day-Fine Project.* Washington, DC: U.S. Department of Justice, 1993.

WINTERS-BROOKE, RAE AND HENNESSEY HAYES. "Assessing the Queensland Community Corrections Risk Needs Inventory." *Current Issues in Criminal Justice* 12 (2001): 288–305.

WITTE, ANN D. *Work Release in North Carolina: The Program and the Process.* Chapel Hill, NC: Institute of Government, 1973.

WITTENBERG, PETER M. "Power, Influence and the Development of Correctional Policy." *Federal Probation* 60 (1996): 43–48.

WITTENBERG, PETER M. "Leadership, Ethics, and Training: Why the Basics Count." *American Jails* 12 (1998): 57–62.

WOMEN'S PRISON ASSOCIATION. *A Study in Neglect: A Report on Women Prisoners.* New York: Women's Prison Association, 1972.

WOOD, PETER B. AND HAROLD G. GRASMICK. "Toward the Development of Punishment Equivalencies: Male and Female Inmates Rate the Severity of Alternative Sanctions Compared to Prison." *Justice Quarterly* 16 (1999): 19–50.

WOOD, WILLIAM T. "Multnomah County Sheriff's Office: Population Release Matrix System." *American Jails* 5 (1991): 52–53.

WOOD, WILLIAM T. "Special Management Inmates in Multnomah County." *American Jails* 9 (1995): 22–26.

WOOLDREDGE, JOHN. "Research Note: A State-Level Analysis of Sentencing Policies and Inmate Crowding in State Prisons." *Crime and Delinquency* 42 (1996): 456–466.

WOOLDREDGE, JOHN, TIMOTHY GRIFFIN, AND TRAVIS PRATT. "Considering Hierarchical Models for Research on Inmate Behavior." *Justice Quarterly* 18 (2001): 203–231.

WOOTEN, HAROLD B. "Public Safety, Crime Reduction, and Crime Prevention: Officers Get It, Will Managers Follow?" *Corrections Management Quarterly* 4 (2000): 34–40.

WORRALL, JOHN L. "Culpability Standards in Section 1983 Litigation against Criminal Justice Officials: When and Why Mental State Matters." *Crime and Delinquency* 47 (2001): 28–59.

WRIGHT, KEVIN N. "Reinventing Corrections." *Corrections Management Quarterly* 2 (1998): 1–88.

WRIGHT, KEVIN N. AND WILLIAM G. SAYLOR. "Male and Female Employees' Perceptions of Prison Work: Is There a Difference?" *Justice Quarterly* 8 (1991): 505–524.

WRIGHT, MARY C. "Pell Grants, Politics and the Penitentiary: Connections Between the Development of U.S. Higher Education and Prisoner Post-Secondary Programs." *The Journal of Correctional Education* 52 (2001): 11–16.

WYNN, JENNIFER. *Inside Rikers: Stories from the World's Largest Penal Colony.* New York: St. Martin's Press, 2001.

YEAGER, MATTHEW G. "Client-Specific Planning: A Status Report." *Criminal Justice Abstracts* (September 2001) 537–549.

YOUNG, VERNATTA D. "All the Women in the Maryland State Penitentiary: 1812–1869." *Prison Journal* 81 (2001): 113–132.

YURKANIN, ANN. "Trend toward Shock Incarceration Increasing among States." *Corrections Today* 50 (1988): 87.

ZACHARIAH, JACK K. *An Overview of Boot Camp Goals, Components, and Results.* Washington, DC: National Institute of Justice, 2002.

ZAITZOW, BARBARA H. "Doing Time: A Case Study of a North Carolina Youth Institution." *Journal of Crime and Justice* 22 (1999): 91–124.

ZASLAW, JAY G. "Young Women in the Juvenile Justice System." *APPA Perspectives* 23 (1999): 33–38.

ZEDLEWSKI, EDWIN. "National Institute of Justice's Community Corrections Portfolio: What's Hot, What's Not." *APPA Perspectives* 23 (1999): 12–14.

ZERILLO, JOHN P. "Build the Minds, Not the Bodies, of Dangerous Inmates." *American Jails* 11 (1997): 67–68.

ZHANG, SHELDON X. "In Search of Hopeful Glimpses: A Critique of Research Strategies in Current Boot Camp Evaluations." *Crime and Delinquency* 44 (1998): 314–334.

ZIEDENBERG, JASON AND VINCENT SCHIRALDI. "The Risks Juveniles Face: Housing Juveniles in Adult Institutions Is Self-Destructive and Self-Defeating." *Corrections Today* 60 (1998): 22–28.

ZIMMER, LYNN E. *Women Guarding Men.* Chicago, IL: University of Chicago Press, 1986.

ZIMMERMAN, SHERWOOD E., RANDY MARTIN, AND THOMAS ROGOSKY. "Developing a Risk Assessment Instrument: Lessons About Validity Relearned." *Journal of Criminal Justice* 29 (2001): 57–66.

ZIMRING, FRANKLIN E., GORDON HAWKINS, AND SAM KAMIN. *Punishment and Democracy: Three Strikes and You're Out in California.* New York: Oxford University Press, 2001.

ZUPAN, LINDA L. *Jails: Reform and the New Generation Philosophy.* Cincinnati, OH: Anderson Publishing Company, 1991.

ZUPAN, LINDA L. "This Jail Is for Rent: The Anatomy of a Deal Too Good to Be True." *American Jails* 6 (1993): 22–32.

Adult Agency Telephone/ Fax/Web Addresses

Alabama	(334) 353-3870	(334) 353-3891	www.agencies.state.al.us/doc/
Alaska	(907) 465-4652	(907) 456-3390	www.correct.state.ak.us
Arizona	(602) 542-5497	(602) 542-1728	http://adcprisoninfo.az.gov
Arkansas	(870) 267-6200	(870) 627-6244	www.state.ar.us/doc
California	(916) 445-7688	(916) 322-2877	www.cdc.state.ca.us
Colorado	(719) 579-9580	(719) 540-4755	www.doc.state.co.us/
Connecticut	(860) 692-7482	(860) 692-7483	www.state.ct.us/doc
Delaware	(302) 539-7601	(302) 739-8221	www.state.de.us/correct
District of Columbia	(202) 673-7316	(202) 332-1470	http://doc.dc.gov
Florida	(850) 488-7480	(850) 922-2848	www.dc.state.fl.us
Georgia	(404) 656-6002	(404) 651-6818	www.dcor.state.ga.us
Hawaii	(808) 587-1350	(808) 587-1282	www.state.hi.us/csd/psd/psd.html
Idaho	(208) 658-2000	(208) 327-7404	www.corr.state.id.us
Illinois	(217) 522-2666	(217) 522-5089	www.idoc.state.il.us
Cook County	(773) 869-2859	(773) 869-2562	www.cookcountysheriff.org/doc/
Indiana	(317) 232-5715	(317) 232-6798	www.state.in.us/indcorrection
Iowa	(515) 242-5703	(515) 281-7345	www.doc.state.ia.us/
Kansas	(785) 296-3317	(785) 296-0014	http://docnet.dc.state.ks.us/
Kentucky	(502) 564-4726	(502) 564-5037	www.cor.state.ky.us
Louisiana	(225) 342-6741	(225) 342-3095	www.corrections.state.la.us
Maine	(207) 287-4360	(207) 287-4370	http://janus.state.me.us/corrections
Maryland	(410) 585-3300	(410) 764-4373	www.dpscs.state.md.us/doc
Massachusetts	(508) 422-3339	(508) 422-3386	www.state.ma.us/doc
Michigan	(517) 373-0720	(517) 373-6883	www.state.mi.us/mdoc/
Minnesota	(651) 642-0282	(651) 642-0223	www.doc.state.mn.us
Mississippi	(601) 359-5600	(601) 359-5680	www.mdoc.state.ms.us
Missouri	(573) 751-2389	(573) 751-4099	www.corrections.state.mo.us
Montana	(406) 444-3930	(406) 444-4920	www.cor.state.mt.us
Nebraska	(402) 471-2654	(402) 479-5623	www.corrections.state.ne.us
Nevada	(775) 887-3216	(775) 687-6715	www.prisons.state.nv.us
New Hampshire	(603) 271-5600	(603) 271-5643	www.state.nh.us/doc
New Jersey	(609) 292-4036	(609) 292-9083	www.state.nj.us/corrections
New Mexico	(505) 827-8709	(505) 827-8220	www.state.nm.us/corrections
New York State	(518) 457-8126	(518) 457-7252	www.docs.state.ny.us
New York City	(212) 266-1212	(212) 266-1219	www.ci.nyc.ny.us/html.doc/home.html
North Carolina	(919) 716-3700	(919) 716-3794	www.doc.state.nc.us
North Dakota	(701) 328-6390	(701) 328-6651	www.state.nd.us/docr
Ohio	(614) 752-1164	(614) 752-1171	www.drc.state.oh.us
Oklahoma	(405) 425-2505	(405) 425-2578	www.doc.state.ok.us
Oregon	(503) 945-0920	(503) 373-1173	www.doc.state.or.us
Pennsylvania	(717) 975-4918	(717) 731-0486	www.cor.state.pa.us
Philadelphia	(215) 685-8201	(215) 685-8577	www.phila.gov/departments/prisons
Rhode Island	(401) 462-2611	(401) 462-2630	www.doc.state.ri.us
South Carolina	(803) 896-8555	(803) 896-3972	www.state.sc.us/doc
South Dakota	(605) 773-3478	(605) 773-3194	www.state.sd.us/corrections/corrections.html
Tennessee	(615) 741-1000	(615) 532-8281	www.state.tn.us/correction
Texas	(936) 437-2101	(936) 537-2123	www.tdcj.state.tx.us
Utah	(801) 265-5500	(801) 265-5726	www.udc.state.ut.us
Vermont	(802) 241-2442	(802) 241-2565	www.doc.state.vt.us/
Virginia	(804) 674-3119	(804) 674-3509	www.vadoc.state.va.us
Washington	(360) 753-1573	(360) 664-4056	www.wa.gov/doc
West Virginia	(304) 558-2036	(304) 558-5934	www.state.wv.us/wvdoc/
Wisconsin	(608) 266-4548	(608) 267-3661	www.wi-doc.com/
Wyoming	(307) 777-7208	(307) 777-7459	http://doc.state.wy.us

Case Index

Ake v. Oklahoma, 470 U.S. 68 (1985), 450

Atkins v. Virginia, 122 S.Ct. 2242 (2002), 452

Austin v. Pennsylvania Department of Corrections, 876 F.Supp. 1437 (11th Cir. 1991), 342

Avery v. Powell, 806 F.Supp. 7 (1992), 401

Baker v. State, 616 So.2d 571 (1993), 154

Baldwin v. New York, 399 U.S. 66 (1970), 638–639

Battle v. Anderson, 447 F.Supp. 516 (1977), 408

Bearden v. Georgia, 461 U.S. 660 (1983), 153–154

Bell v. Wolfish, 441 U.S. 520 (1979), 409, 423, 425, 459

Bettis v. Delo, 14 F.3d 22 (1994), 403

Black v. Romano, 471 U.S. 606 (1985), 153–154

Blackburn v. Snow, 771 F.2d 556 (1985), 405

Booth v. Maryland, 107 S.Ct. 2529 (1987), 81

Bounds v. Smith, 430 U.S. 817 (1977), 410

Bowling v. Enomoto, 514 F.Supp. 201 (1981), 541

Bressman v. Farrier, 825 F.Supp. 231 (1993), 401

Bryson v. Iowa Dist. Court, Iowa, 515 N.W.2d 10 (1994), 401

Burnette v. Phelps, 621 F.Supp. 1157 (1985), 456

California v. Lovercamp, 118 Cal. Rptr. 110 (1974), 590–591

Cannon v. State, 624 So.2d 238 (1993), 157

Clifton v. Robinson, 494 F.Supp. 364 (1980), 405

Coffin v. Reichard, 143 F.2d 443 (1944), 399, 458

Coker v. Georgia, 433 U.S. 584 (1977), 442

Conforti v. State, 800 So.2d 350 (Fla.Dist.App.Nov.) (2001), 156

Cook v. City of New York, 578 F.Supp. 179 (1984), 456

Cooper v. Pate, 382 F.2d 518 (1967), 403

Correctional Services Corporation v. Malesko, 534 U.S. 61 (2001), 377

Demosthenes v. Baal, 495 U.S. 731 (1990), 451

Douglas v. Travis, 737 N.Y.S.2d 165 (N.Y.Supp.App.Div.Jan.) (2002), 510

Duncan v. Louisiana, 391 U.S. 145 (1968), 638

Eddings v. Oklahoma, 455 U.S. 104 (1982), 671

Enmund v. Florida, 458 U.S. 782 (1982), 424

Escobar v. Landwehr, 837 F.Supp. 284 (1993), 403

Estelle v. Gamble, 429 U.S. 97 (1976), 407, 605

Ex parte Franks, 71 S.W.3d 327 (Tex.Crim.App.Dec.) (2001), 510

Ex parte Hull, 312 U.S. 546 (1941), 398, 413, 458

Ex parte Karstendick, 93 U.S. 396 (1876), 285

Ex parte Shores, 195 F. 627 (1912), 285

Fisher v. Winter, 564 F.Supp. 281 (1983), 408

Ford v. Wainwright, 447 U.S. 399 (1986), 450

Friedman v. State of Arizona, 912 F.2d 328 (1990), 404

Furman v. Georgia, 408 U.S. 238 (1972), 390–391, 434, 442, 493

Gagnon v. Scarpelli, 411 U.S. 788 (1973), 152–153, 506

Galvan v. Carothers, 855 F.Supp. 285 (1994), 408

Gardner v. Johnson, 429 F.Supp. 432 (1977), 456

Gates v. Rowland, 39 F.3d 1439 (9th Cir. 1994), 342

Gettleman v. Werner, 377 F.Supp. 22 (1974), 406

Glover v. Johnson, 478 F.Supp. 1075 (1979), 410, 575, 586–587, 617

Gomez v. State, 724 So.2d 1205 (Fla.Dist.App.Nov.) (1998), 153–154

Gregg v. Georgia, 428 U.S. 153 (1976), 390, 434–435, 442

Hackett v. United States, 606 F.2d 319 (1978), 426–427

Hanrahan v. Lane, 747 F.2d. 1137 (1984), 456

*Harris v. Thigpen,*941 F.2d 1495 (1991), 341–342

Hause v. Vaught, 993 F.2d 1079 (1993), 413

Hendrickson v. Griggs, No. 2C 84-3012 (N.D. Iowa, Apr.) (1987), 219

Holt v. Sarver, 306 F.Supp. 362 (1970), 395

Housely v. Dodson, 41 F.3d 597 (1994), 413

Hudson v. Goodlander, 494 F.Supp. 890 (1980), 541

Hudson v. Palmer, 468 U.S. 517 (1984), 405, 423

Hudson v. State, 42 P.3d 150 (Kan.Sup.March) (2002), 510

Hutto v. Finney, 98 S. Ct. 2565 (1978), 456

Inmates, Washington County Jail v. England, 659 F.2d 1081 (1980), 403

In re Gault, 387 U.S. 1 (1967), 637–638

In re Green, 669 F.2d 779 (1981), 390, 398

In re Winship, 397 U.S. 358 (1970), 638

Johnson v. Avery, 393 U.S. 483 (1969), 413–415

Kansas v. Crane, 122 S.Ct. 867 (2002), 515

Kansas v. Hendricks, 117 S.Ct. 2072 (1997), 514

Kennedy v. New York State Department of Correctional Services, (NYS Division of Human Rights, Case No. 3-E-5084-100365E (May, 1990), 541

Kent v. United States, 383 U.S. 541 (1966), 636–637

Lemon v. State, 861 S.W.2d 249 (1993), 158

Marcum v. State, 983 S.W.2d 762 (Tex.App.Feb.) (1999), 156

Martinez Rodriguez v. Jimenez, 409 F.Supp. 582 (1976), 456

McClafin v. Pearce, 743 F.Supp. 1981 (1990), 403

McCorkle v. Johnson, 881 F.2d 993 (11th Cir.) (1989), 403

McGautha v. California, 402 U.S. 183 (1971), 442

McKeiver v. Pennsylvania, 403 U.S. 528 (1971), 638–639, 641

McKnight v. State, 616 So.2d 31 (1993), 157

Medina v. O'Neill, 589 F.Supp. 1028 (1984), 376

Mempa v. Rhay, 389 U.S. 128 (1967), 152, 506

Milonas v. Williams, 691 F.2d 931 (1982), 377

Moore v. State, 623 So.2d 842 (1993), 154–155

Morrissey v. Brewer, 408 U.S. 471 (1972), 152–153, 465, 506–507

Moskowitz v. Wilkinson, 432 F.Supp. 947 (D.Conn.) (1977), 404

Munir v. Scott, 792 F.Supp. 1472 (1992), 404

Nolley v. County of Erie, 776 F.Supp. 715 (W.D.N.Y. 1991), 342

Novak v. Beto, 453 F.2d 661 (1972), 414–415

Owens v. Brierley, 452 F.2d 640 (1971), 456

Payne v. Tennessee, 501 U.S. 808 (1991), 81

Penry v. Johnson, 532 U.S. 782 (2001), 451–452

Penry v. Lynaugh, 492 U.S. 302 (1989), 450–451

People v. Bouyer, 769 N.E.2d 145 (Ill.App.April) (2002), 155

People v. Hipp, 861 S.W.2d 377 (1993), 156–157

People v. Lewis, 502 N.E.2d 988 (1986), 404

People v. Ramos, 48 CrL 1057 (Ill.S.Ct.) (1990), 187

People ex rel. Fryer v. Beaver, 740 N.Y.S.2d 174, (N.Y.Sup.App.Div.March) (2002), 510–511

Preiser v. Rodriguez, 429 U.S. 475 (1973), 416

Procunier v. Martinez, 416 U.S. 396 (1974), 400

Pugh v. Locke, 406 F.Supp. 318 (1976), 456

Quinones v. Nettleship, 773 F.2d 10 (1985), 426

Reynolds v. Sheriff, City of Richmond, 574 F.Supp. 90 (1983), 456

Rhodes v. Chapman, 452 U.S. 337 (1981), 409, 425, 459

Ruffin v. Commonwealth, 62 Va. (21 Gratt) 790 (1871), 391, 398, 506

Ruiz v. Estelle, F.2d 115 (1980), 407–408

Rummel v. Estelle, 445 U.S. 263 (1980), 424–425

Sample v. Borg, 675 F.Supp. 574 (1987), 403

Schall v. Martin, 104 S. Ct. 2403 (1984), 209

Security and Law Enforcement Employees District Council #82 v. Carey, 737 F.2d 187 (1984), 405, 424

Seling v. Young, 121 S.Ct.727 (2001), 514–515

Smith v. Montgomery County, MD, 643 F.Supp. 435 (1986), 456

Smothers v. Gibson, 778 F.2d 470 (1985), 405

Solesbee v. Balkcom, 339 U.S. 9 (1950), 450

Stanford v. Kentucky, 492 U.S. 361 (1989), 440–441, 668, 672

State v. Bergman, 147 CrL 1475 (Ind.Ct.App., 2nd District) (1990), 509

State v. Christian, 588 N.W.2d 881 (S.D.Sup.Jan.) (1999), 158–159

State v. Cofey, 36 P.3d 733 (Alaska App.Dec.) (2001), 511

State v. Hayes, 437 S.E.2d 717 (N.C.App.Dec.) (1993), 154

State v. Jimenez, 49CrL 1140 [NM SupCt] (1991), 110

State v. Lubus, 48 CrL 1173 (Conn.SupCt. (1990), 187–188

State v. Oliver, 588 N.W.2d 412 (Iowa Sup.Dec.) (1998), 156

State v. Tousignant, 43 P.2d 218 (Ariz.App.April) (2002), 157–158

Strickler v. Waters, 989 F.2d 1375 (1993), 413

Sypert v. United States, 559 F.Supp. 546 (1983), 426

Tarlton v. Clark, 441 F.2d. 384 (1971), 498

*Theriault v. Carlson,*339 F.Supp. 375 (N.D. Ga.) (1973), 403

Thompson v. Oklahoma, 108 S. Ct. 2687 (1988), 671–672

Thongvanh v. Thalacker, 17 F.3d 256 (1994), 401

Timm v. Gunter, 913 F.2d 1093 (8th Cir.) (1990), 541

Tisdale v. Dobbs, 807 F.2d 734 (1986), 403

Tucker v. Lambert, 26 P.3d 830 (Or.App.May) (2001), 511

Turner v. Safley, 107 S.Ct. 2254 (1987), 401

Udey v. Kastner, 805 F.2d 1218 (1986), 403

United States v. Arch John Drummond, 967 F.2d 593 (1992), 187

United States v. Bachsian, 4 F.3rd 288 (1993), 154–155

United States v. Cohen, 796 F.2d 20 (1986), 405

United States v. Dawson, 423 U.S. 855 (1975), 405

United States v. Edwards, 960 F.2d 278 (1992), 187

United States v. Insley, 927 F.2d 185 (1991), 187

United States v. Kremer, 280 F.3d 219 (U.S.2ndCir.Feb.) (2002), 158

United States v. Levi, 2 F.2d 842 (1993), 158

United States v. Mills, 704 F.2d 1553 (1983), 405

United States v. Muniz, 374 U.S. 150 (1963), 416

United States v. Noonan, 47 CrL 1287 (3d Cir.) (1990), 509

United States v. Stokes, 286 F.3d 1132 (U.S. 9thCir.April) (2002), 155

United States v. Wickman, 955 F.2d 828 (1992), 187

United States v. Zackular, 945 F.2d 23 (1991), 187

Vandelft v. Moses, 31 F.3d 794 (1994), 412–413

Voss v. Pa. Bd. of Probation & Parole, 788 A.2d 1107 (Pa.Commw.Dec.) (2001), 511–512

Wade v. State, 983 S.W.2d 147 (Ark.App.Nov.) (1998), 158

Walker v. United States, 437 F.Supp. 1081 (1977), 426

Walrath v. United States, 830 F.Supp. 444 (1993), 411, 513

Washington v. Harper, 110 S.Ct. 1028 (1990), 210, 212

Wilkins v. Missouri, 109 S.Ct. 2969 (1989), 440–441, 668, 672

Witherspoon v. Illinois, 391 U.S. 510 (1968), 441–442

Wolff v. McDonnell, 418 U.S. 539 (1974), 400–401

Woodson v. North Carolina, 428 U.S. 280 (1976), 442

Name Index

Abram, Karen M., 606
Abramsky, Sasha, 88
Acker, James R., 654
Ackerman, Robert C., 304
Acoca, Leslie, 614
Adams, William P., 633
Adamson, Christopher, 11–13
Adelman, Stanley E., 378
Administrative Office of the U.S. Courts, 75, 362, 416, 418
Aguirre, Adalberto, 80
Aguirre, Carlos, 324
Alarid, Leanne Fiftal, 4, 427, 630
Albrecht, Hans Jorg, 190
Alderman, Ellen, 425
Alexander, Bruce K., 42
Alexander, Rudolf Jr., 398
Alicie, Sonny, 235
Alleman, Ted, 577
Allison, Tom L., 350
Almada, Laurel, 249
Almvik, Roger, 292
Alozie, Nicholas O., 613
Altschuler, David M., 664
Amarasekara, Kumar, 49
American Correctional Association, 3, 13, 43, 57, 140, 143, 280, 285, 288, 308, 358–362, 371–372, 381, 492, 497, 524–525, 541, 586, 612, 645, 646
American Probation and Parole Association, 117, 562, 565
Amnesty International, 610
Anderson, Dennis B., 500
Anderson, James F., 219, 367, 407
Anderson, Sara L., 500
Angelone, Ron, 603
Anno, Jaye B., 423, 536, 608
Applegate, Brandon K., 212, 235, 331, 443
Applied Research Services, 87
Archambeault, William G., 381
Arizona Department of Corrections, 311, 320, 397
Armstrong, Gaylene Styve, 672
Armstrong, George, 8
Armstrong, Todd A., 650
Armstrong, Troy L., 664
Arnold, Charlotte S., 171, 561, 588
Arnold, Helen, 283
Arrigo, Bruce A., 43, 193, 443
Arrigona, Nancy, 324–325, 640, 652
Ashe, Marie, 48, 326
Associated Press, 8, 58
Atkins, Holly, 212, 235
Auburn, Tim, 563, 565
Augustine, Michelle Campbell, 667
Austin, James, 40, 219, 322, 470, 473, 491, 494, 503, 614, 630

Babyak, Jolene, 300
Backstrand, John A., 214
Backstrom, James C., 647
Bacon, Margaret Hope, 589
Badillo, Herman, 300
Bagaric, Mirko, 49
Baillargeon, Jacques, 358
Baird, S. Christopher, 659, 661
Baker, David W., 443
Baker, Joanna R., 263
Baker, Joanne, 652
Bakken, Timm, 606
Baldus, David C., 421
Balshaw, Kathy Biddle, 214, 340
Banks, Jerry, 556
Barak-Glantz, Israel L., 367–368
Barnhill, Maldine B., 214, 340

Barnes, Harry E., 466
Baro, Agnes L., 340
Baron, Stephen W., 644
Barrineau, H.E., III, 567
Barton, Shannon M., 537
Basta, Joanne, 557
Batchelder, John Stuart, 262
Batiuk, Mary Ellen, 325
Baumer, Eric P., 41
Baunach, Phyllis Jo, 593
Bavon, A., 112
Baxter, E., 305
Bayens, Gerald J., 261
Bayse, D.J., 563–564
Bazemore, Gordon, 18–19, 105, 123
Bean, Philip, 218
Bearn, J., 581
Bedau, Hugo A., 445–446
Beech, Anthony, 83
Beirne, Piers, 9–10
Beck, Allen J., 25, 201, 205–207, 209, 215, 217, 226, 249, 274, 292–294, 469, 480, 574, 576–577, 629
Becker, Fred W., 372, 376
Belbot, Barbara A., 390, 554, 595
Belenko, Steven, 45, 47, 341
Belfrage, Henrik, 319
Bell, Merlyn, 249
Bello, Stephen, 391
Benaquisto, Lucia, 331
Benda, Brent B., 651
Benedict, William Reed, 124
Bennett, Katherine, 289, 538
Benson, Bruce L., 181
Benson, Eric, 629
Berge, Gerald, 307
Bergsmann, Ilene R., 541
Bernardin, John H., 539
Berrueta-Clement, John R., 650
Bessette, J.M., 48
Beyer, Lorraine, 226
Bigger, Phillip J., 552–553
Bilchik, Shay, 599, 645
Birgden, Astrid, 43
Birzer, Michael L., 235
Bittick, John C., 205
Black, Henry Campbell, 113, 425, 565, 625, 632, 645
Black, Shannon, 534
Blackburn, Ronald, 336
Blanchette, Kelly, 306
Blankenship, Michael B., 447
Blauner, Peter, 552
Blevins, L. David, 119
Blinn, Cynthia, 593
Blomberg, Thomas G., 23, 330
Blount, William R., 218
Blow, Frederic C., 119
Blowers, Anita Neuberger, 233
Boari, Nicola, 335
Boccaccini, Marcus T., 449
Boe, Roger, 310–311
Boer, Alesandra, 43, 45, 47
Boer, Douglas P., 45
Boesky, Lisa Melanie, 630
Bohn, Martin J., 305, 308
Boies, John L., 53
Boin, R. Arjen, 338, 358
Bond, Emily L., 661
Bonn, Robert L., 552
Boot Camps Advisor, 148
Boothby, Jennifer L., 335
Bosworth, Kris, 651
Bottomley, A. Keith, 469
Bottoms, Anthony, 29–31, 190

Bouffard, Jeffrey A., 22–23
Bourgoin, Nicolas, 396
Bourque, Blair B., 150
Bowery, Margaret, 372
Boyd, John S., 239
Bradford, Michael, 650
Braithwaite, John, 106
Braithwaite, Ronald, 209
Brame, Robert, 639
Brandt, Gerri Ann, 651
Branham, Lynn S., 416, 421
Braswell, Michael C., 108
Breckenridge, James F., 112
Brenchley, Michael, 367
Brennan, Tim, 241–243
Brettschneider, Corey Lang, 6
Brink, Johann H., 43, 47
Brock, Deon E., 83
Brodsky, Stanley L., 449
Brody, David C., 407
Bronstein, Alvin J., 400–401
Brown, Larry K., 680
Brown, Mark, 305
Brown, Michael, 106
Brown, Randall A., 634
Brown, Robert Jr., 543
Brown, Sammie D., 423, 577
Brown, William B., 217
Browne, Deborah, 627
Brownfield, David, 648, 651
Boutellier, Hans, 142
Bryans, Shane, 538
Bryant, Kendall, 42
Bryl, Jason, 654
Buckley, Sue, 239, 243–244, 257
Buddress, Loren A.N., 188
Buffardi, Harry C., 276
Buigas, Rudy, 606–607
Burdett, Gary, 343
Bureau of Labor Statistics, 524
Burger, Tina, 58
Burke, Lisa Ouimet, 49
Burke, Peggy B., 16, 469–470, 501
Burke, Tod W., 526, 528
Burke, William H., 648
Burkhead, Michael, 82
Burns, Ronald, 150, 334
Burrell, William D., 78, 546
Burt, Grant N., 318
Burton, David L., 630
Butte County Probation Department, 547–548, 552
Butts, Jeffrey A., 322, 633, 636
Bynum, W.F., 581
Byrd, Terry G., 534–535
Byrne, Kenneth, 532
Byrne, Mitchell K., 4, 25, 319
Byrne, Stuart, 4, 25, 319

Cahalan, Margaret W., 204
Caldwell, Michael F., 641
Calhoun, Georgia B., 525, 659, 666
Calhoun, John, 668
California Administrative Office of the Courts, 84
Call, Jack E., 216, 409, 425
Callahan, Charlene M., 654
Cameron, Margaret, 663
Camp, Camille, 3, 31, 43, 45, 77, 86, 88–89, 124, 182, 216, 227, 229, 256, 259, 267, 289, 296, 298–299, 304, 306, 334–335, 338, 358–359, 361–362, 371–372, 375–376, 378–379, 469, 476–478, 480–482, 488–490, 492, 506, 522, 524, 526, 531–532, 537–538, 541, 547, 552, 555, 558, 579, 610, 613, 615, 648

Camp, George, 3, 31, 43, 45, 77, 86, 88–89, 124, 182, 216, 227, 229, 256, 259, 267, 289, 296, 298–299, 304, 306, 334–335, 338, 358–359, 361–362, 371–372, 375–376, 378–379, 469, 476–478, 480–482, 488–490, 492, 506, 522, 524, 526, 531–532, 537–538, 541, 547, 552, 555, 558, 579, 610, 613, 615, 648
Camp, Scott D., 526
Campbell, Justin S., 651, 653
Campbell, Ralph Jr., 549
Caraveo, L. Eduardo, 304
Carbonell, Joyce L., 305, 308
Carlson, Daniel P., 227
Carlson, Eric W., 557–558
Carlson, Joseph R., 605
Carlson, Peter M., 337, 351, 389
Carroll, Leo, 330, 411
Carroll-Burke, Patrick, 467
Carter, Diane, 528
Carter, Keith W., 334–335, 354
Cartier, Jerome, 22
Casarez, Nicole B., 79
Casella, Ronnie, 324
Casey, Karen A., 606
Casper, Marta, 263
Castellano, Thomas C., 633
Caulkins, Jonathan P., 31
Cavadino, Michael, 14
Cavett, Kate, 421
CEGA Services, Inc., 253, 303, 372, 481
Celinska, Katarzyna, 560
Center for Legal Studies, 555
Chamberlain, Patricia, 657
Champion, Dean J., 309–311, 321, 349, 642, 645
Chan, Wendy, 23
Chang, Semoon, 266
Chapman, Jack, 206
Cheeseman, Kelly A., 366, 536, 540
Cheesman, Fred, 400, 416, 418
Chen, Elsa Yee Fang, 57
Cherek, Don R., 611
Chermack, Stephen T., 119
Chesney-Lind, Meda, 332, 599, 665
Christensen, Gary E., 532
Christensen, Wendy, 632
Chuda, Thomas J., 368
Ciancia, James J., 124, 126
Cirincione, Carmen, 241
Clare, Emma, 406
Clark, Cherie L., 142
Clark, Cheryl L., 606
Clark, John, 554
Clark, Michael D., 633, 635
Clasby, Richard, 378
Clay, John, 467
Clayton, Susan L., 406
Clear, Todd R., 78, 168, 296
Clear, Val B., 78
Clement, Priscilla F., 645
Clements, Carl B., 338
Clemmer, D.C., 328–329, 331
Coffey, A.L., 115
Cohen, Stanley, 23, 330
Cohn, Alvin W., 236, 368
Cole, David, 53, 84
Cole, Richard B., 216, 409, 425
Coleman, James E., Jr., 671
Coleman, Ray, 262
Coll, Cynthia Garcia, 423
Colledge, Dale, 150
Collier, Virginia P., 336
Collins, Mary Elizabeth, 644
Collins, William C., 375
Colorado Parole Guidelines Commission, 320
Conley, James R., 259, 338
Conly, Catherine, 586, 588–589
Connecticut Board of Parole, 498
Connecticut Department of Corrections, 560
Connelly, Clare, 49
Connelly, Michael, 566
Conover, Ted, 535
Contact Center, Inc., 456

Contreras, Salvador A., 358
Conway, Peggy, 186
Cook, Sandy, 291, 296, 593
Cooke, Gerald, 668
Corbett, Ronald P., 168, 185
Corley, Mary Ann, 292
Cornelius, Gary F., 43, 201, 237–239, 244, 249, 252–253, 256, 261–262, 267, 558
Correctional Service of Canada, 372
Corrections Compendium, 370, 604
Corrections Digest, 86
Corrections Today, 89, 228–229, 403
Corzine, Jay, 124
Cosgrove, Edward J., 117
Costa, Jeralita, 559
Cotten, Oldenburg Niku U., 591, 608
Cottle, Cindy C., 652
Cowburn, Malcolm, 296
Craissati, Jackie, 83
Crank, John P., 632
Crawford, Adam, 107
Creese, Richard, 581
Creighton, Linda L., 600
Cressey, Donald, 329
Crew, B. Keith, 335
Crews, Gordon A., 351
Cripps, Janice E., 339
Crisanti, Annette S., 43
Crocker, Phyllis L., 448
Crofts, Nick, 226
Cromwell, Paul F., 4, 630
Cross, Marilee, 446
Crowe, Ann H., 666
Cullen, Francis T., 288, 443
Culler, Irving B., 532
Culler, Matthew, 532
Culliver, Concetta C., 588, 595, 605
Cumming, Georgia, 512
Cunniff, Mark A., 256
Cunningham, Mark D., 59, 455
Cushman, Robert C., 113

D'Alessio, Stewart J., 51, 53
Dale, Elizabeth, 427
Daley, Henry W.K., 256, 394, 399
Damphousse, Kelly R., 662
Dana, Davis, 41
D'Anca, Alfred R., 546
Danesh, John, 308
Danni, Kristin A., 76
Davidson, Howard S., 391
Davies, Susanne, 291, 296, 593
Davis, Carol Anne, 577
Davis, Ernest K., 581
Davis, H.C., 292, 427, 585
Davis, James, 609
Davis, Keith, 349–350
Davis, Mark S., 333
Davis, Robert C., 81
Davis, Simon, 111
Davis, Su Perk, 124, 603
Davison, Sophie, 43
Dawson, Roger E., 218
Dean, Charles W., 661
Dear, Greg E., 534
Death Penalty Information Center, 443–444, 447
DeBell, John, 608
Decker, Scott H., 332–334
DeCostanzo, Elaine T., 577
DeFrances, Carol J., 644
DeFronzo, James, 651
DeFuentes, Laura, 325
DeGroot, Anne S., 342, 595, 608
Deis, Jr., Donald R., 381
DeKalb County Court Services, 548
del Carmen, Rolando V., 418, 425, 534, 554–555
Dekleva, Kenneth B., 210
Delaware Statistical Analysis Center, 149
DelGrosso, Ernest J., 552–553
Dell, Colleen Anne, 310–311
Dembo, Richard, 565–566
DeMore, Rosemary, 110

Demuth, Stephen, 56
Dennison, Susan M., 43
Dickey, Walter J., 29, 38
Dickson, William J., 350
Dignan, James, 14
Dixon, Brian G., 23
Dixon, Frank A., 242
Doble, John, 559
Dockerill, John, 337
Dodge, Mary, 580, 604
Dodgson, Kath, 172
Doherty, Diana, 43, 47
Donnelly, S.M., 190
Dooley, Mike, 18–19
Dougherty, Donald M., 611
Douglas, Kevin S., 309
Dowdy, Eric R., 615
Draine, Jeffrey, 108
Drapkin, Martin, 236
Drowota, Claire, 377
DuBay, Tracy, 651
Dubler, Nancy N., 536
Duff, Anthony, 7–8
Duff, Kathleen M., 423
Duggan, Nancy, 558
Dullum, Jane, 170
Dumond, Doris, 661
Durham, Thomas W., 335
Durkee, Daniel, 232–233
Dutton, Donald G., 322
Dysart, Mary Dixie, 680
Dyson, Laronistine, 367, 407
Dziegielewski, Sophia F., 488

Early, Stephen T. Jr., 398
Easteal, Patricia, 291, 410
Eckberg, Deborah A., 556
Eckhart, Dan, 333
Edin, Kathryn, 427
Eggleston, Carolyn Rebecca, 281
Eichor, Perry, 236
Eisenberg, Michael, 324–325
Elis, Lori, 53
Ellenbecker, Mickey, 238
Elliott, Charles, 283
Elliott, William N., 39
Ellsworth, Thomas, 358
Ely, John Frederick, 490
Emerick, Jeanette E., 231–232
Enos, Sandra, 427, 593
Enterkin, Jill, 107
Enuku, Usiwoma Evawoma, 263
Epstein, Irwin, 644
Erez, Edna, 81
Ericson, Nels, 45
Esbensen, Finn-Aage, 651
Espelage, Dorothy, 651
Ethridge, Philip A., 267
Etter, Greg W., 235
Etzioni, Amitai, 350–351
Evans, Donald G., 168
Evans, Jeff, 304
Everett, Ronald S., 53, 84

Fader, Jamie J., 636
Faith, Karlene, 590, 616
Faiver, Kenneth L., 217
Falwell, Sally H., 648, 661
Farabee, David, 22
Farkas, Mary Ann, 366, 534, 538, 540
Farmer, J. Forbes, 300
Farr, Kathryn Ann, 579
Farrell, Amy, 483
Farrington, David P., 639
Farrington, Karen, 6
Faust, Thomas N., 258
Fazel, Seena, 308
Federal Bureau of Prisons, 284
Feeley, Malcolm M., 375
Feeney, Renee, 341–342
Feinman, Clarice, 609
Feld, Barry C., 322, 625, 639–640
Ferguson, Michael, 633

Feucht, Thomas C., 424
Finkelhor, David, 632
Finn, Peter, 264–266, 423
Fiorentini, Gianluca, 335
Firestone, Philip, 47
Fish, Mary, 594
Fisher, Bea, 292
Fisher, Bonnie S., 443
Fisher, Patricia M., 534, 537
Fisher-Giorlando, Marianne, 330, 534
Flaherty, Robert, 424
Flanagan, Timothy J., 289, 538
Flannery, Daniel J., 333
Fleisher, Mark S., 332–334
Fletcher, Beverly R., 577
Fliter, John Allen Jr., 358, 418
Florida Department of Corrections, 126,
    128–130, 132, 334–335, 425
Florida Department of Juvenile Justice, 650
Florida Joint Legislative Management Com-
    mittee, 595, 598
Florida Legislature, 376
Flynn, John M., 261
Flynt, Charles, 238
Fogel, David, 23–24
Folino, Jorge O., 43
Forde, David R., 644
Foster, Burk, 280
Foster, M.J., 87–88
Fowler, Carol R., 443
Fox, James Alan, 668
Fox, Stanford J., 646
Fradella, Henry F., 54, 400, 410
Fraietta, Frank, 19
Frase, Richard S., 88
Fraser, Mark W., 23
Freed, Peter J., 331
Freedman, Estelle B., 581
Freeman, Robert M., 375, 534
French, J.R.P. Jr., 350
Freng, Steve, 227, 534
Frew, David R., 558
Friendship, Caroline, 340
Fruchtman, David A., 78
Fuller, John, 108
Fuller, Lisa G., 595, 599
Fulton, Betsy A., 134, 546, 563
Funk, Stephanie J., 319
Furio, Jennifer, 577

Gabbidon, Shaun L., 378
Gaes, Gerald G., 378
Gaines, Michael, 184
Gainey, Randy R., 186
Gallagher, Patricia, 84
Galperin, Gary J., 210
Galvin, John J., 111
Gammon, Tor, 406
Gardner, Alan, 566
Gardner, Martin R., 396
Garland, David, 7–8
Garnier, Helen E., 662
Garrett, Judith Simon, 389
Garrison, Arthur H., 654
Gartner, Rosemary, 330, 593
Gartrell, John, 82
Garvey, Stephen P., 378, 430, 443
Garza, Pete Jr., 245, 248
Gauger, Glenn, 257
Geer, Tracey M., 310
Geiger, Jeffrey, 307
Gelsthorpe, Loraine, 29–31, 190
Genders, Elaine, 22
Gendreau, Paul, 336
Genovese, Joseph A., 244
Gerber, Jurg, 150
Gest, Ted, 54
Getty, Carol P., 50
Ghetti, Simona, 667
Gibbons, Don C., 214
Giblin, Matthew J., 654
Gido, Rosemary L., 368, 577
Gilbert, Michael J., 236, 267, 375, 379

Gill, Allen, 648
Gill, S. Cary, 603
Gilliard, Darrell K., 215
Gilling, Daniel, 141
Girshick, Lori B., 296
Givelber, Daniel, 51
Glade, George H., 212
Glaser, Brian A., 625, 633, 666
Glaser, Daniel, 504
Glaze, Lauren E., 3, 115, 135, 360, 473, 475,
    478–479, 522, 611
Glazer, Yale, 424
Glick, Barry, 651, 666
Godwin, Tracy M., 563
Goffman, Erving, 274, 291, 330
Goldkamp, John S., 504
Goldsmith, Herb, 651
Goldson, Barry, 667
Goldstein, Harold, 257
Goldstone, Jack A., 335
Goodale, Jeff, 598
Gorton, Joe, 53, 289
Gossweiler, Robert, 41
Gottfredson, Don M., 503, 555
Gottfredson, Michael R., 503, 555
Gould, Larry, 192
Gowen, Darren, 5, 186
Gowdy, Voncile B., 142
Grabowski, Michael, 206, 270
Grann, Martin, 319
Grant, Brian A., 481
Grasmick, Harold G., 600
Gray, Phyllis, 585
Greaves, Lorraine, 583
Green, Dana, 217
Greenberg, David F., 421
Greene, III, John J., 529–530, 545
Greene, Judith, 189, 471, 559
Greene, Susan, 599
Greenfield, Lawrence, 605
Gregoriou, Marcia, 319, 630
Griffin, Marie L., 230, 632
Griffin, Timothy, 338
Griffiths, Curt Taylor, 123
Grimes, Jennifer N., 188, 235
Gross, K. Hawkeye, 329
Gudjonsson, Gisli H., 336, 447
Gunther, Danielle, 248
Gurian, Michael, 241
Gursky, Dan, 290
Guzzi, Mark E., 382

Haddad, Jane, 212
Hadley, Michael L., 105
Haesler, Walter T., 500
Hagan, John, 171
Hahn, Paul H., 233–234, 646
Hairston-Creasie, Finney, 427, 593
Halford, Sally Chandler, 609–610
Halim, Shaheen, 447
Hall, Andy, 396
Hallett, Michael, 106
Halliman, Joseph T., 304, 379–380
Hamberger, L. Kevin, 607
Hamilton, Kate, 144
Hammett, Theodore M., 172, 244
Hampe, Gary D., 76
Han, Mel, 150
Hanbury, Barbara Michelle, 53
Haney, Craig, 599
Hannah-Moffat, Kelly, 306, 410, 599
Hannon, Lance, 651
Hansen, Brian, 647
Hansen, Evan, 237
Hanson, R. Karl, 47
Hanson, Roger A., 256, 394, 399, 400, 416, 418
Harding, Richard W., 376–377, 379, 382
Harju, Beverly J., 39
Harley, D.M., 105
Harlow, Caroline Wolf, 207–208, 212
Harm, Nancy, 593
Harmon, Talia Roitberg, 446
Harrell, Adele, 88

Harries, Keith, 130
Harrington, John, 421
Harris, Andrew J.R., 47
Harris, Patricia M., 150
Harris, Victoria L., 358
Harrison, Lana D., 483
Harrison, Paige M., 25, 206–207, 209, 215,
    217, 249, 274, 292–294, 574, 576–577, 629
Harry, Jennifer L., 473, 543
Hart, Cynthia Baroody, 397
Hart, Stephen D., 309
Hartwell, Stephanie, 498, 604
Hasaballa, Aida Y., 331
Hassell, Kimberly, 632
Haulard, Edgar R., 263
Hausser, Ginger, 405
Hawkins, Darnell F., 12
Hawkins, Gordon, 54, 57
Hayes, Colin, 226
Hayes, Hennessey D., 310, 648
Haynes, Milton, 300
Heckel, Robert V., 644
Heffernan, Esther, 594
Heikes, Joel, 51
Heilbrun, Kirk, 652
Heim, Ted, 232–233
Helfgott, Jacqueline B., 24
Hemmens, Craig, 296, 342, 509, 525, 534, 538
Hennessey, Michael, 218
Henrico County, 253
Henriques, Zelma Weston, 587
Henry, Gary T., 644
Henry, Mark A., 255
Hensley, Christopher, 534, 585
Hepburn, John R., 112
Herman, Susan, 80
Hess, Albert G., 645
Hewitt, Bill, 593
Hicks, Nancy, 289
Higgins, Scott, 88
Higgins-D'Alessandro, Ann, 257
Hill, Cece, 340, 585
Hill, Sarah M., 150
Hillsman, Sally T., 188
Hilte, Ken, 206
Hilton, N. Zoe, 306, 317
Hippensteel, Daryl, 24, 60, 88
Hirsch, Adam J., 10
Hirschel, J. David, 661
Hobbs, Gaynor S., 534
Hobbs, Gillian F., 212, 235
Hobler, Bruce, 263
Hodges, C. Mark, 376
Hodgson, Garrett, 640
Hoefle, Yvonne, 245
Hoffman, Peter B., 505
Hogan, Nancy Lynne, 537
Hoge, Robert D., 314, 639
Hogue, Todd, 336
Hohman, Melinda, 611
Hokanson, Shirley, 585–586
Holcomb, Jefferson E., 445, 447
Hollenhorst, Pamela Stiebs, 337
Hollin, Clive R., 314
Holloway, Linda, 192
Holman, John E., 263
Holt, John, 512
Holt, Norman, 135
Holtfreter, Kristy, 614
Homa, John, 642
Hood, Roger, 429, 443
Hope, Trina L., 662
Horn, Jim, 119
Horn, Martin F., 141, 325, 470
Horn, Rebecca, 607
Horton, Arthur, 634
Houchins, David E., 263
Houston, James G., 5, 86
Hovey, Marcia, 580
Howells, Kevin, 4, 25, 319
Howerton, Mike, 235
Hucklesby, Anthea, 331
Huff, C. Ron, 243

Huff, Corzine Lin, 124
Hughes, Robert, 276
Hughes, Timothy A., 469, 480
Hughes, Tom, 410
Hull, Kim A., 263
Hultberg, John, 367
Human Rights Watch, 326, 339–340, 446
Humphrey, John A., 446
Humphries, Kermit, 501–503
Hunter, Robert J., 207, 226, 235–236, 335
Hunter, Susan M., 423, 579
Hurst, Mallory M., 544, 558
Hurst, Timothy E., 544, 558
Hurtado, Aida, 599
Huskey, Bobbie L., 168
Hutchinson, Virginia, 233, 255–256
Hyams, Joe, 395

Illinois Department of Corrections, 17, 598
Immarigeon, Russ, 599
Inciardi, James A., 607
Ingley, Stephen J., 242
Irwin, John, 56, 213, 304–305, 328–331

Jablecki, Lawrence T., 123
Jackson, Jesse L., Jr., 445
Jackson, Jesse L., Sr., 445
Jackson, Joe, 284
Jackson, Yo, 651
Jacobs, James B., 421–422
Jalazo, Michael, 218
Jarjoura, G. Roger, 124
Jascor, Barb, 526, 528–529
Jeffries, John M., 427
Jiang, Shanbe, 330, 534
Jockusch, Ulrich, 47
Johnson, Kelly D., 219, 630
Johnson, Richard R., 124
Johnson, Robert, 330
Johnson, Sara L., 481
Johnson, W. Wesley, 170, 289, 363, 536, 538
Johnston, G. Wayne, 613
Johnston, Wendy, 181
Johnstone, Gerry, 106
Johnstone, Mark, 121
Jones, Mark, 150, 188, 554–555
Jones, John R., 227
Jones, Joseph F., 214
Jones, Michael A., 661
Jones, Rachel, 538
Jordan, Kathleen B., 591, 608
Joseph, Alfred, 84
Joseph, Gilbert M., 324
Josi, Don A., 426–427, 526, 533–534, 664
Jurich, Sonia, 263
Justice Education Center, Inc., 603

Kaden, Jonathan, 411
Kaiser, Doug, 245
Kakar-Sirpal, Suman, 651
Kamin, Sam, 54, 57
Karberg, Jennifer C., 25, 206–207, 209, 215,
   217, 240, 629
Karp, David R., 105
Kassebaum, Gene G., 112, 591
Katz, Lynne, 634
Kauffman, Kelsey, 421, 583
Kaufman, Gil, 212, 218
Kazura, Kerry, 427
Keeton, Kato B., 48, 244, 341
Keilitz, Susan L., 105
Keiser, George M., 471
Kellam, Leslie, 606
Keller, Ferdinand, 47
Keller, Robert, 422
Kellough, Gail, 61
Kelly, Brian J., 5, 182
Kelly, James, 427
Kelly, William R., 647
Kemshall, Hazel, 513
Kennedy, Caroline, 425
Kennedy, Leslie W., 644
Kennedy, Mary Baldwin, 149
Kennedy, Sofia, 172

Kenny, Dianna T., 45
Keogh, Timothy, 45
Kerle, Ken, 204, 219, 230–231, 237, 244, 541
Kett, Mary, 292
Keyes, David, 336
Keyser, Andrew, 424
Kibblewhite, Karen, 563, 565
Kiekbusch, Richard G., 526
Kilgus, Judith, 380–382
Kilty, Keith M., 84
Kim, Hal, 280
Kimball & Associates, Inc., L. Robert, 258
King, Roy D., 303
Kingery, Leroy V., 244
Kingree, J.B., 209
Kinkade, Patrick T., 289
Kirkish, Patricia, 666
Kirschbaum, Ellen, 586
Kirschner, Stuart M., 210
Klaus, Jon F., 546
Kleiboer, M.A., 190
Klein-Acosta, Donna, 598
Kling, Jeffrey R., 171
Klug, Elizabeth A., 453
Klugiewicz, Gary T., 236
Knauf, Keith, 446
Knight, Barbara B., 398
Knupfer, Anne Meis, 633
Koch Crime Institute, 143, 148
Koegl, Christopher J., 635, 654, 660
Kokorowski, Frank, 227, 534
Kolton, David J.C., 45
Konopa, Jessica B., 563
Konradi, Amanda, 58
Kooy, Thomas J., 260
Koper, Christopher S., 58
Koren, Lawrence, 232–233, 235
Koski, D.D., 262
Kovandzic, Tomislav V., 54
Kposowa, Augustine J., 332
Kramer, John, 611
Kreisher, Kristen, 599
Krienert, Jessie L., 333
Krmpotich, Sharon A., 556
Kronick, Robert F., 501
Kropp, Randall P., 309, 322
Kruittschnitt, Candace, 330, 593
Krumholz, Susan T., 124
Krzycki, Lenny, 445
Kulis, Chester J., 78
Kunzman, E. Eugene, 254
Kytle, Calvin, 668
Kyvsgaard, Britta, 170

Lacy, Michael G., 615
Lambert, Dorothy E., 501
Lambert, Eric G., 533, 537
Lambert, E. Warren, 501
Lambie, Ian, 664
LaMunyon, James W., 252
Lane, Scott D., 611
Lang, Michelle A., 341
Langan, Patrick A., 557
Langston, Denny C., 118
Lankenau, Stephen E., 406
Lappi, Seppala Tapio, 170
Larsson, Paul, 170
Laster, Kathy, 81
Latessa, Edward J., 112
Latta, Robert M., 556
Lattimore, Pamela K., 263
Lauen, Roger J., 285
Law Enforcement Assistance Administration,
   109
Lawrence, Richard, 544
Lea, Susan, 563, 565
Lederman, Cindy S., 634
Lee, Ria J., 652
Lee, Yoon Ho, 325
Lehman, Joseph D., 15–16, 22, 559, 562
Leiber, Michael J., 627, 668
Leon, Ana M., 488
Leonard, Elizabeth Dermody, 576, 587, 607
Leonardi, Thomas J., 558

Leonardson, Gary, 487
Leone, Matthew C., 289
Lerew, Cherise, 651, 653
Lerner, Jimmy A., 326
Leukefeld, Carl G., 112
Levander, Steve, 292
Levin, David J., 557
Levin, Jack, 668
Levine, Murray, 645
Levinson, Robert B., 529–530, 545
Libbus, M. Kay, 244
Liebling, Alison, 283, 525
Liebowitz, Stephen W., 267
Lightfoot, Calvin A., 19
Lindner, Charles, 113, 115, 552
Lipsey, Mark W., 663–664
LIS, Inc., 304
Listman, Shelly Johnson, 112
Locke, Hazen L., 213
Locke, Michelle, 58
Lockwood, Dorothy, 607
LoGalbo, Anthony P., 654
Logan, Gloria, 590
Logan, T.K., 396
Loney, Randolph, 447
Lord, Alex, 340
Love, Bill, 559
Love, Edgar J., 43
Lovegrove, Austin, 325
Lovell, David, 43, 358
Lowe, Craig A., 239
Loza, Fanous Amel, 309
Loza, Wagdy, 309
Lozoff, Bo, 108
Lucas, Weldon G., 213
Lucken, Karol, 187
Lucker, G. William, 181
Luginbuhl, James, 82
Lupton, Gary L., 210
Lurigio, Arthur J., 138, 470, 611–612
Lutze, Faith E., 140–142, 376, 407
Lynch, Mark, 662
Lynett, Elizabeth, 80
Lynn, Peter, 8

Maahs, Jeffrey R., 418, 425, 536
MacDonald, John M., 665
MacDonald, Marnie, 608
MacDougal, Colin, 663
MacKenzie, Doris Layton, 140, 142, 606
MacKinnell, Ian, 84
Mactavish, Marie, 368–371
Maghan, Jess, 303, 305
Maguire, Edward R., 632
Maguire, Kathleen, 31, 39, 49–50, 53, 57, 124,
   140, 172, 186, 188, 210, 215, 229, 236, 239,
   244, 388–389, 443, 488, 490, 574, 576, 611,
   625
Maguire, Mike, 648
Mahaffey, Katherine J., 48
Mahan, Sue, 544, 594, 604, 609–610
Mahoney, Barry, 107
Mailloux, Donna L., 310
Maiuro, Roland D., 112
Mall, Melissa, 533
Maltz, Michael D., 505–506
Manatu, Norma Rupert, 587
Mann, Coramae Richey, 595, 605
Marcus, David K., 48
Maricopa County Arizona Correctional
   Health Services, 244
Marion Superior Court Probation Department,
   120, 132–133
Marker, Nicole, 325
Markowitz, Michael W., 606
Marley, C.W., 481
Marquart, James W., 83, 214, 340, 342, 366,
   536, 540, 577, 608
Marsh, Robert, 406
Martel, Joane, 306
Martin, Jamie S., 427
Martin, Randy, 304, 315, 341
Martin, Sandra L., 591, 608
Martin, Susan E., 42

Martinez, Alma J., 51, 652
Martinson, Robert, 14
Maruna, Shadd, 310
Maruschak, Laura M., 39, 244, 340–341, 430, 433–434, 443, 470, 668
Marvell, Thomas B., 54, 86–87
Marx, Gary T., 185
Maschke, Karen J., 425
Maslach, Christina, 536–537
Massachusetts Department of Corrections, 599
Massachusetts Statistical Analysis Center, 640
Mathiesen, Thomas, 323
Maxey, Joseph W., 585
Maxwell, Christopher D., 576
Maxwell, Gabrielle, 105, 635
Maxwell, Sheila Royo, 576
May, Chris, 181
Mays, G. Larry, 205, 245, 642, 645
Mazerolle, Paul, 41, 319
McCabe, Kimberly A., 119, 336
McCabe, Marita P., 18, 513
McCampbell, Susan W., 268
McCarthy, J., 305, 319
McClellan, Dorothy Spektorov, 598
McClelland, Gary M., 606
McClusky, Cynthia Perez, 641
McCorkle, Jill, 607
McCorkle, Richard C., 149
McCoy, John, 330
McDonald, Douglas C., 189
McGaffigan, Richard P., 611
McGarry, Peggy, 29
McGrath, Robert J., 512
McIntyre, Tom, 268, 400
McKee, Geoffrey R., 667
McKenzie, Dean, 262
McLennan, Rebecca Mary, 284
Meachum, Larry R., 186
Mears, Daniel P., 635, 647
Meehan, Kevin E., 57
Megargee, Edwin I., 305, 308
Meisel, Joshua S., 658
Mello, Michael, 447
Memory, John M., 337
Menghraj, Suzanne, 427
Menifield, Charles E., 642
Mennel, Robert M., 645–646
Messenger, Sheldon, 330
Meyer, Cheryl L., 576
Miers, David, 107
Migliore, Gerry, 552
Miller, Amy, 330, 593
Miller, Arthur F., 488, 490
Miller, Jerome G., 23
Miller, J. Mitchell, 332
Miller, Lisa L., 317
Miller, Marc, 315, 318
Miller, Marilyn J., 416
Miller, Marsha, 263
Miller, Rod, 268
MIller, Susan L., 604
Miller, Tekla Dennison, 289, 562, 565
Mills, Darrell K., 535
Millson, William A., 481
Milovanovic, Dragan, 398
Mirchandani, Kiran, 23
Mitchell, Ojmarrh, 534, 660
Mlinarzik, Joerg, 106
Moke, Paul, 325
Monahan, John, 358
Monday Highlights, 258
Montana Legislative Audit Division, 481
Monterey County Probation Department, 548–549, 552
Montgomery, Mike, 259
Montgomery, Reid H. Jr., 351
Montoya, Louise A., 47
Moody, C.E. Jr., 54, 87
Moon, Dreama G., 577, 606, 608
Moon, Melissa M., 668
Moore, Adrian T., 299
Moore, Delancey H., 243
Moore, Estelle, 336
Moore, Kevin J., 657

Moore, Margaret A., 558–559
Morash, Merry, 614
Morgan, Kathryn D., 554
Morgan, Robert D., 537
Morris, Allison, 105, 586, 635
Morris, Norval, 315, 318, 322–323, 467, 470
Morris, Suzanne M., 218
Mortimer, Ed, 181
Morton, Joann B., 119, 236, 334
Moses, Marilyn C., 559
Motiuk, Larry, 17
Motiuk, Laurence L., 306
Motiuk, Michele S., 47, 257
Moyle, Paul, 372
Moynahan, J.M., 231
Mullen, Rod, 263
Mullings, Janet L., 366, 536, 540
Muraskin, Roslyn, 218
Murray, Christopher, 249
Murton, Tom, 395, 457
Musheno, Michael, 106
Myers, David L., 209, 641
Myers, Laura B., 587
Myers, Wade C., 644

Nadel, Barbara A., 593
Nathan, Pamela, 662
National Council on Crime and Delinquency, 557
National Institute of Corrections, 252
Nelson, Katherine, 241
Nelson, Timothy J., 427
Nesbitt, Charlotte A., 611
Nestrud, Judith T., 234
New Abolitionist, 397
Newell, Tim, 533
Newsweek, 303
New York State Division of Parole, 140, 492
New York State Division of Probation and Correctional Alternatives, 151
Nicholson, Robert A., 606–607
Niemeyer, Mike, 107
Nienstedt, Barbara C., 53, 84
Nink, Carl E., 380–382
Nissen, Laura Burney, 18–19
Norman, Bobby, 266
Norman, Michael D., 77, 213
North Carolina Department of Corrections, 133
Norton-Hawk, Maureen A., 118
Nugent, William R., 106
Nurse, Anne M., 648

O'Brien, Patricia, 470, 586, 611
O'Connell, John P., 171
O'Connor, Patricia E., 274, 291, 296
Office of National Drug Control Policy, 124
Ogan, Guy D., 587
Ogburn, Kevin R., 563–564
Ogilvie, Emma, 662
O'Gorman, J.G., 305
Ohio Department of Rehabilitation and Correction, 513
Okamoto, Duane K., 112
Okun, Peter T.M., 31, 204
Oldenettel, Debra, 634
Oldenstadt, Steven J., 248
Olson, David E., 120, 358, 611
O'Mahony, Paul, 467
O'Meara-Wyman, Kathy, 382
O'Neil, Melinda B., 444
Opata, Josiah, 400
Oraftik, Chuck, 262
O'Rear, Charles E., 526, 528
Oritz, Madeline M., 41
Orlando, Frank, 647
Ormrod, Richard K., 632
O'Shea, Kathleen A., 443
Osofsky, Joy D., 634
Ostermeyer, Melinda, 105
Ostrom, Brian J., 400, 416, 418
O'Sullivan, Sean, 326
Ousey, Graham C.,667
Owen, Barbara, 577, 590, 594–595

Pagani, Linda, 308
Page, Brian T., 539
Palmer, John W., 337, 391, 398–399, 416, 422–423, 583, 598
Palmer, Louis J., Jr., 443, 447, 449
Palomino, Al, 625
Palumbo, Dennis J., 106
Paranal, Rechelle, 427
Parent, Dale, 189
Parks, Evalyn, 557–558
Parrish, David M., 261
Parsons, L.B., 310
Pastore, Ann L., 31, 39, 49–50, 53, 57, 124, 140, 172, 186, 188, 210, 215, 229, 236, 239, 244, 388–389, 443, 488, 490, 574, 576, 611, 625
Patel, Jody, 190
Patel, Kalpana, 340
Patenaude, Allan L., 363, 524, 537
Paternoster, Raymond, 639
Patrick, Diane, 555
Patrick, Steven, 300, 406
Patterline, Brent A., 325
Paulsen, Derek, 534
Payne, Brian K., 186
Peak, Kenneth J., 232
Pearl, Natalie R., 501, 588
Pearson, Christy A., 537
Pease, Ken, 23
Pease, Michael, 494
Pedahzur, Ami, 23
Pelfrey, William V., 540
Pennock, George A., 350
Perez, Joseph F., 268, 400
Perkins, Robin E., 648
Perroncello, Peter, 261
Perrone, Paul, 650
Petersen, David M., 325
Petersen, Rebecca D., 150
Petersilia, Joan M., 16–17, 29, 57, 119–121, 123, 187, 192, 469, 480, 557, 648, 652
Peterson, Michele, 635, 654, 660
Petrocelli, John, 625, 666
Petty, Juleigh, 171
Peugh, Jordon, 45, 47
Peyton, Elizabeth A., 41
Phillips, Richard L., 311
Phillips, Susan, 593
Piehl, Anna Morrison, 475, 499
Pierpoint, Harriet, 559
Pilant, James Alan, 554
Pimlott, Sheryl, 585, 600
Pinard, Georges Franck, 308
Piquero, Alex, 41, 319
Player, Elaine, 22
Plummer, Charles C., 206, 233, 255
Poe-Yamagata, Eileen, 640–641
Pogrebin, Mark R., 240–241, 493, 604
Pojman, Louis P., 15
Polacsek, Michele, 110
Polaschek, Devon L.L., 23
Poletti, Patrizia, 84
Pollitt, Daniel H., 668
Pollock, Joycelyn M., 590, 613
Pollock-Byrne, Joycelyn M., 598
Pontell, Henry N., 248
Poole, Carol, 149
Poole, Eric D., 240–241, 493
Poole, Melissa J., 244
Porporino, Frank J., 538
Potter, Roberto Hugh, 243
Potts, Dennis W., 553
Power, Jacquelyn M., 171
Powers, Jodi, 258
Pratt, John, 305
Pratt, Travis, 338, 536
Prendergast, Michael, 22
Pretrial Services Resource Center, 105
Price, David, 525
Probation Association, 113
Prochnow, Jane, 651
Proctor, Jon L., 493–494
Pullen, Suzanne, 482, 659
Pulitzer, Curtiss, 257
Putkonen, H., 577

Putnam, Mark L., 350
Puzzanchera, C., 642, 663, 666
Pynes, Joan, 539

Quay, Herbert C., 310
Queensland Criminal Justice Commission, 405
Quinlan, J. Michael, 595
Quinn, James F., 192, 263

Rackmill, Stephen J., 186–187, 652–653
Rafter, Nicole Hahn, 16, 574, 580, 583, 599
Ramker, Gerald F., 120
Ranstorp, Magnus, 23
Rapaport, Elizabeth, 447
Rapoza, Samantha, 150
Rasmussen, David W., 181
Rasmussen, Kirsten, 292
Raven, B., 350
Ray, Kenneth A., 382
Reckless, Walter C., 41
Reddington, Frances P., 219, 625
Redlich, Allison D., 667
Reed, Tom, 640
Reid, Gary, 226
Reidy, Thomas J., 59, 455
Reiman, Jeffrey, 15
Reisig, Michael D., 325, 614
Reiss, Albert J. Jr., 607
Reiss, David, 210
Reitzel, Lorraine R., 39
Renzema, Marc, 483
Renzetti, Claire M., 53
Research and Evaluation Associates, Inc., 660
Retford, Mike, 343
Rex, Sue, 29–31, 190
Reynolds, Carl, 408, 456–457
Rhine, Edward E., 362, 651
Richards, Stephen C., 332
Richie, Beth E., 172, 607, 611
Richman, Jack M., 23
Rideau, Wilbert, 280
Riechers, Lisa, 324–325
Rion, Sharon Johnson, 308
Rison, Richard Hall, 595
Riveland, Chase, 15, 303
Rivkind, Nina, 445, 453
Rizzo, Elaine, 526, 528
Roberts, Albert R., 202, 236, 607
Roberts, Cheryl, 172
Roberts, John W., 7, 11, 14, 281, 305, 307, 311
Robertson, James E., 406
Robins, Arthur J., 577
Robinson, David, 538
Robinson, Gwen, 118, 170
Robinson, Kenneth, 111
Roethlisberger, Fritz J., 350
Rogers, Joseph W., 549
Rogers, Richard, 80, 640
Rogers, Robert, 277–278
Rogosky, Thomas, 315
Rohrbach, Louise Ann, 625
Rokach, Ami, 339
Roleff, Tamara L., 388
Rolison, Garry L., 577
Rolland, Mike, 335
Roman, John, 88
Romano, Stephen J., 235
Rosazza, Thomas A., 234
Rose, Winfield H., 642
Rosenblatt, Elihu, 15
Ross, Darrell L., 150, 188, 410
Ross, Jeffrey Ian, 332
Ross, Toby, 642
Roth, Jeffrey A., 58, 607
Rothman, David J., 30
Roulet, Sister Elaine, 600–602
Rountree, Pamela Wilcox, 324
Roush, David W., 661
Roy, Sudipto, 106, 180, 185–186, 188, 235,
  658–659
Rubin, Edward L., 375
Ruck, Martin D., 635, 654
Runda, John C., 362
Rush, Jeffrey, 332

Russell, Betty G., 423, 602
Russell, Brenda, 651
Russell, Jeanne, 606–607
Russo, Joe, 182–183
Rutland, Sandra, 585
Ryan, Timothy, 206, 233, 255

Sabbatine, Ray, 321–322
Safran, David A., 233
Salekin, Randall T., 640
Salerno, Anthony W., 663
Saltzman, Linda E., 243
Salvatore, Ricardo D., 324
Sanborn, Joseph B., Jr., 636
Santa Clara Superior Court, 103–104
Sapp, Allen D., 118
Sarat, Austin, 447–448
Sarre, Rick, 4, 14–16
Savarese, Margaret R., 113, 115
Sawicki, Donna Rau, 636
Saylor, William G., 378, 526, 543
Scarce, Michael, 339
Schaeffer, Beatrix, 637
Scheb, John M., 414
Scheb, John M., Jr., 414
Scheela, Rochelle A., 18
Schellman, George, 216
Schiff, Mara, 105
Schippers, Gerard M., 325
Schiraldi, Vincent, 56, 304–305, 471, 666
Schlank, Anita, 87
Schlossman, Steven, 262
Schmalleger, Frank, 12–13
Schmidt, Annesley K., 172
Schmidt, Rik, 648
Schneider, Michael E., 283, 291
Schneider, Ursula, 335
Scholes, Helen, 577
Schrag, Clarence, 329
Schram, Donna D., 599
Schulz, Holger, 644
Schumacker, Randall E., 500
Schwaner, Shawn L., 505
Schwartz, Ira M., 644
Schwartz, Meryl, 471
Scott, Gregory, 332
Sechrest, Dale K., 113, 426–427, 526,
  533–534, 664
Sechrest, Lee, 310
Segars, Lance, 611
Seidler, Katie, 45
Selke, William, 184, 331, 566
Senese, Jeffrey D., 206
Seng, Magnus, 133, 555, 611
Serin, Ralph C., 310
Sexton, Timothy S., 207, 226, 235–236, 335
Seyko, Ronald J., 106
Seymour, Anne, 559
Seymour, Cynthia B., 427, 593, 599
Shaffer, David R., 210
Shaffer, Deborah Koetzle, 112
Shane-DuBow, Sandra, 53
Shapiro, Brian, 218
Shapiro, Bruce, 445
Shapiro, Carol, 471, 539
Sharbaro, Edward, 422
Shatz, Steven F., 445, 453
Shaw, James W., 142
Shaw, Margaret, 306, 599
Shaw, Michelle, 111
Shearer, Robert A., 370, 553, 566, 587
Shelden, Randall G., 217
Shichor, David, 107, 236, 267, 375, 379
Shine, John, 315
Shook, Chadwick L., 375, 398–399, 405, 407
Shumaker, David M., 644, 667
Sickmund, Melissa, 640–641, 646–647
Sidebottom, Kevin, 235
Sideman, Lawrence M., 586
Siefert, Kristine, 585, 600
Sigler, Robert T., 78, 375, 398–399, 405,
  407
Sigurdson, Herbert R., 238
Sigurdsson, Jon Fridik, 447

Silver, Eric, 317
Silvertstein, Martin, 310
Simmons, Janet L., 306, 317
Simonet, L. John, 210, 217
Simourd, David J., 314
Simourd, Linda, 538
Simpson, Gary J., 430, 443
Simpson, Mark, 315, 485
Sims, Barbara, 278, 368, 525, 533–534, 536,
  540, 545
Singh, Debbie, 18
Skolnick, Jerome, 9
Slabonik, Maria L., 545
Slate, Risdon N., 363, 536, 538
Slatkin, Art, 228, 235
Slavick, Peggy, 149
Slawson, Donna B., 442
Sluder, Richard D., 118, 370, 553, 555
Small, Shawn E., 546
Smandych, Russell C., 279
Smith, Albert G., 553
Smith, Barbara E., 81
Smith, Christopher E., 399
Smith, Lamar, 644
Smith, Linda G., 39
Smith, Robert R., 243
Smith, R.P.P., 376
Smith, Walter R., 530–531
Smykla, John Ortiz, 12–13, 184, 261, 468,
  566, 608–610
Snell, Clete, 270
Snell, Tracy L., 206, 430, 433–434, 443, 470,
  668
Snellenberg, Sidney C., 443
Snyder, Howard N., 627, 629, 639–641, 666
Snyder, T. Richard, 324, 467
Soderlund, Curt, 190
Solomon, Phyllis, 108
Solotaroff, Ivan, 276, 427, 443
Sorensen, Jon R., 83, 455
Souryal, Claire, 85, 140, 142
South Carolina State Reorganization
  Commission, 141
Spalek, Basia, 332
Spapens, A.C., 106
Spelman, William, 118
Spiegel, Allen D., 279
Spiegel, Marc B., 279
Spierenburg, Pieter, 203
Spillane, Joseph, 262
Sprengelmeyer, Peter G., 657
Stack, William R., 242
Stadler, Donald W., 507
Stalans, Loretta J., 133, 555, 644
Staton, Michele, 493
Steadman, Henry J., 218
Steffek, Trisha, 456–457
Steffensmeier, Darrell J., 56, 611
Stein, Judith A., 662
Steinberg, Annie G., 47
Steinhart, David J., 563
Stevens, Dennis J., 368, 593
Stewart, Lee, 581
St. Gerard, Vanessa, 336–337
Stiebs, Pam Hollenhorst, 38
Stiles, Beverly L., 447
Stinchcomb, Jeanne B., 24, 60, 88, 150,
  528–530, 540, 545
Stohr, Mary K., 296, 299, 525, 534, 538, 544
Stolzenberg, Lisa, 51, 53
Stone, Susan, 134
Stoughton, Don, 377
Stougt, Cori, 43
Strada, Frank, 42
Strange, Carolyn, 8
Streib, Victor L., 644, 668
Streifel, Cathy, 611
Stroeber, Rolf, 647
Strom, Kevin J., 644
Strong, Karen Heetderks, 105
Sturges, Judith E., 227, 639, 652
Stutler, Missy, 598
Sullivan, Dennis, 106
Sullivan, Eileen, 241

Sullivan, Judy, 377
Sundt, Jody L., 470
Surette, Ray, 664
Suris, Alina, 253
Sutherland, Edwin H., 41
Swanson, Cheryl, 48, 244, 341
Swanson, Jeffrey W., 17
Swartz, James A., 138
Sweet, Joseph, 658
Sykes, Gresham, 329–331
Szostak, Edward W., 240
Szymanski, Linda, 642

Talty, Richard B., 124, 126
Tartaglini, Aldo J., 233
Tarver, Marsha, 410, 470
Taxman, Faye S., 22–23, 53
Taylor, Jon Marc, 303
Taylor, Mark Lewis, 445
Taylor, Pamela J., 43
Taylor, Terrance J., 632
Taymans, Julianna M., 292
Tchaikovsky, Chris, 593
Teeters, Negley D., 466
Temin, Carolyn Engel, 579, 583
Tengstrom, Anders, 319
Teplin, Linda A., 606
Terry, III, W. Clinton, 150
Tewksbury, Richard A., 262
Texas Criminal Justice Policy Council, 472, 494
Texas Department of Criminal Justice, 123, 133
Thies, Jeanie, 637
Thigpen, Morris L., 423
Thomas, Michael, 204
Thomas, R. Murray, 6
Thomas, Wayne P., 336
Thompson, Joel, 205, 245
Thompson, Kevin, 648, 651
Thornton, David, 340
Thornton, Robert L., 135
Tiefenwerth, Thomas J., 239
Tierney, David W., 18, 513
Tifft, Larry, 106
Tillman, Jack S., 266
Tims, Frank, 112
Tischler, Eric, 630
Tobolowsky, Peggy M., 263
Toch, Hans, 337, 363, 366–367, 370–371, 456
Toepell, Andrea Riesch, 583
Tong, Virginia M., 268, 400
Tonry, Michael, 84, 88, 144, 190, 193, 614
Topham, James, 277
Torbet, Patricia McFall, 642
Torres, Sam, 546, 556
Townsend, Vincent, 236
Tracy, Sarah J., 538
Traskman, Per Ole, 170
Travis, Jeremy, 472
Trevathan, Joseph T., 268
Triplet, Rush, 642
Trounstine, Jean, 604
Tsou, Jonathan Y., 42
Tsunokai, Glenn T., 332
Tubiak, Christine, 488
Tunis, Sandra, 42
Turnbull, Paul J., 41
Turpin-Petrosino, Carolyn, 494
Twill, Sarah E., 488–489

U.K. Home Office, 6
Ulmer, Jeffrey T., 483, 485, 487
Umbreit, Mark S., 191
Underwood, Lee A., 648, 661
Unger, Jennifer B., 625
U.S. Bureau of Justice Assistance, 50
U.S. Bureau of Prisons, 278
U.S. Code Annotated, 288, 566
U.S. Department of Justice Corrections
    Program Office, 303
U.S. General Accounting Office, 188, 472,
    593, 595, 606

U.S. National Institute of Corrections, 340
U.S. National Institute of Justice, 23, 30
U.S. Probation Office, 549, 552
U.S. Sentencing Commission, 363
U.S. Substance Abuse and Mental Health
    Services Administration, 630
Unnithan, N. Prabba, 615
Urratia, Maria Ines, 43
Useem, Bert, 335
Ustad, Karen L., 640
Utah Legislative Auditor General, 661
Utting, David, 4, 30

Vacho, Marla Marino, 588
Van Duin, Menno J., 338
VanHaveren, Richard A., 537
van Kalmthout, Anton, 190
Van Ness, Daniel W., 105
Van Ochten, Marjorie, 543
Van Rybroek, Gregory J., 641
Van Voorhis, Patricia, 300
van Wormer, Katherine, 586
Vanyur, John M., 42
Vardalis, James J., 372, 376
Vaughn, Michael S., 39, 141, 411
Veneziano, Carol, 40, 648
Veneziano, Louis, 648
Vennard, Julie, 4, 30
Ventura, Lois A., 210, 218
Vernon, McCay, 47
Vertone, Leonardo, 647
Vigdal, Gerald L., 537
Vigilante, Kevin C., 607
Vigorita, Michael S., 188–190
Virginia Department of Corrections, 147
Virginia Department of Criminal Justice
    Services, 182
Virginia Policy Design Team, 663
Vitale, Jennifer E., 614
Vito, Gennaro F., 140
Vivian, James E., 49
Vogel, Brenda, 411–412
Vogel, Ronald E., 363, 536, 538
Volunteers in Corrections, 560
Volunteers of America, Inc., 560–561
Von Hirsch, Andrew, 626

Wacquant, Loic, 6, 277
Wadman, Robert C., 77
Waid, Courtney A., 338
Waite, Robert G., 466
Waley-Cohen, Joanna, 7
Walgrave, L., 107
Walker, S. Anne, 562
Walker, Steve, 410, 470
Wallace, Harvey, 410, 470
Walsh, Anthony, 562, 565
Walsh, Arlene, 235
Walters, Glenn D., 39, 263, 299, 305, 488,
    490
Walters, Stephen, 538, 540–541
Waltz, Emily, 259
Wang, Hsiao Ming, 427
Ward, Ann, 337
Ward, David A., 591
Ward, Tony, 262
Warner, Sam, 607
Washington, Jeffrey, 205
Wasserman, Cressida, 80
Watson, Lisa, 608
Watterson, Kathryn, 593
Watts, Jr., J.C., 167
Weatherburn, Don, 652
Webb, Dennis, 235
Weber, Donald E., 648
Webster, Christopher D., 362
Weedon, Joey R., 206
Weiman, David F., 171
Weinrath, Michael, 82
Weisheit, Ralph, 358, 594, 604
Weiss, Joshua M., 39, 309

Welch, Michael, 39, 244, 248
Wellford, Charles, 85
Wells, Dave, 241–243
Wells, Doris T., 537, 539
Welsh, Wayne N., 248–249
West, Angela D., 341
West, Valerie, 421
Western, Bruce, 171
Westervelt, Saundra D., 446
West-Smith, Mary, 493
Wettstein, Robert M., 217
Wheatman, Shannon R., 210
Wheeler, Pat, 604
White, Ahmed A., 372, 382
White, Clem, 18
White, Robert J., 304
Whitehead, John T., 447
Whitfield, Dick, 503
Whitman, Claudia, 562, 565
Whitmore, Robert C., 371
Whitney, Scot, 307
Wicklund, Carl, 192
Wiebush, Richard G., 134
Wikberg, Ron, 280
Wilkinson, Christine, 331, 586
Wilkinson, Reginald A., 471, 473
Williams, Christopher R., 43
Williams, Jimmy J., 261, 608–610
Williams, John, 397
Williams, Marian R., 445, 447
Williams, Shanti, 49
Williams, Vergil L., 594
Willing, Richard, 453, 455
Wilson, David, 332
Wilson, Doris James, 469, 480
Wilson, James Q., 57, 648, 652
Wilson, Sandra Jo, 663–664
Wimbs, Vicki, 235
Wincup, Emma, 585
Winter, Bill, 558
Winter, Melinda M., 254, 308
Winterfield, Laura A., 188
Winters-Brooke, Rae, 310, 648
Witt, Ann Dryden, 263
Witte, Ann D., 483
Wittenberg, Peter M., 237, 356–357
Women's Prison Association, 589
Women's Rights Project, 340
Wood, Peter B., 600
Wood, William T., 210, 242, 257–258
Woodring, Tammy, 209
Woodrow, Jane, 586
Wooldredge, John, 31, 338
Wooten, Harold B., 546
Wordes, Madeline, 634
Worrall, John L., 410
Wortley, Scot, 61
Worzella, Charles, 189
Wright, Kevin N., 351, 363, 526, 543
Wright, Mary C., 263
Wynn, Jennifer, 332

Yarnold, Paul, 133, 555
Yeager, Matthew G., 558
Young, Vernatta D., 680
Yurkanin, Ann, 140

Zachariah, Jack K., 143
Zaitzow, Barbara H., 325
Zapf, Patricia A., 449
Zaslaw, Jay G., 660
Zedlewski, Edwin, 135
Zerillo, John P., 325
Zhang, Sheldon X., 150
Ziedenberg, Jason, 56, 304–305, 666
Zimmer, Lynn E., 541
Zimmerman, Julie, 562, 565
Zimmerman, Sherwood E., 325
Zimring, Franklin E., 54, 57
Zold, Phyllis Ann, 124
Zupan, Linda L., 216, 261, 364

Subject Index

ABC (At-risk Babies Crib), 635
Abolition of parole, 469–470
About Face Program, 148–149
Absconding, 478, 481, 615
  forloughs, 481
  women in ISP, 615
Absolute immunity, 554
ACA Code of Ethics, 530
Acceptance of responsibility, 59, 80
Accreditation of corrections officers,
  233–234, 255, 529–531, 546–547
Act 403 of 2001 (Louisiana), 87–88
Act to Regulate the Treatment and Control of
  Dependent, Neglected and Delinquent
  Children, 646
Actual injury rule, 413
Addams, Jane, 114, 646
Adjudicatory proceedings, 635–636
Adjustment to inmate life measures, 305
Administrative Office of the U.S. Courts,
  75, 115, 362
  functions, 75, 362
  probation, 115
Administrative release, 467
Administrative review of inmate claims, 457
Administration, 226–236, 289–290, 594–598
  jail, 226–236
  prison, 289–290
  women's prisons, 594–598
Admin max, 288
Admin max classification, 306–307
Adult Sex Offender Program (ASOP), 133
Advisory Commission on Intergovernmental
  Relations, 205
Afro-American Society, 330
Age disparities, 84–85
Agency, theory of, 565
Aggravating circumstances, 82–83, 442
  death penalty cases, 442
Aging inmates, 472–473
AIDS (Acquired Immune Deficiency
  Syndrome), 39, 47–48, 239, 243–244,
  340–342, 536, 589, 595, 608
  among jail inmates, 47–48, 239, 243–244, 340
  among state and federal prisoners, 340–342
  constitutional issues, 47–48, 244, 340–342
  female prisoners, 47–48, 340–341, 589,
  595, 608
  job risks working with infected inmates, 536
AIMS (Adult Internal Management System),
  310–311
Alaska Classification Form for Sentenced
  Prisoners, 311–313
Alaska Need Assessment Survey, 315–316
Alcohol-dependent offenders, 218
Alcoholics Anonymous (A.A.), 111, 244
Alston Wilkes Society, 562
Alternative dispute resolution (ADR), 29,
  105–106, 456
  inmate disciplinary councils, 456
Alternative Programs, Inc., 375
American Association of Law Libraries, 412
American Civil Liberties Union (ACLU), 13,
  445, 593
American Correctional Association (ACA),
  13–14, 205, 233–234, 239, 255–256, 281,
  382, 456, 467, 524, 529, 533, 546, 549,
  581, 583, 603, 611
  accreditation standards, 205–206,
  233–234, 239, 546
  formation, 13–14
  goals, 13–14
  history, 467
  inmate litigation support program, 456–457
  privatization, 382

American Correctional Association Division
  of Standards and Accreditation, 205
American Correctional Association
  Professional Education Council, 233
American Jail Association (AJA), 205–206,
  233–234, 242–243, 268, 524, 529, 533
  accreditation programs, 205–206, 233–234
  inmate safety, 242–243
  jail industries, 268
American Law Institute, 673
American Prison Association (APA), 13, 281
American Probation and Parole Association
  (APPA), 117, 533, 546
Americans with Disabilities Act (ADA), 257
Amnesty International, Inc., 13, 444–445, 610
Antecedents to Crime Inventory (ACI), 309–310
Anti-drug legislation, 293–295
  inmate population growth, 293–295
Appointment on merit, 349
Arcene, James, 668
Arizona Cost Model (ACM), 380–381
Arkansas prison scandal, 394–395, 397–398
Arrests, 40, 632–633
  juveniles, 632–633
Arizona Offender Classification System
  (OCS), 320–322
Asian gangs, 332
Assaults against POs, 552–553
Assessment centers, 539–540
Assize, 202
Attention deficit hyperactivity disorder
  (ADHD), 647
Augustus, John, 75, 77, 113, 117
Authoritarian model, 367
Automated management information
  systems (MIS), 243
Automatic waivers, 641
Avenues for civil legal remedies for
  inmates, 415–421
Ayran Brotherhood, 300, 332

Back-door solutions, 335, 472–473, 552
Banishment, 7–9
Barbarism and the death penalty, 445–446
Barfield, Velma, 290, 444
Basic Jail Officer, 528
Bates, Sanford, 284–285
Bay Correctional Facility, 376
Beccaria, Cesare, 9–10, 14, 23, 646
Behavior Alert Classification Identification
  System (B.A.C.I.S.), 242
Belief in Personal Control Scale, 489
Bell, Kyle, 382
Bend-and-spread, 405
Bentham, Jeremy, 9
Beto, Dr. George, 415
Bifurcated trials, 442
"Big Four" prison gangs, 332
BI Incorporated, 172
BJA Jail Work and Industry Center, 268
Black Guerilla Family, 332
Black Muslims, 300, 332, 421–422
  lawsuits filed, 421–422
Body cavity searches, 405–406, 424
Boot camps, 142–150, 606–607
  clientele, 147
  effectiveness, 149–150
  goals, 144–147
  private, 147–148
  rationale, 143–144
  women, 148, 606–607
Bootstrapping, 660
Boston Children's Aid Society, 114
Boston House of Corrections, 113
Brace, Charles Loring, 645

Brady, Ian, 397
Bridewell Workhouse, 7, 202–203
Brockway, Zebulon, 16, 19, 281–283, 468,
  470, 581
Brokers, 47
Brooklyn Plan, 652–653
Buenoano, Judy ("Judi"), 444
Bundy, Ted, 15
Bureaucracy, 349, 367
Bureaucratic model, 348–349, 367
  characteristics, 349
Bureau of Justice Assistance, 268
Bureau of Justice Statistics, 599
Bureau of Labor Statistics, 524
Burgess, Ernest W., 504
Burnout, 536–539
  alleviating, 538–539
  labor turnover, 537–538
  sources, 536–537
Bush, Governor George W., 444

Camp Branch, 508
Campus model, 580–581
Campus-style jail, 252–253
Capital punishment, 427–453, 668–672
  (See Death Penalty)
  juveniles, 668–672
Capone, Al, 300
Career criminals, 40–41
Career escalation, 667
Carroll, Leo, 330
Caseloads of probation/parole officers, 555–558
  assignment models, 557–558
  client success, 556–557
  ideal, 555–556
CD-ROM legal sources, 412–413
Cell searches, 423–424
Census of Institutional Population, 205
Centers for Disease Control, 341
Centralization, 360, 363
Certification, correctional officer, 529–531, 533
Certification, juvenile, 639–645
  hearings, 642
Changing Lives Through Literature, 123–124
Chapman, Kelly, 409
Chessman, Caryl, 391
Children in need of supervision (CHINS),
  627, 632
Children's Center, 600
Children's tribunals, 645–646
Child sexual abusers, 43–47
Chinese banishment, 7
Chivalry hypothesis, 443
Christian reforms, 307–308
  inmate classification, 307–308
Church of England, 7, 202
  jails, 202
Church of the New Song, 403
Citizen's Probation Authority (CPA)
  (Kalamazoo, Michigan), 107
Civil commitments, 512–515
Civil Rights Act, 376–377
Civil rights petitions, 376–378, 409–411, 416
Civil War, 280, 645
  juveniles, 645
  prison development, 280
Clark, Benjamin C., 113
Classical school of criminology, 9–10
Classification, 39–48, 282, 296–308,
  311–314, 666
  functions, 39–48, 311, 314
  juvenile offenders, 666
  prison, 282, 296–308
Classifying offenders, 39–48
Clemmer, Donald, 328–329, 331

Co-corrections, 608–611
    objectives, 609
Code of Ethics, 530
Cognitive Enrichment Advantage, 292
Commission on Accreditation for Corrections
    (CAC), 529–531
Commission on Correctional Certification
    (CCC), 530
Commission on Correctional Curriculum in
    Higher Education, 234
Common law, 631, 645, 670
Community-Based Era, 12
Community control, 126, 128
Community Control II Program, 126–132
Community corrections, 24–30, 167–195
    alternatives, 29–30, 172–195
    characteristics, 29, 169
    clients, 29, 169–170, 172
    elements for effectiveness, 167–168
    functions, 170–172
    goals, 169–170
    issues, 191–195
    philosophy, 29, 168
    types, 172–191
Community Justice Alternatives, 241–242
Community model, 22–23
Community Protection Act of 1990, 514–515
Community reintegration, 119, 168
    community corrections, 168
    probation, 119
Community service orders, 190
Community Services for Women, 613
Community Solutions Act, 167
Community supervision officers, 362
Compensating for sentencing disparities, 473
Compensation for exonerated inmates, 453–455
    amounts by state, 454
Compliance-involvement typology, 351
Comprehensive Crime Control Act of 1984,
    362–363, 469
Compulsory School Act, 646
Concord sentence, 499
Concurrent jurisdiction, 640
Conditional dispositions, 635
Conditional diversion, 108
Conditional releases, 480
Confinement, 399, 660–663
    secure, 660–663
Congregate system, 278–279
Conner, Albert H., 284
Consolidated Youth Services, 359
Constitution of Clarendon, 202
Continuous signalling devices, 181–182
Continuous signalling transmitters, 182
Contraband seizures, 423–424
Contract prisoners, 213, 215–216, 249, 334
Control, 17–18, 49
    sentencing, 49
Controlec, 180
Conventional model, 557
Cook, Rufus R., 113–114
Cooke, Brigitte, 559
Corporal punishment, 8–9, 424
Correctional administration, 363–371
Correctional budgets, 290
Correctional Emergency Response Teams, 235
Correctional models, 18–24
Correctional Program Assessment Inventory,
    135
Correctional Reform Act of 1983, 186
Correctional reforms, 30–31
Correctional Services Corporation, 375,
    377–378
Corrections, 4–5, 10–14, 24–30, 358–371
    community, 24–30
    early origins, 6–10, 10–14
    goals and functions, 14–18
    growth, 292–293
    history, 10–14
    institutional, 24–30
    offender management, 358–371
    religion, 6–7
    types, 24–30

Corrections Compendium surveys, 289, 603–604
Corrections Corporation of America (CCA),
    249, 267, 375–376
    private jail operations, 249
Corrections officers, 523–544, 610–611
    accreditation, 529–531
    certification, 529–531, 533
    characteristics, 525–526
    distinguished from probation and parole
        officers, 523–524
    education, 526–529
    entry requirements, 531–532
    male-female differentials in performance,
        540–544
    men guarding women, 610–611
    negligence and liability issues, 553–555
    numbers, 524–525
    personnel, 524–525
    professionalism, 529–531
    salaries, 531–532
    selection and training, 525–540
    stress, 533–536
    women, 540–544
    women guarding men, 610–611
Corrections and Law Enforcement Family
    Support Program (CLEFS), 538–539
Corrections organization, 358–371
    federal, 360–363
    state, 358–360
Cost-benefit analysis, 86–87
Cothran, Larry, 336
County and Local Detention Vocational
    Certificate, 232–233
Court-ordered inmate population
    reductions, 473, 475
Court-ordered jail improvements, 256
Crime Bill, 57–58, 493
Crime control, 119, 171–172, 188, 472
    community corrections, 171–172
    home confinement, 188
    parole, 472
    probationers, 119
Crime deterrence and parole, 472
Crime prevention and parole, 472
Crime Victims Reparations Act, 191
Criminal contamination, 488
Criminal Detention Facilities Review
    Committees, 266
Criminogenic environment, 119
    probationers, 119
Critical stages, 152
Crofton, Sir Walter, 281–282, 467–468, 470, 581
Cruel and unusual punishment, 376–377,
    406–407, 424–425
Curricula for jail officer training, 232–234
Custodial dispositions, 636
Custodial model, 580–581

Dangerousness, 308–323
    synomous with risk, 308–309
Davis, Richard Allen, 58
Day parole, 483
Day pass, 483
Day reporting centers, 188
Death penalty, 427–453, 668–672
    characteristics of death row inmates,
        430–434
    demographic information, 433–435
    executing females, 443–445
    executions in United States, 430
    juveniles, 668–672
    methods of execution, 439–440
    minimum age, 440–443
    numbers of executions, 434–436
    reasons opposing, 445–453, 668–671
    reasons supporting, 445, 668–671
    states using, 430
    time lapse between conviction and
        execution, 435–439
    trends, 439
    women on death row, 433
Death-qualified jury, 441–442
Death row, 430

Death row inmates, 430–434
    age, 434
    demographic characteristics, 433–435
Debtor's prisons, 6–7
Decarceration, 665
Decentralization, 360, 363
Deciding, Educating, Understanding,
    Counseling, and Evaluation (DEUCE)
    Program, 42
Declaration of Principles, 18, 467
Deferred prosecution, 107, 652–654
Deinstitutionalization of status offenses
    (DSO), 665–666
Deliberate indifference, 236, 255, 407,
    425–427
    inmate issue, 425–427
    jail personnel, 236, 255
Delinquency, 625
Demand waivers, 641
Department of Mental Health Forensic
    Transition Team, 604
Deserts model, 23
Design capacity, 334, 409
Detainees, 213
Detainer warrants, 212–213, 311
Detention centers, 633, 660–663
Determinate sentencing, 50–51
    compared with indeterminate sentencing,
        50–51
Deterrence, 15, 48, 118–119, 445, 472, 648
    death penalty, 445
    juvenile corrections, 648
    parole, 472
    probation, 118–119
    sentencing, 48
Detoxification programs in jails, 244
Dickerson, Denver S., 284
Diderot, Denis, 9
Direct file, 640
Direct supervision jails, 252–253, 261–262
Discipline, 335–337
Discretionary parole, 475
Discretionary waivers, 640
Disposed, 635
Diversion, 5, 29–30, 107–113, 613–614,
    652–654, 665
    conditional, 108
    criticisms, 112–113
    defined, 5, 29, 107
    effectiveness, 111–113
    factors influencing, 109–110
    forms, 108
    functions, 108–109
    juveniles, 652–654, 665
    offense seriousness, 108
    outcomes, 111
    profile of clients, 110–111
    qualifications, 108
    standard, 108
    unconditional, 108
    women, 613–614
Divestiture, 665
DNA tests in inmate exonerations, 453
Domestic violence prevention programs, 607
Dominion, 375
Double-bunking, 259–260, 409, 425
Double-celling, 409, 425
Drug/alcohol dependent offenders, 41–42,
    218, 244
Drug courts, 112
Drug offenders, 472
Drunk tanks, 205
Ducking stool, 11
Duehay, Francis H., 284
Due process clause, 409–411, 413, 421–422
    litigation issue, 421–422

Early release, 466–480
Education furlough, 483
Eighth Amendment, 377, 406–409, 424–425,
    429–430, 605
    death penalty, 429–430
    women's prisons, 605

Electronic monitoring, 172–186
  constitutionality, 185–186
  costs, 182
  criticisms, 183–184
  types, 181–182
Emotional/Social Loneliness Inventory, 489
Employment assistance and community
    corrections, 171
English common law, 645
English Penal Servitude Act, 467
Enlightenment, 9–10
Entry-level correctional officer job
    requirements, 532–533
Equal protection clause, 409–411, 413,
    421–422, 598–599
  litigation issue, 421–422
  women's prisons, 598–599
Ethnicity as a sentencing factor, 84–85
Evaluation research, 135
Evolving standards of decency test, 408
Excessive bail, 406
Exculpatory information, 59
Exhaustion requirement, 416
Exodus Group, 559–560
Experience programs, 663–664
Experiments on prisoners, 394
Expungement order, 509
Extralegal variables, 84–85

Failure to state a claim, 400
False negatives, 318–319, 498–499
False positives, 318–319, 498–499
Family Empowerment Intervention, 566
Family Recovery Embraces Education
    Program, 291–292, 427
Fathers, inmates, 427
Federal Bureau of Prisons (BOP), 3, 19, 42, 249,
    284–288, 296, 299, 335, 337, 361–362,
    375–377, 492, 562, 583, 595, 604, 609
  budget, 361
  established, 19, 284–285
  illegal use of drugs, 42
  numbers, 285–288
  organization, 284–285, 361–362
  overcrowding, 335
Federal Civil Rights Act, 378
Federal corrections, 360–363
Federal Crime Bill, 57–58, 493
Federal detention camps, 288
Federal Habeas Corpus Statute, 416
Federal Juvenile Delinquency Act, 115
Federal medical centers, 288
Federal prison camps, 288
Federal Prison Industries, 378–379
Federal prisoners, 288
  housed in state or local facilities, 288
  prison overcrowding, 288
Federal prisons, 284–291
  compared with state prisons, 284–291
  construction, 288
Federal Tort Claims Act of 1946, 416
  numbers filed, 417
Federal Violent Crime Control and Law
    Enforcement Act of 1994, 57–58
Fee system, 203
Felonies, 38
Felony murder statute, 424
Felony probationers, 119–120
Female boot camps, 606–607
Female gangs, 332
Female inmates, 422–423
  rights, 422–423
Female jail officers, 231, 240–241
Female juveniles, 625, 660–661
  programs, 661
  supervising, 660
Female Offender Regimented Treatment
    Program (FORT), 606–607
Female offenders, 576–579
  characteristics, 576–577
  classification, 577–579
Female probationers and parolees, 611–612
Female prison wardens and superinten-
    dents, 289–290

Fenton, Norman, 370
Fifth Amendment, 411
Filing fees, 418
Financial/community service model, 191
Fines, 188–190
  aggravating and mitigating circumstances
    influencing, 189–190
  types, 189
Firearms in probation/parole officer work,
    552–553
  criticisms, 553
First Amendment, 400–404
First-generation jails, 261
First-offenders, 40
Fishman, Joseph, 204, 326
Five Factor Model of Personality, 305
Fixed indeterminate sentencing, 50
Flat time, 512
Flogging, 278
Florida Community Control II Program,
    126–132
  caseloads, 129
  eligibility requirements, 128–129
  goals, 129
  program requirements, 131
  successfulness, 130, 132
  terms and conditions, 130
Focus groups and jail officer training, 231–232
Force-feeding inmates, 396–397
Force used in jails, 236
Forgotten offenders, 574
Foster homes, 660
Fourth Amendment, 404–406
Fourteenth Amendment, 409–411, 506,
    598–599, 608–611
  co-correctional prisons, 608–611
  women's prisons, 598–599, 608
Fraternal Order of Police, 590
Freedom of Information Act (FOIA), 79
French, James W., 284
Frivolous lawsuits, 390–391, 398, 400, 456–457
Front-door solutions, 109, 335, 552
  diversion, 109
Fry, Elizabeth Gurney, 581
Furloughs, 5, 481–482
  functions, 482
  goals, 481–482
  history, 481

Gangs in jails and prisons, 300, 325
Gangs, juvenile, 641–642, 651
Gaols, 11, 202, 276
GED, 533, 547, 604
  as requirment for corrections employment,
    533, 547
  women's prisons, 604
Gender disparities, 84–85
Gender parity, 611
Gender politics, 447
Geographic information systems (GIS), 130
Get-tough laws, 31, 57, 209, 493
Get-tough movement, 493, 642, 651, 667
Gilmore, Gary, 435
Global Positioning Satellites (GPS), 128,
    130, 182–183
Good-time credits, 31, 50, 281, 337, 466,
    468–469, 480, 499, 512
  alternatives to parole, 31
  controlling inmate violence, 337
  determinate sentencing, 50
  history, 281, 466, 468
  pre-release programs, 480
Good-time laws, 469
Gottfredson, Don M., 504
Graham, Barbara, 443–444
Graunger, Thomas, 668
Great Law of Pennsylvania, 11, 277
Grendon Prison, 19–22
Grievance committees, 289, 456–457
Group homes, 661–662
Guidelines-based sentencing, 51–53

Habeas corpus petitions, 398–399, 411, 416–418
  functions, 399

  numbers filed, 417–418
Habitual offender laws, 54, 157, 424–425, 493
  cruel and unusual punishment, 424–425
  probationers, 157
Halfway houses, 488–490
  costs, 488–489
  criticisms, 490
  functions, 489–490
  origins, 488
  variations, 488–489
  women, 488–489
Hands-off doctrine, 398–399, 506
Hawthorne effect, 350
Hayes, Rutherford B., 13, 281
Health care services in jails, 243–244
Heredity and criminal behavior, 394
High Street Jail, 16, 203
Hinckley, John, 504
HIV/AIDS, 39, 47–48, 243–244, 340–341,
    589, 595, 608
  constitutional issues affecting prisoners,
    244, 340–342
  jail inmates, 243–244
  women's prisons, 589, 595, 608
Holding tanks, 205
Home confinement, 186–188
  criticisms, 187
  eligibility requirements, 187
  goals, 186
  issues, 187–188
Honor farms, 296
Hopper Home, Isaac T., 581, 589
Hostage Recovery Teams, 235
House of Commons, 276
Houses of correction, 7, 499
Howard, John, 276–277, 581
Hubbell, Gaylord, 467, 470
Hull House, 114, 646
Human relations model, 350, 366, 370
Human relations training, 366
Human Rights Act of 1998, 397
Human services approach, 237–238
Hunger strikes by inmates, 213, 396

Ideal types, 367–368
I-Level classification (Interpersonal Maturity
    Level Classification System), 311
Immigration and Naturalization Service, 295
Immunity, 554
Importation model, 329–330, 594
Incapacitation, 15, 49
  sentencing, 49
Incident reports, 320–321
Inculpatory information, 59
Indentured servants, 7
Indeterminate sentencing, 49–50, 468
  law, 468
Index crimes, 574
Industrial Era, 12, 645
  juvenile treatment, 645
In forma pauperis, 418
Informed consent, 394
Informed risk review panels, 87–88
Initial Classification Analysis, 577
In loco parentis, 636
Inmate classification problems, 241–243, 255
Inmate classification systems, 296, 305–308
Inmate control model, 368
Inmate disciplinary councils, 337–338, 456–457
Inmate fathers, 427
Inmate Government Councils, 368
Inmate grievance procedures, 289, 455–457
Inmate litigation explosion, 256
  jail issues, 256
Inmate mothers, 427, 587–589, 593–594
Inmate rights, 391–427
  constitutional basis, 391–411
Inmate violence, 335–337
In-service training, 532–533
In-service training for jail officers, 234–235, 239
Institutional corrections, 24–30
Intake, 633–634
Intensive supervised parole (ISP), 17,
    491–492, 614–616

Intensive supervised probation (ISP), 17, 123–135, 614–616
  alternative programs, 132–135
  caseloads, 124
  clients, 124
  criticisms, 133–134
  program components, 123, 134
  women, 614–616
Intermediate punishments, 118, 121–123, 612–616
  women, 612–616
Intermittent sentences, 141
International Association of Correctional Officers (IACO), 233–234, 238–239
International Community Correction Association, 135
International Halfway House Association (IHHA), 488
Interpersonal relations among jail officers, 240–241
Interstate Commission, 502–503
Interstate compact agreements, 501–503
Interstate Compact for Adult Offender Supervision (ICAOS), 501–502
Interstate Transportation of Dangerous Criminals Act of 2000, 381–382
Inventory of Socially Supportive Behaviors, 489
Inwald Personality Inventory, 549
IQ tests used in corrections, 282
Irish system, 467
Irwin, John, 331
Isolation, 15, 406, 648–650
  juvenile corrections, 648–650
Isolation syndrome, 406

Jail administration, 226–236
  characteristics, 230
  salaries and qualifications, 228–229
Jail and prison overcrowding, 49, 168, 288, 425
  community corrections,168
  sentencing, 49
Jail and Work Industry Symposium, 268
Jail architecture, 258–261
Jail boot camps, 148–149
Jail communications, 231–232
Jail diversion, 108
Jail Education and Treatment Program (JET), 42
Jailhouse lawyers, 390–391, 414–421, 604
  civil remedies, 414–421
  women, 604
Jail lawsuits, 235–236, 245, 255
Jail industries, 268
Jail inmate characteristics, 215–219
Jail Inmate Classification System (JICS), 241–242
Jail inspections, 266
Jail issues, 236–256
  health care services, 243–244
  managing offenders from other jurisdictions, 240
  officer interactions, 240–241
  officer training, 238–239
  overcrowding, 248–253
  quality of personnel, 237–238
  small jail problems, 244–248
  suicides, 253–256
Jail management and operations, 226–227
  county- or state-operated, 226–227
Jail officer recruitment and training, 227–229
  attitudes and work performance, 229–231
  characteristics, 230
  educational qualifications, 232–234
  labor turnover, 227–229
  lawsuits, 234–235
  morale, 230–231
  salaries, 227–229
Jail overcrowding, 88–89, 109, 141, 168, 236, 248–253, 256, 407–408, 472–473
  community corrections, 168
  diversion, 109
  lawsuits, 235–236, 248–249, 256, 407–408
  parole, 472–473
  regional jails, 252
  shock probation, 141

Jail populations, 226
Jail reforms, 256–268
  architecture, 258–261
  court-ordered jail improvements, 256
  direct-supervision jails, 261–262
  jail industries, 268
  inmates with special needs, 257–258
  new-generation jails, 261–262
  privatization of jail operations, 266–268
  vocational/educational provisions, 262–266
Jail removal initiative, 206, 209, 219, 626
Jails, 25, 202–219
  admissions and releases, 206
  average daily population, 206
  census, 204
  distinguished from prisons, 25, 28
  functions, 207–215
  history, 202–206
  juveniles held, 629
  numbers in U.S., 205
Jail sizes, 249, 252
Jail standards, 234–235
Jail statistics, 204
Jail suicides, 219, 253–256
  causes, 253–254
  established prevention policies, 253
Jail training programs, 238–239
Jaworski, Richard, 409
Jeanna's Act, 381–382
Job dissatisfaction, 534–535
Jobs in corrections, 542–543
Judicial immunity, 554
Judicial waivers, 640
Jury, 58
Jury trials, 638
  limitations in juvenile cases, 638
Just-deserts, 49, 445
  death penalty, 445
  sentencing, 49
Just deserts model, 23
Justice and sentencing, 49
Justice model, 23–24
Juvenile arrests, 627–629
Juvenile classification, 660–661, 666
Juvenile corrections, 645–673
  alternatives, 651–664
  future, 666, 672–673
  goals, 646–651
  history, 645–646
  issues, 664–673
Juvenile court, 634–635, 644–645
  leniency, 644–645
Juvenile delinquency, 625–626
Juvenile detention centers, 633, 660–663
Juvenile gangs, 641–642, 651
Juvenile Justice and Delinquency Prevention Act of 1974, 209, 219, 626–627, 665
Juvenile justice system, 630–636
  jurisdiction, 630–632
Juvenile offenders, 219, 624–630
  characteristics, 627–630
  constitutional rights, 636–639
  held in jails, 219, 629–630
  types, 624–625
Juvenile placement, 660–663
Juvenile probation, 654–660
  supervision, 659–660
Juvenile property offenders, 624–625
Juvenile Rehabilitation Administration (JRA), 648
Juvenile Residential Facility Census, 646
Juveniles treated as adults, 666–667

Klaas, Marc, 58
Klaas, Polly, 58
Krenwinkle, Patricia, 493
Krone, Ray, 453–454

Labor turnover among corrections officers, 537–538, 558
LaDow, R.V., 284
Lancaster, Jennie, 290
Large jails, 252
Latent functions of parole, 471

Law Enforcement Assistance Administration (LEAA), 205, 290–291
Law enforcement officers, 5
Law libraries for prisons, 410–414
  cost, 412
  differences in state and federal statutes, 413–414
  form of legal assistance, 411–413
Lawsuit syndrome, 235–236
Legal-rational authority, 349
Legal Services Committee (ACA), 456–457
Legal variables, 84–85
Legislative waivers, 641
Levels of custody, 39, 296–307
Lex talionis, 6, 14
Liability issues in probation/parole officer work, 553–555
Life-without-parole sentences, 54
Linear jails, 261–262
Literacy programs, 291–292
Litigation explosion, 256
Litigation issues, inmate, 421–427
Lockdowns, 303–304
Lockups, 205
Love, Judge Jack, 181

Maconochie, Captain Alexander, 281–282, 466–468, 470
Maconochie's Gentlemen, 467
Magdalen Society, 580
Mail privileges of inmates, 400–401
Maine and parole abolition, 469
Maison de Force (House of Enforcement), 276
Management, jail, 226–236
Management by objectives (MBO), 289
Magaging offenders from other jurisdictions, 240
Mandatory parole, 475
Mandatory probation, 157
Mandatory releases, 480, 512
Mandatory sentencing, 53–58
Mandatory waivers, 640
Manifest functions of parole, 471
Manson, Charles, 309, 493, 504
Manson Family, 615
Marks of commendation, 466–467
Mark system, 281, 466–467
Martinson, Robert, 14
Mass Prison Era, 12
Master control and direct-supervision jails, 262
Matrons, 279
Maxi-maxi classification, 306–307
Maxi-maxi prisons, 303–304
Maximum-security classification, 306
Maximum-security prisons, 299–303
  cost of construction, 298
Mayo, Elton, 350
McGill, Kay, 47
McNeil Island, Washington, 43
Mediation, 105–107, 190
  community corrections, 190
Medical model, 18
Medium jails, 252
Medium-security classification, 306
Medium-security prisons, 299
  cost of construction, 298
Meese, Attorney General Ed, 303
Megajails, 249, 252
Megargee, Edwin, 310
Megargee Inmate Typology, 305
Men guarding women, 610–611
Mentally ill offenders, 43, 210, 212, 217–218, 257–258
  estimates in prisons or jails, 43, 210, 212, 217–218, 257–258
Messenger, Sheldon, 330
Metropolitan correctional centers, 288
Michigan Alcohol Screening Test, 119
Michigan Corrections Officers Training Council, 232–233
Military model, 282
Minnesota Multiphasic Personality Inventory (MMPI), 39, 305, 310, 549
Minimum age of accountability, 631
Minimum due process rights, 507

Minimum-security classification, 306
Minimum-security prisons, 296–298
  cost of construction, 298
MIS (management information systems), 243
Misbehavior report, 320–321
Misclassification problems, 423
Misconduct of jail staff, 255
Misdemeanors, 38
Mitigating circumstances, 83, 442
  death penalty cases, 442
Model Penal Code, 673
Modular jail construction, 261–262
Montesquieu, Charles-Louis de Secondat, 9
Moral Recognition Therapy, 422–423
Mothers Against Drunk Drivers (MADD), 110
Mothers in prison, 593–594
Motions for summary judgments, 400
Motions to dismiss, 400
Multidimensional Treatment Foster Care,
  657–658
Multiple Goal Typology, 150
Murton, Thomas O., 395, 457
Muslims, 403–404
Myers-Briggs Type Indicator (MBTI), 368–370

National Academy of Sciences, 607
National Advisory Commission on Criminal
  Justice Standards and Goals, 289
National Commission for the Protection of
  Human Subjects of Biomedical and
  Behavioral Research, 394
National Congress on Penitentiary and
  Reformatory Discipline, 16, 281
National Correctional Policy on Female
  Offender Services, 611–612
National Council on Crime and Delinquency,
  504
National Council of Juvenile and Family
  Court Judges, 664
National Crime Victimization Survey, 86–87
National Institute of Corrections, 471, 502, 530
National Institute of Corrections Advisory
  Board, 502
National Institute of Corrections Correctional
  Leadership Development Program,
  368–371
National Institute of Corrections, Jails
  Division (NICJD), 233, 255–256
National Institute of Justice, 238, 336, 538
National Jail Census, 1983, 244
National Prison Association, 13, 18, 281,
  467–468, 581, 583
National Sheriffs' Association, 226, 234, 258
Native American inmates, 403
Necessity as a defense to double-bunking, 409
Needs assessment device, 315
Negligence, 425–427, 553–555, 566–567
Nelson, Knox Senator, 395
Net-widening, 106, 112, 133, 142, 652, 659
  diversion, 112, 652
  ISP programs, 133
  juvenile divertees, 652, 659
  probation, 659
  shock probation, 142
New-generation jails, 252, 261–262
New Jersey ISP (Intensive Probation
  Supervision) program, 124–128
  costs, 126
  effectiveness, 126
  expectations, 125
  goals, 124–125
  program elements, 127–128
New penology, 281
New prison construction, 304–305
NIMBY ("not in my back yard") syndrome,
  191–192
1983 National Jail Census, 244
1994 Anti-Crime Bill, 57–58, 493
Nominal dispositions, 635
Nonsecure placement, 660–663
Nonviolent juvenile offenders, 624–625,
  667–668
Norfolk Island, 466–467
Norman Conquest, 11

North, Jeanna, 382
Nuisance lawsuits, 390–391
Numbers game model, 557

Objective jail classification system (OJC),
  255–256
Objective parole criteria, 503–504
Offender accountability and community
  corrections, 171
Offender control, 117–118
Offender management, 358
Offender's sentencing memorandum, 80
Offender's version of events, 80
Offenses, 38–39
Office of Juvenile Justice and Delinqency
  Prevention (OJJDP), 629, 646, 661
Office of Strategic Services (OSS), 539
Once an adult/always an adult provision,
  641–642
On-the-job training, 532–533
Operational capacity, 334
Organizational effectiveness, 349
Oswald, Russell G., 302
Outward Bound, 663–664
Overclassification, 660–661
Overrides, 311

Paraprofessionals, 565–567
  criticisms, 566–567
  legal liabilities, 566–567
  Section 1983 claims, 566–567
  training, 565–566
Parens patriae, 636, 638, 645
Parental banishment, 7–8
Pardons, 469, 480, 509
Parole, 13–14, 465–480
  abolition, 469–470
  functions, 471–473
  goals, 470–471
  history, 466–469
  numbers of parolees, 473–480
  philosophy, 470–471
  program conditions, 490–491
  types, 480–492
Parole abolition, 469–470
Parole board orientations, 503–504
Parole boards, 472, 492–506
  cases that may or may not be reviewed,
    492–493
  composition and diversity, 494–497
  effectiveness, 505–506
  functions, 497–498
  get-tough movement, 493–494, 642
  inmate control, 498–499
  jail and prison overcrowding, 472–473
  objective parole criteria, 503–504
  orientations, 503
  part-time, 496–497
  predicting success or failure, 500–501
  risk assessment, 504–505
  Salient Factor Scores, 504–505
Parole Decision Making Project, 504
Parolees, 473–480
  characteristics, 475–477
  numbers, 473–475
  payment of fees for supervision, 477
  program conditions, 509
  recidivism, 475–476
  rights, 507–512
Parole fees, 477
Parole hearings, 478–480
Parole officers (POs), 4, 523–524, 546–547,
  547–555
  characteristics, 546–547
  distinguished from corrections officers,
    523–524
  duties, 549–552
  negligence and liability issues, 553–555
  firearms use, 547, 552–553
  labor turnover, 558
  risks, 552–553
  salaries, 546–547
  selection requirements, 547–555
Parole plans, 473

Parole programs, 480–492, 544
  criticisms, 545–546
  organization and operation, 544–547
Parole revocation, 506–507
Parole violators, 213, 478–480
  characteristics, 479
Participation hypothesis, 363–365, 536
Participative management, 231–232, 235–236,
  368, 457, 538
  inmate grievance councils, 457
  jail officer training, 231–232, 236
Pataki, Governor George, 473
Peer courts, 635
Pendergraph, Sheriff Jim, 231–232
Penitentiary, 276–278
Penitentiary Act, 276
Penitentiary Era, 12
Penn, William, 11, 19, 203–204, 277
Perry Preschool Project, 650
Persistent felony offenders, 577
Petitions, 632
Philadelphia Society for Alleviating the
  Miseries of Public Prisons, 16, 203
Phillips, Kenneth, 453
Physically handicapped offenders, 47
Plea bargaining, 38, 81, 84, 113
  diversion, 113
Plethysmography, 411
Podular jail designs, 261–262
Police and juveniles, 632–633
Population caps, 256
Post-conviction relief, 414
Post-release parole programs, 487–492
Post-release supervision, 469–470
Power clusters, 356–358
Power in organizations, 350–358
  coercive power, 350
  expert power, 350
  legitimate power, 350
  referent power, 350
  reward power, 350
Predicting parole success or failure, 500–501
Pre-employment screenings, 532
Prejean, Sister Helen, 444
Preliminary hearings, 507
Pre-release programs, 480–487
Presentence investigation, 59
Presentence investigation reports (PSIs),
  59–82, 117
  confidentiality, 79
  contents, 59–60
  functions and uses, 75–76
  influence on judicial decision making, 81–82
  John Augustus's preparation of, 117
  offender's sentencing memorandum, 80
  parole decision making, 76–78
  preparation, 75–76
  private preparation, 78
  sample federal PSI, 68–75
  sample state PSI, 61–67
  victim impact statement, 80–81
Pre-service training, 532–533
President's Commission on Law Enforcement
  and the Administration of Justice, 456, 545
Presumptive/guidelines-based sentencing,
  51–53
Presumptive waivers, 640
Pretrial detention, 207
Pretrial diversion, 107–113 (*See also* Diversion)
  criticisms, 112–113
  effectiveness, 111–113
  factors influencing, 109–110
  functions, 108–109
  outcomes, 111
  profiling divertees, 110–111
  recidivism, 111–112
Pretrial release, 362
Pretrial services, 103–105
Pretrial Services Resource Center, 104–105
Prevention, 15–16, 48, 650–651
  juvenile corrections, 650–651
  sentencing, 48
Preventive detention, 209
Printzlien, Conrad, 652–653

Prison administrators, 371–372
  male-female distribution, 371
  selection and training, 371–372
Prison Climate Survey, 543–544
Prison construction, 304–305
Prisoner classification, 305–308
  religious influence, 305
Prison culture, 291, 326–334, 590–594
  women's prisons, 590–594
Prison design and control, 338–339
Prisoner classification, 304, 307–308, 423–424
  Christian reforms, 307–308
  misclassification problems, 423–424
Prisoner rights issues, 421–427
Prisoners, 291–295
  offense characteristics and sentence
    lengths, 293–294
  sociodemographic characteristics, 293–295
  state and federal inmate population
    growth, 292–293
Prison gangs, 325, 332–334
Prison Industries, 277, 279
  history, 277, 279
Prison issues, 334–342
Prison labor, 11–12, 378–379
Prison Litigation Reform Act of 1995
    (PLRA), 418–421
Prison management styles, 367–368
Prison overcrowding, 88–89, 109, 141, 168,
    288, 334–335, 407–408, 425, 472–473
  community corrections, 168
  diversion, 109
  lawsuits, 407–408, 425
  measuring, 334
  parole, 472–473
  shock probation, 141
Prison privatization, 372–382
  criticisms, 372, 375
  Interstate Transportation of Dangerous
    Criminals Act of 2000, 381–382
  political considerations, 382
  prison labor, 378–379
  prisons for profit, 378–379
  professionalization of administration,
    375–376
  pros and cons, 372, 375
  public accountability, 376–378
  public reaction, 379–381
Prison reform, 276
Prisons, 25, 276–293
  distinguished from jails, 25, 28
  early developments, 284–285
  first, 277
  functions, 323–326
  growth, 276, 292–293
  history, 276–284
  state and federal, 284–291
  types and functions, 284–291, 296–305
Prison wardens and superintendents,
    284–285, 288–289
Privacy, expectation of, 423–425
Privatization of jail operations, 236, 266–268,
    372–375
  pros and cons, 267–268
  sheriffs' opinions, 267
Probation, 14, 113–135
  conditions, 122
  first statute authorizing, 114
  functions, 118–119
  history, 113–116
  juveniles, 115
  philosophy, 117–118
  program conditions, 122–133
  types, 119–135
Probation counselors, 658–659
Probationers, 115, 135–140, 507–512
  characteristics, 136–137
  recidivism, 138, 140
  rights, 152–159, 507–512
Probation officers (POs), 14, 77, 121,
    523–524, 546–555
  characteristics, 546–547
  distinguished from corrections officers,
    523–524

duties, 549–552
  firearms use, 547, 552–553
  labor turnover, 558
  negligence and liability issues, 553–555
  qualifications, 547–549
  risks, 552–553
  rules for reporting probationer program
    rule violations, 151–152
  salaries, 546–547
  selection requirements, 547–555
  supervising male and female clients, 121
Probation programs, 544–547
  criticisms, 545–546
Probation revocation, 150–159, 506
Probation violators, 213
Professionalism, corrections officers,
    529–533, 546–547
Professionalization, 233–234, 241, 533
  administration, 375–376
  corrections officers generally, 533
  jail officers, 233–234, 241
Program eligibility of inmates, 423
Programmed contact devices, 182
Prohibition, 16, 583
Property crimes, 38–39, 624–625
  juveniles, 624–625
Protective custody and jails, 208
Prunty, Warden K.W., 371–372
Psychological Inventory of Criminal Thinking
    Styles (PICTS), 39
Psychological screenings of job applicants,
    532–533
Public accountability and privatization,
    376–378
Public reactions to prison privatization,
    379–381
Public safety and community corrections,
    171–172, 188, 193, 473
  home confinement, 188
  parole, 473
Punishment, 118, 651
  juvenile corrections, 651
  probation, 118
Punitive Era, 12

Quakers, 10, 16, 30, 203–204, 277
Qualified immunity, 416, 554
Quality of jail personnel, 237–238
Quasijudicial immunity, 554

Rabble hypothesis, 213–214
Race as a sentencing factor, 84–84
Racism in prisons, 421–422
Rangel, Mario V., 396–397
Ranges, 307
Rated capacity, 334
Reasonableness test, 398
Recidivism, 41, 121–123, 149, 505–506
  boot camps, 149
  informal standard, 121
  measuring probation and parole
    effectiveness, 121
Reconstruction Period, 645
  juveniles, 645
Red Hannah, 424
Red Light Bandit, 391
Reeves, 11, 202
Referrals, 632
Reformatory Era, 12
Reformatory movement, 16
Reform model, 19
Reformatory model, 580
Regional jails, 252–253
Rehabilitation, 15–16, 19–22, 49, 422–423,
    471, 545, 599–600, 647–647
  corrections, 545
  juveniles, 647–648
  probation and parole, 471, 545
  right of inmates, 422–423
  sentencing, 49
  women's prisons, 599–600
Rehabilitation model, 19–22, 124, 545
Reincarceration, 506

Reintegration, 16–17, 49, 119, 325–326,
    471–472, 647–648
  juvenile, 647–648
  parole, 471–472
  probation, 119
  prison, 325–326
  sentencing, 49
Reintegration model, 22–23
Release from prison, 473, 475
Religion and corrections, 6–7
Reparations, 191
Reparative boards, 559
Resentencing Panels, 126
Restitution, 190–191, 658–659
  juveniles, 658–659
Restorative justice, 105–106
Retribution, 14–15, 48, 445, 651
  death penalty, 445
  juvenile corrections, 651
  sentencing, 48
Retribution model, 23
Reverse waiver hearings, 641
Revocation hearings, 150–152, 506
Revocation of parole or probation, 150–159
Revolutionary War, 203, 466
Reynolds, James Bronson, 115
Riker's Island, 258
Riots in prisons, 277, 300–303, 335–337
  trends, 303, 335–336
Risk, 308–309
Risk assessment, 308–323
  applications, 311–314, 320–323
  effectiveness, 319–320
  institutional placement, 308–323
  parolees, 309, 311, 314
  women, 311
Risk instruments, 308–323
Risk-needs assessment, 320–322
Risk prediction, 315–323, 660–661
  actuarial, 317
  anamnestic, 315, 317
  clinical, 317–318
  juvenile offenders, 660–661
  types, 315–318
Risks and liabilities of corrections work, 536
Role ambiguity, 537
Role conflict, 536
Rolling, Danny Harold, 493
Rosenberg, Ethel, 443–444
Rosenberg, Jerome ("Jerry"), 391–394, 401
Rush, Dr. Benjamin, 16, 277

Sadler, Lloyd Senator, 395
Safe havens, 606
Salient Factor Score Index (SFS 76,
    SFS 81), 504–505
Sawyer, Dr. Kathleen M. Hawk, 285
Screenings of corrections job applicants,
    532–533
Second-generation jails, 261
Section 1983 claims, 376–377, 409–411,
    415–416, 455–456, 566
  against paraprofessionals, 566
  successfulness of filings, 410
Secure placement, 660–663
Seizures of contraband, 423–424
Selection by test, 349
Selection and training of corrections personnel,
    525–544
  criteria, 533
Selective incapacitation, 87, 322–323
Selective release, 323
Self-Appraisal Questionnaire (SAQ), 309
Self-Defense Family, 332
Self-incrimination, 411
Sentence commutations, 455
Sentencing, 48–49
  purposes, 48–49
Sentencing disparities, 31, 84–86, 470–471,
    473
  parole, 470–471, 473
Sentencing guidelines, 31, 51–53, 293
Sentencing hearings, 58–59

Sentencing issues, 84–89
  correctional resources and their limitations, 86
  economics of systemic constraints, 86–88
  jail and prison overcrowding problems, 88–89
  sentencing disparities, 84–86
Sentencing memorandums, 80
Sentencing Reform Act of 1984, 362
Sentencing systems, 49–58
  determinate, 50–51
  indeterminate, 49–50
  mandatory, 53–58
  presumptive or guidelines-based, 51–53
Services delivery and community corrections, 193
Serving time beyond maximum sentences, 512–515
Settlement houses, 114
Sex offenders, 18, 43–47, 133, 310
  numbers in prison population, 45, 47
  risk predictions, 310
  under ISP supervision, 133
Sexual exploitation, 339–340
Sexual harassment in corrections, 240–241, 541–543
Sexually Violent Predator Act (SVPA), 514
SFS 76, 505
SFS 81, 505
Shared-powers model, 367–368
Sheriffs, 11, 202, 226–236
  responsibilities, 226–236
Shock incarceration, 17, 283
Shock parole, 492
Shock probation, 139–142
  effectiveness, 142
  philosophy and objectives, 140–142
Short-term offenders, 208
Sigler, Maurice, 307–308
Silence rule, 278–279
Sirhan Sirhan, 504
Situational offenders, 40
Sixth Amendment claims, 411
Small jails, 244–248, 252–253
Smith, Jay, 455
Smoking ban and inmates, 406
Socialization, 329
Society for the Prevention of Pauperism, 645
Sociodemographic characteristics of prisoners, 293–294
Socioeconomic disparities, 84–85
Solitary confinement, 203–204, 277–278
Spanish Inquisition, 6
Specialization, 349
Specialized caseloads model, 557–558
Special management inmates, 257–258
Special-needs offenders, 193, 257–258, 472–473
  community corrections, 193
  jails, 257–258
  prisoners, 472–473
Special Needs Parole Program, 472–473, 494
Specific release dates, 50
Standard diversion, 108
Standard parole, 490–491
  conditions, 490–491
Standard probation, 119–123
  effectiveness, 121–123
  standardless aspect, 121
Standards for jail officer recruitment and training, 233–234
Stare decisis, 425
State and federal statutes, differences, 413–414
State-operated jails, 205
State prisons, 284–291
  compared with federal prisons, 284–291
  organization, 288–291
Status offenses, 625
Statutory exclusion, 640–641
Statutory releases, 480
Sterilization of prisoners, 394–395
Stress, 533–539
  alleviating, 538–539

labor turnover, 537–538
  relation to burnout, 536–539
  sources, 534–536
Strip searches, 405–406, 424
Stroud, Robert ("Birdman"), 300
Subculture, 291, 326, 331–332
Successfulness of parole, 478
Summary offenses, 38
Superintendent of Prisons, 284
Superintendent of Prisons and Prisoners, 284
Superintendents, 284, 288
Super-max classification, 306–307
Supervised releasees, 362
Supervisory fees and parolees, 477
Sykes, Gresham, 329–331

Tactical response teams, 235
Tate, Sharon, 309
Teaching-Family Treatment Model, 647–648
Teen courts, 635, 654
Temperance Movement, 113
  probation, 113
Temporary release, 483
Test of Adult Basic Education (TABE), 264–266
Therapeutic community, 218
Therapeutic integrity, 149
Therapeutic intervention, 658–659
Therapeutic prison community programs, 22
Third-generation jails, 262
Three Prisons Act, 284
Three Strikes and You're Out!, 30–31, 493
Tickets-of-leave, 467
Tier system, 278
Tort claims, 376–377
Total institution, 291, 330
Totality of circumstances and inmate overcrowding, 409
Total quality management (TQM), 368
Traditional offender categorizations, 40–41
Transfer hearings, 642
Transfers, 639–645
Transportation, 7–8
Treatment Era, 12
Treatment model, 18
Trials, 58
Truancy, 625, 632, 646
Truth-in-sentencing provisions, 226, 499
Tuberculosis (TB), 239, 243–244, 341–342
  jail inmates, 239, 243–244
  prison inmates, 341–342
Tucker, Karla Faye, 444
Tucker telephone, 395, 398
Two-stage hearings in probation/parole revocations, 154, 507

Unconditional diversion, 108
Unconditional releases, 469
Unethical conduct among jail personnel, 255
Uniform Crime Reports (UCR), 39, 86–87
United Chicanos, 332
United Methodist Church, 590
United Nations, 664
U.S. Board of Parole, 362, 469
U.S. Bureau of Census, 646
U.S. Bureau of Prisons, 234, 378, 409
U.S. Bureau of Prisons Choice Program, 262–263
U.S. Census Bureau, 205
  measuring jail populations, 205
U.S. Department of Justice, 360, 362, 479
U.S. Food and Drug Administration, 394
U.S. National Institute on Drug Abuse, 566
U.S. Parole Commission, 362, 504
U.S. Pretrial Services, 362
U.S. Probation Office, 75
U.S. Sentencing Commission, 31, 51, 362–363
  functions, 51, 362–363
U.S. sentencing guidelines, 293, 363
Unsuccessful parolees, 478–480
Utilitarian philosophy, 9

Van Diemen's Land, 466
Van Houton, Leslie, 309, 493, 615–616
Victim impact panels, 110
Victim impact statements (VIS), 80–82
Victim/offender mediation model, 106–107, 191
Victim/reparations model, 191
Victim and Witness Protection Act of 1982, 154, 190
Violent crimes, 38–39
Violent juvenile offenders, 624–625, 641–642,667–668
Vocational/educational provisions in jails, 262–266
Vocational/educational training and community corrections, 171
Voltaire, Francois-Marie Arouet, 9–10
Volunteers, 558–565
  characteristics, 558–559
  criticisms, 562–565
  duties, 559–561
  legal liabilities, 565
  numbers, 562
  rules and regulations 563–565
Votaw, Heber H., 284

Waiver hearings, 642
Waivers, 639–645
Walnut Street Jail, 16, 203–204, 277–278, 305, 307–308, 579, 608
  Auburn State Penitentiary and, 278
  Christian reforms, 307–308
  innovations, 203–204
  Pennsylvania System, 203–204, 277
Warehousing Era, 12
Weber, Max, 349, 367
Welch, Rachel, 579
White, Luther C., 284
Wilderness programs, 663–664
Wilkins, Leslie, 504
Witnesses in protective custody, 207
Women guarding men, 610–611
Women in jails, 39–40
Women and the death penalty, 443–445
Women in corrections, 288–289, 540–544
  compared with men, 543–544
  sexual harassment issues, 541–543
Women's Educational Opportunity Act, 590
Women's Liberation Movement, 443
Women's Movement, 625
Women's Prison Association (WPA), 581, 589
Women's prisons, 579–608
  ACA guidelines for construction, 585
  administration, 594–598
  compared with prisons for men, 598
  construction, 583, 585
  criticisms, 585–588
  culture, 590–594
  history, 579–585
  issues, 598–608
  models of women's prison conditions, 580
  mothers, 593–594
  state and federal institutions (1873–1973), 582
  state and federal institutions (1973–2002), 584
Work furloughs, 467, 483
Workhouses, 202
Work/study release, 5, 482–487
  criticisms, 483–487
  eligibility requirements, 483
  goals, 483
  history, 482–483
Wournos, Aileen Pittman, 444–445
Write-ups, 320–321
Writs of *habeas corpus,* 398–399
Wrongful convictions, 446–447, 453–455
  death penalty, 446–447

Youth courts, 635, 654